APPLET CORRELATION

Applet	Concept Illustrated	Description	Applet Activity
Random numbers	Uses a random number generator to determine the experimental units to be included in a sample.	Generates random numbers from a range of integers specified by the user.	**1.1**, 25; **1.2**, 25; **3.6**, 180; **4.1**, 200; **4.2**, 200; **4.8**, 247
Sample from a population	Assesses how well a sample represents the population and the role that sample size plays in the process.	Produces random sample from population from specified sample size and population distribution shape. Reports mean, median, and standard deviation; applet creates plot of sample.	**4.4**, 214; **4.6**, 238; **4.7**, 252
Sampling distributions	Compares means and standard deviations of distributions; assesses effect of sample size; illustrates undbiasedness.	Simulates repeatedly choosing samples of a fixed size *n* from a population with specified sample size, number of samples, and shape of population distribution. Applet reports means, medians, and standard deviations; creates plots for both.	**5.1**, 290; **5.2**, 290

Long-run probability demonstrations illustrate the concept that theoretical probabilities are long-run experimental probabilities.

Simulating probability of rolling a 6	Investigates relationship between theoretical and experimental probabilities of rolling 6 as number of die rolls increases.	Reports and creates frequency histogram for each outcome of each simulated roll of a fair die. Students specify number of rolls; applet calculates and plots proportion of 6s.	**3.1**, 144; **3.3**, 156; **3.4**, 157, **3.5**, 170
Simulating probability of rolling a 3 or 4	Investigates relationship between theoretical and experimental probabilities of rolling 3 or 4 as number of die rolls increases.	Reports outcome of each simulated roll of a fair die; creates frequency histogram for outcomes. Students specify number of rolls; applet calculates and plots proportion of 3s and 4s.	**3.3**, 156; **3.4**, 157
Simulating the probability of heads: fair coin	Investigates relationship between theoretical and experimental probabilities of getting heads as number of fair coin flips increases.	Reports outcome of each fair coin flip and creates a bar graph for outcomes. Students specify number of flips; applet calculates and plots proportion of heads.	**3.2**, 144; **4.2**, 200
Simulating probability of heads: unfair coin $(P(H) = .2)$	Investigates relationship between theoretical and experimental probabilities of getting heads as number of unfair coin flips increases.	Reports outcome of each flip for a coin where heads is less likely to occur than tails and creates a bar graph for outcomes. Students specify number of flips; applet calculates and plots the proportion of heads.	**4.3**, 214
Simulating probability of heads: unfair coin $(P(H) = .8)$	Investigates relationship between theoretical and experimental probabilities of getting heads as number of unfair coin flips increases.	Reports outcome of each flip for a coin where heads is more likely to occur than tails and creates a bar graph for outcomes. Students specify number of flips; applet calculates and plots the proportion of heads.	**4.3**, 214
Simulating the stock market	Theoretical probabilities are long run experimental probabilities.	Simulates stock market fluctuation. Students specify number of days; applet reports whether stock market goes up or down daily and creates a bar graph for outcomes. Calculates and plots proportion of simulated days stock market goes up.	**4.5**, 215
Mean versus median	Investigates how skewedness and outliers affect measures of central tendency.	Students visualize relationship between mean and median by adding and deleting data points; applet automatically updates mean and median.	**2.1**, 70; **2.2**, 70; **2.3**, 70

WITHDRAWN

(Continued)

Applet	Concept Illustrated	Description	Applet Activity
Standard deviation	Investigates how distribution shape and spread affect standard deviation.	Students visualize relationship between mean and standard deviation by adding and deleting data points; applet updates mean and standard deviation.	**2.4**, 79; **2.5**, 79; **2.6**, 79; **2.7**, 101
Confidence intervals for a mean (the impact of confidence level)	Not all confidence intervals contain the population mean. Investigates the meaning of 95% and 99% confidence.	Simulates selecting 100 random samples from population; finds 95% and 99% confidence intervals for each. Students specify sample size, distribution shape, and population mean and standard deviation; applet plots confidence intervals and reports number and proportion containing true mean.	**6.1**, 314; **6.2**, 314
Confidence intervals for a mean (not knowing standard deviation)	Confidence intervals obtained using the sample standard deviation are different from those obtained using the population standard deviation. Investigates effect of not knowing the population standard deviation.	Simulates selecting 100 random samples from the population and finds the 95% z-interval and 95% t-interval for each. Students specify sample size, distribution shape, and population mean and standard deviation; applet plots confidence intervals and reports number and proportion containing true mean.	**6.3**, 324; **6.4**, 324
Confidence intervals for a proportion	Not all confidence intervals contain the population proportion. Investigates the meaning of 95% and 99% confidence.	Simulates selecting 100 random samples from the population and finds the 95% and 99% confidence intervals for each. Students specify population proportion and sample size; applet plots confidence intervals and reports number and proportion containing true proportion.	**6.5**, 332; **6.6**, 332
Hypothesis tests for a mean	Not all tests of hypotheses lead correctly to either rejecting or failing to reject the null hypothesis. Investigates the relationship between the level of confidence and the probabilities of making Type I and Type II errors.	Simulates selecting 100 random samples from population; calculates and plots t statistic and P-value for each. Students specify population distribution shape, mean, and standard deviation; sample size, and null and alternative hypotheses; applet reports number and proportion of times null hypothesis is rejected at both 0.05 and 0.01 levels.	**7.1**, 373; **7.2**, 384; **7.3**, 384; **7.4**, 384
Hypothesis tests for a proportion	Not all tests of hypotheses lead correctly to either rejecting or failing to reject the null hypothesis. Investigates the relationship between the level of confidence and the probabilities of making Type I and Type II errors.	Simulates selecting 100 random samples from population; calculates and plots z-statistic and P-value for each. Students specify population proportion, sample size, and null and alternative hypotheses; applet reports number and proportion of times null hypothesis is rejected at 0.05 and 0.01 levels.	**7.5**, 400; **7.6**, 401
Correlation by eye	Correlation coefficient measures strength of linear relationship between two variables. Teaches user how to assess strength of a linear relationship from a scattergram.	Computes correlation coefficient r for a set of bivariate data plotted on a scattergram. Students add or delete points and guess value of r; applet compares guess to calculated value.	**11.2**, 654
Regression by eye	The least squares regression line has a smaller SSE than any other line that might approximate a set of bivariate data. Teaches students how to approximate the location of a regression line on a scattergram.	Computes least squares regression line for a set of bivariate data plotted on a scattergram. Students add or delete points and guess location of regression line by manipulating a line provided on the scattergram; applet plots least squares line and displays the equations and the SSEs for both lines.	**11.1**, 629

Statistics

for Business and Economics

EDITION **13**

GLOBAL EDITION

Statistics
for Business and Economics

James T.
MCCLAVE ▪ P. George
BENSON ▪ Terry
SINCICH

Info Tech, Inc.
University of Florida

College of
Charleston

University of South
Florida

Pearson

Harlow, England • London • New York • Boston • San Francisco • Toronto • Sydney • Dubai • Singapore • Hong Kong
Tokyo • Seoul • Taipei • New Delhi • Cape Town • Sao Paulo • Mexico City • Madrid • Amsterdam • Munich • Paris • Milan

Director, Portfolio Management, Math & Statistics: Deirdre Lynch
Portfolio Manager: Patrick Barbera
Portfolio Management Assistant: Justin Billing
Manager, Courseware Content Development, Math & Stats:
  Robert Carroll
Manager, Courseware QA: Mary Durnwald
Associate Acquisitions Editor, Global Edition: Ananya Srivastava
Senior Project Editor, Global Edition: Daniel Luiz
Content Producer: Peggy McMahon
Managing Producer: Scott Disanno
Content Producer, Global Edition: Isha Sachdeva
Manufacturing Controller, Global Edition: Jerry Kataria
Media Producer: Jean Choe

Media Producer, Global Edition: Vikram Kumar
Product Marketing Manager: Kaylee Carlson
Product Marketing Assistant: Jennifer Myers
Senior Author Support/Technology Specialist: Joe Vetere
Manager, Rights and Permissions: Gina Cheselka
Manufacturing Buyer: Carol Melville, RR Donnelley
Associate Director of Design: Blair Brown
Program Design Lead: Barbara T. Atkinson
Text Design, Production Coordination, Composition, and Illustrations:
  Cenveo® Publisher Services
Cover Design: Lumina Datamatics, Inc.
Cover Image: Inzyx/123rf.com

Attributions of third party content appear on page 887, which constitutes an extension of this copyright page.

Pearson Education Limited
KAO Two
KAO Park
Harlow
CM17 9NA
United Kingdom

and Associated Companies throughout the world

Visit us on the World Wide Web at: www.pearsonglobaleditions.com

© Pearson Education Limited 2018

ISBN 10: 1-292-22708-7
ISBN 13: 978-1-292-22708-5

British Library Cataloguing-in-Publication Data
A catalogue record for this book is available from the British Library.

10 9 8 7 6 5 4 3 2 1
20 19 18

Printed in Malaysia (CTP-VVP)

Contents

4   Random Variables and Probability Distributions   213

5   Sampling Distributions   295

6   Inferences Based on a Single Sample: Estimation with Confidence Intervals   330

7   Inferences Based on a Single Sample: Tests of Hypotheses   387

8   Inferences Based on Two Samples: Confidence Intervals and Tests of Hypotheses   452

9   Design of Experiments and Analysis of Variance   522

10 Categorical Data Analysis   599

11 Simple Linear Regression   640

12 Multiple Regression and Model Building   708

13 | Methods for Quality Improvement: Statistical Process Control (Available Online)   13-1

14 | Time Series: Descriptive Analyses, Models, and Forecasting (Available Online)   14-1

Preface

This 13th Global Edition of *Statistics for Business and Economics* is an introductory text emphasizing inference, with extensive coverage of data collection and analysis as needed to evaluate the reported results of statistical studies and make good decisions. As in earlier editions, the text stresses the development of statistical thinking, the assessment of credibility and value of the inferences made from data, both by those who consume and by those who produce them. It assumes a mathematical background of basic algebra.

The text incorporates the following features, developed from the American Statistical Association (ASA) sponsored conferences on *Making Statistics More Effective in Schools of Business* (MSMESB) and ASA's Guidelines for Assessment and Instruction in Statistics Education (GAISE) Project:

- Emphasize statistical literacy and develop statistical thinking
- Use real data in applications
- Use technology for developing conceptual understanding and analyzing data
- Foster active learning in the classroom
- Stress conceptual understanding rather than mere knowledge of procedures
- Emphasize intuitive concepts of probability

New in the 13th Global Edition

- **More than 1,200 exercises, with revisions and updates to 30%.** Many new and updated exercises, based on contemporary business-related studies and real data, have been added. Most of these exercises foster critical thinking skills. The authors analyzed aggregated student usage and performance data from MyLab Statistics for the previous edition of this text. The results of this analysis helped improve the quality and quantity of exercises that matter most to instructors and students.

- **Updated technology.** All printouts from statistical software (Excel 2016/XLSTAT, SPSS, Minitab, and the TI-84 Graphing Calculator) and corresponding instructions for use have been revised to reflect the latest versions of the software.

- **New Statistics in Action Cases.** Two of the 14 Statistics in Action cases are new, each based on real data from a recent business study; several others have been updated.

- **Continued Emphasis on Ethics.** Where appropriate, boxes have been added to emphasize the importance of ethical behavior when collecting, analyzing, and interpreting data with statistics.

- **Business Analytics.** The importance of statistical thinking to successful business analytics is established early in the text.

Content-Specific Substantive Changes to This Edition

- **Chapter 1 (Statistics, Data, and Statistical Thinking).** An introduction to business analytics is now provided in Section 1.7. Here, we establish the value of sound statistical thinking to successful applications of business analytics.

- **Chapter 5 (Sampling Distributions).** After a discussion of the sampling distribution of the sample mean (Section 5.3), we help students decide when to use σ or $\sigma/\sqrt{n}$ in their statistical analysis.

- **Chapter 7 (Tests of Hypothesis).** In the case of testing a population proportion with small samples, exact binomial tests may be applied. We have added material on exact binomial tests to Section 7.6.

- **Chapter 8 (Inferences based on Two Samples).** Sample size formulas for the case of unequal samples have been added to Section 8.5.

- **Chapter 10 (Categorical Data Analysis).** To handle the case of small samples, Fisher's exact test for independence in a 2 × 2 contingency table is now included in Section 10.3.

Hallmark Strengths

We have maintained the pedagogical features of *Statistics for Business and Economics* that we believe make it unique among introductory business statistics texts. These features, which assist the student in achieving an overview of statistics and an understanding of its relevance in both the business world and everyday life, are as follows:

- **Use of Examples as a Teaching Device** Almost all new ideas are introduced and illustrated by data-based applications and examples. We believe that students better understand definitions, generalizations, and theoretical concepts *after* seeing an application. All examples have three components: (1) "Problem," (2) "Solution," and (3) "Look Back" (or "Look Ahead"). This step-by-step process provides students with a defined structure by which to approach problems and enhances their problem-solving skills. The "Look Back/Look Ahead" feature often gives helpful hints to solving the problem and/or provides a further reflection or insight into the concept or procedure that is covered.

- **Now Work** A "Now Work" exercise suggestion follows each example. The Now Work exercise (marked with the [NW] icon in the exercise sets) is similar in style and concept to the text example. This provides students with an opportunity to immediately test and confirm their understanding.

- **Statistics in Action** Each chapter begins with a case study based on an actual contemporary, controversial or high-profile issue in business. Relevant research questions and data from the study are presented and the proper analysis is demonstrated in short "Statistics in Action Revisited" sections throughout the chapter. These motivate students to critically evaluate the findings and think through the statistical issues involved.

- **"Hands-On" Activities for Students** At the end of each chapter, students are provided with an opportunity to participate in hands-on classroom activities, ranging from real data collection to formal statistical analysis. These activities are designed to be performed by students individually or as a class.

- **Applet Exercises.** The text is accompanied by applets (short computer programs), available on the student resource site and in MyLab Statistics. These point-and-click applets allow students to easily run simulations that visually demonstrate some of the more difficult statistical concepts (e.g., sampling distributions and confidence intervals.) Each chapter contains several optional applet exercises in the exercise sets. They are denoted with the following Applet icon: 📊.

- **Real-World Business Cases** Seven extensive business problem-solving cases, with real data and assignments for the student, are provided. Each case serves as a good capstone and review of the material that has preceded it. Typically, these cases follow a group of two or three chapters and require the student to apply the methods presented in these chapters.

- **Real Data–Based Exercises** The text includes more than 1,200 exercises based on applications in a variety of business disciplines and research areas. All applied exercises use current real data extracted from current publications (e.g., newspapers, magazines, current journals, and the Internet). Some students have difficulty learning the mechanics of statistical techniques when all problems are couched in terms of realistic applications. For this reason, all exercise sections are divided into at least four parts:

Learning the Mechanics. Designed as straightforward applications of new concepts, these exercises allow students to test their ability to comprehend a mathematical concept or a definition.

Applying the Concepts—Basic. Based on applications taken from a wide variety of business journals, newspapers, and other sources, these short exercises help students to begin developing the skills necessary to diagnose and analyze real-world problems.

Applying the Concepts—Intermediate. Based on more detailed real-world applications, these exercises require students to apply their knowledge of the technique presented in the section.

Applying the Concepts—Advanced. These more difficult real-data exercises require students to use their critical thinking skills.

Critical Thinking Challenges. Placed at the end of the "Supplementary Exercises" section only, this feature presents students with one or two challenging business problems.

- **Exploring Data with Statistical Computer Software and the Graphing Calculator** Each statistical analysis method presented is demonstrated using output from three leading Windows-based statistical software packages: Excel/XLSTAT, SPSS, and Minitab. Students are exposed early and often to computer printouts they will encounter in today's hi-tech business world.

- **"Using Technology" Tutorials** At the end of each chapter are statistical software tutorials with point-and-click instructions (with screen shots) for Minitab, SPSS, and Excel/XLSTAT. These tutorials are easily located and show students how to best use and maximize statistical software. In addition, output and keystroke instructions for the TI-84 Graphing Calculator are presented.

- **Profiles of Statisticians in History (Biography)** Brief descriptions of famous statisticians and their achievements are presented in side boxes. In reading these profiles, students will develop an appreciation for the statistician's efforts and the discipline of statistics as a whole.

- **Data and Applets** The text is accompanied by a website (www.pearsonglobal editions.com/mcclave) that contains files for all of the data sets marked with an icon 📊 in the text. These include data sets for text examples, exercises, Statistics in Action, and Real-World cases. All data files are saved in multiple formats: Excel, Minitab, and SPSS. This website also contains the applets that are used to illustrate statistical concepts.

Flexibility in Coverage

The text is written to allow the instructor flexibility in coverage of topics. Suggestions for two topics, probability and regression, are given below.

- **Probability and Counting Rules** One of the most troublesome aspects of an introductory statistics course is the study of probability. Probability poses a challenge for instructors because they must decide on the level of presentation, and students find it a difficult subject to comprehend. We believe that one cause for these problems is the mixture of probability and counting rules that occurs in most introductory texts. Consequently, we have included the counting rules (with examples) in an appendix (Appendix B) rather than in the body of Chapter 3. Thus, the instructor can control the level of coverage of probability.

- **Multiple Regression and Model Building** This topic represents one of the most useful statistical tools for the solution of applied problems. Although an entire text could be devoted to regression modeling, we feel that we have presented coverage that is understandable, usable, and much more comprehensive than the presentations in other introductory statistics texts. We devote two full chapters to discussing the major types of inferences that can be derived from a regression analysis, showing how these results appear in the output from statistical software, and, most important, selecting multiple regression models to be used in an analysis. Thus, the instructor has the choice of a one-chapter coverage of simple linear regression (Chapter 11), a two-chapter treatment of simple and multiple regression (excluding the sections on model building in Chapter 12), or complete coverage of regression analysis, including model building and regression diagnostics. This extensive coverage of such useful statistical tools will provide added evidence to the student of the relevance of statistics to real-world problems.

- **Role of Calculus in Footnotes** Although the text is designed for students with a non-calculus background, **footnotes** explain the role of calculus in various derivations. Footnotes are also used to inform the student about some of the theory underlying certain methods of analysis. These footnotes allow additional flexibility in the mathematical and theoretical level at which the material is presented.

Acknowledgments

This book reflects the efforts of a great many people over a number of years. First, we would like to thank the following professors, whose reviews and comments on this and prior editions have contributed to the 13th edition:

Reviewers of the 13th Edition of *Statistics for Business and Economics*

Vivian Jones   *Bethune-Cookman University*
Volodymyr Melnykov   *University of Alabama–Tuscaloosa*
Stephanie Schartel-Dunn   *Missouri Western University*
Balaji Srinivasan   *George Washington University*
Pandu Tadikamalla   *University of Pittsburgh*
Julie Trivitt   *University of Arkansas*

Reviewers of Previous Editions

CALIFORNIA Joyce Curley-Daly, Jim Daly, Robert K. Smidt, *California Polytechnic State University* • Jim Davis, *Golden Gate University* • Carol Eger, *Stanford University* • Paul W. Guy, *California State University, Chico* • Judd Hammack, P. Kasliwal, *California State University, Los Angeles* • Mabel T. King, *California State University, Fullerton* • James Lackritz, *California State University, San Diego* • Beth Rose, *University of Southern California* • Daniel Sirvent, *Vanguard University* **COLORADO** Rick L. Edgeman, Charles F. Warnock, *Colorado State University* • Eric Huggins, *Fort Lewis College* • William J. Weida, *United States Air Force Academy* **CONNECTICUT** Alan E. Gelfand, Joseph Glaz, Timothy J. Killeen, *University of Connecticut* **DELAWARE** Christine Ebert, *University of Delaware* **DISTRICT OF COLUMBIA** Phil Cross, Jose Luis Guerrero-Cusumano, *Georgetown University* • Gaminie Meepagala, *Howard University* **FLORIDA** John M. Charnes, *University of Miami* • C. Brad Davis, *Clearwater Christian College* • Fred Leysieffer, Pi-Erh Lin, Doug Zahn, *Florida State University* • P. V. Rao, *University of Florida* • Laura Reisert, *Florida International University* • Jeffrey W. Steagall, *University of North Florida* • Edna White, *Florida Atlantic University* **GEORGIA** Robert Elrod, *Georgia State University* • Karen Smith, *West Georgia University* **HAWAII** Steve Hora, *University of Hawaii, Hilo* **ILLINOIS** Arunas Dagys, *St. Xavier University* • Edward Minieka, *University of Illinois at Chicago* • Don Robinson, *Illinois State University* • Chipei Tseng, *Northern Illinois University* • Pankaj Vaish, *Arthur Andersen & Company* **IOWA** Dileep Dhavale, *University of Northern Iowa* • William Duckworth II, William Q. Meeker, *Iowa State University* • Tim E. McDaniel, *Buena Vista University* **KANSAS** Paul I. Nelson, *Kansas State University* • Lawrence A. Sherr, *University of Kansas* **KENTUCKY** Richard N. McGrath, *Bowling Green State University* **LOUISIANA** James Willis, *Louisiana State University* **MARYLAND** John F. Beyers, Michael Kulansky, *University of Maryland–University College* • Glenn J. Browne, Mary C. Christman, *University of Maryland* **MASSACHUSETTS** Warren M. Holt, *Southeastern Massachusetts University* • Remus Osan, *Boston University* **MICHIGAN** Atul Agarwal, Petros Ioannatos, *GMI Engineering and Management Institute* • Richard W. Andrews, Peter Lenk, Benjamin Lev, *University of Michigan* • Leszek Gawarecki, *Kettering University* • Toni M. Somers, *Wayne State University* • William Welch, *Saginaw Valley State University* • T. J. Wharton, *Oakland University* **MINNESOTA** Gordon J. Alexander, Donald W. Bartlett, David M. Bergman, Atul Bhatia, Steve Huchendorf, Benny Lo, Karen Lundquist, Vijay Pisharody, Donald N. Steinnes, Robert W. Van Cleave, Steve Wickstrom, *University of Minnesota* • Daniel G. Brick, Leigh Lawton, *University of St. Thomas* • Susan Flach, *General Mills, Inc.* • David

D. Krueger, Ruth K. Meyer, Jan Saraph, Gary Yoshimoto, *St. Cloud State University* • Paula M. Oas, *General Office Products* • Fike Zahroom, *Moorhead State University* **MISSISSIPPI** Eddie M. Lewis, *University of Southern Mississippi* • Alireza Tahai, *Mississippi State University* **MISSOURI** James Holstein, Lawrence D. Ries, *University of Missouri, Columbia* • Marius Janson, L. Douglas Smith, *University of Missouri, St. Louis* • Farroll Tim Wright, *University of Missouri* **NEBRASKA** James Wright, *Chadron State College* **NEW HAMPSHIRE** Ken Constantine, *University of New Hampshire* **NEW JERSEY** Lewis Coopersmith, Cengiz Haksever, *Rider University* • Lei Lei, Xuan Li, Zina Taran, *Rutgers University* • Philip Levine, Leonard Presby, *William Paterson University* **NEW MEXICO** S. Howard Kraye, *University of New Mexico* **NEW YORK** James Czachor, *Fordham-Lincoln Center, AT&T* • Bernard Dickman, *Hofstra University* • Joshua Fogel, *Brooklyn College of City University of New York* • Martin Labbe, *State University of New York, College at New Paltz* • Kenneth Leong, *College of New Rochelle* • Mark R. Marino, *Niagara University/Erie Community College* • G. E. Martin, *Clarkson University* • Thomas J. Pfaff, *Ithaca College* • Gary Simon, *New York University, Stern School of Business* • Rungrudee Suetorsak, *SUNY-Fredonia* **NORTH CAROLINA** Golam Azam, *North Carolina Agricultural & Technical University* • Edward Carlstein, Douglas A. Elvers, *University of North Carolina at Chapel Hill* • Barry P. Cuffe, *Wingate University* • Don Holbert, *East Carolina University* • J. Morgan Jones, *University of North Carolina* • Douglas S. Shafer, *University of North Carolina, Charlotte* **OHIO** William H. Beyer, *University of Akron* • Michael Broida, Tim Krehbiel, *Miami University of Ohio* • Chih-Hsu Cheng, Douglas A. Wolfe, *Ohio State University* • Ronald L. Coccari, *Cleveland State University* • Richard W. Culp, *Wright-Patterson AFB, Air Force Institute of Technology* **OKLAHOMA** Larry Claypool, Brenda Masters, Rebecca Moore, *Oklahoma State University* • Robert Curley, *University of Central Oklahoma* **PENNSYLVANIA** Mohammed Albohali, Douglas H. Frank, *Indiana University of Pennsylvania* • Sukhwinder Bagi, *Bloomsburg University* • Carl Bedell, *Philadelphia College of Textiles and Science* • Ann Hussein, *Philadelphia University* • Behnam Nakhai, *Millersville University* • Rose Prave, *University of Scranton* • Farhad Saboori, *Albright College* • Kathryn Szabet, *LaSalle University* • Christopher J. Zappe, *Bucknell University* **SOUTH CAROLINA** Iris Fetta, Robert Ling, *Clemson University* • Kathleen M. Whitcomb, *University of South Carolina* **TENNESSEE** Francis J. Brewerton, *Middle Tennessee State University* **TEXAS** Larry M. Austin, *Texas Tech University* • Jim Branscome, Robert W. Brobst, Mark Eakin, Grace Esimai, Michael E. Hanna, Craig W. Slinkman, *University of Texas at Arlington* • Katarina Jegdic, *University of Houston–Downtown* • Virgil F. Stone, *Texas A & M University* **VIRGINIA** Edward R. Clayton, *Virginia Polytechnic Institute and State University* **WASHINGTON** June Morita, Kim Tamura, *University of Washington* **WISCONSIN** Ross H. Johnson, *Madison College* **WASHINGTON, D.C.** Keith Ord, *Georgetown University* **CANADA** Clarence Bayne, *Concordia University* • Edith Gombay, *University of Alberta* **TURKEY** Dilek Onkal, *Bilkent University, Ankara* **OTHER** Michael P. Wegmann, *Keller Graduate School of Management*

Other Contributors

Special thanks are due to our supplements authors, Nancy Boudreau and Mark Dummeldinger, both of whom have worked with us for many years. Accuracy checkers Engin Sungur and Joan Saniuk helped ensure a highly accurate, clean text. Finally, the Pearson Education staff of Deirdre Lynch, Patrick Barbera, Christine O'Brien, Karen Wernholm, Joe Vetere, Justin Billing, Peggy McMahon, Barbara Atkinson, Jean Choe, Tiffany Bitzel, and Jennifer Myers, along with Cenveo's Chere Bemelmans and Marilyn Dwyer, helped greatly with all phases of the text development, production, and marketing effort.

Pearson would also like to thank Ralph Scheubrein, Heilbronn University; Alicia Tan, Taylor's University; Hakan Carlqvist, KTH Royal Institute of Technology; Sanjay Nadkarni, Emirates Academy of Hospitality Management; and Pon Subramaniam, American University in Dubai for their work on the Global Edition.

Resources for Success

Student Resources

Student's Solutions Manual, by Nancy Boudreau (Bowling Green State University), provides detailed, worked-out solutions to all odd-numbered text exercises. (ISBN-10: 1-29-222711-7; ISBN-13: 978-1-29-222711-5)

Excel Technology Manual, by Mark Dummeldinger (University of South Florida), provides tutorial instruction and worked-out text examples for Excel. The *Excel Technology Manual* is available for download at pearsonglobaleditions.com/mcclave or within MyLab Statistics.

Business Insight Videos. This series of ten 4- to 7-minute videos, each about a well-known business and the challenges it faces, focuses on statistical concepts as they pertain to the real world. The videos can be downloaded from within MyLab Statistics. Assessment questions to check students' understanding of the videos and answers are available. Contact your Pearson representative for details.

Study Cards for Business Statistics Software. This series of study cards, available for the 2016, 2013, and 2010 versions of Excel® with XLSTAT™ and Data Analysis Toolpak, Minitab® 17 and Express, JMP®, R®, StatCrunch™, and TI-83/84 graphing calculators, provides students with easy, step-by-step guides to the most common business statistics software. Available in MyLab Statistics.

For the Instructor

Instructor's Solutions Manual, by Nancy Boudreau (Bowling Green State University), provides detailed, worked-out solutions to all of the book's exercises. Careful attention has been paid to ensure that all methods of solution and notation are consistent with those used in the core text. Available for download at www.pearsonglobal editions.com/mcclave.

TestGen® (www.pearsoned.com/testgen) enables instructors to build, edit, print, and administer tests using a computerized bank of questions developed to cover all the objectives of the text. TestGen is algorithmically based, allowing instructors to create multiple but equivalent versions of the same question or test with the click of a button. Instructors can also modify test bank questions or add new questions. The software and testbank are available for download from Pearson's Instructor Resource Center.

Technology Resources

On the website www.pearsonglobaleditions.com/mcclave:

- Data sets in multiple formats for text examples, exercises, Statistics in Action, and Making Business Decisions
- Applets support the text by allowing students to easily run simulations that visually demonstrate some of the more challenging statistical concepts discussed.
- Chapter 13: Methods for Quality Improvement: Statistical Process Control
- Chapter 14: Descriptive Analyses, Models, and Forecasting
- Chapter 15: Nonparametric Statistics

MyLab Statistics™ Online Course (access code required)

MyLab Statistics from Pearson is the world's leading online resource for teaching and learning statistics; integrating interactive homework, assessment, and media in a flexible, easy-to-use format. MyLab Statistics is a course management system that helps individual students succeed.

- MyLab Statistics can be implemented successfully in any environment—lab-based, traditional, fully online, or hybrid—and demonstrates the quantifiable difference that integrated usage makes in student retention, subsequent success, and overall achievement.
- MyLab Statistics's comprehensive gradebook automatically tracks students' results on tests, quizzes, homework, and in the study

plan. Instructors can use the gradebook to provide positive feedback or intervene if students have trouble. Gradebook data can be easily exported to a variety of spreadsheet programs, such as Microsoft Excel.

MyLab Statistics provides **engaging experiences** that personalize, stimulate, and measure learning for each student. In addition to the resources below, each course includes a full interactive online version of the accompanying textbook.

- **Personalized Learning:** MyLab Statistics's personalized homework and adaptive and companion study plan features allow your students to work more efficiently, spending time where they really need to.
- **Tutorial Exercises with Multimedia Learning Aids:** The homework and practice exercises in MyLab Statistics align with the exercises in the textbook, and most regenerate algorithmically to give students unlimited opportunity for practice and mastery. Exercises offer immediate helpful feedback, guided solutions, sample problems, animations, videos, statistical software tutorial videos, and eText clips for extra help at point-of-use.
- **Learning Catalytics™:** MyLab Statistics now provides Learning Catalytics—an interactive student response tool that uses students' smartphones, tablets, or laptops to engage them in more sophisticated tasks and thinking.
- **Videos** tie statistics to the real world.
- **Business Insight Videos:** 10 engaging videos show managers at top companies using statistics in their everyday work. Assignable questions encourage discussion.
- **Additional Question Libraries:** In addition to algorithmically regenerated questions that are aligned with your textbook, MyLab Statistics courses come with two additional question libraries:
- **450 exercises** in **Getting Ready for Statistics** cover the developmental math topics

students need for the course. These can be assigned as a prerequisite to other assignments, if desired.
- **1000 exercises** in the **Conceptual Question Library** require students to apply their statistical understanding.
- **StatCrunch™:** MyLab Statistics integrates the web-based statistical software, StatCrunch, within the online assessment platform so that students can easily analyze data sets from exercises and the text. In addition, MyLab Statistics includes access to **www.statcrunch.com**, a vibrant online community where users can access tens of thousands of shared data sets, create and conduct online surveys, perform complex analyses using the powerful statistical software, and generate compelling reports.
- **Statistical Software, Support and Integration:** We make it easy to copy our data sets, from both the eText and the MyLab Statistics questions, into software such as StatCrunch, Minitab®, Excel®, and more. Students have access to a variety of support tools—Technology Tutorial Videos, Technology Study Cards, and Technology Manuals for select titles—to learn how to effectively use statistical software.

MyLab Statistics Accessibility:

- MyLab Statistics is compatible with the JAWS screen reader, and enables multiple-choice, fill-in-the-blank, and free-response problem-types to be read, and interacted with via keyboard controls and math notation input. MyLab Statistics also works with screen enlargers, including ZoomText, MAGic®, and SuperNova. And all MyLab Statistics videos accompanying texts with copyright 2009 and later have closed captioning.
- More information on this functionality is available at http://mystatlab.com/accessibility.

And, MyLab Statistics comes from an **experienced partner** with educational expertise and an eye on the future.

- Knowing that you are using a Pearson product means knowing that you are using quality content. That means that our eTexts are accurate and our assessment tools work. It means we are committed to making MyLab Statistics as accessible as possible.
- Whether you are just getting started with MyLab Statistics, or have a question along the way, we're here to help you learn about our technologies and how to incorporate them into your course.

To learn more about how MyLab Statistics combines proven learning applications with powerful assessment, visit **www.mystatlab.com** or contact your Pearson representative.

MyMathLab® Plus/MyLab Statistics™ Plus

MyLabsPlus combines proven results and engaging experiences from MyMathLab® and MyLab Statistics™ with convenient management tools and a dedicated services team. Designed to support growing math and statistics programs, it includes additional features such as:

- **Batch Enrollment:** Your school can create the login name and password for every student and instructor, so everyone can be ready to start class on the first day. Automation of this process is also possible through integration with your school's Student Information System.
- **Login from your campus portal:** You and your students can link directly from your campus portal into your MyLabsPlus courses. A Pearson service team works with your institution to create a single sign-on experience for instructors and students.
- **Advanced Reporting:** Instructors can review and analyze students' strengths and weaknesses by tracking their performance on tests,

assignments, and tutorials. Administrators can review grades and assignments across all courses on your MyLabsPlus campus for a broad overview of program performance.

- **24/7 Support:** Students and instructors receive 24/7 support, 365 days a year, by email or online chat.

MyLabsPlus is available to qualified adopters. For more information, visit our website at www.mylabsplus.com or contact your Pearson representative.

StatCrunch™

StatCrunch is powerful web-based statistical software that allows users to perform complex analyses, share data sets, and generate compelling reports of their data. The vibrant online community offers tens of thousands of shared data sets for students to analyze.

- **Collect.** Users can upload their own data to StatCrunch or search a large library of publicly shared data sets, spanning almost any topic of interest. Also, an online survey tool allows users to quickly collect data via web-based surveys.
- **Crunch.** A full range of numerical and graphical methods allow users to analyze and gain insights from any data set. Interactive graphics help users understand statistical concepts, and are available for export to enrich reports with visual representations of data.
- **Communicate.** Reporting options help users create a wide variety of visually appealing representations of their data.

Full access to StatCrunch is available with a MyLab Statistics kit, and StatCrunch is available by itself to qualified adopters. StatCrunch Mobile is also now available; just visit www.statcrunch.com from the browser on your smart phone or tablet. For more information, visit our website at www.statcrunch.com, or contact your Pearson representative.

PowerPoint® Lecture Slides provide an outline to use in a lecture setting, presenting definitions, key concepts, and figures from the text. These slides are available within MyLab Statistics or at http://www.pearsonglobaleditions.com/mcclave.

Minitab® 17 and Express: More than 4,000 colleges and universities worldwide use Minitab software because its user-friendly design helps students learn quickly and provides them with a skill-set that's in demand in today's data-driven workforce. Minitab® 17 for PC includes a comprehensive collection of statistical tools to teach beginning through advanced courses. Minitab Express™ for Mac and PC includes all the tools you need for introductory statistics courses. Bundling Minitab software with educational materials ensures students have access to the software they need in the classroom, around campus, and at home. And having 12-month versions of Minitab 17 and Minitab Express available ensures students can use the software for the duration of their course work.

JMP® Student Edition software is statistical discovery software from SAS Institute Inc., the leader in business analytics software and services. JMP® Student Edition is a streamlined version of JMP that provides all the statistics and graphics covered in introductory and intermediate statistics courses.

XLSTAT™ for Pearson. Used by leading businesses and universities, XLSTAT is an Excel® add-in that offers a wide variety of functions to enhance the analytical capabilities of Microsoft® Excel® making it the ideal tool for your everyday data analysis and statistics requirements. XLSTAT™ is compatible with all Excel versions (except Mac 2008). Available for bundling with the text.

Statistics
for Business and Economics

1

CONTENTS

WHERE WE'RE GOING

Introduce the field of statistics (1.1)

Demonstrate how statistics applies to business (1.2)

Introduce the language of statistics and the key elements of any statistical problem (1.3)

Differentiate between population and sample data (1.3)

Differentiate between descriptive and inferential statistics (1.3)

Introduce the key elements of a process (1.4)

Identify the different types of data and data-collection methods (1.5–1.6)

Discover how critical thinking through statistics can help improve our quantitative literacy (1.7)

Statistics, Data, and Statistical Thinking

STATISTICS IN ACTION A 20/20 View of Surveys: Fact or Fiction?

"Did you ever notice that, no matter where you stand on popular issues of the day, you can always find statistics or surveys to back up your point of view–whether to take vitamins, whether daycare harms kids, or what foods can hurt you or save you? There is an endless flow of information to help you make decisions, but is this information accurate, unbiased? John Stossel decided to check that out, and you may be surprised to learn if the picture you're getting doesn't seem quite right, maybe it isn't."

Barbara Walters gave this introduction to a segment of the popular prime-time ABC television program *20/20*. The story was titled "Fact or Fiction?—Exposés of So-Called Surveys." One of the surveys investigated by ABC correspondent John Stossel compared the discipline problems experienced by teachers in the 1940s and those experienced today. The results: In the 1940s, teachers worried most about students talking in class, chewing gum, and running in the halls. Today, they worry most about being assaulted! This information was highly publicized in the print media—in daily newspapers, weekly magazines, gossip columns, the *Congressional Quarterly*, and the *Wall Street Journal*, among others—and referenced in speeches by a variety of public figures, including former First Lady Barbara Bush and former Education Secretary William Bennett.

"Hearing this made me yearn for the old days when life was so much simpler and gentler, but was life that simple then?" asks Stossel. "Wasn't there juvenile delinquency [in the 1940s]? Is the survey true?" With the help of a Yale School of Management professor, Stossel found the original source of the teacher

survey—Texas oilman T. Colin Davis—and discovered it wasn't a survey at all! Davis had simply identified certain disciplinary problems encountered by teachers in a conservative newsletter—a list he admitted was not obtained from a statistical survey, but from Davis's personal knowledge of the problems in the 1940s. ("I was in school then") and his understanding of the problems today ("I read the papers").

Stossel's critical thinking about the teacher "survey" led to the discovery of research that is misleading at best and unethical at worst. Several more misleading (and possibly unethical) surveys, conducted by businesses or special interest groups with specific objectives in mind, were presented on the ABC program. Several are listed below, as well as some recent misleading studies used in product advertisements.

The *20/20* segment ended with an interview of Cynthia Crossen, author of *Tainted Truth: The Manipulation of Fact in America*, an exposé of misleading and biased surveys. Crossen warns, "If everybody is misusing numbers and scaring us with numbers to get us to do something, however good [that something] is, we've lost the power of numbers. Now, we know certain things from research. For example, we know that smoking cigarettes is hard on your lungs and heart, and because we know that, many people's lives have been extended or saved. We don't want to lose the power of information to help us make decisions, and that's what I worry about."

Reported Information (Source)	Actual Study Information
1. Eating oat bran is a cheap and easy way to reduce your cholesterol. (*Quaker Oats*)	Diet must consist of nothing but oat bran to reduce your cholesterol count.
2. One in four American children under age 12 is hungry or at risk of hunger. (*Food Research and Action Center*)	Based on responses to questions: "Do you ever cut the size of meals?" "Do you ever eat less than you feel you should?" "Did you ever rely on limited numbers of foods to feed your children because you were running out of money to buy food for a meal?"
3. There is a strong correlation between a CEO's golf handicap and the company's stock performance: The lower the CEO's handicap (i.e., the better the golfer), the better the stock performs. (*New York Times*, May 31, 1998)	Survey sent to CEOs of 300 largest U.S. companies; only 51 revealed their golf handicaps. Data for several top-ranking CEOs were excluded from the analysis.
4. Prior to the passing of the federal government's health reform act, 30% of employers are predicted to "definitely" or "probably" stop offering health coverage. (*McKinsey & Company Survey*, Feb. 2011)	Online survey of 1,329 private-sector employers in the United States. Respondents were asked leading questions that made it logical to stop offering health insurance.
5. In an advertisement, "more than 80% of dentists surveyed recommend Colgate tooth paste to patients." (*Colgate-Palmolive Company*, Jan. 2007)	The survey allowed each dentist to recommend more than one toothpaste. The Advertising Standards Authority cited and fined Colgate for a misleading ad (implying 80% of dentists recommend Colgate toothpaste in preference to all other brands) and banned the advertisement.
6. An advertisement for Kellogg's Frosted Mini-Wheats claimed that the cereal was "clinically shown to improve kids' attentiveness by nearly 20%." (*Kellogg Company*, 2009)	Only half of the kids in the study showed any improvement in attentiveness; only 1 in 7 improved by 18% or more, and only 1 in 9 improved by 20% or more; kids who ate Frosted Mini-Wheats were compared against kids who had only water. (The Kellogg Company's agreed to pay $4 million to settle suit over false ad claim.)

Reported Information (Source)	Actual Study Information
7. On the basis of a commissioned study, Walmart advertised that it "was responsible for an overall 3.1% decline in consumer prices" and "saves customers over $700 per year." (*Global Insight*, 2005)	The Economic Policy Institute noted that the Global Insight study was based on the retailer's impact on the Consumer Price Index (CPI)—but 60% of the items in the CPI are services, not commodities that can be purchased at Walmart. (Walmart was forced to withdraw the misleading advertisement.)
8. In a survey commissioned by cable provider Comcast, respondents were asked to decide which cable provider, Comcast or DIRECTV, offered more HD channels. Respondents were shown channel lists for DIRECTV (List #387) and Comcast (List #429). (*NAD Case Report No. 5208*, Aug. 25, 2010).	The National Advertising Division (NAD) of the Council of Better Business Bureaus rejected the survey after finding that the higher list number (#429) "served as a subtle, yet effective cue" that Comcast's list contained more channels.

In the following *Statistics in Action Revisited* sections, we discuss several key statistical concepts covered in this chapter that are relevant to misleading surveys like those exposed in the *20/20* program.

STATISTICS IN ACTION REVISITED

- Identifying the population, sample, and inference **(p. 34)**
- Identifying the data-collection method and data type **(p. 44)**
- Critically assessing the ethics of a statistical study **(p. 47)**

1.1 The Science of Statistics

What does *statistics* mean to you? Does it bring to mind batting averages? Gallup polls, unemployment figures, or numerical distortions of facts (lying with statistics!)? Or is it simply a college requirement you have to complete? We hope to persuade you that statistics is a meaningful, useful science whose broad scope of applications to business, government, and the physical and social sciences is almost limitless. We also want to show that statistics can lie only when they are misapplied. Finally, we wish to demonstrate the key role statistics play in critical thinking—whether in the classroom, on the job, or in everyday life. Our objective is to leave you with the impression that the time you spend studying this subject will repay you in many ways.

Although the term can be defined in many ways, a broad definition of *statistics* is the science of collecting, classifying, analyzing, and interpreting information. Thus, a statistician isn't just someone who calculates batting averages at baseball games or tabulates the results of a Gallup poll. Professional statisticians are trained in *statistical science*—that is, they are trained in collecting information in the form of **data,** evaluating it, and drawing conclusions from it. Furthermore, statisticians determine what information is relevant in a given problem and whether the conclusions drawn from a study are to be trusted.

Statistics is the science of data. It involves collecting, classifying, summarizing, organizing, analyzing, and interpreting numerical and categorical information.

In the next section, you'll see several real-life examples of statistical applications in business and government that involve making decisions and drawing conclusions.

1.2 Types of Statistical Applications in Business

BIOGRAPHY

**FLORENCE NIGHTINGALE
(1820–1910)**
The Passionate Statistician

In Victorian England, the "Lady of the Lamp" had a mission to improve the squalid field hospital conditions of the British army during the Crimean War. Today, most historians consider Florence Nightingale to be the founder of the nursing profession. To convince members of the British Parliament of the need for supplying nursing and medical care to soldiers in the field, Nightingale compiled massive amounts of data from the army files. Through a remarkable series of graphs (which included the first "pie chart"), she demonstrated that most of the deaths in the war were due to illnesses contracted outside the battlefield or long after battle action from wounds that went untreated. Florence Nightingale's compassion and self-sacrificing nature, coupled with her ability to collect, arrange, and present large amounts of data, led some to call her the "Passionate Statistician."

Statistics means "numerical descriptions" to most people. Monthly unemployment figures, the failure rate of startup companies, and the proportion of female executives in a particular industry all represent statistical descriptions of large sets of data collected on some phenomenon. Often the data are selected from some larger set of data whose characteristics we wish to estimate. We call this selection process *sampling*. For example, you might collect the ages of a sample of customers of a video streaming services company to estimate the average age of *all* customers of the company. Then you could use your estimate to target the firm's advertisements to the appropriate age group. Notice that statistics involves two different processes: (1) describing sets of data and (2) drawing conclusions (making estimates, decisions, predictions, etc.) about the sets of data based on sampling. So, the applications of statistics can be divided into two broad areas: *descriptive statistics* and *inferential statistics*.

Descriptive statistics utilizes numerical and graphical methods to explore data, i.e., to look for patterns in a data set, to summarize the information revealed in a data set, and to present the information in a convenient form.

Inferential statistics utilizes sample data to make estimates, decisions, predictions, or other generalizations about a larger set of data.

Although we'll discuss both descriptive and inferential statistics in the following chapters, primary theme of the text is **inference.**

Let's begin by examining some business studies that illustrate applications of statistics.

Study 1.1 "Best-Selling Girl Scout Cookies" (Source: www.girlscouts.org): Since 1917, the Girl Scouts of America have been selling boxes of cookies. Currently, there are 12 varieties for sale: Thin Mints, Samoas, Lemonades, Tagalongs, Do-si-dos, Trefoils, Savannah Smiles, Thanks-A-Lot, Dulce de Leche, Cranberry Citrus Crisps, Chocolate Chip, and Thank U Berry Much. Each of the approximately 150 million boxes of Girl Scout cookies sold in 2006 was classified by variety. The results are summarized in Figure 1.1. From the graph, you can clearly see that the best-selling variety is Thin Mints (25%), followed by Samoas (19%) and Tagalongs (13%). Since Figure 1.1 *describes* the variety of categories of the boxes of Girl Scout cookies sold, the graphic is an example of *descriptive statistics*.

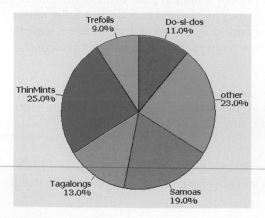

Figure 1.1

Best-selling Girl Scout cookies
Source: Best-Selling Girl Scout Cookies," based on www.girlscouts.org.

Study 1.2 "Executive Compensation vs. Typical Worker Pay" (*Source*: Glassdoor Economic Research, August 25, 2015): How big is the gap between what a firm pays its CEO and what it pays its typical worker? To answer this question, Glassdoor Economic Research compiled data on salaries of executives and workers at S&P 500 firms who filed salary reports with the Securities Exchange Commission (SEC). This information was used to compute the ratio of CEO pay to the typical worker salary at each firm.* The data for the top 10 highest-paid CEOs in the sample of 441 firms in the study are shown in Table 1.1. An analysis of the data for all 441 firms revealed that the "average" ratio of CEO pay to typical worker pay was 205.† In other words, on average, CEOs in the sample earn around 205 times what their firm's typical worker earns. Armed with this sample information, an economist might *infer* that the average ratio of CEO pay to typical worker pay for *all* U.S. firms is 205. Thus, this study is an example of *inferential statistics*.

Table 1.1	Ratio of CEO Compensation to Typical Worker Pay—Top 10 Highest-Paid CEOs				
Employer	Rank	CEO	CEO Pay	Typical Worker Pay	Ratio
Discovery Comm.	1	David M. Zaslav	$156,077,912	$80,000	1,951
Chipotle	2	Steve Ells	$28,924,270	$19,000	1,522
CVS Health	3	Larry J. Merlo	$32,350,733	$27,139	1,192
Walmart	4	C. Douglas McMillon	$25,592,938	$22,591	1,133
Target	5	Brian C. Cornell	$28,164,024	$30,000	939
CBS Corp.	6	Leslie Moonves	$57,175,645	$66,365	862
Bed Bath & Beyond	7	Steven H. Temares	$19,116,040	$26,047	734
Macy's	8	Terry J. Lundgren	$16,497,220	$22,800	724
Gap	9	Glenn Murphy	$16,064,312	$22,800	705
Starbucks	10	Howard D. Schultz	$21,466,454	$32,080	669

Source: From CEO to Worker Pay Ratios: Average CEO Earns 204 Times Median Worker Pay, *Glassdoor Economic Research Blog*, Dr. Andrew Chamberlain. Copyright © by Glassdoor, Inc. Used by permission by Glassdoor, Inc.

Study 1.3 "Does rudeness really matter in the workplace?" (*Academy of Management Journal*, Oct. 2007): Previous studies have established that rudeness in the workplace can lead to retaliatory and counterproductive behavior. However, there has been little research on how rude behaviors influence a victim's task performance. In a recent study, college students enrolled in a management course were randomly assigned to one of two experimental conditions: rudeness condition (45 students) and control group (53 students). Each student was asked to write down as many uses for a brick as possible in 5 minutes; this value (total number of uses) was used as a performance measure for each student. For those students in the rudeness condition, the facilitator displayed rudeness by berating the students in general for being irresponsible and unprofessional (due to a late-arriving confederate). No comments were made about the late-arriving confederate to students in the control group. As you might expect, the researchers discovered that the performance levels for students in the rudeness condition were generally lower than the performance levels for students in the control group; thus, they concluded that rudeness in the workplace negatively affects job performance. As in Study 1.2, this study is an example of the use of inferential statistics. The researchers used data collected on 98 college students in a simulated work environment to make an inference about the performance levels of all workers exposed to rudeness on the job.

---

*The ratio was calculated using the *median* worker salary at each firm. A formal definition of median is given in Chapter 2. For now, think of the median as the *typical* or *middle* worker salary.
†A formal definition of *average* is also given in Chapter 2. Like the median, think of the average as another way to express the *middle* salary.

These studies provide three real-life examples of the uses of statistics in business, economics, and management. Notice that each involves an analysis of data, either for the purpose of describing the data set (Study 1.1) or for making inferences about a data set (Studies 1.2 and 1.3).

1.3 Fundamental Elements of Statistics

Statistical methods are particularly useful for studying, analyzing, and learning about *populations* of *experimental units*.

> An **experimental (or observational) unit** is an object (e.g., person, thing, transaction, or event) upon which we collect data.

> A **population** is a set of units (usually people, objects, transactions, or events) that we are interested in studying.

For example, populations may include (1) *all* employed workers in the United States, (2) *all* registered voters in California, (3) *everyone* who has purchased a particular brand of cellular telephone, (4) *all* the cars produced last year by a particular assembly line, (5) the *entire* stock of spare parts at United Airlines' maintenance facility, (6) *all* sales made at the drive-through window of a McDonald's restaurant during a given year, and (7) the set of *all* accidents occurring on a particular stretch of interstate during a holiday period. Notice that the first three population examples (1–3) are sets (groups) of people, the next two (4–5) are sets of objects, the next (6) is a set of transactions, and the last (7) is a set of events. Also notice that *each set includes all the experimental units in the population* of interest.

In studying a population, we focus on one or more characteristics or properties of the experimental units in the population. We call such characteristics *variables*. For example, we may be interested in the variables age, gender, income, and/or the number of years of education of the people currently unemployed in the United States.

> A **variable** is a characteristic or property of an individual experimental (or observational) unit.

The name *variable* is derived from the fact that any particular characteristic may vary among the experimental units in a population.

In studying a particular variable, it is helpful to be able to obtain a numerical representation for it. Often, however, numerical representations are not readily available, so the process of measurement plays an important supporting role in statistical studies. **Measurement** is the process we use to assign numbers to variables of individual population units. We might, for instance, measure the preference for a food product by asking a consumer to rate the product's taste on a scale from 1 to 10. Or we might measure workforce age by simply asking each worker, "How old are you?" In other cases, measurement involves the use of instruments such as stopwatches, scales, and calipers.

If the population we wish to study is small, it is possible to measure a variable for every unit in the population. For example, if you are measuring the starting salary for all University of Michigan MBA graduates last year, it is at least feasible to obtain every salary. When we measure a variable for every experimental unit of a population, the result is called a **census** of the population. Typically, however, the populations of interest in most applications are much larger, involving perhaps many thousands or even an infinite number of units. Examples of large populations include the seven listed above, as well as all invoices produced in the last year by a *Fortune* 500 company, all potential buyers of a new iPad, and all stockholders of a firm listed on the New York

Stock Exchange. For such populations, conducting a census would be prohibitively time-consuming and/or costly. A reasonable alternative would be to select and study a *subset* (or portion) of the units in the population.

A **sample** is a subset of the units of a population.

For example, suppose a company is being audited for invoice errors. Instead of examining all 15,472 invoices produced by the company during a given year, an auditor may select and examine a sample of just 100 invoices (see Figure 1.2). If he is interested in the variable "invoice error status," he would record (measure) the status (error or no error) of each sampled invoice.

After the variable(s) of interest for every experimental unit in the sample (or population) is (are) measured, the data are analyzed, either by descriptive or by inferential statistical methods. The auditor, for example, may be interested only in *describing* the error rate in the sample of 100 invoices. More likely, however, he will want to use the information in the sample to make *inferences* about the population of all 15,472 invoices.

A **statistical inference** is an estimate or prediction or some other generalization about a population based on information contained in a sample.

That is, we use the information contained in the sample to learn about the larger population. Thus, from the sample of 100 invoices, the auditor may estimate the total number of invoices containing errors in the population of 15,472 invoices. The auditor's inference about the quality of the firm's invoices can be used in deciding whether to modify the firm's billing operations.

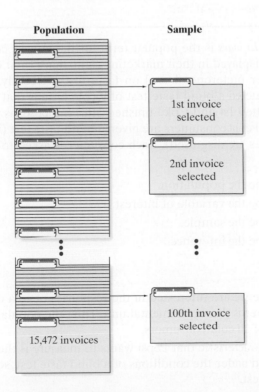

Figure 1.2

A sample of all company invoices

---

*The terms *population* and *sample* are often used to refer to the sets of measurements themselves, as well as to the units on which the measurements are made. When a single variable of interest is being measured, this usage causes little confusion. But when the terminology is ambiguous, we'll refer to the measurements as *population data sets* and *sample data sets*, respectively.

EXAMPLE 1.1

Key Elements of a Statistical Problem— Ages of TV Viewers

Problem According to a report in the *Washington Post* (Sep. 5, 2014), the average age of viewers of television programs broadcast on CBS, NBC, and ABC is 54 years. Suppose a rival network (e.g., FOX) executive hypothesizes that the average age of FOX viewers is less than 54. To test her hypothesis, she samples 200 FOX viewers and determines the age of each.

a. Describe the population.
b. Describe the variable of interest.
c. Describe the sample.
d. Describe the inference.

Solution

a. The population is the set of units of interest to the TV executive, which is the set of all FOX viewers.

b. The age (in years) of each viewer is the variable of interest.

c. The sample must be a subset of the population. In this case, it is the 200 FOX viewers selected by the executive.

d. The inference of interest involves the *generalization* of the information contained in the sample of 200 viewers to the population of all FOX viewers. In particular, the executive wants to *estimate* the average age of the viewers in order to determine whether it is less than 54 years. She might accomplish this by calculating the average age in the sample and using the sample average to estimate the population average.

Look Back A key to diagnosing a statistical problem is to identify the data set collected (in this example, the ages of the 200 FOX TV viewers) as a population or sample.

EXAMPLE 1.2

Key Elements of a Statistical Problem— Pepsi vs. Coca-Cola

Problem *Cola wars* is the popular term for the intense competition between Coca-Cola and Pepsi displayed in their marketing campaigns. Their campaigns have featured claims of consumer preference based on taste tests. Recently, the *Huffington Post* (Nov. 11, 2013) conducted a blind taste test of 9 cola brands that included Coca-Cola and Pepsi. (Pepsi finished 1st and Coke finished 5th.) Suppose, as part of a Pepsi marketing campaign, 1,000 cola consumers are given a blind taste test (i.e., a taste test in which the two brand names are disguised). Each consumer is asked to state a preference for brand A or brand B.

a. Describe the population.
b. Describe the variable of interest.
c. Describe the sample.
d. Describe the inference.

Solution

a. Because we are interested in the responses of cola consumers in a taste test, a cola consumer is the experimental unit. Thus, the population of interest is the collection or set of all cola consumers.

b. The characteristic that Pepsi wants to measure is the consumer's cola preference as revealed under the conditions of a blind taste test, so cola preference is the variable of interest.

c. The sample is the 1,000 cola consumers selected from the population of all cola consumers.

d. The inference of interest is the *generalization* of the cola preferences of the 1,000 sampled consumers to the population of all cola consumers. In particular, the preferences of the consumers in the sample can be used to *estimate* the percentage of all cola consumers who prefer each brand.

Look Back In determining whether the statistical application is inferential or descriptive, we assess whether Pepsi is interested in the responses of only the 1,000 sampled customers (descriptive statistics) or in the responses for the entire population of consumers (inferential statistics).

• **Now Work Exercise 1.25b**

The preceding definitions and examples identify four of the five elements of an inferential statistical problem: a population, one or more variables of interest in a sample, and an inference. But making the inference is only part of the story. We also need to know its **reliability**–that is, how good the inference is. The only way we can be certain that an inference about a population is correct is to include the entire population in our sample. However, because of *resource constraints* (e.g., insufficient time and/or money), we usually can't work with whole populations, so we base our inferences on just a portion of the population (a sample). Consequently, whenever possible, it is important to determine and report the reliability of each inference made. Reliability, then, is the fifth element of inferential statistical problems.

The measure of reliability that accompanies an inference separates the science of statistics from the art of fortune-telling. A palm reader, like a statistician, may examine a sample (your hand) and make inferences about the population (your life). However, unlike statistical inferences, the palm reader's inferences include no measure of reliability.

Suppose, like the TV executive in Example 1.1, we are interested in the *error of estimation* (i.e., the difference between the average age of the population of TV viewers and the average age of a sample of TV viewers). Using statistical methods, we can determine a *bound on the estimation error.* This bound is simply a number that our estimation error (the difference between the average age of the sample and the average age of the population) is not likely to exceed. We'll see in later chapters that bound is a measure of the uncertainty of our inference. The reliability of statistical inferences is discussed throughout this text. For now, we simply want you to realize that an inference is incomplete without a measure of its reliability.

A **measure of reliability** is a statement (usually quantified) about the degree of uncertainty associated with a statistical inference.

Let's conclude this section with a summary of the elements of both descriptive and inferential statistical problems and an example to illustrate a measure of reliability.

Four Elements of Descriptive Statistical Problems

1. The population or sample of interest
2. One or more variables (characteristics of the population or experimental units) that are to be investigated
3. Tables, graphs, or numerical summary tools
4. Identification of patterns in the data

Five Elements of Inferential Statistical Problems

1. The population of interest
2. One or more variables (characteristics of the population or experimental units) that are to be investigated
3. The sample of population units
4. The inference about the population based on information contained in the sample
5. A measure of reliability for the inference

EXAMPLE 1.3

Reliability of an Inference—Pepsi vs. Coca-Cola

Problem Refer to Example 1.2, in which the cola preferences of 1,000 consumers were indicated in a taste test. Describe how the reliability of an inference concerning the preferences of all cola consumers in the Pepsi bottler's marketing region could be measured.

Solution When the preferences of 1,000 consumers are used to estimate the preferences of all consumers in the region, the estimate will not exactly mirror the preferences of the population. For example, if the taste test shows that 56% of the 1,000 consumers chose Pepsi, it does not follow (nor is it likely) that exactly 56% of all cola drinkers in the region prefer Pepsi. Nevertheless, we can use sound statistical reasoning (which is presented later in the text) to ensure that our sampling procedure will generate estimates that are almost certainly within a specified limit of the true percentage of all consumers who prefer Pepsi. For example, such reasoning might assure us that the estimate of the preference for Pepsi from the sample is almost certainly within 5% of the actual population preference. The implication is that the actual preference for Pepsi is between 51% [i.e., $(56 - 5)$%] and 61% [i.e., $(56 + 5)$%]—that is, (56 ± 5)%. This interval represents a measure of reliability for the inference.

Look Back The interval 56 ± 5 is called a *confidence interval*, because we are "confident" that the true percentage of customers who prefer Pepsi in a taste test falls into the range (51, 61). In Chapter 6, we learn how to assess the degree of confidence (e.g., 90% or 95% confidence) in the interval.

STATISTICS IN ACTION

REVISITED

Identifying the Population, Sample, and Inference

Consider the study on the link between a CEO's golf handicap and the company's stock performance, reported in the *New York Times* (May 31, 1998). The newspaper gathered information on golf handicaps of corporate executives obtained from a *Golf Digest* survey sent to CEOs of the 300 largest U.S. companies. (A golf handicap is a numerical "index" that allows golfers to compare skills; the lower the handicap, the better the golfer.) For the 51 CEOs who reported their handicaps, the *New York Times* then determined each CEO's company stock market performance over a 3-year period (measured as a rate-of-return index, from a low value of 0 to a high value of 100). Thus, the experimental unit for the study is a corporate executive, and the two variables measured are golf handicap and stock performance index. Also, the data for the 51 CEOs represent a sample selected from the much larger population of all corporate executives in the United States. (These data are available in the **GLFCEO** file.)

The *New York Times* discovered a "statistical correlation" (a method discussed in Chapter 11) between golf handicap and stock performance. Thus, the newspaper inferred that the better the CEO is at golf, the better the company's stock performance.

 *Data Set:* GLFCEO

1.4	Processes (Optional)

Sections 1.2 and 1.3 focused on the use of statistical methods to analyze and learn about populations, which are sets of *existing* units. Statistical methods are equally useful for analyzing and making inferences about *processes*.

> A **process** is a series of actions or operations that transforms inputs to outputs. A process produces or generates output over time.

The most obvious processes of interest to businesses are those of production or manufacturing. A manufacturing process uses a series of operations performed by

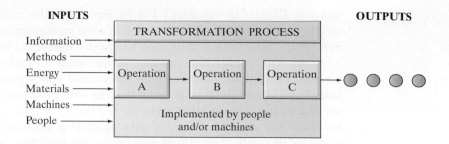

Figure 1.3

Graphical depiction of a manufacturing process

people and machines to convert inputs, such as raw materials and parts, to finished products (the outputs). Examples include the process used to produce the paper on which these words are printed, automobile assembly lines, and oil refineries.

Figure 1.3 presents a general description of a process and its inputs and outputs. In the context of manufacturing, the process in the figure (i.e., the transformation process) could be a depiction of the overall production process or it could be a depiction of one of the many processes (sometimes called *subprocesses*) that exist within an overall production process. Thus, the output shown could be finished goods that will be shipped to an external customer or merely the output of one of the steps or subprocesses of the overall process. In the latter case, the output becomes input for the next subprocess. For example, Figure 1.3 could represent the overall automobile assembly process, with its output being fully assembled cars ready for shipment to dealers. Or, it could depict the windshield assembly subprocess, with its output of partially assembled cars with windshields ready for "shipment" to the next subprocess in the assembly line.

Besides physical products and services, businesses and other organizations generate streams of numerical data over time that are used to evaluate the performance of the organization. Examples include weekly sales figures, quarterly earnings, and yearly profits. The U.S. economy (a complex organization) can be thought of as generating streams of data that include the gross domestic product (GDP), stock prices, and the Consumer Price Index. Statisticians and other analysts conceptualize these data streams as being generated by processes. Typically, however, the series of operations or actions that cause particular data to be realized are either unknown or so complex (or both) that the processes are treated as *black boxes*.

A process whose operations or actions are unknown or unspecified is called a **black box.**

Frequently, when a process is treated as a black box, its inputs are not specified either. The entire focus is on the output of the process. A black box process is illustrated in Figure 1.4.

In studying a process, we generally focus on one or more characteristics, or properties, of the output. For example, we may be interested in the weight or the length of the units produced or even the time it takes to produce each unit. As with characteristics of population units, we call these characteristics *variables*. In studying processes whose output is already in numerical form (i.e., a stream of numbers), the characteristic, or property, represented by the numbers (e.g., sales, GDP, or stock prices) is typically the variable of interest. If the output is not numeric, we use *measurement processes* to assign

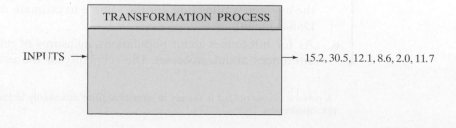

Figure 1.4

A black box process with numerical output

numerical values to variables.* For example, if in the automobile assembly process the weight of the fully assembled automobile is the variable of interest, a measurement process involving a large scale will be used to assign a numerical value to each automobile.

As with populations, we use sample data to analyze and make inferences (estimates, predictions, or other generalizations) about processes. But the concept of a sample is defined differently when dealing with processes. Recall that a population is a set of existing units and that a sample is a subset of those units. In the case of processes, however, the concept of a set of existing units is not relevant or appropriate. Processes generate or create their output *over time*—one unit after another. For example, a particular automobile assembly line produces a completed vehicle every 4 minutes. We define a sample from a process in the box.

Any set of output (object or numbers) produced by a process is also called a **sample.**

Thus, the next 10 cars turned out by the assembly line constitute a sample from the process, as do the next 100 cars or every fifth car produced today.

EXAMPLE 1.4

Key Elements of a Process—Waiting Time at a Fast-Food Window

Problem A particular fast-food restaurant chain has 6,289 outlets with drive-through windows. To attract more customers to its drive-through services, the company is considering offering a 50% discount to customers who wait more than a specified number of minutes to receive their order. To help determine what the time limit should be, the company decided to estimate the average waiting time at a particular drive-through window in Dallas, Texas. For 7 consecutive days, the worker taking customers' orders recorded the time that every order was placed. The worker who handed the order to the customer recorded the time of delivery. In both cases, workers used synchronized digital clocks that reported the time to the nearest second. At the end of the 7-day period, 2,109 orders had been timed.

a. Describe the process of interest at the Dallas restaurant.

b. Describe the variable of interest.

c. Describe the sample.

d. Describe the inference of interest.

e. Describe how the reliability of the inference could be measured.

Solution

a. The process of interest is the drive-through window at a particular fast-food restaurant in Dallas, Texas. It is a process because it "produces," or "generates," meals over time—that is, it services customers over time.

b. The variable the company monitored is customer waiting time, the length of time a customer waits to receive a meal after placing an order. Because the study is focusing only on the output of the process (the time to produce the output) and not the internal operations of the process (the tasks required to produce a meal for a customer), the process is being treated as a black box.

c. The sampling plan was to monitor every order over a particular 7-day period. The sample is the 2,109 orders that were processed during the 7-day period.

d. The company's immediate interest is in learning about the drive-through window in Dallas. They plan to do this by using the waiting times from the sample to make a statistical inference about the drive-through process. In particular, they might use the average waiting time for the sample to estimate the average waiting time at the Dallas facility.

e. As for inferences about populations, measures of reliability can be developed for inferences about processes. The reliability of the estimate of the average waiting

---

*A process whose output is already in numerical form necessarily includes a measurement process as one of its subprocesses.

time for the Dallas restaurant could be measured by a bound on the error of estimation—that is, we might find that the average waiting time is 4.2 minutes, with a bound on the error of estimation of 0.5 minutes. The implication would be that we could be reasonably certain that the true average waiting time for the Dallas process is between 3.7 and 4.7 minutes.

Look Back Notice that there is also a population described in this example: the company's 6,289 existing outlets with drive-through facilities. In the final analysis, the company will use what it learns about the process in Dallas and, perhaps, similar studies at other locations to make an inference about the waiting times in its population of outlets.

● **Now Work Exercise 1.38**

Note that output already generated by a process can be viewed as a population. Suppose a soft-drink canning process produced 2,000 twelve-packs yesterday, all of which were stored in a warehouse. If we were interested in learning something about those 2,000 twelve-packs—such as the percentage with defective cardboard packaging—we could treat the 2,000 twelve-packs as a population. We might draw a sample from the population in the warehouse, measure the variable of interest, and use the sample data to make a statistical inference about the 2,000 twelve-packs, as described in Sections 1.2 and 1.3.

In this optional section, we have presented a brief introduction to processes and the use of statistical methods to analyze and learn about processes. In Chapters 13 and 14 we present an in-depth treatment of these subjects.

1.5 Types of Data

You have learned that statistics is the science of data and that data are obtained by measuring the values of one or more variables on the units in the sample (or population). All data (and hence the variables we measure) can be classified as one of two general types: *quantitative* and *qualitative*.

Quantitative data are data that are measured on a naturally occurring numerical scale.* The following are examples of quantitative data:

1. The temperature (in degrees Celsius) at which each unit in a sample of 20 pieces of heat-resistant plastic begins to melt
2. The current unemployment rate (measured as a percentage) for each of the 50 states
3. The scores of a sample of 150 MBA applicants on the GMAT, a standardized business graduate school entrance exam administered nationwide
4. The number of female executives employed in each of a sample of 75 manufacturing companies

> **Quantitative data** are measurements that are recorded on a naturally occurring numerical scale.

In contrast, qualitative data cannot be measured on a natural numerical scale; they can only be classified into categories.† Examples of qualitative data are as follows:

1. The political party affiliation (Democrat, Republican, or Independent) in a sample of 50 CEOs

---

*Quantitative data can be subclassified as either *interval* or *ratio*. For ratio data, the origin (i.e., the value 0) is a meaningful number. But the origin has no meaning with interval data. Consequently, we can add and subtract interval data, but we can't multiply and divide them. Of the four quantitative data sets listed, (1) and (3) are interval data, while (2) and (4) are ratio data.

†Qualitative data can be subclassified as either *nominal* or *ordinal*. The categories of an ordinal data set can be ranked or meaningfully ordered, but the categories of a nominal data set can't be ordered. Of the four qualitative data sets listed, (1) and (2) are nominal and (3) and (4) are ordinal.

2. The defective status (defective or not) of each of 100 computer chips manufactured by Intel

3. The size of a car (subcompact, compact, midsize, or full-size) rented by each of a sample of 30 business travelers

4. A taste tester's ranking (best, worst, etc.) of four brands of barbecue sauce for a panel of 10 testers

Often, we assign arbitrary numerical values to qualitative data for ease of computer entry and analysis. But these assigned numerical values are simply codes: They cannot be meaningfully added, subtracted, multiplied, or divided. For example, we might code Democrat = 1, Republican = 2, and Independent = 3. Similarly, a taste tester might rank the barbecue sauces from 1 (best) to 4 (worst). These are simply arbitrarily selected numerical codes for the categories and have no utility beyond that.

> **Qualitative data** are measurements that cannot be measured on a natural numerical scale; they can only be classified into one of a group of categories.

EXAMPLE 1.5

Types of Data—Study of a River Contaminated by a Chemical Plant

Problem Chemical and manufacturing plants sometimes discharge toxic-waste materials such as DDT into nearby rivers and streams. These toxins can adversely affect the plants and animals inhabiting the river and the riverbank. The U.S. Army Corps of Engineers conducted a study of fish in the Tennessee River (in Alabama) and its three tributary creeks: Flint Creek, Limestone Creek, and Spring Creek. A total of 144 fish were captured, and the following variables were measured for each:

1. River/creek where each fish was captured
2. Species (channel catfish, largemouth bass, or smallmouth buffalo fish)
3. Length (centimeters)
4. Weight (grams)
5. DDT concentration (parts per million)

These data are saved in the **DDT** file. Classify each of the five variables measured as quantitative or qualitative.

Solution The variables length, weight, and DDT are quantitative because each is measured on a numerical scale: length in centimeters, weight in grams, and DDT in parts per million. In contrast, river/creek and species cannot be measured quantitatively: They can only be classified into categories (e.g., channel catfish, largemouth bass, and smallmouth buffalo fish for species). Consequently, data on river/creek and species are qualitative.

Look Back It is essential that you understand whether data are quantitative or qualitative in nature because the statistical method appropriate for describing, reporting, and analyzing the data depends on the data type (quantitative or qualitative).

● **Now Work Exercise 1.18**

We demonstrate many useful methods for analyzing quantitative and qualitative data in the remaining chapters of the text. But first, we discuss some important ideas on data collection.

1.6 Collecting Data: Sampling and Related Issues

Once you decide on the type of data—quantitative or qualitative—appropriate for the problem at hand, you'll need to collect the data. Generally, you can obtain the data in three different ways:

1. Data from a *published source*
2. Data from a *designed experiment*
3. Data from an *observational study* (e.g., a *survey*)

Sometimes, the data set of interest has already been collected for you and is available in a **published source,** such as a book, journal, newspaper, or Web site. For example, you may want to examine and summarize the unemployment rates (i.e., percentages of eligible workers who are unemployed) in the 50 states of the United States. You can find this data set (as well as numerous other data sets) at your library in the *Statistical Abstract of the United States,* published annually by the U.S. government. Similarly, someone who is interested in monthly mortgage applications for new home construction would find this data set in the *Survey of Current Business,* another government publication. Other examples of published data sources include the *Wall Street Journal* (financial data) and the The *Elias Sports Bureau* (sports information).* The Internet (World Wide Web) provides a medium by which data from published sources are readily available.

A second method of collecting data involves conducting a **designed experiment,** in which the researcher exerts strict control over the units (people, objects, or events) in the study. For example, an often-cited medical study investigated the potential of aspirin in preventing heart attacks. Volunteer physicians were divided into two groups—the *treatment* group and the *control* group. In the treatment group, each physician took one aspirin tablet a day for 1 year, while each physician in the control group took an aspirin-free placebo (no drug) made to look like an aspirin tablet. The researchers, not the physicians under study, controlled who received the aspirin (the treatment) and who received the placebo. As you will learn in Chapter 9, properly designed experiment allows you to extract more information from the data than is possible with an uncontrolled study.

Finally, observational studies can be employed to collect data. In an **observational study,** the researcher observes the experimental units in their natural setting and records the variable(s) of interest. For example, a company psychologist might observe and record the level of "Type A" behavior of a sample of assembly line workers. Similarly, a finance researcher may observe and record the closing stock prices of companies that are acquired by other firms on the day prior to the buyout and compare them to the closing prices on the day the acquisition is announced. Unlike a designed experiment, an observational study is one in which the researcher makes no attempt to control any aspect of the experimental units.

The most common type of observational study is a **survey,** where the researcher samples a group of people, asks one or more questions, and records the responses. Probably the most familiar type of survey is the political poll, conducted by any one of a number of organizations (e.g., Harris, Gallup, Roper, and CNN) and designed to predict the outcome of a political election. Another familiar survey is the Nielsen survey, which provides the major television networks with information on the most watched TV programs. Surveys can be conducted through the mail, with telephone interviews, or with in-person interviews. Although in-person interviews are more expensive than mail or telephone surveys, they may be necessary when complex information must be collected.

A **designed experiment** is a data-collection method where the researcher exerts full control over the characteristics of the experimental units sampled. These experiments typically involve a group of experimental units that are assigned the *treatment* and an untreated (or *control*) group.

An **observational study** is a data-collection method where the experimental units sampled are observed in their natural setting. No attempt is made to control the characteristics of the experimental units sampled. (Examples include *opinion polls* and *surveys*.)

*With published data, we often make a distinction between the *primary source* and *secondary source*. If the publisher is the original collector of the data, the source is primary. Otherwise, the data are secondary source.

Regardless of the data-collection method employed, it is likely that the data will be a sample from some population. And if we wish to apply inferential statistics, we must obtain a *representative sample*.

> A **representative sample** exhibits characteristics typical of those possessed by the population of interest.

For example, consider a political poll conducted during a presidential election year. Assume the pollster wants to estimate the percentage of all 145 million registered voters in the United States who favor the incumbent president. The pollster would be unwise to base the estimate on survey data collected for a sample of voters from the incumbent's own state. Such an estimate would almost certainly be *biased* high; consequently, it would not be very reliable.

The most common way to satisfy the representative sample requirement is to select a simple random sample. A **simple random sample** ensures that every subset of fixed size in the population has the same chance of being included in the sample. If the pollster samples 1,500 of the 145 million voters in the population so that every subset of 1,500 voters has an equal chance of being selected, she has devised a simple random sample.

> A **simple random sample** of n experimental units is a sample selected from the population in such a way that every different sample of size n has an equal chance of selection.

The procedure for selecting a simple random sample typically relies on a **random number generator**. Random number generators are available in table form, online,* and in most statistical software packages. The Excel/XLSTAT, Minitab, and SPSS statistical software packages all have easy-to-use random number generators for creating a random sample. The next two examples illustrate the procedure.

EXAMPLE 1.6

Generating a Simple Random Sample— Selecting Households for a Feasibility Study

Problem Suppose you wish to assess the feasibility of building a new high school. As part of your study, you would like to gauge the opinions of people living close to the proposed building site. The neighborhood adjacent to the site has 711 homes. Use a random number generator to select a simple random sample of 20 households from the neighborhood to participate in the study.

Solution In this study, your population of interest consists of the 711 households in the adjacent neighborhood. To ensure that every possible sample of 20 households selected from the 711 has an equal chance of selection (i.e., to ensure a simple random sample), first assign a number from 1 to 711 to each of the households in the population. These numbers were entered into an Excel worksheet. Now, apply the random number generator of Excel/ XLSTAT, requesting that 20 households be selected without replacement. Figure 1.5 shows one possible set of random numbers generated from XLSTAT. You can see that households numbered 40, 63, 108, . . . , 636 are the households to be included in your sample.

Look Back It can be shown (proof omitted) that there are over 3×10^{38} possible samples of size 20 that can be selected from the 711 households. Random number generators guarantee (to a certain degree of approximation) that each possible sample has an equal chance of being selected.

---

*One of many free online random number generators is available at www.randomizer.org.

	A	B	C	D	E	F	G	H	I	J	K
1	XLSTAT 2011.4.02 - Data sampling - on 11/4/2011 at 10:17:05 AM										
2	Data: Workbook = HOUSEHOLDS.xlsx / Sheet = Sheet1 / Range = Sheet1!$A:$A / 711 rows and 1 column										
3	Sampling method: Random without replacement										
4	Number of samples: 1										
5	Sample size: 20										
6	Seed (random numbers): 4186805										
7											
8											
9	Sampled data:										
10											
11	HOUSEHOLD										
12		40									
13		63									
14		108									
15		153									
16		190									
17		227									
18		283									
19		302									
20		309									
21		371									
22		379									
23		419									
24		434									
25		457									
26		463									
27		489									
28		536									
29		537									
30		560									
31		636									
32											

Figure 1.5

Random selection of 20 households using XLSTAT

● **Now Work Exercise 1.14**

The notion of random selection and randomization is also key to conducting good research with a designed experiment. The next example illustrates a basic application.

EXAMPLE 1.7	**Problem** A designed experiment in the medical field involving human subjects is referred to as a *clinical trial*. One recent clinical trial was designed to determine the potential of using aspirin in preventing heart attacks. Volunteer physicians were randomly divided into two groups—the *treatment* group and the *control* group. Each physician in the treatment group took one aspirin tablet a day for one year, while the physicians in the control group took an aspirin-free placebo made to look identical to an aspirin tablet. Because the physicians did not know which group, treatment or control, they were assigned to, the clinical trial is called a *blind study*. Assume 20 physicians volunteered for the study. Use a random number generator to randomly assign half of the physicians to the treatment group and half to the control group.
Randomization in a Designed Experiment— A Clinical Trial	

Solution Essentially, we want to select a random sample of 10 physicians from the 20. The first 10 selected will be assigned to the treatment group; the remaining 10 will be assigned to the control group. (Alternatively, we could randomly assign each physician, one by one, to either the treatment or the control group. However, this would not guarantee exactly 10 physicians in each group.)

The Minitab random sample procedure was employed, producing the printout shown in Figure 1.6. Numbering the physicians from 1 to 20, we see that physicians 8, 5, 18, 15, 11, 12, 9, 4, 19, and 20 are assigned to receive the aspirin (treatment). The remaining physicians are assigned the placebo (control).

● **Now Work Exercise 1.34e**

↓	C1	C2
	Physician	Treatment
1	1	8
2	2	5
3	3	18
4	4	15
5	5	11
6	6	12
7	7	9
8	8	4
9	9	19
10	10	20
11	11	
12	12	
13	13	
14	14	
15	15	
16	16	
17	17	
18	18	
19	19	
20	20	
21		

Figure 1.6

Minitab Worksheet with Random Assignment of Physicians

In addition to simple random samples, there are more complex random sampling designs that can be employed. These include (but are not limited to) **stratified random sampling, cluster sampling, systematic sampling,** and **randomized response sampling.** Brief descriptions of each follow. (For more details on the use of these sampling methods, consult the references at the end of this chapter.)

Stratified random sampling is typically used when the experimental units associated with the population can be separated into two or more groups of units, called *strata*, where the characteristics of the experimental units are more similar within strata than across strata. Random samples of experimental units are obtained for each strata; then the units are combined to form the complete sample. For example, if you are gauging opinions of voters on a polarizing issue, like government-sponsored health care, you may want to stratify on political affiliation (Republicans and Democrats), making sure that representative samples of both Republicans and Democrats (in proportion to the number of Republicans and Democrats in the voting population) are included in your survey.

Sometimes it is more convenient and logical to sample natural groupings (*clusters*) of experimental units first, and then collect data from all experimental units within each cluster. This involves the use of *cluster sampling*. For example, suppose a marketer for a large upscale restaurant chain wants to find out whether customers like the new menu. Rather than collect a simple random sample of all customers (which would be very difficult and costly to do), the marketer will randomly sample 10 of the 150 restaurant locations (clusters), and then interview all customers eating at each of the 10 locations on a certain night.

Another popular sampling method is *systematic sampling*. This method involves systematically selecting every *k*th experimental unit from a list of all experimental units. For example, every fifth person who walks into a shopping mall could be asked his or her opinion on a business topic of interest. Or, a quality control engineer at a manufacturing plant may select every 10th item produced on an assembly line for inspection.

A fourth alternative to simple random sampling is *randomized response sampling*. This design is particularly useful when the questions of the pollsters are likely to elicit false answers. For example, suppose each person in a sample of wage earners is asked whether he or she ever cheated on an income tax return. A cheater might lie, thus biasing an estimate of the true likelihood of someone cheating on his or her tax return. To circumvent this problem, each person is presented with two questions, one being the object of the survey and the other an innocuous question, such as:

1. Did you ever cheat on your federal income tax return?

2. Did you drink coffee this morning?

One of the questions is chosen at random to be answered by the wage earner by flipping a coin; however, which particular question is answered is unknown to the interviewer. In this way, the random response method attempts to elicit an honest response to a sensitive question. Sophisticated statistical methods are then employed to derive an estimate of the percentage of "yes" responses to the sensitive question.

No matter what type of sampling design you employ to collect the data for your study, be careful to avoid *selection bias*. Selection bias occurs when some experimental units in the population have less chance of being included in the sample than others. This results in samples that are not representative of the population. Consider an opinion poll that employs either a telephone survey or a mail survey. After collecting a random sample of phone numbers or mailing addresses, each person in the sample is contacted via telephone or the mail and a survey conducted. Unfortunately, these types of surveys often suffer from selection bias due to *nonresponse*. Some individuals may not be home when the phone rings, or others may refuse to answer the questions or mail back the questionnaire. As a consequence, no data are obtained for the nonrespondents in the sample. If the nonrespondents and respondents differ greatly on an issue, then *nonresponse bias* exits. For example, those who choose to answer a question on a school board issue may have a vested interest in the outcome of the survey—say, parents with children of school age, schoolteachers whose jobs may be in jeopardy, or citizens whose taxes might be substantially affected. Others with no vested interest may have an opinion on the issue but might not take the time to respond.

> **Selection bias** results when a subset of experimental units in the population has little or no chance of being selected for the sample.

> Consider a sample of experimental units where some units produce data (i.e., responders) and no data is collected on the other units (i.e., nonresponders). **Nonresponse bias** is a type of selection bias that results when the response data differ from the potential data for the nonresponders.

Finally, even if your sample is representative of the population, the data collected may suffer from *measurement error*. That is, the values of the data (quantitative or qualitative) may be inaccurate. In sample surveys, opinion polls, etc., measurement error often results from *ambiguous* or *leading questions*. Consider the survey question: "How often did you change the oil in your car last year?" It is not clear whether the researcher wants to know how often you personally changed the oil in your car or how often you took your car into a service station to get an oil change. The ambiguous question may lead to inaccurate responses. On the other hand, consider the question: "Does the new health plan offer more comprehensive medical services at less cost than the old one?" The way the question is phrased *leads* the reader to believe that the new plan is better and to a "yes" response—a response that is more desirable to the researcher. A better, more neutral way to phrase the question is: "Which health plan offers more comprehensive medical services at less cost, the old one or the new one?"

> **Measurement error** refers to inaccuracies in the values of the data collected. In surveys, the error may be due to ambiguous or leading questions and the interviewer's effect on the respondent.

We conclude this section with two examples involving actual sampling studies.

EXAMPLE 1.8

Method of Data Collection—Survey of Online Shoppers

Problem How do consumers feel about using the Internet for online shopping? To find out, United Parcel Service (UPS) commissioned a nationwide survey of 5,118 U.S. adults who had conducted at least two online transactions in 2015. One finding from the study is that 74% of online shoppers have used a smartphone to do their shopping.

a. Identify the data-collection method.

b. Identify the target population.

c. Are the sample data representative of the population?

Solution

a. The data-collection method is a survey: 5,118 adults completed the questionnaire.

b. Presumably, UPS (who commissioned the survey) is interested in all consumers who have made at least two online transactions in the past year. Consequently, the target population is *all* consumers who use the Internet for online transactions.

c. Because the 5,118 respondents clearly make up a subset of the target population, they do form a sample. Whether or not the sample is representative is unclear because UPS provided no detailed information on how the 5,118 respondents were selected. If the respondents were obtained using, say, random-digit telephone dialing, then the sample is likely to be representative because it is a random sample. However, if the questionnaire was made available to anyone surfing the Internet, then the respondents are *self-selected* (i.e., each Internet user who saw the survey chose whether or not to respond to it). Such a survey often suffers from *nonresponse* bias. It is possible that many Internet users who chose not to respond (or who never saw the questionnaire) would have answered the questions differently, leading to a lower (or higher) sample percentage.

Look Back Any inferences based on survey samples that employ self-selection are suspect due to potential nonresponse bias.

• **Now Work Exercise 1.27**

EXAMPLE 1.9

Representative Data— Price Promotion Study

Problem Marketers use wording such as "was $100, now $80" to indicate a price promotion. The promotion is typically compared to the retailer's previous price or to a competitor's price. A study in the *Journal of Consumer Research* investigated whether between-store comparisons result in greater perceptions of value by consumers than within-store comparisons. Suppose 50 consumers were randomly selected from all consumers in a designated market area to participate in the study. The researchers randomly assigned 25 consumers to read a within-store price promotion advertisement ("was $100, now $80") and 25 consumers to read a between-store price promotion ("$100 there, $80 here"). The consumers then gave their opinion on the value of the discount offer on a 10-point scale (where 1 = lowest value and 10 = highest value). The value opinions of the two groups of consumers were compared.

a. Identify the data-collection method.

b. Are the sample data representative of the target population?

Solution

a. Here, the experimental units are the consumers. Because the researchers controlled which price promotion ad—"within-store" or "between-store"—the experimental units (consumers) were assigned to, a designed experiment was used to collect the data.

b. The sample of 50 consumers was randomly selected from all consumers in the designated market area. If the target population is all consumers in this market, it is likely that the sample is representative. However, the researchers warn that the sample data should not be used to make inferences about consumer behavior in other, dissimilar markets.

Look Back By using randomization in a designed experiment, the researcher is attempting to eliminate different types of bias, including self-selection bias.

• **Now Work Exercise 1.19**

STATISTICS IN ACTION REVISITED

Identifying the Data-Collection Method and Data Type

Refer to the *New York Times* study on the link between a CEO's golf handicap and the company's stock performance. Recall that the newspaper gathered information on golf handicaps of corporate executives obtained from a *Golf Digest* survey that was sent to 300 corporate executives. Thus, the data-collection method is a survey. In addition to golf handicap (a numerical "index" that allows golfers to compare skills), the *Times* measured the CEO's company stock market performance over a 3-year period on a scale of 0 to 100. Because both variables, golf handicap and stock performance, are numerical in nature, they are quantitative data.

📊 *Data Set:* GLFCEO

1.7 Business Analytics: Critical Thinking with Statistics

According to H. G. Wells, author of such science-fiction classics as *The War of the Worlds*
and *The Time Machine*, "*Statistical thinking* will one day be as necessary for efficient
citizenship as the ability to read and write." Written more than a hundred years ago,
Wells's prediction is proving true today.

The growth in data collection associated with scientific phenomena, business operations, and government activities (e.g., marketing, quality control, statistical auditing,
forecasting, etc.) has been remarkable over the past decade. This growth is due, in part,
to technology now capable of capturing lots of data at a high rate, such as information-
sensing mobile devices, cameras, radio-frequency identification (RFID) readers, and
wireless sensor networks. In fact, the term "Big Data" is now commonly used by companies to describe this wealth of information.

However, with big data, comes the need for methods of analysis—**business
analytics**—that ultimately lead to good business decisions. A key to successful applications of business analytics is *quantitative literacy* (i.e., the ability to evaluate data intelli-
gently). Whether the data of interest is "big" or not, each of us has to develop the ability
to use rational thought to interpret and understand the meaning of the data. Business
analytics and quantitative literacy can help you make intelligent decisions, inferences,
and generalizations from data; that is, it helps you *think critically* using statistics. We
term this skill **statistical thinking**.

Business analytics refers to methodologies (e.g., statistical methods) that extract
useful information from data in order to make better business decisions.

Statistical thinking involves applying rational thought and the science of statistics
to critically assess data and inferences. Fundamental to the thought process is that
variation exists in populations and process data.

To gain some insight into the role statistics plays in business analytics, we present
two examples of some misleading or faulty surveys.

EXAMPLE 1.10

**Biased Sample—
Motorcycle Helmet Law**

Problem An article in the *New York Times* considered the question of whether motor-
cyclists should be required by law to wear helmets. In supporting his argument for no
helmets, the editor of a magazine for Harley-Davidson bikers presented the results of
one study that claimed "nine states without helmet laws had a lower fatality rate (3.05
deaths per 10,000 motorcycles) than those that mandated helmets (3.38)" and a survey
that found "of 2,500 bikers at a rally, 98% of the respondents opposed such laws." Based
on this information, do you think it is safer to ride a motorcycle without a helmet? What
further statistical information would you like?

Solution You can use statistical thinking to help you critically evaluate the study. For
example, before you can evaluate the validity of the 98% estimate, you would want to
know how the data were collected. If a survey was, in fact, conducted, it's possible that
the 2,500 bikers in the sample were not selected at random from the target population of all bikers, but rather were "self-selected." (Remember, they were all attending
a rally—a rally likely for bikers who oppose the law.) If the respondents were likely
to have strong opinions regarding the helmet law (e.g., strongly oppose the law), the
resulting estimate is probably biased high. Also, if the selection bias in the sample was
intentional, with the sole purpose to mislead the public, the researchers would be guilty
of **unethical statistical practice**.

You would also want more information about the study comparing the motorcycle fatality rate of the nine states without a helmet law to those states that mandate helmets. Were the data obtained from a published source? Were all 50 states included in the study, or were only certain states selected? That is, are you seeing sample data or population data? Furthermore, do the helmet laws vary among states? If so, can you really compare the fatality rates?

Look Back Questions such as these led a group of mathematics and statistics teachers attending an American Statistical Association course to discover a scientific and statistically sound study on helmets. The study reported a dramatic *decline* in motorcycle crash deaths after California passed its helmet law.

EXAMPLE 1.11

Manipulative or Ambiguous Survey Questions—Satellite Radio Survey

Problem Talk-show host Howard Stern moved his controversial radio program from free, over-the-air (AM/FM) radio to Sirius XM satellite radio. The move was perceived in the industry to boost satellite radio subscriptions. This led American Media Services, a developer of AM/FM radio properties, to solicit a nationwide random-digit dialing phone survey of 1,008 people. The purpose of the survey was to determine how much interest Americans really have in buying satellite radio service. After providing some background on Howard Stern's controversial radio program, one of the questions asked, "How likely are you to purchase a subscription to satellite radio after Howard Stern's move to Sirius?" The result: 86% of the respondents stated that they aren't likely to buy satellite radio because of Stern's move. Consequently, American Media Services concluded that "the Howard Stern Factor is overrated" and that "few Americans expect to purchase satellite radio"—claims that made the headlines of news reports and Web blogs. Do you agree?

Solution First, we need to recognize that American Media Services had a vested interest in the outcome of the survey—the company makes its money from over-the-air broadcast radio stations. Second, although the phone survey was conducted using random-digit dialing, there is no information provided on the response rate. It's possible that nonrespondents (people who were not home or refused to answer the survey questions) tend to be people who use cell phones more than their landline phone and, consequently, are more likely to use the latest in electronic technology, including satellite radio. Finally, the survey question itself is ambiguous. Do the respondents have negative feelings about satellite radio, Howard Stern, or both? If not for Howard Stern's program, would the respondents be more likely to buy satellite radio? To the critical thinker, it's unclear what the results of the survey imply.

Look Back Examining the survey results from the perspective of satellite radio providers, 14% of the respondents indicated that they would be likely to purchase satellite radio. Projecting the 14% back to the population of all American adults, this figure represents about 50 million people; what is interpreted as "few Americans" by American Media Services could be music to the ears of satellite radio providers.

As with many statistical studies, both the motorcycle helmet study and the satellite radio study are based on survey data. Most of the problems with these surveys result from the use of *nonrandom* samples. These samples are subject to potential errors, such as *selection bias, nonresponse bias*, and *measurement error*. Researchers who are aware of these problems and continue to use the sample data to make inferences are practicing *unethical statistics*.

As stated earlier, business analytics relies heavily on statistical thinking to help firms make better business decisions. The role statistics can play in a manager's use of business analytics is displayed in Figure 1.7. Every managerial decision-making problem begins with a real-world problem. This problem is then formulated in managerial terms

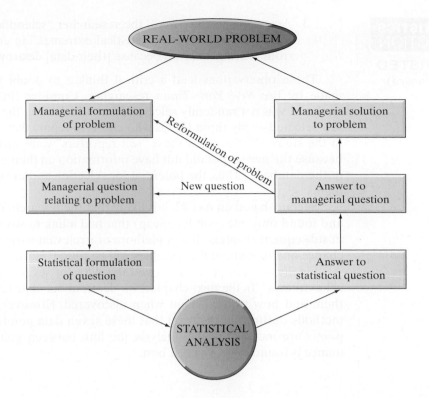

Figure 1.7

Flow diagram showing the role of statistics in business analytics
Source: From *The American Statistician* by George Benson. Copyright © by George Benson. Used by permission of George Benson.

and framed as a managerial question. The next sequence of steps (proceeding counterclockwise around the flow diagram) identifies the role that statistics can play in this process. The managerial question is translated into a statistical question, the sample data are collected and analyzed, and the statistical question is answered. The next step in the process is using the answer to the statistical question to reach an answer to the managerial question. The answer to the managerial question may suggest a reformulation of the original managerial problem, suggest a new managerial question, or lead to the solution of the managerial problem.

One of the most difficult steps in the decision-making process—one that requires a cooperative effort among managers and statisticians—is the translation of the managerial question into statistical terms (for example, into a question about a population). This statistical question must be formulated so that, when answered, it will provide the key to the answer to the managerial question. Thus, as in the game of chess, you must formulate the statistical question with the end result, the solution to the managerial question, in mind.

In the remaining chapters of the text , you'll become familiar with the business analytic tools essential for building a firm foundation in statistics and statistical thinking.

STATISTICS IN ACTION

REVISITED

Critically Assessing the Ethics of a Statistical Study

The *New York Times* reported a strong link between a corporate executive's golf handicap and his/her company's stock performance. Thus, the newspaper inferred that the better the CEO is at golf, the better the company's stock performance will be. To critically assess this study, consider the following facts:

1. *Golf Digest* sent surveys to the CEOs at the 300 largest U.S. firms. Only 74 executives agreed to reveal their golf handicaps. Of these 74 CEOs, the *Times* collected data on stock performance for only 51 of the companies. (The other 23 CEOs were not in the stock performance database used by the newspaper.)

2. The *New York Times* researcher who performed the analysis of the data stated that "for all the different factors I've tested as possible links to predicting which CEOs are going to perform well or poorly, [golf handicap] is certainly one of the ... strongest."

STATISTICS
IN ACTION

REVISTED
(continued)

3. According to the *Times*, the researcher "scientifically sifted out a handful of CEOs because of their statistical extremes," in effect "removing seven CEOs from the final analysis because [their data] destroyed the trend lines."

These observations lead a critical thinker to doubt the validity of the inference made by the *New York Times* researcher. Consider first that the sample of CEOs analyzed was not randomly selected from all CEOs in the United States. In fact, it was self-selected—only those CEOs who chose to report their golf handicap were included in the study. (Not even all these "self-reporters" were included; some were eliminated because the newspaper did not have information on their company's stock performance in the database.) Thus, the potential for selection and/or nonresponse bias is extremely high.

Second, based on fact #2, it is likely that the researcher tested a multitude of factors and found only one (golf handicap) that had a link to stock performance. We will learn in subsequent chapters that a plethora of irrelevant variables are tested statistically, by chance one or more of the variables will be found "statistically significant."

Finally, the researcher removed the data for seven CEOs based on their "statistical extremes." In the next chapter, we learn about statistical "outliers"—how to detect them and how to treat them when discovered. However, it can be shown (using the methods outlined in the text) that these seven data points are not outliers. If the data points are included in the analysis, the link between golf handicap and stock performance is found to be weak, at best.

 *Data Set:* GLFCEO

CHAPTER NOTES

Key Terms

Note: Starred (*) terms are from the optional section in this chapter.

*Black box 35	Qualitative data 38
Big data 45	Quantitative data 37
Business analytics 45	Quantitative literacy 45
Census 30	Randomized response
Cluster sampling 42	sampling 42
Data 27	Random number generator 40
Descriptive statistics 28	Reliability 33
Designed experiment 39	Representative sample 40
Experimental (or observational)	Sample 31
unit 30	Selection bias 43
Inference 28	Simple random sample 40
Inferential statistics 28	Statistical inference 31
Measurement 30	Statistical thinking 45
Measurement error 43	Statistics 27
Measure of reliability 33	Stratified random sampling 42
Nonresponse bias 43	Survey 39
Observational study 39	Systematic sampling 42
Population 30	Unethical statistical practice 45
*Process 34	Variable 30
Published source 39	

Key Ideas

Types of Statistical Applications

Descriptive

1. Identify **population** or **sample** (collection of **experimental units**)
2. Identify **variable(s)**

3. Collect **data**
4. **Describe** data

Inferential

1. Identify **population** (collection of *all* **experimental units**)
2. Identify **variable(s)**
3. Collect **sample** data (*subset* of population)
4. **Inference** about population based on sample
5. **Measure of reliability** for inference

Types of Data

1. **Quantitative** (numerical in nature)
2. **Qualitative** (categorical in nature)

Data-Collection Methods

1. **Observational** (e.g., survey)
2. **Published source**
3. **Designed experiment**

Types of Random Samples

1. **Simple random sample**
2. **Stratified random sample**
3. **Cluster sample**
4. **Systematic sample**
5. **Random response sample**

Problems with Nonrandom Samples

1. **Selection bias**
2. **Nonresponse bias**
3. **Measurement error**

EXERCISES 1.1–1.40

Note: Starred (*) exercises are from the optional section in this chapter.

Learning the Mechanics

1.1 What is statistics?

1.2 Explain the difference between descriptive and inferential statistics.

1.3 List and define the four elements of a descriptive statistics problem.

1.4 List and define the five elements of an inferential statistical analysis.

1.5 List the three major methods of collecting data and explain their differences.

1.6 Explain the difference between quantitative and qualitative data.

1.7 Explain how populations and variables differ.

1.8 Explain how populations and samples differ.

1.9 What is a representative sample? What is its value?

1.10 Why would a statistician consider an inference incomplete without an accompanying measure of its reliability?

*1.11 Give an example of unethical statistical practice.

1.12 Define *statistical thinking*.

1.13 Suppose you have to sort sample units into categories according to their region of origin. The regions are "Africa," "Americas," "Asia," "Europe," and "Oceania." For further analysis with a statistical software, you replace each region name with a numerical code: 1 for Africa, 2 for Americas, and so on. Are the data consisting of the region names qualitative or quantitative? Are the numerical codes qualitative or quantitative? Explain your answer.

1.14 Suppose that a production batch contains 1,000 units and you have to select 10 units for quality assurance. Use a random number generator to select a simple random sample of $n = 10$ from the production batch.

📊 Applet Exercise 1.1

The *Random Numbers* applet generates a list of n random numbers from 1 to N, where n is the size of the sample and N is the size of the population. The list generated often contains repetitions of one or more numbers.

a. Using the applet *Random Numbers*, enter 1 for the minimum value, 10 for the maximum value, and 10 for the sample size. Then click on *Sample*. Look at the results and list any numbers that are repeated and the number of times each of these numbers occurs.

b. Repeat part **a,** changing the maximum value to 20 and keeping the size of the sample fixed at 10. If you still have repetitions, repeat the process, increasing the maximum value by 10 each time but keeping the size of the sample fixed. What is the smallest maximum value for which you had no repetitions?

c. Describe the relationship between the population size (maximum value) and the number of repetitions in the list of random numbers as the population size increases and the sample size remains the same. What can you conclude about using a random number generator to choose a relatively small sample from a large population?

📊 Applet Exercise 1.2

The *Random Numbers* applet can be used to select a random sample from a population, but can it be used to simulate data? In parts **a** and **b,** you will use the applet to create data sets. Then you will explore whether those data sets are realistic.

a. In the activity *Keep the Change* on page 54, a data set called *Amounts Transferred* is described. Use the *Random Numbers* applet to simulate this data set by setting the minimum value equal to 0, the maximum value equal to 99, and the sample size equal to 30. Explain what the numbers in the list produced by the applet represent in the context of the activity. (You may need to read the activity.) Do the numbers produced by the applet seem reasonable? Explain.

b. Use the *Random Numbers* applet to simulate grades on a statistics test by setting the minimum value equal to 0, the maximum value equal to 100, and the sample size equal to 30. Explain what the numbers in the list produced by the applet represent in this context. Do the numbers produced by the applet seem reasonable? Explain.

c. Referring to parts **a** and **b,** why do the randomly generated data seem more reasonable in one situation than in the other? Comment on the usefulness of using a random number generator to produce data.

Applying the Concepts—Basic

1.15 **Performance-based logistics.** In industry, performance-based logistics (PBL) strategies are increasingly popular ways to reduce cost, increase revenue, and attain customer satisfaction. The *Journal of Business Logistics* (Vol. 36, 2015) used the opinions of a sample of 17 upper-level employees of the U.S. Department of Defense and its suppliers to determine the factors that lead to successful PBL projects. The current position (e.g., vice president, manager [mgr.]), type of organization (commercial or government), and years of experience were measured for each employee interviewed. These data are listed below. Identify each variable measured as producing quantitative or qualitative data.

Interviewee	Position	Organization	Experience (years)
1	Vice president	Commercial	30
2	Post production	Government	15
3	Analyst	Commercial	10
4	Senior mgr.	Government	30
5	Support chief	Government	30
6	Specialist	Government	25
7	Senior analyst	Commercial	9
8	Division chief	Government	6
9	Item mgr.	Government	3
10	Senior mgr.	Government	20
11	MRO mgr.	Government	25
12	Logistics mgr.	Government	30
13	MRO mgr.	Commercial	10
14	MRO mgr.	Commercial	5
15	MRO mgr.	Commercial	10
16	Specialist	Government	20
17	Chief	Government	25

1.16 **Jamming attacks on wireless networks.** Terrorists often use wireless networks to communicate. To disrupt these communications, the U.S. military uses jamming attacks on the wireless networks. The *International Journal of Production Economics* (Vol. 172, 2016) described a study of 80 such jamming attacks. The configuration of the wireless network attacked was determined in each case. Configuration consists of network type (WLAN, WSN, or AHN) and number of channels (single- or multi-channel).

a. Suppose the 80 jamming attacks represent all jamming attacks by the U.S. military over the past several years, and these attacks are the only attacks of interest to the researchers. Do the data associated with these 80 attacks represent a population or a sample? Explain.

b. The 80 jamming attacks actually represent a sample. Describe the population for which this sample is representative.

c. Identify the variable "network type" as quantitative or qualitative.

d. Identify the variable "number of channels" as quantitative or qualitative.

e. Explain how to measure number of channels quantitatively.

1.17 **Parking at a university.** Parking at a large university has become a big problem. The university's administrators want to determine the average parking time of its students. An administrator inconspicuously followed 250 students and carefully recorded the time it took them to find a parking spot.

a. What is the population of interest to the university administration?

b. Identify the sample of interest to the university administration.

c. What is the experimental unit of interest to the university administration?

d. What is the variable of interest to the university administration?

1.18 **College application data.** Colleges and universities are requiring an increasing amount of information about applicants before making acceptance and financial aid decisions. Classify each of the following types of data required on a college application as quantitative or qualitative.

a. High school GPA
b. Honors, awards
c. Applicant's score on the SAT or ACT
d. Gender of applicant
e. Parents' income
f. Age of applicant

1.19 **Customer orders at a department store.** A department store receives customer orders through its call center and website. These orders as well as any special orders received in the stores are forwarded to a distribution center where workers pull the items on the orders from inventory, pack them, and prepare the necessary paperwork for the shipping company that will pick up the packages and deliver them to the customers. In order to monitor the subprocess of pulling the items from inventory, one order is checked every 15 minutes to determine whether the worker has pulled the correct item.

a. Identify the process of interest.
b. Identify the variable of interest. Is it quantitative or qualitative?

c. Describe the sample.
d. Describe the inference of interest.
e. How likely is the sample to be representative?

1.20 **Stock prices.** As part of an economics class project, students were asked to randomly select 500 New York Stock Exchange (NYSE) stocks from the Wall Street Journal. They were then asked to summarize the current prices (also referred to as the closing price of the stock for a particular trading date) of the collected stocks using graphical and numerical techniques.

a. Identify the population of interest for this study.
b. Is the variable being collected quantitative or qualitative?
c. Identify the data collection method used in this study.
d. Identify the sample of interest for this study.
e. Identify the experimental unit and variable of interest for this study.

1.21 **Treasury deficit prior to the Civil War.** In *Civil War History* (June 2009), historian Jane Flaherty researched the condition of the U.S. Treasury on the eve of the Civil War in 1861. Between 1854 and 1857 (under President Franklin Pierce), the annual surplus/deficit was +18.8, +6.7, +5.3, and +1.3 million dollars, respectively. In contrast, between 1858 and 1861 (under President James Buchanan), the annual surplus/deficit was −27.3, −16.2, −7.2, and −25.2 million dollars, respectively. Flaherty used these data to aid in portraying the exhausted condition of the U.S. Treasury when Abraham Lincoln took office in 1861. Does this study represent a descriptive or inferential statistical study? Explain.

1.22 **The "lucky store effect" in lottery ticket sales.** In the *American Economic Review* (Vol. 98, 2008), University of Chicago researchers investigated the *lucky store effect* theory in lottery ticket sales, i.e., the theory that a lottery retail store that sold a large-prize-winning ticket will experience greater ticket sales the following week. The researchers examined the weekly ticket sales of all 24,400 active lottery retailers in Texas. The analysis showed that "the week following the sale of [a winning Lotto Texas ticket], the winning store experiences a 12 to 38 percent relative sales increase. . . . " Consequently, the researchers project that future winning lottery retail stores will experience the *lucky store effect*. Is this study an example of descriptive statistics or inferential statistics? Explain.

Applying the Concepts—Intermediate

1.23 **Consumer recycling behavior.** Under what conditions will consumers dispose of recyclable paper in the garbage? This was the question of interest in an article published in the *Journal of Consumer Research* (December, 2013). In one of the studies conducted, the researchers instructed 78 college students to cut an 8.5-×11-inch sheet of paper into eight smaller pieces. Half the students were randomly assigned to list five uses for the cut paper (*usefulness is salient* condition). The students in the other half were asked to list their five favorite TV shows (*control condition*). After completing an unrelated task, all students were asked to dispose of the paper upon leaving. There was a trash bin and a recycling bin outside the door. The researchers kept track of which students recycled and which students disposed of their paper in the garbage. This information was used to test the theory that students in the *usefulness is salient* condition will recycle at a higher rate than students in the *control* condition.

a. Explain why the data-collection method used in this study is a designed experiment.

b. Identify the experimental unit in this study.

c. Identify the variables measured in this study. What type of data (quantitative or qualitative) is produced from each variable? (*Hint:* Two variables are measured.)

d. About 68% of the students in the *usefulness is salient* condition recycled, as compared to 37% of students in the *control* condition. Use this information to make an inference about the population of interest.

1.24 **Who is better at multi-tasking?** In business, employees are often asked to perform a complex task when their attention is divided (i.e., *multi-tasking*). *Human Factors* (May 2014) published a study designed to determine whether video game players are better than non–video game players at multi-tasking. Each in a sample of 60 college students was classified as a video game player or a non-player. Participants entered a street crossing simulator and were asked to cross a busy street at an unsigned intersection. The simulator was designed to have cars traveling at various high rates of speed in both directions. During the crossing, the students also performed a memory task as a distraction. Two variables were measured for each student: (1) a street crossing performance score (measured out of 100 points) and (2) a memory task score (measured out of 20 points). The researchers found no differences in either the street crossing performance or memory task score of video game players and non-gamers. "These results," say the researchers, "suggest that action video game players [and non-gamers] are equally susceptible to the costs of dividing attention in a complex task."

a. Identify the experimental unit for this study.

b. Identify the variables measured as quantitative or qualitative.

c. Is this an application of descriptive statistics or inferential statistics? Explain.

1.25 **Zillow.com estimates of home values.** Zillow.com is a real estate Web site that provides free estimates of the market value of homes. A trio of University of Texas at San Antonio professors compared *Zillow* estimates to actual sale prices of homes and published their results in *The Appraisal Journal* (Winter 2010). The analysis was based on data collected for 2,045 single-family residential properties in Arlington, Texas, that sold during the last 6 months of 2006. Sale price and *Zillow* estimated value (in dollars) were measured for each property. *Zillow* claims that this market has one of its highest-accuracy ratings. However, the research revealed that *Zillow* overestimated the market value by more than 10% for nearly half of the properties.

a. What is the experimental unit for this study?

b. Describe the variables measured in the study. Do these variables produce quantitative or qualitative data?

c. Give a scenario where the 2,045 properties represent a population.

d. If the 2,045 properties represent a representative sample from a population, describe the population.

e. Suppose the relevant population is all single-family residential properties in the United States. Do you believe the 2,045 properties are representative of this population? Explain.

1.26 **Drafting NFL quarterbacks.** The National Football League (NFL) is a lucrative business, generating an annual revenue of about $8 million. One key to becoming a financially successful NFL team is drafting a good quarterback (QB) out of college. The NFL draft allows the worst-performing teams in the previous year the opportunity of selecting the best quarterbacks coming out of college. The *Journal of Productivity Analysis* (Vol. 35, 2011) published a study of how successful NFL teams are in drafting productive quarterbacks. Data were collected for all 331 quarterbacks drafted between 1970 and 2007. Several variables were measured for each QB, including draft position (one of the top 10 players picked, selection between picks 11 and 50, or selected after pick 50), NFL winning ratio (percentage of games won), and QB production score (higher scores indicate more productive QBs). The researchers discovered that draft position is only weakly related to a quarterback's performance in the NFL. They concluded that "quarterbacks taken higher [in the draft] do not appear to perform any better."

a. What is the experimental unit for this study?

b. Identify the type (quantitative or qualitative) of each variable measured.

c. Suppose you want to use this study to project the performance of future NFL QBs. Is this an application of descriptive or inferential statistics? Explain.

1.27 **The economic return to earning an MBA.** What are the economic rewards (e.g., higher salary) to obtaining an MBA degree? This was the question of interest in an article published in the *International Economic Review* (August 2008). The researchers made inferences based on wage data collected for a sample of 3,244 individuals who sat for the Graduate Management Admissions Test (GMAT). (The GMAT exam is required for entrance into most MBA programs.) The following sampling scheme was employed. All those who took the GMAT exam in any of four selected time periods were mailed a questionnaire. Those who responded to the questionnaire were then sent three follow-up surveys (one survey every 3 months). The final sample of 3,244 represents only those individuals who responded to all four surveys. (For example, about 5,600 took the GMAT in one time period; of these, only about 800 responded to all four surveys.)

a. For this study, describe the population of interest.

b. What method was used to collect the sample data?

c. Do you think the final sample is representative of the population? Why or why not? Comment on potential biases in the sample.

1.28 **Corporate sustainability and firm characteristics.** *Corporate sustainability* refers to business practices designed around social and environmental considerations (e.g., "going green"). *Business and Society* (March 2011) published a paper on how firm size and firm type impact sustainability behaviors. The researchers added questions on sustainability to a quarterly survey of Certified Public Accountants (CPAs). The survey was sent to approximately 23,500 senior managers at CPA firms, of which 1,293 senior managers responded. (*Note:* It is not clear how the 23,500 senior managers were selected.) Due to missing data (incomplete survey answers), only 992 surveys were analyzed. These data were used to infer whether larger firms are more likely to report sustainability policies than smaller firms and whether public firms are more likely to report sustainability policies than private firms.

a. Identify the population of interest to the researchers.
b. What method was used to collect the sample data?
c. Comment on the representativeness of the sample.
d. How will your answer to part **c** impact the validity of the inferences drawn from the study?

1.29 **Inspection of highway bridges.** All highway bridges in the United States are inspected periodically for structural deficiency by the Federal Highway Administration (FHWA). Data from the FHWA inspections are compiled into the National Bridge Inventory (NBI). Several of the nearly 100 variables maintained by the NBI are listed below. Classify each variable as quantitative or qualitative.

a. Length of maximum span (feet)
b. Number of vehicle lanes
c. Toll bridge (yes or no)
d. Average daily traffic
e. Condition of deck (good, fair, or poor)
f. Bypass or detour length (miles)
g. Route type (interstate, U.S., state, county, or city)

1.30 **Structurally deficient highway bridges.** Refer to Exercise 1.29. The NBI data were analyzed and the results made available at the FHWA Web site (www.fhwa.dot.gov). Using the FHWA inspection ratings, each of the 608,272 highway bridges in the United States was categorized as structurally deficient, functionally obsolete, or safe. About 13.5% of the bridges were found to be structurally deficient, while 3.5% were functionally obsolete.

a. What is the variable of interest to the researchers?
b. Is the variable of part a quantitative or qualitative?
c. Is the data set analyzed a population or a sample? Explain.
d. How did the NBI obtain the data for the study?

*1.31 **Monitoring product quality.** The Wallace Company of Houston is a distributor of pipes, valves, and fittings to the refining, chemical, and petrochemical industries. The company was a recent winner of the Malcolm Baldrige National Quality Award. One of the steps the company takes to monitor the quality of its distribution process is to send out a survey twice a year to a subset of its current customers, asking the customers to rate the speed of deliveries, the accuracy of invoices, and the quality of the packaging of the products they have received from Wallace.

a. Describe the process studied.
b. Describe the variables of interest.
c. Describe the sample.
d. Describe the inferences of interest.
e. What are some of the factors that are likely to affect the reliability of the inferences?

1.32 **Guilt in decision making.** The effect of guilt emotion on how a decision maker focuses on the problem was investigated in the *Journal of Behavioral Decision Making* (January 2007). A total of 171 volunteer students participated in the experiment, where each was randomly assigned to one of three emotional states (guilt, anger, or neutral) through a reading/writing task. Immediately after

the task, the students were presented with a decision problem (e.g., whether or not to spend money on repairing a very old car). The researchers found that a higher proportion of students in the guilty-state group chose to repair the car than those in the neutral-state and anger-state groups.

a. Identify the population, sample, and variables measured for this study.
b. Identify the data-collection method used.
c. What inference was made by the researcher?
d. In later chapters you will learn that the reliability of an inference is related to the size of the sample used. In addition to sample size, what factors might affect the reliability of the inference drawn in this study?

1.33 **Accounting and Machiavellianism.** *Behavioral Research in Accounting* (January 2008) published a study of Machiavellian traits in accountants. *Machiavellian* describes negative character traits that include manipulation, cunning, duplicity, deception, and bad faith. A questionnaire was administered to a random sample of 700 accounting alumni of a large southwestern university; however, due to nonresponse and incomplete answers, only 198 questionnaires could be analyzed. Several variables were measured, including age, gender, level of education, income, job satisfaction score, and Machiavellian ("Mach") rating score. The research findings suggest that Machiavellian behavior is not required to achieve success in the accounting profession.

a. What is the population of interest to the researcher?
b. What type of data (quantitative or qualitative) is produced by each of the variables measured?
c. Identify the sample.
d. Identify the data-collection method used.
e. What inference was made by the researcher?
f. How might the nonresponses impact the inference?

1.34 **Can money spent on gifts buy love?** Is the gift you purchased for that special someone really appreciated? This was the question of interest to business professors at Stanford University. Their research was published in the *Journal of Experimental Social Psychology* (Vol. 45, 2009). In one study, the researchers investigated the link between engagement ring price (dollars) and level of appreciation of the recipient (measured on a 7-point scale where 1 = "not at all" and 7 = "to a great extent"). Participants for the study were those who used a popular Web site for engaged couples. The Web site's directory was searched for those with "average" American names (e.g., "John Smith," "Sara Jones"). These individuals were then invited to participate in an online survey in exchange for a $10 gift certificate. Of the respondents, those who paid really high or really low prices for the ring were excluded, leaving a sample size of 33 respondents.

a. Identify the experimental units for this study.
b. What are the variables of interest? Are they quantitative or qualitative in nature?
c. Describe the population of interest.
d. Do you believe the sample of 33 respondents is representative of the population? Explain.
e. In a second designed study, the researchers investigated NW whether the link between gift price and level of appreciation is stronger for birthday gift-givers than for birthday gift-receivers. The participants were randomly

assigned to play the role of gift-giver or gift-receiver. Assume that the sample consists of 50 individuals. Use a random number generator to randomly assign 25 individuals to play the gift-receiver role and 25 to play the gift-giver role.

Applying the Concepts—Advanced

1.35 Bank corporate mergers. *Corporate merger* is a means through which one firm (the bidder) acquires control of the assets of another firm (the target). Recently, there was a frenzy of bank mergers in the United States, as the banking industry consolidated into more efficient and more competitive units.
   a. Construct a brief questionnaire (two or three questions) that could be used to query a sample of bank presidents concerning their opinions of why the industry is consolidating and whether it will consolidate further.
   b. Describe the population about which inferences could be made from the results of the survey.
   c. Discuss the pros and cons of sending the questionnaire to all bank presidents versus a sample of 200.

1.36 Random-digit dialing. To ascertain the effectiveness of their advertising campaigns, firms frequently conduct telephone interviews with consumers using *random-digit dialing*. With this approach, a random number generator mechanically creates the sample of phone numbers to be called. Each digit in the phone number is randomly selected from the possible digits 0, 1, 2, . . . , 9. Use the procedure to generate five seven-digit telephone numbers whose first three digits (area code) are 373.

1.37 Current population survey. The employment status (employed or unemployed) of each individual in the U.S. workforce is a set of data that is of interest to economists, businesspeople, and sociologists. To obtain information about the employment status of the workforce, the U.S. Bureau of the Census conducts what is known as the *Current Population Survey*. Each month interviewers visit about 50,000 of the 117 million households in the United States and question the occupants over 14 years of age about their employment status. Their responses enable the Bureau of the Census to *estimate* the percentage of people in the labor force who are unemployed (the *unemployment rate*).
   a. Define the population of interest to the Census Bureau.
   b. What variable is being measured? Is it quantitative or qualitative?
   c. Is the problem of interest to the Census Bureau descriptive or inferential?
   d. In order to monitor the rate of unemployment, it is essential to have a definition of *unemployed*. Different economists and even different countries define it in various ways. Develop your own definition of an "unemployed person." Your definition should answer such questions as: Are students on summer vacation unemployed? Are college professors who do not teach summer school unemployed? At what age are people considered to be eligible for the workforce? Are people who are out of work but not actively seeking a job unemployed?

*1.38 Monitoring the production of soft-drink cans. The Wakefield plant of Coca-Cola and Schweppes Beverages Limited (CCSB) can produce 4,000 cans of soft drink per minute. The automated process consists of measuring and dispensing the raw ingredients into storage vessels to create the syrup, and then injecting the syrup, along with carbon dioxide, into the beverage cans. In order to monitor the subprocess that adds carbon dioxide to the cans, five filled cans are pulled off the line every 15 minutes, and the amount of carbon dioxide in each of these five cans is measured to determine whether the amounts are within prescribed limits.
   a. Describe the process studied.
   b. Describe the variable of interest.
   c. Describe the sample.
   d. Describe the inference of interest.
   e. *Brix* is a unit for measuring sugar concentration. If a technician is assigned the task of estimating the average brix level of all 240,000 cans of beverage stored in a warehouse near Wakefield, will the technician be examining a process or a population? Explain.

1.39 Sampling TV markets for a court case. A recent court case involved a claim of satellite television subscribers obtaining illegal access to local TV stations. The defendant (the satellite TV company) wanted to sample TV markets nationwide and determine the percentage of its subscribers in each sampled market who have illegal access to local TV stations. To do this, the defendant's expert witness drew a rectangular grid over the continental United States, with horizontal and vertical grid lines every .02 degrees of latitude and longitude, respectively. This created a total of 500 rows and 1,000 columns, or $(500)(1,000) = 500,000$ intersections. The plan was to randomly sample 900 intersection points and include the TV market at each intersection in the sample. Explain how you could use a random number generator to obtain a random sample of 900 intersections. Develop at least two plans: one that numbers the intersections from 1 to 500,000 prior to selection and another that selects the row and column of each sampled intersection (from the total of 500 rows and 1,000 columns).

Critical Thinking Challenge

1.40 20/20 survey exposé. Refer to the "Statistics in Action" box of this chapter (p. 25). Recall that the popular prime-time ABC television program *20/20* presented several misleading (and possibly unethical) surveys in a segment titled "Fact or Fiction?—Exposés of So-Called Surveys." The information reported from two of these surveys and several others is listed here (actual survey facts are provided in parentheses).
   • *Quaker Oats study:* Eating oat bran is a cheap and easy way to reduce your cholesterol count. (Fact: Diet must consist of nothing but oat bran to achieve a slightly lower cholesterol count.)
   • *March of Dimes report:* Domestic violence causes more birth defects than all medical issues combined. (Fact: No study—false report.)
   • *American Association of University Women (AAUW) study:* Only 29% of high school girls are happy with themselves, compared to 66% of elementary school girls. (Fact: Of 3,000 high school girls, 29%

responded, "Always true" to the statement "I am happy the way I am." Most answered, "Sort of true" and "Sometimes true.")

- *Food Research and Action Center study:* One in four American children under age 12 is hungry or at risk of hunger. (Fact: Based on responses to questions: "Do you ever cut the size of meals?" and "Do you ever eat less than you feel you should?" and "Did you ever rely on limited numbers of foods to feed your children because you were running out of money to buy food for a meal?")

- *McKinsey survey on the health reform act:* Thirty percent of employers would "definitely" or "probably" stop offering health coverage to their employees if the government-sponsored act is passed. (Fact: Employers were asked leading questions that made it seem logical for them to stop offering insurance. For example, respondents were told that the new health insurance exchanges would become "an easy, affordable way for individuals to obtain health insurance" outside the company. Then they were given examples of how little their workers would pay for

this insurance. Only then were they asked how likely they would be to stop offering health insurance.)

- **a.** Refer to the Quaker Oats study relating oat bran to cholesterol levels. Discuss why it is unethical to report the results as stated.
- **b.** Consider the false March of Dimes report on domestic violence and birth defects. Discuss the type of data required to investigate the impact of domestic violence on birth defects. What data-collection method would you recommend?
- **c.** Refer to the AAUW study of self-esteem of high school girls. Explain why the results of the study are likely to be misleading. What data might be appropriate for assessing the self-esteem of high school girls?
- **d.** Refer to the Food Research and Action Center study of hunger in America. Explain why the results of the study are likely to be misleading. What data would provide insight into the proportion of hungry American children?
- **e.** Refer to the McKinsey survey on the health reform act. Explain what a "leading question" is and why it might produce responses that bias the results.

ACTIVITY 1.1   *Keep the Change:* Collecting Data

Bank of America has a savings program called *Keep the Change*. Each time a customer enrolled in the program uses his or her debit card to make a purchase, the difference between the purchase total and the next higher dollar amount is transferred from the customer's checking account to a savings account. For example, if you were enrolled in the program and used your debit card to purchase a latte for $3.75, then $0.25 would be transferred from your checking to your savings account. For the first 90 days that a customer is enrolled in the program, Bank of America matches the amounts transferred up to $250. In this and subsequent activities, we will investigate the potential benefit to the customer and cost to the bank.

1. Simulate the program by keeping track of all purchases that you make during one week that could be made with a debit card, even if you use a different form of payment. For each purchase, record both the purchase total and the amount that would be transferred from checking to savings with the *Keep the Change* program.

2. You now have two sets of data: *Purchase Totals* and *Amounts Transferred*. Both sets contain quantitative data. For each data set, identify the corresponding naturally occurring numerical scale. Explain why each set has an obvious lower bound but only one set has a definite upper bound.

3. Find the total of the amounts transferred for the one-week period. Because 90 days is approximately 13 weeks, multiply the total by 13 to estimate how much the bank would have to match during the first 90 days. Form a third data set, *Bank Matching*, by collecting the 90-day estimates of all the students in your class. Identify the naturally occurring scale, including bounds, for this set of data.

Keep the data sets from this activity for use in other activities. We suggest you save the data using statistical software (e.g., Minitab) or a graphing calculator.

ACTIVITY 1.2   **Identifying Misleading Statistics**

In the *Statistics in Action* feature at the beginning of this chapter, several examples of false or misleading statistics were discussed. Claims such as *One in four American children under age 12 is hungry or at risk of hunger* are often used to persuade the public or the government to donate or allocate more money to charitable groups that feed the poor. Researchers sometimes claim a relationship exists between two seemingly unrelated quantities such as a CEO's golf handicap and

the company's stock performance; such relationships are often weak at best and of little practical importance. Read the *Statistics in Action* and *Statistics in Action Revisited* features in this chapter before completing this activity.

1. Look for an article in a newspaper or on the Internet in which a large proportion or percentage of a population is purported to be "at risk" of some calamity, as in the

childhood hunger example. Does the article cite a source or provide any information to support the proportion or percentage reported? Is the goal of the article to persuade some individual or group to take some action? If so, what action is being requested? Do you believe that the writer of the article may have some motive for exaggerating the problem? If so, give some possible motives.

2. Look for another article in which a relationship between two seemingly unrelated quantities is purported to exist,

as in the CEO golf handicap and stock performance study. Select an article that contains some information on how the data were collected. Identify the target population and the data-collection method. Based on what is presented in the article, do you believe that the data are representative of the population? Explain. Is the purported relationship of any practical interest? Explain.

References

Careers in Statistics, American Statistical Association, 2011 (www.amstat.org).

Cochran, W. G. *Sampling Techniques*, 3rd ed. New York: Wiley, 1977.

Deming, W. E. *Sample Design in Business Research*. New York: Wiley, 1963.

Dillman, D. A., Smyth, J. D., and Christian, L. M. *Internet, Mail, and Mixed-Mode Surveys: The Tailored Design Method*. New York: Wiley, 2008.

Ethical Guidelines for Statistical Practice, American Statistical Association, 1999 (www.amstat.org).

Hahn, G. J. and Doganaksoy, N. *The Role of Statistics in Business and Industry*. New York: Wiley, 2008.

Huff, D. *How to Lie with Statistics*. New York: Norton, 1982 (paperback 1993).

Hoerl, R. and Snee, R. *Statistical Thinking: Improving Business Performance*. Boston: Duxbury, 2002.

Kish, L. *Survey Sampling*. New York: Wiley, 1965 (paperback, 1995).

Peck, R., Casella, G., Cobb, G., Hoerl, R., Nolan, D., Starbuck, R., and Stern, H. *Statistics: A Guide to the Unknown*, 4th ed. Cengage Learning, 2005.

Scheaffer, R., Mendenhall, W., and Ott, R. L. *Elementary Survey Sampling*, 6th ed. Boston: Duxbury, 2005.

What Is a Survey? American Statistical Association (F. Scheuren, editor), 2nd ed., 2005 (www.amstat.org).

USING TECHNOLOGY

Technology images shown here are taken from SPSS Statistics Professional 23, Minitab 17, XLSTAT, and Excel 2016.

SPSS: Accessing and Listing Data

When you start an SPSS session, you will see a screen similar to Figure 1.S.1. The main portion of the screen is an empty spreadsheet, with columns representing variables and rows representing observations (or cases). The very top of the screen is the SPSS main menu bar, with buttons for the different functions and procedures available in SPSS. Once you have entered data into the spreadsheet, you can analyze the data by clicking the appropriate menu buttons.

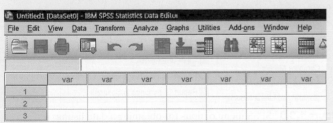

Figure 1.S.1 Initial screen viewed by the SPSS user

Entering Data

Step 1 To create an SPSS data file, enter data directly into the spreadsheet. See Figure 1.S.2, which shows data entered on a variable called "GPA."

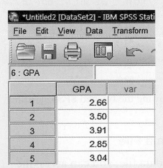

Figure 1.S.2 Data entered into the SPSS spreadsheet

Step 2 Name the variables (columns) by selecting the "Variable View" button at the bottom of the screen and typing in the name of each variable.

Opening an SPSS Data File

If the data have been previously saved as an SPSS (.sav) file, access the data as follows.

Step 1 Click the "File" button on the menu bar, and then click "Open" and "Data," as shown in Figure 1.S.3. A dialog box similar to Figure 1.S.4 will appear.

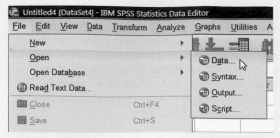

Figure 1.S.3 Options for opening an SPSS data file

Step 2 Specify the location (folder) that contains the data, click on the SPSS data file, and then click "Open" (see Figure 1.S.4). The data will appear in the SPSS spreadsheet, as shown in Figure 1.S.5.

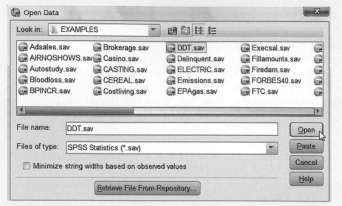

Figure 1.S.4 Selecting the SPSS data file to open

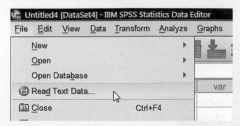

Figure 1.S.5 The SPSS spreadsheet showing the opened SPSS data file

Accessing External Data from a File

If the data are saved in an external data file, you can access the data using the options available in SPSS.

Step 1 Click the "File" button on the menu bar, and then click "Read Text Data," as shown in Figure 1.S.6. A dialog box similar to Figure 1.S.7 will appear.

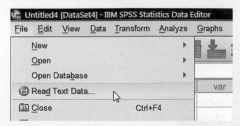

Figure 1.S.6 SPSS options for reading data from an external file

Step 2 Specify the location (folder) that contains the data file, click on the data file, and then click "Open," as shown in Figure 1.S.7. The SPSS Text Import Wizard Opens.

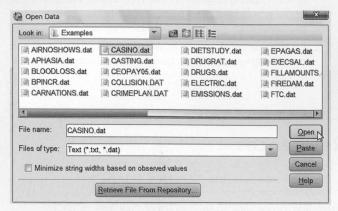

Figure 1.S.7 Selecting the external data file in SPSS

Step 3 The Text Import Wizard is a series of six screen menus. Make the appropriate selections on the screen, and click "Next" to go to the next screen.

Step 4 When finished, click "Finish." The SPSS spreadsheet will reappear with the data from the external data file.

Reminder: The variable (columns) can be named by selecting the "Variable View" button at the bottom of the spreadsheet screen and typing in the name of each variable.

Listing (Printing) Data

Step 1 Click on the "Analyze" button on the SPSS main menu bar, then click on "Reports," and then on "Report Summaries in Rows" (see Figure 1.S.8). The resulting menu, or dialog box, appears as in Figure 1.S.9.

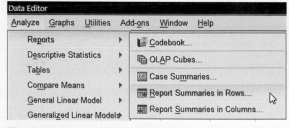

Figure 1.S.8 SPSS menu options for obtaining a data listing

Step 2 Enter the names of the variables you want to print in the "Data Columns" box (you can do this by simply clicking on the variables), check the "Display cases" box at the bottom left, and then click "OK." The printout will show up on your screen.

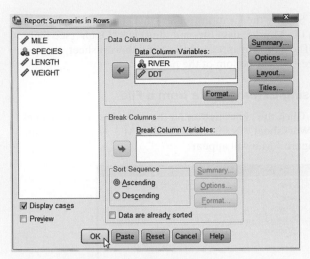

Figure 1.S.9 SPSS data report dialog box

SPSS: Generating a Random Sample

Step 1 Click on "Data" button on the SPSS menu bar and then click on "Select Cases," as shown in Figure 1.S.10. The resulting menu list appears as shown in Figure 1.S.11.

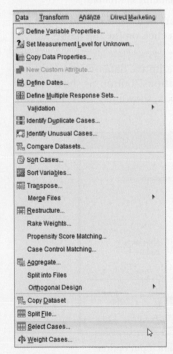

Figure 1.S.10 SPSS menu options for sampling from a data set

Step 2 Select "Random sample of cases" from the list and then click on the "Sample" button. The dialog box shown in Figure 1.S.12 will appear.

Step 3 Specify the sample size there as a percentage of cases or a raw number.

Step 4 Click "Continue" to return to the "Select Cases" dialog box (Figure 1.S.11) and then click "OK." The SPSS spreadsheet will reappear with the selected (sampled) cases.

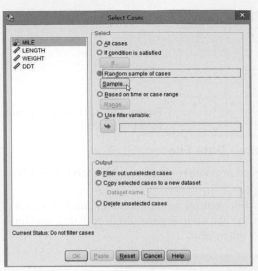

Figure 1.S.11 SPSS options for selecting a random sample

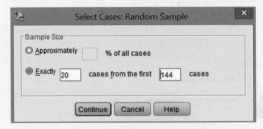

Figure 1.S.12 SPSS random sample dialog box

Minitab: Accessing and Listing Data

When you start a Minitab session, you will see a screen similar to Figure 1.M.1. The bottom portion of the screen is an empty spreadsheet—called a Minitab worksheet—with columns representing variables and rows representing observations (or cases). The very top of the screen is the Minitab main menu bar, with buttons for the different functions and procedures available in Minitab. Once you have entered data into the spreadsheet, you can analyze the data by clicking the appropriate menu buttons. The results will appear in the Session window.

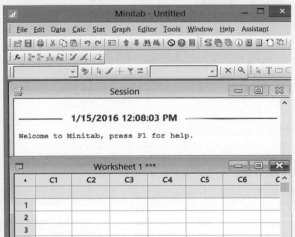

Figure 1.M.1 Initial screen viewed by the Minitab user

Entering Data

Create a Minitab data file by entering data directly into the worksheet. Figure 1.M.2 shows data entered for a variable called "GPA." Name the variables (columns) by typing in the name of each variable in the box below the column number.

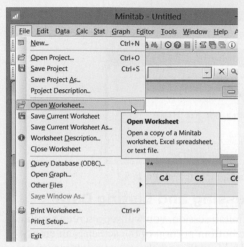

Figure 1.M.2 Data entered into the Minitab worksheet

Opening a Minitab Data File

If the data have been previously saved as a Minitab (.mtw) file, access the data as follows.

Step 1 Click the "File" button on the menu bar, and then click "Open Worksheet," as shown in Figure 1.M.3. A dialog box similar to Figure 1.M.4 will appear.

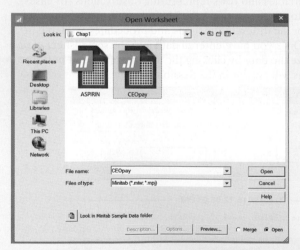

Figure 1.M.3 Options for opening a Minitab data file

Figure 1.M.4 Selecting the Minitab data file to open

Step 2 Specify the location (folder) that contains the data, click on the Minitab data file, and then click "Open" (see Figure 1.M.4). The data will appear in the Minitab worksheet, as shown in Figure 1.M.5 at bottom of the page.

Accessing External Data from a File

Step 1 Click the "File" button on the menu bar, and then click "Open Worksheet," as shown in Figure 1.M.3. A dialog box similar to Figure 1.M.6 will appear.

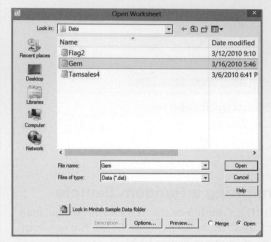

Figure 1.M.6 Selecting the external data file in Minitab

Step 2 Specify the location (folder) that contains the external data file and the file type, and then click on the file name, as shown in Figure 1.M.6.

Step 3 If the data set contains qualitative data or data with special characters, click on the "Options" button, as shown in Figure 1.M.6. The Options dialog box, shown in Figure 1.M.7, will appear.

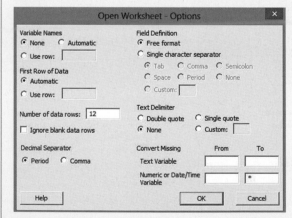

Figure 1.M.7 Selecting the Minitab data input options

↓	C1-T	C2	C3-T	C4	C5	C6	C7
	Employer	Rank	CEO	Total Pay	Median Worker Total Pay	Ratio of CEO Pay to Worker Pay	Overall Company Rating
1	Discovery Comm.	1	David M. Zaslav	$156,077,912	$80,000	1951	3.8
2	Chipotle	2	Steve Ells	$28,924,270	$19,000	1522	3.4
3	CVS Health	3	Larry J. Merlo	$32,350,733	$27,139	1192	2.7
4	Walmart >>	4	C. Douglas McMillon	$25,592,938	$22,591	1133	3.0
5	Target	5	Brian C. Cornell	$28,164,024	$30,000	939	3.2
6	CBS Corp	6	Leslie Moonves	$57,175,645	$66,365	862	3.5
7	Bed Bath & Beyond	7	Steven H. Temares	$19,116,040	$26,047	734	2.9
8	Macy's	8	Terry J. Lundgren	$16,497,220	$22,800	724	3.0
9	Gap	9	Glenn Murphy	$16,064,312	$22,800	705	3.6
10	Starbucks	10	Howard D. Schultz	$21,466,454	$32,080	669	3.8

Figure 1.M.5 The Minitab worksheet showing the opened Minitab data file

Step 4 Specify the appropriate options for the data set, and then click "OK" to return to the "Open Worksheet" dialog box (Figure 1.M.6).

Step 5 Click "Open" and the Minitab worksheet will appear with the data from the external data file.

Reminder: The variables (columns) can be named by typing in the name of each variable in the box under the column number.

Listing (Printing) Data

Step 1 Click on the "Data" button on the Minitab main menu bar, and then click on "Display Data." (See Figure 1.M.8.) The resulting menu, or dialog box, appears as in Figure 1.M.9.

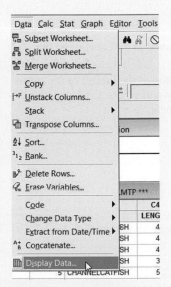

Figure 1.M.8 Minitab options for displaying data

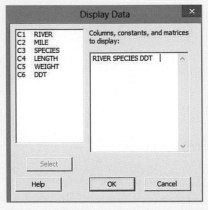

Figure 1.M.9 Minitab Display Data dialog box

Step 2 Enter the names of the variables you want to print in the "Columns, constants, and matrices to display" box (you can do this by simply double clicking on the variables), and then click "OK." The printout will show up on your Minitab session screen.

Minitab: Generating a Random Sample

Step 1 Click on the "Calc" button on the Minitab menu bar and then click on "Random Data," and finally, click on "Sample From Columns," as shown in Figure 1.M.10. The resulting dialog box appears as shown in Figure 1.M.11.

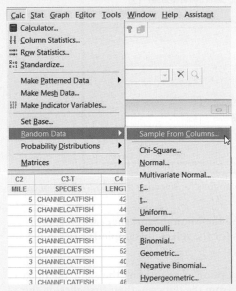

Figure 1.M.10 Minitab menu options for sampling from a data set

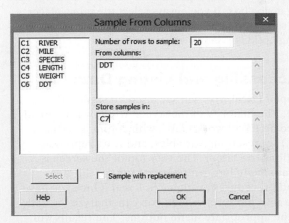

Figure 1.M.11 Minitab options for selecting a random sample from worksheet columns

Step 2 Specify the sample size (i.e., number of rows), the variable(s) to be sampled, and the column(s) where you want to save the sample.

Step 3 Click "OK" and the Minitab worksheet will reappear with the values of the variable for the selected (sampled) cases in the column specified.

In Minitab, you can also generate a sample of case numbers.

Step 1 From the Minitab menu, click on the "Calc" button and then click on "Random Data," and finally, click on the "Uniform" option (see Figure 1.M.10).

Step 2 In the resulting dialog box (shown in Figure 1.M.12), specify the number of cases (rows, i.e., the sample size), and the column where the case numbers selected will be stored.

Figure 1.M.12 Minitab options for selecting a random sample of cases

Step 3 Click "OK" and the Minitab worksheet will reappear with the case numbers for the selected (sampled) cases in the column specified.

[*Note:* If you want the option of generating the same (identical) sample multiple times from the data set, then first click on the "Set Base" option shown in Figure 1.M.10. Specify an integer in the resulting dialog box. If you always select the same integer. Minitab will select the same sample when you choose the random sampling options.]

Excel: Accessing and Listing Data

When you open Excel, you will see a screen similar to Figure 1.E.1. The majority of the screen window is a spreadsheet—called an Excel workbook—with columns (labeled A, B, C, etc.) representing variables, and rows representing observations (or cases). The very top of the screen is the Excel main menu bar, with buttons for the different functions and procedures available in Excel. Once you have entered data into the spreadsheet, you can analyze the data by clicking the appropriate menu buttons. The results will appear in a new workbook.

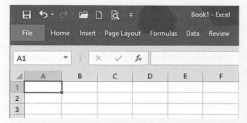

Figure 1.E.1 Initial screen viewed by Excel user

Entering Data

Enter data directly into the appropriate row and column of the spreadsheet. Figure 1.E.2 shows data entered in the first (A) column. Optionally, you can add names for the variables (columns) in the first row of the workbook.

Figure 1.E.2 Data entered into the Excel workbook

Opening an Excel File

If the data have been previously saved as an Excel (.xls) file, access the data as follows.

Step 1 Click the round Office button at the far left of the menu bar, and then click "Open," as shown in Figure 1.E.3. A dialog box similar to Figure 1.E.4 will appear.

Figure 1.E.3 Options for opening an Excel file

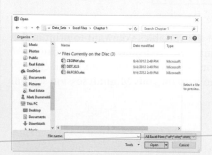

Figure 1.E.4 Selecting the Excel file to open

Step 2 Specify the location (folder) that contains the data, click on the Excel file, and then click "Open" (see Figure 1.E.4). The data will appear in the Excel spreadsheet as shown in Figure 1.E.5.

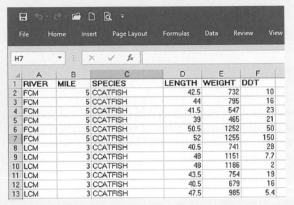

Figure 1.E.5 The Excel spreadsheet showing the opened Excel file

Accessing External Data from a File

Step 1 Click the "Office" button on the menu bar, and then click "Open," as shown in Figure 1.E.3. A dialog box similar to Figure 1.E.6 will appear.

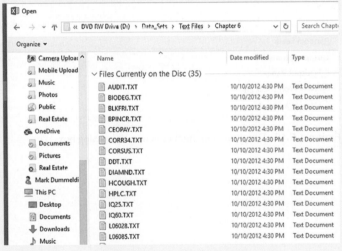

Figure 1.E.6 Selecting the external data file in Excel

Step 2 Specify the location (folder) that contains the external data file and the file type, and then click on the file name and click on "Open," as shown in Figure 1.E.6. The Excel Text Import Wizard opens (Figure 1.E.7).

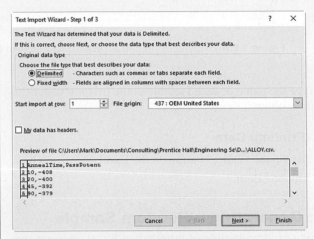

Figure 1.E.7 Excel Text Import Wizard, Screen 1

Step 3 Make the appropriate selections on the screen, and click "Next" to go to the next screen; then click "Next" again.

Step 4 When finished, click "Finish." The Excel workbook will reappear with the data from the external data file.

Naming Variables

Step 1 Select "Insert" from the Excel main menu, and then select "Rows." A blank (empty) row will be added in the first row of the spreadsheet.

Figure 1.E.8 Excel menu options for generating a random sample of numbers

Step 2 Type the name of each variable in the first row under the appropriate column.

Listing (Printing) Data

Step 1 Click on the "Office" button on the Excel main menu bar.

Step 2 Click on "Print."

Excel: Generating a Random Sample

To obtain a random sample of numbers in Excel, perform the following:

Step 1 Select "Data," and then "Data Analysis" from the Excel main menu bar, as shown in Figure 1.E.8 at the top of the page.

Step 2 Select "Random Number Generation" from the Data Analysis dialog box and then click "OK," as shown in Figure 1.E.9.

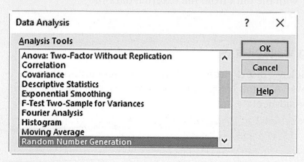

Figure 1.E.9 Excel data analysis tools options: Random number generation

Step 3 In the resulting menu (shown in Figure 1.E.10), specify the number of variables and number of random numbers you want to generate and select "Uniform" for the distribution. Click "OK" to generate the random numbers.

Figure 1.E.10 Excel random number generation dialog box

2

WHERE WE'VE BEEN

Examined the difference between
inferential and descriptive statistics

Described the key elements of a
statistical problem

Learned about the two types of data—
quantitative and qualitative

Discussed the role of statistical thinking
in managerial decision making

WHERE WE'RE GOING

Describe qualitative data using graphs
(2.1)

Describe quantitative data using
graphs (2.2)

Describe quantitative data using
numerical measures (2.3–2.7)

Describe the relationship between two
quantitative variables using graphs
(2.8–2.9)

Detecting descriptive methods that
distort the truth (2.10)

Methods for Describing Sets of Data

STATISTICS IN ACTION   Can Money Buy Love?

*Every day, millions of shoppers hit the stores in full force—both online and on foot—
searching frantically for the perfect gift. . . . Americans [spend] over $30 billion at retail
stores in the month of December alone. [Yet] many dread the thought of buying gifts; they
worry that their purchases will disappoint rather than delight the intended recipients.**

With this paragraph, Stanford University Graduate School of Business researchers
Francis J. Flynn and Gabrielle S. Adams introduce their study "Money Can't Buy Love:
Asymmetric Beliefs About Gift Price and Feelings of Appreciation," published in the
Journal of Experimental Social Psychology (Vol. 45, 2009). The researchers investigated the relationship between the price paid for a gift and the level of appreciation
felt by the recipient. Gift-givers who spend more money on a gift often do so to send
a strong signal of their love to the recipient. The researchers theorized that these gift-
givers would expect the recipient to express a high level of appreciation for the gift.
However, the researchers did not expect gift-recipients to associate a greater level of
appreciation with a higher gift price. That is, "The link between gift price and feelings
of appreciation will be stronger for gift-givers than for gift-recipients."

To test this theory, the researchers conducted an experimental study involving a
representative sample of 237 adults from across the nation. Each subject completed
an online survey in exchange for a $5 gift certificate to a major online retailer. The
survey asked questions about a birthday gift that the subject either received or
gave. The participants were randomly assigned to the role of either gift-giver or

*Source: Republished with permission of Elsevier, from Money can't buy love: Asymmetric beliefs about
gift price and feelings of appreciation in *Journal of Experimental Social Psychology*, Francis J. Flynn
and Gabrielle S. Adams, Volume 45, no. 02, pp. 404–409, 2009; permission conveyed through Copyright
Clearance Center, Inc.

STATISTICS
IN ACTION
(continued)

gift-receiver. (In other words, gift-givers were asked about a birthday gift they recently gave, while gift-recipients were asked about a birthday gift they recently received.) Gifts of cash, gift cards, or gift certificates were excluded from the study. Data were collected on the following variables measured for each participant:

1. *Role* (gift-giver or gift-recipient)
2. *Gender* (male or female)
3. *Gift price* (measured in dollars)
4. *Feeling of appreciation* (measured on a 7-point scale in response to the question: "To what extent do you or does the recipient appreciate this gift?," where 1 = "Not at all," 2 = "A little," 3 = "More than a little," 4 = "Somewhat," 5 = "Moderately so," 6 = "Very much," and 7 = "To a great extent")
5. *Feeling of gratefulness* (measured on a 7-point scale in response to the question: "To what extent do you or does the recipient feel grateful for this gift?," where 1 = "Not at all," 2 = "A little," 3 = "More than a little," 4 = "Somewhat," 5 = "Moderately so," 6 = "Very much," and 7 = "To a great extent")
6. *Overall level of appreciation* (measured as the sum of the two 7-point scales—possible values are 2, 3, 4, . . . , 13, and 14)

These data are saved in the **BUYLOV** file.

The Stanford University researchers' analysis of the data led them to conclude that "gift-givers and gift-receivers disagree about the link between gift price and gift-recipients' feelings of appreciation. Givers anticipated that recipients would appreciate more expensive gifts, but gift-recipients did not base their feelings of appreciation on how much the gift cost."

In the following *Statistics in Action Revisited* sections, we apply the graphical and numerical descriptive techniques of this chapter to the **BUYLOV** data to demonstrate the conclusions reached by the Stanford University researchers.

STATISTICS IN ACTION REVISITED

- Interpreting pie charts and bar graphs **(p. 70)**
- Interpreting histograms **(p. 81)**
- Interpreting numerical descriptive measures **(p. 109)**
- Detecting outliers **(p. 124)**
- Interpreting scatterplots **(p. 130)**

Data Set: BUYLOVE

Suppose you wish to evaluate the managerial capabilities of a class of 400 MBA students based on their Graduate Management Aptitude Test (GMAT) scores. How would you describe these 400 measurements? Characteristics of the data set include the typical or most frequent GMAT score, the variability in the scores, the highest and lowest scores, the "shape" of the data, and whether or not the data set contains any unusual scores. Extracting this information by "eye-balling" the data isn't easy. The 400 scores may provide too many bits of information for our minds to comprehend. Clearly, we need some formal methods for summarizing and characterizing the information in such a data set. Methods for describing data sets are also essential for statistical inference. Most populations make for large data sets. Consequently, we need methods for describing a sample data set that let us make statements (inferences) about the population from which the sample was drawn.

Two methods for describing data are presented in this chapter, one *graphical* and the other *numerical*. Both play an important role in statistics. Section 2.1 presents both graphical and numerical methods for describing qualitative data. Graphical methods for describing quantitative data are presented in Sections 2.2, 2.7, 2.9, and optional Section 2.8; numerical descriptive methods for quantitative data are presented in Sections 2.3–2.6. We end this chapter with a section on the *misuse* of descriptive techniques.

2.1 Describing Qualitative Data

Recall the study of executive compensation by Glassdoor Economic Research firm (see Study 1.2 in Section 1.2). In addition to salary information, personal data on the CEOs was collected, including level of education. Do most CEOs have advanced degrees, such as master's degrees or doctorates? To answer this question, Table 2.1 gives the highest college degree obtained (bachelor's, MBA, master's, law, PhD, or no terminal degree) for each of the CEOs at the 40 top ranked companies (based on ratio of CEOs' pay to workers' pay) in 2015.

Rank	Employer	CEO	Salary ($ millions)	Degree	Age	Ratio
1	Discovery Comm.	David M. Zaslav	156.08	Law	56	1951
2	Chipotle	Steve Ells	28.92	Bachelor's	49	1522
3	CVS Health	Larry J. Merlo	32.35	Bachelor's	60	1192
4	Walmart	C. Douglas McMillon	25.59	MBA	49	1133
5	Target	Brian C. Cornell	28.16	Bachelor's	56	939
6	CBS Corp.	Leslie Moonves	57.18	Bachelor's	66	862
7	Bed Bath & Beyond	Steven H. Temares	19.12	Law	57	734
8	Macy's	Terry J. Lundgren	16.50	Bachelor's	64	724
9	Gap	Art Peck	16.06	MBA	59	705
10	Starbucks	Howard D. Schultz	21.47	Bachelor's	62	669
11	Kroger	W. Rodney McMullen	12.99	Master's	54	636
12	Ross Stores	Barbara Rentler	12.08	Bachelor's	58	632
13	Time Warner Cable	Robert D. Marcus	34.62	Law	50	629
14	Microsoft	Satya Nadella	84.31	MBA	48	615
15	Walt Disney Co.	Robert A. Iger	46.50	Bachelor's	64	587
16	Oracle	Lawrence J. Ellison	67.26	None	71	573
17	Best Buy	Hubert Joly	13.88	Bachelor's	57	552
18	Comcast	Brian L. Roberts	32.96	Bachelor's	56	552
19	Viacom	Philippe P. Dauman	44.33	Law	61	540
20	Walgreens	Gregory D. Wasson	16.73	Bachelor's	57	540
21	UPS	D. Scott Davis	16.99	Bachelor's	63	533
22	Regeneron Pharma	Leonard S. Schleifer	41.97	PhD	63	529
23	Polo Ralph Lauren	Ralph Lauren	24.54	None	76	517
24	Prudential	J. R. Strangfeld	37.48	MBA	61	515
25	Qualcomm	Steven Mollenkopf	60.74	Master's	46	501
26	TJX Companies	Carol Meyrowitz	22.51	Bachelor's	62	501
27	Wynn Resorts	Stephen A. Wynn	25.32	Bachelor's	73	497
28	Staples	Ronald L. Sargent	12.39	MBA	60	488
29	Marriott	Arne M. Sorenson	14.89	Law	56	486
30	Wells Fargo	John G. Stumpf	21.43	MBA	62	484
31	Lowe's	Robert A. Niblock	14.28	Bachelor's	52	480
32	Coca-Cola Company	Muhtar Kent	25.22	MBA	64	460
33	U.S. Bank	Richard K. Davis	19.37	Bachelor's	57	445
34	Mondelez Intl.	Irene Rosenfeld	21.04	PhD	62	427
35	J.P. Morgan	James Dimon	27.70	MBA	59	424
36	Michael Kors	John D. Idol	13.56	None	56	424
37	Cablevision Systems	James L. Dolan	23.70	Bachelor's	60	422
38	GE	Jeffrey R. Immelt	37.25	MBA	59	418
39	Kohl's	Kevin Mansell	9.67	None	62	417
40	Ameriprise	James M. Cracchiolo	24.46	Master's	57	415

Data Set: CEO40

For this study, the variable of interest, highest college degree obtained, is qualitative in nature. Qualitative data are nonnumerical; thus, the value of a qualitative variable can be classified only into categories called *classes*. The possible degree types— bachelor's, MBA, master's, law, PhD, or none—represent the classes for this qualitative variable. We can summarize such data numerically in two ways: (1) by computing the *class frequency*—the number of observations in the data set that fall into each class; or (2) by computing the *class relative frequency*—the proportion of the total number of observations falling into each class.

A **class** is one of the categories into which qualitative data can be classified.

The **class frequency** is the number of observations in the data set falling into a particular class.

The **class relative frequency** is the class frequency divided by the total number of observations in the data set; that is,

$$\text{class relative frequency} = \frac{\text{class frequency}}{n}$$

Examining Table 2.1, we observe that 4 of the 40 best-paid CEOs did not obtain a college degree, 17 obtained bachelor's degrees, 9 MBAs, 3 master's degrees, 2 PhDs, and 5 law degrees. These numbers—4, 17, 9, 3, 2, and 5—represent the class frequencies for the six classes and are shown in the summary table, Figure 2.1, produced using SPSS.

The **class percentage** is the class relative frequency multiplied by 100; that is,

$$\text{class percentage} = (\text{class relative frequency}) \times 100$$

Figure 2.1 also gives the relative frequency of each of the five degree classes. We know that we calculate the relative frequency by dividing the class frequency by the total number of observations in the data set. Thus, the relative frequencies for the five degree types are

$$\text{Bachelor's: } \frac{17}{40} = .425$$

$$\text{Law: } \frac{5}{40} = .125$$

$$\text{Master's: } \frac{3}{40} = .075$$

$$\text{MBA: } \frac{9}{40} = .225$$

$$\text{None: } \frac{4}{40} = .10$$

$$\text{PhD: } \frac{2}{40} = .05$$

These values, expressed as a percentage, are shown in the "Percent" column in the SPSS summary table, Figure 2.1. If we sum the relative frequencies for MBA, master's, law, and PhD, we obtain .225 + .075 + .125 + .05 = .475. Therefore, 47.5% of the 40 best-paid CEOs obtained at least a master's degree (MBA, master's, law, or PhD).

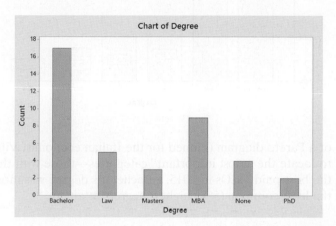

Degree

		Frequency	Percent	Valid Percent	Cumulative Percent
Valid	Bachelor	17	42.5	42.5	42.5
	Law	5	12.5	12.5	55.0
	Masters	3	7.5	7.5	62.5
	MBA	9	22.5	22.5	85.0
	None	4	10.0	10.0	95.0
	PhD	2	5.0	5.0	100.0
	Total	40	100.0	100.0	

Figure 2.1

SPSS Summary Table for Degrees of 40 CEOs

Figure 2.2

Minitab Bar Graph for Degrees of 40 CEOs

BIOGRAPHY

VILFREDO PARETO (1843–1923)
The Pareto Principle

Born in Paris to an Italian aristocratic family, Vilfredo Pareto was educated at the University of Turin, where he studied engineering and mathematics. After the death of his parents, Pareto quit his job as an engineer and began writing and lecturing on the evils of the economic policies of the Italian government. While at the University of Lausanne in Switzerland in 1896, he published his first paper, "Cours d'economie politique." In the paper, Pareto derived a complicated mathematical formula to prove that the distribution of income and wealth in society is not random but that a consistent pattern appears throughout history in all societies. Essentially, Pareto showed that approximately 80% of the total wealth in a society lies with only 20% of the families. This famous law about the "vital few and the trivial many" is widely known as the Pareto principle in economics.

Although the summary table in Figure 2.1 adequately describes the data in Table 2.1, we often want a graphical presentation as well. Figures 2.2 and 2.3 show two of the most widely used graphical methods for describing qualitative data—**bar graphs** and **pie charts.** Figure 2.2 is a bar graph for "highest degree obtained" produced with Minitab. Note that the height of the rectangle, or "bar," over each class is equal to the class frequency. (Optionally, the bar heights can be proportional to class relative frequencies.) In contrast, Figure 2.3 (also created using Minitab) shows the relative frequencies (expressed as a percentage) of the six degree types in a *pie chart.* Note that the pie is a circle (spanning 360°), and the size (angle) of the "pie slice" assigned to each class is proportional to the class relative frequency. For example, the slice assigned to the MBA degree is 22.5% of 360°, or $(.225)(360°) = 81°$.

Before leaving the data set in Table 2.1, consider the bar graph shown in Figure 2.4, produced using SPSS with annotations. Note that the bars for the CEO degree categories are arranged in descending order of height from left to right across the horizontal axis—that is, the tallest bar (MBA) is positioned at the far left and the shortest bar is at the far right. This rearrangement of the bars in a bar graph is called a Pareto diagram. One goal

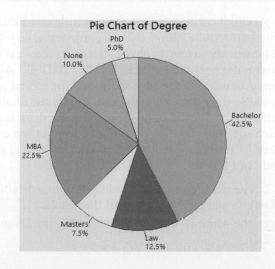

Figure 2.3

Minitab Pie Chart for Degrees of 40 CEOs

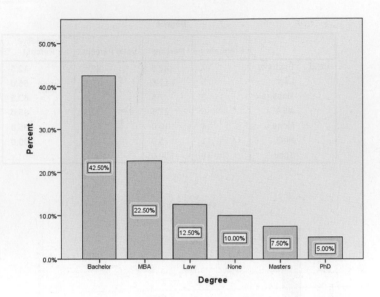

Figure 2.4

SPSS Pareto Diagram for Degrees of 40 CEOs

of a Pareto diagram (named for the Italian economist Vilfredo Pareto) is to make it easy to locate the "most important" categories—those with the largest frequencies. For 40 of the best-paid CEOs in 2015, a Bachelor's degree was most common (42.5%) and a PhD the least common (5%) highest degree obtained.

Summary of Graphical Descriptive Methods for Qualitative Data

Bar graph: The categories (classes) of the qualitative variable are represented by bars, where the height of each bar is either the class frequency, class relative frequency, or class percentage.

Pie chart: The categories (classes) of the qualitative variable are represented by slices of a pie (circle). The size of each slice is proportional to the class relative frequency.

Pareto diagram: A bar graph with the categories (classes) of the qualitative variable (i.e., the bars) arranged by height in descending order from left to right.

Let's look at a practical example that requires interpretation of the graphical results.

EXAMPLE 2.1

Graphing and Summarizing Qualitative Data—Blood Loss Study

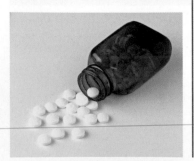

Problem A group of cardiac physicians in southwest Florida have been studying a new drug designed to reduce blood loss in coronary artery bypass operations. Blood loss data for 114 coronary artery bypass patients (some who received a dosage of the drug and others who did not) are saved in the **BLOOD** file. Although the drug shows promise in reducing blood loss, the physicians are concerned about possible side effects and complications. So their data set includes not only the qualitative variable, DRUG, which indicates whether or not the patient received the drug, but also the qualitative variable, COMP, which specifies the type (if any) of complication experienced by the patient. The four values of COMP recorded by the physicians are (1) redo surgery, (2) post-op infection, (3) both, or (4) none.

a. Figure 2.5, generated using SPSS, shows summary tables for the two qualitative variables, DRUG and COMP. Interpret the results.

b. Interpret the Minitab output shown in Figure 2.6 and the SPSS output shown in Figure 2.7.

Solution

a. The top table in Figure 2.5 is a summary frequency table for DRUG. Note that exactly half (57) of the 114 coronary artery bypass patients received the drug and half did not. The bottom table in Figure 2.5 is a summary frequency table for COMP. We see that about 69% of the 114 patients had no complications, leaving about 31% who experienced either a redo surgery, a post-op infection, or both.

DRUG

		Frequency	Percent	Valid Percent	Cumulative Percent
Valid	NO	57	50.0	50.0	50.0
	YES	57	50.0	50.0	100.0
	Total	114	100.0	100.0	

COMP

		Frequency	Percent	Valid Percent	Cumulative Percent
Valid	BOTH	6	5.3	5.3	5.3
	INFECT	15	13.2	13.2	18.4
	NONE	79	69.3	69.3	87.7
	REDO	14	12.3	12.3	100.0
	Total	114	100.0	100.0	

Figure 2.5

SPSS summary tables for DRUG and COMP

b. Figure 2.6 is a Minitab side-by-side bar graph for the data. The four bars on the left represent the frequencies of COMP for the 57 patients who did not receive the drug; the four bars on the right represent the frequencies of COMP for the 57 patients who did receive a dosage of the drug. The graph clearly shows that patients who did not get the drug suffered fewer complications. The exact percentages are displayed in the SPSS summary tables of Figure 2.7. About 56% of the patients who got the drug had no complications, compared with about 83% for the patients who did not get the drug.

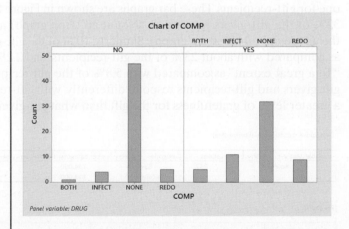

Figure 2.6

Minitab side-by-side bar graphs for COMP, by value of DRUG

COMP

DRUG			Frequency	Percent	Valid Percent	Cumulative Percent
NO	Valid	BOTH	1	1.8	1.8	1.8
		INFECT	4	7.0	7.0	8.8
		NONE	47	82.5	82.5	91.2
		REDO	5	8.8	8.8	100.0
		Total	57	100.0	100.0	
YES	Valid	BOTH	5	8.8	8.8	8.8
		INFECT	11	19.3	19.3	28.1
		NONE	32	56.1	56.1	84.2
		REDO	9	15.8	15.8	100.0
		Total	57	100.0	100.0	

Figure 2.7

SPSS summary tables for COMP by value of DRUG

Look Back Although these results show that the drug may be effective in reducing blood loss, Figures 2.6 and 2.7 imply that patients on the drug may have a higher risk of complications. But before using this information to make a decision about the drug, the physicians will need to provide a measure of reliability for the inference—that is, the physicians will want to know whether the difference between the percentages of patients with complications observed in this sample of 114 patients is generalizable to the population of all coronary artery bypass patients.

● **Now Work Exercise 2.12**

| STATISTICS IN ACTION | **Interpreting Pie Charts and Bar Graphs** |

REVISITED   In the *Journal of Experimental Social Psychology* (Vol. 45, 2009) study on whether money can buy love, Stanford University researchers measured several qualitative (categorical) variables for each of 237 adults: *Gender* (male or female), *Role* (gift-giver or gift-recipient), *Feeling of appreciation for the gift* (measured on an ordinal 7-point scale), and *Feeling of gratefulness for the gift* (measured on an ordinal 7-point scale). We classify the last two variables listed as qualitative, since the numerical values represent distinct response categories (e.g., 1 = "Not at all," 2 = "A little," 3 = "More than a little," 4 = "Somewhat," 5 = "Moderately so," 6 = "Very much," and 7 = "To a great extent") that portray an opinion on how one feels about giving or receiving a gift. Pie charts and bar graphs can be used to summarize and describe the responses for these variables. Recall that the data are saved in the **BUYLOV** file. We used Excel/XLSTAT and SPSS to create pie charts for two of these variables: Role (Figure SIA2.1) and Feeling of Gratefulness (Figure SIA2.2).

First, notice in Figure SIA2.1 that of the 237 adults, 56.5% were gift-givers and 43.5% were gift-recipients. Next, from Figure SIA2.2 you can see that 21.9% of adults responded, "Not at all" to the Feeling of gratefulness question, compared with 3.8% who responded, "To a great extent."

Of interest in the study is whether gift-givers and gift-recipients would respond differently to the Feeling of gratefulness question. We can gain insight into this question by forming bar graphs of the Feeling of gratefulness responses, one graph for gift-givers and one for gift-recipients. These bar graphs are shown in Figure SIA2.3. You can see that about 32% of the gift-givers responded, "Not at all" (top graph) as compared with about 9% of the gift-recipients (bottom graph). Similarly, 10% of the gift-givers responded, "Somewhat" as compared with about 23% of the gift-recipients, and 2.2% of the gift-givers responded, "To a great extent" as compared with 5.8% of the gift-recipients. Thus, it does appear that gift-givers and gift-recipients respond differently, with gift-recipients more likely to express a greater level of gratefulness for the gift than what gift-givers perceive.

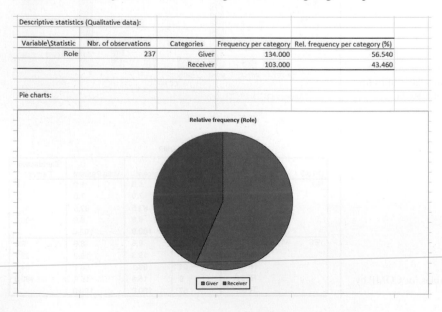

Figure SIA2.1

XLSTAT pie chart for role

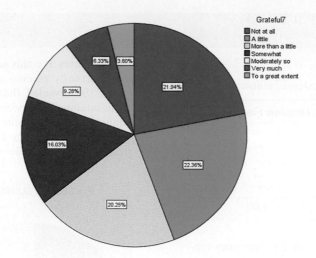

Figure SIA2.2

SPSS pie chart for feeling of
gratefulness

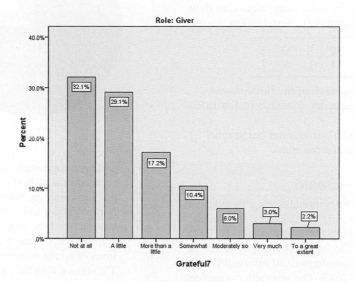

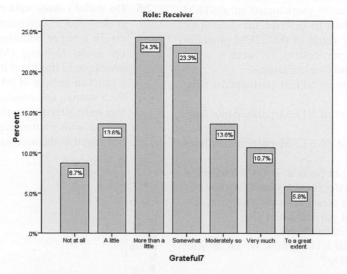

Figure SIA2.3

SPSS bar graphs for feeling of
gratefulness by role

Caution: The information produced in these graphs should be limited to describing
the sample of 237 adults who participated in the study. If one is interested in making inferences about the population of all gift-givers and gift-recipients (as were the
Stanford University researchers), inferential statistical methods need to be applied
to the data. These methods are the topics of later chapters.

 *Data Set:* BUYLOVE

Exercises 2.1–2.17

Learning the Mechanics

2.1 Complete the following table on customer statistics.

Age of Customer	Frequency	Relative Frequency
15 or younger	36	—
16 to 25	96	—
25 to 35	48	—
36 to 50	—	.2
older than 50	12	—
Total	240	1.00

2.2 A qualitative variable is measured for 20 companies randomly sampled and the data are classified into three classes, small (S), medium (M), and large (L), based on the number of employees in each company. The data (observed class for each company) are listed below.

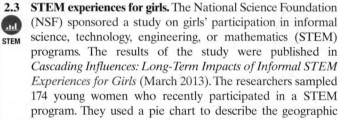

```
S   S   L   M   S   M   M   S   M   S
L   M   S   S   S   S   M   L   S   L
```

a. Compute the frequency for each of the three classes.
b. Compute the relative frequency for each of the three classes.
c. Display the results, part **a**, in a frequency bar graph.
d. Display the results, part **b**, in a pie chart.

Applying the Concepts—Basic

2.3 **STEM experiences for girls.** The National Science Foundation (NSF) sponsored a study on girls' participation in informal science, technology, engineering, or mathematics (STEM) programs. The results of the study were published in *Cascading Influences: Long-Term Impacts of Informal STEM Experiences for Girls* (March 2013). The researchers sampled 174 young women who recently participated in a STEM program. They used a pie chart to describe the geographic location (urban, suburban, or rural) of the STEM programs attended. Of the 174 STEM participants, 107 were in urban areas, 57 in suburban areas, and 10 in rural areas.

a. Determine the proportion of STEM participants from urban areas.
b. Determine the proportion of STEM participants from suburban areas.
c. Determine the proportion of STEM participants from rural areas.
d. Multiply each proportion in parts **a**–**c** by 360 to determine the pie slice size (in degrees) for each location.
e. Use the results, part **d**, to construct a pie chart for geographic location of STEM participants.
f. Interpret the pie slice for urban areas.
g. Convert the pie chart into a bar graph. Which, in your opinion, is more informative?

2.4 **Cable TV subscriptions and "cord cutters."** Has the increasing popularity of smartphones and video streaming over the Internet affected cable and satellite TV subscriptions? This was one of the questions of interest in a recent Pew Research Center survey (December 2015). Telephone (both landline and cell phone) interviews were conducted on a representative sample of 2,001 adults living in the

United States. For this sample, 1,521 adults reported that they currently receive cable or satellite TV service at home, 180 revealed that they have never subscribed to cable/satellite TV service at home, and the remainder (300 adults) admitted that they are "cord cutters," i.e., they canceled the cable/satellite TV service. The results are summarized in the Minitab pie chart shown.

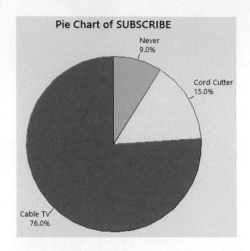

a. According to the pie chart, what proportion of the adults in the sample currently have a cable/satellite TV subscription at home? Verify the accuracy of this proportion using the survey results.
b. Now consider only the 1,821 adults in the sample that have at one time or another subscribed to cable/satellite TV service. Create a graph that compares the proportions of adults who currently subscribe to cable/satellite TV service with the proportion who are "cord cutters."

2.5 **Do social robots walk or roll?** A social (or service) robot is designed to entertain, educate, and care for human users. In a paper published by the *International Conference on Social Robotics* (Vol. 6414, 2010), design engineers investigated the trend in the design of social robots. Using a random sample of 106 social robots obtained through a Web search, the engineers found that 63 were built with legs only, 20 with wheels only, 8 with both legs and wheels, and 15 with neither legs nor wheels. This information is portrayed in the accompanying graph.

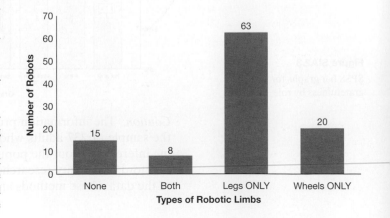

a. What type of graph is used to describe the data?

b. Identify the variable measured for each of the 106 robot designs.

c. Use the graph to identify the social robot design that is currently used the most.

d. Compute class relative frequencies for the different categories shown in the graph.

e. Use the results from part **d** to construct a Pareto diagram for the data.

2.6 Top credit card issuers, by region. *The Nilson Report* (December 2015) published a list of the top 150 credit card issuers worldwide. The issuers (e.g., American Express, MasterCard, Visa) were ranked based on outstanding debt during the year. The table gives a breakdown of the regions in the world served by the top 150 credit card issuers.

Worldwide Region	Number of credit card issuers
Asia-Pacific	48
Canada	10
Europe	34
Latin America	29
Middle East/Africa	3
United States	26
Total	150

a. One of the top 150 credit card issuers is selected at random, and the region it serves is determined. What type of data (quantitative or qualitative) is measured?

b. For each region in the table, calculate the percentage of the 150 top credit card issuers that fall into that region.

c. Use the percentages, part **b**, to construct a relative frequency bar graph for the data summarized in the table.

d. Based on the bar graph, make a statement about the regions that most of the top 150 credit card users serve.

2.7 Microsoft program security issues. To help its users combat malicious attacks (e.g., worms, viruses) on its computer software, Microsoft periodically issues a security bulletin that reports the software affected by the vulnerability. In *Computers & Security* (July 2013), researchers focused on reported security issues with three Microsoft products: Office, Windows, and Explorer

a. In a sample of 50 security bulletins issued in a recent year, 32 reported a security issue with Windows, 6 with Explorer, and 12 with Office. Construct a pie chart to describe the Microsoft products with security issues. Which product had the lowest proportion of security issues?

b. The researchers also categorized the security bulletins according to the expected repercussion of the vulnerability. Categories were Denial of service, Information disclosure, Remote code execution, Spoofing, and Privilege elevation. Suppose that of the 50 bulletins sampled, the following numbers of bulletins were classified into each respective category: 6, 8, 22, 3, 11. Construct a Pareto diagram to describe the expected repercussions from security issues. Based on the graph, what repercussion would you advise Microsoft to focus on?

Applying the Concepts—Intermediate

2.8 Jamming attacks on wireless networks. Refer to the *International Journal of Production Economics* (Vol. 172, 2016) study of U.S. military jamming attacks on wireless networks used by terrorists, Exercise 1.16 (p. 50). Recall that 80 recent jamming attacks were classified according to network type (WLAN, WSN, or AHN) attacked and number of channels (single- or multi-channel) of the network. The results are summarized in the accompanying table.

a. Construct a Pareto diagram for the data. Interpret the results.

b. Construct a pie chart for network type only. Interpret the results.

Network Type/ Number of Channels	Number of Jamming Attacks
WLAN / Single	31
WSN / Single	13
AHN / Single	8
WLAN / Multi	14
WSN / Multi	9
AHN / Multi	5
Total:	80

Source: S. Vadlamani et al., "Jamming Attacks on Wireless Networks: A Taxonomic Survey," *International Journal of Production Economics*, Vol. 172, 2016 (Figure 6).

2.9 The *Apprentice* contestants' performance ratings. *The Apprentice* is a popular TV show that gives the winning contestant the opportunity to work with a famous successful business leader (e.g., Donald Trump in the United States and Lord Alan Sugar in the United Kingdom). A study was conducted to investigate what separates the successful candidates from the losers (*Significance*, April 2015). Data were collected for 159 contestants on the United Kingdom's version of *The Apprentice* over a 10-year period. (For the first 6 years in the study, the prize was a 100,000 pounds per year job with Lord Sugar; in the last 4 years, the prize was a business partnership with Sugar.) Each contestant was rated (on a 20-point scale) based on their performance. In addition, the higher education degree earned by each contestant—no degree, first (bachelor's) degree, or postgraduate degree—was recorded. These data (simulated, based on statistics reported in the article) are saved in the **APPREN** file. Use statistical software to construct a graph that describes the highest degree obtained by the 159 contestants. Interpret the results.

2.10 The economic return to earning an MBA. Refer to the *International Economic Review* (August 2008) study on the economic rewards to obtaining an MBA degree, Exercise 1.27 (p. 51). Job status information was collected for a sample of 3,244 individuals who sat for the GMAT in each of four time periods (waves). Summary information (number of individuals) for Wave 1 (at the time of taking the GMAT) and Wave 4 (7 years later) is provided in the accompanying table. Use a graph to compare and contrast the job status distributions of GMAT takers in Wave 1 and Wave 4.

Job Status	Wave 1	Wave 4
Working, No MBA	2,657	1,787
Working, Have MBA	0	1,372
Not Working, Business School	0	7
Not Working, Other Graduate School	36	78
Not Working, 4-Year Institution	551	0
Total	3,244	3,244

Source: Data from P. Arcidiancono, P. Cooley, and A. Hussey, "The Economic Returns to an MBA," *International Economic Review*, Vol. 49, No. 3, August 2008, Table 1.

2.11 **Profiling UK rental malls.** An analysis of the retail rental levels of tenants of United Kingdom regional shopping malls was published in *Urban Studies* (June 2011). One aspect of the study involved describing the type of tenant typically found at a UK shopping mall. Data were collected for 148 Shopping malls, which housed 1,821 stores. Tenants were categorized into five different-size groups based on amount of floor space: *anchor tenants* (more than 30,000 square feet), *major space users* (between 10,000 and 30,000 sq. ft.), *large standard tenants* (between 4,000 and 10,000 sq. ft.), *small standard tenants* (between 1,500 and 4,000 sq. ft.), and *small tenants* (less than 1,500 sq. ft.). The number of stores in each tenant category was reported as 14, 61, 216, 711, and 819, respectively. Use this information to construct a Pareto diagram for the distribution of tenant groups at UK shopping malls. Interpret the graph.

2.12 **History of corporate acquisitions.** A corporate acquisition occurs when one corporation purchases all the stock shares of another, essentially taking over the other. The *Academy of Management Journal* (August 2008) investigated the performance and timing of corporate acquisitions for a large sample of firms over the years 1980 to 2000. The accompanying data table gives the number of firms sampled and number that announced one or more acquisitions during the years 1980, 1990, and 2000. Construct side-by-side bar charts to describe the firms with and without acquisitions in the 3 years. Compare and contrast the bar charts.

Year	Number of Firms Sampled	Number with Acquisitions
1980	1,963	18
1990	2,197	350
2000	2,778	748

Source: Data from D. N. Iyer and K. D. Miller, "Performance Feedback, Slack, and the Timing of Acquisitions," *Academy of Management Journal,* Vol. 51, No. 4, August 2008, pp. 808–822 (Table 1).

2.13 **Twitter opinions of iPhone 6 features.** What are the features of Apple's iPhone 6 that appeal most to customers? To answer this question, researchers collected data on customer opinions and published the results in *Decision Analytics* (October 2015). The opinions were extracted from a sample of 552 tweets obtained from the social media site Twitter.com. (Any tweet that referred to "iPhone 6" was eligible for selection.) The tweets originated in four cities: San Francisco (138 tweets), New York (182), Los Angeles (89), and Chicago (143). The table below summarizes the opinions on the iPhone 6 camera (excellent, good, or bad) from tweets in each city.

City	Number of Tweets About iPhone 6 Camera		
	Excellent	Good	Bad
San Francisco	14	94	30
New York	18	113	51
Los Angeles	5	51	33
Chicago	0	94	49

Source: S. Hridoy et al., "Localized Twitter Opinion Mining Using Sentiment Analysis," *Decision Analytics*, Vol. 2, No. 8, October 2015 (adapted from Figures 10–13).

a. Create a pie chart to show the proportion of tweets in the sample that originate in the four cities.
b. Create a pie chart to summarize the opinions on the iPhone 6 camera from tweets that originate in San Francisco.
c. Construct side-by-side bar charts to compare the opinions on the iPhone 6 camera for tweets originating in the four cities.
d. Refer to part **c.** What inferences can you make about customer satisfaction with the iPhone 6 camera?

Applying the Concepts—Advanced

2.14 **Museum management.** What criteria do museums use to evaluate their performance? In a worldwide survey reported in *Museum Management and Curatorship* (June 2010), managers of 30 leading museums of contemporary art were asked to provide the performance measure used most often. A summary of the results is provided in the table. The researcher concluded that "there is a large amount of variation within the museum community with regard to . . . performance measurement and evaluation," Do you agree? Use a graph to support your conclusion.

Performance Measure	Number of Museums
Total visitors	8
Paying visitors	5
Big shows	6
Funds raised	7
Members	4

2.15 **Advertising with reader-response cards.** "Reader-response cards" are used by marketers to advertise their product and obtain sales leads. These cards are placed in magazines and trade publications. Readers detach and mail in the cards to indicate their interest in the product, expecting literature or a phone call in return. How effective are these cards (called "bingo cards" in the industry) as a marketing tool? Performark, a Minneapolis business that helps companies close on sales leads, attempted to answer this question by responding to 17,000 card-advertisements placed by industrial marketers in a wide variety of trade publications over a 6-year period. Performark kept track of how long it took for each advertiser to respond. A summary of the response times is given in the next table.

Advertiser's Response Time	Percentage
Never responded	21
13–59 days	33
60–120 days	34
More than 120 days	12
Total	100

a. Describe the variable measured by Performark.

b. These results were displayed in the form of a pie chart. Reconstruct the pie chart from the information given in the table.

c. How many of the 17,000 advertisers never responded to the sales lead?

d. Advertisers typically spend at least a million dollars on a reader-response card marketing campaign. Many industrial marketers feel these "bingo cards" are not worth their expense. Does the information in the pie chart, part **b,** support this contention? Explain why or why not. If not, what information can be gleaned from the pie chart to help potential "bingo card" campaigns?

2.16 **Motivation and right-oriented bias.** Evolutionary theory suggests that motivated decision makers tend to exhibit a right-oriented bias. (For example, if presented with two equally valued brands of detergent on a supermarket shelf, consumers are more likely to choose the brand on the right.) In *Psychological Science* (November 2011), researchers tested this theory using data on all penalty shots attempted in World Cup soccer matches (a total of 204 penalty shots). The researchers believed that goalkeepers, motivated to make a penalty-shot save but with little time to make a decision, would tend to dive to the right. The results of the study (percentages of dives to the left, middle, or right) are provided in the table. Note that the percentages in each row, corresponding to a certain match situation, add to 100%. Use graphs to illustrate the distribution of dives for the three match situations. What inferences can you draw from the graphs?

Match Situation	Dive Left	Stay Middle	Dive Right
Team behind	29%	0%	71%
Tied	48%	3%	49%
Team ahead	51%	1%	48%

Source: Based on M. Roskes et al., "The Right Side? Under Time Pressure, Approach Motivation Leads to Right-Oriented Bias," *Psychological Science*, Vol. 22, No. 11, November 2011 (adapted from Figure 2).

2.17 **Groundwater contamination in wells.** In New Hampshire, about half the counties mandate the use of reformulated gasoline. This has led to an increase in the contamination of groundwater with methyl *tert*-butyl ether (MTBE). *Environmental Science & Technology* (Jan. 2005) reported on the factors related to MTBE contamination in public and private New Hampshire wells. Data were collected for a sample of 223 wells. Three of the variables are qualitative in nature: well class (public or private), aquifer (bedrock or unconsolidated), and detectible level of MTBE (below limit or detect). [*Note:* A detectible level of MTBE occurs if the MTBE value exceeds .2 micrograms per liter.] The data for 11 selected wells are shown in the accompanying table.

Well Class	Aquifer	Detect MTBE
Private	Bedrock	Below Limit
Private	Bedrock	Below Limit
Public	Unconsolidated	Detect
Public	Unconsolidated	Below Limit
Public	Unconsolidated	Below Limit
Public	Unconsolidated	Below Limit
Public	Unconsolidated	Detect
Public	Unconsolidated	Below Limit
Public	Unconsolidated	Below Limit
Public	Bedrock	Detect
Public	Bedrock	Detect

Source: Based on J. D. Ayotte, D. M. Argue, and F. J. McGarry, "Methyl tert-Butyl Ether Occurrence and Related Factors in Public and Private Wells in Southeast New Hampshire," *Environmental Science & Technology*, Vol. 39, No. 1, Jan. 2005, pp. 9–16.

a. Use graphical methods to describe each of the three qualitative variables for all 223 wells.

b. Use side-by-side bar charts to compare the proportions of contaminated wells for private and public well classes.

c. Use side-by-side bar charts to compare the proportions of contaminated wells for bedrock and unconsolidated aquifers.

d. What inferences can be made from the bar charts, parts **a–c?**

2.2 Graphical Methods for Describing Quantitative Data

Recall from Section 1.5 that quantitative data sets consist of data that are recorded on a meaningful numerical scale. For describing, summarizing, and detecting patterns in such data, we can use three graphical methods: **dot plots**, **stem-and-leaf displays**, and **histograms**. Because almost all statistical software packages can produce these graphs, we'll focus here on their interpretations rather than their construction.

For example, suppose a financial analyst is interested in the amount of resources spent by computer hardware and software companies on research and development (R&D). She samples 50 of these high-technology firms and calculates the amount each spent last year on R&D as a percentage of their total revenue. The results are given in

Table 2.2	Percentage of Revenues Spent on Research and Development						
Company	Percentage	Company	Percentage	Company	Percentage	Company	Percentage
1	13.5	14	9.5	27	8.2	39	6.5
2	8.4	15	8.1	28	6.9	40	7.5
3	10.5	16	13.5	29	7.2	41	7.1
4	9.0	17	9.9	30	8.2	42	13.2
5	9.2	18	6.9	31	9.6	43	7.7
6	9.7	19	7.5	32	7.2	44	5.9
7	6.6	20	11.1	33	8.8	45	5.2
8	10.6	21	8.2	34	11.3	46	5.6
9	10.1	22	8.0	35	8.5	47	11.7
10	7.1	23	7.7	36	9.4	48	6.0
11	8.0	24	7.4	37	10.5	49	7.8
12	7.9	25	6.5	38	6.9	50	6.5
13	6.8	26	9.5				

 Data Set: R&D

Table 2.2. As numerical measurements made on the sample of 50 units (the firms), these percentages represent quantitative data. The analyst's initial objective is to summarize and describe these data in order to extract relevant information.

A visual inspection of the data indicates some obvious facts. For example, the smallest R&D percentage is 5.2% (company 45) and the largest is 13.5% (companies 1 and 16). But it is difficult to provide much additional information on the 50 R&D percentages without resorting to some method of summarizing the data. One such method is a dot plot.

Dot Plots

A **dot plot** for the 50 R&D percentages, produced using Minitab, is shown in Figure 2.8. The horizontal axis of Figure 2.8 is a scale for the quantitative variable, percent. The numerical value of each measurement in the data set is located on the horizontal scale by a dot. When data values repeat, the dots are placed above one another, forming a pile at that particular numerical location. As you can see, this dot plot shows that 45 of the 50 R&D percentages (90%) are between 6% and 12%, with most falling between 7% and 9%.

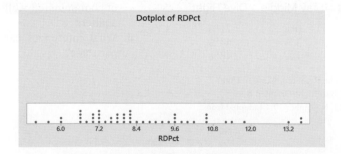

Figure 2.8

Minitab dot plot for 50 R&D percentages

Stem-and-Leaf Display

We used XLSTAT to generate another graphical representation of these same data, a **stem-and-leaf display,** in Figure 2.9. In this display the *stem* is the portion of the measurement (percentage) to the left of the decimal point, while the remaining portion to the right of the decimal point is the *leaf.*

The stems for the data set are listed in the first column of Figure 2.9 from the smallest (5) to the largest (13). Then the leaf for each observation is recorded in the row of the display corresponding to the observation's stem. For example, the leaf 5 of the first observation (13.5) in Table 2.2 is placed in the row corresponding to the stem 13. Similarly, the leaf 4 for the second observation (8.4) in Table 2.2 is recorded in the row corresponding to the stem 8, while the leaf 5 for the third observation (10.5) is recorded

Stem-and-leaf plot (RDPct):

Unit: 1

```
 5 | 2 6 9
 6 | 0 5 5 5 6 8 9 9 9
 7 | 1 1 2 2 4 5 5 7 7 8 9
 8 | 0 0 1 2 2 2 4 5 8
 9 | 0 2 4 5 5 6 7 9
10 | 1 5 5 6
11 | 1 3 7
12 |
13 | 2 5 5
```

Figure 2.9

XLSTAT stem-and-leaf display for 50 R&D percentages

in the row corresponding to the stem 10. (The leaves for these first three observations are shaded in Figure 2.9.) Typically, the leaves in each row are ordered as shown in Figure 2.9.

The stem-and-leaf display presents another compact picture of the data set. You can see at a glance that most of the sampled computer companies (37 of 50) spent between 6.0% and 9.9% of their revenues on R&D, and 11 of them spent between 7.0% and 7.9%. Relative to the rest of the sampled companies, three spent a high percentage of revenues on R&D—in excess of 13%.

The definitions of the stem and leaf can be modified to alter the graphical display. For example, suppose we had defined the stem as the tens digit for the R&D percentage data, rather than the ones and tens digits. With this definition, the stems and leaves corresponding to the measurements 13.5 and 8.4 would be as follows:

Stem	Leaf		Stem	Leaf
1	3		0	8

Note that the decimal portion of the numbers has been dropped. Generally, only one digit is displayed in the leaf.

If you look at the data, you'll see why we didn't define the stem this way. All the R&D measurements fall below 13.5, so all the leaves would fall into just two stem rows—1 and 0—in this display. The picture resulting from using only a few stems would not be nearly as informative as Figure 2.9.

Histograms

A Minitab **histogram** for these 50 R&D measurements is displayed in Figure 2.10. The horizontal axis for Figure 2.10, which gives the percentage amounts spent on R&D for each company, is divided into **class intervals** commencing with the interval (5.0–6.0) and proceeding in intervals of equal size to (13.0–14.0). The vertical axis gives the number (or *frequency*) of the 50 measurements that fall in each class interval. You can see that the class interval (7.0–8.0) (i.e., the class with the highest bar) contains the largest frequency of 11 R&D percentage measurements; the remaining class intervals tend to contain a smaller number of measurements as R&D percentage gets smaller or larger.

Histograms can be used to display either the *frequency* or *relative frequency* of the measurements falling into the class intervals. The class intervals, frequencies, and relative frequencies for the 50 R&D measurements are shown in Table 2.3.* By summing

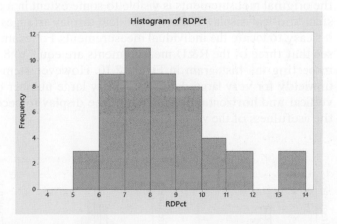

Figure 2.10

Minitab histogram for 50 R&D percentages

*Minitab, like many statistical software packages, will classify an observation that falls on the borderline of a class interval into the next highest class interval. For example, the R&D measurement of 8.0, which falls on the border between the intervals (7.0–8.0) and (8.0–9.0), is classified into the (8.0–9.0) interval. The frequencies in Table 2.3 reflect this convention.

Table 2.3	Class Intervals, Frequencies, and Relative Frequencies for the 50 R&D Measurements		
Class	Class Interval	Class Frequency	Class Relative Frequency
1	5.0–6.0	3	3/50 = .06
2	6.0–7.0	9	9/50 = .18
3	7.0–8.0	11	11/50 = .22
4	8.0–9.0	9	9/50 = .18
5	9.0–10.0	8	8/50 = .16
6	10.0–11.0	4	4/50 = .08
7	11.0–12.0	3	3/50 = .06
8	12.0–13.0	0	0/50 = .00
9	13.0–14.0	3	3/50 = .06
Totals		50	1.00

the relative frequencies in the intervals (6.0–7.0), (7.0–8.0), (8.0–9.0), (9.0–10.0), and (10.0–11.0), we find that .18 + .22 + .18 + .16 + .08 = .82, or 82%, of the R&D measurements are between 6.0 and 11.0. Similarly, summing the relative frequencies in the last two intervals, (12.0–13.0) and (13.0–14.0), we find that 6% of the companies spent over 12.0% of their revenues on R&D. Many other summary statements can be made by further study of the histogram. Note that the sum of all class frequencies will always equal the sample size n.

When interpreting a histogram, consider two important facts. First, the proportion of the total area under the histogram that falls above a particular interval of the horizontal axis is equal to the relative frequency of measurements falling in the interval. For example, the relative frequency for the class interval 7.0–8.0 in Figure 2.10 is .22. Consequently, the rectangle above the interval contains 22% of the total area under the histogram.

Second, imagine the appearance of the relative frequency histogram for a very large set of data (say, a population). As the number of measurements in a data set is increased, you can obtain a better description of the data by decreasing the width of the class intervals. When the class intervals become small enough, a relative frequency histogram will (for all practical purposes) appear as a smooth curve (see Figure 2.11). Some recommendations for selecting the number of intervals in a histogram for smaller data sets are given in the box below Figure 2.11.

While histograms provide good visual descriptions of data sets—particularly very large ones—they do not let us identify individual measurements. In contrast, each of the original measurements is visible to some extent in a dot plot and clearly visible in a stem-and-leaf display. The stem-and-leaf display arranges the data in ascending order, so it's easy to locate the individual measurements. For example, in Figure 2.9, we can easily see that three of the R&D measurements are equal to 8.2, but we can't see that fact by inspecting the histogram in Figure 2.10. However, stem-and-leaf displays can become unwieldy for very large data sets. A very large number of stems and leaves causes the vertical and horizontal dimensions of the display to become cumbersome, diminishing the usefulness of the visual display.

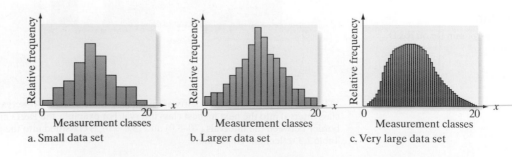

Figure 2.11

Effect of the size of a data set on the outline of a histogram

a. Small data set   b. Larger data set   c. Very large data set

Determining the Number of Classes in a Histogram

Number of Observations in Data Set	Number of Classes
Less than 25	5–6
25–50	7–14
More than 50	15–20

EXAMPLE 2.2

Graphs for a Quantitative Variable— Lost Price Quotes

Problem A manufacturer of industrial wheels suspects that profitable orders are being lost because of the long time the firm takes to develop price quotes for potential customers. To investigate this possibility, 50 requests for price quotes were randomly selected from the set of all quotes made last year, and the processing time was determined for each quote. The processing times are displayed in Table 2.4, and each quote was classified according to whether the order was "lost" or not (i.e., whether or not the customer placed an order after receiving a price quote).

a. Use a statistical software package to create a frequency histogram for these data. Then shade the area under the histogram that corresponds to lost orders. Interpret the result.

b. Use a statistical software package to create a stem-and-leaf display for these data. Then shade each leaf of the display that corresponds to a lost order. Interpret the result.

Solution

a. We used SPSS to generate the frequency histogram in Figure 2.12. Note that 20 classes were formed by the SPSS program. The class intervals are (1.0–2.0), (2.0–3.0), . . . , (20.0–21.0). This histogram clearly shows the clustering of the measurements in the

Table 2.4	**Price Quote Processing Time (Days)**				
Request Number	Processing Time	Lost?	Request Number	Processing Time	Lost?
1	2.36	No	26	3.34	No
2	5.73	No	27	6.00	No
3	6.60	No	28	5.92	No
4	10.05	Yes	29	7.28	Yes
5	5.13	No	30	1.25	No
6	1.88	No	31	4.01	No
7	2.52	No	32	7.59	No
8	2.00	No	33	13.42	Yes
9	4.69	No	34	3.24	No
10	1.91	No	35	3.37	No
11	6.75	Yes	36	14.06	Yes
12	3.92	No	37	5.10	No
13	3.46	No	38	6.44	No
14	2.64	No	39	7.76	No
15	3.63	No	40	4.40	No
16	3.44	No	41	5.48	No
17	9.49	Yes	42	7.51	No
18	4.90	No	43	6.18	No
19	7.45	No	44	8.22	Yes
20	20.23	Yes	45	4.37	No
21	3.91	No	46	2.93	No
22	1.70	No	47	9.95	Yes
23	16.29	Yes	48	4.46	No
24	5.52	No	49	14.32	Yes
25	1.44	No	50	9.01	No

Data Set: QUOTES

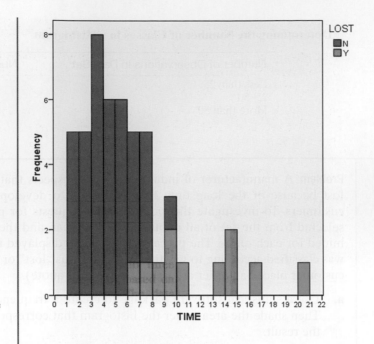

Figure 2.12

SPSS frequency histogram for price quote data

lower end of the distribution (between approximately 1 and 8 days), and the relatively few measurements in the upper end of the distribution (greater than 12 days). The shading of the area of the frequency histogram corresponding to lost orders (green bars) clearly indicates that they lie in the upper tail of the distribution.

b. We used Minitab to generate the stem-and-leaf display in Figure 2.13. Note that the stem (the second column of the printout) consists of the number of whole days (digits to the left of the decimal). The leaf (the third column of the printout) is the tenths digit (first digit after the decimal) of each measurement. Thus, the leaf 2 in the stem 20 (the last row of the printout) represents the time of 20.23 days. Like the histogram, the stem-and-leaf display shows the shaded "lost" orders in the upper tail of the distribution.

Look Back As is usually the case for data sets that are not too large (say, fewer than 100 measurements), the stem-and-leaf display provides more detail than the histogram without being unwieldy. For instance, the stem-and-leaf display in Figure 2.13 clearly indicates that the lost orders are associated with high processing times (as does the histogram in Figure 2.12), and exactly which of the times correspond to lost orders. Histograms are most useful for displaying very large data sets, when the overall shape of the distribution of measurements is more important than the identification of individual measurements. Nevertheless, the message of both graphical displays is clear: Establishing processing time limits may well result in fewer lost orders.

● **Now Work Exercise 2.22**

```
Stem-and-leaf of TIME   N  = 50
Leaf Unit = 0.10

    5    1   24789
   10    2   03569
   18    3   23344699
   24    4   034469
   (6)   5   114579
   20    6   01467
   15    7   24557
   10    8   2
    9    9   049
    6   10   0
    5   11
    5   12
    5   13   4
    4   14   03
    2   15
    2   16   2
    1   17
    1   18
    1   19
    1   20   2
```

Figure 2.13

Minitab stem-and-leaf display for price quote data

Most statistical software packages can be used to generate histograms, stem-and-leaf displays, and dot plots. All three are useful tools for graphically describing data sets. We recommend that you generate and compare the displays whenever you can. You'll find that histograms are generally more useful for very large data sets, while stem-and-leaf displays and dot plots provide useful detail for smaller data sets.

Summary of Graphical Descriptive Methods for Quantitative Data

Dot plot: The numerical value of each quantitative measurement in the data set is represented by a dot on a horizontal scale. When data values repeat, the dots are placed above one another vertically.

Stem-and-leaf display: The numerical value of the quantitative variable is partitioned into a "stem" and a "leaf." The possible stems are listed in order in a column. The leaf for each quantitative measurement in the data set is placed in the corresponding stem row. Leaves for observations with the same stem value are listed in increasing order horizontally.

Histogram: The possible numerical values of the quantitative variable are partitioned into class intervals, where each interval has the same width. These intervals form the scale of the horizontal axis. The frequency or relative frequency of observations in each class interval is determined. A horizontal bar is placed over each class interval, with height equal to either the class frequency or class relative frequency.

STATISTICS IN ACTION

REVISITED

Interpreting Histograms

In the *Journal of Experimental Social Psychology* (Vol. 45, 2009) study on whether money can buy love (p. 63), the researchers randomly assigned participants to the role of either gift-giver or gift-receiver. (Gift-givers, recall, were asked about a birthday gift they recently gave, while gift-recipients were asked about a birthday gift they recently received.) Two quantitative variables were measured for each of the 237 participants: *gift price* (measured in dollars) and *overall level of appreciation for the gift* (measured as the sum of the two 7-point appreciation scales, with higher values indicating a higher level of appreciation). One of the objectives of the research was to investigate whether givers and receivers differ on the price of the gift reported and on the level of appreciation reported. We can explore this phenomenon graphically by forming side-by-side histograms for the quantitative variables, one histogram for gift-givers and one for gift-recipients. These histograms, produced from a Minitab analysis of the data in the **BUYLOV** file, are shown in Figures SIA2.4a and SIA2.4b.

First, examine the histograms for birthday gift price (Figure SIA2.4a). The prices reported by gift-recipients tended to be higher than the prices reported by gift-givers. For example, receivers reported more birthday gift prices of at least $300 than givers, while givers reported more prices of $100 or less than receivers.

Next, examine the histograms for overall level of appreciation (Figure SIA2.4b). For gift-givers, the histogram of appreciation scores is centered around 5 points, while

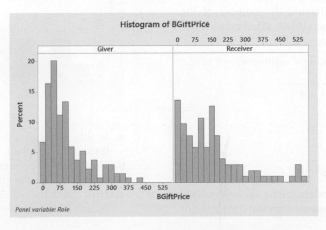

Figure SIA2.4a

Side-by-side histograms for birthday gift price

STATISTICS
IN ACTION
REVISTED
(*continued*)

Figure SIA2.4b
Side-by-side histograms for overall
level of appreciation

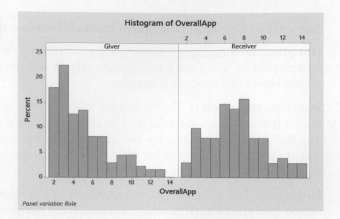

for gift-recipients the histogram is centered higher, at about 8 points. Also from the histograms you can see that about 65% of the givers reported an appreciation level of less than 6 compared with about 28% for gift-recipients. As with the bar graphs in the previous *Statistics in Action Revisited*, it appears that gift-givers and gift-recipients respond differently, with gift-recipients more likely to express a greater level of appreciation for the gift than what gift-givers perceive. In later chapters, we'll learn how to attach a measure of reliability to such an inference.

 *Data Set:* BUYLOV

Exercises 2.18–2.34

Learning the Mechanics

2.18 A company is analyzing the prices at which its items are sold. Graph the relative frequency histogram for the 600 items summarized in the accompanying relative frequency table.

Class Based on Item Price	Relative Frequency
.50 but less than 1.50	.06
1.50 but less than 2.50	.30
2.50 but less than 3.50	.20
3.50 but less than 4.50	.15
4.50 but less than 5.50	.14
5.50 but less than 6.50	.10
6.50 but less than 7.50	.05

2.19 Refer to Exercise 2.18 and calculate the number of the 600 items falling into each of the classes. Then graph a frequency histogram for these data.

2.20 Consider the following stem-and-leaf display shown here.

Stem	Leaf
2	9
3	133
4	122
5	
6	00115

a. Identify the numbers in the original data set represented by the stem and its leaves. Assume that the data was not rounded.

b. Construct a dot plot of the original data set.

c. Now assume that the original data might have been rounded off to the nearest whole number. Identify the interval of the number represented in the first row of the stem-and-leaf display.

2.21 Minitab was used to generate the following histogram:

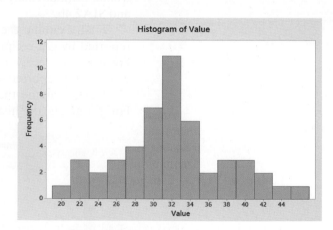

a. Is this a frequency histogram or a relative frequency histogram? Explain.

b. How many measurement classes were used in the construction of this histogram?

c. How many measurements are in the data set described by this histogram?

Applying the Concepts—Basic

2.22 **Stability of compounds in new drugs.** Testing the metabolic stability of compounds used in drugs is the cornerstone of new drug discovery. Two important values computed from the testing phase are the fraction of compound unbound to plasma (*fup*) and the fraction of compound unbound to microsomes (*fumic*). A key formula for assessing stability assumes that the fup/fumic ratio is 1. Pharmacologists at Pfizer Global Research and Development investigated this phenomenon and reported the results in *ACS Medicinal Chemistry Letters* (Vol. 1, 2010). The fup/fumic ratio was determined for each of 416 drugs in the Pfizer database. An SPSS graph describing the fup/fumic ratios is shown below.

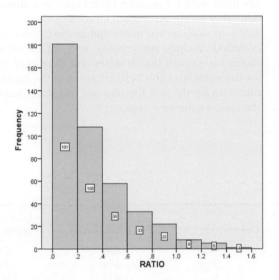

a. What type of graph is displayed?
b. What is the quantitative variable summarized in the graph?
c. Determine the proportion of fup/fumic ratios that fall above 1.
d. Determine the proportion of fup/fumic ratios that fall below .4.

2.23 **Corporate sustainability of CPA firms.** Refer to the *Business and Society* (March 2011) study on the sustainability behaviors of CPA corporations, Exercise 1.28 (p. 51). *Corporate sustainability*, recall, refers to business practices designed around social and environmental considerations. Data on the level of support for corporate sustainability were obtained for 992 senior managers. Level of support was measured quantitatively. Simulation was used to convert the data from the study to a scale ranging from 0 to 160 points, where higher point values indicate a higher level of support for sustainability.

a. A histogram for level of support for sustainability is shown next. What type of histogram is produced, frequency or relative frequency?
b. Use the graph to estimate the percentage of the 992 senior managers who reported a high (100 points or greater) level of support for corporate sustainability.

Minitab histogram for Exercise 2.23

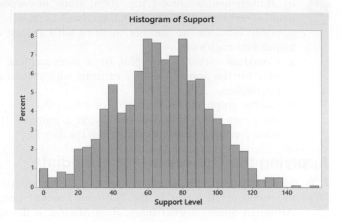

2.24 **Sanitation inspection of cruise ships.** To minimize the potential for gastrointestinal disease outbreaks, all passenger cruise ships arriving at U.S. ports are subject to unannounced sanitation inspections. Ships are rated on a 100-point scale by the Centers for Disease Control and Prevention. A score of 86 or higher indicates that the ship is providing an accepted standard of sanitation. The latest (as of October 2015) sanitation scores for 195 cruise ships are saved in the accompanying file. The first five and last five observations in the data set are listed in the accompanying table.

Cruise Ship	Cruise Line	Score
Adonia	P&O Cruises	96
Adventure of the Seas	Royal Caribbean International	84
AIDAaura	Aida Cruises	86
AIDABella	Aida Cruises	98
AIDAluna	Aida Cruises	87
.		
.		
.		
Voyager of the Seas	Royal Caribbean International	96
Vspbeta	VSP Office Cruise Line	100
Westerdam	Holland America Line	95
Zaandam	Holland America Line	97
Zuiderdam	Holland America Line	100

Source: Data from U.S. Department of Health and Human Services, Centers for Disease Control and Prevention/National Center for Environmental Health and Agency for Toxic Substances and Disease Registry, October 27, 2015.

a. Generate both a stem-and-leaf display and histogram of the data.
b. Use the graphs to estimate the proportion of ships that have an accepted sanitation standard. Which graph did you use?
c. Locate the inspection score of 69 (*Bahama Mama*) on the graph. Which graph did you use?

2.25 **History of corporate acquisitions.** Refer to the *Academy of Management Journal* (Aug. 2008) study of corporate acquisitions from 1980 to 2000, Exercise 2.12 (p. 74). The data file includes the number of firms with at least one acquisition each year.

ACQR

    a. Construct either a dot plot or a stem-and-leaf display for the annual number of firms with at least one acquisition.

    b. On the graph, part **a**, highlight (or circle) the values for the years 1996–2000. Do you detect a pattern? If so, what conclusion can you draw from the data?

Applying the Concepts—Intermediate

2.26 **Most valuable NFL teams.** Each year *Forbes* reports on the value of all teams in the National Football League. Although Spain's soccer team, Real Madrid, is the most valuable team in the world ($3.3 billion), all 32 NFL teams are now worth at least $1 billion. For 2015, *Forbes* reports that the Dallas Cowboys are the most valuable team in the NFL, worth $4 billion. The current values of all 32 NFL teams, as well as the percentage changes in values from 2014 to 2015, debt-to-value ratios, annual revenues, and operating incomes, are listed in the first table below.

NFL

a. Use a graph to describe the distribution of current values for the 32 NFL teams.

b. Use a graph to describe the distribution of the 1-year change in current value for the 32 NFL teams.

c. Use a graph to describe the distribution of debt-to-value ratios for the 32 NFL teams.

d. Use a graph to describe the distribution of the annual revenues for the 32 NFL teams.

e. Use a graph to describe the distribution of operating incomes for the 32 NFL teams.

f. Compare and contrast the graphs, parts **a**–**e**.

2.27 **State SAT scores.** Educators are constantly evaluating the efficacy of public schools in the education and training of American students. One quantitative assessment of change over time is the difference in scores on the SAT, which has been used for decades by colleges and universities as one criterion for admission. Originally, the SAT provided scores in reading and mathematics. Now, three scores are provided: reading, mathematics, and critical writing. SAT scores for each of the 50 states and District of Columbia for the years 2014 and 2010 are saved in the accompanying file. Data for the first five and last two states are shown in the table on the next page.

SATMAT

Rank	Team	Current Value ($ mil)	1-Yr Value Change (%)	Debt/Value (%)	Revenue ($ mil)	Operating Income ($ mil)
1	Dallas Cowboys	4,000	25	5	620	270
2	New England Patriots	3,200	23	7	494	195
3	Washington Redskins	2,850	19	8	439	124.9
4	New York Giants	2,800	33	18	400	105.2
5	San Francisco 49ers	2,700	69	21	427	123.7
6	New York Jets	2,600	44	23	383	118.4
7	Houston Texans	2,500	35	7	383	114.6
8	Chicago Bears	2,450	44	4	352	85.7
9	Philadelphia Eagles	2,400	37	8	370	88.7
10	Green Bay Packers	1,950	42	6	347	63.3
11	Denver Broncos	1,940	34	6	346	65.8
12	Baltimore Ravens	1,930	29	14	345	59.8
13	Pittsburgh Steelers	1,900	41	11	344	54
14	Indianapolis Colts	1,875	34	3	321	90.1
15	Seattle Seahawks	1,870	41	6	334	43.6
16	Miami Dolphins	1,850	42	19	322	41.5
17	Atlanta Falcons	1,670	48	51	303	25.4
18	Minnesota Vikings	1,590	38	31	281	34.5
19	Carolina Panthers	1,560	25	4	325	77.8
20	Arizona Cardinals	1,540	54	10	308	57.2
21	Kansas City Chiefs	1,530	39	5	307	48.6
22	San Diego Chargers	1,525	53	7	304	64.8
23	New Orleans Saints	1,515	36	5	322	70
24	Tampa Bay Buccaneers	1,510	23	12	313	55.2
25	Cleveland Browns	1,500	34	13	313	34.7
26	Tennessee Titans	1,490	28	10	318	50.5
27	Jacksonville Jaguars	1,480	53	7	315	67
28	St. Louis Rams	1,450	56	8	290	34
29	Cincinnati Bengals	1,445	46	7	296	55.5
30	Detroit Lions	1,440	50	19	298	36.1
31	Oakland Raiders	1,430	47	14	285	39
32	Buffalo Bills	1,400	50	14	296	44.2

Source: "The Most Valuable Teams in the NFL," *Forbes*, copyright © September 14, 2015.

Data for Exercise 2.27

	2014			2010		
State	Read	Math	Write	Read	Math	Write
Alabama	547	538	532	556	550	543
Alaska	507	503	475	516	513	489
Arizona	522	525	500	518	524	498
Arkansas	573	571	554	564	564	550
California	498	510	496	501	516	500
Wisconsin	596	608	578	593	603	578
Wyoming	590	599	573	568	565	543

Source: The College Board, 2015.

a. Use graphs to display the SAT mathematics score distributions in 2014 and 2010. How did the distributions of state scores change over the 5-year period?

b. As another method of comparing the 2014 and 2010 SAT mathematics scores, compute the *paired difference* by subtracting the 2010 score from the 2014 score for each state. Summarize these differences with a graph. Compare the results with those of part **a**.

c. Based on the graph, part **b**, what is the largest improvement in SAT mathematics score? Identify the state associated with this improvement.

2.28 **Items arriving and departing a work center.** In a manufacturing plant, a *work center* is a specific production facility that consists of one or more people and/or machines and is treated as one unit for the purposes of capacity requirements for planning and job scheduling. If jobs arrive at a particular work center at a faster rate than they depart, the work center impedes the overall production process and is referred to as a *bottleneck*. The data in the table at the bottom of the page were collected by an operations manager for use in investigating a potential bottleneck work center. Construct dot plots for the two sets of data. Do the dot plots suggest that the work center may be a bottleneck? Explain.

2.29 **Crude oil biodegradation.** In order to protect their valuable resources, oil companies spend millions of dollars researching ways to prevent biodegradation of crude oil. The *Journal of Petroleum Geology* (April 2010) published a study of the environmental factors associated with biodegradation in crude oil reservoirs. Sixteen water specimens were randomly selected from various locations in a reservoir on the floor of a mine. Two of the variables measured were (1) the amount of dioxide (milligrams/liter) present in the water specimen and (2) whether or not oil was present in the water specimen. These data are listed in the accompanying table in the next column. Construct a stem-and-leaf display for the dioxide data. Locate the dioxide levels associated with water specimens that contain oil.

Highlight these data points on the stem-and-leaf display. Is there a tendency for crude oil to be present in water with lower levels of dioxide?

Dioxide Amount	Crude Oil Present
3.3	No
0.5	Yes
1.3	Yes
0.4	Yes
0.1	No
4.0	No
0.3	No
0.2	Yes
2.4	No
2.4	No
1.4	No
0.5	Yes
0.2	Yes
4.0	No
4.0	No
4.0	No

Source: Based on A. Permanyer, J. L. R. Gallego, M. A. Caja, and D. Dessort, "Crude Oil Biodegradation and Environmental Factors at the Riutort Oil Shale Mine, SE Pyrenees," *Journal of Petroleum Geology*, Vol. 33, No. 2, April 2010, (Table 1).

2.30 **Volkswagen emissions scandal.** Recently, the Environmental Protection Agency (EPA) cited Volkswagen (VW) for installing "defeat devices" that allowed VW vehicles to pass emissions inspections for 7 years while emitting 40 times the official limit of nitrogen oxide (NOx). Immediately, speculation began on how many people may have died over this time period due to ambient pollution caused by the excess nitrogen oxide in the air. A study published in *Significance* (December 2015) estimated the number of U.S. deaths attributable to NOx pollution produced from VW vehicles over the 7-year period. The researchers computed the estimate for each of 27 different scenarios

Data for Exercise 2.28

Number of Items Arriving at Work Center per Hour											
155	115	156	150	159	163	172	143	159	166	148	175
151	161	138	148	129	135	140	152	139			

Number of Items Departing Work Center per Hour											
156	109	127	148	135	119	140	127	115	122	99	106
171	123	135	125	107	152	111	137	161			

involving different values of three variables: total distance (in miles) driven by these illegal VW vehicles, the amount by which the VW vehicles exceeded the EPA standard for NOx, and the estimated association between NOx emissions and mortality. The data (simulated from results reported in the study) are listed in the accompanying table.

a. Use a relative frequency histogram to describe the distribution of estimated deaths for the 27 scenarios.

b. Identify the class interval that includes the largest proportion of estimates. Explain why this interval is most likely to include the actual number of deaths attributable to NOx pollution over the 7-years.

10	28	29	5	21	4	15	62	36	42	37	33	68	83
83	67	119	142	150	167	184	201	327	368	477	700	955	

Applying the Concepts—Advanced

2.31 **Is honey a cough remedy?** Does a teaspoon of honey before bed really calm a child's cough? To test the folk remedy, pediatric researchers carried out a designed study conducted over two nights (*Archives of Pediatrics and Adolescent Medicine*, December 2007). A sample of 105 children who were ill with an upper respiratory tract infection and their parents participated in the study. On the first night, the parents rated their children's cough symptoms on a scale from 0 (no problems at all) to 6 (extremely severe) in five different areas. The total symptoms score (ranging from 0 to 30 points) was the variable of interest for the 105 patients. On the second night, the parents were instructed to give their sick child a dosage of liquid "medicine" prior to bedtime. Unknown to the parents, some were given a dosage of dextromethorphan (DM)—an over-the-counter cough medicine—while others were given a similar dose of honey. Also, a third group of parents (the control group) gave their sick children no dosage at all. Again, the parents rated their children's cough symptoms, and the improvement in total cough symptoms score was determined for each child. The data (improvement scores) for the study are shown in the table below, followed (in the next column) by a Minitab dot plot of the data. Notice that the green dots represent the children who received a dose of honey, the red dots represent those who got the DM dosage, and the black dots represent the children in the control group. What conclusions can pediatric researchers draw from the graph? Do you agree with the statement (extracted from the article), "Honey may be a preferable treatment for the cough and sleep difficulty associated with childhood upper respiratory tract infection"?

Data for Exercise 2.31

Honey Dosage:	12	11	15	11	10	13	10	4	15	16	9	14
	10	6	10	8	11	12	12	8	9	5	12	
	12	9	11	15	10	15	9	13	8	12	10	8

DM Dosage:	4	6	9	4	7	7	7	9	12	10	11	6	3
	4	9	12	7	6	8	12	12	4	12	10	15	9
	13	7	10	13	9	4	4						

No Dosage (Control):	5	8	6	1	0	8	12	8	7	7	1	6	7
	7	12	7	9	7	9	5	11	9	5	1	4	3
	6	8	8	6	7	10	9	4	8	7	3		

Source: Based on I. M. Paul et al. "Effect of Honey, Dextromethorphan, and No Treatment on Nocturnal Cough and Sleep Quality for Coughing Children and Their Parents," *Archives of Pediatrics and Adolescent Medicine*, Vol. 161, No. 12, December 2007 (data simulated).

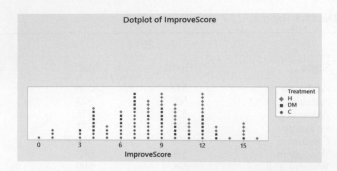
Dotplot of ImproveScore

2.32 **Time in bankruptcy.** Financially distressed firms can gain protection from their creditors while they restructure by filing for protection under U.S. Bankruptcy Codes. In a *prepackaged bankruptcy,* a firm negotiates a reorganization plan with its creditors prior to filing for bankruptcy. This can result in a much quicker exit from bankruptcy than traditional bankruptcy filings. A study of 49 prepackaged bankruptcies was published in *Financial Management* (Spring 1995). For each firm, information was collected on the time (in months) in bankruptcy as well as the results of the board of directors' vote on the type of reorganization plan. Three types of plans were studied: "Joint"—a joint exchange offer with prepackaged bankruptcy solicitation; "Prepack"—prepackaged bankruptcy solicitation only; and "None"—no pre-filing vote held. The data for the 49 firms is provided in the accompanying table.

Reorganization Plan	Time in Bankruptcy (months)						
None	3.9	10.1	4.1	3.0	3.2	4.2	
	2.9	2.4	7.8*	2.6*	2.4		
Prepack	1.5	1.0*	1.9	1.3*	4.1	1.1	1.0*
	3.8	1.0*	1.5	1.0	1.4*	1.2*	3.0*
	1.6*	1.4*	1.1*	1.2	1.5*	2.1*	1.4
	1.7	1.4	2.7	1.2	4.1	2.9*	
Joint	1.4	1.2*	1.2	1.5*	1.4	5.2	4.5*
	2.1	3.9*	1.4*	5.4			

Source: Data from B. L. Betker, "An Empirical Examination of Prepackaged Bankruptcy," *Financial Management*, Vol. 24, No. 1, Spring 1995, p. 6 (Table 2).

a. Construct a stem-and-leaf display for the length of time in bankruptcy for all 49 companies.

b. Summarize the information reflected in the stem-and-leaf display from part **a.** Make a general statement about the length of time in bankruptcy for firms using "prepacks."

c. Select a graphical method that will permit a comparison of the time-in-bankruptcy distributions for the three types or reorganization plans.

d. Firms that were reorganized through a leveraged buyout are identified by an asterisk in the table. Mark these firms on the stem-and-leaf display, part **a.**, by circling their bankruptcy times. Do you observe any pattern in the graph? Explain.

2.33 **Phishing attacks to e-mail accounts.** *Phishing* is the term used to describe an attempt to extract personal/financial information (e.g., PIN numbers, credit card information, bank account numbers) from unsuspecting people through fraudulent e-mail. An article in *Chance* (Summer 2007) demonstrates how statistics can help identify phishing attempts and make e-commerce safer. Data from an actual phishing attack against an organization were used to determine whether the attack may have been an "inside job" that originated within the company. The company set up a publicized e-mail account—called a "fraud box"—that enabled employees to notify them if they suspected an e-mail phishing attack. The interarrival times, i.e., the time differences (in seconds), for 267 fraud box e-mail notifications were recorded and saved in the file. *Chance* showed that if there is minimal or no collaboration or collusion from within the company, the interarrival times would have a frequency distribution similar to the one shown in the accompanying figure. Construct a frequency histogram for the interarrival times. Give your opinion on whether the phishing attack against the organization was an "inside job."

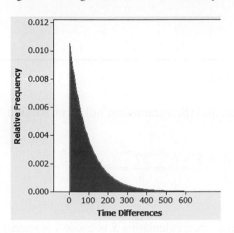

2.34 **Made-to-order delivery times.** Production processes may be classified as *make-to-stock processes* or *make-to-order processes*. Make-to-stock processes are designed to produce a standardized product that can be sold to customers from the firm's inventory. Make-to-order processes are designed to produce products according to customer specifications (Schroeder, *Operations Management*, 2008). In general, performance of make-to-order processes is measured by delivery time—the time from receipt of an order until the product is delivered to the customer. The accompanying data set is a sample of delivery times (in days) for a particular make-to-order firm last year. The delivery times marked by an asterisk are associated with customers who subsequently placed additional orders with the firm.

50*	64*	56*	43*	64*	82*	65*	49*	32*	63*	44*	71
54*	51*	102	49*	73*	50*	39*	86	33*	95	59*	51*
68											

Concerned that they are losing potential repeat customers because of long delivery times, the management would like to establish a guideline for the maximum tolerable delivery time. Use a graphical method to help suggest a guideline. Explain your reasoning.

2.3 Numerical Measures of Central Tendency

When we speak of a data set, we refer to either a sample or a population. If statistical inference is our goal, we'll wish ultimately to use sample **numerical descriptive measures** to make inferences about the corresponding measures for the population.

As you'll see, a large number of numerical methods are available to describe quantitative data sets. Most of these methods measure one of two data characteristics:

1. The **central tendency** of the set of measurements—that is, the tendency of the data to cluster, or center, about certain numerical values (see Figure 2.14a).
2. The **variability** of the set of measurements—that is, the spread of the data (see Figure 2.14b).

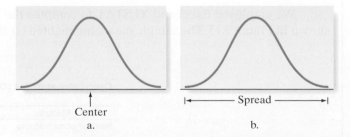

Figure 2.14
Numerical descriptive measures

In this section we concentrate on **measures of central tendency.** In the next section, we discuss measures of variability. The most popular and best-understood measure of central tendency for quantitative data is the arithmetic mean (or simply the mean) of a data set.

The **mean** of a set of quantitative data is the sum of the measurements divided by the number of measurements contained in the data set.

In everyday terms, the mean is the average value of the data set and is often used to represent a "typical" value. We denote the **mean of a sample** of measurements by $\bar{x}$ (read "x-bar") and represent the formula for its calculation as shown in the box below.

Formula for a Sample Mean

$$\bar{x} = \frac{\sum\limits_{i=1}^{n} x_i}{n}$$

[*Note:* $\sum\limits_{i=1}^{n} x_i = (x_1 + x_2 + \cdots + x_n)$. For more details on this summation notation, see Appendix A.]

EXAMPLE 2.3

Calculating the Sample Mean

Problem Calculate the mean of the following five sample measurements: 5, 3, 8, 5, 6.

Solution Using the definition of sample mean and the summation notation, we find

$$\bar{x} = \frac{\sum\limits_{i=1}^{5} x_i}{5} = \frac{5 + 3 + 8 + 5 + 6}{5} = \frac{27}{5} = 5.4$$

Thus, the mean of this sample is 5.4.

Look Back There is no specific rule for rounding when calculating $\bar{x}$ because $\bar{x}$ is specifically defined to be the sum of all measurements divided by n—that is, it is a specific fraction. When $\bar{x}$ is used for descriptive purposes, it is often convenient to round the calculated value of $\bar{x}$ to the number of significant figures used for the original measurements. When $\bar{x}$ is to be used in other calculations, however, it may be necessary to retain more significant figures.

• **Now Work Exercise 2.36**

EXAMPLE 2.4

Finding the Mean on a Printout—R&D Expenditures

Problem Calculate the sample mean for the R&D expenditure percentages of the 50 companies given in Table 2.2 on page 76.

Solution The mean R&D percentage for the 50 companies is denoted

$$\bar{x} = \frac{\sum\limits_{i=1}^{50} x_i}{50}$$

We employed Excel and XLSTAT to compute the mean. The XLSTAT printout is shown in Figure 2.15. The sample mean, highlighted on the printout, is $\bar{x} = 8.492$.

Descriptive statistics (Quantitative data):	
Statistic	**RDPct**
Nbr. of observations	50
Minimum	5.200
Maximum	13.500
Range	8.300
1st Quartile	7.100
Median	8.050
3rd Quartile	9.575
Mean	8.492
Variance (n-1)	3.923
Standard deviation (n-1)	1.981

Figure 2.15

XLSTAT numerical descriptive measures for 50 R&D percentages

Look Back Given this information, you can visualize a distribution of R&D percentages centered in the vicinity $\bar{x} = 8.492$. An examination of the relative frequency histogram (Figure 2.10) confirms that $\bar{x}$ does, in fact, fall near the center of the distribution.

The sample mean $\bar{x}$ will play an important role in accomplishing our objective of making inferences about populations based on sample information. For this reason, we need to use a different symbol for the *mean of a population*–the mean of the set of measurements on every unit in the population. We use the Greek letter μ (mu) for the population mean.

Symbols for the Sample and Population Mean

In this text, we adopt a general policy of using Greek letters to represent population numerical descriptive measures and Roman letters to represent corresponding descriptive measures for the sample. The symbols for the mean are

$$\bar{x} = \text{Sample mean}$$

$$\mu = \text{Population mean*}$$

We'll often use the sample mean $\bar{x}$ to estimate (make an inference about) the population mean, μ. For example, the percentages of revenues spent on R&D by the population consisting of *all* U.S. companies has a mean equal to some value, μ. Our sample of 50 companies yielded percentages with a mean of $\bar{x} = 8.492$. If, as is usually the case, we don't have access to the measurements for the entire population, we could use $\bar{x}$ as an estimator or approximator for μ. Then we'd need to know something about the reliability of our inference—that is, we'd need to know how accurately we might expect $\bar{x}$ to estimate μ. In Chapter 6, we'll find that accuracy depends on two factors:

1. The *size of the sample*. The larger the sample, the more accurate the estimate will tend to be.
2. The *variability,* or *spread, of the data*. All other factors remaining constant, the more variable the data, the less accurate the estimate.

Another important measure of central tendency is the *median*.

The **median** of a quantitative data set is the middle number when the measurements are arranged in ascending (or descending) order.

The median is of most value in describing large data sets. If the data set is characterized by a relative frequency histogram (Figure 2.16), the median is the point on the x-axis such that half the area under the histogram lies above the median and half lies below. [*Note:* In Section 2.2, we observed that the relative frequency associated with a particular interval on the horizontal axis is proportional to the amount of area under the histogram that lies above the interval.] We denote the *median of a sample* by m. Like with the population mean, we use a Greek letter (η) to represent the population median.

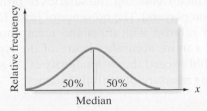

Figure 2.16

Location of the median

---

* The population mean μ is calculated as $\mu = \dfrac{\sum_{i=1}^{N} x_i}{N}$, where N is the population size.

Calculating a Sample Median, m

Arrange the n measurements from smallest to largest.

1. If n is odd, m is the middle number.
2. If n is even, m is the mean of the middle two numbers.

Symbols for the Sample and Population Median

$$m = \text{sample median}$$

$$\eta = \text{population median*}$$

EXAMPLE 2.5

Computing the Median

Problem Consider the following sample of $n = 7$ measurements: 5, 7, 4, 5, 20, 6, 2.

a. Calculate the median m of this sample.

b. Eliminate the last measurement (the 2) and calculate the median of the remaining $n = 6$ measurements.

Solution

a. The seven measurements in the sample are ranked in ascending order: 2, 4, 5, 5, 6, 7, 20. Because the number of measurements is odd, the median is the middle measurement. Thus, the median of this sample is $m = 5$ (the second 5 listed in the sequence).

b. After removing the 2 from the set of measurements, we rank the sample measurements in ascending order as follows: 4, 5, 5, 6, 7, 20. Now the number of measurements is even, so we average the middle two measurements. The median is $m = (5 + 6)/2 = 5.5$.

Look Back When the sample size n is even and the two middle numbers are different (as in part **b**), exactly half of the measurements will fall below the calculated median m. However, when n is odd (as in part **a**), the percentage of measurements that fall below m is approximately 50%. This approximation improves as n increases.

● Now Work Exercise 2.35

In certain situations, the median may be a better measure of central tendency than the mean. In particular, the median is less sensitive than the mean to extremely large or small measurements. Note, for instance, that all but one of the measurements in part **a** of Example 2.5 center about $x = 5$. The single relatively large measurement, $x = 20$, does not affect the value of the median, 5, but it causes the mean, $\bar{x} = 7$, to lie to the right of most of the measurements.

As another example of data for which the central tendency is better described by the median than the mean, consider the salaries of professional athletes (e.g., National Basketball Association players). The presence of just a few athletes (e.g., LeBron James) with extremely high salaries will affect the mean more than the median. Thus, the median will provide a more accurate picture of the typical salary for the professional league. The mean could exceed the vast majority of the sample measurements (salaries), making it a misleading measure of central tendency.

---

*The population median η is calculated like the sample median, but with all N observations in the population arranged from smallest to largest.

EXAMPLE 2.6

Finding the Median on a Printout—R&D Expenditures

Problem Calculate the median for the 50 R&D percentages given in Table 2.2 on page 76. Compare the median to the mean found in Example 2.4.

Solution For this large data set, we again resort to a computer analysis. The median is highlighted on the XLSTAT printout, Figure 2.15. You can see that the median is 8.05. This value implies that half of the 50 R&D percentages in the data set fall below 8.05 and half lie above 8.05.

Note that the mean (8.492) for these data is larger than the median. This fact indicates that the data are **skewed** to the right–that is, there are more extreme measurements in the right tail of the distribution than in the left tail (recall the histogram in Figure 2.10).

Look Back In general, extreme values (large or small) affect the mean more than the median because these values are used explicitly in the calculation of the mean. On the other hand, the median is not affected directly by extreme measurements because only the middle measurement (or two middle measurements) is explicitly used to calculate the median. Consequently, if measurements are pulled toward one end of the distribution (as with the R&D percentages), the mean will shift toward that tail more than the median.

A data set is said to be **skewed** if one tail of the distribution has more extreme observations than the other tail.

A comparison of the mean and the median gives us a general method for detecting skewness in data sets, as shown in the next box. With *rightward skewed* data, the right tail (high end) of the distribution has more extreme observations. These few, but large, measurements tend to pull the mean away from the median toward the right; that is, rightward skewness typically indicates that the mean is greater than the median. Conversely, with *leftward skewed* data, the left tail (low end) of the distribution has more extreme observations. These few, but small, measurements also tend to pull the mean away from the median but toward the left; consequently, leftward skewness typically implies that the mean is smaller than the median.

Detecting Skewness by Comparing the Mean and the Median

If the data set is skewed to the right, then typically the median is less than the mean.

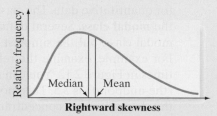

Rightward skewness

If the data set is symmetric, the mean equals the median.

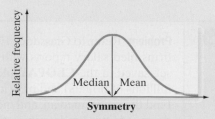

Symmetry

Continued

If the data set is skewed to the left, then typically the mean is less than (to the left of) the median.

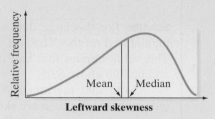

Leftward skewness

A third measure of central tendency is the *mode* of a set of measurements.

> The **mode** is the measurement that occurs most frequently in the data set.

EXAMPLE 2.7

Finding the Mode

Problem Each of 10 taste testers rated a new brand of barbecue sauce on a 10-point scale, where 1 = awful and 10 = excellent. Find the mode for the 10 ratings shown below.

8 7 9 6 8 10 9 9 5 7

Solution Because 9 occurs most often, the mode of the 10 taste-ratings is 9.

Look Back Note that the data are actually qualitative in nature (e.g., "awful," "excellent"). The mode is particularly useful for describing qualitative data. The modal category is simply the category (or class) that occurs most often.

• **Now Work Exercise 2.39**

Because it emphasizes data concentration, the mode is used with quantitative data sets to locate the region in which much of the data are concentrated. A retailer of men's clothing would be interested in the modal neck size and sleeve length of potential customers. The modal income class of the laborers in the United States is of interest to the Labor Department.

For some quantitative data sets, the mode may not be very meaningful. For example, consider the percentages of revenues spent on R&D by 50 companies, Table 2.2. A reexamination of the data reveals that three of the measurements are repeated three times: 6.5%, 6.9%, and 8.2%. Thus, there are three modes in the sample, and none is particularly useful as a measure of central tendency.

A more meaningful measure can be obtained from a relative frequency histogram for quantitative data. The class interval containing the largest relative frequency is called the **modal class.** Several definitions exist for locating the position of the mode within a modal class, but the simplest is to define the mode as the midpoint of the modal class. For example, examine the relative frequency histogram for the price quote processing times in Figure 2.12. You can see that the modal class is the interval (3.0–4.0). The mode (the midpoint) is 3.5. This modal class (and the mode itself) identifies the area in which the data are most concentrated, and in that sense it is a measure of central tendency. However, for most applications involving quantitative data, the mean and median provide more descriptive information than the mode.

EXAMPLE 2.8

Comparing the Mean, Median, and Mode— CEO Salaries

Problem Refer to Glassdoor Economic Research's 2015 list of salaries for 441 CEOs whose firms filed salary reports with the Securities and Exchange Commission (SEC). The data set, saved in the **CEOPAY** file, includes the quantitative variables CEO annual salary (in millions of dollars) and pay (in thousands of dollars) of typical workers at the CEO's firm. Find the mean, median, and mode for both of these variables. Which measure of central tendency is better for describing the distribution of CEO annual salary? Typical worker pay?

Solution Measures of central tendency for the two variables were obtained using SPSS. The means, medians, and modes are displayed at the top of the SPSS printout, Figure 2.17. For CEO salary, the mean, median, and mode are $13.88 million, $11.84 million, and $0, respectively. Note that the mean is much greater than the median, indicating that the data are highly skewed right. This rightward skewness (graphically shown on the histogram for CEO salary in Figure 2.17) is due to several exceptionally high CEO salaries in 2015. Consequently, we would probably want to use the median, $11.84 million, as the "typical" value for annual pay for CEOs at the 441 firms. The mode of $0 is the salary value that occurs most often in the data set, but it is not very descriptive of the "center" of the CEO annual salary distribution. The mode reflects the fact that there were three CEOs who deferred their 2015 pay until the next year.

For typical worker pay, the mean, median, and mode shown are 77.8, 76.9, and 58 thousand dollars, respectively. The mean and median are nearly the same, which is typical of symmetric distributions. Further analysis reveals that 58 is just one of many modes (the lowest one)—another mode (the highest one) is 79. From the histogram on the right in Figure 2.17, you can see that the worker pay distribution is nearly symmetric, and that the modal class includes 75. Consequently, any of the three measures of central tendency could be used to describe the "middle" of the pay distribution.

Look Back The choice of which measure of central tendency to use will depend on the properties of the data set analyzed and on the application. Consequently, it is vital that you understand how the mean, median, and mode are computed.

Statistics

		CEO Salary ($mil)	Worker Pay ($thous)
N	Valid	441	441
	Missing	0	0
Mean		13.8794	77.7922
Median		11.8380	76.9090
Mode		.00	58.00[a]

a. Multiple modes exist. The smallest value is shown

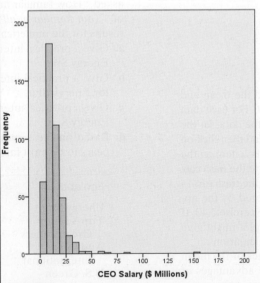

CEO Salary ($ Millions)

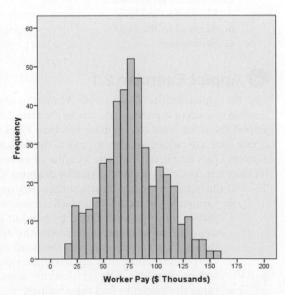

Worker Pay ($ Thousands)

Figure 2.17

SPSS Analysis of CEOs' Salaries and Workers' Pay

Now Work Exercise 2.46a, b

Exercises 2.35–2.55

Learning the Mechanics

2.35 Calculate the mean and median of the following grade
point averages:

NW

$$3.2 \quad 2.5 \quad 2.1 \quad 3.7 \quad 2.8 \quad 2.0$$

2.36 Calculate the mean for samples where
NW
  a. $n = 10, \Sigma x = 85$
  b. $n = 16, \Sigma x = 400$
  c. $n = 45, \Sigma x = 35$
  d. $n = 18, \Sigma x = 242$

2.37 Explain how the relationship between the mean and median provides information about the symmetry or skewness of the data's distribution.

2.38 Parking at a university has become a problem. The university's administrators are interested in determining the
average time it takes a student to find a parking spot. An
administrator inconspicuously followed 190 students and recorded how long it took each of them to find a parking spot.
The durations had a distribution that was skewed to the left.
Based on this information, discuss the relationship between
the mean and the median for the 190 times collected.

2.39 Calculate the mode, mean, and median of the following data:
NW

$$18 \quad 10 \quad 15 \quad 13 \quad 17 \quad 15 \quad 12 \quad 15 \quad 18 \quad 16 \quad 11$$

2.40 Calculate the mean, the median, and the mode for the following samples:
  a. $-2, 0, 5, 5, 5, 10, 11$
  b. $37, 98, 15, 38, 63, 19$
  c. Five food tasters rated a new product either "awful" or
  "excellent." Their ratings were awful, awful, excellent,
  excellent, and awful, respectively.

2.41 Describe how the mean compares to the median for a
distribution as follows:
  a. Skewed to the left
  b. Skewed to the right
  c. Symmetric

📊 Applet Exercise 2.1

Use the applet entitled *Mean versus Median* to find the mean and
median of each of the three data sets in Exercise 2.40. For each data
set, set the lower limit to a number less than all of the data, set the
upper limit to a number greater than all of the data, and then click on
Update. Click on the approximate location of each data item on the
number line. You can get rid of a point by dragging it to the trash can.
To clear the graph between data sets, simply click on the trash can.
  a. Compare the means and medians generated by the applet to those you calculated by hand in Exercise 2.40. If
  there are differences, explain why the applet might give
  values slightly different from the hand calculations.
  b. Despite providing only approximate values of the mean
  and median of a data set, describe some advantages of
  using the applet to find these values.

📊 Applet Exercise 2.2

Use the applet *Mean versus Median* to illustrate your descriptions in Exercise 2.41. For each part **a, b,** and **c,** create a data set
with 10 items that has the given property. Using the applet, verify

that the mean and median have the relationship you described in
Exercise 2.41.

📊 Applet Exercise 2.3

Use the applet *Mean versus Median* to study the effect that an
extreme value has on the difference between the mean and median. Begin by setting appropriate limits and plotting the given
data on the number line provided in the applet.

$$0 \quad 6 \quad 7 \quad 7 \quad 8 \quad 8 \quad 8 \quad 9 \quad 9 \quad 10$$

  a. Describe the shape of the distribution and record the
  value of the mean and median. Based on the shape of
  the distribution, do the mean and median have the relationship that you would expect?
  b. Replace the extreme value of 0 with 2, then 4, and
  then 6. Record the mean and median each time.
  Describe what is happening to the mean as 0 is replaced by higher numbers. What is happening to the
  median? How is the difference between the mean and
  the median changing?
  c. Now replace 0 with 8. What values does the applet give
  you for the mean and the median? Explain why the
  mean and the median should be the same.

Applying the Concepts—Basic

2.42 **Hotels' use of ecolabels.** Ecolabels such as *Energy Star*,
Green Key, and *Audubon International* are used by hotels
to advertise their energy-saving and conservation policies.
The *Journal of Vacation Marketing* (January 2016) published
a study to investigate how familiar travelers are with these
ecolabels and whether travelers believe they are credible. A
sample of 392 adult travelers were administered a questionnaire. One question showed a list of 6 different ecolabels, and
asked, "How familiar are you with this ecolabel, on a scale
of 1 (*not familiar at all*) to 5 (*very familiar*)." Summarized
results for the numerical responses are given in the table.
  a. Give a practical interpretation of the mean response for
  Energy Star.
  b. Give a practical interpretation of the median response
  for Energy Star.
  c. Give a practical interpretation of the response mode for
  Energy Star.
  d. Based on these summary statistics, which ecolabel appears to be most familiar to travelers?

Ecolabel	Mean	Median	Mode
Energy Star	4.44	5	5
TripAdvisor Greenleaders	3.57	4	4
Audubon International	2.41	2	1
U.S. Green Building Council	2.28	2	1
Green Business Bureau	2.25	2	1
Green Key	2.01	1	1

Source: S. Park and M. Millar, "The US Traveler's Familiarity
with and Perceived Credibility of Lodging Ecolabels," *Journal of
Vacation Marketing*, Vol. 22, No. 1, January 2016 (Table 3).

Rank	University	Public/ Private	Academic Reputation Score (100-pt. scale)	Average Financial Aid Awarded	Average Net Cost to Attend	Median Salary During Early Career	% High Meaning*	% STEM† Degrees
1	Harvard University	Private	99	$41,555	$14,455	$61,400	65%	28%
5	Yale University	Private	97	$39,771	$18,479	$60,300	68%	21%
20	University of California Berkeley	Public	79	$16,141	$16,178	$59,500	50%	31%
23	University of Virginia	Public	76	$16,834	$12,672	$54,700	52%	24%
27	Carnegie Mellon University	Private	76	$24,263	$33,257	$64,700	46%	51%
47	Pepperdine University	Private	60	$29,926	$25,345	$48,300	51%	4%

*% high meaning represents the percentage of alumni who say their work makes the world a better place;

†% STEM represents the percentage of degrees awarded in science, technology, engineering, or mathematics.

2.43 Rankings of research universities. Based on factors (e.g., academic reputation, financial aid offerings, overall cost, and success of graduates in the post-college job market)

TOPUNIV

that actual college freshmen said were most important to their college decision, College Choice developed their *2015 Rankings of National Research Universities*. Data for the top 50 universities are saved in the **TOPUNIV** file. Several are listed in the accompanying table above.

a. The *average financial aid awarded* values were determined by recording the financial aid awarded to each freshman who attended the university in 2015. Does this statistic represent a population or sample mean? Interpret this value for Harvard University.

b. The *median salary during early career* values were determined by recording the salaries of a random selection of alumni with 0 to 5 years of experience. Does this statistic represent a population or sample median? Interpret this value for Harvard University.

2.44 Performance of stock screeners. Investment companies provide their clients with automated tools—called *stock*

SCREEN

screeners—to help them select a portfolio of stocks to invest in. The American Association of Individual Investors

(AAII) provides statistics on stock screeners at its Web site, www.aaii.com. The next table lists the annualized percentage return on investment (as compared to the Standard & Poor's 500 Index) for 13 randomly selected stock screeners. (*Note:* A negative annualized return reflects a stock portfolio that performed worse than the S&P 500.)

9.0	−.1	−1.6	14.6	16.0	7.7	19.9	9.8	3.2	24.8	17.6	10.7	9.1

a. Compute the mean for the data set. Interpret its value.

b. Compute the median for the data set. Interpret its value.

2.45 Performance-based logistics. Refer to the *Journal of Business Logistics* (Vol. 36, 2015) study of the factors that

PBL

lead to successful performance-based logistics (PBL) projects, Exercise 1.15 (p. 49). Recall that opinions of a sample of 17 Department of Defense employees and suppliers were solicited during interviews. Demographics (current position, organization type, experience) were recorded for each interviewee and the data listed in the table below.

Interviewee	Position	Organization	Experience (years)
1	Vice president	Commercial	30
2	Postproduction	Government	15
3	Analyst	Commercial	10
4	Senior manager (mgr.)	Government	30
5	Support chief	Government	30
6	Specialist	Government	25
7	Senior analyst	Commercial	9
8	Division chief	Government	6
9	Item mgr.	Government	3
10	Senior mgr.	Government	20
11	MRO mgr.	Government	25
12	Logistics mgr.	Government	30
13	MRO mgr.	Commercial	10
14	MRO mgr.	Commercial	5
15	MRO mgr.	Commercial	10
16	Specialist	Government	20
17	Chief	Government	25

a. Find and interpret the mean years of experience for the 17 interviewees.

b. Find and interpret the median years of experience for the 17 interviewees.

c. Find and interpret the mode of the 17 years of experience values.

2.46 **Surface roughness of oil field pipe.** Oil field pipes are internally coated in order to prevent corrosion. Researchers at the University of Louisiana, Lafayette, investigated the influence that coating may have on the surface roughness of oil field pipes (*Anti-corrosion Methods and Materials,* Vol. 50, 2003). A scanning probe instrument was used to measure the surface roughness of each in a sample of 20 sections of coated interior pipe. The data (in micrometers) are provided in the table.

1.72	2.50	2.16	2.13	1.06	2.24	2.31	2.03	1.09	1.40
2.57	2.64	1.26	2.05	1.19	2.13	1.27	1.51	2.41	1.95

Source: F. Farshed, & T. Pesacreta, "Coated Pipe Interior Surface Roughness as Measured by Three Scanning Probe Instruments," *Anti-corrosion Methods and Materials,* Vol. 50, No. 1, 2003 (Table III).

a. Find and interpret the mean of the sample.

b. Find and interpret the median of the sample.

c. Which measure of central tendency—the mean or the median—best describes the surface roughness of the sampled pipe sections? Explain.

Applying the Concepts—Intermediate

2.47 **Permeability of sandstone during weathering.** Natural stone, such as sandstone, is a popular building construction material. An experiment was carried out to better understand the decay properties of sandstone when exposed to the weather (*Geographical Analysis,* Vol. 42, 2010). Blocks of sandstone were cut into 300 equal-sized slices and the slices randomly divided into three groups of 100 slices each. Slices in Group A were not exposed to any type of weathering; slices in Group B were repeatedly sprayed with a 10% salt solution (to simulate wetting by driven rain) under temperate conditions; and slices in Group C were soaked in a 10% salt solution and then dried (to simulate blocks of sandstone exposed during a wet winter and dried during a hot summer). All sandstone slices were then tested for permeability, measured in milliDarcies (mD). These permeability values measure pressure decay as a function of time. The data for the study (simulated) are saved in the **STONE** file. Measures of central tendency for the permeability measurements of each sandstone group are displayed in the accompanying Minitab printout.

Descriptive Statistics: PermA, PermB, PermC

Variable	N	Mean	Median		Mode	N for Mode
PermA	100	73.62	70.45		59.9, 60, 60.1, 60.4	2
PermB	100	128.54	139.30	146.4, 146.6, 147.9, 148.3		3
PermC	100	83.07	78.65		70.9	3

The data contain at least five mode values.
Only the smallest four are shown.

a. Interpret the mean and median of the permeability measurements for Group A sandstone slices.

b. Interpret the mean and median of the permeability measurements for Group B sandstone slices.

c. Interpret the mean and median of the permeability measurements for Group C sandstone slices.

d. Interpret the mode of the permeability measurements for Group C sandstone slices.

e. The lower the permeability value, the slower the pressure decay in the sandstone over time. Which type of weathering (type B or type C) appears to result in faster decay?

2.48 **Corporate sustainability of CPA firms.** Refer to the *Business and Society* (March 2011) study on the sustainability behaviors of CPA corporations, Exercise 2.23 (p. 83). Recall that level of support for corporate sustainability (measured on a quantitative scale ranging from 0 to 160 points) was obtained for each of 992 senior managers at CPA firms. Numerical measures of central tendency for level of support are shown in the accompanying Minitab printout.

Descriptive Statistics: Support

Variable	N	Mean	Minimum	Median	Maximum	Mode	N for Mode
Support	992	67.755	0.000	68.000	155.000	64	20

a. Locate the mean on the printout. Comment on the accuracy of the statement: "On average, the level of support for corporate sustainability for the 992 senior managers was 67.76 points."

b. Locate the median on the printout. Comment on the accuracy of the statement: "Half of the 992 senior managers reported a level of support for corporate sustainability below 68 points."

c. Locate the mode on the printout. Comment on the accuracy of the statement: "Most of the 992 senior managers reported a level of support for corporate sustainability below 64 points."

d. Based on the values of the measures of central tendency, make a statement about the type of skewness (if any) that exists in the distribution of 992 support levels. Check your answer by examining the histogram shown in Exercise 2.23.

2.49 **Is honey a cough remedy?** Refer to the *Archives of Pediatrics and Adolescent Medicine* (Dec. 2007) study of honey as a remedy for coughing, Exercise 2.31 (p. 86). Recall that the 105 ill children in the sample were randomly divided into three groups: those who received a dosage of an over-the-counter cough medicine (DM), those who received a dosage of honey (H), and those who received no dosage (control group). The coughing improvement scores (as determined by the children's parents) for the patients are reproduced in the next table.

a. Find the median improvement score for the honey dosage group.

Data for Exercise 2.49

Honey Dosage:	12 11 15 11 10 13 10 4 15 16 9 14
	10 6 10 8 11 12 12 8 12 9 11 15
	10 15 9 13 8 12 10 8 9 5 12

| DM Dosage: | 4 6 9 4 7 7 7 9 12 10 11 6 3 4 |
| | 9 12 7 6 8 12 12 4 12 13 7 10 |

No Dosage (Control):	13 9 4 4 10 15 9
	5 8 6 1 0 8 12 8 7 7 1 6 7 7 12
	7 9 7 9 5 11 9 5 6 8
	8 6 7 10 9 4 8 7 3 1 4 3

Source: Based on I. M. Paul et al., "Effect of Honey, Dextromethorphan, and No Treatment on Nocturnal Cough and Sleep Quality for Coughing Children and Their Parents," *Archives of Pediatrics and Adolescent Medicine,* Vol. 161, No. 12, December 2007 (data simulated).

b. Find the median improvement score for the DM dosage group.

c. Find the median improvement score for the control group.

d. Based on the results, parts **a–c,** what conclusions can pediatric researchers draw? (We show how to support these conclusions with a measure of reliability in subsequent chapters.)

2.50 **Crude oil biodegradation.** Refer to the *Journal of Petroleum Geology* (April 2010) study of the environmental factors associated with biodegradation in crude oil reservoirs, Exercise 2.29 (p. 85). Recall that amount of dioxide (milligrams/liter) and presence/absence of crude oil was determined for each of 16 water specimens collected from a mine reservoir. The data are repeated in the accompanying table.

Dioxide Amount	Crude Oil Present
3.3	No
0.5	Yes
1.3	Yes
0.4	Yes
0.1	No
4.0	No
0.3	No
0.2	Yes
2.4	No
2.4	No
1.4	No
0.5	Yes
0.2	Yes
4.0	No
4.0	No
4.0	No

Source: Based on A. Permanyer, J. L. R. Gallego, M. A. Caja, and D. Dessort, "Crude Oil Biodegradation and Environmental Factors at the Riutort Oil Shale Mine, SE Pyrenees," *Journal of Petroleum Geology,* Vol. 33, No. 2, April 2010, (Table 1).

a. Find the mean dioxide level of the 16 water specimens. Interpret this value.

b. Find the median dioxide level of the 16 water specimens. Interpret this value.

c. Find the mode of the 16 dioxide levels. Interpret this value.

d. Find the median dioxide level of the 10 water specimens with no crude oil present.

e. Find the median dioxide level of the 6 water specimens with crude oil present.

f. Compare the results, parts **d** and **e.** Make a statement about the association between dioxide level and presence/absence of crude oil.

2.51 **Symmetric or skewed?** Would you expect the data sets described below to possess relative frequency distributions that are symmetric, skewed to the right, or skewed to the left? Explain.

a. The salaries of all persons employed by a large university

b. The grades on an easy test

c. The grades on a difficult test

d. The amounts of time students in your class studied last week

e. The ages of automobiles on a used-car lot

f. The amounts of time spent by students on a difficult examination (maximum time is 50 minutes)

2.52 **Ranking driving performance of professional golfers.**

PGA
A group of researchers developed a new method for ranking the total driving performance of golfers on the Professional Golf Association (PGA) tour (*The Sport Journal,* Winter 2007). The method requires knowing a golfer's average driving distance (yards) and driving accuracy (percent of drives that land in the fairway). The values of these two variables are used to compute a driving performance index. Data for 40 PGA golfers (as ranked by the new method for a recent tour year) are saved in the accompanying file. The first five and last five observations are listed in the table below.

Rank	Player	Driving Distance (yards)	Driving Accuracy (%)	Driving Performance Index
1	Woods	316.1	54.6	3.58
2	Perry	304.7	63.4	3.48
3	Gutschewski	310.5	57.9	3.27
4	Wetterich	311.7	56.6	3.18
5	Hearn	295.2	68.5	2.82
⋮	⋮	⋮	⋮	⋮
36	Senden	291	66	1.31
37	Mickelson	300	58.7	1.30
38	Watney	298.9	59.4	1.26
39	Trahan	295.8	61.8	1.23
40	Pappas	309.4	50.6	1.17

Source: Based on Frederick Wiseman, Ph.D., Mohamed Habibullah, Ph.D., and Mustafa Yilmaz, Ph.D, "Ranking Driving Performance on the PGA Tour," *Sports Journal,* Vol. 10, No. 1, Winter 2007 (Table 2).

a. Find the mean, median, and mode for the 40 driving performance index values.

b. Interpret each of the measures of central tendency, part **a.**

c. Use the results, part **a,** to make a statement about the type of skewness in the distribution of driving performance indexes. Support your statement with a graph.

Applying the Concepts—Advanced

2.53 **Time in bankruptcy.** Refer to the *Financial Management* (Spring 1995) study of prepackaged bankruptcy filings, Exercise 2.32 (p. 86). Recall that each of 49 firms that negotiated a reorganization plan with its creditors prior to filing for bankruptcy was classified in one of three categories: joint exchange offer with prepack, prepack solicitation only, and no prefiling vote held. Consider the quantitative variable length of time in bankruptcy (months) saved in the accompanying file. Is it reasonable to use a single number (e.g., mean or median) to describe the center of the time-in-bankruptcy distributions? Or should three "centers" be calculated, one for each of the three categories of prepack firms? Explain.

2.54 **Nuclear power plants.** According to the Nuclear Energy Institute (NEI), there were 62 nuclear power plants operating in the United States in 2015. The table at top of the next column lists the 30 states that operate nuclear power plants, the number of plants in each state, and whether the state has passed legislation supporting nuclear energy expansion (regulated) or not (deregulated).
  a. Find the mean, median, and mode of the number of power plants per state. Interpret these values.
  b. Repeat part **a** for the regulated states only.
  c. Repeat part **a** for the deregulated states only.
  d. Compare the results, parts **b** and **c**. What inference can you make about the impact that state regulation has on the number of nuclear power plants?
  e. Eliminate the state with the largest number of power plants from the data set and repeat part **a**. What effect does dropping this measurement have on the measures of central tendency found in part **a**?
  f. Arrange the 30 values in the table from lowest to highest. Next, eliminate the lowest two values and the highest two values from the data set and find the mean of the remaining data values. The result is called a *10% trimmed mean,* because it is calculated after removing the highest 10% and the lowest 10% of the data values. What advantages does a trimmed mean have over the regular arithmetic mean?

State	Status	Number of Power Plants
Alabama	Regulated	2
Arizona	Regulated	1
Arkansas	Regulated	1
California	Regulated	1
Connecticut	Deregulated	1
Florida	Regulated	3
Georgia	Regulated	2
Illinois	Deregulated	6
Iowa	Deregulated	1
Kansas	Regulated	1
Louisiana	Regulated	2
Maryland	Deregulated	1
Massachusetts	Deregulated	1
Michigan	Deregulated	3
Minnesota	Regulated	2
Mississippi	Regulated	1
Missouri	Regulated	1
Nebraska	Regulated	2
New Hampshire	Deregulated	1
New Jersey	Deregulated	3
New York	Deregulated	4
North Carolina	Regulated	3
Ohio	Deregulated	2
Pennsylvania	Deregulated	5
South Carolina	Regulated	4
Tennessee	Regulated	2
Texas	Deregulated	2
Virginia	Regulated	2
Washington	Regulated	1
Wisconsin	Deregulated	1

Source: Nuclear Energy Institute (www.nei.org).

2.55 **Professional athletes' salaries.** The salaries of superstar professional athletes receive much attention in the media. The multimillion-dollar long-term contract is now commonplace among this elite group. Nevertheless, rarely does a season pass without negotiations between one or more of the players' associations and team owners for additional salary and fringe benefits for *all* players in their particular sports.
  a. If a players' association wanted to support its argument for higher "average" salaries, which measure of central tendency do you think it should use? Why?
  b. To refute the argument, which measure of central tendency should the owners apply to the players' salaries? Why?

2.4 Numerical Measures of Variability

Measures of central tendency provide only a partial description of a quantitative data set. The description is incomplete without a **measure of the variability,** or **spread,** of the data set. Knowledge of the data's variability along with its center can help us visualize the shape of a data set as well as its extreme values.

For example, suppose we are comparing the profit margin per construction job (as a percentage of the total bid price) for 100 construction jobs for each of two cost estimators working for a large construction company. The histograms for the two sets of 100 profit margin measurements are shown in Figure 2.18. If you examine the two

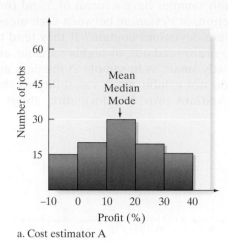
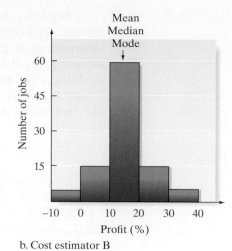

a. Cost estimator A

b. Cost estimator B

Figure 2.18

Profit margin histograms for two cost estimators

histograms, you will notice that both data sets are symmetric with equal modes, medians, and means. However, cost estimator A (Figure 2.18a) has profit margins spread with almost equal relative frequency over the measurement classes, while cost estimator B (Figure 2.18b) has profit margins clustered about the center of the distribution. Thus, estimator B's profit margins are *less variable* than estimator A's. Consequently, you can see that we need a measure of variability as well as a measure of central tendency to describe a data set.

Perhaps the simplest measure of the variability of a quantitative data set is its *range*.

> The **range** of a quantitative data set is equal to the largest measurement minus the smallest measurement.

The range is easy to compute and easy to understand, but it is a rather insensitive measure of data variation when the data sets are large. This is because two data sets can have the same range and be vastly different with respect to data variation. This phenomenon is demonstrated in Figure 2.18. Although the ranges are equal and all central tendency measures are the same for these two symmetric data sets, there is an obvious difference between the two sets of measurements. The difference is that estimator B's profit margins tend to be more stable—that is, to pile up or to cluster about the center of the data set. In contrast, estimator A's profit margins are more spread out over the range, indicating a higher incidence of some high profit margins but also a greater risk of losses. Thus, even though the ranges are equal, the profit margin record of estimator A is more variable than that of estimator B, indicating a distinct difference in their cost-estimating characteristics.

Let's see if we can find a measure of data variation that is more sensitive than the range. Consider the two samples in Table 2.5: Each has five measurements. (We have ordered the numbers for convenience.)

Table 2.5	Two Hypothetical Data Sets	
	Sample 1	Sample 2
Measurements	1, 2, 3, 4, 5	2, 3, 3, 3, 4
Mean	$\bar{x} = \dfrac{1 + 2 + 3 + 4 + 5}{5} = \dfrac{15}{5} = 3$	$\bar{x} = \dfrac{2 + 3 + 3 + 3 + 4}{5} = \dfrac{15}{5} = 3$
Deviations of measurement values from $\bar{x}$	$(1 - 3), (2 - 3), (3 - 3), (4 - 3),$ $(5 - 3),$ or $-2, -1, 0, 1, 2$	$(2 - 3), (3 - 3), (3 - 3), (3 - 3),$ $(4 - 3),$ or $-1, 0, 0, 0, 1$

Note that both samples have a mean of 3 and that we have also calculated the distance and direction, or *deviation*, between each measurement and the mean. What information do these deviations contain? If they tend to be large in magnitude, as in sample 1, the data are spread out, or highly variable, as shown in Figure 2.19a. If the deviations are mostly small, as in sample 2, the data are clustered around the mean, $\bar{x}$, and therefore do not exhibit much variability, as shown in Figure 2.19b. You can see that these deviations provide information about the variability of the sample measurements.

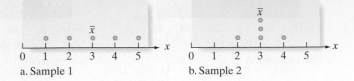

Figure 2.19

Dot plots for two data sets

a. Sample 1   b. Sample 2

The next step is to condense the information in these deviations into a single numerical measure of variability. Averaging the deviations from $\bar{x}$ won't help because the negative and positive deviations cancel; that is, the sum of the deviations (and thus the average deviation) is always equal to zero.

Two methods come to mind for dealing with the fact that positive and negative deviations from the mean cancel. The first is to treat all the deviations as though they were positive, ignoring the sign of the negative deviations. We won't pursue this line of thought because the resulting measure of variability (the mean of the absolute values of the deviations) presents analytical difficulties beyond the scope of this text. A second method of eliminating the minus signs associated with the deviations is to square them. The quantity we can calculate from the squared deviations will provide a meaningful description of the variability of a data set and present fewer analytical difficulties in inference making.

To use the squared deviations calculated from a data set, we first calculate the *sample variance*.

The **sample variance** for a sample of n measurements is equal to the sum of the squared deviations from the mean divided by $(n - 1)$. The symbol s^2 is used to represent the sample variance.

Formula for the Sample Variance

$$s^2 = \frac{\sum\limits_{i=1}^{n} (x_i - \bar{x})^2}{n - 1}$$

Note: A shortcut formula for calculating s^2 is

$$s^2 = \frac{\sum\limits_{i=1}^{n} x_i^2 - \dfrac{\left(\sum\limits_{i=1}^{n} x_i\right)^2}{n}}{n - 1}$$

Referring to the two samples in Table 2.5, you can calculate the variance for sample 1 as follows:

$$s^2 = \frac{(1-3)^2 + (2-3)^2 + (3-3)^2 + (4-3)^2 + (5-3)^2}{5-1}$$

$$= \frac{4+1+0+1+4}{4} = 2.5$$

The second step in finding a meaningful measure of data variability is to calculate the *standard deviation* of the data set.

The **sample standard deviation,** s, is defined as the positive square root of the sample variance, s^2. Thus, $s = \sqrt{s^2}$.

The population variance, denoted by the symbol σ^2 (sigma squared), is the average of the squared distances of the measurements on *all* units in the population from the mean, μ, and σ (sigma) is the square root of this quantity. Because we rarely, if ever, have access to the population data, we do not compute σ^2 or σ. We simply denote these two quantities by their respective symbols.*

Symbols for Variance and Standard Deviation

s^2 = Sample variance

s = Sample standard deviation

σ^2 = Population variance

σ = Population standard deviation

Notice that, unlike the variance, the standard deviation is expressed in the original units of measurement. For example, if the original measurements are in dollars, the variance is expressed in the peculiar units "dollars squared," but the standard deviation is expressed in dollars. Consequently, you can think of s as a "typical" distance of an observation x from its mean, $\bar{x}$.

You may wonder why we use the divisor $(n-1)$ instead of n when calculating the sample variance. Wouldn't using n be more logical so that the sample variance would be the average squared deviation from the mean? The trouble is that using n tends to produce an underestimate of the population variance, σ^2, so we use $(n-1)$ in the denominator to provide the appropriate correction for this tendency.† Because sample statistics such as s^2 are primarily used to estimate population parameters such as σ^2, $(n-1)$ is preferred to n when defining the sample variance.

You now know that the standard deviation measures the variability of a set of data. The larger the standard deviation, the more variable the data. How smaller the standard deviation, the less variable the data. But how can we practically interpret the standard deviation and use it to make inferences? This is the topic of Section 2.5.

---

*The population variance, σ^2, is calculated as $\sigma^2 = \dfrac{\sum\limits_{i=1}^{N}(x_i - \mu)^2}{N}$, where N is the size of the population.

†*Appropriate* here means that s^2 with the divisor $(n-1)$ is an *unbiased estimator* of σ^2. We define and discuss *unbiasedness* of estimators in Chapter 5.

EXAMPLE 2.9

Computing Measures of Variation

Problem Calculate the variance and standard deviation of the following sample: 2, 3, 3, 3, 4. (These data are entered into an Excel spreadsheet, shown in Figure 2.20.)

Solution If you calculate the values of s and s^2 using the formulas in the boxes on pages 100–101, you first need to compute $\bar{x}$. From Figure 2.20 below, we see that $\Sigma x = 15$. Thus, $\bar{x} = \dfrac{\Sigma x}{n} = \dfrac{15}{5} = 3$. Now, for each measurement, find $(x - \bar{x})$ and $(x - \bar{x})^2$, as shown in the Excel spreadsheet.

	A	B	C	D	E
1		X	(X-Xbar)	(X-Xbar)²	
2		2	-1	1	
3		3	0	0	
4		3	0	0	
5		3	0	0	
6		4	1	1	
7					
8	Sum	15	0	2	
9					
10			Variance	0.5	
11					
12			Std. Dev.	0.71	
13					

Figure 2.20

Excel Spreadsheet Showing Variance Calculations

Then we use*

$$s^2 = \frac{\sum_{i=1}^{n}(x - \bar{x})^2}{n - 1} = \frac{2}{5 - 1} = \frac{2}{4} = .5$$

$$s = \sqrt{.5} = .71$$

Look Ahead As the sample size n increases, these calculations can become very tedious. As the next example shows, we can use the computer to find s^2 and s.

● **Now Work Exercise 2.57**

EXAMPLE 2.10

Finding Measures of Variation on a Printout— R&D Expenditures

Problem Use the computer to find the sample variance s^2 and the sample standard deviation s for the 50 companies' percentages of revenues spent on R&D, given in Table 2.2 (p. 76).

Solution The XLSTAT printout describing the R&D percentage data is reproduced in Figure 2.21. The variance and standard deviation, highlighted on the printout, are $s^2 = 3.9228$ and $s = 1.9806$. The value $s = 1.98$ represents a typical deviation of an R&D percentage from the sample mean, $\bar{x} = 8.49\%$. We have more to say about the interpretation of s in the next section.

● **Now Work Exercise 2.67**

Descriptive statistics (Quantitative data):

Statistic	RDPct
Nbr. of observations	50
Minimum	5.200
Maximum	13.500
Range	8.300
1st Quartile	7.100
Median	8.050
3rd Quartile	9.575
Mean	8.492
Variance (n-1)	3.923
Standard deviation (n-1)	1.981

Figure 2.21

XLSTAT numerical descriptive measures for 50 R&D percentages

You now know that the standard deviation measures the variability of a set of data. The larger the standard deviation, the more variable the data. The smaller the standard deviation, the less variable the data. But how can we practically interpret the standard deviation and use it to make inferences? This is the topic of Section 2.5.

*When calculating s^2, how many decimal places should you carry? Although there are no rules for the rounding procedure, it's reasonable to retain twice as many decimal places in s^2 as you ultimately wish to have in s. If you wish to calculate s to the nearest hundredth (two decimal places), for example, you should calculate s^2 to the nearest ten-thousandth (four decimal places).

Exercises 2.56–2.70

Learning the Mechanics

2.56 Answer the following questions about variability of data sets:

a. What is the primary disadvantage of using the range to compare the variability of data sets?

b. Describe the sample variance using words rather than a formula. Do the same with the population variance.

c. Can the variance of a data set ever be negative? Explain. Can the variance ever be smaller than the standard deviation? Explain.

2.57 Calculate the range, variance, and standard deviation for the following samples:
[NW]

a. $4, 2, 1, 0, 1$

b. $1, 6, 2, 2, 3, 0, 3$

c. $8, -2, 1, 3, 5, 4, 4, 1, 3, 3$

d. $0, 2, 0, 0, -1, 1, -2, 1, 0, -1, 1, -1, 0, -3, -2, -1, 0, 1$

2.58 Calculate the variance and standard deviation for samples where

a. $n = 10, \Sigma x^2 = 84, \Sigma x = 20$

b. $n = 40, \Sigma x^2 = 380, \Sigma x = 100$

c. $n = 20, \Sigma x^2 = 18, \Sigma x = 17$.

2.59 Compute $\bar{x}$, s^2, and s for each of the following data sets. If appropriate, specify the units in which your answer is expressed.

a. $3, 1, 10, 10, 4$

b. 8 feet, 10 feet, 32 feet, 5 feet

c. $-1, -4, -3, 1, -4, -4$

d. $\frac{1}{5}$ ounce, $\frac{1}{5}$ ounce, $\frac{1}{5}$ ounce, $\frac{2}{5}$ ounce, $\frac{1}{5}$ ounce, $\frac{4}{5}$ ounce

2.60 Calculate the range, variance, and standard deviation for the following samples:

a. $39, 42, 40, 37, 41$

b. $100, 4, 7, 96, 80, 3, 1, 10, 2$

c. $100, 4, 7, 30, 80, 30, 42, 2$

2.61 Using only integers between 0 and 10, construct two data sets with at least 10 observations each that have the same range but different means. Construct a dot plot for each of your data sets, and mark the mean of each data set on its dot diagram.

2.62 Using only integers between 0 and 10, construct two data sets with at least 10 observations each so that the two sets have the same mean but different variances. Construct dot plots for each of your data sets and mark the mean of each data set on its dot diagram.

2.63 Consider the following sample of five measurements: 2, 1, 1, 0, 3.

a. Calculate the range, s^2, and s.

b. Add 3 to each measurement and repeat part **a.**

c. Subtract 4 from each measurement and repeat part **a.**

d. Considering your answers to parts **a, b,** and **c,** what seems to be the effect on the variability of a data set by adding the same number to or subtracting the same number from each measurement?

📊 Applet Exercise 2.4

Use the applet entitled *Standard Deviation* to find the standard deviation of each of the four data sets in Exercise 2.57. For each data set, set the lower limit to a number less than all of the data, set the upper limit to a number greater than all of the data, and then click on *Update*. Click on the approximate location of each data item on the number line. You can get rid of a point by dragging it to the trash can. To clear the graph between data sets, simply click on the trash can.

a. Compare the standard deviations generated by the applet to those you calculated by hand in Exercise 2.57. If there are differences, explain why the applet might give values slightly different from the hand calculations.

b. Despite providing a slightly different value of the standard deviation of a data set, describe some advantages of using the applet.

📊 Applet Exercise 2.5

Use the applet *Standard Deviation* to study the effect that multiplying or dividing each number in a data set by the same number has on the standard deviation. Begin by setting appropriate limits and plotting the given data on the number line provided in the applet.

$$0 \quad 1 \quad 1 \quad 1 \quad 2 \quad 2 \quad 3 \quad 4$$

a. Record the standard deviation. Then multiply each data item by 2, plot the new data items, and record the standard deviation. Repeat the process, first multiplying each of the original data items by 3 and then by 4. Describe what is happening to the standard deviation as the data items are multiplied by higher numbers. Divide each standard deviation by the standard deviation of the original data set. Do you see a pattern? Explain.

b. Divide each of the original data items by 2, plot the new data, and record the standard deviation. Repeat the process, first dividing each of the original data items by 3 and then by 4. Describe what is happening to the standard deviation as the data items are divided by higher numbers. Divide each standard deviation by the standard deviation of the original data set. Do you see a pattern? Explain.

c. Using your results from parts **a** and **b,** describe what happens to the standard deviation of a data set when each of the data items in the set is multiplied or divided by a fixed number n. Experiment by repeating parts **a** and **b** for other data sets if you need to.

📊 Applet Exercise 2.6

Use the applet *Standard Deviation* to study the effect that an extreme value has on the standard deviation. Begin by setting appropriate limits and plotting the given data on the number line provided in the applet.

$$0 \quad 6 \quad 7 \quad 7 \quad 8 \quad 8 \quad 8 \quad 9 \quad 9 \quad 10$$

a. Record the standard deviation. Replace the extreme value of 0 with 2, then 4, and then 6. Record the standard deviation each time. Describe what is happening to the standard deviation as 0 is replaced by higher numbers.

b. How would the standard deviation of the data set compare to the original standard deviation if the 0 were replaced by 16? Explain.

Applying the Concepts—Basic

2.64 Hotels' use of ecolabels. Refer to the *Journal of Vacation Marketing* (January 2016) study of travelers' familiarity with ecolabels used by hotels, Exercise 2.42 (p. 94). Recall that a sample of 392 adult travelers were shown a list of 6 different ecolabels, and asked, "How familiar are you with this ecolabel, on a scale of 1 (*not familiar at all*) to 5 (*very familiar*)." The mean and standard deviation of the responses for each ecolabel are provided in the table. Which of the ecolabels had the most variation in numerical responses? Explain.

Ecolabel	Mean	Std. Dev.
Energy Star	4.44	0.82
TripAdvisor Greenleaders	3.57	1.38
Audubon International	2.41	1.44
U.S. Green Building Council	2.28	1.39
Green Business Bureau	2.25	1.39
Green Key	2.01	1.30

Source: S. Park and M. Millar, "The US Traveler's Familiarity with and Perceived Credibility of Lodging Ecolabels," *Journal of Vacation Marketing*, Vol. 22, No. 1, January 2016 (Table 3).

2.65 Permeability of sandstone during weathering. Refer to the

STONE *Geographical Analysis* (Vol. 42, 2010) study of the decay properties of sandstone when exposed to the weather, Exercise 2.47 (p. 96). Recall that slices of sandstone blocks were tested for permeability under three conditions: no exposure to any type of weathering (A), repeatedly sprayed with a 10% salt solution (B), and soaked in a 10% salt solution and dried (C). Measures of variation for the permeability measurements (mV) of each sandstone group are displayed in the accompanying Minitab printout.

Descriptive Statistics: PermA, PermB, PermC

Variable	N	StDev	Variance	Minimum	Maximum	Range
PermA	100	14.48	209.53	55.20	122.40	67.20
PermB	100	21.97	482.75	50.40	150.00	99.60
PermC	100	20.05	401.94	52.20	129.00	76.80

a. Find the range of the permeability measurements for Group A sandstone slices. Verify its value using the minimum and maximum values shown on the printout.

b. Find the standard deviation of the permeability measurements for Group A sandstone slices. Verify its value using the variance shown on the printout.

c. Which condition (A, B, or C) has the more variable permeability data?

2.66 Performance of stock screeners. Refer to the American Association of Individual Investors (AAII) statistics on

SCREEN stock screeners, Exercise 2.44 (p. 95). Annualized percentage return on investment (as compared to the Standard & Poor's 500 Index) for 13 randomly selected stock screeners are reproduced in the table.

9.0	−.1	−1.6	14.6	16.0	7.7	19.9	9.8	3.2	24.8	17.6	10.7	9.1

a. Find the range of the data for the 13 stock screeners. Give the units of measurement for the range.

b. Find the variance of the data for the 13 stock screeners. If possible, give the units of measurement for the variance.

c. Find the standard deviation of the data for the 13 stock screeners. Give the units of measurement for the standard deviation.

Applying the Concepts—Intermediate

2.67 Corporate sustainability of CPA firms. Refer to the

CORSUS *Business and Society* (March 2011) study on the sustain-
NW ability behaviors of CPA corporations, Exercise 2.48 (p. 96). Numerical measures of variation for level of support for the 992 senior managers are shown in the accompanying Minitab printout.

Descriptive Statistics: Support

Variable	N	Mean	StDev	Variance	Minimum	Maximum	Range
Support	992	67.755	26.871	722.036	0.000	155.000	155.000

a. Locate the range on the printout. Comment on the accuracy of the statement: "The difference between the largest and smallest values of level of support for the 992 senior managers is 155 points."

b. Locate the variance on the printout. Comment on the accuracy of the statement: "On average, the level of support for corporate sustainability for the 992 senior managers is 722 points."

c. Locate the standard deviation on the printout. Does the distribution of support levels for the 992 senior managers have more or less variation than another distribution with a standard deviation of 50? Explain.

d. Which measure of variation best describes the distribution of 992 support levels? Explain.

2.68 Is honey a cough remedy? Refer to the *Archives of Pediatrics and Adolescent Medicine* (December 2007) study of honey

HCOUGH as a remedy for coughing, Exercise 2.31 (p. 86). The coughing improvement scores (as determined by the children's parents) for the patients in the over-the-counter cough medicine dosage (DM) group, honey dosage group, and control group are reproduced in the accompanying table.

Honey Dosage:	12 11 15 11 10 13 10 4 15 16 9
	14 10 6 10 8 11 12 12 8
	12 9 11 15 10 15 9 13 8 12 10
	8 9 5 12
DM Dosage:	4 6 9 4 7 7 7 9 12 10 11 6
	3 4 9 12 7 6 8 12 12 4 12
	13 7 10 13 9 4 4 10 15 9
No Dosage (Control):	5 8 6 1 0 8 12 8 7 7 1 6
	7 7 12 7 9 7 9 5 11 9 5
	6 8 8 6 7 10 9 4 8 7 3 1 4 3

Source: Based on I. M. Paul et al., "Effect of Honey, Dextromethorphan, and No Treatment on Nocturnal Cough and Sleep Quality for Coughing Children and Their Parents," *Archives of Pediatrics and Adolescent Medicine*, Vol. 161, No. 12, December 2007 (data simulated).

a. Find the standard deviation of the improvement scores for the honey dosage group.

b. Find the standard deviation of the improvement scores for the DM dosage group.

c. Find the standard deviation of the improvement scores for the control group.

d. Based on the results, parts **a–c**, which group appears to have the most variability in coughing improvement scores? The least variability?

2.69 **Active nuclear power plants.** Refer to Exercise 2.54 (p. 98) and the Nuclear Energy Institute's data on the number of nuclear power plants operating in each of 30 states.

NUKES

a. Find the range, variance, and standard deviation of this data set.

b. Eliminate the largest value from the data set and repeat part **a.** What effect does dropping this measurement have on the measures of variation found in part **a?**

c. Eliminate the smallest and largest value from the data set and repeat part **a.** What effect does dropping both of these measurements have on the measures of variation found in part **a?**

Applying the Concepts—Advanced

2.70 **Estimating production time.** A widely used technique for estimating the length of time it takes workers to produce a product is the **time study.** In a time study, the task to be studied is divided into measurable parts, and each is timed with a stopwatch or filmed for later analysis. For each worker, this process is repeated many times for each subtask. Then the average and standard deviation of the time required to complete each subtask are computed for each worker. A worker's overall time to complete the task under study is then determined by adding his or her subtask-time averages (Gaither and Frazier, *Operations Management*, 2001). The data (in minutes) given in the table are the result of a time study of a production operation involving two subtasks.

	Worker A		Worker B	
Repetition	Subtask 1	Subtask 2	Subtask 1	Subtask 2
1	30	2	31	7
2	28	4	30	2
3	31	3	32	6
4	38	3	30	5
5	25	2	29	4
6	29	4	30	1
7	30	3	31	4

a. Find the overall time it took each worker to complete the manufacturing operation under study.

b. For each worker, find the standard deviation of the seven times for subtask 1.

c. In the context of this problem, what are the standard deviations you computed in part **b** measuring?

d. Repeat part **b** for subtask 2.

e. If you could choose workers similar to A or workers similar to B to perform subtasks 1 and 2, which type would you assign to each subtask? Explain your decisions on the basis of your answers to parts **a–d.**

2.5   Using the Mean and Standard Deviation to Describe Data

We've seen that if we are comparing the variability of two samples selected from a population, the sample with the larger standard deviation is the more variable of the two. Thus, we know how to interpret the standard deviation on a relative or comparative basis, but we haven't explained how it provides a measure of variability for a single sample.

To understand how the standard deviation provides a measure of variability of a data set, consider a specific data set and answer the following questions: How many measurements are within 1 standard deviation of the mean? How many measurements are within 2 standard deviations? For a specific data set, we can answer these questions by counting the number of measurements in each of the intervals. However, if we are interested in obtaining a general answer to these questions, the problem is more difficult.

Rules 2.1 and 2.2 give two sets of answers to the questions of how many measurements fall within 1, 2, and 3 standard deviations of the mean. The first, which applies to *any* set of data, is derived from a theorem proved by the Russian mathematician P. L. Chebyshev. The second, which applies to **mound-shaped, symmetric distributions** of data (where the mean, median, and mode are all about the same), is based upon empirical evidence that has accumulated over the years. However, the percentages given for the intervals in Rule 2.2 provide remarkably good approximations even when the distribution of the data is slightly skewed or asymmetric. Note that both rules apply to either population data sets or sample data sets.

Rule 2.1:	Using the Mean and Standard Deviation to Describe Data: Chebyshev's Rule

Chebyshev's Rule applies to *any data set*, regardless of the shape of the frequency distribution of the data.

a. No useful information is provided on the fraction of measurements that fall within 1 standard deviation of the mean [i.e., within the interval $(\bar{x} - s, \bar{x} + s)$ for samples and $(\mu - \sigma, \mu + \sigma)$ for populations].

b. At least $\frac{3}{4}$ will fall within 2 standard deviations of the mean [i.e., within the interval $(\bar{x} - 2s, \bar{x} + 2s)$ for samples and $(\mu - 2\sigma, \mu + 2\sigma)$ for populations].

c. At least $\frac{8}{9}$ of the measurements will fall within 3 standard deviations of the mean [i.e., within the interval $(\bar{x} - 3s, \bar{x} + 3s)$ for samples and $(\mu - 3\sigma, \mu + 3\sigma)$ for populations].

d. Generally, for any number k greater than 1, at least $(1 - 1/k^2)$ of the measurements will fall within k standard deviations of the mean [i.e., within the interval $(\bar{x} - ks, \bar{x} + ks)$ for samples and $(\mu - k\sigma, \mu + k\sigma)$ for populations].

Rule 2.2:	Using the Mean and Standard Deviation to Describe Data: The Empirical Rule

The **Empirical Rule** is a rule of thumb that applies to data sets with frequency distributions that are *mound-shaped and symmetric*, as shown below.

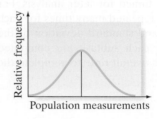

a. Approximately 68% of the measurements will fall within 1 standard deviation of the mean [i.e., within the interval $(\bar{x} - s, \bar{x} + s)$ for samples and $(\mu - \sigma, \mu + \sigma)$ for populations].

b. Approximately 95% of the measurements will fall within 2 standard deviations of the mean [i.e., within the interval $(\bar{x} - 2s, \bar{x} + 2s)$ for samples and $(\mu - 2\sigma, \mu + 2\sigma)$ for populations].

c. Approximately 99.7% (essentially all) of the measurements will fall within 3 standard deviations of the mean [i.e., within the interval $(\bar{x} - 3s, \bar{x} + 3s)$ for samples and $(\mu - 3\sigma, \mu + 3\sigma)$ for populations].

EXAMPLE 2.11

Interpreting the Standard Deviation — R&D Expenditures

Problem The 50 companies' percentages of revenues spent on R&D are repeated in Table 2.6. We have previously shown (see Figure 2.21, p. 102) that the mean and standard deviation of these data (rounded) are 8.49 and 1.98, respectively. Calculate the fraction of these measurements that lie within the intervals $\bar{x} \pm s$, $\bar{x} \pm 2s$, and $\bar{x} \pm 3s$ and compare the results with those predicted by Rules 2.1 and 2.2.

Table 2.6	R&D Percentages for 50 Companies								
13.5	9.5	8.2	6.5	8.4	8.1	6.9	7.5	10.5	13.5
7.2	7.1	9.0	9.9	8.2	13.2	9.2	6.9	9.6	7.7
9.7	7.5	7.2	5.9	6.6	11.1	8.8	5.2	10.6	8.2
11.3	5.6	10.1	8.0	8.5	11.7	7.1	7.7	9.4	6.0
8.0	7.4	10.5	7.8	7.9	6.5	6.9	6.5	6.8	9.5

Data Set: R&D

PAFNUTY L. CHEBYSHEV
(1821–1894)
The Splendid Russian
Mathematician

P. L. Chebyshev was educated in mathematical science at Moscow University, eventually earning his master's degree. Following his graduation, Chebyshev joined St. Petersburg (Russia) University as a professor, becoming part of the well-known "Petersburg math-ematical school." It was here that Chebyshev proved his famous theorem about the probability of a measurement being within k standard deviations of the mean (Rule 2.1). His fluency in French allowed him to gain international recognition in probability theory. In fact, Chebyshev once objected to being described as a "splendid Russian mathematician," saying he surely was a "worldwide math-ematician." One student remem-bered Chebyshev as "a wonderful lecturer" who "was always prompt for class," and "as soon as the bell sounded, he immediately dropped the chalk, and, limping, left the auditorium."

Solution We first form the interval

$$(\bar{x} - s, \bar{x} + s) = (8.49 - 1.98, 8.49 + 1.98) = (6.51, 10.47)$$

A check of the measurements reveals that 34 of the 50 measurements, or 68%, are within 1 standard deviation of the mean.

The next interval of interest,

$$(\bar{x} - 2s, \bar{x} + 2s) = (8.49 - 3.96, 8.49 + 3.96) = (4.53, 12.45),$$

contains 47 of the 50 measurements, or 94%.

Finally, the 3-standard-deviation interval around $\bar{x}$,

$$(\bar{x} - 3s, \bar{x} + 3s) = (8.49 - 5.94, 8.49 + 5.94) = (2.55, 14.43),$$

contains all, or 100%, of the measurements.

In spite of the fact that the distribution of these data is skewed to the right (see Figure 2.10, p. 77), the percentages within 1, 2, and 3 standard deviations (68%, 94%, and 100%) agree very well with the approximations of 68%, 95%, and 99.7% given by the Empirical Rule (Rule 2.2).

Look Back You will find that unless the distribution is extremely skewed, the mound-shaped approximations will be reasonably accurate. Of course, no matter what the shape of the distribution, Chebyshev's Rule (Rule 2.1) ensures that at least 75% and at least 89% of the measurements will lie within 2 and 3 standard deviations of the mean, respectively.

● **Now Work Exercise 2.74**

EXAMPLE 2.12

Check on the Calculation of s—R&D Expenditures

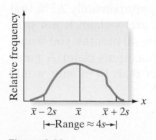

Figure 2.22

The relation between the range and the standard deviation

Problem Chebyshev's Rule and the Empirical Rule are useful as a check on the calcula-tion of the standard deviation. For example, suppose we calculated the standard deviation for the R&D percentages (Table 2.6) to be 3.92. Are there any "clues" in the data that enable us to judge whether this number is reasonable?

Solution The range of the R&D percentages in Table 2.6 is $13.5 - 5.2 = 8.3$. From Chebyshev's Rule and the Empirical Rule we know that most of the measurements (approximately 95% if the distribution is mound-shaped) will be within 2 standard deviations of the mean. And, regardless of the shape of the distribution and the num-ber of measurements, almost all of them will fall within 3 standard deviations of the mean. Consequently, we would expect the range of the measurements to be between 4 (i.e., $\pm 2s$) and 6 (i.e., $\pm 3s$) standard deviations in length (see Figure 2.22).

For the R&D data, this means that s should fall between

$$\frac{\text{Range}}{6} = \frac{8.3}{6} = 1.38 \quad \text{and} \quad \frac{\text{Range}}{4} = \frac{8.3}{4} = 2.08$$

In particular, the standard deviation should not be much larger than $\frac{1}{4}$ of the range, particularly for the data set with 50 measurements. Thus, we have reason to believe that the calculation of 3.92 is too large. A check of our work reveals that 3.92 is the variance s^2, not the standard deviation s (see Example 2.10). We "forgot" to take the square root (a common error); the correct value is $s = 1.98$. Note that this value is between $\frac{1}{6}$ and $\frac{1}{4}$ of the range.

Look Ahead In examples and exercises we'll sometimes use $s \approx \text{range}/4$ to obtain a crude, and usually conservatively large, approximation for s. However, we stress that this is no substitute for calculating the exact value of s when possible.

● **Now Work Exercise 2.75**

In the next example, we use the concepts in Chebyshev's Rule and the Empirical Rule to build the foundation for statistical inference making.

EXAMPLE 2.13

Making a Statistical Inference—Car Battery Guarantee

Problem A manufacturer of automobile batteries claims that the average length of life for its grade A battery is 60 months. However, the guarantee on this brand is for just 36 months. Suppose the standard deviation of the life length is known to be 10 months, and the frequency distribution of the life-length data is known to be mound-shaped.

a. Approximately what percentage of the manufacturer's grade A batteries will last more than 50 months, assuming the manufacturer's claim is true?

b. Approximately what percentage of the manufacturer's batteries will last less than 40 months, assuming the manufacturer's claim is true?

c. Suppose your battery lasts 37 months. What could you infer about the manufacturer's claim?

Solution If the distribution of life length is assumed to be mound-shaped with a mean of 60 months and a standard deviation of 10 months, it would appear as shown in Figure 2.23. Note that we can take advantage of the fact that mound-shaped distributions are (approximately) symmetric about the mean, so that the percentages given by the Empirical Rule can be split equally between the halves of the distribution on each side of the mean.

For example, because approximately 68% of the measurements will fall within 1 standard deviation of the mean, the distribution's symmetry implies that approximately $\frac{1}{2}(68\%) = 34\%$ of the measurements will fall between the mean and 1 standard deviation on each side. This concept is illustrated in Figure 2.23. The figure also shows that 2.5% of the measurements lie beyond 2 standard deviations in each direction from the mean. This result follows from the fact that if approximately 95% of the measurements fall within 2 standard deviations of the mean, then about 5% fall outside 2 standard deviations; if the distribution is approximately symmetric, then about 2.5% of the measurements fall beyond 2 standard deviations on each side of the mean.

a. It is easy to see in Figure 2.23 that the percentage of batteries lasting more than 50 months is approximately 34% (between 50 and 60 months) plus 50% (greater than 60 months). Thus, approximately 84% of the batteries should have life length exceeding 50 months.

b. The percentage of batteries that last less than 40 months can also be easily determined from Figure 2.23. Approximately 2.5% of the batteries should fail prior to 40 months, assuming the manufacturer's claim is true.

c. If you are so unfortunate that your grade A battery fails at 37 months, you can make one of two inferences: either your battery was one of the approximately 2.5% that fail prior to 40 months, or something about the manufacturer's claim is not true. Because the chances are so small that a battery fails before 40 months, you would have good reason to have serious doubts about the manufacturer's claim. A mean smaller than 60 months and/or a standard deviation longer than 10 months would both increase the likelihood of failure prior to 40 months.*

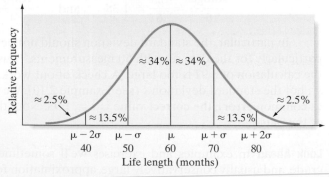

Figure 2.23

Battery life-length distribution: Manufacturer's claim assumed true

---

*The assumption that the distribution is mound-shaped and symmetric may also be incorrect. However, if the distribution were skewed to the right, as life-length distributions often tend to be, the percentage of measurements more than 2 standard deviations *below* the mean would be even less than 2.5%.

Look Back The approximations given in Figure 2.23 are more dependent on the assumption of a mound-shaped distribution than those given by the Empirical Rule (Rule 2.2) because the approximations in Figure 2.23 depend on the (approximate) symmetry of the mound-shaped distribution. We saw in Example 2.11 that the Empirical Rule can yield good approximations even for skewed distributions. This will *not* be true of the approximations in Figure 2.23; the distribution *must* be mound-shaped and approximately symmetric.

Example 2.13 is our initial demonstration of the statistical inference-making process. At this point you should realize that we'll use sample information (in Example 2.13, your battery's failure at 37 months) to make inferences about the population (in Example 2.13, the manufacturer's claim about the life length for the population of all batteries). We'll build on this foundation as we proceed.

STATISTICS IN ACTION

Interpreting Numerical Descriptive Measures

REVISITED   We return to the *Journal of Experimental Social Psychology* (Vol. 45, 2009) study on whether money can buy love for two groups of participants—those assigned the role of gift-giver and those assigned the role of gift-recipient. Recall that the researchers investigated whether givers and receivers differ on the price of the birthday gift reported and on the overall level of appreciation reported. The Minitab descriptive statistics printout for the **BUYLOV** data is displayed in Figure SIA2.5, with means and standard deviations highlighted.

First, we focus on the quantitative variable, *birthday gift price*. The sample mean gift price for givers is $105.84 compared with $149.00 for receivers. Our interpretation is that receivers report a higher average gift price than givers—a difference of about $43.

To interpret the gift price standard deviations (93.47 for givers and 134.5 for receivers), we substitute into the formula, $\bar{x} \perp 2s$, to obtain the following intervals:

Gift-Giver:	$\bar{x} \pm 2s = 105.84 \pm 2(93.47) = 105.84 \pm 186.94 = (-81.1, 292.78)$
Gift-Receiver:	$\bar{x} + 2s = 149.00 \pm 2(134.50) = 149 \pm 269 = (-120, 418)$

Because gift price cannot have a negative value, the two intervals for givers and receivers are more practically given as (0, 293) and (0, 418), respectively. Since the distributions of gift price are not mound-shaped and symmetric (see Figure SIA2.4a), we apply Chebyshev's Rule (Rule 2.1). Thus, we know that at least 75% of the gift-givers in the study reported a gift price between $0 and $293, and at least 75% of the gift-recipients reported a gift price between $0 and $418. You can see that the upper endpoint of the interval for givers lies below that for receivers. Consequently, we can infer that prices reported by gift-recipients tend to be higher than the prices reported by gift-givers. Also, if a gift price of $400 is observed, it is much more likely to be reported by a gift-receiver than a gift-giver.

A similar analysis performed for the variable *overall level of appreciation* yielded the following intervals:

Gift-Giver:	$\bar{x} \pm 2s = 4.985 \pm 2(2.775) = 4.985 \pm 5.55 = (-.565, 10.535)$
Gift-Receiver:	$\bar{x} \pm 2s = 7.165 \pm 2(2.928) = 7.165 \pm 5.856 = (1.309, 13.021)$

Since overall level of appreciation cannot have a value less than 2 and is a whole number, the two intervals for givers and receivers are more practically given as (2, 10) and

Figure SIA2.5

Minitab descriptive statistics for gift price and appreciation level, by role

Descriptive Statistics: BGiftPrice, OverallApp

Variable	Role	N	Mean	StDev	Variance	Minimum	Median	Maximum
BGiftPrice	Giver	134	105.84	93.47	8736.78	2.00	75.50	431.00
	Receiver	103	149.0	134.5	18083.8	1.0	133.0	548.0
OverallApp	Giver	134	4.985	2.775	7.699	2.000	4.000	13.000
	Receiver	103	7.165	2.928	8.571	2.000	7.000	14.000

STATISTICS IN ACTION REVISTED
(continued)

(2, 13), respectively. Applying Chebyshev's Rule, we know that at least 75% of the gift-givers in the study reported an appreciation level between 2 and 10 points, and at least 75% of the gift-recipients reported an appreciation level between 2 and 13 points. Again, the upper endpoint of the interval for givers lies below that for receivers; thus, we infer that overall levels of appreciation reported by gift-recipients tend to be higher than those reported by gift-givers.

Now, how does this information help the researchers determine whether there are "significant" differences in the means for gift-givers and gift-recipients? In Chapters 6 and 7 we present inferential methods that will answer such a question and provide a measure of reliability for the inference.

 *Data Set*: BUYLOV

Exercises 2.71–2.89

Learning the Mechanics

2.71 The output from a statistical software package indicates that the mean and standard deviation of a data set consisting of 200 measurements are $1,500 and $300, respectively.
  a. What are the units of measurement of the variable of interest? Based on the units, what type of data is this: quantitative or qualitative?
  b. What can be said about the number of measurements between $900 and $2,100? Between $600 and $2,400? Between $1,200 and $1,800? Between $1,500 and $2,100?

2.72 For any set of data, what can be said about the percentage of the measurements contained in each of the following intervals?
  a. $\bar{x} - s$ to $\bar{x} + s$
  b. $\bar{x} - 2s$ to $\bar{x} + 2s$
  c. $\bar{x} - 3s$ to $\bar{x} + 3s$

2.73 For a set of data with a mound-shaped relative frequency distribution, what can be said about the percentage of the measurements contained in each of the intervals specified in Exercise 2.72?

2.74 The following is a sample of 25 measurements:

| 7 | 6 | 6 | 11 | 8 | 9 | 11 | 9 | 10 | 8 | 7 | 7 |
| 5 | 9 | 10 | 7 | 7 | 7 | 7 | 9 | 12 | 10 | 10 | 8 | 6 |

  a. Compute $\bar{x}$, s^2, and s for this sample.
  b. Count the number of measurements in the intervals $\bar{x} \pm s$, $\bar{x} \pm 2s$, $\bar{x} \pm 3s$. Express each count as a percentage of the total number of measurements.
  c. Compare the percentages found in part **b** to the percentages given by the Empirical Rule and Chebyshev's Rule.
  d. Calculate the range and use it to obtain a rough approximation for s. Does the result compare favorably with the actual value for s found in part **a**?

2.75 Given a data set with a largest value of 760 and a smallest value of 135, what would you estimate the standard deviation to be? Explain the logic behind the procedure

you used to estimate the standard deviation. Suppose the standard deviation is reported to be 25. Is this feasible? Explain.

Applying the Concepts—Basic

2.76 **Voltage sags and swells.** The power quality of a transformer is measured by the quality of the voltage. Two causes of poor power quality are "sags" and "swells." A sag is an unusual dip and a swell is an unusual increase in the voltage level of a transformer. The power quality of transformers built in Turkey was investigated in *Electrical Engineering* (Vol. 95, 2013). For a sample of 103 transformers built for heavy industry, the mean number of sags per week was 353 and the mean number of swells per week was 184. Assume the standard deviation of the sag distribution is 30 sags per week and the standard deviation of the swell distribution is 25 swells per week.
  a. For a sag distribution with any shape, what proportion of transformers will have between 263 and 443 sags per week? Which rule did you apply and why?
  b. For a sag distribution that is mound-shaped and symmetric, what proportion of transformers will have between 263 and 443 sags per week? Which rule did you apply and why?
  c. For a swell distribution with any shape, what proportion of transformers will have between 109 and 259 swells per week? Which rule did you apply and why?
  d. For a swell distribution that is mound-shaped and symmetric, what proportion of transformers will have between 109 and 259 swells per week? Which rule did you apply and why?

2.77 **Permeability of sandstone during weathering.** Refer to the *Geographical Analysis* (Vol. 42, 2010) study of the decay properties of sandstone when exposed to the weather, Exercises 2.47 and 2.65 (pp. 96 and 104). Recall that slices of sandstone blocks were measured for permeability under three conditions: no exposure to any type of weathering (A), repeatedly sprayed with a 10% salt solution (B), and soaked in a 10% salt solution and dried (C).
  a. Combine the mean (from Exercise 2.47) and standard deviation (from Exercise 2.65) to make a statement about where most of the permeability measurements

for Group A sandstone slices will fall. Which rule did you use to make this inference and why?

b. Repeat part **a** for Group B sandstone slices.

c. Repeat part **a** for Group C sandstone slices.

d. Based on all your analyses, which type of weathering (type A, B, or C) appears to result in faster decay (i.e., higher permeability measurements)?

2.78 **Do social robots walk or roll?** Refer to the *International Conference on Social Robotics* (Vol. 6414, 2010) study on the current trend in the design of social robots, Exercise 2.5 (p. 72). Recall that in a random sample of social robots obtained through a Web search, 28 were built with wheels. The number of wheels on each of the 28 robots is listed in the accompanying table.

ROBOTS

4	4	3	3	3	6	4	2	2	2	1	3	3	3
3	4	4	3	2	8	2	2	3	4	3	3	4	2

Source: Based on S. Chew et al., "Do Social Robots Walk or Roll?" *International Conference on Social Robotics*, Vol. 6414, 2010 (adapted from Figure 2).

a. Generate a histogram for the sample data set. Is the distribution of number of wheels mound-shaped and symmetric?

b. Find the mean and standard deviation for the sample data set.

c. Form the interval, $\bar{x} \pm 2s$.

d. According to Chebychev's Rule, what proportion of sample observations will fall within the interval, part **c?**

e. According to the Empirical Rule, what proportion of sample observations will fall within the interval, part **c?**

f. Determine the actual proportion of sample observations that fall within the interval, part **c**. Even though the histogram, part **a**, is not perfectly symmetric, does the Empirical Rule provide a good estimate of the proportion?

2.79 Parents Against Watching Television. A society called Parents Against Watching Television (PAWT) is primarily concerned with the amount of television viewed by today's youth. It asked 300 parents of elementary school aged children to estimate the number of hours their child spent watching television in any given week. The mean and the standard deviation for their responses were 17 and 3, respectively. PAWT then constructed a stem-and-leaf display for the data, which showed that the distribution of the number of hours was a symmetric, mound-shaped distribution. Identify the interval where you believe approximately 95% of the television viewing times fell in the distribution.

2.80 Motivation of drug dealers. Consider a study of drug dealers and their motivation for participating in the illegal drug market (*Applied Psychology in Criminal Justice*, September 2009). The sample consisted of 100 convicted drug dealers who attended a court-mandated counseling program. Each dealer was scored on the Wanting Recognition (WR) Scale, which provides a quantitative measure of a person's level of need for approval and sensitivity to social situations. (Higher scores indicate a greater need for approval.) The sample of drug dealers had a mean WR score of 39, with a standard deviation of 6. Assume the distribution of WR scores for drug dealers is mound-shaped and symmetric.

a. Give a range of WR scores that will contain about 95% of the scores in the drug dealer sample.

b. What proportion of the drug dealers had WR scores above 51?

c. Give a range of WR sores that contain nearly all the scores in the drug dealer sample.

Applying the Concepts—Intermediate

2.81 **Sanitation inspection of cruise ships.** Refer to the Centers for Disease Control and Prevention listing of the October 2015 sanitation scores for 195 cruise ships, Exercise 2.24 (p. 83).

SANIT

a. Find the mean and standard deviation of the sanitation scores.

b. Calculate the intervals $\bar{x} \pm s, \bar{x} \pm 2s, \bar{x} \pm 3s$.

c. Find the percentage of measurements in the data set that fall within each of the intervals, part **b**. Do these percentages agree with Chebyshev's Rule? The Empirical Rule?

2.82 Volkswagen emissions scandal. Refer to the *Significance* (December 2015) study on estimating the number of U.S. deaths attributable to nitrogen oxide (NOx) pollution produced from illegal VW vehicles, Exercise 2.30 (p. 85). Recall that the researchers computed the estimate for each of 27 different scenarios involving different values of three variables: total distance (in miles) driven by these illegal VW vehicles, the amount by which the VW vehicles exceeded the EPA standard for NOx, and the estimated association between NOx emissions and mortality. The data (simulated from results reported in the study) are reproduced in the accompanying table. Assume that one of the 27 scenarios did, in fact, occur, and that the estimate for this scenario represents the actual number of deaths. Give an interval that will likely contain the number of deaths attributable to NOx pollution over the 7-year period.

VWDEATH

10	28	29	5	21	4	15	62	36	42	37	33	68	83
83	67	119	142	150	167	184	201	327	368	477	700	955	

2.83 Auditing water resources in Australia. Australia has developed a General Purpose Water Accounting (GPWA) reporting system in an effort to provide a financial accounting of water use in the country. The perceptions of potential users of the reports (e.g., water resource managers) were investigated in *Accounting, Auditing & Accountability Journal* (Vol. 29, 2016). Each in a sample of 36 potential users of GPWA reports was asked to complete a survey. Two key survey questions (with possible responses) were as follows:

Q1: Should there be national standards for water reporting? (Yes, No, or Undecided)

Q2: How useful will the GPWA reports be for water users? (1- to 5-point scale, where 1 = not useful at all and 5 = very useful)

The data (simulated from results reported in the journal article) for the 36 potential users are listed in the next table. For those users who believe there should be national standards, give a range that is likely to contain the user's answer to Q2.

User	Q1	Q2
1	Yes	5
2	Yes	4
3	Yes	4
4	Yes	3
5	Undecided	2
6	Yes	4
7	Yes	4
8	Yes	4
9	Yes	4
10	Yes	5
11	Yes	4
12	Yes	4
13	Yes	3
14	Yes	3
15	Yes	3
16	Yes	4
17	Yes	3
18	Yes	4
19	Yes	5
20	Yes	4
21	Undecided	5
22	Yes	4
23	No	2
24	Yes	5
25	Yes	5
26	Yes	5
27	Yes	3
28	Yes	4
29	Yes	5
30	Undecided	5
31	Undecided	5
32	Yes	4
33	Yes	5
34	Undecided	5
35	Yes	5
36	Yes	3

2.84 ***The Apprentice* contestants' performance ratings.** Refer to the *Significance* (April 2015) study of contestants' performance on the popular TV show *The Apprentice*, Exercise 2.9 (p. 73). Recall that each of 159 contestants was rated (on a 20-point scale) based on their performance. The accompanying Minitab printout gives the mean and standard deviation of the contestant ratings, categorized by highest degree obtained (no degree, first degree, or postgraduate degree) and prize (job or partnership with Lord Sugar).

Descriptive Statistics: Rating

Results for Prize = Job

Variable	Degree	N	Mean	StDev	Minimum	Maximum
Rating	First	54	7.796	4.231	1.000	17.000
	None	35	7.457	4.388	1.000	20.000
	Post	10	9.80	4.54	2.00	17.00

Results for Prize = Partner

Variable	Degree	N	Mean	StDev	Minimum	Maximum
Rating	First	33	8.212	4.775	1.000	20.000
	None	21	10.62	4.83	3.00	20.00
	Post	6	6.50	3.33	2.00	12.00

---

a. Give a practical interpretation of the mean rating for contestants with a first (bachelor's) degree who competed for a job with Lord Sugar.

b. Find an interval that captures about 95% of the ratings for contestants with a first (bachelor's) degree who competed for a job with Lord Sugar.

c. An analysis of the data led the researchers to conclude that "when the reward for winning ... was a job, more academically qualified contestants tended to perform less well; however, this pattern is reversed when the prize changed to a business partnership." Do you agree? Explain.

2.85 **Shopping vehicle and judgment.** While shopping at the grocery store, are you more likely to buy a vice product (e.g., a candy bar) when pushing a shopping cart or when carrying a shopping basket? This was the question of interest in a study published in the *Journal of Marketing Research* (December 2011). The researchers believe that when your arm is flexed (as when carrying a basket), you are more likely to choose a vice product than when your arm is extended (as when pushing a cart). To test this theory in a laboratory setting, the researchers recruited 22 consumers and asked each to push his or her hand against a table while being asked a series of shopping questions. Half of the consumers were told to put their arms in a flex position (similar to a shopping basket) and the other half were told to put their arms in an extended position (similar to a shopping cart). Participants were offered several choices between a vice and a virtue (e.g., a movie ticket vs. a shopping coupon, paying later with a larger amount vs. paying now), and a choice score (on a scale of 0 to 100) was determined for each. (Higher scores indicate a greater preference for vice options.) The average choice score for consumers with a flexed arm was 59, while the average for consumers with an extended arm was 43.

a. Suppose the standard deviations of the choice scores for the flexed arm and extended arm conditions are 4 and 2, respectively. Does this information support the researchers' theory? Explain.

b. Suppose the standard deviations of the choice scores for the flexed arm and extended arm conditions are 10 and 15, respectively. Does this information support the researchers' theory? Explain.

2.86 **Buy-side vs. sell-side analysts' earnings forecasts.** Financial analysts who make forecasts of stock prices and recommendations about whether to buy, sell, or hold specific securities can be categorized as either "buy-side" analysts or "sell-side" analysts. A group of Harvard Business School professors compared earnings forecasts of buy-side and sell-side analysts (*Financial Analysts Journal*, July/August 2008). Data were collected on 3,526 forecasts made by buy-side analysts and 58,562 forecasts made by sell-side analysts, and the relative absolute forecast error was determined for each.

a. Frequency distributions for buy-side and sell-side analysts forecast errors (with the sell-side distribution superimposed over the buy-side distribution) are shown in the accompanying figure. Based on the figure, the researchers concluded "that absolute forecast errors for buy-side analysts have a higher mean and variance than those for the sell-side analysts." Do you agree? Explain.

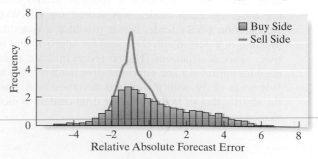

b. The mean and standard deviation of forecast errors for both buy-side and sell-side analysts are given in the following table. For each type of analyst, provide an interval that will contain approximately 95% of the forecast errors. Compare these intervals. Which type of analyst is more likely to have a relative forecast error of +2.00 or higher?

	Buy-Side Analysts	Sell-Side Analysts
Mean	0.85	−0.05
Standard deviation	1.93	0.85

Source: Based on B. Groysberg, P. Healy, and C. Chapman, *Financial Analysis Journal,* Vol. 64, No. 4. July/August 2008 (Table 2).

Applying the Concepts—Advanced

2.87 Land purchase decision. A buyer for a lumber company must decide whether to buy a piece of land containing 5,000 pine trees. If 1,000 of the trees are at least 40 feet tall, the buyer will purchase the land; otherwise, he won't. The owner of the land reports that the height of the trees has a mean of 30 feet and a standard deviation of 3 feet. Based on this information, what is the buyer's decision?

2.88 Improving SAT scores. The National Education Longitudinal Survey (NELS) tracks a nationally representative sample of U.S. students from eighth grade through high school and college. Research published in *Chance* (Winter 2001) examined the Standardized Assessment Test (SAT) scores of 265 NELS students who paid a private tutor to help them improve their scores. The table summarizes the changes in both the SAT–Mathematics and SAT–Verbal scores for these students.

	SAT–Math	SAT–Verbal
Mean change in score	19	7
Standard deviation of score changes	65	49

a. Suppose one of the 265 students who paid a private tutor is selected at random. Give an interval that is likely to contain this student's change in the SAT–Math score.
b. Repeat part **a** for the SAT–Verbal score.

c. Suppose the selected student increased his score on one of the SAT tests by 140 points. Which test, the SAT–Math or SAT–Verbal, is the one most likely to have the 140-point increase? Explain.

2.89 Monitoring weights of flour bags. When it is working properly, a machine that fills 25-pound bags of flour dispenses an average of 25 pounds per fill; the standard deviation of the amount of fill is .1 pound. To monitor the performance of the machine, an inspector weighs the contents of a bag coming off the machine's conveyor belt every half hour during the day. If the contents of two consecutive bags fall more than 2 standard deviations from the mean (using the mean and standard deviation given above), the filling process is said to be out of control, and the machine is shut down briefly for adjustments. The data given in the following table are the weights measured by the inspector yesterday. Assume the machine is never shut down for more than 15 minutes at a time. At what times yesterday was the process shut down for adjustment? Justify your answer.

Time	Weight (pounds)
8:00 A.M.	25.10
8:30	25.15
9:00	24.81
9:30	24.75
10:00	25.00
10:30	25.05
11:00	25.23
11:30	25.25
12:00	25.01
12:30 P.M.	25.06
1:00	24.95
1:30	24.80
2:00	24.95
2:30	25.21
3:00	24.90
3:30	24.71
4:00	25.31
4:30	25.15
5:00	25.20

2.6 Numerical Measures of Relative Standing

We've seen that numerical measures of central tendency and variability describe the general nature of a quantitative data set (either a sample or a population). In addition, we may be interested in describing the *relative* quantitative location of a particular measurement within a data set. Descriptive measures of the relationship of a measurement to the rest of the data are called **measures of relative standing**.

One measure of the relative standing of a measurement is its **percentile ranking,** or **percentile score.** For example, if oil company A reports that its yearly sales are in the 90th percentile of all companies in the industry, the implication is that 90% of all oil companies have yearly sales less than company A's, and only 10% have yearly sales

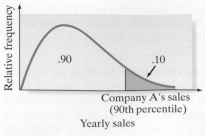

Figure 2.24
Location of 90th percentile for yearly sales of oil companies

exceeding company A's. This is demonstrated in Figure 2.24. Similarly, if the oil company's yearly sales are in the 50th percentile (the median of the data set), 50% of all oil companies would have lower yearly sales and 50% would have higher yearly sales.

Percentile rankings are of practical value only for large data sets. Finding them involves a process similar to the one used in finding a median. The measurements are ranked in order, and a rule is selected to define the location of each percentile. Because we are primarily interested in interpreting the percentile rankings of measurements (rather than finding particular percentiles for a data set), we define the *pth percentile* of a data set.

> For any set of n measurements (arranged in ascending or descending order), the ***pth percentile*** is a number such that p% of the measurements fall below the *pth* percentile and $(100 - p)$% fall above it.

EXAMPLE 2.14

Finding and Interpreting Percentiles—R&D Expenditures

Problem Refer to the percentages spent on R&D by the 50 high-technology firms listed in Table 2.6 (p. 106). A portion of the SPSS descriptive statistics printout is shown in Figure 2.25. Locate the 25th percentile and 95th percentile on the printout and interpret these values.

Solution Both the 25th percentile and 95th percentile are highlighted on the SPSS printout, Figure 2.25. These values are 7.05 and 13.335, respectively. Our interpretations are as follows: 25% of the 50 R&D percentages fall below 7.05 and 95% of the R&D percentages fall below 13.335.

Look Back The method for computing percentiles with small data sets varies according to the software used. As the sample size increases, these percentile values from the different software packages will converge to a single number.

Statistics

RDPCT

N	Valid	50
	Missing	0
Percentiles	5	5.765
	10	6.500
	25	7.050
	50	8.050
	75	9.625
	90	11.280
	95	13.335

Figure 2.25
SPSS percentiles for 50 R&D percentages

● **Now Work Exercise 2.91**

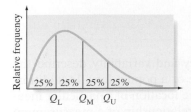

Figure 2.26
The quartiles for a data set

Percentiles that partition a data set into four categories, each category containing exactly 25% of the measurements, are called **quartiles**. The *lower quartile* (Q_L) is the 25th percentile, the *middle quartile* (Q_M) is the median or 50th percentile, and the *upper quartile* (Q_U) is the 75th percentile, as shown in Figure 2.26. Therefore, in Example 2.14, we have (from the SPSS printout, Figure 2.25), $Q_L = 7.05$, $Q_M = 8.05$, and $Q_U = 9.625$. Quartiles will prove useful in finding unusual observations in a data set (Section 2.7).

> The **lower quartile** (Q_L) is the 25th percentile of a data set. The **middle quartile** (Q_M) is the median or 50th percentile. The **upper quartile** (Q_U) is the 75th percentile.

Another measure of relative standing in popular use is the **z-score.** As you can see in the definition of z-score below, the z-score makes use of the mean and standard deviation of the data set in order to specify the relative location of a measurement. Note that the z-score is calculated by subtracting $\bar{x}$ (or μ) from the measurement x and then dividing the result by s (or σ). The final result, the z-score, represents the distance between a given measurement x and the mean, expressed in standard deviations.

The **sample z-score** for a measurement x is

$$z = \frac{x - \bar{x}}{s}$$

The **population z-score** for a measurement x is

$$z = \frac{x - \mu}{\sigma}$$

EXAMPLE 2.15

Finding a z-Score— GMAT Results

Problem A random sample of 2,000 students who sat for the Graduate Management Admission Test (GMAT) is selected. For this sample, the mean GMAT score is $\bar{x} = 540$ points and the standard deviation is $s = 100$ points. One student from the sample, Kara Smith, had a GMAT score of $x = 440$ points. What is Kara's sample z-score?

Solution First, note that Kara's GMAT score lies below the mean score for the 2,000 students (see Figure 2.27). Now we compute

$$z = (x - \bar{x})/s = (440 - 540)/100 = -100/100 = -1.0$$

This z-score implies that Kara Smith's GMAT score is 1.0 standard deviations below the sample mean GMAT score, or, in short, her sample z-score is -1.0.

Look Back The numerical value of the z-score reflects the relative standing of the measurement. A large positive z-score implies that the measurement is larger than almost all other measurements, whereas a large (in magnitude) negative z-score indicates that the measurement is smaller than almost every other measurement. If a z-score is 0 or near 0, the measurement is located at or near the mean of the sample or population.

Figure 2.27
GMAT scores of a sample of test takers

				GMAT Score
240	440	540		840
$\bar{x} - 3s$	Kara Smith's GMAT	$\bar{x}$		$\bar{x} + 3s$

• **Now Work Exercise 2.90**

If we know that the frequency distribution of the measurements is mound-shaped, the following interpretation of the z-score can be given.

Interpretation of z-Scores for Mound-Shaped Distributions of Data

1. Approximately 68% of the measurements will have a z-score between -1 and 1.

2. Approximately 95% of the measurements will have a z-score between -2 and 2.

3. Approximately 99.7% (almost all) of the measurements will have a z-score between -3 and 3.

Note that this interpretation of z-scores is identical to that given by the Empirical Rule for mound-shaped distributions (Rule 2.2). The statement that a measurement falls in the interval $(\mu - \sigma)$ to $(\mu + \sigma)$ is equivalent to the statement that a measurement has a population z-score between -1 and 1 because all measurements between $(\mu - \sigma)$ and $(\mu + \sigma)$ are within 1 standard deviation of μ. These z-scores are displayed in Figure 2.28.

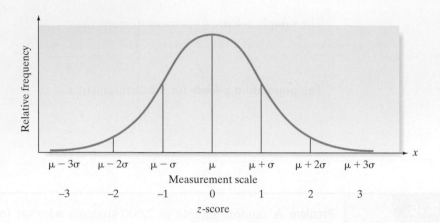

Figure 2.28

Population z-scores for a mound-shaped distribution

Exercises 2.90–2.105

Learning the Mechanics

2.90 Compute the z-score corresponding to each of the following values of x:
a. $x = 40, s = 5, \bar{x} = 30$
b. $x = 90, \mu = 89, \sigma = 2$
c. $\mu = 50, \sigma = 5, x = 50$
d. $s = 4, x = 20, \bar{x} = 30$
e. In parts **a–d**, state whether the z-score locates x within a sample or a population.
f. In parts **a–d**, state whether each value of x lies above or below the mean and by how many standard deviations.

2.91 Give the percentage of measurements in a data set that are above and below each of the following percentiles:
a. 75th percentile
b. 50th percentile
c. 20th percentile
d. 84th percentile

2.92 In terms of percentiles, define Q_L, Q_M and Q_U.

2.93 Compare the z-scores to decide which of the following x values lie the greatest distance above the mean and the greatest distance below the mean.
a. $x = 100, \mu = 50, \sigma = 25$
b. $x = 1, \mu = 4, \sigma = 1$
c. $x = 0, \mu = 200, \sigma = 100$
d. $x = 10, \mu = 5, \sigma = 3$

2.94 Suppose that 40 and 90 are two elements of a population data set and that their z-scores are -2 and 3, respectively. Using only this information, is it possible to determine the population's mean and standard deviation? If so, find them. If not, explain why it's not possible.

Applying the Concepts—Basic

2.95 **Mathematics assessment test scores.** According to the National Center for Education Statistics (2015), scores on a mathematics assessment test for U.S. eighth graders have a mean of 282, a 25th percentile of 258, a 75th percentile of 308, and a 90th percentile of 329. Interpret each of these numerical descriptive measures.

2.96 **Voltage sags and swells.** Refer to the *Electrical Engineering* (Vol. 95, 2013) study of transformer voltage sags and swells, Exercise 2.76 (p. 110). Recall that for a sample of 103 transformers built for heavy industry, the mean number of sags per week was 353 and the mean number of swells per week was 184. Assume the standard deviation of the sag distribution is 30 sags per week and the standard deviation of the swell distribution is 25 swells per week. Suppose one of the transformers is randomly selected and found to have 400 sags and 100 swells in a week.
a. Find the z-score for the number of sags for this transformer. Interpret this value.
b. Find the z-score for the number of swells for this transformer. Interpret this value.

2.97 **Salaries of bachelor's degree graduates.** PayScale, Inc., an online provider of global compensation data, conducts an annual salary survey of bachelor's degree graduates. Three of the many variables measured by PayScale are the graduate's current salary, mid-career salary, and the college or university where they obtained their degree. Descriptive statistics are provided for each of the over 400 colleges and universities that graduates attended. For example, graduates of the University of South Florida (USF) had a mean current salary of $57,000, a median mid-career salary of $48,000, and a mid-career 90th percentile salary of $131,000. Describe the salary distribution of USF bachelor's degree graduates by interpreting each of these summary statistics.

2.98 **Sanitation inspection of cruise ships.** Refer to the October 2015 sanitation levels of cruise ships, Exercise 2.81 (p. 111).
SANIT
a. Give a measure of relative standing for the *TSS Oceanic* score of 73. Interpret the result.
b. Give a measure of relative standing for the *Queen Mary 2* score of 91. Interpret the result.

Applying the Concepts—Intermediate

2.99 **Lead in drinking water.** The U.S. Environmental Protection Agency (EPA) sets a limit on the amount of lead permitted in drinking water. The EPA *Action Level* for lead is .015 milligram per liter (mg/L) of water. Under EPA guidelines, if 90% of a water system's study samples have a lead concentration less than .015 mg/L, the water is considered safe for drinking. I (coauthor Sincich) received a recent report on a study of lead levels in the drinking water of homes in my subdivision. The 90th percentile of the study sample had a lead concentration of .00372 mg/L. Are water customers in my subdivision at risk of drinking water with unhealthy lead levels? Explain.

2.100 **Corporate sustainability of CPA firms.** Refer to the *Business and Society* (March 2011) study on the sustainability behaviors of CPA corporations, Exercise 2.67 (p. 104). Numerical descriptive measures for level of support for corporate sustainability for the 992 senior managers are repeated in the accompanying Minitab printout. One of the managers reported a support level of 155 points. Would you consider this support level to be typical of the study sample? Explain.

Descriptive Statistics: Support

Variable	N	Mean	StDev	Variance	Minimum	Median	Maximum
Support	992	67.755	26.871	722.036	0.000	68.000	155.000

2.101 **Executive networking and firm performance.** Do firms with executive directors who network with executives at other firms perform better? This was one of the questions of interest in a study published in the *Journal of Accounting Public Policy* (Vol. 34, 2015). One measure of firm performance used in the study was annual return on equity (ROE), recorded as a percentage. Data collected over a 5-year period for executive directors at 147 firms yielded the following summary statistics on ROI: mean = 13.93, median = 14.86, 5th percentile = −19.64, 25th percentile = 7.59, 75th percentile = 21.32, 95th percentile = 38.42, and standard deviation = 21.65. Give a practical interpretation of each of these statistics. Then, use this information to draw a sketch of the distribution of the ROI values for the 147 firms.

2.102 **Blue- vs. red-colored exam study.** In a study of how external clues influence performance, university professors gave two different forms of a midterm examination to a large group of introductory students. The questions on the exam were identical and in the same order, but one exam was printed on blue paper and the other on red paper (*Teaching Psychology*, May 1998). Grading only the difficult questions on the exam, the researchers found that

scores on the blue exam had a distribution with a mean of 53% and a standard deviation of 15%, while scores on the red exam had a distribution with a mean of 39% and a standard deviation of 12%. (Assume that both distributions are approximately mound-shaped and symmetric.)
a. Give an interpretation of the standard deviation for the students who took the blue exam.
b. Give an interpretation of the standard deviation for the students who took the red exam.
c. Suppose a student is selected at random from the group of students who participated in the study and the student's score on the difficult questions is 20%. Which exam form is the student more likely to have taken, the blue or the red exam? Explain.

2.103 **Ranking PhD programs in economics.** Thousands of students apply for admission to graduate schools in economics each year with the intention of obtaining a PhD. The *Southern Economic Journal* (April 2008) published a
ECOPHD
guide to graduate study in economics by ranking the PhD programs at 129 colleges and universities. Each program was evaluated according to the number of publications published by faculty teaching in the PhD program and by the quality of the publications. Data obtained from the Social Science Citation Index (SSCI) were used to calculate an overall productivity score for each PhD program. The mean and standard deviation of these 129 productivity scores were then used to compute a z-score for each economics program. Harvard University had the highest z-score ($z = 5.08$) and, hence, was the top-ranked school; Howard University was ranked last because it had the lowest z-score ($z = −0.81$). The data (z-scores) for all 129 economic programs are saved in the data file.
a. Interpret the z-score for Harvard University.
b. Interpret the z-score for Howard University.
c. The authors of the *Southern Economic Journal* article note that "only 44 of the 129 schools have positive z-scores, indicating that the distribution of overall productivity is skewed to the right." Do you agree? (Check your answer by constructing a histogram for the z-scores in the file.)

Applying the Concepts—Advanced

2.104 **Using z-scores for grades.** At one university, the students are given z-scores at the end of each semester rather than the traditional GPAs. The mean and standard deviation of all students' cumulative GPAs, on which the z-scores are based, are 2.7 and .5, respectively.
a. Translate each of the following z-scores to the corresponding GPA: $z = 2.0$, $z = −1.0$, $z = .5$, $z = −2.5$.
b. Students with z-scores below −1.6 are put on probation. What is the corresponding probationary GPA?
c. The president of the university wishes to graduate the top 16% of the students with *cum laude* honors and the top 2.5% with *summa cum laude* honors. Where (approximately) should the limits be set in terms of z-scores? In terms of GPAs? What assumption, if any, did you make about the distribution of the GPAs at the university?

2.105 **Ranking PhD programs in economics (cont'd).** Refer to the *Southern Economic Journal* (April 2008) study of PhD programs in economics, Exercise 2.103. The authors also made the following observation: "A noticeable feature of this skewness is that distinction between schools diminishes as the rank declines. For example, the top-ranked school, Harvard, has a z-score of 5.08, and the fifth-ranked school, Yale, has a z-score of 2.18, a substantial difference. However, . . . , the 70th-ranked school, the University of Massachusetts, has a z-score of –0.43, and the 80th-ranked school, the University of Delaware, has a z-score of –0.50, a very small difference. [Consequently] the ordinal rankings presented in much of the literature that ranks economics departments miss the fact that below a relatively small group of top programs, the differences in [overall] productivity become fairly small." Do you agree?

2.7 Methods for Detecting Outliers: Box Plots and z-Scores

Sometimes it is important to identify inconsistent or unusual measurements in a data set. An observation that is unusually large or small relative to the data values we want to describe is called an *outlier*.

Outliers are often attributable to one of several causes. First, the measurement associated with the outlier may be invalid. For example, the experimental procedure used to generate the measurement may have malfunctioned, the experimenter may have misrecorded the measurement, or the data might have been coded incorrectly in the computer. Second, the outlier may be the result of a misclassified measurement—that is, the measurement belongs to a population different from which the rest of the sample was drawn. Finally, the measurement associated with the outlier may be recorded correctly and be from the same population as the rest of the sample but represent a rare (chance) event. Such outliers occur most often when the relative frequency distribution of the sample data is extremely skewed because such a distribution has a tendency to include extremely large or small observations relative to the others in the data set.

> An observation (or measurement) that is unusually large or small relative to the other values in a data set is called an **outlier.** Outliers typically are attributable to one of the following causes:
>
> 1. The measurement is observed, recorded, or entered into the computer incorrectly.
> 2. The measurement comes from a different population.
> 3. The measurement is correct but represents a rare (chance) event.

Two useful methods for detecting outliers, one graphical and one numerical, are **box plots** and z-scores. The box plot is based on the *quartiles* (defined in Section 2.6) of a data set. Specifically, a box plot is based on the *interquartile range* (IQR), the distance between the lower and upper quartiles:

$$IQR = Q_U - Q_L$$

> The **interquartile range (IQR)** is the distance between the lower and upper quartiles:
>
> $$IQR = Q_U - Q_L$$

An annotated Minitab box plot for the 50 companies' percentages of revenues spent on R&D (Table 2.2) is shown in Figure 2.29.* Note that a rectangle (the box) is drawn, with the top and bottom sides of the rectangle (the **hinges**) drawn at the quartiles Q_L and Q_U, respectively. Recall that Q_L represents the 25th percentile and Q_U

---

*Although box plots can be generated by hand, the amount of detail required makes them particularly well suited for computer generation. We use computer software to generate the box plots in this section.

represents the 75th percentile. By definition, then, the "middle" 50% of the observations—those between Q_L and Q_U—fall inside the box. For the R&D data, these quartiles are at 7.05 and 9.625 (see Figure 2.25, p. 84). Thus,

$$IQR = 9.625 - 7.05 = 2.575$$

The median is shown at 8.05 by a horizontal line within the box.

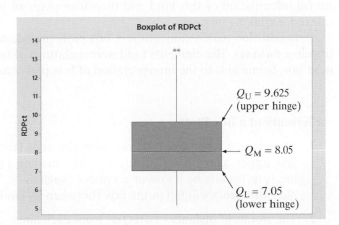

Figure 2.29

Annotated Minitab box plot for 50 R&D percentages

To guide the construction of the "tails" of the box plot, two sets of limits, called **inner fences** and **outer fences,** are used. Neither set of fences actually appears on the box plot. Inner fences are located at a distance of 1.5(IQR) from the hinges. Emanating from the hinges of the box are vertical lines called the **whiskers.** The two whiskers extend to the most extreme observation inside the inner fences. For example, the inner fence on the lower side (bottom) of the R&D percentage box plot is

$$Lower\ inner\ fence = Lower\ hinge - 1.5(IQR)$$
$$= 7.05 - 1.5(2.575)$$
$$= 7.05 - 3.863 = 3.187$$

The smallest measurement in the data set is 5.2, which is well inside this inner fence. Thus, the lower whisker extends to 5.2. Similarly, the upper whisker extends to the most extreme observation inside the upper inner fence, where

$$Upper\ inner\ fence = Upper\ hinge + 1.5(IQR)$$
$$= 9.625 + 1.5(2.575)$$
$$= 9.625 + 3.863 = 13.488$$

The largest measurement inside this fence is the third largest measurement, 13.2. Note that the longer upper whisker reveals the rightward skewness of the R&D distribution.

Values that are beyond the inner fences are deemed *potential outliers* because they are extreme values that represent relatively rare occurrences. In fact, *for mound-shaped distributions, fewer than 1% of the observations are expected to fall outside the inner fences*. Two of the 50 R&D measurements, both at 13.5, fall outside the upper inner fence. Each of these potential outliers is represented by the asterisk (*) at 13.5.

The other two imaginary fences, the outer fences, are defined at a distance 3(IQR) from each end of the box. Measurements that fall beyond the outer fence are represented by 0s (zeros) and are very extreme measurements that require special analysis. Because *less than one-hundredth of 1% (.01% or .0001) of the measurements from mound-shaped distributions are expected to fall beyond the outer fence*, these measurements are considered to be *outliers*. No measurement in the R&D percentage box plot (Figure 2.29) is represented by a 0; thus there are no outliers.

Recall that outliers are extreme measurements that stand out from the rest of the sample and may be faulty: They may be incorrectly recorded observations, members of a population different from the rest of the sample, or, at the least, very unusual measurements from the same population. For example, the two R&D measurements at 13.5 (identified by an asterisk) may be considered outliers. When we analyze these measurements, we find that they are correctly recorded. However, it turns out that both represent R&D expenditures of relatively young and fast-growing companies. Thus, the outlier analysis may have revealed important factors that relate to the R&D expenditures of high-tech companies: their age and rate of growth. Outlier analysis often reveals useful information of this kind and therefore plays an important role in the statistical inference-making process.

In addition to detecting outliers, box plots provide useful information on the variation in a data set. The elements (and nomenclature) of box plots are summarized in the next box. Some aids to the interpretation of box plots are also given.

Elements of a Box Plot*

1. A rectangle (the **box**) is drawn with the ends (the **hinges**) drawn at the lower and upper quartiles (Q_L and Q_U). The median (Q_M) of the data is shown in the box, usually by a line or a symbol (such as "+"). [*Note*: Exactly 50% of the measurements will fall in the box (between Q_L and Q_U).]

2. The points at distances 1.5(IQR) from each hinge define the **inner fences** of the data set. Lines (the **whiskers**) are drawn from each hinge to the most extreme measurement inside the inner fence. Thus,

$$\text{Lower inner fence} = Q_L - 1.5(\text{IQR})$$

$$\text{Upper inner fence} = Q_U + 1.5(\text{IQR})$$

   [*Note*: About 95% to 99% of the measurements will fall within the inner fences.]

3. A second pair of fences, the **outer fences,** are defined at a distance of 3 interquartile ranges, 3(IQR) from the hinges. One symbol (usually "*") is used to represent measurements falling between the inner and outer fences, and another (usually "0") is used to represent measurements beyond the outer fences. Outer fences are not shown unless one or more measurements lie beyond them:

$$\text{Lower outer fence} = Q_L - 3(\text{IQR})$$

$$\text{Upper outer fence} = Q_U + 3(\text{IQR})$$

   [*Note*: Almost all of the measurements will fall within the outer fences.]

4. The symbols used to represent the median and the extreme data points (those beyond the fences) will vary depending on the software you use to construct the box plot. (You may use your own symbols if you are constructing a box plot by hand.) You should consult the program's documentation to determine exactly which symbols are used.

Aids to the Interpretation of Box Plots

1. The line (median) inside the box represents the "center" of the distribution of data.

2. Examine the length of the box. The IQR is a measure of the sample's variability and is especially useful for the comparison of two samples (see Example 2.17).

---

*The originator of the box plot, John Tukey, initially used the constants 1 and 2 in the equations for the inner and outer fences, respectively. Through repetition and experience, Tukey modified the formulas using the constants 1.5 and 3.

3. Visually compare the lengths of the whiskers. If one is clearly longer, the distribution of the data is probably skewed in the direction of the longer whisker.

4. Analyze any measurements that lie beyond the fences. Fewer than 5% should fall beyond the inner fences, even for very skewed distributions. Measurements beyond the outer fences are probably outliers, with one of the following explanations:

   a. The measurement is incorrect. It may have been observed, recorded, or entered into the computer incorrectly.

   b. The measurement belongs to a population different from the population that the rest of the sample was drawn from (see Example 2.17).

   c. The measurement is correct *and* considered a rare observation from the same population as the rest. Generally, we accept this explanation only after carefully ruling out all others.

EXAMPLE 2.16

Interpreting a Box Plot— Lost Price Quotes

Problem In Example 2.2 (p. 79) we analyzed 50 processing times (listed in Table 2.4) for the development of price quotes by the manufacturer of industrial wheels. The intent was to determine whether the success or failure in obtaining the order was related to the amount of time to process the price quotes. Each quote that corresponds to "lost" business was so classified. Use a statistical software package to draw a box plot for all 50 processing times. What does the box plot reveal about the data? Identify any outliers in the data set.

Solution The Minitab box plot printout for these data is shown in Figure 2.30. Note that the upper whisker is much longer than the lower whisker, indicating rightward skewness of the data. However, the most important feature of the data is made very obvious by the box plot: There are four measurements (indicated by asterisks) that are beyond the upper inner fence. Thus, the distribution is extremely skewed to the right, and several measurements—or outliers—need special attention in our analysis. Examination of the data reveals that these four outliers correspond to processing times 14.06, 14.32, 16.29, and 20.23 days.

Look Back Before removing outliers from the data set, a good analyst will make a concerted effort to find the cause of the outliers. We offer an explanation for these processing time outliers in the next example.

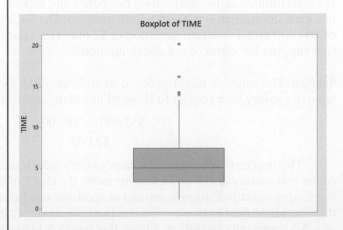

Figure 2.30

Minitab box plot for processing time data

• **Now Work Exercise 2.108**

EXAMPLE 2.17

Comparing Box Plots—Lost Price Quotes

Problem Refer to Example 2.16. The box plot for the 50 processing times (Figure 2.30) does not explicitly reveal the differences, if any, between the set of times corresponding to the success and the set of times corresponding to the failure to obtain the business. Box plots corresponding to the 39 "won" and 11 "lost" bids were generated using SPSS and are shown in Figure 2.31. Interpret them.

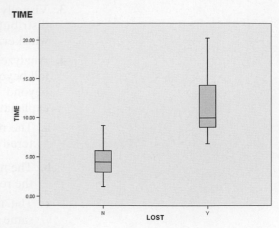

Figure 2.31
SPSS box plots of processing times for won and lost bids

Solution The division of the data set into two parts, corresponding to won and lost bids, eliminates any observations that are beyond the inner fences. Furthermore, the skewness in the distributions has been reduced, as evidenced by the fact that the upper whiskers are only slightly longer than the lower. The box plots also reveal that the processing times corresponding to the lost bids tend to exceed those of the won bids. A plausible explanation for the outliers in the combined box plot (Figure 2.30) is that they are from a different population than the bulk of the times. In other words, there are two populations represented by the sample of processing times—one corresponding to lost bids and the other to won bids.

Look Back The box plots lend support to the conclusion that the price quote processing time and the success of acquiring the business are related. However, whether the visual differences between the box plots generalize to inferences about the populations corresponding to these two samples is a matter for inferential statistics, not graphical descriptions. We'll discuss how to use samples to compare two populations using inferential statistics in Chapter 8.

● **Now Work Exercise 2.112**

The following example illustrates how z-scores can be used to detect outliers and make inferences.

EXAMPLE 2.18

Inference Using z-Scores—Salary Discrimination

Problem Suppose a female bank employee believes that her salary is low as a result of sex discrimination. To substantiate her belief, she collects information on the salaries of her male counterparts in the banking business. She finds that their salaries have a mean of $64,000 and a standard deviation of $2,000. Her salary is $57,000. Does this information support her claim of sex discrimination?

Solution The analysis might proceed as follows: First, we calculate the z-score for the woman's salary with respect to those of her male counterparts. Thus,

$$z = \frac{\$57,000 - \$64,000}{\$2,000} = -3.5$$

The implication is that the woman's salary is 3.5 standard deviations *below* the mean of the male salary distribution. Furthermore, if a check of the male salary data shows that the frequency distribution is mound-shaped, we can infer that very few salaries in this distribution should have a z-score less than −3, as shown in Figure 2.32. Clearly, a z-score of −3.5 represents an outlier. Either this female's salary is from a distribution different from the male salary distribution, or it is a very unusual (highly improbable) measurement from a distribution that is no different from the male salary distribution.

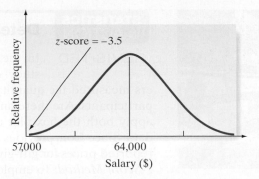

Figure 2.32
Male salary distribution

Look Back Which of the two situations do you think prevails? Statistical thinking would lead us to conclude that her salary does not come from the male salary distribution, lending support to the female bank employee's claim of sex discrimination. A careful investigator should acquire more information before inferring sex discrimination as the cause. We would want to know more about the data-collection technique the woman used and more about her competence at her job. Also, perhaps other factors such as length of employment should be considered in the analysis.

● **Now Work Exercise 2.106**

Examples 2.17 and 2.18 exemplify an approach to statistical inference that might be called the **rare-event approach.** An experimenter hypothesizes a specific frequency distribution to describe a population of measurements. Then a sample of measurements is drawn from the population. If the experimenter finds it unlikely that the sample came from the hypothesized distribution, the hypothesis is concluded to be false. Thus, in Example 2.18 the woman believes her salary reflects discrimination. She hypothesizes that her salary should be just another measurement in the distribution of her male counterparts' salaries if no discrimination exists. However, it is so unlikely that the sample (in this case, her salary) came from the male frequency distribution that she rejects that hypothesis, concluding that the distribution from which her salary was drawn is different from the distribution for the men.

This rare-event approach to inference making is discussed further in later chapters. Proper application of the approach requires a knowledge of probability, the subject of our next chapter.

We conclude this section with some rules of thumb for detecting outliers.

Rules of Thumb for Detecting Outliers*

Box Plots: Observations falling between the inner and outer fences are deemed *suspect outliers*. Observations falling beyond the outer fence are deemed *highly suspect outliers*.

Suspect Outliers	Highly Suspect Outliers
Between $Q_L - 1.5(IQR)$ and $Q_L - 3(IQR)$ or Between $Q_U + 1.5(IQR)$ and $Q_U + 3(IQR)$	Below $Q_L - 3(IQR)$ or Above $Q_U + 3(IQR)$

z-scores: Observations with z-scores greater than 3 in absolute value are considered outliers. For some highly skewed data sets, observations with z-scores greater than 2 in absolute value may be outliers.

Possible Outliers	Outliers
$|z| > 2$	$|z| > 3$

---

*The z score and box plot methods both establish rule-of-thumb limits outside of which a measurement is deemed to be an outlier. Usually, the two methods produce similar results. However, the presence of one or more outliers in a data set can inflate the computed value of s. Consequently, it will be less likely that an errant observation would have a z-score larger than 3 in absolute value. In contrast, the values of the quartiles used to calculate the intervals for a box plot are not affected by the presence of outliers.

Detecting Outliers

In the *Journal of Experimental Social Psychology* (Vol. 45, 2009) study on whether money can buy love, recall that the researchers measured the quantitative variable *birthday gift price* (dollars) for each of the 237 participants. Are there any unusual reported prices in the **BUYLOV** data set? We will apply both the box plot and z-score methods to aid in identifying any outliers in the data. Since from previous analyses, there appears to be a difference in the distribution of reported prices for gift-givers and gift-recipients, we will analyze the data by role.

z-Score Method: To employ the z-score method, we require the mean and standard deviation of the data for each role type. These values were already computed in the previous *Statistics in Action Revisited* section. For gift-givers, $\bar{x} = \$105.84$ and $s = \$93.47$; for gift-recipients, $\bar{x} = \$149.00$ and $s = \$134.50$ (see Figure SIA2.5). Then, the 3-standard-deviation interval for each role is calculated as follows:

Givers: $\bar{x} \pm 3s = 105.84 \pm 3(93.47) = 105.84 \pm 280.41 = (0, 386.25)$

Receivers: $\bar{x} \pm 3s = 149.00 \pm 3(134.50) = 149.00 \pm 403.50 = (0, 552.50)$

(*Note:* Since price cannot be negative, we replaced negative lower endpoints with 0.) If you examine the gift prices for givers reported in the data set, you will find that only one ($431) falls beyond the 3-standard-deviation interval. None of the prices for receivers fall outside the 3-standard-deviation interval. Consequently, if we use the z-score approach, there is only one highly suspect outlier in the gift price data.

Box Plot Method: Box plots for the data are shown in Figure SIA2.6. Although several suspect outliers (asterisks) are shown on the box plot for each role type, there are no highly suspect outliers (zeros) shown. That is, no gift prices fall beyond the outer fences of the box plots.

Figure SIA2.6
Minitab box plots for birthday gift price by role

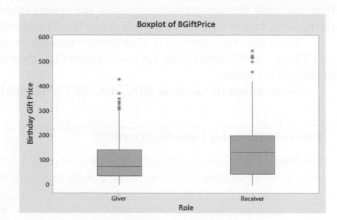

Although not detected by the box plot method, the z-score method did detect one highly suspect outlier—the gift price of $431 reported by a birthday gift-giver. The researchers should investigate whether or not to include this observation in any analysis that leads to an inference about the population of gift-givers. Is the outlier a legitimate value (in which case it will remain in the data set for analysis), or is the outlier associated with a gift-giver who is not a member of the population of interest—say, a person who mistakenly reported on the price of a wedding gift rather than a birthday gift (in which case it will be removed from the data set prior to analysis)?

📊 *Data Set:* BUYLOV

Exercises 2.106–2.121

Learning the Mechanics

2.106 A sample data set has a mean of 57 and a standard deviation of 11. Determine whether each of the following sample measurements are outliers.
a. 65
b. 21
c. 72
d. 98

2.107 Suppose a data set consisting of exam scores has a lower quartile $Q_L = 60$, a median $Q_M = 75$, and an upper quartile $Q_U = 85$. The scores on the exam range from 18 to 100. Without having the actual scores available to you, construct as much of the box plot as possible.

2.108 Consider the horizontal box plot shown below.

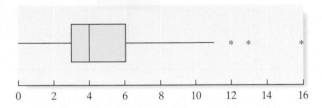

a. What is the median of the data set (approximately)?
b. What are the upper and lower quartiles of the data set (approximately)?
c. What is the interquartile range of the data set (approximately)?
d. Is the data set skewed to the left, skewed to the right, or symmetric?
e. What percentage of the measurements in the data set lie to the right of the median? To the left of the upper quartile?
f. Identify any outliers in the data.

2.109 Consider the following two sample data sets.

Sample A			Sample B		
121	171	158	171	152	170
173	184	163	168	169	171
157	85	145	190	183	185
165	172	196	140	173	206
170	159	172	172	174	169
161	187	100	199	151	180
142	166	171	167	170	188

a. Construct a box plot for each data set.
b. Identify any outliers that may exist in the two data sets.

📊 Applet Exercise 2.7

Use the applet *Standard Deviation* to determine whether an item in a data set may be an outlier. Begin by setting appropriate limits and plotting the data below on the number line provided in the applet.

10 80 80 85 85 85 85 90 90 90 90 90 95 95 95 95 100 100

a. The green arrow shows the approximate location of the mean. Multiply the standard deviation given by the applet by 3. Is the data item 10 more than 3 standard deviations away from the green arrow (the mean)? Can you conclude that the 10 is an outlier?
b. Using the mean and standard deviation from part **a**, move the point at 10 on your plot to a point that appears to be about 3 standard deviations from the mean. Repeat the process in part **a** for the new plot and the new suspected outlier.
c. When you replaced the extreme value in part **a** with a number that appeared to be within 3 standard deviations of the mean, the standard deviation got smaller and the mean moved to the right, yielding a new data set where the extreme value was not within 3 standard deviations of the mean. Continue to replace the extreme value with higher numbers until the new value is within 3 standard deviations of the mean in the new data set. Use trial and error to estimate the smallest number that can replace the 10 in the original data set so that the replacement is not considered to be an outlier.

Applying the Concepts—Basic

2.110 Rankings of research universities. Refer to the College Choice *2015 Rankings of National Research Universities,* Exercise 2.43 (p. 95). Recall that data on academic reputation score, financial aid awarded, and net cost to attend for the top 50 research universities are saved in the **TOPUNIV** file. The 50 academic reputation scores are listed in the accompanying table.

99	92	94	95	97	91	91	92	92	89	84	85	100	87	83
83	89	79	94	79	79	87	76	67	76	76	76	70	74	64
74	69	66	72	65	76	64	65	61	69	62	69	52	64	64
47	60	57	63	62										

a. Find the median, lower quartile, and upper quartile for the data.
b. Find IQR for the data.
c. Graph the data with a box plot.
d. Do you detect any outliers? Suspect outliers?

2.111 Voltage sags and swells. Refer to the *Electrical Engineering* (Vol. 95, 2013) study of power quality (measured by "sags" and "swells") in Turkish transformers, Exercise 2.96 (p. 116). For a sample of 103 transformers built for heavy industry, the mean and standard deviation of the number of sags per week were 353 and 30, respectively; also, the mean and standard deviation of the number of swells per week were 184 and 25, respectively. Consider a transformer that has 400 sags and 100 swells in a week.
a. Would you consider 400 sags per week unusual, statistically? Explain.
b. Would you consider 100 swells per week unusual, statistically? Explain.

2.112 Treating psoriasis with the "Doctorfish of Kangal." Psoriasis is a skin disorder with no known cure and no proven effective pharmacological treatment. An alternative treatment for psoriasis is ichthyotherapy, also known as therapy with the "Doctorfish of Kangal." Fish from the hot pools of Kangal, Turkey, feed on the skin scales of bathers, reportedly reducing the symptoms of psoriasis. In one study, 67 patients diagnosed with psoriasis underwent 3 weeks of ichthyotherapy (*Evidence-Based Research in Complementary and Alternative Medicine,* December 2006). The Psoriasis Area Severity Index (PASI) of each patient was measured both before and after treatment. (The lower the PASI score, the better is the skin condition.) Box plots of the PASI scores, both before (baseline) and after 3 weeks of ichthyotherapy treatment, are shown in the accompanying diagram.

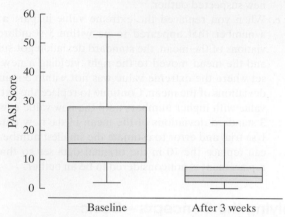

Source: Based on M. Grassberger and W. Hoch, "Ichthyotherapy as Alternative Treatment for Patients with Psoriasis: A Pilot Study," *Evidence-Based Research in Complementary and Alternative Medicine,* December 2006, Vol. 3(4).

a. Find the approximate 25th percentile, the median, and the 75th percentile for the PASI scores before treatment.

b. Find the approximate 25th percentile, the median, and the 75th percentile for the PASI scores after treatment.

c. Comment on the effectiveness of ichthyotherapy in treating psoriasis.

2.113 Budget lapsing at army hospitals. Accountants use the term *budget lapsing* to describe the situation that occurs when unspent funds do not carry over from one budgeting period to the next. Due to budget lapsing, U.S. army hospitals tend to stockpile pharmaceuticals and other supplies toward the end of the fiscal year, leading to a spike in expenditures. This phenomenon was investigated in the *Journal of Management Accounting Research* (Vol. 19, 2007). Data on expenses per full-time equivalent employees for a sample of 1,751 army hospitals yielded the following summary statistics: $\bar{x} = \$6,563$, $m = \$6,232$, $s = \$2,484$, $Q_L = \$5,309$, and $Q_U = \$7,216$.
a. Interpret, practically, the measures of relative standing.
b. Compute the interquartile range, IQR, for the data.
c. What proportion of the 1,751 army hospitals have expenses between \$5,309 and \$7,216?

2.114 Salary offers to MBAs. Consider the top salary offer (in thousands of dollars) received by each member of a sample of 50 MBA students who graduated from the Graduate School of Management at Rutgers, the state university of New Jersey. Descriptive statistics and a box plot for the data are shown on the XLSTAT printouts on the top of next column. [*Note:* The "+" on the box plot represents the location of the mean.]

Statistic	SALARY			
Nbr. of observations	50			
Minimum	35.000			
Maximum	75.000			
Range	40.000			
1st Quartile	45.725			
Median	51.000			
3rd Quartile	58.900			
Mean	52.334			
Variance (n-1)	85.085			
Standard deviation (n-1)	9.224			

Box plots:

Box plot (SALARY)

a. Find and interpret the z-score associated with the highest salary offer, the lowest salary offer, and the mean salary offer. Would you consider the highest offer to be unusually high? Why or why not?

b. Based on the box plot for this data set, which salary offers (if any) are suspect or highly suspect outliers?

Applying the Concepts—Intermediate

2.115 Time in bankruptcy. Refer to the *Financial Management* (Spring 1995) study of 49 firms filing for prepackaged bankruptcies, Exercise 2.32 (p. 86). Recall that three types of "prepack" firms exist: (1) those who hold no prefiling vote, (2) those who vote their preference for a joint solution; and (3) those who vote their preference for a prepack.
a. Construct a box plot for the time in bankruptcy (months) for each type of firm.
b. Find the median bankruptcy times for the three types.
c. How do the variabilities of the bankruptcy times compare for the three types?
d. The standard deviations of the bankruptcy times are 2.47 for "none," 1.72 for "joint," and 0.96 for "prepack." Do the standard deviations agree with the interquartile ranges with regard to the comparison of the variabilities of the bankruptcy times?
e. Is there evidence of outliers in any of the three distributions?

2.116 Corporate sustainability of CPA firms. Refer to the *Business and Society* (March 2011) study on the sustainability behaviors of CPA corporations, Exercise 2.100 (p. 117). Recall that data on the level of support for corporate sustainability were recorded for each of 992 senior managers. One of the managers reported a support level of 155 points. Use both a graph and a numerical technique to determine if this observation is an outlier.

2.117 Sanitation inspection of cruise ships. Refer to Exercise 2.81 (p. 111) and the data on the sanitation levels of passenger cruise ships.

SANIT

a. Use the box plot method to detect any outliers in the data set.

b. Use the z-score method to detect any outliers in the data set.

c. Do the two methods agree? If not, explain why.

2.118 Network server downtime. A manufacturer of network computer server systems is interested in improving its customer support services. As a first step, its marketing department has been charged with the responsibility of summarizing the extent of customer problems in terms of system downtime. The 40 most recent customers were surveyed to determine the amount of downtime (in hours) they had experienced during the previous month. These data are listed in the table.

SERVER

Customer Number	Downtime	Customer Number	Downtime
230	12	250	4
231	16	251	10
232	5	252	15
233	16	253	7
234	21	254	20
235	29	255	9
236	38	256	22
237	14	257	18
238	47	258	28
239	0	259	19
240	24	260	34
241	15	261	26
242	13	262	17
243	8	263	11
244	2	264	64
245	11	265	19
246	22	266	18
247	17	267	24
248	31	268	49
249	10	269	50

a. Construct a box plot for these data. Use the information reflected in the box plot to describe the frequency distribution of the data set. Your description should address central tendency, variation, and skewness.

b. Use your box plot to determine which customers are having unusually lengthy downtimes.

c. Find and interpret the z-scores associated with the customers you identified in part **b.**

2.119 Permeability of sandstone during weathering. Refer to the *Geographical Analysis* (Vol. 42, 2010) study of the decay properties of sandstone when exposed to the weather, Exercise 2.77 (p. 110). Recall that slices of sandstone blocks were tested for permeability under three conditions: no exposure to any type of weathering (A), repeatedly sprayed with a 10% salt solution (B), and soaked in a 10% salt solution and dried (C).

STONE

a. Identify any outliers in the permeability measurements for Group A sandstone slices.

b. Identify any outliers in the permeability measurements for Group B sandstone slices.

c. Identify any outliers in the permeability measurements for Group C sandstone slices.

d. If you remove the outliers detected in parts **a–c,** how will descriptive statistics like the mean, median, and standard deviation be affected? If you are unsure of your answer, carry out the analysis.

Applying the Concepts—Advanced

2.120 Sensor motion of a robot. Researchers at Carnegie Mellon University developed an algorithm for estimating the sensor motion of a robotic arm by mounting a camera with inertia sensors on the arm (*International Journal of Robotics Research*, December 2004). One variable of interest is the error of estimating arm translation (measured in centimeters). Data for 10 experiments are listed in the following table. In each experiment, the perturbation of camera intrinsics and projections were varied. Suppose a trial resulted in a translation error of 4.5 cm. Is this value an outlier for trials with perturbed intrinsics but no perturbed projections? For trials with perturbed projections but no perturbed intrinsics? What type of camera perturbation most likely occurred for this trial?

SENSOR

Trial	Perturbed Intrinsics	Perturbed Projections	Translation Error (cm)
1	Yes	No	1.0
2	Yes	No	1.3
3	Yes	No	3.0
4	Yes	No	1.5
5	Yes	No	1.3
6	No	Yes	22.9
7	No	Yes	21.0
8	No	Yes	34.4
9	No	Yes	29.8
10	No	Yes	17.7

Source: Republished with permission of Sage Publications, Inc. (US), from D. Strelow and S. Singh, "Motion Estimation from Image and Intertial Measurements," *International Journal of Robotics Research*, Vol. 23, No. 12, December 2004 (Table 4). Dennis Strelow, © November 2004; permission conveyed through Copyright Clearance Center, Inc.

2.121 Made-to-order delivery times. Refer to the data on delivery times for a made-to-order product, Exercise 2.34 (p. 87). The delivery times (in days) for a sample of 25 orders are repeated in the accompanying table. (Times marked by an asterisk are associated with customers who subsequently placed additional orders with the company.) Identify any unusual observations (outliers) in the data set, and then use the results to comment on the claim that repeat customers tend to have shorter delivery times than one-time customers.

MTO

50*	64*	56*	43*	64*	82*	65*	49*	32*	63*	44*	71	54*
51*	102	49*	73*	50*	39*	86	33*	95	59*	51*	68	

2.8 Graphing Bivariate Relationships (Optional)

The claim is often made that the crime rate and the unemployment rate are "highly correlated." Another popular belief is that the gross domestic product (GDP) and the rate of inflation are "related." Some people even believe that the Dow Jones Industrial Average and the lengths of fashionable skirts are "associated." The words *correlated*, *related*, and *associated* imply a relationship between two variables—in the examples above, two *quantitative* variables.

One way to describe the relationship between two quantitative variables–called a **bivariate relationship**—is to plot the data in a **scatterplot.** A scatterplot is a two-dimensional graph, with one variable's values plotted along the vertical axis and the other variable's values plotted along the horizontal axis. For example, Figure 2.33 is a scatterplot relating (1) the cost of mechanical work (heating, ventilating, and plumbing) to (2) the floor area of the building for a sample of 26 factory and warehouse buildings. Note that the scatterplot suggests a general tendency for mechanical cost to increase as building floor area increases.

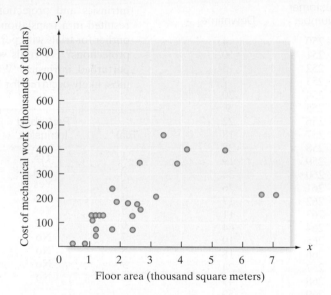

Figure 2.33

Scatterplot of cost vs. floor area

When an increase in one variable is generally associated with an increase in the second variable, we say that the two variables are "positively related" or "positively correlated."* Figure 2.33 implies that mechanical cost and floor area are positively correlated. Alternatively, if one variable has a tendency to decrease as the other increases, we say the variables are "negatively correlated." Figure 2.34 shows hypothetical scatterplots that portray a positive bivariate relationship (Figure 2.34a), a negative bivariate relationship (Figure 2.34b), and a situation where the two variables are unrelated (Figure 2.34c).

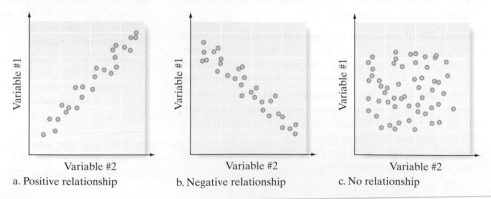

Figure 2.34

Hypothetical bivariate relationship

a. Positive relationship

b. Negative relationship

c. No relationship

*A formal definition of correlation is given in Chapter 11. We will learn that correlation measures the strength of the linear (or straight-line) relationship between two quantitative variables.

EXAMPLE 2.19

Graphing Bivariate Data—Hospital Length of Stay

Problem A medical item used to treat a hospital patient is called a *factor*. For example, factors can be intravenous (IV) tubing, IV fluid, needles, shave kits, bedpans, diapers, dressings, medications, and even code carts. The coronary care unit at Bayonet Point Hospital (St. Petersburg, Florida) recently investigated the relationship between the number of factors used per patient and the patient's length of stay (in days). Data on these two variables for a sample of 50 coronary care patients are given in Table 2.7. Use a scatterplot to describe the relationship between the two variables of interest: number of factors and length of stay.

Table 2.7	Data on Patient's Factors and Length of Stay		
Number of Factors	Length of Stay (days)	Number of Factors	Length of Stay (days)
231	9	354	11
323	7	142	7
113	8	286	9
208	5	341	10
162	4	201	5
117	4	158	11
159	6	243	6
169	9	156	6
55	6	184	7
77	3	115	4
103	4	202	6
147	6	206	5
230	6	360	6
78	3	84	3
525	9	331	9
121	7	302	7
248	5	60	2
233	8	110	2
260	4	131	5
224	7	364	4
472	12	180	7
220	8	134	6
383	6	401	15
301	9	155	4
262	7	338	8

Source: Based on Bayonet Point Hospital, Coronary Care Unit.

Data Set: MEDFAC

Solution Rather than construct the plot by hand, we resort to a statistical software package. The XLSTAT plot of the data in Table 2.7, with length of stay (LOS) on the vertical axis and number of factors (FACTORS) on the horizontal axis, is shown in Figure 2.35.

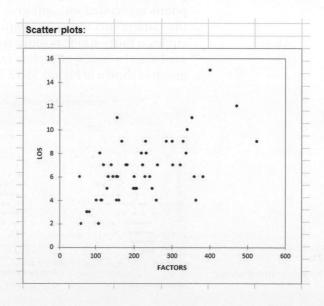

Figure 2.35
XLSTAT scatterplot of data in Table 2.9

Although the plotted points exhibit a fair amount of variation, the scatterplot clearly shows an increasing trend. It appears that a patient's length of stay is positively correlated with the number of factors used in the patient's care.

Look Back If hospital administrators can be confident that the sample trend shown in Figure 2.35 accurately describes the trend in the population, then they may use this information to improve their forecasts of lengths of stay for future patients.

● **Now Work Exercise 2.125**

The scatterplot is a simple but powerful tool for describing a bivariate relationship. However, keep in mind that it is only a graph. No measure of reliability can be attached to inferences made about bivariate populations based on scatterplots of sample data. The statistical tools that enable us to make inferences about bivariate relationships are presented in Chapter 11.

STATISTICS IN ACTION REVISITED **Interpreting Scatterplots**

Refer, again, to the *Journal of Experimental Social Psychology* (Vol. 45, 2009) study on whether money can buy love. Two quantitative variables of interest to the Stanford University researchers were *birthday gift price* (dollars) and *overall level of appreciation for the gift* (measured on a scale from 2 to 14). To investigate a possible relationship between these two variables, we created a scatterplot for the data collected for each of the 237 participants. The Minitab scatterplot is displayed in Figure SIA2.7a.

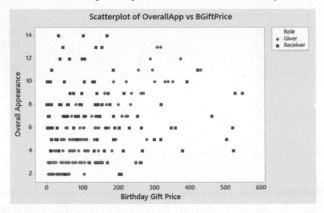

Figure SIA2.7a

Minitab scatterplot of appreciation level vs. gift price

At first glance, the graph appears to show little or no association between appreciation level and gift price. However, if you look closely you will see that the data points associated with gift-givers are plotted with a different symbol (black circle) than the data points associated with gift-recipients (red square). Focusing on just the black circles, a fairly strong positive trend is apparent. To see this trend more clearly, we generated side-by-side scatterplots for the data, one plot for givers and one for receivers. This graph is shown in Figure SIA2.7b.

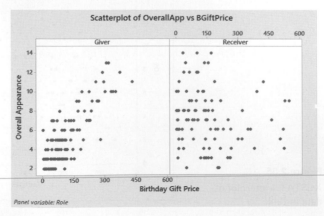

Figure SIA2.7b

Minitab side-by-side scatterplots for the study

The left panel of Figure SIA2.7b shows a fairly strong positive association between appreciation level and gift price for gift-givers. As gift price increases, the gift-giver anticipates that the level of appreciation for the gift will increase. Conversely, the right panel of Figure SIA2.7b shows little or no association between appreciation level and gift price for gift-recipients. This type of analysis led the Stanford University researchers to conclude that "gift-givers and gift-receivers disagree about the link between gift price and gift-recipients' feelings of appreciation. Givers anticipated that recipients would appreciate more expensive gifts, but gift-recipients did not base their feelings of appreciation on how much the gift cost."

In Chapter 11, we show how to attach a measure of reliability to these conclusions.

Exercises 2.122–2.134

Learning the Mechanics

2.122 Construct a scatterplot for the data in the following table.

Variable 1:	5	3	−1	2	7	6	4	0	8
Variable 2:	14	3	10	1	8	5	3	2	12

2.123 Construct a scatterplot for the data in the following table.

Variable 1:	5	1	1.5	2	2.5	3	3.5	4	4.5	5
Variable 2:	2	1	3	4	6	10	9	12	17	17

Applying the Concepts—Basic

2.124 Repair and replacement costs of water pipes. Pipes used in a water distribution network are susceptible to breakage due to a variety of factors. When pipes break, engineers must decide whether to repair or replace the broken pipe. A team of civil engineers estimated the ratio of repair to replacement cost of commercial pipe based on the diameter (in millimeters) of the pipe. (*IHS Journal of Hydraulic Engineering,* September 2012.) Data for a sample of 13 different pipe sizes are provided in the table. Use a scatterplot to aid the engineers in detecting a trend in the data. Does it appear that ratio of repair to replacement cost is strongly associated with pipe size?

DIAMETER	RATIO
80	6.58
100	6.97
125	7.39
150	7.61
200	7.78
250	7.92
300	8.20
350	8.42
400	8.60
450	8.97
500	9.31
600	9.47
700	9.72

Source: C. R. Suribabu and T. R. Neelakantan, "Sizing of Water Distribution Pipes Based on Performance Measure and Breakage-Repair Replacement Economics," *IHS Journal of Hydraulic Engineering,* Vol. 18, No. 3, September 2012 (Table 1).

2.125 In business, do nice guys really finish last? Do "nice guys finish last" in the competitive corporate world? In a study published in *Nature* (March 20, 2008), college students repeatedly played a version of the game "prisoner's dilemma," where competitors choose cooperation, defection, or costly punishment. (Cooperation meant paying 1 unit for the opponent to receive 2 units; defection meant gaining 1 unit at a cost of 1 unit for the opponent; and punishment meant paying 1 unit for the opponent to lose 4 units.) At the conclusion of the games, the researchers recorded the average payoff and the number of times punishment was used against each player. A graph of the data is shown in the accompanying scatterplot. Does it appear that average payoff is associated with punishment use? The researchers concluded that "winners don't punish." Do you agree? Explain.

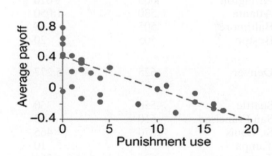

2.126 Lobster trap placement. Strategic placement of lobster traps is one of the keys for a successful lobster fisherman. An observational study of teams fishing for the red spiny lobster in Baja California Sur, Mexico, was conducted and the results published in *Bulletin of Marine Science* (April 2010). Two variables measured for each of eight teams from the Punta Abreojos (PA) fishing cooperative were y = total catch of lobsters (in kilograms) during the season and x = average percentage of traps allocated per day to exploring areas of unknown catch (called *search frequency*). These data are listed in the next table. Graph the data in a scatterplot. What type of trend, if any, do you observe?

Data for Exercise 2.126

Total Catch	Search Frequency
2,785	35
6,535	21
6,695	26
4,891	29
4,937	23
5,727	17
7,019	21
5,735	20

Source: Based on G. G. Shester, "Explaining Catch Variation Among Baja California Lobster Fishers Through Spatial Analysis of Trap-Placement Decisions," *Bulletin of Marine Science,* Vol. 86, No. 2, April 2010 (Table 1), pp. 479–498.

2.127 Does elevation impact hitting performance in baseball?

MLBPKS
The Colorado Rockies play their Major League home baseball games at Coors Field, Denver. Each year, the Rockies are among the leaders in team batting statistics (e.g., home runs, batting average, and slugging percentage). Many baseball experts attribute this phenomenon to the "thin air" of Denver—called the "mile-high" city due to its elevation. *Chance* (Winter 2006) investigated the effects of elevation on slugging percentage in Major League Baseball. Data were compiled on players' composite slugging percentage at each of 29 cities for a recent season, as well as each city's elevation (feet above sea level). The data for selected observations are shown in the table below. Construct a scatterplot of the data for all 29 cities. Do you detect a trend?

City	Slug Pct.	Elevation
Anaheim	.480	160
Arlington	.605	616
Atlanta	.530	1,050
Baltimore	.505	130
Boston	.505	20
⋮	⋮	⋮
Denver	.625	5,277
⋮	⋮	⋮
Seattle	.550	350
San Francisco	.510	63
St. Louis	.570	465
Tampa	.500	10
Toronto	.535	566

Source: J. Schaffer and E. L. Heiny, "The Effects of Elevation on Slugging Percentage in Major League Baseball." *Chance,* Vol. 19, No. 1. Winter 2006 (adapted from Figure 2, p. 30).

2.128 State SAT scores. Refer to Exercise 2.27 (p. 84) and the

SATMAT
data on state SAT scores. Construct a scatterplot for the data, with 2010 Math SAT score on the horizontal axis and 2014 Math SAT score on the vertical axis. What type of trend do you detect?

2.129 Hourly road accidents in India. An analysis of road accident data in India was undertaken, and the results published in the *Journal of Big Data* (Vol. 2, 2015). For a particular cluster of roads, the hourly numbers of accidents totaled over a recent 5-year period are listed in the next table. (These results are adapted from a figure in the journal article.) Create a scatterplot of the data, with number of
ROAD
accidents on the vertical axis and hour on the horizontal axis. What type of trend (if any) do you detect in the data?

Hour	Number
1	125
2	148
3	159
4	270
5	281
6	295
7	302
8	216
9	225
10	353
11	400
12	327

Applying the Concepts—Intermediate

2.130 Spreading rate of spilled liquid. A contract engineer at

LSPILL
DuPont Corp. studied the rate at which a spilled volatile liquid will spread across a surface (*Chemical Engineering Progress,* January 2005). Assume 50 gallons of methanol spills onto a level surface outdoors. The engineer used derived empirical formulas (assuming a state of turbulent-free convection) to calculate the mass (in pounds) of the spill after a period of time ranging from 0 to 60 minutes. The calculated mass values are given in the table. Is there evidence to indicate that the mass of the spill tends to diminish as time increases? Support your answer with a scatterplot.

Time (minutes)	Mass (pounds)
0	6.64
1	6.34
2	6.04
4	5.47
6	4.94
8	4.44
10	3.98
12	3.55
14	3.15
16	2.79
18	2.45
20	2.14
22	1.86
24	1.60
26	1.37
28	1.17
30	0.98
35	0.60
40	0.34
45	0.17
50	0.06
55	0.02
60	0.00

Source: Based on J. Barry, "Estimating Rates of Spreading and Evaporation of Volatile Liquids," *Chemical Engineering Progress,* Vol. 101, No. 1., January 2005, p. 38.

2.131 Performance ratings of government agencies. The U.S.

PARS
Office of Management and Budget (OMB) requires government agencies to produce annual performance and accounting reports (PARS) each year. A research team at George Mason University evaluated the quality of the PARS for 24 government agencies (*The Public Manager,* Summer 2008). Evaluation scores ranged from 12 (lowest)

to 60 (highest). The PARS evaluation scores for two consecutive years are shown in the next table.

Data for Exercise 2.131

Agency	Year 1	Year 2
Transportation	55	53
Labor	53	51
Veterans	51	51
NRC	39	34
Commerce	37	36
HHS	37	35
DHS	37	30
Justice	35	37
Treasury	35	35
GSA	34	40
Agriculture	33	35
EPA	33	36
Social Security	33	33
USAID	32	42
Education	32	36
Interior	32	31
NASA	32	32
Energy	31	34
HUD	31	30
NSF	31	31
State	31	50
OPM	27	28
SBA	22	31
Defense	17	32

Source: J. Ellig and H. Wray, "Performance Ratings of Government Agencies," from Measuring Performance Reporting Quality, *The Public Manager,* Vol. 37.2, Summer 2008, p. 68. Copyright © 2008 by, Jerry Ellig. Used by permission of Jerry Ellig.

a. Construct a scatterplot for the data. Do you detect a trend in the data?

b. Based on the graph, identify one or two agencies that had greater than expected PARS evaluation scores for year 2.

2.132 Most valuable NFL teams. Refer to the *Forbes* listing of the 2015 values of the 32 teams in the National Football League (NFL), Exercise 2.26 (p. 84). Construct a scatterplot to investigate the relationship between 2015 value ($ millions) and operating income ($ millions). Would you recommend that an NFL executive use operating income to predict a team's current value? Explain.

2.133 Best-paid CEOs. Refer to Glassdoor Economic Research firm's 2015 ranking of the 40 best-paid CEOs in Table 2.1 (p. 65). Recall that data were collected on a CEO's current salary, age, and ratio of salary to a typical worker's pay at the firm.

a. Create a scatterplot to relate a CEO's ratio of salary to worker pay to the CEO's age. Comment on the strength of the association between these two variables.

b. Conduct an outlier analysis of the ratio variable. Identify the highly suspect outlier in the data.

c. Remove the highly suspect outlier from the data and recreate the scatterplot of part **a.** What do you observe?

Applying the Concepts—Advanced

2.134 Ranking driving performance of professional golfers. Refer to *The Sport Journal* (Winter 2007) analysis of a new method for ranking the total driving performance of golfers on the PGA tour, Exercise 2.52 (p. 97). Recall that the method uses both the average driving distance (yards) and driving accuracy (percent of drives that land in the fairway). Data on these two variables for the top 40 PGA golfers are saved in the accompanying file. A professional golfer is practicing a new swing to increase his average driving distance. However, he is concerned that his driving accuracy will be lower. Is his concern a valid one? Explain.

2.9 The Time Series Plot (Optional)

Each of the previous sections has been concerned with describing the information contained in a sample or population of data. Often these data are viewed as having been produced at essentially the same point in time. Thus, time has not been a factor in any of the graphical methods described so far.

Data of interest to managers are often produced and monitored over time. Examples include the daily closing price of their company's common stock, the company's weekly sales volume and quarterly profits, and characteristics—such as weight and length—of products produced by the company.

Data that are produced and monitored over time are called **time series data.**

Recall from Section 1.4 that a process is a series of actions or operations that generates output over time. Accordingly, measurements taken of a sequence of units produced by a process—such as a production process—are time series data. In general, any sequence of numbers produced over time can be thought of as being generated by a process. When measurements are made over time, it is important to record both the numerical value and the time or the time period associated with each measurement. With this information, a **time series plot**—sometimes called a **run chart**—can be constructed to describe the time series data and to learn about the process that generated the data.

A time series plot is simply a scatterplot with the measurements on the vertical axis and time or the order in which the measurements were made on the horizontal axis. The plotted points are usually connected by straight lines to make it easier to see the changes and movement in the measurements over time. For example, Figure 2.36 is a time series plot of a particular company's monthly sales (number of units sold per month). And Figure 2.37 is a time series plot of the weights of 30 one-gallon paint cans that were consecutively filled by the same filling head. Notice that the weights are plotted against the order in which the cans were filled rather than some unit of time. When monitoring production processes, it is often more convenient to record the order rather than the exact time at which each measurement was made.

Time series plots reveal the movement (trend) and changes (variation) in the variable being monitored. Notice how sales trend upward in the summer and how the variation in the weights of the paint cans increases over time. This kind of information would not be revealed by stem-and-leaf displays or histograms, as the following example illustrates.

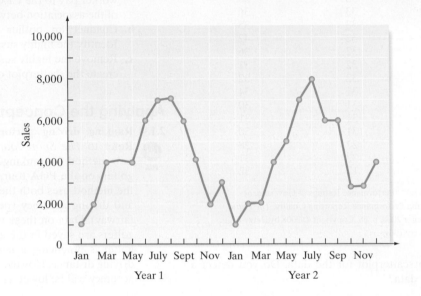

Figure 2.36
Time series plot of company sales

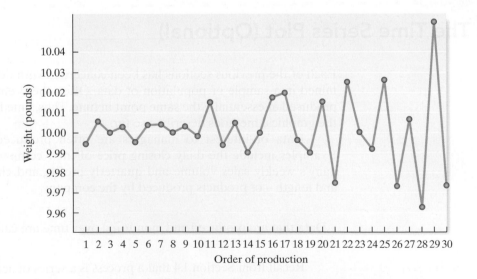

Figure 2.37
Time series plot of paint can weights

EXAMPLE 2.20

Time Series Plot vs. a Histogram—Deming's Example

Problem W. Edwards Deming was one of America's most famous statisticians. He was best known for the role he played after World War II in teaching the Japanese how to improve the quality of their products by monitoring and continually improving their production processes. In his book *Out of the Crisis* (1986), Deming warned against the knee-jerk (i.e., automatic) use of histograms to display and extract information from data. As evidence, he offered the following example.

Fifty camera springs were tested in the order in which they were produced. The elongation of each spring was measured under the pull of 20 grams. Both a time series plot and a histogram were constructed from the measurements. They are shown in Figure 2.38, which has been reproduced from Deming's book. If you had to predict the elongation measurement of the next spring to be produced (i.e., spring 51) and could use only one of the two plots to guide your prediction, which would you use? Why?

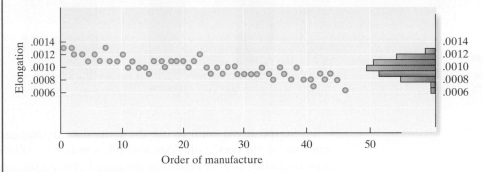

Figure 2.38

Deming's time series plot and histogram

Solution Only the time series plot describes the behavior *over time* of the process that produces the springs. The fact that the elongation measurements are decreasing over time can be gleaned only from the time series plot. Because the histogram does not reflect the order in which the springs were produced, it in effect represents all observations as having been produced simultaneously. Using the histogram to predict the elongation of the 51st spring would very likely lead to an overestimate.

Look Back The lesson from Deming's example is this: For displaying and analyzing data that have been generated over time by a process, the primary graphical tool is the time series plot, not the histogram.

We cover many other aspects of the statistical analysis of time series data in Chapter 14 (available on www.pearsonglobaleditions.com/mcclave).

2.10 Distorting the Truth with Descriptive Techniques

A picture may be "worth a thousand words," but pictures can also color messages or distort them. In fact, the pictures displayed in statistics (e.g., histograms, bar charts, time series plots, etc.) are susceptible to distortion, whether unintentional or as a result of unethical statistical practices. Accordingly, we begin this section by mentioning a few of the pitfalls to watch for when interpreting a chart or a graph. Then we discuss how numerical descriptive measures can be used to distort the truth.

Graphical Distortions

One common way to change the impression conveyed by a graph is to change the scale on the vertical axis, the horizontal axis, or both. For example, consider the data on collisions of large marine vessels operating in European waters over a 5-year period summarized in Table 2.8. Figure 2.39 is a Minitab bar graph showing the frequency of collisions for each of the three locations. The graph shows that "in port" collisions occur more often than collisions "at sea" or collisions in "restricted waters."

Table 2.8	Collisions of Marine Vessels by Location
Location	Number of Ships
At sea	376
Restricted waters	273
In port	478
TOTAL	1,127

Data Set: MARINE

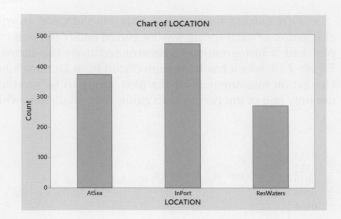

Figure 2.39

Minitab bar graph of vessel collisions by location

Suppose you want to use the same data to exaggerate the difference between the number of "in port" collisions and the number of collisions in "restricted waters." One way to do this is to increase the distance between successive units on the vertical axis—that is, to *stretch* the vertical axis by graphing only a few units per inch. A telltale sign of stretching is a long vertical axis, but this is often hidden by starting the vertical axis at some point above the origin, 0. Such a graph is shown in the SPSS printout, Figure 2.40. By starting the bar chart at 250 collisions (instead of at 0), it appears that the frequency of "in port" collisions is many times larger than the frequency of collisions in "restricted waters."

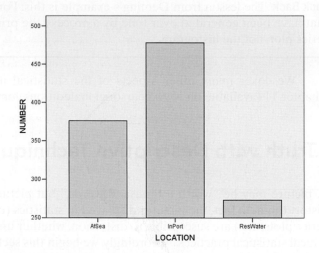

Figure 2.40

SPSS bar graph of vessel collisions by location—adjusted vertical axis

ETHICS in STATISTICS

Intentionally distorting a graph to portray a particular viewpoint is considered *unethical statistical practice*.

Another method of achieving visual distortion with bar graphs is by making the width of the bars proportional to the height. For example, look at the bar chart in Figure 2.41a, which depicts the percentage of a year's total automobile sales attributable to each of four major manufacturers. Now suppose we make both the width and the

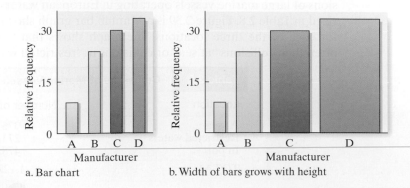

Figure 2.41

Relative share of the automobile market for each of four major manufacturers

a. Bar chart

b. Width of bars grows with height

Production declines again

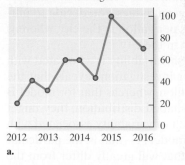

a.

2016: 2nd best year for production

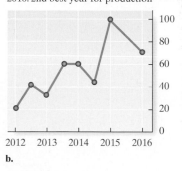

b.

Figure 2.42

Changing the verbal description to change a viewer's interpretation

height grow as the market share grows. This change is shown in Figure 2.41b. The distortion may lead the reader to equate the *area* of the bars with the relative market share of each manufacturer. But the fact is the true relative market share is proportional only to the *height* of the bars.

Sometimes, we do not need to manipulate the graph to distort the impression it creates. Modifying the verbal description that accompanies the graph can change the interpretation that will be made by the viewer. Figure 2.42 provides a good illustration of this ploy. The time series plots show the annual level of production of a firm. The only difference in the two graphs is the headings. The heading "Production declines again" in Figure 2.42a might be used if the firm wants to give the impression that it is under-performing compared to the past (say, in an effort to convince the government that it should not be prosecuted for monopolistic practices). In contrast, the heading "2016: 2nd best year for production" in Figure 2.42b might be intended for stockholders (to give the impression that the firm's stock is a wise investment).

Although we've discussed only a few of the ways that graphs can be used to convey misleading pictures of phenomena, the lesson is clear. Look at all graphical descriptions of data with a critical eye. Particularly, check the axes and the size of the units on each axis. Ignore the visual changes and concentrate on the actual numerical changes indicated by the graph or chart.

Misleading Numerical Descriptive Statistics

The information in a data set can also be distorted by using numerical descriptive measures, as Example 2.21 indicates.

EXAMPLE 2.21

Misleading Descriptive Statistics—Your Average Salary

Problem Suppose you're considering working for a small law firm—one that currently has a senior member and three junior members. You inquire about the salary you could expect to earn if you join the firm. Unfortunately, you receive two answers:

> *Answer A:* The senior member tells you that an "average employee" earns $107,500.
> *Answer B:* One of the junior members later tells you that an "average employee" earns $95,000.

Which answer can you believe?

Solution The confusion exists because the phrase "average employee" has not been clearly defined. Suppose the four salaries paid are $95,000 for each of the three junior members and $145,000 for the senior member. Thus,

$$\text{Mean} = \frac{3(\$95,000) + \$145,000}{4} = \frac{\$430,000}{4} = \$107,500$$

$$\text{Median} = \$95,000$$

You can now see how the two answers were obtained. The senior member reported the mean of the four salaries, and the junior member reported the median. The information you received was distorted because neither person stated which measure of central tendency was being used.

Look Back Based on our earlier discussion of the mean and median, we would probably prefer the median as the measure that best describes the salary of the "average" employee.

Another distortion of information in a sample occurs when *only* a measure of central tendency is reported. Both a measure of central tendency and a measure of variability are needed to obtain an accurate mental image of a data set.

Suppose you want to buy a new car and are trying to decide which of two models to purchase. Because energy and economy are both important issues, you decide to purchase model A because its EPA mileage rating is 32 miles per gallon in the city, whereas the mileage rating for model B is only 30 miles per gallon in the city.

However, you may have acted too quickly. How much variability is associated with the ratings? As an extreme example, suppose that further investigation reveals that the standard deviation for model A mileages is 5 miles per gallon, whereas that for model B is only 1 mile per gallon. If the mileages form a mound-shaped distribution, they might appear as shown in Figure 2.43. Note that the larger amount of variability associated with model A implies that more risk is involved in purchasing model A—that is, the particular car you purchase is more likely to have a mileage rating that will greatly differ from the EPA rating of 32 miles per gallon if you purchase model A, while a model B car is not likely to vary from the 30-miles-per-gallon rating by more than 2 miles per gallon.

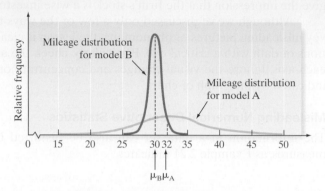

Figure 2.43
Mileage distributions for two car models

We conclude this section with another example on distorting the truth with numerical descriptive measures.

EXAMPLE 2.22

More Misleading Descriptive Statistics— Delinquent Children

Problem *Children out of School in America* is a report on delinquency of school-age children prepared by the Children's Defense Fund (CDF), a government-sponsored organization. Consider the following three reported results of the CDF survey.

- Reported result 1: 25% of the 16- and 17-year-olds in the Portland, Maine, Bayside East Housing Project were out of school. Fact: *Only eight children were surveyed; two were found to be out of school.*

- Reported result 2: Of all the secondary-school students who had been suspended more than once in census tract 22 in Columbia, South Carolina, 33% had been suspended two times and 67% had been suspended three or more times. Fact: *CDF found only three children in that entire census tract who had been suspended; one child was suspended twice and the other two children, three or more times.*

- Reported result 3: In the Portland Bayside East Housing Project, 50% of all the secondary-school children who had been suspended more than once had been suspended three or more times. Fact: *The survey found two secondary-school children had been suspended in that area; one of them had been suspended three or more times.*

Identify the potential distortions in the results reported by the CDF.

Solution In each of these examples, the reporting of percentages (i.e., relative frequencies) instead of the numbers themselves is misleading. No inference we might draw from the cited examples would be reliable. (We'll see how to measure the reliability of estimated percentages in Chapter 6.) In short, either the report should state the numbers alone instead of percentages, or, better yet, it should state that the numbers were too small to report by region.

Look Back If several regions were combined, the numbers (and percentages) would be more meaningful.

ETHICS in STATISTICS

Purposeful reporting of numerical descriptive statistics in order to mislead the target audience is considered *unethical statistical practice.*

Exercises 2.135–2.138

Applying the Concepts—Intermediate

2.135 Museum management. Refer to the *Museum Management and Curatorship* (June 2010) study of how museums evaluate their performance, Exercise 2.14 (p. 74). Recall that managers of 30 museums of contemporary art identified the performance measure used most often. A summary of the results is reproduced in the table. Consider the bar graph shown. Identify two ways in which the bar graph might mislead the viewer by overemphasizing the importance of one of the performance measures.

Performance Measure	Number of Museums	Proportion of Museums
Total visitors	8	.267
Paying visitors	5	.167
Big shows	6	.200
Funds raised	7	.233
Members	4	.133

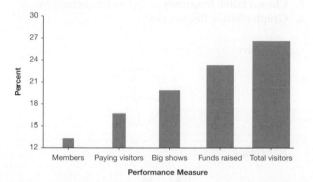

2.136 Volkswagen emissions scandal. Refer to the *Significance* (December 2015) study on estimating the number of U.S. deaths attributable to nitrogen oxide (NOx) pollution produced from illegal VW vehicles, Exercise 2.82 (p. 111). Recall that the researchers computed the estimate for each of 27 different scenarios involving different values of three variables: total distance (in miles) driven by these illegal VW vehicles, the amount by which the VW vehicles exceeded the EPA standard for NOx, and the estimated association between NOx emissions and mortality. Summary statistics for the estimated number of deaths are shown in the accompanying Minitab printout. Suppose the media have requested that the researchers provide a single statistic that best represents the center of the distribution of estimated deaths attributable to NOx pollution produced from the illegal VW vehicles. This statistic will be used to publicize the study findings.

Descriptive Statistics: Deaths

```
Variable  N   Mean  StDev  Minimum   Q1  Median    Q3  Maximum
Deaths    27 163.4 227.4      4.0  29.0   68.0  184.0    955.0
```

a. If you work for Volkswagen and would like to diffuse the media's reaction to the emissions scandal, which statistic would you choose to report and why?

b. If you support an environmental watch group and would like to incite the media to publicize the emissions scandal, which statistic would you choose to report and why?

2.137 Misleading graph. Consider the following graphic, similar to one produced by the *Silicon Alley Insider*, an online publication for business news. The graph is attempting to show the increasing trend in annual revenue produced by Craigslist as compared to the decrease in newspaper classified ad sales.

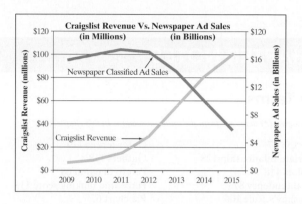

a. Why might the graph be misleading? [*Hint:* Focus on the units of measure on the two vertical axes.]

b. Redraw the graph, but use the same units of measure for both Craigslist revenue and newspaper ad sales. What conclusions can you draw from the redrawn graph?

2.138 BP oil leak. In the summer of 2010, an explosion on the Deepwater Horizon oil drilling rig caused a leak in one of British Petroleum (BP) Oil Company's wells in the Gulf of Mexico. Crude oil rushed unabated for 3 straight months into the Gulf until BP could fix the leak. During the disaster, BP used suction tubes to capture some of the gushing oil. In May of 2011, in an effort to demonstrate the daily improvement in the process, a BP representative presented a graphic on the daily number of 42-gallon barrels (bbl) of oil collected by the suctioning process. A graphic similar to the one used by BP is shown below.

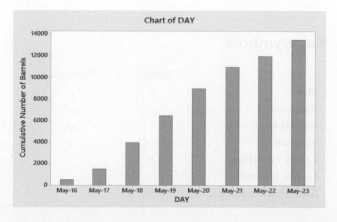

a. Note that the vertical axis represents the "cumulative" number of barrels collected per day. This is calculated by adding the amounts of the previous days' oil collection to the current day's oil collection. Explain why this graph is misleading.

b. Estimates of the actual number of barrels of oil collected per day for each of the 8 days are listed in the accompanying table. Construct a graph for these data that accurately depicts BP's progress in its daily collection of oil. What conclusions can you draw from the graph?

Estimates of Daily Collection of Oil

Day	Number of Barrels (bbl)
May 16	500
May 17	1,000
May 18	3,000
May 19	2,500
May 20	2,500
May 21	2,000
May 22	1,000
May 23	1,500

CHAPTER NOTES

Key Terms

Note: Starred (*) items are from the optional sections in this chapter.

Bar graph 67
*Bivariate relationship 128
Box plots 118
Central tendency 87
Chebyshev's Rule 106
Class 66
Class frequency 66
Class interval 77
Class percentage 66
Class relative frequency 66
Dot plot 75
Empirical Rule 106
Hinges 118
Histogram 77
Inner fences 119
Interquartile range (IQR) 118
Lower quartile 114
Mean 87
Mean of a sample 88
Measures of central tendency 87
Measures of relative standing 113
Measures of variability 98
Median 89
Middle quartile 114
Modal class 92
Mode 92
Mound-shaped distribution 115
Numerical descriptive measures 87

Outer fences 119
Outliers 118
Pareto diagram 68
Percentile ranking/score 113
Pie chart 67
Population z-score 115
pth percentile 114
Quartiles 114
Range 99
Rare-event approach 123
*Run chart 133
Sample standard deviation 101
Sample variance 100
Sample z-score 115
*Scatterplot 128
Skewness 91
Spread 98
Standard deviation 101
Stem-and-leaf display 75
Symmetric distribution 105
*Time series data 133
*Time series plot 133
Time study 105
Upper quartile 114
Variability 87
Variance 100
Whiskers 119
z-score 115

Key Symbols

	Sample	Population
Mean:	$\bar{x}$	μ
Variance:	s^2	σ^2
Std. Dev.:	s	σ
Median:	m or Q_M	η
Lower Quartile:	Q_L	
Upper Quartile:	Q_U	
Interquartile Range:	IQR	

Key Ideas

Describing Qualitative Data

1. Identify **category classes**
2. Determine **class frequencies**
3. **Class relative frequency** = (class frequency)/n
4. **Graph** relative frequencies

Pie Chart:

Bar Graph:

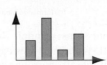

Pareto Diagram:

Graphing Quantitative Data

One Variable

1. Identify class intervals
2. Determine **class interval frequencies**
3. **Class interval relative frequency** = (class interval frequency)/n
4. **Graph** class interval relative frequencies

Dot Plot:

Stem-and-Leaf Display:

```
1 | 3
2 | 2489
3 | 126678
4 | 37
5 | 2
```

Histogram:

Box Plot:

Two Variables

Scatterplot:

Time series plot:

Time

Numerical Description of Quantitative Data

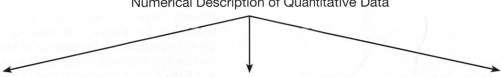

Central Tendency

Mean: $\bar{x} = (\Sigma x_i)/n$

Median: Middle value when data ranked in order

Mode: Value that occurs most often

Variation

Range: Difference between largest and smallest value

Variance:

$$s^2 = \frac{\Sigma(x_i - \bar{x})^2}{n - 1} = \frac{\Sigma x_i^2 - \dfrac{(\Sigma x_i)^2}{n}}{n - 1}$$

Std. Dev.: $s = \sqrt{s^2}$

Interquartile Range: $\text{IQR} = Q_U - Q_L$

Relative Standing

Percentile Score: Percentage of values that fall below x-score

z-score:

$$z = (x - \bar{x})/s$$
$$= (x - \mu)/\sigma$$

Rules for Detecting Quantitative Outliers

Interval	Chebyshev's Rule	Empirical Rule
$\bar{x} \pm s$	At least 0%	$\approx 68\%$
$\bar{x} \pm 2s$	At least 75%	$\approx 95\%$
$\bar{x} \pm 3s$	At least 89%	$\approx$ All

Rules for Detecting Quantitative Outliers

Method	Suspect	Highly Suspect
Box plot:	Values between inner & outer fences	Values beyond outer fences
z-score:	$2 < |z| < 3$	$|z| > 3$

Guide to Selecting the Data Description Method

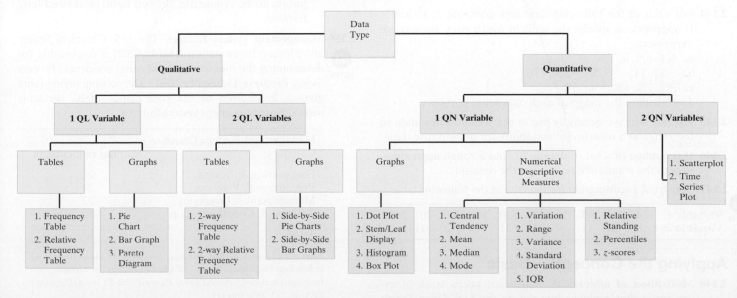

SUPPLEMENTARY EXERCISES 2.139–2.171

Note: Starred (*) exercises refer to the optional sections in this chapter.

Learning the Mechanics

2.139 Construct a relative frequency histogram for the data summarized in the accompanying table.

Measurement Class	Relative Frequency
.00–.75	.02
.75–1.50	.01
1.50–2.25	.03
2.25–3.00	.05
3.00–3.75	.10
3.75–4.50	.14
4.50–5.25	.19
5.25–6.00	.15
6.00–6.75	.12
6.75–7.50	.09
7.50–8.25	.05
8.25–9.00	.04
9.00–9.75	.01

2.140 Discuss the conditions under which the median is preferred to the mean as a measure of central tendency.

2.141 Consider the following three measurements: 0, 4, and 12. Find the z-score for each measurement if they are from a population with a following mean and standard deviation equal to
a. $\mu = 2$ and $\sigma = 1$
b. $\mu = 4$ and $\sigma = 2$
c. $\mu = 8$ and $\sigma = 2$
d. $\mu = 8$ and $\sigma = 8$

2.142 Refer to Exercise 2.141. Assuming all populations are approximately mound-shaped, for parts **a–d**, determine whether the values 0, 4, and 12 are outliers.

2.143 The amount spent on textbooks for the fall term was recorded for a sample of five university students. The following data were observed: $400, $350, $600, $525, and $450. Calculate each of the following values for this data:
a. The sample mean
b. The sample median
c. The sample range
d. The standard deviation

2.144 For each of the following data sets, compute $\bar{x}$, s^2, and s. If appropriate, specify the units in which your answers are expressed.
a. 4, 6, 6, 5, 6, 7
b. −$1, $4, −$3, $0, −$3, −$6
c. $\frac{3}{5}\%, \frac{4}{5}\%, \frac{2}{5}\%, \frac{1}{5}\%, \frac{1}{16}\%$
d. Calculate the range of each data set in parts **a–c**.

2.145 Explain why we generally prefer the standard deviation to the range as a measure of variability for quantitative data.

2.146 If the range of a set of data is 20, find a rough approximation to the standard deviation of the data set.

*2.147 Construct a scattergram for the data in the following table.

Variable 1:	174	268	345	119	400	520	190	448	307	252
Variable 2:	8	10	15	7	22	31	15	20	11	9

Applying the Concepts—Basic

2.148 Motivation of athletes. A statistician keeps track of every serve that a player hits during the U.S. Open Tennis Championship. The statistician reports that the mean serve speed was 100 miles per hour (mph) and the standard deviation of the serve speeds was 15 mph.
a. Suppose the statistician also observes that the distribution of serve speeds was mound-shaped and symmetric. What percentage of the player's serves was between 115 mph and 145 mph?
b. Consider the following serve speeds: 50 mph, 80 mph, and 105 mph. Using the z-score approach for detecting outliers, which of these would represent outliers in the distribution of the player's serve speeds?
c. If nothing is known about the shape of the distribution, what percentage of the player's serve speeds are less than 70 mph?

2.149 Blogs for *Fortune* 500 firms. Web site communication through blogs and forums is a key marketing tool for companies. The *Journal of Relationship Marketing* (Vol. 7, 2008) investigated the prevalence of blogs and forums at *Fortune* 500 firms with both English and Chinese Web sites.
a. Of the firms that provided blogs/forums as a marketing tool, the accompanying table gives a breakdown on the entity responsible for creating the blogs/forums. Use a graphical method to describe the data summarized in the table. Interpret the graph.

Blog/Forum	Percentage of Firms
Created by company	38.5
Created by employees	34.6
Created by third party	11.5
Creator not identified	15.4

Source: Data from K. Mishra and C. Li, "Relationship Marketing in Fortune 500 U.S. and Chinese Web Sites," *Journal of Relationship Marketing,* Vol. 7, No. 1, 2008.

b. In a sample of firms that provide blogs and forums as marketing tools, the mean number of blogs/forums per site was 4.25, with a standard deviation of 12.02. Provide an interval that is likely to contain the number of blogs/forums per site for at least 75% of the *Fortune* 500 firms in the sample.
c. Do you expect the distribution of the number of blogs/forums to be symmetric, skewed right, or skewed left? Explain.

2.150 Management system failures. The U.S. Chemical Safety and Hazard Investigation Board (CSB) is responsible for determining the root cause of industrial accidents (*Process Safety Progress*, December 2004). The accompanying table gives a breakdown of the root causes of 83 incidents caused by management system failures.

Management System Cause Category	Number of Incidents
Engineering & Design	27
Procedures & Practices	24
Management & Oversight	22
Training & Communication	10
Total	83

Source: Based on A. S. Blair, "Management System Failures Identified in Incidents Investigated by the U.S. Chemical Safety and Hazard Investigation Board," *Process Safety Progress,* Vol. 23, No. 4, December 2004, pp. 232–236 (Table 1).

a. Find the relative frequency of the number of incidents for each cause category.

b. Construct a Pareto diagram for the data.

c. From the Pareto diagram, identify the cause categories with the highest (and lowest) relative frequency of incidents.

2.151 Business marketing publications. Business-to-business marketing describes the field of marketing between multiple business entities. The *Journal of Business-to-Business Marketing* (Vol. 15, 2008) produced a pie chart describing the number of business-to-business marketing articles published in all journals, by topical area, between 1971 and 2006. The data used to produce the pie chart are shown in the table.

Area	Number
Global Marketing	235
Sales Management	494
Buyer Behavior	478
Relationships	498
Innovation	398
Marketing Strategy	280
Channels/Distribution	213
Marketing Research	131
Services	136
Total	2,863

Source: Based on Peter J. LaPlaca, "Commentary on 'The Essence of Business Marketing…' by Lichtenthal, Mummalaneni, and Wilson: The JBBM Comes of Age," *Journal of Business-to-Business Marketing*, Vol. 15, No. 2, 2008 (Figure 4), p. 187.

a. Compute the relative frequencies for the nine topical areas shown in the table. Interpret the relative frequency for Buyer Behavior.

b. Use the relative frequencies, part **a**, to construct a pie chart for the data. Why is the slice for Marketing Research smaller than the slice for Sales Management?

*2.152 **U.S. business bankruptcies.** The American Bankruptcy Institute and the National Bankruptcy Research Center monitor the number of business bankruptcy filings each quarter. The table below lists the number of business bankruptcy filings for each quarter of a recent 2-year period.

a. Explain why the data in the table represent time series data.

b. Construct a time series plot for the quarterly number of bankruptcy filings.

c. Do you detect a trend in the time series plot? Explain.

Year	Quarter	Number of Bankruptcies
2011	1	12,376
	2	12,304
	3	11,705
	4	11,149
2012	1	10,998
	2	10,374
	3	9,248
	4	9,231

Source: American Bankruptcy Institute (www.abi.org).

2.153 Crash tests on new cars. The National Highway Traffic Safety Administration (NHTSA) crash-tests new car models to determine how well they protect the driver and front-seat passenger in a head-on collision. The NHTSA has developed a "star" scoring system for the frontal crash test, with results ranging from one star (*) to five stars (*****). The more stars in the rating, the better the level of crash protection in a head-on collision. The NHTSA crash test results for 98 cars (in a recent model year) are stored in the accompanying data file.

a. The driver-side star ratings for the 98 cars are summarized in the Minitab printout shown below. Use the information in the printout to form a pie chart. Interpret the graph.

Tally for Discrete Variables: DRIVSTAR

```
DRIVSTAR  Count   Percent
       2      4      4.08
       3     17     17.35
       4     59     60.20
       5     18     18.37
     N=      98
```

b. One quantitative variable recorded by the NHTSA is driver's severity of head injury (measured on a scale from 0 to 1,500). The mean and standard deviation for the 98 driver head-injury ratings are displayed in the Minitab printout below. Give a practical interpretation of the mean.

Descriptive Statistics: DRIVHEAD

```
Variable  N   Mean   StDev  Minimum   Q1   Median   Q3   Maximum
DRIVHEAD  98  603.7  185.4   216.0   475.0  605.0  724.3  1240.0
```

c. Use the mean and standard deviation to make a statement about where most of the head-injury ratings fall.

d. Find the z-score for a driver head-injury rating of 408. Interpret the result.

2.154 Products "Made in the USA." "Made in the USA" is a claim stated in many product advertisements or on product labels. Advertisers want consumers to believe that the product is manufactured with 100% U.S. labor and materials—which is often not the case. What does "Made in the USA" mean to the typical consumer? To answer this question, a group of marketing professors conducted an experiment at a shopping mall (*Journal of Global Business*, Spring 2002). They asked every fourth adult entrant to the mall to participate in the study. A total of 106 shoppers agreed to answer the question, "'Made in the USA' means what percentage of U.S. labor and materials?" The responses of the 106 shoppers are summarized as follows: "100%" (64 shoppers), "75 to 99%" (20 shoppers), "50 to 74%" (18 shoppers), and "less than 50%" (4 shoppers).

a. What type of data-collection method was used?

b. What type of variable, quantitative or qualitative, is measured?

c. Present the data in graphical form. Use the graph to make a statement about the percentage of consumers who believe "Made in the USA" means 100% U.S. labor and materials.

2.155 Defects in new automobiles. Consider the following data from the automobile industry. All cars produced on a particular day were inspected for defects. The 145 defects found were categorized by type as shown in the accompanying table.

Defect Type	Number
Accessories	50
Body	70
Electrical	10
Engine	5
Transmission	10

a. Construct a Pareto diagram for the data. Use the graph to identify the most frequently observed type of defect.

b. All 70 car body defects were further classified as to type. The frequencies are provided in the following table. Form a Pareto diagram for type of body defect. (Adding this graph to the original Pareto diagram of part **a** is called *exploding the Pareto diagram*.) Interpret the result. What type of body defect should be targeted for special attention?

Body Defect	Number
Chrome	2
Dents	25
Paint	30
Upholstery	10
Windshield	3

2.156 Drivers stopped by police. According to the Bureau of Justice Statistics (September 2013), 80% of all licensed drivers stopped by police are 25 years or older. Give a percentile ranking for the age of 25 years in the distribution of all ages of licensed drivers stopped by police.

Applying the Concepts—Intermediate

2.157 U.S. wine export markets. The Center for International Trade Development (CITD), provides a listing of the top 30 U.S. export markets for sparkling wines. Data on the amount exported (thousands of dollars) and 3-year percentage change for the 30 countries in a recent year are saved in the **WINEX** file. (Data for 5 countries are listed in the table.) Descriptive statistics for these variables are shown in the Minitab printout (next column).

5 of the Top 30 U.S. Sparkling Wine Export Markets

Country	Export ($ Thousands)	3-Year Change (%)
Canada	4952	71.9
Japan	3714	−16.9
Mexico	2104	143.2
Cayman Islands	1576	280.7
United Kingdom	1041	465.8

a. Locate the mean amount exported on the printout and practically interpret its value.

b. Locate the median amount exported on the printout and practically interpret its value.

c. Locate the mean 3-year percentage change on the printout and practically interpret its value.

d. Locate the median 3-year percentage change on the printout and practically interpret its value.

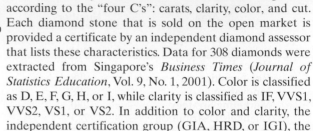

Descriptive Statistics: EXPORT, CHANGE

Variable	N	N*	Mean	StDev	Minimum	Q1	Median	Q3	Maximum	IQR
EXPORT	30	0	653	1113	70	105	231	523	4952	418
CHANGE	28	2	481	1098	−49	21	156	499	5750	478

e. Use the information on the printout to find the range of the amount exported.

f. Locate the standard deviation of the amount exported on the printout.

g. Use the result, part **f**, to find the variance of the amount exported.

h. If one of the top 30 countries is selected at random, give an interval that is likely to include the export amount for this country.

2.158 Color and clarity of diamonds. Diamonds are categorized according to the "four C's": carats, clarity, color, and cut. Each diamond stone that is sold on the open market is provided a certificate by an independent diamond assessor that lists these characteristics. Data for 308 diamonds were extracted from Singapore's *Business Times* (*Journal of Statistics Education*, Vol. 9, No. 1, 2001). Color is classified as D, E, F, G, H, or I, while clarity is classified as IF, VVS1, VVS2, VS1, or VS2. In addition to color and clarity, the independent certification group (GIA, HRD, or IGI), the number of carats and the asking price were recorded.

a. Use a graphical technique to summarize the color and clarity of the 308 diamond stones. What is the color and clarity that occurs most often? Least often?

b. Use a graphical method to describe the carat distribution of all 308 diamonds.

c. Use a graphical method to describe the carat distribution of diamonds certified by the GIA group.

d. Repeat part **c** for the HRD and IGI certification groups.

e. Compare the three carat distributions, parts **c** and **d**. Is there one particular certification group that appears to be assessing diamonds with higher carats than the others?

f. Find and interpret the mean of the data set.

g. Find and interpret the median of the data set.

h. Find and interpret the mode of the data set.

i. Which measure of central tendency best describes the 308 carat values? Explain.

j. Use the mean and standard deviation to form an interval that will contain at least 75% of the carat values in the data set.

k. Construct a scatterplot for the data, with number of carats on the horizontal axis and price on the vertical axis. What type of trend do you detect?

2.159 Hull failures of oil tankers. Owing to several major ocean oil spills by tank vessels, Congress passed the Oil Pollution Act, which requires all tankers to be designed with thicker hulls. Further improvements in the structural design of a tank vessel have been proposed since then, each with the objective of reducing the likelihood of an oil spill and decreasing the amount of outflow in the event of a hull puncture. To aid in this development, *Marine Technology* (Jan. 1995) reported on the spillage amount (in thousands of metric tons) and cause of puncture for 42 major oil spills from tankers and carriers. [*Note:* Cause of puncture is classified as either collision (C), fire/explosion (FE), hull failure (HF), or grounding (G).] The data are saved in the accompanying file.

a. Use a graphical method to describe the cause of oil spillage for the 42 tankers. Does the graph suggest that any one cause is more likely to occur than any other? How is this information of value to the design engineers?

b. Find and interpret descriptive statistics for the 42 spillage amounts. Use this information to form an interval that can be used to predict the spillage amount of the next major oil spill.

2.160 Software defects. The Promise Software Engineering Repository is a collection of data sets available to serve businesses in building predictive software models. One such data set, saved in the accompanying file, contains information on 498 modules of software code. Each module was analyzed for defects and classified as "true" if it contained defective code and "false" if not. Access the data file and produce a bar graph or a pie chart for the defect variable. Use the graph to make a statement about the likelihood of defective software code.

2.161 Velocity of Winchester bullets. The *American Rifleman* (June 1993) reported on the velocity of ammunition fired from the FEG P9R pistol, a 9 mm gun manufactured in Hungary. Field tests revealed that Winchester bullets fired from the pistol had a mean velocity (at 15 feet) of 936 feet per second and a standard deviation of 10 feet per second. Tests were also conducted with Uzi and Black Hills ammunition.

a. Describe the velocity distribution of Winchester bullets fired from the FEG P9R pistol.

b. A bullet, brand unknown, is fired from the FEG P9R pistol. Suppose the velocity (at 15 feet) of the bullet is 1,000 feet per second. Is the bullet likely to be manufactured by Winchester? Explain.

2.162 Time to develop price quotes. A manufacturer of industrial wheels is losing many profitable orders because of the long time it takes the firm's marketing, engineering, and accounting departments to develop price quotes for potential customers. To remedy this problem, the firm's management would like to set guidelines for the length of time each department should spend developing price quotes. To help develop these guidelines, 50 requests for price quotes were randomly selected from the set of price quotes made last year: the processing time (in days) was determined for each price quote for each department. Several observations are displayed in the table below. The price quotes are also classified by whether or not they were "lost" (i.e., whether or not the customer placed an order after receiving the price quote).

Request Number	Marketing	Engineering	Accounting	Lost?
1	7.0	6.2	.1	No
2	.4	5.2	.1	No
3	2.4	4.6	.6	No
4	6.2	13.0	.8	Yes
5	4.7	.9	.5	No
⋮	⋮	⋮	⋮	⋮
46	6.4	1.3	6.2	No
47	4.0	2.4	13.5	Yes
48	10.0	5.3	.1	No
49	8.0	14.4	1.9	Yes
50	7.0	10.0	2.0	No

a. Construct a stem-and-leaf display for the total processing time for each department. Shade the leaves that

correspond to "lost" orders in each of the displays, and interpret each of the displays.

b. Using your results from part **a**, develop "maximum processing time" guidelines for each department that, if followed, will help the firm reduce the number of lost orders.

c. Generate summary statistics for the processing times. Interpret the results.

d. Calculate the z-score corresponding to the maximum processing time guideline you developed in part **b** for each department, and for the total processing time.

e. Calculate the maximum processing time corresponding to a z-score of 3 for each of the departments. What percentage of the orders exceed these guidelines? How does this agree with Chebyshev's Rule and the Empirical Rule?

f. Repeat part **e** using a z-score of 2.

g. Compare the percentage of "lost" quotes with corresponding times that exceed at least one of the guidelines in part **e** to the same percentage using the guidelines in part **f**. Which set of guidelines would you recommend be adopted? Why?

2.163 Trend in Iraq War casualties. While the United States was still actively fighting in the Iraq War, a news media outlet produced a graphic showing a dramatic decline in the annual number of American casualties. The number of deaths for the years 2003, 2004, 2005, and 2006 were (approximately) 475, 850, 820, and 130, respectively.

a. Create a time series plot showing the dramatic decline in the number of American deaths per year.

b. The graphic was based on data collected through February of 2006. Knowing this fact, why is the time series plot misleading?

c. What information would you like to have in order to construct a graph that accurately reflects the trend in American casualties from the Iraq War?

*2.164 History of corporate acquisitions. Refer to the *Academy of Management Journal* (Aug. 2008) study of corporate acquisitions from 1980 to 2000, Exercise 2.12 (p. 74).

a. Construct a time series plot of the number of firms with at least one acquisition.

b. For each year, compute the percentage of sampled firms with at least one acquisition. Then construct a time series plot of these percentages.

c. Which time series plot, part **a** or part **b**, is more informative about the history of corporate acquisitions over time? Explain.

2.165 Radiation levels in homes. In some locations, radiation levels in homes are measured at well above normal background levels in the environment. As a result, many architects and builders are making design changes to ensure adequate air exchange so that radiation will not be "trapped" in homes. In one such location, 50 homes' levels were measured, and the mean level was 10 parts per billion (ppb), the median was 8 ppb, and the standard deviation was 3 ppb. Background levels in this location are at about 4 ppb.

a. Based on these results, is the distribution of the 50 homes' radiation levels symmetric, skewed to the left, or skewed to the right? Why?

b. Use both Chebyshev's Rule and the Empirical Rule to describe the distribution of radiation levels. Which do you think is most appropriate in this case? Why?

c. Use the results from part **b** to approximate the number of homes in this sample that have radiation levels above the background level.

d. Suppose another home is measured at a location 10 miles from the one sampled and has a level of 20 ppb. What is the z-score for this measurement relative to the 50 homes sampled in the other location? Is it likely that this new measurement comes from the same distribution of radiation levels as the other 50? Why? How would you go about confirming your conclusion?

2.166 **Doctors and ethics.** For physicians confronted with ethical dilemmas (e.g., end-of-life issues or treatment of patients without insurance), many hospitals provide ethics consultation services. However, not all physicians take advantage of these services and some refuse to use ethics consultation. The extent to which doctors refuse ethics consults was studied in the *Journal of Medical Ethics* (Vol. 32, 2006). Survey questionnaires were administered to all physicians on staff at a large community hospital in Tampa, Florida, and 118 physicians responded. Several qualitative variables were measured, including *previous use of ethics consultation* ("never used" or "used at least once"), *practitioner specialty* ("medical" or "surgical"), and *future use of ethics consultation* ("yes" or "no").

a. Access the file and generate a graph that describes the level to which the physicians on staff have previously used the ethics consultation services. What proportion of the sampled physicians have never used ethics consultation?

b. Repeat part **a** for *future use of ethics consultation*. What proportion of the sampled physicians state that they will not use the services in the future?

c. Generate side-by-side graphs that illustrate differences in previous use of ethics consultation by medical and surgical specialists. What inference can you make from the graphs?

d. Repeat part **C** for *future use of ethics consultation*.

e. One of the quantitative variables measured in the survey of physicians was *length of time in practice* (i.e., years of experience). The medical researchers hypothesized that older, more experienced physicians would be less likely to use ethics consultation in the future. Generate two graphs to describe the distribution of years of experience—one for physicians who indicated they would use ethics consultation in the future and one for physicians who refused to use ethics consultation. Place the graphs side by side. Is there support for the researchers' assertion? Explain.

f. Find the mean, median, and mode for the *length of time in practice* (i.e., years of experience) variable. Give a practical interpretation of each of these measures of central tendency.

g. Consider only the physicians who would refuse to use ethics consultation in the future. Find the mean, median, and mode for the *length of time in practice* for these physicians. Practically interpret the results.

h. Repeat part **g** for physicians who would use ethics consultation in the future.

i. Use the results, parts **g** and **h**, to comment on the medical researchers' theory.

j. Find the range, variance, and standard deviation for the *length of time in practice* (i.e., years of experience) variable. If possible, give a practical interpretation of each of these measures of variation.

k. Consider only the physicians who would refuse to use ethics consultation in the future. Find the standard deviation for the *length of time in practice* for these physicians.

l. Repeat part **k** for physicians who would use ethics consultation in the future.

m. Use the results, parts **k** and **l**, to compare the variation in the length of time in practice distributions for physicians who would use and who would refuse ethics consultation in the future.

n. In addition to *length of time in practice* (i.e., years of experience), the researchers also measured the *amount of exposure to ethics in medical school* (number of hours) for the sample of 118 physicians. Create a scatterplot for these two variables. Plot years of experience on the vertical axis and amount of exposure to ethics in medical school on the horizontal axis. Comment on the strength of the association between these two variables.

o. Conduct an outlier analysis of the data for the variable *amount of exposure to ethics in medical school*. Identify the highly suspect outlier in the data set.

p. Remove the outlier, part **o,** from the data set and re-create the scatterplot of part **n.** What do you observe?

2.167 **U.S. peanut production.** If not examined carefully, the graphical description of U.S. peanut production shown at the top of the next page can be misleading.

a. Explain why the graph may mislead some readers.

b. Construct an undistorted graph of U.S. peanut production for the given years.

Applying the Concepts—Advanced

2.168 **Investigating the claims of weight-loss clinics.** The U.S. Federal Trade Commission assesses fines and other penalties against weight-loss clinics that make unsupported or misleading claims about the effectiveness of their programs. Brochures from two weight-loss clinics both advertise "statistical evidence" about the effectiveness of their programs. Clinic A claims that the *mean* weight loss during the first month is 15 pounds; Clinic B claims a *median* weight loss of 10 pounds.

a. Assuming the statistics are accurately calculated, which clinic would you recommend if you had no other information? Why?

b. Upon further research, the median and standard deviation for Clinic A are found to be 10 pounds and 20 pounds, respectively, while the mean and standard deviation for Clinic B are found to be 10 and 5 pounds, respectively. Both are based on samples of more than 100 clients. Describe the two clinics' weight-loss distributions as completely as possible given this additional information. What would you recommend to a prospective client now? Why?

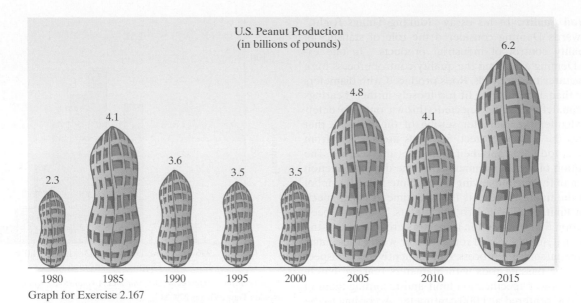

U.S. Peanut Production
(in billions of pounds)

2.3	4.1	3.6	3.5	3.5	4.8	4.1	6.2
1980	1985	1990	1995	2000	2005	2010	2015

Graph for Exercise 2.167

c. Note that nothing has been said about how the sample of clients upon which the statistics are based was selected. What additional information would be important regarding the sampling techniques employed by the clinics?

2.169 Age discrimination study. The Age Discrimination in Employment Act mandates that workers 40 years of age or older be treated without regard to age in all phases of employment (hiring, promotions, firing, etc.). Age discrimination cases are of two types: *disparate treatment* and *disparate impact*. In the former, the issue is whether workers have been intentionally discriminated against. In the latter, the issue is whether employment practices adversely affect the protected class (i.e., workers 40 and over) even though no such effect was intended by the employer. A small computer manufacturer laid off 10 of its 20 software engineers. The ages of all engineers at the time of the layoff are shown below. Analyze the data to determine whether the company may be vulnerable to a disparate impact claim.

Not laid off:	34	55	42	38	42	32	40	40	46	29
Laid off:	52	35	40	41	40	39	40	64	47	44

Critical Thinking Challenges

2.170 No Child Left Behind Act. According to the government, federal spending on K-12 education has increased dramatically over the past 20 years, but student performance has essentially stayed the same. Hence, in 2002, President George Bush signed into law the No Child Left Behind Act, a bill that promised improved student achievement for all U.S. children. *Chance* (Fall 2003) reported on a graphic obtained from the U.S. Department of Education Web site (www.ed.gov) that was designed to support the new legislation. The graphic is reproduced on the previous page. The bars in the graph represent annual federal spending on education, in billions of dollars (left-side vertical axis). The horizontal line represents the annual average fourth-grade

children's reading ability score (right-side vertical axis). Critically assess the information portrayed in the graph. Does it, in fact, support the government's position that our children are not making classroom improvements despite federal spending on education? Use the following facts (divulged in the *Chance* article) to help you frame your answer: (1) The U.S. student population has also increased dramatically over the past 20 years, (2) fourth-grade reading test scores are designed to have an average of 250 with a standard deviation of 50, and (3) the reading test scores of seventh and twelfth graders and the mathematics scores of fourth graders did improve substantially over the past 20 years.

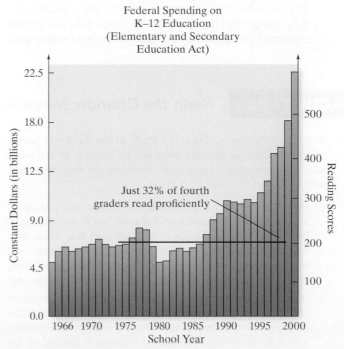

Federal Spending on
K–12 Education
(Elementary and Secondary
Education Act)

Just 32% of fourth graders read proficiently

School Year

Source: Based on U.S. Department of Education.

2.171 Steel rod quality. In his essay "Making Things Right," W. Edwards Deming considered the role of statistics in the quality control of industrial products.* In one example, Deming examined the quality-control process for a manufacturer of steel rods. Rods produced with diameters smaller than 1 centimeter fit too loosely in their bearings and ultimately must be rejected (thrown out). To determine whether the diameter setting of the machine that produces the rods is correct, 500 rods are selected from the day's production and their diameters are recorded. The distribution of the 500 diameters for one day's production is shown in the accompanying figure. Note that the symbol LSL in the figure represents the 1-centimeter lower specification limit of the steel rod diameters. There has been speculation that some of the inspectors are unaware of the trouble that an undersized rod diameter would cause later in the manufacturing process. Consequently, these inspectors may be passing rods with diameters that are barely below the lower specification limit and recording them in the interval centered at 1.000 centimeter. According to the figure, is there any evidence to support this claim? Explain.

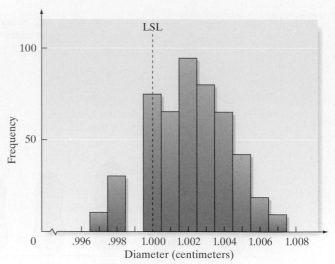

Source: From J. Tanur et al., eds., *Statistics: A Guide to the Unknown.* San Francisco: Holden-Day, 1978, pp. 279–281.

ACTIVITY 2.1   Real Estate Sales

In recent years, the price of real estate in America's major metropolitan areas has skyrocketed. Newspapers usually report recent real estate sales data in their Saturday editions, both hard copies and online. These data usually include the actual prices paid for homes by geographic location during a certain time period, usually a 1-week period 6 to 8 weeks earlier, and some summary statistics, which might include comparisons to real estate sales data in other geographic locations or during other time periods.

1. Locate the real estate sales data in a newspaper for a major metropolitan area. From the information given, identify the time period during which the homes listed were sold. Then describe the way the sales prices are organized. Are they categorized by type of home (single family or condominium), by neighborhood or address, by sales price, etc.?

2. What summary statistics and comparisons are provided with the sales data? Describe several groups of people who might be interested in these data and how each of the summary statistics and comparisons would be helpful to them. Why are the measures of central tendency listed more useful in the real estate market than other measures of central tendency?

3. Based on the lowest and highest sales prices represented in the data, create 10 intervals of equal size and use these intervals to create a relative frequency histogram for the sales data. Describe the shape of the histogram and explain how the summary statistics provided with the data are illustrated in the histogram. Based on the histogram, describe the "typical" home price.

ACTIVITY 2.2   *Keep the Change:* Measures of Central Tendency and Variability

In this activity, we continue our study of the Bank of America *Keep the Change* savings program by looking at the measures of central tendency and variability for the three data sets collected in Activity 1.1 (p. 54).

1. Before performing any calculations, explain why you would expect greater variability in the data set *Purchase Totals* than in *Amounts Transferred*. Then find the mean and median of each of these two data sets. Are the mean and median essentially the same for either of these sets? If so, which one? Can you offer an explanation for these results?

2. Make a histogram for each of the data sets *Amounts Transferred* and *Bank Matching*. Describe any properties of the data that are evident in the histograms. Explain why it is more likely that *Bank Matching* is skewed to the

right than *Amounts Transferred*. Based on your data and histogram, how concerned does Bank of America need to be about matching the maximum amount of $250 for its customers who are college students?

3. Form a fourth data set *Mean Amounts Transferred* by collecting the mean of the data set *Amounts Transferred* for each student in your class. Before performing any calculations, inspect the new data and describe any trends that you notice. Then find the mean and standard deviation of *Mean Amounts Transferred*. How close is the mean to $0.50? Without performing further calculations, determine whether the standard deviation of *Amounts Transferred* is less than or greater than the standard deviation of *Mean Amounts Transferred*. Explain.

Keep your results from this activity for use in other activities.

References

Deming, W. E. *Out of the Crisis*. Cambridge, Mass.: M.I.T. Center for Advanced Engineering Study, 1986.

Gitlow, H., Oppenheim, A., Oppenheim, R., and Levine, D. *Quality Management*, 3rd ed. Homewood, Ill.: Irwin, 2004.

Huff, D. *How to Lie with Statistics*. New York: Norton, 1954.

Ishikawa, K. *Guide to Quality Control,* 2nd ed. Asian Productivity Organization, 1986.

Juran, J. M. *Juran on Quality by Design: The New Steps for Planning Quality into Goods and Services*. New York: The Free Press, 1992.

Tufte, E. R. *Beautiful Evidence*. Cheshire, Conn.: Graphics Press, 2006.

Tufte, E. R. *Envisioning Information*. Cheshire, Conn.: Graphics Press, 1990.

Tufte, E. R. *Visual Display of Quantiative Information*. Cheshire, Conn.: Graphics Press, 1983.

Tufte, E. R. *Visual Explanations*. Cheshire, Conn.: Graphics Press, 1997.

Tukey, J. *Exploratory Data Analysis*. Reading, Mass.: Addison-Wesley, 1977.

Zabel, S. L. "Statistical Proof of Employment Discrimination." *Statistics: A Guide to the Unknown*, 3rd ed. Pacific Grove, Calif.: Wadsworth, 1989.

USING TECHNOLOGY

Technology images shown here are taken from SPSS Statistics Professional 23.0, Minitab 17, XLSTAT, and Excel 2016.

SPSS: Describing Data

Graphing Data

Step 1 Click on the "Graphs" button on the SPSS menu bar and then select "Legacy Dialogs."

Step 2 Click on the graph of your choice (bar, pie, box plot, scatter/dot plot, or histogram) to view the appropriate dialog box. The dialog box for a histogram is shown in Figure 2.S.1.

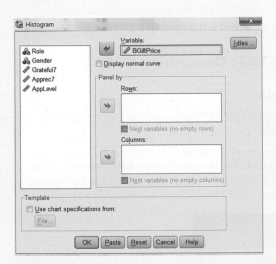

Figure 2.S.1 SPSS histogram dialog box

Step 3 Make the appropriate variable selections and click "OK" to view the graph.

Stem-and-Leaf Plots

Step 1 Select "Analyze" from the main SPSS menu, then "Descriptive Statistics," and then "Explore."

Step 2 In the "Explore" dialog box, select the variable to be analyzed in the "Dependent List" box, as shown in Figure 2.S.2.

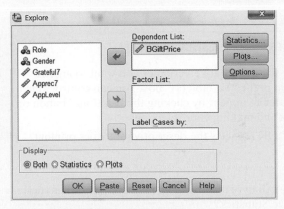

Figure 2.S.2 SPSS explore dialog box

Step 3 Click on either "Both" or "Plots" in the "Display" options and then click "OK" to display the stem-and-leaf graph.

Pareto Diagrams

Step 1 Select "Analyze" from the main SPSS menu, then "Quality Control," and then "Pareto Charts."

Step 2 Click "Define" on the resulting menu and then select the variable to be analyzed and move it to the "Category Axis" box, as shown in Figure 2.S.3.

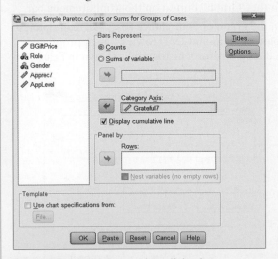

Figure 2.S.3 SPSS Pareto chart dialog box

Step 3 Click "OK" to display the Pareto diagram.

Numerical Descriptive Statistics

Step 1 Click on the "Analyze" button on the main menu bar and then click on "Descriptive Statistics."

Step 2 Select "Descriptives;" the dialog box is shown in Figure 2.S.4.

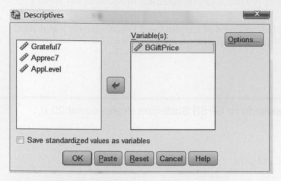

Figure 2.S.4 SPSS descriptive statistics dialog box

Step 3 Select the quantitative variables you want to analyze and place them in the "Variable(s)" box. You can control which descriptive statistics appear by clicking the "Options" button on the dialog box and making your selections.

Step 4 Click "OK" to view the descriptive statistics printout.

Percentiles

Step 1 Select "Analyze" on the main menu bar, and then click on "Descriptive Statistics."

Step 2 Select "Explore" from the resulting menu.

Step 3 In the resulting dialog box (see Figure 2.S.2), select the "Statistics" button and check the "Percentiles" box.

Step 4 Return to the "Explore" dialog box and click "OK" to generate the descriptive statistics.

Minitab: Describing Data

Graphing Data

Step 1 Click on the "Graph" button on the Minitab menu bar.

Step 2 Click on the graph of your choice (bar, pie, scatterplot, histogram, dotplot, or stem-and-leaf) to view the appropriate dialog box. The dialog box for a histogram is shown in Figure 2.M.1.

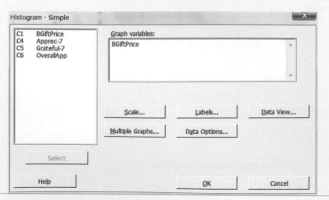

Figure 2.M.1 Minitab histogram dialog box

Step 3 Make the appropriate variable selections and then click "OK" to view the graph.

Numerical Descriptive Statistics

Step 1 Click on the "Stat" button on the main menu bar, click on "Basic Statistics," and then click on "Display Descriptive Statistics." The resulting dialog box appears in Figure 2.M.2.

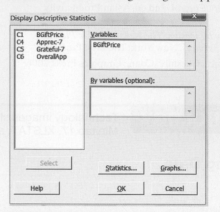

Figure 2.M.2 Minitab descriptive statistics dialog box

Step 2 Select the quantitative variables you want to analyze and place them in the "Variables" box. You can control which descriptive statistics appear by clicking the "Statistics" button on the dialog box and making your selections. (As an option, you can create histograms and dot plots for the data by clicking the "Graphs" button and making the appropriate selections.)

Step 3 Click "OK" to view the descriptive statistics printout.

Excel/XLSTAT: Describing Data

Graphing Data

Step 1 Click the "XLSTAT" button on the Excel main menu bar and then click "Visualizing Data."

Step 2 From the resulting menu (see Figure 2.E.1), select the graph of your choice. For bar graphs, pie charts, stem-and-leaf displays, or box plots, select "Univariate plots"; for histograms, select "Histogram"; and for scatterplots, select "Scatter plots."

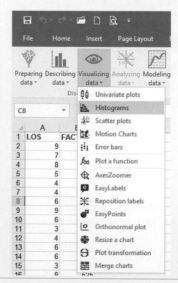

Figure 2.E.1 XLSTAT menu for graphing data

Step 3 When the resulting dialog box appears, highlight the data column(s) you want to graph so that the column information appears in the appropriate entry (see, for example, Figure 2.E.2).

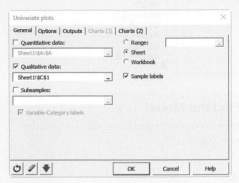

Figure 2.E.2 XLSTAT graphing univariate plots dialog box

Step 4 For univariate plots only, click the "Charts (1)" option for quantitative data or the "Charts (2)" option for qualitative data, and then select the type of graph (e.g., pie chart, bar graph, stem-and-leaf display, or box plot) you want to display. (See Figure 2.E.3.)

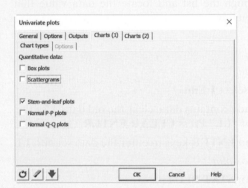

Figure 2.E.3 XLSTAT univariate plots charts options

Step 5 Click "OK," and then "Continue" to display the graph.

Numerical Descriptive Statistics

Step 1 Click the "XLSTAT" button on the Excel main menu bar, click "Describing Data," and then click "Descriptive Statistics."

Step 2 When the resulting dialog box appears, highlight the data column(s) you want to graph so that the column information appears in the quantitative data entry.

Step 3 Click the "Outputs" option, and then select the descriptive statistics you want to produce. (See Figure 2.E.4.)

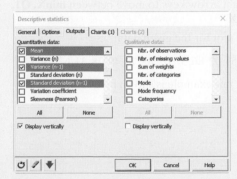

Figure 2.E.4 XLSTAT descriptive statistics outputs options

Step 5 Click "OK," and then "Continue" to display the summary statistics.

TI-84 Graphing Calculator: Describing Data

Histogram from Raw Data

Step 1 *Enter the data*

- Press **STAT** and select **1:Edit**

Note: If the list already contains data, clear the old data. Use the up arrow to highlight "**L1**." Press **CLEAR ENTER**. Use the arrow and **ENTER** keys to enter the data set into **L1.**

Step 2 *Set up the histogram plot*

- Press **2nd** and press **Y =** for **STAT PLOT**
- Press **1** for **Plot1**
- Set the cursor so that **ON** is flashing
- For **Type,** use the arrow and **ENTER** keys to highlight and select the histogram
- For **Xlist,** choose the column containing the data (in most cases, L1)

Note: Press **2nd 1** for **L1.** **Freq** should be set to 1.

- Select the **color** of the bars

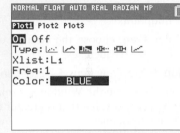

Step 3 *Select your window settings*

- Press **WINDOW** and adjust the settings as follows:

$$X \min = \text{lowest class boundary}$$
$$X \max = \text{highest class boundary}$$
$$X \text{ scl} = \text{class width}$$
$$Y \min = 0$$
$$Y \max \geq \text{greatest class frequency}$$
$$Y \text{ scl} = 1$$
$$X \text{ res} = 1$$

Step 4 *View the graph*

- Press **GRAPH**

Optional *Read class frequencies and class boundaries*

Step You can press **TRACE** to read the class frequencies and class boundaries. Use the arrow keys to move between bars.

Example The following figures show TI-84 window settings and histogram for the following sample data:

86, 70, 62, 98, 73, 56, 53, 92, 86, 37, 62, 83, 78, 49, 78, 37, 67, 79, 57

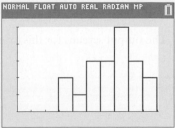

Histogram from a Frequency Table

Step 1 *Enter the data*

- Press **STAT** and select **1:Edit**

Note: If a list already contains data, clear the old data. Use the up arrow to highlight the list name, "**L1**" or "**L2**."

- Press **CLEAR ENTER**
- Enter the midpoint of each class into **L1**
- Enter the class frequencies or relative frequencies into **L2**

Step 2 *Set up the histogram plot*

- Press **2nd** and **Y =** for **STAT PLOT**
- Press **1** for **Plot1**
- Set the cursor so that **ON** is flashing
- For **Type,** use the arrow and **ENTER** keys to highlight and select the histogram
- For **Xlist,** choose the column containing the midpoints
- For **Freq,** choose the column containing the frequencies or relative frequencies

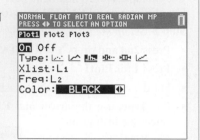

Step 3–4 *Follow steps 3–4 given above.*

Note: To set up the Window for relative frequencies, be sure to set **Ymax** to a value that is greater than or equal to the largest relative frequency.

One-Variable Descriptive Statistics

Step 1 *Enter the data*

- Press STAT and select **1:Edit**

Note: If the list already contains data, clear the old data. Use the up arrow to highlight "**L1**." Press **CLEAR ENTER.**

- Use the arrow and **ENTER** keys to enter the data set into L1

Step 2 *Calculate descriptive statistics*

- Press **STAT**
- Press the right arrow key to highlight **CALC**
- Press **ENTER** for **1-Var Stats**
- Enter the name of the list containing your data
- Press **2nd 1** for **L1** (or **2nd 2** for **L2,** etc.)
- Press arrow down to **Calculate**
- Press **ENTER**

You should see the statistics on your screen. Some of the statistics are off the bottom of the screen. Use the down arrow to scroll through to see the remaining statistics. Use the up arrow to scroll back up.

Example The descriptive statistics for the sample data set

86, 70, 62, 98, 73, 56, 53, 92, 86, 37, 62, 83, 78, 49, 78, 37, 67, 79, 57

The output screens for this example are shown below.

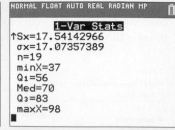

Sorting Data (to Find the Mode)

The descriptive statistics do not include the mode. To find the mode, sort your data as follows:

- Press **STAT**
- Press **2** for **SORTA(**
- Enter the name of the list your data are in. If your data are in **L1,** press **2nd 1**
- Press **ENTER**
- The screen will say: **DONE**
- To see the sorted data, press **STAT** and select **1:Edit**
- Scroll down through the list and locate the data value that occurs most frequently

Box Plot

Step 1 *Enter the data*

- Press **STAT** and select **1:Edit**

Note: If the list already contains data, clear the old data. Use the up arrow to highlight "**L1**." Press **CLEAR ENTER.**

- Use the arrow and **ENTER** keys to enter the data set into **L1**

Step 2 *Set up the box plot*

- Press **2nd Y =** for **STAT PLOT**
- Press **1** for **Plot1**
- Set the cursor so that **"ON"** is flashing
- For **TYPE,** use the right arrow to scroll through the plot icons and select the box plot
- For **XLIST,** choose **L1**
- Set **FREQ** to 1
- Select the **color** of the plot

Step 3 *View the graph*

- Press **ZOOM** and select **9:ZoomStat**

Optional *Read the five-number summary*

- Press **TRACE**
- Use the left and right arrow keys to move between **minX, Q1, Med, Q3,** and **maxX**

Example Make a box plot for the given data:

86, 70, 62, 98, 73, 56, 53, 92, 86, 37, 62, 83, 78, 49, 78, 37, 67, 79, 57

The output screen for this example is shown below.

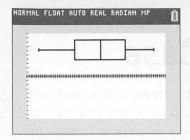

Scatterplots

Step 1 *Enter the data*

- Press **STAT** and select **1:Edit**

Note: If a list already contains data, clear the old data. Use the up arrow to highlight the list name, **"L1"** or **"L2."**

- Press **CLEAR ENTER**

- Enter your *x*-data in **L1** and your *y*-data in **L2**

Step 2 *Set up the scatterplot*

- Press **2nd Y =** for **STAT PLOT**

- Press **1** for **Plot1**

- Set the cursor so that **ON** is flashing

- For **Type,** use the arrow and **ENTER** keys to highlight and select the scatterplot (first icon in the first row)

- For **Xlist,** choose the column containing the *x*-data

- For **Ylist,** choose the column containing the *y*-data

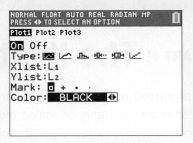

Step 3 *View the scatterplot*

- Press **ZOOM 9** for **ZoomStat**

Example The figures below show a table of data entered on the T1-84 and the scatterplot of the data obtained using the steps given above.

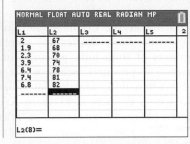
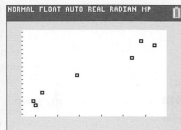

[PART 1] The Kentucky Milk Case

Many products and services are purchased by governments, cities, states, and businesses on the basis of scaled bids, and contracts are awarded to the lowest bidders. This process works extremely well in competitive markets, but it has the potential to increase the cost of purchasing if the markets are noncompetitive or if collusive practices are present.

An investigation that began with a statistical analysis of bids in the Florida school milk market led to the recovery of more than $33,000,000 from dairies that had conspired to rig the bids there. The investigation spread quickly to other states, and to date, settlements and fines from dairies exceed $100.000,000 for school milk bidrigging in 20 other states. This case concerns a school milk bidrigging investigation in Kentucky.

Each year, the Commonwealth of Kentucky invites bids from dairies to supply half-pint containers of fluid milk products for its school districts. The products include whole white milk, low-fat white milk, and low-fat chocolate milk. In 13 school districts in northern Kentucky, the suppliers (dairies) were accused of "price-fixing"— that is, conspiring to allocate the districts so that the "winner" was predetermined. Because these districts are located in Boone, Campbell, and Kenton counties, the geographic market they represent is designated as the "tri-county" market. Over a 9-year period, two dairies—Meyer Dairy and Trauth Dairy—were the only bidders on the milk contracts in the school districts in the tri-county market. Consequently, these two companies were awarded all the milk contracts in the market. (In contrast, a large number of different dairies won the milk contracts for the school districts in the remainder of the northern Kentucky market—called the "surrounding" market.) The

Commonwealth of Kentucky alleged that Meyer and Trauth conspired to allocate the districts in the tri-county market. To date, one of the dairies (Meyer) has admitted guilt, while the other (Trauth) steadfastly maintains its innocence.

The Commonwealth of Kentucky maintains a database on all bids received from the dairies competing for the milk contracts. Some of these data have been made available to you to analyze to determine whether there is empirical evidence of bid collusion in the tri-county market. The data, saved in the **MILK** file, are described in detail below. Some background information on the data and important economic theory regarding bid collusion is also provided. Use this information to guide your analysis. Prepare a professional document that presents the results of your analysis and gives your opinion regarding collusion.

Background Information
Collusive Market Environment

Certain economic features of a market create an environment in which collusion may be found. These basic features include the following:

1. *Few sellers and high concentration.* Only a few dairies control all or nearly all of the milk business in the market.

2. *Homogeneous products.* The products sold are essentially the same from the standpoint of the buyer (i.e., the school district).

3. *Inelastic demand.* Demand is relatively insensitive to price. (*Note:* The quantity of milk required by a school district is primarily determined by school enrollment, not price.)

4. *Similar costs.* The dairies bidding for the milk contracts face similar cost conditions. (*Note:* Approximately 60% of a dairy's production cost is raw milk, which is federally regulated. Meyer and Trauth are dairies of similar size, and both bought their raw milk from the same supplier.)

Although these market structure characteristics create an environment that makes collusive behavior easier, they do not necessarily indicate the existence of collusion. An analysis of the actual bid prices may provide additional information about the degree of competition in the market.

Variable	Type	Description
YEAR	QN	Year in which milk contract awarded
MARKET	QL	Northern Kentucky Market (TRI-COUNTY or SURROUND)
WINNER	QL	Name of winning dairy
WWBID	QN	Winning bid price of whole white milk (dollars per half-pint)
WWQTY	QN	Quantity of whole white milk purchased (number of half-pints)
LFWBID	QN	Winning bid price of low-fat white milk (dollars per half-pints)
LFWQTY	QN	Quantity of low-fat white milk purchased (number of half-pints)
LFCBID	QN	Winning bid price of low-fat chocolate milk (dollars per half-pint)
LFCQTY	QN	Quantity of low-fat chocolate milk purchased (number of half-pints)
DISTRICT	QL	School district number
KYFMO	QN	FMO minimum raw cost of milk (dollars per half-pint)
MILESM	QN	Distance (miles) from Meyer processing plant to school district
MILEST	QN	Distance (miles) from Trauth processing plant to school district
LETDATE	QL	Date on which bidding on milk contract began (month/day/year)

(Number of observations: 392)   *Data Set:* MILK

Collusive Bidding Patterns

The analyses of patterns in sealed bids reveal much about the level of competition, or lack thereof, among the vendors serving the market. Consider the following bid analyses:

1. *Market shares.* A market share for a dairy is the number of milk half-pints supplied by the dairy over a given school year, divided by the total number of half-pints supplied to the entire market. One sign of potential collusive behavior is stable, nearly equal market shares over time for the dairies under investigation.

2. *Incumbency rates.* Market allocation is a common form of collusive behavior in bidrigging conspiracies. Typically, the same dairy controls the same school districts year after year. The incumbency rate for a market in a given school year is defined as the percentage of school districts that are won by the same vendor who won the previous year. An incumbency rate that exceeds 70% has been considered a sign of collusive behavior.

3. *Bid levels and dispersion.* In competitive sealed-bid markets, vendors do not share information about their bids. Consequently, more dispersion or variability among the bids is observed than in collusive markets, where vendors communicate about their bids and have a tendency to submit bids in close proximity to one another in an attempt to make the bidding appear competitive. Furthermore, in competitive markets the bid dispersion tends to be directly proportional to the level of the bid: When bids are submitted at relatively high levels, there is more variability among the bids than when they are submitted at or near marginal cost, which will be approximately the same among dairies in the same geographic market.

4. *Price versus cost/distance.* In competitive markets, bid prices are expected to track costs over time. Thus, if the market is competitive, the bid price of milk should be highly correlated with the raw milk cost. Lack of such a relationship is another sign of collusion. Similarly, bid price should be correlated to the distance the product must travel from the processing plant to the school (due to delivery costs) in a competitive market.

5. *Bid sequence.* School milk bids are submitted over the spring and summer months, generally at the end of one school year and before the beginning of the next. When the bids are examined in sequence in competitive markets, the level of bidding is expected to fall as the bidding season progresses. (This phenomenon is attributable to the learning process that occurs during the season, with bids adjusted accordingly. Dairies may submit relatively high bids early in the season to "test the market," confident that volume can be picked up later if the early high bids lose. But, dairies who do not win much business early in the season are likely to become more aggressive in their bidding as the season progresses, driving price levels down.) Constant or slightly increasing price patterns of sequential bids in a market where a single dairy wins year after year is considered another indication of collusive behavior.

6. *Comparison of average winning bid prices.* Consider two similar markets, one in which bids are possibly rigged and the other in which bids are competitively determined. In theory, the mean winning price in the "rigged" market will be significantly higher than the mean price in the competitive market for each year in which collusion occurs.

155

3

CONTENTS

WHERE WE'VE BEEN

- Identified the objective of inferential statistics: to make inferences about a population based on information in a sample.

- Introduced graphical and numerical descriptive measures for both quantitative and qualitative data.

WHERE WE'RE GOING

- Develop probability as a measure of uncertainty (3.1)

- Introduce basic rules for finding probabilities (3.2–3.6)

- Use probability as a measure of reliability for an inference (3.2–3.6)

- Provide an advanced rule for finding probabilities (3.7)

Probability

STATISTICS IN ACTION   Lotto Buster!

"Welcome to the Wonderful World of Lottery Bu$ters." So began the premier issue of Lottery Buster, *a monthly publication for players of the state lottery games.* Lottery Buster *provides interesting facts and figures on the 44 state lotteries and 2 major multistate lotteries (Mega Millions and Powerball) currently operating in the United States and, more importantly, tips on how to increase a player's odds of winning the lottery.*

New Hampshire, in 1963, was the first state in modern times to authorize a state lottery as an alternative to increasing taxes. (Prior to this time, beginning in 1895, lotteries were banned in America because of corruption.) Since then, lotteries have become immensely popular for two reasons: (1) They lure you with the opportunity to win millions of dollars with a $1 investment, and (2) when you lose, at least you believe your money is going to a good cause. Many state lotteries, such as Florida's, designate a high percentage of lottery revenues to fund state education.

The popularity of the state lottery has brought with it an avalanche of "experts" and "mathematical wizards" (such as the editors of *Lottery Buster*) who provide advice on how to win the lottery—for a fee, of course! Many offer guaranteed "systems" of winning through computer software products with catchy names such as Lotto Wizard, Lottorobics, Win4d, and Lotto-luck.

For example, most knowledgeable lottery players would agree that the "golden rule" or "first rule" in winning lotteries is *game selection*. State lotteries generally offer three types of games: an Instant (scratch-off tickets or online) game, Daily Numbers (Pick-3 or Pick-4), and a weekly Pick-6 Lotto game.

One version of the Instant game involves scratching off the thin opaque covering on a ticket with the edge of a coin to determine whether you have won or

(*continued*)

lost. The cost of a ticket ranges from 50¢ to $5, and the amount won ranges from $1 to $100,000 in most states, and to as much as $1 million in others. *Lottery Buster* advises against playing the Instant game because it is "a pure chance play, and you can win only by dumb luck. No skill can be applied to this game."

The Daily Numbers game permits you to choose either a three-digit (Pick-3) or four-digit (Pick-4) number at a cost of $1 per ticket. Each night, the winning number is drawn. If your number matches the winning number, you win a large sum of money, usually $100,000. You do have some control over the Daily Numbers game (because you pick the numbers that you play), and, consequently, there are strategies available to increase your chances of winning. However, the Daily Numbers game, like the Instant game, is not available for out-of-state play.

To play Pick-6 Lotto, you select six numbers of your choice from a field of numbers ranging from 1 to *N*, where *N* depends on which state's game you are playing. For example, Florida's current Lotto game involves picking six numbers ranging from 1 to 53. The cost of a ticket is $1, and the payoff, if your six numbers match the winning numbers drawn, is $7 million or more, depending on the number of tickets purchased. (To date, Florida has had the largest individual state weekly payoff of over $200 million. The largest multistate lottery payoff was $1,586 billion in Powerball.) In addition to the grand prize, you can win second-, third-, and fourth-prize payoffs by matching five, four, and three of the six numbers drawn, respectively. And you don't have to be a resident of the state to play the state's Lotto game.

In this chapter, several *Statistics in Action Revisited* examples demonstrate how to use the basic concepts of probability to compute the odds of winning a state lottery game and to assess the validity of the strategies suggested by lottery "experts."

STATISTICS IN ACTION REVISITED

Recall that one branch of statistics is concerned with decisions about a population based on sample information. You can see how this is accomplished more easily if you understand the relationship between population and sample—a relationship that becomes clearer if we reverse the statistical procedure of making inferences from sample to population. In this chapter, then, we assume that the population is known and calculate the chances of obtaining various samples from the population. Thus, we show that probability is the reverse of statistics: **In probability, we use the population information to infer the probable nature of the sample.**

Probability plays an important role in inference making. Suppose, for example, you have an opportunity to invest in an oil exploration company. Past records show that out of 10 previous oil drillings (a sample of the company's experiences), all 10 came up dry. What do you conclude? Do you think the chances are better than 50:50 that the company will hit a gusher? Should you invest in this company? Chances are, your answer to these questions will be an emphatic "no." If the company's exploratory prowess is sufficient to hit a producing well 50% of the time, a record of 10 dry wells out of 10 drilled is an event that is just too improbable.

Or suppose you're playing poker with what your opponents assure you is a well-shuffled deck of cards. In three consecutive five-card hands, the person on your right is dealt four aces. Based on this sample of three deals, do you think the cards are being adequately shuffled? Again, your answer is likely to be "no" because dealing three hands of four aces is just too improbable if the cards were properly shuffled.

Note that the decisions concerning the potential success of the oil drilling company and the adequacy of card shuffling both involve knowing the chance—or probability—of a certain sample result. Both situations were contrived so that you could easily conclude that the probabilities of the sample results were small. Unfortunately, the probabilities of many observed sample results are not so easy to evaluate intuitively. For these cases we will need the assistance of a theory of probability.

3.1 Events, Sample Spaces, and Probability

Let's begin our treatment of probability with simple examples that are easily described. With the aid of simple examples, we can introduce important definitions that will help us develop the notion of probability more easily.

Suppose a coin is tossed once and the up face is recorded. The result we see and record is called an *observation*, or *measurement*, and the process of making an observation is called an *experiment*. Notice that our definition of *experiment* is broader than the one used in the physical sciences, where you would picture test tubes, microscopes, and other laboratory equipment. Among other things, statistical experiments may include recording an Internet user's preference for a Web browser, recording a change in the Dow Jones Industrial Average from one day to the next, recording the weekly sales of a business firm, and counting the number of errors on a page of an accountant's ledger. The point is that a statistical experiment can be almost any act of observation as long as the outcome is uncertain.

> An **experiment** is an act or process of observation that leads to a single outcome that cannot be predicted with certainty.

Consider another simple experiment consisting of tossing a die and observing the number on the up face. The six basic possible outcomes to this experiment are as follows:

1. Observe a 1
2. Observe a 2
3. Observe a 3
4. Observe a 4
5. Observe a 5
6. Observe a 6

Note that if this experiment is conducted once, *you can observe one and only one of these six basic outcomes, and the outcome cannot be predicted with certainty*. Also, these possibilities cannot be decomposed into more basic outcomes. Because observing the outcome of an experiment is similar to selecting a sample from a population, the basic possible outcomes to an experiment are called *sample points*.*

> A **sample point** is the most basic outcome of an experiment.

EXAMPLE 3.1

Listing the Sample Points for a Coin–Tossing Experiment

Problem Two coins are tossed, and their up faces are recorded. List all the sample points for this experiment.

Solution Even for a seemingly trivial experiment, we must be careful when listing the sample points. At first glance, we might expect three basic outcomes: Observe two heads, Observe two tails, or Observe one head and one tail. However, further reflection reveals that the last of these, Observe one head and one tail, can be decomposed into two outcomes: Head on coin 1, Tail on coin 2; and Tail on coin 1, Head on coin 2.

A useful tool for illustrating this notion is a **tree diagram.** Figure 3.1 shows a tree diagram for this experiment. At the top of the "tree," there are two branches, representing the two outcomes (*H* or *T*) for the first tossed coin. Each of these outcomes results in two more branches, representing the two outcomes (*H* or *T*) for the second tossed coin. Consequently, after tossing both coins, you can see that we have four sample points.

1. Observe *HH*
2. Observe *HT*
3. Observe *TH*
4. Observe *TT*

---

*Alternatively, the term *simple event* can be used.

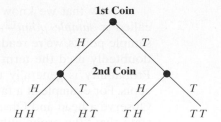

Figure 3.1
Tree diagram for the coin-tossing experiment

where H in the first position means "Head on coin 1," H in the second position means "Head on coin 2," and so on.

Look Back Even if the coins are identical in appearance, there are, in fact, two distinct coins. Thus, the sample points must account for this distinction.

● **Now Work Exercise 3.7a**

We often wish to refer to the collection of all the sample points of an experiment. This collection is called the *sample space* of the experiment. For example, there are six sample points in the sample space associated with the die-toss experiment. The sample spaces for the experiments discussed thus far are shown in Table 3.1.

The **sample space** of an experiment is the collection of all its sample points.

Just as graphs are useful in describing sets of data, a pictorial method for presenting the sample space will often be useful. Figure 3.2 shows such a representation for each of the experiments in Table 3.1. In each case, the sample space is shown as a closed figure, labeled S, containing all possible sample points. Each sample point is represented by a solid dot (i.e., a "point") and labeled accordingly. Such graphical representations are called **Venn diagrams.**

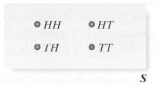

a. Experiment: Observe the up face on a coin

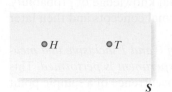

b. Experiment: Observe the up face on a die

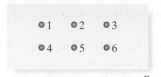

c. Experiment: Observe the up faces on two coins

Figure 3.2
Venn diagrams for the three experiments from Table 3.1

Table 3.1	Experiments and Their Sample Spaces

Experiment: Observe the up face on a coin.
Sample space: **1.** Observe a head
 2. Observe a tail

This sample space can be represented in set notation as a set containing two sample points:

$$S: \{H, T\}$$

where H represents the sample point Observe a head and T represents the sample point Observe a tail.

Experiment: Observe the up face on a die.
Sample space: **1.** Observe a 1
 2. Observe a 2
 3. Observe a 3
 4. Observe a 4
 5. Observe a 5
 6. Observe a 6

This sample space can be represented in set notation as a set of six sample points:

$$S: \{1, 2, 3, 4, 5, 6\}$$

Experiment: Observe the up faces on two coins.
Sample space: **1.** Observe HH
 2. Observe HT
 3. Observe TH
 4. Observe TT

This sample space can be represented in set notation as a set of four sample points:

$$S: \{HH, HT, TH, TT\}$$

Now that we know that an experiment will result in *only one* basic outcome—called a *sample point*—and that the sample space is the collection of all possible sample points, we're ready to discuss the probabilities of the sample points. You've undoubtedly used the term *probability* and have some intuitive idea about its meaning. Probability is generally used synonymously with "chance," "odds," and similar concepts. For example, if a fair coin is tossed, we might reason that both the sample points, Observe a head and Observe a tail, have the same *chance* of occurring. Thus, we might state that "the probability of observing a head is 50%" or "the *odds* of seeing a head are 50:50." Both of these statements are based on an informal knowledge of probability. We'll begin our treatment of probability by using such informal concepts and then later solidify what we mean.

The probability of a sample point is a number between 0 and 1 inclusive that measures the likelihood that the outcome will occur when the experiment is performed. This number is usually taken to be the relative frequency of the occurrence of a sample point in a very long series of repetitions of an experiment.* For example, if we are assigning probabilities to the two sample points (Observe a head and Observe a tail) in the coin-toss experiment, we might reason that if we toss a balanced coin a very large number of times, the sample points Observe a head and Observe a tail will occur with the same relative frequency of .5.

Our reasoning is supported by Figure 3.3. The figure plots the relative frequency of the number of times that a head occurs when simulating (by computer) the toss of a coin N times, where N ranges from as few as 25 tosses to as many as 1,500 tosses of the coin. You can see that when N is large (i.e., $N = 1,500$), the relative frequency is converging to .5. Thus, the probability of each sample point in the coin-tossing experiment is .5.

For some experiments, we may have little or no information on the relative frequency of occurrence of the sample points; consequently, we must assign probabilities to the sample points based on general information about the experiment. For example, if the experiment is to invest in a business venture and to observe whether it succeeds or fails, the sample space would appear as in Figure 3.4.

We are unlikely to be able to assign probabilities to the sample points of this experiment based on a long series of repetitions because unique factors govern each performance of this kind of experiment. Instead, we may consider factors such as the personnel managing the venture, the general state of the economy at the time, the rate

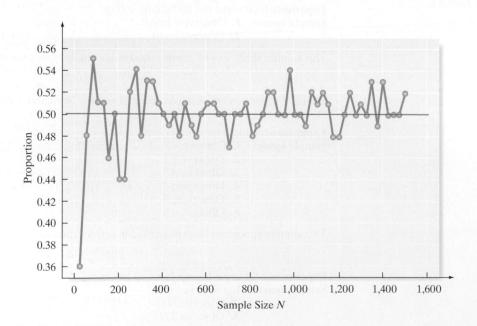

Figure 3.3

Proportion of heads in N coin tosses

---

*The result derives from an axiom in probability theory called the **Law of Large Numbers.** Phrased informally, this law states that the relative frequency of the number of times that an outcome occurs when an experiment is replicated over and over again (i.e., a large number of times) approaches the theoretical probability of the outcome.

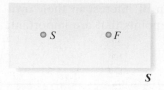

Figure 3.4

Experiment: Invest in a business venture and observe whether it succeeds (*S*) or fails (*F*)

of success of similar ventures, and any other pertinent information. If we finally decide that the venture has an 80% chance of succeeding, we assign a probability of .8 to the sample point Success. This probability can be interpreted as a measure of our degree of belief in the outcome of the business venture; that is, it is a subjective probability. Notice, however, that such probabilities should be based on expert information that is carefully assessed. If not, we may be misled on any decisions based on these probabilities or based on any calculations in which they appear. [*Note*: For a text that deals in detail with the subjective evaluation of probabilities, see Winkler (1972) or Lindley (1985).]

No matter how you assign the probabilities to sample points, the probabilities assigned must obey two rules:

Probability Rules for Sample Points

Let p_i represent the probability of sample point *i*.

1. All sample point probabilities *must* lie between 0 and 1 (i.e., $0 \le p_i \le 1$).
2. The probabilities of all the sample points within a sample space *must* sum to 1 (i.e., $\sum p_i = 1$).

Assigning probabilities to sample points is easy for some experiments. For example, if the experiment is to toss a fair coin and observe the face, we would probably all agree to assign a probability of $\frac{1}{2}$ to the two sample points, Observe a head and Observe a tail. However, many experiments have sample points whose probabilities are more difficult to assign.

EXAMPLE 3.2

Sample Point Probabilities—Hotel Water Conservation

Problem *Going Green* is the term used to describe water conservation programs at hotels and motels. Many hotels now offer their guests the option of participating in these Going Green programs by reusing towels and bed linens. Suppose you randomly select one hotel from a registry of all hotels in Orange County, California, and check whether or not the hotel participates in a water conservation program. Show how this problem might be formulated in the framework of an experiment with sample points and a sample space. Indicate how probabilities might be assigned to the sample points.

Solution The experiment can be defined as the selection of an Orange County hotel and the observation of whether or not a water conservation program is offered to guests at the hotel. There are two sample points in the sample space for this experiment:

C: {The hotel offers a water conservation program.}
N: {The hotel does not offer a water conservation program.}

The difference between this and the coin-toss experiment becomes apparent when we attempt to assign probabilities to the two sample points. What probability should we assign to sample point *C*? If you answer .5, you are assuming that the events *C* and *N* occur with equal likelihood, just like the sample points Heads and Tails in the coin-toss experiment. But assigning sample point probabilities for the hotel water conservation experiment is not so easy. In fact, a recent report by the Orange County Water District stated that 70% of the hotels in the county now participate in a water conservation program of some type. In that case, it might be reasonable to approximate the probability of the sample point *C* as .7 and that of the sample point *N* as .3.

Look Back Here we see that sample points are not always equally likely, so assigning probabilities to them can be complicated—particularly for experiments that represent real applications (as opposed to coin- and die-toss experiments).

● **Now Work Exercise 3.11**

Although the probabilities of sample points are often of interest in their own right, it is usually the probabilities of collections of sample points that are important. Example 3.3 demonstrates this point.

EXAMPLE 3.3

Probability of a Collection of Sample Points—Die-Tossing Experiment

Problem A fair die is tossed, and the up face is observed. If the face is even, you win $1. Otherwise, you lose $1. What is the probability that you win?

Solution Recall that the sample space for this experiment contains six sample points:

$$S: \{1, 2, 3, 4, 5, 6\}$$

Because the die is balanced, we assign a probability of $\frac{1}{6}$ to each of the sample points in this sample space. An even number will occur if one of the sample points, Observe a 2, Observe a 4, or Observe a 6, occurs. A collection of sample points such as this is called an *event*, which we denote by the letter A. Because the event A contains three sample points—each with probability $\frac{1}{6}$—and because no sample points can occur simultaneously, we reason that the probability of A is the sum of the probabilities of the sample points in A. Thus, the probability of A (i.e., the probability that you will win) is $\frac{1}{6} + \frac{1}{6} + \frac{1}{6} = \frac{1}{2}$.

Look Back Based on our notion of probability, $P(A) = \frac{1}{2}$ implies that, *in the long run*, you will win $1 half the time and lose $1 half the time.

• **Now Work Exercise 3.6**

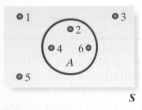

Figure 3.5
Die-toss experiment with event A:
Observe an even number

Figure 3.5 is a Venn diagram depicting the sample space associated with a die-toss experiment and the event A, Observe an even number. The event A is represented by the closed figure inside the sample space S. This closed figure A contains all the sample points that compose it.

To decide which sample points belong to the set associated with an event A, test each sample point in the sample space S. If event A occurs, then that sample point is in the event A. For example, the event A, Observe an even number, in the die-toss experiment will occur if the sample point Observe a 2 occurs. By the same reasoning, the sample points Observe a 4 and Observe a 6 are also in event A.

To summarize, we have demonstrated that an event can be defined in words or it can be defined as a specific set of sample points. This leads us to the following general definition of an event:

> An **event** is a specific collection of sample points. Further, a **simple event** contains only a single sample point, while a **compound event** contains two or more sample points.

EXAMPLE 3.4

The Probability of a Compound Event—Defective Smartphones

Problem Consider an experiment in which two smartphones are randomly selected from an assembly line during manufacturing. The defective status—defective (D) or not (N)—of each is determined. The sample points (outcomes) of the experiment are listed in the table (p. 163), where DD represents the event that the first phone is defective and the second is defective, ND represents the event that the first phone is nondefective and the second is defective, etc. Suppose the correct probabilities associated with the sample points are as shown. [*Note:* The necessary properties of assigning probabilities to sample points are satisfied.] Consider the events

$$A = \{\text{Observe exactly one defective.}\}$$
$$B = \{\text{Observe at least one defective.}\}$$

Calculate the probability of A and the probability of B.

Sample Point	Probability
DD	.010
DN	.045
ND	.045
NN	.900
Total:	1.000

Solution Event A contains the sample points DN and ND; thus, A is a compound event. Because two or more sample points cannot occur at the same time, we can easily calculate the probability of event A by summing the probabilities of the two sample points. Thus, the probability of observing exactly one defective (event A), denoted by the symbol $P(A)$, is

$$P(A) = P(\text{Observe } DN) + P(\text{Observe } ND) = .045 + .045 = .09$$

Similarly, since B represents at least one defective, it contains the sample points: DN, ND, and DD. Thus,

$$P(B) = .045 + .045 + .01 = .10$$

Look Back Again, these probabilities should be interpreted *in the long run*. For example, $P(B) = .10$ implies that if we were to randomly select two smartphones from the assembly line an infinite number of times, we would observe at least one defective in 10% of the pairs.

● **Now Work Exercise 3.3**

The preceding example leads us to a general procedure for finding the probability of an event A:

> **Probability of an Event**
>
> The probability of an event A is calculated by summing the probabilities of the sample points in the sample space for A.

Thus, we can summarize the steps for calculating the probability of any event, as indicated in the next box.

> **Steps for Calculating Probabilities of Events**
>
> **Step 1** Define the experiment; that is, describe the process used to make an observation and the type of observation that will be recorded.
> **Step 2** List the sample points.
> **Step 3** Assign probabilities to the sample points.
> **Step 4** Determine the collection of sample points contained in the event of interest.
> **Step 5** Sum the sample point probabilities to get the event probability.

Applying the Five Steps to Find a Probability— Diversity Training

Problem Diversity training of employees is the latest trend in U.S. business. *USA Today* reported on the primary reasons businesses give for making diversity training part of their strategic planning process. The reasons are summarized in Table 3.2. Assume that one business is selected at random from all U.S. businesses that use diversity training, and the primary reason is determined.

Table 3.2	Primary Reasons for Diversity Training
Reason	Percentage
Comply with personnel policies (CPP)	7
Increase productivity (IP)	47
Stay competitive (SC)	38
Social responsibility (SR)	4
Other (O)	4
Total	100

a. Define the experiment that generated the data in Table 3.2 and list the sample points.

b. Assign probabilities to the sample points.

c. What is the probability that the primary reason for diversity training is business related, that is, related to competition or productivity?

d. What is the probability that social responsibility is not a primary reason for diversity training?

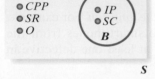

Figure 3.6

Venn diagram for diversity training survey

Solution

a. The experiment is the act of determining the primary reason for diversity training of employees at a U.S. business. The sample points, the simplest outcomes of the experiment, are the five response categories listed in Table 3.2. These sample points are shown in the Venn diagram in Figure 3.6.

b. If, as in Example 3.1, we were to assign equal probabilities in this case, each of the response categories would have a probability of one-fifth, $\frac{1}{5}$, or .20. But, by examining Table 3.2 you can see that equal probabilities are not reasonable here because the response percentages are not even approximately the same in the five classifications. It is more reasonable to assign a probability equal to the response percentage in each class, as shown in Table 3.3.*

c. Let the symbol B represent the event that the primary reason for diversity training is business related. B is not a sample point because it consists of more than one of the response classifications (the sample points). In fact, as shown in Figure 3.6, B consists of two sample points, *IP* and *SC*. The probability of B is defined to be the sum of the probabilities of the sample points in B.

$$P(B) = P(\text{IP}) + P(\text{SC}) = .47 + .38 = .85$$

d. Let *NSR* represent the event that social responsibility is not a primary reason for diversity training. Then *NSR* consists of all sample points except *SR*, and the probability is the sum of the corresponding sample point probabilities:

$$P(NSR) = P(\text{CPP}) + P(\text{IP}) + P(\text{SC}) + P(\text{O})$$
$$= .07 + .47 + .38 + .04 = .96$$

Table 3.3

Sample Point Probabilities for Diversity Training Survey

Sample Point	Probability
CPP	.07
IP	.47
SC	.38
SR	.04
O	.04

---

*The response percentages were based on a sample of U.S. businesses; consequently, these assigned probabilities are estimates of the true population-response percentages. You'll learn how to measure the reliability of probability estimates in Chapter 6.

Look Back The key to solving this problem is to follow the steps outlined in the box. We defined the experiment (Step 1) and listed the sample points (Step 2) in part **a.** The assignment of probabilities to the sample points (Step 3) was done in part **b.** For each probability in parts **c** and **d,** we identified the collection of points in the event (Step 4) and summed their probabilities (Step 5).

● **Now Work Exercise 3.15**

EXAMPLE 3.6

Another Compound Event Probability— Investing in a Successful Venture

Problem You have the capital to invest in two of four ventures, each of which requires approximately the same amount of investment capital. Unknown to you, two of the investments will eventually fail and two will be successful. You research the four ventures because you think that your research will increase your probability of a successful choice over a purely random selection, and you eventually decide on two. If you used none of the information generated by your research and selected two ventures at random, what is the probability that you would select at least one successful venture?

Solution

Step 1: Denote the two successful enterprises as S_1 and S_2 and the two failing enterprises as F_1 and F_2. The experiment involves a random selection of two out of the four ventures, and each possible pair of ventures represents a sample point.

Step 2: The six sample points that make up the sample space are

1. (S_1, S_2) 4. (S_2, F_1)
2. (S_1, F_1) 5. (S_2, F_2)
3. (S_1, F_2) 6. (F_1, F_2)

Step 3: Next, we assign probabilities to the sample points. If we assume that the choice of any one pair is as likely as any other, then the probability of each sample point is $\frac{1}{6}$.

Step 4: The event of selecting at least one of the two successful ventures includes all the sample points except (F_1, F_2).

Step 5: Now, we find

$$P(\text{Select at least one success}) = P(S_1, S_2) + P(S_1, F_1) + P(S_1, F_2) +$$
$$P(S_2, F_1) + P(S_2, F_2)$$
$$= \tfrac{1}{6} + \tfrac{1}{6} + \tfrac{1}{6} + \tfrac{1}{6} + \tfrac{1}{6} = \tfrac{5}{6}$$

Therefore, with a random selection, the probability of selecting at least one successful venture out of two is $\frac{5}{6}$.

The preceding examples have one thing in common: The number of sample points in each of the sample spaces was small; hence, the sample points were easy to identify and list. How can we manage this when the sample points run into the thousands or millions? For example, suppose you wish to select five business ventures from a group of 1,000. Then each different group of five ventures would represent a sample point. How can you determine the number of sample points associated with this experiment?

One method of determining the number of sample points for a complex experiment is to develop a counting system. Start by examining a simple version of the experiment. For example, see if you can develop a system for counting the number of ways to select two ventures from a total of four (this is exactly what was done in Example 3.6). If the ventures are represented by the symbols V_1, V_2, V_3, and V_4, the sample points could be listed in the following pattern:

(V_1, V_2) (V_2, V_3) (V_3, V_4)
(V_1, V_3) (V_2, V_4)
(V_1, V_4)

Note the pattern and now try a more complex situation—say, sampling three ventures out of five. List the sample points and observe the pattern. Finally, see if you can deduce the pattern for the general case. Perhaps you can program a computer to produce the matching and counting for the number of samples of five selected from a total of 1,000.

A second method of determining the number of sample points for an experiment is to use **combinatorial mathematics.** This branch of mathematics is concerned with developing counting rules for given situations. For example, there is a simple rule for finding the number of different samples of 5 ventures selected from 1,000. This rule, called the **Combinations Rule,** is given in the box.

Combinations Rule

A sample of n elements is to be drawn from a set of N elements. Then, the number of different samples possible is denoted by $\binom{N}{n}$ and is equal to

$$\binom{N}{n} = \frac{N!}{n!(N-n)!}$$

where the factorial symbol (!) means that

$$n! = n(n-1)(n-2)\cdots(3)(2)(1)$$

For example, $5! = 5 \cdot 4 \cdot 3 \cdot 2 \cdot 1$. [*Note:* The quantity 0! is defined to be equal to 1.]

EXAMPLE 3.7

Using the Combinations Rule—Selecting 2 Investments from 4

Problem Refer to Example 3.6, where we selected two ventures from four in which to invest. Use the Combinations Rule to determine how many different selections can be made.

Solution For this example, $N = 4$, $n = 2$, and

$$\binom{4}{2} = \frac{4!}{2!2!} = \frac{4 \cdot 3 \cdot 2 \cdot 1}{(2 \cdot 1)(2 \cdot 1)} = \frac{4 \cdot 3}{2 \cdot 1} = \frac{12}{2} = 6$$

Look Back You can see that this agrees with the number of sample points obtained in Example 3.6.

● **Now Work Exercise 3.5**

EXAMPLE 3.8

Using the Combinations Rule—Selecting 5 Investments from 20

Problem Suppose you plan to invest equal amounts of money in each of five business ventures. If you have 20 ventures from which to make the selection, how many different samples of five ventures can be selected from the 20?

Solution For this example, $N = 20$ and $n = 5$. Then the number of different samples of 5 that can be selected from the 20 ventures is

$$\binom{20}{5} = \frac{20!}{5!(20-5)!} = \frac{20!}{5!15!}$$

$$= \frac{20 \cdot 19 \cdot 18 \cdot \cdots \cdot 3 \cdot 2 \cdot 1}{(5 \cdot 4 \cdot 3 \cdot 2 \cdot 1)(15 \cdot 14 \cdot 13 \cdot \cdots \cdot 3 \cdot 2 \cdot 1)} = \frac{20 \cdot 19 \cdot 18 \cdot 17 \cdot 16}{5 \cdot 4 \cdot 3 \cdot 2 \cdot 1} = 15{,}504$$

Look Back You can see that attempting to list all the sample points for this experiment would be an extremely tedious and time-consuming, if not practically impossible, task.

● **Now Work Exercise 3.22**

The Combinations Rule is just one of a large number of counting rules that have been developed by combinatorial mathematicians. This counting rule applies to situations in which the experiment calls for selecting n elements from a total of N elements, without replacing each element before the next is selected. If you are interested in learning other methods for counting sample points for various types of experiments, you will find a few of the basic counting rules in Appendix B. Others can be found in the chapter references.

STATISTICS IN ACTION

REVISITED

The Probability of Winning Lotto

In Florida's state lottery game, called Pick-6 Lotto, you select six numbers of your choice from a set of numbers ranging from 1 to 53. We can apply the Combinations Rule to determine the total number of combinations of 6 numbers selected from 53 (i.e., the total number of sample points [or possible winning tickets]). Here, $N = 53$ and $n = 6$; therefore, we have

$$\binom{N}{n} = \frac{N!}{n!(N-n)!} = \frac{53!}{6!47!}$$
$$= \frac{(53)(52)(51)(50)(49)(48)(47!)}{(6)(5)(4)(3)(2)(1)(47!)}$$
$$= 22,957,480$$

Now, since the Lotto balls are selected at random, each of these 22,957,480 combinations is equally likely to occur. Therefore, the probability of winning Lotto is

$$P(\text{Win 6/53 Lotto}) = 1/(22,957,480) = .00000004356$$

This probability is often stated as follows: The odds of winning the game with a single ticket are 1 in 22,957,480, or 1 in approximately 23 million. For all practical purposes, this probability is 0, implying that you have almost no chance of winning the lottery with a single ticket. Yet each week there is almost always a winner in the Florida Lotto. This apparent contradiction can be explained with the following analogy.

Suppose there is a line of minivans, front to back, from New York City to Los Angeles, California. Based on the distance between the two cities and the length of a standard minivan, there would be approximately 23 million minivans in line. Lottery officials will select, at random, one of the minivans and put a check for $10 million dollars in the glove compartment. For a cost of $1, you may roam the country and select one (and only one) minivan and check the glove compartment. Do you think you will find $10 million in the minivan you choose? You can be almost certain that you won't. But now permit anyone to enter the lottery for $1 and suppose that 50 million people do so. With such a large number of participants, it is very likely that someone will find the minivan with the $10 million—but it almost certainly won't be you! (This example illustrates an axiom in statistics called the Law of Large Numbers. See the footnote at the bottom of p. 160.)

Exercises 3.1–3.29

Learning the Mechanics

3.1 An experiment results in one of the following sample points: E_1, E_2, E_3, or E_4. Find $P(E_4)$ for each of the following cases.
  a. $P(E_1) = .1$, $P(E_2) = .2$, and $P(E_3) = .3$
  b. $P(E_1) = P(E_2) = P(E_3) = P(E_4)$
  c. $P(E_1) = P(E_2) = .1$ and $P(E_3) = P(E_4)$

3.2 The diagram below describes the sample space of a particular experiment and events A and B.

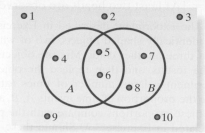

a. What is this type of diagram called?

b. Suppose the sample points are equally likely. Find $P(A)$ and $P(B)$.

c. Suppose $P(1) = P(2) = P(3) = P(4) = \frac{1}{16}$ and $P(5) = P(6) = P(7) = P(8) = P(9) = P(10) = \frac{1}{8}$. Find $P(A)$ and $P(B)$.

3.3 The sample space for an experiment contains five sample points with probabilities as shown in the table. Find the probability of each of the following events:

Sample Points	Probabilities
1	.05
2	.20
3	.30
4	.30
5	.15

A: {Either 1, 2, or 3 occurs.}

B: {Either 1, 3, or 5 occurs.}

C: {4 does not occur.}

3.4 Compute each of the following:

a. $\binom{9}{4}$ b. $\binom{7}{2}$ c. $\binom{4}{4}$

d. $\binom{5}{0}$ e. $\binom{6}{5}$

3.5 Compute the number of ways you can select n elements from N elements for each of the following:

a. $n = 2, N = 5$

b. $n = 3, N = 6$

c. $n = 5, N = 20$

3.6 Two fair dice are tossed, and the face on each die is observed.

a. Use a tree diagram to find the 36 sample points contained in the sample space.

b. Assign probabilities to the sample points in part **a**.

c. Find the probability of each of the following events:

$A = $ {3 showing on each die}

$B = $ {sum of two numbers showing is 7}

$C = $ {sum of two numbers showing is even}

3.7 Three fair coins are tossed and either heads (H) or tails (T) is observed for each coin.

a. List the sample points for this experiment.

b. Assign probabilities to the sample points.

c. Determine the probability of observing each of the following events:

$A = $ [Three heads are observed.]

$B = $ [Exactly two heads are observed.]

$C = $ [At least two heads are observed.]

3.8 Simulate the experiment described in Exercise 3.7 using any five identically shaped objects, two of which are one color and three another color. Mix the objects, draw two, record the results, and then replace the objects. Repeat the experiment a large number of times (at least 100). Calculate the proportion of time events *A*, *B*, and *C* occur. How do these proportions compare with the probabilities you calculated in Exercise 3.7? Should these proportions equal the probabilities? Explain.

📊 Applet Exercise 3.1

Use the applet *Simulating the Probability of Rolling a 6* to explore the relationship between the proportion of 6s rolled on several rolls of a die and the theoretical probability of rolling a 6 on a fair die.

a. To simulate rolling a die one time, click on the *Roll* button on the screen while $n = 1$. The outcome of the roll appears in the list at the right, and the cumulative proportion of 6s for one roll is shown above the graph and as a point on the graph corresponding to 1. Click *Reset* and repeat the process with $n = 1$ several times. What are the possible values of the cumulative proportion of 6s for one roll of a die? Can the cumulative proportion of 6s for one roll of a die equal the theoretical probability of rolling a 6 on a fair die? Explain.

b. Set $n = 10$ and click the *Roll* button. Repeat this several times, resetting after each time. Record the cumulative proportion of 6s for each roll. Compare the cumulative proportions for $n = 10$ with those for $n = 1$ in part **a**. Which tend to be closer to the theoretical probability of rolling a 6 on a fair die?

c. Repeat part **b** for $n = 1,000$, comparing the cumulative proportions for $n = 1,000$ with those for $n = 1$ in part **a** and for $n = 10$ in part **b**.

d. Based on your results for parts **a, b,** and **c**, do you believe that we could justifiably conclude that a die is unfair because we rolled it 10 times and didn't roll any 6s? Explain.

📊 Applet Exercise 3.2

Use the applet *Simulating the Probability of a Head with a Fair Coin* to explore the relationship between the proportion of heads on several flips of a coin and the theoretical probability of getting heads on one flip of a fair coin.

a. Repeat parts **a–c** of Applet Exercise 3.1 for the experiment of flipping a coin and the event of getting heads.

b. Based on your results for part **a**, do you believe that we could justifiably conclude that a coin is unfair because we flipped it 10 times and didn't get any heads? Explain.

Applying the Concepts–Basic

3.9 **Exit poll candidates and voters.** In an exit poll, 45% of voters said that the main issue affecting their choice of candidates was the economy, 35% said national security, and the remaining 20% were not sure. Suppose we select one of the voters who participated in the exit poll at random and ask for the main issue affecting his or her choice of candidates.

a. List the sample points for this experiment.

b. Assign reasonable probabilities to the sample points.

c. What is the probability that the main issue affecting randomly selected voter's choice was either the economy or national security?

3.10 **Do social robots walk or roll?** Refer to the *International Conference on Social Robotics* (Vol. 6414, 2010) study of the trend in the design of social robots, Exercise 2.5 (p. 72). Recall that in a random sample of 106 social (or service) robots designed to entertain, educate, and care for human users, 63 were built with legs only, 20 with wheels only, 8 with both legs and wheels, and 15 with neither legs nor wheels. One of the 106 social robots is randomly selected and the design (e.g., wheels only) is noted.

a. List the sample points for this study.

b. Assign reasonable probabilities to the sample points.

c. What is the probability that the selected robot is designed with wheels?

d. What is the probability that the selected robot is designed with legs?

3.11 Colors of M&M's candies. When they were first produced in 1940, M&M's Plain Chocolate Candies came in only a brown color. Today, M&M's in standard bags come in six colors: brown, yellow, red, blue, orange, and green. According to Mars Corporation, today 24% of all M&M's produced are blue, 20% are orange, 16% are green, 14% are yellow, 13% are brown, and 13% are red. Suppose you purchase a randomly selected bag of M&M's Plain Chocolate Candies and randomly select one of the M&M's from the bag. The color of the selected M&M is of interest.

a. Identify the outcomes (sample points) of this experiment.

b. Assign reasonable probabilities to the outcomes, part **a.**

c. What is the probability that the selected M&M is brown (the original color)?

d. In 1960, the colors red, green, and yellow were added to brown M&Ms. What is the probability that the selected M&M is either red, green, or yellow?

e. In 1995, based on voting by American consumers, the color blue was added to the M&M mix. What is the probability that the selected M&M is not blue?

3.12 Male nannies. In a survey conducted by the International Nanny Association (INA) and reported at the INA Web site (www.nanny.org), 4,176 nannies were placed in a job in a given year. Only 24 of the nannies placed were men. Find the probability that a randomly selected nanny who was placed during the last year is a male nanny (a "mannie").

3.13 Working on summer vacation. Is summer vacation a break from work? Not according to a *Harris Interactive* (July 2013) poll of U.S. adults. The poll found that 61% of the respondents work during their summer vacation, 22% do not work at all while on vacation, and 17% were unemployed. Assuming these percentages apply to the population of U.S. adults, consider the work status during summer vacation of a randomly selected adult.

a. What is the probability that the adult works while on summer vacation?

b. What is the probability that the adult will not work while on summer vacation, either by choice or due to unemployment?

3.14 Mobile access to social media. *The Marketing Management Journal* (Fall 2014) published the results of a designed study to investigate satisfaction with the use of mobile devices to access social media. Mobile device users were classified by gender (male or female) and by the social media they most often (Facebook, Twitter, or YouTube). Consider a similar study in which 10 males and 10 females

were sampled for each of the three social media—a total of 60 mobile device users. One of these users is randomly selected. Of interest is his or her gender and most used social media.

a. Use a tree diagram to determine the possible outcomes (sample points) for this experiment.

b. Why should the probabilities assigned to each outcome be equal? Give the value of this probability.

c. Find the probability that the selected user is a female who accesses Twitter most often.

d. Find the probability that the selected user accesses YouTube most often.

Applying the Concepts—Intermediate

3.15 Performance-based logistics. Refer to the *Journal of Business Logistics* (Vol. 36, 2015) study of performance-based logistics (PBL) strategies, Exercise 1.15 (p. 49). Recall that the study was based on the opinions of a sample of 17 upper-level employees of the U.S. Department of Defense and its suppliers. The current position (e.g., vice president, manager), type of organization (commercial or government), and years of experience for each employee interviewed are listed below. Suppose we randomly select one of these interviewees for more in-depth questioning on PBL strategies.

a. What is the probability that the interviewee works for a government organization?

b. What is the probability that the interviewee has at least 20 years of experience?

Interviewee	Position	Organization	Experience (years)
1	Vice president	Commercial	30
2	Postproduction	Government	15
3	Analyst	Commercial	10
4	Senior manager (mgr.)	Government	30
5	Support chief	Government	30
6	Specialist	Government	25
7	Senior analyst	Commercial	9
8	Division chief	Government	6
9	Item mgr.	Government	3
10	Senior mgr.	Government	20
11	MRO mgr.	Government	25
12	Logistics mgr.	Government	30
13	MRO mgr.	Commercial	10
14	MRO mgr.	Commercial	5
15	MRO mgr.	Commercial	10
16	Specialist	Government	20
17	Chief	Government	25

3.16 Who prepares your tax return? As part of a study on income tax compliance (*Behavioral Research and Accounting*, January 2015), researchers sampled 270 adults at a shopping mall and asked each: "Who usually prepares your tax return?" Their answers (and frequency of responses) are shown in the table (p. 170). Use the information in the table to estimate the probability that a randomly selected adult uses a friend, relative, or professional to prepare his or her income tax return.

Table for Exercise 3.16

Response	Frequency
You	100
Your spouse	16
Equally with spouse	7
Friend or relative	31
Professional help	114
Not required to file	2
TOTAL	270

Source: S. Bhattacharjee, K. Moreno, and D. Salbador, "The Impact of Multiple Tax Returns on Tax Compliance Behavior," *Behavioral Research and Accounting*, Vol. 27, No. 1, January 2015 (from Table 1).

3.17 **Consumer recycling behavior.** Refer to the *Journal of Consumer Research* (December 2013) study of consumer recycling behavior, Exercise 1.23 (p. 50). Recall that 78 college students were asked to dispose of cut paper they used during an exercise. Half the students were randomly assigned to list five uses for the cut paper (*usefulness is salient* condition), while the other half were asked to list their five favorite TV shows (*control* condition). The researchers kept track of which students recycled and which students disposed of their paper in the garbage. Assume that of the 39 students in the *usefulness is salient* condition, 26 recycled; of the 39 students in the *control* condition, 14 recycled. The researchers wanted to test the theory that students in the *usefulness is salient* condition will recycle at a higher rate than students in the *control* condition. Use probabilities to either support or refute the theory.

3.18 **Museum management.** Refer to the *Museum Management and Curatorship* (June 2010) study of the criteria used to evaluate museum performance, Exercise 2.14 (p. 74). Recall that the managers of 30 leading museums of contemporary art were asked to provide the performance measure used most often. A summary of the results is reproduced in the table.

Performance Measure	Number of Museums
Total visitors	8
Paying visitors	5
Big shows	6
Funds raised	7
Members	4

a. If one of the 30 museums is selected at random, what is the probability that the museum uses total visitors or funds raised most often as a performance measure?

b. Consider two museums of contemporary art randomly selected from all such museums. Of interest is whether or not the museums use total visitors or funds raised most often as a performance measure. Use a tree diagram to aid in listing the sample points for this problem.

c. Assign reasonable probabilities to the sample points of part **b.** [*Hint*: Use the probability, part **a,** to estimate these probabilities.]

d. Refer to parts **b** and **c.** Find the probability that both museums use total visitors or funds raised most often as a performance measure.

3.19 **USDA chicken inspection.** The U.S. Department of Agriculture (USDA) reports that, under its standard inspection system, one in every 100 slaughtered chickens passes inspection with fecal contamination.

a. If a slaughtered chicken is selected at random, what is the probability that it passes inspection with fecal contamination?

b. The probability of part **a** was based on a USDA study that found that 306 of 32,075 chicken carcasses passed inspection with fecal contamination. Do you agree with the USDA's statement about the likelihood of a slaughtered chicken passing inspection with fecal contamination?

3.20 **Jamming attacks on wireless networks.** Refer to the *International Journal of Production Economics* (Vol. 172, 2016) study of U.S. military jamming attacks on wireless networks used by terrorists, Exercise 2.8 (p. 73). Recall that 80 recent jamming attacks were classified according to network type (WLAN, WSN, or AHN) attacked and number of channels (single- or multi-channel) of the network. The results are reproduced in the accompanying table.

a. Find the probability that a recent jamming attack involved a single-channel network.

b. Find the probability that a recent jamming attack involved a WLAN network.

Network Type/Number of Channels	Number of Jamming Attacks
WLAN / Single	31
WSN / Single	13
AHN / Single	8
WLAN / Multi	14
WSN / Multi	9
AHN / Multi	5
TOTAL:	80

Source: S. Vadlamani et al., "Jamming Attacks on Wireless Networks: A Taxonomic Survey, "*International Journal of Production Economics*, Vol. 172, 2016 (Figure 6).

3.21 **Randomization in a study of TV commercials.** Gonzaga University professors conducted a study of more than 1,500 television commercials and published their results in the *Journal of Sociology, Social Work and Social Welfare* (Vol. 2, 2008). Commercials from eight networks—ABC, FAM, FOX, MTV, ESPN, CBS, CNN, and NBC—were sampled during an 8-day period, with one network randomly selected each day. The table below shows the actual order determined by random draw:

> ABC—July 6 (Wed)
> FAM—July 7 (Thr)
> FOX—July 9 (Sat)
> MTV—July 10 (Sun)
> ESPN—July 11 (Mon)
> CBS—July 12 (Tue)
> CNN—July 16 (Sat)
> NBC—July 17 (Sun)

a. What is the probability that ESPN was selected on Monday, July 11?

b. Consider the four networks chosen for the weekends (Saturday and Sunday). How many ways could the researchers select four networks from the eight for the weekend analysis of commercials? (Assume that the order of assignment for the four weekend days was immaterial to the analysis.)

c. Knowing that the networks were selected at random, what is the probability that ESPN was one of the four networks selected for the weekend analysis of commercials?

3.22 **Jai-alai bets.** The Quinella bet at the paramutual game of jai-alai consists of picking the jai-alai players that will place first and second in a game *irrespective* of order. In jai-alai, eight players (numbered $1, 2, 3, \ldots, 8$) compete in every game.

   a. How many different Quinella bets are possible?

   b. Suppose you bet the Quinella combination of $2-7$. If the players are of equal ability, what is the probability that you win the bet?

3.23 **Investing in stocks.** From a list of 15 preferred stocks recommended by your broker, you will select three to invest in. How many different ways can you select the three stocks from the 15 recommended stocks?

3.24 **Advertising proposals.** The manager of an advertising department has asked her creative team to propose six new ideas for an advertising campaign for a major client. She will choose three of the six proposals to present to the client. The proposals were named A, B, C, D, E, and F, respectively.

   a. In how many ways can the manager select the three proposals? List the possibilities.

   b. It is unlikely that the manager will *randomly* select three of the six proposals, but if she does, what is the probability that she selects proposals A, D, and E?

3.25 **Volkswagen emissions scandal.** Refer to the *Significance* (December 2015) study estimating the number of U.S. deaths attributable to nitrous oxide pollution (NOx) produced from illegal VW vehicles, Exercise 2.30 (p. 85). The researchers varied the values of three different variables—total distance (in miles) driven by these illegal VW vehicles, the amount by which the VW vehicles exceeded the EPA standard for NOx, and the estimated association between NOx emissions and mortality—to obtain their estimates. Each variable was set at three different levels: Distance (6, 17, and 33 billion miles), Excess amount (15, 30, and 40 times higher than the standard), and Association (.00085, .0019, and .0095 deaths per ton).

   a. How many different combinations of Distance, Excess, and Association are possible? The researchers computed the estimated number of deaths for each of these combinations, which they called *scenarios*.

   b. Refer to part **a.** Suppose the researchers desire to select two of these scenarios for a more detailed analysis. If these scenarios are selected at random, how many possible choices of two are there?

Applying the Concepts—Advanced

3.26 **Drug testing of firefighters.** Hillsborough County, Florida, has 42 fire stations that employ 980 career firefighters and 160 volunteers. Both types of firefighters are drug tested every six months. However, the career firefighters and volunteers are treated as separate populations. For drug testing, 50% of the career firefighters are randomly selected and 50% of the volunteers are randomly selected. Some firefighters at a particular station argue that due to the smaller number of volunteers, an individual volunteer is more likely to be selected in the current sampling scheme than if all the career firefighters and volunteers were combined into a single population and 50% sampled. Do you agree? Explain your reasoning.

$$\left[Hint: \binom{N-1}{n-1} \middle/ \binom{N}{n} = n/N \right]$$

3.27 **Odds of winning a race.** Handicappers for greyhound races express their belief about the probabilities that each greyhound will win a race in terms of **odds.** If the probability of event E is $P(E)$, then the *odds in favor of E* are $P(E)$ to $1 - P(E)$. Thus, if a handicapper assesses a probability of .25 that Oxford Shoes will win its next race, the odds in favor of Oxford Shoes are $\frac{25}{100}$ to $\frac{75}{100}$, or 1 to 3. It follows that the *odds against E* are $1 - P(E)$ to $P(E)$, or 3 to 1 against a win by Oxford Shoes. In general, if the odds in favor of event E are a to b, then $P(E) = a/(a+b)$.

   a. A second handicapper assesses the probability of a win by Oxford Shoes to be $\frac{1}{3}$. According to the second handicapper, what are the odds in favor of Oxford Shoes winning?

   b. A third handicapper assesses the odds in favor of Oxford Shoes to be 1 to 1. According to the third handicapper, what is the probability of Oxford Shoes winning?

   c. A fourth handicapper assesses the odds against Oxford Shoes winning to be 3 to 2. Find this handicapper's assessment of the probability that Oxford Shoes will win.

3.28 **Lead bullets as forensic evidence.** *Chance* (Summer 2004) published an article on the use of lead bullets as forensic evidence in a federal criminal case. Typically, the Federal Bureau of Investigation (FBI) will use a laboratory method to match the lead in a bullet found at the crime scene with unexpended lead cartridges found in possession of the suspect. The value of this evidence depends on the chance of a *false positive* (i.e., the probability that the FBI finds a match given that the lead at the crime scene and the lead in possession of the suspect are actually from two different "melts," or sources). To estimate the false-positive rate, the FBI collected 1,837 bullets that they were confident all came from different melts. The FBI then examined every possible pair of bullets and counted the number of matches using its established criteria. According to *Chance*, the FBI found 693 matches. Use this information to compute the chance of a false positive. Is this probability small enough for you to have confidence in the FBI's forensic evidence?

3.29 **Making your vote count.** Democratic and Republican presidential state primary elections are highlighted by the difference in the way winning candidates are awarded delegates. In Republican states, the winner is awarded all the state's delegates; conversely, the Democratic state winner is awarded delegates in proportion to the percentage of votes. This led to a *Chance* (Fall 2007) article on making your vote count. Consider the following scenario where you are one of five voters (for example, on a county commission where you are one of the five commissioners voting on an issue).

   a. Determine the number of ways the five commissioners can vote, where each commissioner votes either for or against. (These outcomes represent the sample points for the experiment.)

   b. Assume each commissioner is equally likely to vote for or against. Assign reasonable probabilities to the sample points, part **a.**

Table 3.4	Two-Way Table with Percentage of Respondents in Age-Income Classes		
	Income		
Age	<$25,000	$25,000–$50,000	>$50,000
<30 yr	5%	12%	10%
30–50 yr	14%	22%	16%
>50 yr	(B) 8%	10%	3%

(A)

Solution Following the steps for calculating probabilities of events, we first note that the objective is to characterize the income and age distribution of respondents to the mailing. To accomplish this, we define the experiment to consist of selecting a respondent from the collection of all respondents and observing which income and age class he or she occupies. The sample points are the nine different age-income classifications:

E_1: {<30 yr, <$25,000} E_4: {<30 yr, $25,000–$50,000} E_7: {<30 yr, >$50,000}

E_2: {30–50 yr, <$25,000} E_5: {30–50 yr, $25,000–$50,000} E_8: {30–50 yr, >$50,000}

E_3: {>50 yr, <$25,000} E_6: {>50 yr, $25,000–$50,000} E_9: {>50 yr, >$50,000}

Next, we assign probabilities to the sample points. If we blindly select one of the respondents, the probability that he or she will occupy a particular age-income classification is the proportion, or relative frequency, of respondents in the classification. These proportions are given (as percentages) in Table 3.4. Thus,

$$P(E_1) = \text{Relative frequency of respondents in age-income class}$$

$$\{< 30 \text{ yr}, < \$25,000\} = .05$$

$$P(E_2) = .14$$
$$P(E_3) = .08$$
$$P(E_4) = .12$$
$$P(E_5) = .22$$
$$P(E_6) = .10$$
$$P(E_7) = .10$$
$$P(E_8) = .16$$
$$P(E_9) = .03$$

You may verify that the sample points probabilities add to 1.

a. To find $P(A)$, we first determine the collection of sample points contained in event A. Because A is defined as {>$50,000}, we see from Table 3.4 that A contains the three sample points represented by the last column of the table (see shaded area). In other words, the event A consists of the income classification {>$50,000} in all three age classifications. The probability of A is the sum of the probabilities of the sample points in A:

$$P(A) = P(E_7) + P(E_8) + P(E_9) = .10 + .16 + .03 = .29$$

Similarly, B = {≥30 yr} consists of the six sample points in the second and third rows of Table 3.4 (see shaded area):

$$P(B) = P(E_2) + P(E_3) + P(E_5) + P(E_6) + P(E_8) + P(E_9)$$

$$= .14 + .08 + .22 + .10 + .16 + .03 = .73$$

b. The union of events A and B, $A \cup B$, consists of all the sample points in *either A or B or both*—that is, the union of A and B consists of all respondents whose income exceeds \$50,000 *or* whose age is 30 or more. In Table 3.4 this is any sample point found in the third column *or* the last two rows. Thus,

$$P(A \cup B) = .10 + .14 + .22 + .16 + .08 + .10 + .03 = .83$$

c. The intersection of events A and B, $A \cap B$, consists of all sample points in *both A and B*—that is, the intersection of A and B consists of all respondents whose income exceeds \$50,000 *and* whose age is 30 or more. In Table 3.4 this is any sample point found in the third column *and* the last two rows. Thus,

$$P(A \cap B) = .16 + .03 = .19$$

Look Back As with previous problems, the key to finding the probabilities of parts **b** and **c** is to identify the sample points that compose the event of interest. In a two-way table like Table 3.4, the number of sample points will be equal to the number of rows times the number of columns.

● **Now Work Exercise 3.35f–g**

3.3 Complementary Events

A very useful concept in the calculation of event probabilities is the notion of **complementary events:**

> The **complement** of an event A is the event that A does *not* occur—that is, the event consisting of all sample points that are not in event A. We denote the complement of A by A^c.

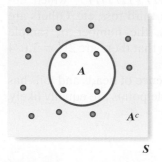

Figure 3.9
Venn diagram of complementary events

An event A is a collection of sample points, and the sample points included in A^c are those not in A. Figure 3.9 demonstrates this idea. Note from the figure that all sample points in S are included in *either A or A^c* and that *no* sample point is in both A and A^c. This leads us to conclude that the probabilities of an event and its complement *must sum to 1:*

> **Rule of Complements**
>
> The sum of the probabilities of complementary events equals 1:
> $P(A) + P(A^c) = 1.$

In many probability problems, calculating the probability of the complement of the event of interest is easier than calculating the event itself. Then, because

$$P(A) + P(A^c) = 1$$

we can calculate $P(A)$ by using the relationship

$$P(A) = 1 - P(A^c)$$

EXAMPLE 3.11

Probability of a Complementary Event— Coin-Toss Experiment

Problem Consider the experiment of tossing fair coins. Define the following event: A: {Observing at least one head}.

a. Find $P(A)$ if 2 coins are tossed.
b. Find $P(A)$ if 10 coins are tossed.

Solution

a. When 2 coins are tossed, we know that the event A: {Observe at least one head.} consists of the sample points

$$A: \{HH, HT, TH\}$$

The complement of A is defined as the event that occurs when A does not occur. Therefore,

$$A^c: \{\text{Observe no heads.}\} = \{TT\}$$

This complementary relationship is shown in Figure 3.10. Since the coins are balanced, we have

$$P(A^c) = P(TT) = \tfrac{1}{4}$$

and

$$P(A) = 1 - P(A^c) = 1 - \tfrac{1}{4} = \tfrac{3}{4}$$

b. We solve this problem by following the five steps for calculating probabilities of events. (See Section 3.1.)

Step 1: Define the experiment. The experiment is to record the results of the 10 tosses of the coin.

Step 2: List the sample points. A sample point consists of a particular sequence of 10 heads and tails. Thus, one sample point is $HHTTTHTHTT$, which denotes head on first toss, head on second toss, tail on third toss, etc. Others are $HTHHHTTTTT$ and $THHTHTHTTH$. Obviously, the number of sample points is very large—too many to list. It can be shown that there are $2^{10} = 1,024$ sample points for this experiment.

Step 3: Assign probabilities. Since the coin is fair, each sequence of heads and tails has the same chance of occurring; therefore, all the sample points are equally likely. Then

$$P(\text{Each sample point}) = \frac{1}{1,024}$$

Step 4: Determine the sample points in event A. A sample point is in A if at least one H appears in the sequence of 10 tosses. However, if we consider the complement of A, we find that

$$A^c = \{\text{No heads are observed in 10 tosses.}\}$$

Thus, A^c contains only one sample point:

$$A^c: \{TTTTTTTTTT\}$$

and $P(A^c) = \dfrac{1}{1,024}$

Step 5: Now we use the relationship of complementary events to find $P(A)$:

$$P(A) = 1 - P(A^c) = 1 - \frac{1}{1,024} = \frac{1,023}{1,024} = .999$$

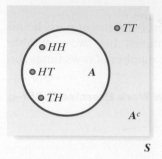

Figure 3.10
Complementary events in the toss of two coins

> **Look Back** In part **a,** we can find $P(A)$ by summing the probabilities of the sample points *HH, HT,* and *TH* in *A*. Many times, however, it is easier to find $P(A^c)$ by using the rule of complements.
>
> **Look Forward** Since $P(A) = .999$ in part **b,** we are virtually certain of observing at least one head in 10 tosses of the coin.
>
> • **Now Work Exercise 3.33e–f**

3.4 The Additive Rule and Mutually Exclusive Events

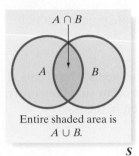

Entire shaded area is $A \cup B$.

Figure 3.11
Venn diagram of union

In Section 3.2 we saw how to determine which sample points are contained in a union and how to calculate the probability of the union by adding the probabilities of the sample points in the union. It is also possible to obtain the probability of the union of two events by using the **additive rule of probability.**

The union of two events will often contain many sample points because the union occurs if either one or both of the events occur. By studying the Venn diagram in Figure 3.11, you can see that the probability of the union of two events, *A* and *B,* can be obtained by summing $P(A)$ and $P(B)$ and subtracting the probability corresponding to $A \cap B$. We must subtract $P(A \cap B)$ because the sample point probabilities in $A \cap B$ have been included twice–once in $P(A)$ and once in $P(B)$. The formula for calculating the probability of the union of two events is given in the next box.

Additive Rule of Probability

The probability of the union of events *A* and *B* is the sum of the probabilities of events *A* and *B* minus the probability of the intersection of events *A* and *B*–that is,

$$P(A \cup B) = P(A) + P(B) - P(A \cap B)$$

EXAMPLE 3.12

Applying the Additive Rule—Hospital Admission Study

Problem Hospital records show that 12% of all patients are admitted for surgical treatment, 16% are admitted for obstetrics, and 2% receive both obstetrics and surgical treatment. If a new patient is admitted to the hospital, what is the probability that the patient will be admitted either for surgery, obstetrics, or both?

Solution Consider the following events:

> *A:* {A patient admitted to the hospital receives surgical treatment.}
>
> *B:* {A patient admitted to the hospital receives obstetrics treatment.}

Then, from the given information,

$$P(A) = .12$$
$$P(B) = .16$$

and the probability of the event that a patient receives both obstetrics and surgical treatment is

$$P(A \cap B) = .02$$

The event that a patient admitted to the hospital receives either surgical treatment, obstetrics treatment, or both is the union $A \cup B$. The probability of $A \cup B$ is given by the additive rule of probability:

$$P(A \cup B) = P(A) + P(B) - P(A \cap B) = .12 + .16 - .02 = .26$$

Thus, 26% of all patients admitted to the hospital receive either surgical treatment, obstetrics treatment, or both.

Look Back From the information given, it is not possible to list and assign probabilities to all the sample points. Consequently, we cannot proceed through the five-step process for finding the probability of an event and must use the additive rule.

● **Now Work Exercise 3.30c**

A very special relationship exists between events A and B when $A \cap B$ contains no sample points. In this case we call the events A and B *mutually exclusive events*.

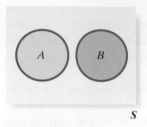

Figure 3.12
Venn diagram of mutually exclusive events

> Events A and B are **mutually exclusive** if $A \cap B$ contains no sample points–that is, if A and B have no sample points in common.

Figure 3.12 shows a Venn diagram of two mutually exclusive events. The events A and B have no sample points in common—that is, A and B cannot occur simultaneously, and $P(A \cap B) = 0$. Thus, we have the important relationship given in the box.

> **Probability of Union of Two Mutually Exclusive Events**
>
> If two events A and B are *mutually exclusive*, the probability of the union of A and B equals the sum of the probabilities of A and B; that is, $P(A \cup B) = P(A) + P(B)$.

> **! CAUTION** The formula just shown is *false* if the events are *not* mutually exclusive. For two nonmutually exclusive events, you must apply the general additive rule of probability.

EXAMPLE 3.13

The Union of Two Mutually Exclusive Events—Coin-Tossing Experiment

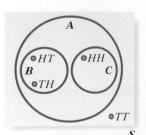

Figure 3.13
Venn diagram for coin-toss experiment

Problem Consider the experiment of tossing two balanced coins. Find the probability of observing *at least* one head.

Solution Define the events

$$A: \{\text{Observe at least one head.}\}$$
$$B: \{\text{Observe exactly one head.}\}$$
$$C: \{\text{Observe exactly two heads.}\}$$

Note that

$$A = B \cup C$$

and that $B \cap C$ contains no sample points (see Figure 3.13). Thus, B and C are mutually exclusive, so that

$$P(A) = P(B \cup C) = P(B) + P(C) = \tfrac{1}{2} + \tfrac{1}{4} = \tfrac{3}{4}$$

Look Back Although this example is very simple, it shows us that writing events with verbal descriptions that include the phrases *at least* or *at most* as unions of mutually exclusive events is very useful. This practice enables us to find the probability of the event by adding the probabilities of the mutually exclusive events.

● **Now Work Exercise 3.38**

STATISTICS IN ACTION

REVISITED

The Probability of Winning a Wheeling System

Refer to Florida's Pick-6 Lotto game in which you select six numbers of your choice from a field of numbers ranging from 1 to 53. In Section 3.1, we learned that the probability of winning Lotto on a single ticket is only 1 in approximately 23 million. The "experts" at *Lottery Buster* recommend many strategies for increasing the odds of winning the lottery. One strategy is to employ a wheeling system. In a complete wheeling system, you select more than six numbers, say, seven, and play every combination of six of those seven numbers.

Suppose you choose to "wheel" the following seven numbers: 2, 7, 18, 23, 30, 32, and 51. Every combination of six of these seven numbers is listed in Table SIA3.1 You can see that there are seven different possibilities. (Use the Combinations Rule with $N = 7$ and $n = 6$ to verify this.) Thus, we would purchase seven tickets (at a cost of $7) corresponding to these different combinations in a complete wheeling system.

To determine if this strategy does, in fact, increase our odds of winning, we need to find the probability that one of these seven combinations occurs during the $\frac{6}{53}$ Lotto draw–that is, we need to find the probability that either Ticket 1 or Ticket 2 or Ticket 3 or Ticket 4 or Ticket 5 or Ticket 6 or Ticket 7 is the winning combination. Note that this probability is stated using the word *or*, implying a union of seven events. Letting T1 represent the event that Ticket 1 wins, and defining T2, T3, . . . , T7 in a similar fashion, we want to find

$$P(\text{T1 or T2 or T3 or T4 or T5 or T6 or T7})$$

Recall (Section 3.1, p. 167) that the 22,957,480 possible combinations in Pick-6 Lotto are mutually exclusive and equally likely to occur. Consequently, the probability of the union of the seven events is simply the sum of the probabilities of the individual events, where each event has probability of 1/(22,957,480):

$$P(\text{win Lotto with 7 wheeled numbers})$$

$$= P(\text{T1 or T2 or T3 or T4 or T5 or T6 or T7})$$

$$= 7/(22,957,480) = .0000003$$

In terms of odds, we now have 3 chances in 10 million of winning the Lotto with the complete wheeling system. The "experts" are correct–our odds of winning Lotto have increased (from 1 in 23 million). However, the probability of winning is so close to 0 we question whether the $7 spent on lottery tickets is worth the negligible increase in odds. In fact, it can be shown that to increase your chance of winning the $\frac{6}{53}$ Lotto to 1 chance in 100 (i.e., .01) using a complete wheeling system, you would have to wheel 26 of your favorite numbers–a total of 230,230 combinations at a cost of $230,230!

Table SIA3.1	Wheeling the Seven Numbers 2, 7, 18, 23, 30, 32, and 51					
Ticket 1:	2	7	18	23	30	32
Ticket 2:	2	7	18	23	30	51
Ticket 3:	2	7	18	23	32	51
Ticket 4:	2	7	18	30	32	51
Ticket 5:	2	7	23	30	32	51
Ticket 6:	2	18	23	30	32	51
Ticket 7:	7	18	23	30	32	51

Exercises 3.30–3.51

Learning the Mechanics

3.30 Suppose $P(A) = .4$, $P(B) = .7$, and $P(A \cap B) = .3$. Find the following probabilities:
a. $P(B^c)$
b. $P(A^c)$
NW c. $P(A \cup B)$

3.31 A number between 1 and 10, inclusive, is randomly chosen, and the events A and B are defined as follows:

A: [The number is even.]

B: [The number is less than 7.]

a. Identify the sample points in the event $A \cup B$.
b. Identify the sample points in the event $A \cap B$.
c. Which expression represents the event that the number is even or less than 7 or both?
d. Which expression represents the event that the number is both even and less than 7?

3.32 A pair of fair dice is tossed. Define the following events:

A: [Exactly one of the dice shows a 1.]
B: [The sum of the numbers on the two dice is even.]

a. Identify the sample points in the events A, B, $A \cap B$, $A \cup B$, and A^c.
b. Find the probabilities of all the events from part **a** by summing the probabilities of the appropriate sample points.
c. Using your result from part **b**, explain why A and B are not mutually exclusive.
d. Find $P(A \cup B)$ using the additive rule. Is your answer the same as in part **b**?

3.33 Consider the Venn diagram below, where
NW
$$P(E_1) = P(E_2) = P(E_3) = \tfrac{1}{5}, P(E_4) = P(E_5) = \tfrac{1}{20},$$
$$P(E_6) = \tfrac{1}{10}, \text{ and } P(E_7) = \tfrac{1}{5}.$$

Find each of the following probabilities:

a. $P(A)$
b. $P(B)$
c. $P(A \cup B)$
d. $P(A \cap B)$
e. $P(A^c)$
f. $P(B^c)$
g. $P(A \cup A^c)$
h. $P(A^c \cap B)$

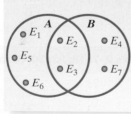

S

3.34 Consider the Venn diagram in the next column, where
$$P(E_1) = .10, P(E_2) = .05, P(E_3) = P(E_4) = .2,$$
$$P(E_5) = .06, P(E_6) = .3, P(E_7) = .06, \text{ and}$$
$$P(E_8) = .03.$$

Find the following probabilities:
a. $P(A^c)$
b. $P(B^c)$
c. $P(A^c \cap B)$
d. $P(A \cup B)$
e. $P(A \cap B)$
f. $P(A^c \cap B^c)$
g. Are events A and B mutually exclusive? Why?

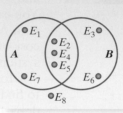

S

3.35 The outcomes of two variables are (Low, Medium, High) and (On, Off), respectively. An experiment is conducted in which the outcomes of each of the two variables are observed. The probabilities associated with each of the six possible outcome pairs are given in the accompanying two-way table.

	Low	Medium	High
On	.50	.10	.05
Off	.25	.07	.03

Consider the following events:

A: {On}
B: {Medium or On}
C: {Off and Low}
D: {High}

a. Find $P(A)$.
b. Find $P(B)$.
c. Find $P(C)$.
d. Find $P(D)$.
e. Find $P(A^c)$.
NW f. Find $P(A \cup B)$.
NW g. Find $P(A \cap C)$.
h. Consider each pair of events (A and B, A and C, A and D, B and C, B and D, C and D). List the pairs of events that are mutually exclusive. Justify your choices.

3.36 Refer to Exercise 3.35. Use the same event definitions to do the following exercises.
a. Write the event that the outcome is "On" and "High" as an intersection of two events.
b. Write the event that the outcome is "Low" or "Medium" as the complement of an event.

📊 Applet Exercise 3.3

Use the applets *Simulating the Probability of Rolling a 6* and *Simulating the Probability of Rolling a 3 or 4* to explore the additive rule for probability.

a. Explain why the applet *Simulating the Probability of Rolling a 6* can also be used to simulate the probability of rolling a 3. Then use the applet with $n = 1,000$ to simulate the probability of rolling a 3. Record the cumulative proportion. Repeat the process to simulate the probability of rolling a 4.

b. Use the applet *Simulating the Probability of Rolling a 3 or 4* with $n = 1,000$ to simulate the probability of rolling a 3 or 4. Record the cumulative proportion.

c. Add the two cumulative proportions from part **a**. How does this sum compare with the cumulative proportion in part **b**? How does this illustrate the additive rule for probability?

📊 Applet Exercise 3.4

Use the applets *Simulating the Probability of Rolling a 6* and *Simulating the Probability of Rolling a 3 or 4* to simulate the probability of the complement of an event.

a. Explain how the applet *Simulating the Probability of Rolling a 6* can also be used to simulate the probability of the event *rolling a 1, 2, 3, 4, or 5*. Then use the applet with $n = 1,000$ to simulate this probability.

b. Explain how the applet *Simulating the Probability of Rolling a 3 or 4* can also be used to simulate the probability of the event *rolling a 1, 2, 5, or 6*. Then use the applet with $n = 1,000$ to simulate this probability.

c. Which applet could be used to simulate the probability of the event *rolling a 1, 2, 3, or 4*? Explain.

Applying the Concepts—Basic

3.37 **Do social robots walk or roll?** Refer to the *International Conference on Social Robotics* (Vol. 6414, 2010) study of the trend in the design of social robots, Exercise 3.10 (p. 168). Recall that in a random sample of 106 social robots, 63 were built with legs only, 20 with wheels only, 8 with both legs and wheels, and 15 with neither legs nor wheels. Use the rule of complements to find the probability that a randomly selected social robot is designed with either legs or wheels.

3.38 **Firefighter glove sizing.** *Human Factors* (December 2015) [NW] published a study on how well firefighter gloves fit. In a group of 586 firefighters who reported their glove size, the researchers determined whether the gloves fit well or poorly, by gender. The data are summarized in the accompanying table. Consider the gender and glove fit status of a randomly selected firefighter.

a. List the sample points for this experiment.

b. Assign reasonable probabilities to these sample points.

c. Find the probability the firefighter is a female.

d. Find the probability the glove fits well.

e. Find the probability the firefighter is a female and has a well-fitting glove.

f. Find the probability the firefighter is a female or has a well-fitting glove.

	Glove Fits Well	Glove Fits Poorly	Totals
Males	415	132	547
Females	19	20	39
Totals	434	152	586

Source: H. Hsiao, et al., "Firefighter Hand Anthropometry and Structural Glove Sizing: A New Perspective," *Human Factors*, Vol. 57, No. 8, December 2015 (Table 6).

3.39 **Study of analysts' forecasts.** The *Journal of Accounting Research* (March 2008) published a study on relationship incentives and degree of optimism among analysts' forecasts. Participants were analysts at either a large or small brokerage firm who made their forecasts either early or late in the quarter. Also, some analysts were only concerned with making an accurate forecast, while others were also interested in their relationship with management. Suppose one of these analysts is randomly selected. Consider the following events:

A = {The analyst is concerned only with making an accurate forecast.}

B = {The analyst makes the forecast early in the quarter.}

C = {The analyst is from a small brokerage firm.}

Describe each of the following events in terms of unions, intersections, and complements (e.g., $A \cup B$, $A \cap B$, A^c, etc.).

a. The analyst makes an early forecast and is concerned only with accuracy.

b. The analyst is not concerned only with accuracy.

c. The analyst is from a small brokerage firm or makes an early forecast.

d. The analyst makes a late forecast and is not concerned only with accuracy.

3.40 **Problems at major companies.** The *Organization Development Journal* (Summer 2006) reported on the results of a survey of human resource officers (HROs) at major employers. The focus of the study was employee behavior, namely, absenteeism and turnover. The study found that 55% of the HROs had problems with employee absenteeism; also, 41% had problems with turnover. Suppose that 22% of the HROs had problems with both absenteeism and turnover. Use this information to find the probability that an HRO selected from the group surveyed had problems with either employee absenteeism or employee turnover.

3.41 **Scanning errors at Walmart.** The National Institute for Standards and Technology (NIST) mandates that for every 100 items scanned through the electronic checkout scanner at a retail store, no more than 2 should have an inaccurate price. A study of the accuracy of checkout scanners at Walmart stores in California was conducted (*Tampa Tribune*, Nov. 22, 2005). Of the 60 Walmart stores investigated, 52 violated the NIST scanner accuracy standard. If one of the 60 Walmart stores is randomly selected, what is the probability that the store does not violate the NIST scanner accuracy standard?

3.42 **Social networking Web sites in the United Kingdom.** In the United States, MySpace and Facebook are considered the two most popular social networking Web sites. In the United Kingdom (UK), the competition for social networking is between MySpace and Bebo. According to Nielsen/NetRatings (April 2006), 4% of UK citizens visit MySpace, 3% visit Bebo, and 1% visit both MySpace and Bebo.

a. Draw a Venn diagram to illustrate the use of social networking sites in the United Kingdom.

b. Find the probability that a UK citizen visits either the MySpace or Bebo social networking site.

c. Use your answer to part **b** to find the probability that a UK citizen does not visit either social networking site.

Applying the Concepts—Intermediate

3.43 Paying monthly bills online. Do most people pay their monthly bills online? *ABA Bank Marketing and Sales* (July-August 2015) reported that 37% of U.S. customers pay their bills online using a personal computer. The table lists the different methods by which customers pay their monthly bills and associated probabilities. Consider the following two events:

A = {Customer does not pay monthly bills online.}

B = {Customer does not pay monthly bills with credit or debit card.}

Payment Method	Probability
Online via personal computer	.37
Write check	.22
Checking account withdrawal	.10
Debit card	.09
Credit card	.07
Cash	.08
Mobile bill account	.04
Online via tablet or e-reader	.03

a. Find $P(A)$.
b. Find $P(B)$.
c. Find $P(A \cap B)$.
d. Use the additive law of probability to find $P(A \cup B)$.

3.44 Fuzzy logic in supply chain management. A branch of mathematics known as *fuzzy logic* was used to improve customer service in supply chain management. (*Decision Analytics*, February 2014.) Customers rate the importance of one service factor relative to another using the following numerical scale: 1 = service factors are equally important, 3 = one factor is moderately more important, 5 = one factor is strongly more important, 7 = one factor is very strongly more important, and 9 = one factor is extremely more important. Fuzzy numbers were developed to allow for variation in customer responses. For example, the fuzzy number $\tilde{1}$ represents an actual response of either 1 or 3; the fuzzy number $\tilde{7}$ represents a response of 5, 7, or 9. Consider the probabilities of the actual responses for each fuzzy number shown in the table.

Fuzzy Response	Probabilities of Actual Responses
$\tilde{1}$	$P(1) = 2/3, P(3) = 1/3$
$\tilde{3}$	$P(1) = 1/3, P(3) = 1/3, P(5) = 1/3$
$\tilde{5}$	$P(3) = 1/3, P(5) = 1/3, P(7) = 1/3$
$\tilde{7}$	$P(5) = 1/3, P(7) = 1/3, P(9) = 1/3$
$\tilde{9}$	$P(7) = 1/3, P(9) = 2/3$

a. If a customer gives a fuzzy response of $\tilde{7}$, what is the probability that the actual response is not a 7?
b. If both $\tilde{5}$ and $\tilde{9}$ represent a possible fuzzy response of a customer, what are the possible actual responses for this customer?

3.45 Study of why EMS workers leave the job. An investigation into why emergency medical service (EMS) workers leave the profession was published in the *Journal of Allied Health* (Fall 2011). The researchers surveyed a sample of 244 former EMS workers, of which 127 were fully compensated while on the job, 45 were partially compensated, and 72 had noncompensated volunteer positions. The numbers of EMS workers who left because of retirement were 7 for fully compensated workers, 11 for partially compensated workers, and 10 for noncompensated volunteers. One of the 244 former EMS workers is selected at random.
a. Find the probability that the former EMS worker was fully compensated while on the job.
b. Find the probability that the former EMS worker was fully compensated while on the job and left due to retirement.
c. Find the probability that the former EMS worker was not fully compensated while on the job.
d. Find the probability that the former EMS worker was either fully compensated while on the job or left due to retirement.

3.46 Stock market participation and IQ. *The Journal of Finance* (December 2011) published a study of whether the decision to invest in the stock market is dependent on IQ. Information on a sample of 158,044 adults living in Finland formed the database for the study. An IQ score (from a low score of 1 to a high score of 9) was determined for each Finnish citizen as well as whether or not the citizen invested in the stock market. The next table gives the number of Finnish citizens in each IQ score/investment category. Suppose one of the 158,044 citizens is selected at random.
a. What is the probability that the Finnish citizen invests in the stock market?
b. What is the probability that the Finnish citizen has an IQ score of 6 or higher?
c. What is the probability that the Finnish citizen invests in the stock market and has an IQ score of 6 or higher?
d. What is the probability that the Finnish citizen invests in the stock market or has an IQ score of 6 or higher?

IQ Score	Invest in Market	No Investment	Totals
1	893	4,659	5,552
2	1,340	9,409	10,749
3	2,009	9,993	12,002
4	5,358	19,682	25,040
5	8,484	24,640	33,124
6	10,270	21,673	31,943
7	6,698	11,260	17,958
8	5,135	7,010	12,145
9	4,464	5,067	9,531
Totals	44,651	113,393	158,044

Source: Based on M. Grinblatt, M. Keloharju, and J. Linnainaa, "IQ and Stock Market Participation," *The Journal of Finance*, Vol. 66, No. 6, December 2011 (adapted from Table 1 and Figure 1).

e. What is the probability that the Finnish citizen does not invest in the stock market?

f. Are the events {Invest in the stock market} and {IQ score of 1} mutually exclusive?

3.47 **Cell phone handoff behavior.** A "handoff" is a term used in wireless communications to describe the process of a cell phone moving from the coverage area of one base station to that of another. Each base station has multiple channels (called color codes) that allow it to communicate with the cell phone. The *Journal of Engineering, Computing and Architecture* (Vol. 3., 2009) published a study of cell phone handoff behavior. During a sample driving trip that involved crossing from one base station to another, the different color codes accessed by the cell phone were monitored and recorded. The table below shows the number of times each color code was accessed for two identical driving trips, each using a different cell phone model. (*Note:* The table is similar to the one published in the article.) Suppose you randomly select one point during the combined driving trips.

	Color Code				
	0	5	b	c	Total
Model 1	20	35	40	0	85
Model 2	15	50	6	4	75
Total	35	85	46	4	160

a. What is the probability that the cell phone was using color code 5?

b. What is the probability that the cell phone was using color code 5 or color code 0?

c. What is the probability that the cell phone used was Model 2 and the color code was 0?

3.48 **Guilt in decision making.** The effect of guilt emotion on how a decision maker focuses on a problem was investigated in the Jan. 2007 issue of the *Journal of Behavioral Decision Making* (see Exercise 1.32, p. 52). A total of 171 volunteer students participated in the experiment, where each was randomly assigned to one of three emotional states (guilt, anger, or neutral) through a reading/writing task. Immediately after the task, students were presented with a decision problem where the stated option had predominantly negative features (e.g., spending money on repairing a very old car). The results (number responding in each category) are summarized in the accompanying table. Suppose one of the 171 participants is selected at random.

Emotional State	Choose Stated Option	Do Not Choose Stated Option	Totals
Guilt	45	12	57
Anger	8	50	58
Neutral	7	49	56
Totals	60	111	171

Source: Based on A. Gangemi and F. Mancini, "Guilt and Focusing in Decision-Making," *Journal of Behavioral Decision Making*, Vol. 20, January. 2007 (Table 2).

a. Find the probability that the respondent is assigned to the guilty state.

b. Find the probability that the respondent chooses the stated option (repair the car).

c. Find the probability that the respondent is assigned to the guilty state and chooses the stated option.

d. Find the probability that the respondent is assigned to the guilty state or chooses the stated option.

3.49 **Likelihood of a tax return audit.** At the beginning of each year, the Internal Revenue Service (IRS) releases information on the likelihood of a tax return being audited. In 2013, the IRS audited 1,242,479 individual tax returns from the total of 145,236,429 filed returns; also, the IRS audited 25,905 returns from the total of 1,924,887 corporation returns filed (*IRS 2014 Data Book*).

a. Suppose an individual tax return is randomly selected. What is the probability that the return was audited by the IRS?

b. Refer to part **a.** Determine the probability that an individual return was not audited by the IRS.

c. Suppose a corporation tax return is randomly selected. What is the probability that the return was audited by the IRS?

d. Refer to part **c.** Determine the probability that a corporation return was not audited by the IRS.

Applying the Concepts—Advanced

3.50 **Galileo's Passedix game.** Passedix is a game of chance played with three fair dice. Players bet whether the sum of the faces shown on the dice will be above or below 10. During the late 16th century, the astronomer and mathematician Galileo Galilei was asked by the Grand Duke of Tuscany to explain why "the chance of throwing a total of 9 with three fair dice was less than that of throwing a total of 10" (*Interstat*, January 2004). The grand duke believed that the chance should be the same because "there are an equal number of partitions of the numbers 9 and 10." Find the flaw in the grand duke's reasoning and answer the question posed to Galileo.

3.51 **Encoding variability in software.** At the 2012 *Gulf Petrochemicals and Chemicals Association (GPCA) Forum,* Oregon State University software engineers presented a paper on modeling and implementing variation in computer software. The researchers employed the compositional choice calculus (CCC)—a formal language for representing, generating, and organizing variation in tree-structured artifacts. The CCC language was compared to two other coding languages—the annotative choice calculus (ACC) and the computational feature algebra (CFA). Their research revealed the following: Any type of expression (e.g., plain expressions, dimension declarations, or lambda abstractions) found in either ACC or CFA can be found in CCC; plain expressions exist in both ACC and CFA; dimension declarations exist in ACC, but not CFA; lambda abstractions exist in CFA, but not ACC. Based on this information, draw a Venn diagram that illustrates the relationships among the three languages. (*Hint:* An expression represents a sample point in the Venn diagram.)

3.5 Conditional Probability

The event probabilities we've been discussing give the relative frequencies of the occurrences of the events when the experiment is repeated a very large number of times. Such probabilities are often called **unconditional probabilities** because no special conditions are assumed, other than those that define the experiment.

Often, however, we have additional knowledge that might affect the likelihood of the outcome of an experiment, so we need to alter the probability of an event of interest. A probability that reflects such additional knowledge is called the **conditional probability** of the event. For example, we've seen that the probability of observing an even number (event A) on a toss of a fair die is $\frac{1}{2}$. But suppose we're given the information that on a particular throw of the die, the result was a number less than or equal to 3 (event B). Would the probability of observing an even number on that throw of the die still be equal to $\frac{1}{2}$? It can't be because making the assumption that B has occurred reduces the sample space from six sample points to three sample points (namely, those contained in event B). This reduced sample space is as shown in Figure 3.14.

Because the sample points for the die-toss experiment are equally likely, each of the three sample points in the reduced sample space is assigned an equal *conditional probability* of $\frac{1}{3}$. Because the only even number of the three in the reduced sample space B is the number 2 and the die is fair, we conclude that the probability that A occurs *given that B occurs* is $\frac{1}{3}$. We use the symbol $P(A|B)$ to represent the probability of event A given that event B occurs. For the die-toss example, $P(A|B) = \frac{1}{3}$.

To get the probability of event A given that event B occurs, we proceed as follows: We divide the probability of the part of A that falls within the reduced sample space B, namely, $P(A \cap B)$, by the total probability of the reduced sample space, namely, $P(B)$. Thus, for the die-toss example with event A: {Observe an even number} and event B: {Observe a number less than or equal to 3}, we find

$$P(A|B) = \frac{P(A \cap B)}{P(B)} = \frac{P(2)}{P(1) + P(2) + P(3)} = \frac{\frac{1}{6}}{\frac{3}{6}} = \frac{1}{3}$$

The formula for $P(A|B)$ is true in general:

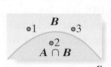

Figure 3.14

Reduced sample space for the die-toss experiment given that event B has occurred

---

Conditional Probability Formula

To find the *conditional probability that event A occurs given that event B occurs*, divide the probability that *both* A and B occur by the probability that B occurs–that is,

$$P(A|B) = \frac{P(A \cap B)}{P(B)} \quad \text{[We assume that } P(B) \neq 0.\text{]}$$

This formula adjusts the probability of $A \cap B$ from its original value in the complete sample space S to a conditional probability in the reduced sample space B. If the sample points in the complete sample space are equally likely, then the formula will assign equal probabilities to the sample points in the reduced sample space, as in the die-toss experiment. If, on the other hand, the sample points have unequal probabilities, the formula will assign conditional probabilities proportional to the probabilities in the complete sample space. This is illustrated by the following practical examples.

EXAMPLE 3.14

The Conditional Probability Formula—Executives Who Cheat at Golf

Problem To develop programs for business travelers staying at convention hotels, a major hotel chain commissioned a study of executives who play golf. The study revealed that 55% of the executives admitted they had cheated at golf. Also, 20% of the executives admitted they had cheated at golf and had lied in business. Given an executive who had cheated at golf, what is the probability that the executive also had lied in business?

Solution Let's define events A and B as follows:

$$A = \{\text{Executive who had cheated at golf}\}$$
$$B = \{\text{Executive who had lied in business}\}$$

From the study, we know that 55% of executives had cheated at golf, so $P(A) = .55$. Now, executives who both cheat at golf (event A) *and* lie in business (event B) represent the compound event $A \cap B$. From the study, $P(A \cap B) = .20$. We want to know the probability that an executive lied in business (event B), given that he or she cheated at golf (event A)–that is, we want to know the conditional probability $P(A|B)$. Applying the preceding conditional probability formula, we have

$$P(B|A) = \frac{P(A \cap B)}{P(A)} = \frac{.20}{.55} = .364$$

Thus, given an executive who had cheated at golf, the probability that the executive also had lied in business is .364.

Look Back One of the keys to correctly applying the formula is to write the information in the study in the form of probability statements involving the events of interest. The word *and* in the statement "cheat at golf *and* lie in business" implies an intersection of the two events, A and B. The word *given* in the phrase "*given* an executive who cheats at golf" implies that event A is the given event.

● **Now Work Exercise 3.60b**

EXAMPLE 3.15

Applying the Conditional Probability Formula to a Two-Way Table— Customer Desire to Buy

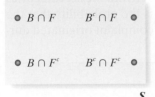

Figure 3.15

Sample space for contacting a sales prospect

Problem Suppose you are interested in the probability of the sale of a large piece of earthmoving equipment. A single prospect is contacted. Let F be the event that the buyer has sufficient money (or credit) to buy the product and let F^c denote the complement of F (the event that the prospect does not have the financial capability to buy the product). Similarly, let B be the event that the buyer wishes to buy the product and let B^c be the complement of that event. Then the four sample points associated with the experiment are shown in Figure 3.15, and their probabilities are given in Table 3.5. Use the sample point probabilities to find the probability that a single prospect will buy, given that the prospect is able to finance the purchase.

Table 3.5	Probabilities of Customer Desire to Buy and Ability to Finance	
	Desire	
	To Buy, B	Not to Buy, B^c
Able to Finance Yes, F	.2	.1
No, F^c	.4	.3

Solution Suppose you consider the large collection of prospects for the sale of your product and randomly select one person from this collection. What is the probability that the person selected will buy the product? In order to buy the product, the customer must be financially able *and* have the desire to buy, so this probability would correspond to the entry in Table 3.5 {To buy, B} and next to {Yes, F}, or $P(B \cap F) = .2$. This is the unconditional probability of the event $B \cap F$.

In contrast, suppose you know that the prospect selected has the financial capability for purchasing the product. Now you are seeking the probability that the customer will buy given (the condition) that the customer has the financial ability to pay. This probability, the conditional probability of B given that F has occurred and denoted by the symbol $P(B|F)$, would be determined by considering only the sample points in the reduced sample space containing the sample points $B \cap F$ and $B^c \cap F$–that is, sample points that imply the prospect is financially able to buy. (This reduced sample space is shaded in Figure 3.16.) From our definition of conditional probability,

$$P(B|F) = \frac{P(B \cap F)}{P(F)}$$

where $P(F)$ is the sum of the probabilities of the two sample points corresponding to $B \cap F$ and $B^c \cap F$ (given in Table 3.5). Then

$$P(F) = P(B \cap F) + P(B^c \cap F) = .2 + .1 = .3$$

and the conditional probability that a prospect buys, given that the prospect is financially able, is

$$P(B|F) = \frac{P(B \cap F)}{P(F)} = \frac{.2}{.3} = .667$$

As we would expect, the probability that the prospect will buy, given that he or she is financially able, is higher than the unconditional probability of selecting a prospect who will buy.

Look Back Note that the conditional probability formula assigns a probability to the event $(B \cap F)$ in the reduced sample space that is proportional to the probability of the event in the complete sample space. To see this, note that the two sample points in the reduced sample space, $(B \cap F)$ and $(B^c \cap F)$, have probabilities of .2 and .1, respectively, in the complete sample space S. The formula assigns conditional probabilities $\frac{2}{3}$ and $\frac{1}{3}$ (use the formula to check the second one) to these sample points in the reduced sample space F so that the conditional probabilities retain the 2-to-1 proportionality of the original sample point probabilities.

● **Now Work Exercise 3.53a–b**

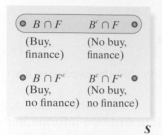

Figure 3.16
Reduced sample space (shaded) containing sample points implying a financially able prospect

---

EXAMPLE 3.16

Applying the Conditional Probability Formula to a Two-Way Table— Customer Complaints

Problem The investigation of consumer product complaints by the Federal Trade Commission (FTC) has generated much interest by manufacturers in the quality of their products. A manufacturer of an electromechanical kitchen utensil conducted an analysis of a large number of consumer complaints and found that they fell into the six categories shown in Table 3.6. If a consumer complaint is received, what is the probability that the cause of the complaint was product appearance given that the complaint originated during the guarantee period?

Table 3.6	Distribution of Product Complaints			
		Reason for Complaint		
Complaint Origin	Electrical	Mechanical	Appearance	Totals
During Guarantee Period	18%	13%	32%	63%
After Guarantee Period	12%	22%	3%	37%
Totals	30%	35%	35%	100%

Solution Let A represent the event that the cause of a particular complaint is product appearance and let B represent the event that the complaint occurred during the guarantee period. Checking Table 3.6, you can see that $(18 + 13 + 32)\% = 63\%$ of the complaints occur during the guarantee period. Hence, $P(B) = .63$. The percentage of complaints that were caused by appearance and occurred during the guarantee period (the event $A \cap B$) is 32%. Therefore, $P(A \cap B) = .32$

Using these probability values, we can calculate the conditional probability $P(A|B)$ that the cause of a complaint is appearance, given that the complaint occurred during the guarantee time:

$$P(A|B) = \frac{P(A \cap B)}{P(B)} = \frac{.32}{.63} = .51$$

Consequently, we can see that slightly more than half the complaints that occurred during the guarantee period were due to scratches, dents, or other imperfections in the surface of the kitchen devices.

Look Back Note that the answer, $\frac{.32}{.63}$, is the proportion for the event of interest A (.32) divided by the row total proportion for the given event B (.63)—that is, it is the proportion of the time A occurs within the given event B.

● **Now Work Exercise 3.62**

3.6 The Multiplicative Rule and Independent Events

The probability of an intersection of two events can be calculated using the multiplicative rule, which employs the conditional probabilities we defined in the previous section. Actually, we have already developed the formula in another context (Section 3.5). You will recall that the formula for calculating the conditional probability of A given B is

$$P(A|B) = \frac{P(A \cap B)}{P(B)}$$

Multiplying both sides of this equation by $P(B)$, we obtain a formula for the probability of the intersection of events A and B. This is often called the **multiplicative rule of probability**.

Multiplicative Rule of Probability

$$P(A \cap B) = P(A)P(B|A) \text{ or, equivalently, } P(A \cap B) = P(B)P(A|B)$$

EXAMPLE 3.17	**Problem** An investor in wheat futures is concerned with the following events:

Applying the Multiplicative Rule— Wheat Futures

B: {U.S. production of wheat will be profitable next year.}

A: {A serious drought will occur next year.}

Based on available information, the investor believes that the probability is .01 that production of wheat will be profitable *assuming* a serious drought will occur in the same year and that the probability is .05 that a serious drought will occur—that is,

$$P(B|A) = .01 \text{ and } P(A) = .05$$

Based on the information provided, what is the probability that a serious drought will occur and that a profit will be made? That is, find $P(A \cap B)$, the probability of the intersection of events A and B.

Solution We want to calculate $P(A \cap B)$. Using the formula for the multiplicative rule, we obtain

$$P(A \cap B) = P(A)P(B|A) = (.05)(.01) = .0005$$

The probability that a serious drought occurs and the production of wheat is profitable is only .0005. As we might expect, this intersection is a very rare event.

Look Back The multiplicative rule can be expressed in two ways: $P(A \cap B) = P(A) \cdot P(B|A)$ or $P(A \cap B) = P(B) \cdot P(A|B)$. Select the formula that involves a given event for which you know the probability (e.g., event B in the example).

● **Now Work Exercise 3.65**

Intersections often contain only a few sample points. In this case, the probability of an intersection is easy to calculate by summing the appropriate sample point probabilities. However, the formula for calculating intersection probabilities is invaluable when the intersection contains numerous sample points, as the next example illustrates.

EXAMPLE 3.18

Applying the Multiplicative Rule— Study of Welfare Workers

Problem A county welfare agency employs 10 welfare workers who interview prospective food stamp recipients. Periodically the supervisor selects, at random, the forms completed by 2 workers to audit for illegal deductions. Unknown to the supervisor, 3 of the workers have regularly been giving illegal deductions to applicants. What is the probability that both of the 2 workers chosen have been giving illegal deductions?

Solution Define the following two events:

$A:$ {First worker selected gives illegal deductions.}
$B:$ {Second worker selected gives illegal deductions.}

We want to find the probability of the event that both selected workers have been giving illegal deductions. This event can be restated as {First worker gives illegal deductions *and* second worker gives illegal deductions}. Thus, we want to find the probability of the intersection, $A \cap B$. Applying the multiplicative rule, we have

$$P(A \cap B) = P(A)P(B|A)$$

To find $P(A)$, it is helpful to consider the experiment as selecting 1 worker from the 10. Then the sample space for the experiment contains 10 sample points (representing the 10 welfare workers), where the 3 workers giving illegal deductions are denoted by the symbol I (I_1, I_2, I_3), and the 7 workers not giving illegal deductions are denoted by the symbol N ($N_1, \ldots, N_7$). The resulting Venn diagram is illustrated in Figure 3.17.

Because the first worker is selected at random from the 10, it is reasonable to assign equal probabilities to the 10 sample points. Thus, each sample point has a probability of $\frac{1}{10}$. The sample points in event A are {$I_1, I_2, I_3,$}—the 3 workers who are giving illegal deductions. Thus,

$$P(A) = P(I_1) + P(I_2) + P(I_3) = \tfrac{1}{10} + \tfrac{1}{10} + \tfrac{1}{10} = \tfrac{3}{10}$$

To find the conditional probability, $P(B|A)$, we need to alter the sample space S. Because we know A has occurred [the first worker selected is giving illegal deductions (say I_3)], only 2 of the 9 remaining workers in the sample space are giving illegal deductions. The Venn diagram for this new sample space (S') is shown in Figure 3.18. Each of these nine sample points is equally likely, so each is assigned a probability of $\frac{1}{9}$. Because the event ($B|A$) contains the sample points {I_1, I_2}, we have

$$P(B|A) = P(I_1) + P(I_2) = \tfrac{1}{9} + \tfrac{1}{9} = \tfrac{2}{9}$$

Substituting $P(A) = \frac{3}{10}$ and $P(B|A) = \frac{2}{9}$ into the formula for the multiplicative rule, we find

$$P(A \cap B) = P(A)P(B|A) = \left(\tfrac{3}{10}\right)\left(\tfrac{2}{90}\right) = \tfrac{6}{90} = \tfrac{1}{15}$$

Thus, there is a 1 in 15 chance that both workers chosen by the supervisor have been giving illegal deductions to food stamp recipients.

Look Back The key words *both* and *and* in the statement "both A and B occur" imply an intersection of two events, which in turn implies that we should *multiply* probabilities to obtain the probability of interest.

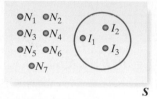

Figure 3.17
Venn diagram for finding $P(A)$

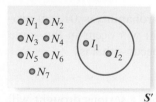

Figure 3.18
Venn diagram for finding $P(B|A)$

● **Now Work Exercise 3.57c**

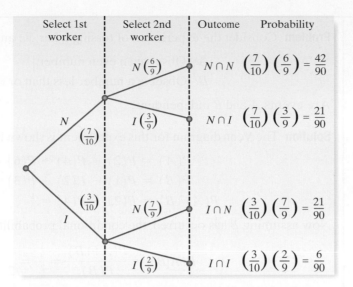

Figure 3.19

Tree diagram for Example 3.18

The sample space approach is only one way to solve the problem posed in Example 3.18. An alternative method employs the tree diagram (introduced in Example 3.1). Tree diagrams are helpful for calculating the probability of an intersection.

To illustrate, a tree diagram for Example 3.18 is displayed in Figure 3.19. The tree begins at the far left with two branches. These branches represent the two possible outcomes N (no illegal deductions) and I (illegal deductions) for the first worker selected. The unconditional probability of each outcome is given (in parentheses) on the appropriate branch—that is, for the first worker selected, $P(N) = \frac{7}{10}$ and $P(I) = \frac{3}{10}$. (These can be obtained by summing sample point probabilities as in Example 3.18.)

The next level of the tree diagram (moving to the right) represents the outcomes for the second worker selected. The probabilities shown here are conditional probabilities because the outcome for the first worker is assumed to be known. For example, if the first worker is giving illegal deductions (I), the probability that the second worker is also giving illegal deductions (I) is $\frac{2}{9}$ because of the 9 workers left to be selected, only 2 remain who are giving illegal deductions. This conditional probability, $\frac{2}{9}$, is shown in parentheses on the bottom branch of Figure 3.19.

Finally, the four possible outcomes of the experiment are shown at the end of each of the four tree branches. These events are intersections of two events (outcome of first worker and outcome of second worker). Consequently, the multiplicative rule is applied to calculate each probability, as shown in Figure 3.19. You can see that the intersection $\{I \cap I\}$ (i.e., the event that both workers selected are giving illegal deductions) has probability $\frac{6}{90} = \frac{1}{15}$—the same value obtained in Example 3.18.

In Section 3.5 we showed that the probability of an event A may be substantially altered by the knowledge that an event B has occurred. However, this will not always be the case. In some instances, the assumption that event B has occurred will *not* alter the probability of event A at all. When this is true, we say that the two events A and B are *independent events.*

Events A and B are **independent events** if the occurrence of B does not alter the probability that A has occurred; that is, events A and B are independent if

$$P(A|B) = P(A)$$

When events A and B are independent, it is also true that

$$P(B|A) = P(B)$$

Events that are not independent are said to be **dependent.**

EXAMPLE 3.19

Checking for Independence—Die-Tossing Experiment

Problem Consider the experiment of tossing a fair die and let

$$A: \{\text{Observe an even number.}\}$$
$$B: \{\text{Observe a number less than or equal to 4.}\}$$

Are events A and B independent?

Solution The Venn diagram for this experiment is shown in Figure 3.20. We first calculate

$$P(A) = P(2) + P(4) + P(6) = \tfrac{1}{2}$$
$$P(B) = P(1) + P(2) + P(3) + P(4) = \tfrac{2}{3}$$
$$P(A \cap B) = P(2) + P(4) = \tfrac{1}{3}$$

Now assuming B has occurred, the conditional probability of A given B is

$$P(A|B) = \frac{P(A \cap B)}{P(B)} = \frac{\tfrac{1}{3}}{\tfrac{2}{3}} = \frac{1}{2} = P(A)$$

Thus, assuming that event B occurring does not alter the probability of observing an even number, $P(A)$ remains $\tfrac{1}{2}$. Therefore, the events A and B are independent.

Look Back Note that if we calculate the conditional probability of B given A, our conclusion is the same:

$$P(B|A) = \frac{P(A \cap B)}{P(A)} = \frac{\tfrac{1}{3}}{\tfrac{1}{2}} = \frac{2}{3} = P(B)$$

• **Now Work Exercise 3.60c**

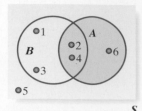

Figure 3.20
Venn diagram for die-toss experiment

BIOGRAPHY

BLAISE PASCAL (1623–1662)
Solver of Chevalier's Dilemma

As a precocious child growing up in France, Blaise Pascal showed an early inclination toward mathematics. Although his father would not permit Pascal to study mathematics before the age of 15 (removing all math texts from his house), at age 12 Pascal discovered on his own that the sum of the angles of a triangle are two right angles.

Pascal went on to become a distinguished mathematician, as well as a physicist, theologian, and the inventor of the first digital calculator. Most historians attribute the beginning of the study of probability to the correspondence between Pascal and Pierre de Fermat in 1654. The two solved the Chevalier's dilemma—a gambling problem related to Pascal by his friend and Paris gambler the Chevalier de Mere. The problem involved determining the expected number of times one could roll two dice without throwing a double 6. (Pascal proved that the breakeven point is 25 rolls.)

EXAMPLE 3.20

Checking for Independence—Consumer Product Complaint Study

Problem Refer to the consumer product complaint study in Example 3.16. The percentages of complaints of various types during and after the guarantee period are shown in Table 3.6. Define the following events:

$$A: \{\text{Cause of complaint is product appearance.}\}$$
$$B: \{\text{Complaint occurred during the guarantee term.}\}$$

Are A and B independent events?

Solution Events A and B are independent if $P(A|B) = P(A)$. We calculated $P(A|B)$ in Example 3.16 to be .51, and from Table 3.6 we see that

$$P(A) = .32 + .03 = .35$$

Therefore, $P(A|B)$ is not equal to $P(A)$, and A and B are dependent events.

• **Now Work Exercise 3.53c**

To gain an intuitive understanding of independence, think of situations in which the occurrence of one event does not alter the probability that a second event will occur. For example, suppose two small companies are being monitored by a financier for possible investment. If the businesses are in different industries and they are otherwise unrelated, then the success or failure of one company may be *independent* of the success or failure of the other—that is, the event that company A fails may not alter the probability that company B will fail.

As a second example, consider an election poll in which 1,000 registered voters are asked their preference between two candidates. Pollsters try to use procedures for selecting a sample of voters so that the responses are independent—that is, the objective of the pollster is to select the sample so the event that one polled voter prefers candidate A does not alter the probability that a second polled voter prefers candidate A.

We will make three final points about independence. The first is that the property of independence, unlike the mutually exclusive property, cannot be shown on or gleaned from a Venn diagram. This means *you can't trust your intuition*. In general, the only way to check for independence is by performing the calculations of the probabilities in the definition.

The second point concerns the relationship between the mutually exclusive and independence properties. Suppose that events A and B are mutually exclusive, as shown in Figure 3.21, and both events have nonzero probabilities. Are these events independent or dependent? That is, does the assumption that B occurs alter the probability of the occurrence of A? It certainly does, because if we assume that B has occurred, it is impossible for A to have occurred simultaneously—that is, $P(A|B) = 0$. Thus, *mutually exclusive events are dependent events* because $P(A) \neq P(A|B)$.

The third point is that the probability of the intersection of independent events is very easy to calculate. Referring to the formula for calculating the probability of an intersection, we find

$$P(A \cap B) = P(A)P(B|A)$$

Thus, because $P(B|A) = P(B)$ when A and B are independent, we have the following useful rule:

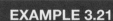

Figure 3.21
Mutually exclusive events
are dependent events

Probability of Intersection of Two Independent Events

If events A and B are independent, the probability of the intersection of A and B equals the product of the probabilities of A and B; that is,

$$P(A \cap B) = P(A)P(B)$$

The converse is also true: If $P(A \cap B) = P(A)P(B)$, then events A and B are independent.

In the die-toss experiment, we showed in Example 3.19 that the events A: {Observe an even number} and B: {Observe a number less than or equal to 4} are independent if the die is fair. Thus,

$$P(A \cap B) = P(A)P(B) = \left(\tfrac{1}{2}\right)\left(\tfrac{2}{3}\right) = \tfrac{1}{3}$$

This agrees with the result that we obtained in the example:

$$P(A \cap B) = P(2) + P(4) = \tfrac{2}{6} = \tfrac{1}{3}$$

EXAMPLE 3.21	
Probability of Independent Events Occurring Simultaneously— Diversity Training Study	**Problem** Refer to Example 3.5 (pp. 164–165). Recall that *USA Today* found that of all U.S. firms that use diversity training, 38% state that their primary reason for using it is to stay competitive. **a.** What is the probability that in a sample of two firms that use diversity training, both primarily use it to stay competitive? **b.** What is the probability that in a sample of 10 firms that use diversity training, all 10 primarily use it to stay competitive?

Solution

a. Let C_1 represent the event that firm 1 gives "stay competitive" as the primary reason for using diversity training. Define C_2 similarly for firm 2. The event that *both* firms give "stay competitive" as their primary reason is the intersection of the two events, $C_1 \cap C_2$. Based on the survey that found that 38% of U.S. firms use diversity training to stay competitive, we could reasonably conclude that $P(C_1) = .38$ and $P(C_2) = .38$. However, in order to compute the probability of $C_1 \cap C_2$ from the multiplicative rule, we must make the assumption that the two events are independent. Because the classification of any firm using diversity training is not likely to affect the classification of another firm, this assumption is reasonable. Assuming independence, we have

$$P(C_1 \cap C_2) = P(C_1)P(C_2) = (.38)(.38) = .1444$$

b. To see how to compute the probability that 10 of 10 firms will give "stay competitive" as their primary reason, first consider the event that 3 of 3 firms give "stay competitive" as the primary reason. Using the notation defined earlier, we want to compute the probability of the intersection $C_1 \cap C_2 \cap C_3$. Again assuming independence of the classifications, we have

$$P(C_1 \cap C_2 \cap C_3) = P(C_1)P(C_2)P(C_3) = (.38)(.38)(.38) = .054872$$

Similar reasoning leads us to the conclusion that the intersection of 10 such events can be calculated as follows:

$$P(C_1 \cap C_2 \cap C_3 \cap \cdots \cap C_{10}) = P(C_1)P(C_2) \cdots P(C_{10}) = (.38)^{10} = .0000628$$

Thus, the probability that 10 of 10 firms all give "stay competitive" as their primary reason for using diversity training is about 63 in 1 million, assuming the events (stated reasons for using diversity training) are independent.

Look Back The very small probability in part **b** makes it extremely unlikely that 10 of 10 firms would give "stay competitive" as their primary reason for diversity training. If this event should actually occur, we would need to reassess our estimate of the probability of .38 used in the calculation. If all 10 firms' reason is staying competitive, then the probability that any one firm gives staying competitive as their reason is much higher than .38. (This conclusion is another application of the rare event approach to statistical inference.)

● **Now Work Exercise 3.74d**

STATISTICS IN ACTION

The Probability of Winning Cash 3 or Play 4

REVISITED   In addition to biweekly Lotto 6/53, the Florida Lottery runs several other games. Two popular daily games are "Cash 3" and "Play 4." In Cash 3, players pay $1 to select three numbers in sequential order, where each number ranges from 0 to 9. If the three numbers selected (e.g., 2-8-4) match exactly the order of the three numbers drawn, the player wins $500. Play 4 is similar to Cash 3, but players must match four numbers (each number ranging from 0 to 9). For a $1 Play 4 ticket (e.g., 3-8-3-0), the player will win $5,000 if the numbers match the order of the four numbers drawn.

During the official drawing for Cash 3, 10 Ping-Pong balls numbered 0, 1, 2, 3, 4, 5, 6, 7, 8, and 9 are placed into each of three chambers. The balls in the first chamber are colored pink, the balls in the second chamber are blue, and the balls in the third chamber are yellow. One ball of each color is randomly drawn, with the official order as pink-blue-yellow. In Play 4, a fourth chamber with orange balls is added, and the official order is pink-blue-yellow-orange. Because the draws of the colored balls are random and independent, we can apply an extension of the rule for the Probability of Intersection of

STATISTICS IN ACTION

REVISITED
(continued)

Two Independent Events to find the odds of winning Cash 3 and Play 4. The probability of matching a numbered ball being drawn from a chamber is $\frac{1}{10}$; therefore,

$$P(\text{Win Cash 3}) = P(\text{match pink}) \text{ AND } (\text{match blue}) \text{ AND } (\text{match yellow})$$
$$= P(\text{match pink}) \times P(\text{match blue}) \times P(\text{match yellow})$$
$$= \left(\tfrac{1}{10}\right)\left(\tfrac{1}{10}\right)\left(\tfrac{1}{10}\right) = \tfrac{1}{1000} = .001$$

$$P(\text{Win Play 4}) = P(\text{match pink AND match blue}$$
$$\text{AND match yellow AND match orange})$$
$$= P(\text{match pink}) \times P(\text{match blue}) \times$$
$$P(\text{match yellow}) \times P(\text{match orange})$$
$$= \left(\tfrac{1}{10}\right)\left(\tfrac{1}{10}\right)\left(\tfrac{1}{10}\right)\left(\tfrac{1}{10}\right)$$
$$= \tfrac{1}{10,000} = .0001$$

Although the odds of winning one of these daily games is much better than the odds of winning Lotto $\frac{6}{53}$, there is still only a 1 in 1,000 chance (for Cash 3) or a 1 in 10,000 chance (for Play 4) of winning the daily game. And the payoffs ($500 or $5,000) are much smaller. In fact, it can be shown that you will lose an average of 50¢ every time you play either Cash 3 or Play 4!

Exercises 3.52–3.80

Learning the Mechanics

3.52 For two events, A and B, $P(A) = .4$, $P(B) = .2$, and $P(A|B) = .6$:
  a. Find $P(A \cap B)$.
  b. Find $P(B|A)$.

3.53 For two events, A and B, $P(A) = .4$, $P(B) = .2$, and
NW $P(A \cap B) = .1$:
  a. Find $P(A|B)$.
  b. Find $P(B|A)$.
  c. Are A and B independent events?

3.54 An experiment results in one of three mutually exclusive events, $A, B,$ or C. It is known that $P(A) = .30, P(B) = .55$, and $P(C) = .15$. Find each of the following probabilities:
  a. $P(A \cup B)$
  b. $P(A \cap C)$
  c. $P(A|B)$
  d. $P(B \cup C)$
  e. Are B and C independent events? Explain.

3.55 For two independent events, A and B, $P(A) = .4$ and $P(B) = .2$:
  a. Find $P(A \cap B)$
  b. Find $P(A|B)$.
  c. Find $P(A \cup B)$

3.56 Two fair coins are tossed, and the following events are defined:

    A: [Observe one head and one tail.]
    B: [Observe at least one head.]

  a. Define the possible sample points and assign probabilities to each.
  b. Draw a Venn diagram for the experiment, showing the sample points and events A and B.
  c. Find $P(A), P(B),$ and $P(A \cap B)$.
  d. Use the formula for conditional probability to find $P(A|B)$ and $P(B|A)$. Verify your answer by inspecting the Venn diagram and using the concept of reduced sample spaces.

3.57 Consider the experiment depicted by the Venn diagram, with the sample space S containing five sample points. The sample points are assigned the following probabilities: $P(E_1) = .20$, $P(E_2) = .30, P(E_3) = .30, P(E_4) = .10, P(E_5) = .10$.

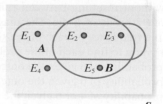

S

  a. Calculate $P(A), P(B),$ and $P(A \cap B)$
  b. Suppose we know that event A has occurred, so that the reduced sample space consists of the three sample points in A—namely, $E_1, E_2,$ and E_3. Use the formula for conditional probability to adjust the probabilities of these three sample points for the knowledge that A has occurred [i.e., $P(E_i|A)$]. Verify that the conditional probabilities are in the same proportion to one another as the original sample point probabilities.
NW   **c.** Calculate the conditional probability $P(B|A)$ in two ways: (1) Add the adjusted (conditional) probabilities of the sample points in the intersection $A \cap B$, as these represent the event that B occurs given that A has occurred; (2) use the formula for conditional probability:

$$P(B|A) = \frac{P(A \cap B)}{P(A)}$$

    Verify that the two methods yield the same result.
  d. Are events A and B independent? Why or why not?

3.58 Two fair dice are tossed, and the following events are defined:

> *A:* {Sum of the numbers showing is odd.}
> *B:* {Sum of the numbers showing is 9, 11, or 12.}

Are events *A* and *B* independent? Why?

3.59 A sample space contains six sample points and events *A, B,* and *C* as shown in the Venn diagram. The probabilities of the sample points are

$$P(1) = .20, P(2) = .05, P(3) = .30, P(4) = .10,$$
$$P(5) = .10, P(6) = .25.$$

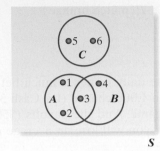

S

a. Which pairs of events, if any, are mutually exclusive? Why?

b. Which pairs of events, if any, are independent? Why?

c. Find $P(A \cup B)$ by adding the probabilities of the sample points and then by using the additive rule. Verify that the answers agree. Repeat for $P(A \cup C)$

📊 Applet Exercise 3.5

Use the applet *Simulating the Probability of Rolling a 6* to simulate conditional probabilities. Begin by running the applet twice with *n* = 10 without resetting between runs. The data on your screen represent 20 rolls of a die. The diagram above the *Roll* button shows the frequency of each of the six possible outcomes. Use this information to find each of the probabilities.

a. The probability of 6 given the outcome is 5 or 6
b. The probability of 6 given the outcome is even
c. The probability of 4 or 6 given the outcome is even
d. The probability of 4 or 6 given the outcome is odd

Applying the Concepts—Basic

3.60 **On-the-job arrogance and task performance.** *Human Performance* (Vol. 23, 2010) published the results of a study that found that arrogant workers are more likely to have poor performance ratings. Suppose that 15% of all full-time workers exhibit arrogant behaviors on the job and that 10% of all full-time workers will receive a poor performance rating. Also, assume that 5% of all full-time workers exhibit arrogant behaviors and receive a poor performance rating. Let *A* be the event that a full-time worker exhibits arrogant behavior on the job. Let *B* be the event that a full-time worker will receive a poor performance rating.

a. Are the events *A* and *B* mutually exclusive? Explain.
b. Find $P(B|A)$.
c. Are the events *A* and *B* independent? Explain.

3.61 **World's largest public companies.** *Forbes* (May 6, 2015) conducted a survey of the 20 largest public companies in

the world. Of these 20 companies, 4 were banking or investment companies based in the United States. A total of 9 U.S. companies were on the top 20 list. Suppose we select one of these 20 companies at random. Given that the company is based in the United States, what is the probability that it is a banking or investment company?

3.62 **Guilt in decision making.** Refer to the *Journal of Behavioral Decision Making* (January 2007) study of the effect of guilt emotion on how a decision maker focuses on a problem, Exercise 3.48 (p. 183). The results (number responding in each category) for the 171 study participants are reproduced in the table below. Suppose one of the 171 participants is selected at random.

Emotional State	Choose Stated Option	Do Not Choose Stated Option	Totals
Guilt	45	12	57
Anger	8	50	58
Neutral	7	49	56
Totals	60	111	171

Source: Based on A. Gangemi and F. Mancini, "Guilt and Focusing in Decision-Making," *Journal of Behavioral Decision Making*, Vol. 20, January 2007 (Table 2).

a. Given that the respondent is assigned to the guilty state, what is the probability that the respondent chooses the stated option?

b. If the respondent does not choose to repair the car, what is the probability that the respondent is in the anger state?

c. Are the events {repair the car} and {guilty state} independent?

3.63 **Blood diamonds.** According to *Global Research News* (March 4, 2014), one-fourth of all rough diamonds produced in the world are *blood diamonds.* (Any diamond that is mined in a war zone—often by children—to finance a warlord's activity, an insurgency, or an invading army's effort is considered a blood diamond.) Also, 90% of the world's rough diamonds are processed in Surat, India, and, of these diamonds one-third are blood diamonds.

a. Find the probability that a rough diamond is not a blood diamond.

b. Find the probability that a rough diamond is processed in Surat and is a blood diamond.

3.64 **Do social robots walk or roll?** Refer to the *International Conference on Social Robotics* (Vol. 6414, 2010) study of the trend in the design of social robots, Exercises 3.10 (p. 168) and 3.37 (p. 181). Recall that in a random sample of 106 social robots, 63 were built with legs only, 20 with wheels only, 8 with both legs and wheels, and 15 with neither legs nor wheels. If a social robot is designed with wheels, what is the probability that the robot also has legs?

3.65 **Shopping with a smartphone.** Each year, United Parcel Service (UPS) commissions a "Pulse of the Online Shopper" survey. The 2015 survey included a sample of 5,118 U.S. shoppers who have made at least two online purchases every three months. The survey revealed that 41% of the shoppers used a smartphone to make a purchase. Of those who made a smartphone purchase, 38% indicated that they preferred the mobile Web site to the full Web site accessed through a computer. Assume these percentages represent actual probabilities for the population of online shoppers. What is the probability that a randomly selected online shopper uses a smartphone to make a purchase and prefers the mobile Web site?

3.66 Identity theft victims. According to *The National Crime Victimization Survey* (September 2015), published by the U.S. Department of Justice, about 17.6 million people were victims of identity theft over the past year. This number represents 7% of all persons age 16 or older in the United States. Of these victims, 86% reported that the identity theft occurred from the unauthorized use of a credit card. Consider a randomly selected person of age 16 or older in the United States.

a. What is the probability that this person was a victim of identity theft?

b. What is the probability that this person was a victim of identity theft that occurred from the unauthorized use of a credit card?

3.67 Study of why EMS workers leave the job. Refer to the *Journal of Allied Health* (Fall 2011) study of why emergency medical service (EMS) workers leave the profession, Exercise 3.45 (p. 182). Recall that in a sample of 244 former EMS workers, 127 were fully compensated while on the job, 45 were partially compensated, and 72 had noncompensated volunteer positions. Also, the numbers of EMS workers who left because of retirement were 7 for fully compensated workers, 11 for partially compensated workers, and 10 for noncompensated volunteers.

a. Given that the former EMS worker was fully compensated while on the job, estimate the probability that the worker left the EMS profession due to retirement.

b. Given that the former EMS worker had a noncompensated volunteer position, estimate the probability that the worker left the EMS profession due to retirement.

c. Are the events {a former EMS worker was fully compensated on the job} and {a former EMS worker left the job due to retirement} independent? Explain.

Applying the Concepts–Intermediate

3.68 Working on summer vacation. Refer to the *Harris Interactive* (July 2013) poll of whether U.S. adults work during summer vacation, Exercise 3.13 (p. 169). Recall that the poll found that 61% of the respondents work during their summer vacation, 22% do not work at all while on vacation, and 17% were unemployed. Also, 38% of those who work while on vacation do so by monitoring their business emails.

a. Given that a randomly selected poll respondent will work while on summer vacation, what is the probability that the respondent will monitor business emails?

b. What is the probability that a randomly selected poll respondent will work while on summer vacation and will monitor business emails?

c. What is the probability that a randomly selected poll respondent will not work while on summer vacation and will monitor business emails?

3.69 Stock market participation and IQ. Refer to *The Journal of Finance* (December 2011) study of whether the decision to invest in the stock market is dependent on IQ, Exercise 3.46 (p. 182). The summary table giving the number of the 158,044 Finnish citizens in each IQ score/investment category is reproduced below. Again, suppose one of the citizens is selected at random.

IQ Score	Invest in Market	No Investment	Totals
1	893	4,659	5,552
2	1,340	9,409	10,749
3	2,009	9,993	12,002
4	5,358	19,682	25,040
5	8,484	24,640	33,124
6	10,270	21,673	31,943
7	6,698	11,260	17,958
8	5,135	7,010	12,145
9	4,464	5,067	9,531
Totals	44,651	113,393	158,044

Source: Based on M. Grinblatt, M. Keloharju, and J. Linnainaa, "IQ and Stock Market Participation," *The Journal of Finance*, Vol. 66, No. 6, December 2011 (data from Table 1 and Figure 1).

a. Given that the Finnish citizen has an IQ score of 6 or higher, what is the probability that he/she invests in the stock market?

b. Given that the Finnish citizen has an IQ score of 5 or lower, what is the probability that he/she invests in the stock market?

c. Based on the results, parts **a** and **b,** does it appear that investing in the stock market is dependent on IQ? Explain.

3.70 Degrees of best-paid CEOs. Refer to the results of the Glassdoor Economic Research (August 25, 2015) survey of the top 40 best-paid CEOs shown in Table 2.1 (p. 65). The data on highest degree obtained are summarized in the SPSS printout below. Suppose you randomly select five of the CEOs (without replacement) and record the highest degree obtained by each.

CE040

Degree

		Frequency	Percent	Valid Percent	Cumulative Percent
Valid	Bachelor	17	42.5	42.5	42.5
	Law	5	12.5	12.5	55.0
	Masters	3	7.5	7.5	62.5
	MBA	9	22.5	22.5	85.0
	None	4	10.0	10.0	95.0
	PhD	2	5.0	5.0	100.0
	Total	40	100.0	100.0	

SPSS Output for Exercise 3.70

a. What is the probability that the highest degree obtained by the first CEO you select is a bachelor's degree?

b. Suppose the highest degree obtained by each of the first four CEOs you select is a bachelor's degree. What is the probability that the highest degree obtained by the fifth CEO you select is a bachelor's degree?

3.71 Ambulance response time. *Geographical Analysis* (Jan. 2010) presented a study of emergency medical service (EMS) ability to meet the demand for an ambulance. In one example, the researchers presented the following scenario. An ambulance station has one vehicle and two demand locations, A and B. The probability that the ambulance can travel to a location in under 8 minutes is .58 for location A and .42 for location B. The probability that the ambulance is busy at any point in time is .3.

a. Find the probability that EMS can meet the demand for an ambulance at location A.

b. Find the probability that EMS can meet the demand for an ambulance at location B.

3.72 Working mothers with children. The U.S. Census Bureau reports a growth in the percentage of mothers in the workforce who have infant children. The following table gives a breakdown of the marital status and working status of mothers with infant children in the year 2014. (The numbers in the table are reported in thousands.) Consider the following events: A = {Mom with infant works}, B = {Mom with infant is married}. Are A and B independent events?

	Working	Not Working
Married	6,027	4,064
No spouse	2,147	1,313

Source: Data from U.S. Census Bureau, Bureau of Labor Statistics, 2014 (Table 4).

3.73 Firefighters' use of gas detection devices. Two deadly gases that can be present in fire smoke are hydrogen cyanide and carbon monoxide. *Fire Engineering* (March 2013) reported the results of a survey of 244 firefighters conducted by the Fire Smoke Coalition. The purpose of the survey was to assess the base level of knowledge of firefighters regarding the use of gas detection devices at the scene of a fire. The survey revealed the following: Eighty percent of firefighters had no standard operating procedures (SOP) for detecting/monitoring hydrogen cyanide in fire smoke; 49% had no SOP for detecting/monitoring carbon monoxide in fire smoke. Assume that 94% of firefighters had no SOP for detecting either hydrogen cyanide or carbon monoxide in fire smoke. What is the probability that a firefighter has no SOP for detecting hydrogen cyanide and no SOP for detecting carbon monoxide in fire smoke?

3.74 Wine quality and soil. The *Journal of Wine Research* (Vol. 21, 2010) published a study of the effects of soil and climate on the quality of wine produced in Spain. The soil at two vineyards—Llarga and Solar—was the focus of the analysis. Wine produced from grapes grown in each of the two vineyards was evaluated for each of three different years (growing seasons) by a wine-tasting panel. Based on the taste tests, the panel (as a group) selected the wine with the highest quality.

a. How many different wines were evaluated by the panel, where one wine was produced for each vineyard/growing season combination?

b. If the wines were all of equal quality, what is the probability that the panel selected a Llarga wine as the wine with the highest quality?

c. If the wines were all of equal quality, what is the probability that the panel selected a wine produced in year 3 as the wine with the highest quality?

NW d. The panel consisted of four different wine tasters who performed the evaluations independently of each other. If the wines were all of equal quality, what is the probability that all four tasters selected a Llarga wine as the wine with the highest quality?

3.75 Are you really being served red snapper? Red snapper is a rare and expensive reef fish served at upscale restaurants. Federal law prohibits restaurants from serving a cheaper, look-alike variety of fish (e.g., vermillion snapper or lane snapper) to customers who order red snapper. Researchers at the University of North Carolina used DNA analysis to examine fish specimens labeled "red snapper" that were purchased from vendors across the country (*Nature*, July 15, 2004). The DNA tests revealed that 77% of the specimens were not red snapper but the cheaper, look-alike variety of fish.

a. Assuming the results of the DNA analysis are valid, what is the probability that you are actually served red snapper the next time you order it at a restaurant?

b. If there are five customers at a chain restaurant, all who have ordered red snapper, what is the probability that at least one customer is actually served red snapper?

3.76 Random shuffling of songs on Spotify. Spotify is a music-streaming service that offers both free and subscription options. Users can create playlists and choose to use Spotify's random shuffling feature to play back the songs. When the shuffling feature was first introduced, many users complained that the algorithm was not working. For example, in a playlist consisting of 2 songs by The White Stripes, 2 by Adele, and 1 by Maroon Five, two possible random orderings of the songs are:

A = {Adele 1, Adele 2, White Stripes 1,
White Stripes 2, Maroon Five}

B = {Adele 2, White Stripes 1, Maroon Five,
White Stripes 2, Adele 1}

a. Find the probability that Adele 1 is selected as the first song to play from the playlist.

b. Given that Adele 1 is selected as the first song, what is the probability that Adele 2 is selected as the second song to play from the playlist?

c. Given that Adele 1 and Adele 2 are the first two songs selected, what is the probability that White Stripes 1 is selected as the third song to play from the playlist?

d. Given that Adele 1, Adele 2, and White Stripes 1 are the first three songs selected, what is the probability that White Stripes 2 is selected as the fourth song to play from the playlist?

e. Given that Adele 1, Adele 2, White Stripes 1 and White Stripes 2 are the first four songs selected, what is the probability that Maroon Five is selected as the last song to play from the playlist?

f. Find the probability of List A by multiplying the probabilities in parts **a–e.**

g. Many users considered List B to be random, but not List A. Demonstrate that the probability of List B is the same as the probability of List A. [*Note:* In response to user complaints, Spotify now uses a different random shuffling algorithm, one that prevents an outcome like List A from occurring.]

Applying the Concepts—Advanced

3.77 **Forensic evidence in a criminal court case.** In our legal system, the use of DNA as forensic evidence is often regarded as the most reliable type of evidence. However, most of the DNA code is the same for all humans. Consequently, assessing the probability of the DNA code that varies among individuals is the key to a successful case. *Chance* (Vol. 28, 2015) published an article on the use of DNA in a criminal case. The evidence found at the crime scene consisted of two alleles (sequences of DNA code), denoted {6/9}. One of these alleles comes from the individual's mother and one from the individual's father, but it is not known which allele—6 or 9—is from which parent. In forensic science, it is assumed that the two outcomes (alleles) are independent.

a. DNA taken from the suspect resulted in a sequence of {6/9}. Given the evidence (E) comes from the suspect, find the probability of a DNA sequence of {6/9}. This probability—denoted $P(E|H_p)$—is used by the prosecution to support a claim of guilt.

b. In the general population, the probability of observing an allele of 6 is .21 and the probability of an allele 9 is .14. Given the evidence (E) comes from a randomly selected person in the general population, find the probability of a DNA sequence of {6/9}. This probability—denoted $P(E|H_d)$—is used by the defense to support the suspect's claim of not guilty.

c. In a court of law, the *likelihood* ratio $P(E|H_p)/P(E|H_d)$ is used to help decide the case. A ratio greater than 1 supports the prosecution, while a ratio less than 1 supports the defendant. Compute this likelihood ratio from the results in parts **a** and **b** and use it to make an inference.

3.78 **Risk of a natural gas pipeline accident.** *Process Safety Progress* (December 2004) published a risk analysis for a natural gas pipeline between Bolivia and Brazil. The most likely scenario for an accident would be natural gas leakage from a hole in the pipeline. The probability that the leak ignites immediately (causing a jet fire) is .01. If the leak does not immediately ignite, it may result in a delayed ignition of a gas cloud. Given no immediate ignition, the probability of delayed ignition (causing a flash fire) is .01. If there is no delayed ignition, the gas cloud will harmlessly disperse. Suppose a leak occurs in the natural gas pipeline. Find the probability that either a jet fire or a flash fire will occur. Illustrate with a tree diagram.

3.79 **Most likely coin-tossing sequence.** In *Parade Magazine*'s (November 26, 2000) column "Ask Marilyn," the following question was posed: "I have just tossed a [balanced] coin 10 times, and I ask you to guess which of the following three sequences was the result. One (and only one) of the sequences is genuine."

> (1) H H H H H H H H H H
> (2) H H T T H T T H H H
> (3) T T T T T T T T T T

a. Demonstrate that prior to actually tossing the coins, the three sequences are equally likely to occur.

b. Find the probability that the 10 coin tosses result in all heads or all tails.

c. Find the probability that the 10 coin tosses result in a mix of heads and tails.

d. Marilyn's answer to the question posed was "Though the chances of the three specific sequences occurring randomly are equal . . . it's reasonable for us to choose sequence (2) as the most likely genuine result." If you know that only one of the three sequences actually occurred, explain why Marilyn's answer is correct. [*Hint:* Compare the probabilities in parts **b** and **c**.]

3.80 **Encryption systems with erroneous ciphertexts.** In cryptography, ciphertext is encrypted or encoded text that is unreadable by a human or computer without the proper algorithm to decrypt it into plain text. The impact of erroneous ciphertexts on the performance of an encryption system was investigated in *IEEE Transactions on Information Forensics and Security* (April 2013). For one data encryption system, the probability of receiving an erroneous ciphertext is assumed to be β, where $0 < \beta < 1$. The researchers showed that if an erroneous ciphertext occurs, the probability of an error in restoring plain text using the decryption system is .5. When no error occurs in the received ciphertext, the probability of an error in restoring plain text using the decryption system is $\alpha\beta$, where $0 < \alpha < 1$. Use this information to give an expression for the probability of an error in restoring plain text using the decryption system.

3.7 Bayes's Rule

An early attempt to employ probability in making inferences is the basis for a branch of statistical methodology known as **Bayesian statistical methods.** The logic employed by the English philosopher Thomas Bayes in the mid-1700s involves converting an unknown conditional probability, say $P(B|A)$, to one involving a known conditional probability, say $P(A|B)$. The method is illustrated in the next example.

EXAMPLE 3.22

**Applying Bayes's
Logic—Intruder
Detection System**

Problem An unmanned monitoring system uses high-tech video equipment and micro-processors to detect intruders. A prototype system has been developed and is in use outdoors at a weapons munitions plant. The system is designed to detect intruders with a probability of .90. However, the design engineers expect this probability to vary with weather conditions. The system automatically records the weather condition each time an intruder is detected. Based on a series of controlled tests, in which an intruder was released at the plant under various weather conditions, the following information is available: Given the intruder was, in fact, detected by the system, the weather was clear 75% of the time, cloudy 20% of the time, and raining 5% of the time. When the system failed to detect the intruder, 60% of the days were clear, 30% cloudy, and 10% rainy. Use this information to find the probability of detecting an intruder, given rainy weather conditions. (Assume that an intruder has been released at the plant.)

Solution Define D to be the event that the intruder is detected by the system. Then D^c is the event that the system fails to detect the intruder. Our goal is to calculate the conditional probability, $P(D|\text{Rainy})$. From the statement of the problem, the following information is available:

$$P(D) = .90 \qquad P(D^c) = .10$$
$$P(\text{Clear}|D) = .75 \qquad P(\text{Clear}|D^c) = .60$$
$$P(\text{Cloudy}|D) = .20 \qquad P(\text{Cloudy}|D^c) = .30$$
$$P(\text{Rainy}|D) = .05 \qquad P(\text{Rainy}|D^c) = .10$$

Note that $P(D|\text{Rainy})$ is not one of the conditional probabilities that is known. However, we can find

$$P(\text{Rainy} \cap D) = P(D)P(\text{Rainy}|D) = (.90)(.05) = .045$$

and

$$P(\text{Rainy} \cap D^c) = P(D^c)P(\text{Rainy}|D^c) = (.10)(.10) = .01$$

using the multiplicative rule of probability. These two probabilities are highlighted on the tree diagram for the problem in Figure 3.22.

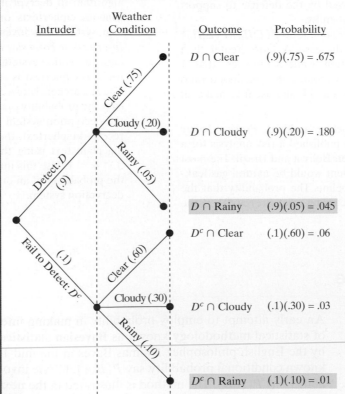

	Weather		
Intruder	Condition	Outcome	Probability

$D \cap$ Clear   (.9)(.75) = .675

$D \cap$ Cloudy   (.9)(.20) = .180

$D \cap$ Rainy   (.9)(.05) = .045

$D^c \cap$ Clear   (.1)(.60) = .06

$D^c \cap$ Cloudy   (.1)(.30) = .03

$D^c \cap$ Rainy   (.1)(.10) = .01

Figure 3.22
Tree diagram for Example 3.22

Now the event Rainy is the union of two mutually exclusive events, $(\text{Rainy} \cap D)$ and $(\text{Rainy} \cap D^c)$. Thus, applying the additive rule of probability, we have

$$P(\text{Rainy}) = P(\text{Rainy} \cap D) + P(\text{Rainy} \cap D^c) = .045 + .01 = .055$$

We now apply the formula for conditional probability to obtain

$$P(D|\text{Rainy}) = \frac{P(\text{Rainy} \cap D)}{P(\text{Rainy})} = \frac{P(\text{Rainy} \cap D)}{P(\text{Rainy} \cap D) + P(\text{Rainy} \cap D^c)}$$

$$= \frac{.045}{.055} = .818$$

Therefore, under rainy weather conditions, the prototype system can detect the intruder with a probability of .818—a value lower than the designed probability of .90.

Look Back One key to solving a problem of this type is recognizing that the conditional probability of interest, $P(D|\text{Rainy})$, is not the same as the conditional probability given, $P(\text{Rainy}|D)$.

● **Now Work Exercise 3.81**

The technique utilized in Example 3.22, called **Bayes's Rule,** can be applied when an observed event A occurs with any one of several mutually exclusive and exhaustive events, $B_1, B_2, \ldots, B_k$. The formula for finding the appropriate conditional probabilities is given in the box.

Bayes's Rule

Given k mutually exclusive and exhaustive events, $B_1, B_2, \ldots, B_k$, such that $P(B_1) + P(B_2) + \cdots + P(B_k) = 1$, and an observed event A, then

$$P(B_i|A) = \frac{P(B_i \cap A)}{P(A)}$$

$$= \frac{P(B_i)P(A|B_i)}{P(B_1)P(A|B_1) + P(B_2)P(A|B_2) + \cdots + P(B_k)P(A|B_k)}$$

In applying Bayes's Rule to Example 3.22 , the observed event $A = \{\text{Rainy}\}$ and the $k = 2$ mutually exclusive and exhaustive events are the complementary events $D = \{\text{intruder detected}\}$ and $D^c = \{\text{intruder not detected}\}$. Hence, the formula

$$P(D|\text{Rainy}) = \frac{P(D)P(\text{Rainy}|D)}{P(D)P(\text{Rainy}|D) + P(D^c) P(\text{Rainy}|D^c)}$$

$$= \frac{(.90)(.05)}{(.90)(.05) + (.10)(.10)} = .818$$

EXAMPLE 3.23

Bayes's Rule Application—Wheelchair Control

Problem Electric wheelchairs are difficult to maneuver for many disabled people. In a paper presented at the *1st International Workshop on Advances in Service Robotics* (March 2003), researchers applied Bayes's Rule to evaluate an "intelligent" robotic controller that aims to capture the intent of the wheelchair user and aid in navigation. Consider the following scenario. From a certain location in a room, a wheelchair user will either (1) turn sharply to the left and navigate through a door, (2) proceed straight to the other side of the room, or (3) turn slightly right and stop at a table. Denote these three events as D (for door), S (for straight), and T (for table). Based on previous trips, $P(D) = .5$, $P(S) = .2$, and $P(T) = .3$. The wheelchair is installed with a robot-controlled joystick. When the user intends to go through the door, he points the joystick straight 30% of the time; when the user intends to go straight, he points the joystick straight 40% of the time; and when the user intends to go to the table, he points the joystick straight 5% of the time. If the wheelchair user points the joystick straight, where is his most likely destination?

Solution Let $J = \{$joystick is pointed straight$\}$. The user intention percentages can be restated as the following conditional probabilities: $P(J|D) = .3$, $P(J|S) = .4$, and $P(J|T) = .05$. Since the user has pointed the joystick straight, we want to find the following probabilities: $P(D|J)$, $P(S|J)$, and $P(T|J)$. Now, the three events, D, S, and T, represent mutually exclusive and exhaustive events, where $P(D) = .5$, $P(S) = .2$, and $P(T) = .3$. Consequently, we can apply Bayes's Rule as follows:

$$P(D|J) = P(J|D) \cdot P(D) / [P(J|D) \cdot P(D) + P(J|S) \cdot P(S) + P(J|T) \cdot P(T)]$$

$$= (.3)(.5) / [(.3)(.5) + (.4)(.2) + (.05)(.3)] = .15/.245 = .612$$

$$P(S|J) = P(J|S) \cdot P(S) / [P(J|D) \cdot P(D) + P(J|S) \cdot P(S) + P(J|T) \cdot P(T)]$$

$$= (.4)(.2) / [(.3)(.5) + (.4)(.2) + (.05)(.3)] = .08/.245 = .327$$

$$P(T|J) = P(J|T) \cdot P(T) / [P(J|D) \cdot P(D) + P(J|S) \cdot P(S) + P(J|T) \cdot P(T)]$$

$$= (.05)(.3) / [(.3)(.5) + (.4)(.2) + (.05)(.3)] = .015/.245 = .061$$

Note that the largest conditional probability is $P(D|J) = .612$. Thus, if the joystick is pointed straight, the wheelchair user is most likely headed through the door.

● **Now Work Exercise 3.88**

Exercises 3.81–3.93

Learning the Mechanics

3.81 Suppose the events B_1 and B_2 are mutually exclusive and complementary events, such that $P(B_1) = .75$ and $P(B_2) = .25$. Consider another event A such that $P(A|B_1) = .3$ and $P(A|B_2) = .5$.
  a. Find $P(B_1 \cap A)$.
  b. Find $P(B_2 \cap A)$.
  c. Find $P(A)$ using the results in parts **a** and **b**.
  d. Find $P(B_1|A)$.
  e. Find $P(B_2|A)$.

3.82 Suppose the events B_1, B_2, and B_3 are mutually exclusive and complementary events, such that $P(B_1) = .2$, $P(B_2) = .4$, and $P(B_3) = .5$. Consider another event A such that $P(A|B_1) = P(A|B_2) = .1$, and $P(A|B_3) = .2$. Use Baye's Rule to find
  a. $P(B_1|A)$
  b. $P(B_2|A)$
  c. $P(B_3|A)$

3.83 Suppose the events B_1, B_2, and B_3 are mutually exclusive and complementary events, such that $P(B_1) = .2$, $P(B_2) = .15$, and $P(B_3) = .65$. Consider another event A such that $P(A) = .4$. If A is independent of B_1, B_2, and B_3, use Bayes's Rule to show that $P(B_1|A) = P(B_1) = .2$.

Applying the Concepts—Basic

3.84 **Confidence of feedback information for improving quality.** In the semiconductor manufacturing industry, a key to improved quality is having confidence in the feedback generated by production equipment. A study of the confidence level of feedback information was published in *Engineering Applications of Artificial Intelligence* (Vol. 26, 2013). At any point in time during the production process, a report can be generated. The report is classified as either "OK" or "not OK." Let A represent the event that an "OK" report is generated in any time period (t). Let B represent the event that an "OK" report is generated in the next time period ($t + 1$). Consider the following probabilities: $P(A) = .8$, $P(B|A) = .9$, and $P(B|A^C) = .5$.
  a. Express the event $B|A$ in the words of the problem.
  b. Express the event $B|A^c$ in the words of the problem.
  c. Find $P(A^c)$.
  d. Find $P(A \cap B)$.
  e. Find $P(A^c \cap B)$.
  f. Use the probabilities, parts **d** and **e**, to find $P(B)$.
  g. Use Bayes' Rule to find $P(A|B)$, i.e., the probability that an "OK" report was generated in one time period (t), given that an "OK" report is generated in the next time period ($t + 1$).

3.85 **Fingerprint expertise.** A study published in *Psychological Science* (August 2011) tested the accuracy of experts and novices in identifying fingerprints. Participants were presented pairs of fingerprints and asked to judge whether the prints in each pair matched. The pairs were presented under three different conditions: prints from the same individual (*match condition*), nonmatching but similar prints (*similar distracter condition*), and nonmatching and very dissimilar prints (*nonsimilar distracter condition*). The percentages of correct decisions made by the two groups under each of the three conditions are listed in the table.

Condition	Fingerprint Experts	Novices
Match	92.12%	74.55%
Similar Distracter	99.32%	44.82%
Nonsimilar Distracter	100%	77.03%

Source: Based on J. M. Tangen, M. B. Thompson, and D. J. McCarthy, "Identifying Fingerprint Expertise," *Psychological Science,* Vol. 22, No. 8, August 2011 (Figure 1).

  a. Given a pair of matched prints, what is the probability that an expert failed to identify the match?

b. Given a pair of matched prints, what is the probability that a novice failed to identify the match?

c. Assume the study included 10 participants, 5 experts and 5 novices. Suppose that a pair of matched prints was presented to a randomly selected study participant and the participant failed to identify the match. Is the participant more likely to be an expert or a novice?

3.86 Tests for Down syndrome. Currently, there are three diagnostic tests available for chromosome abnormalities in a developing fetus. The safest (to both the mother and fetus) and least expensive of the three is the ultrasound test. Two San Diego State University statisticians investigated the accuracy of using ultrasound to test for Down syndrome (*Chance,* Summer 2007). Let D denote that the fetus has a genetic marker for Down syndrome and N denote that the ultrasound test is normal (i.e., no indication of chromosome abnormalities). Then, the statisticians desired the probability $P(D/N)$. Use Bayes's Rule and the following probabilities (provided in the article) to find the desired probability: $P(D) = \frac{1}{180}$, $P(D^c) = \frac{79}{80}$, $P(N|D) = \frac{1}{2}$, $P(N^c|D) = \frac{1}{2}$, $P(N|D^c) = 1$, and $P(N^c|D^c) = 0$.

3.87 Fish contaminated by a plant's toxic discharge. Refer to the U.S. Army Corps of Engineers' study on the DDT contamination of fish in the Tennessee River (Alabama), Example 1.5 (p. 38). Part of the investigation focused on how far upstream the contaminated fish have migrated. (A fish is considered to be contaminated if its measured DDT concentration is greater than 5.0 parts per million.)

a. Considering only the contaminated fish captured from the Tennessee River, the data reveal that 52% of the fish are found between 275 and 300 miles upstream, 39% are found 305 to 325 miles upstream, and 9% are found 330 to 350 miles upstream. Use these percentages to determine the probabilities, $P(275-300)$, $P(305-325)$, and $P(330-350)$.

b. Given that a contaminated fish is found a certain distance upstream, the probability that it is a channel catfish (CC) is determined from the data as $P(CC|275-300) = .775$, $P(CC|305-325) = .77$, and $P(CC|330-350) = .86$. If a contaminated channel catfish is captured from the Tennessee River, what is the probability that it was captured 275–300 miles upstream?

3.88 Errors in estimating job costs. A construction company employs three sales engineers. Engineers 1, 2, and 3 estimate the costs of 30%, 20%, and 50%, respectively, of all jobs bid by the company. For $i = 1, 2, 3$, define E_i to be the event that a job is estimated by engineer i. The following probabilities describe the rates at which the engineers make serious errors in estimating costs:

$P(\text{error}|E_1) = .01$, $P(\text{error}|E_2) = .03$, and

$P(\text{error}|E_3) = .02$

a. If a particular bid results in a serious error in estimating job cost, what is the probability that the error was made by engineer 1?

b. If a particular bid results in a serious error in estimating job cost, what is the probability that the error was made by engineer 2?

c. If a particular bid results in a serious error in estimating job cost, what is the probability that the error was made by engineer 3?

d. Based on the probabilities, parts **a–c**, which engineer is most likely responsible for making the serious error?

Applying the Concepts—Intermediate

3.89 Mining for dolomite. Dolomite is a valuable mineral that is found in sedimentary rock. During mining operations, dolomite is often confused with shale. The radioactivity features of rock can aid miners in distinguishing between dolomite and shale rock zones. For example, if the gamma ray reading of a rock zone exceeds 60 API units, the area is considered to be mostly shale (and is not mined); if the gamma ray reading of a rock zone is less than 60 API units, the area is considered to be abundant in dolomite (and is mined). Data on 771 core samples in a rock quarry collected by the Kansas Geological Survey revealed the following: 476 of the samples are dolomite and 295 of the samples are shale. Of the 476 dolomite core samples, 34 had a gamma ray reading greater than 60. Of the 295 shale core samples, 280 had a gamma ray reading greater than 60. Suppose you obtain a gamma ray reading greater than 60 at a certain depth of the rock quarry. Should this area be mined?

3.90 Nondestructive evaluation. Nondestructive evaluation (NDE) describes methods that quantitatively characterize materials, tissues, and structures by noninvasive means, such as X-ray computed tomography, ultrasonics, and acoustic emission. Recently, NDE was used to detect defects in steel castings (*JOM,* May 2005). Assume that the probability that NDE detects a "hit" (i.e., predicts a defect in a steel casting) when, in fact, a defect exists is .97. (This is often called the *probability of detection.*) Also assume that the probability that NDE detects a hit when, in fact, no defect exists is .005. (This is called the *probability of a false call.*) Past experience has shown a defect occurs once in every 100 steel castings. If NDE detects a hit for a particular steel casting, what is the probability that an actual defect exists?

3.91 Drug testing in the workplace. In Canada, the Supreme Court recently ruled that employees can be tested for drugs only if management has reasonable cause to administer the test. An article in *Chance* (Vol. 28, 2015) focused on the misclassification rates of such drug tests. A *false positive* occurs when a drug test administered to a non–drug user yields a positive result. A *false negative* occurs when a drug test administered to a drug user yields a negative result.

a. The author presented the following scenario: Suppose that 5% of a population of workers consists of drug users. The drug test has a false positive rate (i.e., the probability of a positive drug test given the worker is a non–drug user) of 5% and a false negative rate (i.e., the probability of a negative drug test given the worker is a drug user) of 5%. A worker selected from this population is drug tested and found to have a positive result. What is the probability that the worker is a non–drug user? Apply Bayes' Rule to obtain your answer.

b. Recall that in Canada, drug tests can be administered only with probable cause. Hence, for workers that are tested, it is likely that a high proportion of them use drugs. Now consider a population of workers in which 95% are drug users. Again, assume both the false positive rate and false negative rate of the drug test are 5%. A worker selected from this population is drug tested and found to have a positive result. What is the probability that the worker is a non–drug user?

3.92 Intrusion detection systems. The *Journal of Research of the National Institute of Standards and Technology* (November–December 2003) published a study of a double intrusion detection system with independent systems. If there is an intruder, system A sounds an alarm with probability .9, and system B sounds an alarm with probability .95. If there is no intruder, system A sounds an alarm with probability .2, and system B sounds an alarm with probability .1. Now assume that the probability of an intruder is .4. Also assume that under a given condition (intruder or not), systems A and B operate independently. If both systems sound an alarm, what is the probability that an intruder is detected?

Applying the Concepts—Advanced

3.93 Forensic analysis of JFK assassination bullets. Following the assassination of President John F. Kennedy (JFK) in 1963, the House Select Committee on Assassinations (HSCA)

conducted an official government investigation. The HSCA concluded that although there was a probable conspiracy involving at least one shooter in addition to Lee Harvey Oswald, the additional shooter missed all limousine occupants. A recent analysis of assassination bullet fragments, reported in the *Annals of Applied Statistics* (Vol. 1, 2007), contradicted these findings, concluding that the evidence used by the HSCA to rule out a second assassin is fundamentally flawed. It is well documented that at least two different bullets were the source of bullet fragments found after the assassination. Let E = {bullet evidence used by the HSCA}, T = {two bullets used in the assassination}, and T^c = {more than two bullets used in the assassination}. Given the evidence (E), which is more likely to have occurred—two bullets used (T) or more than two bullets used (T^c)?

a. The researchers demonstrated that the ratio, $P(T|E)/P(T^c|E)$, is less than 1. Explain why this result supports the theory of more than two bullets used in the assassination of JFK.

b. To obtain the result, part **a,** the researchers first showed that

$$P(T|E)/P(T^c|E) = [P(E|T) \cdot P(T)]/[P(E|T^c) \cdot P(T^c)]$$

Demonstrate this equality using Bayes's Rule.

CHAPTER NOTES

Key Terms

Additive rule of probability 177	Multiplicative rule of probability 187
Bayesian statistical methods 197	Mutually exclusive events 178
Bayes's Rule 199	Odds 171
Combinations Rule 166	Probability of an event 163
Combinatorial mathematics 166	Probability rules (sample points) 161
Complement 175	Rule of complements 175
Complementary events 175	Sample point 158
Compound event 172	Sample space 159
Conditional probability 184	Simple event 162
Dependent events 189	Tree diagram 158
Event 162	Two-way table 173
Experiment 158	Unconditional probabilities 184
Independent events 189	Union 172
Intersection 172	Venn diagram 159
Law of Large Numbers 160	

Key Symbols

S	**sample space** (collection of all sample points)
A: {1,2}	set of **sample points in event** A
$P(A)$	**probability** of event A
$A \cup B$	**union** of events A and B (either A or B can occur)
$A \cap B$	**intersection** of events A and B (both A and B occur)
A^c	**complement** of A (event A does not occur)

$A\|B$	event A occurs, **given** event B occurs
$\binom{N}{n}$	number of **combinations** of N elements taken n at a time
$N!$	**N factorial** = $N(N-1)(N-2)\cdots(2)(1)$

Key Ideas

Probability Rules for k Sample Points, $S_1, S_2, S_3, \ldots, S_k$

1. $0 \le P(S_i) \le 1$
2. $\sum P(S_i) = 1$

Combinations Rule

Counting number of samples of n elements selected from N elements

$$\binom{N}{n} = \frac{N!}{n!(N-n)!} = \frac{N(N-1)(N-2)\cdots(N-n+1)}{n(n-1)(n-2)\cdots(2)(1)}$$

Bayes's Rule

For mutually exclusive events $B_1, B_2, \ldots, B_k$, such that $P(B_1) + P(B_2) + \cdots + P(B_k) = 1$,

$$P(B_i|A) = \frac{P(B_i)P(A|B_i)}{P(B_1)P(A|B_1) + P(B_2)P(A|B_2) + \cdots + P(B_k)P(A|B_k)}$$

Guide to Selecting Probability Rules

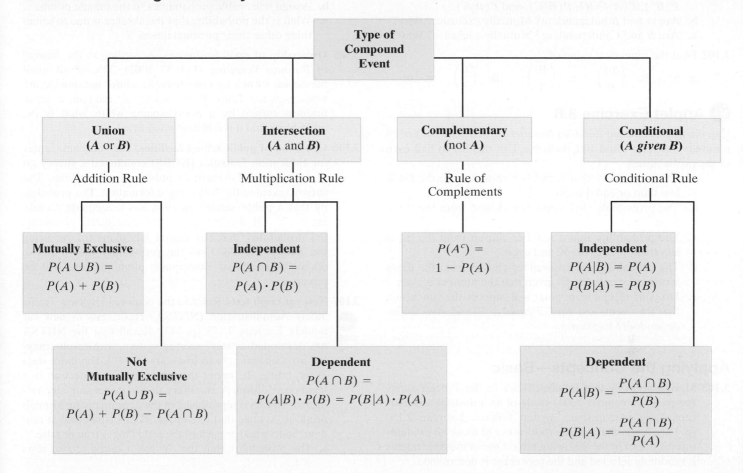

Type of Compound Event

Union (*A* or *B*)	Intersection (*A* and *B*)	Complementary (not *A*)	Conditional (*A* given *B*)
Addition Rule	Multiplication Rule	Rule of Complements	Conditional Rule

Mutually Exclusive
$$P(A \cup B) = P(A) + P(B)$$

Independent
$$P(A \cap B) = P(A) \cdot P(B)$$

$$P(A^c) = 1 - P(A)$$

Independent
$$P(A|B) = P(A)$$
$$P(B|A) = P(B)$$

Not Mutually Exclusive
$$P(A \cup B) = P(A) + P(B) - P(A \cap B)$$

Dependent
$$P(A \cap B) = P(A|B) \cdot P(B) = P(B|A) \cdot P(A)$$

Dependent
$$P(A|B) = \frac{P(A \cap B)}{P(B)}$$
$$P(B|A) = \frac{P(A \cap B)}{P(A)}$$

SUPPLEMENTARY EXERCISES 3.94–3.130

Learning the Mechanics

3.94 Which of the following pairs of events are mutually exclusive? Justify your response.
- **a.** {The next customer entering a retail store is older than 30 years.}, {The next customer entering the same retail store is younger than 20 years.}
- **b.** {The next customer entering a retail store is younger than 20 years.}, {The next customer entering the same retail store will spend more than $900 in purchases.}
- **c.** {The next customer entering the retail store will be older than 70 years and spend more than $900 in purchases.}, {The next customer entering the same retail store will try to steal an item.}

3.95 A sample space consists of three sample points, S_1, S_2, and S_3, with $P(S_1) = .1$, and $P(S_2) = .2$.
- **a.** Assign a probability to S_3 in a way that the three sample points define a valid sample space obeying the two probability rules.
- **b.** If an event $A = \{S_2, S_3\}$, find $P(A)$.

3.96 For two events *A* and *B*, suppose $P(A) = .7$, $P(B) = .5$, and $P(A \cap B) = .4$. Find $P(A \cup B)$.

3.97 Consider two events *A* and *B*, with $P(A) = .1$, $P(B) = .2$, and $P(A \cap B) = 0$.
- **a.** Are *A* and *B* mutually exclusive?
- **b.** Are *A* and *B* independent?

3.98 Two events, *A* and *B*, are independent, with $P(A) = .3$ and $P(B) = .1$.
- **a.** Are *A* and *B* mutually exclusive? Why?
- **b.** Find $P(A|B)$ and $P(B|A)$.
- **c.** Find $P(A \cup B)$.

3.99 Given that $P(A \cap B) = .4$ and $P(A|B) = .8$, find $P(B)$.

3.100 From a production batch with 16 items, 8 items are randomly selected for quality assurance. In how many different ways can the sample be drawn? Suggest an estimate before computing the exact number.

3.101 The Venn diagram below illustrates a sample space containing six sample points and three events, *A*, *B*, and *C*. The probabilities of the sample points are $P(1) = .3$, $P(2) = .2$, $P(3) = .1$, $P(4) = .1$, $P(5) = .1$, and $P(6) = .2$.

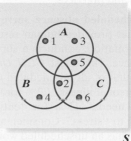

a. Find $P(A \cap B), P(B \cap C), P(A \cup C), P(A \cup B \cup C),$ $P(B^c), P(A^c \cap B), P(B|C),$ and $P(B|A)$.

b. Are A and B independent? Mutually exclusive? Why?

c. Are B and C independent? Mutually exclusive? Why?

3.102 Find the numerical value of

a. $6!$ **b.** $\binom{10}{9}$ **c.** $\binom{10}{1}$ **d.** $\binom{6}{3}$ **e.** $0!$

📊 Applet Exercise 3.6

Use the applet entitled *Random Numbers* to generate a list of 50 numbers between 1 and 100, inclusive. Use this list to find each of the probabilities.

a. The probability that a number chosen from the list is less than or equal to 50

b. The probability that a number chosen from the list is even

c. The probability that a number chosen from the list is less than or equal to 50 and even

d. The probability that a number chosen from the list is less than or equal to 50 given that the number is even

e. Do your results from parts **a–d** support the conclusion that the events *less than or equal to 50* and *even* are independent? Explain.

Applying the Concepts—Basic

3.103 **Management system failures.** Refer to the *Process Safety Progress* (December 2004) study of 83 industrial accidents caused by management system failures, Exercise 2.150 (p. 142). A summary of the root causes of these 83 incidents is reproduced in the following table. One of the 83 incidents is randomly selected and the root cause is determined.

Management System Cause Category	Number of Incidents
Engineering and Design	27
Procedures and Practices	24
Management and Oversight	22
Training and Communication	10
Total	83

Source: Based on A. S. Blair, "Management System Failures Identified in Incidents Investigated by the U.S. Chemical Safety and Hazard Investigation Board," *Process Safety Progress,* Vol. 23, No. 4, December 2004, pp. 232–236 (Table 1).

a. List the sample points for this problem and assign reasonable probabilities to them.

b. Find and interpret the probability that an industrial accident is caused by faulty engineering and design.

c. Find and interpret the probability that an industrial accident is caused by something other than faulty procedures and practices.

3.104 **Workers' unscheduled absence survey.** Each year CCH, Inc., a firm that provides human resources and employment law information, conducts a survey on absenteeism in the workplace. The latest *CCH Unscheduled Absence Survey* found that of all unscheduled work absences, 34% are due to "personal illness," 22% for "family issues," 18% for "personal needs," 13% for "entitlement mentality," and 13% due to "stress." Consider a randomly selected employee who has an unscheduled work absence.

a. List the sample points for this experiment.

b. Assign reasonable probabilities to the sample points.

c. What is the probability that the absence is due to something other than "personal illness"?

3.105 **Ownership of small businesses.** According to the *Journal of Business Venturing* (Vol. 17, 2002), 27% of all small businesses owned by non-Hispanic whites nationwide are women-owned firms. If we select, at random, a small business owned by a non-Hispanic white, what is the probability that it is a male-owned firm?

3.106 **Condition of public school facilities.** The National Center for Education Statistics (NCES) conducted a survey on the condition of America's public school facilities. The survey revealed the following information. The probability that a public school building has inadequate plumbing is .25. Of the buildings with inadequate plumbing, the probability that the school has plans for repairing the building is .38. Find the probability that a public school building has inadequate plumbing and will be repaired.

3.107 **New car crash tests.** Refer to the National Highway Traffic Safety Administration (NHTSA) crash tests of new car models, Exercise 2.153 (p. 143). Recall that the NHTSA has developed a "star" scoring system, with results ranging from one star (*) to five stars (*****). The more stars in the rating, the better the level of crash protection in a head-on collision. A summary of the driver-side star ratings for 98 cars is reproduced in the accompanying Minitab printout. Assume that one of the 98 cars is selected at random. State whether each of the following is true or false.

a. The probability that the car has a rating of two stars is 4.

b. The probability that the car has a rating of four or five stars is .7857.

c. The probability that the car has a rating of one star is 0.

d. The car has a better chance of having a two-star rating than of having a five-star rating.

Tally for Discrete Variables: DRIVSTAR

DRIVSTAR	Count	Percent
2	4	4.08
3	17	17.35
4	59	60.20
5	18	18.37
N=	98	

3.108 **Speeding linked to fatal car crashes.** According to the National Highway Traffic and Safety Administration's National Center for Statistics and Analysis (NCSA), "Speeding is one of the most prevalent factors contributing to fatal traffic crashes" (*NHTSA Technical Report*, August 2005). The probability that speeding is a cause of a fatal crash is .3. Furthermore, the probability that speeding and missing a curve are causes of a fatal crash is .12. Given speeding is a cause of a fatal crash, what is the probability that the crash occurred on a curve?

3.109 **Choosing portable grill displays.** Consider a study of how people attempt to influence the choices of others by offering undesirable alternatives (*Journal of Consumer*

Research, March 2003). Such a phenomenon typically occurs when family members propose a vacation spot, friends recommend a restaurant for dinner, and realtors show the buyer potential homes. In one phase of the study, the researcher had each of 124 college students select showroom displays for portable grills. Five different displays (representing five different-sized grills) were available, but only three displays would be selected. The students were instructed to select the displays to maximize purchases of Grill #2 (a smaller-sized grill).

a. In how many possible ways can the three grill displays that include Grill #2 be selected from the five displays? List the possibilities.

b. The table shows the grill display combinations and the number of each selected by the 124 students. Use this information to assign reasonable probabilities to the different display combinations.

c. Find the probability that a student who participated in the study selected a display combination involving Grill #1.

Grill Display Combination	Number of Students
1-2-3	35
1-2-4	8
1-2-5	42
2-3-4	4
2-3-5	1
2-4-5	34

Source: Based on R. W. Hamilton, "Why Do People Suggest What They Do Not Want? Using Context Effects to Influence Others' Choices," *Journal of Consumer Research*, Vol. 29, No. 4, March 2003 (Table 1).

3.110 Inactive oil and gas structures. U.S. federal regulations require that operating companies clear all inactive offshore oil and gas structures within 1 year after production ceases. Researchers at the Louisiana State University Center for Energy Studies gathered data on both active and inactive oil and gas structures in the Gulf of Mexico (*Oil & Gas Journal*, Jan. 3, 2005). They discovered that the Gulf of Mexico has 2,175 active and 1,225 idle (inactive) structures. The following table breaks down these structures by type (caisson, well protector, or fixed platform). Consider the structure type and active status of one of these oil/gas structures.

	Structure Type			
	Caisson	Well Protector	Fixed Platform	Totals
Active	503	225	1,447	2,175
Inactive	598	177	450	1,225

Source: Data from M. Kaiser, and D. Mesyanzhinov, "Study Tabulates Idle Gulf of Mexico Structures," *Oil & Gas Journal*, Vol. 103, No. 1, January 3, 2005 (Table 2).

a. List the simple events for this experiment.

b. Assign reasonable probabilities to the simple events.

c. Find the probability that the structure is active.

d. Find the probability that the structure is a well protector.

e. Find the probability that the structure is an inactive caisson.

f. Find the probability that the structure is either inactive or a fixed platform.

g. Find the probability that the structure is not a caisson.

3.111 Is a product "green"? A "green" product (e.g., a product built from recycled materials) is one that has minimal impact on the environment and human health. How do consumers determine if a product is "green"? The *2011 ImagePower Green Brands Survey* asked this question of more than 9,000 international consumers. The results are shown in the following table.

Reason for Saying a Product Is Green	Percentage of Consumers
Certification mark on label	45
Packaging	15
Reading information about the product	12
Advertisement	6
Brand Web site	4
Other	18
Total	100

Source: Based on *2011 ImagePower Green Brands Survey*.

a. What method is an international consumer most likely to use to identify a green product?

b. Find the probability that an international consumer identifies a green product by a certification mark on the product label or by the product packaging.

c. Find the probability that an international consumer identifies a green product by reading about the product or from information at the brand's Web site.

d. Find the probability that an international consumer does not use advertisements to identify a green product.

3.112 Monitoring quality of power equipment. *Mechanical Engineering* (February 2005) reported on the need for wireless networks to monitor the quality of industrial equipment. For example, consider Eaton Corp., a company that develops distribution products. Eaton estimates that 90% of the electrical switching devices it sells can monitor the quality of the power running through the device. Eaton further estimates that of the buyers of electrical switching devices capable of monitoring quality, 90% do not wire the equipment up for that purpose. Use this information to estimate the probability that an Eaton electrical switching device is capable of monitoring power quality and is wired up for that purpose.

Applying the Concepts—Intermediate

3.113 Appeals of federal civil trials. The *Journal of the American Law and Economics Association* (Vol. 3, 2001) published the results of a study of appeals of federal civil trials. The following table, extracted from the article, gives a breakdown of 2,143 civil cases that were appealed by either the plaintiff or the defendant. The outcome of the appeal, as well as the type of trial (judge or jury), was determined for each civil case. Suppose one of the 2,143 cases is selected at random and both the outcome of the appeal and type of trial are observed.

	Jury	Judge	Totals
Plaintiff trial win—reversed	194	71	265
Plaintiff trial win— affirmed/ dismissed	429	240	669
Defendant trial win—reversed	111	68	179
Defendant trial win— affirmed/ dismissed	731	299	1,030
Totals	1,465	678	2,143

a. Find $P(A)$, where $A = \{$jury trial$\}$.
b. Find $P(B)$, where $B = \{$plaintiff trial win is reversed$\}$.
c. Are A and B mutually exclusive events?
d. Find $P(A^c)$.
e. Find $P(A \cup B)$.
f. Find $P(A \cap B)$.

3.114 Characteristics of a new product. The long-run success of a business depends on its ability to market products with superior characteristics that maximize consumer satisfaction and that give the firm a competitive advantage (Kotler & Keller, *Marketing Management*, 2015). Ten new products have been developed by a food-products firm. Market research has indicated that the 10 products have the characteristics described by the following Venn diagram:

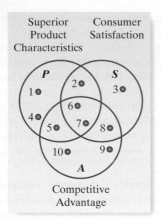

a. Write the event that a product possesses all the desired characteristics as an intersection of the events defined in the Venn diagram. Which products are contained in this intersection?
b. If one of the 10 products were selected at random to be marketed, what is the probability that it would possess all the desired characteristics?
c. Write the event that the randomly selected product would give the firm a competitive advantage or would satisfy consumers as a union of the events defined in the Venn diagram. Find the probability of this union.
d. Write the event that the randomly selected product would possess superior product characteristics and satisfy consumers. Find the probability of this intersection.
e. Two of the 10 products will be selected for an ad campaign. How many different pairs of products are possible?

3.115 Testing a watch manufacturer's claim. A manufacturer of a new SmartWatch claims that the probability of its watch running more than 1 minute slow or 1 minute fast after 1 year of use is .05. A consumer protection agency has purchased four of the manufacturer's watches with the intention of testing the claim.

a. Assuming that the manufacturer's claim is correct, what is the probability that none of the watches are as accurate as claimed?
b. Assuming that the manufacturer's claim is correct, what is the probability that exactly two of the four watches are as accurate as claimed?
c. Suppose that only one of the four tested watches is as accurate as claimed. What inference can be made about the manufacturer's claim? Explain.
d. Suppose that none of the watches tested are as accurate as claimed. Is it necessarily true that the manufacturer's claim is false? Explain.

3.116 Ranking razor blades. The corporations in the highly competitive razor blade industry do a tremendous amount of advertising each year. Corporation G gave a supply of three top-name brands, G, S, and W, to a consumer and asked her to use them and rank them in order of preference. The corporation was, of course, hoping the consumer would prefer its brand and rank it first, thereby giving them some material for a consumer interview advertising campaign. If the consumer did not prefer one blade over any other but was still required to rank the blades, what is the probability that

a. The consumer ranked brand G first?
b. The consumer ranked brand G last?
c. The consumer ranked brand G last and brand W second?
d. The consumer ranked brand W first, brand G second, and brand S third?

3.117 Reliability of gas station air gauges. Tire and automobile manufacturers and consumer safety experts all recommend that drivers maintain proper tire pressure in their cars. Consequently, many gas stations now provide air pumps and air gauges for their customers. In a *Research Note* (Nov. 2001), the National Highway Traffic Safety Administration studied the reliability of gas station air gauges. The next table gives the percentage of gas stations that provide air gauges that overreport the pressure level in the tire.

Station Gauge Pressure	Overreport by 4 psi or More (%)	Overreport by 6 psi or More (%)	Overreport by 8 psi or More (%)
25 psi	16	2	0
35 psi	19	9	0
45 psi	19	14	5
55 psi	20	15	9

a. If the gas station air pressure gauge reads 35 psi, what is the probability that the pressure is overreported by 6 psi or more?
b. If the gas station air pressure gauge reads 55 psi, what is the probability that the pressure is overreported by 8 psi or more?
c. If the gas station air pressure gauge reads 25 psi, what is the probability that the pressure is not overreported by 4 psi or more?
d. Are the events $A = \{$overreport by 4 psi or more$\}$ and $B = \{$overreport by 6 psi or more$\}$ mutually exclusive? Explain.

e. Based on your answer to part **d,** why do the probabilities in the table not sum to 1?

3.118 Which events are independent? Use your intuitive understanding of independence to form an opinion about whether each of the following scenarios represents independent events.

a. The results of consecutive tosses of a coin

b. The opinions of randomly selected individuals in a preelection poll

c. A Major League Baseball player's results in two consecutive at-bats

d. The amount of gain or loss associated with investments in different stocks if these stocks are bought on the same day and sold on the same day 1 month later

e. The amount of gain or loss associated with investments in different stocks that are bought and sold in different time periods, 5 years apart

f. The prices bid by two different development firms in response to a building construction proposal

3.119 Home modifications for wheelchair users. The *American Journal of Public Health* (January 2002) reported on a study of elderly wheelchair users who live at home. A sample of 306 wheelchair users, age 65 or older, were surveyed about whether they had an injurious fall during the year and whether their home features any one of five structural modifications: bathroom modifications, widened doorways/hallways, kitchen modifications, installed railings, and easy-open doors. The responses are summarized in the accompanying table. Suppose we select, at random, one of the 306 surveyed wheelchair users.

Home Features	Injurious Fall(s)	No Falls	Totals
All 5	2	7	9
At least 1 but not all	26	162	188
None	20	89	109
Totals	48	258	306

Source: Based on K. Berg, M. Hines, and S. Allen, "Wheelchair Users at Home: Few Home Modifications and Many Injurious Falls," *American Journal of Public Health*, Vol. 92, No. 1, January 2002 (Table 1).

a. Find the probability that the wheelchair user had an injurious fall.

b. Find the probability that the wheelchair user had all five features installed in the home.

c. Find the probability that the wheelchair user had no falls and none of the features installed in the home.

d. Given the wheelchair user had all five features installed, what is the probability that the user had an injurious fall?

e. Given the wheelchair user had none of the features installed, what is the probability that the user had an injurious fall?

3.120 World Cup soccer match draws. Every 4 years the world's 32 best national soccer teams compete for the World Cup. Run by FIFA (Fédération Internationale de Football Association), national teams are placed into eight groups of four teams, with the group winners advancing to play for the World Cup. *Chance* (Spring 2007) investigated the fairness of the 2006 World Cup draw. Each of the top 8 seeded teams (teams ranked 1–8, called pot 1) were placed into one of the eight groups (named Group A, B, C, D, E, F, G, and H). The remaining 24 teams were assigned to 3 pots of 8 teams each to achieve the best possible geographic distribution between the groups. The teams in pot 2 were assigned to groups as follows: the first team drawn was placed into Group A, the second team drawn was placed in to Group B, etc. Teams in pots 3 and 4 were assigned to the groups in similar fashion. Because teams in pots 2–4 are not necessarily placed there based on their world ranking, this typically leads to a "group of death," i.e., a group involving at least two highly seeded teams where only one can advance.

a. In 2006, Germany (as the host country) was assigned as the top seed in Group A. What is the probability that Paraguay (with the highest ranking in pot 2) was assigned to Group A?

b. Many soccer experts viewed the South American teams (Ecuador and Paraguay) as the most dangerous teams in pot 2. What is the probability one of the South American teams was assigned to Group A?

c. In 2006, Group B was considered the "group of death," with England (world rank 2), Paraguay (highest rank in pot 2), Sweden (2nd highest rank in pot 3), and Trinidad and Tobago. What is the probability that Group B included the team with the highest rank in pot 2 and the team with one of the top two ranks in pot 3?

d. In drawing teams from pot 2, there was a notable exception in 2006. If a South American team (either Ecuador or Paraguay) was drawn into a group with another South American team, it was automatically moved to the next group. This rule impacted Group C (Argentina as the top seed) and Group F (Brazil as the top seed), because they already had South American teams, and groups that followed these groups in the draw. Now Group D included the eventual champion Italy as its top seed. What is the probability that Group D was not assigned one of the dangerous South American teams in pot 2?

3.121 Chance of an Avon sale. The probability that an Avon salesperson sells beauty products to a prospective customer on the first visit to the customer is .4. If the salesperson fails to make the sale on the first visit, the probability that the sale will be made on the second visit is .65. The salesperson never visits a prospective customer more than twice. What is the probability that the salesperson will make a sale to a particular customer?

3.122 Drug testing in athletes. When Olympic athletes are tested for illegal drug use (i.e., doping), the results of a single positive test are used to ban the athlete from competition. *Chance* (Spring 2004) demonstrated the application of Bayes's Rule for making inferences about testosterone abuse among Olympic athletes using the following example: In a population of 1,000 athletes, suppose 100 are illegally using testosterone. Of the users, suppose 50 would test positive for testosterone. Of the nonusers, suppose 9 would test positive.

a. Given that the athlete is a user, find the probability that a drug test for testosterone will yield a positive result. (This probability represents the *sensitivity* of the drug test.)

b. Given the athlete is a nonuser, find the probability that a drug test for testosterone will yield a negative result. (This probability represents the *specificity* of the drug test.)

c. If an athlete tests positive for testosterone, use Bayes's Rule to find the probability that the athlete is really doping. (This probability represents the *positive predictive value* of the drug test.)

3.123 Profile of a sustainable farmer. *Sustainable development or sustainable farming* means finding ways to live and work the Earth without jeopardizing the future. Studies were conducted in five Midwestern states to develop a profile of a sustainable farmer. The results revealed that farmers can be classified along a sustainability scale, depending on whether they are likely (L) or unlikely (U) to engage in the following practices: (1) raise a broad mix of crops; (2) raise livestock; (3) use chemicals sparingly; and (4) use techniques for regenerating the soil, such as crop rotation.

a. List the different sets of classifications that are possible for the four practices (e.g., LUUL).

b. Suppose you are planning to interview farmers across the country to determine the frequency with which they fall into the classification sets you listed for part **a.** Because no information is yet available, assume initially that there is an equal chance of a farmer falling into any single classification set. Using that assumption, what is the probability that a farmer will be classified as unlikely on all four criteria (i.e., classified as a nonsustainable farmer)?

c. Using the same assumption as in part **b,** what is the probability that a farmer will be classified as likely on at least three of the criteria (i.e., classified as a near-sustainable farmer)?

3.124 Evaluating the performance of quality inspectors. The performance of quality inspectors affects both the quality of outgoing products and the cost of the products. A product that passes inspection is assumed to meet quality standards; a product that fails inspection may be reworked, scrapped, or reinspected. Quality engineers at an electric company evaluated performances of inspectors in judging the quality of solder joints by comparing each inspector's classifications of a set of 153 joints with the consensus evaluation of a panel of experts. The results for a particular inspector are shown in the table. One of the 153 solder joints was selected at random.

	Inspector's Judgment	
Committee's Judgment	Joint Acceptable	Joint Rejectable
Joint acceptable	101	10
Joint rejectable	23	19

a. What is the probability that the inspector judged the joint to be acceptable? That the committee judged the joint to be acceptable?

b. What is the probability that both the inspector and the committee judged the joint to be acceptable? That neither judged the joint to be acceptable?

c. What is the probability that the inspector and the committee disagreed? Agreed?

3.125 Using game simulation to teach a course. In *Engineering Management Research* (May 2012), a simulation game approach was proposed to teach concepts in a course on production. The proposed game simulation was for color television production. The products are two color television models, A and B. Each model comes in two colors, red and black. Also, the quantity ordered for each model can be 1, 2, or 3 televisions. The choice of model, color, and quantity is specified on a purchase order card.

a. Using a tree diagram, list how many different purchase order cards are possible. (These are the sample points for the experiment.)

b. Suppose, from past history, that black color TVs are in higher demand than red TVs. For planning purposes, should the engineer managing the production process assign equal probabilities to the simple events, part **a**? Why or why not?

3.126 Patient medical instruction sheets. Physicians and pharmacists sometimes fail to inform patients adequately about the proper application of prescription drugs and about the precautions to take in order to avoid potential side effects. One method of increasing patients' awareness of the problem is for physicians to provide patient medication instruction (PMI) sheets. The American Medical Association, however, has found that only 20% of the doctors who prescribe drugs frequently distribute PMI sheets to their patients. Assume that 20% of all patients receive the PMI sheet with their prescriptions and that 12% receive the PMI sheet and are hospitalized because of a drug-related problem. What is the probability that a person will be hospitalized for a drug-related problem given that the person received the PMI sheet?

3.127 Detecting traces of TNT. University of Florida researchers in the Department of Materials Science and Engineering have invented a technique to rapidly detect traces of TNT (*Today,* Spring 2005). The method, which involves shining a laser light on a potentially contaminated object, provides instantaneous results and gives no false positives. In this application, a false positive would occur if the laser light detects traces of TNT when, in fact, no TNT is actually present on the object. Let A be the event that the laser light detects traces of TNT. Let B be the event that the object contains no traces of TNT. The probability of a false positive is 0. Write this probability in terms of A and B using symbols such as $\cup, \cap,$ and $|$.

Applying the Concepts—Advanced

3.128 The three-dice gambling problem. According to *Significance* (December 2015), the 16th-century mathematician Jerome Cardan was addicted to a gambling game involving tossing three fair dice. One outcome of interest—which Cardan called a "Fratilli"—is when any subset of the three dice sums to 3. For example, the outcome {1, 1, 1} results in 3 when you sum all three dice. Another possible outcome that results in a "Fratilli" is {1, 2, 5}, since the first two dice sum to 3. Likewise, {2, 3, 6} is a "Fratilli," since the second die is a 3. Cardan was an excellent mathematician but calculated the probability of a "Fratilli" incorrectly as $115/216 = .532$.

a. Show that the denominator of Cardan's calculation, 216, is correct. [*Hint*: Knowing that there are 6 possible outcomes for each die, show that the total number of possible outcomes from tossing three fair dice is 216.]

b. One way to obtain a "Fratilli" is with the outcome {1, 1, 1}. How many possible ways can this outcome be obtained?

c. Another way to obtain a "Fratilli" is with an outcome that includes at least one die with a 3. First, find the number of outcomes that do not result in a 3 on any of the dice. [*Hint*: If none of the dice can result in a 3, then there are only 5 possible outcomes for each die.] Now subtract this result from 216 to find the number of outcomes that include at least one 3.

d. A third way to obtain a "Fratilli" is with the outcome {1, 2, 1}, where the order of the individual die outcomes does not matter. How many possible ways can this outcome be obtained?

e. A fourth way to obtain a "Fratilli" is with the outcome {1, 2, 2}, where the order of the individual die outcomes does not matter. How many possible ways can this outcome be obtained?

f. A fifth way to obtain a "Fratilli" is with the outcome {1, 2, 4}, where the order of the individual die outcomes does not matter. How many possible ways can this outcome be obtained? [*Hint:* There are 3 choices for the first die, 2 for the second, and only 1 for the third.]

g. A sixth way to obtain a "Fratilli" is with the outcome {1, 2, 5}, where the order of the individual die outcomes does not matter. How many possible ways can this outcome be obtained? [See *Hint* for part **f.**]

h. A final way to obtain a "Fratilli" is with the outcome {1, 2, 6}, where the order of the individual die outcomes does not matter. How many possible ways can this outcome be obtained? [See *Hint* for part **f.**]

i. Sum the results for parts **b–h** to obtain the total number of possible "Fratilli" outcomes.

j. Compute the probability of obtaining a "Fratilli" outcome. Compare your answer with Cardan's.

3.129 Scrap rate of machine parts. A press produces parts used in the manufacture of large-screen plasma televisions. If the press is correctly adjusted, it produces parts with a scrap rate of 5%. If it is not adjusted correctly, it produces scrap at a 50% rate. From past company records, the machine is known to be correctly adjusted 90% of the time. A quality-control inspector randomly selects one part from those recently produced by the press and discovers it is defective. What is the probability that the machine is incorrectly adjusted?

3.130 Chance of winning at "craps." A version of the dice game "craps" is played in the following manner. A player starts by rolling two balanced dice. If the roll (the sum of the two numbers showing on the dice) results in a 7 or 11, the player wins. If the roll results in a 2 or a 3 (called *craps*), the player loses. For any other roll outcome, the player continues to throw the dice until the original roll outcome recurs (in which case the player wins) or until a 7 occurs (in which case the player loses).

a. What is the probability that a player wins the game on the first roll of the dice?

b. What is the probability that a player loses the game on the first roll of the dice?

c. If the player throws a total of 4 on the first roll, what is the probability that the game ends (win or lose) on the next roll?

3.131 Chance of winning blackjack. Blackjack, a favorite game of gamblers, is played by a dealer and at least one opponent (called a *player*). In one version of the game, 2 cards of a standard 52-card bridge deck are dealt to the player and 2 cards to the dealer. For this exercise, assume that drawing an ace and a face card is called *blackjack*. If the dealer does not draw a blackjack and the player does, the player wins. If both the dealer and player draw blackjack, a "push" (i.e., a tie) occurs.

a. What is the probability that the dealer will draw a blackjack?

b. What is the probability that the player wins with a blackjack?

3.132 Software defects in NASA spacecraft instrument code. Portions of computer software code that may contain undetected defects are called *blind spots*. The issue of blind spots in software code evaluation was addressed at the *8th IEEE International Symposium on High Assurance Software Engineering* (March 2004). The researchers developed guidelines for assessing methods of predicting software defects using data on 498 modules of software code written in "C" language for a NASA spacecraft instrument. One simple prediction algorithm is to count the lines of code in the module; any module with more than 50 lines of code is predicted to have a defect. The accompanying file contains the predicted and actual defect status of all 498 modules. A standard approach to evaluating a software defect prediction algorithm is to form a two-way summary table similar to the one shown here. In the table, *a, b, c,* and *d* represent the number of modules in each cell. Software engineers use these table entries to compute several probability measures, called *accuracy, detection rate, false alarm rate,* and *precision.*

		Module Has Defects	
		False	True
Algorithm	No	*a*	*b*
Predicts Defects	Yes	*c*	*d*

a. *Accuracy* is defined as the probability that the prediction algorithm is correct. Write a formula for *accuracy* as a function of the table values *a, b, c,* and *d*.

b. The *detection rate* is defined as the probability that the algorithm predicts a defect, given that the module actually is a defect. Write a formula for *detection rate* as a function of the table values *a, b, c,* and *d*.

c. The *false alarm rate* is defined as the probability that the algorithm predicts a defect, given that the module actually has no defect. Write a formula for *false alarm rate* as a function of the table values *a, b, c,* and *d*.

d. *Precision* is defined as the probability that the module has a defect, given that the algorithm predicts a defect. Write a formula for *precision* as a function of the table values *a, b, c,* and *d*.

e. Access the accompanying file and compute the values of accuracy, detection rate, false alarm rate, and precision. Interpret the results.

Critical Thinking Challenges

3.133 "Let's Make a Deal." Marilyn vos Savant, who is listed in *Guinness Book of World Records Hall of Fame* for "Highest IQ," writes a weekly column in the Sunday newspaper supplement *Parade Magazine*. Her column, "Ask Marilyn," is devoted to games of skill, puzzles, and mind-bending riddles. In one issue (*Parade Magazine*, February 24, 1991), vos Savant posed the following question:

> Suppose you're on a game show, and you're given a choice of three doors. Behind one door is a car; behind the others, goats. You pick a door—say, #1—and the host, who knows what's behind the doors, opens another door—say #3—which has a goat. He then says to you, "Do you want to pick door #2?" Is it to your advantage to switch your choice?
>
> Marilyn's answer: "Yes, you should switch. The first door has a $\frac{1}{3}$ chance of winning [the car], but the second has a $\frac{2}{3}$ chance [of winning the car]." Predictably, vos Savant's surprising answer elicited thousands of critical

letters, many of them from PhD mathematicians, who disagreed with her. Who is correct, the PhDs or Marilyn?

3.134 Flawed Pentium computer chip. In October 1994, a flaw was discovered in the Pentium microchip installed in personal computers. The chip produced an incorrect result when dividing two numbers. Intel, the manufacturer of the Pentium chip, initially announced that such an error would occur once in 9 billion divisions, or "once in every 27,000 years" for a typical user; consequently, it did not immediately offer to replace the chip.

Depending on the procedure, statistical software packages (e.g., Minitab) may perform an extremely large number of divisions to produce the required output. For heavy users of the software, 1 billion divisions over a short time frame is not unusual. Will the flawed chip be a problem for a heavy Minitab user? [*Note:* Two months after the flaw was discovered, Intel agreed to replace all Pentium chips free of charge.]

ACTIVITY 3.1   *Exit Polls:* **Conditional Probability**

Exit polls are conducted in selected locations as voters leave their polling places after voting. In addition to being used to predict the outcome of elections before the votes are counted, these polls are used to gauge tendencies among voters. The results are usually stated in terms of conditional probabilities.

The table below shows the results of exit polling that suggest men were almost evenly spit on voting for Mitt Romney or Barack Obama, while women were more likely to vote for Obama in the 2012 presidential election. In addition, the table also suggests that more women than men voted in the election. The six percentages in the last three columns represent conditional probabilities where the given event is gender.

2012 Presidential Election, Vote by Gender

	Obama	Romney	Other
Male (47%)	45%	52%	3%
Female (53%)	55%	44%	1%

Source: Data from CNN (www.cnn.com).

1. Find similar exit poll results where the voters are categorized by race, income, education, or some other criterion for a recent national, state, or local election (e.g., the 2016 national election). Choose two different examples and interpret the percentages given as probabilities, or conditional probabilities where appropriate.

2. Use the multiplicative rule of probability to find the probabilities related to the percentages given. [For example, in the table on the left find P(Obama and Male) using the multiplicative rule.] Then interpret each of these probabilities and use them to determine the total percentage of the electorate who voted for each candidate.

3. Describe a situation where a business might use a form of exit polling to gauge customer reaction to a new product or service. Identify the type of business, the product or service, the criterion used to categorize customers, and how the customers' reactions will be determined. Then describe how the results will be summarized as conditional probabilities. How might the results of the poll benefit the business?

ACTIVITY 3.2   *Keep the Change:* **Independent Events**

Once again we return to the Bank of America *Keep the Change* savings program, Activity 1.1 (p. 54). This time we look at whether certain events involving purchase totals and amounts transferred to savings are independent. Throughout this activity, the experiment consists of randomly selecting one purchase from a large group of purchases.

1. Define events A and B as follows:

    A: {Purchase total ends in $0.25.}
    B: {Amount transferred is less that $0.50.}

Explain why events A and B are not independent. Are events A and B mutually exclusive? Use this example to explain the difference between independent events and mutually exclusive events.

2. Now define events A and B in this manner:

    A: {Purchase total is greater than $10.}
    B: {Amount transferred is less than $0.50.}

Do you believe that these events are independent? Explain your reasoning.

3. To investigate numerically whether the events in Question 2 are independent, we will use the data collected in Activity 1.1, page 54. Pool your data with the data from other students or the entire class so that the combined data set represents at least 100 purchases. Complete the table by counting the number of purchases in each category.

Compute appropriate probabilities based on your completed table to test whether the events of Question 2 are independent. If you conclude that the events are not independent, can you explain your conclusion in terms of the original data?

Distribution of Purchases

Transfer Amount	Purchase ≤ $10	Total > $10	Totals
$0.00–$0.49			
$0.99–$0.99			
Totals			

References

Bennett, D. J. *Randomness.* Cambridge, Mass.: Harvard University Press, 1998.

Epstein, R. A. *The Theory of Gambling and Statistical Logic*, rev. ed. New York: Academic Press, 1977.

Feller, W. *An Introduction to Probability Theory and Its Applications*, 3rd ed., Vol. 1. New York: Wiley, 1968.

Lindley, D. V. *Making Decisions*, 2nd ed. London: Wiley, 1985.

Parzen, E. *Modern Probability Theory and Its Applications.* New York: Wiley, 1960.

Wackerly, D., Mendenhall, W., and Scheaffer, R. L. *Mathematical Statistics with Applications,* 7th ed. Boston: Duxbury, 2008.

Williams, B. *A Sampler on Sampling.* New York: Wiley, 1978.

Winkler, R. L. *An Introduction to Bayesian Inference and Decision.* New York: Holt, Rinehart and Winston, 1972.

Wright, G., & Ayton, P., eds. *Subjective Probability.* New York: Wiley, 1994.

USING TECHNOLOGY

Technology images shown here are taken from SPSS Statistics Professional 23.0, Minitab 17, XLSTAT, and Excel 2016.

Note: Automated commands for generating combinations and permutations are not available in SPSS.

Minitab: Combinations and Permutations

Combinations—Choosing *n* Elements from *N* Elements

Step 1 Click "Calc" from the main menu bar, and then select "Calculator."

Step 2 On the resulting dialog box, specify the column you want to store the result in, and then enter "COMBINATIONS(N,n)" in the "Expression" box. (See Figure 3.M.1.)

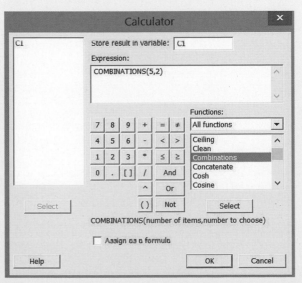

Figure 3.M.1 Minitab calculator dialog box entries for combinations

Step 3 Specify the values of *N* and *n,* as shown in Figure 3.M.1.

Step 4 Click "OK" and the result will appear in the specified column in the Minitab worksheet.

Permutations—Choosing *n* Elements from *N* Elements (See Appendix A for an application.)

Step 1 Click "Calc" from the main menu bar, and then select "Calculator."

Step 2 On the resulting dialog box, specify the column you want to store the result in, and then enter "PERMUTATIONS(N, n)" in the "Expression" box. (See Figure 3.M.2.)

Step 3 Specify the values of *N* and *n,* as shown in Figure 3.M.2.

Step 4 Click "OK" and the result will appear in the specified column in the Minitab worksheet.

Excel: Combinations and Permutations

Combinations—Choosing *n* Elements from *N* Elements

Step 1 Click on the cell in the Excel worksheet where you want the result to appear.

Step 2 In the formula bar, enter "=" followed by "COMBIN(N,n)."

Step 3 Specify the values of *N* and *n,* as shown in Figure 3.E.1.

Step 4 Click "Enter" and the result will appear in the selected cell (see Figure 3.E.1).

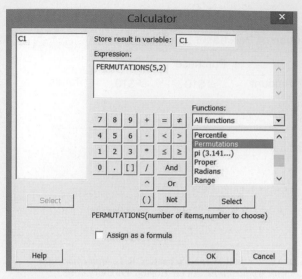

Figure 3.M.2 Minitab calculator dialog box entries for permutations

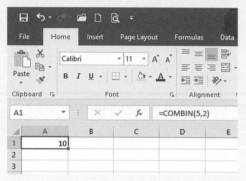

Figure 3.E.1 Excel formula for combinations

Permutations—Choosing *n* Elements from *N* Elements (See Appendix A for an application.)

Step 1 Click on the cell in the Excel worksheet where you want the result to appear.

Step 2 In the formula bar, enter "=" followed by "PERMUT(N,n)."

Step 3 Specify the values of *N* and *n*, as shown in Figure 3.E.2.

Step 4 Click "Enter" and the result will appear in the selected cell (see Figure 3.E.2).

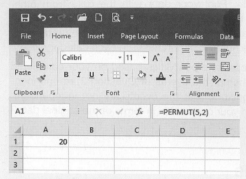

Figure 3.E.2 Excel formula for permutations

TI-84 Graphing Calculator: Combinations and Permutations

Combinations—Choosing *n* Elements from *N* Elements

Step 1 Enter the value of *N*.

Step 2 Press **MATH,** and then select **PROB.**

Step 3 Press **nCr** for combinations.

Step 4 Enter the value of *n;* press **ENTER.**

Permutations—Choosing *n* Elements from *N* Elements (See Appendix A for an application.)

Step 1 Enter the value of *N*.

Step 2 Press **MATH,** and then select **PROB.**

Step 3 Press **nPr** for permutations.

Step 4 Enter the value of *n;* press **ENTER.**

4

CONTENTS

WHERE WE'VE BEEN

Used probability to make an inference about a population from data in an observed sample

Used probability to measure the reliability of the inference

WHERE WE'RE GOING

Develop the notion of a random variable (**4.1**)

Learn that numerical data are observed values of either discrete or continuous random variables (**4.2, 4.5**)

Study two important types of random variables and their probability models: the binomial and normal models (**4.3, 4.6, 4.7**)

Present some additional discrete and continuous random variables (**4.4, 4.8**)

Random Variables and Probability Distributions

STATISTICS IN ACTION

Probability in a Reverse Cocaine Sting: Was Cocaine Really Sold?

The American Statistician *described an interesting application of a discrete probability distribution in a case involving illegal drugs. It all started with a "bust" in a midsized Florida city. During the bust, police seized approximately 500 foil packets of a white, powdery substance, presumably cocaine. Since it is not a crime to buy or sell nonnarcotic cocaine look-alikes (e.g., inert powders), detectives had to prove that the packets actually contained cocaine in order to convict their suspects of drug trafficking. When the police laboratory randomly selected and chemically tested 4 of the packets, all 4 tested positive for cocaine. This finding led to the conviction of the traffickers.*

After the conviction, the police decided to use the remaining foil packets (i.e., those not tested) in reverse sting operations. Two of these packets were randomly selected and sold by undercover officers to a buyer. Between the sale and the arrest, however, the buyer disposed of the evidence. The key question is, Beyond a reasonable doubt, did the defendant really purchase cocaine?

In court, the defendant's attorney argued that his client should not be convicted, because the police could not prove that the missing foil packets contained cocaine. The police contended, however, that since 4 of the original packets tested positive for cocaine, the 2 packets sold in the reverse sting were also highly likely to contain cocaine. In this chapter, two *Statistics in Action Revisited* examples demonstrate how to use probability models to solve the dilemma posed by the police's reverse sting. (The case represented Florida's first cocaine-possession conviction without the actual physical evidence.) (The *American Statistician*, May 1991.)

STATISTICS IN **ACTION** REVISITED

(continued)

- Using the Binomial Model to Solve the Cocaine Sting Case **(p. 237)**
- Using the Hypergeometric Model to Solve the Cocaine Sting Case **(p. 245)**

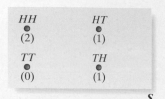

Figure 4.1

Venn diagram for coin-tossing experiment

You may have noticed that many of the examples of experiments in Chapter 3 generated quantitative (numerical) observations. The Consumer Price Index, the unemployment rate, the number of sales made in a week, and the yearly profit of a company are all examples of numerical measurements of some phenomenon. Thus, most experiments have sample points that correspond to values of some numerical variable.

To illustrate, consider the coin-tossing experiment of Chapter 3. Figure 4.1 is a Venn diagram showing the sample points when two coins are tossed and the up faces (heads or tails) of the coins are observed. One possible numerical outcome is the total number of heads observed. These values (0, 1, or 2) are shown in parentheses on the Venn diagram, one numerical value associated with each sample point. In the jargon of probability, the variable "total number of heads observed when two coins are tossed" is called a *random variable*.

> A **random variable** is a variable that assumes numerical values associated with the random outcomes of an experiment, where one (and only one) numerical value is assigned to each sample point.

The term *random variable* is more meaningful than the term *variable* because the adjective *random* indicates that the coin-tossing experiment may result in one of the several possible values of the variable—0, 1, or 2—according to the *random* outcome of the experiment, *HH*, *HT*, *TH*, and *TT*. Similarly, if the experiment is to count the number of customers who use the drive-up window of a bank each day, the random variable (the number of customers) will vary from day to day, partly because of random phenomena that influence whether customers use the drive-up window. Thus, the possible values of this random variable range from 0 to the maximum number of customers the window could possibly serve in a day.

We define two different types of random variables, *discrete* and *continuous*, in Section 4.1. Then we spend the remainder of this chapter discussing specific types of both discrete and continuous random variables and the aspects that make them important in business applications.

4.1   Two Types of Random Variables

Recall that the sample point probabilities corresponding to an experiment must sum to 1. Dividing one unit of probability among the sample points in a sample space and consequently assigning probabilities to the values of a random variable is not always as easy as the examples in Chapter 3 might lead you to believe. If the number of sample points can be completely listed, the job is straightforward. But if the experiment results in an infinite number of numerical sample points that are impossible to list, the task of assigning probabilities to the sample points is impossible without the aid of a probability model. The next three examples demonstrate the need for different probability models depending on the number of values that a random variable can assume.

EXAMPLE 4.1

Values of a Discrete Random Variable—Wine Ratings

Problem A panel of 10 experts for the *Wine Spectator* (a national publication) is asked to taste a new white wine and assign a rating of 0, 1, 2, or 3. A score is then obtained by adding together the ratings of the 10 experts. How many values can this random variable assume?

Solution A sample point is a sequence of 10 numbers associated with the rating of each expert. For example, one sample point is

$$\{1, 0, 0, 1, 2, 0, 0, 3, 1, 0\}$$

[*Note:* Using one of the counting rules in Appendix B, there are a total of $4^{10} = 1,048,576$ sample points for this experiment.] The random variable assigns a score to each one of these sample points by adding the 10 numbers together. Thus, the smallest score is 0 (if all 10 ratings are 0), and the largest score is 30 (if all 10 ratings are 3). Because every integer between 0 and 30 is a possible score, the random variable denoted by the symbol x can assume 31 values. Note that the value of the random variable for the sample point above is $x = 8$.*

Look Back Use of the random variable reduces the amount of information required in the experiment—from over 1 million sample points to 31 values of the random variable. Also, this is an example of a *discrete random variable* because there is a finite number of distinct possible values. Whenever all the possible values a random variable can assume can be listed (or *counted*), the random variable is *discrete*.

EXAMPLE 4.2

Values of a Discrete Random Variable—EPA Application

Problem Suppose the Environmental Protection Agency (EPA) takes readings once a month on the amount of pesticide in the discharge water of a chemical company. If the amount of pesticide exceeds the maximum level set by the EPA, the company is forced to take corrective action and may be subject to penalty. Consider the random variable, x, the number of months before the company's discharge exceeds the EPA's maximum level. What values can x assume?

Solution The company's discharge of pesticide may exceed the maximum allowable level on the first month of testing, the second month of testing, and so on. It is possible that the company's discharge will *never* exceed the maximum level. Thus, the set of possible values for the number of months until the level is first exceeded is the set of all positive integers

$$1, 2, 3, 4, \ldots$$

Look Back If we can list the values of a random variable x, even though the list is never ending, we call the list **countable** and the corresponding random variable *discrete*. Thus, the number of months until the company's discharge first exceeds the limit is a *discrete random variable*.

● **Now Work Exercise 4.4**

EXAMPLE 4.3

Values of a Continuous Random Variable— Another EPA Application

Problem Refer to Example 4.2. A second random variable of interest is the amount x of pesticide (in milligrams per liter) found in the monthly sample of discharge waters from the chemical company. What values can this random variable assume?

Solution Unlike the *number* of months before the company's discharge exceeds the EPA's maximum level, the set of all possible values for the *amount* of discharge *cannot* be listed—that is, it is not countable. The possible values for the amounts of pesticide would correspond to the points on the interval between 0 and the largest possible value the amount of the discharge could attain, the maximum number of milligrams that could occupy 1 liter of volume. (Practically, the interval would be much smaller, say, between 0 and 500 milligrams per liter.)

Look Ahead When the values of a random variable are not countable but instead correspond to the points on some interval, we call it a *continuous random variable*. Thus, the *amount* of pesticide in the chemical plant's discharge waters is a *continuous random variable*.

● **Now Work Exercise 4.5**

---

*The standard mathematical convention is to use a capital letter (e.g., X) to denote the theoretical random variable. The possible values (or realizations) of the random variable are typically denoted with a lower-case letter (e.g., x). Thus, in Example 4.1, the random variable X can take on the values $x = 0, 1, 2, \ldots, 30$. Because this notation can be confusing for introductory statistics students, we simplify the notation by using the lowercase x to represent the random variable throughout.

> Random variables that can assume a *countable* number (finite or infinite) of values are called **discrete.**

> Random variables that can assume values corresponding to any of the points contained in one or more intervals (i.e., values that are infinite and *uncountable*) are called **continuous.**

Several more examples of discrete random variables follow:

1. The number of sales made by a salesperson in a given week: $x = 0, 1, 2, \ldots$
2. The number of consumers in a sample of 500 who favor a particular product over all competitors: $x = 0, 1, 2, \ldots, 500$
3. The number of bids received in a bond offering: $x = 0, 1, 2, \ldots$
4. The number of errors on a page of an accountant's ledger: $x = 0, 1, 2, \ldots$
5. The number of customers waiting to be served in a restaurant at a particular time: $x = 0, 1, 2, \ldots$

Note that each of the examples of discrete random variables begins with the words "The number of...." This wording is very common because the discrete random variables most frequently observed are counts.

We conclude this section with some more examples of continuous random variables:

1. The length of time between arrivals at a hospital clinic: $0 \leq x < \infty$ (infinity)
2. For a new apartment complex, the length of time from completion until a specified number of apartments are rented: $0 \leq x < \infty$
3. The amount of carbonated beverage loaded into a 12-ounce can in a can-filling operation: $0 \leq x \leq 12$
4. The depth at which a successful oil-drilling venture first strikes oil: $0 \leq x \leq c$, where c is the maximum depth obtainable
5. The weight of a food item bought in a supermarket: $0 \leq x \leq 500$ [*Note*: Theoretically, there is no upper limit on x, but it is unlikely that it would exceed 500 pounds.]

Discrete random variables and their probability distributions are discussed in Part I—Sections 4.2–4.4. Continuous random variables and their probability distributions are the topic of Part II—Sections 4.5–4.8.

Exercises 4.1–4.10

Applying the Concepts—Basic

4.1 **Types of random variables.** Which of the following describe continuous random variables? Which describe discrete random variables?

  a. The number of cups of coffee sold in a cafeteria during lunch

  b. The height of a player on a basketball team

  c. The blood pressure levels of a group of students on the day before their final exam

  d. The temperature in degrees Fahrenheit on July 4th in Juneau, Alaska

  e. The number of goals scored in a football game

4.2 **Types of finance random variables.** Security analysts are professionals who devote full-time efforts to evaluating the investment worth of a narrow list of stocks. The following variables are of interest to security analysts. Which are discrete and which are continuous random variables?

  a. The closing price of a particular stock on the New York Stock Exchange

  b. The number of shares of a particular stock that are traded each business day

  c. The quarterly earnings of a particular firm

  d. The percentage change in earnings between last year and this year for a particular firm

  e. The number of new products introduced per year by a firm

f. The time until a pharmaceutical company gains approval from the U.S. Food and Drug Administration to market a new drug

4.3 **NHTSA crash tests.** Refer to the National Highway Traffic Safety Administration (NHTSA) crash tests of new car models, Exercise 2.153 (p. 143). Recall that the NHTSA developed a driver-side "star" scoring system, with results ranging from one star (*) to five stars (*****). The more stars in the rating, the better the level of crash protection in a head-on collision. Suppose that a car is selected from the data and its driver-side star rating is determined. Let x equal the number of stars in the rating. Is x a discrete or continuous random variable?

4.4 **Water in a bottle.** A bottle contains 16 ounces of water. The variable x represents the volume, in ounces, of water remaining in the bottle after the first drink is taken. What are the natural bounds for the values of x? Is x discrete or continuous? Explain.

4.5 **Executive pay.** Refer to Glassdoor Economic Research's list of the top-paid CEOs (Table 1.1, p. 29). One variable saved in the file is the CEO's compensation (in $ millions) in 2015. Is x a discrete or continuous random variable?

Applying the Concepts—Intermediate

4.6 **Banking.** Give an example of a discrete random variable that would be of interest to a banker.

4.7 **Economics.** Give an example of a continuous random variable that would be of interest to an economist.

4.8 **Hotel management.** Give an example of a discrete random variable that would be of interest to the manager of a hotel.

4.9 **Retailing.** Give two examples of discrete random variables that would be of interest to the manager of a clothing store.

4.10 **Stock market.** Give an example of a continuous random variable that would be of interest to a stockbroker.

PART I: DISCRETE RANDOM VARIABLES

4.2 Probability Distributions for Discrete Random Variables

A complete description of a discrete random variable requires that we *specify the possible values the random variable can assume and the probability associated with each value.* To illustrate, consider Example 4.4.

EXAMPLE 4.4

Finding a Probability Distribution— Coin-Tossing Experiment

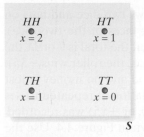

Figure 4.2

Venn diagram for the two-coin-toss experiment

Table 4.1

Probability Distribution for Coin-Toss Experiment: Tabular Form

x	$p(x)$
0	$\frac{1}{4}$
1	$\frac{1}{2}$
2	$\frac{1}{4}$

Problem Recall the experiment of tossing two coins (Section 4.1) and let x be the number of heads observed. Find the probability associated with each value of the random variable x, assuming the two coins are fair. Display these values in a table or graph.

Solution The sample space and sample points for this experiment are reproduced in Figure 4.2. Note that the random variable x can assume values 0, 1, and 2. Recall (from Chapter 3) that the probability associated with each of the four sample points is $\frac{1}{4}$. Then, identifying the probabilities of the sample points associated with each of these values of x, we have

$$P(x = 0) = P(TT) = \tfrac{1}{4}$$
$$P(x = 1) = P(TH) + P(HT) = \tfrac{1}{4} + \tfrac{1}{4} = \tfrac{1}{2}$$
$$P(x = 2) = P(HH) = \tfrac{1}{4}$$

Thus, we now know the values the random variable can assume (0, 1, 2) and how the probability is *distributed over* these values $(\frac{1}{4}, \frac{1}{2}, \frac{1}{4})$. This completely describes the random variable and is referred to as the *probability distribution,* denoted by the symbol $p(x)$.* The probability distribution for the coin-toss example is shown in tabular form in Table 4.1 and in graphical form in Figure 4.3. Because the probability distribution for a discrete random variable is concentrated at specific points (values of x), the graph in Figure 4.3a represents the probabilities as the heights of vertical lines over the corresponding values of x. Although the representation of the probability distribution as a histogram, as in Figure 4.3b, is less precise (because the probability is spread over a unit interval), the histogram representation will prove useful when we approximate probabilities of certain discrete random variables in Section 4.4.

*In standard mathematical notation, the probability that a random variable X takes on a value x is denoted $P(X = x) = p(x)$. Thus, $P(X = 0) = p(0), P(X = 1) = p(1)$, etc. In this introductory text, we adopt the simpler $p(x)$ notation.

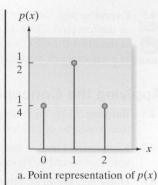
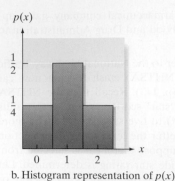

Figure 4.3

Probability distribution for coin-toss experiment: graphical form

a. Point representation of $p(x)$

b. Histogram representation of $p(x)$

Look Ahead We could also present the probability distribution for x as a formula, but this would unnecessarily complicate a very simple example. We give the formulas for the probability distributions of some common discrete random variables later in this chapter.

• **Now Work Exercise 4.16**

> The **probability distribution** of a **discrete random variable** is a graph, table, or formula that specifies the probability associated with each possible value the random variable can assume.

Two requirements must be satisfied by all probability distributions for discrete random variables.

> **Requirements for the Probability Distribution of a Discrete Random Variable, x**
>
> 1. $p(x) \geq 0$ for all values of x
> 2. $\Sigma p(x) = 1$
>
> where the summation of $p(x)$ is over all possible values of x.*

EXAMPLE 4.5

Probability Distribution from a Graph—Playing Craps

Problem Craps is a popular casino game in which a player throws two dice and bets on the outcome (the sum total of the dots showing on the upper faces of the two dice). Consider a $5 wager. On the first toss (called the *come-out* roll), if the total is 7 or 11 the roller wins $5. If the outcome is a 2, 3, or 12, the roller loses $5 (i.e., the roller wins −$5). For any other outcome (4, 5, 6, 8, 9, or 10), a *point* is established and no money is lost or won on that roll (i.e., the roller wins $0). In a computer simulation of repeated tosses of two dice, the outcome x of the come-out roll wager (−$5, $0, or +$5) was recorded. A relative frequency histogram summarizing the results is shown in Figure 4.4. Use the histogram to find the approximate probability distribution of x.

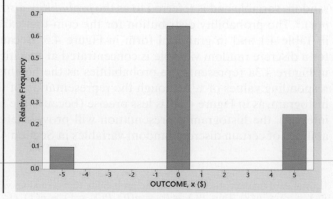

Figure 4.4

Minitab histogram for $5 wager on come-out roll in craps

*Unless otherwise indicated, summations will always be over all possible values of x.

Solution The histogram shows that the relative frequencies of the outcomes $x = -\$5$, $x = \$0$, and $x = \$5$ are .1, .65, and .25, respectively. For example, in repeated tosses of two dice, 25% of the outcomes resulted in a sum of 7 or 11 (a $5 win for the roller). Based on our long-run definition of probability given in Chapter 3, these relative frequencies estimate the probabilities of the three outcomes. Consequently, the approximate probability distribution of x, the outcome of the come-out wager in craps, is $p(-\$5) = .1, p(\$0) = .65$, and $p(\$5) = .25$. Note that these probabilities sum to 1.

Look Back When two dice are tossed, there are a total of 36 possible outcomes. (Can you list these outcomes, or sample points?) Of these, 4 result in a sum of 2, 3, or 12; 24 result in a sum of 4, 5, 6, 8, 9, or 10; and 8 result in a sum of 7 or 11. Using the rules of probability established in Chapter 3, you can show that the actual probability distribution for x is $p(-\$5) = 4/36 = .1111, p(\$0) = 24/36 = .6667$, and $p(\$5) = 8/36 = .2222$.

● **Now Work Exercise 4.11**

Examples 4.4 and 4.5 illustrate how the probability distribution for a discrete random variable can be derived, but for many practical situations, the task is much more difficult. Fortunately, many experiments and associated discrete random variables observed in business possess identical characteristics. Thus, you might observe a random variable in a marketing experiment that possesses the same characteristics as a random variable observed in accounting, economics, or management. We classify random variables according to type of experiment, derive the probability distribution for each of the different types, and then use the appropriate probability distribution when a particular type of random variable is observed in a practical situation. The probability distributions for most commonly occurring discrete random variables have already been derived. This fact simplifies the problem of finding the appropriate probability distributions for the business analyst, as the next example illustrates.

EXAMPLE 4.6
Probability Distribution Using a Formula—Texas Droughts

Problem A drought is a period of abnormal dry weather that causes serious problems in the farming industry of the region. University of Arizona researchers used historical annual data to study the severity of droughts in Texas. (*Journal of Hydrologic Engineering*, September/October 2003.) The researchers showed that the distribution of x, the number of consecutive years that must be sampled until a dry (drought) year is observed, can be modeled using the formula

$$p(x) = (.7)^{x-1}(.3), x = 1, 2, 3, \ldots$$

Find the probability that exactly 3 years must be sampled before a drought year occurs.

Solution We want to find the probability that $x = 3$. Using the formula, we have

$$p(3) = (.7)^{3-1}(.3) = (.7)^2(.3) = (.49)(.3) = .147$$

Thus, there is about a 15% chance that exactly 3 years must be sampled before a drought year occurs in Texas.

Look Back The probability of interest can also be derived using the principles of probability developed in Chapter 3. The event of interest is $N_1 N_2 D_3$, where N_1 represents no drought occurs in the first sampled year, N_2 represents no drought occurs in the second sampled year, and D_3 represents a drought occurs in the third sampled year. The researchers discovered that the probability of a drought occurring in any sampled year is .3 (and, consequently, the probability of no drought occurring in any sampled year is .7). Using the multiplicative rule of probability for independent events, the probability of interest is $(.7)(.7)(.3) = .147$.

● **Now Work Exercise 4.29**

Because probability distributions are analogous to the relative frequency distributions of Chapter 2, it should be no surprise that the mean and standard deviation are useful descriptive measures.

If a discrete random variable x were observed a very large number of times, and the data generated were arranged in a relative frequency distribution, the relative

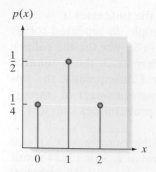

Figure 4.5
Probability distribution for a
two-coin toss

frequency distribution would be indistinguishable from the probability distribution for the random variable. Thus, the probability distribution for a random variable is a theoretical model for the relative frequency distribution of a population. To the extent that the two distributions are equivalent (and we will assume they are), the probability distribution for x possesses a mean μ and a variance σ^2 that are identical to the corresponding descriptive measures for the population. How can you find the mean value for a random variable? We illustrate the procedure with an example.

Examine the probability distribution for x (the number of heads observed in the toss of two fair coins) in Figure 4.5. Try to locate the mean of the distribution intuitively. We may reason that the mean μ of this distribution is equal to 1 as follows: In a large number of experiments—say, 100,000—$\frac{1}{4}$ (or 25,000) should result in $x = 0$, $\frac{1}{2}$ (or 50,000) in $x = 1$, and $\frac{1}{4}$ (or 25,000) in $x = 2$ heads. Therefore, the average number of heads is

$$\mu = \frac{0(25,000) + 1(50,000) + 2(25,000)}{100,000} = 0\left(\tfrac{1}{4}\right) + 1\left(\tfrac{1}{2}\right) + 2\left(\tfrac{1}{4}\right) = 0 + \tfrac{1}{2} + \tfrac{1}{2} = 1$$

Note that to get the population mean of the random variable x, we multiply each possible value of x by its probability $p(x)$ and then sum this product over all possible values of x. The *mean of x* is also referred to as the *expected value of x*, denoted $E(x)$.

The **mean**, or **expected value,** of a discrete random variable x is

$$\mu = E(x) = \sum xp(x)$$

Expected is a mathematical term and should not be interpreted as it is typically used. Specifically, a random variable might never be equal to its "expected value." Rather, the expected value is the mean of the probability distribution or a measure of its central tendency. You can think of μ as the mean value of x in a *very large* (actually, *infinite*) number of repetitions of the experiment, where the values of x occur in proportions equivalent to the probabilities of x.

EXAMPLE 4.7

Finding an Expected Value—An Insurance Application

Problem Suppose you work for an insurance company, and you sell a $10,000 one-year term insurance policy at an annual premium of $290. Actuarial tables show that the probability of death during the next year for a person of your customer's age, sex, health, etc., is .001. What is the expected gain (amount of money made by the company) for a policy of this type?

Solution The experiment is to observe whether the customer survives the upcoming year. The probabilities associated with the two sample points, Live and Die, are .999 and .001, respectively. The random variable you are interested in is the gain x, which can assume the values shown in the following table.

Gain, x	Sample Point	Probability
$290	Customer lives	.999
−$9,710	Customer dies	.001

If the customer lives, the company gains the $290 premium as profit. If the customer dies, the gain is negative because the company must pay $10,000, for a net "gain" of $(290 - 10,000) = -\$9,710$. The expected gain is therefore

$$\mu = E(x) = \sum xp(x)$$
$$= (290)(.999) + (-9,710)(.001) = \$280$$

In other words, if the company were to sell a very large number of one-year $10,000 policies to customers possessing the characteristics previously described, it would (on the average) net $280 per sale in the next year.

Look Back Note that $E(x)$ need not equal a possible value of x—that is, the expected value is $280, but x will equal either $290 or $-$9,710 each time the experiment is performed (a policy is sold and a year elapses). The expected value is a measure of central tendency—and in this case represents the average over a very large number of one-year policies—but is not a possible value of x.

● **Now Work Exercise 4.32a**

We learned in Chapter 2 that the mean and other measures of central tendency tell only part of the story about a set of data. The same is true about probability distributions. We need to measure variability as well. Because a probability distribution can be viewed as a representation of a population, we will use the population variance to measure its variability.

The *population variance* σ^2 is defined as the average of the squared distance of x from the population mean μ. Because x is a random variable, the squared distance, $(x - \mu)^2$, is also a random variable. Using the same logic used to find the mean value of x, we find the mean value of $(x - \mu)^2$ by multiplying all possible values of $(x - \mu)^2$ by $p(x)$ and then summing over all possible x values.* This quantity,

$$E[(x - \mu)^2] = \sum (x - \mu)^2 p(x)$$

is also called the *expected value of the squared distance from the mean;* that is, $\sigma^2 = E[(x - \mu)^2]$. The standard deviation of x is defined as the square root of the variance σ^2.

The **variance** of a **discrete random variable** x is

$$\sigma^2 = E[(x - \mu)^2] = \sum (x - \mu)^2 p(x)$$

The **standard deviation** of a **discrete random variable** is equal to the square root of the variance, i.e., $\sigma = \sqrt{\sigma^2} = \sqrt{\Sigma(x - \mu)^2 p(x)}$.

Knowing the mean μ and standard deviation σ of the probability distribution of x, in conjunction with Chebyshev's Rule (Rule 2.1, p. 106) and the Empirical Rule (Rule 2.2, p. 106), we can make statements about the likelihood that values of x will fall within the intervals $\mu \pm \sigma, \mu \pm 2\sigma$, and $\mu \pm 3\sigma$. These probabilities are given in the box.

Probability Rules for a Discrete Random Variable

Let x be a discrete random variable with probability distribution $p(x)$, mean μ, and standard deviation σ. Then, depending on the shape of $p(x)$, the following probability statements can be made:

	Chebyshev's Rule	Empirical Rule
	Applies to any probability distribution (see Figure 4.6a)	Applies to probability distributions that are mound-shaped and symmetric (see Figure 4.6b)
$P(\mu - \sigma < x < \mu + \sigma)$	≥ 0	$\approx .68$
$P(\mu - 2\sigma < x < \mu + 2\sigma)$	$\geq \frac{3}{4}$	$\approx .95$
$P(\mu - 3\sigma < x < \mu + 3\sigma)$	$\geq \frac{8}{9}$	≈ 1.00

*It can be shown that $E[(x - \mu^2)] = E(x^2) - \mu^2$, where $E(x^2) = \Sigma x^2 p(x)$. Note the similarity between this expression and the shortcut formula $\Sigma(x - \bar{x})^2 = \Sigma x^2 - \frac{(\Sigma x)^2}{n}$ given in Chapter 2.

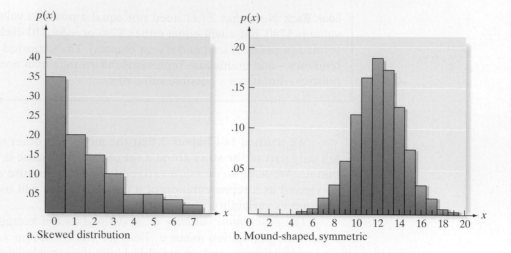

Figure 4.6

Shapes of two probability distributions for a discrete random variable x

a. Skewed distribution

b. Mound-shaped, symmetric

EXAMPLE 4.8

Finding μ and σ — Internet Business Venture

Problem Suppose you invest a fixed sum of money in each of five Internet business ventures. Assume you know that 70% of such ventures are successful, the outcomes of the ventures are independent of one another, and the probability distribution for the number, x, of successful ventures out of five is

x	0	1	2	3	4	5
$p(x)$	.002	.029	.132	.309	.360	.168

a. Find $\mu = E(x)$. Interpret the result.

b. Find $\sigma = \sqrt{E[(x - \mu)^2]}$. Interpret the result.

c. Graph $p(x)$. Locate μ and the interval $\mu \pm 2\sigma$ on the graph. Use either Chebyshev's Rule or the Empirical Rule to approximate the probability that x falls in this interval. Compare this result with the actual probability.

d. Would you expect to observe fewer than two successful ventures out of five?

Solution

a. Applying the formula,

$$\mu = E(x) = \sum xp(x) = 0(.002) + 1(.029) + 2(.132) + 3(.309)$$
$$+ 4(.360) + 5(.168) = 3.50$$

On average, the number of successful ventures out of five will equal 3.5. Remember that this expected value has meaning only when the experiment—investing in five Internet business ventures—is repeated a large number of times.

b. Now we calculate the variance of x:

$$\sigma^2 = E[(x - \mu)^2] = \sum(x - \mu)^2 p(x)$$
$$= (0 - 3.5)^2(.002) + (1 - 3.5)^2(.029) + (2 - 3.5)^2(.132)$$
$$+ (3 - 3.5)^2(.309) + (4 - 3.5)^2(.360) + (5 - 3.5)^2(.168)$$
$$= 1.05$$

Thus, the standard deviation is

$$\sigma = \sqrt{\sigma^2} = \sqrt{1.05} = 1.02$$

This value measures the spread of the probability distribution of x, the number of successful ventures out of five. A more useful interpretation is obtained by answering parts **c** and **d**.

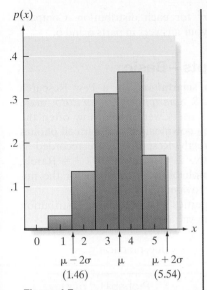

Figure 4.7

Graph of $p(x)$ for Example 4.8

c. The graph of $p(x)$ in histogram form is shown in Figure 4.7 with the mean μ and the interval $\mu \pm 2\sigma = 3.50 \pm 2(1.02) = 3.50 \pm 2.04 = (1.46, 5.54)$ shown on the graph. Note particularly that $\mu = 3.5$ locates the center of the probability distribution. Because this distribution is a theoretical relative frequency distribution that is moderately mound-shaped (see Figure 4.7), we expect (from Chebyshev's Rule) at least 75% and, more likely (from the Empirical Rule), approximately 95% of observed x values to fall in the interval $\mu \pm 2\sigma$—that is, between 1.46 and 5.54. You can see from Figure 4.7 that the actual probability that x falls in the interval $\mu \pm 2\sigma$ includes the sum of $p(x)$ for the values $x = 2$, $x = 3$, $x = 4$, and $x = 5$. This probability is $p(2) + p(3) + p(4) + p(5) = .132 + .309 + .360 + .168 = .969$. Therefore, 96.9% of the probability distribution lies within 2 standard deviations of the mean. This percentage is consistent with both Chebyshev's Rule and the Empirical Rule.

d. Fewer than two successful ventures out of five implies that $x = 0$ or $x = 1$. Because both these values of x lie outside the interval $\mu \pm 2\sigma$, we know from the Empirical Rule that such a result is unlikely (approximate probability of .05). The exact probability, $P(x \le 1)$, is $p(0) + p(1) = .002 + .029 = .031$. Consequently, in a single experiment where we invest in five Internet business ventures, we would not expect to observe fewer than two successful ones.

● **Now Work Exercise 4.17**

Exercises 4.11–4.39

Learning the Mechanics

4.11 A discrete random variable x can assume five possible values: 20, 21, 22, 23, and 24. The following Minitab histogram shows the relative frequency of each value.
  a. What is $p(22)$?
  b. What is the probability that x equals 20 or 24?
  c. What is $P(x \le 23)$?

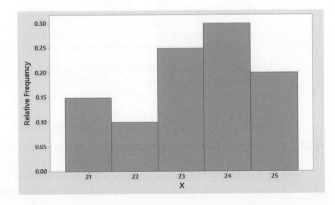

4.12 The random variable x has the following discrete probability distribution:

x	1	3	5	7	9
$p(x)$	.1	.2	.4	.2	.1

  a. List the values x may assume.
  b. What value of x is most probable?
  c. Display the probability distribution as a graph.
  d. Find $P(x = 7)$.
  e. Find $P(x \ge 5)$.
  f. Find $P(x > 2)$.
  g. Find $E(x)$.

4.13 A discrete random variable x can assume five possible values: 2, 3, 5, 8, and 10. Its probability distribution is shown here:

x	2	3	5	8	10
$p(x)$	.10	.20	–	.30	.10

  a. What is $p(5)$?
  b. What is the probability that the random variable x is a value greater than 5?
  c. Find the mean and standard deviation of the distribution.

4.14 Explain why each of the following is or is not a valid probability distribution for a discrete random variable x:

  a.

x	0	1	2	3
$p(x)$	.1	.3	.3	.2

  b.

x	−2	−1	0
$p(x)$	.25	.50	.25

  c.

x	4	9	20
$p(x)$	−.3	.4	.3

  d.

x	2	3	5	6
$p(x)$	.15	.15	.45	.35

4.15 A die is tossed. Let x be the number of spots observed on the upturned face of the die.
  a. Find the probability distribution of x and display it in tabular form.
  b. Display the probability distribution of x in graphical form.

4.16 Toss three fair coins and let x equal the number of heads observed.
  a. Identify the sample points associated with this experiment and assign a value of x to each sample point.

b. Calculate $p(x)$ for each value of x.

c. Construct a graph for $p(x)$.

d. What is $P(x = 2 \text{ or } x = 3)$?

📊 Applet Exercise 4.1

Use the applet *Random Numbers* to generate a list of 25 numbers between 1 and 3, inclusive. Let x represent a number chosen from this list.

a. What are the possible values of x?

b. Write a probability distribution for x in table form.

c. Use the probability distribution in part **b** to find the expected value of x.

d. Let y be a number randomly chosen from the set $\{1, 2, 3\}$. Write a probability distribution for y in table form and use it to find the expected value of y.

e. Compare the expected values of x and y in parts **c** and **d**. Why should these two numbers be approximately the same?

📊 Applet Exercise 4.2

Run the applet *Simulating the Probability of a Head with a Fair Coin* 10 times with $n = 2$, resetting between runs, to simulate flipping two coins 10 times. Count and record the number of heads each time. Let x represent the number of heads on a single flip of the two coins.

a. What are the possible values of x?

b. Use the results of the simulation to write a probability distribution for x in table form and then use it to find the expected value of x.

c. Explain why the expected value in part **b** should be close to 1.

4.17 Consider the probability distribution shown here:
[NW]

x	-4	-3	-2	-1	0	1	2	3	4
$p(x)$	0.2	0.7	.10	.15	.30	.18	.10	.06	.02

a. Calculate μ, σ^2, and σ.

b. Graph $p(x)$. Locate μ, $\mu - 2\sigma$, and $\mu + 2\sigma$ on the graph.

c. What is the probability that x is in the interval $\mu \pm 2\sigma$?

4.18 Consider the discrete probability distribution shown here:

x	1	2	3	4	5
$p(x)$	.1	.2	.2	.3	.2

a. Find $\mu = E(x)$.

b. Find $\sigma = \sqrt{E[(x - \mu)^2]}$.

c. Find the probability that the value of x falls within one standard deviation of the mean. Compare this result to the Empirical Rule.

4.19 Consider the probability distributions shown here:

x	0	1	2		y	0	1	2
$p(x)$	.3	.4	.3		$p(y)$	.1	.8	.1

a. Use your intuition to find the mean for each distribution. How did you arrive at your choice?

b. Which distribution appears to be more variable? Why?

c. Calculate μ and σ^2 for each distribution. Compare these answers with your answers in parts **a** and **b**.

Applying the Concepts—Basic

4.20 **Apps not working on smartphone.** In a Pew Research Center survey titled *U.S. Smartphone Use in 2015*, more than 2,000 smartphone users were asked how often the applications (apps) they downloaded on their cell phones were not working correctly. Responses were recorded as follows: 1 = Frequently, 2 = Occasionally, 3 = Rarely, and 4 = Never. The probability distribution for the numerical response, x, is provided in the table.

a. Verify that the properties of a probability distribution for a discrete random variable are satisfied.

b. Find $P(x > 2)$.

c. Find $E(x)$. Interpret this value, practically.

Response, x		Probability, $p(x)$
1	(Frequently)	.10
2	(Occasionally)	.39
3	(Rarely)	.40
4	(Never)	.11

4.21 **NHTSA crash tests.** Refer to the NHTSA crash tests of new car models, Exercise 4.3 (p. 217). A summary of the driver-side star ratings for the 98 cars in the file is reproduced in the accompanying Minitab printout. Assume that one of the 98 cars is selected at random and let x equal the number of stars in the car's driver-side star rating.

Tally for Discrete Variables: DRIVSTAR

DRIVSTAR	Count	Percent
2	4	4.08
3	17	17.35
4	59	60.20
5	18	18.37
N=	98	

a. Use the information in the printout to find the probability distribution for x.

b. Find $P(x = 5)$.

c. Find $P(x \leq 2)$.

d. Find $\mu = E(x)$ and practically interpret the result.

4.22 **Ages of "dot-com" employees.** The age (in years) distribution for the employees of a highly successful "dot-com" company headquartered in Atlanta is shown in the next table. An employee is to be randomly selected from this population.

Age	20	21	22	23	24	25	26	27	28	29	30	31	32	33
Proportion	.02	.04	.05	.07	.04	.02	.07	.02	.11	.07	.09	.13	.15	.12

Source: Data provided by P. George Benson, University of Charleston.

a. Can the relative frequency distribution in the table be interpreted as a probability distribution? Explain.

b. Graph the probability distribution.

c. What is the probability that the randomly selected employee is over 30 years of age? Over 40 years of age? Under 30 years of age?

d. What is the probability that the randomly selected employee will be 25 or 26 years old?

4.23 **Variable speed limit control for freeways.** A common transportation problem in large cities is congestion on the freeways. In the *Canadian Journal of Civil Engineering* (January 2013), civil engineers investigated the use of variable speed limits (VSL) to control the congestion problem. A portion of an urban freeway was divided into three sections of equal length, and variable speed limits were posted (independently) in each section. Probability distributions of the optimal speed limits for the three sections were determined. For example, one possible set of distributions is as follows (probabilities in parentheses). *Section 1*: 30 mph (.05), 40 mph (.25), 50 mph (.25), 60 mph (.45); *Section 2*: 30 mph (.10), 40 mph (.25), 50 mph (.35), 60 mph (.30); *Section 3*: 30 mph (.15), 40 mph (.20), 50 mph (.30), 60 mph (.35).

a. Verify that the properties of a discrete probability distribution are satisfied for Section 1 of the freeway.

b. Repeat part **a** for Sections 2 and 3 of the freeway.

c. Find the probability that a vehicle traveling at the speed limit in Section 1 will exceed 30 mph.

d. Repeat part **c** for Sections 2 and 3 of the freeway.

4.24 **Choosing portable grill displays.** Refer to the *Journal of Consumer Research* (Mar. 2003) marketing study of influencing consumer choices by offering undesirable alternatives, Exercise 3.109 (p. 204). Recall that each of 124 college students selected showroom displays for portable grills. Five different displays (representing five different-sized grills) were available, but the students were instructed to select only three displays in order to maximize purchases of Grill #2 (a smaller-sized grill). The table shows the grill display combinations and the number of times each was selected by the 124 students. Suppose one of the 124 students is selected at random. Let x represent the sum of the grill numbers selected by this student. (This value is an indicator of the size of the grills selected.)

a. Find the probability distribution for x.

b. What is the probability that x exceeds 10?

Grill Display Combination	Number of Students
1-2-3	35
1-2-4	8
1-2-5	42
2-3-4	4
2-3-5	1
2-4-5	34

Source: Based on R. W. Hamilton, "Why Do People Suggest What They Do Not Want? Using Context Effects to Influence Others' Choices," *Journal of Consumer Research*, Vol. 29, March 2003 (Table 1).

4.25 **Do social robots walk or roll?** Refer to the *International Conference on Social Robotics* (Vol. 6414, 2010) study of the trend in the design of social robots, Exercise 2.3 (p. 72). Recall that in a random sample of 106 social (or service) robots designed to entertain, educate, and care for human users, 63 were built with legs only, 20 with wheels only, 8 with both legs and wheels, and 15 with neither legs nor wheels. Assume the following: Of the 63 robots with legs only, 50 have two legs, 5 have three legs, and 8 have four legs; of the 8 robots with both legs and wheels, all 8 have two legs. Suppose one of the 106 social robots is randomly selected. Let x equal the number of legs on the robot.

a. List the possible values of x.

b. Find the probability distribution of x.

c. Find $E(x)$ and give a practical interpretation of its value.

4.26 **Reliability of a manufacturing network.** A team of industrial management university professors investigated the reliability of a manufacturing system that involves multiple production lines (*Journal of Systems Sciences & Systems Engineering*, March 2013). An example of such a network is a system for producing integrated circuit (IC) cards with two production lines set up in sequence. Items (IC cards) first pass through Line 1, then are processed by Line 2. The probability distribution of the maximum capacity level (x) of each line is shown below. Assume the lines operate independently.

a. Verify that the properties of discrete probability distributions are satisfied for each line in the system.

b. Find the probability that the maximum capacity level for Line 1 will exceed 30 items.

c. Repeat part **b** for Line 2.

d. Now consider the network of two production lines. What is the probability that a maximum capacity level exceeding 30 items is maintained throughout the network? [*Hint:* Apply the multiplicative law of probability for independent events.]

e. Find the mean maximum capacity for each line. Interpret the results practically.

f. Find the standard deviation of the maximum capacity for each line. Then, give an interval for each line that will contain the maximum capacity with probability of at least .75.

Line	Maximum Capacity, x	$p(x)$
1	0	.01
	12	.02
	24	.02
	36	.95
2	0	.002
	35	.002
	70	.996

Applying the Concepts—Intermediate

4.27 **Solar energy cells.** According to the Earth Policy Institute (July 2014), 65% of the world's solar energy cells are manufactured in China. Consider a random sample of five solar energy cells and let x represent the number in the sample that are manufactured in China. In the next section, we show that the probability distribution for x is given by the formula

$$p(x) = \frac{(5!)(.65)^x(.35)^{5-x}}{(x!)(5-x)!}, \text{ where}$$

$$n! = (n)(n-1)(n-2)\cdots(2)(1) \text{ and } 0! = 1$$

a. Explain why x is a discrete random variable.

b. Find $p(x)$ for $x = 0, 1, 2, 3, 4,$ and 5.

c. Show that the properties for a discrete probability distribution are satisfied.

d. Find the probability that at least four of the five solar energy cells in the sample are manufactured in China.

4.28 USDA chicken inspection. In Exercise 3.19 (p. 170) you learned that one in every 100 slaughtered chickens passes USDA inspection with fecal contamination. Consider a random sample of three slaughtered chickens that all pass USDA inspection. Let x equal the number of chickens in the sample that have fecal contamination.

a. Find $p(x)$ for $x = 0, 1, 2, 3$.
b. Graph $p(x)$.
c. Find $P(x \leq 1)$.

4.29 Contaminated gun cartridges. A weapons manufacturer uses a liquid propellant to produce gun cartridges. During the manufacturing process, the propellant can get mixed with another liquid to produce a contaminated cartridge. A University of South Florida statistician, hired by the company to investigate the level of contamination in the stored cartridges, found that 23% of the cartridges in a particular lot were contaminated. Suppose you randomly sample (without replacement) gun cartridges from this lot until you find a contaminated one. Let x be the number of cartridges sampled until a contaminated one is found. It is known that the probability distribution for x is given by the formula

$$p(x) = (.23)(.77)^{x-1}, x = 1, 2, 3, \ldots$$

a. Find $p(1)$. Interpret this result.
b. Find $p(5)$. Interpret this result.
c. Find $P(x \geq 2)$. Interpret this result.

4.30 The "last name" effect in purchasing. The *Journal of Consumer Research* (August 2011) published a study demonstrating the "last name" effect—i.e., the tendency for consumers with last names that begin with a later letter of the alphabet to purchase an item before consumers with last names that begin with earlier letters. To facilitate the analysis, the researchers assigned a number, x, to each consumer based on the first letter of the consumer's last name. For example, last names beginning with "A" were assigned $x = 1$; last names beginning with "B" were assigned $x = 2$; and last names beginning with "Z" were assigned $x = 26$.

a. If the first letters of consumers' last names are equally likely, find the probability distribution for x.
b. Find $E(x)$ using the probability distribution, part **a**. If possible, give a practical interpretation of this value.?
c. Do you believe the probability distribution, part **a**, is realistic? Explain. How might you go about estimating the true probability distribution for x?

4.31 Mailrooms contaminated with anthrax. During autumn 2001, there was a highly publicized outbreak of anthrax cases among U.S. Postal Service workers. In *Chance* (Spring 2002), research statisticians discussed the problem of sampling mailrooms for the presence of anthrax spores. Let x equal the number of mailrooms contaminated with anthrax spores in a random sample of n mailrooms selected from a population of N mailrooms. The researchers showed that the probability distribution for x is given by the formula

$$p(x) = \frac{\binom{k}{x}\binom{N-k}{n-x}}{\binom{N}{n}}$$

where k is the number of contaminated mailrooms in the population. (In Section 4.4 we identify this probability distribution as the *hypergeometric distribution*.) Suppose $N = 100, n = 3$, and $k = 20$.

a. Find $p(0)$.
b. Find $p(1)$.
c. Find $p(2)$.
d. Find $p(3)$.

4.32 Investment risk analysis. The risk of a portfolio of financial assets is sometimes called *investment risk*. In general, investment risk is typically measured by computing the variance or standard deviation of the probability distribution that describes the decision maker's potential outcomes (gains or losses). The greater the variation in potential outcomes, the greater the uncertainty faced by the decision maker; the smaller the variation in potential outcomes, the more predictable the decision maker's gains or losses. The two discrete probability distributions given in the next table were developed from historical data. They describe the potential total physical damage losses next year to the fleets of delivery trucks of two different firms.

Firm A		Firm B	
Loss Next Year	Probability	Loss Next Year	Probability
$ 0	.01	$ 0	.00
500	.01	200	.01
1,000	.01	700	.02
1,500	.02	1,200	.02
2,000	.35	1,700	.15
2,500	.30	2,200	.30
3,000	.25	2,700	.30
3,500	.02	3,200	.15
4,000	.01	3,700	.02
4,500	.01	4,200	.02
5,000	.01	4,700	.01

a. Verify that both firms have the same expected total physical damage loss.
b. Compute the standard deviation of each probability distribution and determine which firm faces the greater risk of physical damage to its fleet next year.

4.33 Ryder Cup miracle in golf. The Ryder Cup is a 3-day golf tournament played between a team of golf professionals from the United States and a team from Europe. A total of 28 matches are played between the teams; one point is awarded to the team winning a match and half a point is awarded to each team if the match ends in a tie (draw). The team with the most points wins the tournament. In 1999, the United States was losing 10 points to 6 when it miraculously won 8.5 of a possible 12 points on the last day of the tournament to seal the win. On the last day, 12 single matches are played. A total of 8.5 points can be won in a variety of ways, as shown in the next table (p. 227). Given one team scores at least 8.5 points on the last day of the tournament, *Chance* (Fall 2009) determined the probabilities of each of these outcomes assuming each team is equally likely to win a match. Let x be the points scored by the winning team on the last day of the tournament when the team scores at least 8.5 points. Find the probability distribution of x.

Table for Exercise 4.33

Wins	Ties	Points	Probability
5	7	8.5	.000123
6	5	8.5	.008823
6	6	9.0	.000456
7	3	8.5	.128030
7	4	9.0	.020086
7	5	9.5	.001257
8	1	8.5	.325213
8	2	9.0	.153044
8	3	9.5	.032014
8	4	10.0	.002514
9	0	9.0	.115178
9	1	9.5	.108400
9	2	10.0	.032901
9	3	10.5	.003561
10	0	10.0	.034552
10	1	10.5	.021675
10	2	11.0	.003401
11	0	11.0	.006284
11	1	11.0	.001972
12	0	12.0	.000518

4.34 Stock market participation and IQ. Refer to *The Journal of Finance* (December 2011) study of whether the decision to invest in the stock market is dependent on IQ, Exercise 3.46 (p. 182). Recall that an IQ score (from a low score of 1 to a high score of 9) was determined for each in a sample of 158,044 Finnish citizens. Also recorded was whether or not the citizen invested in the stock market. The accompanying table gives the number of Finnish citizens in each IQ score/investment category. Which group of Finnish citizens (market investors or noninvestors) has the highest average IQ score?

IQ Score	Invest in Market	No Investment	Totals
1	893	4,659	5,552
2	1,340	9,409	10,749
3	2,009	9,993	12,002
4	5,358	19,682	25,040
5	8,484	24,640	33,124
6	10,270	21,673	31,943
7	6,698	11,260	17,958
8	5,135	7,010	12,145
9	4,464	5,067	9,531
Totals	44,651	113,393	158,044

Source: Based on M. Grinblatt, M. Keloharju, and J. Linnainaa, "IQ and Stock Market Participation," *The Journal of Finance*, Vol. 66, No. 6, December 2011 (data from Table 1 and Figure 1).

4.35 Expected loss due to flood damage. The National Weather Service issues precipitation forecasts that indicate the likelihood of measurable precipitation ($\geq .01$ inch) at a specific point (the official rain gauge) during a given time period. Suppose that if a measurable amount of rain falls during the next 24 hours, a river will reach flood stage and a business will incur damages of $300,000. The National Weather Service has indicated that there is a 30% chance of a measurable amount of rain during the next 24 hours.

a. Construct the probability distribution that describes the potential flood damages.
b. Find the firm's expected loss due to flood damage.

4.36 Expected Lotto winnings. Most states offer weekly lotteries to generate revenue for the state. Despite the long odds of winning, residents continue to gamble on the lottery each week. In SIA, Chapter 3 (p. 167), you learned that the chance of winning Florida's Pick-6 Lotto game is 1 in approximately 23 million. Suppose you buy a $1 Lotto ticket in anticipation of winning the $7 million grand prize. Calculate your expected net winnings. Interpret the result.

Applying the Concepts—Advanced

4.37 Variable speed limit control for freeways. Refer to the *Canadian Journal of Civil Engineering* (January 2013) study of variable speed limits, Exercise 4.23 (p. 225). Recall that a portion of an urban freeway was divided into three sections of equal length, and variable speed limits were posted (independently) in each section. The probability distribution of the optimal speed limit for each section follows (probabilities in parentheses). *Section 1:* 30 mph (.05), 40 mph (.25), 50 mph (.25), 60 mph (.45); *Section 2:* 30 mph (.10), 40 mph (.25), 50 mph (.35), 60 mph (.30); *Section 3:* 30 mph (.15), 40 mph (.20), 50 mph (.30), 60 mph (.35). A vehicle adhering to the speed limit will travel through the three sections of the freeway at a steady (fixed) speed. Let x represent this speed.

a. List the possible values of x.
b. Find $P(x = 30)$. [*Hint:* The event $\{x = 30\}$ is the union of the events $\{x = 30$ in Section 1$\}$, $\{x = 30$ in Section 2$\}$, and $\{x = 30$ in Section 3$\}$. Also, $P(x = 30$ in Section 1$) = P(x = 30 \mid$ Section 1$) \times P($Section 1$)$, where $P($Section 1$) = 1/3$, since the sections are of equal length.]
c. Find the probability distribution for x.
d. What is the probability that the vehicle can travel at least 50 mph through all three sections of the freeway?

4.38 Voter preferences for a committee. A "Condorcet" committee of, say, 3 members, is a committee that is preferred by voters over any other committee of 3 members. A scoring function was used to determine "Condorcet" committees in *Mathematical Social Sciences* (November 2013). Consider a committee with members A, B, and C. Suppose there are 10 voters who each have a preference for a 3-member committee. For example, one voter may prefer a committee made up of members A, C, and G. Then this voter's preference score for the {A, B, C} committee is 2, since 2 of the members (A and B) are on this voter's preferred list. For a 3-member committee, voter preference scores range from 0 (no members on the preferred list) to 3 (all members on the preferred list). The table below shows the preferred lists of 10 voters for a 3-member committee selected from potential members A, B, C, D, E, and G.

Voter:	1	2	3	4	5	6	7	8	9	10
	A	B	A	B	D	C	A	B	A	A
	C	C	B	C	E	E	C	C	B	C
	D	E	D	F	F	G	G	D	C	G

a. Find the preference score for committee {A, B, C} for each voter.

b. For a randomly selected voter, let x represent the preference score for committee {A, B, C}. Determine the probability distribution for x.

c. What is the probability that the preference score, x, exceeds 2?

d. Is {A, B, C} a "Condorcet" committee?

4.39 Parlay card betting. Odds makers try to predict which professional and college football teams will win and by how much (the *spread*). If the odds makers do this accurately, adding the spread to the underdog's score should make the final score a tie. Suppose a bookie will give you $6 for every $1 you risk if you pick the winners in three games (adjusted by the spread) on a "parlay" card. Thus, for every $1 bet, you will either lose $1 or gain $5. What is the bookie's expected earnings per dollar wagered?

4.3   The Binomial Distribution

Many experiments result in *dichotomous* responses—that is, responses for which there exist two possible alternatives, such as Yes-No, Pass-Fail, Defective-Nondefective, or Male-Female. A simple example of such an experiment is the coin-toss experiment. A coin is tossed a number of times, say, 10. Each toss results in one of two outcomes, Head or Tail. Ultimately, we are interested in the probability distribution of x, the number of heads observed. Many other experiments are equivalent to tossing a coin (either balanced or unbalanced) a fixed number n of times and observing the number x of times that one of the two possible outcomes occurs. Random variables that possess these characteristics are called **binomial random variables.**

Public opinion and consumer preference polls (e.g., the CNN, Gallup, and Harris polls) frequently yield observations on binomial random variables. For example, suppose a sample of 100 current customers is selected from a firm's database and each person is asked whether he or she prefers the firm's product (a Head) or prefers a competitor's product (a Tail). Suppose we are interested in x, the number of customers in the sample who prefer the firm's product. Sampling 100 customers is analogous to tossing the coin 100 times. Thus, you can see that consumer preference polls like the one described here are real-life equivalents of coin-toss experiments. We have been describing a **binomial experiment;** it is identified by the following characteristics.

Characteristics of a Binomial Experiment

1. The experiment consists of n identical trials.

2. There are only two possible outcomes on each trial. We will denote one outcome by S (for success) and the other by F (for failure).

3. The probability of S remains the same from trial to trial. This probability is denoted by p, and the probability of F is denoted by q. Note that $q = 1 - p$.

4. The trials are independent.

5. The binomial random variable x is the number of S's in n trials.

EXAMPLE 4.9	

Assessing Whether x Is Binomial—Business Problems

Problem For the following examples, decide whether x is a binomial random variable.

a. You randomly select 3 bonds out of a possible 10 for an investment portfolio. Unknown to you, 8 of the 10 will maintain their present value, and the other 2 will lose value due to a change in their ratings. Let x be the number of the 3 bonds you select that lose value.

b. Before marketing a new product on a large scale, many companies will conduct a consumer preference survey to determine whether the product is likely to be successful. Suppose a company develops a new diet soda and then conducts a taste preference survey in which 100 randomly chosen consumers state their preferences among the new soda and the two leading sellers. Let x be the number of the 100 who choose the new brand over the two others.

c. Some surveys are conducted by using a method of sampling other than simple random sampling (defined in Chapter 3). For example, suppose a television cable company plans to conduct a survey to determine the fraction of households in the city that would use the cable television service. The sampling method is to choose a city block at random and then survey every household on that block. This sampling technique is called *cluster sampling*. Suppose 10 blocks are so sampled, producing a total of 124 household responses. Let x be the number of the 124 households that would use the television cable service.

Solution

a. In checking the binomial characteristics in the box, a problem arises with both characteristic 3 (probabilities remaining the same from trial to trial) and characteristic 4 (independence). The probability that the first bond you pick loses value is clearly $\frac{2}{10}$. Now suppose the first bond you picked was 1 of the 2 that will lose value. This reduces the chance that the second bond you pick will lose value to $\frac{1}{9}$ because now only 1 of the 9 remaining bonds are in that category. Thus, the choices you make are dependent, and therefore x, the number of 3 bonds you select that lose value, is *not* a binomial random variable.

b. Surveys that produce dichotomous responses and use random sampling techniques are classic examples of binomial experiments. In our example, each randomly selected consumer either states a preference for the new diet soda or does not. The sample of 100 consumers is a very small proportion of the totality of potential consumers, so the response of one would be, for all practical purposes, independent of another.* Thus, x is a binomial random variable.

c. This example is a survey with dichotomous responses (Yes or No to the cable service), but the sampling method is not simple random sampling. Again, the binomial characteristic of independent trials would probably not be satisfied. The responses of households within a particular block would be dependent because the households within a block tend to be similar with respect to income, level of education, and general interests. Thus, the binomial model would not be satisfactory for x if the cluster sampling technique were employed.

Look Back Nonbinomial random variables with two outcomes on every trial typically occur because they do not satisfy characteristics 3 or 4 of a binomial experiment.

● **Now Work Exercise 4.48a**

EXAMPLE 4.10	**Problem** A retailer sells both the Apple iPhone and Google Android cell phones online. Assume that 80% of the phones the retailer sells online are iPhones and 20% are Androids.

Deriving the Binomial Probability Distribution in a Purchase Application

a. Use the steps given in Chapter 3 (box on p. 163) to find the probability that all of the next four online cell phone purchases are Androids.

b. Find the probability that three of the next four online cell phone purchases are Androids.

c. Let x represent the number of the next four online cell phone purchases are Androids. Explain why x is a binomial random variable.

d. Use the answers to parts **a** and **b** to derive a formula for $p(x)$, the probability distribution of the binomial random variable x.

---

*In most real-life applications of the binomial distribution, the population of interest has a finite number of elements (trials), denoted N. When N is large and the sample size n is small relative to N, say $n/N \leq .05$, the sampling procedure, for all practical purposes, satisfies the conditions of a binomial experiment.

Solution

a. 1. The first step is to define the experiment. Here we are interested in observing the type of cell phone purchased online by each of the next four (buying) customers: iPhone (*I*) or Android (*A*).

2. Next, we list the sample points associated with the experiment. Each sample point consists of the purchase decisions made by the four online customers. For example, *IIII* represents the sample point that all four purchase iPhones, while *AIII* represents the sample point that customer 1 purchases an Android, while customers 2, 3, and 4 purchase iPhones. The tree diagram, Figure 4.8, shows that there are 16 sample points. These 16 sample points are also listed in Table 4.2.

3. We now assign probabilities to the sample points. Note that each sample point can be viewed as the intersection of four customers' decisions and, assuming the decisions are made independently, the probability of each sample point can be obtained using the multiplicative rule, as follows:

$$
\begin{aligned}
P(IIII) = {}& P[(\text{customer 1 chooses iPhone}) \cap (\text{customer 2 chooses iPhone}) \\
& \cap (\text{customer 3 chooses iPhone}) \cap (\text{customer 4 chooses iPhone})] \\
= {}& P(\text{customer 1 chooses iPhone}) \times P(\text{customer 2 chooses} \\
& \text{iPhone}) \times P(\text{customer 3 chooses iPhone}) \\
& \times P(\text{customer 4 chooses iPhone}) \\
= {}& (.8)(.8)(.8)(.8) = (.8)^4 = .4096
\end{aligned}
$$

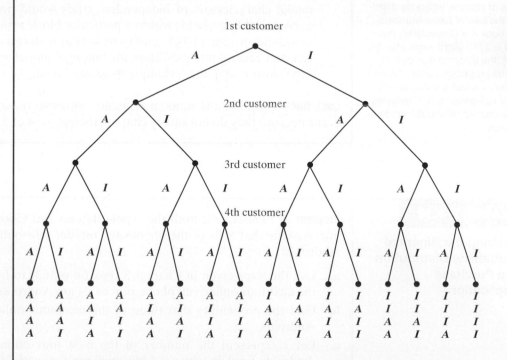

Figure 4.8
Tree diagram showing outcomes for cell phone purchases

Table 4.2	Sample Points for Experiment of Example 4.9			
AAAA	*IAAA*	*IIAA*	*AIII*	*IIII*
	AIAA	*IAIA*	*IAII*	
	AAIA	*IAAI*	*IIAI*	
	AAAI	*AIIA*	*IIIA*	
		AIAI		
		AAII		

All other sample point probabilities are calculated using similar reasoning. For example,

$$P(AIII) = (.2)(.8)(.8)(.8) = (.2)(.8)^3 = .1024$$

You can check that this reasoning results in sample point probabilities that add to 1 over the 16 points in the sample space.

4. Finally, we add the appropriate sample point probabilities to obtain the desired event probability. The event of interest is that all four online customers purchase Androids. In Table 4.2 we find only one sample point, $AAAA$, contained in this event. All other sample points imply that at least one iPhone is purchased. Thus,

$$P(\text{All four purchase Androids.}) = P(AAAA) = (.2)^4 = .0016$$

That is, the probability is only 16 in 10,000 that all four customers purchase Androids.

b. The event that three of the next four online buyers purchase Androids consists of the four sample points in the fourth column of Table 4.2: $IAAA, AIAA, AAIA$, and $AAAI$. To obtain the event probability, we add the sample point probabilities:

$$P(3 \text{ of next 4 customers purchase Androids})$$
$$= P(IAAA) + P(AIAA) + P(AAIA) + P(AAAI)$$
$$= (.2)^3(.8) + (.2)^3(.8) + (.2)^3(.8) + (.2)^3(.8)$$
$$= 4(.2)^3(.8) = .0256$$

Note that each of the four sample point probabilities is the same because each sample point consists of three A's and one I; the order does not affect the probability because the customers' decisions are (assumed) independent.

c. We can characterize the experiment as consisting of four identical trials—the four customers' purchase decisions. There are two possible outcomes to each trial, I or A, and the probability of A, $p = .2$, is the same for each trial. Finally, we are assuming that each customer's purchase decision is independent of all others, so that the four trials are independent. Then it follows that x, the number of the next four purchases that are Androids, is a binomial random variable.

d. The event probabilities in parts **a** and **b** provide insight into the formula for the probability distribution $p(x)$. First, consider the event that three purchases are Androids (part **b**). We found that

$$P(x = 3) = (\text{Number of sample points for which } x = 3)$$
$$\times (.2)^{\text{Number of Androids purchased}} \times (.8)^{\text{Number of iPhones purchased}}$$
$$= 4(.2)^3(.8)^1$$

In general, we can use combinatorial mathematics to count the number of sample points. For example,

Number of sample points for which $x = 3$

$$= \text{Number of different ways of selecting 3 of the 4 trials for } A \text{ purchases}$$
$$= \binom{4}{3} = \frac{4!}{3!(4-3)!} = \frac{4 \cdot 3 \cdot 2 \cdot 1}{(3 \cdot 2 \cdot 1) \cdot 1} = 4$$

The formula that works for any value of x can be deduced as follows. Because

$$P(x = 3) = \binom{4}{3}(.2)^3(.8)^1,$$

then $p(x) = \binom{4}{x}(.2)^x(.8)^{4-x}$

The component $\binom{4}{x}$ counts the number of sample points with x Androids and the component $(.2)^x(.8)^{4-x}$ is the probability associated with each sample point

The graph of $p(x)$ is shown as a probability histogram in Figure 4.9.

To calculate the values of μ and σ, substitute $n = 5$ and $p = .1$ into the following formulas:

$$\mu = np = (5)(.1) = .5$$
$$\sigma = \sqrt{npq} = \sqrt{(5)(.1)(.9)} = \sqrt{.45} = .67$$

To find the interval $\mu - 2\sigma$ to $\mu + 2\sigma$, we calculate

$$\mu - 2\sigma = .5 - 2(.67) = -.84$$
$$\mu + 2\sigma = .5 + 2(.67) = 1.84$$

If the experiment were repeated a large number of times, what proportion of the x observations would fall within the interval $\mu - 2\sigma$ to $\mu + 2\sigma$? You can see from Figure 4.9 that all observations equal to 0 or 1 will fall within the interval. The probabilities corresponding to these values are .5905 and .3280, respectively. Consequently, you would expect $.5905 + .3280 = .9185$, or approximately 91.9%, of the observations to fall within the interval $\mu - 2\sigma$ to $\mu + 2\sigma$.

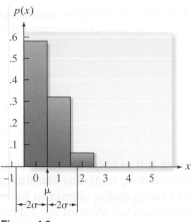

Figure 4.9

The binomial distribution: $n = 5, p = .1$

Look Back This result again emphasizes that for most probability distributions, observations rarely fall more than 2 standard deviations from μ.

● **Now Work Exercise 4.57**

Using Tables and Software to Find Binomial Probabilities

Calculating binomial probabilities becomes tedious when n is large. For some values of n and p, the binomial probabilities have been tabulated in Table I in Appendix D. Part of Table I is shown in Table 4.3; a graph of the binomial probability distribution for $n = 10$ and $p = .10$ is shown in Figure 4.10. Table I actually contains a total of nine tables, labeled (a) through (i), each one corresponding to $n = 5, 6, 7, 8, 9, 10, 15, 20$, and 25. In each of these tables, the columns correspond to values of p, and the rows correspond to values (k) of the random variable x. The entries in the table represent **cumulative binomial probabilities,** $p(x \le k)$. Thus, for example, the entry in the column corresponding to $p = .10$ and the row corresponding to $k = 2$ is .930 (shaded), and its interpretation is

$$P(x \le 2) = P(x = 0) + P(x = 1) + P(x = 2) = .930$$

This probability is also shaded in the graphical representation of the binomial distribution with $n = 10$ and $p = .10$ in Figure 4.10.

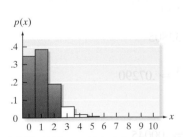

Figure 4.10

Binomial probability distribution for $n = 10$ and $p = .10$; $P(x \le 2)$ shaded

Table 4.3	Reproduction of Part of Table I in Appendix D: Binomial Probabilities for $n = 10$											
	p											
k	.01	.05	.10	.20	.30	.40	.50	.60	.70	.80	.90	.95	.99
0	.904	.599	.349	.107	.028	.006	.001	.000	.000	.000	.000	.000	.000
1	.996	.914	.736	.376	.149	.046	.011	.002	.000	.000	.000	.000	.000
2	1.000	.988	.930	.678	.383	.167	.055	.012	.002	.000	.000	.000	.000
3	1.000	.999	.987	.879	.650	.382	.172	.055	.011	.001	.000	.000	.000
4	1.000	1.000	.998	.967	.850	.633	.377	.166	.047	.006	.000	.000	.000
5	1.000	1.000	1.000	.994	.953	.834	.623	.367	.150	.033	.002	.000	.000
6	1.000	1.000	1.000	.999	.989	.945	.828	.618	.350	.121	.013	.001	.000
7	1.000	1.000	1.000	1.000	.998	.988	.945	.833	.617	.322	.070	.012	.000
8	1.000	1.000	1.000	1.000	1.000	.998	.989	.954	.851	.624	.264	.086	.004
9	1.000	1.000	1.000	1.000	1.000	1.000	.999	.994	.972	.893	.651	.401	.096

You can also use Table I to find the probability that x equals a specific value. For example, suppose you want to find the probability that $x = 2$ in the binomial distribution with $n = 10$ and $p = .10$. This is found by subtraction as follows:

$$P(x = 2) = [P(x = 0) + P(x = 1) + P(x = 2)] - [P(x = 0) + P(x = 1)]$$
$$= P(x \le 2) - P(x \le 1) = .930 - .736 = .194$$

The probability that a binomial random variable exceeds a specified value can be found using Table I and the notion of complementary events. For example, to find the probability that x exceeds 2 when $n = 10$ and $p = .10$, we use

$$P(x > 2) = 1 - P(x \le 2) = 1 - .930 = .070$$

Note that this probability is represented by the unshaded portion of the graph in Figure 4.10.

All probabilities in Table I are rounded to three decimal places. Thus, although none of the binomial probabilities in the table is exactly zero, some are small enough (less than .0005) to round to .000. For example, using the formula to find $P(x = 0)$ when $n = 10$ and $p = .6$, we obtain

$$P(x = 0) = \binom{10}{0}(.6)^0(.4)^{10-0} = .4^{10} = .00010486$$

but this is rounded to .000 in Table I in Appendix D (see Table 4.3).

Similarly, none of the table entries is exactly 1.0, but when the cumulative probabilities exceed .9995, they are rounded to 1.000. The row corresponding to the largest possible value for x, $x = n$, is omitted because all the cumulative probabilities in that row are equal to 1.0 (exactly). For example, in Table 4.3, with $n = 10$, $P(x \le 10) = 1.0$, no matter what the value of p.

Of course, you can also use a statistical software package to find binomial probabilities. The following example further illustrates the use of Table I and statistical software.

| **EXAMPLE 4.13**

Using the Binomial Table and Computer Software—Worker Unionization Problem | **Problem** Suppose a poll of 20 employees is taken in a large company. The purpose is to determine x, the number who favor unionization. Suppose that 60% of all the company's employees favor unionization.

a. Find the mean and standard deviation of x.
b. Use Table I in Appendix D to find the probability that $x \le 10$. Verify this probability using Minitab.
c. Use Table I to find the probability that $x > 12$.
d. Use Table I to find the probability that $x = 11$. Verify this probability using Minitab.
e. Graph the probability distribution of x and locate the interval $\mu \pm 2\sigma$ on the graph. |

Solution

a. The number of employees polled is presumably small compared with the total number of employees in this company. Thus, we may treat x, the number of the 20 who favor unionization, as a binomial random variable. The value of p is the fraction of the total employees who favor unionization; that is, $p = .6$. Therefore, we calculate the mean and variance:

$$\mu = np = 20(.6) = 12$$
$$\sigma^2 = npq = 20(.6)(.4) = 4.8$$
$$\sigma = \sqrt{4.8} = 2.19$$

b. Looking in the $k = 10$ row and the $p = .6$ column of Table I (Appendix D) for $n = 20$, we find the value of .245. Thus,

$$P(x \le 10) = .245$$

Consequently, there is only a .022 probability (i.e., about 2 chances in a hundred) that the first 4 packets will test positive for cocaine and the next 2 packets will test negative for cocaine. A reasonable jury would likely believe that an event with such a small probability is unlikely to occur and conclude that the 2 "lost" packets contained cocaine. In other words, most of us would infer that the defendant in the reverse cocaine sting was guilty of drug trafficking.

(continued)

[*Epilogue:* Several of the defendant's lawyers believed that the .022 probability was too high for jurors to conclude guilt "beyond a reasonable doubt." The argument was made moot, however, when, to the surprise of the defense, the prosecution revealed that the remaining 490 packets had not been used in any other reverse sting operations and offered to test a sample of them. On the advice of the statistician, the defense requested that an additional 20 packets be tested. All 20 tested positive for cocaine! As a consequence of this new evidence, the defendant was convicted by the jury.]

Exercises 4.40–4.60

Learning the Mechanics

4.40 Compute the following:

a. $\dfrac{7!}{3!(7-3)!}$ **b.** $\dbinom{9}{4}$ **c.** $\dbinom{5}{0}$ **d.** $\dbinom{4}{4}$ **e.** $\dbinom{5}{4}$

4.41 Consider the following probability distribution:

$$p(x) = \binom{5}{x}(.7)^x(.3)^{5-x} \quad (x = 0, 1, 2, \ldots, 5)$$

a. Is x a discrete or a continuous random variable?
b. What is the name of this probability distribution?
c. Graph the probability distribution.
d. Find the mean and standard deviation of x.
e. Show the mean and the 2-standard-deviation interval on each side of the mean on the graph you drew in part **c.**

4.42 Suppose x is a binomial random variable with $n = 3$ and $p = .3$.
a. Calculate the value of $p(x)$, $x = 0, 1, 2, 3$, using the formula for a binomial probability distribution.
b. Using your answers to part **a**, give the probability distribution for x in tabular form.

4.43 If x is a binomial random variable, compute $p(x)$ for each of the following cases:
a. $n = 4, x = 2, p = .2$
b. $n = 3, x = 0, p = .7$
c. $n = 5, x = 3, p = .1$
d. $n = 3, x = 1, p = .9$
e. $n = 3, x = 1, q = .3$
f. $n = 4, x = 2, q = .6$

4.44 If x is a binomial random variable, use Table I in Appendix D to find the following probabilities:
a. $P(x = 2)$ for $n = 10, p = .4$
b. $P(x \le 5)$ for $n = 15, p = .6$
c. $P(x > 1)$ for $n = 5, p = .1$
d. $P(x < 10)$ for $n = 25, p = .7$
e. $P(x \ge 10)$ for $n = 15, p = .9$
f. $P(x = 2)$ for $n = 20, p = .2$

4.45 If x is a binomial random variable, calculate μ, σ^2, and σ for each of the following:
a. $n = 25, p = .5$
b. $n = 80, p = .2$
c. $n = 100, p = .6$

d. $n = 70, p = .9$
e. $n = 60, p = .8$
f. $n = 1{,}000, p = .04$

4.46 The binomial probability distribution is a family of probability distributions with each single distribution depending on the values of n and p. Assume that x is a binomial random variable with $n = 4$.
a. Determine a value of p such that the probability distribution of x is symmetric.
b. Determine a value of p such that the probability distribution of x is skewed to the right.
c. Determine a value of p such that the probability distribution of x is skewed to the left.
d. Graph each of the binomial distributions you obtained in parts **a, b,** and **c.** Locate the mean for each distribution on its graph.
e. In general, for what values of p will a binomial distribution be symmetric? Skewed to the right? Skewed to the left?

Applet Exercise 4.3

Use the applets *Simulating the Probability of a Head with an Unfair Coin* $(P(H) = .2)$, and *Simulating the Probability of a Head with an Unfair Coin* $(P(H) = .8)$ to study the mean μ of a binomial distribution.
a. Run each applet mentioned above once with $n = 1{,}000$ and record the cumulative proportions. How will the cumulative proportion for each applet compare with the value of $P(H)$ given for the applet?
b. Using the cumulative proportion from each applet as p, compute $\mu = np$ for each applet where $n = 1{,}000$. What does the value of μ represent in terms of the results from running each applet in part **a**?
c. In your own words, describe what the mean μ of a binomial distribution represents.

Applet Exercise 4.4

Open the applet *Sample from a Population*. On the pull-down menu to the right of the top graph, select *Binary*. Set $n = 10$ as the sample size and repeatedly choose samples from the population. For each sample, record the number of 1s in the sample. Let

x be the number of 1s in a sample of size 10. Explain why x is a binomial random variable.

📊 Applet Exercise 4.5

Use the applet *Simulating the Stock Market* to estimate the probability that the stock market will go up each of the next two days. Repeatedly run the applet for $n = 2$, recording the number of up's each time. Use the proportion of 2s with your results as the estimate of the probability. Compare with the binomial probability where $x = 2, n = 2$, and $p = 0.5$.

Applying the Concepts—Basic

4.47 Working on summer vacation. Recall (Exercise 3.13, p. 169) that a *Harris Interactive* (July 2013) poll found that 22% of U.S. adults do not work at all while on summer vacation. In a random sample of 10 U.S. adults, let x represent the number who do not work during summer vacation.
  a. For this experiment, define the event that represents a "success."
  b. Explain why x is (approximately) a binomial random variable.
  c. Give the value of p for this binomial experiment.
  NW **d.** Find $P(x = 3)$.
  e. Find the probability that 2 or fewer of the 10 U.S. adults do not work during summer vacation.

4.48 Privacy and information sharing. Some grocery stores now offer their customers a free loyalty card that will save money on their purchases. In exchange, the store will keep track of the customer's shopping habits and could potentially sell these data to third parties. A *Pew Internet & American Life Project Survey* (January 2016) revealed that half of all U.S. adults would agree to participate in the loyalty card program. In a random sample of 250 U.S. adults, let x be the number who would participate in the free loyalty card program.
  NW **a.** Explain why x is a binomial random variable (to a reasonable degree of approximation).
  b. What is the value of p? Interpret this value.
  c. What is the expected value of x? Interpret this value.

4.49 The next presidential election. A recent study suggested that 70% of all eligible voters will vote in the next presidential election. Suppose 20 eligible voters are randomly selected from the population of all eligible voters.
  a. Analyze the potential outcomes for the sample using the binomial random variable.
  b. Use a binomial probability table to find the probability that more than 12 of the eligible voters sampled will vote in the next presidential election.
  c. Use a binomial probability table to find the probability that more than 10 but fewer than 16 of the 20 eligible voters sampled will vote in the next presidential election.

4.50 Physicians' opinions on a career in medicine. The Physicians' Foundation reported that 58% of all general practice physicians in the United States do not recommend medicine as a career (*The Physicians' Foundation 2012 Survey of America's Physicians*). Let x represent the number of sampled general practice physicians who do not recommend medicine as a career.

a. Explain why x is approximately a binomial random variable.
  b. Use the Physicians' Foundation report to estimate p for the binomial random variable.
  c. Consider a random sample of 25 general practice physicians. Use p from part **b** to find the mean and standard deviation of x, the number who do not recommend medicine as a career.
  d. For the sample of part **c**, find the probability that at least one general practice physician does not recommend medicine as a career.

4.51 Playing sports related to job pay. Does participation in youth and/or high school sports lead to greater wealth later in life? This was the subject of a recent *Harris POLL* (March 2015). The poll found that 15% of adults who participated in sports now have an income greater than \$100,000. In comparison, 9% of adults who did not participate in sports have an income greater than \$100,000. Consider a random sample of 25 adults, all of whom have participated in youth and/or high school sports.
  NW **a.** What is the probability that fewer than 20 of these adults have an income greater than \$100,000?
  b. What is the probability that between 10 and 20 of these adults have an income greater than \$100,000?
  c. Repeat parts **a** and **b,** but assume that none of the 25 sampled adults participated in youth and/or high school sports.

Applying the Concepts—Intermediate

4.52 Immediate feedback to incorrect exam answers. Researchers from the Educational Testing Service (ETS) found that providing immediate feedback to students answering open-ended questions can dramatically improve students' future performance on exams (*Educational and Psychological Measurement,* Feb. 2010). The ETS researchers used questions from the Graduate Record Examination (GRE) in the experiment. After obtaining feedback, students could revise their answers. Consider one of these questions. Initially, 50% of the students answered the question correctly. After providing immediate feedback to students who had answered incorrectly, 70% answered correctly. Consider a bank of 100 open-ended questions similar to those on the GRE.
  a. In a random sample of 20 students, what is the probability that more than half initially answered the question correctly?
  b. Refer to part **a**. After receiving immediate feedback, what is the probability that more than half of the students answered the question correctly?

4.53 Fingerprint expertise. Refer to the *Psychological Science* (August 2011) study of fingerprint identification, Exercise 3.85 (p. 200). The study found that when presented with prints from the same individual, a fingerprint expert will correctly identify the match 92% of the time. In contrast, a novice will correctly identify the match 75% of the time. Consider a sample of five different pairs of fingerprints, where each pair is a match.
  a. What is the probability that an expert will correctly identify the match in all five pairs of fingerprints?
  b. What is the probability that a novice will correctly identify the match in all five pairs of fingerprints?

4.54 **Making your vote count.** Refer to the *Chance* (Fall 2007) study on making your vote count, Exercise 3.29 (p. 171). Recall the scenario where you are one of five county commissioners voting on an issue, and each commissioner is equally likely to vote for or against.

   a. Your vote counts (i.e., is the decisive vote) only if the other four voters split, two in favor and two against. Use the binomial distribution to find the probability that your vote counts.

   b. If you convince two other commissioners to "vote in bloc" (i.e., you all agree to vote among yourselves first, and whatever the majority decides is the way all three will vote, guaranteeing that the issue is decided by the bloc), your vote counts only if these two commissioners split their bloc votes, one in favor and one against. Again, use the binomial distribution to find the probability that your vote counts.

4.55 **Bridge inspection ratings.** According to the National Bridge Inspection Standard (NBIS), public bridges over 20 feet in length must be inspected and rated every 2 years. The NBIS rating scale ranges from 0 (poorest rating) to 9 (highest rating). University of Colorado engineers used a probabilistic model to forecast the inspection ratings of all major bridges in Denver (*Journal of Performance of Constructed Facilities*, February 2005). For the year 2020, the engineers forecast that 9% of all major Denver bridges will have ratings of 4 or below.

   a. Use the forecast to find the probability that in a random sample of 10 major Denver bridges, at least 3 will have an inspection rating of 4 or below in 2020.

   b. Suppose that you actually observe 3 or more of the sample of 10 bridges with inspection ratings of 4 or below in 2020. What inference can you make? Why?

4.56 **Tax returns audited by the IRS.** According to the Internal Revenue Service (IRS), the chances of your tax return being audited are about 1 in 100 if your income is less than $1 million and 9 in 100 if your income is $1 million or more (*IRS Enforcement and Services Statistics*).

   a. What is the probability that a taxpayer with income less than $1 million will be audited by the IRS? With income $1 million or more?

   b. If five taxpayers with incomes under $1 million are randomly selected, what is the probability that exactly one will be audited? That more than one will be audited?

   c. Repeat part **b** assuming that five taxpayers with incomes of $1 million or more are randomly selected.

   d. If two taxpayers with incomes under $1 million are randomly selected and two with incomes more than $1 million are randomly selected, what is the probability that none of these taxpayers will be audited by the IRS?

   e. What assumptions did you have to make in order to answer these questions using the methodology presented in this section?

4.57 **FDA report on pesticides in food.** Periodically, the Food and Drug Administration (FDA) produces a report as part of its pesticide monitoring program. The FDA's report covers a variety of food items, each of which is analyzed for potentially harmful chemical compounds. Recently, the FDA reported that no pesticides at all were found in 85% of the domestically produced milk, dairy, and egg samples (*Pesticide Monitoring Program: Fiscal Year 2012 Pesticide*

Report, U.S. Food and Drug Administration). Consider a random sample of 800 milk, dairy, and egg items analyzed for the presence of pesticides.

   a. Compute μ and σ for the random variable x, the number of dairy-related items that showed no trace of pesticide.

   b. Based on a sample of 800 dairy-related items, is it likely you would observe less than half without any traces of pesticide? Explain.

Applying the Concepts–Advanced

4.58 **Purchasing decision.** Suppose you are a purchasing officer for a large company. You have purchased 5 million electrical switches, and your supplier has guaranteed that the shipment will contain no more than .1% defectives. To check the shipment, you randomly sample 500 switches, test them, and find that four are defective. Based on this evidence, do you think the supplier has complied with the guarantee? Explain.

4.59 **USGA golf ball specifications.** According to the U.S. Golf Association (USGA), "The diameter of the [golf] ball must not be less than 1.680 inches" (USGA, 2016). The USGA periodically checks the specifications of golf balls by randomly sampling balls from pro shops around the country. Two dozen of each kind are sampled, and if more than three do not meet requirements, that kind of ball is removed from the USGA's approved-ball list.

   a. What assumptions must be made and what information must be known in order to use the binomial probability distribution to calculate the probability that the USGA will remove a particular kind of golf ball from its approved-ball list?

   b. Suppose 10% of all balls produced by a particular manufacturer are less than 1.680 inches in diameter, and assume that the number of such balls, x, in a sample of two dozen balls can be adequately characterized by a binomial probability distribution. Find the mean and standard deviation of the binomial distribution.

   c. Refer to part **b.** If x has a binomial distribution, then so does the number, y, of balls in the sample that meet the USGA's minimum diameter. [*Note*: $x + y = 24$.] Describe the distribution of y. In particular, what are p, q, and n? Also, find $E(y)$ and the standard deviation of y.

4.60 **Network forensic analysis.** A network forensic analyst is responsible for identifying worms, viruses, and infected nodes in the computer network. A new methodology for finding patterns in data that signify infections was investigated in *IEEE Transactions on Information Forensics and Security* (May, 2013). The method uses multiple filters to check strings of information. For this exercise, consider a data string of length 4 bytes (positions), where each byte is either a 0 or a 1 (e.g., 0010). Also, consider two possible strings, named S_1 and S_2. In a simple single-filter system, the probability that S_1 and S_2 differ in any one of the bytes is .5. Derive a formula for the probability that the two strings differ on exactly x of the 4 bytes. Do you recognize this probability distribution?

4.4 Other Discrete Distributions: Poisson and Hypergeometric

Poisson Random Variable

A type of discrete probability distribution that is often useful in describing the number of rare events that will occur in a specific period of time or in a specific area or volume is the **Poisson distribution** (named after the eighteenth-century physicist and mathematician Siméon Poisson). Typical examples of random variables for which the Poisson probability distribution provides a good model are as follows:

1. The number of industrial accidents per month at a manufacturing plant
2. The number of noticeable surface defects (scratches, dents, etc.) found by quality inspectors on a new automobile
3. The parts per million of some toxin found in the water or air emission from a manufacturing plant
4. The number of customer arrivals per unit of time at a supermarket checkout counter
5. The number of death claims received per day by an insurance company
6. The number of errors per 100 invoices in the accounting records of a company

Characteristics of a Poisson Random Variable

1. The experiment consists of counting the number of times a certain event occurs during a given unit of time or in a given area or volume (or weight, distance, or any other unit of measurement).
2. The probability that an event occurs in a given unit of time, area, or volume is the same for all the units.
3. The number of events that occur in one unit of time, area, or volume is independent of the number that occur in any other mutually exclusive unit.
4. The mean (or expected) number of events in each unit is denoted by the Greek letter lambda, λ.

The characteristics of the Poisson random variable are usually difficult to verify for practical examples. The examples given satisfy them well enough that the Poisson distribution provides a good model in many instances. As with all probability models, the real test of the adequacy of the Poisson model is in whether it provides a reasonable approximation to reality—that is, whether empirical data support it.

The probability distribution, mean, and variance for a Poisson random variable are shown in the next box.

Probability Distribution, Mean, and Variance for a Poisson Random Variable*

$$p(x) = \frac{\lambda^x e^{-\lambda}}{x!} \quad (x = 0, 1, 2, \dots)$$

$$\mu = \lambda$$

$$\sigma^2 = \lambda$$

where

λ = Mean number of events during given unit of time, area, volume, etc.

$e = 2.71828\dots$

*The Poisson probability distribution also provides a good approximation to a binomial distribution with mean $\lambda = np$ when n is large and p is small (say, $np \leq 7$).

The calculation of Poisson probabilities is made easier by the use of statistical software, as illustrated in Example 4.14.

EXAMPLE 4.14

Finding Poisson Probabilities—Worker Absenteeism

Problem Suppose the number, x, of a company's employees who are absent on Mondays has (approximately) a Poisson probability distribution. Furthermore, assume that the average number of Monday absentees is 2.6.

a. Find the mean and standard deviation of x, the number of employees absent on Monday.

b. Use Minitab to find the probability that exactly five employees are absent on a given Monday.

c. Use Minitab to find the probability that fewer than two employees are absent on a given Monday.

d. Use Minitab to find the probability that more than five employees are absent on a given Monday.

Solution

a. The mean and variance of a Poisson random variable are both equal to λ. Thus, for this example,

$$\mu = \lambda = 2.6$$
$$\sigma^2 = \lambda = 2.6$$

Then the standard deviation of x is

$$\sigma = \sqrt{2.6} = 1.61$$

Remember that the mean measures the central tendency of the distribution and does not necessarily equal a possible value of x. In this example, the mean is 2.6 absences, and although there cannot be 2.6 absences on a given Monday, the average number of Monday absences is 2.6. Similarly, the standard deviation of 1.61 measures the variability of the number of absences per week. Perhaps a more helpful measure is the interval $\mu \pm 2\sigma$, which in this case stretches from $-.62$ to 5.82. We expect the number of absences to fall in this interval most of the time—with at least 75% relative frequency (according to Chebyshev's Rule) and probably with approximately 95% relative frequency (the Empirical Rule). The mean and the 2-standard-deviation interval around it are shown in Figure 4.13.

b. Since x represents the number of employees absent on a given Monday, we want to find $P(x = 5)$. As with binomial probabilities, tables and computer software give Poisson probabilities of the form $P(x = k)$ or cumulative probabilities of the form $P(x \leq k)$. Setting $\lambda = 2.6$ as an option in Minitab and specifying the value "5" for a Poisson probability, we obtain the value (shaded) shown at the top of the Minitab printout, Figure 4.14:

$$P(x = 5) = .0735$$

c. Here, we want to find $P(x < 2)$. Since x is a discrete whole number, we know that

$$P(x < 2) = P(x \leq 1)$$

This probability is now in the form of a cumulative probability and can be found using statistical software. Setting $\lambda = 2.6$ as an option in Minitab and specifying the value "1" for a cumulative Poisson probability, we obtain the value (shaded) shown in the middle of the Minitab printout, Figure 4.14:

$$P(x < 2) = P(x \leq 1) = .2674$$

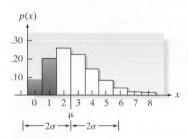

Figure 4.13

Probability distribution for number of Monday absences

Probability Density Function

Poisson with mean = 2.6

```
x   P( X = x )
5    0.0735394
```

Cumulative Distribution Function

Poisson with mean = 2.6

```
x   P( X <= x )
1    0.267385
```

Cumulative Distribution Function

Poisson with mean = 2.6

```
x   P( X <= x )
5    0.950963
```

Figure 4.14

Minitab output for Example 4.14

d. To find the probability that more than five employees are absent on a given Monday, we consider the complementary event

$$P(x > 5) = 1 - P(x \leq 5)$$

Again, we select $\lambda = 2.6$ as an option in Minitab and now specify the value "5" for a cumulative Poisson probability. This yields the probability, .951, shaded at the bottom of the Minitab printout, Figure 4.14. Now, we compute:

$$P(x > 5) = 1 - P(x \leq 5) = 1 - .951 = .049$$

Look Back Note from Figure 4.13 that the probability of part **d** is in the area in the interval $\mu \pm 2\sigma$, or $2.6 \pm 2(1.61) = (-.62, 5.82)$. Then, the number of absences should exceed 5—or, equivalently, should be more than 2 standard deviations from the mean—during only about 4.9% of all Mondays. This percentage agrees remarkably well with that given by the Empirical Rule for mound-shaped distributions, which informs us to expect about 5% of the measurements (values of the random variable x) to lie farther than 2 standard deviations from the mean.

● **Now Work Exercise 4.71**

Hypergeometric Random Variable

The **hypergeometric probability distribution** provides a realistic model for some types of enumerative (countable) data. The characteristics of the hypergeometric distribution are listed in the following box:

Characteristics of a Hypergeometric Random Variable

1. The experiment consists of randomly drawing n elements without replacement from a set of N elements, r of which are S's (for success) and $(N - r)$ of which are F's (for failure).
2. The hypergeometric random variable x is the number of S's in the draw of n elements.

Note that both the hypergeometric and binomial characteristics stipulate that each draw, or trial, results in one of two outcomes. The basic difference between these random variables is that the hypergeometric trials are dependent, while the binomial trials are independent. The draws are dependent because the probability of drawing an S (or an F) is dependent on what occurred on preceding draws.

To illustrate the dependence between trials, we note that the probability of drawing an S on the first draw is r/N. Then the probability of drawing an S on the second draw depends on the outcome of the first. It will be either $(r - 1)/(N - 1)$ or $r/(N - 1)$, depending on whether the first draw was an S or an F. Consequently, the results of the draws represent dependent events.

For example, suppose we define x as the number of women hired in a random selection of three applicants from a total of six men and four women. This random variable satisfies the characteristics of a **hypergeometric random variable** with $N = 10$ and $n = 3$. The possible outcomes on each trial are either the selection of a female (S) or the selection of a male (F). Another example of a hypergeometric random variable is the number x of defective large-screen plasma televisions in a random selection of $n = 4$ from a shipment of $N = 8$. Finally, as a third example, suppose $n = 5$ stocks are randomly selected from a list of $N - 15$ stocks. Then the number x of the five companies selected that pay regular dividends to stockholders is a hypergeometric random variable.

$N = 492$ is the total number of packets in the population

$S = 327$ is the number of successes (cocaine packets) in the population

$n = 2$ is the sample size

$x = 0$ is the number of successes (cocaine packets) in the sample

Again, we substitute into the formula for $p(x)$ to obtain

$$P(x = 0) = p(0) = \frac{\binom{327}{0}\binom{165}{2}}{\binom{492}{2}} = \frac{\left(\frac{327!}{0!327!}\right)\left(\frac{165!}{2!163!}\right)}{\left(\frac{492!}{2!490!}\right)}$$

$$= .112$$

By the multiplicative law of probability, the probability that the first 4 packets test positive for cocaine and the next 2 packets test negative is the product of the two probabilities just given:

$$P(\text{first 4 positive and next 2 negative}) = (.197)(.112)$$

$$= .0221$$

Note that this exact probability is almost identical to the approximate probability computed with the binomial distribution in Section 4.3.

Exercises 4.61–4.83

Learning the Mechanics

4.61 Consider the probability distribution shown here:

$$p(x) = \frac{3^x e^{-3}}{x!} \quad (x = 0, 1, 2, \dots)$$

a. Is x a discrete or continuous random variable? Explain.
b. What is the name of this probability distribution?
c. Graph the probability distribution for $x \le 6$.
d. Find the mean and standard deviation of x.

4.62 Assume that x is a random variable having a Poisson probability distribution with a mean of 1.5. Use statistical software to find the following probabilities:
a. $P(x \le 3)$ b. $P(x \ge 3)$
c. $P(x = 3)$ d. $P(x = 0)$
e. $P(x > 0)$ f. $P(x > 6)$

4.63 Given that x is a hypergeometric random variable, compute $p(x)$ for each of the following cases:
a. $N = 5, n = 3, r = 3, x = 1$
b. $N = 9, n = 5, r = 3, x = 3$
c. $N = 4, n = 2, r = 2, x = 2$
d. $N = 4, n = 2, r = 2, x = 0$

4.64 Given that x is a hypergeometric random variable with $N = 10, n = 5$, and $r = 6$, compute the following:
a. $P(x = 0)$
b. $P(x = 1)$
c. $P(x \le 1)$
d. $P(x \ge 2)$

4.65 Given that x is a random variable for which a Poisson probability distribution provides a good approximation, use statistical software to find the following:

a. $P(x \le 2)$ when $\lambda = 1$
b. $P(x \le 2)$ when $\lambda = 2$
c. $P(x \le 2)$ when $\lambda = 3$
d. What happens to the probability of the event $\{x \le 2\}$ as λ increases from 1 to 3? Is this intuitively reasonable?

4.66 Suppose x is a random variable for which a Poisson probability distribution with $\lambda = 5$ provides a good characterization.
a. Graph $p(x)$ for $x = 0, 1, 2, \dots, 15$.
b. Find μ and σ for x and locate μ and the interval $\mu \pm 2\sigma$ on the graph.
c. What is the probability that x will fall within the interval $\mu \pm 2\sigma$?

4.67 Suppose you plan to sample 10 items from a population of 100 items and would like to determine the probability of observing 4 defective items in the sample. Which probability distribution should you use to compute this probability under the conditions listed here? Justify your answers.
a. The sample is drawn without replacement.
b. The sample is drawn with replacement.

4.68 Given that x is a hypergeometric random variable with $N = 8, n = 4$, and $r = 3$:
a. Display the probability distribution for x in tabular form.
b. Find $P(x \le 2)$.
c. Compute the variance of x.

Applying the Concepts—Basic

4.69 **Do social robots walk or roll?** Refer to the *International Conference on Social Robotics* (Vol. 6414, 2010) study of the trend in the design of social robots, Exercise 4.25

(p. 225). The study found that of 106 social robots, 63 were built with legs only, 20 with wheels only, 8 with both legs and wheels, and 15 with neither legs nor wheels. Suppose you randomly select 10 of the 106 social robots and count the number, x, with neither legs nor wheels.

a. Demonstrate why the probability distribution for x should not be approximated by the binomial distribution.

b. Show that the properties of the hypergeometric probability distribution are satisfied for this experiment.

c. Find μ and σ for the probability distribution for x.

d. Calculate the probability that $x = 2$.

4.70 FDIC bank failures. The Federal Deposit Insurance Corporation (FDIC) normally insures deposits of up to \$100,000 in banks that are members of the Federal Reserve System against losses due to bank failure or theft. Over the last 10 years, the average number of bank failures per year among insured banks was 52 (*FDIC Failed Bank List*, 2016). Assume that x, the number of bank failures per year among insured banks, can be adequately characterized by a Poisson probability distribution with mean 52.

a. Find the expected value and standard deviation of x.

b. In 2010, 157 banks failed. How far (in standard deviations) does $x = 157$ lie above the mean of the Poisson distribution? That is, find the z-score for $x = 157$.

c. In 2015, 8 banks failed. Find $P(x \le 8)$.

4.71 Airline fatalities. Over the past 5 years, U.S. airlines average about 1 fatality per month (U.S. Department of Transportation, *National Transportation Statistics: 2015*). Assume that the probability distribution for x, the number of fatalities per month, can be approximated by a Poisson probability distribution.

a. What is the probability that no fatalities will occur during any given month?

b. What is the probability that one fatality will occur during a month?

c. Find $E(x)$ and the standard deviation of x.

4.72 Male nannies. According to the International Nanny Association (INA), 4,176 nannies were placed in a job during a recent year (www.nanny.org). Of these, only 24 were men. In Exercise 3.12 (p. 169) you found the probability that a randomly selected nanny who was placed during a recent year is a man. Now use the hypergeometric distribution to find the probability that in a random sample of 10 nannies who were placed during a recent year, at least 1 is a man.

4.73 Contaminated gun cartridges. Refer to the investigation of contaminated gun cartridges at a weapons manufacturer, presented in Exercise 4.29 (p. 226). In a sample of 158 cartridges from a certain lot, 36 were found to be contaminated and 122 were "clean." If you randomly select 5 of these 158 cartridges, what is the probability that all 5 will be "clean"?

4.74 Arrivals at an emergency room. Applications of the Poisson distribution were discussed in the *Journal of Case Research in Business and Economics* (December 2014). In one case involving a hospital emergency room, 2 patients arrive on average every 10 minutes. Let x = number of patients arriving at the emergency room in any 10-minute

period. Assume that x has a Poisson distribution with mean 2. What is the probability that more than 4 patients arrive at the emergency room in the next 10 minutes?

Applying the Concepts—Intermediate

4.75 Museum management. Refer to the *Museum Management and Curatorship* (June 2010) study of the criteria used to evaluate museum performance, Exercise 3.18 (p. 170). Recall that the managers of 30 leading museums of contemporary art were asked to provide the performance measure used most often. Of these 30 museums, 8 specified "total visitors" as the performance measure. Consider a random sample of 5 museums selected from the 30. How likely is it that none of the museums in the sample specified "total visitors" as the performance measure?

4.76 Traffic fatalities and sporting events. The relationship between close sporting events and game-day traffic fatalities was investigated in the *Journal of Consumer Research* (December 2011). The researchers found that closer football and basketball games are associated with more traffic fatalities. The methodology used by the researchers involved modeling the traffic fatality count for a particular game as a Poisson random variable. For games played at the winner's location (home court or home field), the mean number of traffic fatalities was .5. Use this information to find the probability that at least three game-day traffic fatalities will occur at the winning team's location.

4.77 Cell phone handoff behavior. Refer to the *Journal of Engineering, Computing and Architecture* (Vol. 3., 2009) study of cell phone handoff behavior, Exercise 3.47 (p. 183). Recall that a "handoff" describes the process of a cell phone moving from one base channel (identified by a color code) to another. During a particular driving trip, a cell phone changed channels (color codes) 85 times. Color code "b" was accessed 40 times on the trip. You randomly select 7 of the 85 handoffs. How likely is it that the cell phone accessed color code "b" only twice for these 7 handoffs?

4.78 Guilt in decision making. The *Journal of Behavioral Decision Making* (January 2007) published a study of how guilty feelings impact on-the-job decisions. In one experiment, 57 participants were assigned to a guilty state through a reading/writing task. Immediately after the task, the participants were presented with a decision problem where the stated option had predominantly negative features (e.g., spending money on repairing a very old car). Of these 57 participants, 45 chose the stated option. Suppose 10 of the 57 guilty-state participants are selected at random. Define x as the number in the sample of 10 who chose the stated option.

a. Find $P(x = 5)$.

b. Find $P(x = 8)$.

c. What is the expected value (mean) of x?

4.79 Flaws in plastic-coated wire. The British Columbia Institute of Technology provides on its Web site (www.math.bcit.ca) practical applications of statistics at mechanical engineering firms. The following is a Poisson application. A roll of plastic-coated wire has an average of .8 flaw per 4-meter length of wire. Suppose a quality-control engineer will sample a 4-meter length of wire from a roll of wire 220 meters in length. If no flaws are found in the sample, the engineer will accept the entire roll of wire.

What is the probability that the roll will be rejected? What assumption did you make to find this probability?

4.80 Making high-stakes insurance decisions. The *Journal of Economic Psychology* (September 2008) published the results of a high-stakes experiment in which subjects were asked how much they would pay for insuring a valuable painting. The painting was threatened by fire and theft, hence, the need for insurance. To make the risk realistic, the subjects were informed that if it rained on exactly 24 days in July, the painting was considered to be stolen; if it rained on exactly 23 days in August, the painting was considered to be destroyed by fire. Although the probability of these two events, "fire" and "theft," was ambiguous for the subjects, the researchers estimated their probabilities of occurrence at .0001. Rain frequencies for the months of July and August were shown to follow a Poisson distribution with a mean of 10 days per month.
  a. Find the probability that it will rain on exactly 24 days in July.
  b. Find the probability that it will rain on exactly 23 days in August.
  c. Are the probabilities, parts **a** and **b**, good approximations to the probabilities of "fire" and "theft"?

Applying the Concepts—Advanced

4.81 Gender discrimination suit. The *Journal of Business & Economic Statistics* (July 2000) presented a case in which a charge of gender discrimination was filed against the U.S. Postal Service. At the time, there were 302 U.S. Postal Service employees (229 men and 73 women) who applied for promotion. Of the 72 employees who were awarded promotion, 5 were female. Make an inference about whether or not females at the U.S. Postal Service were promoted fairly.

4.82 Waiting for a car wash. An automatic car wash takes exactly 5 minutes to wash a car. On average, 10 cars per hour arrive at the car wash. Suppose that 30 minutes before closing time, 5 cars are in line. If the car wash is in continuous use until closing time, is it likely anyone will be in line at closing time?

4.83 Elevator passenger arrivals. A study of the arrival process of people using elevators at a multilevel office building was conducted and the results reported in *Building Services Engineering Research and Technology* (October 2012). Suppose that at one particular time of day, elevator passengers arrive in batches of size 1 or 2 (i.e., either 1 or 2 people arrive at the same time to use the elevator). The researchers assumed that the number of batches, n, arriving over a specific time period follows a Poisson process with mean $\lambda = 1.1$. Now let x_n represent the number of passengers (either 1 or 2) in batch n and assume the batch size has probabilities $p = P(x_n = 1) = .4$ and $q = P(x_n = 2) = .6$. Then, the total number of passengers arriving over a specific time period is $y = x_1 + x_2 + \ldots + x_n$. The researchers showed that if $x_1, x_2, \ldots, x_n$ are independent and identically distributed random variables and also independent of n, then y follows a *compound Poisson* distribution.
  a. Find $P(y = 0)$, i.e., the probability of no arrivals during the time period. [*Hint:* $y = 0$ only when $n = 0$.]
  b. Find $P(y = 1)$, i.e., the probability of only 1 arrival during the time period. [*Hint:* $y = 1$ only when $n = 1$ and $x_1 = 1$.]

PART II: CONTINUOUS RANDOM VARIABLES

4.5 Probability Distributions for Continuous Random Variables

The graphical form of the probability distribution for a **continuous random variable** x is a smooth curve that might appear as shown in Figure 4.17. This curve, a function of x, is denoted by the symbol $f(x)$ and is variously called a **probability density function (pdf),** a **frequency function,** or a **probability distribution.**

The areas under a probability distribution correspond to probabilities for x. For example, the area A beneath the curve between the two points a and b, as shown in Figure 4.17, is the probability that x assumes a value between a and b ($a < x < b$). Because there is no area over a point, say $x = a$, it follows that (according to our model) the probability associated with a particular value of x is equal to 0; that is, $P(x = a) = 0$ and hence $P(a < x < b) = P(a \le x \le b)$. In other words, the probability is the same whether or not you include the endpoints of the interval. Also, because areas over intervals represent probabilities, it follows that the total area under a probability distribution, the probability assigned to all values of x, should equal 1. Note that probability distributions for continuous random variables possess different shapes depending on the relative frequency distributions of real data that the probability distributions are supposed to model.

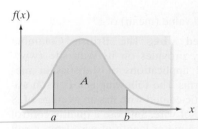

Figure 4.17

A probability distribution $f(x)$ for a continuous random variable x

The **probability distribution for a continuous random variable,** x, can be represented by a smooth curve—a function of x, denoted $f(x)$. The curve is called a **density function** or **frequency function.** The probability that x falls between two values, a and b, i.e., $P(a < x < b)$, is the area under the curve between a and b.

The areas under most probability distributions are obtained by using calculus or numerical methods.* Because these methods often involve difficult procedures, we will give the areas for one of the most common probability distributions in tabular form in Appendix D. Then, to find the area between two values of x, say $x = a$ and $x = b$, you simply have to consult the appropriate table. Of course, you can always use statistical software to find this area.

For each of the continuous random variables presented in this chapter, we will give the formula for the probability distribution along with its mean μ and standard deviation σ. These two numbers will enable you to make some approximate probability statements about a random variable even when you do not have access to a table of areas under the probability distribution.

4.6 The Normal Distribution

One of the most commonly observed continuous random variables has a **bell-shaped** probability distribution (or **bell curve**), as shown in Figure 4.18. It is known as a **normal random variable,** and its probability distribution is called a **normal distribution**.

The normal distribution plays a very important role in the science of statistical inference. Moreover, many business phenomena generate random variables with probability distributions that are very well approximated by a normal distribution. For example, the monthly rate of return for a particular stock is approximately a normal random variable, and the probability distribution for the weekly sales of a corporation might be approximated by a normal probability distribution. The normal distribution might also provide an accurate model for the distribution of scores on an employment aptitude test. You can determine the adequacy of the normal approximation to an existing population by comparing the relative frequency distribution of a large sample of the data to the normal probability distribution. Methods to detect disagreement between a set of data and the assumption of normality are presented in Section 4.7.

The normal distribution is perfectly symmetric about its mean μ, as can be seen in the examples in Figure 4.19. Its spread is determined by the value of its standard deviation σ. The formula for the normal probability distribution is shown in the next box. When plotted, this formula yields a curve like that shown in Figure 4.18.

Note that the mean μ and standard deviation σ appear in this formula, so no separate formulas for μ and σ are necessary. To graph the normal curve, we have to know the numerical values of μ and σ. Computing the area over intervals under the normal

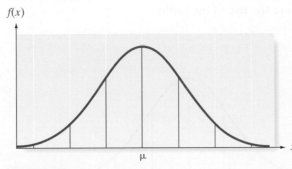

Figure 4.18

A normal probability distribution

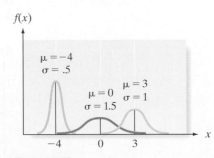

Figure 4.19

Several normal distributions with different means and standard deviations

*Students with knowledge of calculus should note that the probability that x assumes a value in the interval $a < x < b$ is $P(a < x < b) = \int_{a}^{b} f(x)\,dx$, assuming the integral exists. Similar to the requirement for a discrete probability distribution, we require $f(x) \geq 0$ and $\int_{-\infty}^{\infty} f(x)\,dx = 1$.

Probability Distribution for a Normal Random Variable x

Probability density function: $f(x) = \dfrac{1}{\sigma\sqrt{2\pi}} e^{-\left(\frac{1}{2}\right)[(x-\mu)/\sigma]^2}$

where

μ = Mean of the normal random variable x
σ = Standard deviation
π = 3.1415...
e = 2.71828...

$P(x < a)$ is obtained from a table of normal probabilities or using statistical software.

probability distribution is a difficult task.* Consequently, we will use the computed areas listed in Table II in Appendix D. Although there are an infinitely large number of normal curves—one for each pair of values for μ and σ—we have formed a single table that will apply to any normal curve.

Table II is based on a normal distribution with mean $\mu = 0$ and standard deviation $\sigma = 1$, called a *standard normal distribution*. A random variable with a standard normal distribution is typically denoted by the symbol z. The formula for the probability distribution of z is given by

$$f(z) = \dfrac{1}{\sqrt{2\pi}} e^{-\left(\frac{1}{2}\right)z^2}$$

Figure 4.20 shows the graph of a standard normal distribution.

The **standard normal distribution** is a normal distribution with $\mu = 0$ and $\sigma = 1$. A random variable with a standard normal distribution, denoted by the symbol z, is called a *standard normal random variable*.

Because we will ultimately convert all normal random variables to standard normal in order to use Table II to find probabilities, it is important that you learn to use Table II well. A partial reproduction of Table II is shown in Table 4.4. Note that the values of the standard normal random variable z are listed in the left-hand column. The entries in the body of the table give the area (probability) between 0 and z. Examples 4.16 and 4.17 illustrate the use of the table.

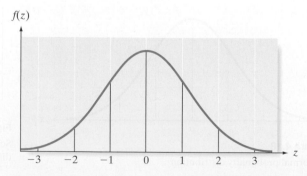

$f(z)$

Figure 4.20

Standard normal distribution:
$\mu = 0, \sigma = 1$

*The student with knowledge of calculus should note that there is not a closed-form expression for $P(a < x < b) = \displaystyle\int_a^b f(x)\,dx$ for the normal probability distribution. The value of this definite integral can be obtained to any desired degree of accuracy by numerical approximation procedures. For this reason, it is tabulated for the user.

Table 4.4	Reproduction of Part of Table II in Appendix D

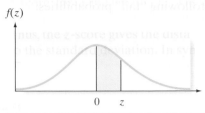

$f(z)$

z	.00	.01	.02	.03	.04	.05	.06	.07	.08	.09
.0	.0000	.0040	.0080	.0120	.0160	.0199	.0239	.0279	.0319	.0359
.1	.0398	.0438	.0478	.0517	.0557	.0596	.0636	.0675	.0714	.0753
.2	.0793	.0832	.0871	.0910	.0948	.0987	.1026	.1064	.1103	.1141
.3	.1179	.1217	.1255	.1293	.1331	.1368	.1406	.1443	.1480	.1517
.4	.1554	.1591	.1628	.1664	.1700	.1736	.1772	.1808	.1844	.1879
.5	.1915	.1950	.1985	.2019	.2054	.2088	.2123	.2157	.2190	.2224
.6	.2257	.2291	.2324	.2357	.2389	.2422	.2454	.2486	.2517	.2549
.7	.2580	.2611	.2642	.2673	.2704	.2734	.2764	.2794	.2823	.2852
.8	.2881	.2910	.2939	.2967	.2995	.3023	.3051	.3078	.3106	.3133
.9	.3159	.3186	.3212	.3238	.3264	.3289	.3315	.3340	.3365	.3389
1.0	.3413	.3438	.3461	.3485	.3508	.3531	.3554	.3577	.3599	.3621
1.1	.3643	.3665	.3686	.3708	.3729	.3749	.3770	.3790	.3810	.3830
1.2	.3849	.3869	.3888	.3907	.3925	.3944	.3962	.3980	.3997	.4015
1.3	.4032	.4049	.4066	.4082	.4099	.4115	.4131	.4147	.4162	.4177
1.4	.4192	.4207	.4222	.4236	.4251	.4265	.4279	.4292	.4306	.4319
1.5	.4332	.4345	.4357	.4370	.4382	.4394	.4406	.4418	.4429	.4441

EXAMPLE 4.16

Using the Standard Normal Table to Find $P(-z_0 < z < z_0)$

Problem Find the probability that the standard normal random variable z falls between -1.33 and 1.33.

Solution The standard normal distribution is shown again in Figure 4.21. Because all probabilities associated with standard normal random variables can be depicted as areas under the standard normal curve, you should always draw the curve and then equate the desired probability to an area.

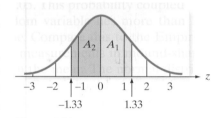

Figure 4.21

Areas under the standard normal curve for Example 4.16

In this example, we want to find the probability that z falls between -1.33 and 1.33, which is equivalent to the area between -1.33 and 1.33, shown shaded in Figure 4.21. Table II provides the area between $z = 0$ and any positive value of z, so that if we look up $z = 1.33$ (the value in the 1.3 row and .03 column, as shown in Table 4.4), we find that the area between $z = 0$ and $z = 1.33$ is .4082. This is the area labeled A_1 in Figure 4.21. To find the area A_2 located between $z = 0$ and $z = -1.33$, we note that the symmetry of the normal distribution implies that the area between $z = 0$ and any point to the left is equal to the area between $z = 0$ and the point equidistant to the right. Thus, in this example, the area between $z = 0$ and $z = -1.33$ is equal to the area between $z = 0$ and $z = 1.33$. That is,

$$A_1 = A_2 = .4082$$

The probability that z falls between -1.33 and 1.33 is the sum of the areas of A_1 and A_2. We summarize in probabilistic notation:

$$P(-1.33 < z < 1.33) = P(-1.33 < z < 0) + P(0 < z < 1.33)$$
$$= A_1 + A_2 = .4082 + .4082 = .8164$$

Look Back Remember that "$<$" and "$\leq$" are equivalent in events involving z because the inclusion (or exclusion) of a single point does not alter the probability of an event involving a continuous random variable.

● **Now Work Exercise 4.87**

equivalent to the event that a standard normal random variable lies between -1.33 and 1.33. We found this probability in Example 4.16 (see Figure 4.21) by doubling the area corresponding to $z = 1.33$ in Table II. That is,

$$P(8 \leq x \leq 12) = P(-1.33 \leq z \leq 1.33) = 2(.4082) = .8164$$

• **Now Work Exercise 4.97**

Table II in Appendix D provides good approximations to probabilities under the normal curve. However, if you do not have access to a normal table, you can always rely on statistical software to compute the desired probability. With most statistical software, you will need to specify the mean and standard deviation of the normal distribution, as well as the key values of the variable for which you desire probabilities. In Example 4.18, we desire $P(8 \leq x \leq 12)$, where $\mu = 10$ and $\sigma = 1.5$. To find this probability using Minitab's normal probability function, we enter 10 for the mean and 1.5 for the standard deviation, and then find two cumulative probabilities: $P(x \leq 12)$ and $P(x < 8)$. These two probabilities are shown (shaded) on the Minitab printout, Figure 4.26. The difference between the two probabilities yields the desired result:

$$P(8 \leq x \leq 12) = P(x \leq 12) - P(x < 8) = .908789 - .0912112 = .8175778$$

Note that this probability agrees with the value computed using Table II to two decimal places. The difference is due to rounding of the probabilities given in Table II.

The steps to follow when calculating a probability corresponding to a normal random variable are shown in the box below.

Cumulative Distribution Function

Normal with mean = 10 and standard deviation = 1.5

```
 x   P( X <= x )
12      0.908789
```

Cumulative Distribution Function

Normal with mean = 10 and standard deviation = 1.5

Figure 4.26

Minitab output with cumulative normal probabilities

```
x   P( X <= x )
8      0.0912112
```

Steps for Finding a Probability Corresponding to a Normal Random Variable

1. Sketch the normal distribution and indicate the mean of the random variable x. Then shade the area corresponding to the probability you want to find.

2. Convert the boundaries of the shaded area from x values to standard normal random variable z values using the formula

$$z = \frac{x - \mu}{\sigma}$$

Show the z values under the corresponding x values on your sketch.

3. Use Table II in Appendix D or statistical software to find the areas corresponding to the z values. If necessary, use the symmetry of the normal distribution to find areas corresponding to negative z values and the fact that the total area on each side of the mean equals .5 to convert the areas to the probabilities of the event you have shaded.

EXAMPLE 4.19

Using Normal Probabilities to Make an Inference–Advertised Gas Mileage

Problem Suppose an automobile manufacturer introduces a new model that has an advertised mean in-city mileage of 27 miles per gallon. Although such advertisements seldom report any measure of variability, suppose you write the manufacturer for the details of the tests, and you find that the standard deviation is 3 miles per gallon. This information leads you to formulate a probability model for the random variable x, the in-city mileage for this car model. You believe that the probability distribution of x can be approximated by a normal distribution with a mean of 27 and a standard deviation of 3.

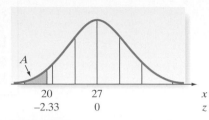

Figure 4.27

Areas under the normal curve for Example 4.19

a. If you were to buy this model of automobile, what is the probability that you would purchase one that averages less than 20 miles per gallon for in-city driving? In other words, find $P(x < 20)$.

b. Suppose you purchase one of these new models and it does get less than 20 miles per gallon for in-city driving. Should you conclude that your probability model is incorrect?

Solution

a. The probability model proposed for x, the in-city mileage, is shown in Figure 4.27. We are interested in finding the area A to the left of 20 because this area corresponds to the probability that a measurement chosen from this distribution falls below 20. In other words, if this model is correct, the area A represents the fraction of cars that can be expected to get less than 20 miles per gallon for in-city driving. To find A, we first calculate the z value corresponding to $x = 20$. That is,

$$z = \frac{x - \mu}{\sigma} = \frac{20 - 27}{3} = -\frac{7}{3} = -2.33$$

Then

$$P(x < 20) = P(z < -2.33)$$

as indicated by the shaded area in Figure 4.27. Because Table II gives areas only to the right of the mean (and because the normal distribution is symmetric about its mean), we look up 2.33 in Table II and find that the corresponding area is .4901. This is equal to the area between $z = 0$ and $z = -2.33$, so we find

$$P(x < 20) = A = .5 - .4901 = .0099 \approx .01$$

According to this probability model, you should have only about a 1% chance of purchasing a car of this make with an in-city mileage under 20 miles per gallon.

b. Now you are asked to make an inference based on a sample—the car you purchased. You are getting less than 20 miles per gallon for in-city driving. What do you infer? We think you will agree that one of two possibilities is true:

1. The probability model is correct. You simply were unfortunate to have purchased one of the cars in the 1% that get less than 20 miles per gallon in the city.

2. The probability model is incorrect. Perhaps the assumption of a normal distribution is unwarranted or the mean of 27 is an overestimate, or the standard deviation of 3 is an underestimate, or some combination of these errors was made. At any rate, the form of the actual probability model certainly merits further investigation.

You have no way of knowing with certainty which possibility is correct, but the evidence points to the second one. We are again relying on the rare-event approach to statistical inference that we introduced earlier. The sample (one measurement in this case) was so unlikely to have been drawn from the proposed probability model that it casts serious doubt on the model. We would be inclined to believe that the model is somehow in error.

Look Back When applying the rare-event approach, the calculated probability must be small (say, less than or equal to .05) in order to infer that the observed event is, indeed, unlikely.

● Now Work Exercise 4.98c

Occasionally you will be given a probability and will want to find the values of the normal random variable that correspond to the probability. For example, suppose the scores on a college entrance examination are known to be normally distributed, and a certain prestigious university will consider for admission only those applicants whose scores exceed the 90th percentile of the test score distribution. To determine the minimum score for admission consideration, you will need to be able to use Table II or statistical software in reverse, as demonstrated in the following example.

EXAMPLE 4.20

Finding a z-value Associated with a Normal Probability

Problem Consider the standard normal distribution, z. Find a value of z, call it z_0, such that:

a. $P(z > z_0) = .10$

b. $P(-z_0 < z < z_0) = .95$

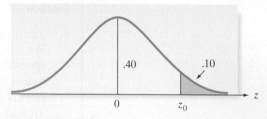

Figure 4.28
Area under the standard normal curve for Example 4.20a

Solution

a. We want to find the value z_0 such that only 10% of the standard normal distribution exceeds z_0 (see Figure 4.28).

We know that the total area to the right of the mean $z = 0$ is .5, which implies that z_0 must lie to the right of (above) 0. To pinpoint the value, we use the fact that the area to the right of z_0 is .10, which implies that the area between $z = 0$ and z_0 is .5 − .1 = .4. But areas between $z = 0$ and some other z value are exactly the types given in Table II. Therefore, we look up the area .4000 in the body of Table II and find that the corresponding z value is (to the closest approximation) $z_0 = 1.28$. The implication is that the point 1.28 standard deviations above the mean is the 90th percentile of a normal distribution.

We can also arrive at this answer using statistical software. In Minitab, we use the inverse cumulative distribution function for a normal random variable and specify the cumulative probability,

$$P(z \leq z_0) = .9$$

The value of z_0 is shown (shaded) on the Minitab printout, Figure 4.29. You can see that this value agrees with our solution using the normal table.

Inverse Cumulative Distribution Function

```
Normal with mean = 0 and standard deviation = 1

P( X <= x )        x
      0.9    1.28155
```

Figure 4.29
Minitab output for Example 4.20a

b. Here we wish to move an equal distance z_0 in the positive and negative directions from the mean $z = 0$ until 95% of the standard normal distribution is enclosed. This means that the area on each side of the mean will be equal to $\frac{1}{2}(.95) = .475$, as shown in Figure 4.30. Because the area between $z = 0$ and z_0 is .475, we look up .475 in the body of Table II to find the value $z_0 = 1.96$. Thus, as we found in the reverse order in part **a**, 95% of a normal distribution lies between -1.96 and 1.96 standard deviations of the mean.

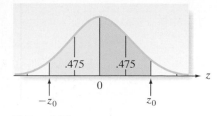

Figure 4.30

Areas under the standard normal curve for Example 4.20b

Look Back As with earlier problems, it is critical to draw correctly the normal probability of interest on the normal curve. Placement of z_0 to the left or right of 0 is the key. Be sure to shade the probability (area) involving z_0. If it does not agree with the probability of interest (i.e., the shaded area is greater than .5 and the probability of interest is smaller than .5), then you need to place z_0 on the opposite side of 0.

➤ **Now Work Exercise 4.89**

Now that you have learned how to find a standard normal z value that corresponds to a specified probability, we demonstrate a practical application in Example 4.21.

EXAMPLE 4.21

Finding a Value of a Normal Random Variable–Paint Manufacturing Application

Problem Suppose a paint manufacturer has a daily production, x, that is normally distributed with a mean of 100,000 gallons and a standard deviation of 10,000 gallons. Management wants to create an incentive bonus for the production crew when the daily production exceeds the 90th percentile of the distribution, in hopes that the crew will, in turn, become more productive. At what level of production should management pay the incentive bonus?

Solution In this example, we want to find a production level, x_0, such that 90% of the daily levels (x values) in the distribution fall below x_0 and only 10% fall above x_0—that is,

$$P(x \leq x_0) = .90$$

Converting x to a standard normal random variable, where $\mu = 100,000$ and $\sigma = 10,000$, we have

$$P(x \leq x_0) = P\left(z \leq \frac{x_0 - \mu}{\sigma}\right)$$

$$= P\left(z \leq \frac{x_0 - 100,000}{10,000}\right) = .90$$

In Example 4.20 (see Figure 4.28) we found the 90th percentile of the standard normal distribution to be $z_0 = 1.28$–that is, we found $P(z \leq 1.28) = .90$. Consequently, we know the production level x_0 at which the incentive bonus is paid corresponds to a z-score of 1.28; that is,

$$\frac{x_0 - 100,000}{10,000} = 1.28$$

If we solve this equation for x_0, we find

$$x_0 = 100,000 + 1.28(10,000) = 100,000 + 12,800 = 112,800$$

This x value is shown in Figure 4.31. Thus, the 90th percentile of the production distribution is 112,800 gallons. Management should pay an incentive bonus when a day's production exceeds this level if its objective is to pay only when production is in the top 10% of the current daily production distribution.

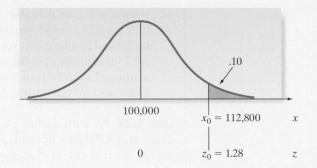

Figure 4.31

Area under the normal curve
for Example 4.21

Look Back As this example shows, in practical applications of the normal table in reverse, first find the value of z_0, then convert the value to the units of x using the z-score formula in reverse.

● **Now Work Exercise 4.99c**

We close this section with one final application of the normal distribution. When n is large, a normal probability distribution may be used to provide a good approximation to the probability distribution of the discrete binomial random variable (Section 4.3). To show how this approximation works, we refer to Example 4.13, in which we used the binomial distribution to model the number x of 20 employees who favor unionization. We assumed that 60% of the company's employees favored unionization. The mean and standard deviation of x were found to be $\mu = 12$ and $\sigma = 2.2$. The binomial distribution for $n = 20$ and $p = .6$ is shown in Figure 4.32 and the approximating normal distribution with mean $\mu = 12$ and standard deviation $\sigma = 2.2$ is superimposed.

As part of Example 4.13, we used Table I to find the probability that $x \le 10$. This probability, which is equal to the sum of the areas contained in the rectangles (shown in Figure 4.32) that correspond to $p(0), p(1), p(2), \ldots, p(10)$, was found to equal .245. The portion of the approximating normal curve that would be used to approximate the area $p(0) + p(1) + p(2) + \cdots + p(10)$ is shaded in Figure 4.32. Note that this shaded area lies to the left of 10.5 (not 10), so we may include all of the probability in the rectangle corresponding to $p(10)$. Because we are approximating a discrete distribution (the binomial) with a continuous distribution (the normal), we call the use of 10.5 (instead of 10 or 11) a **correction for continuity;** that is, we are correcting the discrete distribution so that it can be approximated by the continuous one. The use of the correction for continuity leads to the calculation of the following standard normal z value:

$$z = \frac{x - \mu}{\sigma} = \frac{10.5 - 12}{2.2} = -.68$$

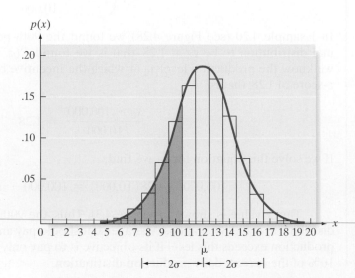

Figure 4.32

Binomial distribution for $n = 20$,
$p = .6$, and normal distribution
with $\mu = 12$, $\sigma = 2.2$

Using Table II, we find the area between $z = 0$ and $z = .68$ to be .2517. Then the probability that x is less than or equal to 10 is approximated by the area under the normal distribution to the left of 10.5, shown shaded in Figure 4.32—that is,

$$P(x \leq 10) \approx P(z \leq -.68) = .5 - P(-.68 < z \leq 0) = .5 - .2517 = .2483$$

The approximation differs only slightly from the exact binomial probability, .245. Of course, when tables of exact binomial probabilities are available, we will use the exact value rather than a normal approximation.

Use of the normal distribution will not always provide a good approximation for binomial probabilities. The following is a useful rule of thumb to determine when n is large enough for the approximation to be effective: *The interval $\mu \pm 3\sigma$ should lie within the range of the binomial random variable x (i.e., 0 to n) in order for the normal approximation to be adequate.* The rule works well because almost all of the normal distribution falls within 3 standard deviations of the mean, so if this interval is contained within the range of x values, there is "room" for the normal approximation to work.

As shown in Figure 4.33a for the preceding example with $n = 20$ and $p = .6$, the interval $\mu \pm 3\sigma = 12 \pm 3(2.2) = (5.4, 18.6)$ lies within the range 0 to 20. However, if we were to try to use the normal approximation with $n = 10$ and $p = .1$, the interval $\mu \pm 3\sigma$ is $1 \pm 3(.95)$, or $(-1.85, 3.85)$. As shown in Figure 4.33b, this interval is not contained within the range of x because $x = 0$ is the lower bound for a binomial random variable. Note in Figure 4.33b that the normal distribution will not "fit" in the range of x, and therefore it will not provide a good approximation to the binomial probabilities.

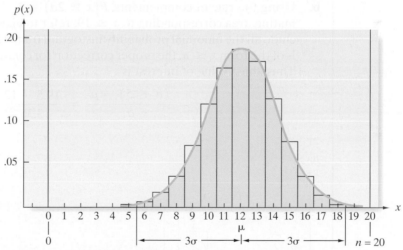

a. $n = 20, p = .6$: Normal approximation is good

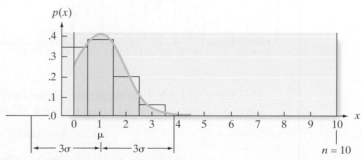

Figure 4.33

Rule of thumb for normal approximation to binomial probabilities

b. $n = 10, p = .1$: Normal approximation is poor

EXAMPLE 4.22

Applying the Normal Approximation to a Binomial Probability—Lot Acceptance Sampling

Problem One problem with any product (e.g., a graphing calculator) that is mass produced is quality control. The process must somehow be monitored or audited to be sure the output of the process conforms to requirements. One method of dealing with this problem is *lot acceptance sampling*, in which items being produced are sampled at various stages of the production process and are carefully inspected. The lot of items from which the sample is drawn is then accepted or rejected, based on the number of defectives in the sample. Lots that are accepted may be sent forward for further processing or may be shipped to customers; lots that are rejected may be reworked or scrapped. For example, suppose a manufacturer of calculators chooses 200 stamped circuits from the day's production and determines x, the number of defective circuits in the sample. Suppose that up to a 6% rate of defectives is considered acceptable for the process.

a. Find the mean and standard deviation of x, assuming the defective rate is 6%.

b. Use the normal approximation to determine the probability that 20 or more defectives are observed in the sample of 200 circuits (i.e., find the approximate probability that $x \geq 20$).

Solution

a. The random variable x is binomial with $n = 200$ and the fraction defective $p = .06$. Thus,

$$\mu = np = 200(.06) = 12$$
$$\sigma = \sqrt{npq} = \sqrt{200(.06)(.94)} = \sqrt{11.28} = 3.36$$

We first note that

$$\mu \pm 3\sigma = 12 \pm 3(3.36) = 12 \pm 10.08 = (1.92, 22.08)$$

lies completely within the range from 0 to 200. Therefore, a normal probability distribution should provide an adequate approximation to this binomial distribution.

b. Using the rule of complements, $P(x \geq 20) = 1 - P(x \leq 19)$. To find the approximating area corresponding to $x \leq 19$, refer to Figure 4.34. Note that we want to include all the binomial probability histogram from 0 to 19, inclusive. Because the event is of the form $x \leq a$, the proper correction for continuity is $a + .5 = 19 + .5 = 19.5$. Thus, the z value of interest is

$$z = \frac{(a + .5) - \mu}{\sigma} = \frac{19.5 - 12}{3.36} = \frac{7.5}{3.36} = 2.23$$

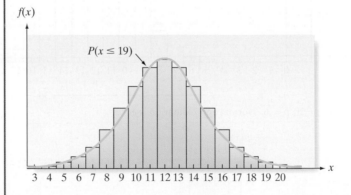

Figure 4.34

Normal approximation to the binomial distribution with $n = 200, p = .06$

Referring to Table II in Appendix D, we find that the area to the right of the mean 0 corresponding to $z = 2.23$ (see Figure 4.35) is .4871. So the area $A = P(z \leq 2.23)$ is

$$A = .5 + .4871 = .9871$$

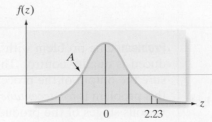

Figure 4.35

Standard normal distribution

Thus, the normal approximation to the binomial probability we seek is

$$P(x \geq 20) = 1 - P(x \leq 19) \approx 1 - .9871 = .0129$$

In other words, the probability is extremely small that 20 or more defectives will be observed in a sample of 200 circuits—*if in fact the true fraction of defectives is .06.*

Look Back If the manufacturer observes $x \geq 20$, the likely reason is that the process is producing more than the acceptable 6% defectives. The lot acceptance sampling procedure is another example of using the rare-event approach to make inferences.

● **Now Work Exercise 4.95**

The steps for approximating a binomial probability by a normal probability are given in the next box.

Using a Normal Distribution to Approximate Binomial Probabilities

1. After you have determined n and p for the binomial distribution, calculate the interval

$$\mu \pm 3\sigma = np \pm 3\sqrt{npq}$$

If the interval lies in the range 0 to n, the normal distribution will provide a reasonable approximation to the probabilities of most binomial events.

2. Express the binomial probability to be approximated in the form $P(x \leq a)$ or $P(x \leq b) - P(x \leq a)$. For example,

$$P(x < 3) = P(x \leq 2)$$

$$P(x \geq 5) = 1 - P(x \leq 4)$$

$$P(7 \leq x \leq 10) = P(x \leq 10) - P(x \leq 6)$$

3. For each value of interest a, the correction for continuity is $(a + .5)$, and the corresponding standard normal z value is

$$z = \frac{(a + .5) - \mu}{\sigma} \quad \text{(See Figure 4.36)}$$

4. Sketch the approximating normal distribution and shade the area corresponding to the probability of the event of interest, as in Figure 4.36. Verify that the rectangles you have included in the shaded area correspond to the event probability you wish to approximate. Using Table II and the z value(s) you calculated in step 3, find the shaded area. This is the approximate probability of the binomial event.

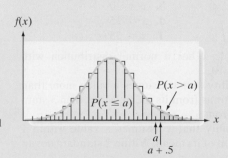

Figure 4.36

Approximating binomial probabilities by normal probabilities

Learning the Mechanics

4.84 Find the area under the standard normal probability distribution between the following pairs of z-scores:
   a. $z = 0$ and $z = 2.00$ **b.** $z = 0$ and $z = 3$
   c. $z = 0$ and $z = 1.5$ **d.** $z = 0$ and $z = .80$

4.85 Find the following probabilities for the standard normal random variable z:
   a. $P(z > 1.46)$ **b.** $P(z < -1.56)$
   c. $P(.67 \leq z < 2.41)$ **d.** $P(-1.96 \leq z < -.33)$
   e. $P(z \geq 0)$ **f.** $P(-2.33 < z < 1.50)$

4.86 Find the following probabilities for the standard normal random variable z:
   a. $P(0 < z < 2.25)$ **b.** $P(-2.25 < z < 0)$
   c. $P(-2.25 < z < 1.25)$ **d.** $P(-2.50 < z < 1.50)$
   e. $P(z < -2.33 \text{ or } z > 2.33)$

4.87 Find each of the following probabilities for the standard normal random variable z:
   a. $P(-1 \leq z \leq 1)$ **b.** $P(-1.96 \leq z \leq 1.96)$
   c. $P(-1.645 \leq z \leq 1.645)$ **d.** $P(-2 \leq z \leq 2)$

4.88 Find a value of the standard normal random variable z, call it z_0, such that
   a. $P(-z_0 \leq z \leq z_0) = .98$ **b.** $P(z \geq z_0) = .05$
   c. $P(z \geq z_0) = .70$ **d.** $P(z \geq z_0) = .025$
   e. $P(z \leq z_0) = .70$

4.89 Find a value of the standard normal random variable z, call it z_0, such that
   a. $P(z \leq z_0) = .2090$
   b. $P(z \leq z_0) = .7090$
   c. $P(-z_0 \leq z < z_0) = .8472$
   d. $P(-z_0 \leq z < z_0) = .1664$
   e. $P(z_0 \leq z \leq 0) = .4798$
   f. $P(-1 < z < z_0)$

4.90 Give the z-score for a measurement from a normal distribution for the following:
   a. 1 standard deviation above the mean
   b. 1 standard deviation below the mean
   c. Equal to the mean
   d. 2.5 standard deviations below the mean
   e. 3 standard deviations above the mean

4.91 Suppose the random variable x is best described by a normal distribution with $\mu = 30$ and $\sigma = 4$. Find the z-score that corresponds to each of the following x values:
   a. $x = 20$ **b.** $x = 30$
   c. $x = 2.75$ **d.** $x = 15$
   e. $x = 35$ **f.** $x = 25$

4.92 The random variable x has a normal distribution with $\mu = 1,000$ and $\sigma = 10$.
   a. Find the probability that x assumes a value more than 2 standard deviations from its mean. More than 3 standard deviations from μ.
   b. Find the probability that x assumes a value within 1 standard deviation of its mean. Within 2 standard deviations of μ.
   c. Find the value of x that represents the 80th percentile of this distribution. The 10th percentile.

4.93 Suppose x is a normally distributed random variable with $\mu = 11$ and $\sigma = 2$. Find each of the following:
   a. $P(10 \leq x \leq 12)$
   b. $P(6 \leq x \leq 10)$
   c. $P(13 \leq x \leq 16)$
   d. $P(7.8 \leq x \leq 12.6)$
   e. $P(x \geq 13.24)$
   f. $P(x \geq 7.62)$

4.94 Suppose x is a normally distributed random variable with $\mu = 50$ and $\sigma = 3$. Find a value of the random variable, call it x_0, such that
   a. $P(x \leq x_0) = .8413$
   b. $P(x > x_0) = .025$
   c. $P(x > x_0) = .95$
   d. $P(41 \leq x < x_0) = .8630$
   e. 10% of the values of x are less than x_0.
   f. 1% of the values of x are greater than x_0.

4.95 Suppose x is a binomial random variable with $p = .4$ and $n = 25$.
   a. Would it be appropriate to approximate the probability distribution of x with a normal distribution? Explain.
   b. Assuming that a normal distribution provides an adequate approximation to the distribution of x, what are the mean and variance of the approximating normal distribution?
   c. Use Table I in Appendix D to find the exact value of $P(x \geq 9)$.
   d. Use the normal approximation to find $P(x \geq 9)$.

4.96 Assume that x is a binomial random variable with $n = 1,000$ and $p = .50$. Use a normal approximation to find each of the following probabilities:
   a. $P(x > 500)$
   b. $P(490 \leq x < 500)$
   c. $P(x > 550)$

📊 Applet Exercise 4.6

Open the applet *Sample from a Population*. On the pull-down menu to the right of the top graph, select *Bell shaped*. The box to the left of the top graph displays the population mean, median, and standard deviation.
   a. Run the applet for each available value of n on the pull-down menu for the sample size. Go from the smallest to the largest value of n. For each value of n, observe the shape of the graph of the sample data and record the mean, median, and standard deviation of the sample.
   b. Describe what happens to the shape of the graph and the mean, median, and standard deviation of the sample as the sample size increases.

Applying the Concepts—Basic

4.97 **Variable life insurance return rates.** With a variable life insurance policy, the rate of return on the investment (i.e., the death benefit) varies from year to year. A study of these variable return rates was published in *International Journal of Statistical Distributions* (Vol. 1, 2015). A transformed ratio of the return rates (x) for two consecutive years was shown to have a normal distribution, with $\mu = 1.5$ and $\sigma = .2$. Use the standard normal table or statistical software to find the following probabilities.

a. $P(1.3 < x < 1.6)$
b. $P(x > 1.4)$
c. $P(x < 1.5)$

4.98 Hotels' use of ecolabels. Refer to the *Journal of Vacation Marketing* (January 2016) study of travelers' familiarity with ecolabels used by hotels, Exercise 2.64 (p. 104). Recall that adult travelers were shown a list of 6 different ecolabels, and asked, "Suppose the response is measured on a continuous scale from 10 (*not familiar at all*) to 50 (*very familiar*)." The mean and standard deviation for the *Energy Star* ecolabel are 44 and 1.5, respectively. Assume the distribution of the responses is approximately normally distributed.

a. Find the probability that a response to *Energy Star* exceeds 43.
b. Find the probability that a response to *Energy Star* falls between 42 and 45.
c. [NW] If you observe a response of 35 to an ecolabel, do you think it is likely that the ecolabel was *Energy Star*? Explain.

4.99 Tomato as a taste modifier. Miraculin—a protein naturally produced in a rare tropical fruit—has the potential to be an alternative low-calorie sweetener. In *Plant Science* (May 2010), a group of Japanese environmental scientists investigated the ability of a hybrid tomato plant to produce miraculin. For a particular generation of the tomato plant, the amount x of miraculin produced (measured in micrograms per gram of fresh weight) had a mean of 105.3 and a standard deviation of 8.0. Assume that x is normally distributed.

a. Find $P(x > 120)$.
b. Find $P(100 < x < 110)$.
c. [NW] Find the value a for which $P(x < a) = .25$.

4.100 Corporate sustainability of CPA firms. Refer to the *Business and Society* (March 2011) study on the sustainability behaviors of CPA corporations, Exercise 2.23 (p. 83). Recall that the level of support for corporate sustainability (measured on a quantitative scale ranging from 0 to 160 points) was obtained for each of 992 senior managers at CPA firms. The accompanying Minitab printout gives the mean and standard deviation for the level of support variable. It can be shown that level of support is approximately normally distributed.

a. Find the probability that the level of support for corporate sustainability of a randomly selected senior manager is less than 40 points.
b. Find the probability that the level of support for corporate sustainability of a randomly selected senior manager is between 40 and 120 points.
c. Find the probability that the level of support for corporate sustainability of a randomly selected senior manager is greater than 120 points.
d. One-fourth of the 992 senior managers indicated a level of support for corporate sustainability below what value?

4.101 Shopping vehicle and judgment. Refer to the *Journal of Marketing Research* (December 2011) study of whether you are more likely to choose a vice product (e.g., a candy bar) when your arm is flexed (as when carrying a shopping basket) than when your arm is extended (as when pushing a shopping cart), Exercise 2.85 (p. 112). The study measured choice scores (on a scale of 0 to 100, where higher scores indicate a greater preference for vice options) for consumers shopping under each of the two conditions. Recall that the average choice score for consumers with a flexed arm was 59, while the average for consumers with an extended arm was 43. For both conditions, assume that the standard deviation of the choice scores is 5. Also assume that both distributions are approximately normally distributed.

a. In the flexed arm condition, what is the probability that a consumer has a choice score of 60 or greater?
b. In the extended arm condition, what is the probability that a consumer has a choice score of 60 or greater?

4.102 Buy-side vs. sell-side analysts' earnings forecasts. Financial analysts who make forecasts of stock prices are categorized as either "buy-side" analysts or "sell-side" analysts. Refer to the *Financial Analysts Journal* (July/August 2008) comparison of earnings forecasts of buy-side and sell-side analysts, Exercise 2.86 (p. 112). The mean and standard deviation of forecast errors for both types of analysts are reproduced in the table. Assume that the distribution of forecast errors are approximately normally distributed.

a. Find the probability that a buy-side analyst has a forecast error of +2.00 or higher.
b. Find the probability that a sell-side analyst has a forecast error of +2.00 or higher.

	Buy-Side Analysts	Sell-Side Analysts
Mean	0.85	−0.05
Standard Deviation	1.93	0.85

Source: Based on B. Groysberg, P. Healy, and C. Chapman, *Financial Analysis Journal*, Vol. 64, No. 4, July/August 2008.

4.103 Blood diamonds. According to *Global Research News* (March 4, 2014), one-fourth of all rough diamonds produced in the world are *blood diamonds*, i.e., diamonds mined to finance war or an insurgency. (See Exercise 3.81, p. 200.) In a random sample of 700 rough diamonds purchased by a diamond buyer, let x be the number that are blood diamonds.

a. Find the mean of x.
b. Find the standard deviation of x.
c. Find the z-score for the value $x = 200$.
d. Find the approximate probability that the number of the 700 rough diamonds that are blood diamonds is less than or equal to 200.

4.104 Privacy and information sharing. Refer to the *Pew Internet & American Life Project Survey* (January 2016), Exercise 4.48 (p. 239). The survey revealed that half of all U.S. adults would agree to participate in a free cost-saving

Descriptive Statistics: Support

```
Variable    N     Mean    StDev    Variance  Minimum  Maximum  Range
Support    992  67.755  26.871   722.036    0.000  155.000  155.000
```

loyalty card program at a grocery store, even if the store could potentially sell these data on the customer's shopping habits to third parties. In a random sample of 250 U.S. adults, let x be the number who would participate in the free loyalty card program.

a. Find the mean of x. (This value should agree with your answer to Exercise 4.48c.)

b. Find the standard deviation of x.

c. Find the z-score for the value $x = 200$.

d. Find the approximate probability that the number of the 250 adults who would participate in the free loyalty card program is less than or equal to 200.

Applying the Concepts—Intermediate

4.105 Executive networking and firm performance. Refer to the *Journal of Accounting Public Policy* (Vol. 34, 2015) study of the impact of executive networking on firm performance, Exercise 2.101 (p. 117). Recall that firm performance was measured as annual return on equity (ROE), recorded as a percentage. The mean ROE for the firms studied was 13.93% and the standard deviation was 21.65%. Assume that these values represent μ and σ for the population ROE distribution and that this distribution is normal. What value of ROE will be exceeded by 80% of the firms?

4.106 Voltage sags and swells. Refer to the *Electrical Engineering* (Vol. 95, 2013) study of the power quality of a transformer, Exercise 2.127 (p. 132). Recall that two causes of poor power quality are "sags" and "swells." (A sag is an unusual dip and a swell is an unusual increase in the voltage level of a transformer.) For Turkish transformers built for heavy industry, the mean number of sags per week was 353 and the mean number of swells per week was 184. As in Exercise 2.127, assume the standard deviation of the sag distribution is 30 sags per week and the standard deviation of the swell distribution is 25 swells per week. Also, assume that the number of sags and number of swells are both normally distributed. Suppose one of the transformers is randomly selected and found to have 400 sags and 100 swells in a week.

a. What is the probability that the number of sags per week is less than 400?

b. What is the probability that the number of swells per week is greater than 100?

4.107 Mean shifts on a production line. *Six Sigma* is a comprehensive approach to quality goal setting that involves statistics. An article in *Aircraft Engineering and Aerospace Technology* (Vol. 76, No. 6, 2004) demonstrated the use of the normal distribution in Six Sigma goal setting at Motorola Corporation. Motorola discovered that the average defect rate for parts produced on an assembly line varies from run to run and is approximately normally distributed with a mean equal to 3 defects per million. Assume that the goal at Motorola is for the average defect rate to vary no more than 1.5 standard deviations above or below the mean of 3. How likely is it that the goal will be met?

4.108 Safety of underground tunnels. Research published in the journal *Tunnelling and Underground Space Technology* (July 2014) evaluated the safety of underground tunnels built in rigid soils. A factor of safety (FS), measured as the ratio of capacity over demand, was determined for three different areas of tunnels made from shotcrete: tunnel face, tunnel walls, and tunnel crown. FS was determined to be normally distributed in each area, with means and standard deviations shown in the table. Tunnel failure is considered to occur when FS is lower than or equal to 1. Which tunnel area is more likely to result in failure? Why?

	Mean (μ)	Standard Deviation (σ)
Tunnel Face	1.2	.16
Tunnel Walls	1.4	.20
Tunnel Crown	2.1	.70

4.109 Hotel guest satisfaction. Refer to the 2015 North American Hotel Guest Satisfaction Index Study, Exercise 4.49 (p. 239). You determined that the probability that a hotel guest was delighted with his or her stay and would recommend the hotel is .12. Suppose a large hotel chain randomly samples 200 of its guests. The chain's national director claims that more than 50 of these guests were delighted with their stay and would recommend the hotel.

a. Under what scenario is the claim likely to be false?

b. Under what scenario is the claim likely to be true?

4.110 Manufacturing hourly pay rate. Government data indicate that the mean hourly wage for manufacturing workers in the United States is $20.10 (Bureau of Labor Statistics, January 2016). Suppose the distribution of manufacturing wage rates nationwide can be approximated by a normal distribution with standard deviation $1.25 per hour. The first manufacturing firm contacted by a particular worker seeking a new job pays $21.40 per hour.

a. If the worker were to undertake a nationwide job search, approximately what proportion of the wage rates would be greater than $21.40 per hour?

b. If the worker were to randomly select a U.S. manufacturing firm, what is the probability the firm would pay more than $21.40 per hour?

c. The population median, call it η, of a continuous random variable x is the value such that $P(x \geq \eta) = P(x \leq \eta) = .5$—that is, the median is the value η such that half the area under the probability distribution lies above η and half lies below it. Find the median of the random variable corresponding to the wage rate and compare it with the mean wage rate.

4.111 Personnel dexterity tests. Personnel tests are designed to test a job applicant's cognitive and/or physical abilities. The Wonderlic IQ test is an example of the former; the Purdue Pegboard speed test involving the arrangement of pegs on a peg board is an example of the latter. A particular dexterity test is administered nationwide by a private testing service. It is known that for all tests administered last year, the distribution of scores was approximately normal with mean 75 and standard deviation 7.5.

a. A particular employer requires job candidates to score at least 80 on the dexterity test. Approximately what percentage of the test scores during the past year exceeded 80?

b. The testing service reported to a particular employer that one of its job candidate's scores fell at the 98th percentile of the distribution (i.e., approximately 98% of the scores were lower than the candidate's, and only 2% were higher). What was the candidate's score?

4.112 California's electoral college votes. During a presidential election, each state is allotted a different number of votes in the Electoral College, depending on population. For example, California is allotted 55 votes (the most) while several states (including the District of Columbia) are allotted 3 votes each (the least). When a presidential candidate wins the popular vote in a state, the candidate wins all the Electoral College votes in that state. To become president, a candidate must win 270 of the total of 538 votes in the Electoral College. *Chance* (Winter 2010) demonstrated the impact on the presidential election of winning California. Assuming a candidate wins California's 55 votes, the number of additional Electoral College votes the candidate will win can be approximated by a normal distribution with $\mu = 241.5$ votes and $\sigma = 49.8$ votes. If a presidential candidate wins the popular vote in California, what are the chances that he or she becomes the next U.S. president?

4.113 Credit/debit card market shares. The following table reports the U.S. credit/debit card industry's market share data for 2015. A random sample of 100 credit/debit card users is to be questioned regarding their satisfaction with their card company. For simplification, assume that each card user carries just one card and that the market share percentages are the percentages of all card customers that carry each brand.

Credit debit Card	Market Share %
Visa	59
MasterCard	26
Discover	2
American Express	13

Source: Based on *Nilson Report* data, June 2015.

a. Propose a procedure for randomly selecting the 100 card users.

b. For random samples of 100 card users, what is the expected number of customers who carry Visa? Discover?

c. What is the approximate probability that half or more of the sample of card users carry Visa? American Express?

d. Justify the use of the normal approximation to the binomial in answering the question in part **c.**

Applying the Concepts—Advanced

4.114 Industrial filling process. The characteristics of an industrial filling process in which an expensive liquid is injected into a container were investigated in the *Journal of Quality Technology* (July 1999). The quantity injected per container is approximately normally distributed with mean 10 units and standard deviation .2 units. Each unit of fill costs $20 per unit. If a container contains less than 10 units (i.e., is underfilled), it must be reprocessed at a cost of $10. A properly filled container sells for $230.

a. Find the probability that a container is underfilled. Not underfilled.

b. A container is initially underfilled and must be reprocessed. Upon refilling, it contains 10.60 units. How much profit will the company make on this container?

c. The operations manager adjusts the mean of the filling process upward to 10.60 units in order to make the probability of underfilling approximately zero. Under these conditions, what is the expected profit per container?

4.115 Executive coaching and meeting effectiveness. Can executive coaching help improve business meeting effectiveness? This was the question of interest in an article published in *Consulting Psychology Journal: Practice and Research* (Vol. 61, 2009). The goal of executive coaching is to reduce content behaviors (e.g., seeking information, disagreeing/attacking) in favor of process behaviors (e.g., asking clarifying questions, summarizing). The study reported that prior to receiving executive coaching, the percentage of observed content behaviors of leaders had a mean of 75% with a standard deviation of 8.5%. In contrast, after receiving executive coaching, the percentage of observed content behaviors of leaders had a mean of 52% with a standard deviation of 7.5%. Assume that the percentage of observed content behaviors is approximately normally distributed for both leaders with and without executive coaching. Suppose you observe 70% content behaviors by the leader of a business meeting. Give your opinion on whether or not the leader has received executive coaching.

4.116 Box plots and the standard normal distribution. What relationship exists between the standard normal distribution and the box-plot methodology (Section 2.8) for describing distributions of data using quartiles? The answer depends on the true underlying probability distribution of the data. Assume for the remainder of this exercise that the distribution is normal.

a. Calculate the values of the standard normal random variable z, call them z_L and z_U, that correspond to the hinges of the box plot—that is, the lower and upper quartiles, Q_L and Q_U—of the probability distribution.

b. Calculate the z values that correspond to the inner fences of the box plot for a normal probability distribution.

c. Calculate the z values that correspond to the outer fences of the box plot for a normal probability distribution.

d. What is the probability that an observation lies beyond the inner fences of a normal probability distribution? The outer fences?

e. Can you better understand why the inner and outer fences of a box plot are used to detect outliers in a distribution? Explain.

4.7 Descriptive Methods for Assessing Normality

In the chapters that follow, we learn how to make inferences about the population based on information in the sample. Several of these techniques are based on the assumption that the population is approximately normally distributed. Consequently, it will be important to determine whether the sample data come from a normal population before we can properly apply these techniques.

Several descriptive methods can be used to check for normality. In this section, we consider the four methods summarized in the box.

Determining Whether the Data Are from an Approximately Normal Distribution

1. Construct either a histogram or stem-and-leaf display for the data and note the shape of the graph. If the data are approximately normal, the shape of the histogram or stem-and-leaf display will be similar to the normal curve, Figure 4.18 (i.e., mound-shaped and symmetric about the mean).

2. Compute the intervals $\bar{x} \pm s$, $\bar{x} \pm 2s$, and $\bar{x} \pm 3s$, and determine the percentage of measurements falling in each. If the data are approximately normal, the percentages will be approximately equal to 68%, 95%, and 100%, respectively.

3. Find the interquartile range, IQR, and standard deviation, s, for the sample, then calculate the ratio IQR/s. If the data are approximately normal, then IQR/$s \approx 1.3$.

4. Examine a *normal probability plot* for the data. If the data are approximately normal, the points will fall (approximately) on a straight line.

The first two methods come directly from the properties of a normal distribution established in Section 4.6. Method 3 is based on the fact that for normal distributions, the z values corresponding to the 25th and 75th percentiles are $-.67$ and $.67$, respectively (see Example 4.17b). Because $\sigma = 1$ for a standard normal distribution,

$$\frac{\text{IQR}}{\sigma} = \frac{Q_U - Q_L}{\sigma} = \frac{.67 - (-.67)}{1} = 1.34$$

The final descriptive method for checking normality is based on a *normal probability plot*. In such a plot, the observations in a data set are ordered from smallest to largest and then plotted against the expected z-scores of observations calculated under the assumption that the data come from a normal distribution. When the data are, in fact, normally distributed, a linear (straight-line) trend will result. A nonlinear trend in the plot suggests that the data are nonnormal.

A **normal probability plot** for a data set is a scatterplot with the ranked data values on one axis and their corresponding expected z-scores from a standard normal distribution on the other axis. [*Note:* Computation of the expected standard normal z-scores is beyond the scope of this text. Therefore, we will rely on available statistical software packages to generate a normal probability plot.]

EXAMPLE 4.23

Checking for Normal Data—EPA Estimated Gas Mileages

Problem The Environmental Protection Agency (EPA) performs extensive tests on all new car models to determine their mileage ratings. The results of 100 EPA tests on a certain new car model are displayed in Table 4.5. Numerical and graphical descriptive measures for the data are shown on the Minitab and SPSS printouts, Figures 4.37a–c. Determine whether the EPA mileage ratings are from an approximate normal distribution.

Table 4.5	EPA Gas Mileage Ratings for 100 Cars (miles per gallon)								
36.3	41.0	36.9	37.1	44.9	36.8	30.0	37.2	42.1	36.7
32.7	37.3	41.2	36.6	32.9	36.5	33.2	37.4	37.5	33.6
40.5	36.5	37.6	33.9	40.2	36.4	37.7	37.7	40.0	34.2
36.2	37.9	36.0	37.9	35.9	38.2	38.3	35.7	35.6	35.1
38.5	39.0	35.5	34.8	38.6	39.4	35.3	34.4	38.8	39.7
36.3	36.8	32.5	36.4	40.5	36.6	36.1	38.2	38.4	39.3
41.0	31.8	37.3	33.1	37.0	37.6	37.0	38.7	39.0	35.8
37.0	37.2	40.7	37.4	37.1	37.8	35.9	35.6	36.7	34.5
37.1	40.3	36.7	37.0	33.9	40.1	38.0	35.2	34.8	39.5
39.9	36.9	32.9	33.8	39.8	34.0	36.8	35.0	38.1	36.9

Data Set: EPAGAS

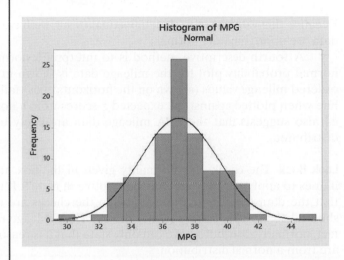

Figure 4.37a

Minitab histogram for gas mileage data

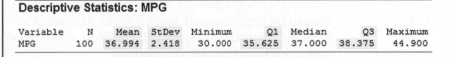

Figure 4.37b

Minitab descriptive statistics for gas mileage data

Descriptive Statistics: MPG

Variable	N	Mean	StDev	Minimum	Q1	Median	Q3	Maximum
MPG	100	36.994	2.418	30.000	35.625	37.000	38.375	44.900

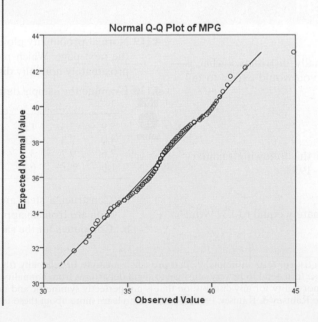

Figure 4.37c

SPSS normal probability plot for gas mileage data

Table 4.6

Describing the 100 EPA Mileage Ratings

Interval	Percentage in Interval
$\bar{x} \pm s = (34.6, 39.4)$	68
$\bar{x} \pm 2s = (32.2, 41.8)$	96
$\bar{x} \pm 3s = (29.8, 44.2)$	99

Solution As a first check, we examine the Minitab histogram of the data shown in Figure 4.37a. Clearly, the mileages fall in an approximately mound-shaped, symmetric distribution centered around the mean of approximately 37 mpg. Note that a normal curve is superimposed on the figure. Therefore, using check #1 in the box, the data appear to be approximately normal.

To apply check #2, we obtain $\bar{x} = 37$ and $s = 2.4$ from the Minitab printout, Figure 4.37b. The intervals $\bar{x} \pm s$, $\bar{x} \pm 2s$, and $\bar{x} \pm 3s$ are shown in Table 4.6, as well as the percentage of mileage ratings that fall in each interval. These percentages agree almost exactly with those from a normal distribution.

Check #3 in the box requires that we find the ratio IQR/s. From Figure 4.37b, the 25th percentile (called Q_1 by Minitab) is $Q_L = 35.625$, and the 75th percentile (labeled Q_3 by Minitab) is $Q_U = 38.375$. Then, IQR $= Q_U - Q_L = 2.75$, and the ratio is

$$\frac{\text{IQR}}{s} = \frac{2.75}{2.4} = 1.15$$

Because this value is approximately equal to 1.3, we have further confirmation that the data are approximately normal.

A fourth descriptive method is to interpret a normal probability plot. An SPSS normal probability plot for the mileage data is shown in Figure 4.37c. Notice that the ordered mileage values (shown on the horizontal axis) fall reasonably close to a straight line when plotted against the expected z-scores from a normal distribution. Thus, check #4 also suggests that the EPA mileage data are likely to be approximately normally distributed.

Look Back The checks for normality given in the box are simple, yet powerful, techniques to apply, but they are only descriptive in nature. It is possible (although unlikely) that the data are nonnormal even when the checks are reasonably satisfied. Thus, we should be careful not to claim that the 100 EPA mileage ratings of Example 4.23 are, in fact, normally distributed. We can only state that it is reasonable to believe that the data are from a normal distribution.*

• **Now Work Exercise 4.120**

As we will learn in Chapter 6, several inferential methods of analysis require the data to be approximately normal. If the data are clearly nonnormal, inferences derived from the method may be invalid. Therefore, it is advisable to check the normality of the data prior to conducting the analysis.

Exercises 4.117–4.131

Learning the Mechanics

4.117 If a population data set is normally distributed, what is the proportion of measurements you would expect to fall within the following intervals?
   a. $\mu \pm \sigma$
   b. $\mu \pm 2\sigma$
   c. $\mu \pm 3\sigma$

4.118 Consider a sample data set with the following summary statistics: $s = 95$, $Q_L = 72$, $Q_U = 195$.
   a. Calculate IQR.
   b. Calculate IQR/s.
   c. Is the value of IQR/s approximately equal to 1.3? What does this imply?

4.119 Normal probability plots for three data sets are shown on the next page. Which plot indicates that the data are approximately normally distributed?

4.120 Examine the sample data in the accompanying table.

NW

L04120

5.9	5.3	1.6	7.4	8.6	1.2	2.1
4.0	7.3	8.4	8.9	6.7	4.5	6.3
7.6	9.7	3.5	1.1	4.3	3.3	8.4
1.6	8.2	6.5	1.1	5.0	9.4	6.4

   a. Construct a stem-and-leaf plot to assess whether the data are from an approximately normal distribution.
   b. Compute s for the sample data.

*Statistical tests of normality that provide a measure of reliability for the inference are available. However, these tests tend to be very sensitive to slight departures from normality (i.e., they tend to reject the hypothesis of normality for any distribution that is not perfectly symmetric and mound-shaped). Consult the references (see Ramsey & Ramsey, 1990) if you want to learn more about these tests.

Normal probability plots for Exercise 4.119

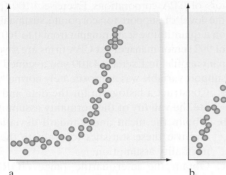

a.

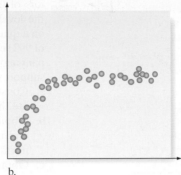

b.

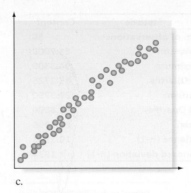

c.

c. Find the values of Q_L and Q_U, then use these values and the value of s from part **b** to assess whether the data come from an approximately normal distribution.

d. Generate a normal probability plot for the data and use it to assess whether the data are approximately normal.

Applying the Concepts—Basic

4.121 *The Apprentice* contestants' performance ratings. Refer to the *Significance* (April 2015) study of contestants' performances on the United Kingdom's version of the TV show, *The Apprentice*, Exercise 2.9 (p. 73). Recall that the performance of each of 159 contestants was rated on a 20-point scale. Contestants were also divided into two groups: those who played for a job and those who played for a business partnership. These data (simulated, based on statistics reported in the article) are saved in the accompanying file. Descriptive statistics for each of the two groups of contestants are displayed in the accompanying Minitab printout.

a. Determine whether the performance ratings of contestants who played for a job are approximately normally distributed.

b. Determine whether the performance ratings of contestants who played for a business partnership are approximately normally distributed.

Descriptive Statistics: Rating

Variable	Prize	N	Mean	StDev	Minimum	Q1	Median	Q3	Maximum	IQR
Rating	Job	99	7.879	4.324	1.000	4.000	8.000	11.000	20.000	7.000
	Partner	60	8.883	4.809	1.000	5.000	8.000	12.000	20.000	7.000

4.122 Shear strength of rock fractures. Understanding the characteristics of rock masses, especially the nature of the fractures, is essential when building dams and power plants. The shear strength of rock fractures was investigated in *Engineering Geology* (May 12, 2010). The Joint Roughness Coefficient (JRC) was used to measure shear strength. Civil engineers collected JRC data for over 750 rock fractures. The results (simulated from information provided in the article) are summarized in the accompanying SPSS histogram. Should the engineers use the normal probability distribution to model the behavior of shear strength for rock fractures? Explain.

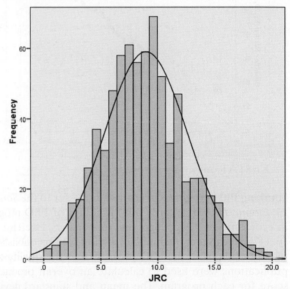

4.123 Drug content assessment. Scientists at GlaxoSmithKline Medicines Research Center used high-performance liquid chromatography (HPLC) to determine the amount of drug in a tablet produced by the company (*Analytical Chemistry*, Dec. 15, 2009). Drug concentrations (measured as a percentage) for 50 randomly selected tablets are listed in the table below and saved in the accompanying file.

a. Descriptive statistics for the drug concentrations are shown at the top of the XLSTAT printout on the next page. Use this information to assess whether the data are approximately normal.

b. An XLSTAT normal probability plot follows. Use this information to assess whether the data are approximately normal.

91.28	92.83	89.35	91.90	82.85	94.83	89.83	89.00	84.62
86.96	88.32	91.17	83.86	89.74	92.24	92.59	84.21	89.36
90.96	92.85	89.39	89.82	89.91	92.16	88.67	89.35	86.51
89.04	91.82	93.02	88.32	88.76	89.26	90.36	87.16	91.74
86.12	92.10	83.33	87.61	88.20	92.78	86.35	93.84	91.20
93.44	86.77	83.77	93.19	81.79				

Source: Based on P. J. Borman, J. C. Marion, I. Damjanov, and P. Jackson, "Design and Analysis of Method Equivalence Studies," *Analytical Chemistry*, Vol. 81, No. 24, December 15, 2009 (Table 3).

Descriptive statistics (Quantitative data):

Statistic	Content
Nbr. of observations	50
Minimum	81.7900
Maximum	94.8300
1st Quartile	87.2725
Median	89.3750
3rd Quartile	91.8800
Mean	89.2906
Variance (n-1)	10.1343
Standard deviation (n-1)	3.1834

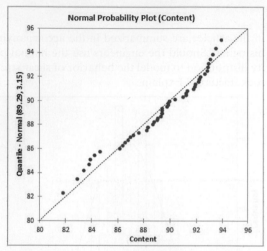

XLSTAT output for Exercise 4.123

4.124 Ranking PhD programs in economics. Refer to the *Southern Economic Journal* (April 2008) rankings of PhD programs in economics at 129 colleges and universities, Exercise 2.103 (p. 117). Recall that the number of publications published by faculty teaching in the PhD program and the quality of the publications were used to calculate an overall productivity score for each program. The mean and standard deviation of these 129 productivity scores were then used to compute a z-score for each economics program. The data (z-scores) for all 129 economic programs are saved in the accompanying file. A Minitab normal probability plot for the z-scores is shown below. Use the graph to assess whether the data are approximately normal.

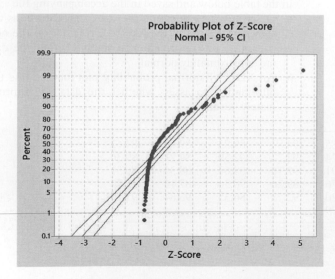

4.125 Corporate sustainability of CPA firms. Refer to the *Business and Society* (March 2011) study on the sustainability behaviors of CPA corporations, Exercise 4.100 (p. 263). Data on the level of support for corporate sustainability (measured on a quantitative scale ranging from 0 to 160 points) for each of 992 senior managers at CPA firms are saved in the accompanying file. In Exercise 4.100 you assumed that the level of support variable was approximately normally distributed.

a. Construct a histogram for the data and use it to evaluate the validity of the normality assumption.

b. Obtain the mean and standard deviation for the data and use these statistics to evaluate the validity of the normality assumption.

c. Obtain the interquartile range (IQR) for the data and use it to evaluate the validity of the normality assumption.

d. Construct a normal probability plot for the data and use it to evaluate the validity of the normality assumption.

Applying the Concepts—Intermediate

4.126 Wear-out of used display panels. Wear-out failure time of electronic components is often assumed to have a normal distribution. Can the normal distribution be applied to the wear-out of used manufactured products, such as colored display panels? A lot of 50 used display panels was purchased by an outlet store. Each panel displays 12 to 18 color characters. Prior to acquisition, the panels had been used for about one-third of their expected lifetimes. The data in the accompanying table (saved in the file) give the failure times (in years) of the 50 used panels. Use the techniques of this section to determine whether the used panel wear-out times are approximately normally distributed.

0.01	1.21	1.71	2.30	2.96	0.19	1.22	1.75	2.30	2.98	0.51
1.24	1.77	2.41	3.19	0.57	1.48	1.79	2.44	3.25	0.70	1.54
1.88	2.57	3.31	0.73	1.59	1.90	2.61	1.19	0.75	1.61	1.93
2.62	3.50	0.75	1.61	2.01	2.72	3.50	1.11	1.62	2.16	2.76
3.50	1.16	1.62	2.18	2.84	3.50					

Source: Based on T. Z. Irony, M. Lauretto, C. Pereira, and J. M. Stern, "A Weibull Wearout Test: Full Bayesian Approach," paper presented at *Mathematical Sciences Colloquium*, Binghamton University, Bringhamton, UK, December 2001.

4.127 Rankings of research universities. Refer to the College Choice *2015 Rankings of National Research Universities*, Exercise 2.110 (p. 125). Data on academic reputation scores for the top 50 research universities (saved in the file) are listed in the accompanying table. Would you recommend using the normal distribution to approximate the distribution of academic reputation scores?

99	92	94	95	97	91	91	92	92	89	84	85	100	87	83
83	89	79	94	79	79	87	76	67	76	76	76	70	74	64
74	69	66	72	65	76	64	65	61	69	62	69	52	64	64
47	60	57	63	62										

4.128 Sanitation inspection of cruise ships. Refer to the data on the October 2015 sanitation scores for 196 cruise ships, first presented in Exercise 2.24 (p. 83). The data are saved in the accompanying file. Assess whether the sanitation scores are approximately normally distributed.

4.129 Ranking driving performance of professional golfers. Refer to *the Sport Journal* (Winter 2007) article on a method for ranking the driving performance of PGA golfers, Exercise 2.52 (p. 97). Recall that the method incorporates a golfer's average driving distance (yards) and driving accuracy (percent of drives that land in the fairway) into a driving performance index. Data on these three variables for the top 40 PGA golfers are saved in the accompanying file. Determine which of these variables—driving distance, driving accuracy, and driving performance index—are approximately normally distributed.

4.130 Permeability of sandstone during weathering. Refer to the *Geographical Analysis* (Vol. 42, 2010) study of the decay properties of sandstone when exposed to the weather, Exercise 2.69 (p. 105). Recall that blocks of sandstone were cut into 300 equal-sized slices, and the slices were randomly divided into three groups of 100 slices each. Slices in Group A were not exposed to any type of weathering; slices in Group B were repeatedly sprayed with a 10% salt solution (to simulate wetting by driven rain) under temperate conditions;

and, slices in Group C were soaked in a 10% salt solution and then dried (to simulate blocks of sandstone exposed during a wet winter and dried during a hot summer). All sandstone slices were then tested for permeability, measured in milliDarcies (mD). The data for the study (simulated) are saved in the accompanying file. Is it plausible to assume that the permeability measurements in any of the three experimental groups are approximately normally distributed?

Applying the Concepts—Advanced

4.131 Chemical composition of gold artifacts. The *Journal of Open Archaeology Data* (Vol. 1, 2012) provided data on the chemical composition of more than 200 pre-Columbian gold and gold-alloy artifacts recovered in the archaeological region inhabited by the Muisca of Colombia (A.D. 600–1800). One of many variables measured was the percentage of copper present in the gold artifacts. Summary statistics for this variable follow: mean = 29.94%, median = 19.75%, standard deviation = 28.37%. Demonstrate why the probability distribution for the percentage of copper in these gold artifacts cannot be normally distributed.

4.8 Other Continuous Distributions: Uniform and Exponential

Uniform Random Variable

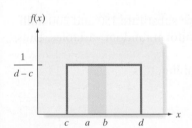

Figure 4.38
The uniform probability distribution

Continuous random variables that appear to have equally likely outcomes over their range of possible values possess a **uniform probability distribution.** For example, if a short exists in a 5-meter stretch of electrical wire, it may have an equal probability of being in any particular 1-centimeter segment along the line. Or if a safety inspector plans to choose a time at random during the four afternoon work hours to pay a surprise visit to a certain area of a plant, then each 1-minute time interval in this 4-work-hour period will have an equally likely chance of being selected for the visit.

Suppose the random variable x can assume values only in an interval $c \le x \le d$. Then the **uniform frequency function** has a rectangular shape, as shown in Figure 4.38. Note that the possible values of x consist of all points in the interval between point c and point d. The height of $f(x)$ is constant in that interval and equals $1/(d - c)$. Therefore, the total area under $f(x)$ is given by

$$\text{Total area of rectangle} = (\text{Base})(\text{Height}) = (d - c)\left(\frac{1}{d - c}\right) = 1$$

The uniform probability distribution provides a model for continuous random variables that are *evenly distributed* over a certain interval—that is, a **uniform random variable** is one that is just as likely to assume a value in one interval as it is to assume a value in any other interval of equal size. There is no clustering of values around any value; instead, there is an even spread over the entire region of possible values.

The uniform distribution is sometimes referred to as the **randomness distribution** because one way of generating a uniform random variable is to perform an experiment in which a point is *randomly selected* on the horizontal axis between the points c and d. If we were to repeat this experiment infinitely often, we would create a uniform probability distribution like that shown in Figure 4.38. The random selection of points in an interval can also be used to generate random numbers such as those in Table I in Appendix B. Recall that random numbers are selected in such a way that every number would have an equal probability of selection. Therefore, random numbers are realizations of a uniform random variable. (Random numbers were used to draw random samples in Section 3.7.) The formulas for the uniform probability distribution, its mean, and its standard deviation are shown in the next box.

Suppose the interval $a < x < b$ lies within the domain of x; that is, it falls within the larger interval $c \leq x \leq d$. Then the probability that x assumes a value within the interval $a < x < b$ is equal to the area of the rectangle over the interval, namely, $(b - a)/(d - c)$.* (See the shaded area in Figure 4.38.)

Probability Distribution for a Uniform Random Variable x

Probability density function: $f(x) = \dfrac{1}{d - c} \quad c \leq x \leq d$

Mean: $\mu = \dfrac{c + d}{2}$ Standard deviation: $\sigma = \dfrac{d - c}{\sqrt{12}}$

$$P(a < x < b) = (b - a)/(d - c), c \leq a < b \leq d$$

EXAMPLE 4.24

Applying the Uniform Distribution—Steel Manufacturing

Problem Suppose the research department of a steel manufacturer believes that one of the company's rolling machines is producing sheets of steel of varying thickness. The thickness is a uniform random variable with values between 150 and 200 millimeters. Any sheets less than 160 millimeters must be scrapped because they are unacceptable to buyers.

a. Calculate and interpret the mean and standard deviation of x, the thickness of the sheets produced by this machine.

b. Graph the probability distribution of x, and show the mean on the horizontal axis. Also show 1- and 2-standard-deviation intervals around the mean.

c. Calculate the fraction of steel sheets produced by this machine that have to be scrapped.

Solution

a. To calculate the mean and standard deviation for x, we substitute 150 and 200 millimeters for c and d, respectively, in the formulas for uniform random variables. Thus,

$$\mu = \frac{c + d}{2} = \frac{150 + 200}{2} = 175 \text{ millimeters}$$

and

$$\sigma = \frac{d - c}{\sqrt{12}} = \frac{200 - 150}{\sqrt{12}} = \frac{50}{3.464} = 14.43 \text{ millimeters}$$

Our interpretations follow:

The average thickness of all manufactured steel sheets is $\mu = 175$ millimeters. From Chebyshev's Rule (Table 2.6, p. 106), we know that at least 75% of the thickness values, x, in the distribution will fall in the interval

$$\mu \pm 2\sigma = 175 \pm 2(14.43)$$
$$= 175 \pm 28.86$$

or between 146.14 and 203.86 millimeters. (This demonstrates, once again, the conservativeness of Chebyshev's Rule because we know that all values of x fall between 150 and 200 millimeters.)

b. The uniform probability distribution is

$$f(x) = \frac{1}{d - c} = \frac{1}{200 - 150} = \frac{1}{50} \quad (150 \leq x \leq 200)$$

---

*The student with knowledge of calculus should note that

$$P(a < x < b) = \int_a^b f(x)d(x) = \int_a^b 1/(d - c)dx = (b - a)/(d - c)$$

The graph of this function is shown in Figure 4.39. The mean and 1- and 2-standard-deviation intervals around the mean are shown on the horizontal axis.

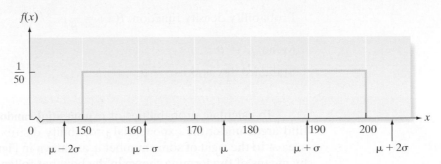

Figure 4.39
Distribution for x in Example 4.24

c. To find the fraction of steel sheets produced by the machine that have to be scrapped, we must find the probability that x, the thickness, is less than 160 millimeters. As indicated in Figure 4.40, we need to calculate the area under the frequency function $f(x)$ between the points $x = 150$ and $x = 160$. Therefore, in this case, $a = 150$ and $b = 160$. Applying the formula in the box, we have

$$P(x < 160) = P(150 < x < 160)$$

$$= \frac{b - a}{d - c} = \frac{160 - 150}{200 - 150} = \frac{10}{50} = \frac{1}{5} = .2$$

That is, 20% of all the sheets made by this machine must be scrapped.

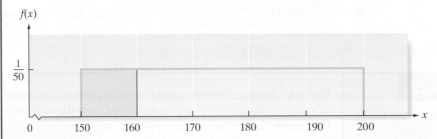

Figure 4.40
Probability that sheet thickness, x, is between 150 and 160 millimeters

Look Back The calculated probability in part **c** is the area of a rectangle with base $160 - 150 = 10$ and height $\frac{1}{50}$. Alternatively, we can find the fraction that has to be scrapped as

$$P(x < 160) = (\text{Base})(\text{Height}) = (10)\left(\frac{1}{50}\right) = \frac{1}{5} = .2$$

Or, we can use statistical software to find the probability, as shown on the Minitab printout, Figure 4.41.

Cumulative Distribution Function

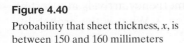

```
Continuous uniform on 150 to 200

   x    P( X <= x )
 160          0.2
```

Figure 4.41
Minitab output for Example 4.24

● **Now Work Exercise 4.142**

Exponential Random Variable

The length of time between emergency arrivals at a hospital, the length of time between breakdowns of manufacturing equipment, and the length of time between catastrophic events (e.g., a stock market crash), are all continuous random phenomena that we might want to describe probabilistically. The length of time or the distance between occurrences of random events like these can often be described by the **exponential probability distribution.** For this reason, the exponential distribution is sometimes called the **waiting-time distribution.** The formula for the exponential probability distribution is shown in the following box, along with its mean and standard deviation.

Unlike the normal distribution, which has a shape and location determined by the values of the two quantities μ and σ, the shape of the exponential distribution is governed by a single quantity: θ. Further, it is a probability distribution with the property that its mean equals its standard deviation. Exponential distributions corresponding to $\theta = .5$, 1, and 2 are shown in Figure 4.42.

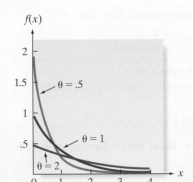

Figure 4.42
Exponential distributions

Probability Distribution for an Exponential Random Variable x

Probability density function: $f(x) = \dfrac{1}{\theta} e^{-x/\theta}$ $(x > 0)$

Mean: $\mu = \theta$

Standard deviation: $\sigma = \theta$

To calculate probabilities of **exponential random variables,** we need to be able to find areas under the exponential probability distribution. Suppose we want to find the area A to the right of some number a, as shown in Figure 4.43. This area can be calculated by means of the formula shown in the box that follows or by using statistical software.

Finding the Area A to the Right of a Number a for an Exponential Distribution*

$$A = P(x \ge a) = e^{-a/\theta}$$

Figure 4.43

The area A to the right of a number a for an exponential distribution

---

EXAMPLE 4.25

Finding an Exponential Probability—Hospital Emergency Arrivals

Problem Suppose the length of time (in hours) between emergency arrivals at a certain hospital is modeled as an exponential distribution with $\theta = 2$. What is the probability that more than 5 hours pass without an emergency arrival?

Solution The probability we want is the area A to the right of $a = 5$ in Figure 4.44. To find this probability, we use the area formula:

$$A = e^{-a/\theta} = e^{-(5/2)} = e^{-2.5}$$

Using a calculator with an exponential function, we find that

$$A = e^{-2.5} = .082085$$

Our exponential model indicates that the probability that more than 5 hours pass between emergency arrivals is about .08 for this hospital.

Look Back The desired probability can also be found with a statistical software package. We accessed the exponential probability function of Minitab, specified a mean of 2, and requested the cumulative probability, $P(x \le 5)$. This probability is shaded in Figure 4.45. Using the rule of complements, the desired probability is

$$P(x > 5) = 1 - P(x \le 5) = 1 - .917915 = .082085$$

Figure 4.44

Area to the right of $a = 5$ for Example 4.25

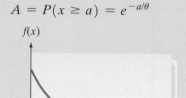

Cumulative Distribution Function

```
Exponential with mean = 2

x    P( X <= x )
5    0.917915
```

Figure 4.45

Minitab output for Example 4.25

• **Now Work Exercise 4.135**

---

*For students with a knowledge of calculus, the shaded area in Figure 4.43 corresponds to the integral $\displaystyle\int_a^b \frac{1}{\theta} e^{-x/\theta}\,dx = -e^{-x/\theta}\Big|_a^\infty = e^{-a/\theta}$.

EXAMPLE 4.26

The Mean and Variance of an Exponential Random Variable— Length of Life of a Microwave Oven

Problem A manufacturer of microwave ovens is trying to determine the length of warranty period it should attach to its magnetron tube, the most critical component in the oven. Preliminary testing has shown that the length of life (in years), x, of a magnetron tube has an exponential probability distribution with $\theta = 6.25$.

a. Find the mean and standard deviation of x.

b. Suppose a warranty period of 5 years is attached to the magnetron tube. What fraction of tubes must the manufacturer plan to replace, assuming that the exponential model with $\theta = 6.25$ is correct?

c. Find the probability that the length of life of a magnetron tube will fall within the interval $\mu - 2\sigma$ to $\mu + 2\sigma$.

Solution

a. Because $\theta = \mu = \sigma$, both μ and σ equal 6.25.

b. To find the fraction of tubes that will have to be replaced before the 5-year warranty period expires, we need to find the area between 0 and 5 under the distribution. This area, A, is shown in Figure 4.46. To find the required probability, we recall the formula

$$P(x > a) = e^{-a/\theta}$$

Using this formula, we find that

$$P(x > 5) = e^{-a/\theta} = e^{-5/6.25} = e^{-.80} = .449329$$

To find the area A, we use the complementary relationship:

$$P(x \le 5) = 1 - P(x > 5) = 1 - .449329 = .550671$$

So approximately 55% of the magnetron tubes will have to be replaced during the 5-year warranty period.

c. We would expect the probability that the life of a magnetron tube, x, falls within the interval $\mu - 2\sigma$ to $\mu + 2\sigma$ to be quite large. A graph of the exponential distribution showing the interval from $\mu - 2\sigma$ to $\mu + 2\sigma$ is given in Figure 4.47. Because the point $\mu - 2\sigma$ lies below $x = 0$, we need to find only the area between $x = 0$ and $x = \mu + 2\sigma = 6.25 + 2(6.25) = 18.75$.

This area, P, which is shaded in Figure 4.47, is

$$P = 1 - P(x > 18.75) = 1 - e^{-18.75/\theta} = 1 - e^{-18.75/6.25} = 1 - e^{-3}$$

Using a calculator, we find that $e^{-3} = .049787$. Therefore, the probability that the life x of a magnetron tube will fall within the interval $\mu - 2\sigma$ to $\mu + 2\sigma$ is

$$P = 1 - e^{-3} = 1 - .049787 = .950213$$

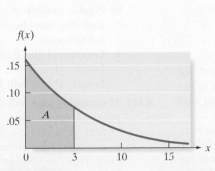

Figure 4.46

Area to the left of $a = 5$ for Example 4.26

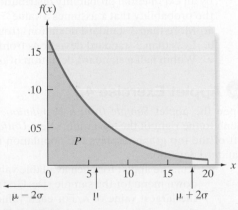

Figure 4.47

Area in the interval $\mu \pm 2\sigma$ for Example 4.26

> **Look Back** You can see that this probability agrees well with the interpretation of a standard deviation given by the Empirical Rule (Table 2.7, p. 129), even though the probability distribution that we were given is not mound-shaped. (It is strongly skewed to the right.)

Exercises 4.132–4.155

Learning the Mechanics

4.132 Suppose x is a random variable best described by a uniform probability distribution with $c = 3$ and $d = 7$.
  a. Find $f(x)$.
  b. Find the mean and standard deviation of x.
  c. Find $P(\mu - \sigma \le x \le \mu + \sigma)$.

4.133 Suppose x is a random variable best described by a uniform probability distribution with $c = 20$ and $d = 45$.
  a. Find $f(x)$.
  b. Find the mean and standard deviation of x.
  c. Graph $f(x)$ and locate μ and the interval $\mu \pm 2\sigma$ on the graph. Note that the probability that x assumes a value within the interval $\mu \pm 2\sigma$ is equal to 1.

4.134 Refer to Exercise 4.133. Find the following probabilities:
  a. $P(20 \le x \le 30)$ **b.** $P(20 < x \le 30)$
  c. $P(x \ge 30)$ **d.** $P(x \ge 45)$
  e. $P(x \le 40)$ **f.** $P(x < 40)$
  g. $P(15 \le x \le 35)$ **h.** $P(21.5 \le x \le 31.5)$

4.135 Suppose x has an exponential distribution with $\theta = 1$. Find the following probabilities:
  [NW]
  a. $P(x > 1)$ **b.** $P(x \le 3)$
  c. $P(x > 1.5)$ **d.** $P(x \le 5)$

4.136 Suppose x has an exponential distribution with $\theta = 2.5$. Find the following probabilities:
  a. $P(x \le 4)$ **b.** $P(x > 5)$
  c. $P(x \le 2)$ **d.** $P(x > 3)$

4.137 The random variable x is best described by a uniform probability distribution with $c = 100$ and $d = 200$. Find the probability that x assumes a value
  a. More than 2 standard deviations from μ.
  b. Less than 3 standard deviations from μ.
  c. Within 2 standard deviations of μ.

4.138 The random variable x can be adequately approximated by an exponential probability distribution with $\theta = 2$. Find the probability that x assumes a value
  a. More than 3 standard deviations from μ.
  b. Less than 2 standard deviations from μ.
  c. Within half a standard deviation of μ.

📊 Applet Exercise 4.7

Open the applet *Sample from a Population*. On the pull-down menu to the right of the top graph, select *Uniform*. The box to the left of the top graph displays the population mean, median, and standard deviation.
  a. Run the applet for each available value of n on the pull-down menu for the sample size. Go from the smallest to the largest value of n. For each value of n, observe the shape of the graph of the sample data and record the mean, median, and standard deviation of the sample.
  b. Describe what happens to the shape of the graph and the mean, median, and standard deviation of the sample as the sample size increases.

📊 Applet Exercise 4.8

Suppose we set the *Random Numbers* applet to generate one number between 1 and 100, inclusive. We let the value of the random variable x be the number generated when the *Sample* button is clicked. Explain why the distribution of x is approximately uniform even though x is a discrete rather than continuous random variable.

Applying the Concepts—Basic

4.139 **Load on timber beams.** Timber beams are widely used in home construction. When the load (measured in pounds) per unit length has a constant value over part of a beam, the load is said to be uniformly distributed over that part of the beam. Uniformly distributed beam loads were used to derive the stiffness distribution of the beam in the *American Institute of Aeronautics and Astronautics Journal* (May 2013). Consider a cantilever beam with a uniformly distributed load between 100 and 115 pounds per linear foot.
  a. What is the probability that a beam load exceeds 110 pounds per linear foot?
  b. What is the probability that a beam load is less than 102 pounds per linear foot?
  c. Find a value L such that the probability that the beam load exceeds L is only .1.

4.140 **Preventative maintenance tests.** The optimal scheduling of preventative maintenance tests of some (but not all) of n independently operating components was developed in *Reliability Engineering and System Safety* (January 2006). The time (in hours) between failures of a component was approximated by an exponential distribution with mean θ.
  a. Suppose $\theta = 1{,}000$ hours. Find the probability that the time between component failures ranges between 1,200 and 1,500 hours.
  b. Again, assume $\theta = 1{,}000$ hours. Find the probability that the time between component failures is at least 1,200 hours.
  c. Given that the time between failures is at least 1,200 hours, what is the probability that the time between failures is less than 1,500 hours?

4.141 **Maintaining pipe wall temperature.** Maintaining a constant pipe wall temperature in some hot-process applications is critical. A technique that utilizes bolt-on trace elements to maintain temperature was presented in the *Journal of Heat Transfer* (November 2000). Without bolt-on trace elements, the pipe wall temperature of a switch condenser used to produce plastic has a uniform distribution ranging from 260° to 290°F. When several bolt-on trace elements are attached to the piping, the wall temperature is uniform from 278° to 285°F.

a. Ideally, the pipe wall temperature should range between 280° and 284°F. What is the probability that the temperature will fall in this ideal range when no bolt-on trace elements are used? When bolt-on trace elements are attached to the pipe?

b. When the temperature is 268°F or lower, the hot liquid plastic hardens (or plates), causing a buildup in the piping. What is the probability of plastic plating when no bolt-on trace elements are used? When bolt-on trace elements are attached to the pipe?

4.142 Detecting anthrax. Researchers at the University of South Florida Center for Biological Defense have developed a safe method for rapidly detecting anthrax spores in powders and on surfaces (*USF Magazine*, Summer 2002). The method has been found to work well even when there are very few anthrax spores in a powder specimen. Consider a powder specimen that has exactly 10 anthrax spores. Suppose that the number of anthrax spores in the sample detected by this method follows an approximate uniform distribution between 0 and 10.

a. Find the probability that 8 or fewer anthrax spores are detected in the powder specimen.

b. Find the probability that between 2 and 5 anthrax spores are detected in the powder specimen.

4.143 Lead in metal shredder residue. On the basis of data collected from metal shredders across the nation, the amount x of extractable lead in metal shredder residue has an approximate exponential distribution with mean $\theta = 2.5$ milligrams per liter (Florida Shredder's Association).

a. Find the probability that x is greater than 2 milligrams per liter.

b. Find the probability that x is less than 5 milligrams per liter.

4.144 Critical-part failures in NASCAR vehicles. In NASCAR races such as the Daytona 500, 43 drivers start the race; however, about 10% of the cars do not finish due to the failure of critical parts. University of Portland professors conducted a study of critical-part failures from 36 NASCAR races (*The Sport Journal*, Winter 2007). The researchers discovered that the time (in hours) until the first critical-part failure is exponentially distributed with a mean of .10 hour.

a. Find the probability that the time until the first critical-part failure is 1 hour or more.

b. Find the probability that the time until the first critical-part failure is less than 30 minutes.

Applying the Concepts—Intermediate

4.145 Social network densities. Social networking sites for business professionals are used to promote one's business. Each social network involves interactions (connections) between members of the network. Researchers define network density as the ratio of actual network connections to the number of possible one-to-one connections. For example, a network with 10 members has $\binom{10}{2} = 45$ total possible connections. If that network has only 5 connections, the network density is $\frac{5}{45} = .111$. Sociologists at the University of Michigan assumed that the density x of

a social network would follow a uniform distribution between 0 and 1 (*Social Networks*, 2010).

a. On average, what is the density of a randomly selected social network?

b. What is the probability that the randomly selected network has a density higher than .7?

c. Consider a social network with only 2 members. Explain why the uniform model would not be a good approximation for the distribution of network density.

4.146 Boeing 787 Dreamliner. An assessment of the new Boeing 787 "Dreamliner" airplane was published in the *Journal of Case Research in Business and Economics* (December 2014). Boeing planned to build and deliver 3,500 of these aircraft within the first 20 years of the 787 program. The researchers used simulation to estimate the number of annual deliveries of 787 airplanes (expressed as a percentage of total Boeing aircraft deliveries during the year). In the fifth year of the program, deliveries were uniformly distributed over the range 2.5% to 5.5%. Assuming the simulated results are accurate, what is the probability that the number of Boeing 787s built and delivered in the fifth year of the program exceeds 4% of the total Boeing aircraft deliveries during the year?

4.147 Soft-drink dispenser. The manager of a local soft-drink bottling company believes that when a new beverage-dispensing machine is set to dispense 7 ounces, it in fact dispenses an amount x at random anywhere between 6.5 and 7.5 ounces inclusive. Suppose x has a uniform probability distribution.

a. Is the amount dispensed by the beverage machine a discrete or a continuous random variable? Explain.

b. Graph the frequency function for x, the amount of beverage the manager believes is dispensed by the new machine when it is set to dispense 7 ounces.

c. Find the mean and standard deviation for the distribution graphed in part **b**, and locate the mean and the interval $\mu \pm 2\sigma$ on the graph.

d. Find $P(x \geq 7)$.

e. Find $P(x < 6)$.

f. Find $P(6.5 \leq x \leq 7.25)$.

g. What is the probability that each of the next six bottles filled by the new machine will contain more than 7.25 ounces of beverage? Assume that the amount of beverage dispensed in one bottle is independent of the amount dispensed in another bottle.

4.148 Phishing attacks to e-mail accounts. Refer to the *Chance* (Summer 2007) article on phishing attacks at a company, Exercise 2.33 (p. 86). Recall that *phishing* describes an attempt to extract personal/financial information through fraudulent e-mail. The company set up a publicized e-mail account—called a "fraud box"—that enabled employees to notify them if they suspected an e-mail phishing attack. If there is minimal or no collaboration or collusion from within the company, the interarrival times (i.e., the time between successive e-mail notifications, in seconds) have an approximate exponential distribution with a mean of 95 seconds.

a. What is the probability of observing an interarrival time of at least 2 minutes?

b. Data for a sample of 267 interarrival times are saved in the accompanying file. Do the data appear to follow an exponential distribution with $\theta = 95$?

4.149 Product failure behavior. An article in *Hotwire* (December 2002) discussed the length of time till failure of a product produced at Hewlett-Packard. At the end of the product's lifetime, the time till failure is modeled using an exponential distribution with mean 500 thousand hours. In reliability jargon this is known as the "wear-out" distribution for the product. During its normal (useful) life, assume the product's time till failure is uniformly distributed over the range 100 thousand to 1 million hours.

  a. At the end of the product's lifetime, find the probability that the product fails before 700 thousand hours.

  b. During its normal (useful) life, find the probability that the product fails before 700 thousand hours.

  c. Show that the probability of the product failing before 830 thousand hours is approximately the same for both the normal (useful) life distribution and the wear-out distribution.

4.150 Cycle availability of a system. In the jargon of system maintenance, *cycle availability* is defined as the probability that the system is functioning at any point in time. The DoD developed a series of performance measures for assessing system cycle availability (*Start*, Vol. 11, 2004). Under certain assumptions about the failure time and maintenance time of a system, cycle availability is shown to be uniformly distributed between 0 and 1. Find the following parameters for cycle availability: mean, standard deviation, 10th percentile, lower quartile, and upper quartile. Interpret the results.

4.151 Gouges on a spindle. A tool-and-die machine shop produces extremely high-tolerance spindles. The spindles are 18-inch slender rods used in a variety of military equipment. A piece of equipment used in the manufacture of the spindles malfunctions on occasion and places a single gouge somewhere on the spindle. However, if the spindle can be cut so that it has 14 consecutive inches without a gouge, then the spindle can be salvaged for other purposes. Assuming that the location of the gouge along the spindle is random, what is the probability that a defective spindle can be salvaged?

4.152 Reliability of CD-ROMs. In *Reliability Ques* (March 2004), the exponential distribution was used to model the lengths of life of CD-ROM drives in a two-drive system. The two CD-ROM drives operate independently, and at least one drive must be operating for the system to operate successfully. Both drives have a mean length of life of 25,000 hours.

  a. The reliability $R(t)$ of a single CD-ROM drive is the probability that the life of the drive exceeds t hours. Give a formula for $R(t)$.

  b. Use the result from part **a** to find the probability that the life of the single CD-ROM drive exceeds 8,760 hours (the number of hours of operation in a year).

  c. The reliability $S(t)$ of the two-drive/CD-ROM system is the probability that the life of at least one drive exceeds t hours. Give a formula for $S(t)$. [*Hint*: Use the rule of complements and the fact that the two drives operate independently.]

  d. Use the result from part **c** to find the probability that the two-drive CD-ROM system has a life whose length exceeds 8,760 hours.

  e. Compare the probabilities you found in parts **b** and **d**.

Applying the Concepts—Advanced

4.153 Acceptance sampling of a product. An essential tool in the monitoring of the quality of a manufactured product is *acceptance sampling*. An acceptance sampling plan involves knowing the distribution of the life length of the item produced and determining how many items to inspect from the manufacturing process. The *Journal of Applied Statistics* (April 2010) demonstrated the use of the exponential distribution as a model for the life length x of an item (e.g., a bullet). The article also discussed the importance of using the median of the lifetime distribution as a measure of product quality, since half of the items in a manufactured lot will have life lengths exceeding the median. For an exponential distribution with mean θ, give an expression for the median of the distribution. (*Hint:* Your answer will be a function of θ.)

4.154 Reliability of a robotic device. The *reliability* of a piece of equipment is frequently defined to be the probability, p, that the equipment performs its intended function successfully for a given period of time under specific conditions (Heizer, Render, and Munson, *Principles of Operations Management*, 2016). Because p varies from one point in time to another, some reliability analysts treat p as if it were a random variable. Suppose an analyst characterizes the uncertainty about the reliability of a particular robotic device used in an automobile assembly line using the following distribution:

$$f(p) = \begin{cases} 1 & 0 \le p \le 1 \\ 0 & \text{otherwise} \end{cases}$$

  a. Graph the analyst's probability distribution for p.

  b. Find the mean and variance of p.

  c. According to the analyst's probability distribution for p, what is the probability that p is greater than .95? Less than .95?

  d. Suppose the analyst receives the additional information that p is definitely between .90 and .95, but that there is complete uncertainty about where it lies between these values. Describe the probability distribution the analyst should now use to describe p.

4.155 Length of life of a halogen bulb. For a certain type of halogen light bulb, an old bulb that has been in use for a while tends to have a longer life than a new bulb. Let x represent the life (in hours) of a new halogen light bulb and assume that x has an exponential distribution with mean $\theta = 250$ hours. According to *Microelectronics and Reliability* (January 1986), the "life" distribution of x is considered *new better than used* (NBU) if

$$P(x > a + b) \le P(x > a)P(x > b)$$

Alternatively, a "life" distribution is considered *new worse than used* (NWU) if

$$P(x > a + b) \ge P(x > a)P(x > b)$$

  a. Show that when $a = 300$ and $b = 200$, the exponential distribution is both NBU and NWU.

  b. Choose any two positive numbers a and b and repeat part **a**.

  c. Show that, in general, for any positive a and b, the exponential distribution with mean θ is both NBU and NWU. Such a "life" distribution is said to be *new same as used*, or *memoryless*. Explain why.

CHAPTER NOTES

Key Terms

Bell curve 249
Bell-shaped distribution 249
Binomial experiment 228
Binomial probability
  distribution 232
Binomial random variable 228
Continuous random variable 216
Correction for continuity 258
Countable 215
Cumulative binomial
  probabilities 234
Discrete random variable 216
Expected value 220
Exponential probability
  distribution 273
Exponential random variable 274
Frequency function 248
Hypergeometric probability
  distribution 243
Hypergeometric random
  variable 243
Mean of a binomial random
  variable 233
Mean of a discrete random
  variable 220
Mean of a hypergeometric ran-
  dom variable 244
Mean of a Poisson random
  variable 241
Normal distribution 249
Normal probability plot 266
Normal random variable 249
Poisson distribution 241
Poisson random variable 241
Probability density
  function(pdf) 248

Probability distribution 248
Probability distribution of a
  discrete random variable 218
Probability distribution of an
  exponential random
  variable 274
Probability distribution of a
  hypergeometric random
  variable 244
Probability distribution of a nor-
  mal random variable 250
Probability distribution of a
  Poisson random variable 241
Probability distribution for a uni-
  form random variable 272
Random variable 214
Randomness distribution 271
Standard deviation of a binomial
  random variable 233
Standard deviation of a discrete
  random variable 221
Standard normal distribution 250
Uniform frequency function 271
Uniform probability
  distribution 271
Uniform random variable 271
Variance of a binomial random
  variable 233
Variance of a discrete random
  variable 221
Variance of a hypergeometric ran-
  dom variable 244
Variance of a Poisson random
  variable 241
Waiting-time distribution 273

Key Symbols

$p(x)$	Probability distribution for discrete random variable, x
$f(x)$	Probability distribution for continuous random variable, x
S	Outcome of binomial trial denoted "success"
F	Outcome of binomial trial denoted "failure"
p	$P(S)$ in binomial trial
q	$P(F)$ in binomial trial $= 1 - p$
e	Constant used in normal and Poisson probability distributions, $e = 2.71828\ldots$
π	Constant used in normal probability distributions, $\pi = 3.1415\ldots$
λ	Mean of Poisson distribution
θ	Mean of exponential distribution

Key Ideas

Properties of Probability Distributions

Discrete Distributions

1. $p(x) \geq 0$

2. $\sum_{\text{all } x} p(x) = 1$

Continuous Distributions

1. $P(x = a) = 0$

2. $P(a < x < b)$ is area under curve between a and b

Normal Approximation to Binomial

x is binomial (n, p)

$$P(x \leq a) \approx P\{z < (a + .5) - \mu\}$$

Methods for Assessing Normality

1. *Histogram*

2. *Stem-and-leaf display*

```
1 | 7
2 | 3389
3 | 245677
4 | 19
5 | 2
```

3. $(IQR)/S \approx 1.3$
4. *Normal probability plot*

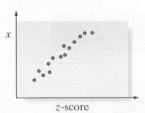

z-score

Key Formulas

Random Variable	Probability Distribution	Mean	Variance
General Discrete:	Table, formula, or graph for $p(x)$	$\displaystyle\sum_{\text{all } x} x \cdot p(x)$	$\displaystyle\sum_{\text{all } x} (x - \mu)^2 \cdot p(x)$
Binomial:	$p(x) = \dbinom{n}{x} p^x q^{n-x}$ $x = 0, 1, 2, \ldots, n$	np	npq
Poisson:	$p(x) = \dfrac{\lambda^x e^{-\lambda}}{x!}$ $x = 0, 1, 2, \ldots$	λ	λ
Hypergeometric	$p(x) = \dfrac{\dbinom{r}{x}\dbinom{N-r}{n-x}}{\dbinom{N}{n}}$	$\dfrac{nr}{N}$	$\dfrac{r(N-r)n(N-n)}{N^2(N-1)}$
Uniform:	$f(x) = 1/(d - c)$ $(c \le x \le d)$	$(c + d)/2$	$(d - c)^2/12$
Normal:	$f(x) = \dfrac{1}{\sigma\sqrt{2\pi}}\, e^{-\frac{1}{2}[(x-\mu)/\sigma]^2}$	μ	σ^2
Exponential	$f(x) = \dfrac{1}{\theta}\, e^{-x/\theta}$	θ	θ^2
Standard Normal:	$f(z) = \dfrac{1}{\sqrt{2\pi}}\, e^{-\frac{1}{2}(z)^2}$ $z = (x - \mu)/\sigma$	$\mu = 0$	$\sigma^2 = 1$

Guide to Selecting a Probability Distribution

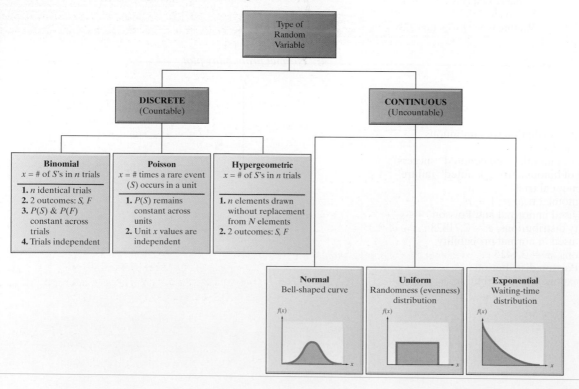

SUPPLEMENTARY EXERCISES 4.156–4.206

Learning the Mechanics

4.156 For each of the following examples, decide whether x is a binomial random variable and explain your decision:

  a. A manufacturer of computer chips randomly selects 100 chips from each hour's production in order to estimate the proportion defective. Let x represent the number of defectives in the 100 sampled chips.

  b. Of five applicants for a job, two will be selected. Although all applicants appear to be equally qualified, only three have the ability to fulfill the expectations of the company. Suppose that the two selections are made at random from the five applicants and let x be the number of qualified applicants selected.

  c. A software developer establishes a support hotline for customers to call in with questions regarding use of the software. Let x represent the number of calls received on the support hotline during a specified workday.

  d. Florida is one of a minority of states with no state income tax. A poll of 1,000 registered voters is conducted to determine how many would favor a state income tax in light of the state's current fiscal condition. Let x be the number in the sample who would favor the tax.

4.157 Given that x is a binomial random variable, compute $p(x)$ for each of the following cases:

  a. $n = 7, x = 3, p = .5$
  b. $n = 4, x = 3, p = .8$
  c. $n = 15, x = 1, p = .1$

4.158 Consider the discrete probability distribution shown here.

x	10	12	18	20
$p(x)$	.2	.3	.1	.4

  a. Calculate μ, σ^2, and σ.
  b. What is $P(x < 15)$?
  c. Calculate $\mu \pm 2\sigma$.
  d. What is the probability that x is in the interval $\mu \pm 2\sigma$?

4.159 Suppose x is a binomial random variable with $n = 20$ and $p = .7$.

  a. Find $P(x = 14)$.
  b. Find $P(x \leq 12)$.
  c. Find $P(x > 12)$.
  d. Find $P(9 \leq x \leq 18)$.
  e. Find $P(8 < x < 18)$.
  f. Find μ, σ^2, and σ.
  g. What is the probability that x is in the interval $\mu \pm 2\sigma$?

4.160 Suppose x is a Poisson random variable. Compute $p(x)$ for each of the following cases:

  a. $\lambda = 2, x = 3$ **b.** $\lambda = 1, x = 4$
  c. $\lambda = .5, x = 2$

4.161 Identify the type of random variable—binomial, Poisson, or hypergeometric—described by each of the following probability distributions:

  a. $p(x) = \dfrac{5^x e^{-5}}{x!}$ $(x = 0, 1, 2, \ldots)$

  b. $p(x) = \binom{6}{x}(.2)^x(.8)^{6-x}$ $(x = 0, 1, 2, \ldots, 6)$

  c. $p(x) = \dfrac{10!}{x!(10 - x)!}(.9)^x(.1)^{10-x}$ $(x = 0, 1, 2, \ldots, 10)$

4.162 Given that x is a hypergeometric random variable, compute $p(x)$ for each of the following cases:

  a. $N = 8, n = 5, r = 3, x = 2$
  b. $N = 6, n = 2, r = 2, x = 2$
  c. $N = 5, n = 4, r = 4, x = 3$

4.163 Which of the following describe discrete random variables, and which describe continuous random variables?

  a. The number of damaged inventory items
  b. The average monthly sales revenue generated by a salesperson over the past year
  c. Square feet of warehouse space a company rents
  d. The length of time a firm must wait before its copying machine is fixed

4.164 Assume that x is a random variable best described by a uniform distribution with $c = 10$ and $d = 90$.

  a. Find $f(x)$.
  b. Find the mean and standard deviation of x.
  c. Graph the probability distribution for x and locate its mean and the interval $\mu \pm 2\sigma$ on the graph.
  d. Find $P(x \leq 60)$.
  e. Find $P(x \geq 90)$.
  f. Find $P(x \leq 80)$.
  g. Find $P(\mu - \sigma \leq x \leq \mu + \sigma)$.
  h. Find $P(x > 75)$.

4.165 Find the following probabilities for the standard normal random variable z:

  a. $P(z \leq 2.1)$
  b. $P(z \geq 2.1)$
  c. $P(z \geq -1.65)$
  d. $P(-2.13 \leq z \leq -.41)$
  e. $P(-1.45 \leq z \leq 2.15)$
  f. $P(z \leq -1.43)$

4.166 Find a z-score, call it z_0, such that

  a. $P(z \leq z_0) = .5080$
  b. $P(z \geq z_0) = .5517$
  c. $P(z \geq z_0) = .1492$
  d. $P(z_0 \leq z \leq .59) = .4773$

4.167 Identify the type of continuous random variable—uniform, normal, or exponential—described by each of the following probability density functions:

  a. $f(x) = (e^{-x/7})/7, x > 0$
  b. $f(x) = 1/20, 5 < x < 25$
  c. $f(x) = \dfrac{e^{-.5[(x-10)/5]^2}}{5\sqrt{2\pi}}$

4.168 Assume that x has an exponential distribution with $\theta = 3$. Find

  a. $P(x \leq 1)$ **b.** $P(x > 1)$
  c. $P(x = 1)$ **d.** $P(x \leq 6)$
  e. $P(2 \leq x \leq 10)$

4.169 The random variable x has a normal distribution with $\mu = 75$ and $\sigma = 10$. Find the following probabilities:

  a. $P(x \leq 80)$ **b.** $P(x \geq 85)$
  c. $P(70 \leq x \leq 75)$ **d.** $P(x > 80)$
  e. $P(x = 78)$ **f.** $P(x \leq 110)$

4.170 Assume that x is a binomial random variable with $n = 100$ and $p = .5$. Use the normal probability distribution to approximate the following probabilities:

a. $P(x \leq 48)$ b. $P(50 \leq x \leq 65)$
c. $P(x \geq 70)$ d. $P(55 \leq x \leq 58)$
e. $P(x = 62)$ f. $P(x \leq 49 \text{ or } x \geq 72)$

4.171 The random variable x has a normal distribution with $\mu = 40$ and $\sigma^2 = 36$. Find a value of x, call it x_0, such that

a. $P(x \geq x_0) = .10$
b. $P(\mu \leq x < x_0) = .40$
c. $P(x < x_0) = .05$
d. $P(x \geq x_0) = .40$
e. $P(x_0 \leq x < \mu) = .45$

Applying the Concepts—Basic

4.172 **Analysis of bottled water.** Is the bottled water you're drinking really purified water? A study of bottled water brands conducted by the Natural Resources Defense Council (NRDC) found that 25% of bottled water is just tap water packaged in a bottle (NRDC report updated, July 2013). Consider a sample of five bottled water brands and let x equal the number of these brands that use tap water.

a. Explain why x is (approximately) a binomial random variable.
b. Give the probability distribution for x as a formula.
c. Find $P(x = 2)$.
d. Find $P(x \leq 1)$.
e. In a random sample of 65 bottled water brands, is it likely that 20 or more brands will contain tap water? Explain.

4.173 **Downloading "apps" to your cell phone.** According to an August 2011 survey by the Pew Internet & American Life Project, nearly 40% of adult cell phone owners have downloaded an application ("app") to their cell phone. The next table gives the probability distribution for x, the number of "apps" used at least once a week by cell phone owners who have downloaded an "app" to their phone. (The probabilities in the table are based on information from the Pew Internet & American Life Project survey.)

Number of "Apps" Used, x	$p(x)$
0	.17
1	.10
2	.11
3	.11
4	.10
5	.10
6	.07
7	.05
8	.03
9	.02
10	.02
11	.02
12	.02
13	.02
14	.01
15	.01
16	.01
17	.01
18	.01
19	.005
20	.005

a. Show that the properties of a probability distribution for a discrete random variable are satisfied.
b. Find $P(x \geq 10)$.
c. Find the mean and variance of x.
d. Give an interval that will contain the value of x with a probability of at least .75.

4.174 **LASIK surgery complications.** According to studies, 1% of all patients who undergo laser surgery (i.e., LASIK) to correct their vision have serious postlaser vision problems (*All About Vision*, 2012). In a sample of 100,000 patients, what is the approximate probability that fewer than 950 will experience serious postlaser vision problems?

4.175 **Requests to a Web server.** According to Brighton Webs LTD, a British company that specializes in data analysis, the arrival time of requests to a Web server within each hour can be modeled by a uniform distribution (www.brighton-webs.co.uk). Specifically, the number of seconds x from the start of the hour that the request is made is uniformly distributed between 0 and 3,600 seconds. Find the probability that a request is made to a Web server sometime during the last 15 minutes of the hour.

4.176 **NASA and rare planet transits.** A "planet transit" is a rare celestial event in which a planet appears to cross in front of its star as seen from Earth. The National Aeronautics and Space Administration (NASA) launched its Kepler mission, designed to discover new planets in the Milky Way by detecting extrasolar planet transits. After 1 year of the mission in which 3,000 stars were monitored, NASA announced that five planet transits had been detected (NASA, American Astronomical Society, January 4, 2010). Assume that the number of planet transits discovered for every 3,000 stars follows a Poisson distribution with $\lambda = 5$. What is the probability that, in the next 3,000 stars monitored by the Kepler mission, more than 10 planet transits will be seen?

4.177 **Hospital patient interarrival times.** The length of time between arrivals at a hospital clinic has an approximately exponential probability distribution. Suppose the mean time between arrivals for patients at a clinic is 4 minutes.

a. What is the probability that a particular interarrival time (the time between the arrival of two patients) is less than 1 minute?
b. What is the probability that the next four interarrival times are all less than 1 minute?
c. What is the probability that an interarrival time will exceed 10 minutes?

4.178 **Dutch elm disease.** A nursery advertises that it has 10 elm trees for sale. Unknown to the nursery, 3 of the trees have already been infected with Dutch elm disease and will die within a year.

a. If a buyer purchases 2 trees, what is the probability that both trees will be healthy?
b. Refer to part **a**. What is the probability that at least 1 of the trees is infected?

4.179 **Tracking missiles with satellite imagery.** The Space-Based Infrared System (SBIRS) uses satellite imagery to detect and track missiles (*Chance*, Summer 2005). The probability that an intruding object (e.g., a missile) will be detected on a flight track by SBIRS is .8. Consider a sample of 20 simulated tracks, each with an intruding object. Let x equal the number of these tracks where SBIRS detects the object.

a. Demonstrate that x is (approximately) a binomial random variable.

b. Give the values of p and n for the binomial distribution.

c. Find $P(x = 15)$, the probability that SBIRS will detect the object on exactly 15 tracks.

d. Find $P(x \geq 15)$, the probability that SBIRS will detect the object on at least 15 tracks.

e. Find $E(x)$ and interpret the result.

4.180 The business of casino gaming. Casino gaming yields over \$35 billion in revenue each year in the United States. *Chance* (Spring 2005) discussed the business of casino gaming and its reliance on the laws of probability. Casino games of pure chance (e.g., craps, roulette, baccarat, and keno) always yield a "house advantage." For example, in the game of double-zero roulette, the expected casino win percentage is 5.26% on bets made on whether the outcome will be either black or red. (This implies that for every \$5 bet on black or red, the casino will earn a net of about 25¢.) It can be shown that in 100 roulette plays on black/red, the average casino win percentage is normally distributed with mean 5.26% and standard deviation 10%. Let x represent the average casino win percentage after 100 bets on black/red in double-zero roulette.

a. Find $P(x > 0)$. (This is the probability that the casino wins money.)

b. Find $P(5 < x < 15)$.

c. Find $P(x < 1)$.

d. If you observed an average casino win percentage of -25% after 100 roulette bets on black/red, what would you conclude?

4.181 Machine repair times. An article in *IEEE Transactions* (March 1990) gave an example of a flexible manufacturing system with four machines operating independently. The repair rates for the machines (i.e., the time, in hours, it takes to repair a failed machine) are exponentially distributed with means $\mu_1 = 1$, $\mu_2 = 2$, $\mu_3 = .5$, and $\mu_4 = .5$, respectively.

a. Find the probability that the repair time for machine 1 exceeds 1 hour.

b. Repeat part **a** for machine 2.

c. Repeat part **a** for machines 3 and 4.

d. If all four machines fail simultaneously, find the probability that the repair time for the entire system exceeds 1 hour.

4.182 Public transit deaths. Millions of suburban commuters use the public transit system (e.g., subway trains) as an alternative to the automobile. While generally perceived as a safe mode of transportation, the average number of deaths per week due to public transit accidents is 5 (Bureau of Transportation Statistics, 2015).

a. Construct arguments both for and against the use of the Poisson distribution to characterize the number of deaths per week due to public transit accidents.

b. For the remainder of this exercise, assume the Poisson distribution is an adequate approximation for x, the number of deaths per week due to public transit accidents. Find $E(x)$ and the standard deviation of x.

c. Based strictly on your answers to part **b,** is it likely that more than 12 deaths occur next week? Explain.

d. Find $P(x > 12)$. Is this probability consistent with your answer to part **c**? Explain.

4.183 On-site treatment of hazardous waste. The Resource Conservation and Recovery Act mandates the tracking and disposal of hazardous waste produced at U.S. facilities. *Professional Geographer* (February 2000) reported the hazardous-waste generation and disposal characteristics of 209 facilities. Only 8 of these facilities treated hazardous waste on-site. Use the hypergeometric distribution to answer the following:

a. In a random sample of 10 of the 209 facilities, what is the expected number in the sample that treat hazardous waste on-site? Interpret this result.

b. Find the probability that 4 of the 10 selected facilities treat hazardous waste on-site.

4.184 When to replace a maintenance system. An article in the *Journal of Quality of Maintenance Engineering* (Vol. 19, 2013) studied the problem of finding the optimal replacement policy for a maintenance system. Consider a system that is tested every 12 hours. The test will determine whether there are any flaws in the system. Assume that the probability of no flaw being detected is .85. If a flaw (failure) is detected, the system is repaired. Following the fifth failed test, the system is completely replaced. Now let x represent the number of tests until the system needs to be replaced.

a. Give the probability distribution for x as a formula.

b. Find the probability that the system needs to be replaced after 8 total tests.

4.185 Software file updates. Software configuration management was used to monitor a software engineering team's performance at Motorola, Inc. (*Software Quality Professional*, Nov. 2004). One of the variables of interest was the number of updates to a file that was changed because of a problem report. Summary statistics for $n = 421$ files yielded the following results: $\bar{x} = 4.71$, $s = 6.09$, $Q_L = 1$, and $Q_U = 6$. Are these data approximately normally distributed? Explain.

4.186 NHTSA crash safety tests. Refer to Exercise 4.21 (p. 224) and the NHTSA crash test data for new cars. One of the variables saved in the accompanying file is the severity of a driver's head injury when the car is in a head-on collision with a fixed barrier while traveling at 35 miles per hour. The more points assigned to the head-injury rating, the more severe the injury. The head-injury ratings can be shown to be approximately normally distributed with a mean of 605 points and a standard deviation of 185 points. One of the crash-tested cars is randomly selected from the data, and the driver's head-injury rating is observed.

a. Find the probability that the rating will fall between 500 and 700 points.

b. Find the probability that the rating will fall between 400 and 500 points.

c. Find the probability that the rating will be less than 850 points.

d. Find the probability that the rating will exceed 1,000 points.

Applying the Concepts—Intermediate

4.187 Errors in measuring truck weights. To help highway planners anticipate the need for road repairs and design future construction projects, data are collected on the estimated volume and weight of truck traffic on specific roadways

(*Transportation Planning Handbook*, 2016) using specialized "weigh-in-motion" equipment. In an experiment involving repeated weighing of a 27,907-pound truck, it was found that the weights recorded by the weigh-in-motion equipment were approximately normally distributed with a mean of 27,315 and a standard deviation of 628 pounds (Minnesota Department of Transportation). It follows that the difference between the actual weight and recorded weight, the error of measurement, is normally distributed with a mean of 592 pounds and a standard deviation of 628 pounds.

a. What is the probability that the weigh-in-motion equipment understates the actual weight of the truck?

b. If a 27,907-pound truck was driven over the weigh-in-motion equipment 100 times, approximately how many times would the equipment overstate the truck's weight?

c. What is the probability that the error in the weight recorded by the weigh-in-motion equipment for a 27,907-pound truck exceeds 400 pounds?

d. It is possible to adjust (or *calibrate*) the weigh-in-motion equipment to control the mean error of measurement. At what level should the mean error be set so the equipment will understate the weight of a 27,907-pound truck 50% of the time? Only 40% of the time?

4.188 Detecting a computer virus attack. *Chance* (Winter 2004) presented basic methods for detecting virus attacks (e.g., Trojan programs or worms) on a network computer that are sent from a remote host. These viruses reach the network through requests for communication (e.g., e-mail, Web chat, or remote log-in) that are identified as "packets." For example, the "SYN flood" virus ties up the network computer by "flooding" the network with multiple packets. Cybersecurity experts can detect this type of virus attack if at least one packet is observed by a network sensor. Assume that the probability of observing a single packet sent from a new virus is only .001. If the virus actually sends 150 packets to a network computer, what is the probability that the virus is detected by the sensor?

4.189 Whistle-blowing among federal employees. *Whistle-blowing* refers to an employee's reporting of wrongdoing by co-workers. A survey found that about 5% of employees contacted had reported wrongdoing during the past 12 months. Assume that a sample of 25 employees in one agency are contacted and let x be the number who have observed and reported wrongdoing in the past 12 months. Assume that the probability of whistle-blowing is .05 for any federal employee over the past 12 months.

a. Find the mean and standard deviation of x. Can x be equal to its expected value? Explain.

b. Write the event that at least 5 of the employees are whistle-blowers in terms of x. Find the probability of the event.

c. If 5 of the 25 contacted have been whistle-blowers over the past 12 months, what would you conclude about the applicability of the 5% assumption to this agency? Use your answer to part **b** to justify your conclusion.

4.190 Ambulance response time. Ambulance response time is measured as the time (in minutes) between the initial call to emergency medical services (EMS) and when the patient is reached by ambulance. *Geographical Analysis* (Vol. 41, 2009) investigated the characteristics of ambulance response time for EMS calls in Edmonton, Alberta. For a particular EMS station (call it Station A), ambulance response time is known to be normally distributed with $\mu = 7.5$ minutes and $\sigma = 2.5$ minutes.

a. Regulations require that 90% of all emergency calls be reached in 9 minutes or less. Are the regulations met at EMS Station A? Explain.

b. A randomly selected EMS call in Edmonton has an ambulance response time of 2 minutes. Is it likely that this call was serviced by Station A? Explain.

4.191 Optimal goal target in soccer. When attempting to score a goal in soccer, where should you aim your shot? Should you aim for a goalpost (as some soccer coaches teach), the middle of the goal, or some other target? To answer these questions, *Chance* (Fall 2009) utilized the normal probability distribution. Suppose the accuracy x of a professional soccer player's shots follows a normal distribution with a mean of 0 feet and a standard deviation of 3 feet. (For example, if the player hits his target, $x = 0$; if he misses his target 2 feet to the right, $x = 2$; and if he misses 1 foot to the left, $x = -1$.) Now, a regulation soccer goal is 24 feet wide. Assume that a goalkeeper will stop (save) all shots within 9 feet of where he is standing; all other shots on goal will score. Consider a goalkeeper who stands in the middle of the goal.

a. If the player aims for the right goalpost, what is the probability that he will score?

b. If the player aims for the center of the goal, what is the probability that he will score?

c. If the player aims for halfway between the right goalpost and the outer limit of the goalkeeper's reach, what is the probability that he will score?

4.192 Marine losses for an oil company. The frequency distribution shown in the table depicts the property and marine losses incurred by a large oil company over the last 2 years. This distribution can be used by the company to predict future losses and to help determine an appropriate level of insurance coverage. In analyzing the losses within an interval of the distribution, for simplification, analysts may treat the interval as a uniform probability distribution (*Research Review*, Summer 1998). In the insurance business, intervals like these are often called *layers*.

Layer	Property and Marine Losses (millions of $)	Frequency
1	0.00–0.01	668
2	0.01–0.05	38
3	0.05–0.10	7
4	0.10–0.25	4
5	0.25–0.50	2
6	0.50–1.00	1
7	1.00–2.50	0

Source: Based on J. M. Cozzolino and P. J. Mikolaj, "Applications of the Piecewise Constant Pareto Distribution," *Research Review*, Summer 1998, pp. 39–59.

a. Use a uniform distribution to model the loss amount in layer 2. Graph the distribution. Calculate and interpret its mean and variance.

b. Repeat part **a** for layer 6.

c. If a loss occurs in layer 2, what is the probability that it exceeds $10,000? That it is under $25,000?

d. If a layer-6 loss occurs, what is the probability that it is between $750,000 and $1,000,000? That it exceeds $900,000? That it is exactly $900,000?

4.193 Reliability of a flow network. The journal Networks periodically publishes studies on the reliability of flow networks. For example, *Networks* (September 2007) provided applications in mobile ad hoc and sensor networks. Consider a similar network with four activities, called arcs. The probability distribution of the capacity x for each of the four arcs is provided in the following table.

Arc 1	x	0	1	2	3
	$p(x)$	.05	.10	.25	.60
Arc 2	x	0	1	2	3
	$p(x)$	.10	.30	.60	0
Arc 3	x	0	1	2	3
	$p(x)$	.05	.25	.70	0
Arc 4	x	0	1	2	3
	$p(x)$	.90	.10	0	0

Source: Adapted from J. Lin, "On Reliability Evaluation of Capacitated-Flow Network in Terms of Minimal Pathsets." *Networks*, Vol. 25, No. 3, May 1995 (Table 1).

a. Verify that the properties of discrete probability distributions are satisfied for each arc capacity distribution.
b. Find the probability that the capacity for Arc 1 will exceed 1.
c. Repeat part **b** for each of the remaining three arcs.
d. Compute μ for each arc and interpret the results.
e. Compute σ for each arc and interpret the results.

4.194 Doctors and ethics. Refer to the *Journal of Medical Ethics* (Vol. 32, 2006) study of the extent to which doctors refuse ethics consultation, Exercise 2.166 (p. 146). Consider a random sample of 10 doctors, each of whom is confronted with an ethical dilemma (e.g., an end-of-life issue or treatment of a patient without insurance). What is the probability that at least two of the doctors refuse ethics consultation? Use your answer to 2.166b to estimate p, the probability that a doctor will refuse to use ethics consultation.

4.195 Flicker in an electrical power system. An assessment of the quality of the electrical power system in Turkey was the topic of an article published in *Electrical Engineering* (March 2013). One measure of quality is the degree to which voltage fluctuations cause light flicker in the system. The perception of light flicker (x) when the system is set at 380 kV was measured periodically (over 10-minute intervals). For transformers supplying heavy industry plants, the light flicker distribution was found to follow (approximately) a normal distribution, with $\mu = 2.2\%$ and $\sigma = .5\%$. If the perception of light flicker exceeds 3%, the transformer is shut down and the system is reset. How likely is it for a transformer supplying a heavy industry plant to be shut down due to light flicker?

4.196 Testing for spoiled wine. Suppose that you are purchasing cases of wine (12 bottles per case) and that, periodically, you select a test case to determine the adequacy of the bottles' seals. To do this, you randomly select and test 3

bottles in the case. If a case contains 1 spoiled bottle of wine, what is the probability that this bottle will turn up in your sample?

4.197 Estimating demand for white bread. A bakery has determined that the number of loaves of its white bread demanded daily has a normal distribution with mean 7,200 loaves and standard deviation 300 loaves. Based on cost considerations, the company has decided that its best strategy is to produce a sufficient number of loaves so that it will fully supply demand on 94% of all days.
a. How many loaves of bread should the company produce?
b. Based on the production in part **a,** on what percentage of days will the company be left with more than 500 loaves of unsold bread?

4.198 Checkout lanes at a supermarket. A team of consultants working for a large national supermarket chain based in the New York metropolitan area developed a statistical model for predicting the annual sales of potential new store locations. Part of their analysis involved identifying variables that influence store sales, such as the size of the store (in square feet), the size of the surrounding population, and the number of checkout lanes. They surveyed 52 supermarkets in a particular region of the country and constructed the relative frequency distribution shown below to describe the number of checkout lanes per store, x.

x	1	2	3	4	5	6	7	8	9	10
Relative Frequency	.01	.04	.04	.08	.10	.15	.25	.20	.08	.05

Source: Based on W. Chow et al., "A Model for Predicting a Supermarket's Annual Sales per Square Foot." Graduate School of Management, Rutgers University, 1994.

a. Why do the relative frequencies in the table represent the approximate probabilities of a randomly selected supermarket having x number of checkout lanes?
b. Find $E(x)$ and interpret its value in the context of the problem.
c. Find the standard deviation of x.
d. According to Chebyshev's Rule (Chapter 2, p. 106), what percentage of supermarkets would be expected to fall within $\mu \pm \sigma$? Within $\mu \pm 2\sigma$?
e. What is the actual number of supermarkets that fall within $\mu \pm \sigma$? $\mu \pm 2\sigma$? Compare your answers with those of part **d.** Are the answers consistent?

4.199 Rating employee performance. Almost all companies utilize some type of year-end performance review for their employees. Human Resources (HR) at the University of Texas Health Science Center provides guidelines for supervisors rating their subordinates. For example, raters are advised to examine their ratings for a tendency to be either too lenient or too harsh. According to HR, "If you have this tendency, consider using a normal distribution—10% of employees (rated) exemplary, 20% distinguished, 40% competent, 20% marginal, and 10% unacceptable." Suppose you are rating an employee's performance on a scale of 1 (lowest) to 100 (highest). Also, assume the ratings follow a normal distribution with a mean of 50 and a standard deviation of 15.
a. What is the lowest rating you should give to an "exemplary" employee if you follow the University of Texas HR guidelines?

b. What is the lowest rating you should give to a "competent" employee if you follow the University of Texas HR guidelines?

4.200 Ship-to-shore transfer times. Lack of port facilities or shallow water may require cargo on a large ship to be transferred to a pier in smaller craft. The smaller craft may have to cycle back and forth from ship to shore many times. Researchers developed models of this transfer process that provide estimates of ship-to-shore transfer times (*Naval Research Logistics*, Vol. 41, 1994). They used an exponential distribution to model the time between arrivals of the smaller craft at the pier.

a. Assume that the mean time between arrivals at the pier is 17 minutes. Give the value of θ for this exponential distribution. Graph the distribution.

b. Suppose there is only one unloading zone at the pier available for the small craft to use. If the first craft docks at 10:00 A.M. and doesn't finish unloading until 10:15 A.M., what is the probability that the second craft will arrive at the unloading zone and have to wait before docking?

Applying the Concepts—Advanced

4.201 How many questionnaires to mail? The probability that a consumer responds to a marketing department's mailed questionnaire is .4. How many questionnaires should be mailed if you want to be reasonably certain that at least 100 will be returned?

4.202 Establishing tolerance limits. The *tolerance limits* for a particular quality characteristic (e.g., length, weight, or strength) of a product are the minimum and/or maximum values at which the product will operate properly. Tolerance limits are set by the engineering design function of the manufacturing operation (*Total Quality Management,* Vol. 11, 2000). The tensile strength of a particular metal part can be characterized as being normally distributed with a mean of 25 pounds and a standard deviation of 2 pounds. The upper and lower tolerance limits for the part are 30 pounds and 21 pounds, respectively. A part that falls within the tolerance limits results in a profit of $10. A part that falls below the lower tolerance limit costs the company $2; a part that falls above the upper tolerance limit costs the company $1. Find the company's expected profit per metal part produced.

4.203 The showcase showdown. On the popular television game show *The Price Is Right,* contestants can play "The Showcase Showdown." The game involves a large wheel with 20 nickel values, 5, 10, 15, 20, . . . , 95, 100, marked on it. Contestants spin the wheel once or twice, with the objective of obtaining the highest total score *without going over a dollar* (*100*). [According to the *American Statistician* (August 1995), the optimal strategy for the first spinner in a three-player game is to spin a second time only if the value of the initial spin is 65 or less.] Let x represent the total score for a single contestant playing "The Showcase Showdown." Assume a "fair" wheel (i.e., a wheel with equally likely outcomes). If the total of the player's spins exceeds 100, the total score is set to 0.

a. If the player is permitted only one spin of the wheel, find the probability distribution for x.

b. Refer to part **a.** Find $E(x)$ and interpret this value.

c. Refer to part **a.** Give a range of values within which x is likely to fall.

d. Suppose the player will spin the wheel twice, no matter what the outcome of the first spin. Find the probability distribution for x.

e. What assumption did you make to obtain the probability distribution, part **d**? Is it a reasonable assumption?

f. Find μ and σ for the probability distribution, part **d.** and interpret the results.

g. Refer to part **d.** What is the probability that in two spins the player's total score exceeds a dollar (i.e., is set to 0)?

h. Suppose the player obtains a 20 on the first spin and decides to spin again. Find the probability distribution for x.

i. Refer to part **h.** What is the probability that the player's total score exceeds a dollar?

j. Given the player obtains a 65 on the first spin and decides to spin again, find the probability that the player's total score exceeds a dollar.

k. Repeat part **j** for different first-spin outcomes. Use this information to suggest a strategy for the one-player game.

4.204 Reliability of a "one-shot" device. A "one-shot" device can be used only once; after use, the device (e.g., a nuclear weapon, space shuttle, automobile air bag) is either destroyed or must be rebuilt. The destructive nature of a one-shot device makes repeated testing either impractical or too costly. Hence, the reliability of such a device must be determined with minimal testing. Consider a one-shot device that has some probability, p, of failure. Of course, the true value of p is unknown, so designers will specify a value of p that is the largest defective rate they are willing to accept. Designers will conduct n tests of the device and determine the success or failure of each test. If the number of observed failures, x, is less than or equal to some specified value, K, then the device is considered to have the desired failure rate. Consequently, the designers want to know the minimum sample size n needed so that observing K or fewer defectives in the sample will demonstrate that the true probability of failure for the one-shot device is no greater than p.

a. Suppose the desired failure rate for a one-shot device is $p = .10$. Also, suppose designers will conduct $n = 20$ tests of the device and conclude that the device is performing to specifications if $K = 1$ (i.e., if 1 or no failures are observed in the sample). Find $P(x \leq 1)$.

b. In reliability analysis, $1 - P(x \leq K)$ is often called the *level of confidence* for concluding that the true failure rate is less than or equal to p. Find the level of confidence for the one-shot device described in part **a.** In your opinion, is this an acceptable level? Explain.

c. Demonstrate that the confidence level can be increased by either (1) increasing the sample size n or (2) decreasing the number K of failures allowed in the sample.

d. Typically, designers want a confidence level of .90, .95, or .99. Find the values of n and K to use so that the designers can conclude (with at least 95% confidence) that the failure rate for the one-shot device of part **a** is no greater than $p = .10$.

[*Note:* The U.S. Department of Defense Reliability Analysis Center (DoD RAC) provides designers with free access to tables and toolboxes that give the minimum sample size n required to obtain a desired confidence level for a specified number of observed failures in the sample.]

Critical Thinking Challenges

4.205 Super weapons development. The U.S. Army is working

MOAGUN

with a major defense contractor (not named here for both confidentiality and security reasons) to develop a "super" weapon. The weapon is designed to fire a large number of sharp tungsten bullets—called flechettes—with a single shot that will destroy a large number of enemy soldiers. (Flechettes are about the size of an average nail, with small fins at one end to stabilize them in flight.) The defense contractor has developed a prototype gun that fires 1,100 flechettes with a single round. In range tests, three 2-feet-wide targets were set up at a distance of 500 meters (approximately 1500 feet) from the weapon. Using a number line as a reference, the centers of the three targets were at 0, 5, and 10 feet, respectively, as shown in the accompanying figure. The prototype gun was aimed at the middle target (center at 5 feet) and fired once. The point x where each of the 1,100 flechettes landed at the 500-meter distance was measured using a horizontal grid. For example, a flechette with a horizontal value of $x = 5.5$ (shown in the figure) hit the middle target, but a flechette with a horizontal value of $x = 2.0$ (also shown in the figure) did not hit any of the three targets. The 1,100 measurements on the random variable x are saved in the accompanying file. (The data are simulated for confidentiality reasons.)

The defense contractor is interested in the likelihood of any one of the targets being hit by a flechette, and in particular, wants to set the gun specifications to maximize the number of target hits. The weapon is designed to have a mean horizontal value, $E(x)$, equal to the aim point (e.g., $\mu = 5$ feet when aimed at the center target). By changing specifications, the contractor can vary the standard deviation, σ. The data file contains flechette measurements for three different range tests—one with a standard deviation of $\sigma = 1$ foot, one with $\sigma = 2$ feet, and one with $\sigma = 4$ feet. Let x_1, x_2, and x_4 represent the random variables for horizontal measurements with $\sigma = 1$, $\sigma = 2$, and $\sigma = 4$, respectively. From past experience, the defense contractor has found that the distribution of the horizontal

flechette measurements is closely approximated by a normal distribution.

a. For each of the three values of σ, use the normal distribution to find the approximate probability that a single flechette shot from the weapon will hit any one of the three targets. [*Hint:* Note that the three targets range from −1 to 1, 4 to 6, and 9 to 11 feet on the horizontal grid.]

b. The actual results of the three range tests are saved in the data file. Use this information to calculate the proportion of the 1,100 flechettes that actually hit each target—called the hit ratio—for each value of σ. How do these actual hit ratios compare with the estimated probabilities of a hit using the normal distribution?

c. If the U.S. Army wants to maximize the chance of hitting the target that the prototype gun is aimed at, what setting should be used for σ? If the Army wants to hit multiple targets with a single shot of the weapon, what setting should be used for σ?

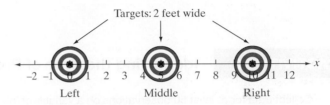

4.206 Space shuttle disaster. On January 28, 1986, the space shuttle *Challenger* exploded, killing all seven astronauts aboard. An investigation concluded that the explosion was caused by the failure of the O ring seal in the joint between the two lower segments of the right solid rocket booster. In a report made 1 year prior to the catastrophe, the National Aeronautics and Space Administration (NASA) claimed that the probability of such a failure was about $\frac{1}{60,000}$, or about once in every 60,000 flights. But a risk-assessment study conducted for the Air Force at about the same time assessed the probability to be $\frac{1}{35}$, or about once in every 35 missions. (*Note:* The shuttle had flown 24 successful missions prior to the disaster.) Given the events of January 28, 1986, which risk assessment—NASA's or the Air Force's—appears to be more appropriate?

ACTIVITY 4.1   *Warehouse Club Memberships:* **Exploring a Binomial Random Variable**

Warehouse clubs are retailers that offer lower prices than traditional retailers, but they sell only to customers who have purchased memberships and often merchandise must be purchased in large quantities. A warehouse club may offer more than one type of membership, such as a regular membership R for a low annual fee and an upgraded membership U for a higher annual fee. The upgraded membership has additional benefits that might include extended shopping hours, additional discounts on certain products, or cash back on purchases.

A local warehouse club has determined that 20% of its customer base has the upgraded membership.

1. What is the probability $P(U)$ that a randomly chosen customer entering the store has an upgraded membership? What is the probability $P(R)$ that a randomly chosen customer entering the store has a regular (not upgraded) membership?

In an effort to sell more upgraded memberships, sales associates are placed at the entrance to the store to explain the benefits of the upgraded membership to customers as they enter. Suppose that in a given time period five customers enter the store.

(continued)

2. Given that 20% of the store's customers have an up-graded membership, how many of the five customers would you expect to have an upgraded membership?

3. Because there are five customers and each customer either has an upgraded membership (U) or does not (R), there are $2^5 = 32$ different possible combinations of membership types among the five customers. List these 32 possibilities.

4. Find the probability of each of the 32 outcomes. Assume that each of the five customers' membership type is independent of each of the other customers' membership type and use your probabilities $P(U)$ and $P(R)$ with the multiplicative rule. For example, $P(RRUUR) = P(R)P(R)P(U)P(U)P(R)$.

5. Notice that $P(URRRR) = P(RURRR) = P(RRURR) = P(RRRUR) = P(RRRRU) = P(U)^1 P(R)^4$ so that P(exactly one U) $= P(URRRR) + P(RURRR) + P(RRURR) + P(RRRUR) + P(RRRRU) = 5P(U)^1 P(R)^4$ where 5 is the number of ways

that exactly one U can occur. Find P(exactly one U). Use similar reasoning to establish that P(no U's) $= 1P(U)^0 P(R)^5$, P(exactly two U's) $= 10P(U)^2 (R)^3$, P(exactly three U's) $= 10P(U)^3 P(R)^2$, P(exactly four U's) $= 5P(U)^4 P(R)^1$, and P(five U's) $= 1P(U)^5 P(R)^0$.

6. Let x be the number of upgraded memberships U in a sample of five customers. Use the results of Part 5 to write a probability distribution for the random variable x in table form. Find the mean and standard deviation of the distribution using the formulas in Section 4.2.

7. Calculate np and $\sqrt{npq}$ where $n = 5$, $p = P(U)$, and $q = P(R)$. How do these numbers compare with the mean and standard deviation of the random variable x in Part 6 and to the expected number of customers with upgraded memberships in Part 1?

8. Explain how the characteristics of a binomial random variable are illustrated in this activity.

ACTIVITY 4.2　Identifying the Type of Probability Distribution

Collect data for at least 50 observations on a variable of interest to you (e.g., scores on a statistics exam, monthly sales of a pre-owned auto dealership, time spent preparing for the GMAT, number of bank failures per year). Be sure to identify the experimental unit prior to beginning your data search.

1. Before you actually collect the data, identify the probability distribution that you believe will be the best model for

the variable you selected. (Be sure to check the properties of the different random variables presented in this chapter.)

2. Enter the data into a statistical software package and graph the distribution. Does the graph match the probability distribution you identified?

References

Deming, W. E. *Out of the Crisis*. Cambridge, Mass.: MIT Center for Advanced Engineering Study, 1986.

Hogg, R. V., McKean, J. W., and Craig, A. T. *Introduction to Mathematical Statistics,* 6th ed. Upper Saddle River, N.J.: Prentice Hall, 2005.

Larsen, R. J., & Marx, M. L. *An Introduction to Mathematical Statistics and Its Applications,* 4th ed. Upper Saddle River, N.J.: Prentice Hall, 2005.

Lindgren, B. W. *Statistical Theory*, 4th ed. New York: Chapman & Hall, 1993.

Ramsey, P. P., & Ramsey, P. H. "Simple tests of normality in small samples," *Journal of Quality Technology,* Vol. 22, 1990.

Wackerly, D., Mendenhall, W., and Scheaffer, R. *Mathematical Statistics with Applications,* 7th ed. North Scituate, Mass.: Duxbury, 2008.

USING **TECHNOLOGY** — Technology images shown here are taken from SPSS Statistics Professional 23.0, Minitab 17, XLSTAT, and Excel 2016.

SPSS: Discrete Probabilities, Continuous Probabilities, and Normal Probability Plots

Discrete and Continuous Probabilities

Step 1 Select "Transform" on the SPSS menu bar and then click on "Compute Variable," as shown in Figure 4.S.1. The resulting dialog box appears as shown in Figure 4.S.2.

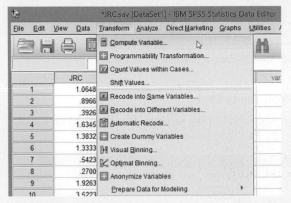

Figure 4.S.1 SPSS menu options for obtaining discrete and continuous probabilities

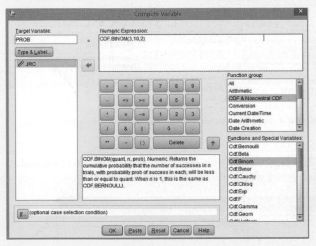

Figure 4.S.2 SPSS compute cumulative binomial probabilities dialog box

Step 2 Specify a name for the "Target Variable."

Step 3 either "CDF" (for cumulative probabilities) or "PDF" (for exact probabilities) in the "Function group" box.

Step 4 Select the appropriate probability distribution in the "Functions and Special Variables" box. (For example, for cumulative probabilities of the binomial, use the function CDF.BINOM. For exact binomial probabilities, use the PDF.BINOM function.)

Step 5 Enter the parameters of the distribution in the "Numeric Expression" box. For example, Figure 4.S.2 shows the cumulative binomial function with parameters of $x = 3$ (the first number in the function), $n = 10$ (the second number), and $p = .2$ (the third number).

Step 6 Click "OK"; SPSS will compute the requested probability (in this example, the cumulative binomial probability that

x is less than or equal to 3) and display it on the SPSS spreadsheet. Similarly, for example, Figure 4.S.3 shows the cumulative normal function with parameters of $x = 3.7$ (the first number in the function), $\mu = 5$ (the second number), and $\sigma = 2$ (the third number). When you click "OK," SPSS will compute the requested probability (in this example, the cumulative normal probability that x is less than 3.7) and display it on the SPSS spreadsheet.

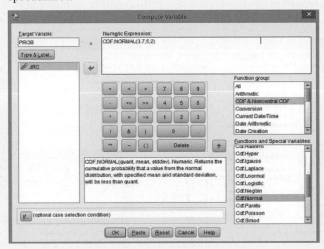

Figure 4.S.3 SPSS compute cumulative normal probabilities dialog box

Normal Probability Plot

Step 1 Select "Analyze" on the SPSS menu bar, and then select "Descriptive Statistics" and "Q-Q Plots," as shown in Figure 4.S.4. The resulting dialog box appears as shown in Figure 4.S.5.

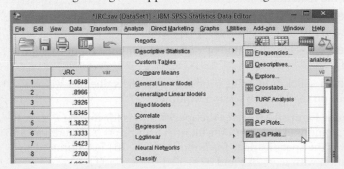

Figure 4.S.4 SPSS options for a normal probability plot

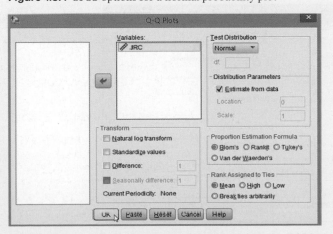

Figure 4.S.5 SPSS normal probability plot dialog box

Step 2 Specify the variable of interest in the "Variables" box and select "Normal" in the "Test Distribution" box.

Step 3 Click "OK" to generate the normal probability plot.

Minitab: Discrete Probabilities, Continuous Probabilities, and Normal Probability Plots

Discrete and Continuous Probabilities

Step 1 Select the "Calc" button on the Minitab menu bar, click on "Probability Distributions," and then finally select the distribution of your choice (e.g., "Binomial"), as shown in Figure 4.M.1.

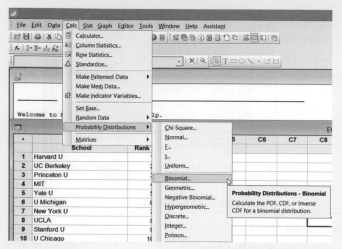

Figure 4.M.1 Minitab menu options for obtaining discrete and continuous probabilities

Step 2 Select either "Probability" or "Cumulative probability" on the resulting dialog box.

Step 3 Specify the parameters of the distribution (e.g., sample size n, probability of success p, μ or σ.)

Step 4 Specify the value of x of interest in the "Input constant" box.

Step 5 Click "OK." The probability for the value of x will appear on the Minitab session window.

[*Note:* Figure 4.M.2 gives the specifications for finding $P(x = 1)$ in a binomial distribution with $n = 5$ and $p = .2$. Figure 4.M.3 gives the specifications for finding $P(x \leq 20)$ in a normal distribution with $\mu = 24.5$ and $\sigma = 3.1$.]

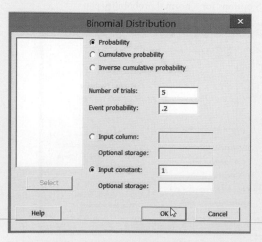

Figure 4.M.2 Minitab binomial distribution dialog box

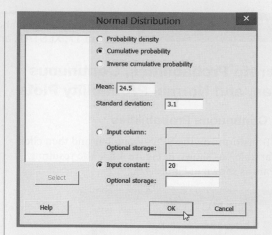

Figure 4.M.3 Minitab normal distribution dialog box

Normal Probability Plot

Step 1 Select "Graph" on the Minitab menu bar and then click on "Probability Plot," as shown in Figure 4.M.4.

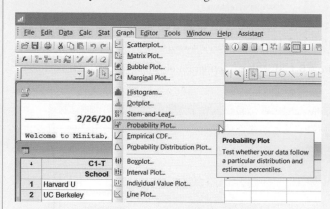

Figure 4.M.4 Minitab options for a normal probability plot

Step 2 Select "Single" (for one variable) on the next box, and the dialog box will appear as shown in Figure 4.M.5.

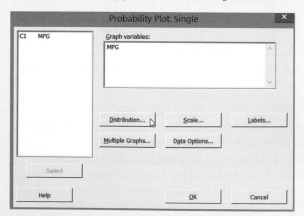

Figure 4.M.5 Minitab normal probability plot dialog box

Step 3 Specify the variable of interest in the "Graph variables" box and then click the "Distribution" button and select the "Normal" option. Click "OK" to return to the Probability Plot dialog box.

Step 4 Click "OK" to generate the normal probability plot.

Excel/XLSTAT: Discrete Probabilities, Continuous Probabilities, and Normal Probability Plots

Discrete and Continuous Probabilities

Step 1 Click on the cell in the Excel worksheet where you want the probability to appear.

Step 2 In the formula bar, enter "=" followed by the appropriate probability function. A list of different probability functions is shown in Figure 4.E.1.

Type of Probability	Excel Function
Binomial Probability, $P(x = a)$	= BINOMDIST (a, n, p, FALSE)
Cumulative Binomial Probability, $P(X \leq a)$	= BINOMDIST (a, n, p, TRUE)
Poisson Probability, $P(X = a)$	= POISSON (a, λ, FALSE)
Cumulative Poisson Probability, $P(x \leq a)$	= POISSON (a, λ, TRUE)
Hypergeometric Probability, $P(x = a)$	= HYPERGEOMDIST (a, n, r, N)
Cumulative Normal Probability, $P(X \leq a)$	= NORMDIST (a, μ, σ, TRUE)
Value of Normal Variable, given Probability p	= NORMINV (p, μ, σ)
Cumulative Exponential Probability, $P(X \leq a)$	= EXPONDIST (a, σ, TRUE)

Note: Probabilities from the uniform distribution function are not available in Excel.

Figure 4.E.1 List of probability functions in Excel

Step 3 Specify the parameters (e.g., n, p, μ, and σ) of the probability distribution as well as a specific value of the random variable (denoted "a") in the probability function on the formula bar, as shown in Figure 4.E.2.

Step 4 Click "Enter" and the probability will appear in the selected cell (see Figure 4.E.2).

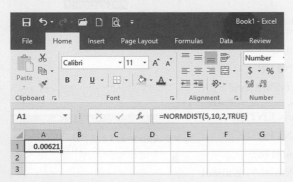

Figure 4.E.2 Normal probability function in Excel

Normal Probability Plot

Step 1 Click the "XLSTAT" button on the Excel main menu bar and then click "Describing Data."

Step 2 From the resulting menu, select "Normality tests" (see Figure 4.E.3).

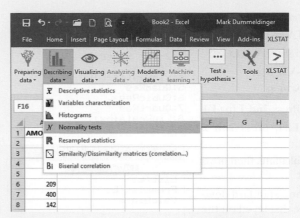

Figure 4.E.3 XLSTAT menu options for describing data

Step 3 When the resulting dialog box appears, highlight the data column(s) you want to graph so that the column information appears in the "Data" entry (see Figure 4.E.4).

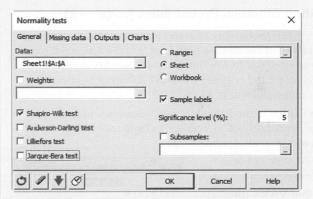

Figure 4.E.4 XLSTAT normality tests dialog box

Step 4 Click the "Charts" tab, and then select "Normal Q-Q plots" on the resulting menu.

Step 5 Click "OK" and then "Continue" to display the normal probability plot.

TI-84 Graphing Calculator: Discrete and Continuous Random Variables Normal Probability Plots

Calculating the Mean and Standard Deviation of a Discrete Random Variable

Step 1 *Enter the data*

• Press **STAT** and select **1:Edit**

Note: If the lists already contain data, clear the old data. Use the up **ARROW** to highlight **L1**

• Press **CLEAR ENTER**

• Use the up **ARROW** to highlight **L2**

• Press **CLEAR ENTER**

• Use the **ARROW** and **ENTER** keys to enter the x values of the variable into **L1**

• Use the **ARROW** and **ENTER** keys to enter the probabilities, $P(x)$, into **L2**

Step 2 *Access the Calc Menu*

- Press **STAT**
- Arrow right to **CALC**
- Select **1-Var Stats**
- Press **ENTER**
- In **List**, Press **2nd 1** for **L1**
- In **FreqList**, press **2nd 2** for **L2**
- Select **Calculate**, then press **ENTER**

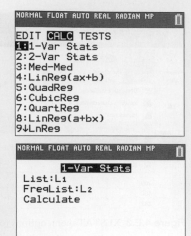

The mean and standard deviation will be displayed on the screen, as well as the quartiles, min, and max.

Calculating Binomial Probabilities I. *P(x = k)*

To compute the probability of k successes in n trials, where p is the probability of success for each trial, use the **binompdf (**command. *Binompdf* stands for "binomial probability density function." This command is under the **DISTR**ibution menu and has the format **binompdf(*n, p, k*).**

Example Compute the probability of 5 successes in 8 trials, where the probability of success for a single trial is 40%. In this example, $n = 8$, $p = .4$, and $k = 5$.

Step 1 *Enter the binomial parameters*

- Press **2nd VARS** for **DISTR**
- Press the down **ARROW** key until **binompdf** is highlighted
- Press **ENTER**
- Enter 8 for **trials**, .4 for **p**, and 5 for **x value**, highlight **Paste**, then press **ENTER**
- Press **ENTER** again
- You should see

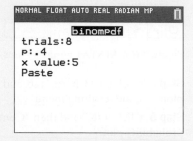

Thus, $P(x = 5)$ is about 12.4%.

II. *P(x ≤ k)*

To compute the probability of k or fewer successes in n trials, where p is the probability of success for each trial, use the **binomcdf(** command. *Binomcdf* stands for "binomial *cumulative* probability density function." This command is under the **DISTR**ibution menu and has the format **binomcdf(*n, p, k*).**

Example Compute the probability of 5 or fewer successes in 8 trails, where the probability of success for a single trial is 40%. In this example, $n = 8$, $p = .4$, and $k = 5$.

Step 2 *Enter the binomial parameters*

- Press **2nd VARS** for **DISTR**
- Press down the **ARROW** key until **binomcdf** is highlighted
- Press **ENTER**
- Enter 8 for **trials**, .4 for **p**, and 5 for **x value**, highlight **Paste**, then press **ENTER**
- Press **ENTER**
- You should see

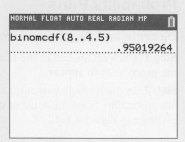

Thus, $P(x \le k)$ is about 95%.

III. *P(x < k), (x > k), (x ≥ k)*

To find the probability of fewer than k successes $P(x < k)$, more than k successes $P(x > k)$, or at least k successes $P(x \ge k)$, variations of the **binomcdf(** command must be used as shown below.

- $P(x < k)$ use **binomcdf(*n, p, k* − 1)**
- $P(x > k)$ use **1 − binomcdf(*n, p, k*)**
- $P(x \ge k)$ use **1 − binomcdf(*n, p, k* − 1)**

Calculating Poisson Probabilities I. *P(x = k)*

To compute $P(x = k)$, the probability of exactly k successes in a specified interval where λ is the mean number of successes *in* the interval, use the **poissonpdf(** command. *Poissonpdf* stands for "Poisson probability density function." This command is under the **DISTR**ibution menu and has the format **poissonpdf( ).**

Example Suppose that the number, x, of reported sightings per week of blue whales is recorded. Assume that x has approximately a Poisson probability distribution and that the average number of weekly sightings is 2.6. Compute the probability that exactly five sightings are made during a given week. In this example, $\lambda = 2.6$ and $k = 5$.

Step 1 *Enter the Poisson parameters*

- Press **2nd VARS** for **DISTR**
- Press the down **ARROW** key until **poissonpdf** is highlighted
- Press **ENTER**
- Enter 2.6 for λ, and 5 for **x values,** highlight **Paste,** then press **ENTER**
- Press **ENTER**
- You should see

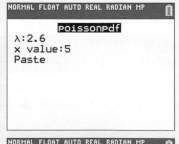

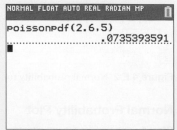

Thus, the $P(x = 5)$ is about 7.4%.

II. $P(x \le k)$

To compute the probability of k or fewer successes in a specified interval, where λ is the mean number of successes in the interval, use the **poissoncdf(** command. *Poissoncdf* stands for "Poisson *cumulative* probability density function." This command is under the *DISTR*ibution menu and has the format **poissoncdf(.**

Example In the preceding example, compute the probability that five or fewer sightings are made during a given week. In this example, $\lambda = 2.6$ and $k = 5$.

Step 2 *Enter the Poisson parameters*

- Press **2nd VARS** for **DISTR**
- Press the down **ARROW** key until **poissoncdf** is highlighted
- Press **ENTER**
- Enter 2.6 for **T**, and 5 for **x value,** highlight **Paste,** then press **ENTER**
- Press **ENTER**
- You should see

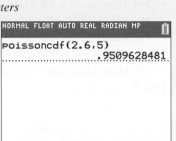

Thus, the $P(x = 5)$ is about 95.1%.

III. $P(x < k)$, $(x > k)$, $(x \ge k)$

To find the probability of fewer than k successes, more than k successes, or at least k successes, variations of the **poissoncdf(** command must be used as shown below.

- $P(x < k)$ use **poissoncdf($\lambda, k - 1$)**
- $P(x > k)$ use $1 -$ **poissoncdf($\lambda, \; k$)**
- $P(x \ge k)$ use $1 -$ **poissoncd($\lambda, k - 1$)**

Graphing the Area Under the Standard Normal Curve

Step 1 *Turn off all plots*

- Press **2nd PRGM** and select **1:ClrDraw**
- Press **ENTER** and "Done" will appear on the screen
- Press **2nd Y=** and select **4:PlotsOff**
- Press **ENTER** and "Done" will appear on the screen

Step 2 *Set the viewing window (Recall that almost all of the area under the standard normal curve falls between −5 and 5. A height of 0.5 is a good choice for Ymax.)*

Note: When entering a negative number, be sure to use the negative sign (−), not the minus sign.

- Set **Xmin** $= -5$
- **Xmax** $= 5$
- **Xscl** $= 1$
- **Ymin** $= 0$
- **Ymax** $= .5$
- **Yscl** $= 0$
- **Xres** $= 1$

Step 3 *View graph*

- Press **2nd VARS**
- Arrow right to **DRAW**
- Press **ENTER** to select **1:ShadeNorm(**
- Enter **lower** limit, **upper** limit, $\mu = 0$ and $\sigma = 1$, and 5 for **x value**
- Select **Draw,** then press **ENTER**

The graph will be displayed along with the area, lower limit, and upper limit.

Thus, $P(z < 1.5) = .9332$.

Nonstandard Normal Probabilities
I. Finding Normal Probabilities Without a Graph

To compute probabilities for a normal distribution, use the **normalcdf(** command. *Normalcdf* stands for "normal cumulative density function." This command is under the **DISTR**ibution menu and has the format **normalcdf(***lower limit, upper limit, mean, standard deviation***).**

Step 1 *Find probability*

- Press **2nd VARS** for **DISTR** and select **Normalcdf(**
- After **Normalcdf(,** type in the lower limit
- Enter **lower** limit, **upper** limit, value of μ and σ
- Select **Paste,** then press **ENTER**
- Press **ENTER**

The probability will be displayed on the screen.

Example What is $P(x < 115)$ for a normal distribution with $\mu = 100$ and $\sigma = 10$?

In this example, the lower limit is 0, the upper limit is 115, the mean is 100, and the standard deviation is 10.

The screen appears as shown here.

Thus, $P(x < 115)$ is .9332.

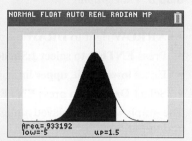

II. Finding Normal Probabilities with a Graph

Step 1 *Turn off all plots*

- Press **Y=** and **CLEAR** all functions from the Y registers
- Press **2nd   Y =** and select **4:PlotsOff**
- Press **ENTER ENTER,** and 'Done' will appear on the screen

Step 2 *Set the viewing window (These values depend on the mean and standard deviation of the data.) Note:* When entering a negative number, be sure to use the negative sign (−), not the minus sign.

- Press **WINDOW**
- Set **Xmin** $= \mu - 5\sigma$
- **Xmax** $= \mu + 5\sigma$
- **Xscl** $= \sigma$
- **Ymin** $= -.125/\sigma$
- **Ymax** $= .5/\sigma$
- **Yscl** $= 1$
- **Xres** $= 1$

Step 3 *View graph*

- Press **2nd VARS**
- **ARROW** right to **DRAW**
- Press **ENTER** to select **1:ShadeNorm(**
- Enter **lower** limit, **upper** limit, value of μ and σ
- Select **Draw**, then press **ENTER**

The graph will be displayed along with the area, lower limit, and upper limit.

Graphing a Normal Probability Plot

Step 1 *Enter the data*

- Press **STAT** and select **1:Edit**

Note: If the list already contains data, clear the old data. Use the up **ARROW** to highlight **L1**.

- Press **CLEAR ENTER**
- Use the **ARROW** and **ENTER** keys to enter the data set into **L1**

Step 2 *Set up the normal probability plot*

- Press **Y=** and **CLEAR** all functions from the Y registers
- Press **2nd** and press **Y=** for **STAT PLOT**
- Press **1** for **Plot 1**
- Set the cursor so that **ON** is flashing
- For **Type**, use the **ARROW** and **ENTER** keys to highlight and select the last graph in the bottom row
- For **Data List**, choose the column containing the data (in most cases, **L1**) (*Note:* Press **2nd 1** for **L1**)
- For **Data Axis**, choose **X** and press **ENTER**

Step 3 *View plot*

- Press **ZOOM 9**

Your data will be displayed against the expected *z*-scores from a normal distribution. If you see a "generally" linear relationship, your data set is approximately normal.

5

WHERE WE'VE BEEN

Learned that the objective of most statistical investigations is inference—that is, making decisions about a population on the basis of information about a sample

Discovered that sample statistics such as the sample mean and sample variance can be used to make decisions

Found that probability distributions for random variables are used to construct theoretical models of populations

WHERE WE'RE GOING

Establish that a sample statistic is a random variable with a probability distribution (5.1)

Define a *sampling distribution* as the probability distribution of a sample statistic (5.1)

Give two important properties of sampling distributions (5.2)

Learn that the sampling distribution of both the sample mean and sample proportion tends to be approximately normal (5.3, 5.4)

Sampling Distributions

STATISTICS IN ACTION   **The Insomnia Pill: Is It Effective?**

More than 15 years ago, neuroscientists at the Massachusetts Institute of Technology (MIT) began experimenting with melatonin—a hormone secreted by the pineal gland in the brain—as a sleep-inducing hormone. Their original study, published in the Proceedings of the National Academy of Sciences *(March 1994), brought encouraging news to insomniacs and travelers who suffer from jet lag: Melatonin was discovered to be effective in reducing sleep onset latency (the amount of time between a person lying down to sleep and the actual onset of stage one sleep). Furthermore, since the hormone is naturally produced, it is nonaddictive.*

Since then, pharmaceutical companies that produce melatonin pills for treating insomnia have received negative reports on the efficacy of the drug. Many people don't think the melatonin pills work. Consequently, the MIT researchers undertook a follow-up study and published their results in *Sleep Medicine Reviews* (February 2005). They reported that commercially available melatonin pills contain too high a dosage of the drug. When the melatonin receptors in the brain are exposed to too much of the hormone, they become unresponsive. The researchers' analysis of all previous studies on melatonin as a sleep inducer confirmed that, taken in small doses, melatonin is effective in reducing sleep onset latency.

In this *Statistics in Action,* our focus is on the original MIT study. Young male volunteers were given various doses of melatonin or a placebo (a dummy medication containing no melatonin). Then they were placed in a dark room at midday and told to close their eyes for 30 minutes. The variable of interest was sleep onset latency (in minutes).

According to the lead investigator, Professor Richard Wurtman, "Our volunteers fall asleep in 5 or 6 minutes on melatonin, while those on placebo take about

15 minutes." Wurtman warned, however, that uncontrolled doses of melatonin could cause mood-altering side effects.

Now, consider a random sample of 40 young males, each of whom is given a dosage of the sleep-inducing hormone melatonin. The times taken (in minutes) to fall asleep for these 40 males are listed in Table SIA5.1 and saved in the **SLEEP** file. The researchers know that with the placebo (i.e., no hormone), the mean sleep onset latency is $\mu = 15$ minutes and the standard deviation is $\sigma = 10$ minutes. They want to use the data to make an inference about the true value of μ for those taking the melatonin. Specifically, the researchers want to know whether melatonin is an effective drug against insomnia.

In this chapter, a *Statistics in Action Revisited* example demonstrates how we can use one of the topics discussed in the chapter—the Central Limit Theorem—to make an inference about the effectiveness of melatonin as a sleep-inducing hormone.

STATISTICS IN ACTION REVISITED

- Making an Inference About the Mean Sleep Onset Latency for Insomnia Pill Takers **(p. 313)**
- Making an Inference About the Proportion of Insomnia Pill Takers with Sleep Onset Latency of Less than 15 Minutes **(p. 319)**

Table SIA5.1	Times Taken (in Minutes) for 40 Male Volunteers to Fall Asleep								
7.6	2.1	1.4	1.5	3.6	17.0	14.9	4.4	4.7	20.1
7.7	2.4	8.1	1.5	10.3	1.3	3.7	2.5	3.4	10.7
2.9	1.5	15.9	3.0	1.9	8.5	6.1	4.5	2.2	2.6
7.0	6.4	2.8	2.8	22.8	1.5	4.6	2.0	6.3	3.2

[Note: These data are simulated sleep times based on summary information provided in the MIT study.]

 Data Set: SLEEP

In Chapter 4, we assumed that we knew the probability distribution of a random variable, and using this knowledge, we were able to compute the mean, variance, and probabilities associated with the random variable. However, in most practical applications, this information is not available. To illustrate, in Example 4.13 (p. 235), we calculated the probability that the binomial random variable x, the number of 20 employees who favor unionization, assumed specific values. To do this, it was necessary to assume some value for p, the proportion of all employees who favor unionization. Thus, for the purposes of illustration, we assumed that $p = .6$ when, in all likelihood, the exact value of p would be unknown. In fact, the probable purpose of taking the poll is to estimate p. Similarly, when we modeled the in-city gas mileage of a certain automobile model in Example 4.21 (p. 257), we used the normal probability distribution with an *assumed* mean and standard deviation of 27 and 3 miles per gallon, respectively. In most situations, the true mean and standard deviation are unknown quantities that have to be estimated. Numerical quantities that describe probability distributions are called *parameters*. Thus, p, the probability of a success in a binomial experiment, and μ and σ, the mean and standard deviation, respectively, of a normal distribution, are examples of parameters.

A **parameter** is a numerical descriptive measure of a population. Because it is based on the observations in the population, its value is almost always unknown.

We have also discussed the sample mean $\bar{x}$, sample variance s^2, sample standard deviation s, and the like, which are numerical descriptive measures calculated from the sample. (See Table 5.1 for a list of the statistics covered so far in this text.) We will often use the information contained in these *sample statistics* to make inferences about the parameters of a population.

A **sample statistic** is a numerical descriptive measure of a sample. It is calculated from the observations in the sample.

Table 5.1	List of Population Parameters and Corresponding Sample Statistics	
	Population Parameter	Sample Statistic
Mean:	μ	$\bar{x}$
Median:	η	m
Variance:	σ^2	s^2
Standard deviation:	σ	s
Binomial proportion:	p	$\hat{p}$

Note that the term *statistic* refers to a *sample* quantity and the term *parameter* refers to a *population* quantity.

Before we can show you how to use sample statistics to make inferences about population parameters, we need to be able to evaluate their properties. Does one sample statistic contain more information than another about a population parameter? On what basis should we choose the "best" statistic for making inferences about a parameter? The purpose of this chapter is to answer these questions.

5.1 The Concept of a Sampling Distribution

If we want to estimate a parameter of a population—say, the population mean μ—we can use a number of sample statistics for our estimate. Two possibilities are the sample mean $\bar{x}$ and the sample median m. Which of these do you think will provide a better estimate of μ?

Before answering this question, consider the following example: Toss a fair die, and let x equal the number of dots showing on the up face. Suppose the die is tossed three times, producing the sample measurements 2, 2, 6. The sample mean is then $\bar{x} = 3.33$, and the sample median is $m = 2$. Since the population mean of x is $\mu = 3.5$, you can see that, for this sample of three measurements, the sample mean $\bar{x}$ provides an estimate that falls closer to μ than does the sample median (see Figure 5.1a). Now suppose we toss the die three more times and obtain the sample measurements 3, 4, 6. Then the mean and median of this sample are $\bar{x} = 4.33$ and $m = 4$, respectively. This time m is closer to μ. (See Figure 5.1b.)

This simple example illustrates an important point: Neither the sample mean nor the sample median will *always* fall closer to the population mean. Consequently, we cannot compare these two sample statistics, or, in general, any two sample statistics, on the basis of their performance for a single sample. Instead, we need to recognize that sample statistics are themselves random variables because different samples can lead to different values for the sample statistics. As random variables, sample statistics must be judged and compared on the basis of their probability distributions (i.e., the *collection* of values and associated probabilities of each statistic that would be obtained if the sampling experiment were repeated a *very large number of times*). We will illustrate this concept with another example.

Suppose it is known that the connector module manufactured for a certain brand of pacemaker has a mean length of $\mu = .3$ inch and a standard deviation of .005 inch. Consider an experiment consisting of randomly selecting 25 recently manufactured connector modules, measuring the length of each, and calculating the sample mean length $\bar{x}$. If this experiment were repeated a very large number of times, the value of $\bar{x}$ would

Figure 5.1

Comparing the sample mean ($\bar{x}$) and sample median (m) as estimators of the population mean (μ)

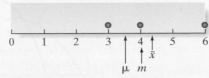

a. Sample 1: $\bar{x}$ is closer than m to μ b. Sample 2: m is closer than $\bar{x}$ to μ

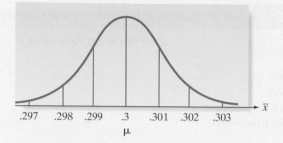

Figure 5.2

Sampling distribution for $\bar{x}$ based on a sample of $n = 25$ length measurements

vary from sample to sample. For example, the first sample of 25 length measurements might have a mean $\bar{x} = .301$, the second sample a mean $\bar{x} = .298$, the third sample a mean $\bar{x} = .303$, etc. If the sampling experiment were repeated a very large number of times, the resulting histogram of sample means would be approximately the probability distribution of $\bar{x}$. If $\bar{x}$ is a good estimator of μ, we would expect the values of $\bar{x}$ to cluster around μ, as shown in Figure 5.2. This probability distribution is called a *sampling distribution* because it is generated by repeating a sampling experiment a very large number of times.

> Consider a sample statistic calculated from a sample of n measurements. The **sampling distribution** of the statistic is the probability distribution of the statistic.

In actual practice, the sampling distribution of a statistic is obtained mathematically or (at least approximately) by simulating the sample on a computer using a procedure similar to that just described.

If $\bar{x}$ has been calculated from a sample of $n = 25$ measurements selected from a population with mean $\mu = .3$ and standard deviation $\sigma = .005$, the sampling distribution (Figure 5.2) provides information about the behavior of $\bar{x}$ in repeated sampling. For example, the probability that you will draw a sample of 25 length measurements and obtain a value of $\bar{x}$ in the interval $.299 \leq \bar{x} \leq .3$ will be the area under the sampling distribution over that interval.

Because the properties of a statistic are typified by its sampling distribution, it follows that to compare two sample statistics, you compare their sampling distributions. For example, if you have two statistics, A and B, for estimating the same parameter (for purposes of illustration, suppose the parameter is the population variance σ^2) and if their sampling distributions are as shown in Figure 5.3, you would choose statistic A in preference to statistic B. You would make this choice because the sampling distribution for statistic A centers over σ^2 and has less spread (variation) than the sampling distribution for statistic B. When you draw a single sample in a practical sampling situation, the probability is higher that statistic A will fall nearer σ^2.

Remember that in practice we will not know the numerical value of the unknown parameter σ^2, so we will not know whether statistic A or statistic B is closer to σ^2 for a sample. We have to rely on our knowledge of the theoretical sampling distributions to choose the best sample statistic and then use it sample after sample. The procedure for finding the sampling distribution for a statistic is demonstrated in Examples 5.1 and 5.2.

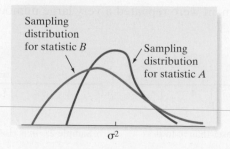

Figure 5.3

Two sampling distributions for estimating the population variance, σ^2

EXAMPLE 5.1

Finding a Sampling Distribution—Coin-Tossing Experiment

Problem In a single toss of a fair coin, let x equal the number of heads observed. Now consider a sample of $n = 2$ tosses. Find the sampling distribution of $\bar{x}$, the sample mean.

Solution For one coin toss, the result is either a head (H) or a tail (T). Thus, the value of x is either $x = 1$ or $x = 0$. The four possible outcomes (sample points) for two coin tosses and corresponding probabilities are listed in Table 5.2. Since a fair coin is tossed, these four possible outcomes are equally likely.

Table 5.2	Outcomes for $n = 2$ Coin Tosses	
Outcome (Toss 1, Toss 2)	Probability	$\bar{x}$
$HH\ (x = 1, x = 1)$	¼	1
$HT\ (x = 1, x = 0)$	¼	.5
$TH\ (x = 0, x = 1)$	¼	.5
$TT\ (x = 0, x = 0)$	¼	0

The value of $\bar{x}$ for each outcome is also listed in Table 5.2. You can see that the values are either 0, .5, or 1. Now, $P(\bar{x} = 1) = P(HH) = \frac{1}{4}$. Similarly, $P(\bar{x} = 0) = P(TT) = \frac{1}{4}$. Finally, using the probability law for unions of mutually exclusive events, $P(\bar{x} = .5) = P(HT \text{ or } TH) = P(HT) + P(TH) = \frac{1}{4} + \frac{1}{4} = \frac{1}{2}$. Thus, the sampling distribution of $\bar{x}$ is:

$\bar{x}$	0	.5	1
$p(\bar{x})$	¼	½	¼

EXAMPLE 5.2

Finding a Sampling Distribution—Come-Out Roll in Craps

Problem Consider the popular casino game of craps, in which a player throws two dice and bets on the outcome (the sum total of the dots showing on the upper faces of the two dice). In Example 4.5 (p. 218), we looked at the possible outcomes of a $5 wager on the first toss (called the *come-out roll*). Recall that if the sum total of the dice is 7 or 11, the roller wins $5; if the total is a 2, 3, or 12, the roller loses $5 (i.e., the roller "wins" $-\$5$); and, for any other total (4, 5, 6, 8, 9, or 10) no money is lost or won on that roll (i.e., the roller wins $0). Let x represent the result of the come-out roll wager ($-\$5$, 0, or $+\$5$). We showed in Example 4.5 that the actual probability distribution of x is:

Outcome of wager, x	-5	0	5
$p(x)$	1/9	6/9	2/9

Now, consider a random sample of $n = 3$ come-out rolls.

a. Find the sampling distribution of the sample mean, $\bar{x}$.
b. Find the sampling distribution of the sample median, m.

Solution The outcomes for every possible sample of $n = 3$ come-out rolls are listed in Table 5.3, along with the sample mean and median. The probability of each sample is obtained using the multiplicative rule. For example, the probability of the sample $(0, 0, 5)$ is $p(0) \cdot p(0) \cdot p(5) = \left(\frac{6}{9}\right)\left(\frac{6}{9}\right)\left(\frac{2}{9}\right) = \frac{72}{729} = .099$. The probability for each sample is also listed in Table 5.3. Note that the sum of these probabilities is equal to 1.

a. From Table 5.3, you can see that $\bar{x}$ can assume the values $-5, -3.33, -1.67, 0, 1.67, 3.33$, and 5. Because $\bar{x} = -5$ occurs only in one sample, $P(\bar{x} = -5) = \frac{1}{729}$. Similarly, $\bar{x} = -3.33$ occurs in three samples, $(-5, -5, 0), (-5, 0, -5)$, and $(0, -5, -5)$. Therefore, $P(\bar{x} = -3.33) = \frac{6}{729} + \frac{6}{729} + \frac{6}{729} = \frac{18}{729}$. Calculating the probabilities of the remaining values of $\bar{x}$ and arranging them in a table, we obtain the following probability distribution:

$\bar{x}$	-5	-3.33	-1.67	0	1.67	3.33	5
$p(\bar{x})$	1/729	18/729	114/729	288/729	228/729	72/729	8/729
	= .0014	= .0247	= .1564	= .3951	= .3127	= .0988	= .0110

Table 5.3	All Possible Samples of $n = 3$ Come-Out Rolls in Craps		
Possible Samples	$\bar{x}$	m	Probability
$-5, -5, -5$	-5	-5	$(1/9)(1/9)(1/9) = 1/729$
$-5, -5, 0$	-3.33	-5	$(1/9)(1/9)(6/9) = 6/729$
$-5, -5, 5$	-1.67	-5	$(1/9)(1/9)(2/9) = 2/729$
$-5, 0, -5$	-3.33	-5	$(1/9)(6/9)(1/9) = 6/729$
$-5, 0, 0$	-1.67	0	$(1/9)(6/9)(6/9) = 36/729$
$-5, 0, 5$	0	0	$(1/9)(6/9)(2/9) = 12/729$
$-5, 5, -5$	-1.67	-5	$(1/9)(2/9)(1/9) = 2/729$
$-5, 5, 0$	0	0	$(1/9)(2/9)(6/9) = 12/729$
$-5, 5, 5$	1.67	5	$(1/9)(2/9)(2/9) = 4/729$
$0, -5, -5$	-3.33	-5	$(6/9)(1/9)(1/9) = 6/729$
$0, -5, 0$	-1.67	0	$(6/9)(1/9)(6/9) = 36/729$
$0, -5, 5$	0	0	$(6/9)(1/9)(2/9) = 12/729$
$0, 0, -5$	-1.67	0	$(6/9)(6/9)(1/9) = 36/729$
$0, 0, 0$	0	0	$(6/9)(6/9)(6/9) = 216/729$
$0, 0, 5$	1.67	0	$(6/9)(6/9)(2/9) = 72/729$
$0, 5, -5$	0	0	$(6/9)(2/9)(1/9) = 12/729$
$0, 5, 0$	1.67	0	$(6/9)(2/9)(6/9) = 72/729$
$0, 5, 5$	3.33	5	$(6/9)(2/9)(2/9) = 24/729$
$5, -5, -5$	-1.67	-5	$(2/9)(1/9)(1/9) = 2/729$
$5, -5, 0$	0	0	$(2/9)(1/9)(6/9) = 12/729$
$5, -5, 5$	1.67	5	$(2/9)(1/9)(2/9) = 4/729$
$5, 0, -5$	0	0	$(2/9)(6/9)(1/9) = 12/729$
$5, 0, 0$	1.67	0	$(2/9)(6/9)(6/9) = 72/729$
$5, 0, 5$	3.33	5	$(2/9)(6/9)(2/9) = 24/729$
$5, 5, -5$	1.67	5	$(2/9)(2/9)(1/9) = 4/729$
$5, 5, 0$	3.33	5	$(2/9)(2/9)(6/9) = 24/729$
$5, 5, 5$	5	5	$(2/9)(2/9)(2/9) = 8/729$

$$Sum = 729/729 = 1$$

This is the sampling distribution for $\bar{x}$ because it specifies the probability associated with each possible value of $\bar{x}$. You can see that the most likely mean outcome after 3 randomly selected come-out rolls is $\bar{x} = \$0$; this result occurs with probability $\frac{288}{729} = .3951$.

b. In Table 5.3, you can see that the median m can assume one of three values: $-5, 0,$ or 5. The value $m = -5$ occurs in 7 different samples. Therefore, $P(m = -5)$ is the sum of the probabilities associated with these 7 samples; that is, $P(m = -5) = \frac{1}{729} + \frac{6}{729} + \frac{2}{729} + \frac{6}{729} + \frac{2}{729} + \frac{6}{729} + \frac{2}{729} = \frac{25}{729}$. Similarly, $m = 0$ occurs in 13 samples and $m = 5$ occurs in 7 samples. These probabilities are obtained by summing the probabilities of their respective sample points. After performing these calculations, we obtain the following probability distribution for the median m:

m	-5	0	5
$p(m)$	$25/729 = .0343$	$612/729 = .8395$	$92/729 = .1262$

Once again, the most likely median outcome after 3 randomly selected come-out rolls is $\bar{x} = \$0$—a result that occurs with probability $\frac{612}{729} = .8395$.

Look Back The sampling distributions of parts **a** and **b** are found by first listing all possible distinct values of the statistic and then calculating the probability of each value. Note that if the values of x were equally likely, the 27 sample points in Table 5.3 would all have the same probability of occurring, namely, $\frac{1}{27}$.

• **Now Work Exercise 5.1**

Examples 5.1 and 5.2 demonstrate the procedure for finding the exact sampling distribution of a statistic when the number of different samples that could be selected from the population is relatively small. In the real world, populations often consist of a large number of different values, making samples difficult (or impossible) to enumerate. When this situation occurs, we may choose to obtain the approximate sampling distribution for a statistic by simulating the sampling over and over again and recording the proportion of times different values of the statistic occur. Example 5.3 illustrates this procedure.

EXAMPLE 5.3

Simulating a Sampling Distribution—Thickness of Steel Sheets

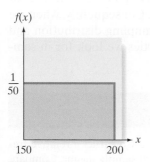

Figure 5.4

Uniform distribution for thickness of steel sheets

Problem Refer to Example 4.24 (p. 272). Recall that the thickness of a steel sheet follows a uniform distribution with values between 150 and 200 millimeters. Suppose we perform the following experiment over and over again: Randomly sample 11 steel sheets from the production line and record the thickness, x, of each. Calculate the two sample statistics

$$\bar{x} = \text{Sample mean} = \frac{\Sigma x}{11}$$

$m = \text{Median} = \text{Sixth sample measurement when the 11 thicknesses}$
$\qquad\qquad\qquad \text{are arranged in ascending order}$

Obtain approximations to the sampling distributions of $\bar{x}$ and m.

Solution Recall from Section 4.8 that the population of thicknesses follows the uniform distribution shown in Figure 5.4. We used Minitab to generate 1,000 samples from this population, each with $n = 11$ observations. Then we compute $\bar{x}$ and m for each sample. Our goal is to obtain approximations to the sampling distributions of $\bar{x}$ and m to find out which sample statistic ($\bar{x}$ or m) contains more information about μ. [*Note*: In this particular example, we *know* the population mean is $\mu = 175$ mm. (See Section 4.8.)] The first 10 of the 1,000 samples generated are presented in Table 5.4. For instance, the first computer-generated sample from the uniform distribution (arranged in ascending order) contains the following thickness measurements: 151, 157, 162, 169, 171, 173, 181, 182, 187, 188, and 193 millimeters. The sample mean $\bar{x}$ and median m computed for this sample are

$$\bar{x} = \frac{151 + 157 + \cdots + 193}{11} = 174.0$$

$m = \text{Sixth ordered measurement} = 173$

The Minitab relative frequency histograms for $\bar{x}$ and m for the 1,000 samples of size $n = 11$ are shown in Figure 5.5. These histograms represent approximations to the true sampling distributions of $\bar{x}$ and m.

Table 5.4	First 10 Samples of $n = 11$ Thickness Measurements from Uniform Distribution												
Sample	Thickness Measurements											Mean	Median
1	173	171	187	151	188	181	182	157	162	169	193	174.00	173
2	181	190	182	171	187	177	162	172	188	200	193	182.09	182
3	192	195	187	187	172	164	164	189	179	182	173	180.36	182
4	173	157	150	154	168	174	171	182	200	181	187	172.45	173
5	169	160	167	170	197	159	174	174	161	173	160	169.46	169
6	179	170	167	174	173	178	173	170	173	198	187	176.55	173
7	166	177	162	171	154	177	154	179	175	185	193	172.09	175
8	164	199	152	153	163	156	184	151	198	167	180	169.73	164
9	181	193	151	166	180	199	180	184	182	181	175	179.27	181
10	155	199	199	171	172	157	173	187	190	185	150	176.18	173

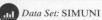 *Data Set:* SIMUNI

Look Back You can see that the values of $\bar{x}$ tend to cluster around μ to a greater extent than do the values of m. Thus, on the basis of the observed sampling distributions, we conclude that $\bar{x}$ contains more information about μ than m does—at least for samples of $n = 11$ measurements from the uniform distribution.

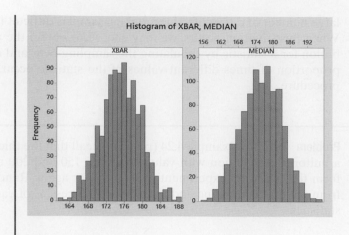

Figure 5.5

Minitab histograms for sample mean and sample median, Example 5.3

• **Now Work Exercise 5.6**

As noted earlier, many sampling distributions can be derived mathematically, but the theory necessary to do this is beyond the scope of this text. Consequently, when we need to know the properties of a statistic, we will present its sampling distribution and simply describe its properties. Several of the important properties we look for in sampling distributions are discussed in the next section.

Exercises 5.1–5.7

Learning the Mechanics

5.1 The probability distribution shown here describes a population of measurements that can assume values of 0, 2, 4, and 6, each of which occurs with the same relative frequency:

x	0	2	4	6
$p(x)$	$\frac{1}{4}$	$\frac{1}{4}$	$\frac{1}{4}$	$\frac{1}{4}$

a. List all the different samples of $n = 2$ measurements that can be selected from this population. For example, $(0, 6)$ is one possible pair of measurements; $(2, 2)$ is another possible pair.

b. Calculate the mean of each different sample listed in part **a**.

c. If a sample of $n = 2$ measurements is randomly selected from the population, what is the probability that a specific sample will be selected?

d. Assume that a random sample of $n = 2$ measurements is selected from the population. List the different values of $\bar{x}$ found in part **b** and find the probability of each. Then give the sampling distribution of the sample mean $\bar{x}$ in tabular form.

e. Construct a probability histogram for the sampling distribution of $\bar{x}$.

5.2 Simulate sampling from the population described in Exercise 5.1 by marking the values of x, one on each of four identical coins (or poker chips, etc.). Place the coins (marked 0, 2, 4, and 6) into a bag, randomly select one, and observe its value. Replace this coin, draw a second coin, and observe its value. Finally, calculate the mean $\bar{x}$ for this sample of $n = 2$ observations randomly selected from the population (Exercise 5.1, part **b**). Replace the coins, mix, and using the same procedure, select a sample of $n = 2$ observations from the population. Record the numbers and calculate $\bar{x}$ for this sample. Repeat this sampling process

until you acquire 100 values of $\bar{x}$. Construct a relative frequency distribution for these 100 sample means. Compare this distribution with the exact sampling distribution of $\bar{x}$ found in part **e** of Exercise 5.1. [*Note:* The distribution obtained in this exercise is an approximation to the exact sampling distribution. But, if you were to repeat the sampling procedure, drawing two coins not 100 times but 10,000 times, the relative frequency distribution for the 10,000 sample means would be almost identical to the sampling distribution of $\bar{x}$ found in Exercise 5.1, part **e**.

5.3 Consider the population described by the probability distribution shown below.

x	1	2	3	4	5
$p(x)$	.2	.3	.2	.2	.1

The random variable x is observed twice. If these observations are independent, verify that the different samples of size 2 and their probabilities are as shown below.

Sample	Probability	Sample	Probability
1, 1	.04	3, 4	.04
1, 2	.06	3, 5	.02
1, 3	.04	4, 1	.04
1, 4	.04	4, 2	.06
1, 5	.02	4, 3	.04
2, 1	.06	4, 4	.04
2, 2	.09	4, 5	.02
2, 3	.06	5, 1	.02
2, 4	.06	5, 2	.03
2, 5	.03	5, 3	.02
3, 1	.04	5, 4	.02
3, 2	.06	5, 5	.01
3, 3	.04		

a. Find the sampling distribution of the sample mean $\bar{x}$.
b. Construct a probability histogram for the sampling distribution of $\bar{x}$.
c. What is the probability that $\bar{x}$ is 4.5 or larger?
d. Would you expect to observe a value of $\bar{x}$ equal to 4.5 or larger? Explain.

5.4 Refer to Exercise 5.3 and find $E(x) = \mu$. Then use the sampling distribution of $\bar{x}$ found in Exercise 5.3 to find the expected value of $\bar{x}$. Note that $E(\bar{x}) = \mu$.

5.5 Refer to Exercise 5.3. Assume that a random sample of $n = 2$ measurements is randomly selected from the population.
a. List the different values that the sample median m may assume and find the probability of each. Then give the sampling distribution of the sample median.
b. Construct a probability histogram for the sampling distribution of the sample median and compare it with the probability histogram for the sample mean (Exercise 5.3, part **b**).

5.6 In Example 5.3 we used a computer to generate 1,000 samples, each containing $n = 11$ observations, from a uniform distribution over the interval from 150 to 200. For this exercise, use a computer to generate 500 samples, each containing $n = 15$ observations, from this population.
a. Calculate the sample mean for each sample. To approximate the sampling distribution of $\bar{x}$, construct a relative frequency histogram for the 500 values of $\bar{x}$.
b. Repeat part **a** for the sample median. Compare this approximate sampling distribution with the approximate sampling distribution of $\bar{x}$ found in part **a**.

5.7 Consider a population that contains values of x equal to $00, 01, 02, 03, \ldots, 96, 97, 98, 99$. Assume that these values of x occur with equal probability. Use a computer to generate 500 samples, each containing $n = 25$ measurements, from this population. Calculate the sample mean $\bar{x}$ and sample variance s^2 for each of the 500 samples.
a. To approximate the sampling distribution of $\bar{x}$, construct a relative frequency histogram for the 500 values of $\bar{x}$.
b. Repeat part **a** for the 500 values of s^2.

5.2 Properties of Sampling Distributions: Unbiasedness and Minimum Variance

The simplest type of statistic used to make inferences about a population parameter is a *point estimator*—a rule or formula that tells us how to use the sample data to calculate a single number that is intended to estimate the value of some population parameter. For example, the sample mean $\bar{x}$ is a point estimator of the population mean μ. Similarly, the sample variance s^2 is a point estimator of the population variance σ^2.

> A **point estimator** of a population parameter is a rule or formula that tells us how to use the sample data to calculate a single number that can be used as an *estimate* of the population parameter.

Often, many different point estimators can be found to estimate the same parameter. Each will have a sampling distribution that provides information about the point estimator. By examining the sampling distribution, we can determine how large the difference between an estimate and the true value of the parameter (called the **error of estimation**) is likely to be. We can also tell whether an estimator is more likely to overestimate or to underestimate a parameter.

EXAMPLE 5.4

Comparing Two Statistics

Problem Suppose two statistics, A and B, exist to estimate the same population parameter θ (theta). (Note that θ could be any parameter: μ, σ^2, σ, etc.) Suppose the two statistics have sampling distributions as shown in Figure 5.6. On the basis of these sampling distributions, which statistic is more attractive as an estimator of θ?

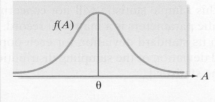

a. Unbiased sample statistic for the parameter θ

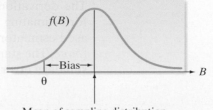

b. Biased sample statistic for the parameter θ

Figure 5.6

Sampling distributions of unbiased and biased estimators

Solution As a first consideration, we would like the sampling distribution to center over the value of the parameter we wish to estimate. One way to characterize this property is in terms of the mean of the sampling distribution. Consequently, we say that a statistic is *unbiased* if the mean of the sampling distribution is equal to the parameter it is intended to estimate. This situation is shown in Figure 5.6a, where the mean μ_A of statistic A is equal to θ. If the mean of a sampling distribution is *not* equal to the parameter it is intended to estimate, the statistic is said to be *biased*. The sampling distribution for a biased statistic is shown in Figure 5.6b. The mean μ_B of the sampling distribution for statistic B is not equal to θ; in fact, it is shifted to the right of θ.

Look Back You can see that biased statistics tend either to overestimate or to underestimate a parameter. Consequently, when other properties of statistics tend to be equivalent, we will choose an unbiased statistic to estimate a parameter of interest.*

● **Now Work Exercise 5.8**

If the sampling distribution of a sample statistic has a mean equal to the population parameter the statistic is intended to estimate, the statistic is said to be an **unbiased estimate** of the parameter.

If the mean of the sampling distribution is not equal to the parameter, the statistic is said to be a **biased estimate** of the parameter.

The standard deviation of a sampling distribution measures another important property of statistics: the spread of these estimates generated by repeated sampling. Suppose two statistics, A and B, are both unbiased estimators of the population parameter. Since the means of the two sampling distributions are the same, we turn to their standard deviations in order to decide which will provide estimates that fall closer to the unknown population parameter we are estimating. Naturally, we will choose the sample statistic that has the smaller standard deviation. Figure 5.7 depicts sampling distributions for A

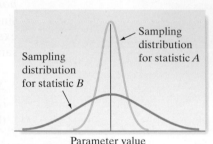

Figure 5.7

Sampling distributions for two unbiased estimators

and B. Note that the standard deviation of the distribution for A is smaller than the standard deviation of the distribution for B, indicating that, over a large number of samples, the values of A cluster more closely around the unknown population parameter than do the values of B. Stated differently, the probability that A is close to the parameter value is higher than the probability that B is close to the parameter value.

In sum, to make an inference about a population parameter, we use the sample statistic with a sampling distribution that is unbiased and has a small standard deviation (usually smaller than the standard deviation of other unbiased sample statistics). The derivation of this sample statistic will not concern us, because the "best" statistic for estimating specific parameters is a matter of record. We will simply present an unbiased estimator with its standard deviation for each population parameter we consider. [*Note:* The standard deviation of the sampling distribution of a statistic is also called the **standard error of the statistic.**]

---

*Unbiased statistics do not exist for all parameters of interest, but they do exist for all the parameters considered in this text.

EXAMPLE 5.5

Biased and Unbiased Estimators–Craps Application

Problem Refer to Example 5.2 and the outcome x of a \$5 wager in craps. We found the sampling distributions of the sample mean $\bar{x}$ and the sample median m for random samples of $n = 3$ dice rolls from a population defined by the following probability distribution:

x	-5	0	5
$p(x)$	$\frac{1}{9}$	$\frac{6}{9}$	$\frac{2}{9}$

The sampling distributions of $\bar{x}$ and m were found to be as follows:

x	-5	-3.33	-1.67	0	1.67	3.33	5
$p(\bar{x})$	$\frac{1}{729}$	$\frac{18}{729}$	$\frac{114}{729}$	$\frac{288}{729}$	$\frac{228}{729}$	$\frac{72}{729}$	$\frac{8}{729}$

m	-5	0	5
$p(m)$	$\frac{25}{729}$	$\frac{612}{729}$	$\frac{92}{729}$

a. Show that $\bar{x}$ is an unbiased estimator of μ in this situation.
b. Show that m is a biased estimator of μ in this situation.

Solution

a. The expected value of a discrete random variable x (see Section 4.3) is defined as $E(x) = \Sigma x p(x)$, where the summation is over all values of x. Then

$$E(x) = \mu = \Sigma x p(x) = (-5)\left(\tfrac{1}{9}\right) + (0)\left(\tfrac{6}{9}\right) + (5)\left(\tfrac{2}{9}\right) = \frac{5}{9} - .556$$

The expected value of the discrete random variable $\bar{x}$ is

$$E(\bar{x}) = \Sigma(\bar{x})p(\bar{x})$$

summed over all values of $\bar{x}$, or

$$E(\bar{x}) = (-5)\left(\tfrac{1}{729}\right) + (-3.33)\left(\tfrac{18}{729}\right) + (-1.67)\left(\tfrac{114}{729}\right) + \cdots + (5)\left(\tfrac{8}{729}\right) = .556$$

Since $E(\bar{x}) = \mu$, $\bar{x}$ is an unbiased estimator of μ.

b. The expected value of the sample median m is

$$E(m) = \Sigma m p(m) = (-5)\left(\tfrac{25}{729}\right) + (0)\left(\tfrac{612}{729}\right) + (5)\left(\tfrac{92}{729}\right) = \frac{335}{729} = .460$$

Since the expected value of m is not equal to μ ($\mu = .556$), the sample median m is a biased estimator of μ.

→ **Now Work Exercise 5.10 a, b, c, d**

EXAMPLE 5.6

Variance of Estimators–Craps Application

Problem Refer to Example 5.5 and find the standard deviations of the sampling distributions of $\bar{x}$ and m. Which statistic would appear to be a better estimator of μ?

Solution The variance of the sampling distribution of $\bar{x}$ (we denote it by the symbol $\sigma_{\bar{x}}^2$) is found to be

$$\sigma_{\bar{x}}^2 = E\{[\bar{x} - E(\bar{x})]^2\} = \Sigma(\bar{x} - \mu)^2 p(\bar{x})$$

where, from Example 5.5,

$$E(\bar{x}) = \mu = .556$$

Then

$$\sigma_{\bar{x}}^2 = (-5 - .556)^2\left(\tfrac{1}{729}\right) + (-3.33 - .556)^2\left(\tfrac{18}{729}\right) + \cdots (5 - .556)^2\left(\tfrac{8}{729}\right)$$

$$= 2.678$$

and

$$\sigma_{\bar{x}} = \sqrt{2.678} = 1.64$$

Similarly, the variance of the sampling distribution of m (we denote it by σ_m^2) is

$$\sigma_m^2 = E\{[m - E(m)]^2\}$$

where, from Example 5.5, the expected value of m is $E(m) = .460$. Then

$$\sigma_m^2 = E\{[m - E(m)]^2\} = \Sigma[m - E(m)]^2 p(m)$$
$$= (-5 - .460)\left(\tfrac{25}{729}\right) + (0 - .460)\left(\tfrac{612}{729}\right) + (5 - .460)\left(\tfrac{92}{729}\right) = 3.801$$

and

$$\sigma_m = \sqrt{3.801} = 1.95$$

Which statistic appears to be the better estimator for the population mean μ, the sample mean $\bar{x}$ or the median m? To answer this question, we compare the sampling distributions of the two statistics. The sampling distribution of the sample median m is biased (i.e., it is located to the left of the mean μ), and its standard deviation $\sigma_m = 1.95$ is larger than the standard deviation of the sampling distribution of $\bar{x}$, $\sigma_{\bar{x}} = 1.64$. Consequently, for the population in question, the sample mean $\bar{x}$ would be a better estimator of the population mean μ than the sample median m would be.

Look Back Ideally, we desire an estimator that is unbiased *and* has the smallest variance among all unbiased estimators. We call this statistic the **minimum-variance unbiased estimator (MVUE)**.

● **Now Work Exercise 5.10 e, f**

Exercises 5.8–5.14

Learning the Mechanics

5.8 Consider the following probability distribution:

x	0	1	4
$p(x)$	$\tfrac{1}{3}$	$\tfrac{1}{3}$	$\tfrac{1}{3}$

a. Find μ and σ^2.
b. Find the sampling distribution of the sample mean $\bar{x}$ for a random sample of $n = 2$ measurements from this distribution.
c. Show that $\bar{x}$ is an unbiased estimator of μ. [*Hint:* Show that $E(\bar{x}) = \Sigma\bar{x}p(\bar{x}) = \mu$.]
d. Find the sampling distribution of the sample variance s^2 for a random sample of $n = 2$ measurements from this distribution.
e. Show that s^2 is an unbiased estimator for σ^2.

5.9 Consider the following probability distribution:

x	2	4	9
$p(x)$	$\tfrac{1}{3}$	$\tfrac{1}{3}$	$\tfrac{1}{3}$

a. Calculate μ for this distribution.
b. Find the sampling distribution of the sample mean $\bar{x}$ for a random sample of $n = 3$ measurements from this distribution, and show that $\bar{x}$ is an unbiased estimator of μ.
c. Find the sampling distribution of the sample median m for a random sample of $n = 3$ measurements from this distribution, and show that the median is a biased estimator of μ.

d. If you wanted to use a sample of three measurements from this population to estimate μ, which estimator would you use? Why?

5.10 Consider the following probability distribution:

x	0	1	2
$p(x)$	$\tfrac{1}{3}$	$\tfrac{1}{3}$	$\tfrac{1}{3}$

a. Find μ.
b. For a random sample of $n = 3$ observations from this distribution, find the sampling distribution of the sample mean.
c. Find the sampling distribution of the median of a sample of $n = 3$ observations from this population.
d. Refer to parts **b** and **c**, and show that both the mean and median are unbiased estimators of μ for this population.
e. Find the variances of the sampling distributions of the sample mean and the sample median.
f. Which estimator would you use to estimate μ? Why?

5.11 Use the computer to generate 500 samples, each containing $n = 25$ measurements, from a population that contains values of x equal to $1, 2, \ldots, 48, 49, 50$. Assume that these values of x are equally likely. Calculate the sample mean $\bar{x}$ and median m for each sample. Construct relative frequency histograms for the 500 values of $\bar{x}$ and the 500 values of m. Use these approximations to the sampling distributions of $\bar{x}$ and m to answer the following questions:
a. Does it appear that $\bar{x}$ and m are unbiased estimators of the population mean? [*Note:* $\mu = 25.5$.]
b. Which sampling distribution displays greater variation?

5.12 Refer to Exercise 5.3.
  a. Show that $\bar{x}$ is an unbiased estimator of μ.
  b. Find $\sigma_{\bar{x}}^2$.
  c. Find the probability that $\bar{x}$ will fall within $2\sigma_{\bar{x}}$ of μ.

5.13 Refer to Exercise 5.3.
  a. Find the sampling distribution of s^2.
  b. Find the population variance σ^2.

  c. Show that s^2 is an unbiased estimator of σ^2.
  d. Find the sampling distribution of the sample standard deviation s.
  e. Show that s is a biased estimator of σ.

5.14 Refer to Exercise 5.5, in which we found the sampling distribution of the sample median. Is the median an unbiased estimator of the population mean μ?

5.3 The Sampling Distribution of the Sample Mean and the Central Limit Theorem

Estimating the mean useful life of automobiles, the mean monthly sales for all iPhone dealers in a large city, and the mean breaking strength of new plastic are practical problems with something in common. In each case, we are interested in making an inference about the mean μ of some population. As we mentioned in Chapter 2, the sample mean $\bar{x}$ is, in general, a good estimator of μ. We now develop pertinent information about the sampling distribution for this useful statistic. We will show that $\bar{x}$ is the minimum-variance unbiased estimator (MVUE) of μ.

EXAMPLE 5.7

Describing the Sampling Distribution of $\bar{x}$

Problem Suppose a population has the uniform probability distribution given in Figure 5.8. The mean and standard deviation of this probability distribution are $\mu = 175$ and $\sigma = 14.43$. (See Section 4.8 for the formulas for μ and σ.) Now suppose a sample of 11 measurements is selected from this population. Describe the sampling distribution of the sample mean $\bar{x}$ based on the 1,000 sampling experiments discussed in Example 5.3.

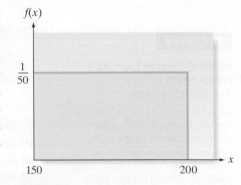

Figure 5.8
Sampled uniform population

Solution You will recall that in Example 5.3 we generated 1,000 samples of $n = 11$ measurements each. The Minitab histogram for the 1,000 sample means is shown in Figure 5.9 with a normal probability distribution superimposed. You can see that this normal probability distribution approximates the computer-generated sampling distribution very well.

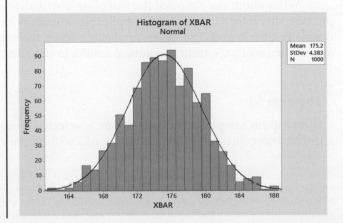

Figure 5.9
Minitab histogram for sample mean in 1,000 samples

To fully describe a normal probability distribution, it is necessary to know its mean and standard deviation. Minitab gives these statistics for the 1,000 $\bar{x}$'s in the upper right corner of the histogram, Figure 5.9. You can see that the mean is 175.2, and the standard deviation is 4.383.

To summarize our findings based on 1,000 samples, each consisting of 11 measurements from a uniform population, the sampling distribution of $\bar{x}$ appears to be approximately normal with a mean of about 175 and a standard deviation of about 4.38.

Look Back Note that the simulated value $\mu_{\bar{x}} = 175.2$ is very close to $\mu = 175$ for the uniform distribution—that is, the simulated sampling distribution of $\bar{x}$ appears to provide an accurate estimate of μ.

The true sampling distribution of $\bar{x}$ has the properties given in the next box, assuming only that a random sample of n observations has been selected from *any* population.

Properties of the Sampling Distribution of $\bar{x}$

1. Mean of sampling distribution equals mean of sampled population, that is, $\mu_{\bar{x}} = E(\bar{x}) = \mu$.

2. Standard deviation of sampling distribution equals

$$\frac{\text{Standard deviation of sampled population}}{\text{Square root of sample size}}$$

That is, $\sigma_{\bar{x}} = \sigma/\sqrt{n}$.*

The standard deviation $\sigma_{\bar{x}}$ is often referred to as the **standard error of the mean.**

You can see that our approximation to $\mu_{\bar{x}}$ in Example 5.7 was precise because property 1 assures us that the mean is the same as that of the sampled population: 175. Property 2 tells us how to calculate the standard deviation of the sampling distribution of $\bar{x}$. Substituting $\sigma = 14.43$, the standard deviation of the sampled uniform distribution, and the sample size $n = 11$ into the formula for $\sigma_{\bar{x}}$, we find

$$\sigma_{\bar{x}} = \frac{\sigma}{\sqrt{n}} = \frac{14.43}{\sqrt{11}} = 4.35$$

Thus, the approximation we obtained in Example 5.7, $\sigma_{\bar{x}} = 4.38$, is very close to the exact value, $\sigma_{\bar{x}} = 4.35$. It can be shown (proof omitted) that the value of $\sigma_{\bar{x}}^2$ is the smallest variance among all unbiased estimators of μ; thus, $\bar{x}$ is the MVUE for μ.

What about the shape of the sampling distribution of $\bar{x}$? Two important theorems provide this information. One is applicable whenever the original population data are normally distributed. The other, applicable when the sample size n is large, represents one of the most important theoretical results in statistics: the **Central Limit Theorem.**

Theorem 5.1

If a random sample of n observations is selected from a population with a normal distribution, the sampling distribution of $\bar{x}$ will be a normal distribution.

---

*If the sample size, n, is large relative to the number, N, of elements in the population (e.g., 5% or more), $\sigma/\sqrt{n}$ must be multiplied by a finite population correction factor, $\sqrt{(N-n)/(N-1)}$. For most sampling situations, this correction factor will be close to 1 and can be ignored.

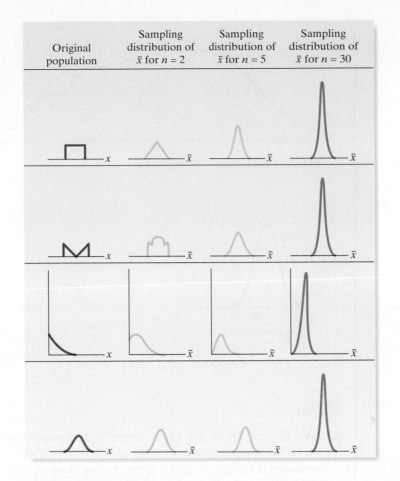

Figure 5.10

Sampling distributions of $\bar{x}$ for different populations and different sample sizes (*Note*: Distributions not drawn to scale. All areas under the curves are equal to 1.)

Theorem 5.2 (Central Limit Theorem)

Consider a random sample of n observations selected from a population (*any* probability distribution) with mean μ and standard deviation σ. Then, when n is sufficiently large, the sampling distribution of $\bar{x}$ will be approximately a normal distribution with mean $\mu_{\bar{x}} = \mu$ and standard deviation $\sigma_{\bar{x}} = \sigma/\sqrt{n}$. The larger the sample size, the better will be the normal approximation to the sampling distribution of $\bar{x}$.*

Thus, for sufficiently large samples, the sampling distribution of $\bar{x}$ is approximately normal. How large must the sample size n be so that the normal distribution provides a good approximation for the sampling distribution of $\bar{x}$? The answer depends on the shape of the distribution of the sampled population, as shown by Figure 5.10. Generally speaking, the greater the skewness of the sampled population distribution, the larger the sample size must be before the normal distribution is an adequate approximation for the sampling distribution of $\bar{x}$. For most sampled populations, sample sizes of $n \geq 30$ will suffice for the normal approximation to be reasonable.

EXAMPLE 5.8	
Using the Central Limit Theorem to Find a Probability	**Problem** Suppose we have selected a random sample of $n = 36$ observations from a population with mean equal to 80 and standard deviation equal to 6. It is known that the population is not extremely skewed.

a. Sketch the relative frequency distributions for the population and for the sampling distribution of the sample mean, $\bar{x}$.

b. Find the probability that $\bar{x}$ will be larger than 82.

*Moreover, because of the Central Limit Theorem, the sum of a random sample on n observations, Σx, will possess a sampling distribution that is approximately normal for large samples. This distribution will have a mean equal to $n\mu$ and a variance equal to $n\sigma^2$. Proof of the Central Limit Theorem is beyond the scope of this book, but it can be found in many mathematical statistics texts.

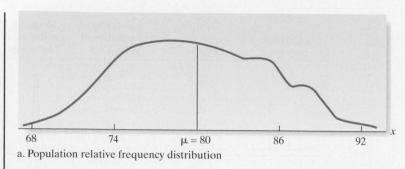

a. Population relative frequency distribution

Figure 5.11

A population relative frequency distribution and the sampling distribution for $\bar{x}$

b. Sampling distribution of $\bar{x}$

Solution

a. We do not know the exact shape of the population relative frequency distribution, but we do know that it should be centered about $\mu = 80$, its spread should be measured by $\sigma = 6$, and it is not highly skewed. One possibility is shown in Figure 5.11a. From the Central Limit Theorem, we know that the sampling distribution of $\bar{x}$ will be approximately normal because the sampled population distribution is not extremely skewed. We also know that the sampling distribution will have mean and standard deviation

$$\mu_{\bar{x}} = \mu = 80 \quad \text{and} \quad \sigma_{\bar{x}} = \frac{\sigma}{\sqrt{n}} = \frac{6}{\sqrt{36}} = 1$$

The sampling distribution of $\bar{x}$ is shown in Figure 5.11b.

b. The probability that $\bar{x}$ will exceed 82 is equal to the darker shaded area in Figure 5.12. To find this area, we need to find the z value corresponding to $\bar{x} = 82$. Recall that the standard normal random variable z is the difference between any normally distributed random variable and its mean, expressed in units of its standard deviation. Because $\bar{x}$ is approximately a normally distributed random variable with mean $\mu_{\bar{x}} = \mu$ and $\sigma_{\bar{x}} = \sigma/\sqrt{n}$, it follows that the standard normal z value corresponding to the sample mean, $\bar{x}$, is

$$z = \frac{(\text{Normal random variable}) - (\text{Mean})}{\text{Standard deviation}} = \frac{\bar{x} - \mu_{\bar{x}}}{\sigma_{\bar{x}}}$$

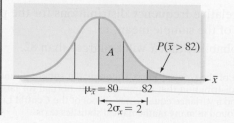

Figure 5.12

The sampling distribution of $\bar{x}$

Therefore, for $\bar{x} = 82$, we have

$$z = \frac{\bar{x} - \mu_{\bar{x}}}{\sigma_{\bar{x}}} = \frac{82 - 80}{1} = 2$$

The area A in Figure 5.12 corresponding to $z = 2$ is given in the table of areas under the normal curve (see Table II in Appendix D) as .4772. Therefore, the tail area corresponding to the probability that $\bar{x}$ exceeds 82 is

$$P(\bar{x} > 82) = P(z > 2) = .5 - .4772 = .0228$$

Look Back The key to finding the probability, part **b,** is to recognize that the distribution of $\bar{x}$ is normal with mean $\mu_{\bar{x}} = \mu$ and $\sigma_{\bar{x}} = \sigma/\sqrt{n}$.

● **Now Work Exercises 5.18–5.19**

EXAMPLE 5.9

Application of the Central Limit Theorem–Testing a Manufacturer's Claim

Problem A manufacturer of automobile batteries claims that the distribution of the lengths of life of its best battery has a mean of 54 months and a standard deviation of 6 months. Recently, the manufacturer has received a rash of complaints from unsatisfied customers whose batteries have died earlier than expected. Suppose a consumer group decides to check the manufacturer's claim by purchasing a sample of 50 of these batteries and subjecting them to tests that determine battery life.

a. Assuming that the manufacturer's claim is true, describe the sampling distribution of the mean lifetime of a sample of 50 batteries.

b. Assuming that the manufacturer's claim is true, what is the probability that the consumer group's sample has a mean life of 52 or fewer months?

Solution

a. Even though we have no information about the shape of the probability distribution of the lives of the batteries, we can use the Central Limit Theorem to deduce that the sampling distribution for a sample mean lifetime of 50 batteries is approximately normally distributed. Furthermore, the mean of this sampling distribution is the same as the mean of the sampled population, which is $\mu = 54$ months according to the manufacturer's claim. Finally, the standard deviation of the sampling distribution is given by

$$\sigma_{\bar{x}} = \frac{\sigma}{\sqrt{n}} = \frac{6}{\sqrt{50}} = .85 \text{ month}$$

Note that we used the claimed standard deviation of the sampled population, $\sigma = 6$ months. Thus, if we assume that the claim is true, the sampling distribution for the mean life of the 50 batteries sampled is as shown in Figure 5.13.

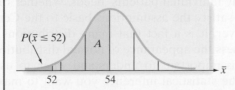

Figure 5.13
Sampling distribution of $\bar{x}$ in Example 5.9 for $n = 50$

b. If the manufacturer's claim is true, the probability that the consumer group observes a mean battery life of 52 or fewer months for their sample of 50 batteries, $P(\bar{x} \leq 52)$, is equivalent to the darker shaded area in Figure 5.13. Because the sampling distribution is approximately normal, we can find this area by computing the standard normal z value:

$$z = \frac{\bar{x} - \mu_{\bar{x}}}{\sigma_{\bar{x}}} = \frac{52 - 54}{.85} = -2.35$$

where $\mu_{\bar{x}}$, the mean of the sampling distribution of $\bar{x}$, is equal to μ, the mean of the lives of the sampled population, and $\sigma_{\bar{x}}$ is the standard deviation of the sampling distribution of $\bar{x}$. Note that z is the familiar standardized distance (z-score) of Section 2.7 and because $\bar{x}$ is approximately normally distributed, it will possess (approximately) the standard normal distribution of Section 4.6.

The area A shown in Figure 5.13 between $\bar{x} = 52$ and $\bar{x} = 54$ (corresponding to $z = -2.35$) is found in Table II in Appendix D to be .4906. Therefore, the area to the left of $\bar{x} = 52$ is

$$P(\bar{x} \leq 52) = .5 - A = .5 - .4906 = .0094$$

Thus, the probability that the consumer group will observe a sample mean of 52 or less is only .0094 if the manufacturer's claim is true.

Look Back If the 50 tested batteries do exhibit a mean of 52 or fewer months, the consumer group will have strong evidence that the manufacturer's claim is untrue because such an event is very unlikely to occur if the claim is true. (This is still another application of the *rare-event approach to statistical inference*.)

● **Now Work Exercise 5.24**

We conclude this section with three final comments on the sampling distribution of $\bar{x}$. First, from the formula $\sigma_{\bar{x}} = \sigma/\sqrt{n}$, we see that the standard deviation of the sampling distribution of $\bar{x}$ gets smaller as the sample size n gets larger. For example, we computed $\sigma_{\bar{x}} = .85$ when $n = 50$ in Example 5.9. However, for $n = 100$, we obtain $\sigma_{\bar{x}} = \sigma/\sqrt{n} = 6/\sqrt{100} = .60$. This relationship will hold true for most of the sample statistics encountered in this text–that is, *the standard deviation of the sampling distribution decreases as the sample size increases*. Consequently, the larger the sample size, the more accurate the sample statistic (e.g., $\bar{x}$) is in estimating a population parameter (e.g., μ). We will use this result in Chapter 6 to help us determine the sample size needed to obtain a specified accuracy of estimation.

Our second comment concerns the Central Limit Theorem. In addition to providing a very useful approximation for the sampling distribution of a sample mean, the *Central Limit Theorem offers an explanation for the fact that many relative frequency distributions of data possess mound-shaped distributions*. Many of the measurements we take in business are really means or sums of a large number of small phenomena. For example, a company's sales for 1 year are the total of the many individual sales the company made during the year. Similarly, we can view the length of time a construction company takes to build a house as the total of the times taken to complete a multitude of distinct jobs, and we can regard the monthly demand for blood at a hospital as the total of the many individual patients' needs. Whether or not the observations entering into these sums satisfy the assumptions basic to the Central Limit Theorem is open to question. However, it is a fact that many distributions of data in nature are mound-shaped and possess the appearance of normal distributions.

Finally, it is important to understand when to use σ or $\sigma/\sqrt{n}$ in your statistical analysis. If the statistical inference you want to make concerns a single value of a random variable—for example, *the life length x of one randomly selected battery*—then use σ, the standard deviation of the probability distribution for x in your calculations. Alternatively, if the statistical inference you want to make concerns the sample mean— for example, *the mean life length $\bar{x}$ for a random sample of n batteries*—then use $\sigma/\sqrt{n}$, the standard deviation of the sampling distribution of $\bar{x}$.

STATISTICS IN ACTION REVISITED

Making an Inference About the Mean Sleep Onset Latency for Insomnia Pill Takers

In a Massachusetts Institute of Technology (MIT) study, each member of a sample of 40 young male volunteers was given a dosage of the sleep-inducing hormone melatonin, placed in a dark room at midday, then instructed to close his eyes for 30 minutes. The researchers measured the time (in minutes) elapsed before each volunteer fell asleep—called sleep onset latency. Recall that the data (shown in Table SIA5.1) are saved in the **SLEEP** file.

Previous research established that with a placebo (i.e., no hormone), the mean sleep onset latency is $\mu = 15$ minutes and the standard deviation is $\sigma = 10$ minutes. If the true value of μ for those taking the melatonin is $\mu < 15$ (i.e., if, on average, the volunteers fall asleep faster with the drug than with the placebo), then the researchers can infer that melatonin is an effective drug against insomnia.

Descriptive statistics for the 40 sleep times are displayed in the SPSS printout shown in Figure SIA5.1. You can see that the mean for the sample is $\bar{x} = 5.935$ minutes. If the drug is not effective in reducing sleep times, then the distribution of sleep times will be no different from the distribution with the placebo. That is, if the drug is not effective, the mean and standard deviation of the population of sleep times are $\mu = 15$ and $\sigma = 10$. If this is true, how likely is it to observe a sample mean that is below 6 minutes?

Descriptive Statistics

	N	Minimum	Maximum	Mean	Std. Deviation
SLEEPTIME	40	1.3	22.8	5.935	5.3917
Valid N (listwise)	40				

Figure SIA5.1

SPSS descriptive statistics for sleep time data

To answer this question, we desire the probability $P(\bar{x} < 6)$. To find this probability, we invoke the Central Limit Theorem. According to the theorem, the sampling distribution of $\bar{x}$ has the following mean and standard deviation:

$$\mu_{\bar{x}} = \mu = 15$$

$$\sigma_{\bar{x}} = \sigma/\sqrt{n} = 10/\sqrt{40} = 1.58$$

The theorem also states that $\bar{x}$ is approximately normally distributed. Therefore, we find the desired probability (using the standard normal table) as follows:

$$P(\bar{x} < 6) = P\left(z < \frac{6 - \mu_{\bar{x}}}{\sigma_{\bar{x}}}\right)$$

$$= P\left(z < \frac{6 - 15}{1.58}\right) = P(z < -5.70) \approx 0$$

In other words, the probability that we observe a sample mean below $\bar{x} = 6$ minutes *if the mean and standard deviation of the sleep times are,* respectively, $\mu = 15$ and $\sigma = 10$ *(i.e., if the drug is not effective),* is almost 0. Therefore, either the drug is not effective and the researchers have observed an extremely rare event (one with almost no chance of happening), or the true value of μ for those taking the melatonin pill is much less than 15 minutes. The rare-event approach to making statistical inferences, of course, would favor the second conclusion. Melatonin appears to be an effective insomnia pill, one that lowers the average time it takes the volunteers to fall asleep.

 Data Set: SLEEP

Exercises 5.15–5.35

Learning the Mechanics

5.15 Will the sampling distribution of $\bar{x}$ always be approximately normally distributed? Explain.

5.16 Suppose a random sample of $n = 25$ measurements is selected from a population with mean μ and standard deviation σ. For each of the following values of μ and σ, give the values of $\mu_{\bar{x}}$ and $\sigma_{\bar{x}}$.
  a. $\mu = 10, \sigma = 3$
  b. $\mu = 100, \sigma = 25$
  c. $\mu = 20, \sigma = 40$
  d. $\mu = 10, \sigma = 100$

5.17 Suppose a random sample of n measurements is selected from a population with mean $\mu = 100$ and variance $\sigma^2 = 100$. For each of the following values of n, give the mean and standard deviation of the sampling distribution of the sample mean $\bar{x}$.
  a. $n = 4$ **b.** $n = 25$
  c. $n = 100$ **d.** $n = 50$
  e. $n = 500$ **f.** $n = 1,000$

5.18 A random sample of $n = 64$ observations is drawn from a population with a mean equal to 20 and a standard deviation equal to 16.
  a. Give the mean and standard deviation of the (repeated) sampling distribution of $\bar{x}$.
  b. Describe the shape of the sampling distribution of $\bar{x}$. Does your answer depend on the sample size?
  c. Calculate the standard normal z-score corresponding to a value of $\bar{x} = 15.5$.
  d. Calculate the standard normal z-score corresponding to $\bar{x} = 23$.

5.19 Refer to Exercise 5.18. Find the probability that
  a. $\bar{x}$ is less than 16.
  b. $\bar{x}$ is greater than 23.
  c. $\bar{x}$ is greater than 25.
  d. $\bar{x}$ falls between 16 and 22.
  e. $\bar{x}$ is less than 14.

5.20 A random sample of $n = 900$ observations is selected from a population with $\mu = 100$ and $\sigma = 10$.
  a. What are the largest and smallest values of $\bar{x}$ that you would expect to see?
  b. How far, at the most, would you expect $\bar{x}$ to deviate from μ?
  c. Did you have to know μ to answer part **b**? Explain.

5.21 A random sample of $n = 100$ observations is selected from a population with $\mu = 30$ and $\sigma = 16$. Approximate the following probabilities:
  a. $P(\bar{x} \geq 28)$
  b. $P(22.1 \leq \bar{x} \leq 26.8)$
  c. $P(\bar{x} \leq 28.2)$
  d. $P(\bar{x} \geq 27.0)$

5.22 Consider a population that contains values of x equal to 0, 1, 2, . . . , 97, 98, 99. Assume that the values of x are equally likely. For each of the following values of n, use a computer to generate 500 random samples and calculate $\bar{x}$ for each sample. For each sample size, construct a relative frequency histogram of the 500 values of $\bar{x}$. What changes occur in the histograms as the value of n increases? What similarities exist? Use $n = 2, n = 5, n = 10, n = 30,$ and $n = 50$.

Applet Exercise 5.1

Open the applet *Sampling Distributions*. On the pull-down menu to the right of the top graph, select *Binary*.
  a. Run the applet for the sample size $n = 10$ and the number of samples $N = 1,000$. Observe the shape of the graph of the sample proportions and record the mean, median, and standard deviation of the sample proportions.
  b. How does the mean of the sample proportions compare with the mean $\mu = 0.5$ of the original distribution?
  c. Compute the standard deviation of the original distribution using the formula $\sigma = \sqrt{np(1 - p)}$ where $n = 1$ and $p = 0.5$. Divide the result by $\sqrt{10}$, the square root of the sample size used in the sampling distribution. How does this result compare with the standard deviation of the sample proportions?
  d. Explain how the graph of the distribution of sample proportions suggests that the distribution may be approximately normal.
  e. Explain how the results of parts **b–d** illustrate the Central Limit Theorem.

Applet Exercise 5.2

Open the applet *Sampling Distributions*. On the pull-down menu to the right of the top graph, select *Uniform*. The box to the left of the top graph displays the population mean, median, and standard deviation of the original distribution.
  a. Run the applet for the sample size $n = 30$ and the number of samples $N = 1,000$. Observe the shape of the graph of the sample means and record the mean, median, and standard deviation of the sample means.
  b. How does the mean of the sample means compare with the mean of the original distribution?
  c. Divide the standard deviation of the original distribution by $\sqrt{30}$, the square root of the sample size used in the sampling distribution. How does this result compare with the standard deviation of the sample proportions?
  d. Explain how the graph of the distribution of sample means suggests that the distribution may be approximately normal.
  e. Explain how the results of parts **b–d** illustrate the Central Limit Theorem.

Applying the Concepts—Basic

5.23 **Voltage sags and swells.** Refer to the *Electrical Engineering* (Vol. 95, 2013) study of the power quality (sags and swells) of a transformer, Exercise 2.76 (p. 110). For transformers built for heavy industry, the distribution of the number of sags per week has a mean of 353 with a standard deviation of 30. Of interest is $\bar{x}$, the sample mean number of sags per week for a random sample of 45 transformers.
  a. Find $E(\bar{x})$ and interpret its value.
  b. Find $Var(\bar{x})$.
  c. Describe the shape of the sampling distribution of $\bar{x}$.
  d. How likely is it to observe a sample mean number of sags per week that exceeds 400?

5.24 **Salary of a travel management professional.** According to the most recent Global Business Travel Association (GBTA) survey, the average base salary of a U.S. travel

management professional is $94,000. Assume that the standard deviation of such salaries is $30,000. Consider a random sample of 50 travel management professionals and let $\bar{x}$ represent the mean salary for the sample.
  a. What is $\mu_{\bar{x}}$?
  b. What is $\sigma_{\bar{x}}$?
  c. Describe the shape of the sampling distribution of $\bar{x}$.
  d. Find the z-score for the value $\bar{x} = 86,660$.
  e. Find $P(\bar{x} > 86,660)$.

5.25 **Corporate sustainability of CPA firms.** Refer to the *Business and Society* (March 2011) study on the sustainability behaviors of CPA corporations, Exercise 1.28 (p. 51). *Corporate sustainability*, recall, refers to business practices designed around social and environmental considerations. The level of support senior managers have for corporate sustainability was measured quantitatively on a scale ranging from 0 to 160 points. The study provided the following information on the distribution of levels of support for sustainability: $\mu = 68$, $\sigma = 27$. Now consider a random sample of 45 senior managers and let $\bar{x}$ represent the sample mean level of support.
  a. Give the value of $\mu_{\bar{x}}$, the mean of the sampling distribution of $\bar{x}$, and interpret the result.
  b. Give the value of $\sigma_{\bar{x}}$, the standard deviation of the sampling distribution of $\bar{x}$, and interpret the result.
  c. What does the Central Limit Theorem say about the shape of the sampling distribution of $\bar{x}$?
  d. Find $P(\bar{x} > 65)$.

5.26 **Critical-part failures in NASCAR vehicles.** Refer to *The Sport Journal* (Winter 2007) analysis of critical-part failures at NASCAR races, Exercise 4.144 (p. 277). Recall that researchers found that the time x (in hours) until the first critical-part failure is exponentially distributed with $\mu = .10$ and $\sigma = .10$. Now consider a random sample of $n = 50$ NASCAR races and let $\bar{x}$ represent the sample mean time until the first critical-part failure.
  a. Find $E(\bar{x})$ and $\text{Var}(\bar{x})$.
  b. Although x has an exponential distribution, the sampling distribution of $\bar{x}$ is approximately normal. Why?
  c. Find the probability that the sample mean time until the first critical-part failure exceeds .13 hour.

5.27 **Tomato as a taste modifier.** Miraculin is a protein naturally produced in a rare tropical fruit that can convert a sour taste into a sweet taste. Refer to the *Plant Science* (May 2010) investigation of the ability of a hybrid tomato plant to produce miraculin, Exercise 4.99 (p. 263). Recall that the amount x of miraculin produced in the plant had a mean of 105.3 micrograms per gram of fresh weight with a standard deviation of 8.0. Consider a random sample of $n = 64$ hybrid tomato plants and let $\bar{x}$ represent the sample mean amount of miraculin produced. Would you expect to observe a value of $\bar{x}$ less than 103 micrograms per gram of fresh weight? Explain.

Applying the Concepts—Intermediate

5.28 **Variable life insurance return rates.** Refer to the *International Journal of Statistical Distributions* (Vol. 1, 2015) study of a variable life insurance policy, Exercise 4.97 (p. 262). Recall that a ratio (x) of the rates of return on the investment for two consecutive years was shown to have a normal distribution, with $\mu = 1.5$ and $\sigma = .2$. Consider a random sample of 100 variable life insurance policies and let $\bar{x}$ represent the mean ratio for the sample.

  a. Find $E(\bar{x})$ and interpret its value.
  b. Find $\text{Var}(\bar{x})$.
  c. Describe the shape of the sampling distribution of $\bar{x}$.
  d. Find the z-score for the value $\bar{x} = 1.52$.
  e. Find $P(\bar{x} > 1.52)$.
  f. Would your answers to parts **a–e** change if the rates (x) of return on the investment for two consecutive years was not normally distributed? Explain.

5.29 **Levelness of concrete slabs.** Geotechnical engineers use water-level "manometer" surveys to assess the levelness of newly constructed concrete slabs. Elevations are typically measured at eight points on the slab; of interest is the maximum differential between elevations. The *Journal of Performance of Constructed Facilities* (February 2005) published an article on the levelness of slabs in California residential developments. Elevation data collected for more than 1,300 concrete slabs *before tensioning* revealed that maximum differential, x, has a mean of $\mu = .53$ inch and a standard deviation of $\sigma = .193$ inch. Consider a sample of $n = 50$ slabs selected from those surveyed and let $\bar{x}$ represent the mean of the sample.
  a. Fully describe the sampling distribution of $\bar{x}$.
  b. Find $P(\bar{x} > .58)$.
  c. The study also revealed that the mean maximum differential of concrete slabs measured *after tensioning and loading* is $\mu = .58$ inch. Suppose the sample data yield $\bar{x} = .59$ inch. Comment on whether the sample measurements were obtained before tensioning or after tensioning and loading.

5.30 **Video game players and divided attention tasks.** *Human Factors* (May 2014) published the results of a study designed to determine whether video game players are better than non–video game players at crossing the street when presented with distractions. Participants (college students) entered a street-crossing simulator. The simulator was designed to have cars traveling at various high rates of speed in both directions. During the crossing, the students also performed a memory task as a distraction. The researchers found that students who are video game players took an average of 5.1 seconds to cross the street, with a standard deviation of .8 second. Assume that the time, x, to cross the street for the population of video game players has $\mu = 5.1$ and $\sigma = .8$. Now consider a sample of 30 students and let $\bar{x}$ represent the sample mean time (in seconds) to cross the street in the simulator.
  a. Find $P(\bar{x} > 5.5)$.
  b. The 30 students in the sample are all non–video game players. What inference can you make about μ and/or σ for the population of non–video game players? Explain.

5.31 **Exposure to a chemical in Teflon-coated cookware.** Perfluorooctanoic acid (PFOA) is a chemical used in Teflon-coated cookware to prevent food from sticking. The EPA is investigating the potential risk of PFOA as a cancer-causing agent (*Science News Online*, August 27, 2005). It is known that the blood concentration of PFOA in people in the general population has a mean of $\mu = 6$ parts per billion (ppb) and a standard deviation of $\sigma = 10$ ppb. *Science News Online* reported on tests for PFOA exposure conducted on a sample of 326 people who live near DuPont's Teflon-making Washington (West Virginia) Works facility.
  a. What is the probability that the average blood concentration of PFOA in the sample is greater than 7.5 ppb?

b. The actual study resulted in $\bar{x} = 300$ ppb. Use this information to make an inference about the true mean μ PFOA concentration for the population of people who live near DuPont's Teflon facility.

5.32 **Rental car fleet evaluation.** National Car Rental Systems, Inc., commissioned the U.S. Automobile Club (USAC) to conduct a survey of the general condition of the cars rented to the public by Hertz, Avis, National, and Budget Rent-a-Car.* USAC officials evaluate each company's cars using a demerit point system. Each car starts with a perfect score of 0 points and incurs demerit points for each discrepancy noted by the inspectors. One measure of the overall condition of a company's cars is the mean of all scores received by the company (i.e., the company's *fleet mean score*). To estimate the fleet mean score of each rental car company, 10 major airports were randomly selected, and 10 cars from each company were randomly rented for inspection from each airport by USAC officials (i.e., a sample of size $n = 100$ cars from each company's fleet was drawn and inspected).

a. Describe the sampling distribution of $\bar{x}$, the mean score of a sample of $n = 100$ rental cars.

b. Interpret the mean of $\bar{x}$ in the context of this problem.

c. Assume $\mu = 30$ and $\sigma = 60$ for one rental car company. For this company, find $P(\bar{x} \geq 45)$.

d. Refer to part **c**. The company claims that their true fleet mean score "couldn't possibly be as high as 30." The sample mean score tabulated by USAC for this company was 45. Does this result tend to support or refute the claim? Explain.

5.33 **Phishing attacks to e-mail accounts.** In Exercise 2.33 (p. 86), you learned that *phishing* describes an attempt to extract personal/financial information from unsuspecting people through fraudulent e-mail. Data from an actual phishing attack against an organization were presented in *Chance* (Summer 2007). The interarrival times, i.e., the time differences (in seconds), for 267 fraud box e-mail notifications, were recorded and are saved in the accompanying file. For this exercise, consider these interarrival times to represent the population of interest.

a. In Exercise 2.33 you constructed a histogram for the interarrival times. Describe the shape of the population of interarrival times.

b. Find the mean and standard deviation of the population of interarrival times.

*Information by personal communication with Rajiv Tandon, corporate vice president and general manager of the Car Rental Division, National Car Rental Systems, Inc., Minneapolis, Minnesota.

c. Now consider a random sample of $n = 40$ interarrival times selected from the population. Describe the shape of the sampling distribution of $\bar{x}$, the sample mean. Theoretically, what are $\mu_{\bar{x}}$ and $\sigma_{\bar{x}}$?

d. Find $P(\bar{x} < 90)$.

e. Use a random number generator to select a random sample of $n = 40$ interarrival times from the population, and calculate the value of $\bar{x}$. (Every student in the class should do this.)

f. Refer to part **e**. Obtain the values of $\bar{x}$ computed by the students and combine them into a single data set. Form a histogram for these values of $\bar{x}$. Is the shape approximately normal?

g. Refer to part **f**. Find the mean and standard deviation of the $\bar{x}$ values. Do these values approximate $\mu_{\bar{x}}$ and $\sigma_{\bar{x}}$, respectively?

Applying the Concepts—Advanced

5.34 **Plastic fill process.** University of Louisville researchers examined the process of filling plastic pouches of dry blended biscuit mix (*Quality Engineering*, Vol. 91, 1996). The current fill mean of the process is set at $\mu = 406$ grams, and the process fill standard deviation is $\sigma = 10.1$ grams. (According to the researchers, "The high level of variation is due to the fact that the product has poor flow properties and is, therefore, difficult to fill consistently from pouch to pouch.") Operators monitor the process by randomly sampling 36 pouches each day and measuring the amount of biscuit mix in each. Consider $\bar{x}$, the mean fill amount of the sample of 36 products. Suppose that on one particular day, the operators observe $\bar{x} = 400.8$. One of the operators believes that this indicates that the true process fill mean μ for that day is less than 406 grams. Another operator argues that $\mu = 406$, and the small value of $\bar{x}$ observed is due to random variation in the fill process. Which operator do you agree with? Why?

5.35 **Handwashing vs. handrubbing.** The *British Medical Journal* (August 17, 2002) published the results of a study to compare the effectiveness of handwashing with soap and handrubbing with alcohol. Health care workers who used handrubbing had a mean bacterial count of 35 per hand with a standard deviation of 59. Health care workers who used handwashing had a mean bacterial count of 69 per hand with a standard deviation of 106. In a random sample of 50 health care workers, all using the same method of cleaning their hands, the mean bacterial count per hand, $\bar{x}$, is less than 30. Give your opinion on whether this sample of workers used handrubbing with alcohol or handwashing with soap.

5.4 The Sampling Distribution of the Sample Proportion

Suppose you want to estimate the proportion of voters in favor of a bill to legalize gambling in your state, or the percentage of store customers who use a store credit card to make a purchase, or the fraction of company CEOs who defer their annual pay. In each case, the data of interest are categorical in nature with two outcomes (e.g., favor or do not favor); consequently, we want to make an inference about a binomial proportion, p.

Just as the sample mean is a good estimator of the population mean, the sample proportion—denoted $\hat{p}$— is a good estimator of the population proportion p. How good the estimator $\hat{p}$ is will depend on the sampling distribution of the statistic. This sampling distribution has properties similar to those of the sampling distribution of $\bar{x}$, as shown in the following example.

EXAMPLE 5.10

Simulating the
Sampling Distribution of
$\hat{p}$—Worker Unionization

Problem Refer to Example 4.13 (p. 235) and the problem of sampling workers to determine whether they are in favor of unionization. We assumed that 60% of all workers at a large plant were, in fact, in favor of unionization. Suppose we will randomly sample 100 plant workers and ask each if he or she is or is not in favor of unionization. Use a computer and statistical software to simulate the sampling distribution of $\hat{p}$, the sample proportion of workers in favor of unionization. What properties do you observe?

Solution Consider a single random sample of 100 workers. If we define a "success" as a worker in favor of unionization, and if 58 of the 100 are in favor of unionization, then our estimate of the binomial proportion p is $\hat{p} = 58/100 = .58$. By repeatedly taking samples in this manner and calculating $\hat{p}$ each time, we can simulate the sampling distribution.

We used SPSS to generate 1,000 samples of size $n = 100$ from a binomial population with probability of success $p = .6$. For each sample, we calculated $\hat{p} = x/n$, where x is the number of successes in the sample. The estimated proportions for the first 20 samples are shown in Table 5.5. An SPSS histogram for all 1,000 estimated proportions is shown in Figure 5.14. This histogram approximates the sampling distribution of $\hat{p}$.

Table 5.5	Results for First 20 Samples of $n = 100$ Workers	
Sample	Number of Success, x	Sample Proportion, $\hat{p}$
1	60	.60
2	58	.58
3	56	.56
4	61	.61
5	54	.54
6	67	.67
7	54	.54
8	55	.55
9	56	.56
10	69	.69
11	59	.59
12	64	.64
13	53	.53
14	65	.65
15	66	.66
16	61	.61
17	60	.60
18	55	.55
19	57	.57
20	61	.61

Figure 5.14

SPSS histogram of 1,000 values of
$\hat{p}$, Example 5.10

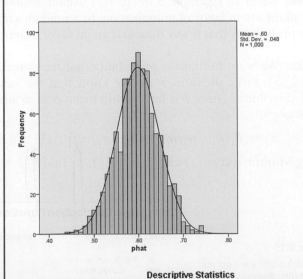

Descriptive Statistics

	N	Minimum	Maximum	Mean	Std. Deviation
phat	1000	.44	.74	.5988	.04823
Valid N (listwise)	1000				

First, note that the sampling distribution appears to be normally distributed. Thus, the sampling distribution of $\hat{p}$ has the same property as the sampling distribution of $\bar{x}$—normally distributed for large n. Second, you can see that the sampling distribution is centered around the value $p = .6$. That is, it appears that the mean of the sampling distribution is equal to p, the proportion being estimated.

Look Back The normal distribution property identified with computer simulation becomes obvious once you recognize that the sample proportion $\hat{p}$ can be written as an average of 0s and 1s, where 1 represents a "success" (a worker in favor of unionization) and 0 represents a "failure" (a worker not in favor of unionization). In the first sample shown in Table 5.5, there were 60 successes and 40 failures; thus

$$\hat{p} = \frac{(60)(1) + (40)(0)}{100} = 60/100 = .60$$

Since $\hat{p}$ is a mean, the Central Limit Theorem can be applied when the sample size n is large.

The true sampling distribution of $\hat{p}$ has the properties listed in the next box.

Sampling Distribution of $\hat{p}$

1. Mean of the sampling distribution is equal to the true binomial proportion, p; that is, $E(\hat{p}) = p$. Consequently, $\hat{p}$ is an unbiased estimator of p.
2. Standard deviation of the sampling distribution is equal to $\sqrt{p(1-p)/n}$; that is, $\sigma_{\hat{p}} = \sqrt{p(1-p)/n}$.
3. For large samples, the sampling distribution is approximately normal. (A sample is considered large if $n\hat{p} \geq 15$ and $n(1-\hat{p}) \geq 15$.)

In Example 5.10, $p = .6$. Thus, the true mean of the sampling distribution of $\hat{p}$ is equal to .6. Also, the true standard deviation of the sampling distribution of $\hat{p}$ is

$$\sigma_{\hat{p}} = \sqrt{p(1-p)/n} = \sqrt{(.6)(.4)/100} = .049$$

Note that our estimates of the mean and standard deviation using simulation—.599 and .048, respectively—closely approximate the true values.

EXAMPLE 5.11

Finding a Probability Involving $\hat{p}$—Workers in Favor of Unionization

Problem Refer to Example 5.10 (p. 317). Again, assume that 60% of all workers at a large plant are in favor of unionization. In a random sample of 100 plant workers, what is the probability that fewer than half are in favor of unionization?

Solution We want to find the probability that the sample proportion is less than .5, i.e., $P(\hat{p} < .5)$. From previous work, we know that the sampling distribution of $\hat{p}$ is normally distributed (since n is large), with mean $p = .6$ and standard deviation $\sigma_{\hat{p}} = .049$. Consequently,

$$P(\hat{p} < .5) = P\{(\hat{p} - p)/\sigma_{\hat{p}} < (.5 - p)/\sigma_{\hat{p}}\} = P\{z < (.5 - .6)/.049\} = P(z < -2.04)$$

Using Minitab software (see Figure 5.15), we find $P(\hat{p} < .5) = P(z < -2.04) = .021$.

Figure 5.15

Minitab output for a normal probability, Example 5.11

```
Cumulative Distribution Function

Normal with mean = 0 and standard deviation = 1

    x    P( X <= x )
-2.04    0.0206752
```

Now Work Exercise 5.39

In the next two chapters, we utilize the sampling distributions of both $\bar{x}$ and $\hat{p}$ to make inferences about population means and proportions.

STATISTICS IN ACTION

REVISITED

Making an Inference About the Proportion of Insomnia Pill Takers with Sleep Onset Latency of Less Than 15 Minutes

We now return to the study on sleep onset latency of volunteers who were given a dosage of the sleep-inducing hormone melatonin. In addition to the time taken to fall asleep in midday, the researchers also recorded whether or not the volunteer took less than 15 minutes to fall asleep. (The variable *LESS15* was recorded as "Yes" or "No" in the **SLEEP** data file.)

Recall that 15 minutes is the average sleep onset latency when no pill (placebo) is taken. Assume that with the placebo, half the volunteers will take less than 15 minutes to fall asleep and half will take more than 15 minutes. (This is assuming the mean of the distribution of sleep onset latency is equal to the median.) If the insomnia drug is truly effective in reducing sleep onset latency, then the true proportion who take less than 15 minutes to fall asleep for all those who take the drug will exceed .5.

The accompanying Minitab printout in Figure SIA5.2 shows that 90% of the 40 male volunteers took less than 15 minutes to fall asleep. Is this enough evidence for the researchers to infer that melatonin is an effective drug against insomnia?

Figure SIA5.2

Minitab Table with Proportion Less Than 15 Minutes

Tally for Discrete Variables: LESS15

LESS15	Count	Percent
No	4	10.00
Yes	36	90.00
N=	40	

As in the previous *Statistics in Action Revisited* section, we can answer this question by finding the probability of the sample result, given the drug is not effective. Here, we want to find the probability that the sample proportion is .9 or higher, given that the true proportion who take less than 15 minutes to fall asleep is only $p = .5$. That is, we desire the probability

$$P(\hat{p} > .9 \,|\, p = .5).$$

According to the Central Limit Theorem, the sampling distribution of $\hat{p}$ is normal, with the following mean and standard deviation:

$$\mu_{\hat{p}} = p = .5 \text{ and } \sigma_{\hat{p}} = \sqrt{p(1-p)/n} = \sqrt{.5(.5)/40} = .079.$$

By converting $\hat{p}$ to a standard normal z value, we find:

$$P(\hat{p} > .9) = P\{z > (.9 - \mu_{\hat{p}})/\sigma_{\hat{p}}\} = P\{z > (.9 - .5)/.079\} = P(z > 5.06) \approx 0$$

Practically, this probability implies that there is almost no chance of observing a sample proportion of .9 or higher *if the true proportion of volunteers who take less than 15 minutes to fall asleep is only $p = .5$ (i.e., if the drug is not effective)*. As in the previous *Statistics in Action Revisited*, either the drug is not effective and the researchers have observed an extremely rare event (one with almost no chance of happening), or the true value of p for those taking the melatonin pill is much higher than .5. We favor the second conclusion and infer (again) that melatonin appears to be an effective insomnia pill.

Exercises 5.36–5.51

Learning the Mechanics

5.36 Suppose a random sample of n measurements is selected from a binomial population with probability of success $p = .2$. For each of the following values of n, give the mean and standard deviation of the sampling distribution of the sample proportion, $\hat{p}$.
  a. $n = 50$
  b. $n = 1,000$
  c. $n = 400$

5.37 Suppose a random sample of $n = 500$ measurements is selected from a binomial population with probability of success p. For each of the following values of p, give the mean and standard deviation of the sampling distribution of the sample proportion, $\hat{p}$.
  a. $p = .1$
  b. $p = .5$
  c. $p = .7$

5.38 A random sample of $n = 80$ measurements is drawn from a binomial population with probability of success .3.
  a. Give the mean and standard deviation of the sampling distribution of the sample proportion, $\hat{p}$.
  b. Describe the shape of the sampling distribution of $\hat{p}$.
  c. Calculate the standard normal z-score corresponding to a value of $\hat{p} = .35$.
  d. Find $P(\hat{p} > .35)$.

5.39 A random sample of $n = 250$ measurements is drawn from a binomial population with probability of success .85.
  a. Find $E(\hat{p})$ and $\sigma_{\hat{p}}$.
  b. Describe the shape of the sampling distribution of $\hat{p}$.
  c. Find $P(\hat{p} < .9)$.

5.40 A random sample of $n = 1,500$ measurements is drawn from a binomial population with probability of success .4. What are the smallest and largest values of $\hat{p}$ you would expect to see?

5.41 Consider a population with values of x equal to 0 or 1. Assume that the values of x are equally likely. For each of the following values of n, use a computer to generate 500 random samples and calculate the sample proportion of 1s observed for each sample. Then construct a histogram of the 500 sample proportions for each sample.
  a. $n = 10$
  b. $n = 25$
  c. $n = 100$
  d. Refer to the histograms, parts **a–c**. What changes occur as the value of n increases? What similarities exist?

Applying the Concepts—Basic

5.42 **Dentists' use of laughing gas.** According to the American Dental Association, 60% of all dentists use nitrous oxide (laughing gas) in their practice. In a random sample of 75 dentists, let $\hat{p}$ represent the proportion who use laughing gas in practice.
  a. Find $E(\hat{p})$.
  b. Find $\sigma_{\hat{p}}$.

  c. Describe the shape of the sampling distribution of $\hat{p}$.
  d. Find $P(\hat{p} > .70)$.

5.43 **Cable TV subscriptions and "cord cutters."** According to a recent *Pew Research Center Survey* (December 2015), 15% of U.S. adults admitted they are "cord cutters," i.e., they canceled the cable/satellite TV service they once subscribed to. (See Exercise 2.4, p. 72) In a random sample of 500 U.S. adults, let $\hat{p}$ represent the proportion who are "cord cutters."
  a. Find the mean of the sampling distribution of $\hat{p}$.
  b. Find the standard deviation of the sampling distribution of $\hat{p}$.
  c. What does the Central Limit Theorem say about the shape of the sampling distribution of $\hat{p}$?
  d. Compute the probability that $\hat{p}$ is less than .12.
  e. Compute the probability that $\hat{p}$ is greater than .10.

5.44 **Do social robots walk or roll?** Refer to the *International Conference on Social Robotics* (Vol. 6414, 2010) study of the trend in the design of social robots, Exercise 2.5 (p. 72). The researchers obtained a random sample of 106 social robots through a Web search and determined the number that were designed with legs, but no wheels. Let $\hat{p}$ represent the sample proportion of social robots designed with legs, but no wheels. Assume that in the population of all social robots, 40% are designed with legs, but no wheels.
  a. Give the mean and standard deviation of the sampling distribution of $\hat{p}$.
  b. Describe the shape of the sampling distribution of $\hat{p}$.
  c. Find $P(\hat{p} > .59)$.
  d. Recall that the researchers found that 63 of the 106 robots were built with legs only. Does this result cast doubt on the assumption that 40% of all social robots are designed with legs, but no wheels? Explain.

5.45 **Working on summer vacation.** According to a *Harris Interactive* (July 2013) poll of U.S. adults, about 60% work during their summer vacation. (See Exercise 3.13, p. 169.) Assume that the true proportion of all U.S. adults who work during summer vacation is $p = .6$. Now consider a random sample of 500 U.S. adults.
  a. What is the probability that between 55% and 65% of the sampled adults work during summer vacation?
  b. What is the probability that over 75% of the sampled adults work during summer vacation?

5.46 **Hospital work-related injuries.** According to an Occupational and Health Safety Administration (OHSA) 2014 report, a hospital is one of the most dangerous places to work. The major cause of injuries that result in missed work was overexertion. Almost half (48%) of the injuries that result in missed work were due to overexertion. Let x be the number of hospital-related injuries caused by overexertion.
  a. Explain why x is approximately a binomial random variable.
  b. Use the OHSA report to estimate p for the binomial random variable of part **a**.

c. Consider a random sample of 100 hospital workers who missed work due to an on-the-job injury. Use the p from part **b** to find the mean and standard deviation of $\hat{p}$, the proportion of the sampled workers who missed work due to overexertion.

d. Refer to part **c.** Find the probability that the sample proportion is less than .40.

Applying the Concepts—Intermediate

5.47 Hotel guest satisfaction. Refer to the results of the 2015 North American Hotel Guest Satisfaction Index Study, Exercise 4.49 (p. 239). Recall that 15% of hotel guests were "delighted" with their experience (giving a rating of 10 out of 10); of these guests, 80% stated they would "definitely" recommend the hotel. In a random sample of 100 hotel guests, find the probability that fewer than 10 were delighted with their stay and would recommend the hotel.

5.48 Stock market participation and IQ. Refer to *The Journal of Finance* (December 2011) study of whether the decision to invest in the stock market is dependent on IQ, Exercise 3.46 (p. 182). The researchers found that the probability of a Finnish citizen investing in the stock market differed depending on IQ score. For those with a high IQ score, the probability is .44; for those with an average IQ score, the probability is .26; and for those with a low IQ score, the probability is .14.

a. In a random sample of 500 Finnish citizens with high IQ scores, what is the probability that more than 150 invest in the stock market?

b. In a random sample of 500 Finnish citizens with average IQ scores, what is the probability that more than 150 invest in the stock market?

c. In a random sample of 500 Finnish citizens with low IQ scores, what is the probability that more than 150 invest in the stock market?

5.49 Fingerprint expertise. Refer to the *Psychological Science* (August 2011) study of fingerprint identification, Exercise 4.53 (p. 239). Recall that when presented with prints from the same individual, a fingerprint expert will correctly identify the match 92% of the time. Consider a forensic database of 1,000 different pairs of fingerprints, where each pair is a match.

a. What proportion of the 1,000 pairs would you expect an expert to correctly identify as a match?

b. What is the probability that an expert will correctly identify fewer than 900 of the fingerprint matches?

5.50 Who prepares your tax return? As part of a study on income tax compliance (*Behavioral Research and Accounting*, January 2015), researchers found that 37% of adult workers prepare their own tax return. Assume that this percentage applies to all U.S. adult workers. Now consider a random sample of 270 adult workers.

a. Find the probability that more than 112 of the workers prepare their own tax return.

b. Find the probability that between 100 and 150 of the workers prepare their own tax return.

5.51 Apps not working on smartphone. In a survey titled *U.S. Smartphone Use in 2015*, 90% of smartphone users indicated that they have had a problem with a downloaded application (app) on their cell phone not working correctly. Assume this percentage applies to all smartphone users in the United States. In a random sample of 75 smartphone users, suppose that fewer than 60 indicate that they have had a problem with an app on their cell phone not working correctly. What inference can you make about the true proportion of smartphone users who have a problem with apps not working on their cell phone?

CHAPTER NOTES

Key Terms

Biased estimate 304
Central Limit Theorem 308
Error of estimation 303
Minimum-variance unbiased estimator (MVUE) 306
Parameter 296

Point estimator 303
Sample statistic 296
Sampling distribution 298
Standard error of the mean 308
Standard error of the statistic 304
Unbiased estimate 304

Key Formulas

	Mean	Standard Deviation	z-score
Sampling distribution of $\bar{x}$:	$\mu_{\bar{x}} = \mu$	$\sigma_{\bar{x}} = \dfrac{\sigma}{\sqrt{n}}$	$z = \dfrac{\bar{x} - \mu_{\bar{x}}}{\sigma_{\bar{x}}}$ $= \dfrac{\bar{x} - \mu}{\sigma/\sqrt{n}}$
Sampling distribution of $\hat{p}$:	p	$\sigma_{\hat{p}} = \sqrt{p(1-p)/n}$	$z = \dfrac{\hat{p} - p}{\sqrt{p(1-p)/n}}$

Key Ideas

Sampling distribution of a statistic—the theoretical probability distribution of the statistic in repeated sampling

Unbiased estimator—a statistic with a sampling distribution mean equal to the population parameter being estimated

Central Limit Theorem—the sampling distribution of the sample mean, $\bar{x}$, or the sample proportion, $\hat{p}$, is approximately normal for large n

$\bar{x}$ is the **minimum-variance unbiased estimator (MVUE)** of μ
$\hat{p}$ is the MVUE of p

Key Symbols

θ	Population parameter (general)
$\mu_{\bar{x}}$	True mean of sampling distribution of $\bar{x}$
$\sigma_{\bar{x}}$	True standard deviation of sampling distribution of $\bar{x}$
p	True mean of sampling distribution of $\hat{p}$
$\sigma_{\hat{p}}$	True standard deviation of sampling distribution of $\ddot{p}$

Generating the Sampling Distribution of $\bar{x}$

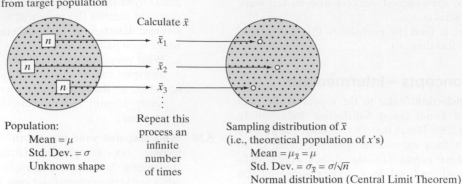

SUPPLEMENTARY EXERCISES 5.52–5.77

Learning the Mechanics

5.52 The standard deviation (or, as it is usually called, the *standard error*) of the sampling distribution for the sample mean, $\bar{x}$, is equal to the standard deviation of the population from which the sample was selected, divided by the square root of the sample size. That is,

$$\sigma_{\bar{x}} = \frac{\sigma}{\sqrt{n}}$$

a. As the sample size is increased, what happens to the standard error of $\bar{x}$? Why is this property considered important?

b. Suppose a sample statistic has a standard error that is not a function of the sample size. In other words, the standard error remains constant as n changes. What would this imply about the statistic as an estimator of a population parameter?

c. Suppose another unbiased estimator (call it A) of the population mean is a sample statistic with a standard error equal to

$$\sigma_A = \frac{\sigma}{\sqrt[3]{n}}$$

Which of the sample statistics, $\bar{x}$ or A, is preferable as an estimator of the population mean? Why?

d. Suppose that the population standard deviation σ is equal to 10 and that the sample size is 64. Calculate the standard errors of $\bar{x}$ and A. Assuming that the sampling distribution of A is approximately normal, interpret the standard errors. Why is the assumption of (approximate) normality unnecessary for the sampling distribution of $\bar{x}$?

5.53 Consider a sample statistic A. As with all sample statistics, A is computed by utilizing a specified function (formula) of the sample measurements. (For example, if A were the sample mean, the specified formula would sum the measurements and divide by the number of measurements.)

a. Describe what we mean by the phrase "the sampling distribution of the sample statistic A."

b. Suppose A is to be used to estimate a population parameter θ. What is meant by the assertion that A is an unbiased estimator of θ?

c. Consider another sample statistic, B. Assume that B is also an unbiased estimator of the population parameter α. How can we use the sampling distributions of A and B to decide which is the better estimator of θ?

d. If the sample sizes on which A and B are based are large, can we apply the Central Limit Theorem and assert that the sampling distributions of A and B are approximately normal? Why or why not?

5.54 A random sample of 40 observations is to be drawn from a large population of measurements. It is known that 30% of the measurements in the population are 1s, 20% are 2s, 20% are 3s, and 30% are 4s.

a. Give the mean and standard deviation of the (repeated) sampling distribution of $\bar{x}$, the sample mean of the 40 observations.

b. Describe the shape of the sampling distribution of $\bar{x}$. Does your answer depend on the sample size?

5.55 A random sample of $n = 68$ observations is selected from a population with $\mu = 19.6$ and $\sigma = 3.2$. Approximate each of the following probabilities:

a. $P(\bar{x} \leq 19.6)$

b. $P(\bar{x} \leq 19)$

c. $P(\bar{x} \geq 20.1)$

d. $P(19.2 \leq \bar{x} \leq 20.6)$

5.56 A random sample of $n = 500$ observations is selected from a binomial population with $p = .35$.

a. Give the mean and standard deviation of the (repeated) sampling distribution of $\hat{p}$, the sample proportion of successes for the 500 observations.

b. Describe the shape of the sampling distribution of $\hat{p}$. Does your answer depend on the sample size?

5.57 A random sample of $n = 300$ observations is selected from a binomial population with $p = .8$. Approximate each of the following probabilities:
  a. $P(\hat{p} < .83)$
  b. $P(\hat{p} > .75)$
  c. $P(.79 < \hat{p} < .81)$

5.58 Use a statistical software package to generate 100 random samples of size $n = 2$ from a population characterized by a normal probability distribution with a mean of 100 and a standard deviation of 10. Compute $\bar{x}$ for each sample, and plot a frequency distribution for the 100 values of $\bar{x}$. Repeat this process for $n = 5, 10, 30$, and 50. How does the fact that the sampled population is normal affect the sampling distribution of $\bar{x}$?

5.59 Use a statistical software package to generate 100 random samples of size $n = 2$ from a population characterized by a uniform probability distribution with $c = 0$ and $d = 10$. Compute $\bar{x}$ for each sample, and plot a frequency distribution for the 100 $\bar{x}$ values. Repeat this process for $n = 5, 10, 30$, and 50. Explain how your plots illustrate the Central Limit Theorem.

5.60 Suppose x equals the number of heads observed when a single coin is tossed; that is, $x = 0$ or $x = 1$. The population corresponding to x is the set of 0s and 1s generated when the coin is tossed repeatedly a large number of times. Suppose we select $n = 2$ observations from this population. (That is, we toss the coin twice and observe two values of x.)
  a. List the three different samples (combinations of 0s and 1s) that could be obtained.
  b. Calculate the value of $\bar{x}$ for each of the samples.
  c. Show that the sample proportion of 1s, $\hat{p}$, is equal to $\bar{x}$.
  d. List the values that $\hat{p}$ can assume, and find the probabilities of observing these values.
  e. Construct a graph of the sampling distribution of $\hat{p}$.

5.61 A random sample of size n is to be drawn from a large population with mean 100 and standard deviation 10, and the sample mean $\bar{x}$ is to be calculated. To see the effect of different sample sizes on the standard deviation of the sampling distribution of $\bar{x}$, plot $\sigma/\sqrt{n}$ against n for $n = 1, 5, 10, 20, 30, 40$, and 50.

Applying the Concepts—Basic

5.62 **Requests to a Web server.** In Exercise 4.175 (p. 282) you learned that Brighton Webs LTD modeled the arrival time of requests to a Web server within each hour, using a uniform distribution. Specifically, the number of seconds x from the start of the hour that the request is made is uniformly distributed between 0 and 3,600 seconds. In a random sample of $n = 60$ Web server requests, let $\bar{x}$ represent the sample mean number of seconds from the start of the hour that the request is made.
  a. Find $E(\bar{x})$ and interpret its value.
  b. Find $\text{Var}(\bar{x})$.
  c. Describe the shape of the sampling distribution of $\bar{x}$.
  d. Find the probability that $\bar{x}$ is between 1,700 and 1,900 seconds.
  e. Find the probability that $\bar{x}$ exceeds 2,000 seconds.

5.63 **Improving SAT scores.** Refer to the *Chance* (Winter 2001) examination of Scholastic Assessment Test (SAT) scores of students who pay a private tutor to help them

improve their results, Exercise 2.88 (p. 113). On the SAT—Mathematics test, these students had a mean score change of +19 points, with a standard deviation of 65 points. In a random sample of 100 students who pay a private tutor to help them improve their results, what is the likelihood that the sample mean score change is less than 10 points?

5.64 **Study of why EMS workers leave the job.** A study of full-time emergency medical service (EMS) workers published in the *Journal of Allied Health* (Fall 2011) found that only about 3% leave their job in order to retire. (See Exercise 3.45, p. 182.) Assume that the true proportion of all full-time EMS workers who leave their job in order to retire is $p = .03$. In a random sample of 1,000 full-time EMS workers, let $\hat{p}$ represent the proportion who leave their job in order to retire.
  a. Describe the properties of the sampling distribution of $\hat{p}$.
  b. Compute $P(\hat{p} < .05)$. Interpret this result.
  c. Compute $P(\hat{p} > .025)$. Interpret this result.

5.65 **Downloading "apps" to your cell phone.** Refer to Exercise 4.173 (p. 282) and the August 2011 survey by the Pew Internet & American Life Project. The study found that 40% of adult cell phone owners have downloaded an application ("app") to their cell phone. Assume this percentage applies to the population of all adult cell phone owners.
  a. In a random sample of 50 adult cell phone owners, how likely is it to find that more than 60% have downloaded an "app" to their cell phone?
  b. Refer to part **a.** Suppose you observe a sample proportion of .62. What inference can you make about the true proportion of adult cell phone owners who have downloaded an "app"?
  c. Suppose the sample of 50 cell phone owners is obtained at a convention for the International Association for the Wireless Telecommunications Industry. How will your answer to part **b** change, if at all?

5.66 **Surface roughness of pipe.** Refer to the *Anti-Corrosion Methods and Materials* (Vol. 50, 2003) study of the surface roughness of oil field pipes, Exercise 2.46 (p. 96). Recall that a scanning probe instrument was used to measure the surface roughness x (in micrometers) of 20 sampled sections of coated interior pipe. Consider the sample mean, $\bar{x}$.
  a. Assume that the surface roughness distribution has a mean of $\mu = 1.8$ micrometers and a standard deviation of $\sigma = .5$ micrometer. Use this information to find the probability that $\bar{x}$ exceeds 1.85 micrometers.
  b. The sample data are reproduced in the following table. Compute $\bar{x}$.
  c. Based on the result, part **b**, comment on the validity of the assumptions made in part **a.**

| 1.72 | 2.50 | 2.16 | 2.13 | 1.06 | 2.24 | 2.31 | 2.03 | 1.09 | 1.40 |
| 2.57 | 2.64 | 1.26 | 2.05 | 1.19 | 2.13 | 1.27 | 1.51 | 2.41 | 1.95 |

Source: Based on Farshad, F., and Pesacreta, T. "Coated pipe interior surface roughness as measured by three scanning probe instruments," *Anti-Corrosion Methods and Materials*, Vol. 50, No. 1, 2003 (Table III).

Applying the Concepts—Intermediate

5.67 **Analysis of supplier lead time.** *Lead time* is the time between a retailer placing an order and having the product available to satisfy customer demand. It includes time for placing the order, receiving the shipment from the supplier, inspecting the units received, and placing them in inventory. Interested in average lead time, μ, for a particular supplier of men's apparel, the purchasing department of a national department store chain randomly sampled 50 of the supplier's lead times and found $\bar{x} = 44$ days.

a. Describe the shape of the sampling distribution of $\bar{x}$.

b. If μ and σ are really 40 and 12, respectively, what is the probability that a second random sample of size 50 would yield $\bar{x}$ greater than or equal to 44?

c. Using the values for μ and σ in part **b,** what is the probability that a sample of size 50 would yield a sample mean within the interval $\mu \pm 2\sigma/\sqrt{n}$?

5.68 **Producing machine bearings.** To determine whether a metal lathe that produces machine bearings is properly adjusted, a random sample of 25 bearings is collected and the diameter of each is measured.

a. If the standard deviation of the diameters of the bearings measured over a long period of time is .001 inch, what is the approximate probability that the mean diameter $\bar{x}$ of the sample of 25 bearings will lie within .0001 inch of the population mean diameter of the bearings?

b. If the population of diameters has an extremely skewed distribution, how will your approximation in part **a** be affected?

5.69 **Quality control.** Refer to Exercise 5.68. The mean diameter of the bearings produced by the machine is supposed to be .5 inch. The company decides to use the sample mean from Exercise 5.68 to decide whether the process is in control (i.e., whether it is producing bearings with a mean diameter of .5 inch). The machine will be considered out of control if the mean of the sample of $n = 25$ diameters is less than .4994 inch or larger than .5006 inch. If the true mean diameter of the bearings produced by the machine is .501 inch, what is the approximate probability that the test will imply that the process is out of control?

5.70 **Length of job tenure.** Researchers at the Terry College of Business at the University of Georgia sampled 344 business students and asked them this question: "Over the course of your lifetime, what is the maximum number of years you expect to work for any one employer?" The sample resulted in $\bar{x} = 19.1$ years. Assume that the sample of students was randomly selected from the 6,000 undergraduate students at the Terry College and that $\sigma = 6$ years.

a. Describe the sampling distribution of $\bar{x}$.

b. If the mean for the 6,000 undergraduate students is $\mu = 18.5$ years, find $P(\bar{x} > 19.1)$.

c. If the mean for the 6,000 undergraduate students is $\mu = 19.5$ years, find $P(\bar{x} > 19.1)$.

d. If $P(\bar{x} > 19.1) = .5$, what is μ?

e. If $P(\bar{x} > 19.1) = .2$, is μ greater than or less than 19.1 years? Explain.

5.71 **Switching banks after a merger.** Banks that merge with others to form "mega-banks" sometimes leave customers dissatisfied with the impersonal service. A poll by the Gallup Organization found 20% of retail customers switched banks after their banks merged with another. One year after the acquisition of First Fidelity by First Union, a random sample of 250 retail customers who had banked with First Fidelity were questioned. Let $\hat{p}$ be the

proportion of those customers who switched their business from First Union to a different bank.

a. Find the mean and the standard deviation of $\hat{p}$.

b. Calculate the interval $E(\hat{p}) \pm 2\sigma_{\hat{p}}$.

c. If samples of size 250 were drawn repeatedly a large number of times and $\hat{p}$ determined for each sample, what proportion of the $\hat{p}$ values would fall within the interval you calculated in part **c**?

5.72 **Piercing rating of fencing safety jackets.** A manufacturer produces safety jackets for competitive fencers. These jackets are rated by the minimum force, in newtons, that will allow a weapon to pierce the jacket. When this process is operating correctly, it produces jackets that have ratings with an average of 840 newtons and a standard deviation of 15 newtons. FIE, the international governing body for fencing, requires jackets to be rated at a minimum of 800 newtons. To check whether the process is operating correctly, a manager takes a sample of 50 jackets from the process, rates them, and calculates $\bar{x}$, the mean rating for jackets in the sample. She assumes that the standard deviation of the process is fixed but is worried that the mean rating of the process may have changed.

a. What is the sampling distribution of $\bar{x}$ if the process is still operating correctly?

b. Suppose the manager's sample has a mean rating of 830 newtons. What is the probability of getting an $\bar{x}$ of 830 newtons or lower if the process is operating correctly?

c. Given the manager's assumption that the standard deviation of the process is fixed, what does your answer to part **b** suggest about the current state of the process (i.e., does it appear that the mean jacket rating is still 840 newtons)?

d. Now suppose that the mean of the process has not changed, but the standard deviation of the process has increased from 15 newtons to 45 newtons. What is the sampling distribution of $\bar{x}$ in this case? What is the probability of getting an $\bar{x}$ of 830 newtons or lower when $\bar{x}$ has this distribution?

5.73 **Errors in filling prescriptions** A large number of preventable errors (e.g., overdoses, botched operations, misdiagnoses) are being made by doctors and nurses in U.S. hospitals. A study of a major metropolitan hospital revealed that of every 100 medications prescribed or dispensed, 1 was in error, but only 1 in 500 resulted in an error that caused significant problems for the patient. It is known that the hospital prescribes and dispenses 60,000 medications per year.

a. What is the expected proportion of errors per year at this hospital? The expected proportion of significant errors per year?

b. Within what limits would you expect the proportion significant errors per year to fall?

5.74 **Purchasing decision.** A building contractor has decided to purchase a load of factory-reject aluminum siding as long as the average number of flaws per piece of siding in a sample of size 35 from the factory's reject pile is 2.1 or less. If it is known that the number of flaws per piece of siding in the factory's reject pile has a Poisson probability distribution with a mean of 2.5, find the approximate probability that the contractor will not purchase a load of siding.

Applying the Concepts—Advanced

5.75 Motivation of drug dealers. Refer to the *Applied Psychology in Criminal Justice* (September 2009) investigation of the personality characteristics of drug dealers, Exercise 2.80 (p. 111). Convicted drug dealers were scored on the Wanting Recognition (WR) Scale—a scale that provides a quantitative measure of a person's level of need for approval and sensitivity to social situations. (Higher scores indicate a greater need for approval.) Based on the study results, we can assume that the WR scores for the population of convicted drug dealers has a mean of 40 and a standard deviation of 5. Suppose that in a sample of 100 people, the mean WR scale score is $\bar{x} = 42$. Is this sample likely to have been selected from the population of convicted drug dealers? Explain.

Critical Thinking Challenges

5.76 Soft-drink bottles. A soft-drink bottler purchases glass bottles from a vendor. The bottles are required to have an internal pressure of at least 150 pounds per square inch (psi). A prospective bottle vendor claims that its production process yields bottles with a mean internal pressure of 157 psi and a standard deviation of 3 psi. The bottler strikes an agreement with the vendor that permits the bottler to sample from the vendor's production process to verify the vendor's claim. The bottler randomly selects 40 bottles from the last 10,000 produced, measures the internal pressure of each, and finds the mean pressure for the sample to be 1.3 psi below the process mean cited by the vendor.

a. Assuming the vendor's claim to be true, what is the probability of obtaining a sample mean this far or farther below the process mean? What does your answer suggest about the validity of the vendor's claim?

b. If the process standard deviation were 3 psi as claimed by the vendor, but the mean were 156 psi, would the observed sample result be more or less likely than in part **a?** What if the mean were 158 psi?

c. If the process mean were 157 psi as claimed, but the process standard deviation were 2 psi, would the sample result be more or less likely than in part **a?** What if instead the standard deviation were 6 psi?

5.77 Fecal pollution at Huntington Beach. California mandates fecal indicator bacteria monitoring at all public beaches. When the concentration of fecal bacteria in the water exceeds a certain limit (400 colony-forming units of fecal coliform per 100 milliliters), local health officials must post a sign (called surf zone posting) warning beachgoers of potential health risks. For fecal bacteria, the state uses a single-sample standard; that is, if the fecal limit is exceeded in a single sample of water, surf zone posting is mandatory. This single-sample standard policy has led to a recent rash of beach closures in California.

A study of the surf water quality at Huntington Beach in California was published in *Environmental Science & Technology* (September 2004). The researchers found that beach closings were occurring despite low pollution levels in some instances, while in others, signs were not posted when the fecal limit was exceeded. They attributed these "surf zone posting errors" to the variable nature of water quality in the surf zone (for example, fecal bacteria concentration tends to be higher during ebb tide and at night) and the inherent time delay between when a water sample is collected and when a sign is posted or removed. In order to prevent posting errors, the researchers recommend using an averaging method, rather than a single sample, to determine unsafe water quality. (For example, one simple averaging method is to take a random sample of multiple water specimens and compare the average fecal bacteria level of the sample with the limit of 400 cfu/100 mL in order to determine whether the water is safe.)

Discuss the pros and cons of using the single-sample standard versus the averaging method. Part of your discussion should address the probability of posting a sign when in fact the water is safe and the probability of posting a sign when in fact the water is unsafe. (Assume that the fecal bacteria concentrations of water specimens at Huntington Beach follow an approximately normal distribution.)

ACTIVITY 5.1   ## Simulating a Sampling Distribution—Cell Phone Usage

[*Note:* This activity is designed for small groups or the entire class.] Consider the length of time a student spends making a cell phone call, sending/retrieving a text message, or accessing e-mail on his/her cell phone. Let *x* represent the length of time, in seconds, for a single cell phone activity (call, text, or e-mail). Here, we are interested in the sampling distribution of $\bar{x}$, the mean length of time for a sample of size *n* cell phone activities.

1. Keep track of the time lengths for all cell phone activities you engage in over the next week.

2. Pool your time length data with data from other class members or the entire class so that the pooled data set has at least 100 observations. Designate someone in the group to calculate the mean and standard deviation of the pooled data set.

3. Devise a convenient way to choose random samples from the pooled data set. (For example, you could assign each observation a number beginning with "1" and use a random number generator to select a sample.)

4. Choose a random sample of size $n = 30$ from the pooled data, and find the mean of the sample. Group members should repeat the process of choosing a sample of size $n = 30$ from the pooled data and finding the sample mean until the group has accumulated at least 25 sample means. (Call this data set *Sample Means*.)

5. Find the mean and standard deviation of the *Sample Means* data set. Also, form a histogram for the *Sample Means* data set. Explain how the Central Limit Theorem is illustrated in this activity.

References

Hogg, R. V., McKean, J. W., and Craig, A. T. *Introduction to Mathematical Statistics,* 6th ed. Upper Saddle River, N.J.: Prentice Hall, 2005.

Larsen, R. J., and Marx, M. L. *An Introduction to Mathematical Statistics and Its Applications,* 4th ed. Upper Saddle River, N.J.: Prentice Hall, 2005.

Lindgren, B. W. *Statistical Theory,* 3rd ed. New York: Macmillan, 1976.

Wackerly, D., Mendenhall, W., and Scheaffer, R. L. *Mathematical Statistics with Applications,* 7th ed. North Scituate, Mass.: Duxbury, 2008.

USING TECHNOLOGY

Technology images shown here are taken from SPSS Statistics Professional 23.0, Minitab 17, XLSTAT, and Excel 2016.

SPSS: Simulating a Sampling Distribution

Generating a sampling distribution with SPSS is not a simple process. The process involves writing code (syntax) in an SPSS program. Consult the SPSS user's guide for help with this feature.

Minitab: Simulating a Sampling Distribution

Step 1 Select "Calc" on the Minitab menu bar, and then click on "Random Data" (see Figure 5.M.1).

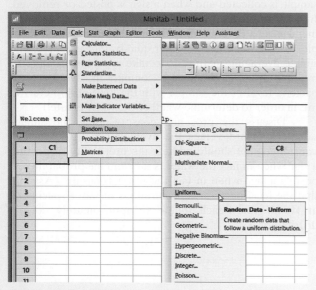

Figure 5.M.1. Minitab options for generating random data

Step 2 On the resulting menu list, click on the distribution of your choice (e.g., "Uniform"). A dialog box similar to the one (the Uniform Distribution) shown in Figure 5.M.2 will appear.

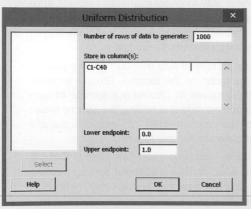

Figure 5.M.2 Minitab dialog box for simulating the uniform distribution

Step 3 Specify the number of samples (e.g., 1,000) to generate in the "Number of rows of data to generate" box and the columns where the data will be stored in the "Store in columns" box. (The number of columns will be equal to the sample size, e.g., 40.) Finally, specify the parameters of the distribution (e.g., the lower and upper range of the uniform distribution). When you click "OK," the simulated data will appear on the Minitab worksheet.

Step 4 Calculate the value of the sample statistic of interest for each sample. To do this, click on the "Calc" button on the Minitab menu bar, and then click on "Row Statistics," as shown in Figure 5.M.3. The resulting dialog box appears in Figure 5.M.4.

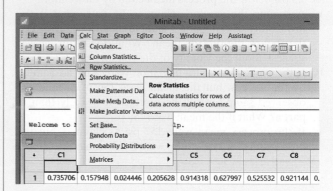

Figure 5.M.3 Minitab selections for generating sample statistics for the simulated data

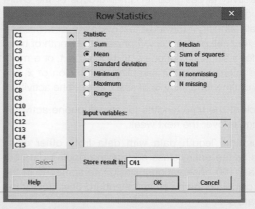

Figure 5.M.4 Minitab row statistics dialog box

Step 5 Check the sample statistic (e.g., the mean) you want to calculate, specify the "Input variables" (or columns), and the column where you want the value of the sample statistic to be saved. Click "OK" and the value of the statistic for each sample will appear on the Minitab worksheet.

[*Note:* Use the Minitab menu choices provided in the Using Technology section in Chapter 2, p. 150, to generate a histogram of the sampling distribution of the statistic or to find the mean and variance of the sampling distribution.]

Excel: Simulating a Sampling Distribution

Step 1 Select "Data" on the main menu bar and then click on "Data Analysis." The resulting menu is shown in Figure 5.E.1.

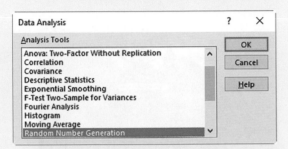

Figure 5.E.1 Excel data analysis menu options

Step 2 Select "Random Number Generation" from the Data Analysis menu and then click "OK." The dialog box in Figure 5.E.2 will appear.

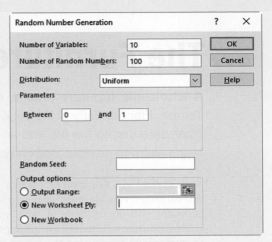

Figure 5.E.2 Excel dialog box for generating uniform random numbers

Step 3 Specify the number of samples (e.g., 10) to generate in the "Number of Variables" box and the sample size of each (e.g., 100) in the "Number of Random Numbers" box.

Step 4 Specify the distribution (e.g., uniform) that the samples will be selected from and the parameters of the distribution.

Step 5 Click "OK"; the random numbers will appear on a new Excel spreadsheet (Figure 5.E.3).

Step 6 Specify a formula for the sample mean on the resulting Excel spreadsheet. For example, the formula "=AVERAGE (A2:J2)" in column "L" computes the mean of the 10 random numbers in each row of the spreadsheet shown in Figure 5.E.3.

Step 7 Once the means of the random samples are computed, you can generate a histogram or summary statistics for the mean by following the steps outlined in Using Technology, Chapter 2.

	A	B	C	D	E	F	G	H	I	J	K	L	M
	L2			f_x	=AVERAGE(A2:J2)								
1	X1	X2	X3	X4	X5	X6	X7	X8	X9	X10		XBAR	
2	0.360546	0.299844	0.676748	0.379192	0.01999	0.610431	0.528581	0.521714	0.351756	0.776666		0.452547	
3	0.226936	0.790551	0.588427	0.532914	0.772332	0.073153	0.900021	0.371502	0.180486	0.344493		0.478082	
4	0.796045	0.961821	0.350017	0.688345	0.185492	0.594684	0.854183	0.547716	0.751762	0.683584		0.641365	
5	0.562395	0.484542	0.797662	0.853572	0.49852	0.23072	0.217963	0.649373	0.841212	0.311136		0.54471	
6	0.754814	0.394024	0.473495	0.020508	0.192541	0.228889	0.987365	0.0347	0.648579	0.866878		0.460179	
7	0.549425	0.438276	0.615833	0.089358	0.534471	0.449202	0.913572	0.519181	0.332621	0.622059		0.5064	
8	0.202704	0.699423	0.236824	0.81109	0.221747	0.010804	0.816309	0.674276	0.39967	0.4579		0.453075	
9	0.682913	0.999542	0.002045	0.855708	0.056215	0.634571	0.46672	0.447951	0.03357	0.301492		0.448073	
10	0.084902	0.488327	0.971648	0.077334	0.684622	0.81579	0.885372	0.822016	0.471816	0.955138		0.625697	
11	0.270913	0.334483	0.686636	0.77459	0.258675	0.519181	0.229713	0.230842	0.502426	0.342906		0.415036	
12	0.915891	0.233528	0.711264	0.864437	0.510758	0.160009	0.230262	0.117313	0.207068	0.051637		0.400217	
13	0.576312	0.127689	0.696585	0.023286	0.335063	0.847896	0.493789	0.916593	0.325816	0.287454		0.463048	
14	0.668111	0.728935	0.439772	0.622761	0.640309	0.848781	0.05884	0.566057	0.199774	0.629109		0.540245	
15	0.460433	0.775933	0.398724	0.330027	0.114902	0.589679	0.479385	0.961486	0.281961	0.859645		0.525217	
16	0.491043	0.057772	0.812037	0.17365	0.752403	0.915342	0.558885	0.242256	0.816126	0.32374		0.514325	
17	0.31016	0.732566	0.091494	0.323222	0.641224	0.330882	0.781701	0.017884	0.599567	0.315287		0.414399	
18	0.29133	0.977386	0.625202	0.418867	0.761498	0.257393	0.61388	0.265389	0.887692	0.570879		0.566952	
19	0.528977	0.158605	0.677206	0.640492	0.46852	0.506088	0.302347	0.26426	0.593554	0.65923		0.479928	
20	0.705496	0.12537	0.82403	0.450484	0.11243	0.87701	0.708518	0.209082	0.11008	0.534196		0.46567	

Figure 5.E.3 Excel formula for computing sample means from random numbers

The Furniture Fire Case

A wholesale furniture retailer stores in-stock items at a large warehouse located in Tampa, Florida. Early in the year, a fire destroyed the warehouse and all the furniture in it. After determining the fire was an accident, the retailer sought to recover costs by submitting a claim to its insurance company.

As is typical in a fire insurance policy of this type, the furniture retailer must provide the insurance company with an estimate of "lost" profit for the destroyed items. Retailers calculate profit margin in percentage form using the Gross Profit Factor (GPF). By definition, the GPF for a single sold item is the ratio of the profit to the item's selling price measured as a percentage, that is,

Item GPF = (Profit/Sales price) × 100%

Of interest to both the retailer and the insurance company is the average GPF for all of the items in the warehouse. Because these furniture pieces were all destroyed, their eventual selling prices and profit values are obviously unknown. Consequently, the average GPF for all the warehouse items is unknown.

One way to estimate the mean GPF of the destroyed items is to use the mean GPF of similar, recently sold items. The retailer sold 3,005 furniture items in the year prior to the fire and kept paper invoices on all sales. Rather than calculate the mean GPF for all 3,005 items (the data were not computerized), the retailer sampled a total of 253 of the invoices and computed the mean GPF for these items. The 253 items were obtained by first selecting a sample of 134 items and then augmenting this sample with a second sample of 119 items. The mean GPFs for the two subsamples were calculated to be 50.6% and 51.0%, respectively, yielding an overall average GPF of 50.8%. This average GPF can be applied to the costs of the furniture items destroyed in the fire to obtain an estimate of the "lost" profit.

According to experienced claims adjusters at the insurance company, the GPF for sale items of the type destroyed in the fire rarely exceeds 48%. Consequently, the estimate of 50.8% appeared to be unusually high. (A 1% increase in GPF for items of this type equates to, approximately, an additional $16,000 in profit.) When the insurance company questioned the retailer on this issue, the retailer responded, "Our estimate was based on selecting two independent, random samples from the population of 3,005 invoices. Because the samples were selected randomly and the total sample size is large, the mean GPF estimate of 50.8% is valid."

A dispute arose between the furniture retailer and the insurance company, and a lawsuit was filed. In one portion of the suit, the insurance company accused the retailer of fraudulently representing their sampling methodology. Rather than selecting the samples randomly, the retailer was accused of selecting an unusual number of "high-profit" items from the population in order to increase the average GPF of the overall sample.

To support their claim of fraud, the insurance company hired a CPA firm to independently assess the retailer's Gross Profit Factor. Through the discovery process, the CPA firm legally obtained the paper invoices for the entire population of 3,005 items sold and input the information into a computer. The selling price, profit, profit margin, and month sold for these 3,005 furniture items are stored in the **FIRE** file, described below.

Your objective in this case is to use these data to determine the likelihood of fraud. Is it likely that a random sample of 253 items selected from the population of 3,005 items would yield a mean GPF of at least 50.8%? Or, is it likely that two independent, random samples of sizes 134 and 119 would yield mean GPFs of at least 50.6% and 51.0%, respectively? (These were the questions posed to a statistician retained by the CPA firm.)

Use the ideas of probability and sampling distributions to guide your analysis.

Prepare a professional document that presents the results of your analysis and gives your opinion regarding fraud. Be sure to describe the assumptions and methodology used to arrive at your findings.

Variable	Type	Description
MONTH	QL	Month in which item was sold in 1991
INVOICE	QN	Invoice number
SALES	QN	Sales price of item in dollars
PROFIT	QN	Profit amount of item in dollars
MARGIN	QN	Profit margin of item = (Profit/Sales) × 100%

 Data Set: FIRE

6

CONTENTS

WHERE WE'VE BEEN

- Learned that populations are characterized by numerical descriptive measures called *parameters*
- Found that decisions about population parameters are based on *statistics* computed from the sample
- Discovered that *inferences* about parameters are subject to uncertainty and that this uncertainty is reflected in the *sampling distribution* of a statistic

---

WHERE WE'RE GOING

- Estimate a population parameter (means, proportion, or variance) based on a large sample selected from the population (6.1)
- Use the sampling distribution of a statistic to form a confidence interval for the population parameter (6.2–6.4, 6.6, 6.7)
- Show how to select the proper sample size for estimating a population parameter (6.5)

Inferences Based on a Single Sample

Estimation with Confidence Intervals

STATISTICS IN ACTION Medicare Fraud Investigations

United States Department of Justice (USDOJ) press release (Feb. 17, 2011): *The Medicare Fraud Strike Force today charged 111 defendants in nine cities, including doctors, nurses, health care company owners and executives, and others, for their alleged participation in Medicare fraud schemes involving more than $225 million in false billing.*

The joint Department of Justice (DOJ) and Health and Human Services (HHS) Medicare Fraud Strike Force is a multi-agency team of federal, state, and local investigators designed to combat Medicare fraud through the use of Medicare data analysis techniques and an increased focus on community policing. More than 700 law enforcement agents from the FBI, HHS-Office of Inspector General (HHS-OIG), multiple Medicaid Fraud Control Units, and other state and local law enforcement agencies participated in today's operation. In addition to making arrests, agents also executed 16 search warrants across the country in connection with ongoing strike force investigations.

In Miami, 32 defendants . . . were charged for their participation in various fraud schemes involving a total of $55 million in false billings for home health care, durable medical equipment and prescription drugs.

Twenty-one defendants . . . were charged in Detroit for schemes to defraud Medicare of more than $23 million. [These] cases involve false claims for home health care, nerve conduction tests, psychotherapy, physical therapy and podiatry.

In Brooklyn, N.Y., 10 individuals . . . were charged with fraud schemes involving $90 million in false billings for physical therapy, proctology services and nerve conduction tests.

STATISTICS IN ACTION

(continued)

Ten defendants were charged in Tampa for participating in schemes involving more than $5 million related to false claims for physical therapy, durable medical equipment and pharmaceuticals.

Nine individuals were charged in Houston for schemes involving $8 million in fraudulent Medicare claims for physical therapy, durable medical equipment, home health care and chiropractor services.

In Dallas, seven defendants were indicted for conspiring to submit $2.8 million in false billing to Medicare related to durable medical equipment and home health care.

Five defendants were charged in Los Angeles for their roles in schemes to defraud Medicare of more than $28 million. [These] cases involve false claims for durable medical equipment and home health care.

In Baton Rouge, La., six individuals were charged for a durable medical equipment fraud scheme involving more than $9 million in false claims.

In Chicago, charges were filed against 11 individuals associated with businesses that have billed Medicare more than $6 million for home health [care], diagnostic testing and prescription drugs.

As the above press release implies, the U.S. Department of Justice (USDOJ) and its Medicare Fraud Strike Force conduct investigations into suspected fraud and abuse of the Medicare system by health care providers. According to published reports, the Strike Force is responsible for 25% of the Medicare fraud charges brought nationwide.

One way in which Medicare fraud occurs is through the use of "upcoding," which refers to the practice of providers coding Medicare claims at a higher level of care than was actually provided to the patient. For example, suppose a particular kind of claim can be coded at three levels, where Level 1 is a routine office visit, Level 2 is a thorough examination involving advanced diagnostic tests, and Level 3 involves performing minor surgery. The amount of Medicare payment is higher for each increased level of claim. Thus, upcoding would occur if Level 1 services were billed at Level 2 or Level 3 payments, or if Level 2 services were billed at Level 3 payment.

The USDOJ relies on sound statistical methods to help identify Medicare fraud. Once the USDOJ has determined that possible upcoding has occurred, it next seeks to further investigate whether it is the result of legitimate practice (perhaps the provider is a specialist giving higher levels of care) or the result of fraudulent action on the part of the provider. To further its investigation, the USDOJ will next ask a statistician to select a sample of the provider's claims. For example, the statistician might determine that a random sample of 52 claims from the 1,000 claims in question will provide a sufficient sample to estimate the overcharge reliably. The USDOJ then asks a health care expert to audit each of the medical files corresponding to the sampled claims and determine whether the level of care matches the level billed by the provider, and, if not, to determine what level should have been billed. Once the audit has been completed, the USDOJ will calculate the overcharge.

In this chapter, we present a recent Medicare fraud case investigated by the USDOJ. Results for the audit of 52 sampled claims, with the amount paid for each claim, the amount disallowed by the auditor, and the amount that should have been paid for each claim, are saved in the **MFRAUD** file.* Knowing that a total of $103,500 was paid for the 1,000 claims, the USDOJ wants to use the sample results to extrapolate the overpayment amount to the entire population of 1,000 claims.

STATISTICS IN ACTION REVISITED

- Estimating the Mean Overpayment **(p. 347)**
- Estimating the Coding Error Rate **(p. 355)**
- Determining Sample Size **(p. 362)**

📊 *Data Set:* MFRAUD

---

*Data provided (with permission) from Info Tech, Inc., Gainesville, Florida.

Look Back Because we know the probability that the interval $\bar{x} \pm 1.96\sigma_{\bar{x}}$ will contain μ is .95, we call the interval estimator a 95% *confidence interval* for μ.

● **Now Work Exercise 6.3a**

The interval $\bar{x} \pm 1.96\sigma_{\bar{x}}$ in Example 6.1 is called a *large-sample* 95% confidence interval for the population mean μ. The term *large-sample* refers to the sample being of sufficiently large size that we can apply the Central Limit Theorem and the normal (z) statistic to determine the form of the sampling distribution of $\bar{x}$. Empirical research suggests that a sample size n exceeding a value between 20 and 30 will usually yield a sampling distribution of $\bar{x}$ that is approximately normal. This result led many practitioners to adopt the rule of thumb that a sample size of $n \geq 30$ is required to use large-sample confidence interval procedures. Keep in mind, though, that 30 is not a magical number and, in fact, is quite arbitrary.

Also, *note that the large-sample interval estimator requires knowing the value of the population standard deviation,* σ. In most (if not nearly all) practical business applications, however, the value of σ will be unknown. For large samples, the fact that σ is unknown poses only a minor problem because the sample standard deviation s provides a very good approximation to σ*. The next example illustrates the more realistic large-sample confidence interval procedure.

EXAMPLE 6.2

Estimating the Mean, σ Unknown–Delinquent Debtors

Problem Refer to Example 6.1 and the problem of estimating μ, the average amount of money owed by a bank's delinquent debtors. The overdue amounts for the $n = 100$ delinquent accounts are shown in Table 6.1. Use the data to find a 95% confidence interval for μ and interpret the result.

Table 6.1	Overdue Amounts (in Dollars) for 100 Delinquent Accounts								
195	243	132	133	209	400	142	312	221	289
221	162	134	275	355	293	242	458	378	148
278	222	236	178	202	222	334	208	194	135
363	221	449	265	146	215	113	229	221	243
512	193	134	138	209	207	206	310	293	310
237	135	252	365	371	238	232	271	121	134
203	178	180	148	162	160	86	234	244	266
119	259	108	289	328	331	330	227	162	354
304	141	158	240	82	17	357	187	364	268
368	274	278	190	344	157	219	77	171	280

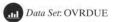 *Data Set:* OVRDUE

	A	B
1		AMOUNT
2		
3	Mean	233.28
4	Standard Error	9.033988
5	Median	222
6	Mode	221
7	Standard Deviation	90.33988
8	Sample Variance	8161.295
9	Kurtosis	0.25481
10	Skewness	0.4768
11	Range	495
12	Minimum	17
13	Maximum	512
14	Sum	23328
15	Count	100
16		

Figure 6.3a

Excel summary statistics for overdue amounts

Solution The large bank almost surely does not know the true standard deviation, σ, of the population of overdue amounts. However, because the sample size is large, we will use the sample standard deviation, s, as an estimate for σ in the confidence interval formula. An Excel printout of summary statistics for the sample of 100 overdue amounts is shown in Figure 6.3a. From the shaded portion of the printout, we find $\bar{x} = 233.28$ and $s = 90.34$. Substituting these values into the interval estimator formula, we obtain:

$$\bar{x} \pm (1.96)\sigma/\sqrt{n} \approx \bar{x} \pm (1.96)s/\sqrt{n} = 233.28 \pm (1.96)(90.34)/\sqrt{100} = 233.28 \pm 17.71$$

Or, (215.57, 250.99). That is, we estimate the mean amount of delinquency for all accounts to fall within the interval $215.57 to $250.99.

Look Back The confidence interval is also shown (highlighted) at the bottom of the Excel/XLSTAT printout, Figure 6.3b. Note that the endpoints of the interval vary slightly from those computed in the example. This is because when σ is unknown and n

---

*In the terminology of Chapter 5, it can be shown that s is an *unbiased* estimator of σ.

is large, the sampling distribution of $\bar{x}$ will deviate slightly from the normal (z) distribution. In practice, these differences can be ignored.

Figure 6.3b

XLSTAT output showing 95% confidence interval for μ, σ unknown

Descriptive statistics (Quantitative data):	
Statistic	**AMOUNT**
Nbr. of observations	100
Minimum	17.0000
Maximum	512.0000
Mean	233.2800
Standard deviation (n-1)	90.3399
Lower bound on mean (95%)	215.3546
Upper bound on mean (95%)	251.2054

● **Now Work Exercise 6.14**

Can we be sure that μ, the true mean, is in the interval (215.57, 250.99) in Example 6.2 ? We cannot be certain, but we can be reasonably confident that it is. This confidence is derived from the knowledge that if we were to draw repeated random samples of 100 measurements from this population and form the interval $\bar{x} \pm 1.96\sigma_{\bar{x}}$ each time, 95% of the intervals would contain μ. We have no way of knowing (without looking at all the delinquent accounts) whether our sample interval is one of the 95% that contains μ or one of the 5% that does not, but the odds certainly favor its containing μ. The probability, .95, that measures the confidence we can place in the interval estimate is called a *confidence coefficient*. The percentage, 95%, is called the *confidence level* for the interval estimate.

> The **confidence coefficient** is the probability that a randomly selected confidence interval encloses the population parameter—that is, the relative frequency with which similarly constructed intervals enclose the population parameter when the estimator is used repeatedly a very large number of times. The **confidence level** is the confidence coefficient expressed as a percentage.

Now we have seen how an interval can be used to estimate a population mean. When we use an interval estimator, we can usually calculate the probability that the estimation *process* will result in an interval that contains the true value of the population mean—that is, the probability that the interval contains the parameter in repeated usage is usually known. Figure 6.4 shows what happens when 10 different samples are drawn from a population, and a confidence interval for μ is calculated from each. The location of μ is indicated by the vertical line in the figure. Ten confidence intervals, each based on one of 10 samples, are shown as horizontal line segments. Note that the confidence intervals move from sample to sample—sometimes containing μ and other times missing μ. *If our confidence level is 95%, then in the long run, 95% of our confidence intervals will contain μ and 5% will not.*

Suppose you wish to choose a confidence coefficient other than .95. Notice in Figure 6.1 that the confidence coefficient .95 is equal to the total area under the sampling distribution, less .05 of the area, which is divided equally between the two tails. Using this idea, we can construct a confidence interval with any desired confidence coefficient by increasing or decreasing the area (call it α) assigned to the tails of the sampling distribution (see Figure 6.5). For example, if we place area $\frac{\alpha}{2}$ in each tail and if $z_{\alpha/2}$ is the z-value such that the area $\frac{\alpha}{2}$ lies to its right, then the confidence interval with confidence coefficient $(1 - \alpha)$ is

$$\bar{x} \pm (z_{\alpha/2})\sigma_{\bar{x}}$$

Figure 6.4

Confidence intervals for μ: 10 samples

Confidence
Interval

1
2
3
4
5
6
7
8
9
10

μ

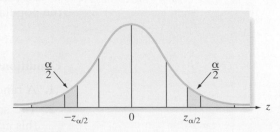

Figure 6.5

Locating $z_{\alpha/2}$ on the standard normal curve

JERZEY NEYMAN (1894–1981)
Speaking Statistics with a Polish Accent

Polish-born Jerzey Neyman was educated at the University of Kharkov (Russia) in elementary mathematics but taught himself graduate mathematics by studying journal articles on the subject. After receiving his doctorate in 1924 from the University of Warsaw (Poland), Neyman accepted a position at University College (London). There, he developed a friendship with Egon Pearson; Neyman and Pearson together developed the theory of hypothesis testing (Chapter 7). In 1934, in a talk to the Royal Statistical Society, Neyman first proposed the idea of interval estimation, which he called *confidence intervals*. (It is interesting that Neyman rarely receives credit in textbooks as the originator of the confidence interval procedure.) In 1938, he immigrated to the United States and the University of California at Berkeley. At Berkeley, he built one of the strongest statistics departments in the country. Jerzey Neyman is considered one of the great founders of modern statistics. He was a superb teacher and innovative researcher who loved his students, always sharing his ideas with them. Neyman's influence on those he met is best expressed by a quote from prominent statistician David Salsburg: "We have all learned to speak statistics with a Polish accent."

The value z_α is defined as the value of the standard normal random variable z such that the area α will lie to its right. In other words, $P(z > z_\alpha) = \alpha$.

To illustrate, for a confidence coefficient of .90, we have $(1 - \alpha) = .90$, $\alpha = .10$, and $\frac{\alpha}{2} = .05$; $z_{.05}$ is the z-value that locates area .05 in the upper tail of the sampling distribution. Recall that Table II in Appendix D gives the areas between the mean and a specified z-value. Because the total area to the right of the mean is .5, we find that $z_{.05}$ will be the z-value corresponding to an area of $.5 - .05 = .45$ to the right of the mean (see Figure 6.6). This z-value is $z_{.05} = 1.645$. The same result may also be obtained using technology. The Minitab printout in Figure 6.7 shows that the z-value that cuts off an upper tail area of .05 is approximately $z_{.05} = 1.645$.

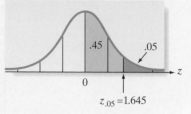

Figure 6.6

The z-value ($z_{.05}$) corresponding to an area equal to .05 in the upper tail of the z-distribution

Figure 6.7

Minitab Output for Finding $z_{.05}$

```
Inverse Cumulative Distribution Function

Normal with mean = 0 and standard deviation = 1

P( X <= x )        x
    0.95      1.64485
```

Confidence coefficients used in practice usually range from .90 to .99. The most commonly used confidence coefficients with corresponding values of α and $z_{\alpha/2}$ are shown in Table 6.2.

Table 6.2	Commonly Used Values of $z_{\alpha/2}$		
Confidence Level			
$100(1 - \alpha)$	α	$\alpha/2$	$z_{\alpha/2}$
90%	.10	.05	1.645
95%	.05	.025	1.960
98%	.02	.01	2.326
99%	.01	.005	2.576

Large-Sample $100(1 - \alpha)$% Confidence Interval for μ, Based on a Normal (z) Statistic

$$\sigma \text{ known}: \bar{x} \pm (z_{\alpha/2})\sigma_{\bar{x}} = \bar{x} \pm (z_{\alpha/2})(\sigma/\sqrt{n})$$

$$\sigma \text{ unknown}: \bar{x} \pm (z_{\alpha/2})\sigma_{\bar{x}} \approx \bar{x} \pm (z_{\alpha/2})(s/\sqrt{n})$$

where $z_{\alpha/2}$ is the z-value corresponding to an area $\frac{\alpha}{2}$ in the tail of a standard normal distribution (see Figure 6.5), $\sigma_{\bar{x}}$ is the standard deviation of the sampling distribution of $\bar{x}$ (also called the **standard error of the mean**), σ is the standard deviation of the population, and s is the standard deviation of the sample.

Conditions Required for a Valid Large-Sample Confidence Interval for μ

1. A random sample is selected from the target population.
2. The sample size n is large (i.e., $n \geq 30$). Due to the Central Limit Theorem, this condition guarantees that the sampling distribution of $\bar{x}$ is approximately normal. (Also, for large n, s will be a good estimator of σ.)

EXAMPLE 6.3

Large-Sample Confidence Interval for μ—Unoccupied Seats per Flight

Problem Unoccupied seats on flights cause airlines to lose revenue. Suppose a large airline wants to estimate its average number of unoccupied seats per flight over the past year. To accomplish this, the records of 225 flights are randomly selected, and the number of unoccupied seats is noted for each of the sampled flights. (The data are saved in the **NOSHOW** file.) Descriptive statistics for the data are displayed in the Minitab printout, Figure 6.8.

Figure 6.8
Minitab confidence interval for mean, Example 6.3

```
Variable    N    Mean   StDev  SE Mean       90% CI
NOSHOWS    225  11.596  4.103   0.274   (11.144, 12.047)
```

Estimate μ, the mean number of unoccupied seats per flight during the past year, using a 90% confidence interval.

Solution The general form of the 90% confidence interval for a population mean is

$$\bar{x} \pm z_{\alpha/2}\sigma_{\bar{x}} = \bar{x} \pm z_{.05}\sigma_{\bar{x}} = \bar{x} \pm 1.645\left(\frac{\sigma}{\sqrt{n}}\right)$$

From Figure 6.8, we find (after rounding) $\bar{x} = 11.6$. Because we do not know the value of σ (the standard deviation of the number of unoccupied seats per flight for all flights of the year), we use our best approximation—the sample standard deviation s. Then the 90% confidence interval is, approximately,

$$11.6 \pm 1.645\left(\frac{4.1}{\sqrt{225}}\right) = 11.6 \pm .45$$

or from 11.15 to 12.05—that is, at the 90% confidence level, we estimate the mean number of unoccupied seats per flight to be between 11.15 and 12.05 during the sampled year. This result is verified (except for rounding) on the right side of the Minitab printout in Figure 6.8.

Look Back We stress that the confidence level for this example, 90%, refers to the procedure used. If we were to apply this procedure repeatedly to different samples, approximately 90% of the intervals would contain μ. Although we do not know whether this particular interval (11.15, 12.05) is one of the 90% that contain μ or one of the 10% that do not, our knowledge of probability gives us "confidence" that the interval contains μ.

● **Now Work Exercise 6.12**

The interpretation of confidence intervals for a population mean is summarized in the next box.

Interpretation of a Confidence Interval for a Population Mean

When we form a $100(1 - \alpha)\%$ confidence interval for μ, we usually express our confidence in the interval with a statement such as, "We can be $100(1 - \alpha)\%$ confident that μ lies between the lower and upper bounds of the confidence interval," where for a particular application, we substitute the appropriate numerical values for the confidence and for the lower and upper bounds. *The statement reflects our confidence in the estimation process rather than in the particular interval that is calculated from the sample data.* We know that repeated application of the same procedure will result in different lower and upper bounds on the interval. Furthermore, we know that $100(1 - \alpha)\%$ of the resulting intervals will contain μ. There is (usually) no way to determine whether any particular interval is one of those that contain μ, or one that does not. However, unlike point estimators, confidence intervals have some measure of reliability, the confidence coefficient, associated with them. For that reason they are generally preferred to point estimators.

Sometimes, the estimation procedure yields a confidence interval that is too wide for our purposes. In this case, we will want to reduce the width of the interval to obtain a more precise estimate of μ. One way to accomplish this is to decrease the confidence coefficient, $1 - \alpha$. For example, reconsider the problem of estimating the mean amount owed, μ, for all delinquent accounts. Recall that for a sample of 100 accounts, $\bar{x} = \$233.28$ and $s = \$90.34$. A 90% confidence interval for μ is

$$\bar{x} \pm 1.645\sigma/\sqrt{n} \approx 233.28 \pm (1.645)(90.34/\sqrt{100}) = 233.28 \pm 14.86$$

or ($218.42, $248.14). You can see that this interval is narrower than the previously calculated 95% confidence interval ($215.57, $250.99). Unfortunately, we also have "less confidence" in the 90% confidence interval. An alternative method used to decrease the width of an interval without sacrificing "confidence" is to increase the sample size n. We demonstrate this method in Section 6.5.

Exercises 6.1–6.22

Learning the Mechanics

6.1 Find $z_{\alpha/2}$ for each of the following:
a. $\alpha = .10$ **b.** $\alpha = .01$
c. $\alpha = .05$ **d.** $\alpha = .20$

6.2 What is the confidence level of each of the following confidence intervals for μ?

a. $\bar{x} \pm 1.96\left(\dfrac{\sigma}{\sqrt{n}}\right)$ **b.** $\bar{x} \pm 1.645\left(\dfrac{\sigma}{\sqrt{n}}\right)$

c. $\bar{x} \pm 2.575\left(\dfrac{\sigma}{\sqrt{n}}\right)$ **d.** $\bar{x} \pm 1.282\left(\dfrac{\sigma}{\sqrt{n}}\right)$

e. $\bar{x} \pm .99\left(\dfrac{\sigma}{\sqrt{n}}\right)$

6.3 A random sample of n measurements was selected from a population with unknown mean μ and known standard deviation σ. Calculate a 95% confidence interval for μ for each of the following situations:
a. $n = 75, \bar{x} = 28, \sigma^2 = 12$
b. $n = 200, \bar{x} = 102, \sigma^2 = 22$
c. $n = 100, \bar{x} = 15, \sigma = .3$
d. $n = 100, \bar{x} = 4.05, \sigma = .83$
e. Is the assumption that the underlying population of measurements is normally distributed necessary to ensure the validity of the confidence intervals in parts **a–d?** Explain.

6.4 A random sample of 90 observations produced a mean $\bar{x} = 25.9$ and a standard deviation $s = 2.7$.
a. Find an approximate 95% confidence interval for the population mean μ.
b. Find an approximate 90% confidence interval for μ.
c. Find an approximate 99% confidence interval for μ.

6.5 A random sample of 70 observations from a normally distributed population possesses a sample mean equal to 26.2 and a sample standard deviation equal to 4.1.
a. Find an approximate 95% confidence interval for μ.
b. What do you mean when you say that a confidence coefficient is .95?
c. Find an approximate 99% confidence interval for μ.

d. What happens to the width of a confidence interval as the value of the confidence coefficient is increased while the sample size is held fixed?
e. Would your confidence intervals of parts **a** and **c** be valid if the distribution of the original population was not normal? Explain.

Applet Exercise 6.1

Use the applet *Confidence Intervals for a Mean (the impact of confidence level)* to investigate the situation in Exercise 6.5 further. For this exercise, assume that $\mu = 2.62$ is the population mean and $\sigma = 4.1$ is the population standard deviation.
a. Using $n = 70$ and the normal distribution with the mean and standard deviation above, run the applet one time. How many of the 95% confidence intervals contain the mean? How many would you expect to contain the mean? How many of the 99% confidence intervals contain the mean? How many would you expect to contain the mean?
b. Which confidence level has a greater frequency of intervals that contain the mean? Is this result what you would expect? Explain.
c. Without clearing, run the applet several more times. What happens to the proportion of 95% confidence intervals that contain the mean as you run the applet more and more? What happens to the proportion of 99% confidence intervals that contain the mean as you run the applet more and more? Interpret these results in terms of the meanings of the 95% confidence interval and the 99% confidence interval.
d. Change the distribution to *right skewed*, clear, and run the applet several more times. Do you get the same results as in part **c**? Would you change your answer to part **e** of Exercise 6.5 ? Explain.

Applet Exercise 6.2

Use the applet *Confidence Intervals for a Mean (the impact of confidence level)* to investigate the effect of the sample size on the proportion of confidence intervals that contain the mean when the underlying distribution is skewed. Set the distribution to *right skewed*, the mean to 10, and the standard deviation to 1.

a. Using $n = 30$, run the applet several times without clearing. What happens to the proportion of 95% confidence intervals that contain the mean as you run the applet more and more? What happens to the proportion of 99% confidence intervals that contain the mean as you run the applet more and more? Do the proportions seem to be approaching the values that you would expect?

b. Clear and run the applet several times using $n = 100$. What happens to the proportions of 95% confidence intervals and 99% confidence intervals that contain the mean this time? How do these results compare with your results in part **a?**

c. Clear and run the applet several times using $n = 1,000$. How do the results compare with your results in parts **a** and **b?**

d. Describe the effect of sample size on the likelihood that a confidence interval contains the mean for a skewed distribution.

6.6 Explain what is meant by the statement, "We are 95% confident that an interval estimate contains μ."

6.7 Explain the difference between an interval estimator and a point estimator for μ.

6.8 The mean and standard deviation of a random sample of n measurements are equal to 33.9 and 3.3, respectively.
a. Find a 95% confidence interval for μ if $n = 100$.
b. Find a 95% confidence interval for μ if $n = 400$.
c. Find the widths of the confidence intervals found in parts **a** and **b**. What is the effect on the width of a confidence interval of quadrupling the sample size while holding the confidence coefficient fixed?

6.9 Will a large-sample confidence interval be valid if the population from which the sample is taken is not normally distributed? Explain.

Applying the Concepts—Basic

6.10 **Heart rate variability of police officers.** Are police officers susceptible to higher-than-normal heart rates? The heart rate variability (HRV) of police officers was the subject of research published in the *American Journal of Human Biology* (January 2014). HRV is defined as the variation in time intervals between heartbeats. A measure of HRV was obtained for each in a sample of 355 Buffalo, N.Y., police officers. (The lower the measure of HRV, the more susceptible the officer is to cardiovascular disease.) For the 73 officers diagnosed with hypertension, a 95% confidence interval for the mean HRV was (4.1, 124.5). For the 282 officers who are not hypertensive, a 95% confidence interval for the mean HRV was (148.0, 192.6).
a. What confidence coefficient was used to generate the confidence intervals?
b. Give a practical interpretation of both 95% confidence intervals. Use the phrase "95% confident" in your answer.
c. When you say you are "95% confident," what do you mean?
d. If you want to reduce the width of each confidence interval, should you use a smaller or larger confidence coefficient? Explain.

6.11 **Tipping points in daily deal transactions?** Online "daily deal" sites (e.g., Groupon) offer customers a voucher to purchase a product at discount prices. However, the number of voucher purchases must exceed a predetermined number before the deal becomes active. This key number is termed the "tipping point" in marketing. Characteristics of the tipping point were investigated in the *Journal of Interactive Marketing* (February 2016). A sample of 2,617 vouchers purchased from daily-deal sites in Korea had a mean tipping point of 112 sales with a standard deviation of 560 sales. The researchers want to estimate the true mean tipping point of all daily deal offerings in Korea with 95% confidence. Find and practically interpret this interval estimate.

6.12 **Corporate sustainability of CPA firms.** *Corporate sustainability* refers to business practices designed around social and environmental considerations. Refer to the *Business and Society* (March 2011) study on the sustainability behaviors of CPA corporations, Exercise 2.23 (p. 83). Recall that the level of support for corporate sustainability (measured on a quantitative scale ranging from 0 to 160 points) was obtained for each in a sample of 992 senior managers at CPA firms. Higher point values indicate a higher level of support for sustainability. The accompanying Minitab printout gives a 90% confidence interval for the mean level of support for all senior managers at CPA firms.

One-Sample T: Support

Variable	N	Mean	StDev	SE Mean	90% CI
Support	992	67.755	26.871	0.853	(66.350, 69.160)

a. Locate the 90% confidence interval on the printout.
b. Use the sample mean and standard deviation on the printout to calculate the 90% confidence interval. Does your result agree with the interval shown on the printout?
c. Give a practical interpretation of the 90% confidence interval.
d. Suppose the CEO of a CPA firm claims that the true mean level of support for sustainability is 75 points. Do you believe this claim? Explain.

6.13 **College dropout study.** Refer to the *American Economic Review* (December 2008) study of college dropouts, Exercise 2.79 (p. 111). Recall that one factor thought to influence the college dropout decision was expected GPA for a student who studied 3 hours per day. In a representative sample of 307 college students who studied 3 hours per day, the mean GPA was $\bar{x} = 3.11$ and the standard deviation was $s = .66$. Of interest is μ, the true mean GPA of all college students who study 3 hours per day.
a. Give a point estimate for μ.
b. Give an interval estimate for μ. Use a confidence coefficient of .98.
c. Comment on the validity of the following statement: "98% of the time, the true mean GPA will fall in the interval computed in part **b**."
d. It is unlikely that the GPA values for college students who study 3 hours per day are normally distributed. In fact, it is likely that the GPA distribution is highly skewed. If so, what impact, if any, does this have on the validity of inferences derived from the confidence interval?

6.14 **Wear-out of used display panels.** Refer to Exercise 4.126 (p. 270) and the study of the wear-out failure time of used colored display panels purchased by an outlet store. Recall that prior to acquisition, the panels had been used for about one-third of their expected lifetimes. The failure times (in years) for a sample of 50 used panels are reproduced in the table. An SPSS printout of the analysis is shown below.

a. Locate a 95% confidence interval for the true mean failure time of used colored display panels on the printout.

b. Give a practical interpretation of the interval, part **a**.

c. In repeated sampling of the population of used colored display panels, where a 95% confidence interval for the mean failure time is computed for each sample, what proportion of all the confidence intervals generated will capture the true mean failure time?

0.01	1.21	1.71	2.30	2.96	0.19	1.22	1.75	2.30	2.98	0.51
1.24	1.77	2.41	3.19	0.57	1.48	1.79	2.44	3.25	0.70	1.54
1.88	2.57	3.31	0.73	1.59	1.90	2.61	1.19	0.75	1.61	1.93
2.62	3.50	0.75	1.61	2.01	2.72	3.50	1.11	1.62	2.16	2.76
3.50	1.16	1.62	2.18	2.84	3.50					

Source: Based on T. Z. Irony, M. Lauretto, C. Pereira, and J. M. Stern, "A Weibull Wearout Test: Full Bayesian Approach," paper presented at *Mathematical Sciences Colloquium*, Binghamton University, Binghamton, UK, December 2001.

Descriptives

			Statistic	Std. Error
FAILTIME	Mean		1.9350	.13133
	95% Confidence Interval for Mean	Lower Bound	1.6711	
		Upper Bound	2.1989	
	5% Trimmed Mean		1.9454	
	Median		1.8350	
	Variance		.862	
	Std. Deviation		.92865	
	Minimum		.01	
	Maximum		3.50	
	Range		3.49	
	Interquartile Range		1.43	
	Skewness		−.008	.337
	Kurtosis		−.755	.662

Applying the Concepts—Intermediate

6.15 **Unethical corporate conduct.** How complicit are entry-level accountants in carrying out an unethical request from their superiors? This was the question of interest in a study published in the journal *Behavioral Research in Accounting* (July 2015). A sample of 86 accounting graduate students participated in the study. After asking the subjects to perform what is clearly an unethical task (e.g., to bribe a customer), the researchers measured each subject's *intention to comply with the unethical request* score. Scores ranged from −1.5 (intention to resist the unethical request) to 2.5 (intention to comply with the unethical request). Summary statistics on the 86 scores follow: $\bar{x} = 2.42, s = 2.84$.

a. Estimate μ, the mean intention to comply score for the population of all entry-level accountants, using a 90% confidence interval.

b. Give a practical interpretation of the interval, part **a**.

c. Refer to part **a**. What proportion of all similarly constructed confidence intervals (in repeated sampling) will contain the true value of μ?

d. Compute the interval, $\bar{x} \pm 2s$. How does the interpretation of this interval differ from that of the confidence interval, part **a**?

6.16 **Shopping on Black Friday.** The day after Thanksgiving—called Black Friday—is one of the largest shopping days in the United States. Winthrop University researchers conducted interviews with a sample of 38 women shopping on Black Friday to gauge their shopping habits and reported the results in the *International Journal of Retail and Distribution Management* (Vol. 39, 2011). One question was, "How many hours do you usually spend shopping on Black Friday?" Data for the 38 shoppers are listed in the accompanying table.

a. Describe the population of interest to the researchers.

b. What is the quantitative variable of interest to the researchers?

c. Use the information in the table to estimate the population mean number of hours spent shopping on Black Friday with a 95% confidence interval.

d. Give a practical interpretation of the interval.

e. A retail store advertises that the true mean number of hours spent shopping on Black Friday is 5.5 hours. Can the store be sued for false advertising? Explain.

6	6	4	4	3	16	4	4	5	6	6	5	5	4
6	5	6	4	5	4	4	4	7	12	5	8	6	10
5	8	8	3	3	8	5	6	10	11			

Source: Based on J. B. Thomas, and C. Peters, "An Exploratory Investigation of Black Friday Consumption Rituals," *International Journal of Retail and Distribution Management,* Vol. 39, No. 7, 2011 (Table I).

6.17 **Executive Compensation Scoreboard.** Refer to the *Glassdoor Economic Research* (August 25, 2015) report on salaries of executives and workers at S&P 500 firms. Recall that the data file contains the salaries (in $ millions) of the 441 CEOs who participated in the survey. Suppose you are interested in estimating the mean salary for these 441 CEOs.

a. What is the target parameter?

b. Obtain a random sample of 50 salaries from the data set.

c. Find the mean of the 50 salaries, part **b**.

d. Verify that the standard deviation for the population of 411 salaries is $\sigma = \$11.36$ million.

e. Use the information, parts **c** and **d**, to form a 99% confidence interval for the true mean salary of the 411 CEOs in the survey.

f. Give a practical interpretation of the interval, part **e**.

g. Find the true mean salary of the 411 CEOs and check to see if this value falls within the 99% confidence interval, part **e**.

6.18 **401(k) Participation rates.** Named for the section of the Internal Revenue Code that authorized them, 401(k) plans permit employees to shift part of their before-tax salaries into investments such as mutual funds. One company, concerned with what it believed was a low employee participation rate in its 401(k) plan, sampled 30 other companies with similar plans and asked for their 401(k) participation rates. The following rates (in percentages) were obtained.

80	76	81	77	82	80	85	60	80	79	82	70
88	85	80	79	83	75	87	78	80	84	72	75
90	84	82	77	75	86						

a. Construct a 90% confidence interval for the mean participation rate for all companies that have 401(k) plans.

b. Interpret the interval in the context of this problem.

c. What assumption is necessary to ensure the validity of this confidence interval?

d. If the company that conducted the sample has a 71% participation rate, can it safely conclude that its rate is below the population mean rate for all companies with 401(k) plans? Explain.

e. If in the data set the 60% had been 80%, how would the center and width of the confidence interval you constructed in part **a** be affected?

6.19 Accounting and Machiavellianism. Refer to the *Behavioral Research in Accounting* (January 2008) study of Machiavellian traits in accountants, Exercise 1.33 (p. 52). Recall that *Machiavellian* describes negative character traits that include manipulation, cunning, duplicity, deception, and bad faith. A Machiavellian ("Mach") rating score was determined for each in a sample of accounting alumni of a large southwestern university. Scores range from a low of 40 to a high of 160, with the theoretical neutral Mach rating score of 100. The 122 purchasing managers in the sample had a mean Mach rating score of 99.6, with a standard deviation of 12.6.

a. From the sample, estimate the true mean Mach rating score of all purchasing managers.

b. Form a 95% confidence interval for the estimate, part **b**.

c. Give a practical interpretation of the interval, part **c**.

d. A director of purchasing at a major firm claims that the true mean Mach rating score of all purchasing managers is 85. Is there evidence to dispute this claim?

6.20 Facial structure of CEOs. In *Psychological Science* (Vol. 22, 2011), researchers reported that a chief executive officer's facial structure can be used to predict a firm's financial performance. The study involved measuring the facial width-to-height ratio (WHR) for each in a sample of 55 CEOs at publicly traded *Fortune* 500 firms. These WHR values (determined by a computer analyzing a photo of the CEO's face) had a mean of $\bar{x} = 1.96$ and a standard deviation of $s = .15$.

a. Find and interpret a 95% confidence interval for μ, the mean facial WHR for all CEOs at publicly traded *Fortune* 500 firms.

b. The researchers found that CEOs with wider faces (relative to height) tended to be associated with firms that had greater financial performance. They based their inference on an equation that uses facial WHR to predict financial performance. Suppose an analyst wants to predict the financial performance of a *Fortune* 500 firm based on the value of the true mean facial WHR of CEOs. The analyst wants to use the value of $\mu = 2.2$. Do you recommend he use this value?

Applying the Concepts—Advanced

6.21 Improving SAT scores. Refer to the *Chance* (Winter 2001) and National Education Longitudinal Survey (NELS) study of 265 students who paid a private tutor to help them improve their SAT scores, Exercise 2.88 (p. 113). The changes in both the SAT–Mathematics and SAT–Verbal scores for these students are reproduced in the table. Suppose the true population mean change in score on one of the SAT tests for all students who paid a private tutor is 15. Which of the two tests, SAT–Mathematics or SAT–Verbal, is most likely to have this mean change? Explain.

	SAT–Math	SAT–Verbal
Mean change in score	19	7
Standard deviation of score changes	65	49

6.22 The "Raid" test kitchen. According to scientists, the cockroach has had 300 million years to develop a resistance to destruction. In a study conducted by researchers for S. C. Johnson & Son, Inc. (manufacturers of Raid and Off!), 5,000 roaches (the expected number in a roach-infested house) were released in the Raid test kitchen. One week later, the kitchen was fumigated, and 16,298 dead roaches were counted, a gain of 11,298 roaches for the 1-week period. Assume that none of the original roaches died during the 1-week period and that the standard deviation of x, the number of roaches produced per roach in a 1-week period, is 1.5. Use the number of roaches produced by the sample of 5,000 roaches to find a 95% confidence interval for the mean number of roaches produced per week for each roach in a typical roach-infested house.

6.3 Confidence Interval for a Population Mean: Student's *t*-Statistic

Federal legislation requires pharmaceutical companies to perform extensive tests on new drugs before they can be marketed. Initially, a new drug is tested on animals. If the drug is deemed safe after this first phase of testing, the pharmaceutical company is then permitted to begin human testing on a limited basis. During this second phase, inferences must be made about the safety of the drug based on information in very small samples.

Suppose a pharmaceutical company must estimate the average increase in blood pressure of patients who take a certain new drug. Assume that only six patients (randomly selected from the population of all patients) can be used in the initial phase of human testing. The use of a *small sample* in making an inference about μ presents two immediate problems when we attempt to use the standard normal z as a test statistic.

WILLIAM S. GOSSET (1876–1937)
Student's t-Distribution

At the age of 23, William Gosset earned a degree in chemistry and mathematics at prestigious Oxford University. He was immediately hired by the Guinness Brewing Company in Dublin, Ireland, for his expertise in chemistry. However, Gosset's mathematical skills allowed him to solve numerous practical problems associated with brewing beer. For example, Gosset applied the Poisson distribution to model the number of yeast cells per unit volume in the fermentation process. His most important discovery was that of the *t*-distribution in 1908. Because most applied researchers worked with small samples, Gosset was interested in the behavior of the mean in the small sample case. He tediously took numerous small sets of numbers, calculated the mean and standard deviation, obtained their *t*-ratio, and plotted the results on graph paper. The shape of the distribution was always the same—the *t*-distribution. Under company policy, employees were forbidden to publish their research results, so Gosset used the pen name *Student* to publish a paper on the subject. Hence, the distribution has been called Student's *t*-distribution.

Problem 1   The shape of the sampling distribution of the sample mean $\bar{x}$ (and the *z*-statistic) now depends on the shape of the population that is sampled. We can no longer assume that the sampling distribution of $\bar{x}$ is approximately normal because the Central Limit Theorem ensures normality only for samples that are sufficiently large.

Solution to Problem 1   According to Theorem 5.1, the sampling distribution of $\bar{x}$ (and *z*) is exactly normal, even for small samples, if the sampled population is normal. It is approximately normal if the sampled population is approximately normal.

Problem 2   The population standard deviation σ is almost always unknown. Although it is still true that $\sigma_{\bar{x}} = \frac{\sigma}{\sqrt{n}}$, the sample standard deviation s may provide a poor approximation for σ when the sample size is small.

Solution to Problem 2   Instead of using the standard normal statistic

$$z = \frac{\bar{x} - \mu}{\sigma_{\bar{x}}} = \frac{\bar{x} - \mu}{\sigma/\sqrt{n}}$$

which requires knowledge of or a good approximation to σ, we define and use the statistic

$$t = \frac{\bar{x} - \mu}{s/\sqrt{n}}$$

in which the sample standard deviation, s, replaces the population standard deviation, σ.

If we are sampling from a normal distribution, the **t-statistic** has a sampling distribution very much like that of the **z-statistic:** mound-shaped, symmetric, with mean 0. The primary difference between the sampling distributions of t and z is that the *t*-statistic is more variable than the z, which follows intuitively when you realize that t contains two random quantities ($\bar{x}$ and s), whereas z contains only one ($\bar{x}$).

The actual amount of variability in the sampling distribution of t depends on the sample size n. A convenient way of expressing this dependence is to say that the *t*-statistic has $(n - 1)$ **degrees of freedom (df).** Recall that the quantity $(n - 1)$ is the divisor that appears in the formula for s^2. This number plays a key role in the sampling distribution of s^2 and appears in discussions of other statistics in later chapters. In particular, the smaller the number of degrees of freedom associated with the *t*-statistic, the more variable will be its sampling distribution.

In Figure 6.9 we show both the sampling distribution of z and the sampling distribution of a *t*-statistic with 4 and 20 df. Note that the *t*-distribution is more variable than the *z*-distribution, and this variability increases as the degrees of freedom decrease. Also, the increased variability of the *t*-statistic means that the *t*-value, t_α, that locates an area α in the upper tail of the *t*-distribution is larger than the corresponding value z_α. For any given value of α, the *t*-value t_α increases as the df decreases. Values of t that

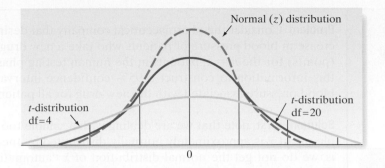

Figure 6.9

Standard normal (z) distribution and t-distributions

will be used in forming small-sample confidence intervals of μ are given in Table III in Appendix D. A partial reproduction of this table is shown in Table 6.3.

Note that t_α values are listed for various degrees of freedom, where α refers to the tail area under the t-distribution to the right of t_α. For example, if we want the t-value with an area of .025 to its right and 4 df, we look in the table under the column $t_{.025}$ for the entry in the row corresponding to 4 df. This entry, $t_{.025} = 2.776$, is highlighted in Figure 6.9. Recall that the corresponding standard normal z-score is $z_{.025} = 1.96$.

The last row of Table III, where df $= \infty$ (infinity), contains the standard normal z-values. This follows from the fact that as the sample size n grows very large, s becomes closer to σ and thus t becomes closer in distribution to z. In fact, when df $= 29$, there is little difference between corresponding tabulated values of z and t. Thus, researchers often choose the arbitrary cutoff of $n = 30$ (df $= 29$) to distinguish between the large-sample and small-sample inferential techniques when σ is unknown.

Table 6.3	Reproduction of Part of Table III in Appendix D

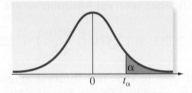

Degrees of Freedom	$t_{.100}$	$t_{.050}$	$t_{.025}$	$t_{.010}$	$t_{.005}$	$t_{.001}$	$t_{.0005}$
1	3.078	6.314	12.706	31.821	63.657	318.13	636.62
2	1.886	2.920	4.303	6.965	9.925	22.326	21.598
3	1.638	2.353	3.182	4.541	5.841	10.213	12.924
4	1.533	2.132	2.776	3.747	4.604	7.173	8.610
5	1.476	2.015	2.571	3.365	4.032	5.893	6.869
6	1.440	1.943	2.447	3.132	3.707	5.208	5.959
7	1.415	1.895	2.365	2.998	3.499	4.785	5.408
8	1.397	1.860	2.306	2.896	3.355	4.501	5.041
9	1.383	1.833	2.262	2.821	3.250	4.297	4.781
10	1.372	1.812	2.228	2.764	3.169	4.144	4.587
11	1.363	1.796	2.201	2.718	3.106	4.025	4.437
12	1.356	1.782	2.179	2.681	3.055	3.930	4.318
13	1.350	1.771	2.160	2.650	3.012	3.852	4.221
14	1.345	1.761	2.145	2.624	2.977	3.787	4.140
15	1.341	1.753	2.131	2.602	2.947	3.733	4.073
⋮	⋮	⋮	⋮	⋮	⋮	⋮	⋮
∞	1.282	1.645	1.960	2.326	2.576	3.090	3.291

EXAMPLE 6.4

A Confidence Interval for μ Using the t-statistic–Blood Pressure Drug

---

Table 6.4

Blood Pressure Increases for $n = 6$ Patients

| 1.7 | 3.0 | .8 | 3.4 | 2.7 | 2.1 |

 *Data Set:* BPINCR

Problem Consider the pharmaceutical company that desires an estimate of the mean increase in blood pressure of patients who take a new drug. The blood pressure increases (points) for the $n = 6$ patients in the human testing phase are shown in Table 6.4. Use this information to construct a 95% confidence interval for μ, the mean increase in blood pressure associated with the new drug for all patients in the population.

Solution First, note that we are dealing with a sample too small to assume that the sample mean $\bar{x}$ is approximately normally distributed by the Central Limit Theorem—that is, we do not get the normal distribution of $\bar{x}$ "automatically" from the Central Limit Theorem when the sample size is small. Instead, the measured variable, in this case the increase in blood pressure, must be normally distributed in order for the distribution of $\bar{x}$ to be normal.

Second, unless we are fortunate enough to know the population standard deviation σ, which in this case represents the standard deviation of *all* the patients' increases in blood pressure when they take the new drug, we cannot use the standard normal z-statistic to form our confidence interval for μ. Instead, we must use the t-distribution, with $(n - 1)$ degrees of freedom.

In this case, $n - 1 = 5$ df, and the t-value is found in Table 6.3 to be $t_{.025} = 2.571$ with 5 df. Recall that the large-sample confidence interval would have been of the form

$$\bar{x} \pm z_{\alpha/2}\sigma_{\bar{x}} = \bar{x} \pm z_{\alpha/2}\frac{\sigma}{\sqrt{n}} = \bar{x} \pm z_{.025}\frac{\sigma}{\sqrt{n}}$$

where 95% is the desired confidence level. To form the interval for a small sample from *a normal distribution, we simply substitute t for z and s for σ in the preceding formula:*

$$\bar{x} \pm t_{\alpha/2}\frac{s}{\sqrt{n}}$$

An SPSS printout showing descriptive statistics for the six blood pressure increases is displayed in Figure 6.10. Note that $\bar{x} = 2.283$ and $s = .950$. Substituting these numerical values into the confidence interval formula, we get

$$2.283 \pm (2.571)\left(\frac{.950}{\sqrt{6}}\right) = 2.283 \pm .997$$

or 1.286 to 3.280 points. Note that this interval agrees (except for rounding) with the confidence interval generated by SPSS in Figure 6.10.

We interpret the interval as follows: We can be 95% confident that the mean increase in blood pressure associated with taking this new drug is between 1.286 and 3.28 points. As with our large-sample interval estimates, our confidence is in the process, not in this particular interval. We know that if we were to repeatedly use this estimation

Descriptives

			Statistic	Std. Error
BPINCR	Mean		2.283	.3877
	95% Confidence Interval for Mean	Lower Bound	1.287	
		Upper Bound	3.280	
	5% Trimmed Mean		2.304	
	Median		2.400	
	Variance		.902	
	Std. Deviation		.9496	
	Minimum		.8	
	Maximum		3.4	
	Range		2.6	
	Interquartile Range		1.625	
	Skewness		−.573	.845
	Kurtosis		−.389	1.741

Figure 6.10

SPSS confidence interval for mean blood pressure increase

procedure, 95% of the confidence intervals produced would contain the true mean μ, *assuming that the probability distribution of changes in blood pressure from which our sample was selected is normal.* The latter assumption is necessary for the small-sample interval to be valid.

Look Back What price did we pay for having to use a small sample to make the inference? First, we had to assume the underlying population was normally distributed, and if the assumption was invalid, our interval might also have been invalid.* Second, we had to form the interval using a *t*-value of 2.571 rather than a *z*-value of 1.96, resulting in a wider interval to achieve the same 95% level of confidence. If the interval from 1.286 to 3.28 is too wide to be of use, then we know how to remedy the situation: increase the number of patients sampled to decrease the interval width (on average).

● **Now Work Exercise 6.24**

The procedure for forming a small-sample confidence interval is summarized in the accompanying boxes.

Small-Sample Confidence Interval for μ, Student's *t*-statistic

$$\sigma \text{ unknown: } \bar{x} \pm t_{\alpha/2}\left(\frac{s}{\sqrt{n}}\right)$$

where $t_{\alpha/2}$ is the *t*-value corresponding to an area $\frac{\alpha}{2}$ in the upper tail of the student's *t*-distribution based on $(n - 1)$ degrees of freedom.

$$\sigma \text{ known: } \bar{x} \pm z_{\alpha/2}\left(\frac{\sigma}{\sqrt{n}}\right)$$

Conditions Required for a Valid Small-Sample Confidence Interval for μ

1. A random sample is selected from the target population.
2. The population has a relative frequency distribution that is approximately normal.

EXAMPLE 6.5

A Small-Sample Confidence Interval for μ—Destructive Sampling

Table 6.5

Number of Characters (in Millions) for $n = 15$ Printhead Tests

1.13	1.55	1.43	.92	1.25
1.36	1.32	.85	1.07	1.48
1.20	1.33	1.18	1.22	1.29

 *Data Set*: PRHEAD

Problem Some quality-control experiments require *destructive sampling* (i.e., the test to determine whether the item is defective destroys the item) in order to measure some particular characteristic of the product. The cost of destructive sampling often dictates small samples. For example, suppose a manufacturer of printers for personal computers wishes to estimate the mean number of characters printed before the printhead fails. Suppose the printer manufacturer tests $n = 15$ randomly selected printheads and records the number of characters printed until failure for each. These 15 measurements (in millions of characters) are listed in Table 6.5, followed by an XLSTAT summary statistics printout in Figure 6.11.

a. Form a 99% confidence interval for the mean number of characters printed before the printhead fails. Interpret the result.

b. What assumption is required for the interval, part **a**, to be valid? Is it reasonably satisfied?

*By *invalid*, we mean that the probability that the procedure will yield an interval that contains μ is not equal to $(1 - \alpha)$. Generally, if the underlying population is approximately normal, then the confidence coefficient will approximate the probability that a randomly selected interval contains μ.

Solution

a. For this small sample $(n = 15)$, we use the t-statistic to form the confidence interval. We use a confidence coefficient of .99 and $n - 1 = 14$ degrees of freedom to find $t_{\alpha/2}$ in Table III :

$$t_{\alpha/2} = t_{.005} = 2.977$$

[*Note:* The small sample forces us to extend the interval almost 3 standard deviations (of $\bar{x}$) on each side of the sample mean in order to form the 99% confidence interval.] From the XLSTAT printout, Figure 6.11, we find $\bar{x} = 1.239$ and $s = .193$. Substituting these values into the confidence interval formula, we obtain

$$\bar{x} \pm t_{.005}\left(\frac{s}{\sqrt{n}}\right) = 1.239 \pm 2.977\left(\frac{.193}{\sqrt{15}}\right)$$

$$= 1.239 \pm .148 \text{ or } (1.091, 1.387)$$

This interval is shown (shaded) at the bottom of the printout, Figure 6.11.

Our interpretation is as follows: The manufacturer can be 99% confident that the printhead has a mean life of between 1.091 and 1.387 million characters. If the manufacturer were to advertise that the mean life of its printheads is (at least) 1 million characters, the interval would support such a claim. Our confidence is derived from the fact that 99% of the intervals formed in repeated applications of this procedure would contain μ.

b. Because n is small, we must assume that the number of characters printed before printhead failure is a random variable from a normal distribution—that is, we assume that the population from which the sample of 15 measurements is selected is distributed normally. One way to check this assumption is to graph the distribution of data in Table 6.5. If the sample data are approximately normal, then the population from which the sample is selected is very likely to be normal. A Minitab stem-and-leaf plot for the sample data is displayed in Figure 6.12. The distribution is mound-shaped and nearly symmetric. Therefore, the assumption of normality appears to be reasonably satisfied.

Look Back Other checks for normality, such as a normal probability plot and the ratio IQR/S, may also be used to verify the normality condition.

● **Now Work Exercise 6.37**

Descriptive statistics (Quantitative data):	
Statistic	**NUMBER**
Nbr. of observations	15
Minimum	0.8500
Maximum	1.5500
Mean	1.2387
Standard deviation (n-1)	0.1932
Lower bound on mean (99%	1.0902
Upper bound on mean (99%	1.3871

Figure 6.11

XLSTAT output showing summary statistics and 95% confidence interval for μ, Example 6.5

```
Stem-and-Leaf Display: NUMBER

Stem-and-leaf of NUMBER  N  = 15
Leaf Unit = 0.010

  1    8   5
  2    9   2
  3   10   7
  5   11   38
 (4)  12   0259
  6   13   236
  3   14   38
  1   15   5
```

Figure 6.12

Minitab stem-and-leaf display of data in Table 6.5

We have emphasized throughout this section that an assumption that the population is approximately normally distributed is necessary for making small-sample inferences about μ when σ is unknown and when using the t-statistic. Although many phenomena do have approximately normal distributions, it is also true that many random phenomena have distributions that are not normal or even mound-shaped. Empirical evidence acquired over the years has shown that confidence intervals based on the t-distribution are rather insensitive to moderate departures from normality—that is, use of the t-statistic when sampling from slightly or moderately skewed mound-shaped populations generally produces credible results; however, for cases in which the distribution is distinctly nonnormal, we must either take a large sample or use a *nonparametric method* (the topic of Chapter 15).

What Do You Do When the Population Relative Frequency Distribution Departs Greatly from Normality?

Answer: Use the nonparametric statistical methods of Chapter 15 (available on the text resource website).

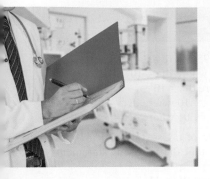

Estimating the Mean Overpayment

Refer to the Medicare fraud investigation described in the *Statistics in Action* (pp. 330–331). Recall that the U.S. Department of Justice (USDOJ) obtained a random sample of 52 claims from a population of 1,000 Medicare claims. For each claim, the amount paid, the amount disallowed (denied) by the auditor, and the amount that should have been paid (allowed) were recorded and saved in the **MFRAUD** file. The USDOJ wants to use these data to calculate an estimate of the overpayment for all 1,000 claims in the population.

One way to do this is to first use the sample data to estimate the mean overpayment per claim for the population, then use the estimated mean to extrapolate the overpayment amount to the population of all 1,000 claims. The difference between the amount paid and the amount allowed by the auditor represents the overpayment for each claim. This value is recorded as the amount denied in the **MFRAUD** file. These overpayment amounts in dollars are listed in the accompanying table.

Minitab software is used to find a 95% confidence interval for μ, the mean overpayment amount. The Minitab printout is displayed in Figure SIA6.1. The 95% confidence interval for μ (highlighted on the printout) is (16.51, 27.13). Thus, the USDOJ can be 95% confident that the mean overpayment amount for the population of 1,000 claims is between $16.51 and $27.13.

Table SIA6.1	Overpayment Amounts (Dollars) for Sample of 52 Claims						
0.00	31.00	0.00	37.20	37.20	0.00	43.40	0.00
37.20	43.40	0.00	37.20	0.00	24.80	0.00	0.00
37.20	0.00	37.20	0.00	37.20	37.20	37.20	0.00
37.20	37.20	0.00	0.00	37.20	0.00	43.40	37.20
0.00	37.20	0.00	37.20	37.20	0.00	37.20	37.20
0.00	37.20	43.40	0.00	37.20	37.20	37.20	0.00
43.40	0.00	43.40	0.00				

 *Data Set:* MFRAUD

```
Variable        N   Mean   StDev  SE Mean      95% CI
Denied_Amount  52  21.82   19.08     2.65  (16.51, 27.13)
```

Figure SIA6.1

Minitab confidence interval for mean overpayment

Now, let x_i represent the overpayment amount for the *i*th claim. If the true mean μ were known, then the total overpayment amount for all 1,000 claims would be equal to

$$\sum_{i=1}^{1,000} x_i = (1,000)\left[\sum_{i=1}^{1,000} x_i\right]/(1,000) = (1,000)\mu$$

Consequently, to estimate the total overpayment amount for the 1,000 claims, the USDOJ will simply multiply the endpoints of the interval by 1,000. This yields the 95% confidence interval ($16,510, $27,130).* Typically, the USDOJ is willing to give the Medicare provider in question the benefit of the doubt by demanding a repayment equal to the lower 95% confidence bound—in this case, $16,510.

*This interval represents an approximation to the true 95% confidence interval for the total amount of overpayment. The precise interval involves use of a continuity correction for population size (see Section 6.6).

Exercises 6.23–6.39

Learning the Mechanics

6.23 Suppose you have selected a random sample of $n = 5$ measurements from a normal distribution. Compare the standard normal z-values with the corresponding t-values if you were forming the following confidence intervals.
  a. 80% confidence interval
  b. 90% confidence interval
  c. 95% confidence interval
  d. 98% confidence interval
  e. 99% confidence interval
  f. Use the table values you obtained in parts **a–e** to sketch the z- and t-distributions. What are the similarities and differences?

📊 Applet Exercise 6.3

Use the applet *Confidence Intervals for a Mean (the impact of not knowing the standard deviation)* to compare proportions of z-intervals and t-intervals that contain the mean for a population that is normally distributed.
  a. Using $n = 5$ and the normal distribution with mean 50 and standard deviation 10, run the applet several times. How do the proportions of z-intervals and t-intervals that contain the mean compare?
  b. Repeat part **a** first for $n = 10$ and then for $n = 20$. Compare your results with those in part **a**.
  c. Describe any patterns you observe between the proportion of z-intervals that contain the mean and the proportion of t-intervals that contain the mean as the sample size increases.

📊 Applet Exercise 6.4

Use the applet *Confidence Intervals for a Mean (the impact of not knowing the standard deviation)* to compare proportions of z-intervals and t-intervals that contain the mean for a population with a skewed distribution.
  a. Using $n = 5$ and the right skewed distribution with mean 50 and standard deviation 10, run the applet several times. How do the proportions of z-intervals and t-intervals that contain the mean compare?
  b. Repeat part **a** first for $n = 10$ and then for $n = 20$. Compare your results with those in part **a**.
  c. Describe any patterns you observe between the proportion of z-intervals that contain the mean and the proportion of t-intervals that contain the mean as the sample size increases.
  d. How does skewedness of the underlying distribution affect the proportions of z-intervals and t-intervals that contain the mean?

6.24 Explain the differences in the sampling distributions of $\bar{x}$ for large and small samples under the following assumptions.
  a. The variable of interest, x, is normally distributed.
  b. Nothing is known about the distribution of the variable x.

6.25 Let t_0 be a particular value of t. Use Table III in Appendix D to find t_0 values such that the following statements are true.

  a. $P(-t_0 < t < t_0) = .95$ where df $= 10$
  b. $P(t \le -t_0 \text{ or } t \ge t_0)$ where df $= 10$
  c. $P(t \le t_0) = .05$ where df $= 10$
  d. $P(t \le -t_0 \text{ or } t \ge t_0) = .10$ where df $= 20$
  e. $P(t \le -t_0 \text{ or } t \ge t_0) = .01$ where df $= 5$

6.26 Let t_0 be a specific value of t. Use Table III in Appendix D to find t_0 values such that the following statements are true.
  a. $P(t \ge t_0) = .025$ where df $= 11$
  b. $P(t \ge t_0) = .01$ where df $= 9$
  c. $P(t \le t_0) = .005$ where df $= 6$
  d. $P(t \le t_0) = .05$ where df $= 18$

6.27 The following random sample was selected from a normal distribution: 4, 6, 3, 5, 9, 3.
  a. Construct a 90% confidence interval for the population mean μ.
  b. Construct a 95% confidence interval for the population mean μ.
  c. Construct a 99% confidence interval for the population mean μ.
  d. Assume that the sample mean $\bar{x}$ and sample standard deviation s remain exactly the same as those you just calculated but are based on a sample of $n = 25$ observations rather than $n = 6$ observations. Repeat parts **a–c**. What is the effect of increasing the sample size on the width of the confidence intervals?

6.28 The following sample of 16 measurements was selected from a population that is approximately normally distributed:

91	80	99	110	95	106	78	121	106	100	97	82
100	83	115	104								

  a. Construct an 80% confidence interval for the population mean.
  b. Construct a 95% confidence interval for the population mean and compare the width of this interval with that of part **a**.
  c. Carefully interpret each of the confidence intervals and explain why the 80% confidence interval is narrower.

Applying the Concepts—Basic

6.29 **Lobster trap placement.** An observational study of teams fishing for the red spiny lobster in Baja California Sur, Mexico, was conducted and the results published in *Bulletin of Marine Science* (April 2010). One of the variables of interest was the average distance separating traps—called *trap spacing*—deployed by the same team of fishermen. Trap-spacing measurements (in meters) for a sample of seven teams of red spiny lobster fishermen are shown in the accompanying table. Of interest is the mean trap spacing for the population of red spiny lobster fishermen fishing in Baja California Sur, Mexico.

93	99	105	94	82	70	86

Source: Based on G. G. Shester, "Explaining Catch Variation Among Baja California Lobster Fishers Through Spatial Analysis of Trap-Placement Decisions," *Bulletin of Marine Science*, Vol. 86, No. 2, April 2010 (Table 1).

a. Identify the target parameter for this study.
b. Compute a point estimate of the target parameter.
c. What is the problem with using the normal (z) statistic to find a confidence interval for the target parameter?
d. Find a 95% confidence interval for the target parameter.
e. Give a practical interpretation of the interval, part **d.**
f. What conditions must be satisfied for the interval, part **d,** to be valid?

6.30 **Radon exposure in Egyptian tombs.** Many ancient Egyptian tombs were cut from limestone rock that contained uranium. Since most tombs are not well ventilated, guards, tour guides, and visitors may be exposed to deadly radon gas. In *Radiation Protection Dosimetry* (December 2010), a study of radon exposure in tombs in the Valley of Kings, Luxor, Egypt (recently opened for public tours), was conducted. The radon levels—measured in becquerels per cubic meter (Bq/m^3)—in the inner chambers of a sample of 12 tombs were determined. Summary statistics follow: $\bar{x} = 3{,}643$ Bq/m^3 and $s = 4{,}487$ Bq/m^3. Use this information to estimate, with 95% confidence, the true mean level of radon exposure in tombs in the Valley of Kings. Interpret the resulting interval.

6.31 **Do social robots walk or roll?** Refer to the *International Conference on Social Robotics* (Vol. 6414, 2010) study on the current trend in the design of social robots, Exercise 2.78 (p. 111). Recall that in a random sample of social robots obtained through a Web search, 28 were built with wheels. The accompanying table shows the number of wheels on each of the 28 robots.
a. Estimate μ, the average number of wheels used on all social robots built with wheels, with 99% confidence.
b. Practically interpret the interval, part **a.**
c. Refer to part **a.** In repeated sampling, what proportion of all similarly constructed confidence intervals will contain the true mean, μ?

| 4 | 4 | 3 | 3 | 3 | 6 | 4 | 2 | 2 | 2 | 1 | 3 | 3 | 3 |
| 3 | 4 | 4 | 3 | 2 | 8 | 2 | 2 | 3 | 4 | 3 | 3 | 4 | 2 |

Source: Based on S. Chew et al., "Do Social Robots Walk or Roll?" *International Conference on Social Robotics,* Vol. 6414, 2010 (adapted from Figure 2).

6.32 Hospital length of stay. Health insurers and the federal government are both putting pressure on hospitals to shorten the average length of stay (LOS) of their patients. The average LOS in the United States is 4.5 days (*Healthcare Cost and Utilization Project Statistical Brief,* October 2014). A random sample of 20 hospitals in one state had a mean LOS of 3.8 days and a standard deviation of 1.2 days.
a. Use a 90% confidence interval to estimate the population mean LOS for the state's hospitals.
b. Interpret the interval in terms of this application.
c. What is meant by the phrase "90% confidence interval"?

6.33 **Repair and replacement costs of water pipes.** Refer to the *IHS Journal of Hydraulic Engineering* (September 2012) study of commercial pipes used in a water distribution network, Exercise 2.124 (p. 131). Of interest was the ratio of repair to replacement cost of the pipe. The ratios for a sample of 13 different pipe sizes are listed in the next table. Assume these data represent a random sample selected

| 6.58 | 6.97 | 7.39 | 7.61 | 7.78 | 7.92 | 8.20 | 8.42 | 8.60 | 8.97 | 9.31 | 9.47 | 9.72 |

Source: C. R. Suribabu and T. R. Neelakantan, "Sizing of water distribution pipes based on performance measure and breakage-repair replacement economics," *IHS Journal of Hydraulic Engineering,* Vol. 18, No. 3, September 2012 (Table 1).

from all possible types of commercial pipe. A Minitab analysis of the data follows.

One-Sample T: RATIO

Variable	N	Mean	StDev	SE Mean	95% CI
RATIO	13	8.226	0.972	0.270	(7.639, 8.814)

a. Locate a 95% confidence interval for the mean ratio of repair to replacement cost for all commercial pipe on the accompanying Minitab printout.
b. A civil engineer claims that the average ratio of repair to replacement cost could be as low as 7.0. Do you agree? Explain.
c. What assumptions about the data are required for the interval, part **a,** to be valid?

Applying the Concepts—Intermediate

6.34 Evaporation from swimming pools. A new formula for estimating the water evaporation from occupied swimming pools was proposed and analyzed in the journal *Heating/Piping/Air Conditioning Engineering* (April 2013). The key components of the new formula are number of pool occupants, area of pool's water surface, and the density difference between room air temperature and the air at the pool's surface. Data were collected from a wide range of pools for which the evaporation level was known. The new formula was applied to each pool in the sample, yielding an estimated evaporation level. The absolute value of the deviation between the actual and estimated evaporation level was then recorded as a percentage. The researchers reported the following summary statistics for absolute deviation percentage: $\bar{x} = 18$, $s = 20$. Assume that the sample contained $n = 15$ swimming pools.
a. Estimate the true mean absolute deviation percentage for the new formula with a 90% confidence interval.
b. The American Society of Heating, Refrigerating, and Air-Conditioning Engineers (ASHRAE) handbook also provides a formula for estimating pool evaporation. Suppose the ASHRAE mean absolute deviation percentage is $\mu = 34\%$. (This value was reported in the article.) On average, is the new formula "better" than the ASHRAE formula? Explain.

6.35 **Oxygen bubbles in molten salt.** Molten salt is used in an electro-refiner to treat nuclear fuel waste. Eventually, the salt needs to be purified (for reuse) or disposed of. A promising method of purification involves oxidation. Such a method was investigated in *Chemical Engineering Research and Design* (March. 2013). An important aspect of the purification process is the rising velocity of oxygen bubbles in the molten salt. An experiment was conducted in which oxygen was inserted (at a designated sparging rate) into molten salt and photographic images of the bubbles were taken. A random sample of 25 images yielded the data on bubble velocity (measured in meters per second) shown in the table. (*Note:* These data are simulated based on information provided in the article.)

0.275	0.261	0.209	0.266	0.265	0.312	0.285	0.317	0.229
0.251	0.256	0.339	0.213	0.178	0.217	0.307	0.264	0.319
0.298	0.169	0.342	0.270	0.262	0.228	0.220		

a. Use statistical software to find a 95% confidence interval for the mean bubble rising velocity of the population. Interpret the result.

b. The researchers discovered that the mean bubble rising velocity is $\mu = .338$ when the sparging rate of oxygen is 3.33×10^{-6}. Do you believe that the data in the table were generated at this sparging rate? Explain.

6.36 **Performance of stock screeners.** In Exercise 2.44 (p. 95) you learned that stock screeners are automated tools used by investment companies to help clients select a portfolio of stocks to invest in. The table below lists the annualized percentage return on investment (as compared to the Standard & Poor's 500 Index) for 13 randomly selected stock screeners provided by the American Association of Individual Investors (AAII).

9.0	−.1	−1.6	14.6	16.0	7.7	19.9	9.8	3.2	24.8	17.6	10.7	9.1

a. Find a 90% confidence interval for the average annualized percentage return on investment of all stock screeners provided by AAII. Interpret the result.

b. Recall that a negative annualized return reflects a stock portfolio that performed worse than the S&P 500. On average, do the AAII stock screeners perform worse or better than the S&P 500? Explain.

c. What assumption about the distribution of the annualized percentage returns on investment is required for the inference, part **b,** to be valid? Is this assumption reasonably satisfied?

6.37 **Minimizing tractor skidding distance.** When planning for a new forest road to be used for tree harvesting, planners must select the location to minimize tractor skidding distance. In the *Journal of Forest Engineering* (July 1999), researchers wanted to estimate the true mean skidding distance along a new road in a European forest. The skidding distances (in meters) were measured at 20 randomly selected road sites. These values are given in the accompanying table.

a. Estimate the true mean skidding distance for the road with a 95% confidence interval.

b. Give a practical interpretation of the interval, part **a.**

c. What conditions are required for the inference, part **b,** to be valid? Are these conditions reasonably satisfied?

d. A logger working on the road claims the mean skidding distance is at least 425 meters. Do you agree?

488	350	457	199	285	409	435	574	439	546
385	295	184	261	273	400	311	312	141	425

Source: Based on J. Tujek and E. Pacola, "Algorithms for Skidding Distance Modeling on a Raster Digital Terrain Model," *Journal of Forest Engineering,* Vol. 10, No. 1, July 1999 (Table 1).

6.38 **Crude oil biodegradation.** Refer to the *Journal of Petroleum Geology* (April 2010) study of the environmental factors associated with biodegradation in crude oil reservoirs, Exercise 2.29 (p. 85). One indicator of biodegradation is the level of dioxide in the water. Recall that 16 water specimens were randomly selected from various locations in a reservoir on the floor of a mine and the amount of dioxide (milligrams/liter) as well as presence of oil was determined for each specimen. These data are reproduced in the next table.

a. Estimate the true mean amount of dioxide present in water specimens that contain oil using a 95% confidence interval. Give a practical interpretation of the interval.

b. Repeat part **a** for water specimens that do not contain oil.

c. Based on the results, parts **a** and **b,** make an inference about biodegradation at the mine reservoir.

Dioxide Amount	Crude Oil Present
3.3	No
0.5	Yes
1.3	Yes
0.4	Yes
0.1	No
4.0	No
0.3	No
0.2	Yes
2.4	No
2.4	No
1.4	No
0.5	Yes
0.2	Yes
4.0	No
4.0	No
4.0	No

Source: Based on A. Permanyer et al., "Crude Oil Biodegradation and Environmental Factors at the Riutort Oil Shale Mine, SE Pyrenees," *Journal of Petroleum Geology,* Vol. 33, No. 2, April 2010 (Table 1).

6.39 **Largest private companies.** IPOs—initial public offerings of stock—create billions of dollars of new wealth for owners, managers, and employees of companies that were previously privately owned. Nevertheless, hundreds of large and thousands of small companies remain privately owned. The revenues of a random sample of 15 firms from *Forbes* 216 Largest Private Companies list are given in the table below.

Company	Revenue (in billions)
Toys, R, Us	$12.4
Pilot Flying J	31.0
Tenaska Energy	12.2
Wawa	9.7
Gulf States Toyota	8.0
Brookshire Grocery	2.5
Sinclair Oil	7.0
Bose	3.4
Mary Kay	4.0
Drummond	2.4
Petco	4.0
SAS	3.1
Forever 21	4.4
Rock Ventures	5.1
Conair	2.3

Source: Data from "America's Largest Private Companies," *Forbes,* October 28, 2015.

a. Describe the population from which the random sample was drawn.

b. Use a 98% confidence interval to estimate the mean revenue of the population of companies in question.

c. Interpret your confidence interval in the context of the problem.

d. What characteristic must the population possess to ensure the appropriateness of the estimation procedure used in part **b**?

e. Suppose *Forbes* reports that the true mean revenue of the 216 companies on the list is $5.0 billion. Is the claim believable?

6.4 Large-Sample Confidence Interval for a Population Proportion

The number of public opinion polls has grown at an astounding rate in recent years. Almost daily, the news media report the results of some poll. Pollsters regularly determine the percentage of people who approve of the president's on-the-job performance, the fraction of voters in favor of a certain candidate, the fraction of customers who prefer a particular product, and the proportion of households that watch a particular TV program. In each case, we are interested in estimating the percentage (or proportion) of some group with a certain characteristic. In this section, we consider methods for making inferences about population proportions when the sample is large.

EXAMPLE 6.6

Estimating a Population Proportion–Preference for Breakfast Cereal

Problem A food-products company conducted a market study by randomly sampling and interviewing 1,000 consumers to determine which brand of breakfast cereal they prefer. Suppose 313 consumers were found to prefer the company's brand. How would you estimate the true fraction of *all* consumers who prefer the company's cereal brand?

Solution In this study, consumers are asked which brand of breakfast cereal they prefer. Note that "brand" is a qualitative variable and that what we are asking is how you would estimate the probability p of success in a binomial experiment, where p is the probability that a chosen consumer prefers the company's brand. One logical method of estimating p for the population is to use the proportion of successes in the sample—that is, we can estimate p by calculating

$$\hat{p} = \frac{\text{Number of consumers sampled who prefer the company's brand}}{\text{Number of consumers sampled}}$$

where $\hat{p}$ is read "p hat." Thus, in this case,

$$\hat{p} = \frac{313}{1,000} = .313$$

Look Back To determine the reliability of the estimator $\hat{p}$, we need to know its sampling distribution—that is, if we were to draw samples of 1,000 consumers over and over again, each time calculating a new estimate $\hat{p}$, what would be the frequency distribution of all the $\hat{p}$ values? Recall (Section 5.4) that the answer lies in viewing $\hat{p}$ as the average, or mean, number of successes per trial over the n trials. If each success is assigned a value equal to 1 and a failure is assigned a value of 0, then the sum of all n sample observations is x, the total number of successes, and $\hat{p} = x/n$ is the average, or mean, number of successes per trial in the n trials. The Central Limit Theorem tells us that the *relative frequency distribution of the sample mean for any population is approximately normal for sufficiently large samples.*

• **Now Work Exercise 6.45a**

The repeated sampling distribution of $\hat{p}$ was the topic of Section 5.4. The characteristics are repeated in the next box and shown in Figure 6.13.

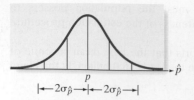

Figure 6.13

Sampling distribution of $\hat{p}$

Properties of the Sampling Distribution of $\hat{p}$

1. The mean of the sampling distribution of $\hat{p}$ is p; that is, $\hat{p}$ is an unbiased estimator of p.
2. The standard deviation of the sampling distribution of $\hat{p}$ is $\sqrt{pq/n}$; that is, $\sigma_{\hat{p}} = \sqrt{pq/n}$, where $q = 1 - p$.
3. For large samples, the sampling distribution of $\hat{p}$ is approximately normal. A sample size is considered large if both $n\hat{p} \geq 15$ and $n\hat{q} \geq 15$.

The fact that $\hat{p}$ is a "sample mean number of successes per trial" allows us to form confidence intervals about p in a manner that is completely analogous to that used for large-sample estimation of μ.

Large-Sample Confidence Interval for p

$$\hat{p} \pm z_{\alpha/2}\sigma_{\hat{p}} = \hat{p} \pm z_{\alpha/2}\sqrt{\frac{pq}{n}} \approx \hat{p} \pm z_{\alpha/2}\sqrt{\frac{\hat{p}\hat{q}}{n}}$$

where $\hat{p} = \dfrac{x}{n}$ and $\hat{q} = 1 - \hat{p}$

Note: When n is large, $\hat{p}$ can approximate the value of p in the formula for $\sigma_{\hat{p}}$.

Conditions Required for a Valid Large-Sample Confidence Interval for p

1. A random sample is selected from the target population.
2. The sample size n is large. (This condition will be satisfied if both $n\hat{p} \geq 15$ and $n\hat{q} \geq 15$. Note that $n\hat{p}$ and $n\hat{q}$ are simply the number of successes and number of failures, respectively, in the sample.)

Thus, if 313 of 1,000 consumers prefer the company's cereal brand, a 95% confidence interval for the proportion of *all* consumers who prefer the company's brand is

$$\hat{p} \pm z_{\alpha/2}\sigma_{\hat{p}} = .313 \pm 1.96\sqrt{\frac{pq}{1,000}}$$

where $q = 1 - p$. Just as we needed an approximation for σ in calculating a large-sample confidence interval for μ, we now need an approximation for p. As Table 6.6 shows, the approximation for p does not have to be especially accurate because the value of $\sqrt{pq}$ needed for the confidence interval is relatively insensitive to changes in p. Therefore, we can use $\hat{p}$ to approximate p. Keeping in mind that $\hat{q} = 1 - \hat{p}$, we substitute these values into the formula for the confidence interval:

$$\hat{p} \pm 1.96\sqrt{\frac{pq}{1,000}} \approx \hat{p} \pm 1.96\sqrt{\frac{\hat{p}\hat{q}}{1,000}}$$

$$= .313 \pm 1.96\sqrt{\frac{(.313)(.687)}{1,000}}$$

$$= .313 \pm .029$$

$$= (.284, .342)$$

Table 6.6		
Values of pq for Several Different Values of p		
p	pq	$\sqrt{pq}$
.5	.25	.50
.6 or .4	.24	.49
.7 or .3	.21	.46
.8 or .2	.16	.40
.9 or .1	.09	.30

The company can be 95% confident that the interval from 28.4% to 34.2% contains the true percentage of *all* consumers who prefer its brand—that is, in repeated construction of confidence intervals, approximately 95% of all samples would produce confidence intervals that enclose p. Note that the guidelines for interpreting a confidence interval about μ also apply to interpreting a confidence interval for p because p is the "population fraction of successes" in a binomial experiment.

EXAMPLE 6.7
Large-Sample Confidence Interval for p—Proportion Optimistic about the Economy

Problem Many public polling agencies conduct surveys to determine the current consumer sentiment concerning the state of the economy. For example, the Bureau of Economic and Business Research (BEBR) at the University of Florida conducts quarterly surveys to gauge consumer sentiment in the Sunshine State. Suppose that the BEBR randomly samples 484 consumers and finds that 157 are optimistic about the state of the economy. Use a 90% confidence interval to estimate the proportion of all consumers in Florida who are optimistic about the state of the economy. Based on the confidence interval, can BEBR infer that a minority of Florida consumers is optimistic about the economy?

Solution The number, x, of the 484 sampled consumers who are optimistic about the Florida economy is a binomial random variable if we can assume that the sample was randomly selected from the population of Florida consumers and that the poll was conducted identically for each sampled consumer.

The point estimate of the proportion of Florida consumers who are optimistic about the economy is

$$\hat{p} = \frac{x}{n} = \frac{157}{484} = .324$$

We first check to be sure that the sample size is sufficiently large that the normal distribution provides a reasonable approximation for the sampling distribution of $\hat{p}$. We require the number of successes in the sample, $n\hat{p}$, and the number of failures, $n\hat{q}$, to both be at least 15. Since the number of successes is $n\hat{p} = 157$ and the number of failures is $n\hat{q} = 327$, we may conclude that the normal approximation is reasonable.

We now proceed to form the 90% confidence interval for p, the true proportion of Florida consumers who are optimistic about the state of the economy:

$$\hat{p} \pm z_{\alpha/2}\sigma_{\hat{p}} = \hat{p} \pm z_{\alpha/2}\sqrt{\frac{pq}{n}} \approx \hat{p} \pm z_{\alpha/2}\sqrt{\frac{\hat{p}\hat{q}}{n}}$$

$$= .324 \pm 1.645\sqrt{\frac{(.324)(.676)}{484}} = .324 \pm .035 = (.289, .359)$$

(This interval is also shown on the Minitab printout, Figure 6.14.) Thus, we can be 90% confident that the proportion of all Florida consumers who are confident about the economy is between .289 and .359. As always, our confidence stems from the fact that 90% of all similarly formed intervals will contain the true proportion p and not from any knowledge about whether this particular interval does.

Figure 6.14

Minitab output showing 95% confidence interval for p, Example 6.7

Test and CI for One Proportion

```
Sample    X    N   Sample p        90% CI
1       157  484  0.324380   (0.289379, 0.359381)

Using the normal approximation.
```

Can we conclude that a minority of Florida consumers is optimistic about the economy based on this interval? If we wished to use this interval to infer that a minority is optimistic, the interval would have to support the inference that p is less than .5—that is, that less than 50% of the Florida consumers are optimistic about the economy. Note that the interval contains only values below .5. Therefore, we can conclude that the true value of p is less than .5 based on this 90% confidence interval.

Look Back   If the confidence interval includes .5 (e.g., an interval from .42 to .54), then we could not conclude that the true proportion of consumers who are optimistic is less than .5. (This is because it is possible that p is as high as .54.)

• **Now Work Exercise 6.45**

We conclude this section with a warning and an illustrative example.

> **CAUTION**   Unless n is extremely large, the large-sample procedure presented in this section performs poorly when p is near 0 or near 1.

The problem stated in the above warning can be illustrated as follows. Suppose you want to estimate the proportion of executives who die from a work-related injury using a sample size of $n = 100$. This proportion is likely to be near 0, say, $p \approx .001$. If so, then $np \approx 100(.001) = .1$ is less than the recommended value of 15 (see Conditions in the box on p. 352). Consequently, a confidence interval for p based on a sample of $n = 100$ will probably be misleading.

To overcome this potential problem, an *extremely* large sample size is required. Because the value of n required to satisfy "extremely large" is difficult to determine, statisticians (see Agresti & Coull, 1998) have proposed an alternative method, based on the Wilson (1927) point estimator of p. The procedure is outlined in the box below. Researchers have shown that this confidence interval works well for any p, even when the sample size n is very small.

Adjusted $(1 - \alpha)$ 100% Confidence Interval for a Population Proportion, p

$$\widetilde{p} \pm z_{\alpha/2}\sqrt{\frac{\widetilde{p}(1 - \widetilde{p})}{n + 4}}$$

where $\widetilde{p} = \frac{x + 2}{n + 4}$ is the adjusted sample proportion of observations with the characteristic of interest, x is the number of successes in the sample, and n is the sample size.

EXAMPLE 6.8

Adjusted Confidence Interval Procedure for p—Injury Rate at a Jewelry Store

Problem   According to the Bureau of Labor Statistics, the probability of injury while working at a jewelry store is less than .01. Suppose that in a random sample of 200 jewelry store workers, 3 were injured on the job. Estimate the true proportion of jewelry store workers who are injured on the job using a 95% confidence interval.

Solution   Let p represent the true proportion of all jewelry store workers who are injured on the job. Because p is near 0, an "extremely large" sample is required to estimate its value using the usual large-sample method. Note that the number of "successes," 3, is less than 15. Thus, we doubt whether the sample size of 200 is large enough to apply the large-sample method. Alternatively, we will apply the adjustment outlined in the box.

Because the number of "successes" (i.e., number of injured jewelry store workers) in the sample is $x = 3$, the adjusted sample proportion is

$$\widetilde{p} = \frac{x + 2}{n + 4} = \frac{3 + 2}{200 + 4} = \frac{5}{204} = .025$$

Note that this adjusted sample proportion is obtained by adding a total of four observations—two "successes" and two "failures"—to the sample data. Substituting $\tilde{p} = .025$ into the equation for a 95% confidence interval, we obtain

$$\tilde{p} \pm 1.96 \sqrt{\frac{\tilde{p}(1 - \tilde{p})}{n + 4}} = .025 \pm 1.96 \sqrt{\frac{(.025)(.975)}{204}}$$
$$= .025 \pm .021$$

or $(.004, .046)$. Consequently, we are 95% confident that the true proportion of jewelry store workers who are injured while on the job falls between .004 and .046.

Look Back If we apply the standard large-sample confidence interval formula, where $\hat{p} = \frac{3}{200} = .015$, we obtain

$$\hat{p} \pm 1.96 \sqrt{\frac{\hat{p}\hat{q}}{200}} = .015 \pm 1.96 \sqrt{\frac{(.015)(.985)}{200}}$$
$$= .015 \pm .017 \text{ or } (-.002, .032)$$

Note that the interval contains negative (nonsensical) values for the true proportion. Such a result is typical when the large-sample method is misapplied.

● Now Work Exercise 6.50

STATISTICS IN ACTION
REVISITED

Estimating the Coding Error Rate

In the previous *Statistics in Action Revisited* (p. 347), we showed how to estimate the mean overpayment amount for claims in a Medicare fraud study. In addition to estimating overcharges, the USDOJ also is interested in estimating the *coding error rate* of a Medicare provider. The coding error rate is defined as the proportion of Medicare claims that are coded incorrectly. Thus, for this inference, the USDOJ is interested in estimating a population proportion, p. Typically, the USDOJ finds that about 50% of the claims in a Medicare fraud case are incorrectly coded.

If you examine the sample data in Table SIA6.1, you can verify that of the 52 audited claims, 31 were determined to be coded incorrectly, resulting in an overcharge. These are the claims with a disallowed amount greater than $0. Therefore, an estimate of the coding error rate, p, for this Medicare provider is

$$\hat{p} = 31/52 = .596$$

A 95% confidence interval for p can be obtained with the use of a confidence interval formula or with statistical software.

The **MFRAUD** file includes a qualitative variable (called "Coding Error") at two levels, where "Yes" represents that the claim is coded incorrectly and "No" represents that the claim is coded correctly. Thus, the USDOJ desires an estimate of the proportion of "Yes" values for the "Coding Error" variable. A confidence interval for the proportion of incorrectly coded claims is highlighted on the accompanying Minitab printout, Figure SIA6.2. The interval, $(.45, .73)$, implies that the true coding error rate for the 1,000 claims in the population falls between .45 and .73, with 95% confidence. Note that the value .5—the proportion of incorrectly coded claims expected by the USDOJ—falls within the 95% confidence interval.

Figure SIA6.2

Minitab confidence interval for coding error rate

```
Event = Yes

Variable       X   N   Sample p        95% CI
Coding_Error  31  52  0.596154  (0.451016, 0.729940)
```

▐ *Data Set:* MFRAUD

Exercises 6.40–6.59

Learning the Mechanics

6.40 Describe the sampling distribution of $\hat{p}$ based on large samples of size n—that is, give the mean, the standard deviation, and the (approximate) shape of the distribution of $\hat{p}$ when large samples of size n are (repeatedly) selected from the binomial distribution with probability of success p.

📊 Applet Exercise 6.5

Use the applet *Confidence Intervals for a Proportion* to investigate the effect of the value of p on the number of confidence intervals that contain the population proportion p for a fixed sample size. For this exercise, use sample size $n = 10$.

a. Run the applet several times without clearing for $p = .1$. What proportion of the 95% confidence intervals contain p? What proportion of the 99% confidence intervals contain p? Do the results surprise you? Explain.

b. Repeat part **a** for each value of p: $p = .2$, $p = .3$, $p = .4$, $p = .5$, $p = .6$, $p = .7$, $p = .8$, and $p = .9$.

c. Which value of p yields the greatest proportion of each type of interval that contain p?

d. Based on your results, what values of p will yield more reliable confidence intervals for a fixed sample size n? Explain.

📊 Applet Exercise 6.6

Use the applet *Confidence Intervals for a Proportion* to investigate the effect of the sample size on the number of confidence intervals that contain the population proportion p for a value of p close to 0 or 1.

a. Run the applet several times without clearing for $p = .5$ and $n = 50$. Record the proportion of the 99% confidence intervals containing p.

b. Now set $p = .1$ and run the applet several times without clearing for $n = 50$. How does the proportion of the 99% confidence intervals containing p compare with that in part **a?**

c. Repeat part **b,** keeping $p = .1$ and increasing the sample size by 50 until you find a sample size that yields a similar proportion of the 99% confidence intervals containing p as that in part **a.**

d. Based on your results, describe how the value of p affects the sample size needed to guarantee a certain level of confidence.

6.41 For the binomial sample information summarized in each part, indicate whether the sample size is large enough to use the methods of this chapter to construct a confidence interval for p.
a. $n = 400, \hat{p} = .10$
b. $n = 50, \hat{p} = .10$
c. $n = 20, \hat{p} = .5$
d. $n = 20, \hat{p} = .3$

6.42 A random sample of size $n = 121$ yielded $\hat{p} = .88$.
a. Is the sample size large enough to use the methods of this section to construct a confidence interval for p? Explain.
b. Construct a 90% confidence interval for p.

c. What assumption is necessary to ensure the validity of this confidence interval?

6.43 A random sample of size $n = 225$ yielded $\hat{p} = .46$.
a. Is the sample size large enough to use the methods of this section to construct a confidence interval for p? Explain.
b. Construct a 95% confidence interval for p.
c. Interpret the 95% confidence interval.
d. Explain what is meant by the phrase "95% confidence interval."

6.44 A random sample of 50 consumers taste-tested a new snack food. Their responses were coded (0: do not like; 1: like; 2: indifferent) and recorded as follows:

SNACK

1	0	0	1	2	0	1	1	0	0
0	1	0	2	0	2	2	0	0	1
1	0	0	0	0	1	0	2	0	0
0	1	0	1	0	0	1	0	1
0	2	0	0	1	1	0	0	0	1

a. Use an 80% confidence interval to estimate the proportion of consumers who like the snack food.
b. Provide a statistical interpretation for the confidence interval you constructed in part **a.**

Applying the Concepts—Basic

6.45 **Customer participation in store loyalty card programs.** Customers who participate in a store's free loyalty card program save money on their purchases but allow the store to keep track of their shopping habits and potentially sell these data to third parties. A *Pew Internet & American Life Project Survey* (January 2016) revealed that half (225) of a random sample of 250 U.S. adults would agree to participate in a store loyalty card program, despite the potential for information sharing.
a. Estimate the true proportion of all U.S. adults who would agree to participate in a store loyalty card program, despite the potential for information sharing.
b. Form a 90% confidence interval around the estimate, part **a.**
c. Provide a practical interpretation of the confidence interval, part **b.** Your answer should begin with, "We are 90% confident ..."
d. Explain the theoretical meaning of the phrase, "We are 90% confident."

6.46 **Crash risk of using cell phones while driving.** Studies have shown that drivers who use cell phones while operating a motor passenger vehicle increase their risk of an accident. To quantify this risk, the *New England Journal of Medicine* (January 2, 2014) reported on the risk of a crash (or near crash) for both novice and expert drivers when using a cell phone. In a sample of 371 cases of novices using a cell phone while driving, 24 resulted in a crash (or near crash). In a sample of 1,467 cases of experts using a cell phone while driving, 67 resulted in a crash (or near crash).
a. Give a point estimate of p, the true crash risk (probability) for novice drivers who use a cell phone while driving.
b. Find a 95% confidence interval for p.

c. Give a practical interpretation of the interval, part **b.**

d. Repeat parts **a–c** for expert drivers.

6.47 **Zillow.com estimates of home values.** Zillow.com is a real estate Web site that provides free estimates of the market value of homes. Refer to *The Appraisal Journal* (Winter 2010) study of the accuracy of Zillow's estimates, Exercise 1.25 (p. 51). Data were collected for a sample of 2,045 single-family residential properties in Arlington, Texas. The researchers determined that Zillow overestimated by more than 10% the market value of 818 of the 2,045 homes. Suppose you want to estimate p, the true proportion of Arlington, Texas, homes with market values that are overestimated by more than 10% by Zillow.

a. Find $\hat{p}$, the point estimate of p.

b. Describe the sampling distribution of $\hat{p}$.

c. Find a 95% confidence interval for p.

d. Give a practical interpretation of the confidence interval, part **c.**

e. Suppose a *Zillow* representative claims that $p = .3$. Is the claim believable? Explain.

6.48 **Do social robots walk or roll?** Refer to the *International Conference on Social Robotics* (Vol. 6414, 2010) study of the trend in the design of social robots, Exercise 5.44 (p. 320). The researchers obtained a random sample of 106 social robots through a Web search and determined that 63 were designed with legs, but no wheels.

a. Find a 99% confidence interval for the proportion of all social robots designed with legs, but no wheels. Interpret the result.

b. In Exercise 5.42, you assumed that 40% of all social robots are designed with legs, but no wheels. Comment on the validity of this assumption.

6.49 **Is Starbucks coffee overpriced?** The *Minneapolis Star Tribune* (August 12, 2008) reported that 73% of Americans say that Starbucks coffee is overpriced. The source of this information was a national telephone survey of 1,000 American adults conducted by Rasmussen Reports.

a. Identify the population of interest in this study.

b. Identify the sample for the study.

c. Identify the parameter of interest in the study.

d. Find and interpret a 95% confidence interval for the parameter of interest.

6.50 **Nannies who are INA certified.** The International Nanny Association (INA) reports that in a sample of 928 in-home child care providers (nannies), 128 have passed the INA Nanny Credential Exam (*2014 International Nanny Association Salary and Benefits Survey*). Use Wilson's adjustment to find a 95% confidence interval for the true proportion of all nannies who have passed the INA certification exam.

Applying the Concepts—Intermediate

6.51 **Cybersecurity survey.** Refer to the *State of Cybersecurity* (2015) survey of firms from around the world, Exercise 1.20 (p. 50). Recall that of the 766 firms that responded to the survey, 628 (or 82%) expect to experience a cyberattack (e.g., a Malware, hacking, or phishing attack) during the year. Estimate the probability of an expected cyberattack at a firm during the year with a 90% confidence interval. Explain how 90% is used as a measure of reliability for the interval.

6.52 **Who prepares your tax return?** Refer to the *Behavioral Research and Accounting* (January 2015) study on income tax compliance, Exercise 5.50 (p. 321). Recall that in a sample of 270 U.S. adult workers, the researchers found that 37% prepare their own tax return.

a. Construct a 99% confidence interval for the true proportion of all U.S. adult workers who prepare their own tax return.

b. Suppose an IRS tax consultant claims that 50% of all U.S. adult workers prepare their own tax return. Make an inference about this claim.

c. According to the researchers, about 70% of the sampled workers were recruited from a shopping mall (where they were reimbursed $5 for their time) and about 30% were full-time workers enrolled in a professional graduate degree program. How might this information impact the inference you made in part **b**?

6.53 **Minority ownership of franchises.** According to a 2011 report for IFA Educational Foundation, 20.5% of all franchised businesses in the United States are minority owned. (This information is based on the U.S. Census Bureau's survey of 27 million business owners.) Suppose that you obtain a sample of 100 franchised businesses located in Mississippi and find that 15 are owned by minorities. Does this result lead you to conclude that the percentage of minority-owned franchises in Mississippi is less than the national value of 20.5%? Explain.

6.54 **Study of aircraft bird-strikes.** As worldwide air traffic volume has grown over the years, the problem of airplanes striking birds and other flying wildlife has increased dramatically. The *International Journal for Traffic and Transport Engineering* (Vol. 3, 2013) reported on a study of aircraft bird strikes at Aminu Kano International Airport in Nigeria. During the survey period, a sample of 44 aircraft bird strikes were analyzed. The researchers found that 36 of the 44 bird strikes at the airport occurred above 100 feet. Suppose an airport air traffic controller estimates that less than 70% of aircraft bird strikes occur above 100 feet. Comment on the accuracy of this estimate. Use a 95% confidence interval to support your inference.

6.55 **Splinting in mountain climbing accidents.** The most common injury that occurs among mountain climbers is trauma to the lower extremity (leg). Consequently, rescuers must be proficient in immobilizing and splinting fractures. In *High Altitude Medicine & Biology* (Vol. 10, 2009), researchers examined the likelihood of mountain climbers needing certain types of splints. A Scottish Mountain Rescue study reported that there was 1 femoral shaft splint needed among 333 live casualties. The researchers will use this study to estimate the proportion of all mountain casualties that require a femoral shaft splint.

a. Is the sample large enough to apply the large-sample estimation method of this section? Show why or why not.

b. Use Wilson's adjustment to find a 95% confidence interval for the true proportion of all mountain casualties that require a femoral shaft splint. Interpret the result.

6.56 **Diamonds sold on the open market.** Refer to the sample of 308 diamond stones that were listed for sale on the open market in Singapore's *Business Times*. Recall that the color of each diamond is classified as D, E, F, G, H, or I, while the clarity of each is classified as VVS1, VVS2, VS1, or VS2.

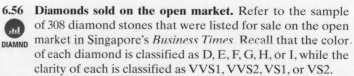

a. Find a 99% confidence interval for the proportion of all diamonds for sale on the open market that are classified as "D" color. Interpret the result.

b. Find a 99% confidence interval for the proportion of all diamonds for sale on the open market that are classified as "VS1" clarity. Interpret the result.

6.57 **Are you really being served red snapper?** Refer to the *Nature* (July 15, 2004) study of fish specimens labeled "red snapper," Exercise 3.75 (p. 196). Recall that federal law prohibits restaurants from serving a cheaper, look-alike variety of fish (e.g., vermillion snapper or lane snapper) to customers who order red snapper. A team of University of North Carolina (UNC) researchers analyzed the meat from each in a sample of 22 "red snapper" fish fillets purchased from vendors across the United States in an effort to estimate the true proportion of fillets that are really red snapper. DNA tests revealed that 17 of the 22 fillets (or 77%) were not red snapper but the cheaper, look-alike variety of fish.

a. Identify the parameter of interest to the UNC researchers.

b. Explain why a large-sample confidence interval is inappropriate to apply in this study.

c. Construct a 95% confidence interval for the parameter of interest using Wilson's adjustment.

d. Give a practical interpretation of the confidence interval.

Applying the Concepts—Advanced

6.58 **Eye shadow, mascara, and nickel allergies.** Pigmented makeup products like mascara and eye shadow may contain metal (e.g., nickel) allergens. Is a nickel allergy more likely to occur in women who report cosmetic dermatitis from using eye shadow or mascara? This was the question of interest in a paper published in the *Journal of the European Academy of Dermatology and Venereology* (June 2010). In a sample of 131 women with cosmetic dermatitis from using eye shadow, 12 were diagnosed with a nickel allergy. In a sample of 250 women with cosmetic dermatitis from using mascara, 25 were diagnosed with a nickel allergy.

a. Compute a 95% confidence interval for the proportion of women with cosmetic dermatitis from using eye shadow who have a nickel allergy. Interpret the result.

b. Compute a 95% confidence interval for the proportion of women with cosmetic dermatitis from using mascara who have a nickel allergy. Interpret the result.

c. Suppose you are informed that the true proportion with a nickel allergy for one of the two groups (eye shadow or mascara) is .12. Can you determine which group is referenced? Explain.

6.59 **U.S. Postal Service's performance.** The U.S. Postal Service (USPS) reports that 95% of first-class mail within the same city is delivered on time (i.e., within 2 days of the time of mailing). To gauge the USPS performance, Price Waterhouse monitored the delivery of first-class mail items between Dec. 10 and Mar. 3—the most difficult delivery season due to bad weather conditions and holidays. In a sample of 332,000 items, Price Waterhouse determined that 282,200 were delivered on time. Comment on the performance of USPS first-class mail service over this time period.

6.5 Determining the Sample Size

Recall (Section 1.6) that one way to collect the relevant data for a study used to make inferences about the population is to implement a designed (planned) experiment. Perhaps the most important design decision faced by the analyst is to determine the size of the sample. We show in this section that the appropriate sample size for making an inference about a population mean or proportion depends on the desired reliability.

Estimating a Population Mean

Consider Example 6.2 (p. 334), in which we estimated the mean overdue amount for all delinquent accounts in a large credit corporation. A sample of 100 delinquent accounts produced the 95% confidence interval $\bar{x} \pm 1.96\sigma_{\bar{x}} \approx 233.28 \pm 17.71$. Consequently, our estimate $\bar{x}$ was within \$17.71 of the true mean amount due, μ, for all the delinquent accounts at the 95% confidence level—that is, the 95% confidence interval for μ was $2(17.71) = \$35.42$ wide when 100 accounts were sampled. This is illustrated in Figure 6.15a.

Now suppose we want to estimate μ to within \$5 with 95% confidence—that is, we want to narrow the width of the confidence interval from \$35.42 to \$10, as shown in Figure 6.15b. How much will the sample size have to be increased to accomplish this? If we want the estimator $\bar{x}$ to be within \$5 of μ, we must have

$$1.96\sigma_{\bar{x}} = 5 \quad \text{or, equivalently,} \quad 1.96\left(\frac{\sigma}{\sqrt{n}}\right) = 5$$

The necessary sample size is obtained by solving this equation for n. To do this, we need an approximation for σ. We have an approximation from the initial sample of

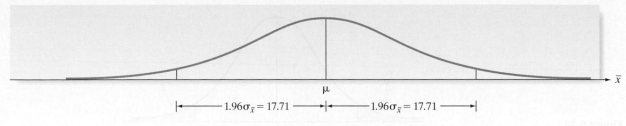

a. $n = 100$

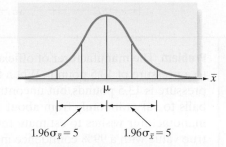

b. $n = 1{,}254$

Figure 6.15

Relationship between sample size and width of confidence interval: delinquent debtors example

100 accounts—namely, the sample standard deviation, $s = 90.34$ (see the Solution to Example 6.2). Thus,

$$1.96\left(\frac{\sigma}{\sqrt{n}}\right) \approx 1.96\left(\frac{s}{\sqrt{n}}\right) = 1.96\left(\frac{90.34}{\sqrt{n}}\right) = 5$$

$$\sqrt{n} = \frac{1.96(90.34)}{5} = 35.413$$

$$n = (35.413)^2 = 1{,}254.1 \approx 1{,}254$$

Approximately 1,254 accounts will have to be randomly sampled to estimate the mean overdue amount μ to within \$5 with (approximately) 95% confidence. The confidence interval resulting from a sample of this size will be approximately \$10 wide (see Figure 6.15b).

In general, we express the reliability associated with a confidence interval for the population mean μ by specifying the **sampling error,** within which we want to estimate μ with $100(1 - \alpha)\%$ confidence. The sampling error (denoted SE), then, is equal to the half-width of the confidence interval, as shown in Figure 6.16.

Sample Size Determination for $100(1 - \alpha)\%$ Confidence Interval for μ

In order to estimate μ with a sampling error SE and with $100(1 - \alpha)\%$ confidence, the required sample size is found as follows:

$$z_{\alpha/2}\left(\frac{\sigma}{\sqrt{n}}\right) = \text{SE}$$

The solution for n is given by the equation

$$n = \left[\frac{(z_{\alpha/2})\sigma}{\text{SE}}\right]^2$$

Note: The value of σ is usually unknown. It can be estimated by the standard deviation, s, from a prior sample. Alternatively, we may approximate the range R of observations in the population, and (conservatively) estimate $\sigma \approx \frac{R}{4}$. In any case, you should round the value of n obtained *upward* to ensure that the sample size will be sufficient to achieve the specified reliability.

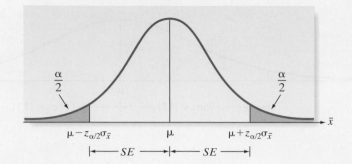

Figure 6.16

Specifying the sampling error as the half-width of a confidence interval

---

EXAMPLE 6.9

Sample Size for Estimating μ—Mean Inflation Pressure of Footballs

Problem The manufacturer of official NFL footballs uses a machine to inflate its new balls to a pressure of 13.5 pounds. When the machine is properly calibrated, the mean inflation pressure is 13.5 pounds, but uncontrollable factors cause the pressures of individual footballs to vary randomly from about 13.3 to 13.7 pounds. For quality-control purposes, the manufacturer wishes to estimate the mean inflation pressure to within .025 pound of its true value with a 99% confidence interval. What sample size should be used?

Solution We desire a 99% confidence interval that estimates μ with a sampling error of SE = .025 pound. For a 99% confidence interval, we have $z_{\alpha/2} = z_{.005} = 2.576$. No previous estimate of s is available; however, we are given that the range of observations is $R = 13.7 - 13.3 = .4$. A conservative estimate (based on Chebychev's Rule) is $\sigma \approx R/4 = .1$. Now we use the formula derived in the box to find the sample size n:

$$n = \left[\frac{(z_{\alpha/2})\sigma}{\text{SE}} \right]^2 = \left[\frac{(2.576)(.1)}{.025} \right]^2 = 106.17$$

We round this up to $n = 107$. Realizing that σ was approximated by $R/4$, we might even advise that the sample size be specified as $n = 110$ to be more certain of attaining the objective of a 99% confidence interval with a sampling error of .025 pound or less.

This result may also be obtained using statistical software. We input $\sigma = .1$, confidence level $(1 - \alpha) = .99$, and margin of error (ME) = .025 into the Minitab *Power and Sample Size* option for estimating a mean and obtained the printout shown in Figure 6.17. The value, $n = 107$, is shaded at the bottom of the printout.

Sample Size for Estimation

Method

Parameter	Mean
Distribution	Normal
Standard deviation	0.1 (population value)
Confidence level	99%
Confidence interval	Two-sided

Results

Margin of Error	Sample Size
0.025	107

Figure 6.17

Minitab Sample Size Output for Example 6.9

Look Back To determine the value of the sampling error SE, look for the value that follows the key words "estimate μ to within…."

Now Work Exercise 6.68

Sometimes the formula will yield a small sample size (say, $n < 30$). Unfortunately, this solution is invalid because the procedures and assumptions for small samples differ from those for large samples, as we discovered in Section 6.3. Therefore, if the formulas yield a small sample size, one simple strategy is to select a sample size $n = 30$.

Estimating a Population Proportion

The method outlined above is easily applied to a population proportion p. To illustrate, in Example 6.6 (p. 351), a company used a sample of 1,000 consumers to estimate the proportion of consumers who prefer its cereal brand. As a follow-up, we obtained the 95% confidence interval, $.313 \pm .029$. Suppose the company wishes to estimate its market share more precisely, say, to within .015 with a 95% confidence interval.

The company wants a confidence interval with a sampling error for the estimate of p of SE = .015. The sample size required to generate such an interval is found by solving the following equation for n (see Figure 6.18):

$$z_{\alpha/2}\sigma_{\hat{p}} = SE \quad \text{or} \quad z_{\alpha/2}\sqrt{\frac{pq}{n}} = .015$$

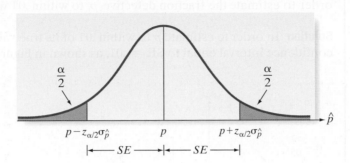

Figure 6.18

Specifying the sampling error of a confidence interval for a population proportion p

Since a 95% confidence interval is desired, the appropriate z-value is $z_{\alpha/2} = z_{.025} = 1.96$. We must approximate the value of the product pq before we can solve the equation for n. As shown in Table 6.6, the closer the values of p and q to .5, the larger the product pq. Thus, to find a conservatively large sample size that will generate a confidence interval with the specified reliability, we generally choose an approximation of p close to .5. In the case of the food-products company, however, we have an initial sample estimate of $\hat{p} = .313$. A conservatively large estimate of pq can therefore be obtained by using, say, $p = .35$. We now substitute into the equation and solve for n:

$$1.96\sqrt{\frac{(.35)(.65)}{n}} = .015$$

$$n = \frac{(1.96)^2(.35)(.65)}{(.015)^2}$$

$$= 3,884.28 \approx 3,885$$

The company must sample about 3,885 consumers to estimate the percentage who prefer its brand to within .015 with a 95% confidence interval.

The procedure for finding the sample size necessary to estimate a population proportion p with a specified sampling error SE is given in the box.

Sample Size Determination for $100(1 - \alpha)\%$ Confidence Interval for p

In order to estimate a binomial probability p with sampling error SE and with $100(1 - \alpha)\%$ confidence, the required sample size is found by solving the following equation for n:

$$z_{\alpha/2}\sqrt{\frac{pq}{n}} = SE$$

The solution for n can be written as follows:

$$n = \frac{(z_{\alpha/2})^2(pq)}{(SE)^2}$$

Note: Because the value of the product pq is unknown, it can be estimated by using the sample fraction of successes, $\hat{p}$, from a prior sample. Remember (Table 6.6) that the value of pq is at its maximum when p equals .5, so you can obtain conservatively large values of n by approximating p by .5 or values close to .5. In any case, you should round the value of n obtained *upward* to ensure that the sample size will be sufficient to achieve the specified reliability.

EXAMPLE 6.10

Sample Size for Estimating p—Fraction of Defective Cell Phones

Problem A cellular telephone manufacturer that entered the postregulation market too quickly has an initial problem with excessive customer complaints and consequent returns of the cell phones for repair or replacement. The manufacturer wants to determine the magnitude of the problem in order to estimate its warranty liability. How many cellular telephones should the company randomly sample from its warehouse and check in order to estimate the fraction defective, p, to within .01 with 90% confidence?

Solution In order to estimate p to within .01 of its true value, we set the half-width of the confidence interval equal to SE $= .01$, as shown in Figure 6.19.

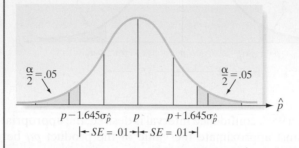

Figure 6.19

Specified reliability for estimate of fraction defective in Example 6.10

The equation for the sample size n requires an estimate of the product pq. We could most conservatively estimate $pq = .25$ (i.e., use $p = .5$), but this may be overly conservative when estimating a fraction defective. A value of .1, corresponding to 10% defective, will probably be conservatively large for this application. The solution is therefore

$$ n = \frac{(z_{\alpha/2})^2(pq)}{(\text{SE})^2} = \frac{(1.645)^2(.1)(.9)}{(.01)^2} = 2{,}435.4 \approx 2{,}436 $$

Thus, the manufacturer should sample 2,436 cellular telephones in order to estimate the fraction defective, p, to within .01 with 90% confidence.

Look Back Remember that this answer depends on our approximation for pq, where we used .09. If the fraction defective is closer to .05 than to .10, we can use a sample of 1,286 cell phones (check this) to estimate p to within .01 with 90% confidence.

● **Now Work Exercise 6.67**

The cost of sampling will also play an important role in the final determination of the sample size to be selected to estimate either μ or p. Although more complex formulas can be derived to balance the reliability and cost considerations, we will solve for the necessary sample size and note that the sampling budget may be a limiting factor. (Consult the references for a more complete treatment of this problem.) Once the sample size n is determined, be sure to devise a sampling plan that will ensure a representative sample is selected from the target population.

STATISTICS IN ACTION

REVISITED

Determining Sample Size

In the previous *Statistics in Action* applications in this chapter, we used confidence intervals (1) to estimate μ, the mean overpayment amount for claims in a Medicare fraud study, and (2) to estimate p, the coding error rate (i.e., proportion of claims that are incorrectly coded) of a Medicare provider. Both of these confidence intervals were based on selecting a random sample of 52 claims from the population of claims handled by the Medicare provider. How does the USDOJ determine how many claims to sample for auditing?

Consider the problem of estimating the coding error rate, p. As stated in a previous *Statistics in Action Revisited*, the USDOJ typically finds that about 50% of the claims in a Medicare fraud case are incorrectly coded. Suppose the USDOJ wants to estimate the true coding error rate of a Medicare provider to within .1 with 95% confidence. How many claims should be randomly sampled for audit in order to attain the desired estimate?

Here, the USDOJ desires a sampling error of SE = .1, a confidence level of $1 - \alpha = .95$ (for which $z_{\alpha/2} = 1.96$), and uses an estimate $p \approx .50$. Substituting these values into the sample size formula (p. 361), we obtain:

$$n = (z_{\alpha/2})^2 (pq)/(\text{SE})^2$$
$$= (1.96)^2 (.5)(.5)/(.1)^2$$
$$= 96.04$$

Consequently, the USDOJ should audit about 97 randomly selected claims to attain a 95% confidence interval for p with a sampling error of .10.

[*Note:* You may wonder why the sample actually used in the fraud analysis included only 52 claims. The sampling strategy employed involved more than selecting a simple random sample; rather, it used a more sophisticated sampling scheme, called stratified random sampling. (See Section 1.6.) The 52 claims represented the sample for just one of the strata.]

Exercises 6.60–6.79

Learning the Mechanics

6.60 If you wish to estimate a population mean with a sampling error of SE = .3 using a 95% confidence interval, and you know from prior sampling that σ^2 is approximately equal to 7.2, how many observations would have to be included in your sample?

6.61 Suppose you wish to estimate a population mean correct to within .20 with probability equal to .90. You do not know σ^2, but you know that the observations will range in value between 30 and 34.
a. Find the approximate sample size that will produce the desired accuracy of the estimate. You wish to be conservative to ensure that the sample size will be ample to achieve the desired accuracy of the estimate. [*Hint:* Using your knowledge of data variation from Section 2.6, assume that the range of the observations will equal 4σ.]
b. Calculate the approximate sample size, making the less conservative assumption that the range of the observations is equal to 6σ.

6.62 In each case, find the approximate sample size required to construct a 95% confidence interval for p that has sampling error of SE = .08.
a. Assume p is near .2.
b. Assume you have no prior knowledge about p, but you wish to be certain that your sample is large enough to achieve the specified accuracy for the estimate.

6.63 The following is a 90% confidence interval for p: (.26, .54). How large was the sample used to construct this interval?

6.64 It costs you $10 to draw a sample of size $n = 1$ and measure the attribute of interest. You have a budget of $1,500.
a. Do you have sufficient funds to estimate the population mean for the attribute of interest with a 95% confidence interval 5 units in width? Assume $\sigma = 14$.
b. If you used a 90% confidence level, would your answer to part **a** change? Explain.

6.65 Suppose you wish to estimate the mean of a normal population using a 95% confidence interval, and you know from prior information that $\sigma^2 \approx 1$.
a. To see the effect of the sample size on the width of the confidence interval, calculate the width of the confidence interval for $n = 16, 25, 49, 100,$ and 400.
b. Plot the width as a function of sample size n on graph paper. Connect the points by a smooth curve and note how the width decreases as n increases.

6.66 If nothing is known about p, .5 can be substituted for p in the sample size formula for a population proportion. But when this is done, the resulting sample size may be larger than needed. Under what circumstances will using $p = .5$ in the sample size formula yield a sample size larger than needed to construct a confidence interval for p with a specified bound and a specified confidence level?

Applying the Concepts—Basic

6.67 **Aluminum cans contaminated by fire.** A gigantic warehouse located in Tampa, Florida, stores approximately 60 million empty aluminum beer and soda cans. Recently, a fire occurred at the warehouse. The smoke from the fire contaminated many of the cans with blackspot, rendering them unusable. A University of South Florida statistician was hired by the insurance company to estimate p, the true proportion of cans in the warehouse that were contaminated by the fire. How many aluminum cans should be randomly sampled to estimate p to within .02 with 90% confidence?

6.68 **Accounting and Machiavellianism.** Refer to the *Behavioral Research in Accounting* (January 2008) study of Machiavellian traits in accountants, Exercise 6.19 (p. 341), where a Mach rating score was determined for each in a sample of accounting alumni who work as purchasing managers. Suppose you want to reduce the width of the 95% confidence interval for the true mean Mach rating score of all purchasing managers you obtained in Exercise 6.19b. How many purchasing managers should be included in the sample if you desire a sampling error of only 1.5 Mach rating points? Use $\sigma \approx 12$ in your calculations.

6.69   **Lobster trap placement.** Refer to the *Bulletin of Marine Science* (April 2010) study of lobster trap placement, Exercise 6.29 (p. 348). Recall that you used a 95% confidence interval to estimate the mean trap spacing (in meters) for the population of red spiny lobster fishermen fishing in Baja California Sur, Mexico. How many teams of fishermen would need to be sampled in order to reduce the width of the confidence interval to 5 meters? Use the sample standard deviation from Exercise 6.29 in your calculation.

6.70   **Evaporation from swimming pools.** Refer to the *Heating/ Piping/Air Conditioning Engineering* (April 2013) study of evaporation from occupied swimming pools, Exercise 6.34 (p. 349). The researchers desired an estimate of the mean absolute value of the deviation between the actual and estimated evaporation level (recorded as a percentage). Using a small sample, the researchers obtained the following summary statistics for absolute deviation percentage $\bar{x} = 18\%, s = 20\%$. How many swimming pools must be sampled to estimate the true mean absolute deviation percentage to within 5% using a 90% confidence interval?

6.71   **Do social robots walk or roll?** Refer to the *International Conference on Social Robotics* (Vol. 6414, 2010) study of the trend in the design of social robots, Exercise 6.48 (p. 357). Recall that you used a 99% confidence interval to estimate the proportion of all social robots designed with legs, but no wheels. How many social robots would need to be sampled in order to estimate the proportion to within .075 of its true value?

6.72   **Study of aircraft bird-strikes.** Refer to the *International Journal for Traffic and Transport Engineering* (Vol. 3, 2013) study of aircraft bird strikes at a Nigerian airport, Exercise 6.54 (p. 357). Recall that an air traffic controller wants to estimate the true proportion of aircraft bird strikes that occur above 100 feet. Determine how many aircraft bird strikes need to be analyzed to estimate the true proportion to within .05 if you use a 95% confidence interval.

Applying the Concepts—Intermediate

6.73   **Bacteria in bottled water.** Is the bottled water you drink safe? The Natural Resources Defense Council warns that the bottled water you are drinking may contain more bacteria and other potentially carcinogenic chemicals than allowed by state and federal regulations. Of the more than 1,000 bottles studied, nearly one-third exceeded government levels (www.nrdc.org). Suppose that the Natural Resources Defense Council wants an updated estimate of the population proportion of bottled water that violates at least one government standard. Determine the sample size (number of bottles) needed to estimate this proportion to within ± 0.01 with 99% confidence.

6.74   **Shopping on Black Friday.** Refer to the *International Journal of Retail and Distribution Management* (Vol. 39, 2011) survey of Black Friday shoppers, Exercise 6.16 (p. 340). One question was, "How many hours do you usually spend shopping on Black Friday?"

   a. How many Black Friday shoppers should be included in a sample designed to estimate the average number of hours spent shopping on Black Friday if you want the estimate to deviate no more than .5 hour from the true mean?

   b. Devise a sampling plan for collecting the data that will likely result in a representative sample.

6.75   **Monitoring phone calls to a toll-free number.** A large food-products company receives about 100,000 phone calls a year from consumers on its toll-free number. A computer monitors and records how many rings it takes for an operator to answer, how much time each caller spends "on hold," and other data. However, the reliability of the monitoring system has been called into question by the operators and their labor union. As a check on the computer system, approximately how many calls should be manually monitored during the next year to estimate the true mean time that callers spend on hold to within 3 seconds with 95% confidence? Answer this question for the following values of the standard deviation of waiting times (in seconds): 10, 20, and 30.

6.76   **Eye shadow, mascara, and nickel allergies.** Refer to the *Journal of the European Academy of Dermatology and Venereology* (June 2010) study of the link between nickel allergies and use of mascara or eye shadow, Exercise 6.58 (p. 358). Recall that two groups of women were sampled— one group with cosmetic dermatitis from using eye shadow and another group with cosmetic dermatitis from using mascara. In either group, how many women would need to be sampled in order to yield an estimate of the population percentage with a nickel allergy that falls no more than 3% from the true value?

6.77   **USGA golf ball tests.** The United States Golf Association (USGA) tests all new brands of golf balls to ensure that they meet USGA specifications. One test conducted is intended to measure the average distance traveled when the ball is hit by a machine called "Iron Byron," a name inspired by the swing of the famous golfer Byron Nelson. Suppose the USGA wishes to estimate the mean distance for a new brand to within 1 yard with 90% confidence. Assume that past tests have indicated that the standard deviation of the distances Iron Byron hits golf balls is approximately 10 yards. How many golf balls should be hit by Iron Byron to achieve the desired accuracy in estimating the mean?

Applying the Concepts—Advanced

6.78   **Is caffeine addictive?** Does the caffeine in coffee, tea, and cola induce an addiction similar to that induced by alcohol, tobacco, heroin, and cocaine? In an attempt to answer this question, researchers at Johns Hopkins University examined 27 caffeine drinkers and found 25 who displayed some type of withdrawal symptoms when abstaining from caffeine. [*Note:* The 27 caffeine drinkers volunteered for the study.] Furthermore, of 11 caffeine drinkers who were diagnosed as caffeine dependent, 8 displayed dramatic withdrawal symptoms (including impairment in normal functioning) when they consumed a caffeine-free diet in a controlled setting. The National Coffee Association claimed, however, that the study group was too small to draw conclusions. Is the sample large enough to estimate the true proportion of caffeine drinkers who are caffeine dependent to within .05 of the true value with 99% confidence? Explain.

6.79   **Preventing production of defective items.** It costs more to produce defective items—because they must be scrapped or reworked—than it does to produce nondefective items. This simple fact suggests that manufacturers should ensure the quality of their products by perfecting their production processes rather than through inspection of finished products (*Out of the Crisis*, Deming, 1986). In order to better understand a particular metal-stamping process, a manufacturer wishes to estimate the mean length of items produced by the process during the past 24 hours.

a. How many parts should be sampled in order to estimate the population mean to within .1 millimeter (mm) with 90% confidence? Previous studies of this machine have indicated that the standard deviation of lengths produced by the stamping operation is about 2 mm.

b. Time permits the use of a sample size no larger than 100. If a 90% confidence interval for μ is constructed using $n = 100$, will it be wider or narrower than would have been obtained using the sample size determined in part **a**? Explain.

c. If management requires that μ be estimated to within .1 mm and that a sample size of no more than 100 be used, what is (approximately) the maximum confidence level that could be attained for a confidence interval that meets management's specifications?

6.6 Finite Population Correction for Simple Random Sampling (Optional)

The large-sample confidence intervals for a population mean μ and a population proportion p presented in the previous sections are based on a simple random sample selected from the target population. Although we did not state it, the procedure also assumes that the number N of measurements (i.e., sampling units) in the population is large relative to the sample size n.

In some sampling situations, the sample size n may represent 5% or perhaps 10% of the total number N of sampling units in the population. When the sample size is large relative to the number of measurements in the population (see the next box), the standard errors of the estimators of μ and p given in Sections 6.2 and 6.4, respectively, should be multiplied by a **finite population correction factor.**

The form of the finite population correction factor depends on how the population variance σ^2 is defined. In order to simplify the formulas of the standard errors, it is common to define σ^2 as division of the sum of squares of deviations by N *rather than by* $N -$ (analogous to the way we defined the sample variance). If we adopt this convention, the finite population correction factor becomes $\sqrt{(N - n)/N}$. Then the estimated standard errors of $\bar{x}$ (the estimator of μ) and $\hat{p}$ (the estimator of p) are as shown in the box.*

Rule of Thumb for Finite Population Correction Factor

Use the finite population correction factor (shown in the next box) when $n/N > .05$.

Simple Random Sampling with Finite Population of Size N
Estimation of the Population Mean

Estimated standard error:

$$\hat{\sigma}_{\bar{x}} = \frac{s}{\sqrt{n}} \sqrt{\frac{N - n}{N}}$$

Approximate 95% confidence interval: $\bar{x} \pm 2\hat{\sigma}_{\bar{x}}$

Estimation of the Population Proportion

Estimated standard error:

$$\hat{\sigma}_{\hat{p}} = \sqrt{\frac{\hat{p}(1 - \hat{p})}{n}} \sqrt{\frac{N - n}{N}}$$

Approximate 95% confidence interval: $\hat{p} \pm 2\hat{\sigma}_{\hat{p}}$

Note: The confidence intervals are "approximate" because we are using 2 to approximate the value $z_{.025} = 1.96$.

---

* The exact finite population correction factor is defined as $\sqrt{\{(N - n)/(N - 1)\}}$. No matter which formula you use, for most surveys and opinion polls, the finite population correction factor is approximately equal to 1 and, if desired, can be safely ignored. However, if $n/N > .05$, the finite population correction factor should be included in the calculation of the standard error.

EXAMPLE 6.11

Applying the Finite Population Correction Factor—Manufacture of Sheet Aluminum Foil

Problem A specialty manufacturer wants to purchase remnants of sheet aluminum foil. The foil, all of which is the same thickness, is stored on 1,462 rolls, each containing a varying amount of foil. To obtain an estimate of the total number of square feet of foil on all the rolls, the manufacturer randomly sampled 100 rolls and measured the number of square feet on each roll. The sample mean was 47.4, and the sample standard deviation was 12.4.

a. Find an approximate 95% confidence interval for the mean amount of foil on the 1,462 rolls.

b. Estimate the total number of square feet of foil on all the rolls by multiplying the confidence interval, part **a**, by 1,462. Interpret the result.

Solution

a. Each roll of foil is a sampling unit, and there are $N = 1,462$ units in the population, and the sample size is $n = 100$. Because $\frac{n}{N} = \frac{100}{1,462} = .068$ exceeds .05, we need to apply the finite population correction factor. We have $n = 100$, $\bar{x} = 47.4$, and $s = 12.4$. Substituting these quantities, we obtain the approximate 95% confidence interval:

$$\bar{x} \pm 2\frac{s}{\sqrt{n}}\sqrt{\frac{(N-n)}{N}} = (47.4) \pm 2\frac{12.4}{\sqrt{100}}\sqrt{\frac{(1,462-100)}{1,462}}$$

$$= 47.4 \pm 2.39$$

or, $(45.01, 49.79)$.

b. For finite populations of size N, the sum of all measurements in the population—called a *population total*—is

$$\sum_{i=1}^{N} x_i = N\mu$$

Because the confidence interval, part **a**, estimates μ, an estimate of the population total is obtained by multiplying the endpoints of the interval by N. For we have

Lower Limit $= N(45.01) = 1,462(45.01) = 65,804.6$

Upper Limit $= N(49.79) = 1,462(49.79) = 72,793.0$

Consequently, the manufacturer estimates the total amount of foil to be in the interval of 65,805 square feet to 72,793 square feet with 95% confidence.

Look Back If the manufacturer wants to adopt a conservative approach, the bid for the foil will be based on the lower confidence limit, 65,805 square feet of foil.

● **Now Work Exercise 6.88a**

Exercises 6.80–6.92

Learning the Mechanics

6.80 Calculate the percentage of the population sampled and the finite population correction factor for each of the following situations.
  a. $n = 1,000, N = 2,500$
  b. $n = 1,000, N = 5,000$
  c. $n = 1,000, N = 10,000$
  d. $n = 1,000, N = 100,000$

6.81 Suppose the standard deviation of the population is known to be $\sigma = 200$. Calculate the standard error of $\bar{x}$ for each of the situations described in Exercise 6.80.

6.82 Suppose $N = 5,000, n = 64$, and $s = 24$.
  a. Compare the size of the standard error of $\bar{x}$ computed with and without the finite population correction factor.
  b. Repeat part **a**, but this time assume $n = 400$.
  c. Theoretically, when sampling from a finite population, the finite population correction factor should always be used in computing the standard error of $\bar{x}$. However, when n is small relative to N, the finite population correction factor is close to 1 and can safely be ignored. Explain how parts **a** and **b** illustrate this point.

6.83 Suppose $N = 10,000$, $n = 2,000$, and $s = 50$.

    a. Compute the standard error of $\bar{x}$ using the finite population correction factor.

    b. Repeat part **a** assuming $n = 4,000$.

    c. Repeat part **a** assuming $n = 10,000$.

    d. Compare parts **a, b,** and **c** and describe what happens to the standard error of $\bar{x}$ as n increases.

    e. The answer to part **c** is 0. This indicates that there is no sampling error in this case. Explain.

6.84 Suppose you want to estimate a population mean, μ, and $\bar{x} = 422$, $s = 14$, $N = 375$, and $n = 40$. Find an approximate 95% confidence interval for μ.

6.85 Suppose you want to estimate a population proportion, p, and $\hat{p} = .42$, $N = 6,000$, and $n = 1,600$. Find an approximate 95% confidence interval for p.

6.86 A random sample of size $n = 30$ was drawn from a population of size $N = 300$. The following measurements were obtained:

L06086

21	33	19	29	22	38	58	29	52	36	37	30
53	37	29	18	35	42	36	41	35	36	33	38
29	38	39	54	42	42						

    a. Estimate μ with an approximate 95% confidence interval.

    b. Estimate p, the proportion of measurements in the population that are greater than 30, with an approximate 95% confidence interval.

Applying the Concepts—Basic

6.87 **NFL player survey.** Researchers at the University of Pennsylvania's Wharton Sports Business Initiative collaborated with the National Football League Players Association (NFLPA) to produce the first NFL Player Survey. Of the 1,696 active NFL players, 1,355 (almost 80%) responded to the survey. One of the survey questions asked, "Who is the coach—professional, college, or high school—that has been the most influential in your career?" Of the 1,355 respondents, 759 selected an NFL (professional) coach.

    a. Construct a 95% confidence interval for the true proportion of active NFL players who select a professional coach as the most influential in their careers.

    b. Why is it necessary to use the continuity correction factor in the construction of the interval, part **a**?

    c. Give a practical interpretation of the interval, part **a**.

6.88 **Magazine subscriber salaries.** Each year, the trade magazine *Quality Progress* publishes a study of subscribers' salaries. One year, the 223 vice presidents sampled had a mean salary of $116,754 and a standard deviation of $39,185. Suppose the goal of the study is to estimate the true mean salary of all vice presidents who subscribe to *Quality Progress*.

    NW   **a.** If 2,193 vice presidents subscribe to *Quality Progress*, estimate the mean with an approximate 95% confidence interval.

    b. Interpret the result.

Applying the Concepts—Intermediate

6.89 **Auditing sampling methods.** Traditionally, auditors have relied to a great extent on sampling techniques, rather than AUDIT 100% audits, to help them test and evaluate the financial records of a client firm. When sampling is used to obtain an estimate of the total dollar value of an account—the account balance—the examination is known as a substantive test (*Audit Sampling—AICPA Audit Guide*, 2015). In order to evaluate the reasonableness of a firm's stated total value of its parts inventory, an auditor randomly samples 100 of the total of 500 parts in stock, prices each part, and reports the results shown in the table.

Part Number	Part Price	Sample Size
002	$ 108	3
101	55	2
832	500	1
077	73	10
688	300	1
910	54	4
839	92	6
121	833	5
271	50	9
399	125	12
761	1,000	2
093	62	8
505	205	7
597	88	11
830	100	19

    a. Give a point estimate of the mean value of the parts inventory.

    b. Find the estimated standard error of the point estimate of part **a**.

    c. Construct an approximate 95% confidence interval for the mean value of the parts inventory.

    d. The firm reported a mean parts inventory value of $300. What does your confidence interval of part **c** suggest about the reasonableness of the firm's reported figure? Explain.

6.90 **Furniture brand familiarity.** A brand name that consumers recognize is a highly valued commodity in any industry. To assess brand familiarity in the furniture industry, NPD (a market research firm) surveyed 1,333 women who head U.S. households that have incomes of $25,000 or more. The sample was drawn from a database of 25,000 households that match the criteria listed above. Of the 10 furniture brands evaluated, La-Z-Boy was the most recognized brand; 70.8% of the respondents indicated they were "very familiar" with La-Z-Boy.

    a. Describe the population being investigated by NPD.

    b. In constructing a confidence interval to estimate the proportion of households that are very familiar with the La-Z-Boy brand, is it necessary to use the finite population correction factor? Explain.

    c. What estimate of the standard error of $\hat{p}$ should be used in constructing the confidence interval of part **b**?

    d. Construct a 90% confidence interval for the true proportion and interpret it in the context of the problem.

6.91 **Invoice errors in a billing system.** In a study of invoice errors in a company's new billing system, an auditor randomly sampled 35 invoices produced by the new system and recorded actual amount (A), invoice amount (I), and the difference (or error), $x = (A - I)$. The results were $\bar{x} = \$1$ and $s = \$124$. At the time that the sample was drawn, the new system had produced 1,500 invoices. Use this information to find an approximate 95% confidence interval for the true mean error per invoice of the new system. Interpret the result.

Applying the Concepts—Advanced

6.92 **Pesticide residue in corn products.** The U.S. Environmental Protection Agency (EPA) bans use of the cancer-causing pesticide ethylene dibromide (EDB) as a fumigant for grain- and flour-milling equipment. EDB was once used to protect against infestation by microscopic roundworms called *nematodes*. The EPA sets maximum safe levels for EDB presence in raw grain, flour, cake mixes, cereals, bread, and other grain products on supermarket shelves and in warehouses. Of the 3,000 corn-related products sold in one state, tests indicated that 15 of a random sample of 175 had EDB residues above the safe level. Will more than 7% of the corn-related products in this state have to be removed from shelves and warehouses? Explain.

6.7 Confidence Interval for a Population Variance (Optional)

In the previous sections, we considered interval estimation for population means or proportions. In this optional section, we discuss a confidence interval for a population variance, σ^2.

Recall Example 1.5 (p. 38) and the U.S. Army Corps of Engineers study of contaminated fish in the Tennessee River, Alabama. It is important for the Corps of Engineers to know how stable the weights of the contaminated fish are. That is, how large is the variation in the fish weights? The key word "variation" indicates that the target population parameter is σ^2, the variance of the weights of all contaminated fish inhabiting the Tennessee River. Of course, the exact value of σ^2 will be unknown. Consequently, the Corps of Engineers wants to estimate its value with a high level of confidence.

Intuitively, it seems reasonable to use the sample variance, s^2, to estimate σ^2. However, unlike with sample means and proportions, the sampling distribution of s^2 does not follow a normal (z) distribution or a Student's t-distribution. Rather, when certain assumptions are satisfied (we discuss these later), the sampling distribution of s^2 possesses approximately a **chi-square (χ^2) distribution.** The chi-square probability distribution, like the t-distribution, is characterized by a quantity called the *degrees of freedom* (df) associated with the distribution. Several chi-square distributions with different df values are shown in Figure 6.20. You can see that unlike z- and t-distributions, the chi-square distribution is not symmetric about 0.

The upper-tail areas for this distribution have been tabulated and are given in Table IV in Appendix D, a portion of which is reproduced in Table 6.7. The table gives the values of χ^2, denoted as χ_α^2, that locate an area of α in the upper tail of the chi-square distribution; that is, $P(\chi^2 > \chi_\alpha^2) = \alpha$. As with the t-statistic, the degrees of freedom associated with s^2 are $(n - 1)$. Thus, for $n = 10$ and an upper-tail value $\alpha = .05$, you will have $n - 1 = 9$ df and $\chi_{.05}^2 = 16.9190$ (highlighted in Table 6.7).

The chi-square distribution is used to find a confidence interval for σ^2, as shown in the box. An illustrative example follows.

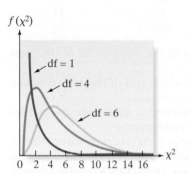

$f(\chi^2)$

df = 1
df = 4
df = 6

0 2 4 6 8 10 12 14 16 χ^2

Figure 6.20
Several χ^2 probability distributions

A $100(1 - \alpha)$ Confidence Interval for σ^2

$$\frac{(n - 1)s^2}{\chi_{\alpha/2}^2} \leq \sigma^2 \leq \frac{(n - 1)s^2}{\chi_{(1-\alpha/2)}^2}$$

where $\chi_{\alpha/2}^2$ and $\chi_{(1-\alpha/2)}^2$ are values corresponding to an area of $\alpha/2$ in the right (upper) and left (lower) tails, respectively, of the chi-square distribution based on $(n - 1)$ degrees of freedom.

Conditions Required for a Valid Confidence Interval for σ^2

1. A random sample is selected from the target population.

2. The population of interest has a relative frequency distribution that is approximately normal.

Table 6.7	Reproduction of Part of Table IV in Appendix D: Critical Values of Chi Square

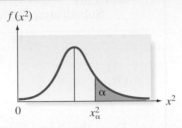

$f(x^2)$

α

0 x^2_α x^2

Degrees of Freedom	$\chi^2_{.100}$	$\chi^2_{.050}$	$\chi^2_{.025}$	$\chi^2_{.010}$	$\chi^2_{.005}$
1	2.70554	3.84146	5.02389	6.63490	7.87944
2	4.60517	5.99147	7.37776	9.21034	10.5966
3	6.25139	7.81473	9.34840	11.3449	12.8381
4	7.77944	9.48773	11.1433	13.2767	14.8602
5	9.23635	11.0705	12.8325	15.0863	16.7496
6	10.6446	12.5916	14.4494	16.8119	18.5476
7	12.0170	14.0671	16.0128	18.4753	20.2777
8	13.3616	15.5073	17.5346	20.0902	21.9550
9	14.6837	16.9190	19.0228	21.6660	23.5893
10	15.9871	18.3070	20.4831	23.2093	25.1882
11	17.2750	19.6751	21.9200	24.7250	25.7569
12	18.5494	21.0261	23.3367	26.2170	28.2995
13	19.8119	22.3621	24.7356	27.6883	29.8194
14	21.0642	23.6848	26.1190	29.1413	31.3193
15	22.3072	24.9958	27.4884	30.5779	32.8013
16	23.5418	26.2862	28.8454	31.9999	34.2672
17	24.7690	27.5871	30.1910	33.4087	35.7185
18	25.9894	28.8693	31.5264	34.8053	37.1564
19	27.2036	30.1435	32.8523	36.1908	38.5822

EXAMPLE 6.12

Estimating σ^2—Weight Variance of Contaminated Fish

Figure 6.21

Minitab descriptive statistics for fish weights, Example 6.12

Problem Refer to the U.S. Army Corps of Engineers study of contaminated fish in the Tennessee River. The Corps of Engineers has collected data for a random sample of 144 fish contaminated with DDT. (The engineers made sure to capture contaminated fish in several different randomly selected streams and tributaries of the river.) The fish weights (in grams) are saved in the **DDT** file. The Army Corps of Engineers wants to estimate the true variation in fish weights to determine whether the fish are stable enough to allow further testing for DDT contamination.

a. Use the sample data to find a 95% confidence interval for the parameter of interest.

b. Determine whether the confidence interval, part **a,** is valid.

Solution

a. Here, the target parameter is σ^2, the variance of the population of weights of contaminated fish. First we need to find the sample variance, s^2, to compute the interval estimate. The Minitab printout, Figure 6.21 gives descriptive statistics for the sample weights saved in the **DDT** file. You can see that $s = 376.5$ grams. Consequently, $s^2 = (376.5)^2 = 141,752.25$.

Descriptive Statistics: WEIGHT

```
Variable    N    Mean   StDev  Minimum  Median  Maximum
WEIGHT    144  1049.7   376.5    173.0  1000.0   2302.0
```

Next, we require the critical values $\chi^2_{\alpha/2}$ and $\chi^2_{(1-\alpha/2)}$ for a chi-square distribution. For a 95% confidence interval, $\alpha = .05$, $\alpha/2 = .025$, and $(1 - \alpha/2) = .975$. Therefore, we need $\chi^2_{.025}$ and $\chi^2_{.975}$. Now, for a sample size $n = 144$, the degrees of freedom associated with the distribution is df $= (n - 1) = 143$. Looking in the df $= 150$ row of Table IV, Appendix D (the row with the df value closest to 143), we find $\chi^2_{.025} = 185.800$ and $\chi^2_{.975} = 117.985$.

Substituting the appropriate values into the formula given in the box, we obtain

$$\frac{(144 - 1)(376.5)^2}{185.500} \le \sigma^2 \le \frac{(144 - 1)(376.5)^2}{117.985}$$

Or,

$$109{,}275 \le \sigma^2 \le 171{,}806$$

Thus, the Army Corps of Engineers can be 95% confident that the variance in weights of the population of contaminated fish ranges between 109,275 and 171,806.

b. According to the box, two conditions are required for the confidence interval to be valid. First, the sample must be randomly selected from the population. The Army Corps of Engineers did, indeed, collect a random sample of contaminated fish, making sure to sample fish from different locations in the Tennessee River. Second, the population data (the fish weights) must be approximately normally distributed. A Minitab histogram for the sampled fish weights (with a normal curve superimposed) is displayed in Figure 6.22. Clearly, the data appear to be approximately normally distributed. Thus, the confidence interval is valid.

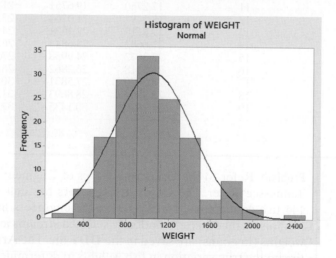

Figure 6.22

Minitab histogram of fish weights, Example 6.12

Look Ahead Will this confidence interval be practically useful in helping the Corps of Engineers decide whether the weights of the fish are stable? Only if it is clear what a weight variance of, say, 150,000 grams^2 implies. Most likely, the Corps of Engineers will want the interval in the same units as the weight measurement—grams. Consequently, a confidence interval for σ, the standard deviation of the population of fish weights, is desired. We demonstrate how to obtain this interval estimate in the next example.

Now Work Exercise 6.98a, b

EXAMPLE 6.13

Estimating σ—Weight Standard Deviation of Contaminated Fish

Problem Refer to Example 6.12. Find a 95% confidence interval for σ, the true standard deviation of the contaminated fish weights.

Solution A confidence interval for σ is obtained by taking the square roots of the lower and upper endpoints of a confidence interval for σ^2. Consequently, the 95% confidence interval for σ is:

$$\sqrt{109{,}275} \le \sigma \le \sqrt{171{,}806}$$

Or,

$$330.5 \le \sigma \le 414.5$$

Thus, the engineers can be 95% confident that the true standard deviation of fish weights is between 330.5 grams and 414.5 grams.

Look Back Suppose the Corps of Engineers' threshold is $\sigma = 500$ grams. That is, if the standard deviation in fish weights is 500 grams or higher, further DDT contamination tests will be suspended due to the unstableness of the fish weights. Since the 95% confidence interval for σ lies below 500 grams, the engineers will continue the DDT contamination tests on the fish.

● **Now Work Exercise 6.98c, d, e, f**

> **! CAUTION** The procedure for estimating either σ^2 or σ requires an assumption regardless of whether the sample size n is large or small (see the condition in the box). The sampled data must come from a population that has an approximate normal distribution. Unlike small-sample confidence intervals for μ based on the t-distribution, *slight to moderate departures from normality will render the chi-square confidence interval for σ^2 invalid.*

Exercises 6.93–6.105

Learning the Mechanics

6.93 For each of the following combinations of confidence interval and degrees of freedom (df), use Table IV in Appendix D to find the values of $\chi^2_{\alpha/2}$ and $\chi^2_{1-\alpha/2}$.
  a. 90% confidence interval with $df = 5$
  b. 95% confidence interval with $df = 13$
  c. 95% confidence interval with $df = 28$
  d. 99% confidence interval with $df = 13$

6.94 Given the following values of $\bar{x}, s$, and n, form a 90% confidence interval for σ^2.
  a. $\bar{x} = 21, s = 2.5, n = 50$
  b. $\bar{x} = 1.3, s = .02, n = 15$
  c. $\bar{x} = 167, s = 31.6, n = 22$
  d. $\bar{x} = 9.4, s = 1.5, n = 5$

6.95 Refer to Exercise 6.94. For each part, **a–d**, form a 90% confidence interval for σ.

6.96 A random sample of $n = 6$ observations from a normal distribution resulted in the data shown in the table. Compute a 95% confidence interval for σ^2.

8	2	3	7	11	6

Applying the Concepts—Basic

6.97 **Oil content of fried sweet potato chips.** The characteristics of sweet potato chips fried at different temperatures were investigated in the *Journal of Food Engineering* (September 2013). A sample of 6 sweet potato slices were fried at 130° using a vacuum fryer. One characteristic of interest to the researchers was internal oil content (measured in millions of grams). The results were: $\bar{x} = 178$ and $s = 11$. The researchers are interested in estimating the variance of the interval oil content measurements for sweet potato chips.
  a. Identify the target parameter, in symbols and words.
  b. Compute a 95% confidence interval for σ^2.

  c. What does it mean to say that the target parameter lies within the interval with "95% confidence"?
  d. What assumption about the data must be satisfied in order for the confidence interval to be valid?
  e. To obtain a practical interpretation of the interval, part **b,** explain why a confidence interval for the standard deviation, σ, is desired.
  f. Use the results, part **b,** to compute a 95% confidence interval for σ. Give a practical interpretation of the interval.

6.98 **Corporate sustainability of CPA firms.** Refer to the *Business and Society* (March 2011) study on the sustainability behaviors of CPA corporations, Exercise 6.12 (p. 339). Recall that the level of support for corporate sustainability (measured on a quantitative scale ranging from 0 to 160 points) was obtained for each in a sample of 992 senior managers at CPA firms. The accompanying Minitab printout gives 90% confidence intervals for both the variance and standard deviation of level of support for all senior managers at CPA firms.

```
Statistics

Variable    N   StDev   Variance
Support    992   26.9      722


90% Confidence Intervals

                          CI for        CI for
Variable   Method          StDev       Variance
Support    Chi-Square   (25.9, 27.9)   (672, 779)
```

  a. Locate the 90% confidence interval for σ^2 on the printout. Interpret the result.
  b. Use the sample variance on the printout to calculate the 90% confidence interval for σ^2. Does your result agree with the interval shown on the printout?
  c. Locate the 90% confidence interval for σ on the printout.

d. Use the result, part **a,** to calculate the 90% confidence interval for σ. Does your result agree with the interval shown on the printout?

e. Give a practical interpretation of the 90% confidence interval for σ.

f. What assumption about the distribution of level of support is required for the inference, part **e,** to be valid? Is this assumption reasonably satisfied? (Use your answer to Exercise 4.125, p. 270.)

6.99 **Facial structure of CEOs.** Refer to the *Psychological Science* (Vol. 22, 2011) study of a chief executive officer's facial structure, Exercise 6.20 (p. 341). Recall that the facial width-to-height ratio (WHR) was determined by computer analysis for each in a sample of 55 CEOs at publicly traded *Fortune* 500 firms, with the following results: $\bar{x} = 1.96, s = .15$.

a. Find and interpret a 95% confidence interval for the standard deviation, σ, of the facial WHR values for all CEOs at publicly traded *Fortune* 500 firms. Interpret the result.

b. For the interval, part **a,** to be valid, the population of WHR values should be distributed how? Draw a sketch of the required distribution to support your answer.

6.100 **Radon exposure in Egyptian tombs.** Refer to the *Radiation Protection Dosimetry* (December 2010) study of radon exposure in tombs carved from limestone in the Egyptian Valley of Kings, Exercise 6.30 (p. 349). The radon levels in the inner chambers of a sample of 12 tombs were determined, yielding the following summary statistics: $\bar{x} = 3,643$ Bq/m³ and $s = 4,487$ Bq/m³. Use this information to estimate, with 95% confidence, the true standard deviation of radon levels in tombs in the Valley of Kings. Interpret the resulting interval.

Applying the Concepts—Intermediate

6.101 **Drug content assessment.** Refer to the *Analytical Chemistry* (Dec. 15, 2009) study of a new method used by GlaxoSmithKline Medicines Research Center to determine the amount of drug in a tablet, Exercise 4.123 (p. 269). Drug concentrations (measured as a percentage) for 50 randomly selected tablets are repeated in the accompanying table. For comparisons against a standard method, the scientists at GlaxoSmithKline desire an estimate of the variability in drug concentrations for the new method. Obtain the estimate for the scientists using a 99% confidence interval. Interpret the interval.

91.28	92.83	89.35	91.90	82.85	94.83	89.83	89.00	84.62
86.96	88.32	91.17	83.86	89.74	92.24	92.59	84.21	89.36
90.96	92.85	89.39	89.82	89.91	92.16	88.67	89.35	86.51
89.04	91.82	93.02	88.32	88.76	89.26	90.36	87.16	91.74
86.12	92.10	83.33	87.31	88.20	92.78	86.35	93.84	91.20
93.44	86.77	83.77	93.19	81.79				

Source: Based on P. J. Borman, J. C. Marion, I. Damjanov, and P. Jackson, "Design and Analysis of Method Equivalence Studies," *Analytical Chemistry*, Vol. 81, No. 24, December 15, 2009 (Table 3).

6.102 **Jitter in a water power system.** *Jitter* is a term used to describe the variation in conduction time of a water power system. Low throughput jitter is critical to successful waterline technology. An investigation of throughput jitter in the opening switch of a prototype system (*Journal of Applied Physics*) yielded the following descriptive statistics on conduction time for $n = 18$ trials: $\bar{x} = 334.8$ nanoseconds, $s = 6.3$ nanoseconds. (Conduction time is defined as the length of time required for the downstream current to equal 10% of the upstream current.)

a. Construct a 95% confidence interval for the true standard deviation of conduction times of the prototype system.

b. Practically interpret the confidence interval, part **a.**

c. A system is considered to have low throughput jitter if the true conduction time standard deviation is less than 7 nanoseconds. Does the prototype system satisfy this requirement? Explain.

6.103 **Lobster trap placement.** Refer to the *Bulletin of Marine Science* (April 2010) observational study of teams fishing for the red spiny lobster in Baja California Sur, Mexico, Exercise 6.29 (p. 348). Trap-spacing measurements (in meters) for a sample of seven teams of red spiny lobster fishermen are repeated in the table. The researchers want to know how variable the trap-spacing measurements are for the population of red spiny lobster fishermen fishing in Baja California Sur, Mexico. Provide the researchers with an estimate of the target parameter using a 99% confidence interval.

93	99	105	94	82	70	86

Source: Based on G. G. Shester, "Explaining Catch Variation Among Baja California Lobster Fishers Through Spatial Analysis of Trap-Placement Decisions," *Bulletin of Marine Science*, Vol. 86, No. 2, April 2010 (Table 1).

6.104 **Phishing attacks on e-mail accounts.** Refer to the *Chance* (Summer 2007) study of an actual phishing attack against an organization, Exercise 5.33 (p. 316). Recall that *phishing* describes an attempt to extract personal/financial information from unsuspecting people through fraudulent e-mail. The interarrival times (in seconds) for 267 fraud box e-mail notifications are saved in the accompanying file. As with Exercise 5.33, consider these interarrival times to represent the population of interest.

a. Obtain a random sample of $n = 10$ interarrival times from the population.

b. Use the sample, part **b,** to obtain an interval estimate of the population variance of the interarrival times. What is the measure of reliability for your estimate?

c. Find the true population variance for the data. Does the interval, part **b,** contain the true variance? Give one reason why it may not.

6.105 **Is honey a cough remedy?** Refer to the *Archives of Pediatrics and Adolescent Medicine* (December 2007) study of honey as a remedy for coughing, Exercise 2.31 (p. 86). Recall that the 105 ill children in the sample were randomly divided into groups. One group received a dosage of an over-the-counter cough medicine (DM); another group received a dosage of honey (H). The coughing improvement scores (as determined by the children's parents) for the patients in the two groups are reproduced in the accompanying table. The pediatric researchers desire information on the variation in coughing improvement scores for each of the two groups.

a. Find a 90% confidence interval for the standard deviation in improvement scores for the honey dosage group.

b. Repeat part **a** for the DM dosage group.

c. Based on the results, parts **a** and **b**, what conclusions can the pediatric researchers draw about which group has the smaller variation in improvement scores? (We demonstrate a more statistically valid method for comparing variances in Chapter 8.)

Honey	11 12 15 11 10 13 10 4 15 16 9 14 10 6 10 11 12 12 8
Dosage:	12 9 11 15 10 15 9 13 8 12 10 9 5 12
DM	4 6 9 4 7 7 7 9 12 10 11 6 3 4 9 12 7 6 8 12
Dosage:	12 4 12 13 7 10 13 9 4 4 10 15 9

Source: Based on I. M. Paul, et al. "Effect of Honey, Dextromethorphan, and No Treatment on Nocturnal Cough and Sleep Quality for Coughing Children and Their Parents," *Archives of Pediatrics and Adolescent Medicine,* Vol. 161, No. 12, December 2007 (data simulated).

CHAPTER NOTES

Key Terms

Note: Asterisks (*) denote items from the optional sections of this chapter.

Key Symbols

θ	General population parameter (theta)
μ	Population mean
σ^2	Population variance
σ	Population standard deviation
p	Population proportion; $P(\text{Success})$ in binomial trial
q	$1 - p$
$\bar{x}$	Sample mean (estimator of μ)
$\hat{p}$	Sample proportion (estimator of p)
$*s^2$	Sample variance (estimator of σ^2)
$\mu_{\bar{x}}$	Mean of the population sampling distribution of $\bar{x}$
$\sigma_{\bar{x}}$	Standard deviation of the sampling distribution of $\bar{x}$
$\sigma_{\hat{p}}$	Standard deviation of the sampling distribution of $\hat{p}$
SE	Sampling error in estimation
α	$(1 - \alpha)$ represents the confidence coefficient
$z_{\alpha/2}$	z-value used in a $100(1 - \alpha)\%$ large-sample confidence interval for μ or p
$t_{\alpha/2}$	Student's t-value used in a $100(1 - \alpha)\%$ small-sample confidence interval for μ
$*N$	Number of observations in the target population
$*\chi_{\alpha/2}^2$	Chi-square value used in a $100(1 - \alpha)\%$ confidence interval for σ^2

Key Ideas/Formulas

Population Parameters, Estimators, and Standard Errors

Parameter (θ)	Estimator $(\hat{\theta})$	Standard Error of Estimator $(\sigma_{\hat{\theta}})$	Estimated Std. Error $(\hat{\sigma}_{\hat{\theta}})$
Mean, μ	$\bar{x}$	$\sigma/\sqrt{n}$	$s/\sqrt{n}$
Proportion, p	$\hat{p}$	$\sqrt{pq/n}$	$\sqrt{\hat{p}\hat{q}/n}$
*Variance, σ^2	s^2	—	—

Confidence Interval: An interval that encloses an unknown population parameter with a certain level of confidence $(1 - \alpha)$

Confidence Coefficient: The probability $(1 - \alpha)$ that a randomly selected confidence interval encloses the true value of the population parameter

Key Words for Identifying the Target Parameter

μ —Mean, Average
p —Proportion, Fraction, Percentage, Rate, Probability
*σ^2 —Variance, Variation, Spread

Commonly Used z-Values for a Large-Sample Confidence Interval

90% CI:	$(1 - \alpha) = .10$	$z_{.05} = 1.645$
95% CI:	$(1 - \alpha) = .05$	$z_{.025} - 1.96$
98% CI:	$(1 - \alpha) = .02$	$z_{.01} = 2.326$
99% CI:	$(1 - \alpha) = .01$	$z_{.005} = 2.576$

Determining the Sample Size n

Estimating μ: $n = (z_{\alpha/2})^2(\sigma^2)/(\text{SE})^2$

Estimating p: $n = (z_{\alpha/2})^2(pq)/(\text{SE})^2$

*Finite Population Correction Factor (use when $n/N > .05$)

Estimating μ: $\widehat{\sigma_{\bar{x}}} = \dfrac{s}{\sqrt{n}}\sqrt{\dfrac{N - n}{N}}$

Estimating p: $\widehat{\sigma_{\hat{p}}} = \sqrt{\dfrac{p(1 - p)}{n}}\sqrt{\dfrac{N - n}{N}}$

Illustrating the Notion of "95% Confidence"

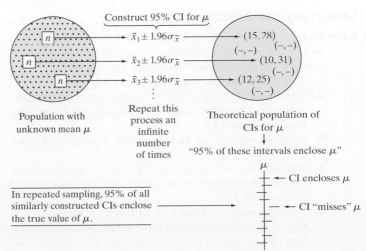

In repeated sampling, 95% of all similarly constructed CIs enclose the true value of μ.

Guide to Forming a Confidence Interval

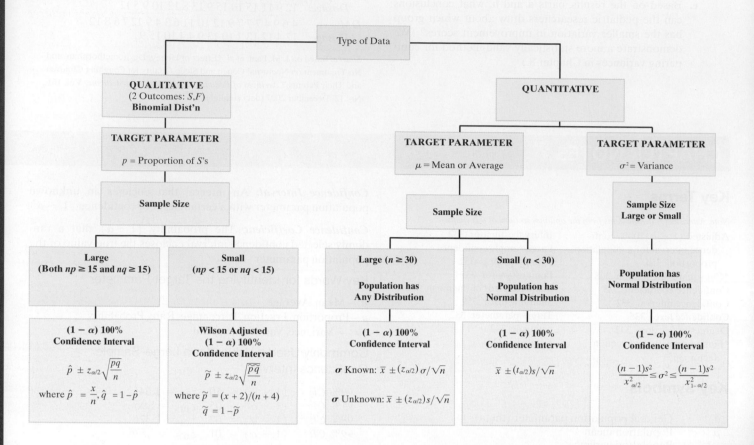

SUPPLEMENTARY EXERCISES 6.106 –6.137

Note: List the assumptions necessary for the valid implementation of the statistical procedures you use in solving all these exercises. Exercises marked with an asterisk (*) are from the optional sections in this chapter.

Learning the Mechanics

6.106 In each of the following instances, determine whether you would use a z- or t-statistic (or neither) to form a 90% confidence interval and then state the appropriate z- or t-statistic value for the confidence interval.

a. Random sample of size $n = 32$ from a normal distribution with a population mean of 60 and population standard deviation of 4.

b. Random sample of size $n = 108$ from an unknown population.

c. Random sample of size $n = 12$ from a normal distribution with sample mean of 83 and sample standard deviation of 2.

d. Random sample of size $n = 24$ from a normal distribution with unknown mean and sample standard deviation of 3.

6.107 Use Table III, Appendix D to determine the t_0 values for each of the following probability statements and their respective degrees of freedom (df).

a. $P(t \leq t_0) = .25$ with $df = 15$
b. $P(t \geq t_0) = .1$ with $df = 8$
c. $P(-t_0 \leq t \leq t_0) = .01$ with $df = 19$
d. $P(-t_0 \leq t \leq t_0) = .05$ with $df = 24$

6.108 In a random sample of 250 people from a city, 148 of them favor apples over other fruits.

a. Use a 90% confidence interval to estimate the true proportion p of people in the population who favor apples over other fruits.

b. How large a sample would be needed to estimate p to be within .15 with 90% confidence?

6.109 A random sample of 225 measurements is selected from a population, and the sample mean and standard deviation are $\bar{x} = 32.5$ and $s = 30.0$, respectively.

a. Use a 99% confidence interval to estimate the mean of the population, μ.

b. How large a sample would be needed to estimate m to within .5 with 99% confidence?

*c. Use a 99% confidence interval to estimate the population variance, σ^2.

d. What is meant by the phrase *99% confidence* as it is used in this exercise?

*6.110 Calculate the finite population correction factor for each of the following situations:
  a. $n = 50, N = 2,000$
  b. $n = 20, N = 100$
  c. $n = 300, N = 1,500$

*6.111 Find $\chi^2_{\alpha/2}$ and $\chi^2_{(1-\alpha/2)}$ from Table IV, Appendix D, for each of the following:
  a. $n = 10, \alpha = .05$
  b. $n = 20, \alpha = .05$
  c. $n = 50, \alpha = .01$

Applying the Concepts—Basic

6.112 Latex allergy in health care workers. Health care workers who use latex gloves with glove powder on a daily basis are particularly susceptible to developing a latex allergy. Each in a sample of 46 hospital employees who were diagnosed with latex allergy based on a skin-prick test reported on their exposure to latex gloves (*Current Allergy & Clinical Immunology,* March 2004). Summary statistics for the number of latex gloves used per week are $\bar{x} = 19.3$, $s = 11.9$.
  a. Give a point estimate for the average number of latex gloves used per week by all health care workers with a latex allergy.
  b. Form a 95% confidence interval for the average number of latex gloves used per week by all health care workers with a latex allergy.
  c. Give a practical interpretation of the interval, part **b.**
  d. Give the conditions required for the interval, part **b,** to be valid.

6.113 General health survey. The Centers for Disease Control and Prevention (CDCP) in Atlanta, Georgia, conducts an annual survey of the general health of the U.S. population as part of its Behavioral Risk Factor Surveillance System. Using random-digit dialing, the CDCP telephones U.S. citizens over 18 years of age and asks them the following four questions:
  1. Is your health generally excellent, very good, good, fair, or poor?
  2. How many days during the previous 30 days was your physical health not good because of injury or illness?
  3. How many days during the previous 30 days was your mental health not good because of stress, depression, or emotional problems?
  4. How many days during the previous 30 days did your physical or mental health prevent you from performing your usual activities?

Identify the parameter of interest for each question.

6.114 Products "Made in the USA." Refer to Exercise 2.154 (p. 143) and the *Journal of Global Business* (Spring 2002) survey to determine what "Made in the USA" means to consumers. Recall that 106 shoppers at a shopping mall in Muncie, Indiana, responded to the question, "Made in the USA" means what percentage of U.S. labor and materials?" Sixty-four shoppers answered, "100%."

a. Define the population of interest in the survey.
b. What is the characteristic of interest in the population?
c. Estimate the true proportion of consumers who believe "Made in the USA" means 100% U.S. labor and materials using a 90% confidence interval.
d. Give a practical interpretation of the interval, part **c.**
e. Explain what the phrase "90% confidence" means for this interval.
f. Compute the sample size necessary to estimate the true proportion to within .05 using a 90% confidence interval.

6.115 Material safety data sheets. The Occupational Safety & Health Administration has required companies that handle hazardous chemicals to complete material safety data sheets (MSDSs). These MSDSs have been criticized for being too hard to understand and complete by workers. A study of 150 MSDSs revealed that only 11% were satisfactorily completed (*Chemical & Engineering News,* February 7, 2005).
  a. Give a point estimate of p, the true proportion of MSDSs that are satisfactorily completed.
  b. Find a 95% confidence interval for p.
  c. Give a practical interpretation of the interval, part **b.**

6.116 Lead and copper in drinking water. Periodically, the Hillsborough County (Florida) Water Department tests the drinking water of homeowners for contaminants such as lead and copper. The lead and copper levels in water specimens collected for a sample of 10 residents of the Crystal Lakes Manors subdivision are shown below, followed by a Minitab printout analyzing the data.

Lead (μg/L)	Copper (mg/L)
1.32	.508
0	.279
13.1	.320
.919	.904
.657	.221
3.0	.283
1.32	.475
4.09	.130
4.45	.220
0	.743

Source: Data from Hillsborough Country Water Department Environmental Laboratory, Tampa, Florida.

Variable	N	Mean	StDev	SE Mean	90% CI
LEAD	10	2.89	3.92	1.24	(0.61, 5.16)
COPPER	10	0.4083	0.2495	0.0789	(0.2637, 0.5529)

a. Locate a 90% confidence interval for the mean lead level in water specimens from Crystal Lakes Manors on the printout.
b. Locate a 90% confidence interval for the mean copper level in water specimens from Crystal Lakes Manors on the printout.
c. Interpret the intervals, parts **a** and **b,** in the words of the problem.
d. Discuss the meaning of the phrase "90% confident."

6.117 Water pollution testing. The EPA wants to test a randomly selected sample of n water specimens and estimate the mean daily rate of pollution produced by a mining operation. If the EPA wants a 95% confidence interval estimate with a sampling error of 1 milligram per liter (mg/L), how many water specimens are required in the sample? Assume prior knowledge indicates that pollution readings in water samples taken during a day are approximately normally distributed with a standard deviation equal to 5 mg/L.

6.118 Bankruptcy effect on U.S. airfares. Both Delta Airlines and USAir filed for bankruptcy. A study of the impact of bankruptcy on the fares charged by U.S. airlines was published in *Research in Applied Economics* (Vol. 2, 2010). The researchers collected data on Orlando-bound airfares for three airlines—Southwest (a stable airline), Delta (just entering bankruptcy at the time), and USAir (emerging from bankruptcy). A large sample of nonrefundable ticket prices was obtained for each airline following USAir's emergence from bankruptcy, and then a 95% confidence interval for the true mean airfare was obtained for each. The results for 7-day advance bookings are shown in the accompanying table.

Airline	95% Confidence Interval
Southwest	($412, $496)
Delta	($468, $500)
USAir	($247, $372)

Source: Based on R. R. Sturm and D. B. Winters, "The Effect of Bankruptcy on U.S. Air Fares," *Research in Applied Economics*, Vol. 2, No. 2, © 2010 Macrothink Institute.

a. What confidence coefficient was used to generate the confidence intervals?

b. Give a practical interpretation of each of the 95% confidence intervals. Use the phrase "95% confident" in your answer.

c. When you say you are "95% confident," what do you mean?

d. If you want to reduce the width of each confidence interval, should you use a smaller or larger confidence coefficient? Explain.

*6.119 Employees with substance abuse problems. According to the New Jersey *Governor's Council for a Drug-Free Workplace Report,* 50 of the 72 sampled businesses that are members of the council admitted that they had employees with substance abuse problems. At the time of the survey, 251 New Jersey businesses were members of the Governor's Council. Use the finite population correction factor to find a 95% confidence interval for the proportion of all New Jersey Governor's Council business members who have employees with substance abuse problems. Interpret the resulting interval.

*6.120 Motivation of drug dealers. Refer to the *Applied Psychology in Criminal Justice* (September 2009) study of the personality characteristics of convicted drug dealers, Exercise 5.75 (p. 325). A random sample of 100 drug dealers had a mean Wanting Recognition (WR) score of 39 points, with a standard deviation of 6 points. The researchers are interested in σ^2, the variation in WR scores for all convicted drug dealers.

a. Identify the target parameter, in symbols and words.

b. Compute a 99% confidence interval for σ^2.

c. What does it mean to say that the target parameter lies within the interval with "99% confidence"?

d. What assumption about the data must be satisfied in order for the confidence interval to be valid?

e. To obtain a practical interpretation of the interval, part **b,** explain why a confidence interval for the standard deviation, σ, is desired.

f. Use the results, part **b,** to compute a 99% confidence interval for σ. Give a practical interpretation of the interval.

*6.121 Budget lapsing at army hospitals. Budget lapsing occurs when unspent funds do not carry over from one budgeting period to the next. Refer to the *Journal of Management Accounting Research* (Vol. 19, 2007) study on budget lapsing at U.S. Army hospitals, Exercise 2.113 (p. 126). Because budget lapsing often leads to a spike in expenditures at the end of the fiscal year, the researchers recorded expenses per full-time equivalent employee for each in a sample of 1,751 army hospitals. The sample yielded the following summary statistics: $\bar{x} = \$6,563$ and $s = \$2,484$. Estimate the mean expenses per full-time equivalent employee of all U.S. Army hospitals using a 90% confidence interval. Interpret the result.

Applying the Concepts—Intermediate

6.122 Size of diamonds sold at retail. Refer to Exercise 2.158 (p. 144) and the *Journal of Statistics Education* data on diamonds saved in the accompanying file. Consider the quantitative variable, number of carats, recorded for each of the 308 diamonds for sale on the open market.

a. Select a random sample of 30 diamonds from the 308 diamonds.

b. Find the mean and standard deviation of the number of carats per diamond for the sample.

c. Use the sample information, part **b,** to construct a 95% confidence interval for the mean number of carats in the population of 308 diamonds.

d. Interpret the phrase *95% confidence* when applied to the interval, part **c.**

e. Refer to the mean of all 308 diamonds you calculated in Exercise 2.157. Does the "population" mean fall within the confidence interval of part **c?**

6.123 Fish contaminated by a plant's discharge. Refer (Example 1.5, p. 38) to the U.S. Army Corps of Engineers data on a sample of 144 contaminated fish collected from the river adjacent to a chemical plant. Estimate the proportion of contaminated fish that are of the channel catfish species. Use a 90% confidence interval and interpret the result.

6.124 Improving the productivity of chickens. Farmers have discovered that the more domestic chickens peck at objects placed in their environment, the healthier and more productive the chickens seem to be. White string has been found to be a particularly attractive pecking stimulus. In one experiment, 72 chickens were exposed to a string stimulus. Instead of white string, blue-colored string was used. The number of pecks each chicken took at the blue string over a specified time interval was recorded. Summary statistics for the 72 chickens were $\bar{x} = 1.13$

pecks, $s = 2.21$ pecks (*Applied Animal Behaviour Science,* October 2000).

a. Estimate the population mean number of pecks made by chickens pecking at blue string using a 99% confidence interval. Interpret the result.

b. Previous research has shown that $\mu = 7.5$ pecks if chickens are exposed to white string. Based on the results, part **a**, is there evidence that chickens are more apt to peck at white string than blue string? Explain.

6.125 Surface roughness of pipe. Refer to the *Anti-corrosion Methods and Materials* (Vol. 50, 2003) study of the surface roughness of coated interior pipe used in oil fields, Exercise 2.46 (p. 96). The data (in micrometers) for 20 sampled pipe sections are reproduced in the accompanying table; a Minitab analysis of the data appears below.

RPIPE

1.72	2.50	2.16	2.13	1.06	2.24	2.31	2.03	1.09	1.40
2.57	2.64	1.26	2.05	1.19	2.13	1.27	1.51	2.41	1.95

Source: Data from F. Farshad and T. Pesacreta, "Coated Pipe Interior Surface Roughness as Measured by Three Scanning Probe Instruments," *Anti-corrosion Methods and Materials,* Vol. 50, No. 1, 2003 (Table III).

a. Locate a 95% confidence interval for the mean surface roughness of coated interior pipe on the accompanying Minitab printout.

b. Would you expect the average surface roughness to be as high as 2.5 micrometers? Explain.

One-Sample T: ROUGH

```
Variable   N    Mean    StDev   SE Mean      95% CI
ROUGH     20  1.88100  0.52391  0.11715  (1.63580, 2.12620)
```

6.126 Interviewing candidates for a job. The costs associated with conducting interviews for a job opening have skyrocketed over the years. According to a Harris Interactive survey, 211 of 502 senior human resources executives at U.S. companies believe that their hiring managers are interviewing too many people to find qualified candidates for the job (*Business Wire,* June 8, 2006).

a. Describe the population of interest in this study.

b. Identify the population parameter of interest, p.

c. Is the sample size large enough to provide a reliable estimate of p?

d. Find and interpret an interval estimate for the true proportion of senior human resources executives who believe that their hiring managers interview too many candidates during a job search. Use a confidence level of 98%.

e. If you had constructed a 90% confidence interval, would it be wider or narrower?

6.127 Overbooking policies for major airlines. Airlines overbook flights in order to reduce the odds of flying with unused seats. An article in *Transportation Research* (Vol. 38, 2002) investigated the optimal overbooking policies for major airlines. One of the variables measured for each airline was the compensation (in dollars) per bumped passenger required to maximize future revenue. Consider the *threshold* levels of compensation for a random sample of 10 major airlines shown in the next table. Estimate the true mean threshold compensation level for all major worldwide airlines using a 90% confidence interval. Interpret the result practically.

OVERBK

825	850	1,210	1,370	1,415
1,500	1,560	1,625	2,155	2,220

Source: Data from Y. Suzuki, "An Empirical Analysis of the Optimal Overbooking Policies for US Major Airlines," *Transportation Research, Part E,* Vol. 38, 2002 (Table 4).

6.128 Paying for music downloads. If you use the Internet, have you ever paid to access or download music? This was one of the questions of interest in a recent *Pew Internet & American Life Project Survey* (October 2010). Telephone interviews were conducted on a representative sample of 1,003 adults living in the United States. For this sample, 506 adults admitted that they have paid to download music.

a. Use the survey information to find a point estimate for the true proportion of U.S. adults who have paid to download music.

b. Find an interval estimate for the proportion, part **a.** Use a 90% confidence interval.

c. Give a practical interpretation of the interval, part **b.** Your answer should begin with "We are 90% confident. . . ."

d. Explain the meaning of the phrase "90% confident."

e. How many more adults need to be sampled to reduce the margin of error in the confidence interval by half?

6.129 Accuracy of price scanners at Walmart. The National Institute for Standards and Technology (NIST) mandates that for every 100 items scanned through the electronic checkout scanner at a retail store, no more than 2 should have an inaccurate price. A study of the accuracy of checkout scanners at Walmart stores in California was conducted. At each of 60 randomly selected Walmart stores, 100 random items were scanned. The researchers found that 52 of the 60 stores had more than 2 items that were inaccurately priced.

a. Give an estimate of p, the proportion of Walmart stores in California that have more than 2 inaccurately priced items per 100 items scanned.

b. Construct a 95% confidence interval for p.

c. Give a practical interpretation of the interval, part **b.**

d. Suppose a Walmart spokesperson claims that 99% of California Walmart stores are in compliance with the NIST mandate on accuracy of price scanners. Comment on the believability of this claim.

e. Are the conditions required for a valid large-sample confidence interval for p satisfied in this application? If not, comment on the validity of the inference in part *d*.

f. Determine the number of Walmart stores that must be sampled in order to estimate the true proportion to within .05 with 90% confidence using the large-sample method.

6.130 Contamination of New Jersey wells. Methyl t-butyl ether (MTBE) is an organic water contaminant that often results from gasoline spills. The level of MTBE (in parts per billion) was measured for a sample of 12 well sites located near a gasoline service station in New Jersey (*Environmental Science & Technology,* January 2005). The data are listed in the accompanying table.

NJGAS

150	367	38	12	11	134
12	251	63	8	13	107

Source: Based on T. Kuder et al., "Enrichment of Stable Carbon and Hydrogen Isotopes During Anaerobic Biodegradation of MTBE: Microcosm and Field Evidence," *Environmental Science & Technology,* Vol. 39, No. 1, January 2005 (Table 1).

a. Give a point estimate for μ, the true mean MTBE level for all well sites located near the New Jersey gasoline service station.

b. Calculate and interpret a 99% confidence interval for μ.

c. What assumptions are required for the interval, part **b**, to be valid? Are these assumptions reasonably satisfied?

6.131 Cell phone use by drivers. Studies have shown that drivers who use cell phones while operating a motor passenger vehicle increase their risk of an accident. Nevertheless, drivers continue to make cell phone calls while driving. A June 2011 *Harris Poll* of 2,163 adults found that 60% (1,298 adults) use cell phones while driving.

a. Give a point estimate of p, the true driver cell phone use rate (i.e., the proportion of all drivers who are using a cell phone while operating a motor passenger vehicle).

b. Find a 95% confidence interval for p.

c. Give a practical interpretation of the interval, part **b**.

d. Determine the margin of error in the interval if the number of adults in the survey is doubled.

6.132 Salmonella poisoning from eating an ice cream bar. Recently, a case of salmonella (bacterial) poisoning was traced to a particular brand of ice cream bar, and the manufacturer removed the bars from the market. Despite this response, many consumers refused to purchase *any* brand of ice cream bars for some period of time after the event (McClave, personal consulting). One manufacturer conducted a survey of consumers 6 months after the outbreak. A sample of 244 ice cream bar consumers was contacted, and 23 respondents indicated that they would not purchase ice cream bars because of the potential for food poisoning.

a. What is the point estimate of the true fraction of the entire market who refuse to purchase bars 6 months after the out-break?

b. Is the sample size large enough to use the normal approximation for the sampling distribution of the estimator of the binomial probability? Justify your response.

c. Construct a 95% confidence interval for the true proportion of the market who still refuses to purchase ice cream bars 6 months after the event.

d. Interpret both the point estimate and confidence interval in terms of this application.

6.133 Salmonella poisoning from eating an ice cream bar (cont'd). Refer to Exercise 6.132. Suppose it is now 1 year after the outbreak of food poisoning was traced to ice cream bars. The manufacturer wishes to estimate the proportion who still will not purchase bars to within .02 using a 95% confidence interval. How many consumers should be sampled?

6.134 Latex allergy in health care workers. Refer to the *Current Allergy & Clinical Immunology* (March 2004) study of health care workers who use latex gloves, Exercise 6.112 (p. 375). In addition to the 46 hospital employees who were diagnosed with a latex allergy based on a skin-prick test, another 37 health care workers were diagnosed with the allergy using a latex-specific serum test. Of these 83 workers with confirmed latex allergy, only 36 suspected that

they had the allergy when asked on a questionnaire. Make a statement about the likelihood that a health care worker with latex allergy suspects he or she actually has the allergy. Attach a measure of reliability to your inference.

Applying the Concepts—Advanced

6.135 Internal auditing of invoices. A firm's president, vice presidents, department managers, and others use financial data generated by the firm's accounting system to help them make decisions regarding such things as pricing, budgeting, and plant expansion. To provide reasonable certainty that the system provides reliable data, internal auditors periodically perform various checks of the system (Horngren, Foster, and Datar, *Cost Accounting: A Managerial Emphasis*, 2005). Suppose an internal auditor is interested in determining the proportion of sales invoices in a population of 5,000 sales invoices for which the "total sales" figure is in error. She plans to estimate the true proportion of invoices in error based on a random sample of size 100.

a. Assume that the population of invoices is numbered from 1 to 5,000 and that every invoice ending with a 0 is in error (i.e., 10% are in error). Use a random number generator to draw a random sample of 100 invoices from the population of 5,000 invoices. For example, random number 456 stands for invoice number 456. List the invoice numbers in your sample and indicate which of your sampled invoices are in error (i.e., those ending in a 0).

b. Use the results of your sample of part **a** to construct a 90% confidence interval for the true proportion of invoices in error.

c. Recall that the true population proportion of invoices in error is equal to .1. Compare the true proportion with the estimate of the true proportion you developed in part **b**. Does your confidence interval include the true proportion?

6.136 Accountants' salary survey. Each year, *Management Accounting* reports the results of a salary survey of the members of the Institute of Management Accountants (IMA). One year, the 2,112 members responding had a salary distribution with a 20th percentile of $35,100; a median of $50,000; and an 80th percentile of $73,000.

a. Use this information to determine the minimum sample size that could be used in next year's survey to estimate the mean salary of IMA members to within $2,000 with 98% confidence. [*Hint*: To estimate s, first apply Chebyshev's Theorem to find k such that at least 60% of the data fall within k standard deviations of μ. Then find $s \approx$ (80th percentile–20th percentile)/$2k$.]

b. Explain how you estimated the standard deviation required for the sample size calculation.

c. List any assumptions you make.

6.137 "Out of control" production process. When companies employ control charts to monitor the quality of their products, a series of small samples is typically used to determine if the process is "in control" during the period of time in which each sample is selected. (We cover quality-control charts in Chapter 13.) Suppose a concrete-block manufacturer samples nine blocks per hour and tests the breaking strength of each. During 1 hour's test, the mean and standard deviation are 985.6 pounds per square inch (psi) and 22.9 psi, respectively. The process is to be considered "out of control" if the true mean strength differs from 1,000 psi. The manufacturer wants to be reasonably certain that the process is really out of control before shutting down the process and trying to determine the problem. What is your recommendation?

Critical Thinking Challenges

6.138 A sampling dispute goes to court. Sampling of Medicare and Medicaid claims by the federal and state agencies who administer those programs has become common practice to determine whether providers of those services are submitting valid claims. (See the *Statistics in Action* for this chapter.) The reliability of inferences based on those samples depends on the methodology used to collect the sample of claims. Consider estimating the true proportion, p, of the population of claims that are invalid. (Invalid claims should not have been reimbursed by the agency.) Of course, to estimate a binomial parameter, p, within a given level of precision we use the formula provided in Section 6.5 to determine the necessary sample size. In a recent actual case, the statistician determined a sample size large enough to ensure that the bound on the error of the estimate would not exceed .05, using a 95% confidence interval. He did so by assuming that the true error rate was $p = .5$, which, as discussed in Section 6.5, provides the maximum sample size needed to achieve the desired bound on the error.

a. Determine the sample size necessary to estimate p to within .05 of the true value using a 95% confidence interval.

b. After the sample was selected and the sampled claims were audited, it was determined that the estimated error rate was $\hat{p} = .20$ and a 95% confidence interval for p was (.15, .25). Was the desired bound on the error of the estimate met?

c. An economist hired by the Medicare provider noted that, since the desired bound on the error of .05 is equal to 25% of the estimated $\hat{p} = .20$ invalid claim rate, the "true" bound on the error was .25, not .05. He argued that a significantly larger sample would be necessary to meet the "relative error" (the bound on the error divided by the error rate) goal of .05, and that the statistician's use of the "absolute error" of .05 was inappropriate, and more sampling was required. The statistician argued that the relative error was a moving target, since it depends on the sample estimate of the invalid claim rate, which cannot be known prior to selecting the sample. He noted that if the estimated invalid claim rate turned out to be larger than .5, the relative error would then be lower than the absolute error bound. As a consequence, the case went to trial over the relative vs. absolute error dispute. Give your opinion on the matter.

[*Note:* The Court concluded that "absolute error was the fair and accurate measure of the margin of error." As a result, a specified absolute bound on the error

continues to be the accepted method for determining the sample size necessary to provide a reliable estimate of Medicare and Medicaid providers' claim submission error rates.]

6.139 Scallops, sampling, and the law. *Interfaces* (March–April 1995) presented the case of a ship that fishes for scallops off the coast of New England. In order to protect baby scallops from being harvested, the U.S. Fisheries and Wildlife Service requires that "the average meat per scallop weigh at least $\frac{1}{36}$ of a pound." The ship was accused of violating this weight standard. Author Arnold Barnett lays out the scenario:

The vessel arrived at a Massachusetts port with 11,000 bags of scallops, from which the harbormaster randomly selected 18 bags for weighing. From each such bag, his agents took a large scoopful of scallops; then, to estimate the bag's average meat per scallop, they divided the total weight of meat in the scoopful by the number of scallops it contained. Based on the 18 [numbers] thus generated, the harbormaster estimated that each of the ship's scallops possessed an average of $\frac{1}{39}$ of a pound of meat (that is, they were about seven percent lighter than the minimum requirement). Viewing this outcome as conclusive evidence that the weight standard had been violated, federal authorities at once confiscated 95 percent of the catch (which they then sold at auction). The fishing voyage was thus transformed into a financial catastrophe for its participants.

The actual scallop weight measurements for each of the 18 sampled bags are listed in the table below. For ease of exposition, Barnett expressed each number as a multiple of $\frac{1}{36}$ of a pound, the minimum permissible average weight per scallop. Consequently, numbers below 1 indicate individual bags that do not meet the standard.

The ship's owner filed a lawsuit against the federal government, declaring that his vessel had fully complied with the weight standard. A Boston law firm was hired to represent the owner in legal proceedings, and Barnett was retained by the firm to provide statistical litigation support and, if necessary, expert witness testimony.

| .93 | .88 | .85 | .91 | .91 | .84 | .90 | .98 | .88 |
| .89 | .98 | .87 | .91 | .92 | .99 | 1.14 | 1.06 | .93 |

Source: Based on A. Barnett, "Misapplications Review: Jail Terms," *Interfaces*, Vol. 25, No. 2, Mar.–Apr. 1995.

a. Recall that the harbormaster sampled only 18 of the ship's 11,000 bags of scallops. One of the questions the lawyers asked Barnett was, "Can a reliable estimate of the mean weight of all the scallops be obtained from a sample of size 18?" Give your opinion on this issue.

b. As stated in the article, the government's decision rule is to confiscate a catch if the sample mean weight of the scallops is less than $\frac{1}{36}$ of a pound. Do you see any flaws in this rule?

c. Develop your own procedure for determining whether a ship is in violation of the minimum-weight restriction. Apply your rule to the data. Draw a conclusion about the ship in question.

ACTIVITY 6.1   Conducting a Pilot Study

Choose a population parameter pertinent to your major area of interest—a population that has an unknown mean, or if the population is binomial, an unknown probability of success. For example, a marketing major may be interested in the proportion of consumers who prefer a certain brand of diet cola. An economics or finance major might want to estimate the mean annual salary of Internet Web site designers. A management major may wish to estimate the proportion of companies that have mandatory sensitivity training for all employees. A pre-med student might desire an estimate of the average number of patients treated daily in the emergency room. An accounting major may want to find the percentage of audits that result in substantive changes to a company's accounting system. We

could continue with examples, but the point should be clear: Choose something of interest to you.

Define the parameter you want to estimate and conduct a *pilot study* to obtain an initial estimate of the parameter of interest and, more importantly, an estimate of the variability associated with the estimator. A pilot study is a small experiment (perhaps 15 to 20 observations) used to gain information about some phenomenon. The purpose of the study is to help plan more elaborate future experiments. Using the results of your pilot study, determine the sample size necessary to estimate the parameter to within a reasonable bound (of your choice) with a 95% confidence interval. Present the results to your class.

References

Agresti, A., and Coull, B. A. "Approximate is better than 'exact' for interval estimation of binomial proportions," *The American Statistician*, Vol. 52, No. 2, May 1998, pp. 119–126.

Arkin, H. *Sampling Methods for the Auditor.* New York: McGraw-Hill, 1982.

Cochran, W. G. *Sampling Techniques*, 3rd ed. New York: Wiley, 1977.

Freedman, D., Pisani, R., and Purves, R. *Statistics.* New York: Norton, 1978.

Kish, L. *Survey Sampling.* New York: Wiley, 1965.

Mendenhall, W., Beaver, R. J., and Beaver, B. *Introduction to Probability and Statistics*, 13th ed. Belmont, CA: Brooks/Cole, 2009.

Wilson, E. G. "Probable inference, the law of succession, and statistical inference," *Journal of the American Statistical Association*, Vol. 22, 1927, pp. 209–212.

USING TECHNOLOGY

Technology images shown here are taken from SPSS Statistics Professional 23.0, Minitab 17, XLSTAT, and Excel 2016.

SPSS: Confidence Intervals

SPSS can be used to obtain one-sample confidence intervals for a population mean and a population proportion, but cannot currently produce confidence intervals for a population variance. Also, sample size calculations are not available in the base SPSS package.

Confidence Interval for a Mean

Step 1 Access the SPSS spreadsheet file that contains the sample data.

Step 2 Click on the "Analyze" button on the SPSS menu bar and then click on "Descriptive Statistics" and "Explore," as shown in Figure 6.S.1.

Step 3 On the resulting dialog box (shown in Figure 6.S.2), specify the quantitative variable of interest in the "Dependent List" and then click on the "Statistics" button.

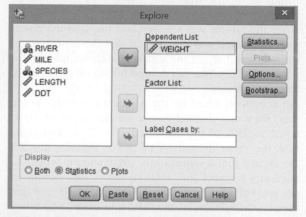

Figure 6.S.2 SPSS explore dialog box

Step 4 Specify the confidence level in the resulting dialog box, as shown in Figure 6.S.3.

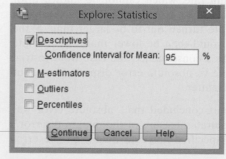

Figure 6.S.3 SPSS explore statistics options

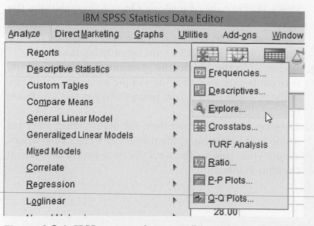

Figure 6.S.1 SPSS menu options—confidence interval for the mean

Step 5 Click "Continue" to return to the "Explore" dialog box and then click "OK" to produce the confidence interval.

Confidence Interval for a Proportion

Step 1 Access the SPSS spreadsheet that contains the qualitative variable of interest.

Step 2 Click on the "Analyze" button on the main menu bar, and then click on "Nonparametric Tests" and "1 Sample" (see Figure 6.S.1).

Step 3 Click the "Fields" option, and then on the resulting dialog box (shown in Figure 6.S.4), move the qualitative (categorical) variable to the "Test Fields" box.

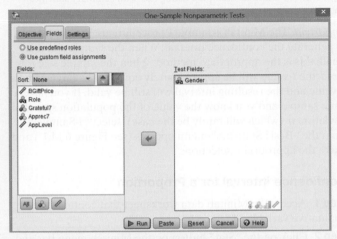

Figure 6.S.4 SPSS field options for binomial confidence interval

Step 4 Click the "Settings" option, and then on the resulting dialog box (shown in Figure 6.S.5), select "Customize Tests" and "Compare observed binary probability to hypothesized (Binomial test)." Then click "Options."

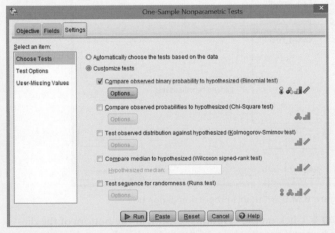

Figure 6.S.5 SPSS settings options for binomial confidence interval

Step 5 On the resulting dialog box (see Figure 6.S.6), click "Likelihood ratio" in the "Confidence Interval" box, click "OK," and then click "Run."

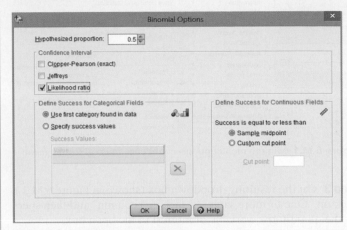

Figure 6.S.6 SPSS binomial options

Step 6 On the resulting output, double click on the "Hypothesis Test Summary" output to display the "Model Viewer" screen, as shown in Figure 6.S.7.

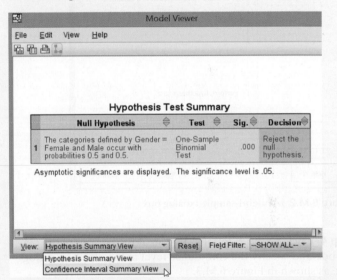

Figure 6.S.7 SPSS model viewer selections for binomial confidence interval

Step 7 At the bottom of the "Model Viewer" screen, select "Confidence Interval Summary View" (as shown in Figure 6.S.7) to view the resulting 95% confidence interval.

Minitab: Confidence Intervals

Minitab can be used to obtain one-sample confidence intervals for a population mean, a population proportion, and a population variance. Also, Minitab has menu options available for determining the sample size.

Confidence Interval for a Mean

Step 1 Access the Minitab data worksheet that contains the quantitative variable of interest.

Step 2 Click on the "Stat" button on the Minitab menu bar and then click on "Basic Statistics" and "1-Sample t," as shown in Figure 6.M.1.

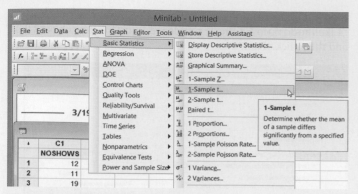

Figure 6.M.1 Minitab menu options–confidence interval for the mean

Step 3 On the resulting dropdown box (shown in Figure 6.M.2.), click on "One or more samples, each in a column" and then specify the quantitative variable of interest in the open box.

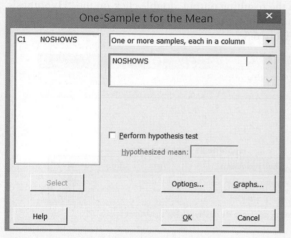

Figure 6.M.2 Minitab 1-sample t dialog box

Step 4 Click on the "Options" button at the bottom of the dialog box and specify the confidence level in the resulting dialog box, as shown in Figure 6.M.3.

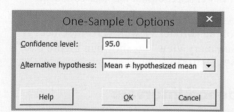

Figure 6.M.3 Minitab 1-sample t options

Step 5 Click "OK" to return to the "1-Sample t" dialog box, and then click "OK" again to produce the confidence interval.

Note: If you want to produce a confidence interval for the mean from summary information (e.g., the sample mean, sample standard deviation, and sample size), click on "Summarized data" in the "1-Sample t" dialog box, as shown in Figure 6.M.4. Enter the values of the summary statistics and then click "OK."

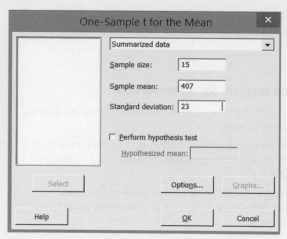

Figure 6.M.4 Minitab 1-sample t dialog box with summary statistics options

Important: The Minitab 1-sample t procedure uses the *t*-statistic to generate the confidence interval. When the sample size *n* is small, this is the appropriate method. When the sample size *n* is large, the *t*-value will be approximately equal to the large-sample *z*-value and the resulting interval will still be valid. If you have a large sample and you know the value of the population standard deviation σ (which will rarely be the case), select "1-Sample z" from the "Basic Statistics" menu options (see Figure 6.M.1) and make the appropriate selections.

Confidence Interval for a Proportion

Step 1 Access the Minitab data worksheet that contains the qualitative variable of interest.

Step 2 Click on the "Stat" button on the Minitab menu bar and then click on "Basic Statistics" and "1 Proportion" (see Figure 6.M.1).

Step 3 On the resulting dropdown box (shown in Figure 6.M.5), click on "One or more samples, each in a column" and then specify the qualitative variable of interest in the open box.

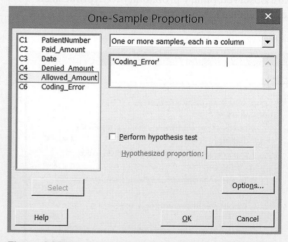

Figure 6.M.5 Minitab 1-proportion dialog box

Step 4 Click on the "Options" button at the bottom of the dialog box and specify the confidence level in the resulting dialog box, as shown in Figure 6.M.6. Also, specify "normal approximation" in the Methods box at the bottom.

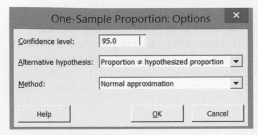

Figure 6.M.6 Minitab 1-proportion dialog box options

Step 5 Click "OK" to return to the "1-Proportion" dialog box and then click "OK" again to produce the confidence interval.

Note: If you want to produce a confidence interval for a proportion from summary information (e.g., the number of successes and the sample size), click on "Summarized data" in the "1-Proportion" dropdown box (see Figure 6.M.7). Enter the value for the number of trials (i.e., the sample size) and the number of events (i.e., the number of successes) and then click "OK."

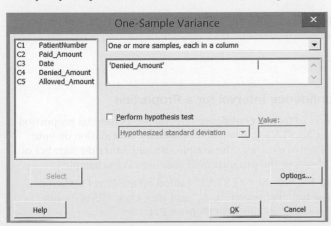

Figure 6.M.7 Minitab 1 Proportion Dialog Box with Summary Statistics Options

Confidence Interval for a Variance

Step 1 Access the Minitab data worksheet that contains the quantitative variable of interest.

Step 2 Click on the "Stat" button on the main Minitab menu bar, and then click on "Basic Statistics" and "1 Variance" (Figure 6.M.1).

Step 3 On the resulting dialog box (shown in Figure 6.M.8), select "One or more samples, each in a column" in the dropdown box, and then specify the quantitative variable of interest in the open box.

Figure 6.M.8 Minitab 1 Variance dialog box

Step 4 Click the "Options" button at the bottom of the dialog box and specify the confidence level in the resulting menu, as shown in Figure 6.M.9.

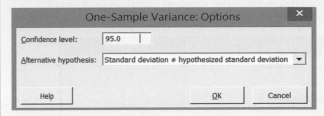

Figure 6.M.9 Minitab 1 Variance options

Step 5 Click "OK" to return to the "1 Variance" dialog box and then click "OK" again to produce the confidence interval.

Note: If you want to produce a confidence interval for a variance from summary information (e.g., the sample variance), select "Sample variance" in the dropdown box of the "1 Variance" dialog box (see Figure 6.M.10). Enter the values of the sample size and sample variance in the appropriate boxes, and then click "OK."

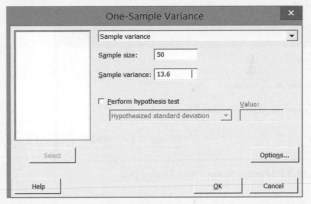

Figure 6.M.10 Minitab 1 Variance dialog box with summary statistics option

Determining the Sample Size

Step 1 Open any Minitab worksheet.

Step 2 Click on the "Stat" button on the Minitab menu bar and then click on "Power and Sample Size" and "Sample Size Estimation," as shown in Figure 6.M.11.

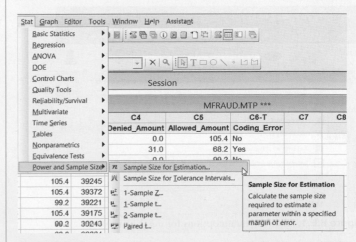

Figure 6.M.11 Minitab Menu Options for Sample Size Determination

Step 3 On the resulting dialog box (see Figure 6.M.12), select either "Mean (normal)" or "Proportion (binomial)" in the Parameter dropdown box, then specify the planned (approximate) value of the standard deviation or proportion, and the margin of error for the confidence interval.

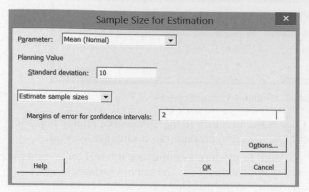

Figure 6.M.12 Minitab Sample Size Dialog Box

Step 4 Click on "Options" at the bottom of the box, and specify the confidence level (as shown in Figure 6.M.13). Click "OK", then "OK" again to view the results.

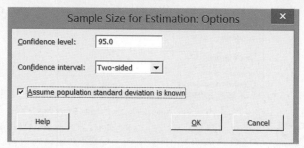

Figure 6.M.13 Minitab Sample Size Dialog Box

Excel/XLSTAT: Confidence Intervals

XLSTAT can produce a confidence interval for a population mean, proportion, and variance. Currently, sample size determinations are not available in XLSTAT.

Confidence Interval for a Mean

Step 1 Click the "XLSTAT" button on the Excel main menu bar, select "Describing data," and then click "Descriptive Statistics," as shown in Figure 6.E.1.

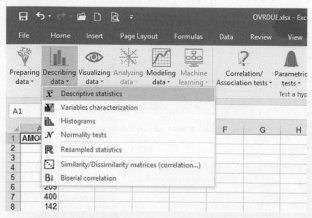

Figure 6.E.1 XLSTAT menu options for descriptive statistics

Step 2 When the resulting dialog box appears, check "Quantitative data" and then highlight the column that contains the values of the quantitative variable you want to analyze so that the column appears in the appropriate entry (see, for example, Figure 6.E.2).

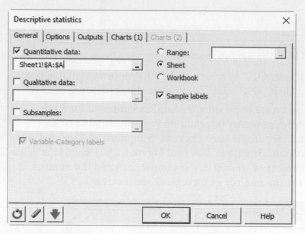

Figure 6.E.2 XLSTAT descriptive statistics dialog box

Step 3 Click the "Options" tab, and then select "Descriptive statistics" and specify the confidence level in the open box, as shown in Figure 6.E.3.

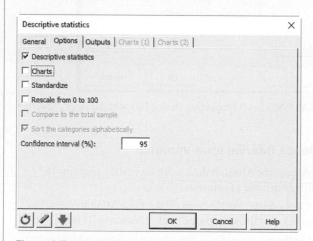

Figure 6.E.3 XLSTAT options for a confidence interval for the mean

Step 4 Click "OK" and then "Continue" to display the confidence interval.

Confidence Interval for a Proportion

[*Note:* To form a confidence interval for a binomial proportion using XLSTAT, you will need summary information on your qualitative data, e.g., the sample size and either the number of successes or the proportion of successes in the sample.]

Step 1 Click the "XLSTAT" button on the Excel main menu bar, select "Parametric tests," and then click "Tests for one proportion," as shown in Figure 6.E.4.

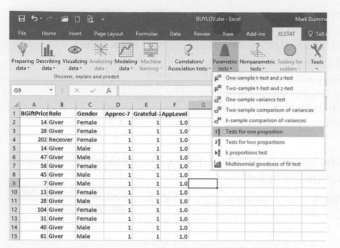

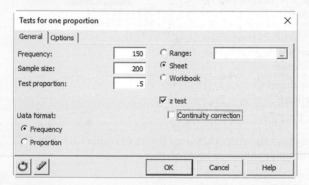

Figure 6.E.4 XLSTAT menu options for a binomial proportion

Step 2 When the resulting dialog box appears, check "Frequency" in the "Data format" area, and then enter the number of successes and the sample size in the "Frequency" and "Sample size" boxes, respectively, as shown in Figure 6.E.5. (Alternatively, you can check "Proportion" in the "Data format" area and enter the sample proportion in the "Test proportion" box.)

Figure 6.E.5 XLSTAT test for one proportion dialog box

Step 3 Click "OK" to display the confidence interval.

Confidence Interval for a Variance

Step 1 Click the "XLSTAT" button on the Excel main menu bar, select "Parametric tests," and then click "One sample variance test." (See Figure 6.E.4).

Step 2 When the resulting dialog box appears, check "Quantitative data" and then highlight the column that contains the values of the quantitative variable you want to analyze so that the column appears in the appropriate entry (see, for example, Figure 6.E.2).

Step 3 Click "OK", then "Continue" to obtain the confidence interval for the variance.

TI-84 Graphing Calculator: Confidence Intervals

The TI-84 can produce confidence intervals for a population mean and proportion. Confidence intervals for a variance and sample size determinations are not available.

Confidence Interval for a Population Mean (Known σ or $n \geq 30$)

Step 1 *Enter the data (skip to Step 2 if you have summary statistics, not raw data)*

- Press **STAT** and select **1:Edit**

Note: If the list already contains data, clear the old data. Use the up **ARROW** to highlight "**L1.**"

- Press **CLEAR ENTER**
- Use the **ARROW** and **ENTER** keys to enter the data set into **L1**

Step 2 *Access the Statistical Tests Menu*

- Press **STAT**
- Arrow right to **TESTS**
- Arrow down to **ZInterval**
- Press **ENTER**

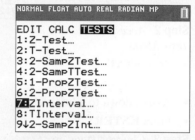

Step 3 *Choose "Data" or "Stats." ("Data" is selected when you have entered the raw data into a List. "Stats" is selected when you are given only the mean, standard deviation, and sample size.)*

- Press **ENTER**

If you selected "Data," enter a value for σ (the best approximation is s, the sample standard deviation)

- Set **List** to **L1**
- Set **Freq** to **1**
- Set **C-Level** to the confidence level
- Arrow down to "**Calculate**"
- Press **ENTER**

If you selected "Stats," enter a value for σ (the best approximation is s, the sample standard deviation)

- Enter the sample mean and sample size
- Set **C-Level** to the confidence level
- Arrow down to "**Calculate**"
- Press **ENTER**

(The bottom screen at right is set up for an example with a standard deviation of 20, a mean of 200, and a sample size of 40.) The confidence interval will be displayed along with the sample mean and the sample size.

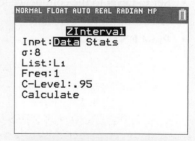

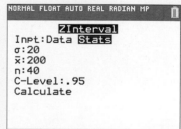

Confidence Interval for a Population Mean ($n < 30$)

Step 1 *Enter the data (skip to Step 2 if you have summary statistics, not raw data)*

- Press **STAT** and select **1:Edit**

Note: If the list already contains data, clear the old data. Use the up **ARROW** to highlight "**L1**."

- Press **CLEAR ENTER**

- Use the **ARROW** and **ENTER** keys to enter the data set into **L1**

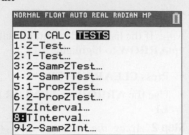

Step 2 *Access the Statistical Tests Menu*

- Press **STAT**

- Arrow right to **TESTS**

- Arrow down to **TInterval**

- Press **ENTER**

Step 3 *Choose "Data" or "Stats." ("Data" is selected when you have entered the raw data into a List. "Stats" is selected when you are given only the mean, standard deviation, and sample size.)*

- Press **ENTER**

- If you selected "Data," set **List** to **L1**

- Set **Freq** to **1**

- Set **C-Level** to the confidence level

- Arrow down to "**Calculate**"

- Press **ENTER**

If you selected "Stats," enter the mean, standard deviation, and sample size.

- Set **C-Level** to the confidence level

- Arrow down to "**Calculate**"

- Press **ENTER**

(The screen here is set up for an example with a mean of 100 and a standard deviation of 10.)

The confidence interval will be displayed with the mean, standard deviation, and sample size.

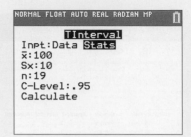

Confidence Interval for a Population Proportion (Large Samples)

Step 1 *Access the Statistical Tests Menu*

- Press **STAT**

- Arrow right to **TESTS**

- Arrow down to **1-PropZInt**

- Press **ENTER**

Step 2 *Enter the values for x, n, and C-Level*

- where x = number of successes

- n = sample size

- **C-Level** = level of Confidence

- Arrow down to "**Calculate**"

- Press **ENTER**

(The screens at the right are set up for an example with $x = 532$, $n = 1{,}100$, and confidence level of .95.)

7

WHERE WE'VE BEEN

Used sample information to provide a *point estimate* of a population parameter

Used the sampling distribution of a statistic to assess the reliability of an estimate through a *confidence interval*

WHERE WE'RE GOING

Introduce the concept of a *test of hypothesis* (7.1–7.2)

Provide a measure of reliability for the hypothesis test, called the *significance level* of the test (7.2, 7.3)

Test a specific value of a population parameter (mean, proportion, or variance) called a *test of hypothesis* (7.4–7.7)

Show how to estimate the reliability of a test (7.8)

Inferences Based on a Single Sample

Tests of Hypotheses

STATISTICS IN ACTION

Diary of a Kleenex® User—How Many Tissues in a Box?

In 1924, Kimberly-Clark Corporation invented a facial tissue for removing cold cream and began marketing it as Kleenex® brand tissues. Today, Kleenex® is recognized as the top-selling brand of tissue in the world. A wide variety of Kleenex® products are available, ranging from extra-large tissues to tissues with lotion. Over the past 80 years, Kimberly-Clark Corporation has packaged the tissues in boxes of different sizes and shapes and varied the number of tissues packaged in each box. For example, typically a family-size box contains 144 two-ply tissues, a cold-care box contains 70 tissues (coated with lotion), and a convenience pocket pack contains 15 miniature tissues.

How does Kimberly-Clark Corp. decide how many tissues to put in each box? According to the *Wall Street Journal,* marketing experts at the company use the results of a survey of Kleenex® customers to help determine how many tissues should be packed in a box. In the mid-1980s, when Kimberly-Clark Corp. developed the cold-care box designed especially for people who have a cold, the company conducted their initial survey of customers for this purpose. Hundreds of customers were asked to keep count of their Kleenex® use in diaries. According to the *Wall Street Journal* report, the survey results left "little doubt that the company should put 60 tissues in each box." The number 60 was "the average number of times people blow their nose during a cold." In 2000, the company increased the number of tissues packaged in a cold-care box to 70 based on the results of a more recent survey.

(*continued*)

From summary information provided in the *Wall Street Journal* article, we constructed a data set that represents the results of a survey similar to the one described above. In the data file named **TISSUE,** we recorded the number of tissues used by each of 250 consumers during a period when they had a cold. We apply the hypothesis-testing methodology presented in this chapter to this data set in several *Statistics in Action Revisited* examples.

STATISTICS IN ACTION REVISITED

● Key Elements of a Hypothesis Test **(p. 397)**

● Testing a Population Mean **(p. 407)**

● Testing a Population Proportion **(p. 423)**

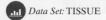 *Data Set:* TISSUE

Suppose you wanted to determine whether the mean waiting time in the drive-through line of a fast-food restaurant is less than 5 minutes, or whether the majority of consumers are optimistic about the economy. In both cases you are interested in making an inference about how the value of a parameter relates to a specific numerical value. Is it less than, equal to, or greater than the specified number? This type of inference, called a **test of hypothesis,** is the subject of this chapter.

We introduce the elements of a test of hypothesis in Sections 7.1–7.3. We then show how to conduct a large-sample test of hypothesis about a population mean in Section 7.4. In Section 7.5 we use small samples to conduct tests about means. Large-sample tests about binomial probabilities are the subject of Section 7.6, and a test about a population variance is covered in Section 7.7. Finally, some advanced methods for determining the reliability of a test are covered in Section 7.8.

7.1 The Elements of a Test of Hypothesis

Suppose building specifications in a certain city require that the average breaking strength of residential sewer pipe be more than 2,400 pounds per foot of length (i.e., per linear foot). Each manufacturer who wants to sell pipe in this city must demonstrate that its product meets the specification. Note that we are interested in making an inference about the mean μ of a population. However, in this example we are less interested in estimating the value of μ than we are in testing a **hypothesis** about its value—that is, *we want to decide whether the mean breaking strength of the pipe exceeds 2,400 pounds per linear foot.*

> A statistical **hypothesis** is a statement about the numerical value of a population parameter.

The method used to reach a decision is based on the rare-event concept explained in earlier chapters. We define two hypotheses: (1) The **null hypothesis** is that which represents the status quo to the party performing the sampling experiment—the hypothesis that will be accepted unless the data provide convincing evidence that it is false. (2) The **alternative,** or **research, hypothesis** is that which will be accepted only if the data provide convincing evidence of its truth. From the point of view of the city conducting the tests, the null hypothesis is that the manufacturer's pipe does *not* meet specifications unless the tests provide convincing evidence otherwise. The null and alternative hypotheses are therefore

Null hypothesis (H_0): $\mu \leq 2{,}400$

(i.e., the manufacturer's pipe does not meet specifications)

Alternative (research) hypothesis (H_a): $\mu > 2{,}400$

(i.e., the manufacturer's pipe meets specifications)

> The **null hypothesis,** denoted H_0, represents the hypothesis that is assumed to be true unless the data provide convincing evidence that it is false. This usually represents the "status quo" or some claim about the population parameter that the researcher wants to test.

> The **alternative (research) hypothesis,** denoted H_a, represents the hypothesis that will be accepted only if the data provide convincing evidence of its truth. This usually represents the values of a population parameter for which the researcher wants to gather evidence to support.

How can the city decide when enough evidence exists to conclude that the manufacturer's pipe meets specifications? Because the hypotheses concern the value of the population mean μ, it is reasonable to use the sample mean $\bar{x}$ to make the inference, just as we did when forming confidence intervals for μ in Sections 6.2 and 6.3. The city will conclude that the pipe meets specifications only when the sample mean $\bar{x}$ convincingly indicates that the population mean exceeds 2,400 pounds per linear foot.

"Convincing" evidence in favor of the alternative hypothesis will exist when the value of $\bar{x}$ exceeds 2,400 by an amount that cannot be readily attributed to sampling variability. To decide, we compute a **test statistic,** i.e., a numerical value computed from the sample. Here, the test statistic is the z-value that measures the distance (in units of the standard deviation) between the value of $\bar{x}$ and the value of μ specified in the null hypothesis. When the null hypothesis contains more than one value of μ, as in this case (H_0: $\mu \leq 2,400$), we use the value of μ closest to the values specified in the alternative hypothesis. The idea is that if the hypothesis that μ *equals* 2,400 can be rejected in favor of $\mu > 2,400$, then μ *less than or equal to* 2,400 can certainly be rejected. Thus, the test statistic is

$$z = \frac{\bar{x} - 2,400}{\sigma_{\bar{x}}} = \frac{\bar{x} - 2,400}{\sigma/\sqrt{n}}$$

Note that a value of $z = 1$ means that $\bar{x}$ is 1 standard deviation above $\mu = 2,400$; a value of $z = 1.5$ means that $\bar{x}$ is 1.5 standard deviations above $\mu = 2,400$; and so on. How large must z be before the city can be convinced that the null hypothesis can be rejected in favor of the alternative and conclude that the pipe meets specifications?

> The **test statistic** is a sample statistic, computed from information provided in the sample, that the researcher uses to decide between the null and alternative hypotheses.

If you examine Figure 7.1, you will note that the chance of observing $\bar{x}$ more than 1.645 standard deviations above 2,400 is only .05—*if in fact the true mean μ is 2,400.* Thus, if the sample mean is more than 1.645 standard deviations above 2,400, either H_0 is true and a relatively rare event has occurred (.05 probability), or H_a is true and the

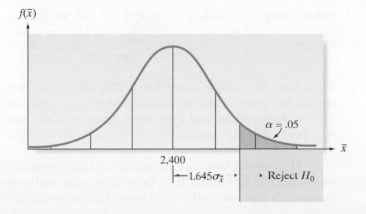

Figure 7.1
The sampling distribution of $\bar{x}$, assuming $\mu = 2,400$

population mean exceeds 2,400. Because we would most likely reject the notion that a rare event has occurred, we would reject the null hypothesis ($\mu \leq 2{,}400$) and conclude that the alternative hypothesis ($\mu > 2{,}400$) is true. What is the probability that this procedure will lead us to an incorrect decision?

Such an incorrect decision—deciding that the null hypothesis is false when in fact it is true—is called a **Type I error.** As indicated in Figure 7.1, the risk of making a Type I error is denoted by the symbol α—that is,

$$\alpha = P(\text{Type I error})$$
$$= P(\text{Rejecting the null hypothesis when in fact the null hypothesis is true})$$

> A **Type I error** occurs if the researcher rejects the null hypothesis in favor of the alternative hypothesis when, in fact, H_0 is true. The probability of committing a Type I error is denoted by α.

In our example,

$$\alpha = P(z > 1.645 \text{ when in fact } \mu = 2{,}400) = .05$$

We now summarize the elements of the test:

$H_0\text{: } \mu \leq 2{,}400$ (Pipe does not meet specifications)

$H_a\text{: } \mu > 2{,}400$ (Pipe meets specifications)

Test statistic: $z = \dfrac{\bar{x} - 2{,}400}{\sigma_{\bar{x}}}$

Rejection region: $z > 1.645$, which corresponds to $\alpha = .05$

Note that the **rejection region** refers to the values of the test statistic for which we will *reject the null hypothesis.*

> The **rejection region** of a statistical test is the set of possible values of the test statistic for which the researcher will reject H_0 in favor of H_a.

To illustrate the use of the test, suppose we test 50 sections of sewer pipe and find the mean and standard deviation for these 50 measurements to be

$$\bar{x} = 2{,}460 \text{ pounds per linear foot}$$
$$s = 200 \text{ pounds per linear foot}$$

As in the case of estimation, we can use s to approximate σ when s is calculated from a large set of sample measurements.

The test statistic is

$$z = \frac{\bar{x} - 2{,}400}{\sigma_{\bar{x}}} = \frac{\bar{x} - 2{,}400}{\sigma/\sqrt{n}} \approx \frac{\bar{x} - 2{,}400}{s/\sqrt{n}}$$

Substituting $\bar{x} = 2{,}460$, $n = 50$, and $s = 200$, we have

$$z \approx \frac{2{,}460 - 2{,}400}{200/\sqrt{50}} = \frac{60}{28.28} = 2.12$$

Therefore, the sample mean lies $2.12\sigma_{\bar{x}}$ above the hypothesized value of μ, 2,400, as shown in Figure 7.2. Because this value of z exceeds 1.645, it falls in the rejection region. That is, we reject the null hypothesis that $\mu = 2{,}400$ and conclude that $\mu > 2{,}400$. Thus, it appears that the company's pipe has a mean strength that exceeds 2,400 pounds per linear foot.

How much faith can be placed in this conclusion? What is the probability that our statistical test could lead us to reject the null hypothesis (and conclude that the company's pipe meets the city's specifications) when in fact the null hypothesis is true?

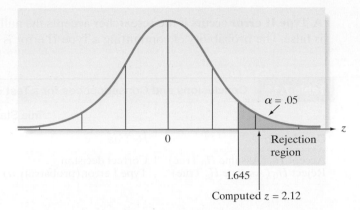

Figure 7.2

Location of the test statistic for a test of the hypothesis $H_0: \mu = 2,400$

EGON S. PEARSON
(1895–1980)
The Neyman-Pearson Lemma

Egon Pearson was the only son of noteworthy British statistician Karl Pearson (see Biography, p. 603). As you might expect, Egon developed an interest in the statistical methods developed by his father and, upon completing graduate school, accepted a position to work for Karl in the Department of Applied Statistics at University College, London. Egon is best known for his collaboration with Jerzey Neyman (see Biography, p. 336) on the development of the theory of hypothesis testing. One of the basic concepts in the Neyman-Pearson approach was that of the "null" and "alternative" hypotheses. Their famous Neyman-Pearson lemma was published in *Biometrika* in 1928. Egon Pearson had numerous other contributions to statistics and was known as an excellent teacher and lecturer. In his last major work, Egon fulfilled a promise made to his father by publishing an annotated version of Karl Pearson's lectures on the early history of statistics.

The answer is $\alpha = .05$—that is, we selected the level of risk, α, of making a Type I error when we constructed the test. Thus, the chance is only 1 in 20 that our test would lead us to conclude the manufacturer's pipe satisfies the city's specifications when in fact the pipe does *not* meet specifications.

Now, suppose the sample mean breaking strength for the 50 sections of sewer pipe turned out to be $\bar{x} = 2,430$ pounds per linear foot. Assuming that the sample standard deviation is still $s = 200$, the test statistic is

$$z = \frac{2,430 - 2,400}{200/\sqrt{50}} = \frac{30}{28.28} = 1.06$$

Therefore, the sample mean $\bar{x} = 2,430$ is only 1.06 standard deviations above the null hypothesized value of $\mu = 2,400$. As shown in Figure 7.3, this value does not fall into the rejection region ($z > 1.645$). Therefore, we know that we cannot reject H_0 using $\alpha = .05$. Even though the sample mean exceeds the city's specification of 2,400 by 30 pounds per linear foot, it does not exceed the specification by enough to provide *convincing* evidence that the *population mean* exceeds 2,400.

Should we accept the null hypothesis $H_0: \mu \leq 2,400$ and conclude that the manufacturer's pipe does not meet specifications? To do so would be to risk a **Type II error**—that of concluding that the null hypothesis is true (the pipe does not meet specifications) when in fact it is false (the pipe does meet specifications). We denote the probability of committing a Type II error by β, and we show in Section 7.8 that β is often difficult to determine precisely. Rather than make a decision (accept H_0) for which the probability of error (β) is unknown, we avoid the potential Type II error by avoiding the conclusion that the null hypothesis is true. Instead, we will simply state that *the sample evidence is insufficient to reject H_0 at $\alpha = .05$.* Because the null hypothesis is the "status-quo" hypothesis, the effect of not rejecting H_0 is to maintain the status quo. In our pipe-testing example, the effect of having insufficient evidence to reject the null hypothesis that the pipe does not meet specifications is probably to prohibit the use of the manufacturer's pipe unless and until there is sufficient evidence that the pipe does

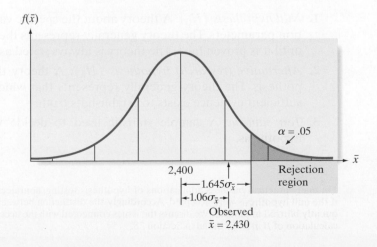

Figure 7.3

Location of test statistic when $\bar{x} = 2,430$

A **Type II error** occurs if the researcher accepts the null hypothesis when, in fact, H_0 is false. The probability of committing a Type II error is denoted by β.

Table 7.1	Conclusions and Consequences for a Test of Hypothesis	
	True State of Nature	
Conclusion	H_0 True	H_a True
Accept H_0 (Assume H_0 True)	Correct decision	Type II error (probability β)
Reject H_0 (Assume H_a True)	Type I error (probability α)	Correct decision

meet specifications—that is, until the data indicate convincingly that the null hypothesis is false, we usually maintain the status quo implied by its truth.

Table 7.1 summarizes the four possible outcomes (i.e., **conclusions**) of a test of hypothesis. The "true state of nature" columns in Table 7.1 refer to the fact that either the null hypothesis H_0 is true or the alternative hypothesis H_a is true. Note that the true state of nature is unknown to the researcher conducting the test. The "decision" rows in Table 7.1 refer to the action of the researcher, assuming that he or she will either conclude that H_0 is true or that H_a is true, based on the results of the sampling experiment. Note that a Type I error can be made *only* when the null hypothesis is rejected in favor of the alternative hypothesis, and a Type II error can be made *only* when the null hypothesis is accepted. Our policy will be to make a decision only when we know the probability of making the error that corresponds to that decision. Because α is usually specified by the analyst, we will generally be able to reject H_0 (accept H_a) when the sample evidence supports that decision. However, because β is usually not specified, *we will generally avoid the decision to accept H_0, preferring instead to state that the sample evidence is insufficient to reject H_0 when the test statistic is not in the rejection region.*

> **!** **CAUTION** Be careful not to "accept H_0" when conducting a test of hypothesis because the measure of reliability, $\beta = P(\text{Type II error})$, is almost always unknown. If the test statistic does not fall into the rejection region, it is better to state the conclusion as "insufficient evidence to reject H_0."*

The elements of a test of hypothesis are summarized in the following box. Note that the first four elements are all specified *before* the sampling experiment is performed. In no case will the results of the sample be used to determine the hypotheses; the data are collected to test the predetermined hypotheses, not to formulate them.

Elements of a Test of Hypothesis

1. *Null hypothesis* (H_0): A theory about the specific values of one or more population parameters. The theory generally represents the status quo, which we adopt until it is proven false. The theory is always stated as H_0: parameter = value.

2. *Alternative (research) hypothesis* (H_a): A theory that contradicts the null hypothesis. The theory generally represents that which we will adopt only when sufficient evidence exists to establish its truth.

3. *Test statistic:* A sample statistic used to decide whether to reject the null hypothesis.

(continued)

---

*In many practical business applications of hypothesis testing, nonrejection leads management to behave as if the null hypothesis were accepted. Accordingly, the distinction between acceptance and nonrejection is frequently blurred in practice. We discuss the issues connected with the acceptance of the null hypothesis and the calculation of β in more detail in Section 7.8.

4. *Rejection region:* The numerical values of the test statistic for which the null hypothesis will be rejected. The rejection region is chosen so that the probability is α that it will contain the test statistic when the null hypothesis is true, thereby leading to a Type I error. The value of α is usually chosen to be small (e.g., .01, .05, or .10) and is referred to as the **level of significance** of the test.

5. *Assumptions:* Clear statement(s) of any assumptions made about the population(s) being sampled.

6. *Experiment and calculation of test statistic:* Performance of the sampling experiment and determination of the numerical value of the test statistic.

7. *Conclusion:*

   a. If the numerical value of the test statistic falls in the rejection region, we reject the null hypothesis and conclude that the alternative hypothesis is true. We know that the hypothesis-testing process will lead to this conclusion incorrectly (Type I error) only $100\alpha\%$ of the time when H_0 is true.

   b. If the test statistic does not fall in the rejection region, we do not reject H_0. Thus, we reserve judgment about which hypothesis is true. We do not conclude that the null hypothesis is true because we do not (in general) know the probability β that our test procedure will lead to an incorrect acceptance of H_0 (Type II error).

As with confidence intervals, the methodology for testing hypotheses varies depending on the target population parameter. In this chapter, we develop methods for testing a population mean, a population proportion, and a population variance. Some key words and the type of data associated with these target parameters are listed in the accompanying box.

Determining the Target Parameter

Parameter	Key Words or Phrases	Type of Data
μ	Mean; average	Quantitative
p	Proportion; percentage; fraction; rate	Qualitative
σ^2	Variance; variability; spread	Quantitative

7.2 Formulating Hypotheses and Setting Up the Rejection Region

In Section 7.1 we learned that the null and alternative hypotheses form the basis for inference using a test of hypothesis. The null and alternative hypotheses may take one of several forms. In the sewer pipe example, we tested the null hypothesis that the population mean strength of the pipe is less than or equal to 2,400 pounds per linear foot against the alternative hypothesis that the mean strength exceeds 2,400—that is, we tested

$$H_0: \mu \leq 2,400 \quad \text{(Pipe does not meet specifications)}$$
$$H_a: \mu > 2,400 \quad \text{(Pipe meets specifications)}$$

This is a **one-tailed** (or **one-sided**) **statistical test** because the alternative hypothesis specifies that the population parameter (the population mean μ in this example) is strictly greater than a specified value (2,400 in this example). If the null hypothesis had been $H_0: \mu \geq 2,400$ and the alternative hypothesis had been $H_a: \mu < 2,400$, the test would still be one-sided because the parameter is still specified to be on "one side" of the null hypothesis value. Some statistical investigations seek to show that the population parameter is *either larger or smaller* than some specified value. Such an alternative hypothesis is called a **two-tailed** (or **two-sided**) **hypothesis.**

While alternative hypotheses are always specified as strict inequalities, such as $\mu < 2{,}400$, $\mu > 2{,}400$, or $\mu \neq 2{,}400$, null hypotheses are usually specified as equalities, such as $\mu = 2{,}400$. Even when the null hypothesis is an inequality, such as $\mu \leq 2{,}400$, we specify $H_0: \mu = 2{,}400$, reasoning that if sufficient evidence exists to show that $H_a: \mu > 2{,}400$ is true when tested against $H_0: \mu = 2{,}400$, then surely sufficient evidence exists to reject $\mu < 2{,}400$ as well. Therefore, the null hypothesis is specified as the value of μ closest to a one-sided alternative hypothesis and as the only value *not* specified in a two-tailed alternative hypothesis. The steps for selecting the null and alternative hypotheses are summarized in the following box.

Steps for Selecting the Null and Alternative Hypotheses

1. Select the *alternative hypothesis* as that which the sampling experiment is intended to establish. The alternative hypothesis will assume one of three forms:

   a. One-tailed, **upper-tailed**   (e.g., $H_a: \mu > 2{,}400$)
   b. One-tailed, **lower-tailed**   (e.g., $H_a: \mu < 2{,}400$)
   c. Two-tailed   (e.g., $H_a: \mu \neq 2{,}400$)

2. Select the *null hypothesis* as the status quo, that which will be presumed true unless the sampling experiment conclusively establishes the alternative hypothesis. The null hypothesis will be specified as that parameter value closest to the alternative in one-tailed tests and as the complementary (or only unspecified) value in two-tailed tests.

$$(\text{e.g., } H_0: \mu = 2{,}400)$$

A **one-tailed test** of hypothesis is one in which the alternative hypothesis is directional and includes the symbol "$<$" or "$>$." Some key words that help you identify the direction are:

$$\begin{aligned}
\textit{Upper-tailed } (>): & \quad \text{"greater than," "larger," "above"} \\
\textit{Lower-tailed } (<): & \quad \text{"less than," "smaller," "below"}
\end{aligned}$$

A **two-tailed test** of hypothesis is one in which the alternative hypothesis does not specify departure from H_0 in a particular direction and is written with the symbol "$\neq$." Some key words that help you identify this nondirectional nature are:

$$\textit{Two-tailed } (\neq): \quad \text{"not equal to," "differs from"}$$

EXAMPLE 7.1

Formulating H_0 and H_a for a Test of a Population Mean— Quality Control

Problem A metal lathe is checked periodically by quality-control inspectors to determine whether it is producing machine bearings with a mean diameter of .5 inch. If the mean diameter of the bearings is larger or smaller than .5 inch, then the process is out of control and must be adjusted. Formulate the null and alternative hypotheses for a test to determine whether the bearing production process is out of control.

Solution The hypotheses must be stated in terms of a population parameter. Here, we define μ as the true mean diameter (in inches) of all bearings produced by the metal lathe. If either $\mu > .5$ or $\mu < .5$, then the lathe's production process is out of control. Because the inspectors want to be able to detect either possibility (indicating that the process is in need of adjustment), these values of μ represent the alternative (or research) hypothesis. Alternatively, because $\mu = .5$ represents an in-control process (the status quo), this represents the null hypothesis. Therefore, we want to conduct the two-tailed test:

$$H_0: \mu = .5 \text{ (i.e., the process is in control)}$$
$$H_a: \mu \neq .5 \text{ (i.e., the process is out of control)}$$

Look Back Here, the alternative hypothesis is not necessarily the hypothesis that the quality-control inspectors desire to support. However, they will make adjustments to the metal lathe settings only if there is strong evidence to indicate that the process is out of control. Consequently, $\mu \neq .5$ must be stated as the alternative hypothesis.

• **Now Work Exercise 7.10a**

EXAMPLE 7.2

Formulating H_0 and H_a for a Test of a Population Proportion—Cigarette Advertisements

Problem Cigarette advertisements are required by federal law to carry the following statement: "Warning: The surgeon general has determined that cigarette smoking is dangerous to your health." However, this warning is often located in inconspicuous corners of the advertisements and printed in small type. Suppose the Federal Trade Commission (FTC) claims that 80% of cigarette consumers fail to see the warning. A marketer for a large tobacco firm wants to gather evidence to show that the FTC's claim is too high, i.e., that fewer than 80% of cigarette consumers fail to see the warning. Specify the null and alternative hypotheses for a test of the FTC's claim.

Solution The marketer wants to make an inference about p, the true proportion of all cigarette consumers who fail to see the surgeon general's warning. In particular, the marketer wants to collect data to show that fewer than 80% of cigarette consumers fail to see the warning, i.e., $p < .80$. Consequently, $p < .80$. represents the alternative hypothesis and $p = .80$ (the claim made by the FTC) represents the null hypothesis. That is, the marketer desires the one-tailed (lower-tailed) test:

$$H_0: p = .80 \text{ (i.e., the FTC's claim is true)}$$
$$H_a: p < .80 \text{ (i.e., the FTC's claim is false)}$$

Look Back Whenever a claim is made about the value of a particular population parameter and the researcher wants to test the claim, believing that it is false, the claimed value will represent the null hypothesis.

• **Now Work Exercise 7.11**

The rejection region for a two-tailed test differs from that for a one-tailed test. When we are trying to detect departure from the null hypothesis in *either* direction, we must establish a rejection region in both tails of the sampling distribution of the test statistic. Figures 7.4a and 7.4b show the one-tailed rejection regions for lower- and upper-tailed tests, respectively. The two-tailed rejection region is illustrated in Figures 7.4c. Note that a rejection region is established in each tail of the sampling distribution for a two-tailed test.

The rejection regions corresponding to typical values selected for α are shown in Table 7.2 for one- and two-tailed tests. Note that the smaller the α you select, the more evidence (the larger the z) you will need before you can reject H_0.

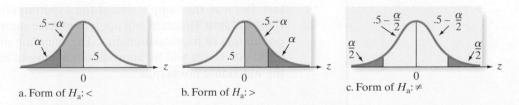

Figure 7.4

Rejection regions corresponding to one- and two-tailed tests

a. Form of H_a: <   b. Form of H_a: >   c. Form of H_a: ≠

Table 7.2	Rejection Regions for Common Values of α		
	Alternative Hypotheses		
	Lower-Tailed	Upper-Tailed	Two-Tailed
$\alpha = .10$	$z < -1.282$	$z > 1.282$	$z < -1.645$ or $z > 1.645$
$\alpha = .05$	$z < 1.645$	$z > 1.645$	$z < -1.96$ or $z > 1.96$
$\alpha = .01$	$z < -2.326$	$z > 2.326$	$z < -2.576$ or $z > 2.576$

Problem A manufacturer of cereal wants to test the performance of one of its filling machines. The machine is designed to discharge a mean amount of 12 ounces per box, and the manufacturer wants to detect any departure from this setting. This quality study calls for randomly sampling 100 boxes from today's production run and determining whether the mean fill for the run is 12 ounces per box. Set up a test of hypothesis for this study, using $\alpha = .01$.

Solution

Step 1: First, we identify the *parameter* of interest. The key word *mean* in the statement of the problem implies that the target parameter is μ, the mean amount of cereal discharged into each box.

Step 2: Next, we set up the *null and alternative hypotheses*. Because the manufacturer wishes to detect a departure from the setting of $\mu = 12$ in either direction, $\mu < 12$ or $\mu > 12$, we conduct a two-tailed statistical test. Following the procedure for selecting the null and alternative hypotheses, we specify as the alternative hypothesis that the mean differs from 12 ounces because detecting the machine's departure from specifications is the purpose of the quality-control study. The null hypothesis is the presumption that the filling machine is operating properly unless the sample data indicate otherwise. Thus,

$H_0: \mu = 12$ (Population mean fill amount is 12 ounces)

$H_a: \mu \neq 12$ (i.e., $\mu < 12$ or $\mu > 12$; machine is under- or overfilling each box)

Step 3: Now we specify the *test statistic*. The test statistic measures the number of standard deviations between the observed value of $\bar{x}$ and the null hypothesized value $\mu = 12$:

$$\text{Test statistic: } z = \frac{\bar{x} - 12}{\sigma_{\bar{x}}}$$

Step 4: Next, we determine the *rejection region*. The rejection region must be designated to detect a departure from $\mu = 12$ in *either* direction, so we will reject H_0 for values of z that are either too small (negative) or too large (positive). To determine the precise values of z that comprise the rejection region, we first select α, the probability that the test will lead to incorrect rejection of the null hypothesis. Then we divide α equally between the lower and upper tails of the distribution of z, as shown in Figure 7.5. In this example, $\alpha = .01$, so $\frac{\alpha}{2} = .005$ is placed in each tail. The areas in the tails correspond to $z = -2.576$ and $z = 2.576$, respectively (from Table 7.2):

Rejection region: $z < -2.576$ or $z > 2.576$ (see Figure 7.5)

Step 5: Finally, we list any *assumptions* about the data necessary for the validity of the test. Because the sample size of the experiment is large enough ($n > 30$), the Central Limit Theorem will apply, and no assumptions need be made about the population of fill measurements. The sampling distribution of the sample mean fill of 100 boxes will be approximately normal regardless of the distribution of the individual boxes' fills.

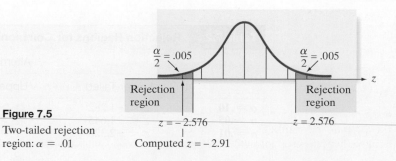

Figure 7.5

Two-tailed rejection
region: $\alpha = .01$

Look Back Note that the test is set up *before* the sampling experiment is conducted. The data are not used to develop the test. Evidently, the manufacturer does not want to disrupt the filling process to adjust the machine, unless the sample data provide very convincing evidence that it is not meeting specifications, because the value of α has been set quite low at .01. If the sample evidence results in the rejection of H_0, the manufacturer will confidently conclude that the machine needs adjustment because there is only a .01 probability of a Type I error.

• **Now Work Exercise 7.10b, c**

Once the test is set up, the manufacturer is ready to perform the sampling experiment and conduct the test. The test is performed in the next section.

STATISTICS IN ACTION

REVISITED

Key Elements of a Hypothesis Test

In Kimberly-Clark Corp.'s survey of people with colds, each of 250 customers was asked to keep count of his or her use of Kleenex® tissues in diaries. One goal of the company was to determine how many tissues to package in a cold-care box of Kleenex®; consequently, the total number of tissues used was recorded for each person surveyed. Since the number of tissues is a quantitative variable, the parameter of interest is either μ, the mean number of tissues used by all customers with colds, or σ^2, the variance of the number of tissues used.

Recall that in 2000, the company increased from 60 to 70 the number of tissues it packages in a cold-care box of Kleenex® tissues. The decision was based on a claim made by marketing experts that the average number of times a person will blow his or her nose during a cold exceeds the previous mean of 60. The key word *average* implies that the parameter of interest is μ, and the marketers are claiming that $\mu > 60$. In order to test the claim, we set up the following null and alternative hypotheses:

$$H_0: \mu = 60 \qquad H_a: \mu > 60$$

We'll conduct this test in the next *Statistics in Action Revisited* on page 407.

Exercises 7.1–7.18

Learning the Mechanics

7.1 Which hypothesis, the null or the alternative, is the status-quo hypothesis? Which is the research hypothesis?

7.2 Which element of a test of hypothesis is used to decide whether to reject the null hypothesis in favor of the alternative hypothesis?

7.3 What is the level of significance of a test of hypothesis?

7.4 What is the difference between Type I and Type II errors in hypothesis testing? How do α and β relate to Type I and Type II errors?

7.5 List the four possible results of the combinations of decisions and true states of nature for a test of hypothesis.

7.6 We reject the null hypothesis when the test statistic falls in the rejection region, but we do not accept the null hypothesis when the test statistic does not fall in the rejection region. Why?

7.7 If you test a hypothesis and reject the null hypothesis in favor of the alternative hypothesis, does your test prove that the alternative hypothesis is correct? Explain.

7.8 For each of the following rejection regions, sketch the sampling distribution for z and indicate the location of the rejection region.
a. $H_0: \mu \leq \mu_0$ and $H_a: \mu > \mu_0$; $\alpha = .1$
b. $H_0: \mu \leq \mu_0$ and $H_a: \mu > \mu_0$; $\alpha = .05$
c. $H_0: \mu \geq \mu_0$ and $H_a: \mu < \mu_0$; $\alpha = .01$
d. $H_0: \mu = \mu_0$ and $H_a: \mu \neq \mu_0$; $\alpha = .05$
e. $H_0: \mu = \mu_0$ and $H_a: \mu \neq \mu_0$; $\alpha = .1$
f. $H_0: \mu = \mu_0$ and $H_a: \mu \neq \mu_0$; $\alpha = .01$
g. For each of the rejection regions specified in parts **a–f**, state the probability notation in z and its respective Type I error value.

Applet Exercise 7.1

Use the applet *Hypothesis Test for a Mean* to investigate the frequency of Type I and Type II errors. For this exercise, use $n = 100$ and the normal distribution with mean 50 and standard deviation 10.

a. Set the null mean equal to 50 and the alternative to *not equal*. Run the applet one time. How many times was the null hypothesis rejected at level .05? In this case, the null hypothesis is true. Which type of error occurred each time the true null hypothesis was rejected? What is the probability of rejecting a true null hypothesis at level .05? How does the proportion of times the null hypothesis was rejected compare with this probability?

b. Clear the applet, then set the null mean equal to 47 and keep the alternative at *not equal.* Run the applet one time. How many times was the null hypothesis *not* rejected at level .05? In this case, the null hypothesis is false. Which type of error occurred each time the null hypothesis was *not* rejected? Run the applet several more times without clearing. Based on your results, what can you conclude about the probability of failing to reject the null hypothesis for the given conditions?

Applying the Concepts—Basic

7.9 **Americans' favorite sport.** *The Harris Poll* (December 2013) conducted an online survey of American adults to determine their favorite sport. Your friend believes professional (National Football League [NFL]) football—with revenue of about $13 billion per year—is the favorite sport for 40% of American adults. Specify the null and alternative hypotheses for testing this belief. Be sure to identify the parameter of interest.

7.10 **Play Golf America program.** The Professional Golf
NW Association (PGA) and *Golf Digest* have developed the Play Golf America program, in which teaching professionals at participating golf clubs provide a free 10-minute lesson to new customers. According to *Golf Digest,* golf facilities that participate in the program gain, on average, $2,400 in greens fees, lessons, or equipment expenditures. A teaching professional at a golf club believes that the average gain in greens fees, lessons, or equipment expenditures for participating golf facilities exceeds $2,400.
a. In order to support the claim made by the teaching professional, what null and alternative hypotheses should you test?
b. Suppose you select $\alpha = .05$. Interpret this value in the words of the problem.
c. For $\alpha = .05$, specify the rejection region of a large-sample test.

7.11 **Student loan default rate.** The national student loan default
NW rate has fluctuated over the past several years. Recently (October 2015) the Department of Education reported the default rate (i.e., the proportion of college students who default on their loans) at .12. Set up the null and alternative hypotheses if you want to determine if the student loan default rate this year is less than .12.

7.12 **A border protection avatar.** The National Center for Border Security and Protection has developed the "Embodied Avatar"—a kiosk with a computer-animated border guard that uses artificial intelligence to scan passports, check fingerprints, read eye pupils, and ask questions of travelers crossing the U.S. border. (*National Defense Magazine,* February 2014.) On the basis of field tests, the avatar's developer claims that the avatar can detect deceitful speech correctly 75% of the time.
a. Identify the parameter of interest.
b. Give the null and alternative hypotheses for testing the claim made by the avatar's developer.
c. Describe a Type I error in the words of the problem.
d. Describe a Type II error in the words of the problem.

7.13 **Calories in school lunches.** A University of Florida economist conducted a study of Virginia elementary school lunch menus. During the state-mandated testing period, school lunches averaged 863 calories (National Bureau of Economic Research, November 2002). The economist claims that after the testing period ends, the average caloric content of Virginia school lunches drops significantly. Set up the null and alternative hypotheses to test the economist's claim.

7.14 **Libor interest rate.** The interest rate at which London banks lend money to one another is called the *London interbank offered rate,* or *Libor.* The British Bankers Association regularly surveys international banks for the Libor rate. One recent report (*Bankrate.com,* March 16, 2016) had the average Libor rate at 1.2% for 1-year loans—a value considered high by many Western banks. Set up the null and alternative hypotheses for testing the reported value.

Applying the Concepts—Intermediate

7.15 **FDA certification of new drugs.** Pharmaceutical companies spend billions of dollars per year on research and development of new drugs. The pharmaceutical company must subject each new drug to lengthy and involved testing before receiving the necessary permission from the Food and Drug Administration (FDA) to market the drug. The FDA's policy is that the pharmaceutical company must provide substantial evidence that a new drug is safe prior to receiving FDA approval, so that the FDA can confidently certify the safety of the drug to potential consumers.
a. If the new drug testing were to be placed in a test of hypothesis framework, would the null hypothesis be that the drug is safe or unsafe? The alternative hypothesis?
b. Given the choice of null and alternative hypotheses in part **a,** describe Type I and Type II errors in terms of this application. Define α and β in terms of this application.
c. If the FDA wants to be very confident that the drug is safe before permitting it to be marketed, is it more important that α or β be small? Explain.

7.16 **Authorizing computer users with palm prints.** Access to computers, email, and Facebook accounts is achieved via a *password*—a collection of symbols (usually letters and numbers) selected by the user. One problem with passwords is that persistent hackers can create programs that enter millions of combinations of symbols into a target system until the correct password is found. An article in *IEEE Pervasive Computing* (October-December 2007) investigated the effectiveness of using palm prints to identify authorized users. For example, a system developed by Palmguard, Inc. tests the hypothesis

H_0: The proposed user is authorized

H_a: The proposed user is unauthorized

by checking characteristics of the proposed user's palm print against those stored in the authorized users' data bank.
a. Define a Type I error and Type II error for this test. Which is the more serious error? Why?
b. Palmguard reports that the Type I error rate for its system is less than 1%, whereas the Type II error rate is .00025%. Interpret these error rates.
c. Another successful security system, the EyeDentifyer, "spots authorized computer users by reading the

one-of-a-kind patterns formed by the network of minute blood vessels across the retina at the back of the eye." The EyeDentifyer reports Type I and II error rates of .01% (1 in 10,000) and .005% (5 in 100,000), respectively. Interpret these rates.

Applying the Concepts—Advanced

7.17 Jury trial outcomes. Sometimes, the outcome of a jury trial defies the "common sense" expectations of the general public (e.g., the 1995 O. J. Simpson verdict and the 2011 Casey Anthony verdict). Such a verdict is more acceptable if we understand that the jury trial of an accused murderer is analogous to the statistical hypothesis-testing process. The null hypothesis in a jury trial is that the accused is innocent. (The status-quo hypothesis in the U.S. system of justice is innocence, which is assumed to be true until proven *beyond a reasonable doubt.*) The alternative hypothesis is guilt, which is accepted only when sufficient evidence exists to establish its truth. If the vote of the jury is unanimous in favor of guilt, the null hypothesis of innocence is rejected, and the court concludes that the accused murderer is guilty. Any vote other than a unanimous one for guilt results in a "not guilty" verdict. The court never accepts the null hypothesis; that is, the court never declares the accused "innocent." A "not guilty" verdict (as in the Casey Anthony case) implies that the court could not find the defendant guilty *beyond a reasonable doubt.*

a. Define Type I and Type II errors in a murder trial.

b. Which of the two errors is the more serious? Explain.

c. The court does not, in general, know the values of α and β; but ideally, both should be small. One of these probabilities is assumed to be smaller than the other in a jury trial. Which one, and why?

d. The court system relies on the belief that the value of α is made very small by requiring a unanimous vote before guilt is concluded. Explain why this is so.

e. For a jury prejudiced against a guilty verdict as the trial begins, will the value of α increase or decrease? Explain.

f. For a jury prejudiced against a guilty verdict as the trial begins, will the value of β increase or decrease? Explain.

7.18 Intrusion detection systems. The *Journal of Research of the National Institute of Standards and Technology* (November–December 2003) published a study of a computer intrusion detection system (IDS). The IDS is designed to provide an alarm whenever unauthorized access (e.g., an intrusion) to a computer system occurs. The probability of the system giving a false alarm (i.e., providing a warning when no intrusion occurs) is defined by the symbol α, while the probability of a missed detection (i.e., no warning given when an intrusion occurs) is defined by the symbol β. These symbols are used to represent Type I and Type II error rates, respectively, in a hypothesis-testing scenario.

a. What is the null hypothesis, H_0?

b. What is the alternative hypothesis, H_a?

c. According to actual data collected by the Massachusetts Institute of Technology Lincoln Laboratory, only 1 in 1,000 computer sessions with no intrusions resulted in a false alarm. For the same system, the laboratory found that only 500 of 1,000 intrusions were actually detected. Use this information to estimate the values of α and β.

7.3 Observed Significance Levels: *p*-Values

According to the statistical test procedure described in Section 7.2, the rejection region and, correspondingly, the value of α are selected prior to conducting the test, and the conclusions are stated in terms of rejecting or not rejecting the null hypothesis. A second method of presenting the results of a statistical test is one that reports the extent to which the test statistic disagrees with the null hypothesis and leaves to the reader the task of deciding whether to reject the null hypothesis. This measure of disagreement is called the *observed significance level* (or *p-value*) for the test.

> The **observed significance level,** or *p*-value, for a specific statistical test is the probability (assuming H_0 is true) of observing a value of the test statistic that is at least as contradictory to the null hypothesis, and supportive of the alternative hypothesis, as the actual one computed from the sample data.

Recall testing H_0: $\mu = 2{,}400$ versus H_a: $\mu = 2{,}400$, where μ is the mean breaking strength of sewer pipe (Section 7.1). The value of the test statistic computed for the sample of $n = 50$ sections of sewer pipe was $z = 2.12$. Because the test is one-tailed—that is, the alternative (research) hypothesis of interest is H_a: $\mu > 2{,}400$—values of the test statistic even more contradictory to H_0 than the one observed would be values larger than $z = 2.12$. Therefore, the observed significance level (*p*-value) for this test is

$$p\text{-value} = P(z > 2.12)$$

or, equivalently, the area under the standard normal curve to the right of $z = 2.12$ (see Figure 7.6).

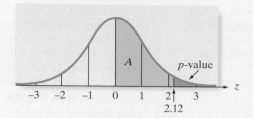

Figure 7.6

Finding the p-value for an upper-tailed test when $z = 2.12$

The area A in Figure 7.6 is given in Table II in Appendix D as .4830. Therefore, the upper-tail area corresponding to $z = 2.12$ is

$$p\text{-value} = .5 - .4830 = .0170$$

Consequently, we say that these test results are "very significant" (i.e., they disagree rather strongly with the null hypothesis, $H_0: \mu = 2,400$, and favor $H_a: \mu > 2,400$). The probability of observing a z-value as large as 2.12 is only .0170, if in fact the true value of μ is 2,400.

If you are inclined to select $\alpha = .05$ for this test, then you would reject the null hypothesis because the p-value for the test, .0170, is less than .05. In contrast, if you choose $\alpha = .01$, you would not reject the null hypothesis because the p-value for the test is larger than .01. Thus, the use of the observed significance level is identical to the test procedure described in the preceding sections except that the choice of α is left to you.

The steps for calculating the p-value corresponding to a test statistic for a population mean are given in the next box.

Steps for Calculating the p-Value for a Test of Hypothesis

1. Determine the value of the test statistic z corresponding to the result of the sampling experiment.

2. **a.** If the test is one-tailed, the p-value is equal to the tail area beyond z in the same direction as the alternative hypothesis. Thus, if the alternative hypothesis is of the form $>$, the p-value is the area to the right of, or above, the observed z-value. Conversely, if the alternative is of the form $<$, the p-value is the area to the left of, or below, the observed z-value. (See Figure 7.7.)

   b. If the test is two-tailed, the p-value is equal to twice the tail area beyond the observed z-value in the direction of the sign of z—that is, if z is positive, the p-value is twice the area to the right of, or above, the observed z-value. Conversely, if z is negative, the p-value is twice the area to the left of, or below, the observed z-value. (See Figure 7.8.)

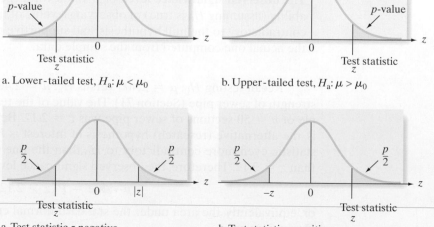

Figure 7.7

Finding the p-value for a one-tailed test

a. Lower-tailed test, $H_a: \mu < \mu_0$

b. Upper-tailed test, $H_a: \mu > \mu_0$

Figure 7.8

Finding the p-value for a two-tailed test: p-value $= 2\left(\frac{p}{2}\right)$

a. Test statistic z negative

b. Test statistic z positive

Problem Consider the one-tailed test of hypothesis, $H_0: \mu = 100$ versus $H_a: \mu > 100$.

a. Suppose the test statistic is $z = 1.44$. Find the *p*-value of the test and the rejection region for the test when $\alpha = .05$. Then show that the conclusion using the rejection region approach will be identical to the conclusion based on the *p*-value.

b. Now suppose the test statistic is $z = 3.01$; find the *p*-value and rejection region for the test when $\alpha = .05$. Again, show that the conclusion using the rejection region approach will be identical to the conclusion based on the *p*-value.

Solution

a. The *p*-value for the test is the probability of observing a test statistic more contradictory to the null hypothesis (i.e., more supportive of the alternative hypothesis) than the value $z = 1.44$. Since we are conducting an upper-tailed test ($H_a: \mu > 100$), the probability we seek is:

$$p\text{-value} = P(z > 1.44) = 1 - P(z < 1.44)$$

The latter probability in the expression is a cumulative probability that can be obtained from the standard normal table (Table II, Appendix D) or using statistical software. The Minitab printout giving this probability is shown in Figure 7.9.

Figure 7.9

Minitab normal probability for Example 7.4a

```
Cumulative Distribution Function

Normal with mean = 0 and standard deviation = 1

    x    P( X ≤ x )
  1.44     0.925066
```

Therefore, we compute

$$p\text{-value} = P(z > 1.44) = 1 - P(z < 1.44) = 1 - .925 = .075$$

This *p*-value is shown on Figure 7.10.

Since $\alpha = .05$ and the test is upper-tailed, the rejection region for the test is $z > 1.645$ (see Table 7.2). This rejection region is also shown in Figure 7.10. Observe that the test statistic ($z = 1.44$) falls outside the rejection region, implying that we fail to reject H_0. Also, $\alpha = .05$ is less than *p*-value $= .075$. This result also implies that we should fail to reject H_0. Consequently, both decision rules agree—there is insufficient evidence to reject H_0.

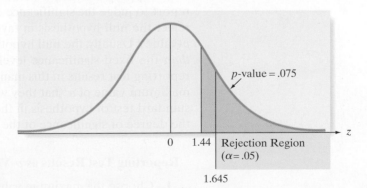

Figure 7.10

Test for Example 7.4a—Fail to reject H_0

b. For $z = 3.01$, the observed significance level of the test is:

$$p\text{-value} = P(z > 3.01) = 1 - P(z < 3.01)$$

A Minitab printout giving the cumulative probability, $P(z < 3.01)$, is shown in Figure 7.11.

Figure 7.11
Minitab normal probability
for Example 7.4b

```
Cumulative Distribution Function

Normal with mean = 0 and standard deviation = 1

  x    P( X ≤ x )
3.01    0.998694
```

Thus, we have

$$p\text{-value} = P(z > 3.01) = 1 - P(z < 3.01) = 1 - .9987 = .0013$$

This p-value is shown on Figure 7.12.

Again, for $\alpha = .05$ and an upper-tailed test, the rejection region is $z > 1.645$. This rejection region is also shown in Figure 7.12. Now the test statistic ($z = 3.01$) falls within the rejection region, leading us to reject H_0. And, $\alpha = .05$ now exceeds the p-value (.0013), which also implies that we should reject H_0. Once again, both decision rules agree—and they always will if the same value of α is used to make the decision.

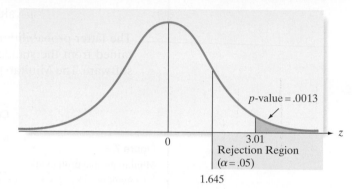

Figure 7.12
Test for Example 7.4b—Reject H_0

Look Ahead Since p-values are easily computed using statistical software, most analysts and researchers utilize the p-value approach to hypothesis testing. In future examples, we will adopt this approach generally, although we'll continue to show the appropriate rejection regions where necessary for illustrative purposes.

● **Now Work Exercise 7.19**

When publishing the results of a statistical test of hypothesis in journals, case studies, reports, and so on, many researchers make use of p-values. Instead of selecting α beforehand and then conducting a test, as outlined in this chapter, the researcher computes (usually with the aid of a statistical software package) and reports the value of the appropriate test statistic and its associated p-value. It is left to the reader of the report to judge the significance of the result (i.e., the reader must determine whether to reject the null hypothesis in favor of the alternative hypothesis, based on the reported p-value). Usually, the null hypothesis is rejected if the observed significance level is *less than* the fixed significance level, α, chosen by the reader. The inherent advantages of reporting test results in this manner are twofold: (1) Readers are permitted to select the maximum value of α that they would be willing to tolerate if they actually carried out a standard test of hypothesis in the manner outlined in this chapter, and (2) a measure of the degree of significance of the result (i.e., the p-value) is provided.

Reporting Test Results as p-Values: How to Decide Whether to Reject H_0

1. Choose the maximum value of α that you are willing to tolerate.

2. If the observed significance level (p-value) of the test is less than the chosen value of α, reject the null hypothesis. Otherwise, do not reject the null hypothesis.

ETHICS in STATISTICS

Selecting the value of α *after* computing the observed significance level (p-value) in order to guarantee a preferred conclusion is considered *unethical statistical practice*.

Note: Some statistical software packages (e.g., SPSS) will conduct only two-tailed tests of hypothesis. For these packages, you obtain the p-value for a one-tailed test, as shown in the box:

Converting a Two-Tailed p-Value from a Printout to a One-Tailed p-Value

$$p = \frac{\text{Reported } p\text{-value}}{2} \quad \text{if} \begin{cases} H_a \text{ is of form} > \text{ and } z \text{ is positive} \\ H_a \text{ is of form} < \text{ and } z \text{ is negative} \end{cases}$$

$$p = 1 - \left(\frac{\text{Reported } p\text{-value}}{2} \right) \quad \text{if} \begin{cases} H_a \text{ is of form} > \text{ and } z \text{ is negative} \\ H_a \text{ is of form} < \text{ and } z \text{ is positive} \end{cases}$$

Exercises 7.19–7.27

Learning the Mechanics

7.19 Consider the test of $H_0\!: \mu = 7$. For each of the following, find the p-value of the test:
  a. $H_a\!: \mu > 7, z = 1.20$
  b. $H_a\!: \mu < 7, z = -1.20$
  c. $H_a\!: \mu \neq 7, z = 1.20$

7.20 If a hypothesis test were conducted using $\alpha = .05$, for which of the following p-values would the null hypothesis be rejected?
  a. .06   **b.** .10
  c. .01   **d.** .001
  e. .251   **f.** .042

7.21 For each α and observed significance level (p-value) pair, indicate whether the null hypothesis would be rejected.
  a. $\alpha = .05, p\text{-value} = .10$
  b. $\alpha = .10, p\text{-value} = .05$
  c. $\alpha = .01, p\text{-value} = .001$
  d. $\alpha = .025, p\text{-value} = .05$
  e. $\alpha = .10, p\text{-value} = .45$

7.22 In a test of the hypothesis $H_0\!: \mu = 50$ versus $H_a\!: \mu > 50$, a sample of $n = 100$ observations possessed mean $\bar{x} = 49.4$ and standard deviation $s = 4.1$. Find and interpret the p-value for this test.

7.23 In a test of $H_0\!: \mu = 100$ against $H_a\!: \mu > 100$, the sample data yielded the test statistic $z = 2.17$. Find and interpret the p-value for the test.

7.24 In a test of the hypothesis $H_0\!: \mu = 10$ versus $H_a\!: \mu \neq 10$, a sample of $n = 50$ observations possessed mean $\bar{x} = 10.7$ and standard deviation $s = 3.1$. Find and interpret the p-value for this test.

7.25 In a test of $H_0\!: \mu = 100$ against $H_a\!: \mu \neq 100$, the sample data yielded the test statistic $z = 2.17$. Find the p-value for the test.

7.26 For each of the following situations, determine the p-value and make the appropriate conclusion.
  a. $H_0\!: \mu \leq 25, H_a\!: \mu > 25, \alpha = .01, z = 2.02$
  b. $H_0\!: \mu \geq 6, H_a\!: \mu < 6, \alpha = .05, z = -1.78$
  c. $H_0\!: \mu = 110, H_a\!: \mu \neq 110, \alpha = .1, z = -1.93$
  d. $H_0\!: \mu = 10, H_a\!: \mu \neq 10, \alpha = .05, z = 1.96$

7.27 An analyst tested the null hypothesis that $\mu \geq 20$ against the alternative hypothesis that $\mu < 20$. The analyst reported a p-value of .06. What is the smallest value of α for which the null hypothesis would be rejected?

7.4 Test of Hypothesis About a Population Mean: Normal (z) Statistic

When testing a hypothesis about a population mean μ, the test statistic we use will depend on whether the sample size n is large (say, $n \geq 30$) or small, and whether or not we know the value of the population standard deviation, σ. In this section, we consider the large-sample case.

Because the sample size is large, the Central Limit Theorem guarantees that the sampling distribution of $\bar{x}$ is approximately normal. Consequently, the test statistic for a test based on large samples will be based on the normal z-statistic. Although the z-statistic requires that we know the true population standard deviation σ, we rarely if ever know σ. However, we established in Chapter 6 that when n is large, the sample standard deviation s provides a good approximation to σ, and the z-statistic can be approximated as follows:

$$z = \frac{\bar{x} - \mu_0}{\sigma_{\bar{x}}} = \frac{\bar{x} - \mu_0}{\sigma / \sqrt{n}} \approx \frac{\bar{x} - \mu_0}{s / \sqrt{n}}$$

where μ_0 represents the value of μ specified in the null hypothesis.

The setup of a large-sample test of hypothesis about a population mean is summarized in the following boxes. Both the one- and two-tailed tests are shown.

Conditions Required for a Valid Large-Sample Hypothesis Test for μ

1. A random sample is selected from the target population.
2. The sample size n is large (i.e., $n \geq 30$). (Due to the Central Limit Theorem, this condition guarantees that the test statistic will be approximately normal regardless of the shape of the underlying probability distribution of the population.)

Large-Sample Test of Hypothesis about μ Based on a Normal (z) Statistic

	σ known	σ unknown
Test statistic:	$z_c = \dfrac{(\bar{x} - \mu_0)}{(\sigma/\sqrt{n})}$	$z_c = \dfrac{(\bar{x} - \mu_0)}{(s/\sqrt{n})}$

	One-Tailed Tests		Two-Tailed Test
	$H_0: \mu = \mu_0$	$H_0: \mu = \mu_0$	$H_0: \mu = \mu_0$
	$H_a: \mu < \mu_0$	$H_a: \mu > \mu_0$	$H_a: \mu \neq \mu_0$
Rejection region:	$z_c < -z_\alpha$	$z_c > z_\alpha$	$|z_c| > z_{\alpha/2}$
p-value:	$P(z < z_c)$	$P(z > z_c)$	$2P(z > z_c)$ if z_c is positive
			$2P(z < z_c)$ if z_c is negative

Decision: Reject H_0 if $\alpha > p$-value or if test statistic (z_c) falls in rejection region where $P(z > z_\alpha) = \alpha$, $P(z > z_{\alpha/2}) = \alpha/2$, and $\alpha = P(\text{Type I error}) = P(\text{Reject } H_0 | H_0 \text{ true})$.

[*Note:* The symbol for the numerical value assigned to μ under the null hypothesis is μ_0.]

Once the test has been set up, the sampling experiment is performed and the test statistic and corresponding p-value are calculated. The next box reviews possible conclusions for a test of hypothesis, depending on the result of the sampling experiment.

Possible Conclusions for a Test of Hypothesis

1. If the calculated test statistic falls in the rejection region (or, $\alpha > p$-value), reject H_0 and conclude that the alternative hypothesis H_a is true. State that you are rejecting H_0 at the α level of significance. Remember that the confidence is in the testing *process,* not in the particular result of a single test.
2. If the test statistic does not fall in the rejection region (or, $\alpha < p$-value), conclude that the sampling experiment does not provide sufficient evidence to reject H_0 at the α level of significance. [Generally, we will not "accept" the null hypothesis unless the probability β of a Type II error has been calculated (see Section 7.8).]

EXAMPLE 7.5

Carrying Out a Hypothesis Test for μ– Mean Amount of Cereal in a Box

Problem Refer to the quality-control test set up in Example 7.3 (p. 396). Recall that a machine is designed to discharge a mean of 12 ounces of cereal per box. A sample of 100 boxes yielded the fill amounts (in ounces) shown in Table 7.3. Use these data to conduct the following test:

$$H_0: \mu = 12 \quad \text{(Population mean fill amount is 12 ounces)}$$
$$H_a: \mu \neq 12 \quad \text{(Machine is under- or overfilling the box)}$$

Table 7.3		Fill Amounts from Quality-Control Tests							
12.3	12.2	12.9	11.8	12.1	11.7	11.8	11.3	12.0	11.7
11.0	12.7	11.2	11.8	11.4	11.3	11.5	12.1	12.5	11.7
12.3	11.7	11.6	11.6	11.1	12.1	12.4	11.4	11.6	11.4
10.9	11.0	11.5	11.6	11.6	11.4	11.9	11.1	11.7	12.1
12.2	11.7	11.6	11.4	12.4	11.0	11.8	12.9	13.2	11.5
11.5	12.0	11.9	11.8	12.5	11.8	12.4	12.0	12.2	12.4
11.8	12.6	11.8	11.8	11.5	12.0	12.7	11.5	11.0	11.8
11.2	12.6	12.0	12.6	12.0	12.0	12.5	12.0	12.8	11.8
12.6	12.4	10.9	12.0	11.9	11.6	11.3	12.1	11.8	12.2
12.2	11.5	12.7	11.5	11.0	11.7	12.5	11.6	11.3	11.1

Data Set: CEREAL

Descriptive Statistics: FILL

```
Variable    N    Mean   StDev  Minimum      Q1  Median      Q3  Maximum
FILL      100  11.851   0.512   10.900  11.500  11.800  12.200   13.200
```

Figure 7.13

Minitab descriptive statistics for fill amounts, Example 7.5

Solution To carry out the test, we need to find the values of $\bar{x}$ and s. These values, $\bar{x} = 11.851$ and $s = .512$, are shown (highlighted) on the Minitab printout, Figure 7.13. Now, we substitute these sample statistics into the test statistic and obtain:

$$z = \frac{\bar{x} - 12}{\sigma_{\bar{x}}} = \frac{\bar{x} - 12}{\sigma / \sqrt{n}} = \frac{11.851 - 12}{\sigma / \sqrt{100}}$$

$$\approx \frac{11.851 - 12}{s/10} = \frac{-.149}{.512/10} = -2.91$$

The implication is that the sample mean, 11.851, is (approximately) 3 standard deviations below the null hypothesized value of 12.0 in the sampling distribution of $\bar{x}$. You can see in Figure 7.5 that this value of z is in the lower-tail rejection region, which consists of all values of $z < -2.576$. These sample data provide sufficient evidence to reject H_0 and conclude, at the $\alpha = .01$ level of significance, that the mean fill differs from the specification of $\mu = 12$ ounces. It appears that the machine is, on average, underfilling the boxes.

Look Back Three points about the test of hypothesis in this example apply to all statistical tests:

1. Because z is less than -2.576, it is tempting to state our conclusion at a significance level lower than $\alpha = .01$. We resist the temptation because the level of α is determined before the sampling experiment is performed. If we decide that we are willing to tolerate a 1% Type I error rate, the result of the sampling experiment should have no effect on that decision. In general, *the same data should not be used both to set up and to conduct the test.*

2. When we state our conclusion at the .01 level of significance, we are referring to the failure rate of the procedure, not the result of this particular test. We know that the test procedure will lead to the rejection of the null hypothesis only 1% of the time when in fact $\mu = 12$. Therefore, *when the test statistic falls in the rejection region, we infer that the alternative $\mu \neq 12$ is true and express our confidence in the procedure by quoting the α level of significance, or the $100(1 - \alpha)\%$ confidence level.*

3. Although a test may lead to a "statistically significant" result (i.e., rejecting H_0 at significance level α, as in the test above), it may not be "practically significant." For example, suppose the quality-control study tested $n = 100,000$ cereal boxes, resulting in $\bar{x} = 11.995$ and $s = .5$. Now, a two-tailed hypothesis test of H_0: $\mu = 12$ results in a test statistic of $z = \dfrac{(11.995 - 12)}{.5/\sqrt{100,000}} = -3.16.$

This result at $\alpha = .01$ leads us to "reject H_0" and conclude that the mean, μ, is "statistically different" from 12. However, for all practical purposes, the sample mean, $\bar{x} = 11.995$, and hypothesized mean, $\mu = 12$, are the same. Because the result is not "practically significant," the company is not likely to spend money fixing a machine that, for all practical purposes, is dispensing an average of 12 ounces of cereal into the boxes. Consequently, *not all "statistically significant" results are "practically significant."*

● **Now Work Exercise 7.34**

EXAMPLE 7.6

Using p-Values—Test of Mean Filling Weight

Problem Find the observed significance level (*p*-value) for the test of the mean filling weight in Examples 7.3 and 7.5. Interpret the result.

Solution Again, we are testing $H_0: \mu = 12$ ounces versus $H_a: \mu \neq 12$ ounces. The observed value of the test statistic in Example 7.5 was $z = -2.91$, and any value of z less than -2.91 or greater than 2.91 (because this is a two-tailed test) would be even more contradictory to H_0. Therefore, the observed significance level for the test is

$$p\text{-value} = P(z < -2.91 \text{ or } z > 2.91) = P(|z| > 2.91)$$

Thus, we calculate the area below the observed z-value, $z = -2.91$, and double it. Consulting Table II in Appendix D, we find that $P(z < -2.91) = .5 - .4982 = .0018$. Therefore, the *p*-value for this two-tailed test is

$$2P(z < -2.91) = 2(.0018) = .0036$$

This *p*-value can also be obtained using statistical software. The rounded *p*-value is shown (highlighted) on the Minitab printout, Figure 7.14. Since $\alpha = .01$ is greater than $p\text{-value} = .0036$, our conclusion is identical to that in Example 7.5—reject H_0.

Figure 7.14

Minitab test of mean fill amount, Example 7.6

```
One-Sample T: FILL

Test of µ = 12 vs ≠ 12

Variable    N    Mean    StDev  SE Mean        95% CI          T      P
FILL      100  11.8510  0.5118  0.0512  (11.7495, 11.9525)  -2.91  0.004
```

Look Back We can interpret this *p*-value as a strong indication that the machine is not filling the boxes according to specifications because we would observe a test statistic this extreme or more extreme only 36 in 10,000 times if the machine were meeting specifications ($\mu = 12$). The extent to which the mean differs from 12 could be better determined by calculating a confidence interval for μ.

● **Now Work Exercise 7.25**

EXAMPLE 7.7

Using p-Values—Test of Mean Hospital Length of Stay

Problem Knowledge of the amount of time a patient occupies a hospital bed—called *length of stay* (LOS)—is important for allocating resources. At one hospital, the mean LOS was determined to be 5 days. A hospital administrator believes the mean LOS may now be less than 5 days due to a newly adopted managed health care system. To check this, the LOSs (in days) for 100 randomly selected hospital patients were recorded; these data are listed in Table 7.4. Suppose we want to test the hypothesis that the true mean length of stay at the hospital is less than 5 days; that is,

$$H_0: \mu = 5 \,(\text{Mean LOS after adoption is 5 days})$$

$$H_a: \mu < 5 \,(\text{Mean LOS after adoption is less than 5 days})$$

Assuming that $\sigma = 3.68$, use the data in the table to conduct the test at $\alpha = .05$.

Table 7.4		Lengths of Stay for 100 Hospital Patients							
2	3	8	6	4	4	6	4	2	5
8	10	4	4	4	2	1	3	2	10
1	3	2	3	4	3	5	2	4	1
2	9	1	7	17	9	9	9	4	4
1	1	1	3	1	6	3	3	2	5
1	3	3	14	2	3	9	6	6	3
5	1	4	6	11	22	1	9	6	5
2	2	5	4	3	6	1	5	1	6
17	1	2	4	5	4	4	3	2	3
3	5	2	3	3	2	10	2	4	2

Data Set: LOS

Solution The data were entered into a computer and Minitab was used to conduct the analysis. The Minitab printout for the lower-tailed test is displayed in Figure 7.15. Both the test statistic, $z = -1.28$, and the *p*-value of the test, $p = .101$, are highlighted on the Minitab printout. Since the *p*-value exceeds our selected α value, $\alpha = .05$, we cannot reject the null hypothesis. Hence, there is insufficient evidence (at $\alpha = .05$) to conclude that the true mean LOS at the hospital is less than 5 days.

One-Sample Z: LOS

```
Test of μ = 5 vs < 5
The assumed standard deviation = 3.68

Variable    N   Mean   StDev  SE Mean  95% Upper Bound     Z      P
LOS        100  4.530  3.678   0.368            5.135  -1.28  0.101
```

Figure 7.15

Minitab lower-tailed test of mean LOS, Example 7.7

Look Back A hospital administrator, desirous of a mean length of stay less than 5 days, may be tempted to select an α level that leads to a rejection of the null hypothesis *after* determining *p*-value = .101. There are two reasons one should resist this temptation. First, the administrator would need to select $\alpha > .101$ (say, $\alpha = .15$) in order to conclude that $H_a: \mu < 5$ is true. A Type I error rate of 15% is considered too large by most researchers. Second, and more importantly, such a strategy is considered unethical statistical practice. (See marginal note, p. 402.)

Now Work Exercise 7.32

In the next section, we demonstrate how to conduct a test for μ when the sample size is small. The procedure is essentially the same as with a large sample; however, we will need to make some assumptions about the population data.

STATISTICS IN ACTION

REVISITED

Testing a Population Mean

Refer to Kimberly-Clark Corporation's survey of 250 people who kept a count of their use of Kleenex® tissues in diaries (p. 387). We want to test the claim made by marketing experts that μ, the average number of tissues used by people with colds, is greater than 60 tissues. That is, we want to test

$$H_0: \mu = 60 \quad H_a: > 60$$

We will select $\alpha = .05$ as the level of significance for the test.

The survey results for the 250 sampled Kleenex® users are stored in the **TISSUE** data file. A Minitab analysis of the data yielded the printout displayed in Figure SIA7.1.

The observed significance level of the test, highlighted on the printout, is *p*-value ≈ 0. Since this *p*-value is less than $\alpha = .05$, we have sufficient evidence to reject H_0; therefore, we conclude that the mean number of tissues used by a person with a cold is greater than 60 tissues. This result supports the company's decision to put 70 tissues in a cold-care box of Kleenex.

One-Sample T: NUMUSED

Test of μ = 60 vs > 60

Variable	N	Mean	StDev	SE Mean	95% Lower Bound	T	P
NUMUSED	250	68.68	25.03	1.58	66.06	5.48	0.000

Figure SIA7.1
Minitab test of $\mu = 60$ for Kleenex survey

 *Data Set:* TISSUE

Exercises 7.28–7.46

Learning the Mechanics

7.28 Consider the test $H_0: \mu = 70$ versus $H_a: \mu > 70$ using a large sample of size $n = 400$. Assume $\sigma = 20$.
  a. Describe the sampling distribution of $\bar{x}$.
  b. Find the value of the test statistic if $\bar{x} = 72.5$.
  c. Refer to part **b.** Find the p-value of the test.
  d. Find the rejection region of the test for $\alpha = .01$.
  e. Refer to parts **c** and **d.** Use the p-value approach to make the appropriate conclusion.
  f. Repeat part **e,** but use the rejection region approach.
  g. Do the conclusions, parts **e** and **f,** agree?

7.29 Suppose you are interested in conducting the statistical test of $H_0: \mu = 255$ against $H_a: \mu > 255$, and you have decided to use the following decision rule: Reject H_0 if the sample mean of a random sample of 81 items is more than 270. Assume that the standard deviation of the population is 63.
  a. Express the decision rule in terms of z.
  b. Find α, the probability of making a Type I error, by using this decision rule.

7.30 A random sample of 80 observations from a population with population mean 198 and population standard deviation of 15 yielded a sample mean of 190.
  a. Construct a hypothesis test with the alternative hypothesis that $\mu < 198$ at 1% significance level. Interpret your results.
  b. Construct a hypothesis test with the alternative hypothesis that $\mu \neq 198$ at 1% significance level. Interpret your results.
  c. State the Type I error you might make in parts **a** and **b.**

7.31 A random sample of 64 observations produced the following summary statistics: $\bar{x} = .323$ and $s^2 = .034$.
  a. Test the null hypothesis that $\mu = .36$ against the alternative hypothesis that $\mu < .36$ using $\alpha = .10$.
  b. Test the null hypothesis that $\mu = .36$ against the alternative hypothesis that $\mu \neq .36$ using $\alpha = .10$. Interpret the result.

Applet Exercise 7.2

Use the applet *Hypotheses Test for a Mean* to investigate the effect of the underlying distribution on the proportion of Type I errors. For this exercise use $n = 100$, mean = 50, standard deviation = 10, null mean = 50, and alternative <.
  a. Select the normal distribution and run the applet several times without clearing. What happens to the proportion of times the null hypothesis is rejected at the .05 level as the applet is run more and more times?
  b. Clear the applet and then repeat part **a** using the right skewed distribution. Do you get similar results? Explain.
  c. Describe the effect that the underlying distribution has on the probability of making a Type I error.

Applet Exercise 7.3

Use the applet *Hypotheses Test for a Mean* to investigate the effect of the underlying distribution on the proportion of Type II errors. For this exercise use $n = 100$, mean = 50, standard deviation = 10, null mean = 52, and alternative <.
  a. Select the normal distribution and run the applet several times without clearing. What happens to the proportion of times the null hypothesis is rejected at the .01 level as the applet is run more and more times? Is this what you would expect? Explain.
  b. Clear the applet and then repeat part **a** using the right skewed distribution. Do you get similar results? Explain.
  c. Describe the effect that the underlying distribution has on the probability of making a Type II error.

Applet Exercise 7.4

Use the applet *Hypotheses Test for a Mean* to investigate the effect of the null mean on the probability of making a Type II error. For this exercise use $n = 100$, mean = 50, standard deviation = 10, and alternative < with the normal distribution. Set the null mean to 55 and run the applet several times without clearing. Record the proportion of Type II errors that occurred at the .01 level. Clear the applet and repeat for null means of 54, 53, 52, and 51. What can you conclude about the probability of a Type II error as the null mean gets closer to the actual mean? Can you offer a reasonable explanation for this?

Applying the Concepts—Basic

7.32 Corporate sustainability of CPA firms. Refer to the *Business and Society* (March 2011) study on the sustainability behaviors of CPA corporations, Exercise 6.12 (p. 339). Recall that the level of support for corporate

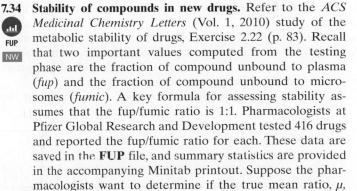

A	B	C	D	E	F	G	H

XLSTAT 2016.04.32229 - One-sample t-test and z-test

Theoretical mean: 75

Significance level (%): 5

Summary statistics ▼ ►

Summary statistics:

Variable	Observations	Minimum	Maximum	Mean	Std. deviation
Support	992	0.000	155.000	67.755	26.871

One-sample z-test / Two-tailed test:

95% confidence interval on the mean:
(66.083, 69.427)

Difference	-7.2450
z (Observed value)	-8.4920
|z| (Critical value)	1.9600
p-value (Two-tailed)	< 0.0001
alpha	0.05

Test interpretation:

H0: The difference between the means is equal to 0.

Ha: The difference between the means is different from 0.

As the computed p-value is lower than the significance level alpha=0.05, one should reject the null hypothesis H0, and accept the alternative hypothesis Ha.

The risk to reject the null hypothesis H0 while it is true is lower than 0.01%.

XLSTAT output for Exercise 7.32

sustainability (measured on a quantitative scale ranging from 0 to 160 points) was obtained for each in a sample of 992 senior managers at CPA firms. The data (where higher point values indicate a higher level of support for sustainability) are saved in the accompanying file. The CEO of a CPA firm claims that the true mean level of support for sustainability is 75 points.

a. Specify the null and alternative hypotheses for testing this claim.

b. For this problem, what is a Type I error? A Type II error?

c. The XLSTAT printout shown above gives the results of the test. Locate the test statistic and *p*-value on the printout.

d. At $\alpha = .05$, give the appropriate conclusion.

e. What assumptions, if any, about the distribution of support levels must hold true in order for the inference derived from the test to be valid? Explain.

7.33 Packaging of a children's health food. Can packaging of a healthy food product influence children's desire to consume the product? This was the question of interest in an article published in the *Journal of Consumer Behaviour* (Vol. 10, 2011). A fictitious brand of a healthy food product—sliced apples—was packaged to appeal to children (a smiling cartoon apple was on the front of the package). The researchers showed the packaging to a sample of 408 school children and asked each whether he or she was willing to eat the product. Willingness to eat was measured on a 5-point scale, with 1 = "not willing at all" and 5 = "very willing." The data are summarized as follows: $\bar{x} = 3.69$, $s = 2.44$. Suppose the researchers knew that the mean willingness to eat an actual brand of sliced apples (which is not packaged for children) is $\mu = 3$.

a. Conduct a test to determine whether the true mean willingness to eat the brand of sliced apples packaged for children exceeded 3. Use $\alpha = .05$ to make your conclusion.

b. The data (willingness to eat values) are not normally distributed. How does this impact (if at all) the validity of your conclusion in part **a**? Explain.

7.34 Stability of compounds in new drugs. Refer to the *ACS Medicinal Chemistry Letters* (Vol. 1, 2010) study of the metabolic stability of drugs, Exercise 2.22 (p. 83). Recall that two important values computed from the testing phase are the fraction of compound unbound to plasma (*fup*) and the fraction of compound unbound to microsomes (*fumic*). A key formula for assessing stability assumes that the fup/fumic ratio is 1:1. Pharmacologists at Pfizer Global Research and Development tested 416 drugs and reported the fup/fumic ratio for each. These data are saved in the **FUP** file, and summary statistics are provided in the accompanying Minitab printout. Suppose the pharmacologists want to determine if the true mean ratio, μ, differs from 1.

a. Specify the null and alternative hypotheses for this test.

b. Descriptive statistics for the sample ratios are provided in the Minitab printout on page 410. Note that the sample mean, $\bar{x} = .327$ is less than 1. Consequently, a pharmacologist wants to reject the null hypothesis. What are the problems with using such a decision rule?

c. Locate values of the test statistic and corresponding *p*-value on the printout.

d. Select a value of α, the probability of a Type I error. Interpret this value in the words of the problem.

e. Give the appropriate conclusion, based on the results of parts **c** and **d**.

Minitab Output for Exercise 7.34

```
Test of μ = 1 vs ≠ 1

Variable   N    Mean   StDev  SE Mean      95% CI         T      P
RATIO     416  0.3269  0.2915  0.0143  (0.2988, 0.3550)  -47.09  0.000
```

f. What conditions must be satisfied for the test results to be valid?

7.35 **Facial structure of CEOs.** Refer to the *Psychological Science* (Vol. 22, 2011) study on using a chief executive officer's facial structure to predict a firm's financial performance, Exercise 6.20 (p. 341). Recall that the facial width-to-height ratio (WHR) for each in a sample of 55 CEOs at publicly traded *Fortune* 500 firms was determined. The sample resulted in $\bar{x} = 1.96$ and $s = .15$. An analyst wants to predict the financial performance of a *Fortune* 500 firm based on the value of the true mean facial WHR of CEOs. The analyst wants to use the value of $\mu = 2.2$. Do you recommend he use this value? Conduct a test of hypothesis for μ to help you answer the question. Specify all the elements of the test: H_0, H_a, test statistic, p-value, α, and your conclusion.

7.36 **Trading skills of institutional investors.** The trading skills of institutional stock investors were quantified and analyzed in *The Journal of Finance* (April 2011). The study focused on "round-trip" trades, i.e., trades in which the same stock was both bought and sold in the same quarter. Consider a random sample of 200 round-trip trades made by institutional investors. Suppose the sample mean rate of return is 2.95% and the sample standard deviation is 8.82%. If the true mean rate of return of round-trip trades is positive, then the population of institutional investors is considered to have performed successfully.

a. Specify the null and alternative hypotheses for determining whether the population of institutional investors performed successfully.
b. Find the rejection region for the test using $\alpha = .05$.
c. Interpret the value of α in the words of the problem.
d. A Minitab printout of the analysis is shown below. Locate the test statistic and p-value on the printout. [*Note:* For large samples, $z \approx t$.]
e. Give the appropriate conclusion in the words of the problem.

```
Test of μ = 0 vs > 0

 N    Mean   StDev  SE Mean  95% Lower Bound    T      P
200  2.950   8.820   0.624       1.919        4.73   0.000
```

7.37 **Producer's and consumer's risk.** In quality-control applications of hypothesis testing, the null and alternative hypotheses are frequently specified as

H_0: The production process is performing satisfactorily.

H_a: The process is performing in an unsatisfactory manner.

Accordingly, α is sometimes referred to as the *producer's risk,* while β is called the *consumer's risk* (Stevenson, *Operations Management,* 2014). An injection molder produces plastic golf tees. The process is designed to produce tees with a mean weight of .250 ounce. To investigate whether the injection molder is operating satisfactorily,

40 tees were randomly sampled from the last hour's production. Their weights (in ounces) are listed in the following table.

.247	.251	.254	.253	.253	.248	.253	.255	.256	.252
.253	.252	.253	.256	.254	.256	.252	.251	.253	.251
.253	.253	.248	.251	.253	.256	.254	.250	.254	.255
.249	.250	.254	.251	.251	.255	.251	.253	.252	.253

a. Write H_0 and H_a in terms of the true mean weight of the golf tees, μ.
b. Access the data and find $\bar{x}$ and s.
c. Calculate the test statistic.
d. Find the p-value for the test.
e. Locate the rejection region for the test using $\alpha = .01$.
f. Do the data provide sufficient evidence to conclude that the process is not operating satisfactorily?
g. In the context of this problem, explain why it makes sense to call α the producer's risk and β the consumer's risk.

Applying the Concepts—Intermediate

7.38 **Unethical corporate conduct.** Refer to the *Behavioral Research in Accounting* (July 2015) study of unethical corporate conduct, Exercise 6.15 (p. 340). Recall that each in a sample of 86 accounting graduate students was asked to perform an unethical task (e.g., to bribe a customer), and each subject's *intention to comply with the unethical request* score was measured. [Scores ranged from -1.5 (intention to resist the unethical request) to 2.5 (intention to comply with the unethical request)]. Summary statistics on the 86 scores follow: $\bar{x} = 2.42$, $s = 2.84$. One researcher, of the opinion that subjects will tend to perform the unethical task, believes the population mean intention score μ will exceed 2. Do the data support this belief? Test using $\alpha = .01$.

7.39 **Time required to complete a task.** When a person is asked, "How much time will you require to complete this task?" cognitive theory posits that people (e.g., a business consultant) will typically underestimate the time required. Would the opposite theory hold if the question was phrased in terms of how much work could be completed in a given amount of time? This was the question of interest to researchers writing in *Applied Cognitive Psychology* (Vol. 25, 2011). For one study conducted by the researchers, each in a sample of 40 University of Oslo students was asked how many minutes it would take to read a 32-page report. In a second study, 42 students were asked how many pages of a lengthy report they could read in 48 minutes. (The students in either study did not actually read the report.) Numerical descriptive statistics (based on summary information published in the article) for both studies are provided in the accompanying table.

	Estimated Time (minutes)	Estimated Number of Pages
Sample size, n	40	42
Sample mean, $\bar{x}$	60	28
Sample standard deviation, s	41	14

a. The researchers determined that the actual mean time it takes to read the report is $\mu = 48$ minutes. Is there evidence to support the theory that the students, on average, overestimated the time it would take to read the report? Test using $\alpha = .10$.

b. The researchers also determined that the actual mean number of pages of the report that is read within the allotted time is $\mu = 32$ pages. Is there evidence to support the theory that the students, on average, underestimated the number of report pages that could be read? Test using $\alpha = .10$.

c. The researchers noted that the distribution of both estimated time and estimated number of pages is highly skewed (i.e., not normally distributed). Does this fact impact the inferences derived in parts **a** and **b**? Explain.

7.40 **Time spent in fitness center.** The owner of a fitness center wants to compare the time his customers spend on each visit to his center during working hours and the time they spend on each visit outside of working hours. He conducted a survey on his customers. The following table records the summary of his findings.

Time Period	Sample size (number of customer)	Mean time spent (in hours)	Standard deviation
During working hours	100	1.97	20.65
Outside working hours	150	3.05	6.02

a. Determine if the customers spent less than 2 hours per visit during working hours at a 5% significance level.

b. Determine if the customers spent more than 2.5 hours per visit outside of working hours at a 5% significance level.

7.41 **Point spreads of NFL games.** During the National Football League (NFL) season, Las Vegas odds makers establish a point spread on each game for betting purposes. For example, the Carolina Panthers were established as 3.5-point favorites over the eventual champion Denver Broncos in the 2016 Super Bowl. The final scores of NFL games were compared against the final point spreads established by the odds makers in *Chance* (Fall 1998). The difference between the game outcome and point spread (called a *point-spread error*) was calculated for 240 NFL games. The mean and standard deviation of the point-spread errors are $\bar{x} = -1.6$ and $s = 13.3$. Use this information to test the hypothesis that the true mean point-spread error for all NFL games differs from 0. Conduct the test at $\alpha = .01$ and interpret the result.

7.42 **Revenue for a full-service funeral.** According to the National Funeral Directors Association (NFDA), the nation's 19,000 funeral homes collected an average of $7,180 per full-service funeral in 2014 (www.nfda.org). A random sample of 36 funeral homes reported revenue data for the current year. Among other measures, each reported its average fee for a full-service funeral. These data (in thousands of dollars) are shown in the following table.

7.4	9.4	5.3	8.4	7.5	6.5	6.2	8.3	6.7
11.6	6.3	5.9	6.7	5.8	5.2	6.4	6.0	7.4
7.2	6.6	6.3	5.3	6.6	5.6	8.4	7.2	7.4
5.8	6.3	6.1	7.0	7.2	6.1	5.4	7.4	6.6

a. What are the appropriate null and alternative hypotheses to test whether the average full-service fee of U. S. funeral homes this year is less than $7,180?

b. Conduct the test at $\alpha = .05$. Do the sample data provide sufficient evidence to conclude that the average fee this year is lower than in 2014?

c. In conducting the test, was it necessary to assume that the population of average full-service fees was normally distributed? Justify your answer.

7.43 **Buy-side vs. sell-side analysts' earnings forecasts.** Refer to the *Financial Analysts Journal* (July/August 2008) study of earnings forecasts of buy-side and sell-side analysts, Exercise 2.86 (p. 112). Recall that data were collected on 3,526 forecasts made by buy-side analysts and 58,562 forecasts made by sell-side analysts, and the relative absolute forecast error was determined for each. A positive forecast error indicates that the analyst is overestimating earnings, while a negative forecast error implies that the analyst is underestimating earnings. Summary statistics for the forecast errors in the two samples are reproduced in the table below.

	Buy-Side Analysts	Sell-Side Analysts
Mean	0.85	−0.05
Standard Deviation	1.93	0.85

Source: Based on B. Groysberg, P. Healy, and C. Chapman, "Buy-Side vs. Sell-Side Analysts' Earnings Forecast," *Financial Analysts Journal*, Vol. 64, No. 4, July/August 2008.

a. Conduct a test (at $\alpha = .01$) to determine if the true mean forecast error for buy-side analysts is positive. Use the observed significance level (*p*-value) of the test to make your decision and state your conclusion in the words of the problem.

b. Conduct a test (at $\alpha = .01$) to determine if the true mean forecast error for sell-side analysts is negative. Use the observed significance level (*p*-value) of the test to make your decision and state your conclusion in the words of the problem.

7.44 **Solder-joint inspections.** Current technology uses high-resolution X-rays and lasers for inspection of solder-joint defects on printed circuit boards (PCBs) (*Global SMT & Packaging*, April 2008). A particular manufacturer of laser-based inspection equipment claims that its product can inspect on average at least 10 solder joints per second when the joints are spaced .1 inch apart. The equipment was tested by a potential buyer on 48 different PCBs. In each case, the equipment was operated for exactly 1 second. The number of solder joints inspected on each run follows:

10	9	10	10	11	9	12	8	8	9	6	10
7	10	11	9	9	13	9	10	11	10	12	8
9	9	9	7	12	6	9	10	10	8	7	9
11	12	10	0	10	11	12	9	7	9	9	10

a. The potential buyer wants to know whether the sample data refute the manufacturer's claim. Specify the null and alternative hypotheses that the buyer should test.

b. In the context of this exercise, what is a Type I error? A Type II error?

c. Conduct the hypothesis test you described in part **a** and interpret the test's results in the context of this exercise. Use $\alpha = .05$.

Applying the Concepts—Advanced

7.45 Managers who engage in "coopetition." In business, firms that both cooperate and compete with other firms are described as engaging in "coopetition." A study published in *Industrial Marketing Management* (February 2016) examined the level of external tension experienced by managers who engage in coopetition. External tension (measured on a 20-point scale) was recorded for each in a sample of 1,532 managers, all from firms that were engaged in coopetition. The sample mean tension was $\bar{x} = 10.82$ and the sample standard deviation was $s = 3.04$.

a. Conduct a test (using $\alpha = .05$) to determine if the true mean external tension level of all managers who engage in coopetition differs from 10.5 points.

b. Find a 95% confidence interval for the true mean external tension level of all managers who engage in coopetition.

c. Explain how the confidence interval of part **b** can be used to infer whether or not the true mean differs from 10.5.

d. The test, part **a**, yields a "statistically significant" result. Use the confidence interval, part **b**, and the fact that external tension is measured on a 20-point scale to comment on whether the result is "practically significant."

7.46 Salaries of postgraduates. The *Economics of Education Review* (Vol. 21, 2002) published a paper on the relationship between education level and earnings. The data for the research were obtained from the National Adult Literacy Survey of more than 25,000 respondents. The survey revealed that males with a postgraduate degree have a mean salary of $61,340 (with standard error $s_{\bar{x}} = \$2,185$), while females with a postgraduate degree have a mean of $32,227 (with standard error $s_{\bar{x}} = \$932$).

a. The article reports that a 95% confidence interval for μ_M, the population mean salary of all males with postgraduate degrees, is ($57,050, $65,631). Based on this interval, is there evidence to say that μ_M differs from $60,000? Explain.

b. Use the summary information to test the hypothesis that the true mean salary of males with postgraduate degrees differs from $60,000. Use $\alpha = .05$.

c. Explain why the inferences in parts **a** and **b** agree.

d. The article reports that a 95% confidence interval for μ_F, the population mean salary of all females with postgraduate degrees, is ($30,396, $34,058). Based on this interval, is there evidence to say that μ_F differs from $33,000? Explain.

e. Use the summary information to test the hypothesis that the true mean salary of females with postgraduate degrees differs from $33,000. Use $\alpha = .05$.

f. Explain why the inferences in parts **d** and **e** agree.

7.5 Test of Hypothesis About a Population Mean: Student's *t*-Statistic

A manufacturing operation consists of a single-machine-tool system that produces an average of 15.5 transformer parts every hour. After undergoing a complete overhaul, the system was monitored by observing the number of parts produced in each of 17 randomly selected 1-hour periods. The mean and standard deviation for the 17 production runs are

$$\bar{x} = 15.42 \qquad s = .16$$

Does this sample provide sufficient evidence to conclude that the true mean number of parts produced every hour by the overhauled system differs from 15.5?

This inference can be placed in a test of hypothesis framework. We establish the preoverhaul mean as the null hypothesized value and use a two-tailed alternative that the true mean of the overhauled system differs from the preoverhaul mean:

$H_0: \mu = 15.5$ (Mean of overhauled system equals 15.5 parts per hour)

$H_a: \mu \neq 15.5$ (Mean of overhauled system differs from 15.5 parts per hour)

Recall from Section 6.3 that when we are faced with making inferences about a population mean using the information in a small sample, two problems emerge:

1. The normality of the sampling distribution for $\bar{x}$ does not follow from the Central Limit Theorem when the sample size is small. We must assume that the distribution of measurements from which the sample was selected is approximately normally distributed in order to ensure the approximate normality of the sampling distribution of $\bar{x}$.

2. If the population standard deviation σ is unknown, as is usually the case, then we cannot assume that s will provide a good approximation for σ when the sample size is small. Instead, we must use the *t*-distribution rather than the standard normal *z*-distribution to make inferences about the population mean μ.

Therefore, as the test statistic of a small-sample test of a population mean, we use the *t*-statistic:

$$\text{Test statistic: } t = \frac{\bar{x} - \mu_0}{s/\sqrt{n}} = \frac{\bar{x} - 15.5}{s/\sqrt{n}}$$

where μ_0 is the null hypothesized value of the population mean μ. In our example, $\mu_0 = 15.5$.

To find the rejection region, we must specify the value of α, the probability that the test will lead to rejection of the null hypothesis when it is true, and then consult either the *t*-table (Table III in Appendix D) or use computer software. Using $\alpha = .05$, the two-tailed rejection region is

$$\text{Rejection region: } t_{\alpha/2} = t_{.025} = 2.120 \text{ with } n - 1 = 16 \text{ df}$$

$$\text{Reject } H_0 \text{ if } t < -2.120 \text{ or } t > 2.120$$

The rejection region is shown in Figure 7.16.

We are now prepared to calculate the test statistic and reach a conclusion:

$$t = \frac{\bar{x} - \mu_0}{s/\sqrt{n}} = \frac{15.42 - 15.50}{.16/\sqrt{n}} = \frac{-.08}{.0388} = -2.06$$

Because the calculated value of *t* does not fall in the rejection region (Figure 7.16), we cannot reject H_0 at the $\alpha = .05$ level of significance. Based on the sample evidence, we should not conclude that the mean number of parts produced per hour by the over-hauled system differs from 15.5.

It is interesting that the calculated *t*-value, -2.06, is *less than* $-z_{.05} = -1.96$. The implication is that if we had *incorrectly* used a *z*-statistic for this test, we would have rejected the null hypothesis at $\alpha = .05$, concluding that

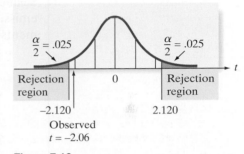

Figure 7.16
Two-tailed rejection region for small-sample *t*-test

the mean production per hour of the over-hauled system differs from 15.5 parts. The important point is that the statistical procedure to be used must always be closely scrutinized, with all the assumptions understood. Many statistical distortions are the result of misapplications of otherwise valid procedures.

The technique for conducting a small-sample test of hypothesis about a population mean is summarized in the following box.

Small-Sample Test of Hypothesis about μ Based on Student's *t*-Statistic

Test statistic: $$t_c = \frac{(\bar{x} - \mu_0)}{(s\sqrt{n})}$$

	One-Tailed Tests		Two-Tailed Test
	$H_0: \mu = \mu_0$	$H_0: \mu = \mu_0$	$H_0: \mu = \mu_0$
	$H_a: \mu < \mu_0$	$H_a: \mu > \mu_0$	$H_a: \mu \neq \mu_0$
Rejection region:	$t_c < -t_\alpha$	$t_c > t_\alpha$	$\lvert t_c \rvert > t_{\alpha/2}$
p-value:	$P(t < t_c)$	$P(t > t_c)$	$2P(t > t_c)$ if t_c is positive
			$2P(t < t_c)$ if t_c is negative

Decision: Reject H_0 if $\alpha > p$-value or if test statistic (t_c) falls in rejection region where $P(t > t_\alpha) = \alpha$, $P(t > t_{\alpha/2}) = \alpha/2$, $\alpha = P(\text{Type I error}) = P(\text{Reject } H_0 | H_0 \text{ true})$, and t is based on $(n - 1)$ degrees of freedom.

[*Note:* The symbol for the numerical value assigned to μ under the null hypothesis is μ_0.]

Conditions Required for a Valid Small-Sample Hypothesis Test for μ

1. A random sample is selected from the target population.
2. The population from which the sample is selected has a distribution that is approximately normal.

EXAMPLE 7.8

Small-Sample Test for μ—Does a New Engine Meet Air Pollution Standards?

Problem A major car manufacturer wants to test a new engine to determine whether it meets new air pollution standards. The mean emission μ of all engines of this type must be less than 20 parts per million of carbon. Ten engines are manufactured for testing purposes, and the emission level of each is determined. The data (in parts per million) are listed in Table 7.5.

Do the data supply sufficient evidence to allow the manufacturer to conclude that this type of engine meets the pollution standard? Assume that the production process is stable and the manufacturer is willing to risk a Type I error with probability $\alpha = .01$.

Table 7.5	Emission Levels for Ten Engines								
15.6	16.2	22.5	20.5	16.4	19.4	19.6	17.9	12.7	14.9

Data Set: CARBON

Solution The manufacturer wants to support the research hypothesis that the mean emission level μ for all engines of this type is less than 20 parts per million. The elements of this small-sample one-tailed test are

$$H_0: \mu = 20 \qquad \text{(Mean emission level equals 20 ppm)}$$

$$H_a: \mu < 20 \qquad \text{(Mean emission level is less than 20 ppm—i.e., engine meets pollution standard)}$$

Test statistic: $t = \dfrac{\bar{x} - 20}{s/\sqrt{n}}$

Rejection region: For $\alpha = .01$ and df $= n - 1 = 9$, the one-tailed rejection region (see Figure 7.17) is $t < -t_{.01} = -2.821$.

Assumption: The relative frequency distribution of the population of emission levels for all engines of this type is approximately normal. Based on the shape of the Minitab stem-and-leaf display of the data shown in Figure 7.18, this assumption appears to be reasonably satisfied.

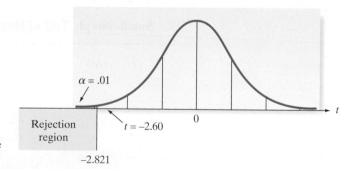

Figure 7.17

A *t*-distribution with 9 df and the rejection region for Example 7.8

To calculate the test statistic, we entered the data into a computer and analyzed it using Minitab. The Minitab printout is shown in Figure 7.18. From the printout, we obtain $\bar{x} = 17.57$, $s = 2.95$. Substituting these values into the test statistic formula, we get

$$t = \frac{\bar{x} - 20}{s/\sqrt{n}} = \frac{17.57 - 20}{2.95/\sqrt{10}} = -2.60$$

Because the calculated t falls outside the rejection region (see Figure 7.17), the manufacturer cannot reject H_0. There is insufficient evidence to conclude that $\mu < 20$ parts per million. Consequently, we cannot conclude that the new engine type meets the pollution standard.

Stem-and-Leaf Display: E-LEVEL

```
Stem-and-leaf of E-LEVEL   N  = 10
Leaf Unit = 1.0

  1    1  2
  3    1  45
 (3)   1  667
  4    1  99
  2    2  0
  1    2  2
```

One-Sample T: E-LEVEL

```
Test of µ = 20 vs < 20
```

Variable	N	Mean	StDev	SE Mean	95% Upper Bound	T	P
E-LEVEL	10	17.570	2.952	0.934	19.281	-2.60	0.014

Figure 7.18

Minitab analysis of 10 emission levels, Example 7.8

Look Back Are you satisfied with the reliability associated with this inference? The probability is only $\alpha = .01$ that the test would support the research hypothesis if, in fact, it were false.

● **Now Work Exercise 7.50a, b**

EXAMPLE 7.9

The *p*-Value for a Small-Sample Test of μ

Problem Find the observed significance level for the test described in Example 7.8. Interpret the result.

Solution The test of Example 7.8 was a lower-tailed test: H_0: $\mu = 20$ versus H_a: $\mu < 20$. Because the value of t computed from the sample data was $t = -2.60$, the observed significance level (or *p*-value) for the test is equal to the probability that t would assume a value less than or equal to -2.60 if, in fact, H_0 were true. This is equal to the area in the lower tail of the t-distribution (shaded in Figure 7.19).

One way to find this area (i.e., the *p*-value for the test) is to consult the t-table (Table III in Appendix D). Unlike the table of areas under the normal curve, Table III gives only the t-values corresponding to the areas .100, .050, .025, .010, .005, .001, and .0005. Therefore, we can only approximate the *p*-value for the test. Because the observed t-value was based on 9 degrees of freedom, we use the df = 9 row in Table III and move across the row until we reach the t-values that are closest to the observed $t = -2.60$. [*Note:* We ignore the minus sign.]

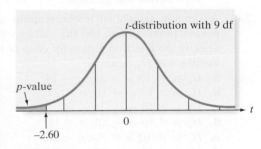

Figure 7.19

The observed significance level for the test of Example 7.8

The t-values corresponding to *p*-values of .010 and .025 are 2.821 and 2.262, respectively. Because the observed t-value falls between $t_{.010}$ and $t_{.025}$, the *p*-value for the test lies between .010 and .025. In other words, $.010 < p\text{-value} < .025$. Thus, we would reject the null hypothesis, H_0: $\mu = 20$ parts per million, for any value of α larger than .025 (the upper bound of the *p*-value).

A second, more accurate, way to obtain the *p*-value is to use a statistical software package to conduct the test of hypothesis. The Minitab printout shown in Figure 7.18 gives both the test statistic (-2.60) and *p*-value (.014).

You can see that the actual *p*-value of the test falls within the bounds obtained from Table III. Based on the actual *p*-value, we will reject H_0: $\mu = 20$ in favor of H_a: $\mu < 20$ for any α level larger than .014. Since $\alpha = .01$ in Example 7.8, we fail to reject the null hypothesis.

● **Now Work Exercise 7.50c**

Small-sample inferences typically require more assumptions and provide less information about the population parameter than do large-sample inferences. Nevertheless, the *t*-test is a method of testing a hypothesis about a population mean of a normal distribution when only a small number of observations are available. What can be done if you know that the population relative frequency distribution is decidedly nonnormal, say, highly skewed?

What Can Be Done if the Population Relative Frequency Distribution Departs Greatly from Normal?

Answer: Use one of the nonparametric statistical methods of Chapter 15.

Exercises 7.47–7.63

Learning the Mechanics

7.47 **a.** Consider testing $H_0: \mu = 80$. Under what conditions should you use the *t*-distribution to conduct the test?
b. In what ways are the distributions of the *z*-statistic and *t*-test statistic alike? How do they differ?

7.48 For each of the following rejection regions, sketch the sampling distribution of *t* and indicate the location of the rejection region on your sketch:
a. $t > 1.440$ where df $= 6$
b. $t < -1.782$ where df $= 12$
c. $t < -2.060$ or $t > 2.060$ where df $= 25$
d. For each of parts **a–c**, what is the probability that a Type I error will be made?

7.49 A random sample of *n* observations is selected from a normal population to test the null hypothesis that $\mu = 10$. Specify the rejection region for each of the following combinations of H_a, α, and *n:*
a. $H_a: \mu \neq 10; \alpha = .05; n = 14$
b. $H_a: \mu > 10; \alpha = .01; n = 24$
c. $H_a: \mu > 10; \alpha = .10; n = 9$
d. $H_a: \mu < 10; \alpha = .01; n = 12$
e. $H_a: \mu \neq 10; \alpha = .10; n = 20$
f. $H_a: \mu < 10; \alpha = .05; n = 4$

7.50 A sample of five measurements, randomly selected from a normally distributed population, resulted in the following summary statistics: $\bar{x} = 4.8$, $s = 1.3$.
a. Test the null hypothesis that the mean of the population is 6 against the alternative hypothesis, $\mu < 6$. Use $\alpha = .05$.
b. Test the null hypothesis that the mean of the population is 6 against the alternative hypothesis, $\mu \neq 6$. Use $\alpha = .05$.
c. Find the observed significance level for each test.

7.51 Suppose you are testing a hypothesis for a sample of 25 people for the null hypothesis $H_0: \mu \leq 85$ versus the alternative hypothesis $H_a: \mu > 85$. The population standard deviation is unknown and the test results into a *p*-value $= .0292$.
a. Justify why the *t*-statistic would be more suitable for this test.

b. Make an appropriate conclusion about the test at a 5% significance level.
c. Determine the *p*-value if this test were to be conducted for a two-tailed test with $H_a: \mu \neq 85$ and make a conclusion at the 5% significance level.

Applying the Concepts—Basic

7.52 **Performance-based logistics.** Refer to the *Journal of Business Logistics* (Vol. 36, 2015) study of the factors that lead to successful performance-based logistics projects, Exercise 2.45 (p. 95). Recall that opinions of a sample of Department of Defense (DOD) employees and suppliers were solicited during interviews. Data on years of experience for the 6 commercial suppliers interviewed are listed in the accompanying table. Assume these 6 interviewees represent a random sample selected from all DOD commercial suppliers. Consider the claim, "On average, commercial suppliers of the DOD have over 5 years of experience."

30	10	9	10	5	10

a. Give the null and alternative hypotheses for testing the claim.
b. Find the test statistic for the hypothesis test.
c. Give the rejection region for the hypothesis test, using $\alpha = .05$.
d. State the appropriate conclusion for the hypothesis test.
e. A Minitab printout giving the test results is shown below. Find and interpret the *p*-value of the test.

```
Test of μ = 5 vs > 5

Variable    N   Mean   StDev  SE Mean  95% Lower Bound    T      P
Experience  6   12.33  8.87   3.62                 5.04   2.03   0.049
```

Minitab Output for Exercise 7.52

7.53 **Accidents at construction sites.** In a study published in the *Business & Economics Research Journal* (April 2015), occupational accidents at three construction sites in Turkey were monitored. The total numbers of accidents at the three randomly selected sites were 51, 104, and 37.

Summary statistics for these three sites are: $\bar{x} = 64$ and $s = 35.3$. Suppose an occupational safety inspector claims that the average number of occupational accidents at all Turkish construction sites is less than 70.

a. Set up the null and alternative hypotheses for the test.

b. Find the rejection region for the test using $\alpha = .01$.

c. Compute the test statistic.

d. Give the appropriate conclusion for the test.

e. What conditions are required for the test results to be valid?

7.54 Lobster trap placement. Refer to the *Bulletin of Marine Science* (April 2010) observational study of lobster trap placement by teams fishing for the red spiny lobster in Baja California Sur, Mexico, Exercise 6.29 (p. 348). Trap-spacing measurements (in meters) for a sample of seven teams of red spiny lobster fishermen are reproduced in the accompanying table. Let μ represent the average of the trap-spacing measurements for the population of red spiny lobster fishermen fishing in Baja California Sur, Mexico. In Exercise 6.29 you computed the mean and standard deviation of the sample measurements to be $\bar{x} = 89.9$ meters and $s = 11.6$ meters, respectively. Suppose you want to determine if the true value of μ differs from 95 meters.

93	99	105	94	82	70	86

Source: Based on G. G. Shester, "Explaining Catch Variation Among Baja California Lobster Fishers Through Spatial Analysis of Trap-Placement Decisions," *Bulletin of Marine Science,* Vol. 86, No. 2, April 2010 (Table 1), pp. 479–498.

a. Specify the null and alternative hypotheses for this test.

b. Since $\bar{x} = 89.9$ is less than 95, a fisherman wants to reject the null hypothesis. What are the problems with using such a decision rule?

c. Compute the value of the test statistic.

d. Find the approximate *p*-value of the test.

e. Select a value of α, the probability of a Type I error. Interpret this value in the words of the problem.

f. Give the appropriate conclusion, based on the results of parts **d** and **e**.

g. What conditions must be satisfied for the test results to be valid?

h. In Exercise 6.29 you found a 95% confidence interval for μ. Does this interval support your conclusion in part **f**?

7.55 Radon exposure in Egyptian tombs. Refer to the *Radiation Protection Dosimetry* (December 2010) study of radon exposure in Egyptian tombs, Exercise 6.30 (p. 349). The radon levels—measured in becquerels per cubic meter (Bq/m^3)—in the inner chambers of a sample of 12 tombs are listed in the table shown below. For the safety of the guards and visitors, the Egypt Tourism Authority (ETA) will temporarily close the tombs if the true mean level of radon exposure in the tombs rises to 6,000 Bq/m^3. Consequently, the ETA wants to conduct a test to determine if the true mean level of radon exposure in the tombs is less than 6,000 Bq/m^3, using a Type I error probability of .10. An SPSS analysis of the data is shown at the bottom of the page. Specify all the elements of the test: H_0, H_a, test statistic, *p*-value, α, and your conclusion.

50	910	180	580	7800	4000
390	12100	3400	1300	11900	1100

7.56 Performance of stock screeners. Recall, from Exercise 6.36 (p. 350), that stock screeners are automated tools used by investment companies to help clients select a portfolio of stocks to invest in. The data on the annualized percentage return on investment (as compared to the Standard & Poor's 500 Index) for 13 randomly selected stock screeners provided by the American Association of Individual Investors (AAII) are repeated in the accompanying table. You want to determine whether μ, the average annualized return for all AAII stock screeners, is positive (which implies that the stock screeners perform better, on average, than the S&P 500). An XLSTAT printout of the analysis is shown on the top of page 418.

9.0	−.1	−1.6	14.6	16.0	7.7	19.9	9.8	3.2	24.8	17.6	10.7	9.1

a. State H_0 and H_a for this test.

b. Locate the values of $\bar{x}$ and s on the printout, and then use these values to compute the test statistic. Verify that your calculation is correct by comparing it with the test statistic value shown on the printout.

c. Locate the observed significance level (*p*-value) on the printout.

d. Give the appropriate conclusion if you test using $\alpha = .05$.

e. What assumption about the data must hold in order for the inference derived from the test to be valid?

One-Sample Statistics

	N	Mean	Std. Deviation	Std. Error Mean
RADON	12	3642.50	4486.929	1295.265

One-Sample Test

	Test Value = 6000					
					95% Confidence Interval of the Difference	
	t	df	Sig. (2-tailed)	Mean Difference	Lower	Upper
RADON	-1.820	11	.096	-2357.500	-5208.36	493.36

SPSS output for Exercise 7.55

A	B	C	D	E	F	G
	XLSTAT 2016.04.32229 - One-sample t-test and z-test					
	Theoretical mean: 0					
	Significance level (%): 5					
	Summary statistics ▼ ▶					
	Summary statistics:					
	Variable	Observations	Minimum	Maximum	Mean	Std. deviation
	RETURN	13	-1.600	24.800	10.823	7.711
	One-sample z-test / Upper-tailed test:					
	95% confidence interval on the mean:					
	(7.3051, +Inf)					
	Difference	10.8231				
	z (Observed value)	5.0604				
	z (Critical value)	1.6449				
	p-value (one-tailed)	< 0.0001				
	alpha	0.05				

XLSTAT output for Exercise 7.56

Applying the Concepts—Intermediate

7.57 **Oxygen bubble velocity in a purification process.** Refer to the *Chemical Engineering Research and Design* (March 2013) study of a method of purifying nuclear fuel waste, Exercise 6.35 (p. 349). Recall that the process involves oxidation in molten salt and tends to produce oxygen bubbles with a rising velocity. To monitor the process, the researchers collected data on bubble velocity (measured in meters per second) for a random sample of 25 photographic bubble images. These data (simulated) are reproduced in the accompanying table. When oxygen is inserted into the molten salt at a rate (called the *sparging rate*) of 3.33×10^{-6}, the researchers discovered that the true mean bubble rising velocity is $\mu = .338$.

a. Conduct a test of hypothesis to determine if the true mean bubble rising velocity for the population from which the sample is selected is $\mu = .338$. Use $\alpha = .10$.

b. Based on the test results, part **a,** do you believe that the data in the table were generated at the sparging rate of 3.33×10^{-6}? Explain.

0.275	0.261	0.209	0.266	0.265	0.312	0.285	0.317	0.229
0.251	0.256	0.339	0.213	0.178	0.217	0.307	0.264	0.319
0.298	0.169	0.342	0.270	0.262	0.228	0.220		

7.58 **Shopping vehicle and judgment.** Refer to the *Journal of Marketing Research* (December 2011) study of grocery store shoppers' judgments, Exercise 2.85 (p. 112). For one part of the study, 11 consumers were told to put their arm in a flex position (similar to carrying a shopping basket) and then each consumer was offered several choices between a vice product and a virtue product (e.g., a movie ticket vs. a shopping coupon, pay later with a larger amount vs. pay now). Based on these choices, a vice choice score was determined on a scale of 0 to 100 (where higher scores indicate a greater preference for vice options). The data in the next table are (simulated) choice scores for the 11 consumers. Suppose that the average choice score for consumers with an extended arm position (similar to pushing a shopping cart) is known to be $\mu = 50$. The researchers theorize that the mean choice score for consumers shopping with a flexed arm will be higher than 43 (reflecting their higher propensity to select a vice product) Test the theory at $\alpha = .05$.

56	76	62	57	55	61	62	43	57	61	58

7.59 **Minimizing tractor skidding distance.** Refer to the *Journal of Forest Engineering* (July 1999) study of minimizing tractor skidding distances along a new road in a European forest, Exercise 6.37 (p. 350). The skidding distances (in meters) were measured at 20 randomly selected road sites. The data are repeated below. Recall that a logger working on the road claims the mean skidding distance is at least 425 meters. Is there sufficient evidence to refute this claim? Use $\alpha = .10$.

488	350	457	199	285	409	435	574	439	546
385	295	184	261	273	400	311	312	141	425

Source: Based on J. Tujek and E. Pacola, "Algorithms for Skidding Distance Modeling on a Raster Digital Terrain Model," *Journal of Forest Engineering,* Vol. 10, No. 1, July 1999 (Table 1).

7.60 **Crude oil biodegradation.** Refer to the *Journal of Petroleum Geology* (April 2010) study of the environmental factors associated with biodegradation in crude oil reservoirs, Exercise 6.38 (p. 350). Recall that 16 water specimens were randomly selected from various locations in a reservoir on the floor of a mine and that the amount of dioxide (milligrams/liter)—a measure of biodegradation—as well as presence of oil were determined for each specimen. These data are reproduced in the accompanying table.

a. Conduct a test to determine if the true mean amount of dioxide present in water specimens that contained oil was less than 3 milligrams/liter. Use $\alpha = .10$.

b. Repeat part **a** for water specimens that did not contain oil.

Dioxide Amount	Crude Oil Present
3.3	No
0.5	Yes
1.3	Yes
0.4	Yes
0.1	No
4.0	No
0.3	No
0.2	Yes
2.4	No
2.4	No
1.4	No
0.5	Yes
0.2	Yes
4.0	No
4.0	No
4.0	No

Source: Based on A. Permanyer et al., "Crude Oil Biodegradation and Environmental Factors at the Riutort Oil Shale Mine, SE Pyrenees," *Journal of Petroleum Geology,* Vol. 33, No. 2, April 2010 (Table 1).

7.61 **Increasing hardness of polyester composites.** Polyester resins reinforced with fiberglass are used to fabricate wall panels of restaurants. It is theorized that adding cement kiln dust (CKD) to the polyester composite will increase wall panel hardness. In a study published in *Advances in Applied Physics* (Vol. 2, 2014), hardness (joules [J] per squared centimeters) was determined for three polyester composite mixtures that used a 40% CKD weight ratio. The hardness values were reported as 83, 84, and 79 J/cm^2. Research has shown that the mean hardness value of polyester composite mixtures that use a 20% CKD weight ratio is $\mu = 76$ J/cm^2. In your opinion, does using a 40% CKD weight ratio increase the mean hardness value of polyester composite mixtures? Support your answer statistically.

7.62 **Nuclear power plants.** Refer to the Nuclear Energy Institute's list of all states with active nuclear power plants, Exercise 2.54 (p. 98). The data on number of power plants per state are reproduced in the accompanying table. Note that states not listed have 0 active nuclear power plants.

NUKES

a. Compute the average number of power plants per state for all 50 states. Explain why this value represents μ, the population mean number of active power plants per state.

b. Use a random number generator to select a random sample of 5 from the 50 states. Give the number of active nuclear power plants for each of these 5 states.

c. Use the sample data, part **b**, to test the claim that the mean number of active nuclear power plants operating in all states differs from 1.24? Test using $\alpha = .10$.

d. Give at least two reasons why you may have falsely rejected the null hypothesis in part **c**. [*Hint:* Consider the sample size and the conditions required for a valid small-sample test.]

	State	Number
1	Alabama	2
2	Arizona	1
3	Arkansas	1
4	California	1
5	Connecticut	1
6	Florida	3
7	Georgia	2
8	Illinois	6
9	Iowa	1
10	Kansas	1

	State	Number
11	Louisiana	2
12	Maryland	1
13	Massachusetts	1
14	Michigan	3
15	Minnesota	2
16	Mississippi	1
17	Missouri	1
18	Nebraska	2
19	New Hampshire	1
20	New Jersey	3
21	New York	4
22	North Carolina	3
23	Ohio	2
24	Pennsylvania	5
25	South Carolina	4
26	Tennessee	2
27	Texas	2
28	Virginia	2
29	Washington	1
30	Wisconsin	1

Source: Nuclear Energy Institute (www.nei.org).

Applying the Concepts—Advanced

7.63 **Arsenic in smelters.** The Occupational Safety and Health Act (OSHA) allows issuance of engineering standards to ensure safe workplaces for all Americans. The maximum allowable mean level of arsenic in smelters, herbicide production facilities, and other places where arsenic is used is .004 milligram per cubic meter of air. Suppose smelters at two plants are being investigated to determine whether they are meeting OSHA standards. Two analyses of the air are made at each plant, and the results (in milligrams per cubic meter of air) are shown in the table. A claim is made that the OSHA standard is violated at Plant 2 but not at Plant 1. Do you agree?

OSHA

Plant 1		Plant 2	
Observation	Arsenic Level	Observation	Arsenic Level
1	.01	1	.05
2	.005	2	.09

7.6 Large-Sample Test of Hypothesis About a Population Proportion

Inferences about population proportions (or percentages) are often made in the context of the probability, *p*, of "success" for a binomial distribution. We saw how to use large samples from *binomial* distributions to form confidence intervals for *p* in Section 6.4. We now consider tests of hypotheses about *p*.

For example, consider the problem of *insider trading* in the stock market. Insider trading is the buying and selling of stock by an individual privy to inside information in a company, usually a high-level executive in the firm. The Securities and Exchange Commission (SEC) imposes strict guidelines about insider trading so that all investors can have equal access to information that may affect the stock's price. An investor wishing to test the effectiveness of the SEC guidelines monitors the market for a period of a year and records the number of times a stock price increases the day following a significant purchase of stock by an insider. For a total of 576 such transactions, the stock increased the following day 327 times. Does this sample provide evidence that the stock price may be affected by insider trading?

We first view this as a binomial experiment, with the 576 transactions as the trials, and with success representing an increase in the stock's price the following day. Let p represent the probability that the stock price will increase following a large insider purchase. If the insider purchase has no effect on the stock price (that is, if the information available to the insider is identical to that available to the general market), then the investor expects the probability of a stock increase to be the same as that of a decrease, or $p = .5$. On the other hand, if insider trading affects the stock price (indicating that the market has not fully accounted for the information known to the insiders), then the investor expects the stock either to decrease or to increase more than half the time following significant insider transactions; that is, $p \neq .5$.

We can now place the problem in the context of a test of hypothesis:

$$H_0: p = .5 \text{ (Probability of stock increase equals .5—}$$
$$\text{i.e., insider purchase has no effect on stock price)}$$

$$H_a: p \neq .5 \text{ (Probability of stock increase differs from .5—}$$
$$\text{i.e., insider trading effects stock price)}$$

Recall (Section 5.4) that the sample proportion, $\hat{p}$, is really just the sample mean of the outcomes of the individual binomial trials and, as such, is approximately normally distributed (for large samples) according to the Central Limit Theorem. Thus, for large samples, we can use the standard normal z as the test statistic:

$$\textit{Test statistic: } z = \frac{\text{Sample proportion} - \text{Null hypothesized proportion}}{\text{Standard deviation of sample proportion}}$$

$$= \frac{\hat{p} - p_0}{\sigma_{\hat{p}}}$$

where we use the symbol p_0 to represent the null hypothesized value of p.

Rejection region: We use the standard normal distribution to find the appropriate rejection region for the specified value of α. Using $\alpha = .05$, the two-tailed rejection region is

$$z < -z_{\alpha/2} = -z_{.025} = -1.96 \text{ or } z > z_{\alpha/2} = z_{.025} = 1.96$$

See Figure 7.20.

We are now prepared to calculate the value of the test statistic. Before doing so, we want to be sure that the sample size is large enough to ensure that the normal approximation for the sampling distribution of $\hat{p}$ is reasonable. Recall from Section 6.4 that we require both np and nq to be at least 15. Because the null hypothesized value, p_0, is assumed to be the true value of p until our test procedure indicates otherwise, we check to see if $np_0 \geq 15$ and $nq_0 \geq 15$ (where $q_0 = 1 - p_0$). Now, $np_0 = (576)(.5) = 288$ and $nq_0 = (576)(.5) = 288$; therefore, the normal distribution will provide a reasonable approximation for the sampling distribution of $\hat{p}$.

Returning to the hypothesis test at hand, the proportion of the sampled transactions that resulted in a stock increase is

$$\hat{p} = \frac{327}{576} = .568$$

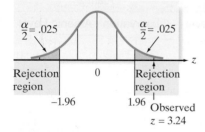

Figure 7.20

Rejection region for insider trading example

Finally, we calculate the number of standard deviations (the z-value) between the sampled and hypothesized values of the binomial proportion:

$$z = \frac{\hat{p} - p_0}{\sigma_{\hat{p}}} = \frac{\hat{p} - p_0}{\sqrt{p_0 q_0/n}} = \frac{.568 - .5}{.021} = \frac{.068}{.021} = 3.24$$

The implication is that the observed sample proportion is (approximately) 3.24 standard deviations above the null hypothesized proportion .5 (Figure 7.20). Therefore, we reject the null hypothesis, concluding at the .05 level of significance that the true probability of an increase or decrease in a stock's price differs from .5 the day following insider purchase of the stock. It appears that an insider purchase significantly increases the probability that the stock price will increase the following day. (To estimate the magnitude of the probability of an increase, a confidence interval can be constructed.)

The test of hypothesis about a population proportion p is summarized in the next box. Note that the procedure is entirely analogous to that used for conducting large-sample tests about a population mean.

Large-Sample Test of Hypothesis about p: Normal (z) Statistic

Test statistic:
$$z_c = \frac{(\hat{p} - p_0)}{\sigma_{\hat{p}}} = \frac{(\hat{p} - p_0)}{\sqrt{(p_0 q_0 / n)}}$$

	One-Tailed Tests		Two-Tailed Test
	$H_0: p = p_0$	$H_0: p = p_0$	$H_0: p = p_0$
	$H_a: p < p_0$	$H_a: p > p_0$	$H_a: p \neq p_0$
Rejection region:	$z_c < -z_\alpha$	$z_c > z_\alpha$	$\|z_c\| > z_{\alpha/2}$
p-value:	$P(z < z_c)$	$P(z > z_c)$	$2P(z > z_c)$ if z_c is positive
			$2P(t < z_c)$ if z_c is negative

Decision: Reject H_0 if $\alpha > p$-value or if test statistic (z_c) falls in rejection region where $P(z > z_\alpha) = \alpha$, $P(z > z_{\alpha/2}) = \alpha/2$, and $\alpha = P(\text{Type I error}) = P(\text{Reject } H_0 | H_0 \text{ true})$.

[*Note:* The symbol for the numerical value assigned to p under the null hypothesis is p_0.]

Conditions Required for a Valid Large-Sample Hypothesis Test for p

1. A random sample is selected from a binomial population.
2. The sample size n is large. (This condition will be satisfied if both $np_0 \geq 15$ and $nq_0 \geq 15$.)

EXAMPLE 7.10

Hypothesis Test for p—Proportion of Defective Batteries

Problem The reputations (and hence sales) of many businesses can be severely damaged by shipments of manufactured items that contain a large percentage of defectives. For example, a manufacturer of alkaline batteries may want to be reasonably certain that fewer than 5% of its batteries are defective. Suppose 300 batteries are randomly selected from a very large shipment; each is tested, and 10 defective batteries are found. Does this provide sufficient evidence for the manufacturer to conclude that the fraction defective in the entire shipment is less than .05? Use $\alpha = .01$.

Solution The objective of the sampling is to determine whether there is sufficient evidence to indicate that the fraction defective, p, is less than .05. Consequently, we will test the null hypothesis that $p = .05$ against the alternative hypothesis that $p < .05$. The elements of the test are

$$H_0: p = .05 \text{ (Fraction of defective batteries equals .05)}$$

$$H_a: p < .05 \text{ (Fraction of defective batteries is less than .05)}$$

Test statistic: $z = \dfrac{\hat{p} - p_0}{\sigma_{\hat{p}}}$

Rejection region: $z < -z_{.01} = -2.326$ (see Figure 7.21)

Before conducting the test, we check to determine whether the sample size is large enough to use the normal approximation to the sampling distribution of $\hat{p}$. Because $np_0 = (300)(.05) = 15$ and $nq_0 = (300)(.95) = 285$ are both at least 15, the normal approximation will be adequate.

We now calculate the test statistic:

$$z = \frac{\hat{p} - .05}{\sigma_{\hat{p}}} = \frac{(10/300) - .05}{\sqrt{p_0 q_0 / n}} = \frac{.03333 - .05}{\sqrt{p_0 q_0 / 300}}$$

Notice that we use p_0 to calculate $\sigma_{\hat{p}}$ because, in contrast to calculating $\sigma_{\hat{p}}$ for a confidence interval, the test statistic is computed on the assumption that the null hypothesis is true—that is, $p = p_0$. Therefore, substituting the values for $\hat{p}$ and p_0 into the z-statistic, we obtain

$$z \approx \frac{-.01667}{\sqrt{(.05)(.95)/300}} = \frac{-.01667}{.0126} = -1.32$$

As shown in Figure 7.21, the calculated z-value does not fall in the rejection region. Therefore, there is insufficient evidence at the .01 level of significance to indicate that the shipment contains fewer than 5% defective batteries.

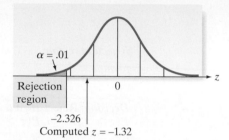

Figure 7.21

Rejection region for Example 7.10

-2.326

Computed $z = -1.32$

• **Now Work Exercise 7.64a, b**

EXAMPLE 7.11

The *p*-Value for a Test About a Population Proportion *p*

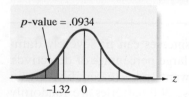

p-value = .0934

-1.32 0

Figure 7.22

The observed significance level for Example 7.11

Problem In Example 7.10 we found that we did not have sufficient evidence, at the $\alpha = .01$ level of significance, to indicate that the fraction defective p of alkaline batteries was less than $p = .05$. How strong was the weight of evidence favoring the alternative hypothesis ($H_a: p < .05$)? Find the observed significance level for the test.

Solution The computed value of the test statistic z was $z = -1.32$. Therefore, for this lower-tailed test, the observed significance level is

$$\text{Observed significance level} = P(z \le -1.32)$$

This lower-tail area is shown in Figure 7.22. The area between $z = 0$ and $z = 1.32$ is given in Table II in Appendix D as .4066. Therefore, the observed significance level is $.5 - .4066 = .0934$.

Note: The observed significance level can also be obtained with statistical software. The Minitab printout shown in Figure 7.23 gives the *p*-value (highlighted).

Test and CI for One Proportion

Test of p = 0.05 vs p < 0.05

Sample	X	N	Sample p	95% Upper Bound	Z-Value	P-Value
1	10	300	0.033333	0.050380	-1.32	0.093

Using the normal approximation.

Figure 7.23

Minitab lower-tailed test of *p*, Example 7.11

Look Back Although we did not reject $H_0: p = .05$ at $\alpha = .01$, the probability of observing a z-value as small as or smaller than -1.32 is only .0934 if, in fact, H_0 is true. Therefore, we would reject H_0 if we choose $\alpha = .10$ (because the observed significance level is less than .10), and we would not reject H_0 (the conclusion of Example 7.10) if we choose $\alpha = .05$ or $\alpha = .01$.

• **Now Work Exercise 7.64c**

Small Samples

Because most surveys and studies employ large samples, the large-sample testing procedure based on the normal (z) statistic presented here will be appropriate for making inferences about a population proportion. *However, in the case of small samples (where either np_0 or nq_0 is less than 15), tests for a population proportion based on the z-statistic may not be valid—especially when conducting one-tailed tests.* A test of proportions that can be applied to small samples utilizes the binomial, rather than the normal, distribution. These are called *exact binomial tests* because the exact (rather than approximate) p-value for the test is computed based on the binomial distribution.

For example, consider testing $H_0: p = .6$ against $H_a: p < .6$, where p is the true proportion of all employees at a large company who favor unionization. Suppose that in a survey of $n = 20$ employees (randomly selected from all employees of the company), $x = 10$ favor unionization. Is this sufficient evidence at $\alpha = .05$ to reject the null hypothesis?

First, note that $p_0 = .6$ and $np_0 = 20(.6) = .12$ is less than 15; consequently, we require a small-sample test of binomial proportions. Now, we observed $x = 10$ employees in favor of unionization. Then, by definition (see p. 399), the observed significance level (p-value) of this lower-tailed test will be equal to the probability of observing 10 or fewer employees in favor of unionization, given the true population proportion in favor of unionization is $p = .6$. That is,

$$p\text{-value} = P(x \leq 10 \,|\, p = .6)$$

In Example 4.13 (p. 235), we found this binomial probability using Minitab. The Minitab printout is reproduced below in Figure 7.24. You can see that the p-value $= .245$. Since $\alpha = .05 < p$-value, we fail to reject the null hypothesis.

Two of the statistical software packages presented in this text—Minitab and SPSS—have procedures for conducting exact binomial tests in the case of small samples.

Figure 7.24

Minitab Output with p-Value for Exact Binomial Test

Cumulative Distribution Function

```
Binomial with n = 20 and p = 0.6

 x   P( X ≤ x )
10    0.244663
```

| STATISTICS IN ACTION | **Testing a Population Proportion** |

REVISITED

In the previous *Statistics in Action Revisited* (p. 407), we investigated Kimberly-Clark Corporation's assertion that the company should put more than 60 tissues in a cold-care box of Kleenex® tissues. We did this by testing the claim that the mean number of tissues used by a person with a cold is $\mu = 60$, using data collected from a survey of 250 Kleenex® users. Another approach to the problem is to consider the proportion of Kleenex® users who use more than 60 tissues when they have a cold. Now the population parameter of interest is p, the proportion of all Kleenex® users who use more than 60 tissues when they have a cold.

Kimberly-Clark Corporation's belief that the company should put more than 60 tissues in a cold-care box will be supported if over half of the Kleenex® users surveyed used more than 60 tissues (i.e., if $p > .5$). Is there evidence to indicate that the population proportion exceeds .5? To answer this question, we set up the following null and alternative hypotheses:

$$H_0: p = .5 \quad H_a: p > .5$$

Recall that the survey results for the 250 sampled Kleenex® users are stored in the **TISSUE** data file. In addition to the number of tissues used by each person, the file contains a qualitative variable—called USED60—representing whether the person used fewer or more than 60 tissues. (The values of USED60 in the data set are "LESS" or "MORE.") A Minitab analysis of this variable yielded the printout displayed in Figure SIA7.2.

On the Minitab printout, x represents the number of the 250 people with colds who used more than 60 tissues. Note that $x = 154$. This value is used to compute the test statistic $z = 3.67$, highlighted on the printout. The p-value of the test, also highlighted on the printout, is p-value $= .000$. Since this value is less than $\alpha = .05$, there is sufficient evidence (at $\alpha = .05$) to reject H_0; we conclude that the proportion of all Kleenex® users who use more than 60 tissues when they have a cold exceeds 5. This conclusion supports again the company's decision to put more than 60 tissues in a cold-care box of Kleenex.

Test and CI for One Proportion: USED60

Test of p = 0.5 vs p > 0.5

Event = MORE

Variable	X	N	Sample p	95% Lower Bound	Z-Value	P-Value
USED60	154	250	0.616000	0.565404	3.67	0.000

Using the normal approximation.

Figure SIA7.2

Minitab test of $p = .5$ for Kleenex survey

Data Set: TISSUE

Exercises 7.64–7.81

Learning the Mechanics

7.64 Suppose a random sample of 100 observations from a binomial population gives a value of $\hat{p} = .63$ and you wish to test the null hypothesis that the population parameter p is equal to .70 against the alternative hypothesis that p is less than .70.

a. Noting that $\hat{p} = .63$, what does your intuition tell you? Does the value of $\hat{p}$ appear to contradict the null hypothesis?

b. Use the large-sample z-test to test $H_0: p = .70$ against the alternative hypothesis, $H_a: p < .70$. Use $\alpha = .05$. How do the test results compare with your intuitive decision from part **a**?

c. Find and interpret the observed significance level of the test you conducted in part **b**.

7.65 Suppose the sample in Exercise 7.64 has produced $\hat{p} = .83$ and we wish to test $H_0: p = .9$ against the alternative $H_a: p < .9$.

a. Calculate the value of the z-statistic for this test.

b. Note that the numerator of the z-statistic $(\hat{p} - p_0 = .83 - .90 = -.07)$ is the same as for Exercise 7.64. Considering this, why is the absolute value of z for this exercise larger than that calculated in Exercise 7.64?

c. Complete the test using $\alpha = .05$ and interpret the result.

d. Find the observed significance level for the test and interpret its value.

7.66 A two-tailed test was conducted with the null and alternative hypotheses stated being $H_0: p = .69$ against $H_a: p \neq .69$, respectively, with a sample size of 150. The test results were $z = -.98$ and two-tailed p-value $= .327$

a. Determine the conditions required for a valid large-sample test.

b. How would the p-value change if the alternative hypothesis was one-tailed, $H_a: p < .69$ at a 5% significance level? Interpret this p-value.

7.67 Refer to Exercise 6.44 (p. 356), in which 50 consumers taste-tested a new snack food. Their responses (where $0 =$ do not like; $1 =$ like; $2 =$ indifferent) are reproduced below.

a. Test $H_0: p = .5$ against $H_a: p > .5$, where p is the proportion of customers who do not like the snack food. Use $\alpha = .10$.

b. Find the observed significance level of your test.

1	0	0	1	2	0	1	1	0	0	0	1
0	2	0	2	2	0	0	1	1	0	0	0
0	1	0	2	0	0	0	1	0	0	1	0
0	1	0	1	0	2	0	0	1	1	0	0
0	1										

7.68 For the binomial sample sizes and null hypothesized values of p in each part, determine whether the sample size is large enough to use the normal approximation methodology presented in this section to conduct a test of the null hypothesis $H_0: p = p_0$.

a. $n = 900, p_0 = .975$ **b.** $n = 125, p_0 = .01$

c. $n = 40, p_0 = .75$ **d.** $n = 15, p_0 = .75$

e. $n = 12, p_0 = .62$

Applet Exercise 7.5

Use the applet *Hypotheses Test for a Proportion* to investigate the relationships between the probabilities of Type I and

Type II errors occurring at levels .05 and .01. For this exercise, use $n = 100$, true $p = 0.5$, and alternative *not equal*.

a. Set null $p = .5$. What happens to the proportion of times the null hypothesis is rejected at the .05 level and at the .01 level as the applet is run more and more times? What type of error has occurred when the null hypothesis is rejected in this situation? Based on your results, is this type of error more likely to occur at level .05 or at level .01? Explain.

b. Set null $p = .6$. What happens to the proportion of times the null hypothesis is *not* rejected at the .05 level and at the .01 level as the applet is run more and more times? What type of error has occurred when the null hypothesis is *not* rejected in this situation? Based on your results, is this type of error more likely to occur at level .05 or at level .01? Explain.

c. Use your results from parts **a** and **b** to make a general statement about the probabilities of Type I and Type II errors at levels .05 and .01.

📊 Applet Exercise 7.6

Use the applet *Hypotheses Test for a Proportion* to investigate the effect of the true population proportion p on the probability of a Type I error occurring. For this exercise, use $n = 100$, and alternative *not equal*.

a. Set true $p = .5$ and null $p = .5$. Run the applet several times and record the proportion of times the null hypothesis is rejected at the .01 level.

b. Clear the applet and repeat part **a** for true $p = .1$ and null $p = .1$. Then repeat one more time for true $p = .01$ and null $p = .01$.

c. Based on your results from parts **a** and **b,** what can you conclude about the probability of a Type I error occurring as the true population proportion gets closer to 0?

Applying the Concepts—Basic

7.69 Customer participation in store loyalty card programs. Customers who participate in a store's free loyalty card program save money on their purchases, but allow the store to keep track of the customer's shopping habits and potentially sell these data to third parties. A *Pew Internet & American Life Project Survey* (January 2016) revealed that 225 of a random sample of 250 U.S. adults would agree to participate in a store loyalty card program, despite the potential for information sharing. Let p represent the true proportion of all customers who would participate in a store loyalty card program.

a. Compute a point estimate of p.

b. Consider a store owner who claims that more than 80% of all customers would participate in a loyalty card program. Set up the null and alternative hypotheses for testing whether the true proportion of all customers who would participate in a store loyalty card program exceeds .8.

c. Compute the test statistic for part **b**.

d. Find the rejection region for the test if $\alpha = .01$.

e. Find the p-value for the test.

f. Make the appropriate conclusion using the rejection region.

g. Make the appropriate conclusion using the p-value.

7.70 Fraud survey of Asia-Pacific firms. The opinions of employees at Asia-Pacific firms regarding fraud, bribery, and corruption in the workplace were elicited in the *2015 Asia-Pacific (APAC) Fraud Survey*. Interviews were conducted with a sample 1,508 employees of large APAC companies. One question concerned whether or not the employee's company had implemented a "whistle-blower" hotline—that is, a phone number that an employee can call to report fraud or other types of misconduct without fear of retribution. The 2015 survey found that 680 of the 1,508 respondents' companies had not implemented a whistle-blower hotline. In comparison, 436 of the 681 respondents in the 2013 survey reported their companies had not implemented a whistle-blower hotline.

a. Test $H_0: p = .5$ against $H_a: p < .5$ using data from the 2015 survey and $\alpha = .05$. Give a practical interpretation of the results.

b. Test $H_0: p = .5$ against $H_a: p > .5$ using data from the 2013 survey and $\alpha = .05$. Give a practical interpretation of the results.

7.71 TV subscription streaming. "Streaming" of television programs is trending upward. According to *The Harris Poll* (August 26, 2013), over one-third of American's qualify as "subscription streamers," i.e., those who watch streamed TV programs through a subscription service such as Netflix, Hulu Plus, or Amazon Prime. The poll included 2,242 adult TV viewers, of which 785 are subscription streamers. On the basis of this result, can you conclude that the true fraction of adult TV viewers who are subscription streamers differs from one-third? Carry out the test using a Type I error rate of $\alpha = .10$. Be sure to give the null and alternative hypotheses tested, test statistic value, rejection region or p-value, and conclusion.

7.72 Gummi Bears: Red or yellow? Companies that produce candies typically offer different colors of their candies to provide consumers a choice. Presumably, the consumer will choose one color over another because of taste. *Chance* (Winter 2010) presented an experiment designed to test this taste theory. Students were blindfolded and then given a red or yellow Gummi Bear to chew. (Half the students were randomly assigned to receive the red Gummi Bear and half to receive the yellow Bear. The students could not see what color Gummi Bear they were given.) After chewing, the students were asked to guess the color of the candy based on the flavor. Of the 121 students who participated in the study, 97 correctly identified the color of the Gummi Bear.

a. If there is no relationship between color and Gummi Bear flavor, what proportion of the population of students would correctly identify the color?

b. Specify the null and alternative hypotheses for testing whether color and flavor are related.

c. Carry out the test and give the appropriate conclusion at $\alpha = .01$. Use the p-value of the test, shown on the accompanying SPSS printout, to make your decision.

Binomial Test

		Category	N	Observed Prop.	Test Prop.	Exact Sig. (2-tailed)
ID_Color	Group 1	Yes	97	.80	.50	.000
	Group 2	No	24	.20		
	Total		121	1.00		

7.73 Toothpaste brands with the ADA seal. *Consumer Reports* evaluated and rated 46 brands of toothpaste. One attribute examined in the study was whether or not a toothpaste

ADA

brand carries an American Dental Association (ADA) seal verifying effective decay prevention. The data for the 46 brands (coded 1 = ADA seal, 0 = no ADA seal) are listed here.

0	0	0	0	0	0	1	1	1	0	0	1
0	1	0	0	0	0	1	1	1	0	1	1
1	1	0	0	0	0	0	1	0	0	1	1
1	0	1	0	1	1	1	0	0	0		

a. Give the null and alternative hypotheses for testing whether the true proportion of toothpaste brands with the ADA seal verifying effective decay prevention is less than .5.
b. Locate the p-value on the Minitab printout below.
c. Make the appropriate conclusion using $\alpha = .10$.

Test and CI for One Proportion: ADAseal

```
Test of p = 0.5 vs p < 0.5

Event = 1

Variable   X   N  Sample p  95% Upper Bound  Z-Value  P-Value
ADAseal   20  46  0.434783         0.555007    -0.88    0.188

Using the normal approximation.
```

7.74 Vacation-home owners. The National Association of Realtors (NAR) reported the results of an April 2015 survey of home buyers. In a random sample of 1,971 residential properties purchased during the year, 414 were purchased as a vacation home. Five years ago, 10% of residential properties were vacation homes.

a. Do the survey results allow the NAR to conclude (at $\alpha = .01$) that the percentage of all residential properties purchased for vacation homes is greater than 10%?
b. In a previous year, the NAR sent the survey questionnaire to a nationwide sample of 45,000 new home owners, of which 1,982 responded to the survey. How might this bias the results? [Note: In the most recent survey, the NAR used a more valid sampling method.]

Applying the Concepts—Intermediate

7.75 Organic-certified coffee. Coffee markets that conform to organic standards focus on the environmental aspects of coffee growing, such as the use of shade trees and a reduced reliance on chemical pesticides. A study of organic coffee growers was published in *Food Policy* (Vol. 36, 2010). In a representative sample of 845 coffee growers from southern Mexico, 417 growers were certified to sell to organic coffee markets while 77 growers were transitioning to become organic certified. In the United States, 60% of coffee growers are organic certified. Is there evidence to indicate that fewer than 60% of the coffee growers in southern Mexico are either organic certified or transitioning to become organic certified? State your conclusion so that there is only a 5% chance of making a Type I error.

7.76 Dehorning of dairy calves. For safety reasons, calf dehorning has become a routine practice at dairy farms. A report by Europe's Standing Committee on the Food Chain and Animal Health (SANKO) stated that 80% of European dairy farms carry out calf dehorning. A later study, published in the *Journal of Dairy Science* (Vol. 94,

2011), found that in a sample of 639 Italian dairy farms, 515 dehorned calves. Does the *Journal of Dairy Science* study support or refute the figure reported by SANKO? Explain.

7.77 Effectiveness of skin cream. Pond's Age-Defying Complex, a cream with alpha hydroxy acid, advertised that it could reduce wrinkles and improve the skin. In a study published in *Archives of Dermatology* (June 1996), 33 middle-aged women used a cream with alpha hydroxy acid for 22 weeks. At the end of the study period, a dermatologist judged whether each woman exhibited skin improvement. The results for the 33 women (where I = improved skin and N = no improvement) are listed in the next table. [*Note:* Pond's recently discontinued the production of this cream product, replacing it with Age-Defying Towelettes.]

a. Do the data provide sufficient evidence to conclude that the cream improved the skin of more than 60% of middle-aged women? Test using $\alpha = .05$.
b. Find and interpret the p-value of the test.

I	I	N	I	N	N	I	I	I	I	I
N	I	I	N	I	I	I	N	I	N	I
I	I	I	I	N	I	N	I	I	N	

7.78 Detection of motorcycles while driving. Motorcycle fatalities have increased dramatically over the past decade. As a result, manufacturers of powered two-wheelers (PTWs) are tweaking their design in order to improve visibility by automobile drivers. The factors that impact the visibility of PTWs on the road were investigated in *Accident Analysis and Prevention* (Vol. 44, 2012). A visual search study was conducted in which viewers were presented with pictures of driving scenarios and asked to identify the presence or absence of a PTW. Of interest to the researchers is the detection rate, i.e., the proportion of pictures showing a PTW in which the viewer actually detected the presence of the PTW. Suppose that, in theory, the true detection rate for pictures of PTWs is .70. The study revealed that in a sample of 2,376 pictures that included a PTW, only 1,554 were detected by the viewers. Use this result to test the theory at $\alpha = .10$.

7.79 Smart TVs. According to *Nielsen's Television Audience Report* (2015), 29% of households in the $75,000 income bracket own a Smart TV with Internet and video streaming access. Develop a sampling plan that will allow you to test this claim. Identify the target population, experimental units, variable to be measured, parameter of interest, null and alternative hypotheses, and the form of the test statistic.

Applying the Concepts—Advanced

7.80 Choosing portable grill displays. Refer to the *Journal of Consumer Research* (March 2003) experiment on influencing the choices of others by offering undesirable alternatives, Exercise 3.23 (p. 171). Recall that each of 124 college students selected three portable grills from five to display on the showroom floor. The students were instructed to include Grill #2 (a smaller-sized grill) and select the remaining two grills in the display to maximize purchases of Grill #2. If the six possible grill display combinations (1-2-3, 1-2-4, 1-2-5, 2-3-4, 2-3-5, and 2-4-5) were selected at random, then the proportion of students selecting any display was $\frac{1}{6} = .167$.

One theory tested by the researcher was that the students would tend to choose the three-grill display so that Grill #2 was a compromise between a more desirable and a less desirable grill (i.e., display 1-2-3, 1-2-4, or 1-2-5). Of the 124 students, 85 selected a three-grill display that was con-sistent with this theory. Use this in-formation to test the theory proposed by the researcher at $\alpha = .05$.

7.81 **The Pepsi Challenge.** "Take the Pepsi Challenge" was a famous marketing campaign used by the Pepsi-Cola Company. Coca-Cola drinkers participated in a blind taste test where they were asked to taste unmarked cups of Pepsi and Coke and were asked to select their favorite. In one Pepsi television commercial, an announcer stated that "in recent blind taste tests, more than half the Diet Coke drinkers surveyed said they preferred the taste of Diet Pepsi." Suppose 100 Diet Coke drinkers took the Pepsi Challenge and 56 preferred the taste of Diet Pepsi. Determine if more than half of all Diet Coke drinkers selected Diet Pepsi in the blind taste test. Select α to minimize the probability of a Type I error. What were the consequences of the test results from Coca-Cola's perspective?

7.7   Test of Hypothesis About a Population Variance

Although many practical problems involve inferences about a population mean (or pro-portion), it is sometimes of interest to make an inference about a population variance, σ^2. To illustrate, a quality-control supervisor in a cannery knows that the exact amount each can contains will vary because there are certain uncontrollable factors that affect the amount of fill. The mean fill per can is important, but equally important is the varia-tion of fill. If σ^2, the variance of the fill, is large, some cans will contain too little and others too much. Suppose regulatory agencies specify that the standard deviation of the amount of fill should be less than .1 ounce. To determine whether the process is meeting this specification, the supervisor randomly selects 10 cans and weighs the contents of each. The results are given in Table 7.6.

Table 7.6	Fill Weights (in Ounces) of 10 Cans								
16.00	16.06	15.95	16.04	16.10	16.05	16.02	16.03	15.99	16.02

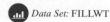 *Data Set:* FILLWT

Do these data provide sufficient evidence to indicate that the variability is as small as desired? To answer this question, we need a procedure for testing a hypothesis about σ^2.

Intuitively, it seems that we should compare the sample variance σ^2 with the hypothesized value of σ^2 (or s with σ) to make a decision about the population's variability. The quantity

$$\frac{(n-1)s^2}{\sigma^2}$$

is known to have a **chi-square** (χ^2) **sampling distribution** when the population from which the sample is taken is *normally distributed*. (Chi-square distributions were intro-duced in Section 6.6.)

Since the distribution of $\frac{(n-1)s^2}{\sigma^2}$ is known, we can use this quantity as a test sta-tistic in a test of hypothesis for a population variance, as illustrated in the next example.

BIOGRAPHY

FRIEDRICH R. HELMERT (1843–1917)
Helmert Transformations

German Friedrich Helmert studied engineering sciences and mathematics at Dresden University, where he earned his PhD, then accepted a position as a professor of geodesy—the scientific study of the earth's size and shape—at the technical school in Aachen. Helmert's mathematical solutions to geodesy problems led him to several statistics-related discoveries. His greatest statistical contribution occurred in 1876, when he was the first to prove that the sampling distribution of the sample variance, s^2, is a chi-square distribution. Helmert used a series of mathematical transformations to obtain the distribution of s^2—transformations that have since been named "Helmert transformations" in his honor. Later in life, Helmert was appointed professor of advanced geodesy at the prestigious University of Berlin and director of the Prussian Geodesic Institute.

EXAMPLE 7.12

Test for σ^2—Fill Weight Variance

Problem   Refer to the fill weights for the sample of ten 16-ounce cans in Table 7.6. Do the data provide sufficient evidence to indicate that the true standard deviation σ of the fill measurements of all 16-ounce cans is less than .1 ounce?

Solution   Here, we want to test whether $\sigma < .1$. Because the null and alternative hypotheses must be stated in terms of σ^2 rather than σ, we want to test the null hypothesis that $\sigma^2 = (.1)^2 = .01$ against the alternative that $\sigma^2 < .01$. Therefore, the elements of the test are

$H_0: \sigma^2 = .01$ (Fill variance equals .01—i.e., process specifications are not met)

$H_a: \sigma^2 < .01$ (Fill variance is less than .01—i.e., process specifications are met)

$$\text{Test statistic: } \chi^2 = \frac{(n-1)s^2}{\sigma^2}$$

Assumption: The distribution of the amounts of fill is approximately normal.

Rejection region: The smaller the value of s^2 we observe, the stronger the evidence in favor of H_a. Thus, we reject H_0 for "small values" of the test statistic. Recall (Section 6.6) that the chi-square distribution depends on $(n-1)$ degrees of freedom. With $\alpha = .05$ and $(n-1) = 9$ df, the χ^2 value for rejection is found in Table IV and pictured in Figure 7.25. We will reject H_0 if $\chi^2 < 3.32511$.

[*Note:* The area given in Table IV is the area to the *right* of the numerical value in the table. Thus, to determine the lower-tail value, which has $\alpha = .05$ to its *left*, we used the $\chi^2_{.95}$ column in Table IV.]

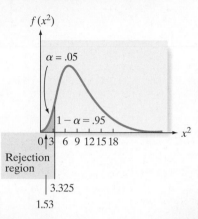

Figure 7.25
Rejection region for Example 7.12

Test and CI for One Variance: WEIGHT

Method

Null hypothesis	$\sigma = 0.1$
Alternative hypothesis	$\sigma < 0.1$

The chi-square method is only for the normal distribution.
The Bonett method is for any continuous distribution.

Statistics

Variable	N	StDev	Variance
WEIGHT	10	0.0412	0.00169

95% One-Sided Confidence Intervals

Variable	Method	Upper Bound for StDev	Upper Bound for Variance
WEIGHT	Chi-Square	0.0677	0.00458
	Bonett	0.0732	0.00536

Tests

Variable	Method	Test Statistic	DF	P-Value
WEIGHT	Chi-Square	1.52	9	0.003
	Bonett	—	—	0.010

Figure 7.26
Minitab analysis of fill weight variance, Example 7.12

A Minitab analysis of the data in Table 7.6 is displayed in Figure 7.26. The value of s (highlighted) on the printout is $s = .0412$. Substituting into the formula for the test statistic, we have

$$\chi^2 = \frac{(n-1)s^2}{\sigma^2} = \frac{9(.0412)^2}{.01} = 1.53$$

Because the test statistic falls into the rejection region, we reject H_0 in favor of H_a—that is, the supervisor can conclude that the variance σ^2 of the population of all amounts of fill is less than .01 ($\sigma < .1$) with probability of a Type I error equal to $\alpha = .05$. If this procedure is repeatedly used, it will incorrectly reject H_0 only 5% of the time. Thus, the quality-control supervisor is confident in the decision that the cannery is operating within the desired limits of variability.

Look Back Note that both the test statistic (rounded) and the lower-tailed p-value of the test (.003) are highlighted at the bottom of the printout, Figure 7.26. Because $\alpha = .05$ exceeds the p-value, our decision to reject H_0 is confirmed.

● **Now Work Exercise 7.87**

One-tailed and two-tailed tests of hypothesis for σ^2 are given in the following box.

Large-Sample Test of Hypothesis about σ^2: Chi-Square Statistic

Test statistic: $$\chi_c^2 = \frac{(n-1)s^2}{\sigma_0^2}$$

	One-Tailed Tests		Two-Tailed Test
	$H_0: \sigma^2 = \sigma_0^2$	$H_0: \sigma^2 = \sigma_0^2$	$H_0: \sigma^2 = \sigma_0^2$
	$H_a: \sigma^2 < \sigma_0^2$	$H_a: \sigma^2 > \sigma_0^2)$	$H_a: \sigma^2 \neq \sigma_0^2$
Rejection region:	$\chi_c^2 < \chi_{(1-\alpha)}^2$	$\chi_c^2 > \chi_\alpha^2$	$\chi_c^2 < \chi_{(1-\alpha/2)}^2$ or $\chi_c^2 > \chi_{\alpha/2}^2$
p-value:	$P(\chi^2 < \chi_c^2)$	$P(\chi^2 > \chi_c^2)$	$2 \min\{P(\chi^2 < \chi_c^2), P(\chi^2 > \chi_c^2)\}$

Decision: Reject H_0 if $\alpha > p$-value or if test statistic (χ_c^2) falls in rejection region where $P(\chi^2 > \chi_\alpha^2) = \alpha$, $P(\chi^2 < \chi_{(1-\alpha)}^2) = \alpha$, $\alpha = P(\text{Type I error}) = P(\text{Reject } H_0|H_0 \text{ true})$ and the chi-square distribution is based on $(n-1)$ degrees of freedom.

[*Note*: The symbol for the numerical value assigned to σ^2 under the null hypothesis is σ_0^2.]

Conditions Required for a Valid Hypothesis Test for σ^2

1. A random sample is selected from the target population.
2. The population from which the sample is selected has a distribution that is approximately normal.

❗ **CAUTION:** The procedure for conducting a hypothesis test for σ^2 in the above examples requires an assumption regardless of whether the sample size n is large or small. We must assume that the population from which the sample is selected has an approximate normal distribution. Unlike small-sample tests for μ based on the t-statistic, *slight to moderate departures from normality will render the chi-square test invalid.*

Exercises 7.82–7.95

Learning the Mechanics

7.82 Let χ_0^2 be a particular value of χ^2. Find the value of χ_0^2 such that
 a. $P(\chi^2 > \chi_0^2) = .10$ for $n = 12$
 b. $P(\chi^2 > \chi_0^2) = .05$ for $n = 9$
 c. $P(\chi^2 > \chi_0^2) = .025$ for $n = 5$

7.83 A random sample of n observations is selected from a normal population to test the null hypothesis that $\sigma^2 = 25$. Specify the rejection region for each of the following combinations of H_a, α, and n:
 a. H_a: $\sigma^2 \neq 25$; $\alpha = .05$; $n = 16$
 b. H_a: $\sigma^2 > 25$; $\alpha = .01$; $n = 23$
 c. H_a: $\sigma^2 > 25$; $\alpha = .10$; $n = 15$
 d. H_a: $\sigma^2 < 25$; $\alpha = .01$; $n = 13$
 e. H_a: $\sigma^2 \neq 25$; $\alpha = .10$; $n = 7$
 f. H_a: $\sigma^2 < 25$; $\alpha = .05$; $n = 25$

7.84 A random sample of seven measurements gave $\bar{x} = 9.4$ and $s^2 = 4.84$.
 a. What assumptions must you make concerning the population in order to test a hypothesis about σ^2?
 b. Suppose the assumptions in part **a** are satisfied. Test the null hypothesis, $\sigma^2 = 1$, against the alternative hypothesis, $\sigma^2 > 1$. Use $\alpha = .05$.
 c. Test the null hypothesis that $\sigma^2 = 1$ against the alternative hypothesis that $\sigma^2 \neq 1$. Use $\alpha = .05$.

7.85 Refer to Exercise 7.84. Suppose we had $n = 100$, $\bar{x} = 9.4$, and $s^2 = 4.84$.
 a. Test the null hypothesis, H_0: $\sigma^2 = 1$, against the alternative hypothesis, H_a: $\sigma^2 > 1$.
 b. Compare your test result with that of Exercise 7.84.

7.86 In a test for population variance, the null hypothesis is H_0: $\sigma^2 \geq 20$ versus the alternative hypothesis H_a: $\sigma^2 < 20$. If a random sample of $n = 5$ produced the following measurements: 15, 19, 9, 14, and 25. Conduct the test at the 5% level of significance.

Applying the Concepts—Basic

7.87 **Trading skills of institutional investors.** Refer to *The Journal of Finance* (April 2011) analysis of trading skills of institutional investors, Exercise 7.36 (p. 410). Recall that the study focused on "round-trip" trades, i.e., trades in which the same stock was both bought and sold in the same quarter. In a random sample of 200 round-trip trades made by institutional investors, the sample standard deviation of the rates of return was 8.82%. One property of a consistent performance of institutional investors is a small variance in the rates of return of round-trip trades, say, a standard deviation of less than 10%.
 a. Specify the null and alternative hypotheses for determining whether the population of institutional investors performs consistently.
 b. Find the rejection region for the test using $\alpha = .05$.
 c. Interpret the value of α in the words of the problem.
 d. A Minitab printout of the analysis is shown (next column). Locate the test statistic and p-value on the printout.

 e. Give the appropriate conclusion in the words of the problem.
 f. What assumptions about the data are required for the inference to be valid?

Test and CI for One Variance

```
Method

Null hypothesis          σ = 10
Alternative hypothesis   σ < 10

The chi-square method is only for the normal distribution.
The Bonett method cannot be calculated with summarized data.


Statistics

  N   StDev   Variance
200    8.82      77.8


Tests

                         Test
Method        Statistic    DF   P-Value
Chi-Square       154.81    199    0.009
```

7.88 **Lobster trap placement.** Refer to the *Bulletin of Marine Science* (April 2010) observational study of lobster trap placement by teams fishing for the red spiny lobster in Baja California Sur, Mexico, Exercise 7.54 (p. 417). Trap-spacing measurements (in meters) for a sample of seven teams of red spiny lobster fishermen are repeated in the table. (These measurements are for the BT cooperative in the accompanying data file.) The researchers want to know whether σ^2, the variation in the population of trap-spacing measurements, is larger than 10 m². They will conduct a test of hypothesis using $\alpha = .05$.

93	99	105	94	82	70	86

Source: Based on G. G. Shester, "Explaining Catch Variation Among Baja California Lobster Fishers Through Spatial Analysis of Trap-Placement Decisions," *Bulletin of Marine Science,* Vol. 86, No. 2, April 2010 (Table 1), pp. 479–498.

 a. Specify the null and alternative hypotheses for this test.
 b. Find the variance of the sample data, s^2.
 c. Note that $s^2 > 10$. Consequently, a fisherman wants to reject the null hypothesis. What are the problems with using such a decision rule?
 d. Compute the value of the test statistic.
 e. Use statistical software to find the p-value of the test.
 f. Give the appropriate conclusion.
 g. What conditions must be satisfied for the test results to be valid?

7.89 **Golf tees produced from an injection mold.** Refer to Exercise 7.37 (p. 410) and the weights of tees produced by an injection mold process. If operating correctly, the process will produce tees with a weight variance of .000004 (ounces)². If the weight variance differs from .000004, the injection molder is out of control.

a. Set up the null and alternative hypotheses for testing whether the injection mold process is out of control.

b. Use the data saved in the accompanying file to conduct the test, part **a**. Use $\alpha = .01$.

c. What conditions are required for inferences derived from the test to be valid? Are they reasonably satisfied?

7.90 **Oil content of fried sweet potato chips.** Refer to the *Journal of Food Engineering* (September 2013) study of the characteristics of sweet potato chips fried at different temperatures, Exercise 6.97 (p. 371). Recall that a sample of 6 sweet potato slices were fried at 130° using a vacuum fryer, and the internal oil content (gigagrams [Gg]) was measured for each slice. The results were: $\bar{x} = .178$ Gg and $s = .011$ Gg.

a. Conduct a test of hypothesis to determine if the standard deviation, σ, of the population of internal oil contents for sweet potato slices fried at 130° differs from .1. Use $\alpha = .05$.

b. In Exercise 6.97, you formed a 95% confidence interval for the true standard deviation of the internal oil content distribution for the sweet potato chips. Use this interval to make an inference about whether $\sigma = .1$. Does the result agree with the test, part **a**?

Applying the Concepts—Intermediate

7.91 **Strand bond performance of pre-stressed concrete.** An

FORCE experiment was carried out to investigate the strength variability of pre-stressed, bonded concrete after anchorage failure has occurred, and the results were published in *Engineering Structures* (June 2013). The maximum strand force, measured in kilonewtons (kN), achieved after anchorage failure for 12 pre-stressed concrete strands is given in the accompanying table. Can you infer that the true variance of the maximum strand forces that occur after anchorage failure is less than 25 kN^2? Test using $\alpha = .10$.

158.2	161.5	166.5	158.4	159.9	161.9	162.8	161.2	160.1	175.6	168.8	163.7

7.92 **Drug content assessment.** Refer to the *Analytical Chemistry* (December 15, 2009) study of a new method used by GlaxoSmithKline Medicines Research Center to determine the amount of drug in a tablet, Exercise 6.101 (p. 372). Drug concentrations (measured as a percentage) for 50 randomly selected tablets are repeated in the accompanying table. The standard method of assessing drug content yields a concentration variance of 9. Can the scientists at GlaxoSmithKline conclude that the new method of determining drug concentration is less variable than the standard method? Test using $\alpha = .01$.

91.28	92.83	89.35	91.90	82.85	94.83	89.83	89.00	84.62
86.96	88.32	91.17	83.86	89.74	92.24	92.59	84.21	89.36
90.96	92.85	89.39	89.82	89.91	92.16	88.67	89.35	86.51
89.04	91.82	93.02	88.32	88.76	89.26	90.36	87.16	91.74
86.12	92.10	83.33	87.61	88.20	92.78	86.35	93.84	91.20
93.44	86.77	83.77	93.19	81.79				

Source: Based on P. J. Borman, J. C. Marion, I. Damjanov, and P. Jackson, "Design and Analysis of Method Equivalence Studies," *Analytical Chemistry*, Vol. 81, No. 24, December 15, 2009 (Table 3).

7.93 **Jitter in a water power system.** Refer to the *Journal of Applied Physics* investigation of throughput jitter in the opening switch of a prototype water power system, Exercise 6.102 (p. 372). Recall that low throughput jitter is critical to successful waterline technology. An analysis of conduction time for a sample of 18 trials of the prototype system yielded $\bar{x} = 334.8$ nanoseconds and $s = 6.3$ nanoseconds. (Conduction time is defined as the length of time required for the downstream current to equal 10% of the upstream current.) A system is considered to have low throughput jitter if the true conduction time standard deviation is less than 7 nanoseconds. Does the prototype system satisfy this requirement? Test using $\alpha = .01$.

7.94 **Cooling method for gas turbines.** During periods of high electricity demand, especially during the hot summer months, the power output from a gas turbine engine can drop dramatically. One way to counter this drop in power is by cooling the inlet air to the gas turbine. An increasingly popular cooling method uses high-pressure inlet fogging. The performance of a sample of 67 gas turbines augmented with high-pressure inlet fogging was investigated in the *Journal of Engineering for Gas Turbines and Power* (January 2005). One measure of performance is heat rate (kilojoules per kilowatt per hour). Heat rates for the 67 gas turbines are listed in the table below. Suppose that standard gas turbines have heat rates with a standard deviation of 1,500 kJ/kWh. Is there sufficient evidence to indicate that the heat rates of the augmented gas turbine engine are more variable than the heat rates of the standard gas turbine engine? Test using $\alpha = .05$.

14622	13196	11948	11289	11964	10526	10387	10592	10460	10086
14628	13396	11726	11252	12449	11030	10787	10603	10144	11674
11510	10946	10508	10604	10270	10529	10360	14796	12913	12270
11842	10656	11360	11136	10814	13523	11289	11183	10951	9722
10481	9812	9669	9643	9115	9115	11588	10888	9738	9295
9421	9105	10233	10186	9918	9209	9532	9933	9152	9295
16243	14628	12766	8714	9469	11948	12414			

Data for Exercise 7.94

Applying the Concepts—Advanced

7.95 Why do small firms export? The *Journal of Small Business Management* (Vol. 40, 2002) published a study of what motivates small firms to export. In a survey of 137 exporting firms, each CEO was asked to respond to the statement "Management believes that the firm can achieve economies of scale by exporting" on a scale of 1 (strongly disagree) to 5 (strongly agree). Summary statistics for the $n = 137$ scale scores were reported as $\bar{x} = 3.85$ and $s = 1.5$.

a. Explain why the researcher will be unable to conclude that the true mean scale score exceeds 3.5 if the standard deviation of the scale scores is too large.

b. Give the largest value of the true standard deviation, σ, for which you will reject the null hypothesis $H_0: \mu = 3.5$ in favor of the alternative hypothesis $H_a: \mu > 3.5$ using $\alpha = .01$.

c. Based on the study results, is there evidence (at $\alpha = .01$) to indicate that σ is smaller than the value you determined in part **b**?

d. The scale scores for the sample of 137 small firms are unlikely to be normally distributed. Does this invalidate the inference made about μ in part **b**? About σ in part **c**?

7.8 Calculating Type II Error Probabilities: More About β (Optional)

In our introduction to hypothesis testing in Section 7.1, we showed that the probability of committing a Type I error, α, can be controlled by the selection of the rejection region for the test. Thus, when the test statistic falls in the rejection region and we make the decision to reject the null hypothesis, we do so knowing the error rate for incorrect rejections of H_0. The situation corresponding to accepting the null hypothesis, and thereby risking a Type II error, is not generally as controllable. For that reason, we adopted a policy of nonrejection of H_0 when the test statistic does not fall in the rejection region, rather than risking an error of unknown magnitude.

To see how β, the probability of a Type II error, can be calculated for a test of hypothesis, recall the example in Section 7.1 in which a city tests a manufacturer's sewer pipe to see whether it meets the requirement that the mean strength exceeds 2,400 pounds per linear foot. The setup for the test is as follows:

$$H_0: \mu = 2{,}400$$
$$H_a: \mu > 2{,}400$$

Test statistic: $z = \dfrac{\bar{x} - 2{,}400}{\sigma/\sqrt{n}}$

Rejection region: $z > 1.645$ for $\alpha = .05$

Figure 7.27a shows the rejection region for the **null distribution**—that is, the distribution of the test statistic assuming the null hypothesis is true. The area in the rejection region is .05, and this area represents α, the probability that the test statistic leads to rejection of H_0 when in fact H_0 is true.

The Type II error probability β is calculated assuming that the null hypothesis is false because it is defined as the *probability of accepting H_0 when it is false*. Because H_0 is false for any value of μ exceeding 2,400, one value of β exists for each possible value of μ greater than 2,400 (an infinite number of possibilities). Figure 7.27b–d show three of the possibilities, corresponding to alternative hypothesis values of μ equal to 2,425, 2,450, and 2,475, respectively. Note that β is the area in the *nonrejection* (or *acceptance*) *region* in each of these distributions and that β decreases as the true value of μ moves farther from the null hypothesized value of $\mu = 2{,}400$. This is sensible because the probability of incorrectly accepting the null hypothesis should decrease as the distance between the null and alternative values of μ increases.

In order to calculate the value of β for a specific value of μ in H_a, we proceed as follows:

1. Calculate the value of $\bar{x}$ that corresponds to the border between the acceptance and rejection regions. For the sewer pipe example, this is the value of $\bar{x}$ that lies 1.645 standard deviations above $\mu = 2{,}400$ in the sampling distribution of $\bar{x}$.

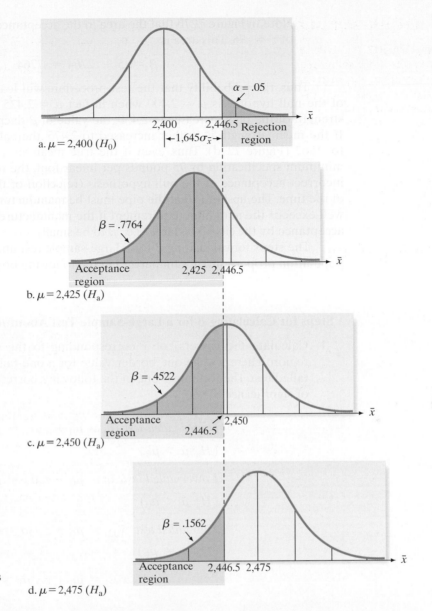

Figure 7.27

Values of α and β for various values of μ

a. $\mu = 2,400 \ (H_0)$

b. $\mu = 2,425 \ (H_a)$

c. $\mu = 2,450 \ (H_a)$

d. $\mu = 2,475 \ (H_a)$

Denoting this value by $\bar{x}_0$, corresponding to the largest value of $\bar{x}$ that supports the null hypothesis, we find (recalling that $s = 200$ and $n = 50$)

$$\bar{x}_0 = \mu_0 + 1.645\sigma_{\bar{x}} = 2,400 + 1.645\left(\frac{\sigma}{\sqrt{n}}\right)$$

$$\approx 2,400 + 1.645\left(\frac{s}{\sqrt{n}}\right) = 2,400 + 1.645\left(\frac{200}{\sqrt{50}}\right)$$

$$= 2,400 + 1.645(28.28) = 2,446.5$$

2. For a particular alternative distribution corresponding to a value of μ, denoted by μ_a, we calculate the z-value corresponding to $\bar{x}_0$, the border between the rejection and acceptance regions. We then use this z-value and Table II in Appendix D to determine the area in the *acceptance region* under the alternative distribution. This area is the value of β corresponding to the particular alternative μ_a. For example, for the alternative $\mu_a = 2,425$, we calculate

$$z = \frac{\bar{x}_0 - 2,425}{\sigma_{\bar{x}}} = \frac{\bar{x}_0 - 2,425}{\sigma/\sqrt{n}}$$

$$\approx \frac{\bar{x}_0 - 2,425}{\sigma_{\bar{x}}} = \frac{2,446.5 - 2,425}{28.28} = .76$$

Note in Figure 7.27b that the area in the acceptance region is the area to the left of $z = .76$. This area is

$$\beta = .5 + .2764 = .7764$$

Thus, the probability that the test procedure will lead to an incorrect acceptance of the null hypothesis $\mu = 2{,}400$ when in fact $\mu = 2{,}425$ is about .78. As the average strength of the pipe increases to 2,450, the value of β decreases to .4522 (Figure 7.27c). If the mean strength is further increased to 2,475, the value of β is further decreased to .1562 (Figure 7.27d). Thus, even if the true mean strength of the pipe exceeds the minimum specification by 75 pounds per linear foot, the test procedure will lead to an incorrect acceptance of the null hypothesis (rejection of the pipe) approximately 16% of the time. The upshot is that the pipe must be manufactured so that the mean strength well exceeds the minimum requirement if the manufacturer wants the probability of its acceptance by the city to be large (i.e., β to be small).

The steps for calculating β for a large-sample test about a population mean and a population proportion are summarized in the following boxes.

Steps for Calculating β for a Large-Sample Test About μ

1. Calculate the value(s) of $\bar{x}$ corresponding to the border(s) of the rejection region. There will be one border value for a one-tailed test and two for a two-tailed test. The formula is one of the following, corresponding to a test with level of significance α:

    Upper-tailed test: $\bar{x}_0 = \mu_0 + z_\alpha \sigma_{\bar{x}} \approx \mu_0 + z_\alpha \left(\dfrac{s}{\sqrt{n}} \right)$
    $(H_a: \mu > \mu_0)$

    Lower-tailed test: $\bar{x}_0 = \mu_0 - z_\alpha \sigma_{\bar{x}} \approx \mu_0 - z_\alpha \left(\dfrac{s}{\sqrt{n}} \right)$
    $(H_a: \mu < \mu_0)$

    Two-tailed test: $\bar{x}_{0,L} = \mu_0 - z_{\alpha/2} \sigma_{\bar{x}} \approx \mu_0 - z_{\alpha/2} \left(\dfrac{s}{\sqrt{n}} \right)$
    $(H_a: \mu \neq \mu_0)$

    $\bar{x}_{0,U} = \mu_0 + z_{\alpha/2} \sigma_{\bar{x}} \approx \mu_0 + z_{\alpha/2} \left(\dfrac{s}{\sqrt{n}} \right)$

2. Specify the value of μ_a in the alternative hypothesis for which the value of β is to be calculated. Then convert the border value(s) of $\bar{x}_0$ to z-value(s) using the alternative distribution with mean μ_a. The general formula for the z-value is

    $$z = \frac{\bar{x}_0 - \mu_a}{\sigma_{\bar{x}}}$$

3. Sketch the alternative distribution (centered at μ_a), and shade the area in the acceptance (nonrejection) region. Use the z-statistic(s) and Table II of Appendix D to find the shaded area, which is β.

    Lower-tailed test: $\beta = P\left(z > \dfrac{\bar{x}_0 - \mu_a}{\sigma_{\bar{x}}} \right)$
    $(H_a: \mu < \mu_0)$

    Upper-tailed test: $\beta = P\left(z < \dfrac{\bar{x}_0 - \mu_a}{\sigma_{\bar{x}}} \right)$
    $(H_a: \mu > \mu_0)$

    Two-tailed test: $\beta = P\left(\dfrac{\bar{x}_{0,L} - \mu_a}{\sigma_{\bar{x}}} < z < \dfrac{\bar{x}_{0,U} - \mu_a}{\sigma_{\bar{x}}} \right)$
    $(H_a: \mu \neq \mu_0)$

Steps for Calculating β for a Large-Sample Test About p

1. Calculate the value(s) of $\hat{p}$ corresponding to the border(s) of the rejection region. There will be one border for a one-tailed test and two for a two-tailed test. The formula is one of the following, corresponding to a test with level of significance α.

Upper-tailed test: $\hat{p}_0 = p_0 + z_\alpha \sigma_p = p_0 + z_\alpha \sqrt{\dfrac{p_0 q_0}{n}}$

$(H_a: p > p_0)$

Lower-tailed test: $\hat{p}_0 = p_0 - z_\alpha \sigma_p = p_0 + z_\alpha \sqrt{\dfrac{p_0 q_0}{n}}$

$(H_a: p < p_0)$

Two-tailed test: $\hat{p}_{0,L} = p_0 - z_{\alpha/2} \sigma_p = p_0 - z_{\alpha/2} \sqrt{\dfrac{p_0 q_0}{n}}$

$(H_a: p \neq p_0)$

$$\hat{p}_{0,U} = p_0 + z_{\alpha/2} \sigma_p = p_0 + z_{\alpha/2} \sqrt{\dfrac{p_0 q_0}{n}}$$

2. Specify the value of p_a in the alternative hypothesis for which the value of β is to be calculated. Then covert the border values of $\hat{p}_0$ to z-value(s), using the alternative distribution with mean p_a. The general formula for the z-value is:

$$z = (\hat{p}_0 - p_a)/\sigma_p = \frac{\hat{p}_0 - p_a}{\sqrt{\dfrac{p_a q_a}{n}}}$$

3. Sketch the alternative distribution (centered at p_a), and shade the area in the acceptance (nonrejection) region. Use the z-statistic(s) and Table II of Appendix D to find the shaded area, which is β.

Upper-tailed test: $\beta = P\left(z < \dfrac{\hat{p}_0 - p_a}{\sqrt{\dfrac{p_a q_a}{n}}} \right)$

$(H_a: p > p_0)$

Lower-tailed test: $\beta = P\left(z > \dfrac{\hat{p}_0 - p_a}{\sqrt{\dfrac{p_a q_a}{n}}} \right)$

$(H_a: p < p_0)$

Two-tailed test: $\beta = P\left(\dfrac{\hat{p}_{0,L} - p_a}{\sqrt{\dfrac{p_a q_a}{n}}} < z < \dfrac{\hat{p}_{0,U} - p_a}{\sqrt{\dfrac{p_a q_a}{n}}} \right)$

$(H_a: p \neq p_0)$

Following the calculation of β for a particular value of the parameter in H_a you should interpret the value in the context of the hypothesis-testing application. It is often useful to interpret the value of $1 - \beta$, which is known as the **power of the test** corresponding to a particular alternative, say, μ_a for a population mean. Since β is the probability of accepting the null hypothesis when the alternative hypothesis is true with $\mu = \mu_a$, $1 - \beta$ is the probability of the complementary event, or the probability of rejecting the null hypothesis when the alternative $H_a: \mu = \mu_a$ is true. That is, the power $(1 - \beta)$ measures the likelihood that the test procedure will lead to the correct decision (reject H_0) for a particular value of the mean (or proportion) in the alternative hypothesis.

> The **power of a test** is the probability that the test will correctly lead to the rejection of the null hypothesis for a particular value of μ or p in the alternative hypothesis. The power is equal to $(1 - \beta)$ for the particular alternative considered.

For example, in the sewer pipe example we found that $\beta = .7764$ when $\mu = 2,425$. This is the probability that the test leads to the (incorrect) acceptance of the null hypothesis when $\mu = 2,425$. Or, equivalently, the power of the test is $1 - .7764 = .2236$, which means that the test will lead to the (correct) rejection of the null hypothesis only 22% of the time when the pipe exceeds specifications by 25 pounds per linear foot. When the manufacturer's pipe has a mean strength of 2,475 (that is, 75 pounds per linear foot in excess of specifications), the power of the test increases to $1 - .1562 = .8438$—that is, the test will lead to the acceptance of the manufacturer's pipe 84% of the time if $\mu = 2,475$.

EXAMPLE 7.13	**Problem** Recall the quality-control study in Example 7.5, in which we tested to determine whether a cereal box filling machine was deviating from the specified mean fill of $\mu = 12$ ounces. The test setup is repeated here:

The Power of a Test— Quality-Control Study

$$H_0: \mu = 12$$

$$H_a: \mu \neq 12 \text{ (i.e., } \mu < 12 \text{ or } \mu > 12\text{)}$$

Test statistic: $z = \dfrac{\bar{x} - 12}{\sigma_{\bar{x}}}$

Rejection region: $z < -1.96$ or $z > 1.96$ for $\alpha = .05$

$z < -2.575$ or $z > 2.575$ for $\alpha = .01$

Note that two rejection regions have been specified corresponding to values of $\alpha = .05$ and $\alpha = .01$, respectively. Assume that $n = 100$ and $s = .5$.

a. Suppose the machine is underfilling the boxes by an average of .1 ounce (i.e., $\mu = 11.9$). Calculate the values of β corresponding to the two rejection regions. Discuss the relationship between the values of α and β.

b. Calculate the power of the test for each of the rejection regions when $\mu = 11.9$.

Solution

a. We first consider the rejection region corresponding to $\alpha = .05$. The first step is to calculate the border values of $\bar{x}$ corresponding to the two-tailed rejection region, $z < -1.96$ or $z > 1.96$:

$$\bar{x}_{0,L} = \mu_0 - 1.96\sigma_{\bar{x}} \approx \mu_0 - 1.96\left(\frac{s}{\sqrt{n}}\right) = 12 - 1.96\left(\frac{.5}{10}\right) = 11.902$$

$$\bar{x}_{0,U} = \mu_0 + 1.96\sigma_{\bar{x}} \approx \mu_0 + 1.96\left(\frac{s}{\sqrt{n}}\right) = 12 + 1.96\left(\frac{.5}{10}\right) = 12.098$$

These border values are shown in Figure 7.28a.

Next, we convert these values to z-values in the alternative distribution with $\mu_a = 11.9$:

$$z_L = \frac{x_{0,L} - \mu_a}{\sigma_{\bar{x}}} \approx \frac{11.902 - 11.9}{.05} = .04$$

$$z_U = \frac{x_{0,U} - \mu_a}{\sigma_{\bar{x}}} \approx \frac{12.098 - 11.9}{.05} = 3.96$$

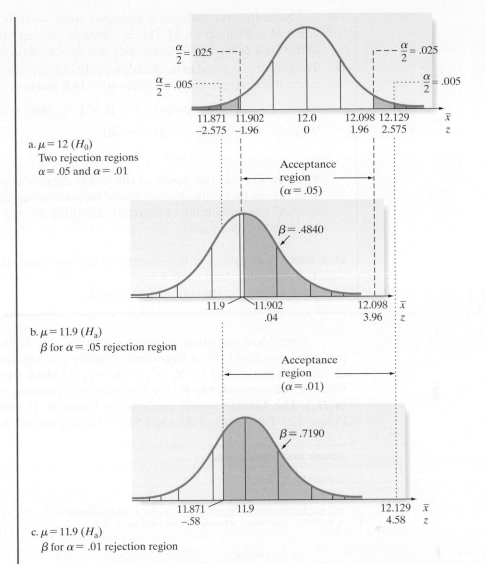

a. $\mu = 12$ (H_0)
Two rejection regions
$\alpha = .05$ and $\alpha = .01$

b. $\mu = 11.9$ (H_a)
β for $\alpha = .05$ rejection region

Figure 7.28

Calculation of β for filling machine process, Example 7.13

c. $\mu = 11.9$ (H_a)
β for $\alpha = .01$ rejection region

These z-values are shown in Figure 7.28b: You can see that the acceptance (or non-rejection) region is the area between them. Using Table II in Appendix D, we find that the area between $z = 0$ and $z = .04$ is .0160, and the area between $z = 0$ and $z = 3.96$ is (approximately) .5 (because $z = 3.96$ is off the scale of Table II). Then the area between $z = .04$ and $z = 3.96$ is, approximately,

$$\beta = .5 - .0160 = .4840$$

Thus, the test with $\alpha = .05$ will lead to a Type II error about 48% of the time when the machine is underfilling, on average, by .1 ounce.

For the rejection region corresponding to $\alpha = .01$, $z < -2.575$, or $z > 2.575$, we find

$$\bar{x}_{0,L} = 12 - 2.575\left(\frac{.5}{10}\right) = 11.871$$

$$\bar{x}_{0,U} = 12 + 2.575\left(\frac{.5}{10}\right) = 12.129$$

These border values of the rejection region are shown in Figure 7.28c.

Converting these two border values to z-values in the alternative distribution with $\mu_a = 11.9$, we find $z_L = -.58$ and $z_U = 4.58$. The area between these values is, approximately,

$$\beta = P(-.58 < z < 4.58) = .2190 + .5 = .7190$$

Thus, the chance that the test procedure with $\alpha = .01$ will lead to an incorrect acceptance of H_0 is about 72%.

Note that the value of β increases from .4840 to .7190 when we decrease the value of α from .05 to .01. This is a general property of the relationship between α and β: *as α is decreased (increased), β is increased (decreased)*.

b. The power is defined to be the probability of (correctly) rejecting the null hypothesis when the alternative is true. When $\mu = 11.9$ and $\alpha = .05$, we find

$$\text{Power} = 1 - \beta = 1 - .4840 = .5160$$

When $\mu = 11.9$ and $\alpha = .01$, we find

$$\text{Power} = 1 - \beta = 1 - .7190 = .2810$$

You can see that the power of the test is decreased as the level of α is decreased. This means that as the probability of incorrectly rejecting the null hypothesis is decreased, the probability of correctly accepting the null hypothesis for a given alternative is also decreased.

Look Back A key point of this example is that the value of α must be selected carefully, with the realization that a test is made less capable of detecting departures from the null hypothesis when the value of α is decreased.

● **Now Work Exercise 7.102**

Note: Most statistical software packages now have options for computing the power of standard tests of hypothesis. Usually you will need to specify the type of test (z-test or t-test), form of H_a ($<$, $>$, or $\neq$), standard deviation, sample size, and the value of the parameter in H_a (or the difference between the value in H_0 and the value in H_a). The Minitab power analysis for Example 7.13 when $\alpha = .05$ is displayed in Figure 7.29. The power of the test (.516) is highlighted on the printout.

Power and Sample Size

```
1-Sample Z Test

Testing mean = null (versus ≠ null)
Calculating power for mean = null + difference
α = 0.05  Assumed standard deviation = 0.5
```

Figure 7.29

Minitab power analysis for Example 7.13

Difference	Sample Size	Power
0.1	100	0.516005

We have shown that the probability of committing a Type II error, β, is inversely related to α (Example 7.13) and that the value of β decreases as the value of μ_a moves farther from the null hypothesis value (sewer pipe example). The sample size n also affects β. Remember that the standard deviation of the sampling distribution of $\bar{x}$ is inversely proportional to the square root of the sample size ($\sigma_{\bar{x}} = \sigma/\sqrt{n}$). Thus, as illustrated in Figure 7.30, the variability of both the null and alternative sampling distributions is decreased as n is increased. If the value of α is specified and remains fixed, the value of β decreases as n increases, as illustrated in Figure 7.30. Conversely, the power of the test for a given alternative hypothesis is increased as the sample size is increased. The properties of β and power are summarized in the box.

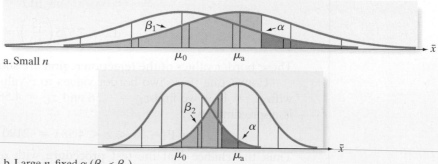

Figure 7.30

Relationship between α, β, and n

a. Small n

b. Large n, fixed α ($\beta_2 < \beta_1$)

Properties of β and Power

1. For fixed n and α, the value of β decreases, and the power increases as the distance between the specified null value μ_0 (or, p_0) and the specified alternative value μ_a (or, p_a) increases (see Figure 7.27).

2. For fixed n and values of μ_0 and μ_a (or, p_0 and p_a), the value of β increases, and the power decreases as the value of α is decreased (see Figure 7.28).

3. For fixed α and values of μ_0 and μ_a (or, p_0 and p_a), the value of β decreases, and the power increases as the sample size n is increased (see Figure 7.30).

Exercises 7.96–7.107

Learning the Mechanics

7.96 **a.** List three factors that will increase the power of a test.
  b. What is the relationship between β, the probability of committing a Type II error, and the power of a test?

7.97 Suppose you want to test $H_0: \mu = 500$ against $H_a: \mu > 500$ using $\alpha = .05$. The population in question is normally distributed with standard deviation 100. A random sample of size $n = 25$ will be used.
  a. Sketch the sampling distribution of $\bar{x}$, assuming that H_0 is true.
  b. Find the value of $\bar{x}_0$, that value of $\bar{x}$ above which the null hypothesis will be rejected. Indicate the rejection region on your graph of part **a**. Shade the area above the rejection region and label it α.
  c. On your graph of part **a**, sketch the sampling distribution of $\bar{x}$ if $\mu = 550$. Shade the area under this distribution that corresponds to the probability that $\bar{x}$ falls in the nonrejection region when $\mu = 550$. Label this area β.
  d. Find β.
  e. Compute the power of this test for detecting the alternative $H_a: \mu = 550$.

7.98 Refer to Exercise 7.97.
  a. If $\mu = 575$ instead of 550, what is the probability that the hypothesis test will incorrectly fail to reject H_0? That is, what is β?
  b. If $\mu = 575$, what is the probability that the test will correctly reject the null hypothesis? That is, what is the power of the test?
  c. Compare β and the power of the test when $\mu = 575$ with the values you obtained in Exercise 7.97 for $\mu = 550$. Explain the differences.

7.99 It is desired to test $H_0: \mu = 75$ against $H_a: \mu < 75$ using $\alpha = .10$. The population in question is uniformly distributed with standard deviation 15. A random sample of size 49 will be drawn from the population.
  a. Describe the (approximate) sampling distribution of $\bar{x}$ under the assumption that H_0 is true.
  b. Describe the (approximate) sampling distribution of $\bar{x}$ under the assumption that the population mean is 70.
  c. If μ were really equal to 70, what is the probability that the hypothesis test would lead the investigator to commit a Type II error?
  d. What is the power of this test for detecting the alternative $H_a: \mu = 70$?

7.100 Refer to Exercise 7.99.
  a. Find β for each of the following values of the population mean: 74, 72, 70, 68, and 66.
  b. Plot each value of β you obtained in part **a** against its associated population mean. Show β on the vertical axis and μ on the horizontal axis. Draw a curve through the five points on your graph.
  c. Use your graph of part **b** to find the approximate probability that the hypothesis test will lead to a Type II error when $\mu = 73$.
  d. Convert each of the β values you calculated in part **a** to the power of the test at the specified value of μ. Plot the power on the vertical axis against μ on the horizontal axis. Compare the graph of part **b** with the *power curve* of this part.
  e. Examine the graphs of parts **b** and **d**. Explain what they reveal about the relationships among the distance between the true mean μ and the null hypothesized mean μ_0, the value of β, and the power.

7.101 In testing the hypotheses $H_0: p \le .32$ against $H_a: p > .32$, suppose you found that the number of successes in a sample of 120 observations was 48.
  a. Justify whether this test meets the conditions required for a valid large-sample test where the sampling distribution is approximately normal.
  b. Determine the expected value and the standard error value for the assumptions made in part **a**.
  c. Find the β value if p has a real value of .4 at the 5% significance level and interpret your finding.
  d. Find the β value if p has a real value of .28 at the 5% significance level and interpret your finding.

Applying the Concepts—Intermediate

7.102 **Square footage of new California homes.** The average size of single-family homes built in the United States is 2,600 square feet (U.S. Census Bureau, 2015). A random sample of 100 new homes sold in California yielded the following size information: $\bar{x} = 2{,}717$ square feet and $s = 257$ square feet.
  a. Assume the average size of U.S. homes is known with certainty. Do the sample data provide sufficient evidence to conclude that the mean size of California homes built exceeds the national average? Test using $\alpha = .01$.
  b. Suppose the actual mean size of new California homes was 2,700 square feet. What is the power of the test in part **a** to detect this 100-square-foot difference?

c. If the California mean were actually 2,650 square feet, what is the power of the test in part **a** to detect this 50-square-foot difference?

7.103 Manufacturers that practice sole sourcing. If a manufacturer (the vendee) buys all items of a particular type from a particular vendor, the manufacturer is practicing *sole sourcing* (Schonberger and Knod, *Operations Management*, 2001). As part of a sole-sourcing arrangement, a vendor agrees to periodically supply its vendee with sample data from its production process. The vendee uses the data to investigate whether the mean length of rods produced by the vendor's production process is truly 5.0 millimeters (mm) or more, as claimed by the vendor and desired by the vendee.

a. If the production process has a standard deviation of .01 mm, the vendor supplies $n = 100$ items to the vendee, and the vendee uses $\alpha = .05$ in testing $H_0: \mu = 5.0$ mm against $H_a: \mu < 5.0$ mm, what is the probability that the vendee's test will fail to reject the null hypothesis when in fact $\mu = 4.9975$ mm? What is the name given to this type of error?

b. Refer to part **a**. What is the probability that the vendee's test will reject the null hypothesis when in fact $\mu = 5.0$? What is the name given to this type of error?

c. What is the power of the test to detect a departure of .0025 mm below the specified mean rod length of 5.0 mm?

7.104 Customer participation in store loyalty card programs. Refer to the *Pew Internet & American Life Project Survey* (January 2016) study of 250 store customers and their participation in a store loyalty card program, Exercise 7.69 (p. 425). Recall that a store owner claimed that more than 80% of all customers would participate in a loyalty card program. You conducted a test of $H_0: p = .8$ versus $H_a: p > .8$ using $\alpha = .01$. What is the probability that the test results will support the claim if, in fact, the true percentage of customers who would participate in a loyalty card program is 79%?

7.105 Gummi Bears: Red or yellow? Refer to the *Chance* (Winter 2010) experiment to determine if color of a Gummi Bear is related to its flavor, Exercise 7.72 (p. 425). You tested the null hypothesis of $p = .5$ against the two-tailed alternative hypothesis of $p \neq .5$ using $\alpha = .01$, where p represents the true proportion of blind folded students who correctly identified the color of the Gummi Bear. Recall that of the 121 students who participated in the study, 97 correctly identified the color. Find the power of the test if the true proportion is $p = .65$.

7.106 Fuel economy of the Honda Civic. According to the Environmental Protection Agency (EPA) *Fuel Economy Guide,* the 2016 Honda Civic automobile obtains a mean of 39 miles per gallon (mpg) on the highway. Suppose Honda claims that the EPA has underestimated the Civic's mileage. To support its assertion, the company selects $n = 50$ model 2016 Civic cars and records the mileage obtained for each car over a driving course similar to the one used by the EPA. The following data resulted: $\bar{x} = 41.3$ mpg, $s = 6.4$ mpg.

a. If Honda wishes to show that the mean mpg for 2016 Civic autos is greater than 39 mpg, what should the alternative hypothesis be? The null hypothesis?

b. Do the data provide sufficient evidence to support the auto manufacturer's claim? Test using $\alpha = .05$. List any assumptions you make in conducting the test.

c. Calculate the power of the test for the mean values of 39.5, 40, 40.5, 41, and 41.5, assuming $s = 6.4$ is a good estimate of σ.

d. Plot the power of the test on the vertical axis against the mean on the horizontal axis. Draw a curve through the points.

e. Use the power curve of part **d** to estimate the power for the mean value $\mu = 40.75$. Calculate the power for this value of μ and compare it with your approximation.

f. Use the power curve to approximate the power of the test when $\mu = 44$. If the true value of the mean mpg for this model is really 44, what (approximately) are the chances that the test will fail to reject the null hypothesis that the mean is 39?

7.107 Solder-joint inspections. Refer to Exercise 7.44 (p. 411), in which the performance of a particular type of laser-based inspection equipment was investigated. Assume that the standard deviation of the number of solder joints inspected on each run is 1.2. If $\alpha = .05$ is used in conducting the hypothesis test of interest using a sample of 48 circuit boards, and if the true mean number of solder joints that can be inspected is really equal to 9.5, what is the probability that the test will result in a Type II error?

CHAPTER NOTES

Key Terms

Note: Asterisks (*) denote items from the optional sections of this chapter.

Alternative (research) hypothesis 389	One-tailed (one-sided) statistical test 394
Chi-square sampling distribution 427	*Power of the test 435
Conclusions 392	Rejection region 390
Hypothesis 388	Test of hypothesis 388
Level of significance 393	Test statistic 389
Lower-tailed test 394	Two-tailed (two-sided) hypothesis 394
Null distribution 432	Type I error 390
Null hypothesis 389	Type II error 392
Observed significance level (*p*-value) 399	Upper-tailed test 394

Key Symbols

μ	Population mean
p	Population proportion, $P(\text{Success})$, in binomial trial
σ^2	Population variance
$\bar{x}$	Sample mean (estimator of μ)
$\hat{p}$	Sample proportion (estimator of p)
s^2	Sample variance (estimator of σ^2)
H_0	Null hypothesis
H_a	Alternative hypothesis
μ_0	Hypothesized value of population mean
p_0	Hypothesized value of population proportion
σ_0^2	Hypothesized value of population variance
α	Probability of a Type I error

β Probability of a Type II error
χ^2 Chi-square (sampling distribution of s^2 for normal data)

Key Ideas

Key Words for Identifying the Target Parameter

μ — Mean, Average
p — Proportion, Fraction, Percentage, Rate, Probability
σ^2 — Variance, Variability, Spread

Elements of a Hypothesis Test

1. *Null hypothesis* (H_0)
2. *Alternative hypothesis* (H_a)
3. *Test statistic* (z, t, *or* χ^2)
4. *Significance level* (α)
5. *p-value*
6. *Conclusion*

Probabilities in Hypothesis Testing

$\alpha = P(\textbf{Type I Error}) = P(\text{Reject } H_0 \text{ when } H_0 \text{ is true})$
$\beta = P(\textbf{Type II Error}) = P(\text{Accept } H_0 \text{ when } H_0 \text{ is false})$
$1 - \beta = \textbf{Power of a Test} = P(\text{Reject } H_0 \text{ when } H_0 \text{ is false})$

Forms of Alternative Hypothesis

Lower-tailed: $H_a: \mu < \mu_0$
Upper-tailed: $H_a: \mu > \mu_0$
Two-tailed: $H_a: \mu \neq \mu_0$

Using p-Values to Make Conclusions

1. Choose significance level (α)
2. Obtain p-value of the test
3. If $\alpha >$ p-value, reject H_0

Guide to Selecting a One-Sample Hypothesis Test

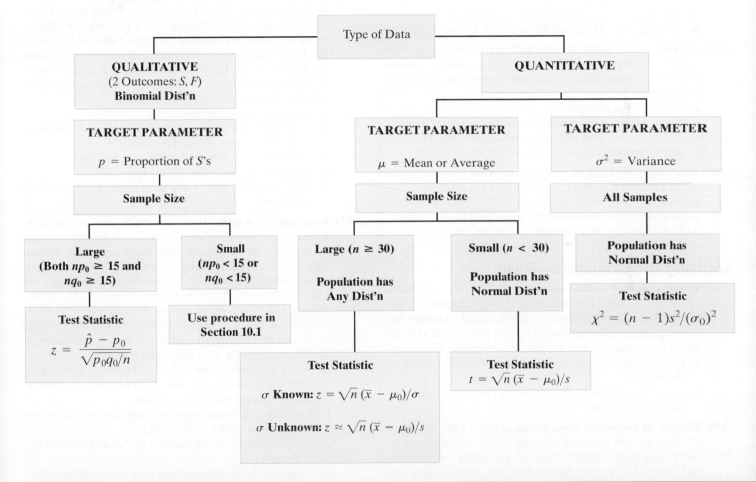

Note: List the assumptions necessary for the valid implementation of the statistical procedures you use in solving all these exercises. Exercises marked with an asterisk (*) are from the optional section in this chapter.

Learning the Mechanics

7.108 Specify the differences between a large-sample and small-sample test of hypothesis about a population mean μ. Focus on the assumptions and test statistics.

7.109 *Complete the following statement:* The smaller the p-value associated with a test of hypothesis, the stronger the support for the _____ hypothesis. Explain your answer.

7.110 Which of the elements of a test of hypothesis can and should be specified *prior* to analyzing the data that are to be used to conduct the test?

7.111 If you select a very small value for α when conducting a hypothesis test, will β tend to be big or small? Explain.

7.112 If the rejection of the null hypothesis of a particular test would cause your firm to go out of business, would you want α to be small or large? Explain.

7.113 A simple random sample of 25 observations was selected from a normal population. The mean and standard deviation of this sample are 20 and 5, respectively.
  a. Test $H_0: \mu = 22$ against $H_a: \mu \neq 22$ at the 10% significance level.
  b. Test $H_0: \mu \geq 22$ against $H_a: \mu < 22$ at the 1% significance level.

7.114 A random sample of 175 measurements possessed a mean $\bar{x} = 8.2$ and a standard deviation $s = .79$.
  a. Test $H_0: \mu = 8.3$ against $H_a: \mu \neq 8.3$. Use $\alpha = .05$.
  b. Test $H_0: \mu = 8.4$ against $H_a: \mu \neq 8.4$. Use $\alpha = .05$.
  c. Test $H_0: \sigma = 1$ against $H_a: \sigma \neq 1$. Use $\alpha = .05$.
  *d. Find the power of the test, part **a**, if $\mu_a = 8.5$.

7.115 A random sample of $n = 200$ observations from a binomial population yields $\hat{p} = .29$.
  a. Test $H_0: p = .35$ against $H_a: p < .35$. Use $\alpha = .05$.
  b. Test $H_0: p = .35$ against $H_a: p \neq .35$. Use $\alpha = .05$.

7.116 A t-test is conducted for the null hypothesis $H_0: \mu = 10$ versus the alternative $H_a: \mu > 10$ for a random sample of $n = 17$ observations. The test results are $t = 1.174$, p-value $= .1288$.
  a. Interpret the p-value.
  b. What assumptions are necessary for the validity of this test?
  c. Calculate and interpret the p-value, assuming the alternative hypothesis was instead $H_a: \mu \neq 10$.

7.117 A random sample of 41 observations from a normal population possessed a mean $\bar{x} = 88$ and a standard deviation $s = 6.9$.
  a. Test $H_0: \sigma^2 = 30$ against $H_a: \sigma^2 > 30$. Use $\alpha = .05$.
  b. Test $H_0: \sigma^2 = 30$ against $H_a: \sigma^2 \neq 30$. Use $\alpha = .05$.

Applying the Concepts—Basic

7.118 **Effectiveness of online courses.** The Survey of Online Learning, "Grade Level: Tracking Online Education in the United States, 2014," reported that 74% of college leaders believe that their online education courses are as good as or superior to courses that use traditional, face-to-face instruction.
  a. Give the null hypothesis for testing the claim made by the survey.
  b. Give the rejection region for a two-tailed test conducted at $\alpha = .01$.

7.119 **History of corporate acquisitions.** Refer to the *Academy of Management Journal* (August 2008) investigation of the performance and timing of corporate acquisitions, Exercise 2.12 (p. 74). Recall that the investigation discovered that in a random sample of 2,778 firms, 748 announced one or more acquisitions during the year 2000. Does the sample provide sufficient evidence to indicate that the true percentage of all firms that announced one or more acquisitions during the year 2000 is less than 30%? Use $\alpha = .05$ to make your decision.

7.120 **Latex allergy in health care workers.** Refer to the *Current Allergy & Clinical Immunology* (March 2004) study of $n = 46$ hospital employees who were diagnosed with a latex allergy from exposure to the powder on latex gloves, Exercise 6.112 (p. 375). The number of latex gloves used per week by the sampled workers is summarized as follows: $\bar{x} = 19.3$ and $s = 11.9$. Let μ represent the mean number of latex gloves used per week by all hospital employees. Consider testing $H_0: \mu = 20$ against $H_a: \mu < 20$.
  a. Give the rejection region for the test at a significance level of $\alpha = .01$.
  b. Calculate the value of the test statistic.
  c. Use the results, parts **a** and **b**, to make the appropriate conclusion.

7.121 **Latex allergy in health care workers (cont'd).** Refer to Exercise 7.120. Let σ^2 represent the variance in the number of latex gloves used per week by all hospital employees. Consider testing $H_0: \sigma^2 = 100$ against $H_a: \sigma^2 \neq 100$.
  a. Give the rejection region for the test at a significance level of $\alpha = .01$.
  b. Calculate the value of the test statistic.
  c. Use the results, parts **a** and **b**, to make the appropriate conclusion.

7.122 **"Made in the USA" survey.** Refer to the *Journal of Global Business* (Spring 2002) study of what "Made in the USA" means to consumers, Exercise 2.154 (p. 143). Recall that 64 of 106 randomly selected shoppers believed "Made in the USA" means 100% of labor and materials are from the United States. Let p represent the true proportion of consumers who believe "Made in the USA" means 100% of labor and materials are from the United States.
  a. Calculate a point estimate for p.
  b. A claim is made that $p = .70$. Set up the null and alternative hypotheses to test this claim.
  c. Calculate the test statistic for the test, part **b**.
  d. Find the rejection region for the test if $\alpha = .01$.
  e. Use the results, parts **c** and **d**, to make the appropriate conclusion.

7.123 **Beta value of a stock.** The "beta coefficient" of a stock is a measure of the stock's volatility (or risk) relative to the market as a whole. Stocks with beta coefficients greater than 1 generally bear greater risk (more volatility) than the market, whereas stocks with beta coefficients less than 1 are less risky (less volatile) than the overall market (Alexander, Sharpe, and Bailey, *Fundamentals of Investments*, 2000). A random sample of 15 high-technology stocks was selected at the end of 2009, and the mean and standard deviation of the beta coefficients were calculated: $\bar{x} = 1.23$, $s = .37$.
  a. Set up the appropriate null and alternative hypotheses to test whether the average high-technology stock is riskier than the market as a whole.
  b. Establish the appropriate test statistic and rejection region for the test. Use $\alpha = .10$.
  c. What assumptions are necessary to ensure the validity of the test?
  d. Calculate the test statistic and state your conclusion.
  e. What is the approximate p-value associated with this test? Interpret it.
  f. Conduct a test to determine if the variance of the stock beta values differs from .15. Use $\alpha = .05$.

7.124 **Accuracy of price scanners at Walmart.** Refer to Exercise 6.129 (p. 377) and the study of the accuracy of checkout scanners at Walmart stores in California. Recall that the National Institute for Standards and Technology (NIST) mandates that for every 100 items scanned through the electronic checkout scanner at a retail store, no more than two should have an inaccurate price. A study of random items purchased at California Walmart stores found that 8.3% had the wrong price (*Tampa Tribune,* Nov. 22, 2005). Assume that the study included 1,000 randomly selected items.

a. Identify the population parameter of interest in the study.

b. Set up H_0 and H_a for a test to determine if the true proportion of items scanned at California Walmart stores exceeds the 2% NIST standard.

c. Find the test statistic and rejection region (at $\alpha = .05$) for the test.

d. Give a practical interpretation of the test.

e. What conditions are required for the inference, part **d**, to be valid? Are these conditions met?

7.125 Paying for music downloads. If you use the Internet, have you ever paid to access or download music? This was one of the questions of interest in a *Pew Internet & American Life Project Survey* (October 2010). In a representative sample of 755 adults who use the Internet, 506 admitted that they have paid to download music. Let *p* represent the true proportion of all Internet-using adults who have paid to download music.

a. Compute a point estimate of *p*.

b. Set up the null and alternative hypotheses for testing whether the true proportion of all Internet-using adults who have paid to download music exceeds .7.

c. Compute the test statistic for part **b**.

d. Find the rejection region for the test if $\alpha = .01$.

e. Find the *p*-value for the test.

f. Make the appropriate conclusion using the rejection region.

g. Make the appropriate conclusion using the *p* value.

7.126 Size of diamonds sold at retail. Refer to the *Journal of Statistics Education* data on diamonds saved in the file. In Exercise 6.122 (p. 376) you selected a random sample of 30 diamonds from the 308 diamonds and found the mean and standard deviation of the number of carats per diamond for the sample. Let μ represent the mean number of carats in the population of 308 diamonds. Suppose you want to test $H_0: \mu = .6$ against $H_a: \mu \neq .6$.

a. In the words of the problem, define a Type I error and a Type II error.

b. Use the sample information to conduct the test at a significance level of $\alpha = .05$.

c. Conduct the test, part **b**, using $\alpha = .10$.

d. What do the results suggest about the choice of α in a test of hypothesis?

7.127 Accounting and Machiavellianism. Refer to the *Behavioral Research in Accounting* (January 2008) study of Machiavellian traits in accountants, Exercise 6.19 (p. 341). A Mach rating score was determined for each in a random sample of 122 purchasing managers, with the following results: $\bar{x} = 99.6, s = 12.6$. Recall that a director of purchasing at a major firm claims that the true mean Mach rating score of all purchasing managers is 85.

a. Suppose you want to test the director's claim. Specify the null and alternative hypotheses for the test.

b. Give the rejection region for the test using $\alpha = .10$.

c. Find the value of the test statistic.

d. Use the result, part **c**, to make the appropriate conclusion.

Applying the Concepts—Intermediate

7.128 Consumers' use of discount coupons. In 1894, druggist Asa Candler began distributing handwritten tickets to his customers for free glasses of Coca-Cola at his soda fountain. That was the genesis of the discount coupon. In 1975, it was estimated that 65% of U.S. consumers regularly used discount coupons when shopping. In a more recent consumer survey, 81% said they regularly redeem coupons (NCH Marketing Services 2015 Consumer Survey). Assume the recent survey consisted of a random sample of 1,000 shoppers.

a. Does the survey provide sufficient evidence that the percentage of shoppers using cents-off coupons exceeds 65%? Test using $\alpha = .05$.

b. Is the sample size large enough to use the inferential procedures presented in this section? Explain.

c. Find the observed significance level for the test you conducted in part **a** and interpret its value.

7.129 Errors in medical tests. Medical tests have been developed to detect many serious diseases. A medical test is designed to minimize the probability that it will produce a "false positive" or a "false negative." A *false positive* refers to a positive test result for an individual who does not have the disease, whereas a false negative is a negative test result for an individual who does have the disease.

a. If we treat a medical test for a disease as a statistical test of hypothesis, what are the null and alternative hypotheses for the medical test?

b. What are the Type I and Type II errors for the test? Relate each to false positives and false negatives.

c. Which of the errors has graver consequences? Considering this error, is it more important to minimize α or β? Explain.

7.130 Drivers' use of the Lincoln Tunnel. The Lincoln Tunnel (under the Hudson River) connects suburban New Jersey to midtown Manhattan. On Mondays at 8:30 A.M., the mean number of cars waiting in line to pay the Lincoln Tunnel toll is 1,220. Because of the substantial wait during rush hour, the Port Authority of New York and New Jersey is considering raising the amount of the toll between 7:30 and 8:30 A.M. to encourage more drivers to use the tunnel at an earlier or later time. Suppose the Port Authority experiments with peak-hour pricing for 6 months, increasing the toll from $4 to $7 during the rush hour peak. On 10 different workdays at 8:30 A.M. aerial photographs of the tunnel queues are taken and the number of vehicles counted. The results follow:

| 1,260 | 1,052 | 1,201 | 942 | 1,062 | 999 | 931 | 849 | 867 | 735 |

Analyze the data for the purpose of determining whether peak-hour pricing succeeded in reducing the average number of vehicles attempting to use the Lincoln Tunnel during the peak rush hour.

7.131 Point spreads of NFL games. Refer to the *Chance* (Fall 1998) study of point-spread errors in NFL games, Exercise 7.41 (p. 411). Recall that the difference between the actual game outcome and the point spread established by odds makers—the point-spread error—was calculated for 240 NFL games. The results are summarized as follows: $\bar{x} = -1.6, s = 13.3$. Suppose the researcher wants to know whether the true standard deviation of the point-spread errors exceeds 15. Conduct the analysis using $\alpha = .10$.

7.132 Improving the productivity of chickens. Refer to the *Applied Animal Behaviour Science* (October 2000) study of the color of string preferred by pecking domestic chickens, Exercise 6.124 (p. 376). Recall that $n = 72$ chickens were exposed to blue string and the number of pecks each chicken took at the string over a specified time interval had a mean of $\bar{x} = 1.13$ pecks and a standard deviation of $s = 2.21$ pecks. Also recall that previous research had shown that $\mu = 7.5$ pecks if chickens are exposed to white string.

a. Conduct a test (at $\alpha = .01$) to determine if the true mean number of pecks at blue string is less than $\mu = 7.5$ pecks.

b. In Exercise 6.122, you used a 99% confidence interval as evidence that chickens are more apt to peck at white string than blue string. Do the test results, part **a,** support this conclusion? Explain.

7.133 Are manufacturers satisfied with trade promotions? Sales promotions that are used by manufacturers to entice retailers to carry, feature, or push the manufacturer's products are called *trade promotions.* A survey of 132 manufacturers conducted by Nielsen found that 36% of the manufacturers were satisfied with their spending for trade promotions (*Survey of Trade Promotion Practices,* 2004). Is this sufficient evidence to reject a previous claim by the American Marketing Association that no more than half of all manufacturers are dissatisfied with their trade promotion spending?

a. Conduct the appropriate hypothesis test at $\alpha = .02$. Begin your analysis by determining whether the sample size is large enough to apply the testing methodology presented in this chapter.

b. Report the observed significance level of the test and interpret its meaning in the context of the problem.

c. Calculate β, the probability of a Type II error, if in fact 55% of all manufacturers are dissatisfied with their trade promotion spending.

7.134 Arresting shoplifters. Shoplifting in the United States costs retailers about $35 million a day. Despite the seriousness of the problem, the National Association of shoplifting Prevention (NASP) claims that only 50% of all shoplifters are turned over to police (www.shopliftingprevention.org). A random sample of 40 U.S. retailers were questioned concerning the disposition of the most recent shoplifter they apprehended. A total of 24 were turned over to police. Do these data provide sufficient evidence to contradict the NASP?

a. Conduct a hypothesis test to answer the question of interest. Use $\alpha = .05$.

b. Is the sample size large enough to use the inferential procedure of part **a**?

c. Find the observed significance level of the hypothesis test in part **a.** Interpret the value.

d. For what values of α would the observed significance level be sufficient to reject the null hypothesis of the test you conducted in part **b**?

*7.135 **Arresting shoplifters (cont'd).** Refer to Exercise 7.134.

a. Describe a Type II error in terms of this application.

b. Calculate the probability β of a Type II error for this test, assuming that the true fraction of shoplifters turned over to the police is $p = .55$.

c. Suppose the number of retailers sampled is increased from 40 to 100. How does this affect the probability of a Type II error for $p = .55$?

7.136 Frequency marketing programs by restaurants. To instill customer loyalty, airlines, hotels, rental car companies, and credit card companies (among others) have initiated *frequency marketing programs* that reward their regular customers. A large fast-food restaurant chain wished to explore the profitability of such a program. They randomly selected 12 of their 1,200 restaurants nationwide and instituted a frequency program that rewarded customers with a $5.00 gift certificate after every 10 meals purchased at full price. They ran the trial program for 3 months. The restaurants not in the sample had an average increase in profits of $1,050 over the previous 3 months, whereas the restaurants in the sample had the following changes in profit.

$2,232.90	$ 545.47	$3,440.70	$1,809.10
$6,552.70	$4,798.70	$2,965.00	$2,610.70
$3,381.30	$1,591.40	$2,376.20	−$2,191.00

Note that the last number is negative, representing a decrease in profits.

a. Specify the appropriate null and alternative hypotheses for determining whether the mean profit change for restaurants with frequency programs was significantly greater (in a statistical sense) than $1,050.

b. Conduct the test of part **b** using $\alpha = .05$. Does it appear that the frequency program would be profitable for the company if adopted nationwide?

7.137 EPA limits on vinyl chloride. The EPA sets an airborne limit of 5 parts per million (ppm) on vinyl chloride, a colorless gas used to make plastics, adhesives, and other chemicals. It is both a carcinogen and a mutagen (New Jersey Department of Health, *Hazardous Substance Fact Sheet,* 2010). A major plastics manufacturer, attempting to control the amount of vinyl chloride its workers are exposed to, has given instructions to halt production if the mean amount of vinyl chloride in the air exceeds 3.0 ppm. A random sample of 50 air specimens produced the following statistics: $\bar{x} = 3.1$ ppm, $s = .5$ ppm.

a. Do these statistics provide sufficient evidence to halt the production process? Use $\alpha = .01$.

b. If you were the plant manager, would you want to use a large or a small value for α for the test in part **a**? Explain.

c. Find the p-value for the test and interpret its value.

*7.138 **EPA limits vinyl chloride (cont'd).** Refer to Exercise 7.137.

a. In the context of the problem, define a Type II error.

b. Calculate β for the test described in part **a** of Exercise 7.137, assuming that the true mean is $\mu = 3.1$ ppm.

c. What is the power of the test to detect a departure from the manufacturer's 3.0 ppm limit when the mean is 3.1 ppm?

d. Repeat parts **b** and **c,** assuming that the true mean is 3.2 ppm. What happens to the power of the test as the plant's mean vinyl chloride level departs further from the limit?

*7.139 **EPA limits on vinyl chloride (cont'd).** Refer to Exercises 7.137 and 7.138.

a. Suppose an α-value of .05 is used to conduct the test. Does this change favor halting production? Explain.

b. Determine the value of β and the power for the test when $\alpha = .05$ and $\mu = 3.1$.

c. What happens to the power of the test when α is increased?

7.140 Unemployment and a reduced workweek. In an effort to increase employment, France mandated in February 2000 that all companies with 20 or more employees reduce the workweek to 35 hours. The economic impact of the short-ened workweek was analyzed in *Economic Policy* (July 2008). The researchers focused on several key variables such as hourly wages, dual-job holdings, and level of employment. Assume that in the year prior to the 35-hour-workweek law, unemployment in France was at 12%. Suppose that in a random sample of 500 French citizens (eligible workers) taken several years after the law was enacted, 53 were un-employed. Conduct a test of hypothesis to determine if the French unemployment rate dropped after the enactment of the 35-hour-workweek law. Test using $\alpha = .05$.

7.141 Do ball bearings conform to specifications? It is essential in the manufacture of machinery to use parts that conform to specifications. In the past, diameters of the ball bear-ings produced by a certain manufacturer had a variance of .00156. To cut costs, the manufacturer instituted a less expensive production method. The variance of the diam-eters of 100 randomly sampled bearings produced by the new process was .00211. Do the data provide sufficient evi-dence to indicate that diameters of ball bearings produced by the new process are more variable than those produced by the old process?

7.142 Feminized faces in TV commercials. Television commer-cials most often employ females or "feminized" males to pitch a company's product. Research published in *Nature* (August 27 1998) revealed that people are, in fact, more attracted to "feminized" faces, regardless of gender. In one experiment, 50 human subjects viewed both a Japanese fe-male face and a Caucasian male face on a computer. Using special computer graphics, each subject could morph the faces (by making them more feminine or more masculine) until they attained the "most attractive" face. The level of feminization x (measured as a percentage) was measured.

a. For the Japanese female face, $\bar{x} = 10.2\%$ and $s = 31.3\%$. The researchers used this sample infor-mation to test the null hypothesis of a mean level of feminization equal to 0%. Verify that the test statistic is equal to 2.3.

b. Refer to part **a**. The researchers reported the *p*-value of the test as $p = .021$. Verify and interpret this result.

c. For the Caucasian male face, $\bar{x} = 15.0\%$ and $s = 25.1\%$. The researchers reported the test statistic (for the test of the null hypothesis stated in part **a**) as 4.23 with an associated *p*-value of approximately 0. Verify and interpret these results.

7.143 Water distillation with solar energy. In countries with a wa-ter shortage, converting salt water to potable water is big business. The standard method of water distillation is with a single-slope solar still. Several enhanced solar energy water distillation systems were investigated in *Applied Solar Energy* (Vol. 46, 2010). One new system employs a sun-tracking meter and a step-wise basin. The new system was tested over 3 randomly selected days at a location in

DISTLL

Amman, Jordan. The daily amounts of distilled water col-lected by the new system over the 3 days were 5.07, 5.45, and 5.21 liters per square meter (l/m^2). Suppose it is known that the mean daily amount of distilled water collected by the standard method at the same location in Jordan is $\mu = 1.4 \ l/m^2$.

a. Set up the null and alternative hypotheses for de-termining whether the mean daily amount of dis-tilled water collected by the new system is greater than 1.4.

b. For this test, give a practical interpretation of the value $\alpha = .10$.

c. Find the mean and standard deviation of the distilled water amounts for the sample of 3 days.

d. Use the information from part **c** to calculate the test statistic.

e. Find the observed significance level (*p*-value) of the test.

f. State, practically, the appropriate conclusion.

Applying the Concepts—Advanced

7.144 Ages of cable TV shoppers. Cable TV's Home Shopping Network (HSN) reports that the average age of its shop-pers is 52 years. Suppose you want to test the null hy-pothesis, $H_0: \mu = 52$, using a sample of $n = 50$ cable TV shoppers.

a. Find the *p*-value of a two-tailed test if $\bar{x} = 53.3$ and $s = 7.1$.

b. Find the *p*-value of an upper-tailed test if $\bar{x} = 53.3$ and $s = 7.1$.

c. Find the *p*-value of a two-tailed test if $\bar{x} = 53.3$ and $s = 10.4$.

d. For each of the tests, parts **a–c**, give a value of α that will lead to a rejection of the null hypothesis.

e. If $\bar{x} = 53.3$, give a value of s that will yield a two-tailed *p*-value of .01 or less.

7.145 Factors that inhibit learning in marketing. What factors in-hibit the learning process in the classroom? To answer this question, researchers at Murray State University surveyed 40 students from a senior-level marketing class (*Marketing Education Review*). Each student was given a list of factors and asked to rate the extent to which each factor inhibited the learning process in courses offered in their depart-ment. A 7-point rating scale was used, where 1 = "not at all" and 7 = "to a great extent." The factor with the high-est rating was instructor related: "Professors who place too much emphasis on a single right answer rather than overall thinking and creative ideas." Summary statistics for the student ratings of this factor are $\bar{x} = 4.70$, $s = 1.62$.

a. Conduct a test to determine if the true mean rating for this instructor-related factor exceeds 4. Use $\alpha = .05$. Interpret the test results.

b. Examine the results of the study from a practical view, then discuss why "statistically significant" does not al-ways imply "practically significant."

c. Because the variable of interest, rating, is measured on a 7-point scale, it is unlikely that the population of rat-ings will be normally distributed. Consequently, some analysts may perceive the test, part **a**, to be invalid and search for alternative methods of analysis. Defend or refute this argument.

7.146 Testing the placebo effect. The *placebo effect* describes the phenomenon of improvement in the condition of a patient taking a placebo—a pill that looks and tastes real but contains no medically active chemicals. Physicians at a clinic in La Jolla, California, gave what they thought were drugs to 7,000 asthma, ulcer, and herpes patients. Although the doctors later learned that the drugs were really placebos, 70% of the patients reported an improved condition. Use this information to test (at $\alpha = .05$) the placebo effect at the clinic. Assume that if the placebo is ineffective, the probability of a patient's condition improving is .5.

Critical Thinking Challenge

7.147 The hot tamale caper. "Hot tamales" are chewy, cinnamon-flavored candies. A bulk vending machine is known to dispense, on average, 15 hot tamales per bag with a standard deviation of 3 per bag. *Chance* (Fall 2000) published an article on a classroom project in which students were required to purchase bags of hot tamales from the machine and count the number of candies per bag. One student group claimed they purchased five bags that had the following candy counts: 25, 23, 21, 21, and 20. These data are saved in the file. There was some question as to whether the students had fabricated the data. Use a hypothesis test to gain insight into whether or not the data collected by the students were fabricated. Use a level of significance that gives the benefit of the doubt to the students.

ACTIVITY 7.1   *Challenging a Company's Claim:* Tests of Hypotheses

Use the Internet or a newspaper or magazine to find an example of a claim made by a company about the reliability or efficiency of one of its products. In this activity, you represent a consumer group that believes the claim may be false.

1. In your example, what kinds of evidence might exist that would cause one to suspect that the claim might be false and therefore worthy of a statistical study? Be specific. If the claim were false, how would consumers be hurt?

2. Describe what data are relevant and how those data may be collected.

3. Explain the steps necessary to reject the company's claim at level α. State the null and alternative hypotheses. If you reject the claim, does it mean that the claim is false?

4. If you reject the claim when the claim is actually true, what type of error has occurred? What is the probability of this error occurring?

5. If you were to file a lawsuit against the company based on your rejection of its claim, how might the company use your results to defend itself?

ACTIVITY 7.2   *Keep the Change:* Tests of Hypotheses

In this activity, we will test claims that the mean amount transferred for any single purchase is $0.50 and that the mean amount that Bank of America matches for a customer during the first 90 days of enrollment is at least $25. We will be working with data sets from Activity 1.1, page 54 and Activity 2.2, page 148.

1. Based on the assumption that all transfer amounts between $0.00 and $0.99 seem to be equally likely to occur, one may conclude that the mean of the amounts transferred is about $0.50. Explain how someone who doesn't believe this conclusion would use a test of hypothesis to argue that the conclusion is false.

2. Suppose that your original data set *Amounts Transferred* from Activity 1.1 represents a random sample of amounts transferred for all Bank of America customers' purchases. Does your sample meet the requirements for performing either a large-sample or a small-sample test of hypothesis about the population mean? Explain. If your data meet the criteria for one of the tests, perform that test at $\alpha = .05$.

3. Use the pooled data set of *Amounts Transferred* from Activity 4.2 to represent a random sample of amounts transferred for all Bank of America customers' purchases. Explain how the conditions for the large-sample test of hypothesis about a population mean are met. Then perform the test at $\alpha = .05$. Do your results suggest that the mean may be something other than $0.50? Explain.

4. A friend suggests to you that the mean amount the bank matches for a customer during the first 90 days is at least $25. Explain how you could use a test of hypothesis to argue that your friend is wrong.

5. Suppose that your data set *Bank Matching* from Activity 1.1 represents a random sample of all Bank of America customers' bank matching. Perform an appropriate test of hypothesis at $\alpha = .05$ against your friend's claim. Assume that the underlying distribution is normal, if necessary. Does the test provide evidence that your friend's claim is false?

Keep the results from this activity for use in other activities.

References

Snedecor, G. W., and Cochran, W. G. *Statistical Methods,* 7th ed. Ames, IA: Iowa State University Press, 1980.

Wackerly, D., Mendenhall, W., and Scheaffer, R. *Mathematical Statistics with Applications,* 7th ed. Belmont, CA: Thomson, Brooks/Cole, 2008.

SPSS: Tests of Hypotheses

Note: SPSS cannot currently conduct a test for a population variance.

Testing μ

Step 1 Access the SPSS spreadsheet file that contains the sample data.

Step 2 Click on the "Analyze" button on the SPSS menu bar and then click on "Compare Means" and "One-Sample T Test," as shown in Figure 7.S.1.

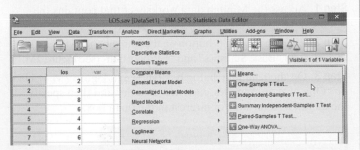

Figure 7.S.1 SPSS menu options for a test on a mean

Step 3 On the resulting dialog box (shown in Figure 7.S.2), specify the quantitative variable of interest in the "Test Variable(s)" box and the value of μ_0 for the null hypothesis in the "Test Value" box.

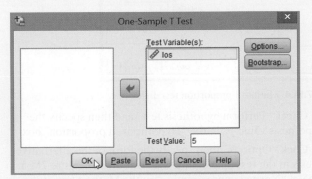

Figure 7.S.2 SPSS 1-sample *t*-test for mean dialog box

Step 4 Click "OK." SPSS will automatically conduct a two-tailed test of hypothesis.

Important Note: The SPSS one-sample *t*-procedure uses the *t*-statistic to conduct the test of hypothesis. When the sample size *n* is small, this is the appropriate method. When the sample size *n* is large, the *t*-value will be approximately equal to the large-sample *z*-value and the resulting test will still be valid.

Testing p

Step 1 Access the SPSS spreadsheet file that contains the sample data.

Step 2 Click on the "Analyze" button on the SPSS menu bar, then click on "Nonparametric Tests," "Legacy Dialogs," and "Binomial" (see Figure 7.S.3).

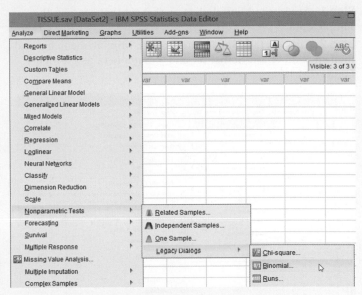

Figure 7.S.3 SPSS menu options for test on a proportion

Step 3 On the resulting dialog box (shown in Figure 7.S.4), specify the binomial variable of interest in the "Test Variable List" box and the value of p_0 for the null hypothesis in the "Test Proportion" box.

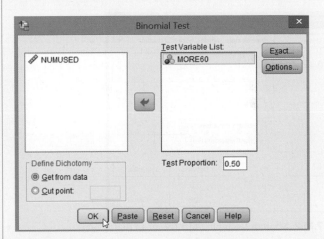

Figure 7.S.4 SPSS binomial test for proportion dialog box

Step 4 Click "OK." to generate the two-tailed test of hypothesis.

Important: SPSS requires the binomial variable to be entered as a quantitative variable. Typically, this is accomplished by entering two numerical values (e.g., 0 and 1) for the two outcomes of the variable. If the data have been entered in this fashion, select the "Get from data" option in the "Define Dichotomy" area of the dialog box.

You can also create the two outcome values for a quantitative variable by selecting the "Cut point" option in the "Define Dichotomy" area and specifying a numerical value. All values of the variables less than or equal to the cut point value are assigned to one group (success), and all other values are assigned to the other group (failure).

Minitab: Tests of Hypotheses

Testing μ

Step 1 Access the Minitab data worksheet that contains the sample data.

Step 2 Click on the "Stat" button on the Minitab menu bar and then click on "Basic Statistics" and "1-Sample t," as shown in Figure 7.M.1.

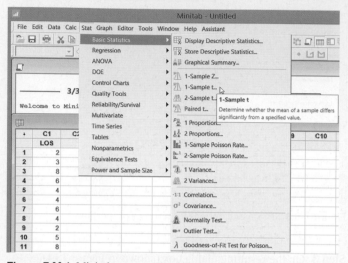

Figure 7.M.1 Minitab menu options for a test on a mean

Step 3 On the resulting dialog box (shown in Figure 7.M.2), click on "One or more samples, each in a column" and then specify the quantitative variable of interest in the open box.

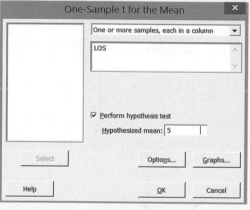

Figure 7.M.2 Minitab 1-sample *t*-test for mean dialog box

Step 4 Check "Perform hypothesis test" and then specify the value of μ_0 for the null hypothesis in the "Hypothesized mean" box.

Step 5 Click on the "Options" button at the bottom of the dialog box and specify the form of the alternative hypothesis, as shown in Figure 7.M.3.

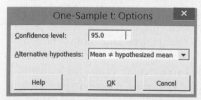

Figure 7.M.3 Minitab 1-sample *t*-test options

Step 6 Click "OK" to return to the "1-Sample t" dialog box and then click "OK" again to produce the hypothesis test.

Note: If you want to produce a test for the mean from summary information (e.g., the sample mean, sample standard deviation, and sample size), click on "Summarized data" in the "1-Sample t" dialog box, enter the values of the summary statistics and μ_0, and then click "OK."

Important: The Minitab one-sample *t*-procedure uses the *t*-statistic to generate the hypothesis test. When the sample size *n* is small, this is the appropriate method. When the sample size *n* is large, the *t*-value will be approximately equal to the large-sample *z*-value, and the resulting test will still be valid. If you have a large sample and you know the value of the population standard deviation σ (which is rarely the case), select "1-Sample Z" from the "Basic Statistics" menu options (see Figure 7.M.1) and make the appropriate selections.

Testing *p*

Step 1 Access the Minitab data worksheet that contains the sample data.

Step 2 Click on the "Stat" button on the Minitab menu bar and then click on "Basic Statistics" and "1 Proportion" (see Figure 7.M.1).

Step 3 On the resulting dialog box (shown in Figure 7.M.4), click on "One or more samples, each in a column" and then specify the qualitative variable of interest in the open box.

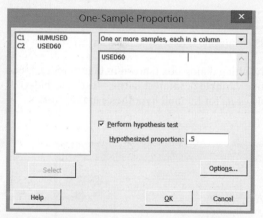

Figure 7.M.4 Minitab 1 proportion test dialog box

Step 4 Check "Perform hypothesis test" and then specify the null hypothesis value p_0 in the "Hypothesized proportion" box.

Step 5 Click "Options," then specify the form of the alternative hypothesis in the resulting dialog box, as shown in Figure 7.M.5. Also, select "Normal approximation" in the Method box at the bottom.

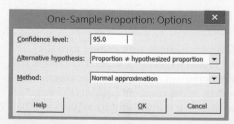

Figure 7.M.5 Minitab 1 proportion test options

Step 6 Click "OK" to return to the "1 Proportion" dialog box and then click "OK" again to produce the test results.

Note: If you want to produce a confidence interval for a proportion from summary information (e.g., the number of successes and the sample size), click on "Summarized data" in the "1 Proportion" dialog box (see Figure 7.M.4). Enter the value for the number of trials (i.e., the sample size) and the number of events (i.e., the number of successes), and then click "OK."

Testing σ^2

Step 1 Access the Minitab data worksheet that contains the sample data set.

Step 2 Click on the "Stat" button on the Minitab menu bar and then click on "Basic Statistics" and "1 Variance" (see Figure 7.M.1).

Step 3 Once the resulting dialog box appears (see Figure 7.M.6), click on "One or more samples, each in a column" and then specify the quantitative variable of interest in the open box.

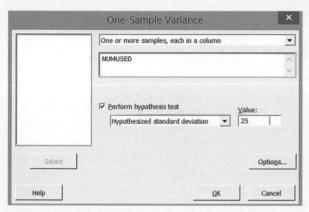

Figure 7.M.6 Minitab 1 variance test dialog box

Step 4 Check "Perform hypothesis test" and specify the null hypothesis value of the standard deviation σ_0 in the open box.

Step 5 Click on the "Options" button at the bottom of the dialog box and specify the form of the alternative hypothesis (similar to Figure 7.M.3).

Step 6 Click "OK" twice to produce the hypothesis test.

Note: If you want to produce a test for the variance from summary information (e.g., the sample standard deviation and sample size), click on "Summarized data" in the "1 Variance" dialog box (Figure 7.M.6) and enter the values of the summary statistics.

Excel/XLSTAT: Tests of Hypotheses

Testing μ

Step 1 Click the "XLSTAT" button on the Excel main menu bar, select "Parametric tests," and then click "One-sample t-test and z-test," as shown in Figure 7.E.1.

Step 2 When the resulting dialog box appears, highlight the column that contains the values of the quantitative variable you want to analyze so that the column appears in the appropriate "Data" entry (see, for example, Figure 7.E.2).

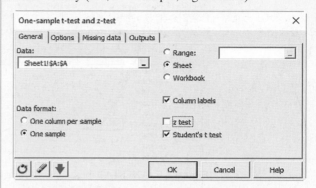

Figure 7.E.2 XLSTAT test mean dialog box

Step 3 Click the "Options" tab, then specify the form of the alternative hypothesis, value of the hypothesized (theoretical) mean, and the value of α (significance level) in the appropriate boxes, as shown in Figure 7.E.3.

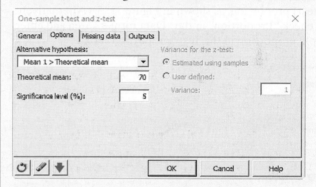

Figure 7.E.3 XLSTAT options for testing a mean

Step 4 Click "OK," then "Continue" to display the test results.

Testing p

[*Note:* To conduct a test of hypothesis for a binomial proportion using XLSTAT, you will need summary information on your qualitative data, e.g., the sample size and either the number of successes or proportion of successes in the sample.]

Step 1 Click the "XLSTAT" button on the Excel main menu bar, select "Parametric tests," and then click "Tests for one proportion," as shown in Figure 7.E.4.

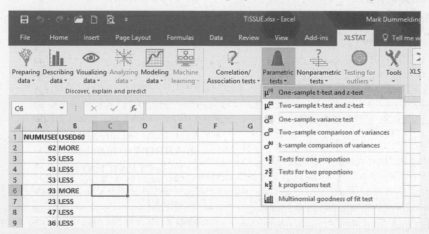

Figure 7.E.1 XLSTAT menu options for testing a mean

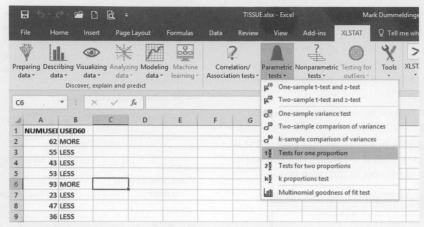

Figure 7.E.4 XLSTAT menu options for a binomial proportion

Step 2 When the resulting dialog box appears, check "Frequency" in the "Data format" area, enter the number of successes and the sample size in the "Frequency" and "Sample size" boxes, respectively, and then specify the value of the hypothesized (test) proportion, as shown in Figure 7.E.5. (Alternatively, you can check "Proportion" in the "Data format" area and enter the sample proportion in the Test "proportion" box.)

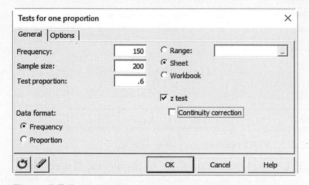

Figure 7.E.5 XLSTAT test for proportion dialog box

Step 3 Click the "Options" tab, specify the form of the alternative hypothesis, and then enter "0" for the hypothesized difference and the value of α (significance level) in the appropriate boxes, as shown in Figure 7.E.6.

Figure 7.E.6 XLSTAT options for testing a proportion

Step 4 Click "OK" to display the test results.

Testing σ^2

Step 1 Click the "XLSTAT" button on the Excel main menu bar, select "Parametric tests," and then click "One-sample variance test" (see menu options in Figure 7.E.1).

Step 2 When the resulting dialog box appears, highlight the column that contains the values of the quantitative variable you want to analyze so that the column appears in the appropriate "Data" entry (similar to Figure 7.E.2).

Step 3 Click the "Options" tab and then specify the form of the alternative hypothesis, the value of the hypothesized (theoretical) variance, and the value of α (significance level) in the appropriate boxes, as shown in Figure 7.E.7.

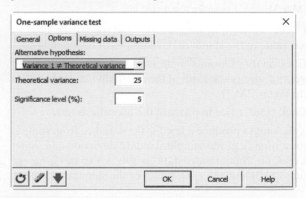

Figure 7.E.7 XLSTAT Options for Testing a Variance

Step 4 Click "OK," and then "Continue" to display the test results.

TI-84 Graphing Calculator: Tests of Hypotheses

Note: The TI-84 graphing calculator cannot currently conduct a test for a population variance.

Testing μ

Step 1 *Enter the Data (Skip to Step 2 if you have summary statistics, not raw data)*

• Press **STAT** and select **1:Edit**

Note: If the list already contains data, clear the old data. Use the up **ARROW** to highlight "**L1.**"

• Press **CLEAR ENTER**

• Use the **ARROW** and **ENTER** keys to enter the data set into **L1**

Step 2 *Access the Statistical Tests Menu*

• Press **STAT**

- Arrow right to **TESTS**
- Press **ENTER** to select either **Z-Test** (if large sample and σ known) or **T-Test** (if small sample and σ unknown)

Step 3 *Choose "**Data**" or "**Stats.**" ("Data" is selected when you have entered the raw data into a List. "Stats" is selected when you are given only the mean, standard deviation, and sample size.)*

- Press **ENTER**

If you selected "Data," enter the values for the hypothesis test where $\mu_0 = $ the value for μ in the null hypothesis, $\sigma = $ assumed value of the population standard deviation.

- Set **List** to **L1**
- Set **Freq** to **1**
- Use the **ARROW** to highlight the appropriate alternative hypothesis
- Press **ENTER**
- Arrow down to **"Calculate"**
- Press **ENTER**

If you selected "Stats," enter the values for the hypothesis test where $\mu_0 = $ the value for μ in the null hypothesis, $\sigma = $ assumed value of the population standard deviation.

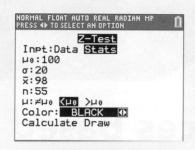

- Enter the sample mean, sample standard deviation, and sample size
- Use the **ARROW** to highlight the appropriate alternative hypothesis
- Press **ENTER**
- Arrow down to **"Calculate"**
- Press **ENTER**

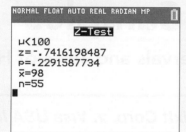

The chosen test will be displayed as well as the z (or t) test statistic, the p-value, the sample mean, and the sample size.

Testing p

Step 1 *Enter the Data (Skip to Step 2 if you have summary statistics, not raw data)*

- Press **STAT** and select **1:Edit**

Note: If the list already contains data, clear the old data. Use the up **ARROW** to highlight **"L1."**

- Press **CLEAR ENTER**
- Use the **ARROW** and **ENTER** keys to enter the data set into **L1**

Step 2 *Access the Statistical Tests Menu*

- Press **STAT**
- Arrow right to **TESTS**
- Press **ENTER** after selecting **1-Prop Z Test**

Step 3 *Enter the hypothesized proportion p_0, the number of success x, and the sample size n*

- Use the **ARROW** to highlight the appropriate alternative hypothesis
- Press **ENTER**
- Arrow down to **"Calculate"**
- Press **ENTER**

The chosen test will be displayed as well as the z-test statistic and the p-value.

8

WHERE WE'VE BEEN

- Explored two methods for making statistical inferences: *confidence intervals* and *tests of hypotheses*

- Studied confidence intervals and tests for a single population mean μ, a single population proportion p, and a single population variance σ^2

- Learned how to select the sample size necessary to estimate a population parameter with a specified margin of error

WHERE WE'RE GOING

- Learn how to identify the target parameter for comparing two populations (8.1)

- Learn how to compare two population means using confidence intervals and tests of hypotheses (8.2–8.3)

- Apply these inferential methods to problems where we want to compare two population proportions or two population variances (8.4, 8.6)

- Determine the sizes of the samples necessary to estimate the difference between two population parameters with a specified margin of error (8.5)

Inferences Based on Two Samples

Confidence Intervals and Tests of Hypotheses

STATISTICS IN ACTION   *ZixIt Corp. v. Visa USA Inc.* — A Libel Case

The National Law Journal *(Aug. 26–Sep. 2, 2002) reported on an interesting court case involving ZixIt Corp., a start-up Internet credit card clearing center. ZixIt claimed that its new online credit card processing system would allow Internet shoppers to make purchases without revealing their credit card numbers. This claim violated the established protocols of most major credit card companies, including Visa. Without the company's knowledge, a Visa vice president for technology research and development began writing emails and Web site postings on a Yahoo! message board for ZixIt investors, challenging ZixIt's claim and urging investors to sell their ZixIt stock. The Visa executive posted more than 400 emails and notes before he was caught. Once it was discovered that a Visa executive was responsible for the postings, ZixIt filed a lawsuit against Visa Corp., alleging that Visa—using the executive as its agent—had engaged in a "malicious two-part scheme to disparage and interfere with ZixIt" and its efforts to market the new online credit card processing system. In the libel case ZixIt asked for $699 million in damages.*

Dallas lawyers Jeff Tillotson and Mike Lynn, of the law firm Lynn, Tillotson & Pinker, were hired to defend Visa in the lawsuit. The lawyers, in turn, hired Dr. James McClave (coauthor of this text) as their expert statistician. McClave testified in court on an "event study" he did matching the Visa executive's email postings with movement of ZixIt's stock price the next business day. McClave's testimony, showing that there was an equal number of days when the stock went up as went down after a posting, helped the lawyers representing Visa to prevail in the case.

STATISTICS IN ACTION

(continued)

The National Law Journal reported that, after two-and-a-half days of deliberation, "the jurors found [the Visa executive] was not acting in the scope of his employment and that Visa had not defamed ZixIt or interfered with its business."

In this chapter, we demonstrate several of the statistical analyses McClave used to infer that the Visa executive's postings had no effect on ZixIt's stock price. The daily ZixIt stock prices as well as the timing of the Visa executive's postings are saved in the **ZIXVSA** file.* We apply the statistical methodology presented in this chapter to this data set in two *Statistics in Action Revisited* examples.

STATISTICS IN ACTION REVISITED

- Comparing Mean Price Changes **(p. 463)**
- Comparing Proportions **(p. 486)**

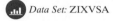 *Data Set:* ZIXVSA

8.1 Identifying the Target Parameter

Many experiments involve a comparison of two populations. For instance, a realtor may want to estimate the difference in mean sales price between city and suburban homes. A consumer group might test whether two major brands of food freezers differ in the average amount of electricity they use. A television market researcher wants to estimate the difference in the proportions of younger and older viewers who regularly watch a popular TV program. A golf ball supplier may be interested in comparing the variability in the distance that two competing brands of golf balls travel when struck with the same club. In this chapter, we consider techniques for using two samples to compare the populations from which they were selected.

The same procedures that are used to estimate and test hypotheses about a single population can be modified to make inferences about two populations. As in Chapters 6 and 7, the methodology used will depend on the sizes of the samples and the parameter of interest (i.e., the *target parameter*). Some key words and the type of data associated with the parameters covered in this chapter are listed in the box.

Determining the Target Parameter

Parameter	Key Words or Phrases	Type of Data
$\mu_1 - \mu_2$	Mean difference; difference in averages	Quantitative
$p_1 - p_2$	Difference between proportions, percentages, fractions, or rates; compare proportions	Qualitative
$(\sigma_1)^2/(\sigma_2)^2$	Ratio of variances; difference in variability or spread; compare variation	Quantitative

You can see that the key words *difference* and *compare* help identify the fact that two populations are to be compared. For the examples given above, the words *mean* in *mean sales price* and *average* in *average amount of electricity* imply that the target parameter is the difference in population means, $\mu_1 - \mu_2$. The word *proportions* in *proportions of younger and older viewers* indicates that the target parameter is the difference in proportions, $p_1 - p_2$. Finally, the key word *variability* in *variability in the distance* identifies the ratio of population variances, $(\sigma_1)^2/(\sigma_2)^2$, as the target parameter.

As with inferences about a single population, the type of data (quantitative or qualitative) collected on the two samples is also indicative of the target parameter. With quantitative data, you are likely to be interested in comparing the means or variances of

*Data provided (with permission) from Info Tech, Inc., Gainesville, Florida.

the data. With qualitative data with two outcomes (success or failure), a comparison of the proportions of successes is likely to be of interest.

We consider methods for comparing two population means in Sections 8.2 and 8.3. A comparison of population proportions is presented in Section 8.4 and population variances in Section 8.6. We show how to determine the sample sizes necessary for reliable estimates of the target parameters in Section 8.5.

8.2 Comparing Two Population Means: Independent Sampling

In this section we develop both large-sample and small-sample methodologies for comparing two population means. In the large-sample case, we use the z-statistic (where $z \approx t$ when the population variances are unknown), while in the small-sample case we use the t-statistic.

Large Samples

EXAMPLE 8.1

Large-Sample Confidence Interval for $(\mu_1 - \mu_2)$—Comparing Mean Car Prices

Problem In recent years, the United States and Japan have engaged in intense negotiations regarding restrictions on trade between the two countries. One of the claims made repeatedly by U.S. officials is that many Japanese manufacturers price their goods higher in Japan than in the United States, in effect subsidizing low prices in the United States by extremely high prices in Japan. According to the U.S. argument, Japan accomplishes this by keeping competitive U.S. goods from reaching the Japanese marketplace.

An economist decided to test the hypothesis that higher retail prices are being charged for Japanese automobiles in Japan than in the United States. She obtained independent random samples of 50 retail sales in the United States and 50 retail sales in Japan over the same time period and for the same model of automobile and converted the Japanese sales prices from yen to dollars using current conversion rates. The data, saved in the **AUTOS** file, are listed in Table 8.1. Form a 95% confidence interval for the difference between the population mean retail prices of this automobile model for the two countries. Interpret the result.

Solution Recall that the general form of a large-sample confidence interval for a single mean μ is $\bar{x} \pm z_{\alpha/2}\sigma_{\bar{x}}$—that is, we add and subtract $z_{\alpha/2}$ standard deviations of the sample estimate, $\bar{x}$, to the value of the estimate. We employ a similar procedure to form the confidence interval for the difference between two population means.

Let μ_1 represent the mean of the population of retail sales prices for this car model sold in the United States. Let μ_2 be similarly defined for retail sales in Japan. We wish to form a confidence interval for $(\mu_1 - \mu_2)$. An intuitively appealing estimator for

Table 8.1	Automobile Retail Prices (Thousands of Dollars)								
USA Sales:	28.2	26.2	27.2	28.7	28.4	26.6	24.9	26.8	22.1	20.8
	28.5	25.5	26.2	26.3	28.2	29.5	23.2	26.8	22.9	27.2
	28.2	26.3	26.8	26.4	28.6	25.6	27.1	28.1	28.9	29.0
	27.3	28.8	24.9	26.7	30.3	27.1	24.6	27.2	23.0	28.4
	26.9	23.3	26.3	25.9	26.6	27.6	26.0	27.1	24.6	28.0
Japan Sales:	28.5	24.0	28.2	31.1	23.9	28.7	24.9	26.4	26.3	28.0
	26.8	29.8	27.3	26.6	24.9	26.3	26.5	25.4	27.6	30.1
	26.4	28.0	27.5	28.4	29.8	24.8	28.2	26.7	30.2	26.2
	30.4	27.9	25.5	25.4	27.7	27.1	27.9	27.4	28.2	26.2
	28.5	26.9	27.6	24.4	31.6	28.6	26.2	24.3	22.5	30.0

Data Set: AUTOS

Group Statistics

	COUNTRY	N	Mean	Std. Deviation	Std. Error Mean
PRICE	USA	50	26596.00	1981.440	280.218
	JAPAN	50	27236.00	1974.093	279.179

Independent Samples Test

		Levene's Test for Equality of Variances		t-test for Equality of Means					95% Confidence Interval of the Difference	
		F	Sig.	t	df	Sig. (2-tailed)	Mean Difference	Std. Error Difference	Lower	Upper
PRICE	Equal variances assumed	.118	.732	-1.618	98	.109	-640.000	395.554	-1424.964	144.964
	Equal variances not assumed			-1.618	97.999	.109	-640.000	395.554	-1424.964	144.964

Figure 8.1

SPSS summary statistics and confidence interval for automobile price study

$(\mu_1 - \mu_2)$ is the difference between the sample means, $(\bar{x}_1 - \bar{x}_2)$. Thus, we will form the confidence interval of interest by

$$(\bar{x}_1 - \bar{x}_2) \pm z_{\sigma/2} \sigma_{(\bar{x}_1 - \bar{x}_2)}$$

Assuming the two samples are independent, the standard deviation of the difference between the sample means is

$$\sigma_{(\bar{x}_1 - \bar{x}_2)} = \sqrt{\frac{\sigma_1^2}{n_1} + \frac{\sigma_2^2}{n_2}} \approx \sqrt{\frac{s_1^2}{n_1} + \frac{s_2^2}{n_2}}$$

Note that we have substituted s_1^2 and s_2^2 for the usually unknown values of σ_1^2 and σ_2^2, respectively. With large samples, this will be a good approximation.

Summary statistics for the car sales data are displayed in the SPSS printout, Figure 8.1. Note that $\bar{x}_1 = \$26,596$, $\bar{x}_2 = \$27,236$, $s_1 = \$1,981$, and $s_2 = \$1,974$. Using these values and noting that $\alpha = .05$ and $z_{.025} = 1.96$, we find that the 95% confidence interval is, approximately,

$$(26,596 - 27,236) \pm 1.96\sqrt{\frac{(1,981)^2}{50} + \frac{(1,974)^2}{50}} = -640 \pm (1.96)(396)$$

$$= -640 \pm 776$$

or $(-1416, 136)$. This interval is also given at the bottom of Figure 8.1. (Differences in the results are due to rounding and normal approximation.)

Using this estimation procedure over and over again for different samples, we know that approximately 95% of the confidence intervals formed in this manner will enclose the difference in population means $(\mu_1 - \mu_2)$. Therefore, we are highly confident that the difference in mean retail prices in the United States and Japan is between $-\$1,416$ and $\$136$. Because 0 falls in this interval, it is possible for the difference to be 0 (i.e., for $\mu_1 = \mu_2$); thus, the economist cannot conclude that a significant difference exists between the mean retail prices in the two countries.

Look Back If the confidence interval for $(\mu_1 - \mu_2)$ contains all positive numbers [e.g., $(527, 991)$], then we would conclude that the difference between the means is positive and that $\mu_1 > \mu_2$. Alternatively, if the interval contains all negative numbers [e.g., $(-722, -145)$], then we would conclude that the difference between the means is negative and that $\mu_1 < \mu_2$.

> **Now Work Exercise 8.3a**

The justification for the procedure used in Example 8.1 to estimate $(\mu_1 - \mu_2)$ relies on the properties of the sampling distribution of $(\bar{x}_1 - \bar{x}_2)$. The performance of the estimator in repeated sampling is pictured in Figure 8.2, and its properties are summarized in the box on the next page.

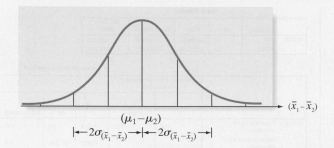

Figure 8.2

Sampling distribution of $(\bar{x}_1 - \bar{x}_2)$

Properties of the Sampling Distribution of $(\bar{x}_1 - \bar{x}_2)$

1. The mean of the sampling distribution $(\bar{x}_1 - \bar{x}_2)$ is $(\mu_1 - \mu_2)$.

2. If the two samples are independent, the standard deviation of the sampling distribution is

$$\sigma_{(\bar{x}_1 - \bar{x}_2)} = \sqrt{\frac{\sigma_1^2}{n_1} + \frac{\sigma_2^2}{n_2}}$$

where σ_1^2 and σ_2^2 are the variances of the two populations being sampled, and n_1 and n_2 are the respective sample sizes. We also refer to $\sigma_{(\bar{x}_1 - \bar{x}_2)}$ as the **standard error** of the statistic $(\bar{x}_1 - \bar{x}_2)$.

3. The sampling distribution of $(\bar{x}_1 - \bar{x}_2)$ is approximately normal for *large samples* by the Central Limit Theorem.

In Example 8.1, we noted the similarity in the procedures for forming a large-sample confidence interval for one population mean and a large-sample confidence interval for the difference between two population means. When we are testing hypotheses, the procedures are again very similar. The general large-sample procedures for forming confidence intervals and testing hypotheses about $(\mu_1 - \mu_2)$ are summarized in the following boxes.

Large, Independent Samples Confidence Interval for $(\mu_1 - \mu_2)$: Normal (z) Statistic

σ_1^2 and σ_2^2 known: $(\bar{x}_1 - \bar{x}_2) \pm z_{\alpha/2}\sigma_{(\bar{x}_1 - \bar{x}_2)} = (\bar{x}_1 - \bar{x}_2) \pm z_{\alpha/2}\sqrt{\dfrac{\sigma_1^2}{n_1} + \dfrac{\sigma_2^2}{n_2}}$

σ_1^2 and σ_2^2 unknown: $(\bar{x}_1 - \bar{x}_2) \pm z_{\alpha/2}\sigma_{(\bar{x}_1 - \bar{x}_2)} \approx (\bar{x}_1 - \bar{x}_2) \pm z_{\alpha/2}\sqrt{\dfrac{s_1^2}{n_1} + \dfrac{s_2^2}{n_2}}$

Large, Independent Samples Test of Hypothesis for $(\mu_1 - \mu_2)$: Normal (z) Statistic

One-Tailed Test	Two-Tailed Test
$H_0: (\mu_1 - \mu_2) = D_0$	$H_0: (\mu_1 - \mu_2) = D_0$
$H_a: (\mu_1 - \mu_2) < D_0$	$H_a: (\mu_1 - \mu_2) \neq D_0$
[or $H_a: (\mu_1 - \mu_2) > D_0$]	

where $D_0 =$ Hypothesized~normal difference between the means (this difference is often hypothesized to be equal to 0)

Test statistic:

$$z = \frac{(\bar{x}_1 - \bar{x}_2) - D_0}{\sigma_{(\bar{x}_1 - \bar{x}_2)}} \quad \text{where} \quad \sigma_{(\bar{x}_1 - \bar{x}_2)} = \sqrt{\frac{\sigma_1^2}{n_1} + \frac{\sigma_2^2}{n_2}} \text{ if } \sigma_1^2 \text{ and } \sigma_2^2 \text{ are known}$$

$$\approx \sqrt{\frac{s_1^2}{n_1} + \frac{s_2^2}{n_2}} \text{ if } \sigma_1^2 \text{ and } \sigma_2^2 \text{ are unknown}$$

One-Tailed Test	Two-Tailed Test
Rejection region: $z < -z_\alpha$	*Rejection region:* $\|z\| > z_{\alpha/2}$
[or $z > z_\alpha$ when $H_a: (\mu_1 - \mu_2) > D_0$]	
p-value $= P(z < z_c)$ [or $P(z > z_c)$]	*p-value* $= 2P(z > \|z_c\|)$
where z_c is the calculated value of the test statistic.	

Conditions Required for Valid Large-Sample Inferences About $(\mu_1 - \mu_2)$

1. The two samples are randomly selected in an independent manner from the two target populations.
2. The sample sizes, n_1 and n_2, are both large (i.e., $n_1 \geq 30$ and $n_2 \geq 30$). [Due to the Central Limit Theorem, this condition guarantees that the sampling distribution of $(\bar{x}_1 - \bar{x}_2)$ will be approximately normal regardless of the shapes of the underlying probability distributions of the populations. Also, s_1^2 and s_2^2 will provide good approximations to σ_1^2 and σ_2^2 when the samples are both large.]

EXAMPLE 8.2

Large-Sample Test for $(\mu_1 - \mu_2)$—Comparing Mean Car Prices

Problem Refer to the study of retail prices of an automobile sold in the United States and Japan, Example 8.1. Another way to compare the mean retail prices for the two countries is to conduct a test of hypothesis. Use the information on the SPSS printout, Figure 8.1, to conduct the test. Use $\alpha = .05$.

Solution Again, we let μ_1 and μ_2 represent the population mean retail sales prices in the United States and Japan, respectively. If the claim made by the U.S. government is true, then the mean retail price in Japan will exceed the mean in the United States [i.e., $\mu_1 < \mu_2$ or $(\mu_1 - \mu_2) < 0$]. Thus, the elements of the test are as follows:

$H_0: (\mu_1 - \mu_2) = 0$ (i.e., $\mu_1 = \mu_2$; note that $D_0 = 0$ for this hypothesis test)

$H_a: (\mu_1 - \mu_2) < 0$ (i.e., $\mu_1 < \mu_2$)

Test statistic: $z = \dfrac{(\bar{x}_1 - \bar{x}_2) - D_0}{\sigma_{(\bar{x}_1 - \bar{x}_2)}} = \dfrac{(\bar{x}_1 - \bar{x}_2) - 0}{\sigma_{(\bar{x}_1 - \bar{x}_2)}}$

Rejection region: $z < -z_{.05} = -1.645$ (see Figure 8.3)

Substituting the summary statistics given in Figure 8.1 into the test statistic, we obtain

$$z = \frac{(\bar{x}_1 - \bar{x}_2) - 0}{\sigma_{(x_1 - x_2)}} = \frac{(26{,}596 - 27{,}236)}{\sqrt{\dfrac{\sigma_1^2}{n_1} + \dfrac{\sigma_2^2}{n_2}}}$$

$$\approx \frac{-640}{\sqrt{\dfrac{s_1^2}{n_1} + \dfrac{s_2^2}{n_2}}} = \frac{-640}{\sqrt{\dfrac{(1{,}981)^2}{50} + \dfrac{(1{,}974)^2}{50}}} = \frac{-640}{396} = -1.62$$

This value of the test statistic is shown (highlighted) at the bottom of the SPSS printout, Figure 8.1 (p. 455).

As you can see in Figure 8.3, the calculated z-value does not fall in the rejection region. Therefore, the samples do not provide sufficient evidence, at $\alpha = .05$, for the economist to conclude that the mean retail price in Japan exceeds that in the United States.

Look Back First, note that this conclusion agrees with the inference drawn from the 95% confidence interval in Example 8.1. Generally, however, a confidence interval will provide more information on the difference in means than a test. A test can detect only whether or not a difference between the means exists, while the confidence interval provides information on the magnitude of the difference. Second, a one-tailed hypothesis test and a confidence interval (which is two-tailed) may not always agree. However, a two-tailed test of hypothesis and a confidence interval will *always* give the same inference about the target parameter, as long as the value of α is the same for both.

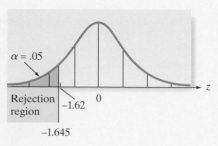

Figure 8.3

Rejection region for Example 8.2

EXAMPLE 8.3

The *p*-Value of a Test for $(\mu_1 - \mu_2)$

Problem Find the observed significance level for the test in Example 8.2. Interpret the result.

Solution The alternative hypothesis in Example 8.2, H_a: $(\mu_1 - \mu_2) < 0$, required a lower one-tailed test using

$$z = \frac{\bar{x}_1 - \bar{x}_2}{\sigma_{(\bar{x}_1 - \bar{x}_2)}}$$

as a test statistic. Because the approximate *z*-value calculated from the sample data was -1.62, the observed significance level (*p*-value) for the lower-tailed test is the probability of observing a value of *z* more contradictory to the null hypothesis as $z = -1.62$; that is,

$$p\text{-value} = P(z < -1.62)$$

This probability is computed assuming H_0 is true and is equal to the shaded area shown in Figure 8.4.

The tabulated area corresponding to $z = 1.62$ in Table II in Appendix D is .4474. Therefore, the observed significance level of the test is

$$p\text{-value} \approx .5 - .4474 = .0526$$

Because our selected α value, .05, is less than this *p*-value, we have insufficient evidence to reject H_0: $(\mu_1 - \mu_2) = 0$ in favor of H_a: $(\mu_1 - \mu_2) < 0$.

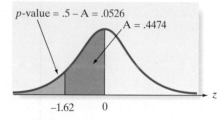

Figure 8.4

The observed significance level for Example 8.2

Look Back The *p*-value of the test is more easily obtained from a statistical software package. A Minitab printout for the hypothesis test is displayed in Figure 8.5. The one-tailed *p*-value, highlighted on the printout, is .054, which agrees (to two decimals) with our approximated *p*-value. (*Note*: Minitab uses the *t*-distribution as an approximation to the *z*-distribution to determine the *p*-value.)

Two-Sample T-Test and CI: USA, JAPAN

```
Two-sample T for USA vs JAPAN

          N    Mean   StDev   SE Mean
USA       50   26596   1981      280
JAPAN     50   27236   1974      279


Difference = μ (USA) – μ (JAPAN)
Estimate for difference:   –640
95% upper bound for difference:   17
T-Test of difference = 0 (vs <): T-Value = –1.62   P-Value = 0.054   DF = 97
```

Figure 8.5

Minitab analysis for comparing U.S. and Japan mean auto prices

● **Now Work Exercise 8.3b**

Small Samples

When comparing two population means with small samples (say, $n_1 < 30$ or $n_2 < 30$), the methodology of the previous three examples is invalid. The reason? When the sample sizes are small, estimates of σ_1^2 and σ_2^2 are unreliable, and the Central Limit Theorem (which guarantees that the z-statistic is normal) can no longer be applied. But as in the case of a single mean (Section 7.5), we use the familiar Student's t-distribution.

To use the t-distribution, both sampled populations must be approximately normally distributed with equal population variances, and the random samples must be selected independently of each other. The normality and equal variances assumptions imply relative frequency distributions for the populations that would appear as shown in Figure 8.6.

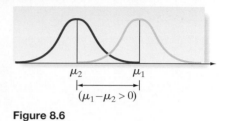

Figure 8.6

Assumptions for the two-sample t: (1) normal populations, (2) equal variances

Because we assume the two populations have equal variances ($\sigma_1^2 = \sigma_2^2 = \sigma^2$), it is reasonable to use the information contained in *both* samples to construct a **pooled sample estimator of σ^2** for use in confidence intervals and test statistics.* Thus, if s_1^2 and s_2^2 are the two sample variances (both estimating the variance σ^2 common to both populations), the pooled estimator of σ^2, denoted as s_p^2, is

$$s_p^2 = \frac{(n_1 - 1)s_1^2 + (n_2 - 1)s_2^2}{(n_1 - 1) + (n_2 - 1)} = \frac{(n_1 - 1)s_1^2 + (n_2 - 1)s_2^2}{n_1 + n_2 - 2}$$

or

$$s_p^2 = \frac{\overbrace{\sum(x_1 - \bar{x}_1)^2}^{\text{From sample 1}} + \overbrace{\sum(x_2 - \bar{x}_2)^2}^{\text{From sample 2}}}{n_1 + n_2 - 2}$$

where x_1 represents a measurement from sample 1 and x_2 represents a measurement from sample 2. Recall that the term *degrees of freedom* was defined in Section 6.2 as 1 less than the sample size. Thus, in this case, we have $(n_1 - 1)$ degrees of freedom for sample 1 and $(n_2 - 1)$ degrees of freedom for sample 2. Because we are pooling the information on σ^2 obtained from both samples, the degrees of freedom associated with the pooled variance s_p^2 is equal to the sum of the degrees of freedom for the two samples, namely, the denominator of s_p^2; that is, $(n_1 - 1) + (n_2 - 1) = n_1 + n_2 - 2$.

Note that the second formula given for s_p^2 shows that the pooled variance is simply a *weighted* average of the two sample variances, s_1^2 and s_2^2. The weight given each variance is proportional to its degrees of freedom. If the two variances have the same number of degrees of freedom (i.e., if the sample sizes are equal), then the pooled variance is a simple average of the two sample variances. The result is an average or "pooled" variance that is a better estimate of σ^2 than either s_1^2 or s_2^2 alone.

Both the confidence interval and the test of hypothesis procedures for comparing two population means with small samples are summarized in the following boxes.

Small, Independent Samples Confidence Interval for $(\mu_1 - \mu_2)$: Student's t-Statistic

$$(\bar{x}_1 - \bar{x}_2) \pm t_{\alpha/2}\sqrt{s_p^2\left(\frac{1}{n_1} + \frac{1}{n_2}\right)}$$

where $s_p^2 = \dfrac{(n_1 - 1)s_1^2 + (n_2 - 1)s_2^2}{n_1 + n_2 - 2}$

and $t_{\alpha/2}$ is based on $(n_1 + n_2 - 2)$ degrees of freedom.

---

*s_p^2 can be shown to be the minimum-variance unbiased estimator (MVUE) of σ^2 when $\sigma^2 = \sigma_1^2 = \sigma_2^2$.

Small, Independent Samples Test of Hypothesis for $(\mu_1 - \mu_2)$: Student's t-Statistic

One-Tailed Test	Two-Tailed Test
H_0: $(\mu_1 - \mu_2) = D_0$	H_0: $(\mu_1 - \mu_2) = D_0$
H_a: $(\mu_1 - \mu_2) < D_0$	H_a: $(\mu_1 - \mu_2) \neq D_0$
[or H_a: $(\mu_1 - \mu_2) > D_0$]	

$$\text{Test statistic: } t = \frac{(\bar{x}_1 - \bar{x}_2) - D_0}{\sqrt{s_p^2 \left(\dfrac{1}{n_1} + \dfrac{1}{n_2} \right)}}$$

One-Tailed Test	Two-Tailed Test
Rejection region: $t < -t_\alpha$	Rejection region: $|t| > t_{\alpha/2}$
[or $t > t_\alpha$ when H_a: $(\mu_1 - \mu_2) > D_0$]	
p-value $= P(t < t_c)$ [or $P(t > t_c)$]	p-value $= 2P(t > |t_c|)$

where t_α and $t_{\alpha/2}$ are based on $(n_1 + n_2 - 2)$ degrees of freedom and t_c is the calculated value of the test statistic.

Conditions Required for Valid Small-Sample Inferences About $(\mu_1 - \mu_2)$

1. The two samples are randomly selected in an independent manner from the two target populations.

2. Both sampled populations have distributions that are approximately normal.

3. The population variances are equal (i.e., $\sigma_1^2 = \sigma_2^2$).

EXAMPLE 8.4

Small-Sample Confidence Interval for $(\mu_1 - \mu_2)$—Managerial Success

Problem Behavioral researchers have developed an index designed to measure managerial success. The index (measured on a 100-point scale) is based on the manager's length of time in the organization and his or her level within the firm; the higher the index, the more successful the manager. Suppose a researcher wants to compare the average success index for two groups of managers at a large manufacturing plant. Managers in group 1 engage in a high volume of interactions with people outside the manager's work unit. (Such interactions include phone and face-to-face meetings with customers and suppliers, outside meetings, and public relations work.) Managers in group 2 rarely interact with people outside their work unit. Independent random samples of 12 and 15 managers are selected from groups 1 and 2, respectively, and the success index of each is recorded. The results of the study are given in Table 8.2.

a. Use the data in the table to estimate the true mean difference between the success indexes of managers in the two groups. Use a 95% confidence interval.

b. Interpret the interval, part **a.**

c. What assumptions must be made so that the estimate is valid? Are they reasonably satisfied?

Table 8.2	Managerial Success Indexes for Two Groups of Managers										
	Group 1						Group 2				
	Interaction with Outsiders						Few Interactions				
	65	58	78	60	68	69	62	53	36	34	56	50
	66	70	53	71	63	63	42	57	46	68	48	42
							52	53	43			

Two-Sample T-Test and CI: SUCCESS, GROUP

```
Two-sample T for SUCCESS

GROUP   N    Mean   StDev   SE Mean
1       12   65.33   6.61      1.9
2       15   49.47   9.33      2.4


Difference = μ (1) - μ (2)
Estimate for difference:  15.87
95% CI for difference:  (9.29, 22.45)
T-Test of difference = 0 (vs ≠): T-Value = 4.97   P-Value = 0.000   DF = 25
Both use Pooled StDev = 8.2472
```

Figure 8.7

Minitab printout for Example 8.4

Solution

a. For this experiment, let μ_1 and μ_2 represent the mean success index of group 1 and group 2 managers, respectively. Then, the objective is to obtain a 95% confidence interval for $(\mu_1 - \mu_2)$.

The first step in constructing the confidence interval is to obtain summary statistics (e.g., $\bar{x}$ and s) on the success index for each group of managers. The data of Table 8.2 were entered into a computer, and Minitab was used to obtain these descriptive statistics. The Minitab printout appears in Figure 8.7. Note that $\bar{x}_1 = 65.33, s_1 = 6.61, \bar{x}_2 = 49.47$, and $s_2 = 9.33$.

Next, we calculate the pooled estimate of variance:

$$s_p^2 = \frac{(n_1 - 1)s_1^2 + (n_2 - 1)s_2^2}{n_1 + n_2 - 2}$$

$$= \frac{(12 - 1)(6.61)^2 + (15 - 1)(9.33)^2}{12 + 15 - 2} = 67.97$$

where s_p^2 is based on $(n_1 + n_2 - 2) = (12 + 15 - 2) = 25$ degrees of freedom. Also, we find $t_{\alpha/2} = t_{.025} = 2.06$ (based on 25 degrees of freedom) from Table III in Appendix D.

Finally, the 95% confidence interval for $(\mu_1 - \mu_2)$, the difference between mean managerial success indexes for the two groups, is

$$(\bar{x}_1 - \bar{x}_2) \pm t_{\alpha/2}\sqrt{s_p^2\left(\frac{1}{n_1} + \frac{1}{n_2}\right)} = 65.33 - 49.47 \pm t_{.025}\sqrt{67.97\left(\frac{1}{12} + \frac{1}{15}\right)}$$

$$= 15.86 \pm (2.06)(3.19)$$

$$= 15.86 \pm 6.58$$

or $(9.28, 22.44)$. This interval agrees (except for rounding) with the one shown at the bottom of the Minitab printout, Figure 8.7.

b. Notice that the confidence interval includes positive differences only. Consequently, we are 95% confident that $(\mu_1 - \mu_2)$ exceeds 0. In fact, we estimate the mean success index, μ_1, for managers with a high volume of outsider interaction (group 1) to be anywhere between 9.28 and 22.44 points higher than the mean success index, μ_2, of managers with few interactions (group 2).

c. To properly use the small-sample confidence interval, the following assumptions must be satisfied:

1. The samples of managers are randomly and independently selected from the populations of group 1 and group 2 managers.

2. The success indexes are normally distributed for both groups of managers.

3. The variance of the success indexes is the same for the two populations (i.e., $\sigma_1^2 = \sigma_2^2$).

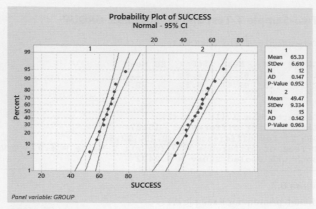

Figure 8.8

Minitab normal probability plots for manager success index

The first assumption is satisfied, based on the information provided about the sampling procedure in the problem description. To check the plausibility of the remaining two assumptions, we resort to graphical methods. Figure 8.8 is a Minitab printout that displays normal probability plots for the success indexes of the two samples of managers. The near straight-line trends on both plots indicate that the success index distributions are approximately mound-shaped and symmetric. Consequently, each sample data set appears to come from a population that is approximately normal.

One way to check assumption #3 is to test the null hypothesis H_0: $\sigma_1^2 = \sigma_2^2$. This test is covered in Section 8.6. Another approach is to examine box plots for the sample data. Figure 8.9 is a Minitab printout that shows side-by-side vertical box plots for the success indexes in the two samples. Recall from Section 2.7 that the box plot represents the "spread" of a data set. The two box plots appear to have about the same spread (we verify this finding with a test of hypothesis in Section 8.6); thus, the samples appear to come from populations with approximately the same variance.

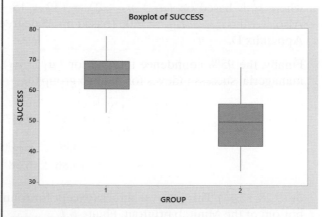

Figure 8.9

Minitab box plots for manager success index

Look Back All three assumptions appear to be reasonably satisfied for this application of the small-sample confidence interval.

● **Now Work Exercise 8.7**

The two-sample t-statistic is a powerful tool for comparing population means when the assumptions are satisfied. It has also been shown to retain its usefulness when the sampled populations are only approximately normally distributed. And when the sample sizes are equal, the assumption of equal population variances can be relaxed— that is, if $n_1 = n_2$, then σ_1^2 and σ_2^2 can be quite different, and the test statistic will still possess, approximately, a Student's t-distribution. In the case where $\sigma_1^2 \neq \sigma_2^2$ and $n_1 \neq n_2$, an approximate small-sample confidence interval or test can be obtained by modifying the degrees of freedom associated with the t-distribution.

The next box gives the approximate small-sample procedures to use when the assumption of equal variances is violated. The test for the "unequal sample sizes" case is based on Satterthwaite's (1946) approximation. When using statistical software to produce the results, be sure to select the "unequal variances" option (or de-select the "assume equal variances" option).

Approximate Small-Sample Procedures when $\sigma_1^2 \neq \sigma_2^2$

1. **Equal sample sizes** $(n_1 = n_2 = n)$
   Confidence interval: $(\bar{x}_1 - \bar{x}_2) \pm t_{\alpha/2} \sqrt{(s_1^2 + s_1^2)/n}$
   Test statistic for H_0: $(\mu_1 - \mu_2) = 0$: $t = (\bar{x}_2 - \bar{x}_2)/\sqrt{(s_1^2 + s_2^2)/n}$
   where t is based on $\nu = n_1 + n_2 - 2 = 2(n - 1)$ degrees of freedom.

2. **Unequal sample sizes** $(n_1 \neq n_2)$
   Confidence interval: $(\bar{x}_1 - \bar{x}_2) \pm t_{\alpha/2}\sqrt{(s_1^2/n_1) + (s_2^2/n_2)}$
   Test statistic for H_0: $(\mu_1 - \mu_2) = 0$: $t = (\bar{x}_1 - \bar{x}_2)/\sqrt{(s_1^2/n_1) + (s_2^2/n_2)}$
   where t is based on degrees of freedom equal to

   $$\nu = \frac{(s_1^2/n_1 + s_2^2/n_2)^2}{\dfrac{(s_1^2/n_1)^2}{n_1 - 1} + \dfrac{(s_1^2/n_2)^2}{n_2 - 1}}$$

Note: The value of ν will generally not be an integer. Round ν down to the nearest integer to use the t-table.

When the assumptions are clearly not satisfied, you can select larger samples from the populations or you can use other available statistical tests (nonparametric statistical tests, which are described in Chapter 15).

What Should You Do if the Assumptions Are Not Satisfied?

Answer: If you are concerned that the assumptions are not satisfied, use the Wilcoxon rank sum test for independent samples to test for a shift in population distributions. See Chapter 15.

STATISTICS IN ACTION **Comparing Mean Price Changes**

REVISITED   Refer to the *ZixIt v. Visa* court case described in the Statistics in Action (pp. 452–453). Recall that a Visa executive wrote email and made Web site postings in an effort to undermine a new online credit card processing system developed by ZixIt. ZixIt sued Visa for libel, asking for $699 million in damages. An expert statistician, hired by the defendants (Visa), performed an "event study" in which he matched the Visa executive's email postings with movement of ZixIt's stock price the next business day. The data were collected daily from September 1 to December 30, 1999 (an 83-day period) and are available in the **ZIXVSA** file. In addition to daily closing price (dollars) of ZixIt stock, the file contains a variable for whether or not the Visa executive posted an email and the change in price of the stock the following business day. During the 83-day period, the executive posted email on 43 days and had no postings on 40 days.

Two-Sample T-Test and CI: PriceChange, Posting

```
Two-sample T for PriceChange

Posting   N    Mean   StDev   SE Mean
NO        40   -0.13   3.46     0.55
POST      43    0.06   2.20     0.34


Difference = μ (NO) - μ (POST)
Estimate for difference:  -0.188
95% CI for difference:  (-1.470, 1.093)
T-Test of difference = 0 (vs ≠): T-Value = -0.29   P-Value = 0.770   DF = 65
```

Figure SIA8.1

Minitab comparison of two price change means

If the daily postings by the Visa executive had a negative impact on ZixIt stock, then the average price change following nonposting days should exceed the average price change following posting days. Consequently, one way to analyze the data is to conduct a comparison of two population means through either a confidence interval or a test of hypothesis. Here, we let μ_1 represent the mean price change of ZixIt stock following all nonposting days and μ_2 represent the mean price change of ZixIt stock following posting days. If, in fact, the charges made by ZixIt are true, then μ_1 will exceed μ_2. However, if the data do not support ZixIt's claim, then we will not be able to reject the null hypothesis $H_0: (\mu_1 - \mu_2) = 0$ in favor of $H_a: (\mu_1 - \mu_2) > 0$. Similarly, if a confidence interval for $(\mu_1 - \mu_2)$ contains the value 0, then there will be no evidence to support ZixIt's claim.

Because both sample sizes ($n_1 = 40$ and $n_2 = 43$) are large, we can apply the large-sample z-test or large-sample confidence interval procedure for independent samples. A Minitab printout for this analysis is shown in Figure SIA8.1. Both the 95% confidence interval and p-value for a two-tailed test of hypothesis are highlighted on the printout. Note that the 95% confidence interval, $(-\$1.47, \$1.09)$, includes the value \$0, and the p-value for the two-tailed hypothesis test (.770) implies that the two population means are not significantly different. Also, interestingly, the sample mean price change after posting days ($\bar{x}_1 = \$.06$) is small and positive, while the sample mean price change after nonposting days ($\bar{x}_2 = -\$.13$) is small and negative, totally contradicting ZixIt's claim.

The statistical expert for the defense presented these results to the jury, arguing that the "average price change following posting days is small and similar to the average price change following nonposting days" and "the difference in the means is not statistically significant."

Note: The statistician also compared the mean ZixIt trading volume (number of ZixIt stock shares traded) after posting days with the mean trading volume after nonposting days. These results are shown in Figure SIA8.2. You can see that the 95% confidence interval for the difference in mean trading volume (highlighted) includes 0, and the p-value for a two-tailed test of hypothesis for a difference in means (also highlighted) is not statistically significant. These results were also presented to the jury in defense of Visa.

Two-Sample T-Test and CI: VolumeAfter, Posting

```
Two-sample T for VolumeAfter

Posting   N    Mean     StDev    SE Mean
NO        40   719645   430837   68121
POST      43   578665   333921   50922


Difference = μ (NO) - μ (POST)
Estimate for difference:  140980
95% CI for difference:  (-28526, 310485)
T-Test of difference = 0 (vs ≠): T-Value = 1.66   P-Value = 0.102   DF = 73
```

Figure SIA8.2

Minitab comparison of two trading volume means analysis

Data Set: ZIXVSA

Learning the Mechanics

8.1 The purpose of this exercise is to compare the variability of $\bar{x}_1$ and $\bar{x}_2$ with the variability of $(\bar{x}_1 - \bar{x}_2)$.

   a. Suppose the first sample is selected from a population with mean $\mu_1 = 150$ and variance $\sigma_1^2 = 900$. Within what range should the sample mean vary about 95% of the time in repeated samples of 100 measurements from this distribution? That is, construct an interval extending 2 standard deviations of $\bar{x}_1$ on each side of μ_1.

   b. Suppose the second sample is selected independently of the first from a second population with mean $\mu_2 = 150$ and variance $\sigma_2^2 = 1,600$. Within what range should the sample mean vary about 95% of the time in repeated samples of 100 measurements from this distribution? That is, construct an interval extending 2 standard deviations of $\bar{x}_2$ on each side of μ_2.

   c. Now consider the difference between the two sample means $(\bar{x}_1 - \bar{x}_2)$. What are the mean and standard deviation of the sampling distribution of $(\bar{x}_1 - \bar{x}_2)$?

   d. Within what range should the difference in sample means vary about 95% of the time in repeated independent samples of 100 measurements each from the two populations?

   e. What, in general, can be said about the variability of the difference between independent sample means relative to the variability of the individual sample means?

8.2 Independent random samples from two populations with standard deviations $\sigma_1 = 2$ and $\sigma_2 = 8$, respectively, are selected. The sample sizes and the sample means are recorded in the following table:

Sample 1	Sample 2
$n_1 = 58$	$n_2 = 62$
$\bar{x}_1 = 17.5$	$\bar{x}_2 = 16.23$

   a. Calculate the standard error of the sampling distribution for Sample 1.

   b. Calculate the standard error of the sampling distribution for Sample 2.

   c. Suppose you were to calculate the difference between the sample means $(\bar{x}_1 - \bar{x}_2)$. Find the mean and standard error of the sampling distribution of $(\bar{x}_1 - \bar{x}_2)$.

   d. Will the statistic $(\bar{x}_1 - \bar{x}_2)$ be normally distributed?

8.3 In order to compare the means of two populations, independent random samples of 400 observations are selected from each population, with the following results:

Sample 1	Sample 2
$\bar{x}_1 = 5,275$	$\bar{x}_2 = 5,240$
$s_1 = 150$	$s_2 = 200$

   a. Use a 95% confidence interval to estimate the difference between the population means $(\mu_1 - \mu_2)$. Interpret the confidence interval.

   b. Test the null hypothesis $H_0: (\mu_1 - \mu_2) = 0$ versus the alternative hypothesis $H_a: (\mu_1 - \mu_2) \neq 0$. Give the significance level of the test and interpret the result.

   c. Suppose the test in part **b** was conducted with the alternative hypothesis $H_a: (\mu_1 - \mu_2) > 0$. How would your answer to part **b** change?

   d. Test the null hypothesis $H_0: (\mu_1 - \mu_2) = 25$ versus $H_a: (\mu_1 - \mu_2) \neq 25$. Give the significance level and interpret the result. Compare your answer with the test conducted in part **b**.

   e. What assumptions are necessary to ensure the validity of the inferential procedures applied in parts **a–d**?

8.4 To use the t-statistic to test for a difference between the means of two populations, what assumptions must be made about the two populations? About the two samples?

8.5 Two populations are described in each of the following cases. In which cases would it be appropriate to apply the small-sample t-test to investigate the difference between the population means?

   a. Population 1: Normal distribution with variance σ_1^2. Population 2: Skewed to the right with variance $\sigma_2^2 = \sigma_1^2$.

   b. Population 1: Normal distribution with variance σ_1^2. Population 2: Normal distribution with variance $\sigma_2^2 \neq \sigma_1^2$.

   c. Population 1: Skewed to the left with variance σ_1^2. Population 2: Skewed to the left with variance $\sigma_2^2 = \sigma_1^2$.

   d. Population 1: Normal distribution with variance σ_1^2. Population 2: Normal distribution with variance $\sigma_2^2 = \sigma_1^2$.

   e. Population 1: Uniform distribution with variance σ_1^2. Population 2: Uniform distribution with variance $\sigma_2^2 = \sigma_1^2$.

8.6 Assume that $\sigma_1^2 = \sigma_2^2 = \sigma^2$. Calculate the pooled estimator of σ^2 for each of the following cases:

   a. $s_1^2 = 120, s_2^2 = 100, n_1 = n_2 = 25$

   b. $s_1^2 = 12, s_2^2 = 20, n_1 = 20, n_2 = 10$

   c. $s_1^2 = .15, s_2^2 = .20, n_1 = 6, n_2 = 10$

   d. $s_1^2 = 3,000, s_2^2 = 2,500, n_1 = 16, n_2 = 17$

   Note that the pooled estimate is a weighted average of the sample variances. To which of the variances does the pooled estimate fall nearer in each of the above cases?

8.7 Independent random samples from normal populations produced the results shown in the next table.

Sample 1	Sample 2
1.2	4.2
3.1	2.7
1.7	3.6
2.8	3.9
3.0	

   a. Calculate the pooled estimate of σ^2.

   b. Do the data provide sufficient evidence to indicate that $\mu_2 > \mu_1$? Test using $\alpha = .10$.

   c. Find a 90% confidence interval for $(\mu_1 - \mu_2)$.

   d. Which of the two inferential procedures, the test of hypothesis in part **b** or the confidence interval in part **c**, provides more information about $(\mu_1 - \mu_2)$?

8.8 Two independent random samples have been selected—100 observations from population 1 and 100 from population 2. Sample means $\bar{x}_1 = 26.6$ and $\bar{x}_2 = 15.5$ were obtained. From previous experience with these populations, it is known that the variances are $\sigma_1^2 = 9$ and $\sigma_2^2 = 16$.

a. Find $\sigma_{(\bar{x}_1 - \bar{x}_2)}$.

b. Sketch the approximate sampling distribution for $(\bar{x}_1 - \bar{x}_2)$, assuming $(\mu_1 - \mu_2) = 10$.

c. Locate the observed value of $(\bar{x}_1 - \bar{x}_2)$ on the graph you drew in part **b**. Does it appear that this value contradicts the null hypothesis $H_0: (\mu_1 - \mu_2) = 10$?

d. Use the z-table to determine the rejection region for the test of $H_0: (\mu_1 - \mu_2) = 10$ against $H_0: (\mu_1 - \mu_2) \neq 10$. Use $\alpha = .05$.

e. Conduct the hypothesis test of part **d** and interpret your result.

f. Construct a 95% confidence interval for $(\mu_1 - \mu_2)$. Interpret the interval.

g. Which inference provides more information about the value of $(\mu_1 - \mu_2)$—the test of hypothesis in part **e** or the confidence interval in part **f**?

8.9 Independent random samples of $n_1 = 233$ and $n_2 = 312$ are selected from two populations and used to test the hypothesis $H_0: (\mu_1 - \mu_2) = 0$ against the alternative $H_a: (\mu_1 - \mu_2) \neq 0$.

a. The two-tailed p-value of the test is .1150. Interpret this result.

b. If the alternative hypothesis had been $H_a: (\mu_1 - \mu_2) < 0$, how would the p-value change? Interpret the p-value for this one tailed test.

8.10 Independent random samples from approximately normal populations produced the results shown below.

L08010

Sample 1				Sample 2			
52	33	42	44	52	43	47	56
41	50	44	51	62	53	61	50
45	38	37	40	56	52	53	60
44	50	43		50	48	60	55

a. Do the data provide sufficient evidence to conclude that $(\mu_2 - \mu_1) > 10$? Test using $\alpha = .01$.

b. Construct a 98% confidence interval for $(\mu_2 - \mu_1)$. Interpret your result.

8.11 Independent random samples selected from two normal populations produced the sample means and standard deviations shown below.

Sample 1	Sample 2
$n_1 = 17$	$n_2 = 12$
$\bar{x}_1 = 5.4$	$\bar{x}_2 = 7.9$
$s_1 = 3.4$	$s_2 = 4.8$

a. Conduct the test $H_0: (\mu_1 - \mu_2) = 0$ against $H_a: (\mu_1 - \mu_2) \neq 0$. Interpret the results.

b. Estimate $(\mu_1 - \mu_2)$ using a 95% confidence interval.

Applying the Concepts—Basic

8.12 **Lobster trap placement.** Refer to the *Bulletin of Marine Science* (April 2010) study of lobster trap placement, Exercise 6.29 (p. 348). Recall that the variable of interest was the average distance separating traps—called

TRAPS

trapspacing—deployed by teams of fishermen. The trap-spacing measurements (in meters) for a sample of seven teams from the Bahia Tortugas (BT) fishing cooperative are repeated in the table. In addition, trap-spacing measurements for eight teams from the Punta Abreojos (PA) fishing cooperative are listed. For this problem, we are interested in comparing the mean trap-spacing measurements of the two fishing cooperatives.

BT Cooperative:	93	99	105	94	82	70	86	
PA Cooperative:	118	94	106	72	90	66	153	98

Source: Based on G. G. Shester, "Explaining Catch Variation Among Baja California Lobster Fishers Through Spatial Analysis of Trap-Placement Decisions," *Bulletin of Marine Science*, Vol. 86, No. 2, April 2010 (Table 1).

a. Identify the target parameter for this study.

b. Compute a point estimate of the target parameter.

c. What is the problem with using the normal (z) statistic to find a confidence interval for the target parameter?

d. Find a 90% confidence interval for the target parameter.

e. Use the interval, part **d**, to make a statement about the difference in mean trap-spacing measurements of the two fishing cooperatives.

f. What conditions must be satisfied for the inference, part **e**, to be valid?

8.13 **Last name and acquisition timing.** The speed with which consumers decide to purchase a product was investigated in the *Journal of Consumer Research* (August 2011). The researchers theorized that consumers with last names that begin with letters later in the alphabet will tend to acquire items faster than those whose last names begin with letters earlier in the alphabet—called the *last name effect*. MBA students were offered free tickets to an event for which there was a limited supply of tickets. The first letter of the last name of those who responded to an email offer in time to receive the tickets was noted as well as the response time (measured in minutes). The researchers compared the response times for two groups of MBA students: (1) those with last names beginning with one of the first nine letters of the alphabet and (2) those with last names beginning with one of the last nine letters of the alphabet. Summary statistics for the two groups are provided in the table.

	First 9 Letters: A–I	Last 9 Letters: R–Z
Sample size:	25	25
Mean response time (minutes):	25.08	19.38
Standard deviation (minutes):	10.41	7.12

Source: Based on K. A. Carlson and J. M. Conrad, "The Last Name Effect: How Last Name Influences Acquisition Timing," *Journal of Consumer Research*, Vol. 38, No. 2, August 2011.

a. Construct a 95% confidence interval for the difference between the true mean response times for MBA students in the two groups.

b. Based on the interval, part **a**, which group has the shorter mean response time? Does this result support the researchers' *last name effect* theory? Explain.

8.14 **Employees' test scores.** A company sent its employees to attend two different English courses. The company is interested in knowing if there is any difference between the two courses attended by its employees. When the employees returned from the courses, the company asked them to take a common test. The summary statistics of the test results of each of the two English courses are recorded in the following table:

Course 1	Course 2
$n_1 = 50$	$n_2 = 50$
$\bar{x}_1 = 75.1$	$\bar{x}_2 = 72.1$
$s_1 = 12.8$	$s_2 = 14.6$

a. Identify the parameter(s) that would help the company determine the difference between the two courses.

b. State the appropriate null and alternative hypotheses that the company would like to test.

c. After conducting the hypothesis test at the 5% significance level, the company found the p-value = .327. Interpret this result for the company.

8.15 **Performance-based logistics.** Refer to the *Journal of Business Logistics* (Vol. 36, 2015) study of the factors that lead to successful performance-based logistics projects, Exercise 2.45 (p. 95). Recall that opinions of a sample of Department of Defense (DOD) employees and suppliers were solicited during interviews. Data on years of experience for the 6 commercial suppliers interviewed and the 11 government employees interviewed are listed in the accompanying table. Assume these samples were randomly and independently selected from the populations of DOD employees and commercial suppliers. Consider the following claim: "On average, commercial suppliers of the DOD have less experience than government employees."

Commercial:	30	10	9	10	5	10					
Government:	15	30	30	25	6	3	20	25	30	20	25

a. Give the null and alternative hypotheses for testing the claim.

b. An XLSTAT printout giving the test results is shown at the bottom of the page. Find and interpret the p-value of the test using $\alpha = .05$.

c. What assumptions about the data are required for the inference, part **b**, to be valid? Check these assumptions graphically using the data in the **PBL** file.

8.16 **Drug content assessment.** Refer to Exercise 4.123 (p. 269) and the *Analytical Chemistry* (Dec. 15, 2009) study in which scientists used high-performance liquid chromatography to determine the amount of drug in a tablet. Twenty-five tablets were produced at each of two different, independent sites. Drug concentrations (measured as a percentage) for the tablets produced at the two sites are listed in the table below. The scientists want to know whether there is any difference between the mean drug concentration in tablets produced at Site 1 and the corresponding mean at Site 2. Use the Minitab printout (next page) to help the scientists draw a conclusion.

Site 1

91.28	92.83	89.35	91.90	82.85	94.83	89.83	89.00	84.62
86.96	88.32	91.17	83.86	89.74	92.24	92.59	84.21	89.36
90.96	92.85	89.39	89.82	89.91	92.16	88.67		

Site 2

89.35	86.51	89.04	91.82	93.02	88.32	88.76	89.26	90.36
87.16	91.74	86.12	92.10	83.33	87.61	88.20	92.78	86.35
93.84	91.20	93.44	86.77	83.77	93.19	81.79		

Source: P. J. Borman, J. C. Marion, I. Damjanov, and P. Jackson, "Design and Analysis of Method Equivalence Studies," *Analytical Chemistry,* Vol. 81, No. 24, December 15, 2009 (Table 3). Republished with permission of American Chemical Society; permission conveyed through Copyright Clearance Center, Inc.

Summary statistics:

Variable	Observations	Minimum	Maximum	Mean	Std. deviation
Experience	Commercial	6	5.0000	30.0000	12.3333	8.8694
Experience	Government	11	3.0000	30.0000	20.8182	9.3682

t-test for two independent samples / Lower-tailed test:

95% confidence interval on the difference between the means:

	(-Inf ,	-0.2951)

Difference	-8.4848
t (Observed value)	-1.8162
t (Critical value)	-1.7531
DF	15
p-value (one-tailed)	0.0447
alpha	0.05

XLSTAT Output for Exercise 8.15

Two-Sample T-Test and CI: Content, Site

```
Two-sample T for Content

Site   N   Mean   StDev   SE Mean
1      25  89.55  3.07    0.61
2      25  89.03  3.34    0.67


Difference = μ (1) - μ (2)
Estimate for difference:  0.515
95% CI for difference:  (-1.308, 2.338)
T-Test of difference = 0 (vs ≠): T-Value = 0.57  P-Value = 0.573  DF = 48
Both use Pooled StDev = 3.2057
```

Minitab output for Exercise 8.16

8.17 **Buy-side vs. sell-side analysts' earnings forecasts.** Refer to the *Financial Analysts Journal* (Jul./Aug. 2008) study of financial analysts' forecast earnings, Exercise 2.86 (p. 112). Recall that data were collected on 3,526 forecasts made by buy-side analysts and 58,562 forecasts made by sell-side analysts, and the relative absolute forecast error was determined for each. The mean and standard deviation of forecast errors for both types of analysts are given in the table.

	Buy-Side Analysts	Sell-Side Analysts
Sample Size	3,526	58,562
Mean	0.85	−0.05
Standard Deviation	1.93	0.85

Source: B. Groysberg, P. Healy, and C. Chapman, "Buy-Side vs. Sell-side Analysts' Earnings Forecasts," *Financial Analysts Journal,* Vol. 64, No. 4, July/August 2008.

a. Construct a 95% confidence interval for the difference between the mean forecast error of buy-side analysts and the mean forecast error of sell-side analysts.

b. Based on the interval, part **a,** which type of analysis has the greater mean forecast error? Explain.

c. What assumptions about the underlying populations of forecast errors (if any) are necessary for the validity of the inference, part **b**?

Applying the Concepts—Intermediate

8.18 **Homework assistance for accounting students.** How much assistance should accounting professors provide students for completing homework? Is too much assistance counterproductive? These were some of the questions of interest in a *Journal of Accounting Education* (Vol. 25, 2007) article. A total of 75 junior-level accounting majors who were enrolled in Intermediate Financial Accounting participated in an experiment. All students took a pretest on a topic not covered in class; then each was given a homework problem to solve on the same topic. However, the students were randomly assigned different levels of assistance on the homework. Some (20 students) were given the completed solution, some (25 students) were given check figures at various steps of the solution, and the rest (30 students) were given no help. After finishing the homework, each student was given a posttest on the subject. One of the variables of interest to the researchers was the knowledge gain (or, test score improvement), measured as the difference between the posttest and pretest scores.

The sample mean knowledge gains for the three groups of students are provided in the table.

	No Solutions	Check Figures	Completed Solutions
Sample Size	30	25	20
Sample Mean	2.43	2.72	1.95

Source: Based on T. M. Lindquist and L. M. Olsen, "How Much Help, Is Too Much Help? An Experimental Investigation of the Use of Check Figures and Completed Solutions in Teaching Intermediate Accounting," *Journal of Accounting Education,* Vol. 25, No. 3, 2007, pp. 103–117 (Table 1, Panel B).

a. The researchers theorized that as the level of homework assistance increased, the test score improvement from pretest to posttest would decrease. Do the sample means reported in the table support this theory?

b. What is the problem with using only the sample means to make inferences about the population mean knowledge gains for the three groups of students?

c. The researchers conducted a statistical test of hypothesis to compare the mean knowledge gain of students in the "no solutions" group with the mean knowledge gain of students in the "check figures" group. Based on the theory, part **a,** set up the null and alternative hypotheses for the test.

d. The observed significance level of the t-test of part c was reported as .8248. Using $\alpha = .05$, interpret this result.

e. The researchers conducted a statistical test of hypothesis to compare the mean knowledge gain of students in the "completed solutions" group with the mean knowledge gain of students in the "check figures" group. Based on the theory, part **a,** set up the null and alternative hypotheses for the test.

f. The observed significance level of the *t*-test of part **e** was reported as .1849. Using $\alpha = .05$, interpret this result.

g. The researchers conducted a statistical test of hypothesis to compare the mean knowledge gain of students in the "no solutions" group with the mean knowledge gain of students in the "completed solutions" group. Based on the theory, part **a,** set up the null and alternative hypotheses for the test.

h. The observed significance level of the *t*-test of part **g** was reported as .2726. Using $\alpha = .05$, interpret this result.

8.19 **Comparing taste-test rating protocols.** Taste-testers of new food products are presented with several competing food samples and asked to rate the taste of each on a 9-point scale (where 1 = "dislike extremely" and 9 = "like extremely"). In the *Journal of Sensory Studies* (June 2014), food scientists compared two different taste-testing protocols. The sequential monadic (SM) method presented the samples one-at-a-time to the taster in a random order, while the rank rating (RR) method presented the samples to the taster all at once, side-by-side. Consider the following experiment (similar to the one conducted in the journal): 50 consumers of apricot jelly were asked to taste-test five different varieties. Half the testers used the SM protocol and half used the RR protocol during testing. In a second experiment, 50 consumers of cheese were asked to taste-test four different varieties. Again, half the testers used the SM protocol and half used the RR protocol during testing. For each product (apricot jelly and cheese), the mean taste scores of the two protocols (SM and RR) were compared. The results are shown in the accompanying tables.

Apricot Jelly (Taste means)				*Cheese* (Taste means)			
Variety	RR	SM	P-value	Variety	RR	SM	P-value
A	6.8	6.4	.488	A	5.2	4.4	.013
B	6.9	6.7	.721	B	5.9	5.3	.065
C	5.3	5.4	.983	C	5.6	4.7	.002
D	6.7	6.4	.585	D	7.5	6.7	.034
E	6.4	6.1	.499				

a. Consider the five varieties of apricot jelly. Identify the varieties for which you can conclude that "the mean taste scores of the two protocols (SM and RR) differ significantly at $\alpha = .05$."

b. Consider the four varieties of cheese. Identify the varieties for which you can conclude that "the mean taste scores of the two protocols (SM and RR) differ significantly at $\alpha = .05$."

c. Explain why the taste-test scores do not need to be normally distributed for the inferences, parts **a** and **b**, to be valid.

8.20 **Producer willingness to supply biomass.** The conversion of biomass to energy is critical for producing transportation fuels. How willing are producers to supply biomass products such as cereal straw, corn stover, and surplus hay? To answer this question, economists conducted a survey of producers in both mid-Missouri and southern Illinois (*Biomass and Energy*, Vol. 36, 2012). Independent samples of 431 Missouri producers and 508 Illinois producers participated in the survey. Each producer was asked to give the maximum proportion of hay produced that he or she would be willing to sell to the biomass market. Summary statistics for the two groups of producers are listed in the table. Does the mean amount of surplus that hay producers are willing to sell to the biomass market differ for the two areas, Missouri and Illinois? Use $\alpha = .05$ to make the comparison.

	Missouri Producers	Illinois Producers
Sample Size	431	508
Mean Amount of Hay (%)	21.5	22.2
Standard Deviation (%)	33.4	34.9

Source: Based on I. Altman and D. Sanders, "Producer Willingness and Ability to Supply Biomass: Evidence from the U.S. Midwest," *Biomass and Energy,* Vol. 36, No. 8, 2012 (Tables 3 and 7).

8.21 **Does rudeness really matter in the workplace?** Studies have established that rudeness in the workplace can lead to retaliatory and counterproductive behavior. However, there has been little research on how rude behaviors influence a victim's task performance. Such a study was conducted, with the results published in the *Academy of Management Journal* (Oct. 2007). College students enrolled in a management course were randomly assigned to one of two experimental conditions: rudeness condition (45 students) and control group (53 students). Each student was asked to write down as many uses for a brick as possible in 5 minutes. For those students in the rudeness condition, the facilitator displayed rudeness by generally berating students for being irresponsible and unprofessional (due to a late-arriving confederate). No comments were made about the late-arriving confederate to students in the control group. The number of different uses for a brick was recorded for each of the 98 students and is shown below. Conduct a statistical analysis (at $\alpha = .01$) to determine if the true mean performance level for students in the rudeness condition is lower than the true mean performance level for students in the control group.

8.22 **Service without a smile.** "Service with a smile" is a slogan that many businesses adhere to. However, there are some jobs (e.g., those of judges, law enforcement officers, pollsters) that require neutrality when dealing with the public. An organization will typically provide "display rules" to guide employees on what emotions they should use when interacting with the public. A *Journal of Applied*

Data for Exercise 8.21

Control Group:

1	24	5	16	21	7	20	1	9	20	19	10	23	16	0	4	9	13	17	13	0	2	12	11	7	3	11
1	19	9	12	18	5	21	30	15	4	2	12	11	10	13	11	3	6	10	13	16	12	28	19	12	20	

Rudeness Condition:

4	11	18	11	9	6	5	11	9	12	7	5	7	3	11	1	9	11	10	7	8	9	10	7
11	4	13	5	4	7	8	3	8	15	9	16	10	0	7	15	13	9	2	13	10			

Data for Exercise 8.22

Positive Display Rule:

2	4	3	3	3	3	4	4	4	4	4	4	4	4	4	4	4	4	4	4	5
4	4	4	4	4	4	4	4	4	4	4	4	4	4	4	5	5	5	5	5	
5	5	5	5	5	5	5	5	5	5	5	5	5	5	5	5	5	5	5	5	5
5	5	5	5	5	5	5	5	5	5	5	5	5	5	5	5	5				

Neutral Display Rule:

3	3	2	1	2	1	1	1	2	2	1	2	2	2	3	2	2	1	2
2	2	2	2	1	2	2	2	2	2	2	1	2	2	2	2	2	2	
3	2	1	2	2	2	1	2	1	2	2	3	2	2	2	2	2	2	
2	2	2	2	1	2	2	2	2	2									

Psychology (Vol. 96, 2011) study compared the results of surveys conducted using two different types of display rules: positive (requiring a strong display of positive emotions) and neutral (maintaining neutral emotions at all times). In this designed experiment, 145 undergraduate students were randomly assigned to either a positive display rule condition ($n_1 = 78$) or a neutral display rule condition ($n_2 = 67$). Each participant was trained on how to conduct the survey using the display rules. As a manipulation check, the researchers asked each participant to rate, on a scale of 1 = "strongly agree" to 5 = "strongly disagree," the statement, "This task requires me to be neutral in my expressions."

a. If the manipulation of the participants was successful, which group should have the larger mean response? Explain.

b. The data for the study (simulated based on information provided in the journal article) are listed in the table above. Access the data and run an analysis to determine if the manipulation was successful. Conduct a test of hypothesis using $\alpha = .05$.

c. What assumptions, if any, are required for the inference from the test to be valid?

8.23 **Is honey a cough remedy?** Refer to the *Archives of Pediatrics and Adolescent Medicine* (Dec. 2007) study of honey as a children's cough remedy, Exercise 2.31 (p. 86). Children who were ill with an upper respiratory tract infection and their parents participated in the study. Parents were instructed to give their sick child a dosage of liquid "medicine" prior to bedtime. Unknown to the parents, some were given a dosage of dextromethorphan (DM)—an over-the-counter cough medicine—while others were given a similar dose of honey. (*Note*: A third group gave their children no medicine.) Parents then rated their children's cough symptoms, and the improvement in total cough symptoms score was determined for each child. The data (improvement scores) for the 35 children in the DM dosage group and the 35 children in the honey dosage group are reproduced in the next table. Do you agree with the statement (extracted from the article), "Honey may be a preferable treatment for the cough and sleep difficulty associated with childhood upper respiratory tract infection"? Use the comparison of two means methodology presented in this section to answer the question.

Honey Dosage:

12	11	15	11	10	13	10	4	15	16	9	14	10	6	10	8	11	
12	12	8	12	9	11	15	10	15	9	13	8	12	10	8	9	5	12

DM Dosage:

4	6	9	4	7	7	7	9	12	10	11	6	3	4	9	7	8	
12	12	4	12	13	7	10	13	9	4	4	10	15	9	12	6		

Source: I. M. Paul et al., "Effect of Honey, Dextromethorphan, and No Treatment on Nocturnal Cough and Sleep Quality for Coughing Children and Their Parents," *Archives of Pediatrics and Adolescent Medicine*, Vol. 161, No. 12, December 2007 (data simulated).

8.24 **Gender diversity of board of directors.** The gender diversity of a large corporation's board of directors was studied in *Accounting & Finance* (December 2015). In particular, the researchers wanted to know whether firms with a nominating committee would appoint more female directors than firms without a nominating committee. One of the key variables measured at each corporation was the percentage of board directors who are female. In a sample of 491 firms with a nominating committee, the mean percentage was 7.5%; in an independent sample of 501 firms without a nominating committee, the mean percentage was 4.3%.

a. To answer the research question, the researchers compared the mean percentage of female board directors at firms with a nominating committee with the corresponding percentage at firms without a nominating committee using an independent samples test. Set up the null and alternative hypotheses for this test.

b. The test statistic was reported as $z = 5.51$ with a corresponding *p*-value of .0001. Interpret this result if $\alpha = .05$.

c. Do the population percentages for each type of firm need to be normally distributed for the inference, part **b**, to be valid? Why or why not?

d. To assess the practical significance of the test, part **b**, construct a 95% confidence interval for the difference between the true mean percentages at firms with and without a nominating committee. Interpret the result. [*Hint*: Use the difference between the sample means and the value of the test statistic to solve for the standard error of the difference between the sample means.]

Applying the Concepts—Advanced

8.25 Ages of self-employed immigrants. Is self-employment for immigrant workers a faster route to economic advancement in the country? This was one of the questions studied in research published in the *International Journal of Manpower* (Vol. 32, 2011). One aspect of the study involved comparing the ages of self-employed and wage-earning immigrants. The researcher found that in Sweden, native wage earners tend to be younger than self-employed natives. However, immigrant wage earners tend to be older than self-employed immigrants. This inference was based on summary statistics for male Swedish immigrants shown in the table.

	Self-Employed Immigrants	Wage-Earning Immigrants
Sample Size	870	84,875
Mean Age (years)	44.88	46.79

Source: Based on L. Andersson, "Occupational Choice and Returns to Self-Employment Among Immigrants," *International Journal of Manpower*, Vol. 32, No. 8, 2011 (Table I).

a. Based on the information given, why is it impossible to provide a measure of reliability for the inference "Self-employed immigrants are younger, on average, than wage-earning immigrants in Sweden"?

b. What information do you need to obtain a measure of reliability for the inference, part **a**?

c. Give a value of the test statistic that would lead you to conclude that the true mean age of self-employed immigrants is less than the true mean age of wage-earning immigrants if you are willing to risk a Type I error rate of .01.

d. Assume that σ, the standard deviation of the ages, is the same for both self-employed and wage-earning immigrants. Give an estimate of σ that would lead you to conclude that the true mean age of self-employed immigrants is less than the true mean age of wage-earning immigrants using $\alpha = .01$.

e. Is the true value of σ likely to be larger or smaller than the one you calculated in part **d**?

8.3 Comparing Two Population Means: Paired Difference Experiments

Suppose you want to compare the mean daily sales of two restaurants located in the same city. If you were to record the restaurants' total sales for each of 12 randomly selected days during a 6-month period, the results might appear as shown in Table 8.3. Do these data provide evidence of a difference between the mean daily sales of the two restaurants?

We want to test the null hypothesis that the mean daily sales, μ_1 and μ_2, for the two restaurants are equal against the alternative hypothesis that they differ; that is,

$$H_0: (\mu_1 - \mu_2) = 0$$
$$H_a: (\mu_1 - \mu_2) \neq 0$$

Many researchers mistakenly use the *t*-statistic for two independent samples (Section 8.2) to conduct this test. The analysis is shown on the Excel/XLSTAT printout, Figure 8.10. The test statistic, $t = .38$, is highlighted on the printout, as well as the *p*-value of the test, *p*-value $= .7047$. At $\alpha = .10$, the *p*-value exceeds α. Thus, from *this*

Table 8.3	Daily Sales for Two Restaurants	
Day	Restaurant 1 (x_1)	Restaurant 2 (x_2)
1 (Wednesday)	$1,005	$ 918
2 (Saturday)	2,073	1,971
3 (Tuesday)	873	825
4 (Wednesday)	1,074	999
5 (Friday)	1,932	1,827
6 (Thursday)	1,338	1,281
7 (Thursday)	1,449	1,302
8 (Monday)	759	678
9 (Friday)	1,905	1,782
10 (Monday)	693	639
11 (Saturday)	2,106	2,049
12 (Tuesday)	981	933

📊 *Data Set: SALES2*

Summary statistics:

Variable	Observations	Minimum	Maximum	Mean	Std. deviation
SALES1	12	693.0000	2106.0000	1349.0000	530.0744
SALES2	12	639.0000	2049.0000	1267.0000	516.0370

t-test for two independent samples / Two-tailed test:

95% confidence interval on the difference between the means:
  (−360.8877 , 524.8877)

Difference	82.0000
t (Observed value)	0.3840
|t| (Critical value)	2.0739
DF	22
p-value (Two-tailed	0.7047
alpha	0.05

Figure 8.10

Excel/XLSTAT printout of an invalid analysis of the data in Table 8.3

analysis we might conclude that insufficient evidence exists to infer that there is a difference in mean daily sales for the two restaurants.

If you carefully examine the data in Table 8.3, however, you will find this conclusion difficult to accept. The sales of restaurant 1 exceed those of restaurant 2 *for every one of the randomly selected 12 days.* This, in itself, is strong evidence to indicate that μ_1 differs from μ_2, and we will subsequently confirm this fact. Why, then, was the *t*-test unable to detect this difference? The answer is, *the independent samples* t-*test is not a valid procedure to use with this set of data.*

The *t*-test is inappropriate because the assumption of independent samples is invalid. We have randomly chosen *days;* thus, once we have chosen the sample of days for restaurant 1, we have *not* independently chosen the sample of days for restaurant 2. The dependence between observations within days can be seen by examining the pairs of daily sales, which tend to rise and fall together as we go from day to day. This pattern provides strong visual evidence of a violation of the assumption of independence required for the two-sample *t*-test of Section 8.2. Also, substituting $s_1^2 = 530.07$ and $s_2^2 = 516.04$ (obtained from the printout, Figure 8.10) into the formula for s_p^2, we obtain

$$s_p^2 = \frac{(n_1 - 1)s_1^2 + (n_2 - 1)s_2^2}{n_1 + n_2 - 2}$$

$$= \frac{(12 - 1)(530.07)^2 + (12 - 1)(516.04)^2}{12 + 12 - 2} = 273,635.7$$

Thus, there is a *large variation within samples* (reflected by the large value of s_p^2) in comparison with the relatively *small difference between the sample means.* Because s_p^2 is so large, the *t*-test of Section 8.2 is unable to detect a possible difference between μ_1 and μ_2.

We now consider a valid method of analyzing the data of Table 8.3. In Table 8.4, we add the column of differences between the daily sales of the two restaurants, $d = x_1 - x_2$. We can regard these daily differences in sales as a random sample of all daily differences, past and present. Then we can use this sample to make inferences about the mean of the population of differences, μ_d, which is equal to the difference $(\mu_1 - \mu_2)$—that is, the mean of the population (and sample) of differences equals the difference between the population (and sample) means. Thus, our test becomes

$$H_0: \mu_d = 0 \ [\text{i.e., } (\mu_1 - \mu_2) = 0]$$
$$H_a: \mu_d \neq 0 \ [\text{i.e., } (\mu_1 - \mu_2) \neq 0]$$

Table 8.4	Daily Sales and Differences for Two Restaurants		
Day	Restaurant 1 (x_1)	Restaurant 2 (x_2)	Difference $d = x_1 - x_2$
1 (Wednesday)	$1,005	$ 918	$ 87
2 (Saturday)	2,073	1,971	102
3 (Tuesday)	873	825	48
4 (Wednesday)	1,074	999	75
5 (Friday)	1,932	1,827	105
6 (Thursday)	1,338	1,281	57
7 (Thursday)	1,449	1,302	147
8 (Monday)	759	678	81
9 (Friday)	1,905	1,782	123
10 (Monday)	693	639	54
11 (Saturday)	2,106	2,049	57
12 (Tuesday)	981	933	48

The test statistic is a one-sample t (Section 7.5) because we are now analyzing a single sample of differences for small n:

$$\text{Test statistic: } t = \frac{\bar{d} - 0}{s_d / \sqrt{n_d}}$$

where $\bar{d}$ = Sample mean difference
s_d = Sample standard deviation of differences
n_d = Number of differences = number of pairs

Assumptions: The population of differences in daily sales is approximately normally distributed. The sample differences are randomly selected from the population differences. [*Note:* We do not need to make the assumption that $\sigma_1^2 = \sigma_2^2$.]

Rejection region: At significance level $\alpha = .05$, we will reject H_0 if $|t| > t_{.05}$, where $t_{.05}$ is based on $(n_d - 1)$ degrees of freedom.

Referring to Table III in Appendix D, we find the t-value corresponding to $\alpha = .025$ and $n_d - 1 = 12 - 1 = 11$ df to be $t_{.025} = 2.201$. Then we will reject the null hypothesis if $|t| > 2.201$ (see Figure 8.11). Note that the number of degrees of freedom has decreased from $n_1 + n_2 - 2 = 22$ to 11 when we use the paired difference experiment rather than the two independent random samples design.

Summary statistics for the $n = 12$ differences are shown on the Minitab printout, Figure 8.12. Note that $\bar{d} = 82.0$ and $s_d = 32.0$ (rounded). Substituting these values into the formula for the test statistic, we have

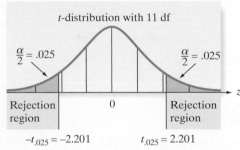

Figure 8.11

Rejection region for restaurant sales example

$$t = \frac{\bar{d} - 0}{s_d / \sqrt{n_d}} = \frac{82}{32 / \sqrt{12}} = 8.88$$

Because this value of t falls in the rejection region, we conclude (at $\alpha = .05$) that the difference in population mean daily sales for the two restaurants differs from 0. We can reach the same conclusion by noting that the p-value of the test, highlighted in Figure 8.12,

```
Paired T for SALES1 - SALES2

              N    Mean   StDev   SE Mean
SALES1       12    1349    530       153
SALES2       12    1267    516       149
Difference   12   82.00   31.99      9.23

95% CI for mean difference: (61.68, 102.32)
T-Test of mean difference = 0 (vs ≠ 0):  T-Value = 8.88   P-Value = 0.000
```

Figure 8.12

Minitab analysis of differences in daily restaurant sales

is approximately 0. The fact that $(\bar{x}_1 - \bar{x}_2) = \bar{d} = \$82.00$ strongly suggests that the mean daily sales for restaurant 1 exceed the mean daily sales for restaurant 2.

This kind of experiment, in which observations are paired and the differences are analyzed, is called a **paired difference experiment.** In many cases, a paired difference experiment can provide more information about the difference between population means than an independent samples experiment. The idea is to compare population means by comparing the differences between pairs of experimental units (objects, people, etc.) that were very similar prior to the experiment. The differencing removes sources of variation that tend to inflate σ^2. For instance, in the restaurant example, the day-to-day variability in daily sales is removed by analyzing the differences between the restaurants' daily sales. Making comparisons within groups of similar experimental units is called **blocking,** and the paired difference experiment is an example of a **randomized block experiment.** In our example, the days represent the blocks.

Some other examples for which the paired difference experiment might be appropriate are the following:

1. Suppose you want to estimate the difference $(\mu_1 - \mu_2)$ in mean price per gallon between two major brands of premium gasoline. If you choose two independent random samples of stations for each brand, the variability in price due to geographic location may be large. To eliminate this source of variability, you could choose pairs of stations of similar size, one station for each brand, in close geographic proximity and use the sample of differences between the prices of the brands to make an inference about $(\mu_1 - \mu_2)$.

2. A college placement center wants to estimate the difference $(\mu_1 - \mu_2)$ in mean starting salaries for men and women graduates who seek jobs through the center. If it independently samples men and women, the starting salaries may vary because of their different college majors and differences in grade point averages. To eliminate these sources of variability, the placement center could match male and female job seekers according to their majors and grade point averages. Then the differences between the starting salaries of each pair in the sample could be used to make an inference about $(\mu_1 - \mu_2)$.

3. To compare the performance of two automobile salespeople, we might test a hypothesis about the difference $(\mu_1 - \mu_2)$ in their respective mean monthly sales. If we randomly choose n_1 months of salesperson 1's sales and independently choose n_2 months of salesperson 2's sales, the month-to-month variability caused by the seasonal nature of new car sales might inflate s_p^2 and prevent the two-sample t-statistic from detecting a difference between μ_1 and μ_2, if such a difference actually exists. However, by taking the difference in monthly sales for the two salespeople for each of n months, we eliminate the month-to-month variability (seasonal variation) in sales, and the probability of detecting a difference between μ_1 and μ_2, if a difference exists, is increased.

The hypothesis-testing procedures and the method of forming confidence intervals for the difference between two means using a paired difference experiment are summarized in the following boxes for both large and small n.

Paired Difference Confidence Interval for $\mu_d = (\mu_1 - \mu_2)$

Large Sample, Normal (z) Statistic:

$$\bar{d} \pm z_{\alpha/2} \frac{\sigma_d}{\sqrt{n_d}} \approx \bar{d} \pm z_{\alpha/2} \frac{s_d}{\sqrt{n_d}}$$

Small Sample, Student's t-Statistic:

$$\bar{d} \pm t_{\alpha/2} \frac{s_d}{\sqrt{n_d}}$$

where $t_{\alpha/2}$ is based on $(n_d - 1)$ degrees of freedom.

Paired Difference Test of Hypothesis for $\mu_d = (\mu_1 - \mu_2)$

One-Tailed Test	Two-Tailed Test
$H_0: \mu_d = D_0$	$H_0: \mu_d = D_0$
$H_a: \mu_d < D_0$	$H_a: \mu_d \neq D_0$
[or $H_a: \mu_d > D_0$]	

Large Sample, Normal (z) Statistic

Test statistic: $z = \dfrac{\bar{d} - D_0}{\sigma_d/\sqrt{n_d}} \approx \dfrac{\bar{d} - D_0}{s_d/\sqrt{n_d}}$

Rejection region: $z < -z_\alpha$	Rejection region: $\|z\| > z_{\alpha/2}$
[or $z > z_\alpha$ when $H_a: \mu_d > D_0$]	
p-value $= P(z < z_c)$ [or $P(z > z_c)$]	p-value $= 2P(z > \|z_c\|)$

where z_c is the calculated value of the test statistic.

Small Sample, Student's t-Statistic

Test statistic: $t = \dfrac{d - D_0}{s_d/\sqrt{n_d}}$

Rejection region: $t < -t_\alpha$	Rejection region: $\|t\| > t_{\alpha/2}$
[or $t > t_\alpha$ when $H_a: \mu_d > D_0$]	
p-value $= P(t < t_c)$ [or $P(t > t_c)$]	p-value $= 2P(t > \|t_c\|)$

where t_α and $t_{\alpha/2}$ are based on $(n_d - 1)$ degrees of freedom and t_c is the calculated value of the test statistic.

Conditions Required for Valid Large-Sample Inferences About μ_d

1. A random sample of differences is selected from the target population of differences.
2. The sample size n_d is large (i.e., $n_d \geq 30$). (By the Central Limit Theorem, this condition guarantees that the test statistic will be approximately normal regardless of the shape of the underlying probability distribution of the population.)

Conditions Required for Valid Small-Sample Inferences About μ_d

1. A random sample of differences is selected from the target population of differences.
2. The population of differences has a distribution that is approximately normal.

EXAMPLE 8.5

Confidence Interval for μ_d—Comparing Mean Salaries of Males and Females

Problem An experiment is conducted to compare the starting salaries of male and female college graduates who find jobs. Pairs are formed by choosing a male and a female with the same major and similar grade point averages (GPAs). Suppose a random sample of 10 pairs is formed in this manner and the starting annual salary of each person is recorded. The results are shown in Table 8.5. Compare the mean starting salary, μ_1, for males with the mean starting salary, μ_2, for females using a 95% confidence interval. Interpret the results.

Table 8.5	Data on Annual Salaries for Matched Pairs of College Graduates		
Pair	Male x_1	Female x_2	Difference $d = x_1 - x_2$
1	$29,300	$28,800	$ 500
2	41,500	41,600	−100
3	40,400	39,800	600
4	38,500	38,500	0
5	43,500	42,600	900
6	37,800	38,000	−200
7	69,500	69,200	300
8	41,200	40,100	1,100
9	38,400	38,200	200
10	59,200	58,500	700

📊 *Data Set:* PAIRS

Solution Because the data on annual salary are collected in pairs of males and females matched on GPA and major, a paired difference experiment is performed. To conduct the analysis, we first compute the differences between the salaries, as shown in Table 8.5. Summary statistics for these $n = 10$ differences are displayed in the Minitab printout, Figure 8.13.

```
Paired T for MALE - FEMALE

             N   Mean  StDev  SE Mean
MALE        10  43930  11665     3689
FEMALE      10  43530  11617     3674
Difference  10    400    435      137


95% CI for mean difference: (89, 711)
T-Test of mean difference = 0 (vs ≠ 0): T-Value = 2.91   P-Value = 0.017
```

Figure 8.13

Minitab analysis of salary differences

The 95% confidence interval for $\mu_d = (\mu_1 - \mu_2)$ for this small sample is

$$\overline{d} \pm t_{\alpha/2} \frac{s_d}{\sqrt{n_d}}$$

where $t_{\alpha/2} = t_{.025} = 2.262$ (obtained from Table III Appendix D) is based on $n_d - 1 = 9$ degrees of freedom. Substituting the values of $\overline{d} = 400$ and $s_d = 435$ shown on the printout, we obtain

$$\overline{d} \pm t_{.025} \frac{s_d}{\sqrt{n_d}} = 400 \pm 2.262 \left(\frac{435}{\sqrt{10}} \right)$$

$$= 400 \pm 311 = (\$89, \$711)$$

[*Note:* This interval is also shown on the Minitab printout, Figure 8.13.] Our interpretation is that the true mean difference between the starting salaries of males and females falls between $89 and $711, with 95% confidence. Because the interval falls above 0, we infer that $\mu_1 - \mu_2 > 0$; that is, that the mean salary for males exceeds the mean salary for females.

Look Back Remember that $\mu_d = \mu_1 - \mu_2$. So, if $\mu_d > 0$, then $\mu_1 > \mu_2$. Alternatively, if $\mu_d < 0$, then $\mu_1 < \mu_2$.

● **Now Work Exercise 8.39**

To measure the amount of information about $(\mu_1 - \mu_2)$ gained by using a paired difference experiment in Example 8.5 rather than an independent samples experiment, we can compare the relative widths of the confidence intervals obtained by the two methods. A 95% confidence interval for $(\mu_1 - \mu_2)$ using the paired difference

Group Statistics

	GENDER	N	Mean	Std. Deviation	Std. Error Mean
SALARY	M	10	43930.00	11665.148	3688.844
	F	10	43530.00	11616.946	3673.601

Independent Samples Test

		Levene's Test for Equality of Variances		t-test for Equality of Means					95% Confidence Interval of the Difference	
		F	Sig.	t	df	Sig. (2-tailed)	Mean Difference	Std. Error Difference	Lower	Upper
SALARY	Equal variances assumed	.000	.991	.077	18	.940	400.000	5206.046	-10537.496	11337.496
	Equal variances not assumed			.077	18.000	.940	400.000	5206.046	-10537.509	11337.509

Figure 8.14

SPSS analysis of salaries, assuming independent samples

experiment is, from Example 8.5, ($89, $711). If we mistakenly analyzed the same data as though this were an independent samples experiment,* we would first obtain the descriptive statistics shown in the SPSS printout, Figure 8.14.

Then we would substitute the sample means and standard deviations shown on the printout into the formula for a 95% confidence interval for $(\mu_1 - \mu_2)$ using independent samples:

$$(\bar{x}_1 - \bar{x}_2) \pm t_{.025}\sqrt{s_p^2\left(\frac{1}{n_1} + \frac{1}{n_2}\right)}$$

where

$$s_p^2 = \frac{(n_1 - 1)s_1^2 + (n_2 - 1)s_2^2}{n_1 + n_2 - 2}$$

SPSS performed these calculations and obtained the interval $(-\$10,537.50, \$11,337.50)$. This interval is highlighted in Figure 8.14.

Notice that the independent samples interval includes 0. Consequently, if we were to use this interval to make an inference about $(\mu_1 - \mu_2)$, we would incorrectly conclude that the mean starting salaries of males and females do not differ! You can see that the confidence interval for the independent sampling experiment is about five times wider than for the corresponding paired difference confidence interval. Blocking out the variability due to differences in majors and grade point averages significantly increases the information about the difference in male and female mean starting salaries by providing a much more accurate (smaller confidence interval for the same confidence coefficient) estimate of $(\mu_1 - \mu_2)$.

You may wonder whether conducting a paired difference experiment is always superior to an independent samples experiment. The answer is—most of the time but not always. We sacrifice half the degrees of freedom in the t-statistic when a paired difference design is used instead of an independent samples design. This is a loss of information, and unless this loss is more than compensated for by the reduction in variability obtained by blocking (pairing), the paired difference experiment will result in a net loss of information about $(\mu_1 - \mu_2)$. Thus, we should be convinced that the pairing will significantly reduce variability before performing the paired difference experiment. Most of the time this will happen.

One final note: The pairing of the observations is determined before the experiment is performed (that is, by the *design* of the experiment). A paired difference experiment is *never* obtained by pairing the sample observations after the measurements have been acquired.

ETHICS in STATISTICS

In a two-group analysis, intentionally pairing observations after the data have been collected in order to produce a desired result is considered *unethical statistical practice.*

What Do You Do When the Assumption of a Normal Distribution for the Population of Differences Is Not Satisfied?

Answer: Use the Wilcoxon signed rank test for the paired difference design (Chapter 15).

---

*This is done only to provide a measure of the increase in the amount of information obtained by a paired design in comparison to an unpaired design. Actually, if an experiment is designed using pairing, an unpaired analysis would be invalid because the assumption of independent samples would not be satisfied.

Exercises 8.26–8.42

Learning the Mechanics

8.26 A paired difference experiment produced the following results:

$$n_d = 38 \quad \bar{x}_1 = 92 \quad \bar{x}_2 = 95.5 \quad \bar{d} = -3.5 \quad s_d^2 = 21$$

a. Determine the values of z for which the null hypothesis, $\mu_1 - \mu_2 = 0$, would be rejected in favor of the alternative hypothesis, $\mu_1 - \mu_2 < 0$. Use $\alpha = .10$.

b. Conduct the paired difference test described in part **a**. Draw the appropriate conclusions.

c. What assumptions are necessary so that the paired difference test will be valid?

d. Find a 90% confidence interval for the mean difference μ_d.

e. Which of the two inferential procedures, the confidence interval of part **d** or the test of hypothesis of part **b**, provides more information about the differences between the population means?

8.27 A paired difference experiment yielded n_d pairs of observations. In each case, what is the rejection region for testing $H_0: \mu_d > 2$?

a. $n_d = 12, \alpha = .05$
b. $n_d = 24, \alpha = .10$
c. $n_d = 4, \alpha = .025$
d. $n_d = 80, \alpha = .01$

8.28 The data for a random sample of six paired observations are shown in the next table.

NW

L08028

a. Calculate the difference between each pair of observations by subtracting observation 2 from observation 1. Use the differences to calculate $\bar{d}$ and s_d^2.

b. If μ_1 and μ_2 are the means of populations 1 and 2, respectively, express μ_d in terms of μ_1 and μ_2.

Pair	Sample from Population 1 (Observation 1)	Sample from Population 2 (Observation 2)
1	7	4
2	3	1
3	9	7
4	6	2
5	4	4
6	8	7

c. Form a 95% confidence interval for μ_d.

d. Test the null hypothesis $H_0: \mu_d = 0$ against the alternative hypothesis $H_a: \mu_d \neq 0$. Use $\alpha = .05$.

8.29 The data for a random sample of 10 paired observations are shown in the table below.

L08029

Pair	Sample from Population 1	Sample from Population 2
1	19	24
2	25	27
3	31	36
4	52	53
5	49	55
6	34	34
7	59	66
8	47	51
9	17	20
10	51	55

a. If you wish to test whether these data are sufficient to indicate that the mean for population 2 is larger than that for population 1, what are the appropriate null and alternative hypotheses? Define any symbols you use.

b. Conduct the test, part **a**, using $\alpha = .10$.

c. Find a 90% confidence interval for μ_d. Interpret this result.

d. What assumptions are necessary to ensure the validity of this analysis?

8.30 A paired difference experiment yielded the following results:

$$n_d = 7 \quad \Sigma d = -7 \quad \Sigma d^2 = 35$$

a. Determine whether these data are sufficient to infer whether the two population means differ at the 10% significance level.

b. Calculate the p-value for the analysis in part **a** and interpret your result.

c. Justify the assumption you made in your analysis in part **a**.

Applying the Concepts—Basic

8.31 **Summer weight-loss camp.** Camp Jump Start is an 8-week summer camp for overweight and obese adolescents. Counselors develop a weight-management program for each camper that centers on nutrition education and physical activity. To justify the cost of the camp, counselors must provide empirical evidence that the weight-management program is effective. In a study published in *Pediatrics* (April 2010), the body mass index (BMI) was measured for each of 76 campers both at the start and end of camp. Summary statistics on BMI measurements are shown in the table.

	Mean	Standard Deviation
Starting BMI	34.9	6.9
Ending BMI	31.6	6.2
Paired Differences	3.3	1.5

Source: Based on J. Huelsing, N. Kanafani, J. Mao, and N. H. White, "Camp Jump Start: Effects of a Residential Summer Weight-Loss Camp for Older Children and Adolescents," *Pediatrics*, Vol. 125, No. 4, April 2010 (Table 3).

a. Give the null and alternative hypotheses for determining whether the mean BMI at the end of camp is less than the mean BMI at the start of camp.

b. How should the data be analyzed, as an independent samples test or as a paired difference test? Explain.

c. Calculate the test statistic using the formula for an independent samples test. (*Note:* This is *not* how the test should be conducted.)

d. Calculate the test statistic using the formula for a paired difference test.

e. Compare the test statistics, parts **c** and **d**. Which test statistic provides more evidence in support of the alternative hypothesis?

f. The p-value of the test, part **d**, was reported as $p < .0001$. Interpret this result, assuming $\alpha = .01$.

g. Do the differences in BMI values need to be normally distributed in order for the inference, part **f**, to be valid? Explain.

h. Find a 99% confidence interval for the true mean change in BMI for Camp Jump Start campers. Interpret the result.

8.32 **Performance ratings of government agencies.** The U.S. Office of Management and Budget (OMB) requires government agencies to produce annual performance and accounting reports (PARS) each year. A research team at George Mason University evaluated the quality of the PARS for 24 government agencies (*The Public Manager,* Summer 2008), where evaluation scores ranged from 12 (lowest) to 60 (highest). The accompanying file contains evaluation scores for all 24 agencies for two consecutive years. (See Exercise 2.131, p. 132.) Data for a random sample of five of these agencies are shown in the accompanying table. Suppose you want to conduct a paired difference test to determine whether the true mean evaluation score of government agencies in year 2 exceeds the true mean evaluation score in year 1.

Agency	Year 1 Score	Year 2 Score
GSA	34	40
Agriculture	33	35
Social Security	33	33
USAID	32	42
Defense	17	32

Source: J. Ellig and H. Wray, "Measuring Performance Reporting Quality," *The Public Manager,* Vol. 37, No. 2, Summer 2008 (p. 66). Copyright © 2008 by Jerry Ellig. Used by permission of Jerry Ellig.

a. Explain why the data should be analyzed using a paired difference test.

b. Compute the difference between the year 2 score and the year 1 score for each sampled agency.

c. Find the mean and standard deviation of the differences, part **b**.

d. Use the summary statistics, part **c**, to find the test statistic.

e. Give the rejection region for the test using $\alpha = .10$.

f. Make the appropriate conclusion in the words of the problem.

8.33 **Twinned drill holes.** A traditional method of verifying mineralization grades in mining is to drill twinned holes, i.e., the drilling of a new hole, or "twin," next to an earlier drill hole. The use of twinned drill holes was investigated in *Exploration and Mining Geology* (Vol. 18, 2009). Geologists use data collected at both holes to estimate the total amount of heavy minerals (THM) present at the drilling site. The data in the following table (based on information provided in the journal article) represent THM percentages for a sample of 15 twinned holes drilled at a diamond mine in Africa. The geologists want to know if there is any evidence of a difference in the true THM means of all original holes and their twin holes drilled at the mine.

a. Explain why the data should be analyzed as paired differences.

b. Compute the difference between the "1st Hole" and "2nd Hole" measurements for each drilling location.

c. Find the mean and standard deviation of the differences, part **b**.

d. Use the summary statistics, part **c**, to find a 90% confidence interval for the true mean difference ("1st Hole" minus "2nd Hole") in THM measurements.

e. Interpret the interval, part **d**. Can the geologists conclude that there is no evidence of a difference in the true THM means of all original holes and their twin holes drilled at the mine?

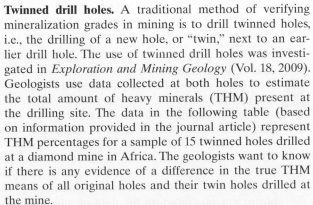

Location	1st Hole	2nd Hole
1	5.5	5.7
2	11.0	11.2
3	5.9	6.0
4	8.2	5.6
5	10.0	9.3
6	7.9	7.0
7	10.1	8.4
8	7.4	9.0
9	7.0	6.0
10	9.2	8.1
11	8.3	10.0
12	8.6	8.1
13	10.5	10.4
14	5.5	7.0
15	10.0	11.2

8.34 **Packaging of a children's health food.** Refer to the *Journal of Consumer Behaviour* (Vol. 10, 2011) study of packaging of a children's health food product, Exercise 7.33 (p. 409). Recall that a fictitious brand of a healthy food product—sliced apples—was packaged to appeal to children. The researchers compared the appeal of this fictitious brand to the appeal of a commercially available brand of sliced apples, which was not packaged for children. Each of 408 schoolchildren rated both brands on a 5-point "willingness to eat" scale, with 1 = "not willing at all" and 5 = "very willing." The fictitious brand had a sample mean score of 3.69, while the commercially available brand had a sample mean score of 3.00. The researchers wanted to compare the population mean score for the fictitious brand, μ_F, with the population mean score for the commercially available brand, μ_C. They theorized that μ_F would be greater than μ_C.

a. Specify the null and alternative hypotheses for the test.

b. Explain how the researchers should analyze the data and why.

c. The researchers reported a test statistic value of 5.71. Interpret this result. Use $\alpha = .05$ to make your conclusion.

d. Find the approximate *p*-value of the test.

e. Could the researchers have tested at $\alpha = .01$ and arrived at the same conclusion?

8.35 **"I am not selling anything" surveys.** To improve response rates in telephone surveys, interviewers are often instructed by the polling company to state, "I am not selling anything" at the outset of the call. The effectiveness of this strategy was investigated in the *International Journal of Public Opinion Research* (Winter 2004). The sample consisted of 29 different telephone surveys. However, in each survey about half the people were contacted by interviewers using the "I am not selling anything" introduction and the other half were contacted by interviewers using the standard introduction. Thus, for each of the 29 surveys, both the "not selling" and standard interviewing techniques were employed. Summary statistics on response rates (proportion of people called who actually responded to the survey questions) are given in the accompanying table. The goal of the researchers was to compare the mean response rates of the two interviewing methods with the specific purpose to determine if the mean response rate for "not selling" was higher than that for the standard.

	"Not selling" Introduction	Standard Introduction
Number of Surveys	29	29
Mean Response Rate	.262	.246
Standard Deviation	.12	.11

Source: Republished with permission of Oxford Publishing Limited, from E. D. De Leeuw and J. J. Hox, "I Am Not Selling Anything: 29 Experiments in Telephone Introductions," *International Journal of Public Opinion Research*, Vol. 16, No. 4, Winter 2004, pp. 464–473 (Table 1). Permission conveyed through Copyright Clearance Center, Inc.

a. Explain why the data should be analyzed as a paired difference experiment.

b. Analyze the data in the table using the independent samples *t*-test. Do you detect a significant difference between the mean response rates of the two methods using $\alpha = .05$?

c. The researchers applied the paired difference *t* procedure and obtained an observed significance level of *p*-value = .001. Interpret this result if $\alpha = 0.5$.

d. Compare the inferences you made in parts **b** and **c**.

8.36 **Consumers' attitudes toward advertising.** The two most common marketing tools used for product advertising are ads on television and ads in a print magazine. Consumers' attitudes toward television and magazine advertising were investigated in the *Journal of Advertising* (Vol. 42, 2013). In one experiment, each in a sample of 159 college students was asked to rate both the television and the magazine marketing tool on a scale of 1 to 7 points according to whether the tool was a good example of advertising, a typical form of advertising, and a representative form of advertising. Summary statistics for these "typicality" scores are provided in the following table. One objective is to compare the mean ratings of TV and magazine advertisements.

a. The researchers analyzed the data using a paired-samples *t*-test. Explain why this is the most valid method of analysis. Give the null and alternative hypotheses for the test.

b. The researchers reported a paired *t*-value of 6.96 with an associated *p*-value of .001 and stated that the "mean difference between television and magazine advertising was statistically significant." Explain what this means in the context of the hypothesis test.

c. To assess whether the result is "practically significant," we require a confidence interval for the mean difference. Although this interval was not reported in the article, you can compute it using the information provided in the table. Find a 95% confidence interval for the mean difference and interpret the result. What is your opinion regarding whether the two means are "practically significant."

	TV Ad Rating	Magazine Ad Rating	Difference Between TV and Magazine Ad Rating
Sample mean	6.49	6.04	.45
Sample standard deviation	.65	.87	.815

Source: H. S. Jin and R. J. Lutz, "The Typicality and Accessibility of Consumer Attitudes Toward Television Advertising: Implications for the Measurement of Attitudes Toward Advertising in General," *Journal of Advertising*, Vol. 42, No. 4, 2013 (from Table 1).

Applying the Concepts—Intermediate

8.37 **Taking "power naps" during work breaks.** Lack of sleep costs companies about $18 billion a year in lost productivity, according to the National Sleep Foundation. In recognition of this problem, many companies now make quiet rooms available for employees to take "power naps" during work breaks (*U.S. News & World Report*, November 15, 2010). Consider a major airline that encourages reservation agents to nap during their breaks. The accompanying table lists the number of complaints received about each of a sample of 10 reservation agents during the 6 months before naps were encouraged and during the 6 months after the policy change.

NAPS

a. Do the data present sufficient evidence to conclude that the new napping policy reduced the mean number of customer complaints about reservation agents? Test using $\alpha = .05$.

b. What assumptions must hold to ensure the validity of the test?

c. What variables, not controlled in the study, could lead to an invalid conclusion?

Operator	Before Policy	After Policy
1	10	5
2	3	0
3	16	7
4	11	4
5	8	6
6	2	4
7	1	2
8	14	3
9	5	5
10	6	1

8.38 **Acidity of mouthwash.** Acid has been found to be a primary cause of dental caries (cavities). It is theorized that oral mouthwashes contribute to the development of caries due to the antiseptic agent oxidizing into acid over time. This theory was tested in the *Journal of Dentistry, Oral Medicine and Dental Education* (Vol. 3, 2009). Three bottles of mouthwash, each of a different brand, were randomly selected from a drugstore. The pH level (where lower pH levels indicate higher acidity) of each bottle was measured on the date of purchase and after 30 days. The data are shown in the table on the next page. Conduct an analysis to determine if the mean initial pH level of mouthwash differs significantly from the mean pH level after 30 days. Use $\alpha = .05$ as your level of significance.

Data for Exercise 8.38

Mouthwash Brand	Initial pH	Final pH
LMW	4.56	4.27
SMW	6.71	6.51
RMW	5.65	5.58

Source: Based on K. L. Chunhye and B. C. Schmitz, "Determination of pH, Total Acid, and Total Ethanol in Oral Health Products: Oxidation of Ethanol and Recommendations to Mitigate Its Association with Dental Caries," *Journal of Dentistry, Oral Medicine and Dental Education,* Vol. 3, No. 1, 2009 (Table 1).

8.39 **Solar energy generation along highways.** The potential of using solar panels constructed above national highways to generate energy was explored in the *International Journal of Energy and Environmental Engineering* (December 2013). Two-layer solar panels (with 1 meter separating the panels) were constructed above sections of both east-west and north-south highways in India. The amount of energy (kilowatt-hours) supplied to the country's grid by the solar panels above the two types of highways was determined each month. The data for several randomly selected months are provided in the table. The researchers concluded that the "two-layer solar panel energy generation is more viable for the north-south oriented highways as compared to east-west oriented roadways." Compare the mean solar energy amounts generated for the two types of highways using a 95% confidence interval. Does the interval support the researchers' conclusion?

Month	East-West	North-South
February	8658	8921
April	7930	8317
July	5120	5274
September	6862	7148
October	8608	8936

Source: P. Sharma and T. Harinarayana, "Solar Energy Generation Potential Along National Highways," *International Journal of Energy and Environmental Engineering,* Vol. 49, No. 1, December 2013 (Table 3).

8.40 **Impact of red light cameras on car crashes.** To combat red-light-running crashes many states have installed red light cameras at dangerous intersections to photograph the license plates of vehicles that run the red light. How effective are photo-red enforcement programs in reducing red-light-running crash incidents at intersections? The Virginia Department of Transportation (VDOT) conducted a comprehensive study of its photo-red enforcement program. In one portion of the study, the VDOT provided crash data both before and after installation of red light cameras at several intersections. The data (measured as the number of crashes caused by red light running per intersection per year) for 13 intersections in Fairfax County, Virginia, are given in the table. Analyze the data for the VDOT. What do you conclude?

Intersection	Before Camera	After Camera
1	3.60	1.36
2	0.27	0
3	0.29	0
4	4.55	1.79
5	2.60	2.04
6	2.29	3.14
7	2.40	2.72

Intersection	Before Camera	After Camera
8	0.73	0.24
9	3.15	1.57
10	3.21	0.43
11	0.88	0.28
12	1.35	1.09
13	7.35	4.92

Source: Based on "Research Report: The Impact of Red Light Cameras (Photo-Red Enforcement) on Crashes in Virginia" from Virginia Transportation Research Council.

8.41 **Evaluating a new drug.** Merck Research Labs conducted an experiment to evaluate the effect of a new drug using the single-T swim maze. Nineteen impregnated dam rats were captured and allocated a dosage of 12.5 milligrams of the drug. One male and one female rat pup were randomly selected from each resulting litter to perform in the swim maze. Each pup was placed in the water at one end of the maze and allowed to swim until it escaped at the opposite end. If the pup failed to escape after a certain period of time, it was placed at the beginning of the maze and given another chance. The experiment was repeated until each pup accomplished three successful escapes. The table below reports the number of swims required by each pup to perform three successful escapes. Is there sufficient evidence of a difference between the mean number of swims required by male and female pups? Conduct the test (at $\alpha = .10$). Comment on the assumptions required for the test to be valid.

Litter	Male	Female	Litter	Male	Female
1	8	5	11	6	5
2	8	4	12	6	3
3	6	7	13	12	5
4	6	3	14	3	8
5	6	5	15	3	4
6	6	3	16	8	12
7	3	8	17	3	6
8	5	10	18	6	4
9	4	4	19	9	5
10	4	4			

Source: Copyright © 2012 by Merck Research Laboratories.

Applying the Concepts—Advanced

8.42 **Alcoholic fermentation in wines.** Determining alcoholic fermentation in wine is critical to the wine-making process. Must/wine density is a good indicator of the fermentation point because the density value decreases as sugars are converted into alcohol. For decades, winemakers have measured must/wine density with a hydrometer. Although accurate, the hydrometer employs a manual process that is very time-consuming. Consequently, large wineries are searching for more rapid measures of density measurement. An alternative method uses the hydrostatic balance instrument (similar to the hydrometer but digital). A winery in Portugal collected the must/wine density measurements for white wine samples randomly selected from the fermentation process for a recent harvest. For each sample, the density of the wine at 20°C was measured with both the hydrometer and the hydrostat balance. The densities for 40 wine samples are saved in the file. The first five and last five observations are shown in the table (next page). The winery will use the alternative method of measuring wine density only if it can be demonstrated that the mean difference between the density measurements of the two methods does not exceed .002. Perform the analysis for the winery. Provide the winery with a written report of your conclusions.

Sample	Hydrometer	Hydrostatic
5	1.10263	1.10518
⋮	⋮	⋮
36	1.08084	1.08097
37	1.09452	1.09431
38	0.99479	0.99498
39	1.00968	1.01063
40	1.00684	1.00526

Source: Cooperative Cellar of Borba (*Adega Cooperative de Borba*), Portugal.

Sample	Hydrometer	Hydrostatic
1	1.08655	1.09103
2	1.00270	1.00272
3	1.01393	1.01274
4	1.09467	1.09634

8.4 Comparing Two Population Proportions: Independent Sampling

Suppose a personal water craft (PWC) manufacturer wants to compare the potential market for its products in the northeastern United States to the market in the southeastern United States. Such a comparison would help the manufacturer decide where to concentrate sales efforts. Using telephone directories, the company randomly chooses 1,000 households in the southeast (SE) and 1,000 households in the northeast (NE) and determines whether each household plans to buy a PWC within the next 5 years. The objective is to use this sample information to make an inference about the difference $(p_1 - p_2)$ between the proportion p_1 of *all* households in the SE and the proportion p_2 of *all* households in the NE that plan to purchase a PWC within 5 years.

The two samples represent independent binomial experiments. (See Section 4.3 for the characteristics of binomial experiments.) The binomial random variables are the numbers x_1 and x_2 of the 1,000 sampled households in each area that indicate they will purchase a PWC within 5 years. The results are summarized in Table 8.6.

We can now calculate the sample proportions $\hat{p}_1$ and $\hat{p}_2$ of the households in the SE and NE, respectively, that are prospective buyers:

Table 8.6	Results of Telephone Survey
SE	NE
$n_1 = 1,000$	$n_2 = 1,000$
$x_1 = 42$	$x_2 = 24$

$$\hat{p}_1 = \frac{x_1}{n_1} = \frac{42}{1,000} = .042$$

$$\hat{p}_2 = \frac{x_2}{n_2} = \frac{24}{1,000} = .024$$

The difference between the sample proportions $(\hat{p}_1 - \hat{p}_2)$ makes an intuitively appealing point estimator of the difference between the population parameters $(p_1 - p_2)$. For our example, the estimate is

$$(\hat{p}_1 - \hat{p}_2) = .042 - .024 = .018$$

To judge the reliability of the estimator $(\hat{p}_1 - \hat{p}_2)$, we must observe its performance in repeated sampling from the two populations—that is, we need to know the sampling distribution of $(\hat{p}_1 - \hat{p}_2)$. The properties of the sampling distribution are given in the next box. Remember that $\hat{p}_1$ and $\hat{p}_2$ can be viewed as means of the number of successes per trial in the respective samples, so the Central Limit Theorem applies when the sample sizes are large.

Properties of the Sampling Distribution of $(p_1 - p_2)$

1. The mean of the sampling distribution of $(\hat{p}_1 - \hat{p}_2)$ is $(p_1 - p_2)$; that is,

$$E(\hat{p}_1 - \hat{p}_2) = p_1 - p_2$$

Thus, $(\hat{p}_1 - \hat{p}_2)$ is an unbiased estimator of $(p_1 - p_2)$.

2. The standard deviation of the sampling distribution of $(\hat{p}_1 - \hat{p}_2)$ is

$$\sigma_{(\hat{p}_1 - \hat{p}_2)} = \sqrt{\frac{p_1 q_1}{n_1} + \frac{p_2 q_2}{n_2}}$$

3. If the sample sizes n_1 and n_2 are large (see Section 6.4 for a guideline), the sampling distribution of $(\hat{p}_1 - \hat{p}_2)$ is approximately normal.

Because the distribution of $(\hat{p}_1 - \hat{p}_2)$ in repeated sampling is approximately normal, we can use the z-statistic to derive confidence intervals for $(p_1 - p_2)$ or test a hypothesis about $(p_1 - p_2)$.

For the PWC example, a 95% confidence interval for the difference $(p_1 - p_2)$ is

$$(\hat{p}_1 - \hat{p}_2) \pm 1.96\sigma_{(\hat{p}_1 - \hat{p}_2)} \quad \text{or} \quad (\hat{p}_1 - \hat{p}_2) \pm 1.96\sqrt{\frac{p_1 q_1}{n_1} + \frac{p_2 q_2}{n_2}}$$

The quantities $p_1 q_1$ and $p_2 q_2$ must be estimated to complete the calculation of the standard deviation $\sigma_{(\hat{p}_1 - \hat{p}_2)}$ and hence the calculation of the confidence interval. In Section 6.4 we showed that the value of pq is relatively insensitive to the value chosen to approximate p. Therefore, $\hat{p}_1 \hat{q}_1$ and $\hat{p}_2 \hat{q}_2$ will provide satisfactory estimates to approximate $p_1 q_1$ and $p_2 q_2$, respectively. Then

$$\sqrt{\frac{p_1 q_1}{n_1} + \frac{p_2 q_2}{n_2}} \approx \sqrt{\frac{\hat{p}_1 \hat{q}_1}{n_1} + \frac{\hat{p}_2 \hat{q}_2}{n_2}}$$

and we will approximate the 95% confidence interval by

$$(\hat{p}_1 - \hat{p}_2) \pm 1.96\sqrt{\frac{\hat{p}_1 \hat{q}_1}{n_1} + \frac{\hat{p}_2 \hat{q}_2}{n_2}}$$

Substituting the sample quantities yields

$$(.042 - .024) \pm 1.96\sqrt{\frac{(.042)(.958)}{1,000} + \frac{(.024)(.976)}{1,000}}$$

or, $.018 \pm .016$. Thus, we are 95% confident that the interval from .002 to .034 contains $(p_1 - p_2)$. We infer that there are between .2% and 3.4% more households in the southeast than in the northeast that plan to purchase PWCs in the next 5 years.

The general form of a confidence interval for the difference $(p_1 - p_2)$ between population proportions is given in the following box.

Large-Sample $(1 - \alpha)$% Confidence Interval for $(p_1 - p_2)$: Normal (z) Statistic

$$(\hat{p}_1 - \hat{p}_2) \pm z_{\alpha/2}\sigma_{(\hat{p}_1 - \hat{p}_2)} = (\hat{p}_1 - \hat{p}_2) \pm z_{\alpha/2}\sqrt{\frac{p_1 q_1}{n_1} + \frac{p_2 q_2}{n_2}}$$

$$\approx (\hat{p}_1 - \hat{p}_2) \pm z_{\alpha/2}\sqrt{\frac{\hat{p}_1 \hat{q}_1}{n_1} + \frac{\hat{p}_2 \hat{q}_2}{n_2}}$$

Conditions Required for Valid Large-Sample Inferences About $(p_1 - p_2)$

1. The two samples are randomly selected in an independent manner from the two target populations.

2. The sample sizes, n_1 and n_2, are both large so that the sampling distribution of $(\hat{p}_1 - \hat{p}_2)$ will be approximately normal. (This condition will be satisfied if both $n_1 \hat{p}_1 \geq 15$, $n_1 \hat{q}_1 \geq 15$, and $n_2 \hat{p}_2 \geq 15$, $n_2 \hat{q}_2 \geq 15$.)

The z-statistic,

$$z = \frac{(\hat{p}_1 - \hat{p}_2) - (p_1 - p_2)}{\sigma_{(\hat{p}_1 - \hat{p}_2)}}$$

is used to test the null hypothesis that $(p_1 - p_2)$ equals some specified difference, say, D_0. For the special case where $D_0 = 0$—that is, where we want to test the null hypothesis $H_0: (p_1 - p_2) = 0$ (or, equivalently, $H_0: p_1 = p_2$)—the best estimate of $p_1 = p_2 = p$ is obtained by dividing the total number of successes $(x_1 + x_2)$ for the two samples by the total number of observations $(n_1 + n_2)$; that is,

$$\hat{p} = \frac{x_1 + x_2}{n_1 + n_2} \quad \text{or} \quad \hat{p} = \frac{n_1\hat{p}_1 + n_2\hat{p}_2}{n_1 + n_2}$$

The second equation shows that $\hat{p}$ is a weighted average of $\hat{p}_1$ and $\hat{p}_2$, with the larger sample receiving more weight. If the sample sizes are equal, then $\hat{p}$ is a simple average of the two sample proportions of successes.

We now substitute the weighted average $\hat{p}$ for both p_1 and p_2 in the formula for the standard deviation of $(\hat{p}_1 - \hat{p}_2)$:

$$\sigma_{(\hat{p}_1 - \hat{p}_2)} = \sqrt{\frac{p_1 q_1}{n_1} + \frac{p_2 q_2}{n_2}} \approx \sqrt{\frac{\hat{p}\hat{q}}{n_1} + \frac{\hat{p}\hat{q}}{n_2}} = \sqrt{\hat{p}\hat{q}\left(\frac{1}{n_1} + \frac{1}{n_2}\right)}$$

The test is summarized in the next box.

Large-Sample Test of Hypothesis About $(p_1 - p_2)$: Normal (z) Statistic

One-Tailed Test	Two-Tailed Test
$H_0: (p_1 - p_2) = 0$*	$H_0: (p_1 - p_2) = 0$
$H_a: (p_1 - p_2) \neq 0$	$H_a: (p_1 - p_2) \neq 0$
$\quad$[or $H_a: (p_1 - p_2) > 0$]	

$$\text{Test statistic: } z = \frac{(\hat{p}_1 - \hat{p}_2)}{\sigma_{(\hat{p}_1 - \hat{p}_2)}}$$

Rejection region: $z < -z_\alpha$	Rejection region: $|z| > z_{\alpha/2}$
$\quad$[or $z > z_\alpha$ when $H_a: (p_1 - p_2) > 0$]	
p-value $= P(z < z_c)$ [or $P(z > z_c)$]	p-value $= 2P(z > |z_c|)$

where z_c is the calculated value of the test statistic.

$$\text{Note: } \sigma_{(\hat{p}_1 - \hat{p}_2)} = \sqrt{\frac{p_1 q_1}{n_1} + \frac{p_2 q_2}{n_2}} \approx \sqrt{\hat{p}\hat{q}\left(\frac{1}{n_1} + \frac{1}{n_2}\right)}, \text{ where } \hat{p} = \frac{x_1 + x_2}{n_1 + n_2}.$$

EXAMPLE 8.6

Large-Sample Test About $(p_1 - p_2)$—Comparing Car Repair Rates

Problem A consumer advocacy group wants to determine whether there is a difference between the proportions of the two leading automobile models that need major repairs (more than $500) within 2 years of their purchase. A sample of 400 two-year owners of model 1 is contacted, and a sample of 500 two-year owners of model 2 is contacted. The numbers x_1 and x_2 of owners who report that their cars needed major repairs within the first 2 years are 53 and 78, respectively. Test the null hypothesis that no difference exists between the proportions in populations 1 and 2 needing major repairs against the alternative that a difference does exist. Use $\alpha = .10$.

---

*The test can be adapted to test for a difference $D_0 \neq 0$. Because most applications call for a comparison of p_1 and p_2, implying $D_0 = 0$, we will confine our attention to this case.

Solution If we define p_1 and p_2 as the true proportions of model 1 and model 2 owners, respectively, whose cars needed major repairs within 2 years, the elements of the test are

$$H_0: (p_1 - p_2) = 0$$

$$H_a: (p_1 - p_2) \neq 0$$

Test statistic: $z = \dfrac{(\hat{p}_1 - \hat{p}_2) - 0}{\sigma_{(\hat{p}_1 - \hat{p}_2)}}$

Rejection region $(\alpha = .10)$: $|z| > z_{\alpha/2} = z_{.05} = 1.645$ (see Figure 8.15)

We now calculate the sample proportions of owners who needed major car repairs,

$$\hat{p}_1 = \frac{x_1}{n_1} = \frac{53}{400} = .1325$$

$$\hat{p}_2 = \frac{x_2}{n_2} = \frac{78}{500} = .1560$$

Then

$$z = \frac{(\hat{p}_1 - \hat{p}_2) - 0}{\sigma_{(\hat{p}_1 - \hat{p}_2)}} \approx \frac{(\hat{p}_1 - \hat{p}_2)}{\sqrt{\hat{p}\hat{q}\left(\dfrac{1}{n_1} + \dfrac{1}{n_2}\right)}}$$

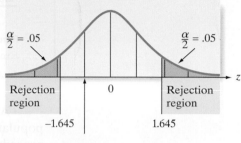

Figure 8.15
Rejection region for Example 8.6

where

$$\hat{p} = \frac{x_1 + x_2}{n_1 + n_2} = \frac{53 + 78}{400 + 500} = .1456$$

Note that $\hat{p}$ is a weighted average of $\hat{p}_1$ and $\hat{p}_2$, with more weight given to the larger sample of model 2 owners.

Thus, the computed value of the test statistic is

$$z = \frac{.1325 - .1560}{\sqrt{(.1456)(.8544)\left(\dfrac{1}{400} + \dfrac{1}{500}\right)}} = \frac{-.0235}{.0237} = -.99$$

The samples provide insufficient evidence at $\alpha = .10$ to detect a difference between the proportions of the two models that needed repairs within 2 years.

Look Back Even though 2.35% more sampled owners of model 2 found they needed major repairs, this difference is less than 1 standard deviation ($z = -.99$) from the hypothesized zero difference between the true proportions. Thus, a 95% confidence interval for $(p_1 - p_2)$ would include 0—also implying no evidence of a difference.

● **Now Work Exercise 8.49**

EXAMPLE 8.7

Finding the Observed Significance Level of a Test for $p_1 - p_2$

Problem Use a statistical software package to conduct the test in Example 8.6. Find and interpret the p-value of the test.

Solution We entered the sample sizes (n_1 and n_2) and number of successes (x_1 and x_2) into Excel/XLSTAT and obtained the printout shown in Figure 8.16. The test statistic for this two-tailed test is shaded on the printout, as well as the observed significance level (p-value). Note that p-value = .3205 exceeds $\alpha = .10$. Consequently, there is no evidence of a difference between the true population proportions.

z-test for two proportions / Two-tailed test:			
95% confidence interval on the difference between the proportions:			
(-0.0695 , 0.0225)			
Difference	-0.0235		
z (Observed value)	-0.9934		
z (Critical value)	1.9600		
p-value (Two-tailed)	0.3205		
alpha	0.05		

Figure 8.16

Excel/XLSTAT printout for test of two proportions

As with a single population proportion, most studies designed to compare two population proportions employ large samples; consequently, the large-sample testing procedure based on the normal (z) statistic presented here will be appropriate for making inferences about $p_1 - p_2$. *However, in the case of small samples, tests for $p_1 - p_2$ based on the z-statistic may not be valid.* A test to compare proportions that can be applied to small samples utilizes *Fisher's exact test.* We discuss this method in an optional section in Chapter 10.

What Do You Do in the Small-Sample Case When Comparing Two Population Proportions?

Answer: Use Fisher's exact test (Chapter 10).

STATISTICS IN ACTION

Comparing Proportions

REVISITED   In the first *Statistics in Action Revisited* in this chapter (p. 463), we demonstrated how the expert statistician used a comparison of two means to defend Visa in a libel case. Recall that ZixIt claimed that a Visa executive's email postings had a negative impact on ZixIt's attempt to develop a new online credit card processing system. Here, we demonstrate another way to analyze the data, one successfully presented in court by the statistician.

In addition to daily closing price and trading volume of ZixIt stock, the **ZIXVSA** file also contains a qualitative variable that indicates whether the stock price increased or not (decreased or stayed the same) on the following day. This variable was created by the statistician to compare the proportion of days on which ZixIt stock went up for posting and nonposting days. Let p_1 represent the proportion of days where the ZixIt stock price increased following all nonposting days and p_2 represent the proportion of days where the ZixIt stock price increased following posting days. Then, if the charges made by ZixIt were true (i.e., that postings had a negative impact on ZixIt stock), p_1 will exceed p_2. Thus, a comparison of two population proportions is appropriate. Recall that during the 83-day period of interest, the executive posted emails on 43 days and had no postings on 40 days. Again, both sample sizes ($n_1 = 40$ and $n_2 = 43$) are large, so we can apply the large-sample z-test or large-sample confidence interval procedure for independent samples. (Can you demonstrate this?) A Minitab printout for this analysis is shown in Figure SIA8.3.

From the printout you can see that following the 40 nonposting days, the price increased on 20 days; following the 43 posting days, the stock price increased on 18 days. Thus, the sample proportions are $p_1 = 20/40 = .5$ and $p_2 = 18/43 = .42$. Are these

---

Test and CI for Two Proportions: Up/Down, Posting

```
Event = UP

Posting   X    N   Sample p
NO       20   40   0.500000
POST     18   43   0.418605


Difference = p (NO) - p (POST)
Estimate for difference:  0.0813953
95% CI for difference:  (-0.132500, 0.295291)
Test for difference = 0 (vs ≠ 0):  Z = 0.75   P-Value = 0.456

Fisher's exact test: P-Value = 0.513
```

Figure SIA8.3

Minitab comparison of two proportions analysis

sample proportions different enough for us to conclude that the population proportions are different and that ZixIt's claim was true? Not according to the statistical analysis. Note that the 95% confidence interval for $(p_1 - p_2)$, $(-.133, .295)$, includes the value 0, and the p-value for the two-tailed test of $H_0: (p_1 - p_2) = 0$, p-value $= .456$, exceeds, say, $\alpha = .05$. Both imply that the two population proportions are not significantly different. Also, neither sample proportion is significantly different from .5. (Can you demonstrate this?) Consequently, in courtroom testimony, the statistical expert used these results to conclude that "the direction of ZixIt's stock price movement following days with postings is random, just like days with no postings."

Data Set: ZIXVSA

Exercises 8.43–8.60

Learning the Mechanics

8.43 Consider making an inference about $p_1 - p_2$, where there are x_1 successes in n_1 binomial trials and x_2 successes in n_2 binomial trials.
   a. Describe the distributions of x_1 and x_2.
   b. Explain why the Central Limit Theorem is important in finding an approximate distribution for $(\hat{p}_1 - \hat{p}_2)$.

8.44 For each of the following values of α, find the values of z for which $H_0: (p_1 - p_2) = 0$ would be rejected in favor of $H_a: (p_1 - p_2) < 0$.
   a. $\alpha = .01$ **b.** $\alpha = .025$
   c. $\alpha = .05$ **d.** $\alpha = .10$

8.45 In each case, determine whether the sample sizes are large enough to conclude that the sampling distribution of $(\hat{p}_1 - \hat{p}_2)$ is approximately normal.
   a. $n_1 = 12, n_2 = 14, \hat{p}_1 = .42, \hat{p}_2 = .57$
   b. $n_1 = 12, n_2 = 14, \hat{p}_1 = .92, \hat{p}_2 = .86$
   c. $n_1 = n_2 = 30, \hat{p}_1 = .70, \hat{p}_2 = .73$
   d. $n_1 = 100, n_2 = 250, \hat{p}_1 = .93, \hat{p}_2 = .97$
   e. $n_1 = 125, n_2 = 200, \hat{p}_1 = .08, \hat{p}_2 = .12$

8.46 Construct a 95% confidence interval for $(p_1 - p_2)$ in each of the following situations:
   a. $n_1 = 400, \hat{p}_1 = .65; n_2 = 400, \hat{p}_2 = .58$
   b. $n_1 = 180, \hat{p}_1 = .31; n_2 = 250, \hat{p}_2 = .25$
   c. $n_1 = 100, \hat{p}_1 = .46; n_2 = 120, \hat{p}_2 = .61$

8.47 Independent random samples, each containing 800 observations, were selected from two binomial populations. The samples from populations 1 and 2 produced 320 and 400 successes, respectively.
   a. Test $H_0: (p_1 - p_2) = 0$ against $H_a: (p_1 - p_2) > 0$. Use $\alpha = .05$.
   b. Test $H_0: (p_1 - p_2) = 0$ against $H_a: (p_1 - p_2) \neq 0$. Use $\alpha = .01$.
   c. Test $H_0: (p_1 - p_2) = 0$ against $H_a: (p_1 - p_2) < 0$. Use $\alpha = .01$.
   d. Form a 90% confidence interval for $(p_1 - p_2)$.

8.48 Random samples of size $n_1 = 400$ and $n_2 = 500$ were drawn from populations 1 and 2, respectively. The samples yielded $x_1 = 105$ and $x_2 = 140$. Test $H_0: p_1 - p_2 \geq 0$ against $H_a: p_1 - p_2 < 0$ at the 1% level of significance.

Applying the Concepts—Basic

8.49 **The "winner's curse" in auction bidding.** In auction bidding, the "winner's curse" is the phenomenon of the winning (or highest) bid price being above the expected value of the item being auctioned. *The Review of Economics and Statistics* (Aug. 2001) published a study on whether bid experience impacts the likelihood of the winner's curse occurring. Two groups of bidders in a sealed-bid auction were compared: (1) super-experienced bidders and (2) less-experienced bidders. In the super-experienced group, 29 of 189 winning bids were above the item's expected value; in the less-experienced group, 32 of 149 winning bids were above the item's expected value.

a. Find an estimate of p_1, the true proportion of super-experienced bidders who fell prey to the winner's curse.

b. Find an estimate of p_2, the true proportion of less-experienced bidders who fell prey to the winner's curse.

c. Construct a 90% confidence interval for $p_1 - p_2$.

d. Give a practical interpretation of the confidence interval, part **c**. Make a statement about whether bid experience impacts the likelihood of the winner's curse occurring.

8.50 **Redeeming coupons from text messages.** Many companies now use text messaging on cell phones as a means of marketing their products. One way to do this is to send a redeemable discount coupon (called an m-coupon) via a text. The redemption rate of m-coupons—the proportion of coupons redeemed—was the subject of an article in the *Journal of Marketing Research* (October 2015). In a two-year study, over 8,000 mall shoppers participated by signing up to receive m-coupons. The researchers were interested in comparing the redemption rates of m-coupons for different products. In a sample of 2,447 m-coupons for products sold at a milkshake store, 79 were redeemed; in a sample of 6,619 m-coupons for products sold at a donut store, 72 were redeemed.

a. Compute the redemption rate for the sample of milkshake m-coupons.

b. Compute the redemption rate for the sample of donut m-coupons.

c. Give a point estimate for the difference between the true redemption rates.

d. Form a 90% confidence interval for the difference between the true redemption rates. Give a practical interpretation of the result.

e. Explain the meaning of the phrase "90% confident" in your answer to part **d**.

f. Based on the interval, part **d**, is there a "statistically" significant difference between the redemption rates? (Recall that a result is "statistically" significant if there is evidence to show that the true difference in proportions is not 0.)

g. Assume the true difference between redemption rates must exceed .01 (i.e., 1%) for the researchers to consider the difference to be "practically" significant. Based on the interval, part **c**, is there a "practically" significant difference between the redemption rates?

8.51 **Producer willingness to supply biomass.** Refer to the *Biomass and Energy* (Vol. 36, 2012) study of the willingness of producers to supply biomass products such as surplus hay, Exercise 8.20 (p. 469). Recall that independent samples of Missouri producers and Illinois producers were surveyed. Another aspect of the study focused on the services producers were willing to supply. One key service involves windrowing (mowing and piling) of hay. Of the 558 Missouri producers surveyed, 187 were willing to offer windrowing services; of the 940 Illinois producers surveyed, 380 were willing to offer windrowing services. The researchers want to know if the proportion of producers who were willing to offer windrowing services to the biomass market differs for the two areas, Missouri and Illinois.

a. Specify the parameter of interest to the researchers.

b. Set up the null and alternative hypotheses for testing whether the proportion of producers who were willing to offer windrowing services differs in Missouri and Illinois.

c. A Minitab analysis of the data is shown below. Locate the test statistic on the printout.

d. Give the rejection region for the test using $\alpha = .01$.

e. Locate the p-value of the test on the printout.

f. Make the appropriate conclusion using both the p-value and rejection region approach. Your conclusions should agree.

Test and CI for Two Proportions

```
Sample    X    N   Sample p
1        187  558  0.335125
2        380  940  0.404255


Difference = p (1) - p (2)
Estimate for difference:  -0.0691299
99% CI for difference:  (-0.135079, -0.00318070)
Test for difference = 0 (vs ≠ 0):  Z = -2.67  P-Value = 0.008

Fisher's exact test: P-Value = 0.008
```

8.52 **Web survey response rates.** Response rates to Web surveys are typically low, partially due to users starting but not finishing the survey. The factors that influence response rates were investigated in *Survey Methodology* (December 2013). In a designed study, Web users were directed to participate in one of several surveys with different formats. For example, one format utilized a welcome screen with a white background and another format utilized a welcome screen with a red background. The "break-off rates," i.e., the proportion of sampled users who break off the survey before completing all questions, for the two formats are provided in the table.

	White Welcome Screen	Red Welcome Screen
Number of Web users	190	183
Number who break off survey	49	37
Break-off rate	.258	.202

Source: R. Haer and N. Meidert, "Does the First Impression Count? Examining the Effect of the Welcome Screen Design on the Response Rate," *Survey Methodology,* Vol. 39, No. 2, December 2013 (Table 4.1).

a. Verify the values of the break-off rates shown in the table.

b. The researchers theorize that the true break-off rate for Web users of the red welcome screen will be lower than the corresponding break-off rate for the white welcome screen. Give the null and alternative hypotheses for testing this theory.

c. Compute the test statistic for the test.

d. Find the p-value of the test.

e. Make the appropriate conclusion using $\alpha = .10$.

8.53 **Hospital administration of malaria patients.** One of the most serious health problems in India is malaria. Consequently, Indian hospital administrators must have the resources to treat the high volume of malaria patients that are admitted. Research published in the *National Journal of Community Medicine* (Vol. 1, 2010) investigated whether the malaria admission rate is higher in some months than in others. In a sample of 192 hospital patients admitted in January, 32 were treated for malaria.

In an independent sample of 403 patients admitted in May (4 months later), 34 were treated for malaria.

a. Describe the two populations of interest in this study.

b. Give a point estimate of the difference in the malaria admission rates in January and May.

c. Find a 90% confidence interval for the difference in the malaria admission rates in January and May.

d. Based on the interval, part **c**, can you conclude that a difference exists in the true malaria admission rates in January and May? Explain.

Applying the Concepts—Intermediate

8.54 Traffic sign maintenance. The Federal Highway Administration (FHWA) recently issued new guidelines for maintaining and replacing traffic signs. Civil engineers at North Carolina State University conducted a study of the effectiveness of various sign maintenance practices developed to adhere to the new guidelines and published the results in the *Journal of Transportation Engineering* (June 2013). One portion of the study focused on the proportion of traffic signs that fail the minimum FHWA retroreflectivity requirements. Of 1,000 signs maintained by the North Carolina Department of Transportation (NCDOT), 512 were deemed failures. Of 1,000 signs maintained by county-owned roads in North Carolina, 328 were deemed failures. Conduct a test of hypothesis to determine whether the true proportions of traffic signs that fail the minimum FHWA retroreflectivity requirements differ depending on whether the signs are maintained by the NCDOT or by the county. Test using $\alpha = .05$.

8.55 Salmonella in produce. Salmonella infection is the most common type of bacterial food-borne illness in the United States. How prevalent is salmonella in produce grown in the major agricultural region of Monterey, California? Researchers from the U.S. Department of Agriculture (USDA) conducted tests for salmonella in produce grown in the region and published their results in *Applied and Environmental Microbiology* (April 2011). In a sample of 252 cultures obtained from water used to irrigate the region, 18 tested positive for salmonella. In an independent sample of 476 cultures obtained from the region's wildlife (e.g., birds), 20 tested positive for salmonella. Is this sufficient evidence for the USDA to state that the prevalence of salmonella in the region's water differs from the prevalence of salmonella in the region's wildlife? Use $\alpha = .01$ to make your decision.

8.56 Angioplasty's benefits challenged. More than 1 million heart patients each year undergo an angioplasty. The benefits of an angioplasty were challenged in a study of 2,287 patients (2007 Annual Conference of the American College of Cardiology, New Orleans). All the patients had substantial blockage of the arteries but were medically stable. All were treated with medication such as aspirin and beta-blockers. However, half the patients were randomly assigned to get an angioplasty and half were not. After 5 years, the researchers found that 211 of the 1,145 patients in the angioplasty group had subsequent heart attacks compared with 202 of 1,142 patients in the medication-only group. Do you agree with the study's conclusion, "There was no significant difference in the rate of heart attacks for the two groups"? Support your answer with a 95% confidence interval.

8.57 Entrepreneurial careers of MBA alumni. Are African American MBA students more likely to begin their careers as entrepreneurs than white MBA students? This was a question of interest to the Graduate Management Admission Council (GMAC). *GMAC Research Reports* (Oct. 3, 2005) published the results of a survey of MBA alumni. Of the 1,304 African Americans who responded to the survey, 209 reported their employment status after graduation as self-employed or a small business owner. Of the 7,120 whites who responded to the survey, 356 reported their employment status after graduation as self-employed or a small business owner. Use this information to answer the research question.

8.58 Predicting software defects. Refer to the PROMISE Software Engineering Repository data on 498 modules of software code written in "C" language for a NASA spacecraft instrument, saved in the file. (See Exercise 3.132, p. 209). Recall that the software code in each module was evaluated for defects; 49 were classified as "true" (i.e., module has defective code), and 449 were classified as "false" (i.e., module has correct code). Consider these to be independent random samples of software code modules. Researchers predicted the defect status of each module using the simple algorithm, "If number of lines of code in the module exceeds 50, predict the module to have a defect." The accompanying SPSS printout shows the number of modules in each of the two samples that were predicted to have defects (PRED_LOC = "yes") and predicted to have no defects (PRED_LOC = "no"). Now, define the *accuracy rate* of the algorithm as the proportion of modules that were correctly predicted. Compare the accuracy rate of the algorithm when applied to modules with defective code with the accuracy rate of the algorithm when applied to modules with correct code. Use a 99% confidence interval.

DEFECT * PRED_LOC Crosstabulation

Count

		PRED_LOC		
		no	yes	Total
DEFECT	false	400	49	449
	true	29	20	49
Total		429	69	498

Applying the Concepts—Advanced

8.59 Vulnerability of relying party Web sites. When you sign on to your Facebook account, you are granted access to more than 1 million *relying party* (RP) Web sites. Vulnerabilities in this sign-on system may permit an attacker to gain unauthorized access to your profile, allowing the attacker to impersonate you on the RP Web site. Computer and systems engineers investigated the vulnerability of relying party Web sites and presented their results at the *Proceedings of the 5th AMC Workshop on Computers & Communication Security* (October 2012). RP Web sites were categorized as server-flow or client-flow Web sites. Of the 40 server-flow sites studied, 20 were found to be vulnerable to impersonation attacks. Of the 54 client-flow sites examined, 41 were found to be vulnerable to impersonation attacks. Give your opinion on whether a client-flow Web site is more likely to be vulnerable to an impersonation attack than a server-flow Web site. If so, how much more likely?

8.60 Religious symbolism in TV commercials. Gonzaga University professors conducted a study of television commercials and published their results in the *Journal of Sociology, Social Work and Social Welfare* (Vol. 2, 2008). The key research question was as follows: "Do television advertisers use religious symbolism to sell goods and services?" In a sample of 797 TV commercials collected ten years earlier, only 16 commercials used religious symbolism. Of the sample of 1,499 TV commercials examined in the more recent study, 51 commercials used religious symbolism. Conduct an analysis to determine if the percentage of TV commercials that use religious symbolism has changed over time. If you detect a change, estimate the magnitude of the difference and attach a measure of reliability to the estimate.

8.5 Determining the Required Sample Size

You can find the appropriate sample size to estimate the difference between a pair of parameters with a specified sampling error (SE) and degree of reliability by using the method described in Section 6.5 — that is, to estimate the difference between a pair of parameters correct to within SE units with confidence level $(1 - \alpha)$, let $z_{\alpha/2}$ standard deviations of the sampling distribution of the estimator equal SE. Then solve for the sample size. To do this, you have to solve the problem for a specific ratio between n_1 and n_2. Most often, you will want to have equal sample sizes—that is, $n_1 = n_2 = n$. We will illustrate the procedure with two examples.

EXAMPLE 8.8

Finding the Sample Sizes for Estimating $(\mu_1 - \mu_2)$—Comparing Mean Crop Yields

Problem New fertilizer compounds are often advertised with the promise of increased crop yields. Suppose we want to compare the mean yield μ_1 of wheat when a new fertilizer is used with the mean yield μ_2 with a fertilizer in common use. The estimate of the difference in mean yield per acre is to be correct to within .25 bushel with a confidence coefficient of .95. If the sample sizes are to be equal, find $n_1 = n_2 = n$, the number of 1-acre plots of wheat assigned to each fertilizer.

Solution To solve the problem, you need to know something about the variation in the bushels of yield per acre. Suppose from past records you know the yields of wheat possess a range of approximately 10 bushels per acre. You could then approximate $\sigma_1 = \sigma_2 = \sigma$ by letting the range equal 4σ. Thus,

$$4\sigma \approx 10 \text{ bushels}$$
$$\sigma \approx 2.5 \text{ bushels}$$

The next step is to solve the equation

$$z_{\alpha/2}\sigma_{(\bar{x}_1 - \bar{x}_2)} = SE \quad \text{or} \quad z_{\alpha/2}\sqrt{\frac{\sigma_1^2}{n_1} + \frac{\sigma_2^2}{n_2}} = SE$$

for n, where $n = n_1 = n_2$. Because we want the estimate to lie within SE = .25 of $(\mu_1 - \mu_2)$ with confidence coefficient equal to .95, we have $z_{\alpha/2} = z_{.025} = 1.96$. Then, letting $\sigma_1 = \sigma_2 = 2.5$ and solving for n, we have

$$1.96\sqrt{\frac{(2.5)^2}{n} + \frac{(2.5)^2}{n}} = .25$$

$$1.96\sqrt{\frac{2(2.5)^2}{n}} = .25$$

$$n = 768.32 \approx 769 \text{ (rounding up)}$$

Consequently, you will have to sample 769 acres of wheat for each fertilizer to estimate the difference in mean yield per acre to within .25 bushel.

Look Back Because $n = 769$ would necessitate extensive and costly experimentation, you might decide to allow a larger sampling error (say, SE = .50 or SE = 1) to reduce the sample size, or you might decrease the confidence coefficient. The point is that we can obtain an idea of the experimental effort necessary to achieve a specified precision in our final estimate by determining the approximate sample size *before* the experiment is started.

● **Now Work Exercise 8.62a**

EXAMPLE 8.9

Finding the Sample Sizes for Estimating $(p_1 - p_2)$—Comparing Defect Rates of Two Machines

Problem A production supervisor suspects a difference exists between the proportions p_1 and p_2 of defective items produced by two different machines. Experience has shown that the proportion defective for each of the two machines is in the neighborhood of .03. If the supervisor wants to estimate the difference in the proportions to within .005 using a 95% confidence interval, how many items must be randomly sampled from the production of each machine? (Assume that the supervisor wants $n_1 = n_2 = n$.)

Solution In this sampling problem, the sampling error is SE = .005, and for the specified level of reliability, $(1 - \alpha) = .95$, $z_{\alpha/2} = z_{.025} = 1.96$. Then, letting $p_1 = p_2 = .03$ and $n_1 = n_2 = n$, we find the required sample size per machine by solving the following equation for n:

$$z_{\alpha/2}\sigma_{(\hat{p}_1 - \hat{p}_2)} = SE$$

or

$$z_{\alpha/2}\sqrt{\frac{p_1 q_1}{n_1} + \frac{p_2 q_2}{n_2}} = SE$$

$$1.96\sqrt{\frac{(.03)(.97)}{n} + \frac{(.03)(.97)}{n}} = .005$$

$$1.96\sqrt{\frac{2(.03)(.97)}{n}} = .005$$

$$n = 8{,}943.2$$

Look Back This large n will likely result in a tedious sampling procedure. If the supervisor insists on estimating $(p_1 - p_2)$ correct to within .005 with 95% confidence, approximately 9,000 items will have to be inspected for each machine.

● **Now Work Exercise 8.61a**

You can see from the calculations in Example 8.9 that $\sigma_{(\hat{p}_1 - \hat{p}_2)}$ (and hence the solution, $n_1 = n_2 = n$) depends on the actual (but unknown) values of p_1 and p_2. In fact, the required sample size $n_1 = n_2 = n$ is largest when $p_1 = p_2 = .5$. Therefore, if you have no prior information on the approximate values of p_1 and p_2, use $p_1 = p_2 = .5$ in the formula for $\sigma_{(\hat{p}_1 - \hat{p}_2)}$. If p_1 and p_2 are in fact close to .5, then the values of n_1 and n_2 that you have calculated will be correct. If p_1 and p_2 differ substantially from .5, then your solutions for n_1 and n_2 will be larger than needed. Consequently, using $p_1 = p_2 = .5$ when solving for n_1 and n_2 is a conservative procedure because the sample sizes n_1 and n_2 will be at least as large as (and probably larger than) needed.

The procedures for determining the sample sizes necessary for estimating $(\mu_1 - \mu_2)$ or $(p_1 - p_2)$ for the case $n_1 = n_2$ and for μ_d in a paired difference experiment are given in the boxes that follow.

Determination of Sample Size for Estimating $(\mu_1 - \mu_2)$: Equal Sample Size Case

To estimate $(\mu_1 - \mu_2)$ with a given sampling error SE and with confidence level $(1 - \alpha)$, use the following formula to solve for equal sample sizes that will achieve the desired reliability:

$$n_1 = n_2 = \frac{(z_{\alpha/2})^2 (\sigma_1^2 + \sigma_2^2)}{(SE)^2}$$

You will need to substitute estimates for the values of σ_1^2 and σ_2^2 before solving for the sample size. These estimates might be sample variances s_1^2 and s_2^2 from prior sampling (e.g., a pilot sample) or from an educated (and conservatively large) guess based on the range—that is, $s \approx R/4$.

Determination of Sample Size for Estimating $(p_1 - p_2)$: Equal Sample Size Case

To estimate $(p_1 - p_2)$ with a given sampling error SE and with confidence level $(1 - \alpha)$, use the following formula to solve for equal sample sizes that will achieve the desired reliability:

$$n_1 = n_2 = \frac{(z_{\alpha/2})^2(p_1q_1 + p_2q_2)}{(SE)^2}$$

You will need to substitute estimates for the values of p_1 and p_2 before solving for the sample size. These estimates might be based on prior samples, obtained from educated guesses, or, most conservatively, specified as $p_1 = p_2 = .5$.

Determination of Sample Size for Estimating μ_d

To estimate μ_d to within a given sampling error SE and with confidence level $(1 - \alpha)$, use the following formula to solve for the number of pairs, n_d, that will achieve the desired reliability:

$$n_d = (z_{\alpha/2})^2(\sigma_d^2)/(SE)^2$$

You will need to substitute an estimate for the value of σ_d, the standard deviation of the paired differences, before solving for the sample size.

Note: When estimating either $(\mu_1 - \mu_2)$ or $(p_1 - p_2)$, you may desire one sample size to be a multiple of the other, e.g., $n_2 = a(n_1)$, where a is an integer. For example, you may want to sample twice as many experimental units in the second sample as in the first. Then $a = 2$ and $n_2 = 2(n_1)$. For this unequal sample size case, slight adjustments are made to the computing formulas. These formulas (proof omitted) are provided below for convenience.

Adjustment to Sample Size Formula for Estimating $(\mu_1 - \mu_2)$ When $n_2 = a(n_1)$

$$n_1 = \frac{(z_{\alpha/2})^2(a\sigma_1^2 + \sigma_2^2)}{a(SE)^2} \qquad n_2 = a(n_1)$$

Adjustment to Sample Size Formula for Estimating $(p_1 - p_2)$ When $n_2 = a(n_1)$

$$n_1 = \frac{(z_{\alpha/2})^2(ap_1q_1 + p_2q_2)}{a(SE)^2} \qquad n_2 = a(n_1)$$

Exercises 8.61–8.72

Learning the Mechanics

8.61 Assuming that $n_1 = n_2$, find the sample sizes needed to estimate $(p_1 - p_2)$ for each of the following situations:

NW **a.** Sampling error = .01 with 99% confidence. Assume that $p_1 \approx .4$ and $p_2 \approx .7$.

b. A 90% confidence interval of width .05. Assume that there is no prior information available to obtain approximate values of p_1 and p_2.

c. Sampling error = .03 with 90% confidence. Assume that $p_1 \approx .2$ and $p_2 \approx .3$.

8.62 Find the appropriate values of n_1 and n_2 (assume $n_1 = n_2$) needed to estimate $(\mu_1 - \mu_2)$ for each of the following situations:

NW **a.** A sampling error equal to 3.2 with 95% confidence. From prior experience it is known that $\sigma_1 \approx 15$ and $\sigma_2 \approx 17$.

b. A sampling error equal to 8 with 99% confidence. The range of each population is 60.

c. A 90% confidence interval of width 1.0. Assume that $\sigma_1^2 \approx 5.8$ and $\sigma_2^2 \approx 7.5$.

8.63 Suppose you want to estimate the difference between two population means correct to within 1.8 with a 95% confidence interval. If prior information suggests that the population variances are approximately equal to $\sigma_1^2 = \sigma_2^2 = 14$ and you want to select independent random samples of equal size from the populations, how large should the sample sizes, n_1 and n_2, be?

8.64 Enough money has been budgeted to collect independent random samples of size $n_1 = n_2 = 100$ from populations 1 and 2 to estimate $(\mu_1 - \mu_2)$. Prior information indicates that $\sigma_1 = \sigma_2 = 10$. Have sufficient funds been allocated to construct a 90% confidence interval for $(\mu_1 - \mu_2)$ of width 5 or less? Justify your answer.

Applying the Concepts—Basic

8.65 **Last name and acquisition timing.** Refer to the *Journal of Consumer Research* (August 2011) study of the *last name effect* in acquisition timing, Exercise 8.13 (p. 466). Recall that the mean response times (in minutes) to acquire free tickets were compared for two groups of MBA students—those students with last names beginning with one of the first nine letters of the alphabet and those with last names beginning with one of the last nine letters of the alphabet. How many MBA students from each group would need to be selected to estimate the difference in mean times to within 2 minutes of its true value with 95% confidence? (Assume equal sample sizes were selected for each group and that the response time standard deviation for both groups is $\sigma \approx 9$ minutes.)

8.66 **Homework assistance for accounting students.** Refer to the *Journal of Accounting Education* (Vol. 25, 2007) study of providing homework assistance to accounting students, Exercise 8.18 (p. 468). Recall that one group of students was given a completed homework solution and another group was given only check figures at various steps of the solution. The researchers wanted to compare the average test score improvement of the two groups. How many students should be sampled in each group to estimate the difference in the averages to within .5 point with 99% confidence? Assume that the standard deviations of the test score improvements for the two groups are approximately equal to 1.

8.67 **Vulnerability of relying party Web sites.** Refer to the *Proceedings of the 5th AMC Workshop on Computers & Communication Security* (October 2012) study of the vulnerability of relying party (RP) Web sites, Exercise 8.59 (p. 489). Recall that the Web sites were categorized as server-flow or client-flow Web sites. The researchers want to estimate the true difference between the proportion of server-flow Web sites vulnerable to attack and the corresponding proportion of client-flow Web sites with a 95% confidence interval. They want to know how many Web sites of each type they need to sample to obtain an estimate that is no more than .15 from the true difference.

a. Identify the parameter of interest for this study.

b. What is the desired confidence level?

c. What is the desired sampling error?

d. Find the sample size required to obtain the desired estimate. Assume $n_1 = n_2$.

e. Repeat part **d**, but now assume that twice as many Web sites will be sampled from the population of server-flow Web sites as from the population of client-flow Web sites, i.e., assume $n_1 = 2n_2$.

8.68 **Conducting a political poll.** A pollster wants to estimate the difference between the proportions of men and women who favor a particular national candidate using a 90% confidence interval of width .04. Suppose the pollster has no prior information about the proportions. If equal numbers of men and women are to be polled, how large should the sample sizes be?

Applying the Concepts—Intermediate

8.69 **Shared leadership in airplane crews.** Refer to the *Human Factors* (March 2014) study of shared leadership by the cockpit and cabin crews of a commercial airplane, Exercise 8.14 (p. 466). Recall that each crew was rated as working either successfully or unsuccessfully as a team. Then, during a simulated flight, the number of leadership functions exhibited per minute was determined for each individual crew member. One objective was to compare the mean leadership scores for successful and unsuccessful teams. How many crew members would need to be sampled from successful and unsuccessful teams to estimate the difference in means to within .05 with 99% confidence? Assume you will sample twice as many members from successful teams as from unsuccessful teams. Also, assume that the variance of the leadership scores for both groups is approximately .04.

8.70 **Solar energy generation along highways.** Refer to the *International Journal of Energy and Environmental Engineering* (December 2013) study of solar energy generation along highways, Exercise 8.39 (p. 481). Recall that the researchers compared the mean monthly amount of solar energy generated by east-west– and north-south–oriented solar panels using a matched-pairs experiment. However, a small sample of only five months was used for the analysis. How many more months would need to be selected to estimate the difference in means to within 25 kilowatt-hours with a 90% confidence interval? Use the information provided in the **SOLAR** file to find an estimate of the standard error required to carry out the calculation.

8.71 **Angioplasty's benefits challenged.** Refer to the study of patients with substantial blockage of the arteries presented at the 2007 Annual Conference of the American College of Cardiology, Exercise 8.56 (p. 489). Recall that half the patients were randomly assigned to get an angioplasty and half were not. The researchers compared the proportion of patients with subsequent heart attacks for the two groups and reported no significant difference between the two proportions. Although the study involved over 2,000 patients, the sample size may have been too small to detect a difference in heart attack rates.

a. How many patients must be sampled in each group to estimate the difference in heart attack rates to within .015 with 95% confidence? (Use summary data from Exercise 8.56 in your calculation.)

b. Comment on the practicality of carrying out the study with the sample sizes determined in part **a.**

c. Comment on the practical significance of the difference detected in the confidence interval for the study, part **a.**

8.72 **Traffic sign maintenance.** Refer to the *Journal of Transportation Engineering* (June 2013) study of traffic sign maintenance in North Carolina, Exercise 8.54 (p. 489). Recall that the proportion of signs on NCDOT-maintained roads that fail minimum requirements was compared to the corresponding proportion for signs on county-owned roads. How many signs should be sampled from each maintainer to estimate the difference between the proportions to within .03 using a 90% confidence interval? Assume the same number of signs will be sampled from NCDOT-maintained roads and county-owned roads.

8.6 Comparing Two Population Variances: Independent Sampling

Many times, it is of practical interest to use the techniques developed in this chapter to compare the means or proportions of two populations. However, there are also important instances when we wish to compare two population variances. For example, when two devices are available for producing precision measurements (scales, calipers, thermometers, etc.), we might want to compare the variability of the measurements of the devices before deciding which one to purchase. Or when two standardized tests can be used to rate job applicants, the variability of the scores for both tests should be taken into consideration before deciding which test to use.

For problems like these, we need to develop a statistical procedure to compare population variances. The common statistical procedure for comparing population variances, σ_1^2 and σ_2^2, makes an inference about the ratio $\frac{\sigma_1^2}{\sigma_2^2}$. In this section, we will show how to test the null hypothesis that the ratio $\frac{\sigma_1^2}{\sigma_2^2}$ equals 1 (the variances are equal) against the alternative hypothesis that the ratio differs from 1 (the variances differ):

$$H_0: \frac{\sigma_1^2}{\sigma_2^2} = 1 \quad (\sigma_1^2 = \sigma_2^2)$$

$$H_a: \frac{\sigma_1^2}{\sigma_2^2} \neq 1 \quad (\sigma_1^2 \neq \sigma_2^2)$$

To make an inference about the ratio $\frac{\sigma_1^2}{\sigma_2^2}$, it seems reasonable to collect sample data and use the ratio of the sample variances, $\frac{s_1^2}{s_2^2}$. We will use the test statistic

$$F = \frac{s_1^2}{s_2^2}$$

To establish a rejection region for the test statistic, we need to know the sampling distribution of $\frac{s_1^2}{s_2^2}$. As you will subsequently see, the sampling distribution of $\frac{s_1^2}{s_2^2}$ is based on two of the assumptions already required for the t-test:

1. The two sampled populations are normally distributed.

2. The samples are randomly and independently selected from their respective populations.

When these assumptions are satisfied and when the null hypothesis is true (that is, $\sigma_1^2 = \sigma_2^2$), the sampling distribution of $F = \frac{s_1^2}{s_2^2}$ is the **F-distribution** with $(n_1 - 1)$ numerator degrees of freedom and $(n_2 - 1)$ denominator degrees of freedom, respectively. The shape of the F-distribution depends on the degrees of freedom associated with s_1^2 and s_2^2—that is, on $(n_1 - 1)$ and $(n_2 - 1)$. An F-distribution with 7 and 9 df is shown in Figure 8.17. As you can see, the distribution is skewed to the right because $\frac{s_1^2}{s_2^2}$ cannot be less than 0 but can increase without bound.

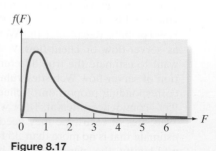

Figure 8.17

An F-distribution with 7 numerator and 9 denominator degrees of freedom

We need to be able to find F-values corresponding to the tail areas of this distribution to establish the rejection region for our test of hypothesis because we expect the ratio F of the sample variances to be either very large or very small when the population variances are unequal. The upper-tail F-values for $\alpha = .10, .05, .025,$ and $.01$ can be found in Tables V, VI, VII, and VIII in Appendix D. Table VI is partially reproduced in Table 8.7. It gives F-values that correspond to $\alpha = .05$ upper-tail areas for different degrees of freedom ν_1 for the numerator sample variance, s_1^2, whereas the rows correspond to the degrees of freedom ν_2 for the denominator sample variance, s_2^2. Thus, if the numerator degrees of freedom is $\nu_1 = 7$ and the denominator degrees of freedom is $\nu_2 = 9$, we look in the seventh column and ninth row to find $F_{.05} = 3.29$. As shown in Figure 8.18, $\alpha = .05$ is the tail area to the right of 3.29 in the F-distribution with 7 and 9 df—that is, if $\sigma_1^2 = \sigma_2^2$, then the probability that the F-statistic will exceed 3.29 is $\alpha = .05$.

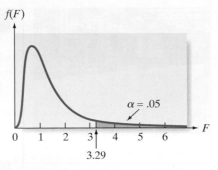

Figure 8.18

An F-distribution for $\nu_1 = 7$ df and $\nu_2 = 9$ df; $\alpha = .05$

Table 8.7	Reproduction of Part of Table VI in Appendix D: Percentage Points of the *F*-Distribution, $\alpha = .05$

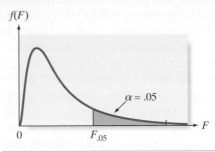

					Numerator Degrees of Freedom				
ν_1	ν_2	1	2	3	4	5	6	7	8	9
	1	161.4	199.5	215.7	224.6	230.2	234.0	236.8	238.9	240.5
	2	18.51	19.00	19.16	19.25	19.30	19.33	19.35	19.37	19.38
	3	10.13	9.55	9.28	9.12	9.01	8.94	8.89	8.85	8.81
	4	7.71	6.94	6.59	6.39	6.26	6.16	6.09	6.04	6.00
	5	6.61	5.79	5.41	5.19	5.05	4.95	4.88	4.82	4.77
	6	5.99	5.14	4.76	4.53	4.39	4.28	4.21	4.15	4.10
	7	5.59	4.74	4.35	4.12	3.97	3.87	3.79	3.73	3.68
	8	5.32	4.46	4.07	3.84	3.69	3.58	3.50	3.44	3.39
	9	5.12	4.26	3.86	3.63	3.48	3.37	3.29	3.23	3.18
	10	4.96	4.10	3.71	3.48	3.33	3.22	3.14	3.07	3.02
	11	4.84	3.98	3.59	3.36	3.20	3.09	3.01	2.95	2.90
	12	4.75	3.89	3.49	3.25	3.11	3.00	2.91	2.85	2.80
	13	4.67	3.81	3.41	3.18	3.03	2.92	2.83	2.77	2.71
	14	4.60	3.74	3.34	3.11	2.96	2.85	2.76	2.70	2.65

Denominator Degrees of Freedom

EXAMPLE 8.10

An *F*-Test Application—Comparing Paper Mill Production Variation

Problem A manufacturer of paper products wants to compare the variation in daily production levels at two paper mills. Independent random samples of days are selected from each mill, and the production levels (in units) are recorded. The data are shown in Table 8.8. Do these data provide sufficient evidence to indicate a difference in the variability of production levels at the two paper mills? (Use $\alpha = .10$.)

Table 8.8	Production Levels at Two Paper Mills							
Mill 1:	34	18	28	21	40	23	29	
	25	10	38	32	22	22		
Mill 2:	31	13	27	19	22	18	23	22	21
	18	15	24	13	19	18	19	23	13

Data Set: PAPER

Solution Let

$$\sigma_1^2 = \text{Population variance of production levels at mill 1}$$

$$\sigma_2^2 = \text{Population variance of production levels at mill 2}$$

The hypotheses of interest, then, are

$$H_0: \frac{\sigma_1^2}{\sigma_2^2} = 1 \qquad (\sigma_1^2 = \sigma_2^2)$$

$$H_a: \frac{\sigma_1^2}{\sigma_2^2} \neq 1 \qquad (\sigma_1^2 \neq \sigma_2^2)$$

The nature of the F-tables given in Appendix D affects the form of the test statistic. To form the rejection region for a two-tailed F-test, we want to make certain that the upper tail is used because only the upper-tail values of F are shown in the tables in Appendix D. To accomplish this, *we will always place the larger sample variance in the numerator of the F-test statistic.* This doubles the tabulated value for α because we double the probability that the F-ratio will fall in the upper tail by always placing the larger sample variance in the numerator—that is, we establish a one-tailed rejection region by putting the larger variance in the numerator rather than establishing rejection regions in both tails.

Thus, for our example, we have a numerator s_1^2 with df $= \nu_1 = n_1 - 1 = 12$ and a denominator s_2^2 with df $= \nu_2 = n_2 - 1 = 17$. Therefore, the test statistic will be

$$F = \frac{\text{Larger sample variance}}{\text{Smaller sample variance}} = \frac{s_1^2}{s_2^2}$$

and we will reject $H_0: \sigma_1^2 = \sigma_2^2$ for $\alpha = .10$ when the calculated value of F exceeds the tabulated value:

$$F_{\alpha/2} = F_{.05} = 2.38 \qquad \text{(see Figure 8.19)}$$

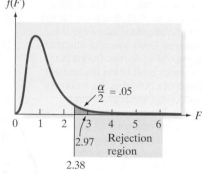

Figure 8.19
Rejection region for Example 8.10

To calculate the value of the test statistic, we require the sample variances. Summary statistics for the data in Table 8.8 are shown on the Minitab printout, Figure 8.20. The sample standard deviations (shaded) are $s_1 = 8.36$ and $s_2 = 4.85$. Therefore,

$$F = \frac{s_1^2}{s_2^2} = \frac{(8.36)^2}{(4.85)^2} = 2.97$$

This test statistic value is also shaded at the bottom of the printout.

When we compare this result with the rejection region shown in Figure 8.19, we see that $F = 2.97$ falls in the rejection region. Therefore, the data provide sufficient evidence to indicate that the population variances differ. It appears that the variation in production levels at mill 1 tends to be higher than the variation at mill 2.

Look Back What would you have concluded if the value of F calculated from the samples had not fallen in the rejection region? Would you have concluded that the null hypothesis of equal variances is true? No, because then you risk the possibility of a Type II error (accepting

Test and CI for Two Variances: LEVEL vs MILL

Method

Null hypothesis   Variance(1) / Variance(2) = 1
Alternative hypothesis   Variance(1) / Variance(2) ≠ 1
Significance level   α = 0.05

F method was used. This method is accurate for normal data only.

Statistics

```
                                      95% CI for
MILL   N   StDev   Variance           Variances
1     13   8.360    69.897     (35.942, 190.465)
2     18   4.849    23.516     (13.242,  52.851)
```

Ratio of standard deviations = 1.724
Ratio of variances = 2.972

95% Confidence Intervals

```
                            CI for
               CI for StDev  Variance
Method           Ratio        Ratio
F          (1.026, 3.049)  (1.052, 9.299)
```

Figure 8.20

Minitab Output with
F-Test for Equal
Variances

Tests

```
                        Test
Method  DF1  DF2  Statistic  P-Value
F        12   17     2.97      0.040
```

H_0 if H_a is true) without knowing the value of β, the probability of accepting H_0: $\sigma_1^2 = \sigma_2^2$ if, in fact, it is false. Because we will not consider the calculation of β for specific alternatives in this text, when the F-statistic does not fall in the rejection region, we simply conclude that insufficient sample evidence exists to refute the null hypothesis that $\sigma_1^2 = \sigma_2^2$.

● **Now Work Exercise 8.78a**

The F-test for equal population variances is summarized in the following boxes.*

F-Test for Equal Population Variances

One-Tailed Test	Two-Tailed Test>
H_0: $\sigma_1^2 = \sigma_2^2$	H_0: $\sigma_1^2 = \sigma_2^2$
H_a: $\sigma_1^2 < \sigma_2^2$ (or H_a: $\sigma_1^2 > \sigma_2^2$)	H_a: $\sigma_1^2 \neq \sigma_2^2$
Test statistic:	*Test statistic:*
$F = \dfrac{s_2^2}{s_1^2}$	$F = \dfrac{\text{Larger sample variance}}{\text{Smaller sample variance}}$
$\left(\text{or } F = \dfrac{s_1^2}{s_2^2} \text{ when } H_a: \sigma_1^2 > \sigma_2^2\right)$	$= \dfrac{s_1^2}{s_2^2} \text{ when } s_1^2 > s_2^2$
	$\left(\text{or } \dfrac{s_2^2}{s_1^2} \text{ when } s_2^2 > s_1^2\right)$
Rejection region:	*Rejection region:*
$F > F_\alpha$	$F > F_{\alpha/2}$
$p\text{-value} = P(F > F_c)$	$p\text{-value} = P(F^* < 1/F_c) + P(F > F_c)$

where F_c is the calculated value of the test statistic, F is based on v_1 numerator df and v_2 denominator df, and F^* is based on v_2 numerator df and v_1 denominator df.

*Although a test of a hypothesis of equality of variances is the most common application of the F-test, it can also be used to test a hypothesis that the ratio between the population variances is equal to some specified value: H_0: $\sigma_1^2/\sigma_2^2 = k$. The test is conducted in exactly the same way as specified in the box, except that we use the test statistic

$$F = \frac{s_1^2}{s_2^2}\left(\frac{1}{k}\right)$$

> **Conditions Required for a Valid *F*-Test for Equal Variances**
>
> 1. Both sampled populations are normally distributed.
> 2. The samples are random and independent.

EXAMPLE 8.11

The Observed Significance Level of an *F*-Test

Problem Find the *p*-value for the test in Example 8.10 using the *F*-tables in Appendix D. Compare this with the exact *p*-value obtained from a computer printout.

Solution Because the observed value of the *F*-statistic in Example 8.10 was 2.97, the observed significance level of the test would equal the probability of observing a value of *F* at least as contradictory to $H_0: \sigma_1^2 = \sigma_2^2$ as $F = 2.97$, if, in fact, H_0 is true. Because we give the *F*-tables in Appendix D only for values of α equal to .10, .05, .025, and .01, we can only approximate the observed significance level. Checking Tables VII and VIII, we find $F_{.025} = 2.82$ and $F_{.01} = 3.46$. Because the observed value of *F* exceeds $F_{.025}$ but is less than $F_{.01}$, the observed significance level for the test is less than $2(.025) = .05$ but greater than $2(.01) = .02$—that is,

$$.02 < p\text{-value} < .05$$

The exact *p*-value of the test is shown at the bottom of the Minitab printout, Figure 8.20. This value (highlighted) is .04.

Look Back We double the α value shown in Tables VII and VIII because this is a two-tailed test.

● **Now Work Exercise 8.78b**

As a final application, consider the comparison of population variances as a check of the assumption $\sigma_1^2 = \sigma_2^2$ needed for the two-sample *t*-test. Rejection of the null hypothesis $\sigma_1^2 = \sigma_2^2$ would indicate that the assumption is invalid. [*Note:* Nonrejection of the null hypothesis does *not* imply that the assumption is valid.] We illustrate with an example.

EXAMPLE 8.12

Checking the Assumption of Equal Variances

Problem In Example 8.4 (Section 8.2) we used the two-sample *t*-statistic to compare the success indexes of two groups of managers. The data are repeated in Table 8.9 for convenience. The use of the *t*-statistic was based on the assumption that the population variances of the managerial success indexes were equal for the two groups. Conduct a test of hypothesis to check this assumption at $\alpha = .10$.

Table 8.9	Managerial Success Indexes for Two Groups of Managers										
	Group 1						Group 2				
	Interaction with Outsiders						Few Interactions				
	65	58	78	60	68	69	62	53	36	34	56	50
	66	70	53	71	63	63	42	57	46	68	48	42
							52	53	43			

.ıl *Data Set:* SUCCESS

Solution We want to test

$$H_0: \sigma_1^2 = \sigma_2^2$$
$$H_a: \sigma_1^2 \neq \sigma_2^2$$

This F-test is shown on the Excel/XLSTAT printout, Figure 8.21. Both the test statistic, $F = .5$, and two-tailed p-value, p-value $= .2554$, are highlighted on the printout. Because $\alpha = .10$ is less than the p-value, we do not reject the null hypothesis that the population variances of the success indexes are equal. It is here that the temptation to misuse the F-test is strongest. *We cannot conclude that the data justify the use of the t-statistic.* This is equivalent to accepting H_0, and we have repeatedly warned against this conclusion because the probability of a Type II error, β, is unknown. The α level of .10 protects us only against rejecting H_0 if it is true. This use of the F-test may prevent us from abusing the t-procedure when we obtain a value of F that leads to a rejection of the assumption that $\sigma_1^2 = \sigma_2^2$. But when the F-statistic does not fall in the rejection region, we know little more about the validity of the assumption than before we conducted the test.

Summary statistics:

Variable	Observations	Minimum	Maximum	Mean	Std. deviation
GROUP1	12	53.0000	78.0000	65.3333	6.6104
GROUP2	15	34.0000	68.0000	49.4667	9.3340

Fisher's F-test / Two-tailed test:

90% confidence interval on the ratio of variances:

(0.1955, 1.3736)

Ratio	0.5016
F (Observed value)	0.5016
F (Critical value)	2.5655
DF1	11
DF2	14
p-value (Two-tailed)	0.2554
alpha	0.1

Figure 8.21

Excel/XLSTAT analysis for testing assumption of equal variances

Look Back A 90% confidence interval for the ratio σ_1^2/σ_2^2 is shown in the middle of the Excel/XLSTAT printout of Figure 8.21. Note that the interval (.196, 1.374) includes 1; hence, we cannot conclude that the ratio differs from 1. Thus, the confidence interval leads to the same conclusion as the two-tailed test does: There is insufficient evidence of a difference between the population variances.

●　**Now Work Exercise 8.84**

What Do You Do if the Assumption of Normal Population Distributions Is Not Satisfied?

Answer: The F-test is much less robust (i.e., much more sensitive) to departures from normality than the t-test for comparing the population means (Section 8.2). If you have doubts about the normality of the population frequency distributions, use a **nonparametric method** (e.g., *Levene's test*) for comparing the two population variances. This method can be found in the nonparametric statistics texts listed in the references for Chapter 15.

Exercises 8.73–8.88

Learning the Mechanics

8.73 Use Tables V, VI, VII, and VIII in Appendix D to find each
NW   of the following F-values:
   a. $F_{.05}$ where $\nu_1 = 9$ and $\nu_2 = 6$
   b. $F_{.01}$ where $\nu_1 = 18$ and $\nu_2 = 14$
   c. $F_{.025}$ where $\nu_1 = 11$ and $\nu_2 = 4$
   d. $F_{.10}$ where $\nu_1 = 20$ and $\nu_2 = 5$

8.74 Given ν_1 and ν_2, find the following probabilities:
   a. $\nu_1 = 2, \nu_2 = 30, P(F \geq 5.39)$
   b. $\nu_1 = 24, \nu_2 = 10, P(F < 2.74)$
   c. $\nu_1 = 7, \nu_2 = 1, P(F \leq 236.8)$
   d. $\nu_1 = 40, \nu_2 = 40, P(F > 2.11)$

8.75 Identify the rejection region for each of the following
   cases. Assume $\nu_1 = 7$ and $\nu_2 = 9$.
   a. $H_a: \sigma_1^2 < \sigma_2^2, \alpha = .05$
   b. $H_a: \sigma_1^2 > \sigma_2^2, \alpha = .01$
   c. $H_a: \sigma_1^2 \neq \sigma_2^2, \alpha = .1$ with $s_1^2 > s_2^2$
   d. $H_a: \sigma_1^2 < \sigma_2^2, \alpha = .025$

8.76 Random samples of size $n_1 = 21$ and $n_2 = 31$ were drawn
   from populations 1 and 2, respectively. For each of the
   following cases, determine the test statistic and appropriate decision for a two-tailed test of the null hypothesis
   $H_0: \sigma_1^2 = \sigma_2^2$ against $H_a: \sigma_1^2 \neq \sigma_2^2$ at $\alpha = .05$.
   a. $s_1^2 = 500, s_2^2 = 900$ **b.** $s_1^2 = .13, s_2^2 = .05$
   c. $s_1^2 = 3, s_2^2 = 8$ **d.** $s_1^2 = .19, s_2^2 = .15$

8.77 Specify the appropriate rejection region for testing
   $H_0: \sigma_1^2 = \sigma_2^2$ in each of the following situations:
   a. $H_a: \sigma_1^2 > \sigma_2^2; \alpha = .05, n_1 = 25, n_2 = 20$
   b. $H_a: \sigma_1^2 < \sigma_2^2; \alpha = .05, n_1 = 10, n_2 = 15$
   c. $H_a: \sigma_1^2 \neq \sigma_2^2; \alpha = .10, n_1 = 21, n_2 = 31$
   d. $H_a: \sigma_1^2 < \sigma_2^2; \alpha = .01, n_1 = 31, n_2 = 41$
   e. $H_a: \sigma_1^2 \neq \sigma_2^2; \alpha = .05, n_1 = 7, n_2 = 16$

8.78 Independent random samples were selected from each of
NW   two normally distributed populations, $n_1 = 12$ from population 1 and $n_2 = 27$ from population 2. The means and
   variances for the two samples are shown in the table.

Sample 1	Sample 2
$n_1 = 12$	$n_2 = 27$
$\bar{x}_1 = 31.7$	$\bar{x}_2 = 37.4$
$s_1^2 = 3.87$	$s_2^2 = 8.75$

   a. Test the null hypothesis $H_0: \sigma_1^2 = \sigma_2^2$ against the alternative hypothesis $H_a: \sigma_1^2 \neq \sigma_2^2$. Use $\alpha = .10$.
   b. Find and interpret the approximate p-value of the test.

8.79 Independent random samples were selected from each of
   two normally distributed populations, $n_1 = 6$ from popula-
L08079   tion 1 and $n_2 = 5$ from population 2. The data are shown
   in the table.

Sample 1	Sample 2
3.1	2.3
4.4	1.4
1.2	3.7
1.7	8.9
.7	5.5
3.4	

   a. Test $H_0: \sigma_1^2 = \sigma_2^2$ against $H_a: \sigma_1^2 < \sigma_2^2$. Use $\alpha = .01$.
   b. Find and interpret the approximate p-value of the test.

Applying the Concepts—Basic

8.80 **Lobster trap placement.** Refer to the *Bulletin of Marine
   Science* (April 2010) study of lobster trap placement,
TRAPS   Exercise 8.12 (p. 466). The data are repeated here. You used
   the small-sample t-statistic to form a confidence interval
   for the difference between the mean trap-spacing measurements of the two fishing cooperatives. This method requires
   the variance of the population of trap spacings for the BT
   cooperative, $(\sigma_{BT})^2$, to be the same as the population variance for the PA cooperative, $(\sigma_{PA})^2$.

BT Cooperative:	93	99	105	94	82	70	86	
PA Cooperative:	118	94	106	72	90	66	153	98

Source: G. G. Shester, "Explaining Catch Variation Among Baja California
Lobster Fishers Through Spatial Analysis of Trap-Placement Decisions,"
Bulletin of Marine Science, Vol. 86, No. 2, April 2010 (Table 1).

   a. Set up the null and alternative hypotheses for testing
   the equality of variances.
   b. Find the sample variances for the two cooperatives.
   c. Compute the test statistic.
   d. Find the approximate p-value of the test.
   e. Make the appropriate conclusion using $\alpha = .01$.

8.81 **Performance-based logistics.** Refer to the *Journal of
   Business Logistics* (Vol. 36, 2015) study of the factors that
PBL   lead to successful performance-based logistics projects,
   Exercise 8.15 (p. 467). You used the data in the **PBL** file
   to test whether commercial suppliers have less experience, on average, than government employees. Due to
   small samples ($n_1 = 6$ commercial suppliers and $n_2 = 11$
   government employees), the test requires the variance of
   experience to be the same for the two populations.
   a. Set up the null and alternative hypotheses for a formal
   test of this assumption.
   b. Find the value of the test statistic on the accompanying
   XLSTAT printout.
   c. Locate the p-value of the test on the printout.
   d. Using $\alpha = .05$, give the appropriate conclusion. Does the
   result agree with your answer to 8.14c?

Summary statistics:

Variable	Observations	Minimum	Maximum	Mean	Std. deviation
Experience | Commercial	6	5.0000	30.0000	12.3333	8.8694
Experience | Government	11	3.0000	30.0000	20.8182	9.3682

Fisher's F-test / Two-tailed test:

95% confidence interval on the ratio of variances:
(0.2116, 5.9331)

Ratio	0.8963	
F (Observed value)	0.8963	
F (Critical value)	4.2361	
DF1	5	
DF2	10	
p-value (Two-tailed)	0.9617	
alpha	0.05	

8.82 Mental health of workers and the unemployed. A study in the *Journal of Occupational and Organizational Psychology* investigated the relationship of employment status and mental health. A sample of working and unemployed people was selected, and each person was given a mental health examination using the General Health Questionnaire (GHQ), a widely recognized measure of mental health. Although the article focused on comparing the mean GHQ levels, a comparison of the variability of GHQ scores for employed and unemployed men and women is of interest as well.

a. In general terms, what does the amount of variability in GHQ scores tell us about the group?

b. What are the appropriate null and alternative hypotheses to compare the variability of the mental health scores of the employed and unemployed groups? Define any symbols you use.

c. The standard deviation for a sample of 142 employed men was 3.26, while the standard deviation for 49 unemployed men was 5.10. Conduct the test you set up in part **b** using $\alpha = .05$. Interpret the results.

d. What assumptions are necessary to ensure the validity of the test?

8.83 Drug content assessment. Refer to Exercise 8.16 (p. 467) and the *Analytical Chemistry* (Dec. 15, 2009) study in which scientists used high-performance liquid chromatography to determine the amount of drug in a tablet. Recall that 25 tablets were produced at each of two different, independent sites. The researchers want to determine if the two sites produced drug concentrations with different variances. A Minitab printout of the analysis follows. Locate the test statistic and p-value on the printout. Use these values and $\alpha = .05$ to conduct the appropriate test for the researchers.

```
Test and CI for Two Variances: Content vs Site

Method

Null hypothesis          σ(1) / σ(2) = 1
Alternative hypothesis   σ(1) / σ(2) ≠ 1
Significance level       α = 0.05

F method was used. This method is accurate for normal data only.


Statistics

                            95% CI for
Site   N  StDev  Variance     StDevs
1      25  3.067    9.406   (2.395, 4.267)
2      25  3.339   11.147   (2.607, 4.645)

Ratio of standard deviations = 0.919
Ratio of variances = 0.844


95% Confidence Intervals

                           CI for
         CI for StDev     Variance
Method      Ratio          Ratio
F       (0.610, 1.384)  (0.372, 1.915)


Tests

                       Test
Method  DF1  DF2  Statistic  P-Value
F        24   24     0.84     0.681
```

Applying the Concepts—Intermediate

8.84 Last name and acquisition timing. Refer to the *Journal of Consumer Research* (August 2011) study of the *last name effect* in acquisition timing, Exercise 8.13 (p. 466). Recall that the mean response times (in minutes) to acquire free tickets were compared for two groups of MBA students—those students with last names beginning with one of the first 9 letters of the alphabet and those with last names beginning with one of the last 9 letters of the alphabet. Summary statistics for the two groups are repeated in the table.

	First 9 Letters: A–I	Last 9 Letters: R–Z
Sample size:	25	25
Mean response time (minutes):	25.08	19.38
Standard deviation (minutes):	10.41	7.12

Source: K. A. Carlson and J. M. Conrad, "The Last Name Effect: How Last Name Influences Acquisition Timing," *Journal of Consumer Research,* Vol. 38, No. 2, August 2011.

a. Find a 95% confidence interval for the ratio of the true variances in response times for the two groups on the printout and interpret the result.

b. On the basis of the interval, can you conclude that one group has a larger variance in response time than the other? Explain.

c. How does your answer to part **b** affect the inference you made regarding the difference in mean response times in Exercise 8.13?

8.85 Analyzing human inspection errors. Tests of product quality using human inspectors can lead to serious inspection error problems (*Journal of Quality Technology*). To evaluate the performance of inspectors in a new company, a quality manager had a sample of 12 novice inspectors evaluate 200 finished products. The same 200 items were evaluated by 12 experienced inspectors. The quality of each item—whether defective or nondefective—was known to the manager. The table lists the number of inspection errors (classifying a defective item as nondefective or vice versa) made by each inspector.

Novice Inspectors				Experienced Inspectors			
30	35	26	40	31	15	25	19
36	20	45	31	28	17	19	18
33	29	21	48	24	10	20	21

a. Prior to conducting this experiment, the manager believed the variance in inspection errors was lower for experienced inspectors than for novice inspectors. Do the sample data support her belief? Test using $\alpha = .05$.

b. What is the appropriate p-value of the test you conducted in part **a**?

8.86 Oil content of fried sweet potato chips. Refer to the *Journal of Food Engineering* (September 2013) study of the characteristics of fried sweet potato chips, Exercise 7.90 (p. 431). Recall that a sample of 6 sweet potato slices fried at 130° using a vacuum fryer yielded the following statistics on internal oil content (measured in gigagrams [Gg]): $\bar{x}_1 = .178$ Gg and $s_1 = .011$ Gg. A second sample of 6 sweet potato slices was obtained, but these were subjected to a two-stage frying process (again, at 130°) in an attempt to improve texture and appearance. Summary statistics on internal oil content for this second sample follows: $\bar{x}_2 = .140$ Gg and $s_2 = .002$ Gg. Using a t-test, the researchers want to compare the mean internal oil content of sweet potato chips fried with the two methods. Do you recommend the researchers carry out this analysis? Explain.

8.87 Shopping vehicle and judgment. Refer to the *Journal of Marketing Research* (December 2011) study of shopping cart design, Exercise 2.85 (p. 112). Recall that design engineers want to know whether the mean choice of vice-over-virtue score is higher when a consumer's arm is flexed (as when carrying a shopping basket) than when the consumer's arm is extended (as when pushing a shopping cart). The average choice score for the $n_1 = 11$ consumers with a flexed arm was $\bar{x}_1 = 59$, while the average for the $n_2 = 11$ consumers with an extended arm was $\bar{x}_2 = 43$. In which scenario is the assumption required for a *t*-test to compare means more likely to be violated, $s_1 = 4$ and $s_2 = 2$, or, $s_1 = 10$ and $s_2 = 15$? Explain.

8.88 Is honey a cough remedy? Refer to the *Archives of Pediatrics and Adolescent Medicine* (Dec. 2007) study of honey as a children's cough remedy, Exercise 8.23 (p. 470). The data (cough improvement scores) for the 33 children in the DM dosage group and the 35 children in the honey dosage group are reproduced in the table below. In Exercise 8.23, you used a comparison of two means to determine whether "honey may be a preferable treatment for the cough and sleep difficulty associated with childhood upper respiratory tract infection." The researchers also want to know if the variability in coughing improvement scores differs for the two groups. Conduct the appropriate analysis, using $\alpha = .10$.

Honey Dosage:	12	11	15	11	10	13	10	4	15	16	9	14	10	6	10	11	12	15
	12	9	11	15	10	9	13	8	12	10	8	9	5	12	8	12	8	
DM Dosage:	4	6	9	4	7	7	7	9	12	10	11	3	9	7	8	12	12	
	13	7	10	13	9	4	4	10	15	9	6	4	12	6	12	4		

Source: I. M. Paul et al., "Effect of Honey, Dextromethorphan, and No Treatment on Nocturnal Cough and Sleep Quality for Coughing Children and Their Parents," *Archives of Pediatrics and Adolescent Medicine*, Vol. 161, No. 12, December 2007 (data simulated).

CHAPTER NOTES

Key Terms

Blocking 474
F-distribution 494
Nonparametric method 499
Paired difference experiment 474
Pooled sample estimator of σ^2 459

Randomized block experiment 474
Sampling error 490
Standard error 456

Key Symbols

$\mu_1 - \mu_2$	Difference between population means
μ_d	Paired difference in population means
$p_1 - p_2$	Difference between population proportions
$\frac{\sigma_1^2}{\sigma_2^2}$	Ratio of population variances
D_0	Hypothesized value of difference
$\bar{x}_1 - \bar{x}_2$	Difference between sample means
$\bar{d}$	Mean of sample differences
$\hat{p}_1 - \hat{p}_2$	Difference between sample proportions
$\frac{s_1^2}{s_2^2}$	Ratio of sample variances
$\sigma_{(\bar{x}_1 - \bar{x}_2)}$	Standard error for $\bar{x}_1 - \bar{x}_2$
$\sigma_{\bar{d}}$	Standard error for $\bar{d}$
$\sigma_{(\hat{p}_1 - \hat{p}_2)}$	Standard error for $\hat{p}_1 - \hat{p}_2$
F_α	Critical value for *F*-distribution
ν_1	Numerator degrees of freedom for *F*-distribution
ν_2	Denominator degrees of freedom for *F*-distribution
SE	Sampling error in estimation

Key Ideas

Key Words for Identifying the Target Parameter

$\mu_1 - \mu_2$	Difference in means or averages
μ_d	Paired difference in means or averages
$p_1 - p_2$	Difference in proportions, fractions, percentages, rates
$\frac{\sigma_1^2}{\sigma_2^2}$	Ratio (or difference) in variances, spreads

Determining the Sample Size

Estimating $\mu_1 - \mu_2$: $n_1 = n_2 = (z_{\alpha/2})^2(\sigma_1^2 + \sigma_2^2)/(\text{SE})^2$
Estimating $p_1 - p_2$: $n_1 = n_2 = (z_{\alpha/2})^2(p_1q_1 + p_2q_2)/(\text{SE})^2$
Estimating μ_d: $n_d = (z_{\alpha/2})^2(\sigma_d)^2/(\text{SE})^2$

Conditions Required for Inferences About $\mu_1 - \mu_2$

Large samples:
1. Independent random samples
2. $n_1 \geq 30, n_2 \geq 30$

Small samples:
1. Independent random samples
2. Both populations normal
3. $\sigma_1^2 = \sigma_2^2$

Conditions Required for Inferences About $\frac{\sigma_1^2}{\sigma_2^2}$

Large or small samples:
1. Independent random samples
2. Both populations normal

Conditions Required for Inferences About μ_d

Large samples:
1. Random sample of paired differences
2. $n_d \geq 30$

Small samples:
1. Random sample of paired differences
2. Population of differences is normal

Conditions Required for Inferences About $p_1 - p_2$

Large samples:
1. Independent random samples
2. $n_1p_1 \geq 15, n_1q_1 \geq 15$
3. $n_2p_2 \geq 15, n_2q_2 \geq 15$

Using a Confidence Interval for $(\mu_1 - \mu_2)$ or $(p_1 - p_2)$ to Determine Whether a Difference Exists

1. If the confidence interval includes all *positive* numbers $(+, +)$: $\rightarrow$ Infer $\mu_1 > \mu_2$ or $p_1 > p_2$
2. If the confidence interval includes all *negative* numbers $(-, -)$: $\rightarrow$ Infer $\mu_1 < \mu_2$ or $p_1 < p_2$
3. If the confidence interval includes 0 $(-, +)$: $\rightarrow$ Infer no evidence of a difference

Guide to Selecting a Two-Sample Hypothesis Test and Confidence Interval

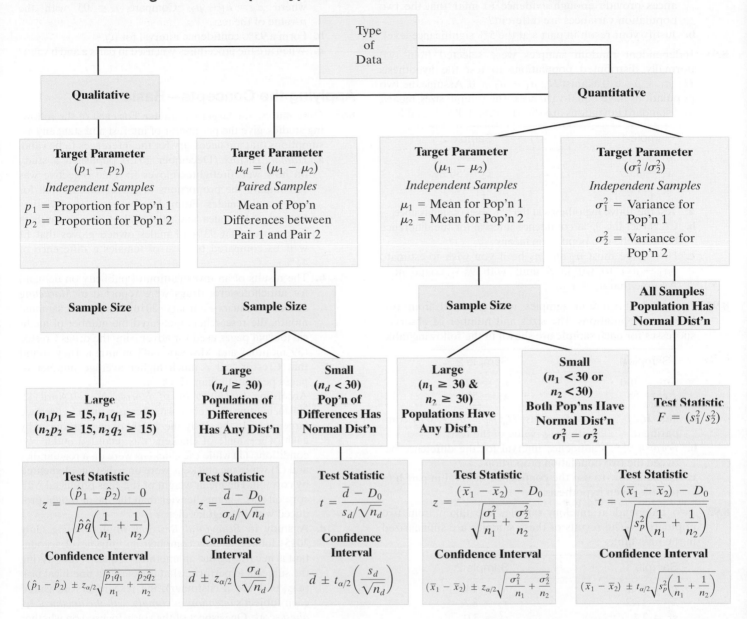

SUPPLEMENTARY EXERCISES 8.89–8.123

Learning the Mechanics

8.89 List the assumptions necessary for each of the following inferential techniques:

a. Large-sample inferences about the difference $(\mu_1 - \mu_2)$ between population means using a two-sample z-statistic

b. Small-sample inferences about $(\mu_1 - \mu_2)$ using an independent samples design and a two-sample t-statistic

c. Small-sample inferences about $(\mu_1 - \mu_2)$ using a paired difference design and a single-sample t-statistic to analyze the differences

d. Large-sample inferences about the differences $(p_1 - p_2)$ between binomial proportions using a two-sample z-statistic

e. Inferences about the ratio $\frac{\sigma_1^2}{\sigma_2^2}$ of two population variances using an F-test.

8.90 Two independent random samples were selected from normally distributed populations to conduct an experiment on the variability of responses of two different experimental procedures that may or may not be the same. The sample sizes, means, and variances are shown in the following table.

Sample 1	Sample 2
$n_1 = 14$	$n_2 = 16$
$\bar{x}_1 = 44$	$\bar{x}_2 = 41$
$s_1^2 = 569.2$	$s_2^2 = 810$

a. At the 10% level of significance, do the samples' variances provide enough evidence to infer that the two population variances are different?

b. Justify your result in part **a** at the 5% significance level.

8.91 Independent random samples were selected from two normally distributed populations to test the hypothesis $H_0: \mu_1 - \mu_2 \geq 0$ against $H_a: \mu_1 - \mu_2 < 0$. Assume the two populations have equal variances. The sample sizes, means, and standard deviations are shown in the following table.

Sample 1	Sample 2
$n_1 = 10$	$n_2 = 15$
$\bar{x}_1 = 43.3$	$\bar{x}_2 = 50.2$
$s_1 = 18.3$	$s_2 = 15.2$

a. Test the above hypotheses at the 5% level of significance.

b. Construct the 95% confidence interval for the difference between the two population means.

c. How large must n_1 and n_2 be if you wish to estimate $(\mu_1 - \mu_2)$ to within 5 units with 95% confidence? Assume that $n_1 = n_2$.

8.92 Independent random samples were selected from two binomial populations. The sizes and number of observed successes for each sample are shown in the following table.

Sample 1	Sample 2
$n_1 = 100$	$n_2 = 125$
$x_1 = 58$	$x_2 = 50$

a. Test $H_0: p_1 - p_2 = 0$ against $H_a: p_1 - p_2 \neq 0$ by comparing $\alpha = .05$ with the p-value of the test.

b. Form a 95% confidence interval for the difference between the two population proportions.

c. Explain how to use the confidence interval in part **b** to test the given hypothesis.

8.93 Two independent random samples are taken from two populations. The results of these samples are summarized in the next table.

Sample 1	Sample 2
$n_1 = 135$	$n_2 = 148$
$\bar{x}_1 = 12.2$	$\bar{x}_2 = 8.3$
$s_1^2 = 2.1$	$s_2^2 = 3.0$

a. Form a 90% confidence interval for $(\mu_1 - \mu_2)$.

b. Test $H_0: (\mu_1 - \mu_2) = 0$ against $H_a: (\mu_1 - \mu_2) \neq 0$ by comparing $\alpha = .01$ with the p-value of the test.

c. What sample sizes would be required if you wish to estimate $(\mu_1 - \mu_2)$ to within .2 with 90% confidence? Assume that $n_1 = n_2$.

8.94 A random sample of five pairs of observations were selected, one of each pair from a population with mean μ_1, the other from a population with mean μ_2. The data are shown in the accompanying table.

Pair	Value from Population 1	Value from Population 2
1	28	22
2	31	27
3	24	20
4	30	27
5	22	20

a. Test the null hypothesis $H_0: \mu_d = 0$ against $H_a: \mu_d \neq 0$, where $\mu_d = \mu_1 - \mu_2$. Compare $\alpha = .05$ with the p-value of the test.

b. Form a 95% confidence interval for μ_d.

c. When are the procedures you used in parts **a** and **b** valid?

Applying the Concepts—Basic

8.95 **Determining the target parameter.** For each of the following studies, give the parameter of interest and state any assumptions that are necessary for the inferences to be valid.

a. *Human Factors* (December 2015) published a study on how well firefighter gloves fit. One objective was to compare the proportions of gloves that fit well for males and females. From data collected for 586 firefighters (546 males and 40 females), the researchers determined that 93% of males owned gloves that fit well, as compared to 49% of females a difference of 44%.

b. The results of an investigation of publicity on demand for anticholesterol drugs were reported in *Marketing Science* (January-February 2016). For each sampled month, the researchers measured the number of medical journal pages used for advertising the drugs Crestor (39 months) and Mevacor (142 months). They found that Crestor had a much higher average number of pages per month than Mevacor.

c. According to *University of Florida News* (April 11, 2001), feeding chickens corn oil causes them to produce larger eggs. In the study, the weight of eggs produced by each of a sample of chickens was recorded under two conditions: (1) while the chickens were on a regular diet and (2) while the chickens were on a diet supplemented by corn oil. The mean weight of the eggs produced with corn oil was 3 grams heavier than the mean weight produced with the regular diet.

d. A study in *Behavioral Research in Accounting* (July 2015) looked at how complicit an entry-level accountant is in carrying out an unethical request. After asking the subjects to perform what is clearly an unethical task (e.g., to bribe a customer), the researchers measured each subject's *intention to comply with the unethical request* score. One aspect of the study focused on whether the variability in the scores differed depending on the subject's impulsivity level (high or low).

8.96 **Financial incentives for college students.** A study reported in *Inside Higher Education News* (May 22, 2006) found that financial incentives can improve low-income college students' grades and retention. As part of their "Opening Doors" program, a Louisiana community college offered to pay students $1,000 per semester on condition that they maintain at least half-time enrollment and at least a 2.0 grade point average (GPA).

a. About 61% of Opening Doors students enrolled full time as opposed to about 52% of traditional students. Identify the target parameter for this comparison.

b. The mean GPA of Opening Doors students was 2.3 as compared to the mean GPA of 2.1 for traditional students. Identify the target parameter for this comparison.

8.97 **Rating service at five-star hotels.** A study published in the *Journal of American Academy of Business, Cambridge* (March 2002) examined whether the perception of service quality at five-star hotels in Jamaica differed by gender. Hotel guests were randomly selected from the lobby and restaurant areas and asked to rate 10 service-related items (e.g., "The personal attention you received from our employees"). Each item was rated on a 5-point scale (1 = "much worse than I expected," 5 = "much better than I expected"), and the sum of the items for each guest was determined. A summary of the guest scores is provided in the table.

Gender	Sample Size	Mean Score	Standard Deviation
Males	127	39.08	6.73
Females	114	38.79	6.94

a. Construct a 90% confidence interval for the difference between the population mean service-rating scores given by male and female guests at Jamaican five-star hotels.
b. Conduct a test to determine if the service-rating score variances differ by gender. Use $\alpha = .10$
c. Use the results, parts a and b, to make an inference about whether the perception of service quality at five-star hotels in Jamaica differs by gender.

8.98 Hull failures of oil tankers. Refer to the *Marine Technology* (Jan. 1995) study of major oil spills from tankers and carriers, Exercise 2.159 (p. 144). The data for the 42 recent spills are saved in the accompanying file.

HULL

a. Construct a 90% confidence interval for the difference between the mean spillage amount of accidents caused by collision and the mean spillage amount of accidents caused by fire/explosion. Interpret the result.
b. Conduct a test of hypothesis to compare the mean spillage amount of accidents caused by grounding with the corresponding mean of accidents caused by hull failure. Use $\alpha = .05$.
c. Refer to parts a and b. State any assumptions required for the inferences derived from the analyses to be valid. Are these assumptions reasonably satisfied?
d. Conduct a test of hypothesis to compare the variation in spillage amounts for accidents caused by collision and accidents caused by grounding. Use $\alpha = .02$.

8.99 Effectiveness of teaching software. The U.S. Department of Education (DOE) conducted a national study of the effectiveness of educational software. In one phase of the study, a sample of 1,516 first-grade students in classrooms that used educational software was compared with a sample of 1,103 first-grade students in classrooms that did not use the technology. In its *Report to Congress,* the DOE concluded that "[mean] test scores [of students on the SAT reading test] were not significantly higher in classrooms using reading ... software products" than in classrooms that did not use educational software.
a. Identify the parameter of interest to the DOE.
b. Specify the null and alternative hypotheses for the test conducted by the DOE.
c. The *p*-value for the test was reported as .62. Based on this value, do you agree with the conclusion of the DOE? Explain.

8.100 Durability of shock absorbers. A manufacturer of automobile shock absorbers was interested in comparing the durability of its shocks with that of the shocks produced by

SHOCK

its biggest competitor. To make the comparison, one of the manufacturer's and one of the competitor's shocks were randomly selected and installed on the rear wheels of each of six cars. After the cars had been driven 20,000 miles, the strength of each test shock was measured, coded, and recorded. Results of the examination are shown in the table.

Car Number	Manufacturer's Shock	Competitor's Shock
1	8.8	8.4
2	10.5	10.1
3	12.5	12.0
4	9.7	9.3
5	9.6	9.0
6	13.2	13.0

a. Explain why the data are collected as matched pairs.
b. Do the data present sufficient evidence to conclude that there is a difference in the mean strength of the two types of shocks after 20,000 miles of use? Use $\alpha = .05$.
c. Find the approximate observed significance level for the test and interpret its value.
d. What assumptions are necessary to apply a paired difference analysis to the data?
e. Construct a 95% confidence interval for μ_d. Interpret the confidence interval.
f. Suppose the data are based on independent random samples. Construct a 95% confidence interval for $(\mu_1 - \mu_2)$. Interpret your result.
g. Compare the confidence intervals you obtained in parts e and f. Which is wider? To what do you attribute the difference in width? Assuming in each case that the appropriate assumptions are satisfied, which interval provides you with more information about $(\mu_1 - \mu_2)$? Explain.
h. Are the results of an unpaired analysis valid if the data come from a paired experiment?

8.101 NHTSA new car crash tests. Refer to the National Highway Traffic Safety Administration (NHTSA) crash-test data for new cars saved in the **CRASH** file. Crash-test dummies were placed in the driver's seat and front passenger's seat of a new car model, and the car was steered by remote control into a head-on collision with a fixed barrier while traveling at 35 miles per hour. Two of the variables measured for each of the 98 new cars in the data set are (1) the severity of the driver's chest injury and (2) the severity of the passenger's chest injury. (The more points assigned to the chest injury rating, the more severe the injury.) Suppose the NHTSA wants to determine whether the true mean driver chest injury rating exceeds the true mean passenger chest injury rating and, if so, by how much.

CRASH

a. State the parameter of interest to the NHTSA.
b. Explain why the data should be analyzed as matched pairs.
c. Find a 99% confidence interval for the true difference between the mean chest injury ratings of drivers and front-seat passengers.
d. Interpret the interval, part c. Does the true mean driver chest injury rating exceed the true mean passenger chest injury rating? If so, by how much?
e. What conditions are required for the analysis to be valid? Do these conditions hold for these data?

8.102 Diamonds sold at retail. Refer to the data for 308 diamonds saved in the file. Two quantitative variables in the data set are number of carats and selling price. One of the qualitative variables is the independent certification body that assessed each of the stones. Three certification bodies were used: GIA, IGI, and HRD. The Minitab printout shown below gives the means and standard deviations of the quantitative variables for each certification body.

Descriptive Statistics: CARAT, PRICE

Variable	CERT	N	Mean	StDev
CARAT	GIA	151	0.6723	0.2456
	HRD	79	0.8129	0.1831
	IGI	78	0.3665	0.2163
PRICE	GIA	151	5310	3247
	HRD	79	7181	2898
	IGI	78	2267	2121

a. Construct a 95% confidence interval for the difference between the mean carat size of diamonds certified by GIA and the mean carat size of diamonds certified by HRD.

b. Interpret the result, part **a.** Specifically, which (if either) of the two population means compared is larger and by how much?

c. Construct a 95% confidence interval for the difference between the mean carat size of diamonds certified by GIA and the mean carat size of diamonds certified by IGI.

d. Interpret the result, part **c.** Specifically, which (if either) of the two population means is larger and by how much?

e. Construct a 95% confidence interval for the difference between the mean selling price of diamonds certified by HRD and the mean selling price of diamonds certified by IGI.

f. Interpret the result, part **e.** Specifically, which (if either) of the two population means is larger and by how much?

g. Conduct a test to determine whether the variation in carat size differs for diamonds certified by GIA and diamonds certified by HRD. Use $\alpha = .05$.

h. Conduct a test to determine whether the variation in carat size differs for diamonds certified by GIA and diamonds certified by IGI. Use $\alpha = .05$.

i. Conduct a test to determine whether the variation in selling price differs for diamonds certified by HRD and diamonds certified by IGI. Use $\alpha = .05$.

j. Use a statistical software package (and the data in the accompanying file) to determine whether the assumption of normally distributed data for each certification group is reasonably satisfied.

8.103 Children's recall of TV ads. A study examined children's recall and recognition of television advertisements (*Journal of Advertising*, Spring 2006). Two groups of children were shown a 60-second commercial for Sunkist FunFruit Rock-n-Roll Shapes. One group (the A/V group) was shown the ad with both audio and video; the second group (the video only group) was shown only the video portion of the commercial. Following the viewing, the children were asked to recall 10 specific items from the ad. The number of the 10 items recalled correctly by each child is summarized in the table. The researchers theorized that "children who receive an audiovisual presentation will have the same level of mean recall of ad information as those who receive only the visual aspects of the ad."

Video Only Group	A/V Group
$n_1 = 20$	$n_2 = 20$
$\bar{x}_1 = 3.70$	$\bar{x}_2 = 3.30$
$s_1 = 1.98$	$s_2 = 2.13$

Source: Based on J. K. Maher, M. Y. Hu, and R. H. Kolbe, "Children's Recall of Television Ad Elements," *Journal of Advertising*, Spring 2006, Volume 35(1).

a. Set up the appropriate null and alternative hypotheses to test the researchers' theory.

b. Find the value of the test statistic.

c. Give the rejection region for $\alpha = .10$.

d. Make the appropriate inference. What can you say about the researchers' theory?

e. The researchers reported the p-value of the test as p-value = .542. Interpret this result.

f. What conditions are required for the inference to be valid?

g. Conduct a test of equal variances using $\alpha = .05$.

8.104 Is steak your favorite barbeque food? July is National Grilling Month in the United States. On July 1, 2008, *The Harris Poll #70* reported on a survey of Americans' grilling preferences. When asked about their favorite food prepared on a barbeque, 662 of 1,250 randomly sampled Democrats preferred steak, as compared to 586 of 930 randomly sampled Republicans.

a. Give a point estimate for the proportion of all Democrats who prefer steak as their favorite barbeque food.

b. Give a point estimate for the proportion of all Republicans who prefer steak as their favorite barbeque food.

c. Give a point estimate for the difference between the proportions of all Democrats and all Republicans who prefer steak as their favorite barbeque food.

d. Construct a 95% confidence interval for the difference between the proportions of all Democrats and all Republicans who prefer steak as their favorite barbeque food.

e. Give a practical interpretation of the interval, part **d.**

f. Explain the meaning of the phrase 95% confident in your answer to part **e.**

8.105 Planning habits survey. *American Demographics* (January 2002) reported the results of a survey on the planning habits of men and women. In response to the question, "What is your preferred method of planning and keeping track of meetings, appointments, and deadlines?," 56% of the men and 46% of the women answered, "Keep them in my head." A nationally representative sample of 1,000 adults participated in the survey; therefore, assume that 500 were men and 500 were women.

a. Set up the null and alternative hypotheses for testing whether the percentage of men who prefer keeping track of appointments in their head is larger than the corresponding percentage of women.

b. Compute the test statistic for the test.

c. Give the rejection region for the test using $\alpha = .01$.

d. Find the p-value for the test.

e. Make the appropriate conclusion.

8.106 Turnover rates in the United States and Japan. High job turnover rates are often associated with high product defect rates because high turnover rates mean more inexperienced workers who are unfamiliar with the company's product lines (Stevenson, *Production/Operations Management*, 2000). In a study, five Japanese and five U.S. plants that manufacture air conditioners were randomly sampled; their turnover rates are listed in the table.

U.S. Plants	Japanese Plants
7.11%	3.52%
6.06	2.02
8.00	4.91
6.87	3.22
4.77	1.92

a. Do the data provide sufficient evidence to indicate that the mean annual percentage turnover for U.S. plants exceeds the corresponding mean percentage for Japanese plants? Test using $\alpha = .05$.

b. Find and interpret the observed significance level of the test you conducted in part **a.**

c. List any assumptions you made in conducting the hypothesis test of part **a.** Comment on their validity for this application.

8.107 Smartphone usage differs by gender. The role of the smartphone in modern life was investigated by a *Compete Pulse* (November 2011) survey. A total of 251 male and 284 female smartphone users were interviewed in the sample. One of the objectives was to compare male and female smartphone users. For example, 48% of men conduct financial transactions on their phone, as compared to 60% of women. Also, 42% of men watch streaming content (movies/TV) on their phone, as compared to 35% of women.

a. Describe the two populations of interest in the survey.

b. Give an estimate of the proportion of men and the proportion of women who conduct financial transactions on a smartphone.

c. Find a 90% confidence interval for the difference between the proportions of men and women who conduct financial transactions on a smartphone.

d. From your answer to part **c,** can you conclude that men are less likely than women to conduct financial transactions on a smartphone? Explain.

e. Give an estimate of the proportion of men and the proportion of women who watch streaming content on their smartphone.

f. Conduct a test to determine whether the proportions of men and women who watch streaming content on their phone differ. Use $\alpha = .10$.

Applying the Concepts—Intermediate

8.108 Life expectancies of working women and housewives. Is housework hazardous to your health? A study in *Public Health Reports* compared the life expectancies of 25-year-old white women in the labor force with those who are housewives. How large a sample would have to be taken from each group in order to be 95% confident that the estimate of difference in average life expectancies for the two groups is within 1 year of the true difference in average life expectancies? Assume that equal sample sizes will be selected from the two groups and that the standard deviation for both groups is approximately 15 years.

8.109 Comparing purchasers and nonpurchasers of toothpaste. Marketing strategists would like to predict consumer response to new products and their accompanying promotional schemes. Consequently, studies that examine the differences between buyers and nonbuyers of a product are of interest. One classic study conducted by Shuchman and Riesz (*Journal of Marketing Research*) was aimed at characterizing the purchasers and nonpurchasers of Crest toothpaste. The researchers demonstrated that both the mean household size (number of persons) and mean household income were significantly larger for purchasers than for nonpurchasers. A similar study used independent random samples of size 20 and yielded the data shown in the following table on the age of the householder primarily responsible for buying toothpaste.

a. Do the data present sufficient evidence to conclude there is a difference in the mean age of purchasers and nonpurchasers? Use $\alpha = .10$.

b. What assumptions are necessary in order to answer part **a?**

c. Find the observed significance level for the test and interpret its value.

d. Calculate and interpret a 90% confidence interval for the difference between the mean ages of purchasers and nonpurchasers.

Purchasers						Nonpurchasers					
34	35	23	44	52	46	28	22	44	33	55	63
28	48	28	34	33	52	45	31	60	54	53	58
41	32	34	49	50	45	52	52	66	35	25	48
29	59					59	61				

8.110 Testing electronic circuits. Japanese researchers have developed a compression/depression method of testing electronic circuits based on Huffman coding (*IEICE Transactions on Information & Systems*, January 2005). The new method is designed to reduce the time required for input decompression and output compression—called the *compression ratio*. Experimental results were obtained by testing a sample of 11 benchmark circuits (all of different sizes) from a SUN Blade 1000 workstation. Each circuit was tested using the standard compression/depression method and the new Huffman-based coding method, and the compression ratio was recorded. The data are given in the accompanying table. Compare the two methods with a 95% confidence interval. Which method has the smaller mean compression ratio?

Circuit	Standard Method	Huffman-Coding Method
1	.80	.78
2	.80	.80
3	.83	.86
4	.53	.53
5	.50	.51
6	.96	.68
7	.99	.82
8	.98	.72
9	.81	.45
10	.95	.79
11	.99	.77

Source: Based on H. Ichihara, M. Shintani, and T. Inoue, "Huffman-Based Test Response Coding," *IEICE Transactions on Information & Systems*, Vol. E88-D, No. 1, January 2005 (Table 3).

8.111 Racial profiling by the LAPD. *Racial profiling* is a term used to describe any police action that relies on ethnicity rather than behavior to target suspects engaged in criminal activities. Does the Los Angeles Police Department (LAPD) invoke racial profiling in stops and searches of LA drivers? This question was addressed in *Chance* (Spring 2006).

a. Data on stops and searches of both African American and white drivers are summarized in the accompanying table. Conduct a test (at $\alpha = .05$) to determine if there is a disparity in the proportions of African American and white drivers who are searched by the LA police after being stopped.

b. The LAPD defines a *hit rate* as the proportion of searches that result in a discovery of criminal activity. Use the data in the table to estimate the disparity in the hit rates for African American and white drivers using a 95% confidence interval. Interpret the results.

Race	Number Stopped	Number Searched	Number of "Hits"
African American	61,688	12,016	5,134
White	106,892	5,312	3,006

Source: Based on L. S. Khadjavi, "Driving While Black in the City of Angels," *Chance*, Vol. 19, No. 2.

8.112 State SAT scores. Refer to Exercise 2.27 (p. 84) and the data on average math SAT scores for each of the 50 states and District of Columbia for the years 2014 and 2010. The data are saved in the file. (The first five observations and last two observations in the data set are shown in the table below.)

State	2014	2010
Alabama	538	550
Alaska	503	513
Arizona	525	524
Arkansas	571	564
California	510	516
Wisconsin	608	603
Wyoming	599	565

Source: The College Board, 2015.

a. In Exercise 2.27c, you computed the *paired differences* of SAT scores by subtracting the 2010 score from the 2014 score for each state. Find the mean of these 51 paired differences. This value is μ_d, the mean difference in SAT scores for the population of 50 states and the District of Columbia.

b. Explain why there is no need to employ the confidence interval or test procedures of this section to make an inference about μ_d.

c. Now, suppose the 50 paired differences of part a represent a sample of SAT score differences for 50 randomly selected high school students. Use the data in the file to make an inference about whether the true mean SAT score of high school students in 2014 differs from the true mean in 2010. Use a confidence level of .90.

8.113 Rat damage to sugarcane fields. Poisons are used to prevent rat damage in sugarcane fields. The U.S. Department of Agriculture is investigating whether the rat poison should be located in the middle of the field or on the outer perimeter. One way to answer this question is to determine where the greater amount of damage occurs. If damage is measured by the proportion of cane stalks that have been damaged by rats, how many stalks from each section of the field should be sampled to estimate the true difference between proportions of stalks damaged in the two sections to within .02 with 95% confidence?

8.114 Environmental impact study. Some power plants are located near rivers or oceans so that the available water can be used for cooling the condensers. Suppose that, as part of an environmental impact study, a power company wants to estimate the difference in mean water temperature between the discharge of its plant and the offshore waters. How many sample measurements must be taken at each site to estimate the true difference between means to within .2°C with 95% confidence? Assume that the range in readings will be about 4°C at each site and the same number of readings will be taken at each site.

8.115 Instrument precision. When new instruments are developed to perform chemical analyses of products (food, medicine, etc.), they are usually evaluated with respect to two criteria: accuracy and precision. *Accuracy* refers to the ability of the instrument to identify correctly the nature and amounts of a product's components. *Precision* refers to the consistency with which the instrument will identify the components of the same material. Thus, a large variability in the identification of a single batch of a product indicates a lack of precision. Suppose a pharmaceutical firm is considering two brands of an instrument designed to identify the components of certain drugs. As part of a comparison of precision, 10 test-tube samples of a well-mixed batch of a drug are selected and then 5 are analyzed by instrument A and 5 by instrument B. The data shown below are the percentages of the primary component of the drug given by the instruments. Do these data provide evidence of a difference in the precision of the two machines? Use $\alpha = .10$.

Instrument A	Instrument B
43	46
48	49
37	43
52	41
45	48

8.116 Cooling method for gas turbines. Refer to the *Journal of Engineering for Gas Turbines and Power* (January 2005) study of gas turbines augmented with high-pressure inlet fogging, Exercise 7.94 (p. 431). The researchers classified gas turbines into three categories: traditional, advanced, and aeroderivative. Summary statistics on heat rate (kilojoules per kilowatt per hour) for each of the three types of gas turbines are shown in the Minitab printout (at the top of the next page).

a. Is there sufficient evidence of a difference between the mean heat rates of traditional augmented gas turbines and aeroderivative augmented gas turbines? Test using $\alpha = .05$.

Descriptive Statistics: HEATRATE

```
Variable  ENGINE        N    Mean  StDev  Minimum  Maximum
HEATRATE  Advanced     21    9764    639     9105    11588
          Aeroderiv     7   12312   2652     8714    16243
          Traditional  39   11544   1279    10086    14796
```

Minitab output for Exercise 8.116

b. Is there sufficient evidence of a difference between the mean heat rates of advanced augmented gas turbines and aeroderivative augmented gas turbines? Test using $\alpha = .05$.

c. Conduct a test (at $\alpha = .05$) for equality of heat rate variances for traditional and aeroderivative augmented gas turbines. Use the result to make a statement about the validity of the inference derived in part **a**.

d. Conduct a test (at $\alpha = .05$) for equality of heat rate variances for advanced and aeroderivative augmented gas turbines. Use the result to make a statement about the validity of the inference derived in part **b**.

8.117 Average housing space per person. Even though Japan is an economic superpower, Japanese workers are in many ways worse off than their U.S. and European counterparts. For example, the estimated average housing space per person (in square feet) is 645 in the United States but only 344 in Japan (Diawa House Industry, Co., Japan). Suppose a team of economists and sociologists from the United Nations plans to reestimate the difference in the mean housing space per person for U.S. and Japanese workers. Assume that equal sample sizes will be used for each country and that the standard deviation is 35 square feet for Japan and 80 for the United States. How many people should be sampled in each country to estimate the difference to within 10 square feet with 95% confidence?

8.118 Positive spillover effects from self-managed work teams. To improve quality, productivity, and timeliness, many American industries employ self-managed work teams (SMWTs). Because SMWTs require that employees be trained in interpersonal skills, they can have potential positive spillover effects on a worker's family life. The link between SMWT work characteristics and workers' perceptions of positive spillover into family life was investigated in the *Quality Management Journal* (Summer 1995). Survey data were collected from 114 AT&T employees who work in SMWTs at an AT&T technical division. The workers were divided into two groups: (1) those who reported positive spillover of work skills to family life and (2) those who did not report positive work spillover. The two groups were compared on a variety of job and demographic characteristics, one of which was the use of creative ideas (measured on a 7-point scale, where the larger the number, the more of the characteristic indicated). The data (simulated from summary information provided in the *Quality Management Journal* article) are saved in the file.

a. One comparison of interest to the researchers is whether the mean creative use of ideas scale score for employees who report positive spillover of work skills to family life differs from the mean scale score for employees who did not report positive work spillover. Give the null and alternative hypotheses that will allow the researchers to make the comparison.

b. Discuss whether it is appropriate to apply the large-sample z-test to test the hypotheses, part **a**.

c. The results of the test are shown in the SPSS printout below. Interpret these results. Make the appropriate conclusion using $\alpha = .05$.

SPSS output for Exercise 8.118

Independent Samples Test

| | | Levene's Test for Equality of Variances | | t-test for Equality of Means | | | | | | |
| | | | | | | | | | 95% Confidence Interval of the Difference | |
		F	Sig.	t	df	Sig. (2-tailed)	Mean Difference	Std. Error Difference	Lower	Upper
CREATIVE	Equal variances assumed	16.479	.000	8.565	112	.000	.808	.094	.621	.994
	Equal variances not assumed			8.847	108.727	.000	.808	.091	.627	.988

Minitab output for Exercise 8.118

Test and CI for Two Proportions: GENDER, GROUP

```
Event = MALE

GROUP     X   N   Sample p
NOSPILL  59  67   0.880597
SPILLOV  39  47   0.829787


Difference = p (NOSPILL) - p (SPILLOV)
Estimate for difference:  0.0508098
95% CI for difference:  (-0.0817519, 0.183371)
Test for difference = 0 (vs ≠ 0):  Z = 0.77  P-Value = 0.442

Fisher's exact test: P-Value = 0.585
```

d. A 95% confidence interval for the difference between the mean use of creative ideas scale scores is shown in the last column of the SPSS printout. Interpret this interval. Does the inference derived from the confidence interval agree with that from the hypothesis test?

e. The data also include the qualitative variable, Gender, for each worker. The researchers want to know whether the proportion of male workers in the two groups are significantly different. A Minitab printout of the analysis is also shown at the bottom of p. 509. Fully interpret the results in the words of the problem.

Applying the Concepts—Advanced

8.119 Impact of gender on advertising. How does gender affect the type of advertising that proves to be most effective? An article in the *Journal of Advertising Research* (May/June 1990) makes reference to numerous studies that conclude males tend to be more competitive with others than with themselves. To apply this conclusion to advertising, the author created two ads promoting a new brand of soft drink:

> *Ad 1:* Four men are shown competing in racquetball
> *Ad 2:* One man is shown competing against himself in racquetball

The author hypothesized that the first ad would be more effective when shown to males. To test this hypothesis, 43 males were shown both ads and asked to measure their attitude toward the advertisement (Aad), their attitude toward the brand of soft drink (Ab), and their intention to purchase the soft drink (Intention). Each variable was measured using a 7-point scale, with higher scores indicating a more favorable attitude. The results are shown in the table below. Do you agree with the author's hypothesis?

	Sample Means		
	Aad	Ab	Intention
Ad 1	4.465	3.311	4.366
Ad 2	4.150	2.902	3.813
Level of Significance	$p = .091$	$p = .032$	$p = .050$

8.120 Salaries of postgraduates. Refer to the *Economics of Education Review* (Vol. 21, 2002) study of the relationship between education level and earnings, Exercise 7.46 (p. 412). A National Adult Literacy Survey revealed that males with a postgraduate degree had a sample mean salary of $61,340 (with standard error $s_{\bar{x}_M} = \$2,185$), while females with a postgraduate degree had a sample mean salary of $32,227 (with standard error $s_{\bar{x}_F} = \$932$). Let μ_M represent the population mean salary of all males with postgraduate degrees and μ_F represent the population mean salary of all females with postgraduate degrees.

a. Set up the null and alternative hypotheses for determining whether μ_M exceeds μ_F.

b. Calculate the test statistic for the test, part **a.** [*Note:* $s_{\bar{x}_M - \bar{x}_F} = \sqrt{(s_{\bar{x}_M}^2 + s_{\bar{x}_F}^2)}.]$

c. Find the rejection region for the test using $\alpha = .01$.

d. Use the results, parts **b** and **c,** to make the appropriate conclusion.

8.121 Gambling in public high schools. With the rapid growth in legalized gambling in the United States, there is concern that the involvement of youth in gambling activities is also increasing. Consider a study of the rates of gambling among Minnesota public school students (*Journal of Gambling Studies,* Winter 2001). Based on survey data, the accompanying table shows the percentages of ninth-grade boys who gambled weekly or daily on any game (e.g., cards, sports betting, lotteries) for two different years.

a. Are the percentages of ninth-grade boys who gambled weekly or daily on any game in the 2 years significantly different? (Use $\alpha = .01$.)

b. The article states that "because of the large sample sizes, even small differences may achieve statistical significance, so interpretations of the differences should include a judgment regarding the magnitude of the difference and its public health significance." Do you agree with this statement? If not, why not? If so, obtain a measure of the magnitude of the difference between the 2 years and attach a measure of reliability to the difference.

	Year 1	Year 7
Number of Ninth-Grade Boys in Survey	21,484	23,199
Number Who Gambled Weekly/Daily	4,684	5,313

8.122 CareerBank.com annual salary survey. CareerBank.com conducts an annual salary survey of accounting, finance, and banking professionals. For one survey, data were collected for 2,800 responses submitted online by professionals across the country who voluntarily responded to CareerBank.com's Web-based survey. Salary comparisons were made by gender, education, and marital status. Some of the results are shown in the accompanying table.

	Males	Females
Mean Salary	$69,848	$52,012
Number of Respondents	1,400	1,400

a. Suppose you want to make an inference about the difference between the mean salaries of male and female accounting/finance/banking professionals at a 95% level of confidence. Why is this impossible to do using the information in the table?

b. Give values of the missing standard deviations that would lead you to conclude that the mean salary for males is significantly higher than the mean salary for females at a 95% level of confidence.

c. In your opinion, are the sample standard deviations, part **b,** reasonable values for the salary data? Explain.

d. How does the data-collection method impact any inferences derived from the data?

Critical Thinking Challenges

8.123 Facility layout study. Facility layout and material flow-path design are major factors in the productivity analysis of automated manufacturing systems. Facility layout is concerned with the location arrangement of machines and buffers for work-in-process. Flowpath design is concerned with the direction of manufacturing material flows (e.g., unidirectional or bidirectional; Lee, Lei, and Pinedo, *Annals of Operations Research,* 1997). A manufacturer of printed circuit boards is interested in evaluating two alternative existing layout and flowpath designs. The output of each design was monitored for 8 consecutive working days. The data (shown here) are saved in the file. Design 2 appears to be superior to Design 1. Do you agree? Explain fully.

Working Days	Design 1 (units)	Design 2 (units)
8/16	1,220	1,273
8/17	1,092	1,363
8/18	1,136	1,342
8/19	1,205	1,471
8/20	1,086	1,299
8/23	1,274	1,457
8/24	1,145	1,263
8/25	1,281	1,368

ACTIVITY 8.1   *Box Office Receipts:* Comparing Population Means

Use the Internet to find the daily box office receipts for two different hit movies during the first 8 weeks after their releases. In this activity, you will compare the mean daily box office receipts of these movies in two different ways.

1. Independently select random samples of size $n = 30$ from the data sets for each of the movies' daily box office receipts. Find the mean and standard deviation of each sample. Then find a confidence interval for the difference of the means.

2. Now pair the data for the two movies by day, that is, the box office receipts for the day of release for each movie are paired, the box office receipts for each movie's second day are paired, and so forth. Calculate the difference in box office receipts for each day and select a random sample of size $n = 30$ from the daily differences. Then find a confidence interval for the sample mean.

3. Compare the confidence intervals from Exercises 1 and 2. Explain how the sampling for the paired difference experiment is different from the independent sampling. How might this sampling technique yield a better comparison of the two means in the box office example?

4. Compute the actual means for the daily box office receipts for each of the movies and then find the difference of the means. Does the difference of the means lie in both confidence intervals you found? Is the exact difference remarkably closer to one of the estimates? Explain.

ACTIVITY 8.2   *Keep the Change:* Inferences Based on Two Samples

In this activity, you will compare the mean amounts transferred for two different Bank of America customers as well as design some studies that might help the marketing department determine where to allocate more of its advertising budget. You will be working with data sets from Activity 1.1, *Keep the Change: Collecting Data,* on page 54.

1. You will need to work with another student in the class on this exercise. Each of you should use your data set *Amounts Transferred* from the Chapter 1 Activity as a random sample from a theoretically larger set of all your amounts ever transferred. Then the means and standard deviations of your data sets will be the sample means and standard deviations. Write a confidence interval for the difference of the two means at the 95% level. Does the interval contain 0? Are your mean amounts transferred significantly different? Explain.

2. Design a study to determine whether there is a significant difference in the mean amount of Bank of America matches for customers in California enrolled in the program and the mean amount of Bank of America matches for customers in Florida enrolled in the program. Be specific about sample sizes, tests used, and how a conclusion will be reached. How might the results of this study help Bank of America estimate costs in the program?

3. Design a study to determine whether there is a significant difference in the percentage of Bank of America customers in California enrolled in the program and the percentage of Bank of America customers in Florida enrolled in the program. Be specific about sample sizes, tests used, and how a conclusion will be reached. How might the results of this study help Bank of America's marketing department?

Keep the results from this activity for use in other activities.

References

Freedman, D., Pisani, R., and Purves, R. *Statistics.* New York: W. W. Norton and Co., 1978.

Gibbons, J. D. *Nonparametric Statistical Inference,* 2nd ed. New York: McGraw-Hill, 1985.

Hollander, M., and Wolfe, D. A. *Nonparametric Statistical Methods.* New York. Wiley, 1973.

Koehler, K. *Snedecor and Cochran's Statistical Methods,* 9th ed. New York: Blackwell Publishing, 2012.

Mendenhall, W., Beaver, R. J., and Beaver, B. M. *Introduction to Probability and Statistics,* 13th ed. Belmont, CA: Brooks/Cole, 2009.

Satterthwaite, F. W. "An approximate distribution of estimates of variance components," *Biometrics Bulletin,* Vol. 2, 1946, pp. 110–114.

Steel, R. G. D., and Torrie, J. H. *Principles and Procedures of Statistics,* 2nd ed. New York: McGraw-Hill, 1980.

USING TECHNOLOGY   Technology images shown here are taken from SPSS Statistics Professional 23.0, Minitab 17, XLSTAT, and Excel 2016.

SPSS: Two-sample Inferences

SPSS can be used to make two-sample inferences about $\mu_1 - \mu_2$ for independent samples, μ_d for paired samples, $p_1 - p_2$, and $\frac{\sigma_1^2}{\sigma_2^2}$.

Comparing Means with Independent Samples

Step 1 Access the SPSS spreadsheet file that contains the sample data. The data file should contain one quantitative variable (which the means will be calculated on) and one qualitative variable with either two numerical coded values (e.g., 1 and 2) or two short categorical levels (e.g., "yes" and "no"). These two values represent the two groups or populations to be compared.

Step 2 Click on the "Analyze" button on the SPSS menu bar and then click on "Compare Means" and "Independent-Samples T Test," as shown in Figure 8.S.1.

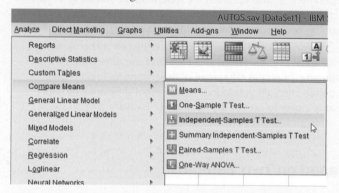

Figure 8.S.1 SPSS menu options for comparing two means

Step 3 On the resulting dialog box (shown in Figure 8.S.2), specify the quantitative variable of interest in the "Test Variable(s)" box and the qualitative variable in the "Grouping Variable" box.

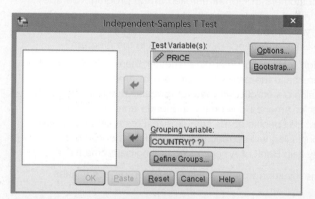

Figure 8.S.2 SPSS independent-samples T test dialog box

Step 4 Click the "Define Groups" button and specify the values of the two groups in the resulting dialog box (see Figure 8.S.3).

Figure 8.S.3 SPSS define groups dialog box

Step 5 Click "Continue" to return to the "Independent-Samples T Test" dialog screen. Without any further menu selections, SPSS will automatically conduct a two-tailed test of the null hypothesis, $H_0: \mu_1 - \mu_2 = 0$.

Step 6 If you want to generate a confidence interval for $\mu_1 - \mu_2$, click the "Options" button and specify the confidence level on the resulting menu screen, as shown in Figure 8.S.4. Click "Continue" to return to the "T Test" dialog box.

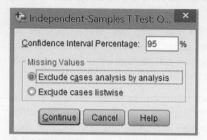

Figure 8.S.4 SPSS options dialog box

Step 7 Click "OK" to generate the SPSS printout.

Important Note: The SPSS two-sample t-procedure uses the t-statistic to conduct the test of hypothesis. When the sample sizes are small, this is the appropriate method. When the sample sizes are large, the t-value will be approximately equal to the large-sample z-value, and the resulting test will still be valid.

Comparing Means with Paired Samples

Step 1 Access the SPSS spreadsheet file that contains the sample data. The data file should contain two quantitative variables–one with the data values for the first group (or population) and one with the data values for the second group.

(*Note:* The sample size should be the same for each group.)

Step 2 Click on the "Analyze" button on the SPSS menu bar and then click on "Compare Means" and "Paired-Samples T Test" (see Figure 8.S.1).

Step 3 On the resulting dialog box (shown in Figure 8.S.5), specify the two quantitative variables of interest in the "Paired Variables" box. Without any further menu selections, SPSS will automatically conduct a two-tailed test of the null hypothesis, $H_0: \mu_d = 0$.

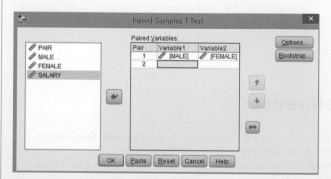

Figure 8.S.5 SPSS paired-samples dialog box

Step 4 If you want to generate a confidence interval for μ_d, click the "Options" button and specify the confidence level on the resulting menu screen (as shown in Figure 8.S.4). Click "Continue" to return to the "Paired-Samples" dialog box.

Step 5 Click "OK" to generate the SPSS printout.

Comparing Proportions with Independent Samples

Step 1 SPSS requires summary data to compare population proportions. Create a data file with three variables (columns)—(1) SAMPLE, (2) OUTCOME, and (3) NUMBER—and four rows. Each row will give the sample number, outcome (success or failure), and number of observations. For example, Figure 8.S.6 shows the data file for a problem with 60 out of 100 successes for sample 1 and 50 out of 100 successes for sample 2.

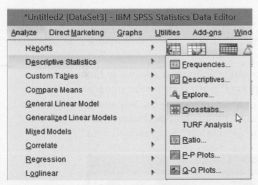

	SAMPLE	OUTCOME	NUMBER	va
1	1	S	60	
2	1	F	42	
3	2	S	50	
4	2	F	51	
5				

Figure 8.S.6 SPSS data file for comparing two proportions

Step 2 Click on the "Data" button on the SPSS menu bar and then click on "Weight Cases". Enter the "Number" variable into the "Frequency Variable" box, then click "OK."

Step 3 Click on the "Analyze" button on the SPSS menu bar and then click on "Descriptive Statistics" and "Crosstabs." (See Figure 8.S.7.)

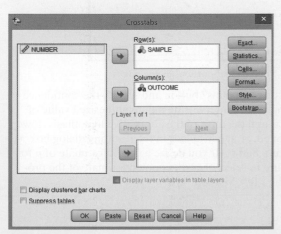

Figure 8.S.7 SPSS menu options for comparing two proportions

Step 4 On the resulting menu, specify "SAMPLE" in the "Row" box and "OUTCOME" in the "Column(s)" box as shown in Figure 8.S.8. Also, click the "Statistics" option button and select "Chi-square," then click the "Cells" option button and select "Observed Counts" and "Row Percentages."

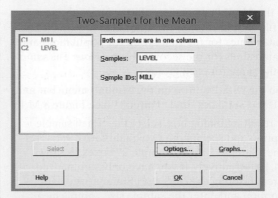

Figure 8.S.8 SPSS menu options for comparing two proportions

Step 5 Click "Continue," then click "OK." On the resulting SPSS printout, look for the *p*-value associated with the "Likelihood Ratio" test (this is equivalent to the large-sample *z*-test).

Comparing Variances with Independent Samples

Follow the steps outlined for "Comparing Means with Independent Samples" above. On the resulting SPSS printout, there will be an *F*-test for comparing population variances. (This test, called Levene's Test, is a nonparametric test that is similar to the *F*-test presented in the text.)

Minitab: Two-Sample Inferences

Minitab can be used to make two-sample inferences about $\mu_1 - \mu_2$ or independent samples, μ_d for paired samples, $p_1 - p_2$ and $\frac{\sigma_1^2}{\sigma_2^2}$.

Comparing Means with Independent Samples

Step 1 Access the Minitab worksheet that contains the sample data.

Step 2 Click on the "Stat" button on the Minitab menu bar and then click on "Basic Statistics" and "2-Sample t," as shown in Figure 8.M.1. The resulting dialog box appears as shown in Figure 8.M.2.

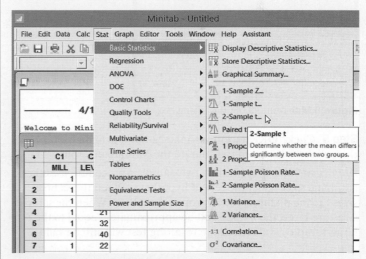

Figure 8.M.1 Minitab menu options for comparing two means

Figure 8.M.2 Minitab 2-sample *t* dialog box

Step 3a If the worksheet contains data for one quantitative variable (which the means will be computed on) and one qualitative variable (which represents the two groups or populations), select "Both samples are in one column" and then specify the quantitative variable in the "Samples" area and the qualitative variable in the "Sample IDs" area. (See Figure 8.M.2.)

Step 3b If the worksheet contains the data for the first sample in one column and the data for the second sample in another column, select "Each sample is in its own column" and then specify the "Sample 1" and "Sample 2" variables. Alternatively, if you have only summarized data (i.e., sample sizes, sample means, and sample standard deviations), select "Summarized data" and enter these summarized values in the appropriate boxes.

Step 4 Click the "Options" button on the Minitab "2-Sample t" dialog box. Specify the confidence level for a confidence interval, the null hypothesized value of the difference, $\mu_1 - \mu_2$, and the form of the alternative hypothesis (lower-tailed, two-tailed, or upper-tailed) in the resulting dialog box, as shown in Figure 8.M.3. Check the "Assume equal variances" box for a small sample t-test, leave it unchecked for a large sample z-test.

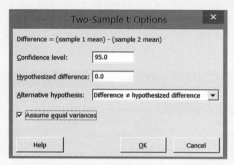

Figure 8.M.3 Minitab options dialog box

Step 5 Click "OK" to return to the "2-Sample t" dialog box and then click "OK" again to generate the Minitab printout.

Important Note: The Minitab two-sample t-procedure uses the t-statistic to conduct the test of hypothesis. When the sample sizes are small, this is the appropriate method. When the sample sizes are large, the t-value will be approximately equal to the large-sample z-value, and the resulting test will still be valid.

Comparing Means with Paired Samples

Step 1 Access the Minitab worksheet that contains the sample data. The data file should contain two quantitative variables—one with the data values for the first group (or population) and one with the data values for the second group. (*Note:* The sample size should be the same for each group.)

Step 2 Click on the "Stat" button on the Minitab menu bar and then click on "Basic Statistics" and "Paired t" (see Figure 8.M.1).

Step 3 On the resulting dialog box, select the "Each sample is in a column" option and specify the two quantitative variables of interest in the "Sample 1" and "Sample 2" boxes, as shown in Figure 8.M.4. [Alternatively, if you have only summarized data of the paired differences, select the "Summarized data (differences)" option and enter the sample size, sample mean, and sample standard deviation in the appropriate boxes.]

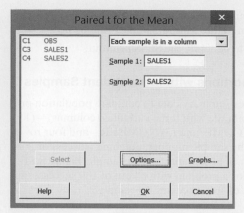

Figure 8.M.4 Minitab paired-samples t dialog box

Step 4 Click the "Options" button and specify the confidence level for a confidence interval, the null hypothesized value of the difference, μ_d, and the form of the alternative hypothesis (lower-tailed, two-tailed, or upper-tailed) in the resulting dialog box. (See Figure 8.M.3.)

Step 5 Click "OK" to return to the "Paired t" dialog box and then click "OK" again to generate the Minitab printout.

Comparing Proportions with Large Independent Samples

Step 1 Access the Minitab worksheet that contains the sample data.

Step 2 Click on the "Stat" button on the Minitab menu bar and then click on "Basic Statistics" and "2 Proportions," as shown in Figure 8.M.1.

Step 3 On the resulting dialog box (shown in Figure 8.M.5), select the data option ("Both samples are in one column" or "Each sample is in its own column" or "Summarized data") and make the appropriate menu choices. (Figure 8.M.5 shows the menu options when you select "Summarized data.")

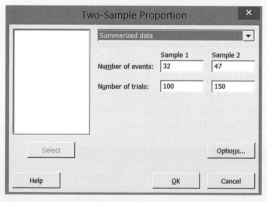

Figure 8.M.5 Minitab 2 proportions dialog box

Step 4 Click the "Options" button and specify the confidence level for a confidence interval, the null hypothesized value of the difference, and the form of the alternative hypothesis (lower-tailed, two-tailed, or upper-tailed) in the resulting dialog box, as shown in Figure 8.M.6. (If you desire a pooled estimate of p for the test, be sure to select "Use the pooled estimate of the proportion" in the "Test Method" box.)

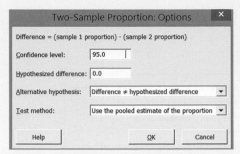

Figure 8.M.6 Minitab 2 proportions options

Step 5 Click "OK" to return to the "2 Proportions" dialog box and then click "OK" again to generate the Minitab printout.

Comparing Variances with Independent Samples

Step 1 Access the Minitab worksheet that contains the sample data.

Step 2 Click on the "Stat" button on the Minitab menu bar and then click on "Basic Statistics" and "2 Variances" (Figure 8.M.1).

Step 3 On the resulting dialog box (shown in Figure 8.M.7), the menu selections and options are similar to those for the two-sample *t*-test.

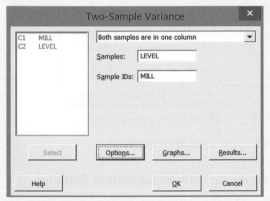

Figure 8.M.7 Minitab 2 variances dialog box

Step 4 Click "OK" to produce the Minitab *F*-test printout.

Excel/XLSTAT: Two-Sample Inferences

Comparing Means with Independent Samples

Step 1 Click the "XLSTAT" button on the Excel main menu bar, select "Parametric tests," and then click "Two-sample t-test and z-test," as shown in Figure 8.E.1.

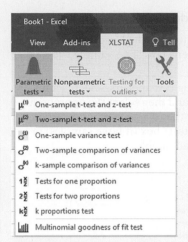

Figure 8.E.1 XLSTAT menu options for testing a mean

Step 2 When the resulting dialog box appears, select the proper "Data format" (e.g., "One column per variable"), and then select the appropriate columns (e.g., one column for the variable being analyzed and one for the variable that represents the two different samples). Also, check the "z test" box (if large samples) or the "Student's t test" box (if small samples). See, for example, Figure 8.E.2.

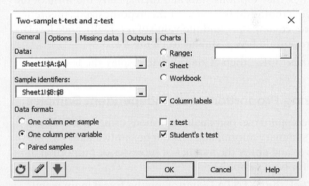

Figure 8.E.2 XLSTAT two-sample test dialog box

Step 3 Click the "Options" tab, then specify the form of the alternative hypothesis, the value of the hypothesized (theoretical) difference in means, and the value of α (significance level) in the appropriate boxes, as shown in Figure 8.E.3.

Figure 8.E.3 XLSTAT options for comparing two means

Step 4 Click "OK," then "Continue" to display the test results.

Comparing Means with Independent Samples

Step 1   Click the "XLSTAT" button on the Excel main menu bar, select "Parametric tests," then click "Two-sample t-test and z-test," as shown in Figure 8.E.1.

Step 2   When the resulting dialog box appears, select "Paired samples" as the "Data format," and then select the appropriate columns containing the data for the two samples, as shown in Figure 8.E.4. Also, check the "z test" box (if large samples) or the "Student's t test" box (if small samples).

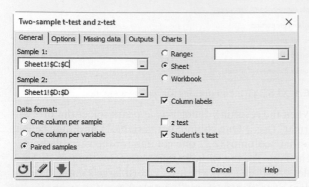

Figure 8.E.4   XLSTAT options for paired samples

Step 3   Click the "Options" tab, and then specify the form of the alternative hypothesis, the value of the hypothesized (theoretical) difference in means, and the value of α (significance level) in the appropriate boxes, similar to Figure 8.E.3.

Step 4   Click "OK," then "Continue" to display the test results.

Comparing Proportions with Independent Samples

[*Note:* To compare two binomial proportions using XLSTAT, you will need summary information on your qualitative data, e.g., the sample sizes and either the number of successes or proportion of successes for both samples.]

Step 1   Click the "XLSTAT" button on the Excel main menu bar, select "Parametric tests," then click "Tests for two proportions," as shown in Figure 8.E.5.

Figure 8.E.5   XLSTAT menu options for comparing proportions

Step 2   When the resulting dialog box appears, check "Frequencies" in the "Data format" area, then enter the number of successes and the sample size for each sample in the appropriate boxes, as shown in Figure 8.E.6. (Alternatively, you can

check "Proportions" in the "Data format" area and enter the sample proportions.)

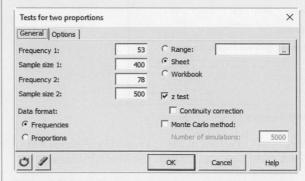

Figure 8.E.6   XLSTAT test for two proportions dialog box

Step 3   Click the "Options" tab, specify the form of the alternative hypothesis, and then enter "0" for the hypothesized difference and the value of α (significance level) in the appropriate boxes, as shown in Figure 8.E.7.

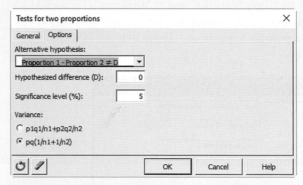

Figure 8.E.7   XLSTAT options for testing proportions

Step 4   Click "OK" to display the test results.

Comparing Variances with Independent Samples

Step 1   Click the "XLSTAT" button on the Excel main menu bar, select "Parametric tests," then click "Two-sample comparison of variances" (see Figure 8.E.1).

Step 2   When the resulting dialog box appears, select the proper "Data format" (e.g., "One column per variable"), and then select the appropriate columns (e.g., one column for the variable being analyzed and one for the variable that represents the two different samples). Also, check the "Fisher's F-test" box, as shown in Figure 8.E.8.

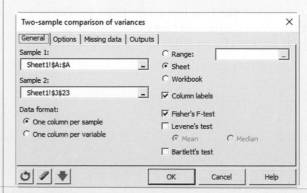

Figure 8.E.8   XLSTAT two-sample variance test dialog box

Step 3 Click the "Options" tab, and then specify the form of the alternative hypothesis, the value of the hypothesized (theoretical) ratio of variances, and the value of α (significance level) in the appropriate boxes, as shown in Figure 8.E.9.

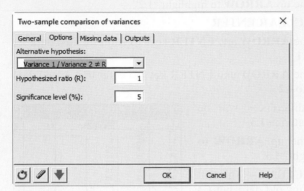

Figure 8.E.9 XLSTAT options for comparing two variances

Step 4 Click "OK," then "Continue" to display the test results.

TI-83/TI-84 Graphing Calculator:

Two-Sample Inferences

The TI-84 graphing calculator can be used to conduct tests and form confidence intervals for the difference between two means with independent samples, the difference between two means with matched pairs, the difference between two proportions for large independent samples, and the ratio of two variances.

Confidence Interval for $\mu_1 - \mu_2$

Step 1 *Enter the data (Skip to Step 2 if you have summary statistics, not raw data)*

- Press **STAT** and select **1:Edit**

Note: If the lists already contain data, clear the old data. Use the up **ARROW** to highlight "**L1.**"

- Press **CLEAR ENTER**
- Use the up **ARROW** to highlight "**L2**"
- Press **CLEAR ENTER**
- Use the **ARROW** and **ENTER** keys to enter the first data set into **L1**
- Use the **ARROW** and **ENTER** keys to enter the second data set into **L2**

Step 2 *Access the Statistical Tests Menu*

- Press **STAT**
- Arrow right to **TESTS**
- Arrow down to **2-SampTInt**
- Press **ENTER**

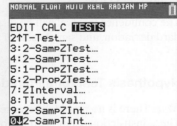

Step 3 *Choose "**Data**" or "**Stats**" ("Data" is selected when you have entered the raw data into the Lists. "Stats" is selected when you are given only the means, standard deviations, and sample sizes.)*

- Press **ENTER**
- If you selected "Data," set **List1** to **L1** and **List2** to **L2**
- Set **Freq1** to **1** and set **Freq2** to **1**
- Set **C-Level** to the confidence level
- If you are assuming that the two populations have equal variances, select **Yes** for **Pooled**
- If you are not assuming equal variances, select **No**
- Press **ENTER**
- Arrow down to "**Calculate**"
- Press **ENTER**
- If you selected "Stats," enter the means, standard deviations, and sample sizes
- Set **C-Level** to the confidence level
- If you are assuming that the two populations have equal variances, select **Yes** for **Pooled**
- If you are not assuming equal variances, select **No**
- Press **ENTER**
- Arrow down to "**Calculate**"
- Press **ENTER**

(The accompanying screen is set up for an example with a mean of 100, a standard deviation of 10, and a sample size of 15 for the first data set and a mean of 105, a standard deviation of 12, and a sample size of 18 for the second data set.)

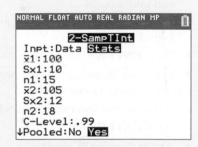

The confidence interval will be displayed with the degrees of freedom, the sample statistics, and the pooled standard deviation (when appropriate).

Hypothesis Test for $\mu_1 - \mu_2$

Step 1 *Enter the data (Skip to Step 2 if you have summary statistics, not raw data)*

- Press **STAT** and select **1:Edit**

Note: If the lists already contain data, clear the old data. Use the up **ARROW** to highlight "**L1.**"

- Press **CLEAR ENTER**
- Use the up **ARROW** to highlight "**L2**"
- Press **CLEAR ENTER**
- Use the **ARROW** and **ENTER** keys to enter the first data set into **L1**
- Use the **ARROW** and **ENTER** keys to enter the second data set into **L2**

Step 2 *Access the Statistical Tests Menu*

- Press **STAT**
- Arrow right to **TESTS**

- Arrow down to **2-SampTTest**
- Press **ENTER**

Step 3 *Choose "Data" or "Stats" ("Data" is selected when you have entered the raw data into the Lists. "Stats" is selected when you are given only the means, standard deviations, and sample sizes.)*

- Press **ENTER**
- If you selected "Data," set **List1** to **L1** and **List2** to **L2**
- Set **Freq1** to 1 and set **Freq2** to 1
- Use the **ARROW** to highlight the appropriate alternative hypothesis
- Press **ENTER**
- If you are assuming that the two populations have equal variances, select **Yes** for **Pooled**
- If you are not assuming equal variances, select **No**
- Press **ENTER**
- Arrow down to "**Calculate**"
- Press **ENTER**
- If you selected "**Stats,**" enter the means, standard deviations, and sample sizes
- Use the **ARROW** to highlight the appropriate alternative hypothesis
- Press **ENTER**
- If you are assuming that the two populations have equal variances, select **Yes** for **Pooled**
- If you are not assuming equal variances, select **No**
- Press **ENTER**
- Arrow down to "**Calculate**"
- Press **ENTER**

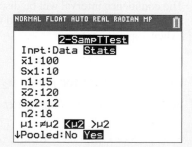

(The screen at the right is set up for an example with a mean of 100, a standard deviation of 10, and a sample size of 15 for the first data set and a mean of 120, a standard deviation of 12, and a sample size of 18 for the second data set.)

The results of the hypothesis test will be displayed with the *p*-value, degrees of freedom, the sample statistics, and the pooled standard deviation (when appropriate).

Confidence Interval for a Paired Difference Mean

Note: There is no paired difference option on the calculator. These instructions demonstrate how to calculate the differences and then use the 1-sample *t*-interval.

Step 1 *Enter the data and calculate the differences.*

- Press **STAT** and select **1:Edit**

Note: If the lists already contain data, clear the old data. Use the up **ARROW** to highlight "**L1.**"

- Press **CLEAR ENTER**
- Use the up **ARROW** to highlight "**L2**"
- Press **CLEAR ENTER**
- Use the **ARROW** and **ENTER** keys to enter the first data set into **L1**
- Use the **ARROW** and **ENTER** keys to enter the second data set into **L2**
- The differences will be calculated in **L3**
- Use the up **ARROW** to highlight "**L3**"
- Press **CLEAR**— This will clear any old data, but **L3** will remain highlighted
- To enter the equation $L3 = L1 - L2$, use the following keystrokes:
- Press **2ND** "**1**" (this will enter L1)
- Press the **MINUS** button
- Press **2ND** "**2**" (this will enter L2)
- Notice the equation at the bottom of the screen.)
- Press **ENTER** (the differences should be calculated in L3)

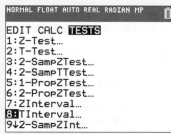

Step 2 *Access the Statistical Tests Menu*

- Press **STAT**
- Arrow right to **TESTS**
- Arrow down to **TInterval** (**even for large-sample case**)
- Press **ENTER**

Step 3 *Choose "Data"*

- Press **ENTER**
- Set **List** to **L3**
- Set **Freq** to 1
- Set **C-Level** to the confidence level
- Arrow down to "**Calculate**"
- Press **ENTER**

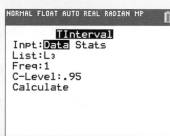

The confidence interval will be displayed with the mean, standard deviation, and sample size of the differences.

Hypothesis Test for a Paired Difference Mean

Note: There is no paired difference option on the calculator. These instructions demonstrate how to calculate the differences and then use the 1-sample *t*-test.

Step 1 *Enter the data and calculate the differences.*

- Press **STAT** and select **1:Edit**

Note: If the lists already contain data, clear the old data. Use the up **ARROW** to highlight "**L1.**"

- Press **CLEAR ENTER**
- Use the up **ARROW** to highlight "**L2**"
- Press **CLEAR ENTER**
- Use the **ARROW** and **ENTER** keys to enter the first data set into **L1**
- Use the **ARROW** and **ENTER** keys to enter the second data set into **L2**
- The differences will be calculated in **L3**
- Use the up **ARROW** to highlight "**L3**"
- Press **CLEAR**—this will clear any old data, but **L3** will remain highlighted
- To enter the equation L3 = L1 − L2, use the following keystrokes:
- Press **2ND** "**1**" (this will enter L1)
- Press the **MINUS** button
- Press **2ND** "**2**" (this will enter L2)

(Notice the equation at the bottom of the screen.)

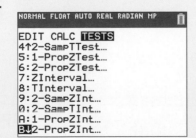

- Press **ENTER** (the differences should be calculated in L3)

Step 2 *Access the Statistical Tests Menu*

- Press **STAT**
- Arrow right to **TESTS**
- Arrow down to **T-Test** (even for large-sample case)
- Press **ENTER**

Step 3 *Choose "Data"*

- Press **ENTER**
- Enter the values for the hypothesis test, where μ_0 = the value for μ_d in the null hypothesis
- Set **List** to **L3**
- Set **Freq** to **1**
- Use the **ARROW** to highlight the appropriate alternative hypothesis
- Press **ENTER**
- Arrow down to "**Calculate**"
- Press **ENTER**

The test statistic and the *p*-value will be displayed, as well as the sample mean, standard deviation, and sample size of the differences.

Confidence Interval for $(p_1 - p_2)$

Step 1 *Access the Statistical Tests Menu*

- Press **STAT**
- Arrow right to **TESTS**
- Arrow down to **2-PropZInt**

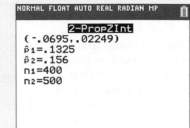

- Press **ENTER**

Step 2 *Enter the values from the sample information and **the confidence level***

where x_1 = number of successes in the first sample (e.g., 53)
n_1 = sample size for the first sample (e.g., 400)
x_2 = number of successes in the second sample (e.g., 78)
n_2 = sample size for the second sample (e.g., 500)

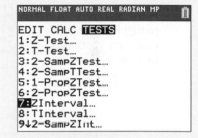

- Set **C-Level** to the confidence level
- Arrow down to "**Calculate**"
- Press **ENTER**

Hypothesis Test for $(p_1 - p_2)$

Step 1 *Access the Statistical Tests Menu*

- Press **STAT**
- Arrow right to **TESTS**
- Arrow down to **2-PropZ-Test**
- Press **ENTER**

Step 2 *Enter the values from the sample information and **select the alternative hypothesis***

where x_1 = number of successes in the first sample (e.g., 53)
n_1 = sample size for the first sample (e.g., 400)
x_2 = number of successes in the second sample (e.g., 78)
n_2 = sample size for the second sample (e.g., 500)

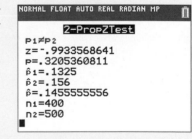

- Use the **ARROW** to highlight the appropriate alternative hypothesis
- Press **ENTER**
- Arrow down to "**Calculate**"
- Press **ENTER**

Hypothesis Test for $\left(\dfrac{\sigma_1^2}{\sigma_2^2}\right)$

Step 1 *Enter the data (Skip to Step 2 if you have summary statistics, not raw data)*

- Press **STAT** and select **1:Edit**

Note: If the lists already contain data, clear the old data. Use the up **ARROW** to highlight "**L1**."

- Press **CLEAR ENTER**
- Use the up **ARROW** to highlight "**L2**"
- Press **CLEAR ENTER**
- Use the **ARROW** and **ENTER** keys to enter the first data set into **L1**

- Use the **ARROW** and **ENTER** keys to enter the second data set into **L2**

Step 2 *Access the Statistical Tests Menu*

- Press **STAT**
- Arrow right to **TESTS**
- Arrow down to **2-SampFTest**
- Press **ENTER**

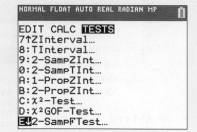

Step 3 *Choose "Data" or "Stats" ("Data" is selected when you have entered the raw data into the Lists. "Stats" is selected when you are given only the means, standard deviations, and sample sizes.)*

- Press **ENTER**
- If you selected "Data"
  - Set **List1** to **L1** and **List2** to **L2**
  - Set **Freq1** to **1** and set **Freq2** to **1**
  - Use the **ARROW** to highlight the appropriate alternative hypothesis
  - Press **ENTER**

- Arrow down to "**Calculate**"
- Press **ENTER**
- If you selected "Stats," enter the standard deviations and sample sizes
  - Use the **ARROW** to highlight the appropriate alternative hypothesis
  - Press **ENTER**
  - Arrow down to "**Calculate**"
  - Press **ENTER**

The results of the hypothesis test will be displayed with the *p*-value and the input data used.

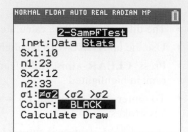

[PART II] The Kentucky Milk Case

In The Kentucky Milk Case—Part I, you used graphical and numerical descriptive statistics to investigate bid collusion in the Kentucky school milk market. This case expands your previous analyses, incorporating inferential statistical methodology. The three areas of your focus are described below. (See p. 155 for the file layout of the **MILK** data.) Again, you should prepare a professional document that presents the results of the analyses and any implications regarding collusionary practices in the tri-county Kentucky milk market.

1. *Incumbency rates.* Recall from Part I that market allocation (where the same dairy controls the same school districts year after year) is a common form of collusive behavior in bid-rigging conspiracies. Market allocation is typically gauged by the incumbency rate for a market in a given school year—defined as the percentage of school districts that are won by the same milk vendor who won the previous year. Past experience with milk bids in a competitive market reveals that a "normal" incumbency rate is about .7—that is, 70% of the school districts are expected to purchase their milk from the same vendor who supplied the milk the previous year. In the 13-district tri-county Kentucky market, 13 vendor transitions potentially exist each year. Over the 1985–1988 period (when bid collusion was alleged to have occurred), there were 52 potential vendor transitions. Based on the actual number of vendor transitions that occurred each year and over the 1985–1988 period, make an inference regarding bid collusion.

2. *Bid price dispersion.* Recall that in competitive, sealed-bid markets, more dispersion or variability among the bids is observed than in collusive markets. (This is due to conspiring vendors sharing information about their bids.) Consequently, if collusion exists, the variation in bid prices in the tri-county market should be significantly smaller than the corresponding variation in the surrounding market. For each milk product, conduct an analysis to compare the bid price variances of the two markets each year. Make the appropriate inferences.

3. *Average winning bid price.* According to collusion theorists, the mean winning bid price in the "rigged" market will exceed the mean winning bid price in the competitive market for each year in which collusion occurs. In addition, the difference between the competitive average and the "rigged" average tends to grow over time when collusionary tactics are employed over several consecutive years. For each milk product, conduct an analysis to compare the winning bid price means of the tri-county and surrounding markets each year. Make the appropriate inferences.

 Data Set: MILK

9

WHERE WE'VE BEEN

- Presented methods for estimating and testing hypotheses about a single population mean
- Presented methods for comparing two population means

WHERE WE'RE GOING

- Discuss the critical elements in the design of a sampling experiment (9.1)
- Learn how to set up three of the more popular experimental designs for comparing more than two population means: *completely randomized, randomized block,* and *factorial designs* (9.2, 9.4, 9.5)
- Show how to analyze data collected from a designed experiment using a technique called an *analysis of variance* (9.2, 9.4, 9.5)
- Present a follow-up analysis to an ANOVA: Ranking means (9.3)

Design of Experiments and Analysis of Variance

STATISTICS IN ACTION

Tax Compliance Behavior—Factors That Affect Your Level of Risk Taking When Filing Your Federal Tax Return

According to the Internal Revenue Service (IRS), the amount of uncollected but legally owed federal taxes is more than $450 billion each year. Time *magazine (March 27, 2013) estimates that "the single biggest contributor to [this] tax gap—accounting for 84% of it—are people who simply under-report their income." Most taxpayers are aware that the IRS has auditing procedures in place to detect noncompliance with the tax law (e.g., intentionally underreporting income, taking bogus deductions, hiding assets) and that, if caught, the offender risks both heavy monetary penalties and criminal charges. Yet, this type of risk-taking behavior continues to occur each tax season.*

Are there certain factors that influence the level of risk taking when filing a federal or state income tax return? This was the question of interest in a study published in *Behavioral Research in Accounting* (January 2015). The researchers—professors at Virginia Polytechnic Institute (VPI) and Northeastern University (NU)—theorized that a taxpayer's level of risk taking will vary depending on whether the taxpayer owes money or will receive a refund. Prior research has found that taxpayers with pending payments due on a single tax return tend to report more aggressively (i.e., take more risks) than taxpayers with pending refunds. The current research by the VPI and NU professors extended this idea by examining a taxpayer's behavior under two conditions: filing of a single tax return and filing of multiple tax returns (e.g., both a federal and a state return).

The researchers applied prospect theory to predict that a taxpayer's aggressiveness will be greater when filing multiple returns when a refund is due (as compared to a single return), but will be less when filing multiple returns with a net payment

(continued)

due (as compared to a single return). In other words, a taxpayer is willing to take more risks when filing multiple returns than when filing a single return as long as he or she is due a refund; however, the taxpayer will take fewer risks when filing multiple returns than when filing a single return if he or she owes money. These predictions are summarized in the following two propositions:

Proposition 1: Taxpayers' aggressiveness will shift up (more risk taking) when a net refund on multiple returns is due as compared to a net refund on a single return.

Proposition 2: Taxpayers' aggressiveness will shift down (less risk taking) when a net payment due is on multiple returns as compared to a net refund on a single return.

The researchers designed an experiment to test the two propositions. Subjects for the study were taxpayers, recruited either from a shopping mall or from a professional graduate degree program. Each taxpayer was randomly assigned to one of four experimental conditions: (1) filing a single federal tax return with a refund due, (2) filing a single federal tax return with a payment due, (3) filing multiple (federal and state) tax returns with a net refund due, and (4) filing multiple (federal and state) tax returns with a net payment due. See Figure SIA9.1. For this *Statistics in Action*, assume that 60 taxpayers were assigned to each condition, yielding a total sample size of 240.*

	Net Refund Due	Net Payment Due
Single Return	Condition 1	Condition 2
Multiple Returns	Condition 3	Condition 4

Figure SIA9.1

Layout of experimental design

After reading a description of his or her tax situation (condition), each subject was given an estimate of the refund or payment due. Subjects were then informed of an opportunity for an additional deduction on their federal return as the result of a new tax law change. This deduction would either increase the net refund or decrease the net payment due. Subjects were also told that the IRS might interpret the new law differently and disallow the deduction. Therefore, some risk was associated with taking the deduction. If the deduction was disallowed, they would have to pay back the taxes saved along with interest and penalties. Finally, with all this information, each participant responded, on a nine-point scale, to whether he or she would take the additional deduction (1 = *definitely would not take the deduction*; 9 = *definitely would take the deduction*). The researchers used this variable to capture taxpayers' compliance behavior.

The data for the 240 subjects (simulated from information provided in the journal article) are saved in the **TAX** file. In the *Statistics in Action Revisited* sections that follow, we illustrate how to analyze these data to test the researchers' propositions about a taxpayer's compliance behavior.

STATISTICS IN ACTION REVISITED

- Testing the Equality of the Tax Compliance Behavior Means for the Four Experimental Conditions **(p. 540)**
- Ranking the Tax Compliance Behavior Means for the Four Experimental Conditions **(p. 551)**
- Investigating the Effects of Tax Position (Refund or Payment) and Returns Filed (Single or Multiple) on the Tax Compliance Behavior Mean **(p. 578)**

Most of the data analyzed in previous chapters were collected in *observational* sampling experiments rather than *designed* sampling experiments. In *observational studies*, the analyst has little or no control over the variables under study and merely observes their values. In contrast, *designed experiments* are those in which the analyst attempts

---

* In the actual study, the number of taxpayers assigned to each of the four conditions were 53, 60, 82, and 75 respectively.

to control the levels of one or more variables to determine their effect on a variable of interest. When properly designed, such experiments allow the analyst to determine whether a change in the controlled variable causes a change in the response variable, that is, it allows one to infer *cause and effect*. Although many practical business situations do not present the opportunity for such control, it is instructive, even for observational experiments, to have a working knowledge of the analysis and interpretation of data that result from designed experiments and to know the basics of how to design experiments when the opportunity arises.

We first present the basic elements of an experimental design in Section 9.1. We then discuss three of the simpler, and more popular, experimental designs in Section 9.2, 9.4, and 9.5. In Section 9.3 we show how to rank the population means, from smallest to largest.

9.1 Elements of a Designed Experiment

Certain elements are common to almost all designed experiments, regardless of the specific area of application. For example, the *response* is the variable of interest in the experiment. The response might be the Graduate Management Admission Test (GMAT) score of a business graduate student, the total sales of a firm last year, or the total income of a particular household this year. The response is also called the *dependent variable*. Typically, the response variable is quantitative in nature since one of the objectives of a designed experiment is to compare response variable means.

> The **response variable** is the variable of interest to be measured in the experiment. We also refer to the response as the **dependent variable**. Typically, the response/dependent variable is quantitative in nature.

The intent of most statistical experiments is to determine the effect of one or more variables on the response. These variables are usually referred to as the *factors* in a designed experiment. Factors are either *quantitative* or *qualitative*, depending on whether the variable is measured on a numerical scale or not. For example, we might want to explore the effect of the qualitative factor Gender on the response GMAT score. In other words, we want to compare the GMAT scores of male and female business graduate students. Or, we might wish to determine the effect of the quantitative factor Number of salespeople on the response Total sales for retail firms. Often two or more factors are of interest. For example, we might want to determine the effect of the quantitative factor Number of wage earners and the qualitative factor Location on the response Household income.

> **Factors** are those variables whose effect on the response is of interest to the experimenter. **Quantitative factors** are measured on a numerical scale, whereas **qualitative factors** are those that are not (naturally) measured on a numerical scale. Factors are also referred to as **independent variables.**

Levels are the values of the factors that are used in the experiment. The levels of qualitative factors are categorical in nature. For example, the levels of Gender are Male and Female, and the levels of Location might be North, East, South, and West.* The levels of quantitative factors are numerical values. For example, the Number of salespeople may have levels 1, 3, 5, 7, and 9. The factor Years of education may have levels 8, 12, 16, and 20.

---

*The levels of a qualitative variable may bear numerical labels. For example, the Locations could be numbered 1, 2, 3, and 4. However, in such cases, the numerical labels for a qualitative variable will usually be codes representing categorical levels.

Factor levels are the values of the factor used in the experiment.

When a *single factor* is employed in an experiment, the *treatments* of the experiment are the levels of the factor. For example, if the effect of the factor Gender on the response GMAT score is being investigated, the treatments of the experiment are the two levels of Gender—Female and Male. Or, if the effect of the Number of wage earners on Household income is the subject of the experiment, the numerical values assumed by the quantitative factor Number of wage earners are the treatments. If *two or more factors* are used in an experiment, the treatments are the factor-level combinations used. For example, if the effects of the factors Gender and Socioeconomic Status (SES) on the response GMAT score are being investigated, the treatments are the combinations of the levels of Gender and SES used; thus (Female, high SES), (Male, high SES), and (Female, low SES) would all be treatments.

The **treatments** of an experiment are the factor-level combinations used.

The objects on which the response variable and factors are observed are the *experimental units*. For example, GMAT score, College GPA, and Gender are all variables that can be observed on the same experimental unit—a business graduate student. Or, the Total sales, the Earnings per share, and the Number of salespeople can be measured on a particular firm in a particular year, and the firm-year combination is the experimental unit. The Total income, the Number of female wage earners, and the Location can be observed for a household at a particular point in time, and the household-time combination is the experimental unit. Every experiment, whether observational or designed, has experimental units on which the variables are observed. However, the identification of the experimental units is more important in designed experiments, when the experimenter must actually sample the experimental units and measure the variables.

An **experimental unit** is the object on which the response and factors are observed or measured.*

When the specification of the treatments and the method of assigning the experimental units to each of the treatments are controlled by the analyst, the study is said to be *designed*. In contrast, if the analyst is just an observer of the treatments on a sample of experimental units, the study is *observational*. For example, if you give one randomly selected group of employees a training program and withhold it from another randomly selected group to evaluate the effect of the training on worker productivity, then you are designing a study. If, on the other hand, you compare the productivity of employees with college degrees with the productivity of employees without college degrees, the study is observational.

A **designed study** is one for which the analyst controls the specification of the treatments and the method of assigning the experimental units to each treatment. An **observational study** is one for which the analyst simply observes the treatments and the response on a sample of experimental units.

The diagram in Figure 9.1 provides an overview of the experimental process and a summary of the terminology introduced in this section. Note that the experimental unit is at the core of the process. The method by which the sample of experimental units is selected from the population determines the type of experiment. The level of every factor (the treatment) and the response are all variables that are observed or measured on each experimental unit.

*Recall (Chapter 1) that the set of all experimental units is the population.

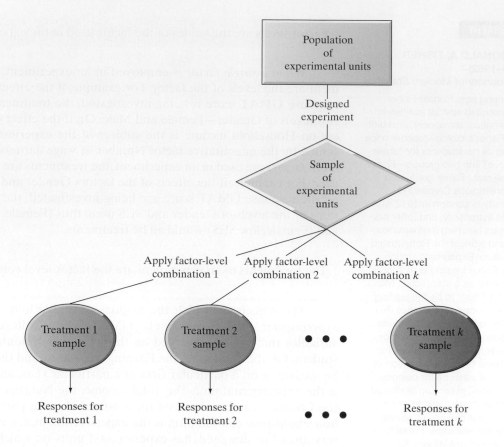

Figure 9.1

Designed experiment: Process and terminology

EXAMPLE 9.1

Key Elements of a Designed Experiment— Testing Golf Ball Brands

Problem The USGA (United States Golf Association) regularly tests golf equipment to ensure that it conforms to USGA standards. Suppose it wishes to compare the mean distance traveled by four different brands of golf balls when struck by a driver (the club used to maximize distance). The following experiment is conducted: 10 balls of each brand are randomly selected. Each is struck by "Iron Byron" (the USGA's golf robot named for the famous golfer Byron Nelson) using a driver, and the distance traveled is recorded. A layout of the experimental design is portrayed in Figure 9.2 Identify each of the following elements in this experiment: response, factors, factor types, levels, treatments, and experimental units.

Brand A	Brand B	Brand C	Brand D
—	—	—	—
—	—	—	—
—	—	—	—
⋮	⋮	⋮	⋮
—	—	—	—

> Distances for 10 randomly selected balls from Brand B lot

Figure 9.2

Layout of designed study for Example 9.1

Solution The response is the variable of interest, Distance traveled. The only factor being investigated is the Brand of golf ball, and it is nonnumerical and therefore qualitative. The four brands (say A, B, C, and D) represent the levels of this factor. Because only one factor is used, the treatments are the four levels of this factor—that is, the four brands.

The experimental unit is a golf ball; more specifically, it is a golf ball at a particular position in the striking sequence, because the distance traveled can be recorded only when the ball is struck, and we would expect the distance to be different (due to random factors such as wind resistance, landing place, and so forth) if the same ball is struck a second time. Note that 10 experimental units are sampled for each treatment, generating a total of 40 observations.

Look Back This study, like many real applications, is a blend of designed and observational: The analyst cannot control the assignment of the brand to each golf ball (observational), but he or she can control the assignment of each ball to the position in the striking sequence (designed).

● **Now Work Exercise 9.5**

EXAMPLE 9.2

A Two-Factor Experiment—Testing Golf Ball Brands

Problem Suppose the USGA is interested in comparing the mean distances the four brands of golf balls travel when struck by a five-iron and by a driver. Ten balls of each brand are randomly selected, five to be struck by the driver and five by the five-iron. Identify the elements of the experiment and construct a schematic diagram similar to Figure 9.1 to provide an overview of this experiment.

Solution The response is the same as in Example 9.1—Distance traveled. The experiment now has two factors: Brand of golf ball and Club used. There are four levels of Brand (A, B, C, and D) and two of Club (driver and five-iron, or 1 and 5). Treatments are factor-level combinations, so there are $4 \times 2 = 8$ treatments in this experiment: (A, 1), (A, 5), (B, 1), (B, 5), (C, 1), (C, 5), (D, 1), and (D, 5). The experimental units are still the golf balls. Note that five experimental units are sampled per treatment, generating 40 observations. The experiment is summarized in Figure 9.3.

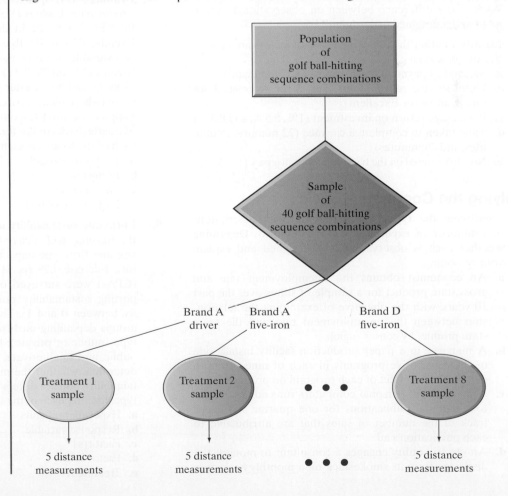

Figure 9.3

Two-factor golf experiment summary: Example 9.2

> **Look Back** Whenever there are two or more factors in an experiment, remember to combine the levels of the factors—one level from each factor—to obtain the treatments.
>
> • **Now Work Exercise 9.10**

Our objective in designing a study is usually to maximize the amount of information obtained about the relationship between the treatments and the response. Of course, we are almost always subject to constraints on budget, time, and even the availability of experimental units. Nevertheless, designed studies are generally preferred to observational studies. Not only do we have better control of the amount and quality of the information collected, but we also avoid the biases inherent in observational studies in the selection of the experimental units representing each treatment. Inferences based on observational studies always carry the implicit assumption that the sample has no hidden bias that was not considered in the statistical analysis. Better understanding of the potential problems with observational studies is a by-product of our study of experimental design in the remainder of this chapter.

Exercises 9.1–9.14

Learning the Mechanics

9.1 What are the treatments for a designed experiment that uses one qualitative factor with four levels—A, B, C, and D?

9.2 What are the treatments for a designed experiment with two factors, one qualitative with two levels (A and B) and one quantitative with five levels (50, 60, 70, 80, and 90)?

9.3 What is the difference between an observational experiment and a designed experiment?

9.4 Identify whether the following levels of factors are qualitative or quantitative.
   a. Method of payment (cash, check, and credit card)
   b. Hotel service rating (1 for Fair, 2 for Average, 3 for Good, and 4 for Excellent)
   c. Percentage return on investment (1%, 5.5%, and 8.3%)
   d. Time taken to complete a car race (22 minutes, 25 minutes, and 29 minutes)
   e. Number printed on the back of a football jersey (1, 2, 3, etc.)

Applying the Concepts—Basic

9.5 **Identifying the type of experiment.** Brief descriptions of a number of experiments are given next. Determine whether each is observational or designed and explain your reasoning.
   a. An economist obtains the unemployment rate and gross state product for a sample of states over the past 10 years, with the objective of examining the relationship between the unemployment rate and the gross state product by census region.
   b. A manager in a paper production facility installs one of three incentive programs in each of nine plants to determine the effect of each program on productivity.
   c. A marketer of personal computers runs ads in each of four national publications for one quarter and keeps track of the number of sales that are attributable to each publication's ad.
   d. An electric utility engages a consultant to monitor the discharge from its smokestack on a monthly basis over

a 1-year period to relate the level of sulfur dioxide in the discharge to the load on the facility's generators.
   e. Intrastate trucking rates are compared before and after governmental deregulation of prices changed, with the comparison also taking into account distance of haul, goods hauled, and the price of diesel fuel.

9.6 **Drafting NFL quarterbacks.** Refer to the *Journal of Productivity Analysis* (Vol. 35, 2011) study of how successful NFL teams are in drafting productive quarterbacks, Exercise 1.26 (p. 51). Recall that the researchers measured two variables for each of the 331 quarterbacks drafted between 1970 and 2007: (1) Draft position (Top 10, between picks 11 and 50, or after pick 50) and (2) QB production score (where higher scores indicate more productive QBs). Suppose we want to compare the mean production score of quarterbacks in the three draft position groups. Identify each of the following elements for this study:
   a. Response variable
   b. Factor(s)
   c. Treatments
   d. Experimental units

9.7 **Corporate sustainability and firm characteristics.** Refer to the *Business and Society* (March 2011) study on how firm size and firm type impact corporate sustainability behaviors, Exercise 1.28 (p. 51). Certified Public Accountants (CPAs) were surveyed on their firms' likelihood of reporting sustainability policies (measured as a probability between 0 and 1). The CPAs were divided into four groups depending on firm size (large or small) and firm type (public or private): large/public, large/private, small/public, and small/private. One goal of the analysis was to determine whether the mean likelihood of reporting sustainability policies differs depending on firm size and firm type. Identify each of the following elements for this study:
   a. Experimental units
   b. Response variable
   c. Factor(s)
   d. Factor levels
   e. Treatments

9.8 Accounting and Machiavellianism. A study of Machiavellian traits in accountants was published in *Behavioral Research in Accounting* (January 2008). Recall (from Exercise 1.33, p. 52) that *Machiavellian* describes negative character traits such as manipulation, cunning, duplicity, deception, and bad faith. A Mach rating score was determined for each in a sample of accounting alumni of a large southwestern university. The accountants were then classified as having high, moderate, or low Mach rating scores. For one portion of the study, the researcher investigated the impact of both Mach score classification and gender on the average income of an accountant. For this experiment, identify each of the following:

a. Experimental unit
b. Response variable
c. Factors
d. Levels of each factor
e. Treatments

9.9 Can money spent on gifts buy love? Refer to the *Journal of Experimental Social Psychology* (Vol. 45, 2009) study of whether buying gifts truly buys love, Exercise 1.34 (p. 52). Recall that study participants were randomly assigned to play the role of gift-giver or gift-receiver. Gift-receivers were asked to provide the level of appreciation (measured on a 7-point scale where 1 = "not at all" and 7 = "to a great extent") they had for the last birthday gift they received from a loved one. Gift-givers were asked to recall the last birthday gift they gave to a loved one and to provide the level of appreciation the loved one had for the gift. The researchers wanted to know if the average level of appreciation is higher for birthday gift-givers than for birthday gift-receivers.

a. Why is this study designed?
b. Specify the key elements of the study: experimental unit, response variable, factor, and treatments.

Applying the Concepts—Intermediate

9.10 Value perceptions of consumers. Refer to the *Journal of Consumer Research* study of whether between-store comparisons result in greater perceptions of value by consumers than within-store comparisons, Example 1.9 (p. 44). Recall that 50 consumers were randomly selected from all consumers in a designated market area to participate in the study. The researchers randomly assigned 25 consumers to read a within-store price promotion advertisement ("was $100, now $80") and 25 consumers to read a between-store price promotion ("$100 there, $80 here"). The consumers then gave their opinion on the value of the discount offer on a 10-point scale (where 1 = lowest value and 10 = highest value). The goal was to compare the average discount values of the two groups of consumers.

a. What is the response variable for this study?
b. What are the treatments for this study?
c. What is the experimental unit for this study?

9.11 Value perceptions of consumers (cont'd). Refer to Exercise 9.10. In addition to the factor, Type of advertisement (within-store price promotion and between-store price promotion), the researchers also investigated the impact of a second factor—Location where ad is read (at home or in the store). About half of the consumers who were assigned to the within-store price promotion read the ad at home, and the other half read the ad in the store. Similarly, about half of the consumers who were assigned to the between-store price promotion read the ad at home, and the other half read the ad in the store. In this second experiment, the goal was to compare the average discount values of the groups of consumers created by combining Type of advertisement with Location.

a. How many treatments are involved in this experiment?
b. Identify the treatments.

9.12 Reducing stress in livestock transported to market. Livestock that are transported long distances for slaughter or market often lose weight due to stress. The *Animal Science Journal* (May 2014) investigated the use of ascorbic acid (AA) to reduce the stress in goats during transportation. Twenty-four healthy Boer goats were randomly divided into four groups (A, B, C, and D) of six animals each. Goats in group A were administered a dosage of AA 30 minutes prior to transportation; goats in group B were administered a dosage of AA 30 minutes following transportation; group C goats were not given any AA prior to or following transportation; and goats in group D were not given any AA and were not transported. Weight was measured before and after transportation and the weight loss (in kilograms) determined for each goat. The researchers discovered that mean weight loss is reduced in goats administered AA. For this study, identify each of the following:

a. Experimental unit
b. Response variable
c. Factor
d. Factor levels

9.13 Mixed gender decision-making groups. In business, a group of executives is often assigned to make key decisions. The *American Journal of Political Science* (April 2014) published a study on a woman's impact on mixed-gender deliberating groups. The researchers randomly assigned subjects to one of several 5-member decision-making groups. The groups' gender composition varied as follows: 0 females, 1 female, 2 females, 3 females, 4 females, or 5 females. Each group was then randomly assigned to utilize one of two types of decision rules: unanimous or majority rule. Ten groups were created for each of the $6 \times 2 = 12$ combinations of gender composition and decision rule. One variable of interest, measured for each group, was the number of words spoken by women on a certain topic per 1,000 total words spoken during the deliberations.

a. Why is this experiment considered a designed study?
b. Identify the experimental unit and dependent variable in this study.
c. Identify the factors for this study. Give the levels of each factor.
d. How many treatments are in this study? List them.

Applying the Concepts—Advanced

9.14 Testing a new pain-reliever tablet. Paracetamol is the active ingredient in drugs designed to relieve mild to moderate pain and fever. To save costs, pharmaceutical companies are looking to produce paracetamol tablets from locally available materials. The properties of paracetamol tablets derived from khaya gum were studied in the *Tropical Journal of Pharmaceutical Research* (June 2003). Three factors believed to affect the properties of paracetamol tablets are (1) the nature of the binding agent, (2) the concentration of the binding agent, and (3) the relative density of the tablet. In the experiment, binding agent was set at two levels (khaya gum and PVP), binding concentration at two levels (.5% and 4.0%), and relative density at two levels (low and high). One of the dependent variables investigated in the study was tablet dissolution

time (i.e., the amount of time [in minutes] for 50% of the tablet to dissolve). The goal of the study was to determine the effect of binding agent, binding concentration, and relative density on mean dissolution time.

a. Identify the dependent (response) variable in the study.

b. What are the factors investigated in the study? Give the levels of each.

c. How many treatments are possible in the study? List them.

9.2 The Completely Randomized Design: Single Factor

The simplest experimental design, a *completely randomized design,* consists of the *independent random selection* of experimental units representing each treatment. For example, we could independently select random samples of 20 female and 15 male high school seniors to compare their mean SAT scores. Or, we could independently select random samples of 30 households from each of four census districts to compare the mean income per household among the districts. In both examples, our objective is to compare treatment means by selecting random, independent samples for each treatment.

> Consider an experiment that involves a single factor with k treatments. A **completely randomized design** is a design in which the experimental units are randomly assigned to the k treatments or in which independent random samples of experimental units are selected for each treatment.*

<table>
<tr><td>

EXAMPLE 9.3

Assigning Treatments in a Completely Randomized Design— Bottled Water Brands Study

</td><td>

Problem Suppose we want to compare the taste preferences of consumers for three different brands of bottled water (say, Brands A, B, and C) using a random sample of 15 bottled water consumers. Set up a completely randomized design for this purpose—that is, assign the experimental units to the treatments for this design.

Solution In this study, the experimental units are the 15 consumers, and the treatments are the three brands of bottled water. One way to set up the completely randomized design is to randomly assign one of the three brands to each consumer to taste. Then we could measure (say, on a 1-to-10-point scale) the taste preference of each consumer. A good practice is to assign the same number of consumers to each brand—in this case, five consumers to each of the three brands. (When an equal number of experimental units are assigned to each treatment, we call the design a **balanced design.**)

A random number generator or statistical software can be used to make the random assignments. Figure 9.4 is a Minitab worksheet showing the random assignments made with the Minitab "Random Data" function. You can see that Minitab randomly reordered the 15 consumers, then randomly assigned the first five reordered consumers (numbered 15, 8, 10, 7, 3) to taste Brand A, the next five (numbered 4, 13, 11, 9, 5) to taste Brand B, and the last five (numbered 1, 12, 14, 2, 6) to taste Brand C.

Look Back In some experiments, it will not be possible to randomly assign treatments to the experimental units or vice versa—the units will already be associated with one of the treatments. (For example, if the treatments are Male and Female, you cannot change a person's gender.) In this case, a completely randomized design is one where you select independent random samples of experimental units from each treatment.

</td></tr>
</table>

*We use *completely randomized* design to refer to both designed and observational studies. Thus, the only requirement is that the experimental units to which treatments are applied (designed) or on which treatments are observed (observational) are independently selected for each treatment.

Figure 9.4

Minitab random assignments of consumers to brands

	C1	C2	C3	C4	C5	C6
	Consumer	ReOrder	BrandA	BrandB	BrandC	
1	1	15	15	4	1	
2	2	8	8	13	12	
3	3	10	10	11	14	
4	4	7	7	9	2	
5	5	3	3	5	6	
6	6	4				
7	7	13				
8	8	11				
9	9	9				
10	10	5				
11	11	1				
12	12	12				
13	13	14				
14	14	2				
15	15	6				

CRD3Brands.mtw ***

• **Now Work Exercise 9.24d**

The objective of a completely randomized design is usually to compare the treatment means. If we denote the true, or population, means of the k treatments as $\mu_1, \mu_2, \ldots, \mu_k$, then we will test the null hypothesis that the treatment means are all equal against the alternative that at least two of the treatment means differ:

$$H_0: \mu_1 = \mu_2 = \cdots = \mu_k$$

H_a: At least two of the k treatment means differ

The μ's might represent the means of *all* female and male high school seniors' SAT scores or the means of *all* households' income in each of four census regions.

To conduct a statistical test of these hypotheses, we will use the means of the independent random samples selected from the treatment populations using the completely randomized design—that is, we compare the k sample means, $\bar{x}_1, \bar{x}_2, \ldots, \bar{x}_k$.

Table 9.1	SAT Scores for High School Students
Females	Males
530	490
560	520
590	550
620	580
650	610

Data Set: HSSAT1

For example, suppose you select independent random samples of five female and five male high school seniors and record their SAT scores. The data are shown in Table 9.1. A Minitab analysis of the data, shown in Figure 9.5, reveals that the sample mean SAT scores (shaded) are 590 for females and 550 for males. Can we conclude that the population of female high school students scores higher, on average, than the population of male students?

Descriptive Statistics: Females, Males

Figure 9.5

Minitab descriptive statistics for data in Table 9.1

```
Variable  N   Mean   StDev  Variance  Minimum  Maximum
Females   5   590.0   47.4   2250.0    530.0    650.0
Males     5   550.0   47.4   2250.0    490.0    610.0
```

To answer this question, we must consider the amount of sampling variability among the experimental units (students). The SAT scores in Table 9.1 are depicted in the dot plot shown in Figure 9.6. Note that the difference between the sample means is small relative to the

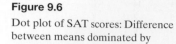

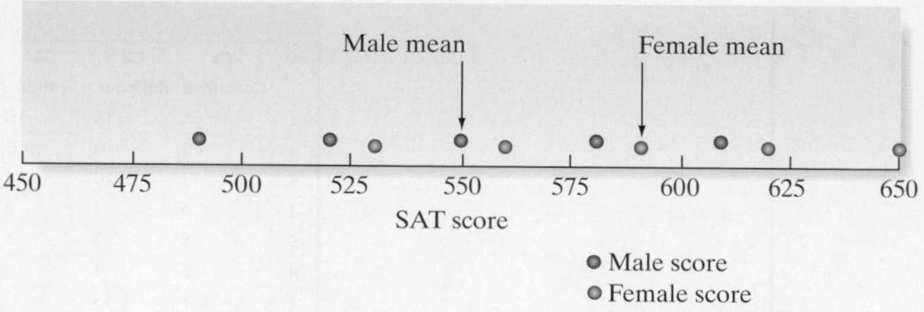

Figure 9.6

Dot plot of SAT scores: Difference between means dominated by sampling variability

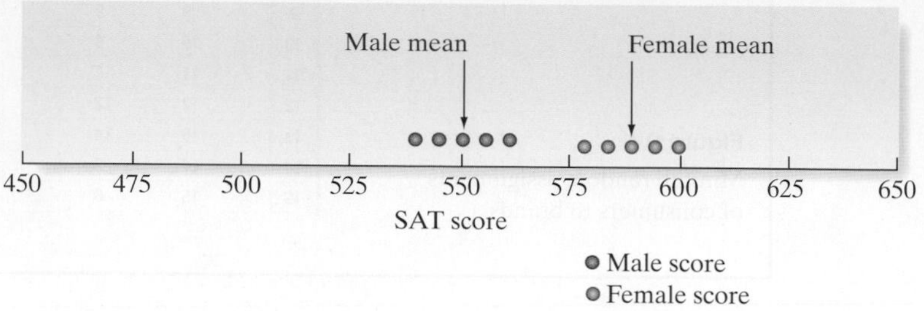

Figure 9.7

Dot plot of SAT scores: Difference between means large relative to sampling variability

sampling variability of the scores within the treatments, namely, Female and Male. We would be inclined not to reject the null hypothesis of equal population means in this case.

In contrast, if the data are as depicted in the dot plot of Figure 9.7, then the sampling variability is small relative to the difference between the two means. We would be inclined to favor the alternative hypothesis that the population means differ in this case.

Now Work Exercise 9.17a

You can see that the key is to compare the difference between the treatment means with the amount of sampling variability. To conduct a formal statistical test of the hypotheses requires numerical measures of the difference between the treatment means and the sampling variability within each treatment. The variation between the treatment means is measured by the **Sum of Squares for Treatments (SST),** which is calculated by squaring the distance between each treatment mean and the overall mean of *all* sample measurements, then multiplying each squared distance by the number of sample measurements for the treatment, and finally, adding the results over all treatments. For the data in Table 9.1, the overall mean is 570. Thus, we have:

$$\text{SST} = \sum_{i=1}^{k} n_i (\bar{x}_i - \bar{x})^2 = 5(550 - 570)^2 + 5(590 - 570)^2 = 4{,}000$$

In this equation we use $\bar{x}$ to represent the overall mean response of all sample measurements—that is, the mean of the combined samples. The symbol n_i is used to denote the sample size for the ith treatment. You can see that the value of SST is 4,000 for the two samples of five female and five male SAT scores depicted in Figures 9.6 and 9.7.

Next, we must measure the sampling variability within the treatments. We call this the **Sum of Squares for Error (SSE)** because it measures the variability around the treatment means that is attributed to sampling error. The value of SSE is computed by summing the squared distance between each response measurement and the corresponding treatment mean and then adding the squared differences over all measurements in the entire sample:

$$\text{SSE} = \sum_{j=1}^{n_1} (x_{1j} - \bar{x}_1)^2 + \sum_{j=1}^{n_2} (x_{2j} - \bar{x}_2)^2 + \cdots + \sum_{j=1}^{n_k} (x_{kj} - \bar{x}_k)^2$$

Here, the symbol x_{1j} is the jth measurement in sample 1, x_{2j} is the jth measurement in sample 2, and so on. This rather complex-looking formula can be simplified by recalling the formula for the sample variance, s^2, given in Chapter 2:

$$s^2 = \sum_{i=1}^{n} \frac{(x_i - \bar{x})^2}{n - 1}$$

Note that each sum in SSE is simply the numerator of s^2 for that particular treatment. Consequently, we can rewrite SSE as

$$SSE = (n_1 - 1)s_1^2 + (n_2 - 1)s_2^2 + \cdots + (n_k - 1)s_k^2$$

where $s_1^2, s_2^2, \ldots, s_k^2$ are the sample variances for the k treatments. For the SAT scores in Table 9.1, the Minitab printout (Figure 9.5) shows that $s_1^2 = 2{,}250$ (for females) and $s_2^2 = 2{,}250$ (for males); then we have

$$SSE = (5 - 1)(2{,}250) + (5 - 1)(2{,}250) = 18{,}000$$

To make the two measurements of variability comparable, we divide each by the degrees of freedom to convert the sums of squares to mean squares. First, the **Mean Square for Treatments (MST)**, which measures the variability among the treatment means, is equal to

$$MST = \frac{SST}{k - 1} = \frac{4{,}000}{2 - 1} = 4{,}000$$

where the number of degrees of freedom for the k treatments is $(k - 1)$. Next, the **Mean Square for Error (MSE)**, which measures the sampling variability within the treatments, is

$$MSE = \frac{SSE}{n - k} = \frac{18{,}000}{10 - 2} = 2{,}250$$

Finally, we calculate the ratio of MST to MSE—an *F*-statistic:

$$F = \frac{MST}{MSE} = \frac{4{,}000}{2{,}250} = 1.78$$

These quantities—MST, MSE, and *F*—are shown (highlighted) on the Minitab printout displayed in Figure 9.8.

Values of the *F*-statistic near 1 indicate that the two sources of variation, between treatment means and within treatments, are approximately equal. In this case, the difference between the treatment means may well be attributable to sampling error, which provides little support for the alternative hypothesis that the population treatment means differ. Values of *F* well in excess of 1 indicate that the variation among treatment means well exceeds that within treatments and therefore support the alternative hypothesis that the population treatment means differ.

When does *F* exceed 1 by enough to reject the null hypothesis that the means are equal? This depends on the degrees of freedom for treatments and for error and on the value of α selected for the test. We compare the calculated *F*-value to a table of *F*-values (Tables V–VIII in Appendix D) with $v_1 = (k - 1)$ degrees of freedom in the numerator and $v_2 = (n - k)$ degrees of freedom in the denominator and corresponding to a Type I error probability of α. For the SAT score example, the *F*-statistic has $v_1 = (2 - 1) = 1$ numerator degree of freedom and $v_2 = (10 - 2) = 8$ denominator degrees of freedom. Thus, for $\alpha = .05$, we find (Table VI in Appendix D)

$$F_{.05} = 5.32$$

The implication is that MST would have to be 5.32 times greater than MSE before we could conclude at the .05 level of significance that the two population treatment

One-way ANOVA: Females, Males

Source	DF	SS	MS	F	P
Factor	1	4000	4000	1.78	0.219
Error	8	18000	2250		
Total	9	22000			

S = 47.43   R-Sq = 18.18%   R-Sq(adj) = 7.95%

Figure 9.8

Minitab printout with ANOVA results for data in Table 9.1

means differ. Because the data yielded $F = 1.78$, our initial impressions from the dot plot in Figure 9.6 are confirmed—there is insufficient information to conclude that the mean SAT scores differ for the populations of female and male high school seniors. The rejection region and the calculated F-value are shown in Figure 9.9.

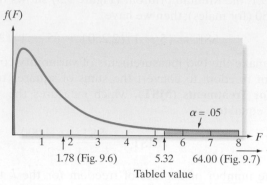

Figure 9.9

Rejection region and calculated F-values for SAT score samples

Table 9.2	
SAT Scores for High School Students Shown in Figure 9.7	
Females	Males
580	540
585	545
590	550
595	555
600	560

 *Data Set*: HSSAT2

In contrast, consider the dot plot in Figure 9.7. The SAT scores depicted in this dot plot are listed in Table 9.2, followed by Minitab descriptive statistics in Figure 9.10. Note that the sample means for females and males, 590 and 550, respectively, are the same as in the previous example. Consequently, the variation between the means is the same, namely, MST = 4,000. However, the variation within the two treatments appears to be considerably smaller. In fact, Figure 9.10 shows that $s_1^2 = 62.5$ and $s_2^2 = 62.5$. Thus, the variation within the treatments is measured by

$$\text{SSE} = (5 - 1)(62.5) + (5 - 1)(62.5) = 500$$

$$\text{MSE} = \frac{\text{SSE}}{n - k} = \frac{500}{8} = 62.5 \text{ (shaded on Figure 9.10)}$$

Then the F-ratio is

$$F = \frac{\text{MST}}{\text{MSE}} = \frac{4,000}{62.5} = 64.0 \text{ (shaded on Figure 9.10)}$$

Again, our visual analysis of the dot plot is confirmed statistically: $F = 64.0$ well exceeds the tabled F-value, 5.32, corresponding to the .05 level of significance. We would therefore reject the null hypothesis at that level and conclude that the SAT mean score of males differs from that of females.

Now Work Exercise 9.17b–h

The **analysis of variance F-test** for comparing treatment means is summarized in the next box.

Descriptive Statistics: Females, Males

Variable	N	Mean	StDev	Variance	Minimum	Maximum
Females	5	590.00	7.91	62.50	580.00	600.00
Males	5	550.00	7.91	62.50	540.00	560.00

One-way ANOVA: Females, Males

Source	DF	SS	MS	F	P
Factor	1	4000.0	4000.0	64.00	0.000
Error	8	500.0	62.5		
Total	9	4500.0			

Figure 9.10

Minitab descriptive statistics and ANOVA results for data in Table 9.2

ANOVA *F*-Test to Compare *k* Treatment Means: Completely Randomized Design

$$H_0: \mu_1 = \mu_2 = \cdots = \mu_k$$

H_a: At least two treatment means differ

Test statistic: $F = \dfrac{\text{MST}}{\text{MSE}}$

Rejection region: $F > F_\alpha$

p-value: $P(F > F_c)$

where F_c is the calculated value of the test statistic and F_α is based on $(k - 1)$ numerator degrees of freedom (associated with MST) and $(n - k)$ denominator degrees of freedom (associated with MSE).

Conditions Required for a Valid ANOVA *F*-Test: Completely Randomized Design

1. The samples are randomly selected in an independent manner from the *k* treatment populations. (This can be accomplished by randomly assigning the experimental units to the treatments.)
2. All *k* sampled populations have distributions that are approximately normal.
3. The *k* population variances are equal (i.e., $\sigma_1^2 = \sigma_2^2 = \sigma_3^2 = \cdots = \sigma_k^2$).

Computational formulas for MST and MSE are given in Appendix C. We will rely on some of the many statistical software packages available to compute the *F* statistic, concentrating on the interpretation of the results rather than their calculations.

EXAMPLE 9.4

Conducting an ANOVA *F*-Test—Comparing Golf Ball Brands

Problem Suppose the USGA wants to compare the mean distances associated with four different brands of golf balls when struck with a driver. A completely randomized design is employed, with Iron Byron, the USGA's robotic golfer, using a driver to hit a random sample of 10 balls of each brand in a random sequence. The distance is recorded for each hit, and the results are shown in Table 9.3, organized by brand.

a. Set up the test to compare the mean distances for the four brands. Use $\alpha = .10$.

b. Use statistical software to obtain the test statistic and *p*-value. Interpret the results.

Table 9.3	Results of Completely Randomized Design: Iron Byron Driver			
	Brand A	Brand B	Brand C	Brand D
	251.2	263.2	269.7	251.6
	245.1	262.9	263.2	248.6
	248.0	265.0	277.5	249.4
	251.1	254.5	267.4	242.0
	260.5	264.3	270.5	246.5
	250.0	257.0	265.5	251.3
	253.9	262.8	270.7	261.8
	244.6	264.4	272.9	249.0
	254.6	260.6	275.6	247.1
	248.8	255.9	266.5	245.9
Sample Means	250.8	261.1	270.0	249.3

Data Set: GLFCRD

Solution

a. To compare the mean distances of the four brands, we first specify the hypotheses to be tested. Denoting the population mean of the *i*th brand by μ_i, we test

$$H_0: \mu_1 = \mu_2 = \mu_3 = \mu_4$$

H_a: The mean distances differ for at least two of the brands

The test statistic compares the variation among the four treatment (Brand) means with the sampling variability within each of the treatments.

$$\text{Test statistic: } F = \frac{\text{MST}}{\text{MSE}}$$

$$\text{Rejection region: } F > F_\alpha = F_{.10}$$

with $v_1 = (k - 1) = 3$ df and $v_2 = (n - k) = 36$ df

From Table V in Appendix D, we find $F_{.10} \approx 2.25$ for 3 and 36 df. Thus, we will reject H_0 if $F > 2.25$. (See Figure 9.11.)

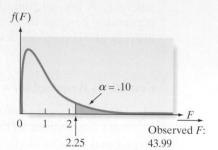

Figure 9.11

F-test for completely randomized design: Golf ball experiment

The assumptions necessary to ensure the validity of the test are as follows:

1. The samples of 10 golf balls for each brand are selected randomly and independently.
2. The probability distributions of the distances for each brand are normal.
3. The variances of the distance probability distributions for each brand are equal.

b. The Excel printout for the data in Table 9.3 resulting from this completely randomized design is given in Figure 9.12. The values of the mean squares, MST = 931.46 and MSE = 21.175, are highlighted on the printout. The F-ratio, 43.99, also highlighted on the printout, exceeds the tabled value of 2.25. We therefore reject the null hypothesis at the .10 level of significance, concluding that at least two of the brands differ with respect to mean distance traveled when struck by the driver.

We can also arrive at the appropriate conclusion by noting that the observed significance level of the F-test (highlighted on the printout) is approximately 0. This implies that we would reject the null hypothesis that the means are equal at any reasonably selected α level.

	A	B	C	D	E	F	G
1	Anova: Single Factor						
2							
3	SUMMARY						
4	*Groups*	*Count*	*Sum*	*Average*	*Variance*		
5	BrandA	10	2507.8	250.78	22.42178		
6	BrandB	10	2610.6	261.06	14.94711		
7	BrandC	10	2699.5	269.95	20.25833		
8	BrandD	10	2493.2	249.32	27.07289		
9							
10							
11	ANOVA						
12	*Source of Variation*	*SS*	*df*	*MS*	*F*	*P-value*	*F crit*
13	Between Groups	2794.389	3	931.4629	43.98875	3.97E-12	2.866266
14	Within Groups	762.301	36	21.17503			
15							
16	Total	3556.69	39				

Figure 9.12

Excel printout for ANOVA of golf ball distance data

[*Note:* Excel uses exponential notation to display the p-value. The value 3.97E-12 is equal to .00000000000397.]

Look Ahead Now that we know the mean driving distances differ, a logical follow-up question is: "Which ball brand travels farthest, on average, when hit with a driver?" In Section 9.3 we present a method for ranking treatment means in an ANOVA.

● **Now Work Exercise 9.21**

Table 9.4	General ANOVA Summary Table for a Completely Randomized Design			
Source	df	SS	MS	F
Treatments	$k - 1$	SST	$MST = \dfrac{SST}{k - 1}$	$\dfrac{MST}{MSE}$
Error	$n - k$	SSE	$MSE = \dfrac{SSE}{n - k}$	
Total	$n - 1$	SS(Total)		

The results of an **analysis of variance (ANOVA)** can be summarized in a simple tabular format similar to that obtained from the Excel printout in Example 9.4. The general form of the table is shown in Table 9.4, where the symbols df, SS, and MS stand for degrees of freedom, Sum of Squares, and Mean Square, respectively. Note that the two sources of variation, Treatments and Error, add to the Total Sum of Squares, SS(Total). The ANOVA summary table for Example 9.4 is given in Table 9.5, and the partitioning of the Total Sum of Squares into its two components is illustrated in Figure 9.13.

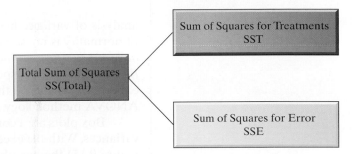

Figure 9.13

Partitioning of the Total Sum of Squares for the completely randomized design

Table 9.5	ANOVA Summary Table for Example 9.4				
Source	df	SS	MS	F	p-Value
Brands	3	2,794.39	931.46	43.99	.0000
Error	36	762.30	21.18		
Total	39	3,556.69			

EXAMPLE 9.5

Checking the ANOVA Assumptions

Problem Refer to the completely randomized design ANOVA conducted in Example 9.4. Are the assumptions required for the test approximately satisfied?

Solution The assumptions for the test are repeated below.

1. The samples of golf balls for each brand are selected randomly and independently.
2. The probability distributions of the distances for each brand are normal.
3. The variances of the distance probability distributions for each brand are equal.

Since the sample consisted of 10 randomly selected balls of each brand and the robotic golfer Iron Byron was used to drive all the balls, the first assumption of independent random samples is satisfied. To check the next two assumptions, we will employ two graphical methods presented in Chapter 2: histograms and box plots. A Minitab histogram of driving distances for each brand of golf ball is shown in Figure 9.14, followed by SPSS box plots in Figure 9.15.

The normality assumption can be checked by examining the histograms in Figure 9.14. With only 10 sample measurements for each brand, however, the displays are not very informative. More data would need to be collected for each brand before we could assess whether the distances come from normal distributions. Fortunately,

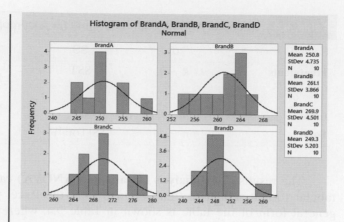

Figure 9.14

Minitab histograms for golf ball distances

analysis of variance has been shown to be a very **robust method** when the assumption of normality is not satisfied exactly—that is, *moderate departures from normality do not have much effect on the significance level of the ANOVA F-test or on confidence coefficients.* Rather than spend the time, energy, or money to collect additional data for this experiment to verify the normality assumption, we will rely on the robustness of the ANOVA methodology.

Box plots are a convenient way to obtain a rough check on the assumption of equal variances. With the exception of a possible outlier for Brand D (indicated by a circle in Figure 9.15) the box plots in Figure 9.15 show that the spread of the distance measurements is about the same for each brand. Because the sample variances appear to be the same, the assumption of equal population variances for the brands is probably satisfied. Although robust with respect to the normality assumption, ANOVA is *not robust* with respect to the equal variances assumption. Departures from the assumption of equal population variances can affect the associated measures of reliability (e.g., *p*-values and confidence levels). Fortunately, the effect is slight when the sample sizes are equal, as in this experiment.

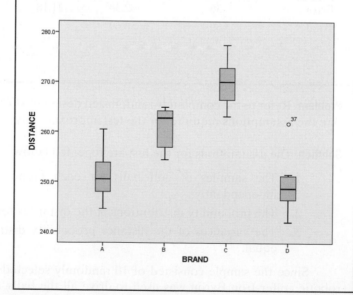

Figure 9.15

SPSS box plots for golf ball distances

Now Work Exercise 9.28

Although graphs can be used to check the ANOVA assumptions, as in Example 9.5, no measures of reliability can be attached to these graphs. When you have a plot that is unclear as to whether or not an assumption is satisfied, you can use formal statistical tests, which are beyond the scope of this text. (Consult the references for information on these tests.) When the validity of the ANOVA assumptions is in doubt, nonparametric statistical methods are useful.

What Do You Do When the Assumptions Are Not Satisfied for an ANOVA for a Completely Randomized Design?

Answer: Use a nonparametric statistical method such as the Kruskal-Wallis *H*-test of Section 15.5.

The procedure for conducting an analysis of variance for a completely randomized design is summarized in the following box. Remember that the hallmark of this design is independent random samples of experimental units associated with each treatment. We discuss a design with dependent samples in Section 9.4.

Steps for Conducting an ANOVA for a Completely Randomized Design

1. Be sure the design is truly completely randomized, with independent random samples for each treatment.

2. Check the assumptions of normality and equal variances.

3. Create an ANOVA summary table that specifies the variability attributable to treatments and error, making sure that it leads to the calculation of the *F*-statistic for testing the null hypothesis that the treatment means are equal in the population. Use a statistical software program to obtain the numerical results. (If no such package is available, use the calculation formulas in Appendix C.)

4. If the *F*-test leads to the conclusion that the means differ,

   a. Conduct a multiple comparisons procedure for as many of the pairs of means as you wish to compare (see Section 9.3). Use the results to summarize the statistically significant differences among the treatment means.

   b. If desired, form confidence intervals for one or more individual treatment means.

5. If the *F*-test leads to the nonrejection of the null hypothesis that the treatment means are equal, consider the following possibilities:

   a. The treatment means are equal—that is, the null hypothesis is true.

   b. The treatment means really differ, but other important factors affecting the response are not accounted for by the completely randomized design. These factors inflate the sampling variability, as measured by MSE, resulting in smaller values of the *F*-statistic. Either increase the sample size for each treatment or use a different experimental design (as in Section 9.4) that accounts for the other factors affecting the response.

Note: Be careful not to automatically conclude that the treatment means are equal because the possibility of a Type II error must be considered if you accept H_0.

We conclude this section by making two important points about an analysis of variance. First, recall that we performed a hypothesis test for the difference between two means in Section 8.2 using a two-sample *t*-statistic for two independent samples. When two independent samples are being compared, the two-tailed *t*- and *F*-tests are equivalent. To see this, apply the formula for *t* to the two samples of SAT scores in Table 9.2:

$$t = \frac{\bar{x}_1 - \bar{x}_2}{\sqrt{s_p^2 \left(\frac{1}{n_1} + \frac{1}{n_2} \right)}} = \frac{590 - 550}{\sqrt{(62.5) \left(\frac{1}{5} + \frac{1}{5} \right)}} = \frac{40}{5} = 8$$

Here, we used the fact that $s_p^2 = $ MSE, which you can verify by comparing the formulas. Note that the calculated *F* for these samples ($F = 64$) equals the square of the calculated *t* for the same samples ($t = 8$). Likewise, the critical *F*-value (5.32) equals the square of the critical *t*-value at the two-sided .05 level of significance

($t_{.025} = 2.306$ with 8 df). Because both the rejection region and the calculated values are related in the same way, the tests are equivalent. Moreover, the assumptions that must be met to ensure the validity of the t- and F-tests are the same:

1. The probability distributions of the populations of responses associated with each treatment must all be approximately normal.
2. The probability distributions of the populations of responses associated with each treatment must have equal variances.
3. The samples of experimental units selected for the treatments must be random and independent.

In fact, the only real difference between the tests is that the F-test can be used to compare *more than two* treatment means, whereas the t-test is applicable to two samples only.

For our second point, refer to Example 9.4. Our conclusion that at least two of the brands of golf balls have different mean distances traveled when struck with a driver leads naturally to the following questions: Which of the brands differ? How are the brands ranked with respect to mean distance?

One way to obtain this information is to construct a confidence interval for the difference between the means of any pair of treatments using the method of Section 8.2. For example, if a 95% confidence interval for $(\mu_A - \mu_C)$ in Example 9.4 is found to be $(-24, -13)$, we are confident that the mean distance for Brand C exceeds the mean for Brand A (because all differences in the interval are negative). Constructing these confidence intervals for all possible brand pairs will allow you to rank the brand means. A method for conducting these *multiple comparisons*—one that controls for Type I errors—is presented in Section 9.3.

STATISTICS IN ACTION REVISITED

Testing the Equality of the Tax Compliance Behavior Means for the Four Experimental Conditions

We now consider the *Behavioral Research in Accounting* (January 2015) study of the factors that impact the level of risk taking when filing a federal or state income tax return. Recall that the researchers designed an experiment in which 240 subjects (taxpayers) were randomly assigned to one of four experimental conditions: (1) filing a single federal tax return with a refund due, (2) filing a single federal tax return with a payment due, (3) filing multiple (federal and state) tax returns with a net refund due, and (4) filing multiple (federal and state) tax returns with a net payment due. (See Figure SIA9.1, p. 523) After being informed that an additional deduction on their federal return—one that the IRS might disallow—would either increase the net refund or decrease the net payment due, the subject's tax compliance behavior score was measured on a nine-point scale (1 = *definitely would not take the deduction;* 9 = *definitely would take the deduction*).

According to the researchers' theory, the mean tax compliance behavior score will vary depending on whether a single return or multiple returns are filed and whether a net refund or net payment is due. Proposition 1 states that the mean for taxpayers in Condition 3 (multiple returns/refund due) will exceed the mean for taxpayers in Condition 1 (single return/refund due). Proposition 2 states that the mean for taxpayers in Condition 4 (multiple returns/payment due) will be lower than the mean for taxpayers in Condition 2 (single return/payment due).

As a first, basic approach to testing these propositions, we will run an ANOVA for a completely randomized design with four treatments (conditions) and with 20 subjects (taxpayers) in each treatment. The dependent variable in the ANOVA is the tax compliance behavior score. Let μ_j represent the true mean tax compliance behavior score for Condition j. Then the null and alternative hypotheses for the ANOVA test are

$$H_0: \mu_1 = \mu_2 = \mu_3 = \mu_4$$
$$H_a: \text{At least two } \mu_j\text{'s differ}$$

A conclusion of "fail to reject H_0" (i.e., insufficient evidence of differences in the means) would not support the researchers' propositions. A conclusion of "reject H_0" (i.e., sufficient evidence of differences in the means) would provide, at minimum, partial support for the researchers' propositions.

The data in the **TAX** file were analyzed using Minitab. The results are displayed in the Minitab printout, Figure SIA9.2.

One-way ANOVA: (1)Ref-Single, (2)Pay-Single, (3)Ref-Multi, (4)Pay-Multi

Method

```
Null hypothesis          All means are equal
Alternative hypothesis   At least one mean is different
Significance level       α = 0.05
```

Equal variances were assumed for the analysis.

Factor Information

```
Factor   Levels  Values
Factor        4  (1)Ref-Single, (2)Pay-Single, (3)Ref-Multi, (4)Pay-Multi
```

Analysis of Variance

```
Source   DF   Adj SS   Adj MS   F-Value   P-Value
Factor    3    40.98   13.661      2.85     0.038
Error   236  1131.00    4.792
Total   239  1171.98
```

Model Summary

```
      S   R-sq   R-sq(adj)   R-sq(pred)
2.18915  3.50%       2.27%        0.20%
```

Means

```
Factor          N   Mean   StDev       95% CI
(1)Ref-Single  60  3.850   2.399  (3.293, 4.407)
(2)Pay-Single  60  4.783   2.643  (4.227, 5.340)
(3)Ref-Multi   60  4.917   2.002  (4.360, 5.473)
(4)Pay-Multi   60  4.417   1.555  (3.860, 4.973)
```

Pooled StDev = 2.18915

Figure SIA9.2

Minitab ANOVA for comparing tax compliance behavior means

The ANOVA F-value (shaded on the printout) is $F = 2.85$; the corresponding p-value (also shaded) is p-value $= .038$. Since a Type I error rate of $\alpha = .05$ exceeds the p-value, there is sufficient evidence to conclude that, for the population of taxpayers, the mean tax compliance behavior means differ in some fashion.

Does this conclusion fully support the researchers' propositions? That is, can we conclude from this analysis that $\mu_3 > \mu_1$ (Proposition 1) and that $\mu_4 < \mu_2$ (Proposition 2)? A check of the sample means (highlighted at the bottom of Figure SIA9.2) seems to support both propositions. To see this more clearly, examine the graph of the sample means in Figure SIA9.3. Notice that when a refund is due (see red dotted line in the figure) the sample mean response for multiple returns exceeds the sample mean for a single return, just as predicted by the researchers in Proposition 1. Similarly, when a payment is due (see blue solid line in the figure) the sample mean response for multiple returns is lower than the sample mean for a single return, just as predicted by the researchers in Proposition 2.

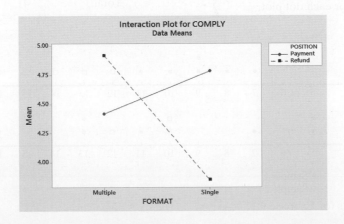

Figure SIA9.3

Minitab graph of tax compliance behavior means

Unfortunately, we cannot attach a measure of reliability to these inferences, since they are based on sample means only. All we can conclude (from the ANOVA) is that at least two of the population tax compliance behavior means differ at $\alpha = .05$.

In the following two *Statistics in Action Revisited* sections (Section 9.3 and Section 9.5), we extend the analysis of this section and apply inferential methods that show support for the researchers' propositions.

Exercises 9.15–9.34

Learning the Mechanics

9.15 Use Tables V, VI, VII, and VIII in Appendix D to find each of the following *F*-values:
   a. $F_{.05}, v_1 = 4, v_2 = 4$
   b. $F_{.01}, v_1 = 4, v_2 = 4$
   c. $F_{.10}, v_1 = 30, v_2 = 40$
   d. $F_{.025}, v_1 = 15, v_2 = 12$

9.16 Use Appendix tables V, VI, VII, and VII to estimate the *p*-values for the following cases:
   a. $F = 6.29; v_1 = 5, v_2 = 10$
   b. $F = 2.84; v_1 = 3, v_2 = 5$
   c. $F = 7.21; v_1 = 7, v_2 = 6$
   d. $F = 2.98; v_1 = 4, v_2 = 12$

9.17 Consider dot plots 1 and 2 shown below. Assume that the two [NW] samples represent independent, random samples corresponding to two treatments in a completely randomized design.
   a. In which plot is the difference between the sample means small relative to the variability within the sample observations? Justify your answer.
   b. Calculate the treatment means (i.e., the means of samples 1 and 2) for both dot plots.
   c. Use the means to calculate the Sum of Squares for Treatments (SST) for each dot plot.
   d. Calculate the sample variance for each sample and use these values to obtain the Sum of Squares for Error (SSE) for each dot plot.
   e. Calculate the Total Sum of Squares [SS(Total)] for the two dot plots by adding the Sums of Squares for Treatments and Error. What percentage of SS(Total) is accounted for by the treatments—that is, what percentage of the Total Sum of Squares is the Sum of Squares for Treatments—in each case?
   f. Convert the Sums of Squares for Treatments and Error to mean squares by dividing each by the appropriate number of degrees of freedom. Calculate the *F*-ratio of the Mean Square for Treatments (MST) to the Mean Square for Error (MSE) for each dot plot.

   g. Use the *F*-ratios to test the null hypothesis that the two samples are drawn from populations with equal means. Use $\alpha = .05$.
   h. What assumptions must be made about the probability distributions corresponding to the responses for each treatment to ensure the validity of the *F*-tests conducted in part **g**?

9.18 Refer to Exercise 9.17. Conduct a two-sample *t*-test (Section 8.2) of the null hypothesis that the two treatment means are equal for each dot plot. Use $\alpha = .05$ and two-tailed tests. In the course of the test, compare each of the following with the *F*-tests in Exercise 9.17:
   a. The pooled variances and the MSEs
   b. The *t*- and *F*-test statistics
   c. The tabled values of *t* and *F* that determine the rejection regions
   d. The conclusions of the *t*- and *F*-tests
   e. The assumptions that must be made to ensure the validity of the *t*- and *F*-tests

9.19 Refer to Exercises 9.17 and 9.18. Complete the following ANOVA table for each of the two dot plots:

Source	df	SS	MS	F
Treatments				
Error				
Total				

9.20 A partially completed ANOVA table for a completely randomized design is shown here:

Source	df	SS	MS	F
Treatments	6	17.5	—	—
Error	—	—	—	
Total	41	46.5		

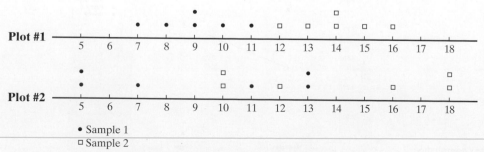

• Sample 1
□ Sample 2

Dot plots for Exercise 9.17

a. Complete the ANOVA table.

b. How many treatments are involved in the experiment?

c. What is the total sample size, n, for the experiment?

d. Use a random number generator to randomly assign each experimental unit to one of the treatments. Assume the sample size will be the same for each treatment.

e. Do the data provide sufficient evidence to indicate a difference among the population means? Test using $\alpha = .10$.

f. Find the approximate observed significance level for the test in part **c** and interpret it.

g. Suppose that $\bar{x}_1 = 3.7$ and $\bar{x}_2 = 4.1$. Do the data provide sufficient evidence to indicate a difference between μ_1 and μ_2? Assume that there are six observations for each treatment. Test using $\alpha = .10$.

h. Refer to part **g.** Find a 90% confidence interval for $(\mu_1 - \mu_2)$. [*Hint:* Use $s = \sqrt{\text{MSE}}$ as an estimate of both σ_1 and σ_2.]

i. Refer to part **g.** Find a 90% confidence interval for μ_1. [*Hint:* Use $s = \sqrt{\text{MSE}}$ as an estimate of σ_1.]

9.21 The data in the next table resulted from an experiment that used a completely randomized design.

NW

L09021

Treatment 1	Treatment 2	Treatment 3
3.8	5.4	1.3
1.2	2.0	0.7
4.1	4.8	2.2
5.5	3.8	
2.3		

a. Use statistical software (or the appropriate calculation formulas in Appendix C) to complete the following ANOVA table:

Source	df	SS	MS	F
Treatments				
Error				
Total				

b. Test the null hypothesis that $\mu_1 = \mu_2 = \mu_3$, where μ_i represents the true mean for treatment i, against the alternative that at least two of the means differ. Use $\alpha = .01$.

Applying the Concepts—Basic

9.22 **How workers respond to wage cuts.** A randomized field experiment was carried out to determine how workers respond to wage cuts and the results published in *Institute for the Study of Labor: Discussion Paper Series* (March 2011). A company formed teams of two employees to sell promotional cards at the same hourly wage. After a short period of time on the job, teams were unknowingly randomly assigned to one of three treatments. In the "unilateral wage cut" treatment, one worker's pay was cut by 25%; in the "general wage cut" treatment, both workers' pay was cut by 25%; and in the "baseline" treatment, neither worker received a pay cut. The variable of interest was the decrease in the number of promotional cards sold after implementation of the pay cuts. The researchers wanted to know if the average decrease in cards sold differed depending on whether one or more of the workers received a pay cut.

a. Identify the type of experimental design used in the study.

b. Identify the dependent variable of interest.

c. What is the factor in this experiment? The factor levels?

d. Specify the null hypothesis of interest to the researchers.

e. The ANOVA F-test was carried out and resulted in a p-value less than .001. Interpret these results using $\alpha = .01$.

9.23 **Using Twitter in the classroom.** Can Twitter be used to enhance student learning and engagement in a university classroom? This was the question of interest in a study published in the *Journal of Marketing Education* (December 2015). A sample of 411 undergraduate students enrolled in either a first-year marketing or fashion course participated in the study. On the first day of class, students were asked to self-assess their Twitter skill level as 1, 2, 3, 4, or 5, where $1 = poor$ and $5 = excellent$. Students were then informed that Twitter would be used as a communication and learning tool throughout the duration of the course. Twitter use sessions were regularly scheduled, and each student was required to submit a paper describing his or her actual Twitter activity and personal learning outcomes using the technology. At the end of the semester, the researchers measured several variables for each student, including the number of actual tweets submitted and whether the student would continue to use Twitter as a learning tool (measured on a 5-point scale). The means of the variables were compared across the five Twitter skill levels for males and females separately. The ANOVA results are summarized in the table below.

Dependent Variable		Twitter Skill Level Means					F	p-Value
		Poor	2	3	4	Excellent		
# Tweets	*Males*	20.0	13.4	14.8	16.1	19.2	1.17	.331
	Females	14.6	16.9	15.3	16.1	15.7	0.56	.731
Continue Using	*Males*	3.89	2.74	3.52	3.78	3.83	2.21	.062
	Females	2.97	3.16	3.71	3.82	3.74	3.34	.006

Source: B. West, H. Moore, and B. Barry, "Beyond the Tweet: Using Twitter to Enhance Engagement, Learning, and Success Among First-Year Students," *Journal of Marketing Education*, Vol. 37, No. 3, December 2015 (from Table 4). Copyright © 2015 by Sage Publications, Inc. (US). Used by permission of Sage Publications, Inc. (US)

a. For each of the four ANOVAs conducted, specify the response variable, treatments, and null and alternative hypotheses tested.

b. Using $\alpha = .05$, practically interpret the results of each test.

9.24 Evaluation of flexography printing plates. Flexography is a printing process used in the packaging industry. The process is popular, since it is cost-effective and can be used to print on a variety of surfaces (e.g., paperboard, foil, and plastic). A study was conducted to determine if flexography exposure time has an impact on the quality of the printing (*Journal of Graphic Engineering and Design,* Vol. 3, 2012). Four different exposure times were studied: 8, 10, 12, and 14 minutes. A sample of 36 print images were collected at each exposure time level, for a total of 144 print images. The measure of print quality used was dot area (hundreds of dots per square millimeter). The data were subjected to an analysis of variance, with partial results shown in the accompanying table.

Source	df	SS	MS	F	p-Value
Exposure	3	.010	—	—	<.001
Error	140	.029	—		
Total	143	.039			

a. Compute the missing entries in the ANOVA table.

b. Is there sufficient evidence to indicate that mean dot area differs depending on the exposure time? Use $\alpha = .05$.

9.25 Performance of a bus depot. The performances of public bus depots in India were evaluated and ranked in the *International Journal of Engineering Science and Technology* (February 2011). A survey was administered to 150 customers selected randomly and independently at each of three different bus depots (Depot 1, Depot 2, and Depot 3); thus, the total sample consisted of 450 bus customers. Based on responses to 16 different items (e.g., bus punctuality, seat comfort, luggage service, etc.), a performance score (out of 100 total points) was calculated for each customer. The average performance scores were compared across the three bus depots using an analysis of variance. The ANOVA *F*-test resulted in a *p*-value of .0001.

a. Give details (experimental units, dependent variable, factor, treatments) on the experimental design utilized in this study.

b. The researchers concluded that the "mean customer performance scores differed across the three bus depots at a 95% confidence level." Do you agree?

9.26 Making high-stakes insurance decisions. The *Journal of Economic Psychology* (September 2008) published the results of a high-stakes experiment where subjects (university students) were asked how much they would pay for insuring a valuable painting. The painting was threatened by both fire and theft, hence, the need for insurance. Of interest was the amount the subject was willing to pay (WTP) for insurance (thousands of dollars). For one part of the experiment, a total of 252 subjects were randomly assigned to one of three groups. Group 1 subjects ($n_1 = 84$) were informed of the hazards (both fire and theft) but were not told the exact probabilities of the hazards occurring. These subjects provided a separate WTP value for fire and theft. Group 2 subjects ($n_2 = 84$) were also informed of the hazards (fire/theft) and were not told the exact probabilities of the hazards occurring. However, these subjects provided a single WTP value covering both fire and theft. Group 3 subjects ($n_3 = 84$) were told of the hazards in sequential order (fire first, then theft). After being given the exact probability of fire occurring, the subjects provided a WTP value for fire. Then they were given the exact probability of theft occurring and were asked to provide a WTP value for theft. The researchers investigated whether the mean total WTP value differed for the three groups.

a. Explain why the experimental design employed is a completely randomized design.

b. Identify the dependent (response) variable and treatments for the design.

c. Give the null and alternative hypotheses of interest to the researchers.

d. Use a random number generator to randomly assign each of the 252 subjects to one of the three groups. Be sure to assign 84 subjects to each group. [NW]

9.27 Contingent valuation of homes in contaminated areas. Contingent valuation (CV) is a method of estimating property values that uses survey responses from potential homeowners. CV surveys were employed to determine the impact of contamination on property values in the *Journal of Real Estate Research* (Vol. 27, 2005). Homeowners were randomly selected from each of seven states—Kentucky, Pennsylvania, Ohio, Alabama, Illinois, South Carolina, and Texas. Each homeowner was asked to estimate the property value of a home located in an area contaminated by petroleum leaking from underground storage tanks (LUST). The dependent variable of interest was the LUST discount percentage (i.e., the difference between the current home value and estimated LUST value, as a percentage). The researchers were interested in comparing the mean LUST discount percentages across the seven states.

a. Give the null and alternative hypotheses of interest to the researchers.

b. An ANOVA summary table is shown below. Use the information provided to conduct the hypothesis test, part **a.** Use $\alpha = .10$.

Source	df	SS	MS	F-Value	p-Value
States	6	.1324	.0221	1.60	0.174
Error	59	.8145	.0138		
Total	65	.9469			

Applying the Concepts—Intermediate

9.28 Study of recall of TV commercials. Do TV shows with violence and sex impair memory for commercials? To answer this question, Iowa State researchers conducted a designed experiment in which 324 adults were randomly assigned to one of three viewer groups of 108 participants each (*Journal of Applied Psychology,* June 2002). One group watched a TV program with a violent content code (V) rating, the second group viewed a show with a sex content code (S) rating, and the last group watched a neutral TV program with neither a V nor an S rating. Nine commercials were embedded into each TV show. After viewing the program, each participant was scored on his or her recall of the brand names in the commercial messages, with scores ranging from 0 (no brands recalled) to 9 (all [NW] ADREC brands recalled). The data (simulated from information provided in the article) are saved in the accompanying file. The researchers compared the mean recall scores of the three viewing groups with an analysis of variance for a completely randomized design.

a. Identify the experimental units in the study.

b. Identify the dependent (response) variable in the study.

c. Identify the factor and treatments in the study.

d. The sample mean recall scores for the three groups were $\bar{x}_v = 2.08$, $\bar{x}_s = 1.71$, and $\bar{x}_{\text{Neutral}} = 3.17$. Explain why one should not draw an inference about differences in the population mean recall scores on the basis of only these summary statistics.

e. An ANOVA on the data yielded the results shown in the Minitab printout below. Locate the test statistic and *p*-value on the printout.

f. Interpret the results from part **e**, using $\alpha = 0.01$. What can the researchers conclude about the three groups of TV ad viewers?

g. Check that the ANOVA assumptions are reasonably satisfied.

One-way ANOVA: VIOLENT, SEX, NEUTRAL

```
Analysis of Variance

Source   DF   Adj SS   Adj MS   F-Value   P-Value
Factor    2    123.3   61.633    20.45     0.000
Error   321    967.4    3.014
Total   323   1090.6


Model Summary

      S    R-sq   R-sq(adj)   R-sq(pred)
1.73596   11.30%     10.75%        9.64%
```

9.29 Do the media influence your attitude toward tanning? Dermatologists' primary recommendation to prevent skin cancer is minimal exposure to the sun. Yet, models used in product advertisements are typically well tanned. Do such advertisements influence a consumer's attitude toward tanning? University of California and California State University researchers designed an experiment to investigate this phenomenon and published their results in *Basic and Applied Social Psychology* (May 2010). College student participants were randomly assigned to one of three conditions: (1) view product advertisements featuring models with a tan, (2) view product advertisements featuring models without a tan, or (3) view products advertised with no models (control group). The objective was to determine whether the mean attitude toward tanning differs across the three conditions. A tanning attitude index (measured on a scale of 0 to 5 points) was recorded for each participant. The results are summarized in the accompanying table.

	Tanned Models	Models with No Tan	No Models
Sample Size	56	56	56
Mean	2.40	2.11	2.50
Standard Deviation	.85	.73	.82

Source. Based on H. Mahler et al., "Effects of Media Images on Attitudes Toward Tanning," *Basic and Applied Social Psychology*, Vol. 32, No. 2, May 2010 (adapted from Table 1).

a. Identify the type of experimental design utilized by the researchers.

b. Identify the experimental units, dependent variable, and treatments for the design.

c. Set up the null hypothesis for a test to compare the treatment means.

d. The sample means shown in the table are obviously different. Explain why the researchers should not use these means alone to test the hypothesis, part **c**.

e. The researchers conducted an ANOVA on the data and reported the following results: $F = 3.60$, *p*-value $= .03$. Carry out the test, part **c**. Use $\alpha = .05$ to draw your conclusion.

f. What assumptions are required for the inferences derived from the test to be valid?

9.30 **Homework assistance for accounting students.** Refer to the *Journal of Accounting Education* (Vol. 25, 2007) study of assisting accounting students with their homework, Exercise 8.18 (p. 468). A total of 75 junior-level accounting majors who were enrolled in Intermediate Financial Accounting participated in the experiment. Recall that students took a pretest on a topic not covered in class and then each was given a homework problem to solve on the same topic. A completely randomized design was employed, with students randomly assigned to receive one of three different levels of assistance on the homework: (1) the completed solution, (2) check figures at various steps of the solution, and (3) no help at all. After finishing the homework, each student was given a posttest on the subject. The response variable of interest to the researchers was the knowledge gain (or, test score improvement), measured as the difference between the posttest and pretest scores. The data (simulated from descriptive statistics published in the article) are saved in the accompanying file.

a. Give the null and alternative hypotheses tested in an analysis of variance of the data.

b. Summarize the results of the analysis in an ANOVA table.

c. Interpret the results, practically. Does your conclusion agree with the inferences drawn in Exercise 8.18?

9.31 **Improving driving performance while fatigued.** Long-haul truck drivers are often asked to drive while fatigued. Can a secondary task—such as a word association task—improve the performance of a fatigued driver? This was the question of interest in a *Human Factors* (May 2014) study. The researchers used a driving simulator to obtain their data. Each of 40 college students was assigned to drive a long distance in the simulator. However, the student-drivers were divided into four groups of 10 drivers each. Group 1 performed the verbal task continuously (*continuous verbal condition*); Group 2 performed the task only at the end of the drive (*late verbal condition*); Group 3 did not perform the task at all (*no verbal condition*); and, Group 4 listened to a program on the car radio (*radio show condition*). At the end of the simulated drive, drivers were asked to recall billboards that they saw along the way. The percentage of billboards recalled by each student-driver is provided in the next table. Use the information in the accompanying SPSS printout to determine if the mean recall percentage differs for student-drivers in the four groups. Test using $\alpha = .01$.

Data for Exercise 9.31

Continuous Verbal	Late Verbal	No Verbal	Radio Show
14	57	64	37
63	64	83	45
10	66	54	87
29	18	59	62
37	95	60	14
60	52	39	46
43	58	56	59
4	92	73	45
36	85	78	45
47	47	73	50

SPSS Output for Exercise 9.31

ANOVA

RECALL

	Sum of Squares	df	Mean Square	F	Sig.
Between Groups	5921.700	3	1973.900	5.388	.004
Within Groups	13189.400	36	366.372		
Total	19111.100	39			

9.32 **Is honey a cough remedy?** Pediatric researchers carried out a designed study to test whether a teaspoon of honey before bed calms a child's cough and published their results in *Archives of Pediatrics and Adolescent Medicine* (December 2007). (This experiment was first described in Exercise 2.31, p. 86.) A sample of 105 children who were ill with an upper respiratory tract infection and their parents participated in the study. On the first night, the parents rated their children's cough symptoms on a scale from 0 (no problems at all) to 6 (extremely severe) in five different areas. The total symptoms score (ranging from 0 to 30 points) was the variable of interest for the 105 patients. On the second night, the parents were instructed to give their sick children a dosage of liquid "medicine" prior to bedtime. Unknown to the parents, some were given a dosage of dextromethorphan (DM)—an over-the-counter cough medicine—while others were given a similar dose of honey. Also, a third group of parents (the control group) gave their sick children no dosage at all. Again, the parents rated their children's cough symptoms, and the improvement in total cough symptoms score was determined for each child. The data (improvement scores) for the study are shown in the accompanying table. The goal of the researchers was to compare the mean improvement scores for the three treatment groups.

a. Identify the type of experimental design employed. What are the treatments?

b. Conduct an analysis of variance on the data and interpret the results.

c. Check the validity of the ANOVA assumptions.

Honey Dosage:	12	11	15	11	10	13	10	4	15	16	9	14
	10	6	10	8	11	12	12	8	12	9	11	15
	10	15	9	13	8	12	10	8	9	5	12	
DM Dosage:	4	6	9	4	7	7	7	9	12	10	11	
	6	3	4	9	12	7	6	8	12	12	4	
	12	13	7	10	13	9	4	4	10	15	9	
No Dosage (Control):	5	8	6	1	0	8	12	8	7	7	1	6
	7	7	12	7	9	5	11	9	5	6	8	8
	6	7	10	9	4	8	7	3	1	4	3	

Source: I. M. Paul et al., "Effect of Honey, Dextromethorphan, and No Treatment On Nocturnal Cough and Sleep Quality for Coughing Children and Their Parents," *Archives of Pediatrics and Adolescent Medicine,* Vol. 161, No. 12, December 2007 (data simulated).

9.33 **Commercial eggs produced from different housing systems.** In the production of commercial eggs in Europe, four different types of housing systems for the chickens are used: cage, barn, free range, and organic. The characteristics of eggs produced from the four housing systems were investigated in *Food Chemistry* (Vol. 106, 2008). Twenty-eight commercial grade A eggs were randomly selected from supermarkets—10 of which were produced in cages, 6 in barns, 6 with free range, and 6 organic. A number of quantitative characteristics were measured for each egg, including shell thickness (millimeters), whipping capacity (percent overrun), and penetration strength (newtons). The data (simulated from summary statistics provided in the journal article) are saved in the accompanying file. For each characteristic, the researchers compared the means of the four housing systems. Minitab descriptive statistics and ANOVA printouts for each characteristic are shown below. Fully interpret the results. Identify the characteristics for which the housing systems differ.

Descriptive Statistics: THICKNESS, OVERRUN, STRENGTH

Variable	HOUSING	N	Mean	StDev	Minimum	Maximum
THICKNESS	BARN	6	0.50000	0.01414	0.48000	0.52000
	CAGE	10	0.4230	0.0350	0.3700	0.4700
	FREE	6	0.5017	0.0279	0.4700	0.5500
	ORGANIC	6	0.4817	0.0387	0.4300	0.5200
OVERRUN	BARN	6	513.33	8.38	501.00	526.00
	CAGE	10	480.60	12.91	462.00	502.00
	FREE	6	517.50	8.17	510.00	531.00
	ORGANIC	6	529.17	10.65	511.00	544.00
STRENGTH	BARN	6	39.333	1.120	37.600	40.300
	CAGE	10	37.320	2.127	33.000	40.200
	FREE	6	37.17	3.79	31.50	40.60
	ORGANIC	6	35.97	3.04	32.60	40.20

One-way ANOVA: THICKNESS versus HOUSING

Source	DF	SS	MS	F	P
HOUSING	3	0.034291	0.011430	11.74	0.000
Error	24	0.023377	0.000974		
Total	27	0.057668			

One-way ANOVA: OVERRUN versus HOUSING

Source	DF	SS	MS	F	P
HOUSING	3	10788	3596	31.36	0.000
Error	24	2752	115		
Total	27	13540			

One-way ANOVA: STRENGTH versus HOUSING

Source	DF	SS	MS	F	P
HOUSING	3	35.12	11.71	1.70	0.193
Error	24	164.82	6.87		
Total	27	199.94			

Minitab output for Exercise 9.33

Applying the Concepts—Advanced

9.34 **Banning controversial sports team sponsors.** Successful marketing of professional sports franchises involves finding sponsors that appeal to the team's fans. The *Journal of Marketing Research* (October 2015) published a study that investigated the impact of banning a controversial sponsor (e.g., one that manufactures an alcoholic beverage) on a soccer team's success. Data were collected for 43 English soccer clubs over a 30-year period, where each club-year represents a market. The clubs were divided into four types: (1) clubs that had banned alcohol sponsors but now have other sponsors, (2) clubs that had banned alcohol sponsors and now have no other sponsors, (3) clubs that did not have banned alcohol sponsors but now have other sponsors, and (4) clubs that did not have banned alcohol sponsors and now have no other sponsors. To assess the impact of an alcohol ban in a market, the researchers computed the *matching value loss (MVL)*, a numerical measure used to estimate the value lost between a club and a sponsor if a ban is implemented. The table below gives summary statistics for the matching value loss for the four club types in 177 markets. The mean matching value losses of the four types were compared using an analysis of variance. Although the ANOVA table was not provided in the article, sufficient information is provided to reconstruct it.

Club Type	Sample Size (No. of markets)	Mean MVL	Standard Deviation
Banned/Others	55	8.52	1.01
Banned/No Others	39	8.55	.94
No Bans/Others	28	6.63	.31
No Bans/No Others	55	6.38	.38

Source: Y. Yang and A. Goldfarb, "Banning Controversial Sponsors: Understanding Equilibrium Outcomes When Sports Sponsorships Are Viewed as Two-Sided Matches," *Journal of Marketing Research*, Vol. 52, October 2015 (from Table 7).

a. Compute SST for the ANOVA, using the formula (see p. 532)

$$SST = \sum_{i=1}^{4} n_i (\bar{x}_i - \bar{x})^2$$

where $\bar{x}$ is the overall mean MVL of clubs in all 177 markets. [*Hint*: $\bar{x} = (\sum_{i=1}^{4} n_i(\bar{x}_i))/177$.]

b. Recall that SSE for the ANOVA can be written as

$$SSE = (n_1 - 1)s_1^2 + (n_2 - 1)s_2^2 + (n_3 - 1)s_3^2 + (n_4 - 1)s_4^2$$

where s_1^2, s_2^2, s_3^2 and s_4^2 are the sample variances associated with the four treatments. Compute SSE for the ANOVA.

c. Use the results from parts **a** and **b** to construct the ANOVA table.

d. Is there sufficient evidence (at $\alpha = .01$) of differences among the mean market value losses of clubs in the four types?

e. Comment on the validity of the ANOVA assumptions. How might this affect the results of the study?

9.3 Multiple Comparisons of Means

Consider a completely randomized design with three treatments, A, B, and C. Suppose we determine that the treatment means are statistically different via the ANOVA F test of Section 9.2. To complete the analysis, we want to rank the three treatment means. As mentioned in Section 9.2, we start by placing confidence intervals on the difference between various pairs of treatment means in the experiment. In the three-treatment experiment, for example, we would construct confidence intervals for the following differences: $\mu_A - \mu_B, \mu_A - \mu_C,$ and $\mu_B - \mu_C$.

> **Determining the Number of Pairwise Comparisons of Treatment Means**
>
> In general, if there are k treatment means, there are
>
> $$c = \frac{k(k-1)}{2}$$
>
> pairs of means that can be compared.

If we want to have $100(1 - \alpha)\%$ confidence that each of the c confidence intervals contains the true difference it is intended to estimate, we must use a smaller value of α for each individual confidence interval than we would use for a single interval. For example, suppose we want to rank the means of the three treatments, A, B, and C, with 95% confidence that all three confidence intervals comparing the means contain the true differences between the treatment means. Then each individual confidence interval will need to be constructed using a level of significance smaller than $\alpha = .05$ in order to have 95% confidence that the three intervals collectively include the true differences.*

Now Work Exercise 9.35

---

*The reason each interval must be formed at a higher confidence level than that specified for the collection of intervals can be demonstrated as follows:

$P\{$At least one of c intervals fails to contain the true difference$\}$
$= 1 - P\{$All c intervals contain the true differences$\}$
$= 1 - (1 - \alpha)^c \geq \alpha$

Thus, to make this probability of at least one failure equal to α, we must specify the individual levels of significance to be less than α.

To make **multiple comparisons of a set of treatment means,** we can use a number of procedures that, under various assumptions, ensure that the overall confidence level associated with all the comparisons remains at or above the specified $100(1 - \alpha)\%$ level. Three widely used techniques are the Bonferroni, Scheffé, and Tukey methods. For each of these procedures, the risk of making a Type I error applies to the comparisons of the treatment means in the experiment; thus, the value of α selected is called an **experimentwise error rate** (in contrast to a **comparisonwise error rate**).

> For a single comparison of two means in a designed experiment, the probability of making a Type I error (i.e., the probability of concluding that a difference in the means exists, given that the means are the same) is called a **comparisonwise error rate (CER).**

> For multiple comparisons of means in a designed experiment, the probability of making at least one Type I error (i.e., the probability of concluding that at least one difference in means exists, given that the means are all the same) is called an **experimentwise error rate (EER).**

The choice of a multiple comparisons method in ANOVA will depend on the type of experimental design used and the comparisons of interest to the analyst. For example, **Tukey** (1949) developed his procedure specifically for pairwise comparisons when the sample sizes of the treatments are equal. The **Bonferroni method** (see Miller, 1981), like the Tukey procedure, can be applied when pairwise comparisons are of interest; however, Bonferroni's method does not require equal sample sizes. **Scheffé** (1953) developed a more general procedure for comparing all possible linear combinations of treatment means (called *contrasts*). Consequently, when making pairwise comparisons, the confidence intervals produced by Scheffé's method will generally be wider than the Tukey or Bonferroni confidence intervals.

The formulas for constructing confidence intervals for differences between treatment means using the Tukey, Bonferroni, or Scheffé method are provided in Appendix C. However, because these procedures (and many others) are available in the ANOVA programs of most statistical software packages, we use the computer to conduct the analysis. The programs generate a confidence interval for the difference between two treatment means for all possible pairs of treatments based on the experimentwise error rate (α) selected by the analyst.

EXAMPLE 9.6

Ranking Treatment Means—Golf Ball Experiment

Problem Refer to the completely randomized design of Example 9.4, in which we concluded that at least two of the four brands of golf balls are associated with different mean distances traveled when struck with a driver.

a. Use Tukey's multiple comparisons procedure to rank the treatment means with an overall confidence level of 95%.

b. Estimate the mean distance traveled for balls manufactured by the brand with the highest rank.

Solution

a. To rank the treatment means with an overall confidence level of .95, we require the experimentwise error rate of $\alpha = .05$. The confidence intervals generated by Tukey's method appear at the top of the SPSS printout, Figure 9.16. [*Note:* SPSS uses the number 1 for Brand A, 2 for Brand B, etc.] For any pair of means, μ_i and μ_j, SPSS computes two confidence intervals—one for $(\mu_i - \mu_j)$ and one for $(\mu_j - \mu_i)$. Only one of these intervals is necessary to decide whether the means differ significantly.

Multiple Comparisons

Dependent Variable: DISTANCE

Tukey HSD

(I) BRANDNUM	(J) BRANDNUM	Mean Difference (I-J)	Std. Error	Sig.	95% Confidence Interval Lower Bound	95% Confidence Interval Upper Bound
1	2	-10.2800*	2.0579	.000	-15.822	-4.738
	3	-19.1700*	2.0579	.000	-24.712	-13.628
	4	1.4600	2.0579	.893	-4.082	7.002
2	1	10.2800*	2.0579	.000	4.738	15.822
	3	-8.8900*	2.0579	.001	-14.432	-3.348
	4	11.7400*	2.0579	.000	6.198	17.282
3	1	19.1700*	2.0579	.000	13.628	24.712
	2	8.8900*	2.0579	.001	3.348	14.432
	4	20.6300*	2.0579	.000	15.088	26.172
4	1	-1.4600	2.0579	.893	-7.002	4.082
	2	-11.7400*	2.0579	.000	-17.282	-6.198
	3	-20.6300*	2.0579	.000	-26.172	-15.088

*. The mean difference is significant at the 0.05 level.

Homogeneous Subsets

DISTANCE

Tukey HSD[a]

BRANDNUM	N	Subset for alpha = 0.05 — 1	Subset for alpha = 0.05 — 2	Subset for alpha = 0.05 — 3
4	10	249.320		
1	10	250.780		
2	10		261.060	
3	10			269.950
Sig.		.893	1.000	1.000

Means for groups in homogeneous subsets are displayed.

a. Uses Harmonic Mean Sample Size = 10.000.

Figure 9.16

SPSS printout of Tukey's multiple comparisons for the golf ball data

In this example, we have $k = 4$ brand means to compare. Consequently, the number of relevant pairwise comparisons—that is, the number of nonredundant confidence intervals—is $c = 4(3)/2 = 6$. These six intervals, highlighted in Figure 9.16, are given in Table 9.6.

Table 9.6	Pairwise Comparisons for Example 9.6
Brand Comparison	**Confidence Interval**
$(\mu_A - \mu_B)$	$(-15.82, -4.74)$
$(\mu_A - \mu_C)$	$(-24.71, -13.63)$
$(\mu_A - \mu_D)$	$(-4.08, 7.00)$
$(\mu_B - \mu_C)$	$(-14.43, -3.35)$
$(\mu_B - \mu_D)$	$(6.20, 17.28)$
$(\mu_C - \mu_D)$	$(15.09, 26.17)$

We are 95% confident that the intervals *collectively* contain all the differences between the true brand mean distances. Note that intervals that contain 0, such as the Brand A–Brand D interval from −4.08 to 7.00, do not support a conclusion that the true brand mean distances differ. If both endpoints of the interval are positive, as with the Brand B–Brand D interval from 6.20 to 17.28, the implication is that the first Brand (B) mean distance exceeds the second (D). Conversely, if both endpoints of the interval are negative, as with the Brand A–Brand C interval from −24.71 to −13.63, the implication is that the second Brand (C) mean distance exceeds the first Brand (A) mean distance.

A convenient summary of the results of the Tukey multiple comparisons is a listing of the brand means from highest to lowest, with a solid horizontal line connecting those that are *not* significantly different. This summary is shown in Figure 9.17. A similar summary is shown at the bottom of the SPSS printout, Figure 9.16. The interpretation is that Brand C's mean distance exceeds all others; Brand B's mean exceeds that of Brands A and D; and the means of Brands A and D do not differ significantly. All these inferences are made simultaneously with 95% confidence, the overall confidence level of the Tukey multiple comparisons.

Figure 9.17

Summary of Tukey multiple comparisons

Mean:	249.3	250.8	261.1	270.0
Brand:	D	A	B	C

b. Brand C is ranked highest; thus, we want a confidence interval for μ_C. Because the samples were selected independently in a completely randomized design, a confidence interval for an individual treatment mean is obtained with the one-sample t confidence interval of Section 6.3, using the mean square for error, MSE, as the measure of sampling variability for the experiment. A 95% confidence interval on the mean distance traveled by Brand C (apparently the "longest ball" of those tested), is

$$\bar{x}_C \pm t_{.025}\sqrt{\frac{MSE}{n}}$$

where $n = 10$, $t_{.025} \approx 2$ (based on 36 degrees of freedom), and MSE = 21.175 (obtained from the Excel printout, Figure 9.12). Substituting, we obtain

$$270.0 \pm (2)\sqrt{\frac{21.175}{10}} = 270.0 \pm 2.9 \text{ or } (267.1, 272.9)$$

Thus, we are 95% confident that the true mean distance traveled for Brand C is between 267.1 and 272.9 yards, when hit with a driver by Iron Byron.

Look Back The easiest way to create a summary table like the one in Figure 9.17 is to first list the treatment means in rank order. Begin with the largest mean and compare it with (in order) the second largest mean, the third largest mean, and so on, by examining the appropriate confidence intervals shown on the computer printout. If a confidence interval contains 0, then connect the two means with a line. (These two means are not significantly different.) Continue in this manner by comparing the second largest mean with the third largest, fourth largest, and so on, until all possible $c = \frac{(k)(k+1)}{2}$ comparisons are made.

● **Now Work Exercise 9.39**

Remember that the Tukey method—designed for comparing pairs of treatment means with equal sample sizes—is just one of numerous multiple comparisons procedures available. Another technique may be more appropriate for the experimental design you employ. Consult the references for details on these other methods and when they should be applied. Guidelines for using the Tukey, Bonferroni, and Scheffé methods are given in the box.

ETHICS in STATISTICS

Running several different multiple comparisons methods and reporting only the one that produces a desired outcome, without regard to the experimental design, is considered *unethical statistical practice*.

Guidelines for Selecting a Multiple Comparisons Method in ANOVA

Method	Treatment Sample Sizes	Types of Comparisons
Tukey	Equal	Pairwise
Bonferroni	Equal or unequal	Pairwise or general contrasts (number of contrasts known)
Scheffé	Equal or unequal	General contrasts

Note: For equal sample sizes and pairwise comparisons, Tukey's method will yield simultaneous confidence intervals with the smallest width, and the Bonferroni intervals will have smaller widths than the Scheffé intervals.

STATISTICS IN ACTION REVISITED

Ranking the Tax Compliance Behavior Means for the Four Experimental Conditions

We again return to the *Behavioral Research in Accounting* (January 2015) study of the factors that affect the level of risk taking when filing a federal or state income tax return. At the end of Section 9.2, we used an ANOVA for a completely randomized design to compare the mean tax compliance behavior score for taxpayers in four different experimental conditions: (1) filing a single federal tax return with a refund due, (2) filing a single federal tax return with a payment due, (3) filing multiple (federal and state) tax returns with a net refund due, and (4) filing multiple (federal and state) tax returns with a net payment due. The ANOVA *F*-test revealed that significant differences exist among the four means.

Now, we follow up this ANOVA with multiple comparisons of the tax condition (treatment) means. This analysis will allow the researchers to rank the means and ultimately determine if there is support for the two propositions hypothesized in the journal article. Since the sample sizes associated with the four conditions are equal, and because we desire pairwise comparisons of the means, the method with the highest power (i.e., the one with the greatest chance of detecting a difference when differences actually exist) is Tukey's multiple comparisons method. Also, this method explicitly controls the comparisonwise error rate (i.e., the overall Type I error rate). For this problem there are four treatments (tax conditions). Consequently, there are $c = k(k - 1)/2 = 4(3)/2 = 6$ comparisons of interest.

Again, let the symbol μ_j represent the population mean tax compliance behavior score for taxpayers in Condition *j*. Then, the six comparisons we desire are as follows: $(\mu_1 - \mu_2)$, $(\mu_1 - \mu_3)$, $(\mu_1 - \mu_4)$, $(\mu_2 - \mu_3)$, $(\mu_2 - \mu_4)$, and $(\mu_3 - \mu_4)$. We used Excel/XLSTAT to perform the multiple comparisons for the data saved in the **TAX** file. The results—using an experimentwise error rate of .05—are shown in Figure SIA9.4. Based on the confidence intervals for the differences in means, XLSTAT determines which means are significantly different. Treatments with the same letter in the "Groups" column are not significantly different.

The overlapping letter "A" at the bottom of Figure SIA9.4 implies that Conditions 3, 2, and 4 do not have significantly different means. Similarly, the overlapping letter "B" implies that Conditions 2, 4, and 1 do not have significantly different means. The only two tax conditions found to have significantly different tax compliance behavior means are Conditions 3 and 1 (since they do not have the same "Group" letter). These inferences can be made with an overall 5% chance of a Type I error.

CONDITION / Tukey (HSD) / Analysis of the differences between the categories with a confidence interval of 95%:

Contrast	Difference	Standardized difference	Critical value	Pr > Diff	Significant
(3)Ref-Multi vs (1)Ref-Single	1.0667	2.6688	2.5874	0.0403	Yes
(3)Ref-Multi vs (4)Pay-Multi	0.5000	1.2510	2.5874	0.5951	No
(3)Ref-Multi vs (2)Pay-Single	0.1333	0.3336	2.5874	0.9872	No
(2)Pay-Single vs (1)Ref-Single	0.9333	2.3352	2.5874	0.0931	No
(2)Pay-Single vs (4)Pay-Multi	0.3667	0.9174	2.5874	0.7956	No
(4)Pay-Multi vs (1)Ref-Single	0.5667	1.4178	2.5874	0.4895	No
Tukey's d critical value:			3.6592		

Category	LS means	Groups		
(3)Ref-Multi	4.9167	A		
(2)Pay-Single	4.7833	A	B	
(4)Pay-Multi	4.4167	A	B	
(1)Ref-Single	3.8500		B	

Figure SIA9.4

XLSTAT Multiple Comparisons of Tax Compliance Behavior Means

Since the Condition 3 mean (4.92) exceeds the Condition 1 mean (3.85), there is evidence to support the researchers' first proposition, namely, that the mean for taxpayers filing multiple returns with a net refund due will exceed the mean for taxpayers filing a single return with a net refund due, i.e., $\mu_3 > \mu_1$. However, the researchers' second proposition, namely, that the mean for taxpayers filing multiple returns with a net payment due will be lower than the mean for taxpayers filing a single return with a payment due (i.e., $\mu_4 < \mu_2$) cannot be supported based on the multiple comparisons. Although the sample mean for Condition 4 is smaller than the sample mean for Condition 2, there is no significant difference between the means.

In the *Statistics in Action Revisited* in the last section of this chapter, we apply a more complex ANOVA method—one that takes into account the two factors Tax Position (Refund or Payment Due) and Return Format (Single or Multiple)—to test the researchers' propositions.

Exercises 9.35–9.49

Learning the Mechanics

9.35 Consider a completely randomized design with k treatments. Assume all pairwise comparisons of treatment means are to be made using a multiple comparisons procedure. Determine the total number of pairwise comparisons for the following values of k.
- **a.** $k = 3$ **b.** $k = 5$
- **c.** $k = 4$ **d.** $k = 10$

9.36 Define an experimentwise error rate.

9.37 Define a comparisonwise error rate.

9.38 The Tukey method to compare four treatment means produced the following 95% confidence coefficient intervals. Identify which of the following pairwise comparisons are significantly different and which are not. Explain your reason.
- **a.** $.29 \le \mu_2 - \mu_1 \le 4.47$
- **b.** $-2.25 \le \mu_3 - \mu_1 \le 1.83$
- **c.** $-3.74 \le \mu_1 - \mu_4 \le -1.86$
- **d.** $-1.13 \le \mu_2 - \mu_3 \le .54$

9.39 A multiple comparison procedure for comparing four treatment means produced the confidence intervals shown here. Rank the means from smallest to largest. Which means are significantly different?

$(\mu_1 - \mu_2)$: $(2, 15)$

$(\mu_1 - \mu_3)$: $(4, 7)$

$(\mu_1 - \mu_4)$: $(-10, 3)$

$(\mu_2 - \mu_3)$: $(-5, 11)$

$(\mu_2 - \mu_4)$: $(-12, -6)$

$(\mu_3 - \mu_4)$: $(-8, -5)$

Applying the Concepts—Basic

9.40 **How workers respond to wage cuts.** Refer to the *Institute for the Study of Labor: Discussion Paper Series* (March 2011) study of how workers respond to wage cuts, Exercise 9.22 (p. 543). Recall that teams of workers were divided into three wage cut groups: "unilateral wage cut," "general wage cut," and "baseline" (no wage cut). The researchers determined that the average decrease in promotional cards sold differed depending on the wage cut treatment group. Now the researchers want to rank the treatment means by making all possible pairwise comparisons.
- **a.** How many pairwise comparisons make up this phase of the study? List them.

- **b.** Why is a multiple comparisons procedure like Tukey's recommended for the analysis?
- **c.** The confidence interval for the difference between the means for "baseline" and "general wage cut," i.e., for $(\mu_{baseline} - \mu_{general})$, includes only positive values. Interpret this result.

9.41 **Evaluation of flexography printing plates.** Refer to the *Journal of Graphic Engineering and Design* (Vol. 3, 2012) study of the quality of flexography printing, Exercise 9.24 (p. 544). Recall that four different exposure times were studied—8, 10, 12, and 14 minutes—and that the measure of print quality used was dot area (hundreds of dots per square millimeter). Tukey's multiple comparisons procedure (at an experimentwise error rate of .05) was used to rank the mean dot areas of the four exposure times. The results are summarized below. Which exposure time yields the highest mean dot area? Lowest?

Mean Dot Area:	.571	.582	.588	.594
Exposure Time: (minutes)	12	10	14	8

9.42 **Guilt in decision making.** The effect of guilt emotion on how a decision maker focuses on a problem was investigated in the January 2007 issue of the *Journal of Behavioral Decision Making* (see Exercise 3.48, p. 183). A sample of 77 volunteer students participated in one portion of the experiment, where each was randomly assigned to one of three emotional states (guilt, anger, or neutral) through a reading/writing task. Immediately after the task, students were presented with a decision problem where the stated option had predominantly negative features (e.g., spending money on repairing a very old car). Prior to making the decision, the researchers asked each subject to list possible, more attractive alternatives. The researchers then compared the mean number of alternatives listed across the three emotional states with an analysis of variance for a completely randomized design. A partial ANOVA summary table is shown below.

Source	df	F-Value	p-Value
Emotional State	2	22.68	0.001
Error	74		
Total	76		

- **a.** What conclusion can you draw from the ANOVA results?

b. A multiple comparisons of means procedure was applied to the data using an experimentwise error rate of .05. Explain what the .05 represents.

c. The multiple comparisons yielded the following results. What conclusion can you draw?

Sample mean:	1.90	2.17	4.75
Emotional state:	Angry	Neutral	Guilt

9.43 **Performance of a bus depot.** Refer to the *International Journal of Engineering Science and Technology* (February 2011) study of public bus depot performance, Exercise 9.25 (p. 544). Recall that 150 customers provided overall performance ratings at each of three different bus depots (Depot 1, Depot 2, and Depot 3). The average performance scores were determined to be significantly different at $\alpha = .05$ using an ANOVA F-test. The sample mean performance scores were reported as $\bar{x}_1 = 67.17$, $\bar{x}_2 = 58.95$, and $\bar{x}_3 = 44.49$. The researchers employed the Bonferroni method to rank the three performance means using an experimentwise error rate of .05. Adjusted 95% confidence intervals for the differences between each pair of treatment means are shown in the table. Use this information to rank the mean performance scores at the three bus depots.

Comparison	Adjusted 95% CI
$(\mu_1 - \mu_2)$	(1.50, 14.94)
$(\mu_1 - \mu_3)$	(15.96, 29.40)
$(\mu_2 - \mu_3)$	(7.74, 21.18)

9.44 **Do the media influence your attitude toward tanning?** Refer to the *Basic and Applied Social Psychology* (May 2010) study of whether product advertisements influence consumers' attitudes toward tanning, Exercise 9.29 (p. 545). Recall that college students were randomly assigned to one of three conditions—view product advertisements featuring models with a tan, view product advertisements featuring models without a tan, or view products advertised with no models. An ANOVA F-test revealed that the mean attitude toward tanning differed across the conditions. The researchers followed up this analysis with a multiple comparisons of means using an experimentwise error rate of .05. These results are summarized below. Fully interpret the results. Does it appear that the type of product advertisement can influence a consumer's attitude toward tanning?

Mean:	2.11	2.40	2.50
Condition:	Models/No Tan	Tanned Models	No Models

Applying the Concepts—Intermediate

9.45 **Baking properties of pizza cheese.** Due to its unique stretchability, mozzarella is the most commonly used pizza cheese by pizzerias. How do the baking properties of mozzarella compare with those of other pizza cheese options? This was the question of interest in a study published in the *Journal of Food Science* (August 2014). Seven different cheeses were compared: mozzarella, cheddar, Colby, Edam, Emmental, Gruyère, and provolone. A pizza was baked with each of the different cheeses; then images of the pizzas were taken with a digital video camera. From these images, the researchers calculated the color change index (CCI)—a measure of cheese color uniformity—for sampled digital pixels. The mean CCI values of the seven cheeses were compared using a completely randomized design ANOVA.

a. Identify the treatments for this experiment.

b. Identify the dependent variable for this experiment.

c. The ANOVA F-test resulted in a p-value $< .05$. Practically interpret this result.

d. How many different pairwise comparisons of cheeses are possible?

e. A multiple comparisons procedure with an experimentwise error rate of .05 was applied to the data, revealing the following results. What conclusions can you draw from these results?

Mean CCI:	.10	.15	.15	.18	.19	.30	3.62
Cheese:	Colby	Edam	Emmental	Cheddar	Gruyère	Provolone	Mozzarella

9.46 **Study of recall of TV commercials.** Refer to the *Journal of Applied Psychology* (June 2002) completely randomized design study to compare the mean commercial recall scores of viewers of three TV programs, presented in Exercise 9.28 (p. 544). Recall that one program had a violent content code (V) rating, one had a sex content code (S) rating, and one was a neutral TV program. Using Tukey's method, the researchers conducted multiple comparisons of the three mean recall scores.

a. How many pairwise comparisons were made in this study?

b. The multiple comparison procedure was applied to the data and the results are shown in the Minitab printout at the top of the next page. An experimentwise error rate of .05 was used. Locate the confidence interval for the comparison of the V and S groups. Interpret this result practically.

c. Repeat part **b** for the remaining comparisons. Which of the groups has the largest mean recall score?

d. In the journal article, the researchers concluded that "memory for [television] commercials is impaired after watching violent or sexual programming." Do you agree?

9.47 **Effectiveness of sales closing techniques.** Refer to the *B2B Marketing Insider* (Oct. 7, 2010) comparison of six sales closing techniques, Exercise 9.31 (p. 545). Assume the "level of trust" means for prospects of salespeople using each of the six closing techniques are listed in the table. A multiple comparisons of means analysis was conducted (at $\alpha = .05$), with the results shown in the accompanying table. Fully interpret the results.

Treatments: Closing Technique	Mean Level of Trust	Differing Treatments
1. No close	4.70	1 from 5 and 6
2. Financial close	4.50	2 from 6
3. Time Line close	4.40	No differences
4. Sympathy close	4.35	No differences
5. The Visual close	4.00	5 from 1
6. Thermometer close	3.95	6 from 1 and 2

Tukey Pairwise Comparisons

```
Grouping Information Using the Tukey Method and 95% Confidence

Factor    N    Mean   Grouping
NEUTRAL   108  3.167  A
VIOLENT   108  2.083    B
SEX       108  1.713    B

Means that do not share a letter are significantly different.

Tukey Simultaneous Tests for Differences of Means

                       Difference   SE of                        Adjusted
Difference of Levels   of Means     Difference    95% CI        T-Value  P-Value
SEX - VIOLENT            -0.370      0.236     (-0.923, 0.183)    -1.57    0.260
NEUTRAL - VIOLENT        1.083       0.236     ( 0.530, 1.636)     4.59    0.000
NEUTRAL - SEX            1.454       0.236     ( 0.901, 2.007)     6.15    0.000

Individual confidence level = 98.01%
```

Minitab output for Exercise 9.46

9.48 Is honey a cough remedy? Refer to the *Archives of Pediatrics and Adolescent Medicine* (December 2007) study of treatments for children's cough symptoms, Exercise 9.32 (p. 546). Do you agree with the statement (extracted from the article), "Honey may be a preferable treatment for the cough and sleep difficulty associated with childhood upper respiratory tract infection"? Perform a multiple comparisons of means to answer the question.

9.49 Commercial eggs produced from different housing systems. Refer to the *Food Chemistry* (Vol. 106, 2008) study of four different types of egg housing systems, Exercise 9.33 (p. 546). Recall that you analyzed the data file and discovered that the mean shell thickness (millimeters) differed for cage, barn, free range, and organic egg housing systems. A multiple comparisons of means was conducted using the Bonferroni method with an experimentwise

error rate of .05. The results are displayed in the SPSS printout below.

a. Locate the confidence interval for $(\mu_{CAGE} - \mu_{BARN})$ on the printout and interpret the result.

b. Locate the confidence interval for $(\mu_{CAGE} - \mu_{FREE})$ on the printout and interpret the result.

c. Locate the confidence interval for $(\mu_{CAGE} - \mu_{ORGANIC})$ on the printout and interpret the result.

d. Locate the confidence interval for $(\mu_{BARN} - \mu_{FREE})$ on the printout and interpret the result.

e. Locate the confidence interval for $(\mu_{BARN} - \mu_{ORGANIC})$ on the printout and interpret the result.

f. Locate the confidence interval for $(\mu_{FREE} - \mu_{ORGANIC})$ on the printout and interpret the result.

g. Based on the results, parts **a–f,** provide a ranking of the housing system means. Include the experimentwise error rate as a statement of reliability.

Multiple Comparisons

THICKNESS
Bonferroni

(I) HOUSE	(J) HOUSE	Mean Difference (I-J)	Std. Error	Sig.	95% Confidence Interval	
					Lower Bound	Upper Bound
CAGE	BARN	-.07867*	.01612	.000	-.1250	-.0323
	FREE	-.07700*	.01612	.000	-.1233	-.0307
	ORGANIC	-.05867*	.01612	.008	-.1050	-.0123
BARN	CAGE	.07867*	.01612	.000	.0323	.1250
	FREE	.00167	.01802	1.000	-.0501	.0535
	ORGANIC	.02000	.01802	1.000	-.0318	.0718
FREE	CAGE	.07700*	.01612	.000	.0307	.1233
	BARN	-.00167	.01802	1.000	-.0535	.0501
	ORGANIC	.01833	.01802	1.000	-.0335	.0701
ORGANIC	CAGE	.05867*	.01612	.008	.0123	.1050
	BARN	-.02000	.01802	1.000	-.0718	.0318
	FREE	-.01833	.01802	1.000	-.0701	.0335

*. The mean difference is significant at the 0.05 level.

9.4 The Randomized Block Design

If the completely randomized design results in nonrejection of the null hypothesis that the treatment means differ because the sampling variability (as measured by MSE) is large, we may want to consider an experimental design that better controls the variability. In contrast to the selection of independent samples of experimental units specified by the completely randomized design, the *randomized block design* uses experimental units that are *matched sets,* assigning one from each set to each treatment. The matched sets of experimental units are called *blocks.* The theory behind the randomized block design is that the sampling variability of the experimental units in each block will be reduced, in turn reducing the measure of error, MSE.

> The **randomized block design** consists of a two-step procedure:
>
> 1. Matched sets of experimental units, called **blocks,** are formed, each block consisting of k experimental units (where k is the number of treatments). The b blocks should consist of experimental units that are as similar as possible.
>
> 2. One experimental unit from each block is randomly assigned to each treatment, resulting in a total of $n = bk$ responses.

For example, if we wish to compare the SAT scores of female and male high school seniors, we could select independent random samples of five females and five males, and analyze the results of the completely randomized design as outlined in Section 9.2. Or, we could select matched pairs of females and males according to their scholastic records and analyze the SAT scores of the pairs. For instance, we could select pairs of students with approximately the same GPAs from the same high school. Five such pairs (blocks) are depicted in Table 9.7. Note that this is just a *paired difference experiment,* first discussed in Section 8.3.

Table 9.7	Randomized Block Design: SAT Score Comparison		
Block	Female SAT Score	Male SAT Score	Block Mean
1 (school A, 2.75 GPA)	540	530	535
2 (school B, 3.00 GPA)	570	550	560
3 (school C, 3.25 GPA)	590	580	585
4 (school D, 3.50 GPA)	640	620	630
5 (school E, 3.75 GPA)	690	690	690
Treatment Mean	606	594	

 *Data Set:* HSSAT3

As before, the variation between the treatment means is measured by squaring the distance between each treatment mean and the overall mean, multiplying each squared distance by the number of measurements for the treatment, and summing over treatments:

$$\text{SST} = \sum_{i=1}^{k} b(\bar{x}_{T_i} - \bar{x})^2$$

$$= 5(606 - 600)^2 + 5(594 - 600)^2 = 360$$

where $\bar{x}_{T_i}$ represents the sample mean for the ith treatment, b (the number of blocks) is the number of measurements for each treatment, and k is the number of treatments.

The blocks also account for some of the variation among the different responses—that is, just as SST measures the variation between the female and male means, we can calculate a measure of variation among the five block means representing different schools and scholastic abilities. Analogous to the computation of SST, we sum the squares of the differences between each block mean and the overall mean, multiplying each squared difference by the number of measurements for each block, and sum over blocks to calculate the **Sum of Squares for Blocks (SSB)**:

$$\text{SSB} = \sum_{i=1}^{b} k(\bar{x}_{B_i} - \bar{x})^2$$

$$= 2(535 - 600)^2 + 2(560 - 600)^2 + 2(585 - 600)^2$$
$$+ 2(630 - 600)^2 + 2(690 - 600)^2$$
$$= 30{,}100$$

where $\bar{x}_{B_i}$ represents the sample mean for the ith block and k (the number of treatments) is the number of measurements in each block. As we expect, the variation in SAT scores attributable to schools and levels of scholastic achievement is apparently large.

Now, we want to compare the variability attributed to treatments with that which is attributed to sampling variability. In a randomized block design, the sampling variability is measured by subtracting that portion attributed to treatments and blocks from the Total Sum of Squares, SS(Total). The total variation is the sum of squared differences of each measurement from the overall mean:

$$
\begin{aligned}
SS(\text{Total}) &= \sum_{i=1}^{n} (x_i - \bar{x})^2 \\
&= (540 - 600)^2 + (530 - 600)^2 + (570 - 600)^2 + (550 - 600)^2 \\
&\quad + \cdots + (690 - 600)^2 \\
&= 30{,}600
\end{aligned}
$$

Then the variation attributable to sampling error is found by subtraction:

$$
SSE = SS(\text{Total}) - SST - SSB = 30{,}600 - 360 - 30{,}100 = 140
$$

In summary, the Total Sum of Squares—30,600—is divided into three components: 360 attributed to treatments (Gender), 30,100 attributed to blocks (Scholastic ability and School), and 140 attributed to sampling error.

The mean squares associated with each source of variability are obtained by dividing the sum of squares by the appropriate number of degrees of freedom. The partitioning of the Total Sum of Squares and the total degrees of freedom for a randomized block experiment is summarized in Figure 9.18.

To determine whether we can reject the null hypothesis that the treatment means are equal in favor of the alternative that at least two of them differ, we calculate

$$
MST = \frac{SST}{k - 1} = \frac{360}{2 - 1} = 360
$$

$$
MSE = \frac{SSE}{n - b - k + 1} = \frac{140}{10 - 5 - 2 + 1} = 35
$$

The F-ratio that is used to test the hypothesis is

$$
F = \frac{360}{35} = 10.29
$$

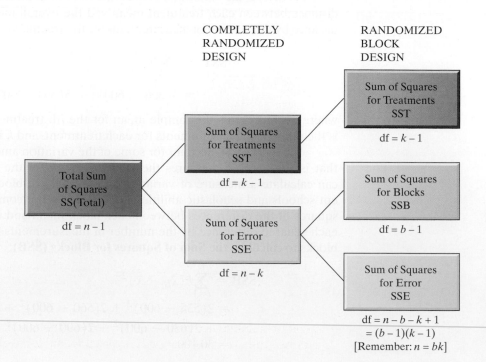

Figure 9.18

Partitioning of the total sum of squares for the randomized block design

Comparing this ratio with the tabled F-value corresponding to $\alpha = .05$, $v_1 = (k - 1) = 1$ degree of freedom in the numerator, and $v_2 = (n - b - k + 1) = 4$ degrees of freedom in the denominator, we find that

$$F = 10.29 > F_{.05} = 7.71$$

which indicates that we should reject the null hypothesis and conclude that the mean SAT scores differ for females and males. All of these calculations, of course, can be obtained using statistical software. The output for the Minitab analysis of the data in Table 9.7 is shown in Figure 9.19. The values of SST, SSE, MST, MSE, and F are highlighted on the printout.

Figure 9.19

Minitab printout with ANOVA results for the data in Table 9.7

Two-way ANOVA: SAT versus GENDER, BLOCK

Source	DF	SS	MS	F	P
GENDER	1	360	360	10.29	0.033
BLOCK	4	30100	7525	215.00	0.000
Error	4	140	35		
Total	9	30600			

Comment: If you review Section 8.3, you will find that the analysis of a paired difference experiment results in a one-sample t-test on the differences between the treatment responses within each block. Applying the procedure to the differences between female and male scores in Table 9.7, we find

$$t = \frac{\bar{x}_d}{s_d/\sqrt{n_d}} = \frac{12}{\sqrt{70}/\sqrt{5}} = 3.207$$

At the .05 level of significance with $(n_d - 1) = 4$ degrees of freedom,

$$t = 3.21 > t_{.025} = 2.776$$

Since $t^2 = (3.207)^2 = 10.29$ and $t^2_{.025} = (2.776)^2 = 7.71$, we find that the paired difference t-test and the ANOVA F-test are equivalent, with both the calculated test statistics and the rejection region related by the formula $F = t^2$. The difference between the tests is that the paired difference t-test can be used to compare only two treatments in a randomized block design, whereas the F-test can be applied to *two or more* treatments in a randomized block design.

The F-test is summarized in the following box.

ANOVA F-Test to Compare k Treatment Means: Randomized Block Design

H_0: $\mu_1 = \mu_2 = \cdots = \mu_k$

H_a: At least two treatment means differ

Test statistic: $F = \dfrac{\text{MST}}{\text{MSE}}$

Rejection region: $F > F_\alpha$

p-value: $P(F > F_c)$

where F_c is the calculated value of the test statistic and F_α is based on $(k - 1)$ numerator degrees of freedom and $(n - b - k + 1)$ denominator degrees of freedom.

Conditions Required for a Valid ANOVA F-Test: Randomized Block Design

1. The b blocks are randomly selected, and all k treatments are applied (in random order) to each block.

2. The distributions of observations corresponding to all bk block-treatment combinations are approximately normal.

3. The bk block-treatment distributions have equal variances.

Note that the assumptions concern the probability distributions associated with each block-treatment combination. The experimental unit selected for each combination is assumed to have been randomly selected from all possible experimental units for that combination, and the response is assumed to be normally distributed with the same variance for each of the block-treatment combinations. For example, the F-test comparing female and male SAT score means requires the scores for each combination of gender and scholastic ability (e.g., females with 3.25 GPA from School C) to be normally distributed with the same variance as the other combinations employed in the experiment.

For those who are interested, the calculation formulas for randomized block designs are given in Appendix C. Throughout this section, we will rely on statistical software packages to analyze randomized block designs and to obtain the necessary ingredients for testing the null hypothesis that the treatment means are equal.

EXAMPLE 9.7

Experimental Design Principles

Problem Refer to Examples 9.4–9.6. Suppose the USGA wants to compare the mean distances associated with the four brands of golf balls when struck by a driver but wishes to employ human golfers rather than the robot Iron Byron. Assume that 10 balls of each brand are to be used in the experiment.

a. Explain how a completely randomized design could be employed.

b. Explain how a randomized block design could be employed.

c. Which design is likely to provide more information about the differences among the brand mean distances?

Solution

a. Because the completely randomized design calls for independent samples, we can employ such a design by randomly selecting 40 golfers and then randomly assigning 10 golfers to each of the four brands. Finally, each golfer will strike the ball of the assigned brand, and the distance will be recorded. The design is illustrated in Figure 9.20a.

b. The randomized block design employs blocks of relatively homogeneous experimental units. For example, we could randomly select 10 golfers and permit each golfer to hit four balls, one of each brand, in a random sequence. Then each golfer is a block, with each treatment (brand) assigned to each block (golfer). The design is summarized in Figure 9.20b.

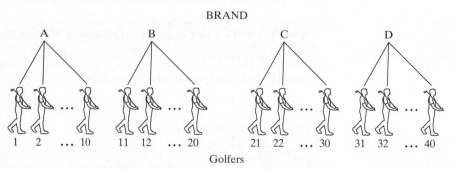

BRAND

Golfers

a. Completely randomized design

BRAND

		A	B	C	D
	1	Hit 3	Hit 1	Hit 4	Hit 2
	2	Hit 2	Hit 4	Hit 3	Hit 1
Golfers	⋮	⋮	⋮	⋮	⋮
	10	Hit 4	Hit 3	Hit 1	Hit 2

b. Randomized block design

Figure 9.20

Illustration of completely randomized design and randomized block design: comparison of four golf ball brands

c. Because we expect much more variability among distances generated by "real" golfers than by Iron Byron, we would expect the randomized block design to control the variability better than the completely randomized design—that is, with 40 different golfers, we would expect the sampling variability among the measured distances within each brand to be greater than that among the four distances generated by each of 10 golfers hitting one ball of each brand.

● **Now Work Exercise 9.54**

EXAMPLE 9.8

Randomized Block Design—Comparing Golf Ball Brands

Problem Refer to Example 9.7. Suppose the randomized block design of part **b** is employed, employing a random sample of 10 golfers, with each golfer using a driver to hit four balls, one of each brand, in a random sequence.

a. Set up a test of the research hypothesis that the brand mean distances differ. Use $\alpha = .05$.

b. The data for the experiment are given in Table 9.8. Use statistical software to analyze the data and conduct the test set up in part **a.**

Solution

a. We want to test whether the data in Table 9.8 provide sufficient evidence to conclude that the brand mean distances differ. Denoting the population mean of the ith brand by μ_i, we test

$$H_0: \mu_1 = \mu_2 = \mu_3 = \mu_4$$
$$H_a: \text{The mean distances differ for at least two of the brands.}$$

The test statistic compares the variation among the four treatment (brand) means with the sampling variability within each of the treatments.

$$Test\ statistic: F = \frac{\text{MST}}{\text{MSE}}$$

Rejection region: $F > F_\alpha = F_{.05}$, with $v_1 = (k - 1) = 3$ numerator degrees of freedom and $v_2 = (n - k - b + 1) = 27$ denominator degrees of freedom. From Table VI in Appendix D, we find $F_{.05} = 2.96$. Thus, we will reject H_0 if $F > 2.96$.

The assumptions necessary to ensure the validity of the test are as follows: (1) The probability distributions of the distances for each brand–golfer combination are normal. (2) The variances of the distance probability distributions for each brand–golfer combination are equal.

Table 9.8	Distance Data for Randomized Block Design			
Golfer (Block)	Brand A	Brand B	Brand C	Brand D
1	202.4	203.2	223.7	203.6
2	242.0	248.7	259.8	240.7
3	220.4	227.3	240.0	207.4
4	230.0	243.1	247.7	226.9
5	191.6	211.4	218.7	200.1
6	247.7	253.0	268.1	244.0
7	214.8	214.8	233.9	195.8
8	245.4	243.6	257.8	227.9
9	224.0	231.5	238.2	215.7
10	252.2	255.2	265.4	245.2
Sample Means	227.0	233.2	245.3	220.7

Data Set: GLFRBD

b. Minitab was used to analyze the data in Table 9.8, and the result is shown in Figure 9.21. The values of MST and MSE (highlighted on the printout) are 1,099.6 and 20.2, respectively. The F-ratio for Brand (also highlighted on the printout) is $F = 54.31$, which exceeds the tabled value of 2.96. We therefore reject the null hypothesis at the $\alpha = .05$ level of significance, concluding that at least two of the brands differ with respect to mean distance traveled when struck by the driver.

```
Analysis of Variance for DISTANCE

Source   DF      SS       MS      F       P
BRAND     3    3298.7   1099.6  54.31   0.000
GOLFER    9   12073.9   1341.5  66.26   0.000
Error    27     546.6     20.2
Total    39   15919.2


S = 4.49947    R-Sq = 96.57%    R-Sq(adj) = 95.04%
```

Figure 9.21

Minitab randomized block design ANOVA: golf ball brand comparison

Look Back The result of part **b** can also be obtained by noting that the observed significance level of the test, highlighted on the printout, is $p \approx 0$.

● **Now Work Exercise 9.55**

The results of an ANOVA can be summarized in a simple tabular format, similar to that used for the completely randomized design in Section 9.2. The general form of the table is shown in Table 9.9, and that for Example 9.8 is given in Table 9.10. Note that the randomized block design is characterized by three sources of variation—Treatments, Blocks, and Error—which sum to the Total Sum of Squares. We hope that employing blocks of experimental units will reduce the error of variability, thereby making the test for comparing treatment means more powerful.

When the F-test results in the rejection of the null hypothesis that the treatment means are equal, we will usually want to compare the various pairs of treatment means to determine which specific pairs differ. We can employ a multiple comparisons procedure as in Section 9.3. The number of pairs of means to be compared will again be $c = \frac{k(k-1)}{2}$, where k is the number of treatment means. In Example 9.8, $c = \frac{4(3)}{2} = 6$; that is, there are six pairs of golf ball brand means to be compared.

Table 9.9	General ANOVA Summary Table for a Randomized Block Design			
Source	df	SS	MS	F
Treatments	$k - 1$	SST	MST	MST/MSE
Blocks	$b - 1$	SSB	MSB	
Error	$n - k - b + 1$	SSE	MSE	
Total	$n - 1$	SS(Total)		

Table 9.10	ANOVA Table for Example 9.8				
Source	df	SS	MS	F	p
Treatments (brand)	3	3,298.7	1,099.6	54.31	.000
Blocks (golfer)	9	12,073.9	1,341.5		
Error	27	546.6	20.2		
Total	39	15,919.2			

EXAMPLE 9.9

Ranking Treatment Means in a Randomized Block Design—Golf Ball Study

Problem Apply Bonferroni's procedure to the data in Example 9.8. Use an experiment-wise error rate (EER) of .05 to rank the mean distances of the four golf ball brands. Interpret the results.

Solution We used Excel/XLSTAT to obtain the rankings of the means with Bonferroni's method. The XLSTAT printout is shown in Figure 9.22. Since there are $k = 4$ treatments (brands) in this design, there are $c = \frac{4(3)}{2} = 6$ pairwise comparisons of brand means to be analyzed. These comparisons (contrasts) are shown at the top of Figure 9.22. Rather than give a confidence interval for each comparison, XLSTAT provides information to determine whether the two means being compared are significantly different. You can see that when EER $= .05$, all six comparisons yield significant differences. (This is equivalent to stating that none of the six confidence intervals contain 0.) Consequently, with overall 95% confidence we can conclude that the true mean driving distances for all four golf ball brands differ from each other.

The bottom of Figure 9.22 gives the rankings of the four brands as well as the sample mean driving distances. (Note that each brand is associated with a different group letter.) So, with overall 95% confidence, we have $\mu_C > \mu_B > \mu_A > \mu_D$.

BRAND / Bonferroni / Analysis of the differences between the categories with a confidence interval of 95%:

Contrast	Difference	Standardized difference	Critical value	Pr > Diff	Significant
BrandD vs BrandC	-24.6000	-12.2253	2.8469	< 0.0001	Yes
BrandD vs BrandB	-12.4500	-6.1872	2.8469	< 0.0001	Yes
BrandD vs BrandA	-6.3200	-3.1408	2.8469	0.0041	Yes
BrandA vs BrandC	-18.2800	-9.0845	2.8469	< 0.0001	Yes
BrandA vs BrandB	-6.1300	-3.0464	2.8469	0.0051	Yes
BrandB vs BrandC	-12.1500	-6.0381	2.8469	< 0.0001	Yes
Modified significance level:			0.0083		

Category	Mean	Groups			
BrandD	220.7300	A			
BrandA	227.0500		B		
BrandB	233.1800			C	
BrandC	245.3300				D

Figure 9.22

XLSTAT output of Bonferroni rankings of golf ball brand means

● **Now Work Exercise 9.57d**

Unlike the completely randomized design, the randomized block design cannot, in general, be used to estimate individual treatment means. Whereas the completely randomized design employs a random sample for each treatment, the randomized block design does not necessarily employ a random sample of experimental units for each treatment. The experimental units within the blocks are assumed to be randomly selected, but the blocks themselves may not be randomly selected.

We can, however, test the hypothesis that the block means are significantly different. We simply compare the variability attributable to differences among the block means with that associated with sampling variability. The ratio of MSB to MSE is an F-ratio similar to that formed in testing treatment means. The F-statistic is compared with a tabled value for a specific value of α, with numerator degrees of freedom $(b - 1)$ and denominator degrees of freedom $(n - k - b + 1)$. The test is usually given on the same printout as the test for treatment means. Refer to the Minitab printout in Figure 9.21 and note that the test statistic for comparing the block means is

$$F = \frac{MSB}{MSE} = \frac{MS(Golfers)}{MS(Error)} = \frac{1,341.5}{20.2} = 66.26$$

with a p-value of .000. Because $\alpha = .05$ exceeds this p-value, we conclude that the block means are different. The results of the test are summarized in Table 9.11.

In the golf example, the test for block means confirms our suspicion that the golfers vary significantly; therefore, use of the block design was a good decision. However, be careful not to conclude that the block design was a mistake if the F-test for blocks does not result in rejection of the null hypothesis that the block means are the same.

Table 9.11	ANOVA Table for Randomized Block Design: Test for Blocks Included				
Source	df	SS	MS	F	p
Treatments (brands)	3	3,298.7	1,099.6	54.31	.000
Blocks (golfers)	9	12,073.9	1,341.5	66.26	.000
Error	27	546.6	20.2		
Total	39	15,919.2			

Remember that the possibility of a Type II error exists, and we are not controlling its probability as we are the probability α of a Type I error. If the experimenter believes that the experimental units are more homogeneous within blocks than between blocks, then he or she should use the randomized block design regardless of the results of a single test comparing the block means.

The procedure for conducting an analysis of variance for a randomized block design is summarized in the next box. Remember that the hallmark of this design is using blocks of homogeneous experimental units in which each treatment is represented.

Steps for Conducting an ANOVA for a Randomized Block Design

1. Be sure the design consists of blocks (preferably, blocks of homogeneous experimental units) and that each treatment is randomly assigned to one experimental unit in each block.

2. If possible, check the assumptions of normality and equal variances for all block-treatment combinations. [*Note:* This may be difficult to do because the design will likely have only one observation for each block-treatment combination.]

3. Create an ANOVA summary table that specifies the variability attributable to Treatments, Blocks, and Error, which leads to the calculation of the F-statistic to test the null hypothesis that the treatment means are equal in the population. Use a statistical software package or the calculation formulas in Appendix C to obtain the necessary numerical ingredients.

4. If the F-test leads to the conclusion that the means differ, use the Bonferroni, Tukey, or similar procedure to conduct multiple comparisons of as many of the pairs of means as you wish. Use the results to summarize the statistically significant differences among the treatment means. Remember that, in general, the randomized block design cannot be used to form confidence intervals for individual treatment means.

5. If the F-test leads to the nonrejection of the null hypothesis that the treatment means are equal, several possibilities exist:

   a. The treatment means are equal—that is, the null hypothesis is true.

   b. The treatment means really differ, but other important factors affecting the response are not accounted for by the randomized block design. These factors inflate the sampling variability, as measured by MSE, resulting in smaller values of the F-statistic. Either increase the sample size for each treatment or conduct an experiment that accounts for the other factors affecting the response (as in Section 9.5). Do not automatically reach the former conclusion because the possibility of a Type II error must be considered if you accept H_0.

6. If desired, conduct the F-test of the null hypothesis that the block means are equal. Rejection of this hypothesis lends statistical support to using the randomized block design.

Note: It is often difficult to check whether the assumptions for a randomized block design are satisfied. There is usually only one observation for each block-treatment combination. When you feel these assumptions are likely to be violated, a nonparametric procedure is advisable.

> **What Do You Do When Assumptions Are Not Satisfied for the Analysis of Variance for a Randomized Block Design?**
>
> *Answer:* Use a nonparametric statistical method such as the Friedman F_r test of Section 15.6.

Exercises 9.50–9.63

Learning the Mechanics

9.50 A randomized block design yielded the following partial ANOVA table.

Source	SS	df	MS	F
Treatments	—	3	—	—
Blocks	2761.5	5	—	—
Error	—	—	73.087	—
Total	4308.1	23		

a. Find the sum of squares for the treatments and the error term.

b. Find the mean of squares for the treatments and the blocks.

c. Specify the null and alternative hypotheses you would use to compare the treatment means.

d. What test statistic should be used to conduct the hypothesis of part **c**?

e. Specify the rejection region for the test in parts **c** and **d** at the 1% significance level.

f. Can we infer at the 1% significance level that the treatment means are different?

g. If the SSE is zero and the SSB is not equal to zero, can we conduct the randomized block design of the analysis of variance? Explain.

9.51 An experiment was conducted using a randomized block design. The data from the experiment are displayed in the following table.

L09051

	Block		
Treatment	1	2	3
1	2	3	5
2	8	6	7
3	7	6	5

a. Fill in the missing entries in the ANOVA table.

Source	df	SS	MS	F
Treatments	2	21.5555		
Blocks	2			
Error	4			
Total	8	30.2222		

b. Specify the null and alternative hypotheses you would use to investigate whether a difference exists among the treatment means.

c. What test statistic should be used in conducting the test of part **b**?

d. Describe the Type I and Type II errors associated with the hypothesis test of part **b**.

e. Conduct the hypothesis test of part **b** using $\alpha = .05$.

9.52 A randomized block design was used to compare the mean responses for three treatments. Four blocks of three homogeneous experimental units were selected, and each treatment was randomly assigned to one experimental unit within each block. The data are shown below, followed by an SPSS ANOVA printout for this experiment.

	Block			
Treatment	1	2	3	4
A	3.4	5.5	7.9	1.3
B	4.4	5.8	9.6	2.8
C	2.2	3.4	6.9	.3

Tests of Between-Subjects Effects

Dependent Variable: RESPONSE

Source	Type III Sum of Squares	df	Mean Square	F	Sig.
Corrected Model	83.781[a]	5	16.756	141.935	.000
Intercept	238.521	1	238.521	2020.412	.000
TREATMENT	12.032	2	6.016	50.958	.000
BLOCK	71.749	3	23.916	202.586	.000
Error	.708	6	.118		
Total	323.010	12			
Corrected Total	84.489	11			

a. R Squared = .992 (Adjusted R Squared = .985)

Multiple Comparisons

Dependent Variable: RESPONSE

Tukey HSD

(I) TREATMENT	(J) TREATMENT	Mean Difference (I-J)	Std. Error	Sig.	95% Confidence Interval	
					Lower Bound	Upper Bound
A	B	-1.125*	.2430	.009	-1.870	-.380
	C	1.325*	.2430	.004	.580	2.070
B	A	1.125*	.2430	.009	.380	1.870
	C	2.450*	.2430	.000	1.705	3.195
C	A	-1.325*	.2430	.004	-2.070	-.580
	D	-2.450*	.2430	.000	-3.195	-1.705

Based on observed means.

The error term is Mean Square(Error) = .118.

*. The mean difference is significant at the 0.05 level.

a. Use the printout to fill in the entries in the following ANOVA table.

Source	df	SS	MS	F
Treatments				
Blocks				
Error				
Total				

b. Do the data provide sufficient evidence to indicate that the treatment means differ? Use $\alpha = .05$.

c. Do the data provide sufficient evidence to indicate that blocking was effective in reducing the experimental error? Use $\alpha = .05$.

d. Use the printout to rank the treatment means at $\alpha = .05$.

e. What assumptions are necessary to ensure the validity of the inferences made in parts **b, c,** and **d**?

9.53 Suppose an experiment employing a randomized block design has four treatments and nine blocks, for a total of $4 \times 9 = 36$ observations. Assume that the Total Sum of Squares for the response is SS(Total) = 500. For each of the following partitions of SS(Total), test the null hypothesis that the treatment means are equal and test the null hypothesis that the block means are equal. Use $\alpha = .05$ for each test.

a. The Sum of Squares for Treatments (SST) is 20% of SS(Total), and the Sum of Squares for Blocks (SSB) is 30% of SS(Total).

b. SST is 50% of SS(Total), and SSB is 20% of SS(Total).

c. SST is 20% of SS(Total), and SSB is 50% of SS(Total).

d. SST is 40% of SS(Total), and SSB is 40% of SS(Total).

e. SST is 20% of SS(Total), and SSB is 20% of SS(Total).

Applying the Concepts—Basic

9.54 **Making high-stakes insurance decisions.** Refer to the *Journal of Economic Psychology* (Sep. 2008) study on high-stakes insurance decisions, Exercise 9.26 (p. 544). A second experiment involved only the group 2 subjects. In part A of the experiment, these 84 subjects were informed of the hazards (both fire and theft) of owning a valuable painting but were not told the exact probabilities of the hazards occurring. The subjects then provided an amount they were willing to pay (WTP) for insuring the painting. In part B of the experiment, these same subjects were informed of the exact probabilities of the hazards (fire and theft) of owning a valuable sculpture. The subjects then provided a WTP amount for insuring the sculpture. The researchers were interested in comparing the mean WTP amounts for the painting and the sculpture.

a. Explain why the experimental design employed is a randomized block design.

b. Identify the dependent (response) variable, treatments, and blocks for the design.

c. Give the null and alternative hypotheses of interest to the researchers.

9.55 **Peer mentor training at a firm.** Peer mentoring occurs when a more experienced employee provides one-on-one support and knowledge sharing with a less experienced

employee. The *Journal of Managerial Issues* (Spring 2008) published a study of the impact of peer mentor training at a large software company. Participants were 222 employees who volunteered to attend a 1-day peer mentor training session. One variable of interest was the employee's level of competence in peer mentoring (measured on a 7-point scale). The competence level of each trainee was measured at three different times in the study: 1 week before training, 2 days after training, and 2 months after training. One goal of the experiment was to compare the mean competence levels of the three time periods.

a. Explain why these data should be analyzed using a randomized block design. As part of your answer, identify the blocks and the treatments.

b. A partial ANOVA table for the experiment is shown below. Explain why there is enough information in the table to make conclusions.

Source	df	SS	MS	F-Value	p-Value
Time Period	2	—	—	—	0.001
Blocks	221	—	—	—	0.001
Error	442	—	—		
Total	665	—			

c. State the null hypothesis of interest to the researcher.

d. Make the appropriate conclusion.

e. A multiple comparisons of means for the three time periods (using an experimentwise error rate of .10) is summarized below. Fully interpret the results.

Sample mean:	3.65	4.14	4.17
Time period:	*before*	*2 months after*	*2 days after*

9.56 **Solar energy generation along highways.** The potential of solar panels on roofs built above national highways as a source of solar energy was investigated in the *International Journal of Energy and Environmental Engineering* (December, 2013). Computer simulation was used to estimate the monthly solar energy (kilowatt-hours) generated from solar panels installed across a 200-kilometer stretch of highway in India. Each month, the simulation was run under each of four conditions: single-layer solar panels, double-layer solar panels 1 meter apart, double-layer solar panels 2 meters apart, and double-layer solar panels 3 meters apart. The data for 12 months are shown in the table. To compare the mean solar energy values generated by the four panel configurations, a randomized block design ANOVA was conducted. A Minitab printout of the analysis is provided on the next page.

Month	Single Layer	Double Layer		
		1-meter	2-meters	3-meters
January	7,308	8,917	9,875	10,196
February	6,984	8,658	9,862	9,765
March	7,874	9,227	11,092	11,861
April	7,328	7,930	9,287	10,343
May	7,089	7,605	8,422	9,110
June	5,730	6,350	7,069	7,536
July	4,531	5,120	5,783	6,179
August	4,587	5,171	5,933	6,422
September	5,985	6,862	8,208	8,925

Month	Single Layer	Double Layer		
		1-meter	2-meters	3-meters
October	7,051	8,608	10,008	10,239
November	6,724	8,264	9,238	9,334
December	6,883	8,297	9,144	9,808

Source: Republished with permission of Springer, from P. Sharma and T. Harinarayana, "Solar Energy Generation Potential Along National Highways," *International Journal of Energy and Environmental Engineering*, Vol. 49, No. 1, December 2013 (Table 3). Permission conveyed through Copyright Clearance Center, Inc.

```
Analysis of Variance for Energy

Source     DF      SS        MS       F      P
Condition   3   49730750  16576917  115.54  0.000
Month      11   90618107   8238010   57.42  0.000
Error      33    4734730    143477
Total      47  145083587


S = 378.783   R-Sq = 96.74%   R-Sq(adj) = 95.35%
```

Minitab Output for Exercise 9.56

a. Identify the dependent variable, treatments, and blocks for this experiment.

b. What null hypothesis would you test to compare the mean solar energy values generated by the four panel configurations?

c. Carry out the test, part **b.** Give the F-value and associated p-value.

d. What conclusion can you draw from the analysis?

9.57 **Interactive video games and physical fitness.** Wii Fit is an interactive video game marketed to consumers who want to increase their physical fitness level. The effectiveness of Wii Fit activities relative to other physical activities was investigated in the *Journal of Physical Activity and Health* (Vol. 7, 2010). A sample of 15 young adults (ages 21–38 years) participated in the study. Each adult completed a total of eight activities—rest, handheld gaming, Wii yoga, Wii muscle conditioning, Wii balance, Wii aerobics, brisk treadmill walking, and treadmill jogging. At the end of each session, the heart rate (beats per minute) of the participant was recorded. Since the goal was to compare mean heart rates across the eight activities, and since each adult completed all activities, a randomized block design ANOVA was conducted.

a. Identify the treatments for this experiment.

b. Identify the blocks for this experiment.

c. The ANOVA F-test for treatments resulted in a p-value of .001. Interpret this result using $\alpha = .01$.

d. Multiple comparisons (with an experimentwise error rate of .05) of the mean heart rates for the eight activities revealed the following. (*Note:* Means with the same letter are not significantly different.) Provide a ranking of the treatment means.

	Mean Heart Rate
Rest	58.3 a
Handheld gaming	65.6 a
Wii balance	76.7 b
Wii yoga	77.6 b
Wii muscle conditioning	82.4 b
Wii aerobics	94.5 b
Brisk treadmill walking	108.3 c
Treadmill jogging	153.7 d

9.58 **Taste testing scales.** Before marketing a new food product, companies evaluate the palatability of the food item using a numerical taste test scale. For example, the Hedonic 9-point scale uses the following ratings: 1 = dislike extremely, 2 = dislike very much, 3 = dislike moderately, 4 = dislike slightly, 5 = neither like nor dislike, 6 = like slightly, 7 = like moderately, 8 = like very much, and 9 = like extremely. Another scale, called the general Labeled Magnitude Scale (gLMS) uses ratings that range from –100 (for strongest imaginable dislike) to +100 (for strongest imaginable like). Both of these scales were applied to food items in a study published in the *Journal of Food Science* (February 2014). Students and staff at the University of Florida taste-tested five food/beverage items: black coffee (BC), cheesecake (CC), grapefruit juice (GF), orange juice (OJ), and pepperoni (PP). Half ($n = 200$) of the subjects used the 9-point scale and half ($n = 200$) used gLMS to rate each of the food items. (These ratings, simulated from information provided in the article, are saved in the **TASTE** file.) One of the objectives of the research was to compare the average 9-point taste ratings of the five food/beverage items.

a. Explain why these data should be analyzed using an ANOVA for a randomized block design. Identify the treatments, blocks, and dependent variable for this design.

b. An Excel/XLSTAT printout of the ANOVA is shown below, followed by a multiple comparisons of food item means summary. Interpret the results, practically.

c. Refer to part **b.** Perform a similar analysis for the data on the gLMS rating scale. Again, interpret the results, practically.

Regression of variable Hedonic9:					
Analysis of variance:					
Source	DF	Sum of squares	Mean squares	F	Pr > F
Model	203	3823.6770	18.8358	9.6599	< 0.0001
Error	796	1552.1140	1.9499		
Corrected	999	5375.7910			
Computed against model Y=Mean(Y)					

Type III Sum of Squares analysis:					
Source	DF	Sum of squares	Mean squares	F	Pr > F
Taster	199	436.9910	2.1959	1.1262	0.1369
Food	4	3386.6860	846.6715	434.2146	< 0.0001

Food / Bonferroni / Analysis of the differences between the categories with a confidence interval of 95%:				
Category	Mean		Groups	
BC	3.0750	A		
GF	3.3700	A		
PP	6.6500		B	
OJ	6.7850		B	
CC	7.3850			C

Applying the Concepts—Intermediate

9.59 **A new method of evaluating health care research reports.** When evaluating research reports in health care, a popular tool is the Assessment of Multiple Systematic Reviews (AMSTAR). AMSTAR, which incorporates

11 items (questions), has been widely accepted by professional health associations. A group of dental researchers has revised the assessment tool and named it R-AMSTAR (*The Open Dentistry Journal*, Vol. 4, 2010). The revised assessment tool was validated on five systematic reviews (named R1, R2, R3, R4, and R5) on rheumatoid arthritis. For each review, scores on the 11 R-AMSTAR items (all measured on a 4-point scale) were obtained. The data are shown in the table at the bottom of the page.

a. One goal of the study was to compare the mean item scores of the five reviews. Set up the null and alternative hypotheses for this test.

b. Examine the data in the table and explain why a randomized block ANOVA is appropriate to apply.

c. The Minitab output for a randomized block ANOVA of the data (with Review as treatments and Item as blocks) appears below. Interpret the *p*-values of the tests shown.

d. The Minitab printout also reports the results of a Tukey multiple comparison analysis of the five Review means. Which pairs of means are significantly different? Do these results agree with your conclusion in part **c**?

e. The experimentwise error rate used in the analysis of part **d** is .05. Interpret this value.

General Linear Model: SCORE versus REVIEW, ITEM

```
Analysis of Variance

Source   DF  Adj SS  Adj MS  F-Value  P-Value
  REVIEW   4   2.518  0.6295     1.22    0.319
  ITEM    10  43.500  4.3500     8.41    0.000
Error     40  20.682  0.5170
Total     54  66.700

Model Summary

      S   R-sq  R-sq(adj)  R-sq(pred)
0.719059  68.99%    58.14%      41.38%


Grouping Information Using the Tukey Method and 95% Confidence

REVIEW   N    Mean  Grouping
R5      11  3.18182  A
R2      11  3.04545  A
R3      11  2.86364  A
R4      11  2.86364  A
R1      11  2.54545  A

Means that do not share a letter are significantly different.
```

9.60 **Reducing on-the-job stress.** Plant therapists believe that plants can reduce on-the-job stress. A Kansas State PLANTS University study was conducted to investigate this phenomenon. Two weeks prior to final exams, 10 undergraduate students took part in an experiment to determine what effect the presence of a live plant, a photo of a plant, or absence of a plant has on a student's ability to relax while isolated in a dimly lit room. Each student participated in three sessions—one with a live plant, one with a plant photo, and one with no plant (control).* During each session, finger temperature was measured at 1-minute intervals for 20 minutes. Because increasing finger temperature indicates an increased level of relaxation, the maximum temperature (in degrees) was used as the response variable. For example, one student's finger measured 95.6° in the "Live Plant" condition, 92.6° in the "Plant Photo" condition, and 96.6° in the "No Plant" condition. The temperatures under the three conditions for the other nine students follow: Student 2 (95.6°, 94.8°, 96.0°), Student 3 (96.0°, 97.2°, 96.2°), Student 4 (95.2°, 94.6°, 95.7°), Student 5 (96.7°, 95.5°, 94.8°), Student 6 (96.0°, 96.6°, 93.5°), Student 7 (93.7°, 96.2°, 96.7°), Student 8 (97.0°, 95.8°, 95.4°), Student 9 (94.9°, 96.6°, 90.5°), Student 10 (91.4°, 93.5°, 96.6°). These data (based on data from Elizabeth Schreiber, Department of Statistics, Kansas State University, Manhattan, Kansas) are saved in the accompanying file. Conduct an ANOVA and make the proper inferences at $\alpha = .10$.

9.61 **Irrelevant facial similarity effects on judgment.** Facial simi- larity to previously encountered persons can be a potential MORPH source of bias in decision making. For example, in a job interview, the interviewer should judge the job candidate solely on his or her qualifications, not on whether the candidate looks similar to a previously rejected candidate. Research published in *Experimental Psychology* (January 2014) investigated irrelevant facial similarity effects on judgment. Subjects (university students) were trained to evaluate employees' suitability for a job on a scale of 0 (not at all suitable) to 100 (very suitable). Then each subject rated each of three different job applicants. Each subject saw a picture of the applicant as well as a summary of the employee's application documents. Unknown to the subject, all the applicants were given average qualifications, but one applicant's picture was morphed to look similar to a candidate who had been given a low rating during training (low-performance morph) and another was morphed to look similar to a candidate who had been given a

Data for Exercise 9.59

Review	Item 1	Item 2	Item 3	Item 4	Item 5	Item 6	Item 7	Item 8	Item 9	Item 10	Item 11
R1	4.0	1.0	4.0	2.0	3.5	3.5	3.5	3.5	1.0	1.0	1.0
R2	3.5	2.5	4.0	4.0	3.5	4.0	3.5	2.5	3.5	1.5	1.0
R3	4.0	4.0	3.5	4.0	1.5	2.5	3.5	3.5	2.5	1.5	1.0
R4	3.5	2.0	4.0	4.0	2.0	4.0	3.5	3.0	3.5	1.0	1.0
R5	3.5	4.0	4.0	3.0	2.5	4.0	4.0	4.0	2.5	1.0	2.5

Source: J. Kung et al., "From Systematic Reviews to Clinical Recommendations to Clinical-Based Health Care: Validation of Revised Assessment of Multiple Systematic Reviews (R-AMSTAR) for Grading of Clinical Relevance," *The Open Dentistry Journal*, Vol. 4, 2010 (Table 2). Copyright © Kung et al.; Licensee Bentham Open.

*The experiment is simplified for this exercise. The actual experiment involved 30 students who participated in 12 sessions.

high rating during training (high-performance morph). The third candidate was given a neutral photo—one that had not been seen before by the subjects. Suitability data (simulated based on information provided in the article) for 10 subjects rating each of the 3 candidates are provided in the table. Are there differences in the mean ratings of the three candidates? If so, which candidate (low, neutral, or high) received the highest mean rating?

Subject	Low	Neutral	High
1	52	55	57
2	46	55	49
3	61	61	64
4	52	45	53
5	26	25	30
6	43	47	50
7	47	48	44
8	54	56	59
9	77	82	91
10	41	50	49

9.62 **Stress in cows prior to slaughter.** What is the level of stress (if any) that cows undergo prior to being slaughtered? To answer this question, researchers designed an experiment involving cows bred in Normandy, France (*Applied Animal Behaviour Science,* June 2010). The heart rate (beats per minute) of a cow was measured at four different pre-slaughter phases—(1) first phase of visual contact with pen mates, (2) initial isolation from pen mates for prepping, (3) restoration of visual contact with pen mates, and (4) first contact with human prior to slaughter. Data for eight cows (simulated from information provided in the article) are shown in the accompanying table. The researchers analyzed the data using an analysis of variance for a randomized block design. Their objective was to determine whether the mean heart rate of cows differed in the four pre-slaughter phases.

	PHASE			
COW	1	2	3	4
1	124	124	109	107
2	100	98	98	99
3	103	98	100	106
4	94	91	98	95
5	122	109	114	115
6	103	92	100	106
7	98	80	99	103
8	120	84	107	110

Source: Based on *Applied Animal Behaviour Science.*

a. Identify the treatments and blocks for this experimental design.

b. Conduct the appropriate analysis using a statistical software package. Summarize the results in an ANOVA table.

c. Is there evidence of differences among the mean heart rates of cows in the four pre-slaughter phases? Test using $\alpha = .05$.

Coating systems characteristics for Exercise 9.63

d. If warranted, conduct a multiple comparisons procedure to rank the four treatment means. Use an experimentwise error rate of $\alpha = .05$.

Applying the Concepts—Advanced

9.63 **Anticorrosive behavior of steel coated with epoxy.** Organic coatings that use epoxy resins are widely used for protecting steel and metal against weathering and corrosion. Researchers at National Technical University (Athens, Greece) examined the steel anticorrosive behavior of different epoxy coatings formulated with zinc pigments in an attempt to find the epoxy coating with the best corrosion inhibition (*Pigment & Resin Technology,* Vol. 32, 2003). The experimental units were flat, rectangular panels cut from steel sheets. Each panel was coated with one of four different coating systems, S1, S2, S3, and S4. Three panels were prepared for each coating system. (These panels are labeled S1-A, S1-B, S1-C, S2-A, S2-B, . . . , S4-C.) The characteristics of the four coating systems are listed at the bottom of the page.

Each coated panel was immersed in deionized and deaerated water and then tested for corrosion. Because exposure time is likely to have a strong influence on anticorrosive behavior, the researchers attempted to remove this extraneous source of variation through the experimental design. Exposure times were fixed at 24 hours, 60 days, and 120 days. For each of the coating systems, one panel was exposed to water for 24 hours, one exposed to water for 60 days, and one exposed to water for 120 days in random order. The design is illustrated in the accompanying table.

Exposure Time	Coating System/Panel Exposed
24 hours	S1-A, S2-C, S3-C, S4-B
60 days	S1-C, S2-A, S3-B, S4-A
120 days	S1-B, S2-B, S3-A, S4-C

Following exposure, the corrosion rate (nanoamperes per square centimeter) was determined for each panel. The lower the corrosion rate, the greater the anticorrosion performance of the coating system. The data are shown in the next table. Are there differences among the epoxy treatment means? If so, which of the epoxy coating systems yields the lowest corrosion rate?

Exposure Time	System S1	System S2	System S3	System S4
24 hours	6.7	7.5	8.2	6.1
60 days	8.7	9.1	10.5	8.3
120 days	11.8	12.6	14.5	11.8

Source: Republished with permission of Emerald Group Publishing Limited, from N. Kouloumbi, P. Pantazopoulou, and P. Moundoulas, "Anticorrosion Performance of Epoxy Coatings on Steel Surface Exposed to Deionized Water," *Pigment & Resin Technology,* Vol. 32, No. 2, 2003, pp. 89–99 (Table II). Permission conveyed through Copyright Clearance Center, Inc.

Coating System	1st Layer	2nd Layer
S1	Zinc dust	Epoxy paint, 100 micrometers thick
S2	Zinc phosphate	Epoxy paint, 100 micrometers thick
S3	Zinc phosphate with mica	Finish layer, 100 micrometers thick
S4	Zinc phosphate with mica	Finish layer, 200 micrometers thick

9.5   Factorial Experiments: Two Factors

All of the experiments discussed in Sections 9.2–9.4 were **single-factor experiments.** The treatments were levels of a single factor, with the sampling of experimental units performed using either a completely randomized or a randomized block design. However, most responses are affected by more than one factor, and we will therefore often wish to design experiments involving more than one factor.

Consider an experiment in which the effects of two factors on the response are being investigated. Assume that factor A is to be investigated at a levels and factor B at b levels. Recalling that treatments are factor-level combinations, you can see that the experiment has, potentially, ab treatments that could be included in the experiment. A *complete factorial experiment* is one in which all possible ab treatments are employed.

> A **complete factorial experiment** is one in which every factor-level combination is employed—that is, the number of treatments in the experiment equals the total number of factor-level combinations.

For example, suppose the USGA wants to determine not only the relationship between distance and brand of golf ball but also between distance and the club used to hit the ball. If they decide to use four brands and two clubs (say, driver and five-iron) in the experiment, then a complete factorial would call for employing all $4 \times 2 = 8$ Brand-Club combinations. This experiment is referred to more specifically as a *complete 4 × 2 factorial*. A layout for a two-factor factorial experiment (we are henceforth referring to a *complete factorial* when we use the term *factorial*) is given in Table 9.12. The factorial experiment is also referred to as a **two-way classification** because it can be arranged in the row-column format exhibited in Table 9.12.

Table 9.12	Schematic Layout of Two-Factor Factorial Experiment				
		Factor B at b Levels			
	Level	1	2	3	... b
	1	Trt. 1	Trt. 2	Trt. 3	... Trt. b
	2	Trt. $b + 1$	Trt. $b + 2$	Trt. $b + 3$	... Trt. $2b$
Factor A at a **Levels**	3	Trt. $2b + 1$	Trt. $2b + 2$	Trt. $2b + 3$	... Trt. $3b$
	⋮	⋮	⋮	⋮	... ⋮
	a	Trt. $(a - 1)b + 1$	Trt. $(a - 1)b + 2$	Trt. $(a - 1)b + 3$	... Trt. ab

To complete the specification of the experimental design, the treatments must be assigned to the experimental units. If the assignment of the ab treatments in the factorial experiment is random and independent, the design is completely randomized. For example, if the machine Iron Byron is used to hit 80 golf balls, 10 for each of the eight Brand-Club combinations, in a random sequence, the design would be completely randomized. In the remainder of this section, we confine our attention to factorial experiments employing completely randomized designs.

If we employ a completely randomized design to conduct a factorial experiment with ab treatments, we can proceed with the analysis in exactly the same way as we did in Section 9.2—that is, we calculate (or let the computer calculate) the measure of treatment mean variability (MST) and the measure of sampling variability (MSE) and use the F-ratio of these two quantities to test the null hypothesis that the treatment means are equal. However, if this hypothesis is rejected, so that we conclude some differences exist among the treatment means, important questions remain. Are both factors affecting the response or only one? If both, do they affect the response independently, or do they interact to affect the response?

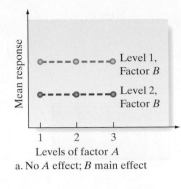

a. No A effect; B main effect

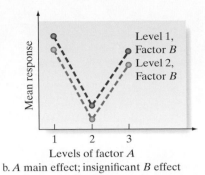

b. A main effect; insignificant B effect

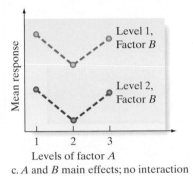

c. A and B main effects; no interaction

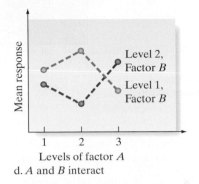

d. A and B interact

Figure 9.23

Illustration of possible treatment effects: factorial experiment

For example, suppose the distance data indicate that at least two of the eight treatment (Brand-Club combinations) means differ in the golf experiment. Does the brand of ball (factor A) or the club used (factor B) affect mean distance, or do both affect it? Several possibilities are shown in Figure 9.23. In Figure 9.23a, the brand means are equal (only three are shown for the purpose of illustration), but the distances differ for the two levels of factor B (Club). Thus, there is no effect of Brand on distance, but a Club main effect is present. In Figure 9.23b, the Brand means differ, but the Club means are equal for each Brand. Here a Brand main effect is present, but no effect of Club is present.

Figures 9.23c and 9.23d illustrate cases in which both factors affect the response. In Figure 9.23c, the mean distances between Clubs does not change for the three Brands, so that the effect of Brand on distance is independent of Club—that is, the two factors Brand and Club *do not interact*. In contrast, Figure 9.23d shows that the difference between mean distances between Clubs varies with Brand. Thus, the effect of Brand on distance depends on Club, and therefore the two factors *do interact*.

To determine the nature of the treatment effect, if any, on the response in a factorial experiment, we need to break the treatment variability into three components: Interaction between Factors A and B, Main Effect of Factor A, and Main Effect of Factor B. The **Factor Interaction** component is used to test whether the factors combine to affect the response, while the **Factor Main Effect** components are used to determine whether the factors separately affect the response.

Now Work Exercise 9.71c

The partitioning of the Total Sum of Squares into its various components is illustrated in Figure 9.24. Notice that at stage 1, the components are identical to those in the one-factor, completely randomized designs of Section 9.2; the Sums of Squares for Treatments and Error sum to the Total Sum of Squares. The degrees of freedom for treatments is equal to $(ab - 1)$, one less than the number of treatments. The degrees of freedom for error is equal to $(n - ab)$, the total sample size minus the number of treatments. Only at stage 2 of the partitioning does the factorial experiment differ from those previously discussed. Here we divide the Treatments Sum of Squares into its three components: Interaction and the two Main Effects. These components can then be used to test the nature of the differences, if any, among the treatment means.

There are a number of ways to proceed in the testing and estimation of factors in a factorial experiment. We present one approach in the next box.

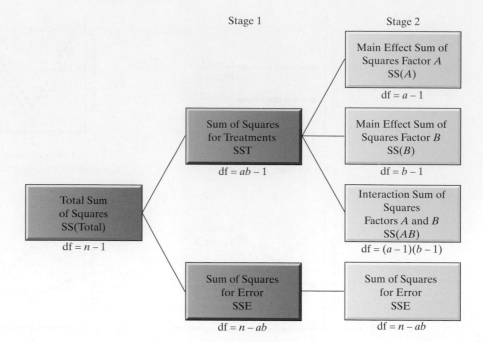

Stage 1   Stage 2

Figure 9.24

Partitioning the Total Sum of Squares for a two-factor factorial

Procedure for Analysis of Two-Factor Factorial Experiment

1. Partition the Total Sum of Squares into the Treatments and Error components (stage 1 of Figure 9.24). Use either a statistical software package or the calculation formulas in Appendix C to accomplish the partitioning.

2. Use the F-ratio of Mean Square for Treatments to Mean Square for Error to test the null hypothesis that the treatment means are equal.*

   a. If the test results in nonrejection of the null hypothesis, consider refining the experiment by increasing the number of replications or introducing other factors. Also consider the possibility that the response is unrelated to the two factors.

   b. If the test results in rejection of the null hypothesis, then proceed to step 3.

3. Partition the Treatments Sum of Squares into the Main Effect and Interaction Sum of Squares (stage 2 of Figure 9.24). Use either a statistical software package or the calculation formulas in Appendix C to accomplish the partitioning.

4. Test the null hypothesis that factors A and B do not interact to affect the response by computing the F-ratio of the Mean Square for Interaction to the Mean Square for Error.

   a. If the test results in nonrejection of the null hypothesis, proceed to step 5.

   b. If the test results in rejection of the null hypothesis, conclude that the two factors interact to affect the mean response. Then proceed to step 6a.

5. Conduct tests of two null hypotheses that the mean response is the same at each level of factor A and factor B. Compute two F-ratios by comparing the Mean Square for each Factor Main Effect with the Mean Square for Error.

   a. If one or both tests result in rejection of the null hypothesis, conclude that the factor affects the mean response. Proceed to step 6b.

*Some analysts prefer to proceed directly to test the interaction and main effect components, skipping the test of treatment means. We begin with this test to be consistent with our approach in the one-factor completely randomized design.

b. If both tests result in nonrejection, an apparent contradiction has occurred. Although the treatment means apparently differ (step 2 test), the interaction (step 4) and main effect (step 5) tests have not supported that result. Further experimentation is advised.

6. Compare the means:
   a. If the test for interaction (step 4) is significant, use a multiple comparisons procedure to compare any or all pairs of the treatment means.

   b. If the test for one or both main effects (step 5) is significant, use a multiple comparisons procedure to compare the pairs of means corresponding to the levels of the significant factor(s).

We assume the completely randomized design is a balanced design, meaning that the same number of observations are made for each treatment—that is, we assume that r experimental units are randomly and independently selected for each treatment. The numerical value of r must exceed 1 in order to have any degrees of freedom with which to measure the sampling variability. [Note that if $r = 1$, then $n = ab$, and the degrees of freedom associated with Error (Figure 9.24) is df $= n - ab = 0$.] The value of r is often referred to as the number of **replicates** of the factorial experiment because we assume that all ab treatments are repeated, or replicated, r times. Whatever approach is adopted in the analysis of a factorial experiment, several tests of hypotheses are usually conducted. The tests are summarized in the next box.

ANOVA Tests Conducted for Factorial Experiments: Completely Randomized Design, r Replicates per Treatment

Test for Treatment Means

H_0: No difference among the ab treatment means
H_a: At least two treatment means differ

Test statistic: $F = \dfrac{\text{MST}}{\text{MSE}}$

Rejection region: $F > F_\alpha$
p-value: $P(F > F_c)$

where F_c is the calculated value of the test statistic and F is based on $(ab - 1)$ numerator and $(n - ab)$ denominator degrees of freedom [*Note*: $n = abr$.]

Test for Factor Interaction

H_0: Factors A and B do not interact to affect the response mean.
H_a: Factors A and B do interact to affect the response mean.

Test statistic: $F = \dfrac{\text{MS}(AB)}{\text{MSE}}$

Rejection region: $F > F_\alpha$
p-value: $P(F > F_c)$
where F is based on $(a - 1)(b - 1)$ numerator and $(n - ab)$ denominator degrees of freedom

Test for Main Effect of Factor A

H_0: No difference among the a mean levels of factor A
H_a: At least two factor A mean levels differ

Test statistic: $F = \dfrac{\text{MS}(A)}{\text{MSE}}$

Rejection region: $F > F_\alpha$
p-value: $P(F > F_c)$
where F is based on $(a - 1)$ numerator and $(n - ab)$ denominator degrees of freedom

Test for Main Effect of Factor B

H_0: No difference among the b mean levels of factor B
H_a: At least two factor B mean levels differ

Test statistic: $F = \dfrac{MS(B)}{MSE}$

Rejection region: $F > F_\alpha$
p-value: $P(F > F_c)$

where F is based on $(b - 1)$ numerator and $(n - ab)$ denominator degrees of freedom

---

Conditions Required for Valid F-Tests in Factorial Experiments

1. The response distribution for each factor-level combination (treatment) is normal.
2. The response variance is constant for all treatments.
3. Random and independent samples of experimental units are associated with each treatment.

EXAMPLE 9.10

Conducting a Factorial ANOVA—Golf Ball Study

Problem The USGA is interested in knowing whether the difference in distance traveled by any two golf ball brands depends on the club used. Consequently, the USGA tests four different brands (A, B, C, D) of golf balls and two different clubs (driver, five-iron) in a completely randomized design. Each of the eight Brand-Club combinations (treatments) is randomly and independently assigned to four experimental units, each experimental unit consisting of a specific position in the sequence of hits by Iron Byron. The distance response is recorded for each of the 32 hits, and the results are shown in Table 9.13.

Table 9.13	Distance Data for 4 × 2 Factorial Golf Experiment			
			Brand	
		A	B	C	D
Club	Driver	226.4	238.3	240.5	219.8
		232.6	231.7	246.9	228.7
		234.0	227.7	240.3	232.9
		220.7	237.2	244.7	237.6
	Five-Iron	163.8	184.4	179.0	157.8
		179.4	180.6	168.0	161.8
		168.6	179.5	165.2	162.1
		173.4	186.2	156.5	160.3

Data Set: GLFAC1

a. Use a statistical software package to partition the Total Sum of Squares into the components necessary to analyze this 4 × 2 factorial experiment.

b. Conduct the appropriate ANOVA tests and interpret the results of your analysis. Use $\alpha = .10$ for each test you conduct.

c. If appropriate, conduct multiple comparisons of the treatment means. Use an experimentwise error rate of .10. Illustrate the comparisons with a graph.

Solution

a. The SPSS printout that partitions the Total Sum of Squares [i.e., SS(Total)] for this factorial experiment is given in Figure 9.25. The value SS(Total) = 34,482.049,

Tests of Between-Subjects Effects

Dependent Variable: DISTANCE

Source	Type III Sum of Squares	df	Mean Square	F	Sig.
Corrected Model	33659.809[a]	7	4808.544	140.354	.000
Intercept	1306778.611	1	1306778.611	38142.983	.000
BRAND	800.736	3	266.912	7.791	.001
CLUB	32093.111	1	32093.111	936.752	.000
BRAND * CLUB	765.961	3	255.320	7.452	.001
Error	822.240	24	34.260		
Total	1341260.660	32			
Corrected Total	34482.049	31			

a. R Squared = .976 (Adjusted R Squared = .969)

Figure 9.25

SPSS ANOVA for factorial experiment on golf ball data

shown as "Corrected Total SS" at the bottom of the printout, is partitioned into the "Corrected Model" (i.e., Treatment) and Error Sums of Squares. Note that SST = 33,659.09 (with 7 df) and SSE = 822.24 (with 24 df) add to SS(Total) (with 31 df). The Treatment Sum of Squares, SST, is further divided into Main Effect (Brand and Club) and Interaction Sum of Squares. These values, highlighted on Figure 9.25, are SS(Brand) = 800.7 (with 3 df), SS(Club) = 32,093.1 (with 1 df), and SS(Brand × Club) = 766.0 (with 3 df).

b. Once partitioning is accomplished, our first test is

H_0: The eight treatment means are equal.

H_a: At least two of the eight means differ.

Test statistic: $F = \dfrac{MST}{MSE} = 140.354$ (top line of printout)

Observed significance level: $p = .000$ (top line of printout)

Because $\alpha = .10$ exceeds p, we reject this null hypothesis and conclude that at least two of the Brand-Club combinations differ in mean distance.

After accepting the hypothesis that the treatment means differ, and therefore that the factors Brand and/or Club somehow affect the mean distance, we want to determine how the factors affect the mean response. We begin with a test of interaction between Brand and Club:

H_0: The factors Brand and Club do not interact to affect the mean response.

H_a: Brand and Club interact to affect mean response.

Test statistic: $F = \dfrac{MS(AB)}{MSE} = \dfrac{MS(\text{Brand} \times \text{Club})}{MSE}$

$= \dfrac{255.32}{34.26} = 7.452$ (bottom of printout)

Observed significance level: $p = .001$ (bottom of printout)

Because $\alpha = .10$ exceeds the p-value, we conclude that the factors Brand and Club interact to affect mean distance.

Because the factors interact, we do not test the main effects for Brand and Club. Instead, we compare the treatment means in an attempt to learn the nature of the interaction in part **c.**

c. Rather than compare all $8(7)/2 = 28$ pairs of treatment means, we test for differences only between pairs of brands within each club. That differences exist *between* clubs can be assumed. Therefore, only $4(3)/2 = 6$ pairs of means need to be compared for each club, or a total of 12 comparisons for the two clubs. The results of these comparisons using Tukey's method with an experimentwise error rate of $\alpha = .10$ for each club are displayed in the SPSS printout, Figure 9.26. For each club, the brand means are listed in descending order in Figure 9.26, and those not significantly different are listed in the same "Homogeneous Subset" column.

CLUB=5IRON
Tukey HSD[a,b]

BRAND	N	Subset 1	Subset 2
D	4	160.500	
C	4	167.175	
A	4	171.300	
B	4		182.675
Sig.		.103	1.000

Means for groups in homogeneous subsets are displayed.
Based on observed means.
The error term is Mean Square(Error) = 36.108.

a. Uses Harmonic Mean Sample Size = 4.000.

b. Alpha = .10.

CLUB=DRIVER
Tukey HSD[a,b]

BRAND	N	Subset 1	Subset 2
A	4	228.425	
D	4	229.750	
B	4	233.725	233.725
C	4		243.100
Sig.		.570	.146

Means for groups in homogeneous subsets are displayed.
Based on observed means.
The error term is Mean Square(Error) = 32.412.

a. Uses Harmonic Mean Sample Size = 4.000.

b. Alpha = .10.

Figure 9.26

SPSS ranking of brand means for each level of club

As shown in Figure 9.26, the picture is unclear with respect to Brand means. For the five-iron (top of Figure 9.26), the Brand B mean significantly exceeds all other brands. However, when hit with a driver (bottom of Figure 9.26), Brand B's mean is not significantly different from any of the other brands. The Club × Brand interaction can be seen in the SPSS plot of means in Figure 9.27. Note that the difference between the mean distances of the two clubs (driver and five-iron) varies depending on brand. The biggest difference appears for Brand C, while the smallest difference is for Brand B.

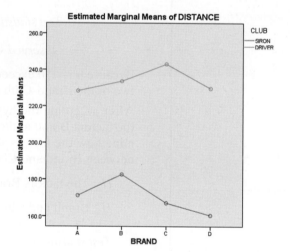

Figure 9.27

SPSS means plot for factorial golf ball experiment

Look Back Note the nontransitive nature of the multiple comparisons. For example, for the driver, the Brand C mean can be "the same" as the Brand B mean, and the Brand B mean can be "the same" as the Brand D mean, and yet the Brand C mean can significantly exceed the Brand D mean. The reason lies in the definition of "the same"—we must be careful not to conclude two means are equal simply because they are placed in the same subgroup or connected by a vertical line. The line indicates only that *the connected means are not significantly different.* You should conclude (at the overall α level of significance) only that means not connected are different, while withholding judgment on those that are connected. The picture of which means differ and by how much will become clearer as we increase the number of replicates of the factorial experiment.

Now Work Exercise 9.72

As with completely randomized and randomized block designs, the results of a factorial ANOVA are typically presented in an ANOVA summary table. Table 9.14 gives the general form of the ANOVA table, while Table 9.15 gives the ANOVA table for the golf ball data analyzed in Example 9.10. A two-factor factorial is characterized by four sources of variation—Factor A, Factor B, $A \times B$ interaction, and Error—which sum to the total Sum of Squares.

Table 9.14	General ANOVA Summary Table for a Two-Factor Factorial Experiment with r Replicates, where Factor A Has a Levels and Factor B Has b Levels			
Source	df	SS	MS	F
A	$a - 1$	SSA	MSA	MSA/MSE
B	$b - 1$	SSB	MSB	MSB/MSE
AB	$(a - 1)(b - 1)$	SSAB	MSAB	MSAB/MSE
Error	$ab(r - 1)$	SSE	MSE	
Total	$n - 1$	SS(Total)		

Table 9.15	ANOVA Summary Table for Example 9.10			
Source	df	SS	MS	F
Brand	1	32,093.11	32,093.11	936.75
Club	3	800.74	266.91	7.79
Interaction	3	765.96	255.32	7.45
Error	24	822.24	34.26	
Total	31	34,482.05		

EXAMPLE 9.11

More Practice on Conducting a Factorial Analysis—Golf Ball Study

Problem Refer to Example 9.10. Suppose the same factorial experiment is performed on four other brands (E, F, G, and H), and the results are as shown in Table 9.16. Repeat the factorial analysis and interpret the results.

Table 9.16	Distance Data for Second Factorial Golf Experiment				
		Brand			
		E	F	G	H
Club	**Driver**	238.6	261.4	264.7	235.4
		241.9	261.3	262.9	239.8
		236.6	254.0	253.5	236.2
		244.9	259.9	255.6	237.5
	Five-Iron	165.2	179.2	189.0	171.4
		156.9	171.0	191.2	159.3
		172.2	178.0	191.3	156.6
		163.2	182.7	180.5	157.4

Data Set: GLFAC2

Solution The Minitab printout for the second factorial experiment is shown in Figure 9.28. We conduct several tests, as outlined in the box on page 571.

General Linear Model: DISTANCE versus BRAND, CLUB

```
Analysis of Variance

Source       DF    Adj SS    Adj MS   F-Value   P-Value
  BRAND       3    3410.3    1136.8     46.21     0.000
  CLUB        1   46443.9   46443.9   1887.94     0.000
  BRAND*CLUB  3     105.2      35.1      1.42     0.260
Error        24     590.4      24.6
Total        31   50549.8

Model Summary

      S     R-sq   R-sq(adj)   R-sq(pred)
4.95987   98.83%      98.49%       97.92%
```

Figure 9.28

Minitab analysis for second factorial golf experiment

Test for Equality of Treatment Means

Note that Minitab (unlike SPSS) does not automatically conduct the F-test for treatment differences. Consequently, to conduct this test, we must first calculate the Sum of Squares for Treatments. Using the Sums of Squares for Brands, Clubs, and Interaction (Brand*Club) shown on the printout, we obtain

$$SS(Treatments) = SS(Clubs) + SS(Brands) + SS(Interaction)$$
$$= 46,443.9 + 3,410.3 + 105.2 = 49,959.4$$

For this 4×2 factorial experiment, there are eight treatments. Then

$$MS(Treatments) = SS(Treatments)/(8 - 1) = 49,959.4/7 = 7,137.1$$

The test statistic is

$$F = MS(Treatments)/MSE = 7,137.1/24.6 = 290.1$$

Because this F-value exceeds the critical value of $F_{.10} = 1.98$ (obtained from Table V in Appendix D), we reject the null hypothesis of no treatment differences and conclude that at least two of the Brand-Club combinations have significantly different mean distances.

Test for Interaction

Next, we test for interaction between Brand and Club:

$$F = \frac{MS(Brand \times Club)}{MSE} = 1.42 \text{ (highlighted on the printout)}$$

Because this F-ratio does not exceed the tabled value of $F_{.10} = 2.33$ with 3 and 24 df (obtained from Table V in Appendix D), we cannot conclude at the .10 level of significance that the factors interact. In fact, note that the observed significance level (on the Minitab printout) for the test of interaction is .26. Thus, at any level of significance lower than $\alpha = .26$, we could not conclude that the factors interact. We therefore test the main effects for Brand and Club.

Test for Brand Main Effect

We first test the Brand main effect:

H_0: No difference exists among the true Brand mean distances.
H_a: At least two Brand mean distances differ.

Test statistic: $F = \dfrac{MS(Brand)}{MSE} = \dfrac{1,136.77}{24.60} = 46.21$ (highlighted on the printout)

Observed significance level: $p = .000$ (highlighted on the printout)

Since $\alpha = .10$ exceeds the p-value, we conclude that at least two of the brand means differ. We will subsequently determine which brand means differ using Tukey's multiple comparisons procedure. But first, we want to test the Club main effect.

Test for Club Main Effect

H_0: No differences exist between the Club mean distances.
H_a: The Club mean distances differ.

Test statistic: $F = \dfrac{MS(Club)}{MSE} = \dfrac{46,443.9}{24.60} = 1,887.94$

Observed significance level: $p = .000$

Since $\alpha = .10$ exceeds the p-value, we conclude that the two clubs are associated with different mean distances. Because only two levels of Club were used in the experiment, this F-test leads to the inference that the mean distance differs for two clubs. It is no surprise (to golfers) that the mean distance for balls hit with the driver is significantly greater than the mean distance for those hit with the five-iron.

Ranking of Means

To determine which of the Brands' mean distances differ, we want to compare the $k = 4$ Brand means using Tukey's method at $\alpha = .10$. The results of these multiple comparisons are displayed in the Minitab printout, Figure 9.29. Minitab computes simultaneous 90% confidence intervals for the $c = 4(3)/2 = 6$ possible comparisons of the form $\mu_i - \mu_j$. These intervals are highlighted on the printout. Any interval that does not include 0 implies a significant difference between the two treatment means.

A summary of these pairwise comparisons is shown at the top of the Minitab printout. You can see that Brands G and F are associated with significantly greater mean distances than Brands E and H, but we cannot distinguish between Brands G and F or between Brands E and H.

```
Grouping Information Using the Tukey Method and 90% Confidence

BRAND   N      Mean    Grouping
G       8   223.587    A
F       8   218.437    A
E       8   202.437          B
H       8   199.200          B

Means that do not share a letter are significantly different.


Tukey Simultaneous Tests for Differences of Means

Difference
of BRAND     Difference    SE of      Simultaneous               Adjusted
Levels       of Means    Difference      90% CI        T-Value    P-Value
F - E           16.00       2.48    ( 10.00,  22.00)     6.45       0.000
G - E           21.15       2.48    ( 15.15,  27.15)     8.53       0.000
H - E            3.24       2.48    ( -9.23,   2.76)    -1.31       0.568
G - F            5.15       2.48    ( -0.85,  11.15)     2.08       0.189
H - F          -19.24       2.48    (-25.23, -13.24)    -7.76       0.000
H - G          -24.39       2.48    (-30.38, -18.39)    -9.83       0.000

Individual confidence level = 97.65%
```

Figure 9.29

Minitab printout with Tukey multiple comparisons for brand

Look Back Because the interaction between Brand and Club was not significant, we conclude that this difference among brands applies to both clubs. The sample means for all Club-Brand combinations are shown in Figure 9.30 and appear to support the conclusions of the tests and comparisons. Note that the Brand means maintain their relative positions for each Club—brands F and G dominate brands E and H for both the driver and the five-iron.

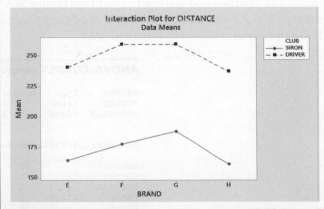

Figure 9.30

Minitab means plot for second factorial golf ball experiment

● **Now Work Exercise 9.74**

The analysis of factorial experiments can become complex if the number of factors is increased. Even the two-factor experiment becomes more difficult to analyze if some factor combinations have different numbers of observations than others. We have provided an introduction to these important experiments using two-factor factorials with equal numbers of observations for each treatment. Although similar principles apply to most factorial experiments, you should consult the references for this chapter and at the end of the book if you need to design and analyze more complex factorials.

Investigating the Effects of Tax Position (Refund or Payment) and Returns Filed (Single or Multiple) on the Tax Compliance Behavior Mean

STATISTICS IN ACTION REVISITED

In the previous two *Statistics in Action Revisited* sections, we analyzed data from the *Behavioral Research in Accounting* (January, 2015) study using an ANOVA for a completely randomized design with a single factor. The factor, Condition, had four levels: (1) filing a single federal tax return with a refund due, (2) filing a single federal tax return with a payment due, (3) filing multiple (federal and state) tax returns with a net refund due, and (4) filing multiple (federal and state) tax returns with a net payment due. The results provided useful information on the tax compliance behavior means of the four conditions. The researchers, however, designed the experiment as a 2×2 factorial, with Tax Position (the first factor) at two levels (Refund or Payment due) and Return Format (the second factor) at two levels (Single or Multiple returns). (See, again, Figure SIA9.1.)

Analyzing these data using an ANOVA for a factorial design not only will allow the researchers to compare the means of the $2 \times 2 = 4$ treatments (conditions) but will also provide insight into whether the effect of Tax Position on tax compliance behavior differs depending on Return Format—that is, interaction between the two factors. Why investigate factor interaction? Recall the two propositions from the journal article:

Proposition 1: Taxpayers' aggressiveness will shift up (more risk taking) when a net refund on multiple returns is due as compared to a net refund on a single return.

Proposition 2: Taxpayers' aggressiveness will shift down (less risk taking) when a net payment due is on multiple returns as compared to a net refund on a single return.

In Proposition 1, the researchers believe that the mean tax compliance behavior will be *higher* for multiple returns than for a single return, given that the taxpayer is due a *net refund*. In contrast, Proposition 2 states that the mean tax compliance behavior will be *lower* for multiple returns than for a single return, given that the taxpayer owes a *net payment*. Together, the propositions predict an interaction between Return Format (Single or Multiple) and Tax Position (Net Refund or Payment).

We discovered in an earlier *Statistics in Action Revisited* section that the pattern of the sample means appears to support both of these propositions and an interaction between Tax Position and Return Format (see Figure SIA9.3). Here, we provide the results for the 2×2 factorial ANOVA, and specifically, conduct the test for interaction. The Minitab output is shown in Figure SIA9.5.

Figure SIA9.5

Minitab output for 2×2 factorial ANOVA of tax compliance behavior means

```
ANOVA: COMPLY versus FORMAT, POSITION

Factor     Type    Levels  Values
FORMAT     fixed        2  Multiple, Single
POSITION   fixed        2  Payment, Refund


Analysis of Variance for COMPLY

Source          DF       SS       MS     F      P
FORMAT           1    7.350    7.350  1.53  0.217
POSITION         1    2.817    2.817  0.59  0.444
FORMAT*POSITION  1   30.817   30.817  6.43  0.012
Error          236 1131.000    4.792
Total          239 1171.983

S = 2.18915   R-Sq = 3.50%   R-Sq(adj) = 2.27%
```

The p-value for testing factor interaction (highlighted on the printout) is .012. Since this p-value is less than $\alpha = .05$, there is sufficient evidence of interaction between Tax Position and Return Format.

Does this result support both propositions? Not necessarily. The result implies that the difference in means between a single return filed and multiple returns filed depends on whether the taxpayer is due a refund or owes a payment. However, the interaction test alone does not provide insight into to which of the two means (multiple vs. single returns) is larger at each level of Tax Position (refund or payment), only that the difference in means is not the same. This information is provided by Tukey's multiple comparisons procedure and the accompanying adjusted confidence intervals for the differences in means. We learned in the previous *Statistics in Action Revisited* (see Figure SIA9.4) that the mean for taxpayers filing multiple returns with a net refund due does, in fact, exceed the mean for taxpayers filing a single return with a net refund due—supporting Proposition 1. However, the mean for taxpayers filing multiple returns with a net payment due is not significantly different than the mean for taxpayers filing a single return with a payment due. Thus, although the sample means are in the right direction, there is not sufficient statistical evidence to support Proposition 2.

Exercises 9.64–9.81

Learning the Mechanics

9.64 Suppose you conduct a 4 × 3 factorial experiment.
  a. How many factors are used in the experiment?
  b. Can you determine the factor type(s)—qualitative or quantitative—from the information given? Explain.
  c. Can you determine the number of levels used for each factor? Explain.
  d. Describe a treatment for this experiment and determine the number of treatments used.
  e. What problem is caused by using a single replicate of this experiment? How is the problem solved?

9.65 The partially completed ANOVA for a 3 × 2 factorial experiment with two replications is shown below.

Source	SS	df	MS	F
A	48	—	39	—
B	65	—	—	—
AB	34	—	17	—
Error	—	—	—	—
Total	347	25		

  a. Complete the ANOVA table.
  b. Conduct a hypothesis test at the 10% significance level to determine if differences exist among the treatment means.
  c. Based on your finding in part **b**, do you need to determine whether these factors interact to affect the response mean? If so, suggest the next test you would need to conduct.
  d. Is it easier to interpret main effects when the interaction component is not significant in a two-way ANOVA? Explain.
  e. Test to determine if factors A and B interact at the 10% significance level.
  f. Does the result of the interaction test warrant further testing? Explain.

9.66 The partially complete ANOVA table given next is for a two-factor factorial experiment.

Source	df	SS	MS	F
Treatments	7	4.1	—	—
A	3	—	.75	—
B	1	.95	—	—
AB	—	—	.30	—
Error	—	—	—	
Total	23	6.5		

  a. Give the number of levels for each factor.
  b. How many observations were collected for each factor-level combination?
  c. Complete the ANOVA table.
  d. Test to determine whether the treatment means differ. Use $\alpha = .10$.
  e. Conduct the tests of factor interaction and main effects, each at the $\alpha = .10$ level of significance. Which of the tests are warranted as part of the factorial analysis? Explain.

9.67 The following two-way table gives data for a 2 × 3 factorial experiment with two observations for each factor-level combination.

 L09067

	Level	Factor B		
		1	2	3
Factor A	1	3.1, 4.0	4.6, 4.2	6.4, 7.1
	2	5.9, 5.3	2.9, 2.2	3.3, 2.5

  a. Identify the treatments for this experiment. Calculate and plot the treatment means, using the response variable as the y-axis and the levels of factor B as the x-axis. Use the levels of factor A as plotting symbols. Do the treatment means appear to differ? Do the factors appear to interact?
  b. The Minitab ANOVA printout for this experiment is shown on the next page. Sum the appropriate sums of squares and test to determine whether the treatment means differ at the $\alpha = .05$ level of significance. Does the test support your visual interpretation from part **a**?
  c. Does the result of the test in part **b** warrant a test for interaction between the two factors? If so, perform it using $\alpha = .05$.

Minitab Output for Exercise 9.67

```
Analysis of Variance for Response

Source   DF       SS       MS       F       P
A         1   4.4408   4.4408   18.06   0.005
B         2   4.1267   2.0633    8.39   0.018
A*B       2  18.0067   9.0033   36.62   0.000
Error     6   1.4750   0.2458
Total    11  28.0492


S = 0.495816   R-Sq = 94.74%   R-Sq(adj) = 90.36%
```

d. Do the results of the previous tests warrant tests of the two factor main effects? If so, perform them using $\alpha = .05$.

e. Interpret the results of the tests. Do they support your visual interpretation from part **a**?

9.68 The next table gives data for a 2×2 factorial experiment with two observations per factor-level combination.

L09068

		Factor B	
	Level	1	2
Factor A	1	29.6, 35.2	47.3, 42.1
	2	12.9, 17.6	28.4, 22.7

a. Identify the treatments for this experiment. Calculate and plot the treatment means, using the response variable as the y-axis and the levels of factor B as the x-axis. Use the levels of factor A as plotting symbols. Do the treatment means appear to differ? Do the factors appear to interact?

b. Use the computational formulas in Appendix C to create an ANOVA table for this experiment.

c. Test to determine whether the treatment means differ at the $\alpha = .05$ level of significance. Does the test support your visual interpretation from part **a**?

d. Does the result of the test in part **b** warrant a test for interaction between the two factors? If so, perform it using $\alpha = .05$.

e. Do the results of the previous tests warrant tests of the two factor main effects? If so, perform them using $\alpha = .05$. Yes.

f. Interpret the results of the tests. Do they support your visual interpretation from part **a**?

g. Given the results of your tests, which pairs of means, if any, should be compared?

9.69 Suppose a 3×3 factorial experiment is conducted with three replications. Assume that SS(Total) = 1,000. For each of the following scenarios, form an ANOVA table, conduct the appropriate tests, and interpret the results.

a. The Sum of Squares of factor A main effect [SS(A)] is 20% of SS(Total), the Sum of Squares for factor B main effect [SS(B)] is 10% of SS(Total), and the Sum of Squares for interaction [SS(AB)] is 10% of SS(Total).

b. SS(A) is 10%, SS(B) is 10%, and SS(AB) is 50% of SS(Total).

c. SS(A) is 40%, SS(B) is 10%, and SS(AB) is 20% of SS(Total).

d. SS(A) is 40%, SS(B) is 40%, and SS(AB) is 10% of SS(Total).

Applying the Concepts—Basic

9.70 **Dynamics of the buyer-seller relationship.** An article in *Industrial Marketing Management* (January 2016) investigated the dynamics of the buyer-seller relationship—in particular, the relationship between a large software development company (the seller) and a large mobile telecommunications firm (the buyer). On the basis of interviews with employees of both firms involved in the transaction, the researchers identified two factors that drive the buyer-seller dynamic: (1) Adaptation of sales process (high or low) and (2) Knowledge of buying process (high or low). The four combinations of Adaptation and Knowledge (with descriptions of the buyer-seller adaptation dynamic) are shown in the table. Consider an experiment in which you want to determine the effects of these two factors on final sales price. Data on final sales price will be collected for each of the four types of buyer-seller adaptation dynamics and an ANOVA performed.

	High Knowledge	*Low Knowledge*
High Adaptation	Strategic adaptation	Proactive adaptation
Low Adaptation	Reactive adaptation	Ad hoc adaptation

a. Identify the experimental design used.

b. How many treatments are in this experiment? Name them.

c. If factor interaction is detected, what can you conclude?

d. Suppose no factor interaction is detected, but a main effect for Knowledge is detected. What can you conclude?

9.71 **Job satisfaction of STEM Faculty.** Are university faculty members in Science, Technology, Engineering, and Math (STEM) disciplines more satisfied with their job than non-STEM faculty? And if so, does this difference vary depending on gender? These were some of the questions of interest in a study published in the *Journal of Women and Minorities in Science and Engineering* (Vol. 18, 2012). A sample of 215 faculty members at a large public university participated in a survey. One question asked the degree to which the faculty member was satisfied with university policies and procedures. Responses were recorded on a 5-point numerical scale, with 1 = strongly disagree to 5 = strongly agree. Each participant was categorized according to gender (male or female) and discipline (STEM or non-STEM). Thus, a 2×2 factorial design was utilized.

a. Identify the treatments for this experiment.

b. For this study, what does it mean to say that discipline and gender interact?

c. A plot of the treatment means is shown below. Based on this graph only, would you say that discipline and gender interact?

d. Construct a partial ANOVA table for this study. (Give the sources of variation and degrees of freedom.)

e. The journal article reported the F-test for interaction as F = 4.10 with p-value = .04. Interpret these results.

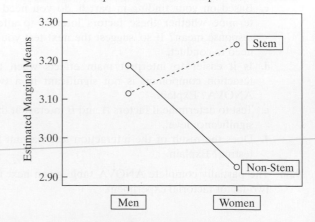

9.72 Eggshell quality in laying hens. Introducing calcium into a hen's diet can improve the shell quality of the eggs laid. One way to do this is with a limestone diet. In *Animal Feed Science and Technology* (June 2010), researchers investigated the effect of hen's age and limestone diet on eggshell quality. Two different diets were studied—fine limestone (FL) and coarse limestone (CL). Hens were classified as either younger hens (24–36 weeks old) or older hens (56–68 weeks old). The study used 120 younger hens and 120 older hens. Within each age group, half the hens were fed a fine limestone diet and the other half a coarse limestone diet. Thus, there were 60 hens in each of the four combinations of age and diet. The characteristics of the eggs produced from the laying hens were recorded, including shell thickness.

a. Identify the type of experimental design employed by the researchers.

b. Identify the factors and the factor levels (treatments) for this design.

c. Identify the experimental unit.

d. Identify the dependent variable.

e. The researchers found no evidence of factor interaction. Interpret this result, practically.

f. The researchers found no evidence of a main effect for hen's age. Interpret this result, practically.

g. The researchers found statistical evidence of a main effect for limestone diet. Interpret this result, practically.

(*Note:* The mean shell thickness for eggs produced by hens on a CL diet was larger than the corresponding mean for hens on an FL diet.)

9.73 Corporate social responsibility study. The importance that consumers place on the social responsibility of firms has grown over the past decade. As a consequence, corporations are developing more socially responsible strategies and procedures (e.g., corporate sustainability, fair-trade policies). The perceptions consumers have of these strategies were investigated in the *Journal of Marketing* (November 2009). Undergraduate marketing students were provided information on a firm's irresponsible behaviors as well as public statements made by the firm to promote its corporate social responsibility policy. Each student then rated the level of hypocrisy in the statements on a 7-point scale. Students were divided into groups depending on the type of *statement* they were given (concrete or abstract) and on the *order of information* provided (statement first or corporate behavior first). The researchers analyzed the data using a 2 × 2 factorial design.

a. Identify the factors and treatments in this experiment.

b. An ANOVA *F*-test for the interaction between statement type and order of information was found to be significant (p-value $< .01$). Practically interpret this result.

NW c. The means for the four treatments are shown in the table. Graph these means to demonstrate the nature of the interaction.

d. Based on the result, part **b**, advise the researchers on whether or not they should perform main effect tests.

Statement Type	Order of Information	Treatment Mean
Concrete	Statement first	5.90
Concrete	Behavior first	4.60
Abstract	Statement first	5.33
Abstract	Behavior first	5.26

9.74 Purchase of fair-trade products. "Just-world" theory proposes that people receive the rewards and/or punishments that they deserve. Marketing researchers examined just-world theory in the context of fair trade (*Journal of Marketing*, January 2012). In particular, the researchers wanted to know if manipulating market conditions has an impact on whether consumers purchase fair-trade products. A designed experiment with two manipulated market factors was employed. One factor was *justice reparation potential* (low or high); a second factor was *producer need* (moderate or high). A sample of business students was divided into four groups—34 students were randomly assigned to each of the $2 \times 2 = 4$ market condition treatments. After reading a news article and press release that manipulated their condition, students reported on their intention to purchase a fair-trade product. Intention was measured on a scale ranging from 0 to 6 points. The data for all 136 students (simulated based on information provided in the journal article) are saved in the accompanying file. An ANOVA for the data is shown in the accompanying Minitab printout.

```
Analysis of Variance for INT

Source     DF       SS       MS       F       P
JRP         1    1.360    1.360    1.25   0.266
NEED        1    0.622    0.622    0.57   0.451
JRP*NEED    1   22.405   22.405   20.55   0.000
Error     132  143.948    1.091
Total     135  168.335


S = 1.04428    R-Sq = 14.49%    R-Sq(adj) = 12.54%
```

a. For this designed experiment, explain (practically) what it means to have factor interaction.

b. Conduct the *F*-test for factor interaction using $\alpha = .01$. What do you conclude?

c. In the journal article, the researchers reported on the ANOVA *F*-tests for main effects. Is this necessary? Explain.

d. A plot of the sample means for the four treatments is shown below in the Minitab graph. Explain why this graph supports your answer to part **b**.

e. The researchers hypothesized that when justice restoration potential is low, fair-trade purchase intentions will be lower when Need is high rather than moderate. Conversely, when justice restoration potential is high, purchase intentions will be greater when Need is high rather than moderate. Is there evidence to support this theory?

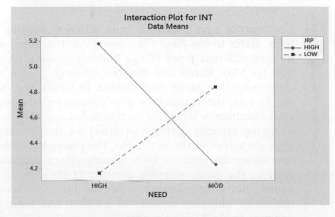

Applying the Concepts—Intermediate

9.75 Temptation in consumer choice. Are you willing to pay more for a tempting vice option (e.g., eating a hamburger, surfing the Internet) than a virtuous option (e.g., eating broccoli, reading the newspaper)? The costs and benefits of consumer temptation choice were investigated in the *Journal of Marketing Research* (February 2012). In one experiment, the researchers used a 2 × 2 factorial design involving a sample of 180 consumers. The first factor varied as to whether consumers were asked to imagine ordering a steak (*vice*) or organic pasta (*virtue*) at a restaurant. The second factor varied as to whether the restaurant described was *homogeneous* in its offerings (either "only tasty, less healthy dishes like steak" or "only healthy, less tasty dishes like organic pasta") or offered a *mixed menu* (both "tasty, less healthy dishes like steak" and "healthy, less tasty dishes like organic pasta"). Consumers were randomly assigned to one of the four order/menu conditions and then asked to give the maximum amount (in dollars) they would be willing to pay for their choice. A partial ANOVA table for the data is shown below.

Source	df	F-Value	p-Value
Order (vice/virtue)	–	–	–
Menu (homogeneous/mixed)	–	–	–
Order × Menu	–	11.25	<.001
Error	–		
Total	179		

a. Fill in the missing degrees of freedom values in the ANOVA table.

b. Give a practical interpretation of the test for interaction using $\alpha = .05$.

c. The F-values (and corresponding p-values) missing in the table were not provided in the journal article. Are these results required to complete the analysis of the data? Explain.

d. In a follow-up to the ANOVA, the researchers compared the mean willing to pay values for the homogeneous and mixed-menu conditions at each level of the order condition. In the virtue condition, the mean for the homogeneous menu ($11.08) was significantly lower than the mean for the mixed menu ($13.26). In the vice condition, the mean for the homogeneous menu ($17.11) was significantly higher than the mean for the mixed menu ($15.00). Demonstrate why these results support your answer to part **b.** Illustrate with a graph.

9.76 Commercial eggs produced from different housing systems. Refer to the *Food Chemistry* (Vol. 106, 2008) study of four different types of egg housing systems, Exercise 9.33 (p. 546). Recall that the four housing systems were cage, barn, free range, and organic. In addition to housing system, the researchers also determined the weight class (medium or large) for each sampled egg. The data on whipping capacity (percent overrun) for the 28 sampled eggs are shown in the next table. The researchers want to investigate the effect of both housing system and weight class on the mean whipping capacity of the eggs. In particular, they want to know whether the difference between the mean whipping capacity of medium and large eggs depends on the housing system.

EGGS

Housing	Wtclass	Overrun (%)
Cage	M	495, 462, 488, 471, 471
	L	502, 472, 474, 492, 479
Free	M	513, 510, 510
	L	520, 531, 521
Barn	M	515, 516, 514
	L	526, 501, 508
Organic	M	532, 511, 527
	L	530, 544, 531

a. Identify the factors and treatments for this experiment.

b. Use statistical software to conduct an ANOVA on the data. Report the results in an ANOVA table.

c. Is there evidence of interaction between housing system and weight class? Test using $\alpha = .05$. [*Hint:* Due to an unbalanced design, you will need to analyze the data using the general linear model procedure of your statistical software.] What does this imply, practically?

d. Interpret the main effect test for housing system (using $\alpha = .05$). What does this imply, practically?

e. Interpret the main effect test for weight class (using $\alpha = .05$). What does this imply, practically?

9.77 Consumer recycling behavior. Under what conditions will consumers dispose of recyclable paper in the garbage? This was the question of interest in an article published in the *Journal of Consumer Research* (December 2013). In one of the studies conducted, the researchers provided each of 160 college students with a sheet of paper and a pair of scissors to evaluate. Half the students were randomly assigned an extra-large sheet of paper and the other half a half-sheet of paper. Within each group, half the students were asked to cut the paper into four pieces while the other half did not cut the paper. After completing an unrelated task (evaluating the scissors), all students were asked to describe the extent to which "the paper was like garbage" (as opposed to being recyclable) on a 5-point scale. The researchers analyzed the data as a 2 × 2 factorial design, with Paper Size (extra-large or half-sheet) and Paper Distortion (cut paper or not) as the two factors. The resulting partial ANOVA table is shown below.

Source	df	F	p-Value
Size	1	11.50	< .001
Distortion	1	22.07	< .001
Size × Distortion	1	7.52	< .010
Error	153		
Total	156		

a. Identify the treatments in this experiment.

b. Using $\alpha = .05$, is there sufficient evidence of Paper Size by Paper Distortion interaction? Give a practical interpretation of this result.

c. Based on the result, part **a,** should the researchers conduct the main effect tests for Paper Size and Paper Distortion? Explain.

d. The means of the four treatments were ranked using a multiple comparisons method (EER = .05). Interpret the results shown below.

1.49	1.61	1.84	2.95
No Cut, Extra-large	No Cut, Half-sized	Cut, Extra-large	Cut, Half-sized

9.78 Eyewitnesses and mugshots. Criminologists investigated whether mugshot group size (the number of mugshots shown at one time) has an effect on selections made by an eyewitness to a crime (*Applied Psychology in Criminal Justice*, April 2010). A sample of 90 college students was shown a video of a simulated theft. Shortly thereafter, each student was shown 180 mugshots and asked to select a photo that most closely resembled the thief. (Multiple photos could be selected.) The students were randomly assigned to view either 3, 6, or 12 mugshots at a time. Within each mugshot group size, the students were further randomly divided into three sets. In the first set, the researchers focused on the selections made in the first 60 photos shown; in the second set, the focus was on selections made in the middle 60 photos shown; and in the third set, selections made in the last 60 photos were recorded. The dependent variable of interest was the number of mugshot selections. Simulated data for this 3×3 factorial ANOVA, with mugshot group size at three levels (3, 6, or 12 photos) and photo set at three levels (first 60, middle 60, and last 60) are saved in the accompanying file. Fully analyze the data for the researchers. In particular, the researchers want to know if mugshot group size has an effect on the mean number of selections, and, if so, which group size leads to the most selections. Also, are there a higher number of selections made in the first 60, middle 60, or last 60 photos viewed?

9.79 TV ad recall study. Refer to the *Journal of Applied Psychology* (June 2002) study of the effect of violence and sex on a television viewer's ability to recall a TV commercial, Exercise 9.28 (p. 544). Recall that 324 adults were randomly assigned to one of three TV content groups, with 108 subjects in each group. One group watched a TV program with a violent content code (V) rating; the second group viewed a show with a sex content code (S) rating; and the last group watched a neutral TV program. Commercials were imbedded into each TV show, and after the participants viewed the show, the advertisement recall score was measured for each participant. In addition, the researchers recorded whether or not the subject had previously seen the commercial. The layout for the full experimental design is shown in the accompanying schematic. Note that there are two factors in this experiment—TV content group at three levels and watched commercial before status at two levels—and the design is a 3×2 factorial. The researchers want to know whether the two factors, TV content group and watched commercial before status, impact mean recall score. Conduct a two-way factorial analysis of variance on the data saved in the accompanying file. The researchers concluded that (1) the Neutral TV content group has the highest mean recall score, but that there is no significant difference between the mean recall scores of the Violent and Sex content groups and (2) there is no significant difference between the mean recall scores of those who had previously watched the commercial and those who had not. Do you agree?

Layout of Experimental Design for TV Ad Recall Study

	TV Content Group		
	Violent (V)	Sex (S)	Neutral (N)
Watched commercial before: *Yes*	$n = 48$	$n = 60$	$n = 54$
No	$n = 60$	$n = 48$	$n = 54$

Applying the Concepts—Advanced

9.80 On the trail of the cockroach. Knowledge of how cockroaches forage for food is valuable for companies that develop and manufacture roach bait and traps. Many entomologists believe, however, that the navigational behavior of cockroaches scavenging for food is random. D. Miller of Virginia Tech University challenged the "random-walk" theory by designing an experiment to test a cockroach's ability to follow a trail of their fecal material (*Explore*, Research at the University of Florida, Fall 1998).

A methanol extract from roach feces—called a *pheromone*—was used to create a chemical trail. German cockroaches were released at the beginning of the trail, one at a time, and a video surveillance camera was used to monitor the roach's movements. In addition to the trail containing the fecal extract (the treatment), a trail using methanol only (the control) was created. To determine if trail-following ability differed among cockroaches of different age, sex, and reproductive status, four roach groups were used in the experiment: adult males, adult females, gravid (pregnant) females, and nymphs (immatures). Twenty roaches of each type were randomly assigned to the treatment trail, and 10 of each type were randomly assigned to the control trail. Thus, a total of 120 roaches were used in the experiment. The movement pattern of each cockroach was measured (in "pixels") as the average trail deviation. The data for the 120 cockroaches in the study are stored in the accompanying file. (The first 5 and last 5 observations in the data set are listed here.) Conduct a complete analysis of the data. Determine whether roaches can distinguish between the fecal extract and control trail and whether trail-following ability differs according to age, sex, and reproductive status.

Trail Deviation	Roach Group	Trail
3.1	Adult Male	Extract
42.0	Adult Male	Control
6.2	Adult Male	Extract
22.7	Adult Male	Control
34.0	Adult Male	Extract
⋮	⋮	⋮
23.8	Nymph	Extract
5.1	Nymph	Extract
3.8	Nymph	Extract
3.1	Nymph	Extract
2.8	Nymph	Extract

9.81 Impact of flavor name on consumer choice. Do consumers react favorably to products with ambiguous colors or names? Marketing Professors E. G. Miller and B. E. Kahn investigated this phenomenon in the *Journal of Consumer Research* (June 2005). As a "reward" for participating in an unrelated experiment, 100 consumers were told they could have some jelly beans available in several cups on a table. Half the consumers were assigned to take jelly beans with common descriptive flavor names (e.g., watermelon green), while the other half were assigned to take jelly beans with ambiguous flavor names (e.g., monster green). Within each group, half of the consumers took the jelly beans and left (low cognitive load condition), while the other half were distracted with additional questions designed to distract them while they were taking their jelly beans (high cognitive load condition). Consequently, a 2×2 factorial experiment was employed—with Flavor Name (common or ambiguous) and Cognitive Load (low or high) as the two factors—with 25 consumers assigned to each of four treatments. The dependent variable of interest was the number of jelly beans taken by each consumer. The means and standard deviations of the four treatments are shown in the accompanying table.

	Ambiguous		Common	
	Mean	Std. Dev.	Mean	Std. Dev.
Low load	18.0	15.0	7.8	9.5
High load	6.1	9.5	6.3	10.0

Source: Based on E. G. Miller and B. E. Kahn, "Shades of Meaning: The Effect of Color and Flavor Names on Consumer Choice," *Journal of Consumer Research*, Vol. 32, No. 1, June 2005 (Table 1).

a. Calculate the total of the $n = 25$ measurements for each of the four categories in the 2×2 factorial experiment.

b. Calculate the correction for mean, CM. (See Appendix C for computational formulas.)

c. Use the results of parts **a** and **b** to calculate the sums of squares for Load, Name, and Load $\times$ Name interaction.

d. Calculate the sample variance for each treatment. Then calculate the sum of squares of deviations within each sample for the four treatments.

e. Calculate SSE. (*Hint:* SSE is the pooled sum of squares for the deviations calculated in part **d**.)

f. Now that you know SS(Load), SS(Name), SS(Load $\times$ Name), and SSE, find SS(Total).

g. Summarize the calculations in an ANOVA table.

h. The researchers reported the F-value for Load $\times$ Name interaction as $F = 5.34$. Do you agree?

i. Conduct a complete analysis of these data. Use $\alpha = .05$ for any inferential techniques you employ. Illustrate your conclusions graphically.

j. What assumptions are necessary to ensure the validity of the inferential techniques you used? State them in terms of this experiment.

CHAPTER NOTES

Key Terms

Analysis of variance (ANOVA) 537
Balanced design 530
Blocks 555
Bonferroni multiple comparisons procedure 548
Comparisonwise error rate (CER) 548
Complete factorial experiment 568
Completely randomized design 530
Dependent variable 524
Designed study 525
Experimental unit 525
Experimentwise error rate (EER) 548
Factor interaction 569
Factor levels 525
Factor main effect 569
Factors 524
F-statistic 533
F-test 534
Independent variables 524
Mean Square for Error (MSE) 533

Mean Square for Treatments (MST) 533
Multiple comparisons of a set of treatment means 548
Observational study 525
Qualitative factors 524
Quantitative factors 524
Randomized block design 555
Replicates 571
Response variable 524
Robust method 538
Scheffé multiple comparisons procedure 550
Single-factor experiment 568
Sum of Squares for Blocks (SSB) 555
Sum of Squares for Error (SSE) 532
Sum of Squares for Treatments (SST) 532
Treatments 525
Tukey multiple comparisons procedure 550
Two-way classification 568

Key Symbols/Notation

ANOVA	Analysis of variance
SST	Sum of Squares for Treatments
MST	Mean Square for Treatments
SSB	Sum of Squares for Blocks
MSB	Mean Square for Blocks
SSE	Sum of Squares for Error
MSE	Mean Square for Error
$a \times b$ factorial	Factorial design with one factor at a levels and the other factor at b levels
SS(A)	Sum of Squares for main effect factor A
MS(A)	Mean Square for main effect factor A
SS(B)	Sum of Squares for main effect factor B
MS(B)	Mean Square for main effect factor B
SS(AB)	Sum of Squares for factor $A \times B$ interaction
MS(AB)	Mean Square for factor $A \times B$ interaction

Key Ideas

Key Elements of a Designed Experiment

1. *Response (dependent) variable*—quantitative
2. *Factors*—quantitative or qualitative
3. *Factor levels (values of factors)*—selected by the experimenter
4. *Treatments*—combinations of factor levels
5. *Experimental units*—assign treatments to experimental units and measure response for each

Balanced design
Sample sizes for each treatment are equal.

Tests for main effects in a factorial design
Only appropriate if the test for factor interaction is nonsignificant.

Robust method
Slight to moderate departures from normality do not have impact on validity of the ANOVA results.

Conditions Required for Valid *F*-Test in a Completely Randomized Design

1. All k treatment populations are approximately normal.
2. $\sigma_1^2 = \sigma_2^2 = \cdots = \sigma_k^2$

Conditions Required for Valid *F*-Test in a Randomized Block Design

1. All treatment-block populations are approximately normal.
2. All treatment-block populations have the same variance.

Conditions Required for Valid *F*-Tests in a Complete Factorial Design

1. All treatment populations are approximately normal.
2. All treatment populations have the same variance.

Multiple Comparisons of Means Methods

Number of pairwise comparisons with *k* treatment means
$$c = k(k - 1)/2$$

Tukey method:
1. Balanced design
2. Pairwise comparisons of means

Bonferroni method:
1. Either balanced or unbalanced design
2. Pairwise comparisons of means

Scheffé method:
1. Either balanced or unbalanced design
2. General contrasts of means

Experimentwise error rate (EER)
Risk of making at least one Type I error when making multiple comparisons of means in ANOVA

Guide to Selecting the Experimental Design

Guide to Conducting Anova *F*-Tests

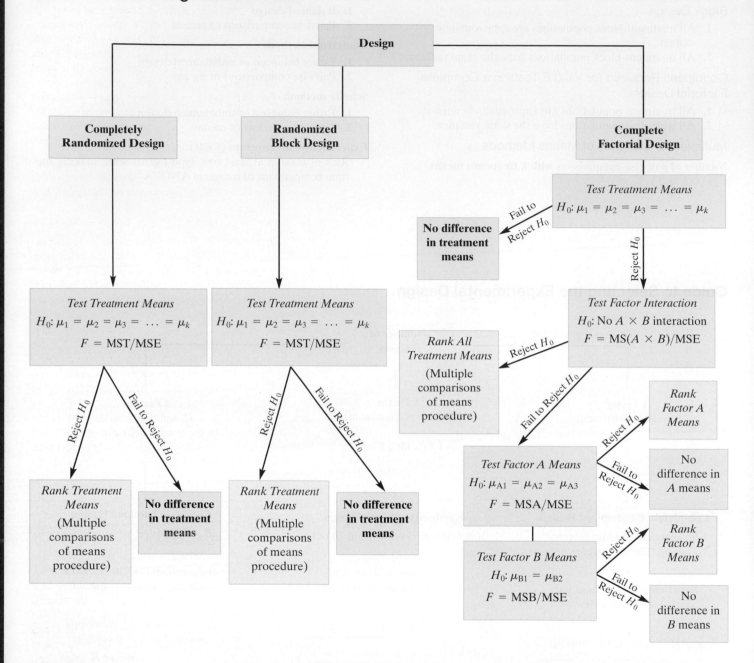

SUPPLEMENTARY EXERCISES 9.82–9.109

Learning the Mechanics

9.82 What is the difference between a one-way ANOVA and a two-way ANOVA?

9.83 Explain the difference between an experiment that employs a completely randomized design and one that employs a randomized block design.

9.84 What are the treatments in a two-factor experiment, with factor *A* at three levels and factor *B* at two levels?

9.85 Why does the experimentwise error rate of a multiple comparisons procedure differ from the significance level

for each comparison (assuming the experiment has more than two treatments)?

9.86 A completely randomized design is used to compare four treatment means. The data are shown in the table.

L09086

Treatment 1	Treatment 2	Treatment 3	Treatment 4
8	6	9	12
10	9	10	13
9	8	8	10
10	8	11	11
11	7	12	11

a. Given that SST $= 36.95$ and SS(Total) $= 62.55$, complete an ANOVA table for this experiment.

b. Is there evidence that the treatment means differ? Use $\alpha = .10$.

c. Place a 90% confidence interval on the mean response for treatment 4.

9.87 An experiment employing a randomized block design was conducted to compare the mean responses for four treatments—A, B, C, and D. The treatments were randomly assigned to the four experimental units in each of five blocks. The data are shown in the following table.

Treatment	Block				
	1	2	3	4	5
A	8.6	7.5	8.7	9.8	7.4
B	7.3	6.3	7.3	8.4	6.3
C	9.1	8.3	9.0	9.9	8.2
D	9.3	8.2	9.2	10.0	8.4

a. Given that SS(Total) $= 22.31$ and SS(Block) $= 10.688$ and SSE $= .288$, complete an ANOVA table for the experiment.

b. Do the data provide sufficient evidence to indicate a difference among treatment means? Test using $\alpha = .05$.

c. Does the result of the test in part **b** warrant further comparison of the treatment means? If so, how many pairwise comparisons need to be made?

d. Is there evidence that the block means differ? Use $\alpha = .05$.

9.88 The following table shows a partially completed ANOVA table for a two-factor factorial experiment.

Source	SS	df	MS	F
A	5	2	–	–
B	56	4	–	–
A × B	–	–	.125	.0417
Error	–	–	3	
Total	107	29		

a. Complete the ANOVA table.

b. For the above ANOVA table, indicate the appropriate null and alternative hypotheses for determining whether differences exist among the treatment means and identify the degrees of freedom.

c. Test the hypotheses stated in part **b** at the 5% significance level.

d. Based on your finding in part **c**, is further testing warranted? If so, conduct the test at the 5% significance level.

Applying the Concepts—Basic

9.89 **Robots trained to behave like ants.** Robotic researchers investigated whether robots could be trained to behave like ants in an ant colony (*Nature*, August 2000). Robots were trained and randomly assigned to "colonies" (i.e., groups) consisting of 3, 6, 9, or 12 robots. The robots were assigned the task of foraging for "food" and to recruit another robot when they identified a resource-rich area. One goal of the experiment was to compare the mean energy expended (per robot) of the four different colony sizes.

a. What type of experimental design was employed?

b. Identify the treatments and the dependent variable.

c. Set up the null and alternative hypotheses of the test.

d. The following ANOVA results were reported: $F = 7.70$, numerator df $= 3$, denominator df $= 56$, p-value $< .001$. Conduct the test at a significance level of $\alpha = .05$ and interpret the result.

e. Multiple comparisons of mean energy expended for the four colony sizes were conducted using an experiment-wise error rate of .05. The results are summarized below.

Sample mean:	.97	.95	.93	.80
Group size:	3	6	9	12

How many pairwise comparisons are conducted in this analysis?

f. Refer to part **e**. Interpret the results shown in the table.

9.90 **Ethics of salespeople.** Within marketing, the area of personal sales has long suffered from a poor ethical image, particularly in the eyes of college students. An article in *Journal of Business Ethics* (Vol. 15, 1996) investigated whether such opinions by college students are a function of the type of sales job (high tech vs. low tech) and/or the sales task (new account development vs. account maintenance). Four different samples of college students were confronted with the four different situations (new account development in a high-tech sales task, new account development in a low-tech sales task, account maintenance in a high-tech sales task, and account maintenance in a low-tech sales task) and were asked to evaluate the ethical behavior of the salesperson on a 7-point scale ranging from 1 (not a serious ethical violation) to 7 (a very serious ethical violation). Identify each of the following elements of the experiment:

a. Response   **b.** Factor(s) and factor level(s)

c. Treatments   **d.** Experimental units

9.91 **Impact of paper color on exam scores.** A study published in *Teaching Psychology* (May 1998) examined how external clues influence student performance. Undergraduate students were randomly assigned to one of four different midterm examinations. Form 1 was printed on blue paper and contained difficult questions, while form 2 was also printed on blue paper but contained simple questions. Form 3 was printed on red paper, with difficult questions; form 4 was printed on red paper with simple questions. The researchers were interested in the impact that Color (red or blue) and Question (simple or difficult) had on mean exam score.

Form	Color	Question	Mean Score
1	Blue	Difficult	53.3
2	Blue	Simple	80.0
3	Red	Difficult	39.3
4	Red	Simple	73.6

a. What experimental design was employed in this study? Identify the factors and treatments.

b. The researchers conducted an ANOVA and found a significant interaction between Color and Question (p-value $< .03$). Interpret this result.

c. The sample mean scores (percentage correct) for the four exam forms are listed in the table above. Plot the four means on a graph to illustrate the Color × Question interaction.

9.92 Study of mutual fund performance. Mutual funds are classified as large-cap funds, medium-cap funds, or small-cap funds, depending on the capitalization of the companies in the fund. Hawaii Pacific University researchers investigated whether the average performance of a mutual fund is related to capitalization size (*American Business Review*, January 2002). Independent random samples of 30 mutual funds were selected from each of the three fund groups, and the 90-day rate of return was determined for each fund. The data for the 90 funds were subjected to an analysis of variance, with the results shown in the ANOVA summary table below.

Source	df	SS	MS	F	p-Value
Fund group	2	409.566	204.783	6.965	.002
Error	87	2,557.860	29.401		
Total	89	2,967.426			

Source: S. W. Shi and M. J. Seiler, "Growth and Value Style Comparison of U.S. Stock Mutual Funds," *American Business Review*, January 2002 (Table 3). Published by American Business Review, © 2002.

a. State the null and alternative hypotheses for the ANOVA.

b. Give the rejection region for the test using $\alpha = .01$.

c. Make the appropriate conclusion using either the test statistic or the *p*-value.

9.93 Study of mutual fund performance. Refer to Exercise 9.92. Using an experimentwise error rate of .05, Tukey confidence intervals for the difference between mean rates of return for all possible pairs of fund types are given below.

Comparison	Tukey Confidence Interval
$\mu_{Large} - \mu_{Medium}$	$(-.1847, 5.3807)$
$\mu_{Large} - \mu_{Small}$	$(2.4426, 8.0080)$
$\mu_{Medium} - \mu_{Small}$	$(-.1554, 5.4100)$

a. Why is the Tukey multiple comparisons method preferred over another method?

b. Is there a significant difference between the treatment means for large-cap and medium-cap mutual funds? Explain.

c. Is there a significant difference between the treatment means for large-cap and small-cap mutual funds? Explain.

d. Is there a significant difference between the treatment means for medium-cap and small-cap mutual funds? Explain.

e. Use your answers to parts **b–d** to rank the treatment means.

f. Give a measure of reliability for the inference in part **e**.

9.94 *Fortune's* E-50 list. The *Fortune* E-50 is a listing of the top 50 electronic commerce and Internet-based companies, as determined by *Fortune* magazine each year. *Fortune* groups the companies into four categories: (1) e-companies, (2) Internet software and service, (3) Internet hardware, and (4) Internet communication. Consider a study to compare the mean rates of return for the stock of companies in the four *Fortune* categories. Because the age of an electronic commerce or Internet-based company

may have an impact on rate of return, the study is designed to remove any age variation. Four 1-year-old companies, four 3-year-old companies, and four 5-year-old companies were selected; within each age group, one company was randomly selected from category 1, one from category 2, one from category 3, and one from category 4.

a. What type of experimental design is employed?

b. Identify the key elements of the experiment (i.e., treatments, blocks, response variable, and experimental unit).

9.95 Income and road rage. Is a driver's propensity to engage in road rage related to his or her income? Researchers at Mississippi State University attempted to answer this question by conducting a survey of a representative sample of over 1,000 U.S. adult drivers (*Accident Analysis and Prevention*, Vol. 34, 2002). Based on how often each driver engaged in certain road rage behaviors (e.g., making obscene gestures at, tailgating, and thinking about physically hurting another driver), a road rage score was assigned. (Higher scores indicate a greater pattern of road rage behavior.) The drivers were also grouped by annual income: under \$30,000, between \$30,000 and \$60,000, and over \$60,000. The data were subjected to an analysis of variance, with the results summarized in the table.

Income Group	Sample Size	Mean Road Rage Score
Under \$30,000	379	4.60
\$30,000 to \$60,000	392	5.08
Over \$60,000	267	5.15

ANOVA Results: *F*-value = 3.90 *p*-value < .01

Source: Republished with permission of Elsevier, from *Accident Analysis and Prevention*, Elisabeth Wells Parker; Jennifer Ceminsky; Victoria Hallberg; Ronald W Snow; Gregory Dunaway; Shawn Guiling; Marsha Williams; Bradley Anderson, Volume 34, Issue 3, pp. 271–278, 2016; permission conveyed through Copyright Clearance Center, Inc.

a. Is there evidence to indicate that the mean road rage score differs for the three income groups? Test using $\alpha = .05$.

b. An experimentwise error rate of .01 was used to rank the three means. Give a practical interpretation of this error rate.

c. How many pairwise comparisons are necessary to compare the three means? List them.

d. A multiple comparisons procedure revealed that the means for the income groups \$30,000–\$60,000 and over \$60,000 were not significantly different. All other pairs of means were found to be significantly different. Summarize these results in table form.

e. Which of the comparisons of part **c** will yield a confidence interval that does not contain 0?

9.96 Forecasting electrical consumption. Two different methods of forecasting monthly electrical consumption were compared and the results published in *Applied Mathematics and Computation* (Vol. 186, 2007). The two methods were Artificial Neural Networks (ANN) and Time Series Regression (TSR). Forecasts were made using each method for each of 4 months. These forecasts were also compared with the actual monthly consumption values. A layout of the design is shown in the next table. The researchers want to compare the mean electrical consumption values of the ANN forecast, TSR forecast, and Actual consumption.

Month	ANN Forecast	TSR Forecast	Actual Consumption
1	—	—	—
2	—	—	—
3	—	—	—
4	—	—	—
Sample Mean	13.480	13.260	13.475

a. Identify the experimental design employed in the study.

b. A partial ANOVA table for the study is provided below. Fill in the missing entries.

Source	df	SS	MS	F-Value	p-Value
Forecast Method	—	—	.195	2.83	.08
Month	3	—	10.780	—	<.01
Error	—	.414	.069		
Total	11	33.144			

c. Use the information in the table to conduct the appropriate ANOVA F-test using $\alpha = .05$. State your conclusion in the words of the problem.

9.97 Baker's vs. brewer's yeast. The *Electronic Journal of Biotechnology* (Dec. 15, 2003) published an article on a comparison of two yeast extracts, baker's yeast and brewer's yeast. Brewer's yeast is a surplus by-product obtained from a brewery, hence it is less expensive than primary-grown baker's yeast. Samples of both yeast extracts were prepared at four different temperatures (45, 48, 51, and 54°C); thus, a 2×4 factorial design with yeast extract at two levels and temperature at four levels was employed. The response variable was the autolysis yield (recorded as a percentage).

a. How many treatments are included in the experiment?

b. An ANOVA found sufficient evidence of factor interaction at $\alpha = .05$. Interpret this result practically.

c. Give the null and alternative hypotheses for testing the main effects of yeast extract and temperature.

d. Explain why the tests, part **c**, should not be conducted.

e. Multiple comparisons of the four temperature means were conducted for each of the two yeast extracts. Interpret the results shown below.

Baker's yeast:	Mean yield (%):	41.1	47.5	48.6	50.3
	Temperature (°C):	54	45	48	51
Brewer's yeast:	Mean yield (%):	39.4	47.3	49.2	49.6
	Temperature (°C):	54	51	48	45

Applying the Concepts—Intermediate

9.98 A managerial decision problem. A direct-mail company assembles and stores paper products (envelopes, letters, brochures, order cards, etc.) for its customers. The company estimates the total number of pieces received in a shipment by estimating the weight per piece and then weighing the entire shipment. The company is unsure whether the sample of pieces used to estimate the mean weight per piece should be drawn from a single carton, or whether it is worth the extra time required to pull a few pieces from several cartons. To aid management in making a decision, eight brochures were pulled from each of five cartons of a typical shipment and weighed. The weights (in pounds) are shown in the table.

Carton 1	Carton 2	Carton 3	Carton 4	Carton 5
.01851	.01872	.01869	.01899	.01882
.01829	.01861	.01853	.01917	.01895
.01844	.01876	.01876	.01852	.01884
.01859	.01886	.01880	.01904	.01835
.01854	.01896	.01880	.01923	.01889
.01853	.01879	.01882	.01905	.01876
.01844	.01879	.01862	.01924	.01891
.01833	.01879	.01860	.01893	.01879

a. Identify the response, factor(s), treatments, and experimental units.

b. Do these data provide sufficient evidence to indicate differences in the mean weight per brochure among the five cartons?

c. What assumptions must be satisfied in order for the test of part **b** to be valid?

d. Use Tukey's method to compare all pairs of means, with $\alpha = .05$ as the overall level of significance.

e. Given the results, make a recommendation to management about whether to sample from one carton or from many cartons.

9.99 Ethics of downsizing. A major strategic alternative for many U.S. firms is to reduce the size of their workforce, i.e., to "downsize." The ethics of downsizing decisions from the employees' perspective was investigated in the *Journal of Business Ethics* (Vol. 18, 1999). The researchers surveyed a sample of 209 employees who were enrolled in an Executive MBA Program or weekend program at one of three Colorado universities. These individuals were divided into five distinct groups, depending on their job situation at a previous or current firm. The groups were named (1) Casualties, (2) Survivors, (3) Implementors/casualties, (4) Implementors/survivors, and (5) Formulators. The sampled employees completed a questionnaire on their ethical perceptions of downsizing. One item asked employees to respond to the statement: "It is unethical for a downsizing decision to be announced or implemented on or prior to a major holiday." Responses were measured using a 5-point Likert scale, where 1 = strongly agree, 2 = agree, 3 = neutral, 4 = disagree, and 5 = strongly disagree. Data on both the qualitative variable "Group" and the quantitative variable "Ethics response" are saved in the accompanying file. The researchers' goal was to determine if any differences exist among the mean ethics scores for the five groups.

a. The data were analyzed using an ANOVA for a completely randomized design. Identify the factor, treatments, response variable, and experimental units for this design.

b. Specify the null and alternative hypotheses tested.

c. A Minitab printout of the ANOVA is displayed on the next page. Can you conclude that the mean ethics scores of the five groups of employees are significantly different? Explain.

One-way ANOVA: CASUAL, SURVIVE, IMPCAS, IMPSUR, FORMUL

```
Analysis of Variance

Source   DF  Adj SS  Adj MS  F-Value  P-Value
Factor    4   40.84  10.210     9.85    0.000
Error   204  211.35   1.036
Total   208  252.19

Model Summary

      S   R-sq   R-sq(adj)   R-sq(pred)
1.01786  16.19%     14.55%       12.00%

Means

Factor    N   Mean  StDev        95% CI
CASUAL   47  1.787  0.832   (1.495, 2.080)
SURVIVE  71  1.845  1.023   (1.607, 2.083)
IMPCAS   27  1.593  0.636   (1.206, 1.979)
IMPSUR   33  2.545  1.301   (2.196, 2.895)
FORMUL   31  2.871  1.176   (2.511, 3.231)

Pooled StDev = 1.01786
```

Minitab output for Exercise 9.99

d. Access the data and check that the assumptions required for the ANOVA F-test are reasonably satisfied.

e. Multiple comparisons of the treatment (group) means were conducted using the Bonferroni method with an experimentwise error rate of .05. Explain why the Bonferroni method is preferred over another multiple comparisons method (e.g., Tukey or Scheffé).

f. Refer to part e. Determine the number of pairwise comparisons for this analysis.

g. The sample mean ethics scores for the five groups and Bonferroni rankings are summarized below. Identify the groups with the significantly largest mean ethics scores.

1.59	1.79	1.84	2.45	2.87
Implementors/ casualties Group 3	Casualties Group 1	Survivors Group 2	Implementors/ survivors Group 4	Formulators Group 5

9.100 **Absentee rates at a jeans plant.** A plant that manufactures denim jeans in the United Kingdom introduced a computerized automated handling system. The new system delivers garments to the assembly line operators by means of an overhead conveyor. Although the automated system minimizes operator handling time, it inhibits operators from working ahead and taking breaks from their machine. A study in *New Technology, Work, and Employment* (July 2001) investigated the impact of the new handling system on worker absentee rates at the jeans plant. One theory is that the mean absentee rate will vary by day of the week, as operators decide to indulge in 1-day absences to relieve work pressure. Nine weeks were randomly selected, and the absentee rate (percentage of workers absent) determined for each day (Monday through Friday) of the workweek. The data are listed in the table at the top of the next column. Conduct a complete analysis of the data to determine whether the mean absentee rate differs across the 5 days of the workweek.

Data for Exercise 9.100

Week	Mon	Tues	Wed	Thur	Fri
1	5.3	0.6	1.9	1.3	1.6
2	12.9	9.4	2.6	0.4	0.5
3	0.8	0.8	5.7	0.4	1.4
4	2.6	0.0	4.5	10.2	4.5
5	23.5	9.6	11.3	13.6	14.1
6	9.1	4.5	7.5	2.1	9.3
7	11.1	4.2	4.1	4.2	4.1
8	9.5	7.1	4.5	9.1	12.9
9	4.8	5.2	10.0	6.9	9.0

Source: Based on J. J. Boggis, "The Eradication of Leisure," *New Technology, Work, and Employment,* Vol. 16, No. 2, July 2001, pp. 118–129 (Table 3).

9.101 **Effectiveness of sales closing techniques.** Industrial sales professionals have long debated the effectiveness of various sales closing techniques. For example, a University of Akron study investigated the impact of five different closing techniques and a no-close condition on the level of a sales prospect's trust in the salesperson (*Industrial Marketing Management*, September 1996). More recently, a *B2B Marketing Insider* blog (October 7, 2010) examined five currently-used sales closing techniques. Consider the following study. Sales scenarios are presented to a sample of 230 purchasing executives. Each subject received one of the five closing techniques or a scenario in which no close was achieved. After reading the sales scenario, each executive was asked to rate his/her level of trust in the salesperson on a 7-point scale. The table reports the six treatments employed in the study and the number of subjects receiving each treatment.

Treatments: Closing Techniques	Sample Size
1. No close	35
2. Financial close	35
3. Time Line close	30
4. Sympathy close	40
5. The Visual close	35
6. Thermometer close	55

Source: Based on J. M. Hawes, "Do Closing Techniques Diminish Prospect Trust?" from *Industrial Marketing Management,* September 1996, Vol. 25(5).

a. Consider the following hypotheses:

H_0: The salesperson's level of prospect trust is not influenced by the choice of closing method.

H_a: The salesperson's level of prospect trust is influenced by the choice of closing method.

Rewrite these hypotheses in the form required for an analysis of variance.

b. Assume the ANOVA F-statistic is $F = 2.21$. Is there sufficient evidence to reject H_0 at $\alpha = .05$?

c. What assumptions must be met for the test of part a to be valid?

d. Would you classify this experiment as observational or designed? Explain.

9.102 **Insomnia and education.** Many workers suffer from stress and chronic insomnia. Is insomnia related to education status? Researchers at the Universities of Memphis, Alabama at Birmingham, and Tennessee investigated this question in the *Journal of Abnormal Psychology*

(February 2005). Adults living in Tennessee were selected to participate in the study using a random-digit telephone dialing procedure. In addition to insomnia status (normal sleeper or chronic insomnia), the researchers classified each participant into one of four education categories (college graduate, some college, high school graduate, and high school dropout). One dependent variable of interest to the researchers was a quantitative measure of daytime functioning called the Fatigue Severity Scale (FSS). The data were analyzed as a 2 × 4 factorial experiment, with Insomnia status and Education level as the two factors.

a. Determine the number of treatments for this study. List them.

b. The researchers reported that "the Insomnia × Education interaction was not statistically significant." Practically interpret this result. (Illustrate with a graph.)

c. The researchers discovered that the sample mean FSS for people with insomnia was greater than the sample mean FSS for normal sleepers, and this difference was statistically significant. Practically interpret this result.

d. The researchers reported that the main effect of Education was statistically significant. Practically interpret this result.

e. Refer to part **d.** In a follow-up analysis, the sample mean FSS values for the four Education levels were compared using Tukey's method ($\alpha = .05$), with the results shown below. What do you conclude?

Mean:	3.3	3.6	3.7	4.2
	College	*Some*	*HS*	*HS*
Education:	*graduate*	*college*	*graduate*	*dropout*

9.103 **Diamonds sold at retail.** Refer to the *Journal of Statistics Education* study of 308 diamonds for sale on the open market, Exercise 2.157 (p. 144). Recall that the file contains information on the quantitative variables, size (number of carats) and price (in dollars), and on the qualitative variables, color (D, E, F, G, H, and I), clarity (IF, VS1, VS2, VVS1, and VVS2), and independent certification group

(GIA, HRD, or IGI). Select one of the quantitative variables and one of the qualitative variables.

a. Set up the null and alternative hypotheses for determining whether the means of the quantitative variable differ for the levels of the qualitative variable.

b. Use the data to conduct the test, part **a,** at $\alpha = 10$. State the conclusion in the words of the problem.

c. Check any assumptions required for the methodology used in part **b** to be valid.

d. Follow up the analysis with multiple comparisons of the treatment means. Use an experimentwise error rate of .05. Interpret the results practically.

9.104 **Participation in a company's walking program.** A study was conducted to investigate the effect of prompting in a walking program instituted at a large corporation (*Health Psychology*, March 1995). Five groups of walkers—27 in each group—agreed to participate by walking for 20 minutes at least one day per week over a 24-week period. The participants were prompted to walk each week via telephone calls, but different prompting schemes were used for each group. Walkers in the control group received no prompting phone calls; walkers in the "frequent/low" group received a call once a week with low structure (i.e., "just touching base"); walkers in the "frequent/high" group received a call once a week with high structure (i.e., goals are set); walkers in the "infrequent/low" group received a call once every 3 weeks with low structure; and walkers in the "infrequent/high" group received a call once every 3 weeks with high structure. The table at the bottom of the page lists the number of participants in each group who actually walked the minimum requirement each week for weeks 1, 4, 8, 12, 16, and 24. The data were subjected to an analysis of variance for a randomized block design, with the five walker groups representing the treatments and the six time periods (weeks) representing the blocks.

Source	df	SS	MS	F	p-Value
Prompt	4	1185.000	—	—	0.0000
Week	—	386.400	77.28000	10.40	0.0001
Error	20	148.600	7.43000		
Totals	29	1720.00			

Table for Exercise 9.104

Week	Control	Frequent/Low	Frequent/High	Infrequent/Low	Infrequent/High
1	7	23	25	21	19
4	2	19	25	10	12
8	2	18	19	9	9
12	2	7	20	8	2
16	2	18	18	8	7
24	1	17	17	7	6

Source: D. N. Lombard, T. N. Lombard, and R. A. Winett, "Walking to Meet Health Guidelines: The Effect of Prompting Frequency and Prompt Structure," *Health Psychology*, Vol. 14, No. 2, March 1995, p. 167 (Table 2).

Turkey Ranking for Exercise 9.104

Mean:	2.67	9.17	10.50	17.00	20.67
Prompt:	*Control*	*Infr./High*	*Infr./Low*	*Frequent/Low*	*Frequent/High*

a. What is the purpose of blocking on weeks in this study?
b. Fill in the missing entries on the ANOVA summary table shown.
c. Is there sufficient evidence of a difference in the mean number of walkers per week among the five walker groups? Use $\alpha = .05$.
d. Tukey's technique was used to compare all pairs of treatment means with an experimentwise error rate of $\alpha = .05$. The rankings are shown at the bottom of the page. Interpret these results.
e. What assumptions must hold to ensure the validity of the inferences in parts **c** and **d**?

9.105 Manager's trust and job-related tension. Research published in *Accounting, Organizations and Society* (Vol. 19, 1994) investigated whether the effects of different performance evaluation styles (PES) on the level of job-related tension is affected by trust. Three performance evaluation styles were considered. Each is related to the way in which accounting information is used for the purpose of evaluation. The three styles are budget-constrained (BC), profit-conscious (PC), and the nonaccounting style (NA), which focuses on factors such as quality of output and attitude toward the job. Consider a questionnaire (similar to the one used in the study) administered to 200 managers. It measures the performance evaluation style of each manager's superior (on a 10-point scale), the manager's job-related tension, and the manager's level of trust (low, medium, and high) in his or her superior. These data were used to produce the partial ANOVA table and table of treatment means shown next.

Source	df	SS	MS	F
PES	2	4.35	–	–
Trust	–	15.20	–	–
PES × trust	4	3.50	–	–
Error	191	–		
Total	199	301.55		

		Performance Evaluation Style		
		BC	PC	NA
Trust	Low	6.5 ($n = 30$)	6.2 ($n = 20$)	6.3 ($n = 20$)
	Medium	5.5 ($n = 25$)	5.6 ($n = 30$)	5.3 ($n = 15$)
	High	4.6 ($n = 20$)	4.8 ($n = 25$)	4.7 ($n = 15$)

Source: Based on A. Ross, "Trust as a Moderator of the Effect of Performance Evaluation Style on Job-Related Tension: A Research Note," from *Accounting, Organizations, and Society,* October 1994, Volume 19(7).

a. Describe the treatments of this study.
b. Complete the ANOVA table.
c. Investigate the presence of an interaction effect by conducting the appropriate hypothesis test using $\alpha = .05$.
d. Use a plot of treatment means to investigate the interaction effect. Interpret your results. Are your results of parts **c** and **d** consistent?

e. Given your answers to parts **c** and **d,** should the *F*-tests for the two main effects be conducted?

9.106 Testing the effectiveness of supermarket sales strategies.

SUPMKT
Factorial designs are commonly employed in marketing research to evaluate the effectiveness of sales strategies. At one supermarket, two of the factors were price level (regular, reduced price, cost to supermarket) and Display level (normal display space, normal display space plus end-of-aisle display, twice the normal display space). A 3×3 complete factorial design was employed, where each treatment was applied three times to a particular product at a particular supermarket. The dependent variable of interest was unit sales for the week. (To minimize treatment carryover effects, each treatment was preceded and followed by a week in which the product was priced at its regular price and was displayed in its normal manner.) The next table reports the data collected.

a. How many treatments are considered in this study?
b. Do the data indicate that the mean sales differ among the treatments? Test using $\alpha = .10$.
c. Is the test of interaction between the factors price and Display warranted as a result of the test in part **b**? If so, conduct the test using $\alpha = .10$.
d. Are the tests of the main effects for Price and Display warranted as a result of the previous tests? If so, conduct them using $\alpha = .10$.
e. Which pairs of treatment means should be compared as a result of the tests in parts **b–d**?

		Price		
		Regular	Reduced	Cost to Supermarket
Display	Normal	989 / 1,025 / 1,030	1,211 / 1,215 / 1,182	1,577 / 1,559 / 1,598
	Normal Plus	1,191 / 1,233 / 1,221	1,860 / 1,910 / 1,926	2,492 / 2,527 / 2,511
	Twice Normal	1,226 / 1,202 / 1,180	1,516 / 1,501 / 1,498	1,801 / 1,833 / 1,852

Applying the Concepts—Advanced

9.107 Testing a new insect repellent. Traditionally, people protect themselves from mosquito bites by applying insect repellent to their skin and clothing. Research suggests that permethrin, an insecticide with low toxicity to humans, can provide protection from mosquitoes. A study in the *Journal of the American Mosquito Control Association* (March 1995) investigated whether a tent sprayed with a commercially available 1% permethrin formulation would protect people, both inside and outside the tent, against biting mosquitoes. Two canvas tents—one treated with permethrin, the other untreated—were positioned 25 meters apart on flat, dry ground in an area infested with mosquitoes. Eight people participated in the experiment, with four randomly assigned to each tent. Of the four stationed at each tent, two were randomly assigned to stay inside the tent (at opposite corners) and two to stay outside the tent (at opposite corners). During a specified 20-minute period during the night, each person kept count of the number of mosquito bites received. The goal of the study was to determine the effect of both Tent type (treated or untreated) and Location (inside or outside the tent) on the mean mosquito bite count.

a. What type of design was employed in the study?

b. Identify the factors and treatments.

c. Identify the response variable.

d. The study found statistical evidence of interaction between Tent type and Location. Give a practical interpretation of this result.

9.108 **Exam performance study.** The *Teaching of Psychology* (August 1998) published a study of whether a practice test helps students prepare for a final exam. Undergraduate students were grouped according to their class standing and whether they attended a review session or took a practice test prior to the final exam. The experimental design was a 3×2 factorial design, with Class Standing at three levels (low, medium, or high) and Exam Preparation at two levels (practice exam or review session). There were 22 students in each of the $3 \times 2 = 6$ treatment groups. After completing the final exam, each student rated his/her exam preparation on an 11-point scale ranging from 0 (not helpful at all) to 10 (extremely helpful). The data for this experiment (simulated from summary statistics provided in the article) are saved in the accompanying file. (The first 5 and last 5 observations in the data set are listed below.) Conduct a complete analysis of variance of the helpfulness ratings data, including (if warranted) multiple comparisons of means. Do your findings support the research conclusion that "students at all levels of academic ability benefit from a . . . practice exam"?

 PRACEX

Exam Preparation	Class Standing	Helpfulness Rating
Practice	Low	6
Practice	Low	7
Practice	Low	7
Practice	Low	5
Practice	Low	3
⋮	⋮	⋮
Review	High	5
Review	High	2
Review	High	5
Review	High	4
Review	High	3

Source: Republished with permission of Sage Publications, Inc. (US), from W. R. Balch, "Practice Versus Review Exams and Final Exam Performance," *Teaching of Psychology*, Vol. 25, No. 3. Permission conveyed through Copyright Clearance Center, Inc.

Critical Thinking Challenge

9.109 **Pollutants at a housing development.** Polycyclic aromatic hydrocarbons (PAHs)—formed during the incomplete burning of oil, gas, or coal—are considered to be potential dangerous pollutants by the Environmental Protection Agency (EPA). Consider an actual developer who purchased a large parcel of land in Florida that he planned to turn into a residential community. Because the parcel turned out to have significant deposits of PAHs, the developer was required to remove these pollutants from the

site prior to commencing development. The clean-up was completed, but the housing bubble burst and the development was a bust. The developer blamed the failure of his plan on the discovery of the pollutants, and filed suit against two industries (named Industry A and B) that were within 25 miles of the site. Although both industries produced PAH waste materials as part of their industrial processes, both denied responsibility for the pollution. Experts were hired to investigate the degree of similarity between pollutants at the industrial sites and those at the development site. Soil specimens were collected at each of four locations: 7 at the housing development site, 8 at Industry A, 5 at Industry B, and 2 at Industry C. Two different molecular diagnostic ratios for measuring the level of PAH in soil were determined for each soil specimen. These data are displayed in the accompanying table.

Soil Specimen	SITE	RATIO PAH1	PAH2
1	Development	0.620	1.040
2	Development	0.630	1.020
3	Development	0.660	1.070
4	Development	0.670	1.180
5	Development	0.610	1.020
6	Development	0.670	1.090
7	Development	0.660	1.100
8	IndustryA	0.620	0.950
9	IndustryA	0.660	1.090
10	IndustryA	0.700	0.960
11	IndustryA	0.560	0.970
12	IndustryA	0.560	1.000
13	IndustryA	0.570	1.030
14	IndustryA	0.600	0.970
15	IndustryA	0.580	1.015
16	IndustryB	0.770	1.130
17	IndustryB	0.720	1.110
18	IndustryB	0.560	0.980
19	IndustryB	0.705	1.130
20	IndustryB	0.670	1.140
21	IndustryC	0.675	1.115
22	IndustryC	0.650	1.060

a. A biochemical expert hired by Industry A chose to analyze the data using a series of *t*-tests for comparing two means. That is, he conducted a two-sample *t*-test (Section 8.2) using $\alpha = .05$ for each possible pair of sites: Industry A vs. Industry B, Industry A vs. Industry C, Industry A vs. Development, Industry B vs. Industry C, Industry B vs. Development, and Industry C vs. Development. The results of these 6 *t*-tests for the second PAH ratio variable led the expert to conclude that (1) mean PAH2 ratio at the development site is *statistically different* from the corresponding mean at Industry A and (2) the mean PAH2 ratio at the development site is not *statistically different* from the corresponding mean at Industry B. Use the data in the **PAH** file to replicate these results.

b. The inferences derived in part **a** led the expert to argue that the source of the PAH contamination at the housing development site is more likely to have been derived from Industry A than from Industry B. A statistician, hired to rebut this testimony, argued that the analysis (and subsequent inference) was flawed. Explain why.

c. Propose a better, more statistically valid, method of analyzing the data. Conduct this analysis for both dependent variables, PAH Ratio 1 and PAH Ratio 2. What do you conclude?

d. According to the statistician's court testimony, "the results provide clear evidence that these samples are simply too small to make a reliable determination about the sites' similarity or dissimilarity with respect to [PAH] diagnostic ratios." The statistician went on

to conclude that "the small samples relied upon by [the biochemical expert] shed no light on the issue of whether [Industry A and Industry B] are similar or dissimilar to the [development] site." Do you agree? [*Concluding Note:* The trial judge ultimately decided that the biochemist's statistical analyses and his opinions based on them would be excluded from the evidence used to decide the case. As of this date, the issue of responsibility for the pollution has still not been decided.]

ACTIVITY 9.1   Designed vs. Observational Experiments

In this activity, you will revisit Activity 8.1 and Activity 8.2 (p. 511) and consider two new but similar experiments.

1. Explain why both of the situations in Activity 8.1 and Activity 8.2 are observational experiments. What key elements of a designed experiment are missing in each situation?

2. A movie company wishes to measure the effect of advertising on box office receipts. Thirty U.S. cities with similar demographics are chosen for an experiment. The 30 cities are randomly divided into three groups of 10 cities. In each city a trailer for a new film will be run on a local cable station during prime time in the week leading up to the release of the film. In the first group of 10 cities the trailer will be run 500 times, in the second group the trailer will be run 1,000 times, and in the third group it will be run 1,500 times. The company will collect the box office receipts for the opening weekend of the film in each city and compare the mean box office receipts.

   Explain why this is a designed experiment. Identify the factor and the response variable. Is the factor quantitative or qualitative? Identify the factor levels and the experimental units. What part of choosing the cities is not necessarily random? Explain why it might be difficult to randomize this part of the experiment.

3. Suppose Bank of America wants to determine whether e-mail and postcard reminders of the benefits of the *Keep*

the Change program result in customers using their debit cards more often. A random sample of customers is chosen and split into four groups. The customers in one group are sent an e-mail reminder, those in the second group are sent a postcard, the customers in the third group are sent both, and those in the last group are sent neither. The bank keeps track of how many more times each customer uses his/her debit card in the 2 weeks after the reminders are sent as compared to the 2 weeks before the reminders are sent. The means for the four groups are compared.

   Explain why this is a designed experiment. Identify the factors and the response variable. Is the factor quantitative or qualitative? Identify the factor levels, the treatments, and the experimental units. Comparing this experiment with that in Exercise 2, why is it more realistic to choose a random sample for the experiment?

4. For each of the designed experiments in Exercises 2 and 3, rework the experiment to have a randomized block design. Explain how you will choose your experimental units from each population. Then describe the criteria you would use to split the experimental units into matched sets. How do you determine which experimental unit in each matched set receives each level of treatment? What data are collected and how are the data compared? Do you believe that there is any benefit to the block design? Explain.

References

Cochran, W. G., and Cox, G. M. *Experimental Designs*, 2nd ed. New York: Wiley, 1957.

Hsu, J. C. *Multiple Comparisons: Theory and Methods*. London: Chapman & Hall, 1996.

Koehler, K. *Snedecor and Cochran's Statistical Methods*, 9th ed. New York: Blackwell Publishing, 2012.

Kramer, C. Y. "Extension of multiple range tests to group means with unequal number of replications," *Biometrics*, Vol. 12, 1956, pp. 307–310.

Kutner, M., Nachtsheim, C., Neter, J., and Li, W. *Applied Linear Statistical Models*, 5th ed. New York: McGraw-Hill/Irwin, 2005.

Mason, R. L., Gunst, R. F., and Hess, J. L. *Statistical Design and Analysis of Experiments*. New York: Wiley, 1989.

Mendenhall, W. *Introduction to Linear Models and the Design and Analysis of Experiments*. Belmont, Calif.: Wadsworth, 1968.

Miller, R. G., Jr. *Simultaneous Statistical Inference*. New York: Springer-Verlag, 1981.

Scheffé, H. "A method for judging all contrasts in the analysis of variance," *Biometrica*, Vol. 40, 1953, pp. 87–104.

Scheffé, H. *The Analysis of Variance*. New York: Wiley, 1959.

Steele, R. G. D., and Torrie, J. H. *Principles and Procedures of Statistics: A Biometrical Approach*, 2nd ed. New York: McGraw-Hill, 1980.

Tukey, J. "Comparing individual means in the analysis of variance," *Biometrics*, Vol. 5, 1949, pp. 99–114.

Winer, B. J. *Statistical Principles in Experimental Design*, 2nd ed. New York: McGraw-Hill, 1971.

USING TECHNOLOGY | Technology images shown here are taken from SPSS Statistics Professional 23.0, Minitab 17, XLSTAT, and Excel 2016.

SPSS: Analysis of Variance

SPSS can conduct ANOVAs for all three types of experimental designs discussed in this chapter: completely randomized, randomized block, and factorial designs.

Completely Randomized Design

Step 1 Access the SPSS spreadsheet file that contains the sample data. The data file should contain one quantitative variable (the response, or dependent, variable) and one factor variable with at least two levels. (These values must be numbers, e.g., 1, 2, 3, . . .)

Step 2 Click on the "Analyze" button on the SPSS menu bar, then click on "Compare Means" and "One-Way ANOVA," as shown in Figure 9.S.1.

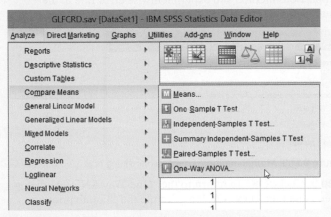

Figure 9.S.1 SPSS menu options for one-way ANOVA

Step 3 In the resulting dialog box (shown in Figure 9.S.2), specify the response variable under "Dependent List" and the factor variable under "Factor."

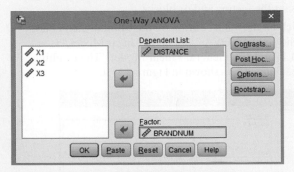

Figure 9.S.2 SPSS one-way ANOVA dialog box

Step 4 Click the "Post Hoc" button and select a multiple comparisons method and experimentwise error rate in the resulting dialog box (see Figure 9.S.3).

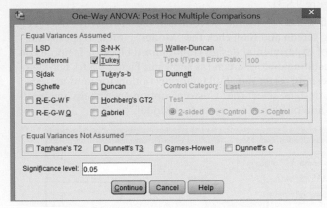

Figure 9.S.3 SPSS multiple comparisons dialog box

Step 5 Click "Continue" to return to the "One-Way ANOVA" dialog screen and then click "OK" to generate the SPSS printout.

Randomized Block and Factorial Designs

Step 1 Access the SPSS spreadsheet file that contains the sample data. The data file should contain one quantitative variable (the response, or dependent, variable) and at least two other variables that represent the factors and/or blocks.

Step 2 Click on the "Analyze" button on the SPSS menu bar and then click on "General Linear Model" and "Univariate," as shown in Figure 9.S.4.

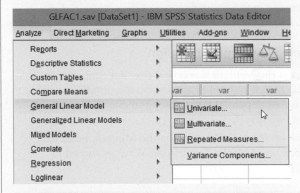

Figure 9.S.4 SPSS menu options for two-way ANOVA

Step 3 On the resulting dialog box (Figure 9.S.5), specify the response variable under "Dependent Variable" and the factor variable(s) and block variable under "Fixed Factor(s)."

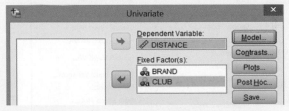

Figure 9.S.5 SPSS two-way ANOVA dialog box

Step 4 Click the "Post Hoc" button and select the factor variable of interest, a multiple comparisons method, and experimentwise error rate in the resulting dialog box (similar to Figure 9.S.3).

Step 5 Click "Continue" to return to the "Two-Way ANOVA" dialog screen and then click the "Model" button to specify the type of experimental design (randomized block or factorial) on the resulting dialog screen (as shown in Figure 9.S.6). For factorial designs, select the "Full factorial" option; for randomized block designs, select the "Custom" option and specify the treatment and blocking factors under "Model."

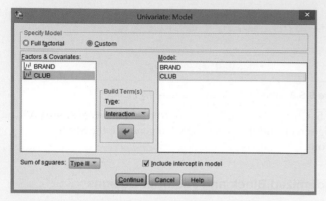

Figure 9.S.6 SPSS design (model) specification box

Step 6 Click "Continue" to return to the "Two-Way ANOVA" dialog screen and then click "OK" to generate the SPSS printout.

Minitab: Analysis of Variance

Minitab can conduct ANOVAs for all three types of experimental designs discussed in this chapter: completely randomized, randomized block, and factorial designs.

Completely Randomized Design

Step 1 Access the Minitab worksheet file that contains the sample data. The data file should contain one quantitative variable (the response, or dependent, variable) and one factor variable with at least two levels.

Step 2 Click on the "Stat" button on the Minitab menu bar and then click on "ANOVA" and "One-Way," as shown in Figure 9.M.1.

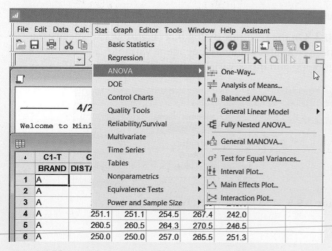

Figure 9.M.1 Minitab menu options for one-way ANOVA

Step 3 On the resulting dialog screen (Figure 9.M.2), specify the response variable in the "Response" box and the factor variable in the "Factor" box.

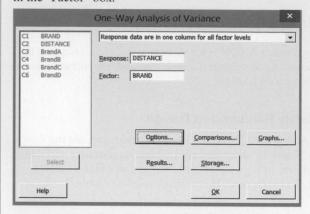

Figure 9.M.2 Minitab one-way ANOVA dialog box

Step 4 Click the "Comparisons" button and select a multiple comparisons method and experimentwise error rate in the resulting dialog box (see Figure 9.M.3).

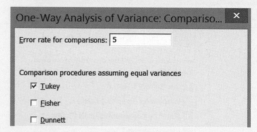

Figure 9.M.3 Minitab multiple comparisons dialog box

Step 5 Click "OK" to return to the "One-Way ANOVA" dialog screen and then click "OK" to generate the Minitab printout.

Randomized Block and Factorial Designs

Step 1 Access the Minitab worksheet file that contains the sample data. The data file should contain one quantitative variable (the response, or dependent, variable) and two other variables that represent the factors and/or blocks.

Step 2 Click on the "Stat" button on the Minitab menu bar and then click on "ANOVA," "General Linear Model," (see Figure 9.M.1) and "Fit General Linear Model." The resulting dialog screen appears as shown in Figure 9.M.4.

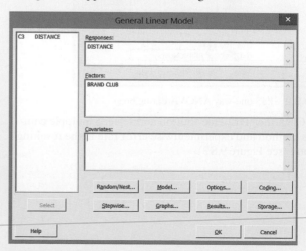

Figure 9.M.4 Minitab two-way ANOVA dialog box

Step 3 Specify the response variable in the "Response" box and the two factor variables in the "Factor" box. If the design is a randomized block, no further selections are necessary. If the design is factorial, click "Model." In the resulting dialog box (see Figure 9.M.5), highlight the two factors and click "Add" Interaction, then "OK".

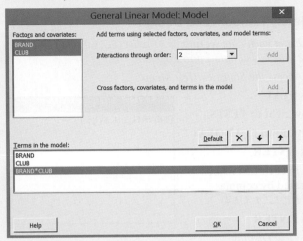

Figure 9.M.5 Minitab ANOVA Model dialog box

Step 4 Click "OK" to generate the Minitab printout.

Note: Multiple comparisons of treatment means are obtained by selecting "Stat," "ANOVA," "General Linear Model," and then "Comparisons." On the resulting dialog box, select the comparisons method (e.g., Tukey) and the factor (or factors) for which means will be compared. Press "OK" to view the results.

Excel/XLSTAT: Analysis of Variance

XLSTAT can conduct ANOVAs for all three types of experimental designs discussed in this chapter: completely randomized design, randomized block design, and two-factor factorial designs. The Excel workbook file should include a column for the quantitative dependent (response) variable, and columns for the qualitative factors.

Completely Randomized Design

Step 1 Click the "XLSTAT" button on the Excel main menu bar, select "Modeling Data," then click "ANOVA," as shown in Figure 9.E.1.

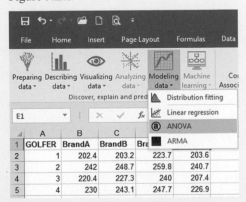

Figure 9.E.1 XLSTAT menu options for analysis of variance

Step 2 When the resulting dialog box appears, enter the appropriate column for the quantitative dependent variable in the "Y / Dependent variables" box and the appropriate column for the qualitative factor variable in the "X / Explanatory variables" box. (*Note:* Be sure to check "Qualitative" and enter the factor column in this box.) See, for example, Figure 9.E.2.

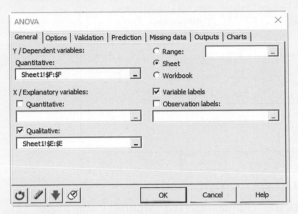

Figure 9.E.2 XLSTAT ANOVA dialog box

Step 3 Click the "Outputs" tab and then the "Means" tab to run a multiple comparisons of means. On the resulting dialog box, check "Pairwise comparisons," then select the method (e.g., Tukey), as shown in Figure 9.E.3. [*Note:* The default EER is .05. If you want to change the EER value, click the "Options" tab on the ANOVA dialog box and specify a different confidence interval percentage (e.g., 90%).]

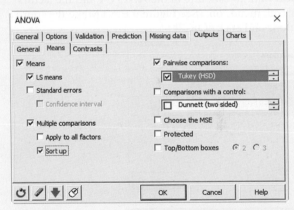

Figure 9.E.3 XLSTAT output options for analysis of variance

Step 4 Click "OK," then "Continue" to display the test results.

Randomized Block and Factorial Designs

Step 1 Click the "XLSTAT" button on the Excel main menu bar, select "Modeling Data," then click "ANOVA," as shown in Figure 9.E.1.

Step 2 When the resulting dialog box appears, enter the appropriate column for the quantitative dependent variable in the "Y / Dependent variables" box and the appropriate columns for the qualitative factor variables in the "X / Explanatory variables" box. (*Note:* Be sure to check "Qualitative" and enter the factor columns in this box.) See, for example, Figure 9.E.2.

Step 3 To run a factorial ANOVA, click the "Options" tab and check "Interactions" on the resulting screen, as shown in Figure 9.E.4. [*Note:* Do not check "Interactions" when running a randomized block ANOVA.]

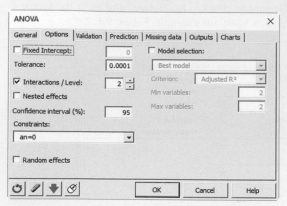

Figure 9.E.4 XLSTAT ANOVA options

Step 4 Click the "Outputs" tab and "Multiple Comparisons" tabs to run a multiple comparisons of means. On the resulting dialog box, check "Pairwise comparisons," then select the method (e.g., Tukey), as shown in Figure 9.E.3. [*Note:* The default EER is .05. If you want to change the EER value, click the "Options" tab on the ANOVA dialog box and specify a different confidence interval percentage (e.g., 90%).]

Step 5 Click "OK," then "Continue" to display the test results. [*Note:* For two-factor designs, XLSTAT will prompt you to select the effects you want to estimate in the ANOVA and the factors you want to rank means on. (See Figure 9.E.5.) Make the appropriate selections and click "OK."]

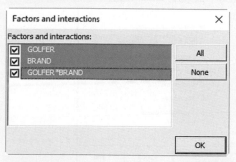

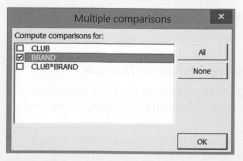

Figure 9.E.5 XLSTAT ANOVA model selections

TI-84 Graphing Calculator: Analysis of Variance

The TI-84 graphing calculator can be used to compute a one-way ANOVA for a completely randomized design but not a two-way ANOVA for either a randomized block or factorial design.

Completely Randomized Design

Step 1 *Enter each data set into its own list (i.e., sample 1 into L1, sample 2 into L2, sample 3 into L3, etc.).*

Step 2 *Access the Statistical Test Menu*

- Press **STAT**
- Arrow right to **TESTS**
- Arrow down to **ANOVA(**
- Press **ENTER**
- Type in each List name separated by commas (*e.g., L1, L2, L3, L4*)
- Press **ENTER**

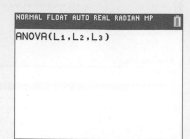

Step 3 *View Display*

The calculator will display the *F*-test statistic, as well as the *p*-value, the factor degrees of freedom, sum of squares, mean square, and by arrowing down, the Error degrees of freedom, sum of squares, mean square, and the pooled standard deviation.

10

WHERE WE'VE BEEN

Presented methods for making inferences about the population proportion associated with a two-level qualitative variable (i.e., a binomial variable)

Presented methods for making inferences about the difference between two binomial proportions

WHERE WE'RE GOING

Discuss qualitative (i.e., categorical) data with more than two outcomes (10.1)

Present a *chi-square* hypothesis test for comparing the category proportions associated with a single qualitative variable—called a *one-way analysis* (10.2)

Present a *chi-square* hypothesis test for relating two qualitative variables—called a *two-way analysis* (10.3)

Caution about the misuse of chi-square tests (10.4)

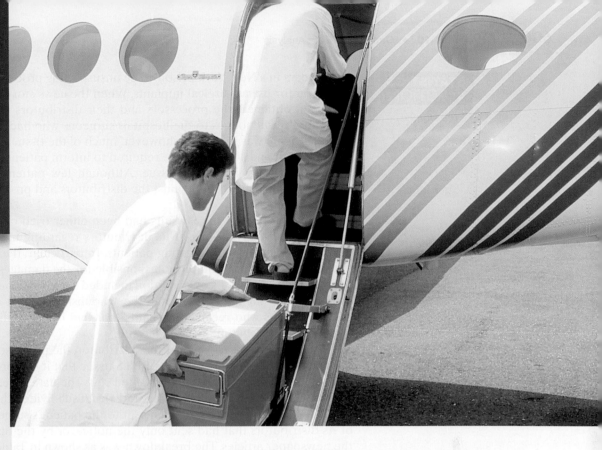

Categorical Data Analysis

STATISTICS IN ACTION The Illegal Transplant Tissue Trade—Who Is Responsible for Paying Damages?

According to Organ and Tissue Transplantation and Alternatives *(January 1, 2011), published by BCC Research, "The global market for transplantation products, devices, and pharmaceuticals was valued at nearly $54 billion in 2010 and is projected to grow at an 8.3% compound annual growth rate to reach $80 billion in 2015." In other words, the worldwide tissue transplant market is big business. Here in the United States, tissue implants are routinely performed to aid patients in various types of surgery, including joint replacements, spinal surgery, sports-related surgeries (tendons and ligaments), and others.**

The process of obtaining a tissue transplant involves several parties. First, of course, is the donor, who has agreed to have tissue removed upon death and whose family has approved the donation. The tissue is then "harvested" by an approved tissue bank. Next, the harvested tissue is sent to a processor, who sterilizes the tissue. Finally, the processor either sends it directly to the hospital/surgeon doing the implant or sends it to a distributor, who inventories the tissue and ultimately sends it on to the hospital/surgeon. The entire process is highly regulated by the Federal Trade Commission (FTC), particularly the harvesting and processing aspects.

Given this background, we consider an actual case that began in the early 2000s when the owner of a tissue bank—Biomedical Tissue Services (BTS)—became a ringleader of a group of funeral home directors that harvested tissue illegally and without the permission of donors or their families. In some cases the cadavers were cancerous or infected with HIV or hepatitis, all of which would, of course, disqualify them as donors. BTS then sent the tissue to processors without divulging that it had obtained the tissue illegally. (*Note:* The owner is currently serving a sentence of

*Source: "Organ and Tissue Transplantations," BBC Research Report.

18–24 years in a New York prison.) The unsuspecting processors sterilized the tissue and sent it on for use as surgical implants. When the news story broke about how the tissue had been obtained, the processors and their distributors were required to send FTC-mandated recall notices to the hospitals/surgeons who had received the tissue. Some of the BTS tissue was recovered; however, much of the tissue had already been implanted, and hospitals and surgeons were required to inform patients who had received implants of the potentially infectious tissue. Although few patients subsequently became infected, a number filed suit against the distributors and processors (and BTS) asking for monetary damages.

After the bulk of the lawsuits had been either tried or settled, a dispute arose between a processor and one of its distributors regarding ultimate responsibility for the payment of damages to litigating patients. In particular, the processor claimed that the distributor should be held more responsible for the damages, since in its recall package, the distributor had of its own volition included some salacious, inflammatory newspaper articles describing in graphic detail the "ghoulish" acts that had been committed. None of the patients who received implants that had been sterilized by this processor ever became infected, but many still filed suit.

To establish its case against the distributor, the processor collected data on the patients who had received implants of BTS tissue that it had processed and on the number of those patients who subsequently filed suit: The data revealed that of a total of 8,914 patients, 708 filed suit. A consulting statistician subdivided this information according to whether the recall notice had been sent to the patient's surgeon by the processor or one of its distributors that had sent only the notice, or by the distributor that had included the newspaper articles. The breakdown was as shown in Table SIA10.1:

Table SIA10.1	Data for the Tainted Tissue Case*	
Recall Notice Sender	Number of Patients	Number of Lawsuits
Processor/Other distributor	1,751	51
Distributor in question	6,163	657
Totals	8,914	708

Source: Info Tech, Inc.

Do these data provide evidence of a difference in the probability that a patient would file a lawsuit depending on which party sent the recall notice? If so, and if the probability is significantly higher for the distributor in question, then the processor can argue in court that the distributor who sent the inflammatory newspaper articles is more responsible for the damages.

We apply the statistical methodology presented in this chapter to solve the case of the illegal transplant tissue in the following *Statistics in Action Revisited* example.

STATISTICS IN ACTION REVISITED

• Testing Whether Likelihood of a Lawsuit Is Related to Recall Notice Sender **(p. 618)**

10.1 Categorical Data and the Multinomial Experiment

Recall from Section 1.5 that observations on a qualitative variable can be categorized only. For example, consider the highest level of education attained by each in a group of salespersons. Level of education is a qualitative variable, and each salesperson would fall in one and only one of the following five categories: some high school, high school diploma, some college, college degree, and graduate degree. The result of the categorization would be a count of the numbers of salespersons falling into the respective categories.

*For confidentiality purposes, the parties in the case cannot be identified. Permission to use the data in this *Statistics in Action* has been granted by the consulting statistician.

When the qualitative variable results in one of two responses (yes or no, success or failure, favor or do not favor, etc.), the data—called *counts*—can be analyzed using the binomial probability distribution discussed in Section 4.3. However, qualitative variables, such as level of education, that allow for more than two categories for a response are much more common, and these must be analyzed using a different method.

Qualitative data that fall in more than two categories often result from a **multinomial experiment.** The characteristics for a multinomial experiment with k outcomes are described in the box. You can see that the binomial experiment of Chapter 4 is a multinomial experiment with $k = 2$.

Properties of the Multinomial Experiment

1. The experiment consists of n identical trials.

2. There are k possible outcomes to each trial. These outcomes are called **classes, categories,** or **cells.**

3. The probabilities of the k outcomes, denoted by $p_1, p_2, \ldots, p_k$, remain the same from trial to trial, where $p_1 + p_2 + \cdots + p_k = 1$.

4. The trials are independent.

5. The random variables of interest are the **cell counts,** $n_1, n_2, \ldots, n_k$, of the number of observations that fall in each of the k classes.

EXAMPLE 10.1

Identifying a Multinomial Experiment

Problem Consider the problem of determining the highest level of education attained by each of $n = 100$ salespersons at a large company. Suppose we categorize level of education into one of five categories—some high school, high school diploma, some college, college degree, and graduate degree—and count the number of the 100 salespeople that fall into each category. Is this a multinomial experiment to a reasonable degree of approximation?

Solution Checking the five properties of a multinomial experiment shown in the box, we have the following:

1. The experiment consists of $n = 100$ identical trials, where each trial is to determine the highest level of education of a salesperson.

2. There are $k = 5$ possible outcomes to each trial corresponding to the five education-level categories.

3. The probabilities of the $k = 5$ outcomes, p_1, p_2, p_3, p_4, and p_5, remain (to a reasonable degree of approximation) the same from trial to trial, where p_i represents the true probability that a salesperson attains level of education i.

4. The trials are independent (i.e., the education level attained by one salesperson does not affect the level attained by any other salesperson).

5. We are interested in the count of the number of salespeople who fall into each of the five categories. These five *cell counts* are denoted n_1, n_2, n_3, n_4, and n_5.

Thus, the properties of a multinomial experiment are satisfied.

In this chapter, we are concerned with the analysis of categorical data—specifically, the data that represent the counts for each category of a multinomial experiment. In Section 10.2, we learn how to make inferences about category probabilities for data classified according to a single qualitative (or categorical) variable. Then, in Section 10.3, we consider inferences about category probabilities for data classified according to two qualitative variables. The statistic used for these inferences is one that possesses, approximately, the familiar chi-square distribution.

10.2 Testing Category Probabilities: One-Way Table

In this section, we consider a multinomial experiment with k outcomes that correspond to categories of a *single* qualitative variable. The results of such an experiment are summarized in a **one-way table.** The term *one-way* is used because only one variable is classified. Typically, we want to make inferences about the true proportions that occur in the k categories based on the sample information in the one-way table.

To illustrate, suppose a large supermarket chain conducts a consumer-preference survey by recording the brand of bread purchased by customers in its stores. Assume the chain carries three brands of bread—two major brands (A and B) and its own store brand. The brand preferences of a random sample of 150 consumers are observed, and the number preferring each brand is tabulated; the resulting count data appear in Table 10.1.

Note that our consumer-preference survey satisfies the properties of a multinomial experiment for the qualitative variable brand of bread. The experiment consists of randomly sampling $n = 150$ buyers from a large population of consumers containing an unknown proportion p_1 who prefer brand A, a proportion p_2 who prefer brand B, and a proportion p_3 who prefer the store brand. Each buyer represents a single trial that can result in one of three outcomes: The consumer prefers brand A, B, or the store brand with probabilities $p_1, p_2,$ and p_3, respectively. (Assume that all consumers will have a preference.) The buyer preference of any single consumer in the sample does not affect the preference of another; consequently, the trials are independent. And, finally, you can see that the recorded data are the number of buyers in each of three consumer-preference categories. Thus, the consumer-preference survey satisfies the five properties of a multinomial experiment.

In the consumer-preference survey, and in most practical applications of the multinomial experiment, the k outcome probabilities $p_1, p_2, \ldots, p_k$ are unknown, and we typically want to use the survey data to make inferences about their values. The unknown probabilities in the consumer-preference survey are

$$p_1 = \text{Proportion of all buyers who prefer brand A}$$
$$p_2 = \text{Proportion of all buyers who prefer brand B}$$
$$p_3 = \text{Proportion of all buyers who prefer the store brand}$$

For example, to decide whether the consumers have a preference for any of the brands, we will want to test the null hypothesis that the brands of bread are equally preferred (that is, $p_1 = p_2 = p_3 = \frac{1}{3}$) against the alternative hypothesis that one brand is preferred (that is, at least one of the probabilities $p_1, p_2,$ and p_3 exceeds $\frac{1}{3}$). Thus, we want to test

$H_0: p_1 = p_2 = p_3 = \frac{1}{3}$ (no preference)

$H_a:$ At least one of the proportions exceeds $\frac{1}{3}$ (a preference exists)

If the null hypothesis is true and $p_1 = p_2 = p_3 = \frac{1}{3}$, the expected value (mean value) of the number of customers who prefer brand A is given by

$$E_1 = np_1 = (n)\tfrac{1}{3} = (150)\tfrac{1}{3} = 50$$

Similarly, $E_2 = E_3 = 50$ if the null hypothesis is true and no preference exists.

The following test statistic—the **chi-square test**—measures the degree of disagreement between the data and the null hypothesis:

$$\chi^2 = \frac{[n_1 - E_1]^2}{E_1} + \frac{[n_2 - E_2]^2}{E_2} + \frac{[n_3 - E_3]^2}{E_3}$$
$$= \frac{(n_1 - 50)^2}{50} + \frac{(n_2 - 50)^2}{50} + \frac{(n_3 - 50)^2}{50}$$

Note that the farther the observed numbers $n_1, n_2,$ and n_3 are from their expected value (50), the larger χ^2 will become—that is, large values of χ^2 imply that the null hypothesis is false.

Table 10.1
Results of Consumer Preference Survey

A	B	Store Brand
61	53	36

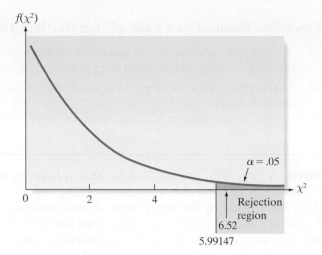

Figure 10.1

Rejection region for consumer-preference survey

KARL PEARSON (1857–1936)
The Father of Statistics

While attending college, London-born Karl Pearson exhibited a wide range of interests, including mathematics, physics, religion, history, socialism, and Darwinism. After earning a law degree at Cambridge University and a PhD in political science at the University of Heidelberg (Germany), Pearson became a professor of applied mathematics at University College in London. His 1892 book, *The Grammar of Science,* illustrated his conviction that statistical data analysis lies at the foundation of all knowledge; consequently, many consider Pearson to be the "father of statistics." A few of Pearson's many contributions to the field include introducing the term *standard deviation* and its associated symbol (σ), developing the distribution of the correlation coefficient, cofounding and editing the prestigious statistics journal *Biometrika,* and (what many consider his greatest achievement) creating the first chi-square "goodness-of-fit" test. Pearson inspired his students (including his son, Egon, and William Gossett) with his wonderful lectures and enthusiasm for statistics.

We have to know the distribution of χ^2 in repeated sampling before we can decide whether the data indicate that a preference exists. When H_0 is true, χ^2 can be shown to have (approximately) the chi-square distribution of Section 6.6. For this one-way classification, the χ^2 distribution has $(k - 1)$ degrees of freedom.* The rejection region for the consumer-preference survey for $\alpha = .05$ and $k - 1 = 3 - 1 = 2$ df is

$$\text{Rejection region: } \chi^2 > \chi^2_{.05}$$

The value of $\chi^2_{.05}$ (found in Table IV in Appendix D) is 5.99147. (See Figure 10.1.) The computed value of the test statistic is

$$\chi^2 = \frac{(n_1 - 50)^2}{50} + \frac{(n_2 - 50)^2}{50} + \frac{(n_3 - 50)^2}{50}$$
$$= \frac{(61 - 50)^2}{50} + \frac{(53 - 50)^2}{50} + \frac{(36 - 50)^2}{50} = 6.52$$

Since the computed $\chi^2 = 6.52$ exceeds the critical value of 5.99147, we conclude at the $\alpha = .05$ level of significance that a consumer preference exists for one or more of the brands of bread.

Now that we have evidence to indicate that the proportions $p_1, p_2,$ and p_3 are unequal, we can make inferences concerning their individual values using the methods of Section 6.4. [*Note:* We cannot use the methods of Section 8.4 to compare two proportions because the cell counts are dependent random variables.] The general form for a test of a hypothesis concerning multinomial probabilities is shown in the next box.

A Test of a Hypothesis About Multinomial Probabilities: One-Way Table

$$H_0: p_1 = p_{1,0}, p_2 = p_{2,0}, \ldots, p_k = p_{k,0}$$

where $p_{1,0}, p_{2,0}, \ldots, p_{k,0}$ represent the hypothesized values of the multinomial probabilities.

H_a: At least one of the multinomial probabilities does not equal its hypothesized value.

Test statistic: $\chi^2 = \sum \dfrac{[n_i - E_i]^2}{E_i}$

where $E_i = np_{i,0}$ is the **expected cell count**—that is, the expected number of outcomes of type i assuming that H_0 is true. The total sample size is n.

$$\text{Rejection region: } \chi^2 > \chi^2_\alpha$$
$$\text{p-value: } P(\chi^2 > \chi^2_c)$$

where χ^2_α has $(k - 1)$ df and χ^2_c is the computed value of the test statistic.

---

* The derivation of the degrees of freedom for χ^2 involves the number of linear restrictions imposed on the count data. In the present case, the only constraint is that $\Sigma n_i = n$, where n (the sample size) is fixed in advance. Therefore, df $= k - 1$. For other cases, we will give the degrees of freedom for each usage of χ^2 and refer the interested reader to the references for more detail.

Conditions Required for a Valid χ^2 Test: One-Way Table

1. A multinomial experiment has been conducted. This is generally satisfied by taking a random sample from the population of interest.

2. The sample size n is large. This is satisfied if for every cell, the expected cell count E_i will be equal to 5 or more.*

EXAMPLE 10.2

A One-Way χ^2 Test— Evaluating a Firm's Merit-Increase Plan

Problem A large firm has established what it hopes is an objective system of deciding on annual pay increases for its employees. The system is based on a series of evaluation scores determined by the supervisors of each employee. Employees with scores above 80 receive a merit pay increase, those with scores between 50 and 80 receive the standard increase, and those below 50 receive no increase. The firm designed the plan with the objective that, on the average, 25% of its employees would receive merit increases, 65% would receive standard increases, and 10% would receive no increase. After 1 year of operation using the new plan, the distribution of pay increases for a random sample of 600 company employees was as shown in Table 10.2. Test at the $\alpha = .01$ level to determine whether these data indicate that the distribution of pay increases differs significantly from the proportions established by the firm.

Solution Define the population proportions for the three pay increase categories to be

$$p_1 = \text{Proportion of employees who receive no pay increase}$$
$$p_2 = \text{Proportion of employees who receive a standard increase}$$
$$p_3 = \text{Proportion of employees who receive a merit increase}$$

Then the null hypothesis representing the distribution of percentages in the firm's proposed plan is

$$H_0: p_1 = .10, p_2 = .65, p_3 = .25$$

and the alternative is

H_a: At least two of the proportions differ from the firm's proposed plan.

Now, we have

$$Test\,statistic: \chi^2 = \sum \frac{[n_i - E_i]^2}{E_i}$$

where

$$E_1 = np_{1,0} = 600(.10) = 60$$
$$E_2 = np_{2,0} = 600(.65) = 390$$
$$E_3 = np_{3,0} = 600(.25) = 150$$

Since all these values are larger than 5, the χ^2 approximation is appropriate. Also, since the employees were randomly selected, the properties of the multinomial distribution are satisfied.

Rejection region: For $\alpha = .01$ and df $= k - 1 = 2$, reject H_0 if $\chi^2 > \chi^2_{.01}$, where (from Table IV in Appendix D) $\chi^2_{.01} = 9.21034$.

We now calculate the test statistic:

$$\chi^2 = \frac{(42 - 60)^2}{60} + \frac{(365 - 390)^2}{390} + \frac{(193 - 150)^2}{150} = 19.33$$

Table 10.2

Distribution of Pay Increases

None	Standard	Merit
42	365	193

 *Data Set:* PAYINC

---

*The assumption that all expected cell counts are at least 5 is necessary to ensure that the χ^2 approximation is appropriate. Exact methods for conducting the test of a hypothesis exist and may be used for small expected cell counts, but these methods are beyond the scope of this text. Also, some researchers relax this assumption somewhat, requiring expected cell counts to be at least 1 and no more than 20% to be less than 5.

This value exceeds the table value of χ^2 (9.21034); therefore, the data provide strong evidence ($\alpha = .01$) that the company's actual pay plan distribution differs from its proposed plan.

The χ^2 test can also be conducted using statistical software. Figure 10.2 is an Excel/XLSTAT printout of the analysis of the data in Table 10.2; note that the p-value of the test is reported as less than .0001. Because $\alpha = .01$ exceeds this p-value, there is sufficient evidence to reject H_0.

Figure 10.2

Excel/XLSTAT multinomial chi-square test for data in Table 10.2

Chi-square test:	
Chi-square (Observed value)	19.3292
Chi-square (Critical value)	5.9915
DF	2
p-value	< 0.0001
alpha	0.05

Look Back If the conclusion for the χ^2 test is "fail to reject H_0," then there is insufficient evidence to conclude that the actual pay plan distribution differs from the proposed plan as stated in H_0. Be careful not to "accept H_0" and conclude that $p_1 = .10$, $p_2 = .65$, and $p_3 = .25$. The probability (β) of a Type II error is unknown.

• **Now Work Exercise 10.7a**

If we focus on one particular outcome of a multinomial experiment, we can use the methods developed in Section 6.4 for a binomial proportion to establish a confidence interval for any one of the multinomial probabilities.* For example, if we want a 95% confidence interval for the proportion of the company's employees who will receive merit increases under the new system, we calculate

$$\hat{p}_3 \pm 1.96\sigma_{\hat{p}_3} \approx \hat{p}_3 \pm 1.96\sqrt{\frac{\hat{p}_3(1 - \hat{p}_3)}{n}} \qquad \text{where } \hat{p}_3 = \frac{n_3}{n} = \frac{193}{600} = .32$$

$$= .32 \pm 1.96\sqrt{\frac{(.32)(1 - .32)}{600}} = .32 \pm .04$$

Thus, we estimate that between 28% and 36% of the firm's employees will qualify for merit increases under the new plan. It appears that the firm will have to raise the requirements for merit increases in order to achieve the stated goal of a 25% employee qualification rate.

Exercises 10.1–10.18

Learning the Mechanics

10.1 Use Table IV in Appendix D to estimate the p-value for each of the following cases.
 a. $\chi^2 = 19.35$, $k = 10$
 b. $\chi^2 = 11.8$, $k = 7$
 c. $\chi^2 = 35.1$, $k = 13$

10.2 What are the characteristics of a multinomial experiment? Compare the characteristics with those of a binomial experiment.

10.3 What conditions must n satisfy to make the χ^2 test valid?

10.4 A multinomial experiment with $k = 3$ cells and $n = 320$ produced the data shown in the following one-way table. Do these data provide sufficient evidence to contradict the null hypothesis that $p_1 = .25$, $p_2 = .25$, and $p_3 = .50$? Test using $\alpha = .05$.

L10004

	Cell		
	1	2	3
n_i	78	60	182

*Note that focusing on one outcome has the effect of lumping the other $(k - 1)$ outcomes into a single group. Thus, we obtain, in effect, two outcomes—or a binomial experiment.

10.5 A multinomial experiment with $k = 4$ cells and $n = 205$ produced the data shown in the one-way table below.

L10005

	Cell			
	1	2	3	4
n_i	43	56	59	47

a. Do these data provide sufficient evidence to conclude that the multinomial probabilities differ? Test using $\alpha = .05$.

b. What are the Type I and Type II errors associated with the test of part **a?**

c. Construct a 95% confidence interval for the multinomial probability associated with cell 3.

Applying the Concepts—Basic

10.6 **Cable TV subscriptions and "cord cutters."** Refer to the *Pew Research Center Survey* (December 2015) of current and former cable/satellite TV customers, Exercise 2.4 (p. 72). In a representative sample of 2,001 adults living in the United States, 1,521 reported that they currently receive cable or satellite TV service at home; 180 revealed that they have never subscribed to cable/satellite TV service at home; and the remainder (300 adults) admitted that they are "cord cutters," i.e., they canceled the cable/satellite TV service. Suppose a major cable TV provider claims that in the population of all U.S. adults, 75% currently subscribe to cable/satellite TV service, 10% never have subscribed, and 15% are "cord cutters."

CABLETV

a. If the true percentages of U.S. adults in each subscriber status group are as claimed by the cable TV provider, how many of the sampled adults would you expect to find in each subscriber category?

b. Give the null hypothesis for testing the cable TV provider's claim.

c. Find the chi-square test statistic for testing the null hypothesis, part **b.**

d. Find the rejection region for the test if $\alpha = .05$.

e. Find the p-value of the test.

f. Give the appropriate conclusion for the test in the words of the problem.

10.7 **Do social robots walk or roll?** Refer to the *International Conference on Social Robotics* (Vol. 6414, 2010) study of how engineers design social robots, Exercise 2.5 (p. 72). In a random sample of 106 social robots obtained through a Web search, the researchers found that 63 were built with legs only, 20 with wheels only, 8 with both legs and wheels, and 15 with neither legs nor wheels. Prior to obtaining

NW

SOCROB

these sample results, a robot design engineer stated that 50% of all social robots produced have legs only, 30% have wheels only, 10% have both legs and wheels, and 10% have neither legs nor wheels.

a. Explain why the data collected for each sampled social robot are categorical in nature.

b. Specify the null and alternative hypotheses for testing the design engineer's claim.

c. Assuming the claim is true, determine the number of social robots in the sample that you expect to fall into each design category.

d. Use the results to compute the chi-square test statistic.

e. Make the appropriate conclusion using $\alpha = .05$.

10.8 **Rankings of MBA programs.** *Business Ethics* (Fall 2005) published rankings of master in business administration (MBA) programs worldwide. Each of 30 business schools was rated according to student exposure to social and environmental issues in the classroom. Ratings ranged from 1 star (lowest-rated group) to 5 stars (highest-rated group). A summary of the star ratings assigned to the 30 MBA programs is reproduced in the table.

MBASTR

Criteria	5 stars	4 stars	3 stars	2 stars	1 star	Total
Student Exposure	2	9	14	5	0	30

Source: Based on the source D. Biello, "MBA Programs for Social and Environmental Stewardship," *Business Ethics,* Fall 2005, p. 25.

a. Identify the categorical variable (and its levels) measured in this study.

b. How many of the sampled MBA programs would you expect to observe in each star rating category if there are no differences in the category proportions in the population of all MBA programs?

c. Specify the null and alternative hypotheses for testing whether there are differences in the star rating category proportions in the population of all MBA programs.

d. Calculate the χ^2 test statistic for testing the hypotheses in part **c.**

e. Give the rejection region for the test using $\alpha = .05$.

f. Use the results, parts **d** and **e,** to make the appropriate conclusion.

g. Find and interpret a 95% confidence interval for the proportion of all MBA programs that are ranked in the three-star category.

10.9 **Museum management.** Refer to the *Museum Management and Curatorship* (June 2010) worldwide survey of 30 leading museums of contemporary art, Exercise 2.14 (p. 74).

MMC

Chi-Square Goodness-of-Fit Test for Observed Counts in Variable: Number

Using category names in PERFORM Measure

Category	Observed	Test Proportion	Expected	Contribution to Chi-Sq
Total visitors	8	0.2	6	0.666667
Paying visitors	5	0.2	6	0.166667
Big shows	6	0.2	6	0.000000
Funds raised	7	0.2	6	0.166667
Members	4	0.2	6	0.666667

N	DF	Chi-Sq	P-Value
30	4	1.66667	0.797

Minitab output for Exercise 10.9

Recall that each museum manager was asked to provide the performance measure used most often for internal evaluation. A summary of the results is provided in the table (next column). The data were analyzed using a chi-square test for a multinomial experiment. The results are shown in the Minitab printout on the previous page.

Performance Measure	Number of Museums
Total visitors	8
Paying visitors	5
Big shows	6
Funds raised	7
Members	4

NW
a. Is there evidence to indicate that one performance measure is used more often than any of the others? Test using $\alpha = .10$.
b. Find a 90% confidence interval for the proportion of museums worldwide that use total visitors as their performance measure. Interpret the result.

10.10 Offshoring companies. "Offshoring" is a term that describes a company's practice of relocating jobs and/or production to another country to reduce labor costs. *The Journal of Applied Business Research* (January/February 2011) published a study on the phenomenon of offshoring and how prevalent it is worldwide. The article included the results from a recent survey of CEOs at U.S. firms, where each CEO was asked about his or her firm's position on offshoring. A summary of the results (similar to the actual study) is shown in the accompanying table.

OFSHR1

Firm's Position	Number of Firms
Currently offshoring	126
Not currently offshoring, but plan to do so in the future	72
Offshored in the past, but no more	30
Offshoring not applicable	372
Total	600

a. Identify the qualitative variable of interest (and its levels) for this study.
b. Are the proportions of U.S. firms in the four offshoring position categories significantly different? Conduct the appropriate chi-square test using $\alpha = .05$.
c. Construct a 95% confidence interval for the proportion of U.S. firms who are currently offshoring. Interpret the result.

Applying the Concepts—Intermediate

10.11 Tourists' view of destination image. Tourism Web sites such as Trip Advisor provide a medium for online marketing of a travel destination. Actual tourists' evaluations and reviews of this marketing tool—called destination image—were assessed in a study published in the *Journal of Destination Marketing & Management* (October 2015). The study focused on a sample of 505 tourists who submitted posts on TripAdvisor about The Historic Areas of Istanbul (Turkey) page. The researchers classified each post according to destination image component: Cognitive (awareness of the destination), Affective (feelings toward the destination), or Conative (action taken). The results are summarized in the accompanying table. On the basis of

DIMAGE

the sample data, can you conclude that in the population of posts to a travel destination Web site there are no differences in the percentages of posts classified into the three destination image categories? Test using $\alpha = .10$.

Destination Image	Frequency	Percentage (%)
Cognitive	338	66.9
Affective	112	22.2
Conative	55	10.9

Source: Republished with permission of Elsevier, from S. Kladou and E. Mavragani, "Assessing Destination Image: An Online Marketing Approach and the Case of TripAdvisor," *Journal of Destination Marketing & Management*, Vol. 4, October 2015 (Table 2). Permission conveyed through Copyright Clearance Center, Inc.

10.12 Traffic sign maintenance. Refer to the *Journal of Transportation Engineering* (June 2013) study of traffic sign maintenance, Exercise 8.54 (p. 489). Recall that civil engineers estimated the proportion of traffic signs maintained by the North Carolina Department of Transportation (NCDOT) that fail minimum retroreflectivity requirements. The researchers were also interested in the proportions of NCDOT signs with background colors white (regulatory signs), yellow (warning/caution), red (stop/yield/wrong way), and green (guide/information). In a random sample of 1,000 road signs maintained by the NCDOT, 373 were white, 447 were yellow, 88 were green, and 92 were red. Suppose that NCDOT stores new signs in a warehouse for use as replacement signs; of these, 35% are white, 45% are yellow, 10% are green, and 10% are red. Does the distribution of background colors for all road signs maintained by NCDOT match the color distribution of signs in the warehouse? Test using $\alpha = .05$.

NCDOT

10.13 Mobile device typing strategies. Text messaging on mobile devices (e.g., cell phones, smartphones) often requires typing in awkward positions that may lead to health issues. A group of Temple University public health professors investigated this phenomenon and published their results in *Applied Ergonomics* (March 2012). One portion of the study focused on the typing styles of mobile device users. Typing style was categorized as (1) device held with both hands/both thumbs typing, (2) device held with right hand/right thumb typing, (3) device held with left hand/left thumb typing, (4) device held with both hands/right thumb typing, (5) device held with left hand/right index finger typing, or (6) other. In a sample of 859 college students observed typing on their mobile devices, the professors observed 396, 311, 70, 39, 18, and 25, respectively, in the six categories. Is this sufficient evidence to conclude that the proportions of mobile device users in the six texting style categories differ? Use $\alpha = .10$ to answer the question.

TXTMS1

10.14 Profiling UK rental malls. Refer to the *Urban Studies* (June 2011) analysis of tenants renting space in United Kingdom regional shopping malls, Exercise 2.11 (p. 74). Recall that tenants were categorized into five different-size groups based on amount of floor space: *anchor tenants* (more than 30,000 sq. ft.), *major space users* (between 10,000 and 30,000 sq. ft.), *large standard tenants* (between 4,000 and 10,000 sq. ft.), *small standard tenants* (between 1,500 and 4,000 sq. ft.), and *small tenants* (less than 1,500 sq. ft.). Suppose that a UK mall developer believes that the proportions of tenants in each category are .01, .05, .10, .40,

UKMALL

and .44, respectively. In the actual study, 1,821 stores were sampled and the number of stores in each tenant category was reported as 14, 61, 216, 711, and 819, respectively. Use this information to test the mall developer's belief (at $\alpha = .01$). What do you conclude?

10.15 **Coupon user study.** A hot topic in marketing research is the exploration of a technology-based self-service (TBSS) encounter, e.g., ATMs, automated hotel checkout, online banking, and express package tracking. Marketing Professor Dan Ladik (University of Suffolk) investigated a customer's motivation to use a TBSS developed for a firm's discount coupons. The coupon users received the coupons in one of three ways—mail only (nontechnology user), Internet only (TBSS user), and both mail and Internet. One of the variables of interest in the study was *Type of coupon user.* In particular, the professor wants to know if the true proportions of mail only, Internet only, and both mail and Internet users differ. In a sample of 440 coupon users, the professor discovered that 262 received coupons via only mail, 43 via only the Internet, and 135 via both mail and Internet. Conduct the appropriate analysis for the professor. Use $\alpha = .01$.

10.16 **Cell phone user survey.** If you subscribe to a cell phone plan, how many different cell phone numbers do you own? This was one question of interest in *Public Opinion Quarterly* (Vol. 70, No. 5, 2006). According to the Current Population Survey (CPS) Cell Phone Supplement, 51% of cell phone plans have only one cell number, 37% have two numbers, 9% have three numbers, and 3% have four or more numbers. An independent survey of 943 randomly selected cell phone users found that 473 pay for only one number, 334 pay for two numbers, 106 pay for three numbers, and 30 pay for four or more numbers. Conduct a test to determine if the data from the independent survey contradict the percentages reported by the CPS Cell Phone Supplement. Use $\alpha = .01$.

Applying the Concepts—Advanced

10.17 **Overloading in the trucking industry.** Although illegal, overloading is common in the trucking industry. A state highway planning agency (Minnesota Department of Transportation) monitored the movements of overweight trucks on an interstate highway using an unmanned, computerized scale that is built into the highway. Unknown to the truckers, the scale weighed their vehicles as they passed over it. Each day's proportion of 1 week's total truck traffic (five-axle tractor truck semitrailers) is shown in the first column of the table below. During the same week, the number of overweight trucks per day is given in the second column. This information is saved in the accompanying file. The planning agency would like to know whether the number of overweight trucks per week is distributed over the 7 days of the week in direct proportion to the volume of truck traffic. Test using $\alpha = .05$.

Day	Proportion	Number
Monday	.191	90
Tuesday	.198	82
Wednesday	.187	72
Thursday	.180	70
Friday	.155	51
Saturday	.043	18
Sunday	.046	31

10.18 **Political representation of religious groups.** Do those elected to the U.S. House of Representatives really "represent" their constituents demographically? This was a question of interest in *Chance* (Summer 2002). One of several demographics studied was religious affiliation. The accompanying table gives the proportion of the U.S. population for several religions, as well as the number of the 435 seats in the House of Representatives that are affiliated with that religion. Give your opinion on whether or not the House of Representatives is statistically representative of the religious affiliations of their constituents in the United States.

Religion	Proportion of U.S. Population	Number of Seats in House
Catholic	.28	117
Methodist	.04	61
Jewish	.02	30
Other	.66	227
Totals	1.00	435

10.3 Testing Category Probabilities: Two-Way (Contingency) Table

In Section 10.1, we introduced the multinomial probability distribution and considered data classified according to a single qualitative criterion. We now consider multinomial experiments in which the data are classified according to two criteria—that is, *classification with respect to two qualitative factors.*

For example, consider a study published in the *Journal of Marketing* on the impact of using celebrities in television advertisements. The researchers investigated the relationship between gender of a viewer and the viewer's brand awareness. Three hundred TV viewers were asked to identify products advertised by male celebrity spokespersons. The data are summarized in the two-way table shown in Table 10.3. This table is called a **contingency table;** it presents multinomial count data classified on two scales, or **dimensions, of classification**—namely, gender of viewer and brand awareness.

Table 10.3	Contingency Table for Marketing Example			
		Gender		
		Male	Female	Totals
Brand Awareness	Could Identify Product	95	41	136
	Could Not Identify Product	50	114	164
	Totals	145	155	300

Data Set: CELEB

The symbols representing the cell counts for the multinomial experiment in Table 10.3 are shown in Table 10.4a; and the corresponding cell, row, and column probabilities are shown in Table 10.4b. Thus, n_{11} represents the number of viewers who are male and could identify the brand, and p_{11} represents the corresponding cell probability. Note the symbols for the row and column totals and also the symbols for the probability totals. The latter are called **marginal probabilities** for each row and column. The marginal probability p_{r1} is the probability that a TV viewer identifies the product; the marginal probability p_{c1} is the probability that the TV viewer is male. Thus,

$$p_{r1} = p_{11} + p_{12} \quad \text{and} \quad p_{c1} = p_{11} + p_{21}$$

We can see, then, that this really is a multinomial experiment with a total of 300 trials, $(2)(2) = 4$ cells or possible outcomes, and probabilities for each cell as shown in Table 10.4b. If the 300 TV viewers are randomly chosen, the trials are considered independent, and the probabilities are viewed as remaining constant from trial to trial.

Suppose we want to know whether the two classifications, gender and brand awareness, are dependent—that is, if we know the gender of the TV viewer, does that information give us a clue about the viewer's brand awareness? In a probabilistic sense, we know (Chapter 3) that independence of events A and B implies $P(AB) = P(A)P(B)$. Similarly, in the contingency table analysis, if the **two classifications are independent**, the probability that an item is classified in any particular cell of the table is the product of the corresponding marginal probabilities. Thus, under the hypothesis of independence, in Table 10.4b, we must have

$$p_{11} = p_{r1}p_{c1}, \quad p_{21} = p_{r2}p_{c1}$$
$$p_{12} = p_{r1}p_{c_2}, \quad p_{22} = p_{r2}p_{c2}$$

Table 10.4a	Observed Counts for Contingency Table 10.3			
		Gender		
		Male	Female	Totals
Brand Awareness	Could Identify Product	n_{11}	n_{12}	R_1
	Could Not Identify Product	n_{21}	n_{22}	R_2
	Totals	C_1	C_2	n

Table 10.4b	Probabilities for Contingency Table 10.3			
		Gender		
		Male	Female	Totals
Brand Awareness	Could Identify Product	p_{11}	p_{12}	p_{r1}
	Could Not Identify Product	p_{21}	p_{22}	p_{r2}
	Totals	p_{c1}	p_{c2}	1

To test the hypothesis of independence, we use the same reasoning employed in the one-dimensional tests of Section 10.2. First, we calculate the *expected*, or *mean, count in each cell*, assuming that the null hypothesis of independence is true. We do this by noting that the expected count in a cell of the table is just the total number of multinomial trials, n, times the cell probability. Recall that n_{ij} represents the **observed count** in the cell located in the ith row and jth column. Then the expected cell count for the upper left-hand cell (first row, first column) is

$$E_{11} = np_{11}$$

or, when the null hypothesis (the classifications are independent) is true,

$$E_{11} = np_{r1}p_{c1}$$

Since these true probabilities are not known, we estimate p_{r1} and p_{c1} by the proportions $\hat{p}_{r1} = R_1/n$ and $\hat{p}_{c1} = C_1/n$, where R_1 and C_1 represent the totals for row 1 and column 1, respectively. Thus, the estimate of the expected value E_{11} is

$$\hat{E}_{11} = n\left(\frac{R_1}{n}\right)\left(\frac{C_1}{n}\right) = \frac{R_1C_1}{n}$$

Similarly, for each i, j,

$$\hat{E}_{ij} = \frac{(\text{Row total})(\text{Column total})}{\text{Total sample size}}$$

Thus,

$$\hat{E}_{12} = \frac{R_1C_2}{n}$$

$$\hat{E}_{21} = \frac{R_2C_1}{n}$$

$$\hat{E}_{22} = \frac{R_2C_2}{n}$$

Finding Expected Cell Counts for a Two-Way Contingency Table

The estimate of the expected number of observations falling into the cell in row i and column j is given by

$$\hat{E}_{ij} = \frac{R_iC_j}{n}$$

where R_i = total for row i, C_j = total for column j, and n = sample size.

Using the data in Table 10.3, we find

$$\hat{E}_{11} = \frac{R_1C_1}{n} = \frac{(136)(145)}{300} = 65.73$$

$$\hat{E}_{12} = \frac{R_1C_2}{n} = \frac{(136)(155)}{300} = 70.27$$

$$\hat{E}_{21} = \frac{R_1C_2}{n} = \frac{(164)(145)}{300} = 79.27$$

$$\hat{E}_{22} = \frac{R_1C_2}{n} = \frac{(164)(155)}{300} = 84.73$$

These estimated expected values are more easily obtained using computer software. Figure 10.3 is a Minitab printout of the analysis, with expected values highlighted.

Tabulated Statistics: AWARE, GENDER

```
Using frequencies in NUMBER


Rows: AWARE    Columns: GENDER

            Female   Male   All

ID-Product      41     95   136
             70.27  65.73

No-ID          114     50   164
             84.73  79.27

All            155    145   300

Cell Contents:        Count
                      Expected count


Pearson Chi-Square = 46.135, DF = 1, P-Value = 0.000
Likelihood Ratio Chi-Square = 47.362, DF = 1, P-Value = 0.000


Fisher's exact test: P-Value =  0.0000000
```

Figure 10.3

Minitab contingency table analysis of data in Table 10.3

We now use the χ^2 statistic to compare the observed and expected (estimated) counts in each cell of the contingency table:

$$\chi^2 = \frac{[n_{11} - \hat{E}_{11}]^2}{\hat{E}_{11}} + \frac{[n_{12} - \hat{E}_{12}]^2}{\hat{E}_{12}} + \frac{[n_{21} - \hat{E}_{21}]^2}{\hat{E}_{21}} + \frac{[n_{22} - \hat{E}_{22}]^2}{\hat{E}_{22}}$$

$$= \sum \frac{[n_{ij} - \hat{E}_{ij}]^2}{\hat{E}_{ij}}$$

(*Note:* The use of Σ in the context of a contingency table analysis refers to a sum over all cells in the table.)

Substituting the data of Table 10.3 into this expression, we get

$$\chi^2 = \frac{(95 - 65.73)^2}{65.73} + \frac{(41 - 70.27)^2}{70.27} + \frac{(50 - 79.27)^2}{79.27} + \frac{(114 - 84.73)^2}{84.73} = 46.14$$

Note that this value is also shown (highlighted) in Figure 10.3.

Large values of χ^2 imply that the observed counts do not closely agree, and hence, the hypothesis of independence is false. To determine how large χ^2 must be before it is too large to be attributed to chance, we make use of the fact that the sampling distribution of χ^2 is approximately a χ^2 probability distribution when the classifications are independent.

When testing the null hypothesis of independence in a two-way contingency table, the appropriate degrees of freedom will be $(r - 1)(c - 1)$, where r is the number of rows and c is the number of columns in the table. For the brand awareness example, the degrees of freedom for χ^2 are $(r - 1)(c - 1) = (2 - 1)(2 - 1) = 1$. Then, for $\alpha = .05$, we reject the hypothesis of independence when

$$\chi^2 > \chi^2_{.05} = 3.8146$$

Because the computed $\chi^2 = 46.14$ exceeds the value 3.84146, we conclude that viewer gender and brand awareness are dependent events. This result may also be obtained by noting that the *p*-value of the test (highlighted in Figure 10.3) is approximately 0.

The pattern of **dependence** can be seen more clearly by expressing the data as percentages. We first select one of the two classifications to be used as the base variable. In the preceding example, suppose we select gender of the TV viewer as the classificatory variable to be the base. Next, we represent the responses for each level of the second categorical variable (brand awareness in our example) as a percentage of the subtotal for the base variable. For example, from Table 10.3, we convert the response for males who identify the brand (95) to a percentage of the total number of male viewers (145)—that is,

$$\left(\tfrac{95}{145}\right)100\% = 65.5\%$$

The conversions of all Table 10.3 entries are similarly computed, and the values are shown in Table 10.5. The value shown at the right of each row is the row's total expressed as a percentage of the total number of responses in the entire table. Thus, the percentage of TV viewers who identify the product is $\left(\tfrac{136}{300}\right)100\% = 45.3\%$ (rounded to the nearest 10th of a percent).

Table 10.5	Percentage of TV Viewers Who Identify Brand, by Gender			
		Gender		
		Male	Female	Totals
Brand Awareness	Could Identify Product	65.5	26.5	45.3
	Could Not Identify Product	34.5	73.5	54.7
	Totals	100	100	100

If the gender and brand awareness variables are independent, then the percentages in the cells of the table are expected to be approximately equal to the corresponding row percentages. Thus, we would expect the percentages who identify the brand for each gender to be approximately 45% if the two variables are independent. The extent to which each gender's percentage departs from this value determines the dependence of the two classifications, with greater variability of the row percentages meaning a greater degree of dependence. A plot of the percentages helps summarize the observed pattern. In the SPSS bar graph in Figure 10.4, we show the gender of the viewer (the base variable) on the horizontal axis, and the percentages of TV viewers who identify the brand (green bars) on the vertical axis. The "expected" percentage under the assumption of independence is shown as a horizontal line.

Figure 10.4 clearly indicates the reason that the test resulted in the conclusion that the two classifications in the contingency table are dependent. The percentage of male TV viewers who identify the brand promoted by a male celebrity is more than twice as high as the percentage of female TV viewers who identify the brand.* Statistical measures of the degree of dependence and procedures for making comparisons of pairs of levels for classifications are available. They are beyond the scope of this text but can be found in the references. We will, however, use descriptive summaries such as Figure 10.4 to examine the degree of dependence exhibited by the sample data.

The general form of a two-way contingency table containing r rows and c columns (called an $r \times c$ contingency table) is shown in Table 10.6. Note that the observed count in the (ij) cell is denoted by n_{ij}, the ith row total is R_i, the jth column total is C_j, and the

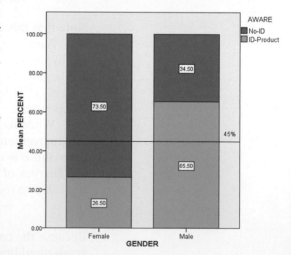

Figure 10.4

SPSS bar graph showing percent of viewers who identify TV product

*Another way to make this comparison is to make an inference about the difference $(p_1 - p_2)$, where p_1 is the proportion of males who identify the brand and p_2 is the corresponding proportion for females, using the methods in Chapter 8. In fact, a χ^2 analysis for a 2×2 contingency table is equivalent to a test of the null hypothesis, $H_0: p_1 - p_2 = 0$, against the two-sided alternative $H_a: p_1 - p_2 \neq 0$.

Table 10.6	General $r \times c$ Contingency Table					
Column	1	2	$\cdots$	c	Row Totals
1	n_{11}	n_{12}	$\cdots$	n_{1c}	R_1
2	n_{21}	n_{22}	$\cdots$	n_{2c}	R_2
Row $\vdots$	$\vdots$	$\vdots$		$\vdots$	$\vdots$
r	n_{r1}	n_{r2}	$\cdots$	n_{rc}	R_r
Column Totals	C_1	C_2	$\cdots$	C_c	n

total sample size is n. Using this notation, we give the general form of the contingency table test for independent classifications in the next box.

General Form of a Two-Way (Contingency) Table Analysis: χ^2 Test for Independence

H_0: The two classifications are independent.
H_a: The two classifications are dependent.

Test statistic: $\chi^2 = \sum \dfrac{[n_{ij} - \hat{E}_{ij}]^2}{\hat{E}_{ij}}$

where $\hat{E}_{ij} = \dfrac{R_i C_j}{n}$

Rejection region: $\chi^2 > \chi^2_\alpha$
p-value: $P(\chi^2 > \chi^2_c)$
where χ^2_α has $(r - 1)(c - 1)$ df and χ^2_c is the computed value of the test statistic.

Conditions Required for a Valid χ^2 Test: Contingency Table

1. The n observed counts are a random sample from the population of interest. We may then consider this to be a multinomial experiment with $r \times c$ possible outcomes.

2. The sample size, n, will be large enough so that, for every cell, the estimated expected count, $\hat{E}_{ij}$, will be equal to 5 or more.

EXAMPLE 10.3

Conducting a Two-Way Analysis—Broker Rating and Customer Income

Problem A large brokerage firm wants to determine whether the service it provides to affluent clients differs from the service it provides to lower-income clients. A sample of 500 clients is selected, and each client is asked to rate his or her broker. The results are shown in Table 10.7.

a. Test to determine whether there is evidence that broker rating and customer income are dependent. Use $\alpha = .05$.

b. Graph the data and describe the patterns revealed. Is the result of the test supported by the plot?

Solution

a. The first step is to obtain estimated expected cell frequencies under the assumption that the classifications are independent. Rather than compute these values by hand, we resort to statistical software. The Excel/XLSTAT printout of the analysis of Table 10.7 is displayed in Figure 10.5. Each cell in the "Theoretical frequencies" table of Figure 10.5 contains the expected frequency in that cell. Note that $\hat{E}_{11}$, the estimated expected count for the Outstanding, Under \$30,000 cell, is 53.86.

Table 10.7	Survey Results (Observed Clients), Example 10.3			

		Client's Income			
		Under $30,000	$30,000–$60,000	Over $60,000	Totals
Broker Rating	Outstanding	48	64	41	153
	Average	98	120	50	268
	Poor	30	33	16	79
	Totals	176	217	107	500

Data Set: BROKER

Test of independence between the rows and the columns (RATING / INCOME):

Chi-square (Observed value)	4.2777
Chi-square (Critical value)	9.4877
DF	4
p-value	0.3697
alpha	0.05

Observed frequencies (RATING / INCOME):

	1:UND30K	2:30K-60K	3:OVR60K	Total
1:OUTSTANDING	48	64	41	153
2:AVERAGE	98	120	50	268
3:POOR	30	33	16	79
Total	176	217	107	500

Theoretical frequencies (RATING / INCOME):

	1:UND30K	2:30K-60K	3:OVR60K	Total
1:OUTSTANDING	53.8560	66.4020	32.7420	153
2:AVERAGE	94.3360	116.3120	57.3520	268
3:POOR	27.8080	34.2860	16.9060	79
Total	176	217	107	500

Percentages / Column (RATING / INCOME):

	1:UND30K	2:30K-60K	3:OVR60K	Total
1:OUTSTANDING	27.2727	29.4931	38.3178	30.6000
2:AVERAGE	55.6818	55.2995	46.7290	53.6000
3:POOR	17.0455	15.2074	14.9533	15.8000
Total	100	100	100	100

Figure 10.5

XLSTAT contingency table analysis for brokerage data

Similarly, the estimated expected count for the Outstanding, $30,000–$60,000 cell is $\hat{E}_{12} = 66.40$. Because all the estimated expected cell frequencies are greater than 5, the χ^2 approximation for the test statistic is appropriate. Assuming the clients chosen were randomly selected from all clients of the brokerage firm, the characteristics of the multinomial probability distribution are satisfied.

The null and alternative hypotheses we want to test are

H_0: The rating a client gives his or her broker is independent of client's income.

H_a: Broker rating and client income are dependent.

The test statistic, $\chi^2 = 4.28$, is highlighted at the top of the printout, as is the observed significance level (p-value) of the test. Because $\alpha = .05$ is less than $p = .370$, we fail to reject H_0. This survey does not support the firm's alternative hypothesis that affluent clients receive different broker service than lower-income clients. (Note that we could not reject H_0 even with $\alpha = .10$.)

b. The broker rating frequencies are expressed as percentages of income category frequencies in the bottom table of the XLSTAT printout, Figure 10.5. The expected percentages under the assumption of independence are shown in the "Total" column of the printout. A Minitab side-by-side bar graph of the data is shown in Figure 10.6. Note that the response percentages deviate only slightly from those expected under the assumption of independence, supporting the result of the test in part **a**—that is, neither the descriptive plot nor the statistical test provides evidence that the rating given for broker services depends on (varies with) the customer's income.

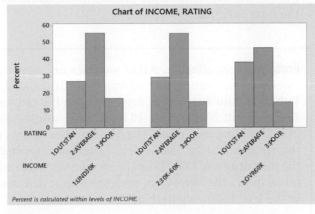

Figure 10.6

Minitab side-by-side bar graph for brokerage data

● **Now Work Exercise 10.24**

Contingency Tables with Fixed Marginals

In the *Journal of Marketing* study on celebrities in TV ads, a single random sample was selected from the target population of all TV viewers and the outcomes—values of gender and brand awareness—were recorded for each viewer. For this type of study, the researchers had no *apriori* knowledge of how many observations would fall into the categories of the qualititative variables. In other words, prior to obtaining the sample, the researchers did not know how many males or how many brand identifiers would make up the sample. Oftentimes, it is advantageous to select a random sample from each of the levels of one of the qualitative variables.

For example, in the *Journal of Marketing* study, the researchers may want to be sure of an equivalent number of males and females in their sample. Consequently, they will select independent random samples of 150 males and 150 females. (In fact, this was the sampling plan for the actual study.) Summary data for this type of study yield a **contingency table with fixed marginals** since the column totals for one qualitative variable (e.g., gender) are known in advance.* The goal of the analysis does not change—determine whether the two qualitative variables (e.g., gender and brand awareness) are dependent.

The procedure for conducting a chi-square analysis for a contingency table with fixed marginals is identical to the one outlined above, since it can be shown (proof omitted) that the χ^2 test statistic for this type of sampling also has an approximate chi-square distribution with $(r - 1)(c - 1)$ degrees of freedom. One reason why you might choose this alternative sampling plan is to obtain sufficient observations in each cell of the contingency table to ensure that the chi-square approximation is valid. Remember, this will usually occur when the expected cell counts are all greater than or equal to 5. By selecting a large sample (150 observations) for each gender in the *Journal of Marketing* study, the researchers improved the odds of obtaining large expected cell counts in the contingency table.

*Data from this type of study are also known as *product binomial data*.

Exact Tests for Independence in a Contingency Table

The procedure for testing independence in a contingency table is an "approximate" test because the χ^2 test statistic has an approximate chi-square probability distribution. The larger the sample, the better the test's approximation. For this reason, the test is often called an *asymptotic* test. For small samples (i.e., samples that produce contingency tables with one or more cells that have an expected number less than 5), the *p*-value from the asymptotic chi-square test may not be a good estimate of the actual (exact) *p*-value of the test. In this case, we can employ a technique proposed by R. A. Fisher (1935).

For 2 × 2 contingency tables, Fisher developed a procedure for computing the exact *p*-value for the test of independence—called **Fisher's exact test.** The method, which utilizes the hypergeometric probability distribution of Chapter 4 (p. 243), is illustrated in the next example.

EXAMPLE 10.4

Exact Test for a 2 × 2 Contingency Table—AIDS Vaccine Application

HIVVAC1

Problem New, effective AIDS vaccines are now being developed using the process of "sieving," i.e., sifting out infections with some strains of HIV. A Harvard School of Public Health statistician demonstrated how to test the efficacy of an HIV vaccine in *Chance* (Fall 2000). Table 10.8 gives the results of a preliminary HIV vaccine trial in a 2 × 2 contingency table. The vaccine was designed to eliminate a particular strain of the virus, called the "MN strain." The trial consisted of 7 AIDS patients vaccinated with the new drug and 31 AIDS patients who were treated with a placebo (no vaccination). The table shows the number of patients who tested positive and negative for the MN strain in the trial follow-up period.

Table 10.8	Contingency Table for Example 10.4		
	MN STRAIN		
PATIENT GROUP	Positive	Negative	TOTALS
Unvaccinated	22	9	31
Vaccinated	2	5	7
TOTALS	24	14	38

a. Conduct a test to determine whether the vaccine is effective in treating the MN strain of HIV. Use $\alpha = .05$.

b. Are the assumptions for the test, part **a**, satisfied?

c. Consider the hypergeometric probability

$$\binom{7}{2}\binom{31}{22} \div \binom{38}{24} = \frac{\frac{7!}{2!5!}\frac{31!}{22!9!}}{\frac{38!}{24!14!}} = .04378$$

This represents the probability that 2 out of 7 vaccinated AIDS patients test positive and 22 out of 31 unvaccinated patients test positive, i.e., the *probability of the contingency table* result, given the null hypothesis of independence is true. Two contingency tables (with the same marginal totals as the original table) that are more contradictory to the null hypothesis of independence than the observed table are shown in Tables 10.9a and 10.9b. Use the hypergeometric formula to find the probability of each of these contingency tables.

HIVVAC2

Table 10.9a	Alternative Contingency Table for Example 10.4		
	MN STRAIN		
PATIENT GROUP	Positive	Negative	TOTALS
Unvaccinated	23	8	31
Vaccinated	1	6	7
TOTALS	24	14	38

Table 10.9b	Alternative Contingency Table for Example 10.4		
	MN STRAIN		
PATIENT GROUP	Positive	Negative	TOTALS
Unvaccinated	24	7	31
Vaccinated	0	7	7
TOTALS	24	14	38

d. The p-value of Fisher's exact test is the probability of observing a result at least as contradictory to the null hypothesis as the observed contingency table, given the same marginal totals. Sum the three probabilities of part **c** to obtain the p-value of Fisher's exact test. Interpret this value in the context of the vaccine trial.

Solution

a. If the vaccine is effective in treating the MN strain of HIV, then the proportion of HIV-positive patients in the vaccinated group will be smaller than the corresponding proportion for the unvaccinated group. That is, the two variables, patient group and strain test result, will be dependent. Consequently, we conducted a chi-square test for independence on the data of Table 10.8. An SPSS printout of the analysis is displayed in Figure 10.7. The approximate p-value of the test (highlighted on the printout) is .036. Since this value is less than $\alpha = .05$, we reject the null hypothesis of independence and conclude that the vaccine has an effect on the proportion of patients who test positive for the MN strain of HIV.

b. The asymptotic chi-square test of part **a** is a large-sample test. Our assumption is that the sample will be large enough so that the expected cell counts are all greater than or equal to 5. These expected cell counts are highlighted on the SPSS printout, Figure 10.7. Note that two cells have expected numbers that are less than 5. Consequently, the large-sample assumption is not satisfied. Therefore, the p-value produced from the test may not be a reliable estimate of the true p-value.

c. With the hypergeometric formula, the probability that the Table 10.9a result, given the null hypothesis of independence is true, is:

$$\binom{7}{1}\binom{31}{23} \div \binom{38}{24} = \frac{\frac{7!}{1!6!}\frac{31!}{23!8!}}{\frac{38!}{24!14!}} = .00571$$

Similarly, the probability of the contingency table in Table 10.9b, is:

$$\binom{7}{0}\binom{31}{24} \div \binom{38}{24} = \frac{\frac{7!}{0!7!}\frac{31!}{24!7!}}{\frac{38!}{24!14!}} = .00027$$

GROUP * MNSTRAIN Crosstabulation

			MNSTRAIN		Total
			NEG	POS	
GROUP	UNVAC	Count	9	22	31
		Expected Count	11.4	19.6	31.0
	VACC	Count	5	2	7
		Expected Count	2.6	4.4	7.0
Total		Count	14	24	38
		Expected Count	14.0	24.0	38.0

Chi-Square Tests

	Value	df	Asymp. Sig. (2-sided)	Exact Sig. (2-sided)	Exact Sig. (1-sided)
Pearson Chi-Square	4.411[b]	1	.036		
Continuity Correction[a]	2.777	1	.096		
Likelihood Ratio	4.289	1	.038		
Fisher's Exact Test				.077	.050
N of Valid Cases	38				

a. Computed only for a 2x2 table

b. 2 cells (50.0%) have expected count less than 5. The minimum expected count is 2.58.

Figure 10.7

SPSS Contingency Table Analysis for Table 10.8

d. To obtain the *p*-value of Fisher's exact test, we sum contingency table probabilities for all possible contingency tables that give a result *at least* as contradictory to the null hypothesis as the observed contingency table. Since the contingency tables in Table 10.9 are the only two possible tables that give a more contradictory result, we add their hypergeometric probabilities to the hypergeometric probability for Table 10.8 to obtain the exact *p*-value for a test of independence:

$$p\text{-value} = .04378 + .00571 + .00027 = .04976.$$

Since this exact *p*-value is less than $\alpha = .05$, we reject the null hypothesis of independence; there is sufficient evidence to reliably conclude that the vaccine is effective in treating the MN strain of HIV. Fisher's exact *p*-value for this test, *p*-value = $.04976 \approx .050$, can be more easily obtained using statistical software. It is shown (highlighted) under the "Exact Sig (1-sided)" column at the bottom of the SPSS printout in Figure 10.7.

Look Back Fisher's exact test *p*-value for the contingency table, Table 10.3, is shown at the bottom of the associated Minitab printout, Figure 10.3.

• **Now Work Exercise 10.26**

Because it is so easily obtained using statistical software, apply Fisher's exact test (rather than the asymptotic chi-square test) when analyzing a 2 × 2 contingency table. Fisher's procedure can also be applied to a more general 2 × c contingency table (i.e., a table with 2 levels of one categorical variable and c levels of the other). Statistical software is programmed to compute the exact *p*-value of these tests.

Testing Whether Likelihood of a Lawsuit Is Related to Recall Notice Sender

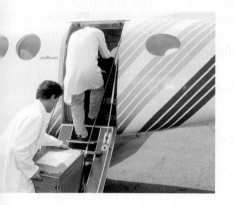

We return to the case involving tainted transplant tissue (see p. 599). Recall that a processor of the tainted tissue filed a lawsuit against a tissue distributor, claiming that the distributor was more responsible than the processor for paying damages to litigating transplant patients. Why? Because the distributor in question had sent recall notices (as required by the FTC) to hospitals and surgeons with unsolicited newspaper articles describing in graphic detail the "ghoulish" acts that had been committed. According to the processor, by including the articles in the recall package, this distributor inflamed the tissue recipients, increasing the likelihood that the patients would file a lawsuit.

To prove its case in court, the processor needed to establish a statistical link between the likelihood of a lawsuit and the sender of the recall notice. More specifically, can the processor show that the probability of a lawsuit is higher for the patients of surgeons who received the recall notice with the inflammatory articles than for the patients of surgeons who only received the recall notice?

A statistician serving as an expert consultant for the processor reviewed data for the 7,914 patients who received recall notices (of which 708 filed suit). These data are saved in the **GHOUL1** file. For each patient, the file contains information on the SENDER of the recall notice (Processor or Distributor) and whether or not a LAWSUIT was filed (Yes or No). Since both of these variables are qualitative, and we want to know whether the probability of a LAWSUIT depended on the SENDER of the recall notice, a contingency table analysis is appropriate.

Figure SIA10.1 shows the Minitab contingency table analysis. The null and alternative hypotheses for the test are

$$H_0: \text{Lawsuit and Sender are independent}$$
$$H_a: \text{Lawsuit and Sender are dependent}$$

Both the chi-square test statistic (100.5) and *p*-value of the test (.000) are highlighted on the printout. If we conduct the test at $\alpha = .01$, there is sufficient evidence to reject H_0.

```
Tabulated statistics: SENDER, LAWSUIT

Rows: SENDER    Columns: LAWSUIT

                 No      Yes     All

Distributor     5506      657    6163
                89.34    10.66  100.00
                5612      551    6163
                1.989   20.244      *

Processor       1700       51    1751
                97.09     2.91  100.00
                1594      157    1751
                7.001   71.252      *

All             7206      708    7914
                91.05     8.95  100.00
                7206      708    7914
                   *        *       *


Cell Contents:     Count
                   % of Row
                   Expected count
                   Contribution to Chi-square

Pearson Chi-Square = 100.485, DF = 1, P-Value = 0.000
Likelihood Ratio Chi-Square = 124.748, DF = 1, P-Value = 0.000
```

Figure SIA10.1

Minitab contingency table analysis—likelihood of lawsuit vs. recall notice sender

That is, the data provide evidence to indicate that the likelihood of a tainted transplant patient filing a lawsuit is associated with the sender of the recall notice.

To determine which sender had the higher percentage of patients to file a lawsuit, examine the row percentages (highlighted) in the contingency table of Figure SIA10.1 You can see that of the 1,751 patients sent recall notices by the processor, 51 (or 2.91%) filed lawsuits. In contrast, of the 6,163 patients sent recall notices by the distributor in question, 657 (or 10.66%) filed lawsuits. Thus, the probability of a patient filing a lawsuit was almost five times higher for the distributor's patients than for the processor's patients.

Before testifying on these results in court, the statistician decided to do one additional analysis: He eliminated from the sample data any patients whose surgeon had been sent notices by both parties. Why? Since these patients' surgeons received both recall notices, the underlying reason for filing a lawsuit would be unclear. Did the patient file simply because he or she received tainted transplant tissue, or was the filing motivated by the inflammatory articles that accompanied the recall notice? After eliminating these patients, the data looked like that shown in Table SIA10.2. A Minitab contingency table analysis on this reduced data set (saved in the **GHOUL2** file) is shown in Figure SIA10.2.

As in the previous analysis, the chi-square test statistic (110.2) and *p*-value of the test (.000)—both highlighted on the printout—imply that the likelihood of a tainted transplant patient filing a lawsuit is associated with the sender of the recall notice, at $\alpha = .01$. Also, the percentage of patients filing lawsuits when sent a recall notice by the distributor (10.62%) is again five times higher than the percentage of patients filing lawsuits when sent a recall notice by the processor (2.04%).

The results of both analyses were used to successfully support the processor's claim in court. Nonetheless, we need to point out one caveat to the contingency table analyses. Be careful not to conclude that the data are proof that the inclusion of the inflammatory articles *caused* the probability of litigation to increase. Without controlling all

Table SIA10.2	Data for the Tainted Tissue Case, Dual Recall Notices Eliminated		
Recall Notice Sender		Number of Patients	Number of Lawsuits
Processor/Other distributor		1,522	31
Distributor in question		5,705	606
Totals		7,227	637

Source: Info Tech, Inc.

Tabulated statistics: SENDER, LAWSUIT

```
Rows: SENDER    Columns: LAWSUIT

                  No      Yes      All

Distributor     5099      606     5705
                89.38    10.62   100.00
                5202      503     5705
                2.045   21.160       *

Processor       1491       31     1522
                97.96     2.04   100.00
                1388      134     1522
                7.667   79.315       *

All             6590      637     7227
                91.19     8.81   100.00
                6590      637     7227
                   *        *        *

Cell Contents:       Count
                     % of Row
                     Expected count
                     Contribution to Chi-square
```

Figure SIA10.2

Minitab contingency table analysis, with dual recall notices eliminated

```
Pearson Chi-Square = 110.187, DF = 1, P-Value = 0.000
Likelihood Ratio Chi-Square = 144.862, DF = 1, P-Value = 0.000
```

possible variables that may relate to filing a lawsuit (e.g., a patient's socioeconomic status, whether or not a patient has filed a lawsuit in the past), we can only say that the two qualitative variables, lawsuit status and recall notice sender, are statistically associated. However, the fact that the likelihood of a lawsuit was almost five times higher when the notice was sent by the distributor shifts the burden of proof to the distributor to explain why this occurred and to convince the court that it should not be held accountable for paying the majority of the damages.

Alternative Analysis: As mentioned in a footnote in this section (p. 612), a 2×2 contingency table analysis is equivalent to a comparison of two population proportions. In the tainted tissue case, we want to compare p_1, the proportion of lawsuits filed by patients who were sent recall notices by the processor, with p_2, the proportion of lawsuits filed by patients who were sent recall notices by the distributor who included the inflammatory articles. Both a test of the null hypothesis, H_0: $(p_1 - p_2) = 0$, and a 95% confidence interval for the difference, $(p_1 - p_2)$ using the reduced sample data, are shown (highlighted) on the Minitab printout, Figure SIA10.3.

Test and CI for Two Proportions

```
Sample    X     N   Sample p
1        31   1522   0.020368
2       606   5705   0.106223

Difference = p (1) - p (2)
Estimate for difference:  -0.0858547
95% CI for difference:  (-0.0965452, -0.0751641)
Test for difference = 0 (vs not = 0):   Z = -10.50   P-Value = 0.000

Fisher's exact test: P-Value = 0.000
```

Figure SIA10.3

Minitab output with 95% confidence interval and test for difference in proportions of lawsuits filed

The *p*-value for the test (.000) indicates that the two proportions are significantly different at $\alpha = 05$. The 95% confidence interval, $(-.097, -.075)$, shows that the proportion of lawsuits associated with patients who were sent recall notices from the distributor ranges between .075 and .097 higher than the corresponding proportion for the processor. Both results support the processor's case, namely, that the patients who were sent recall notices with the inflammatory news articles were more likely to file a lawsuit than those who were sent only recall notices.

Exercises 10.19–10.39

Learning the Mechanics

10.19 State the most accurate statement that can be made about the p-value for each of the following cases where the contingency table contains r rows and c columns.
  a. $r = 4, c = 5, \chi^2 = 22.18$
  b. $r = 4, c = 3, \chi^2 = 22.18$
  c. $r = 3, c = 2, \chi^2 = 5.51$

10.20 Consider the 2×3 (i.e., $r = 2$ and $c = 3$) contingency table shown below.

L10020

		Column		
		1	2	3
Row	1	9	34	53
	2	16	30	25

  a. Specify the null and alternative hypotheses that should be used in testing the independence of the row and column classifications.
  b. Specify the test statistic and the rejection region that should be used in conducting the hypothesis test of part **a**. Use $\alpha = .01$.
  c. Assuming the row classification and the column classification are independent, find estimates for the expected cell counts.
  d. Conduct the hypothesis test of part **a**. Interpret your result.

10.21 Refer to Exercise 10.20.
  a. Convert the frequency responses to percentages by calculating the percentage of each column total falling in each row. Also convert the row totals to percentages of the total number of responses. Display the percentages in a table.
  b. Create a bar graph with row 1 percentage on the vertical axis and column number on the horizontal axis. Show the row 1 total percentage as a horizontal line on the graph.
  c. What pattern do you expect to see if the rows and columns are independent? Does the plot support the result of the test of independence in Exercise 10.20?

10.22 Test the null hypothesis of independence of the two classifications, A and B, in the 3×3 contingency table shown below. Test using $\alpha = .05$.

L10022

		B		
		B_1	B_2	B_3
	A_1	40	72	42
A	A_2	63	53	70
	A_3	31	38	30

10.23 Refer to Exercise 10.22.
  a. Convert the responses to percentages by calculating the percentage of each B class total falling into each A classification.
  b. Calculate the percentage of the total number of responses that constitute each of the A classification totals.
  c. Create a bar graph with row A_1 percentage on the vertical axis and B classification on the horizontal axis. Does

the graph support the result of the test of hypothesis in Exercise 10.22? Explain.
  d. Repeat part **c** for the row A_2 percentages.
  e. Repeat part **c** for the row A_3 percentages.

Applying the Concepts—Basic

10.24 Safety of hybrid cars. According to the Highway Loss Data Institute (HLDI), "Hybrid [automobiles] have a safety edge over their conventional twins when it comes to shielding their occupants from injuries in crashes" (*HLDI Bulletin*, Sept. 2011). Consider data collected by the HLDI on Honda Accords. In a sample of 50,132 collision claims for conventional Accords, 5,364 involved injuries; in a sample of 1,505 collision claims for hybrid Accords, 137 involved injuries. You want to use this information to determine whether the injury rate for hybrid Accords is less than the injury rate for conventional Accords.
  a. Identify the two qualitative variables measured for each Honda Accord collision claim.
  b. Form a contingency table for this data, giving the number of claims in each combination of the qualitative variable categories.
  c. Give H_0 and H_a for testing whether injury rate for collision claims depends on Accord model (hybrid or conventional).
  d. Find the expected number of claims in each cell of the contingency table, assuming that H_0 is true.
  e. Compute the χ^2 test statistic and compare your answer with the test statistic shown on the accompanying XLSTAT printout (below).
  f. Find the rejection region for the test using $\alpha = .05$ and compare your answer to the critical value shown on the accompanying XLSTAT printout.

Results for the variables Model and Claim:

Contingency table (Model / Claim):

	Injury	No Injury
Conventional	5364	44768
Hybrid	137	1368

Test of independence between the rows and the columns (Model / Claim):

Chi-square (Observed value)	3.9139
Chi-square (Critical value)	3.8415
DF	1
p-value	0.0479
alpha	0.05

  g. Make the appropriate conclusion using both the rejection region method and the p-value (shown on the XLSTAT printout).
  h. Find a 95% confidence interval for the difference between the injury rates of conventional and hybrid Honda Accords. (See Section 10.3.) Use the interval to determine whether the injury rate for hybrid Accords is less than the injury rate for conventional Accords.

10.25 Purchasing souvenirs. A major tourist activity is shopping. Travel researchers estimate that nearly one-third of total travel expenditures are used on shopping for souvenirs (*Journal of Travel Research,* May 2011). To investigate the impact of gender on souvenir shopping, a survey of 3,200 tourists was conducted. One question asked how often the tourist purchases photographs, postcards, or paintings of the region visited. Responses were recorded as "Always," "Often," "Occasionally," or "Rarely or Never." The table shows the percentages of tourists responding in each category, by gender.

Photos, Postcards, Paintings	Male Tourist	Female Tourist
Always	16%	28%
Often	27	31
Occasionally	35	29
Rarely or never	22	12
Totals	100%	100%

Source: H. Wilkins, "Souvenirs: What and Why We Buy," *Journal of Travel Research,* Vol. 50, No. 3, May 2011 (adapted from Table 2).

a. Based on the percentages shown in the table, do you think male and female tourists differ in their responses to purchasing photographs, postcards, or paintings? Why are these percentages alone insufficient to draw a conclusion about the true response category proportions?

b. Assume that 1,500 males and 1,700 females participated in the survey. Use these sample sizes and the percentages in the table to compute the counts of tourists in each of the Response/Gender categories. This represents the contingency table for the study.

c. Specify the null and alternative hypotheses for testing whether male and female tourists differ in their responses to purchasing photographs, postcards, or paintings.

d. An SPSS printout of the contingency table analysis is shown below. Locate the test statistic and *p*-value on the printout.

e. Make the appropriate conclusion using $\alpha = .01$.

RESPONSE * GENDER Crosstabulation

			Female	Male	Total
			GENDER		
RESPONSE	1:Always	Count	476	240	716
		Expected Count	380.4	335.6	716.0
	2:Often	Count	527	405	932
		Expected Count	495.1	436.9	932.0
	3:Occasionally	Count	493	525	1018
		Expected Count	540.8	477.2	1018.0
	4:Rarely/Never	Count	204	330	534
		Expected Count	283.7	250.3	534.0
Total		Count	1700	1500	3200
		Expected Count	1700.0	1500.0	3200.0

Chi-Square Tests

	Value	df	Asymp. Sig. (2-sided)
Pearson Chi-Square	112.433[a]	3	.000
Likelihood Ratio	113.788	3	.000
N of Valid Cases	3200		

a. 0 cells (0.0%) have expected count less than 5. The minimum expected count is 250.31.

10.26 Tourists' view of destination image. Refer to the *Journal of Destination Marketing & Management* (October 2015) study of tourist destination image, Exercise 10.11 (p. 607).

Recall that the study analyzed the posts submitted on TripAdvisor about The Historic Areas of Istanbul (Turkey) page. In addition to destination image component, the researchers also classified each post according to Type of comment (positive only, negative only, or both positive and negative) and Gender of the poster (male or female). An analysis of the data collected for the sample of 125 tourists who identified their gender is provided in the accompanying Excel/XLSTAT printout.

a. Specify the null and alternative hypotheses for testing whether Type of comment posted to TripAdvisor depends on Gender.

b. Locate the *p*-value of the chi-square test for independence on the XLSTAT printout. Compare this value with $\alpha = .10$ and make the appropriate conclusion.

c. Examine the expected (theoretical) cell counts shown on the printout and read the accompanying note at the bottom of the output. Explain why the inference you made in part **b** may be invalid.

d. Apply Fisher's exact test for the contingency table. Use the exact *p*-value shown at the bottom of the printout. What do you conclude?

Observed frequencies (GENDER / COMMENT):

	Both	Negative	Positive	Total
Female	15	2	31	48
Male	11	5	61	77
Total	26	7	92	125

Theoretical frequencies (GENDER / COMMENT):

	Both	Negative	Positive	Total
Female	9.9840	2.6880	35.3280	48.0000
Male	16.0160	4.3120	56.6720	77.0000
Total	26	7	92	125

Test of independence between the rows and the columns (Chi-square):

Chi-square (Observed value)	5.2376
Chi-square (Critical value)	5.9915
DF	2
p-value	0.0729
alpha	0.05

Theoretical counts lower than 5 have been detected.
To safely use the Chi-square test based on the Chi-square approximation, the theoretical counts should not be lower than 5.

Fisher's exact test:

p-value (Two-tailed)	0.0746
alpha	0.05

10.27 Are travel professionals equitably paid? *Business Travel News* (July 28, 2014) reported the results of its annual Travel Manager Salary & Attitude survey. A total of 248 travel professionals, 76 males and 172 females, participated in the survey. One question asked for the travel professional's opinion on the fairness of his/her salary. Responses were classified as "salary too low," "equitable/fair," or "paid well." The table below gives a breakdown of the responses in each category by gender.

	Males	Females
Salary too low	24	84
Equitable/fair	38	69
Paid well	14	19
Totals	76	172

a. Find the proportion of male travel professionals who believe their salary is too low and compare it with the proportion of female travel professionals who believe their salary is too low.

b. Repeat part **a** but compare the proportions who believe their salary is equitable/fair.

c. Repeat part **a** but compare the proportions who believe they are paid well.

d. Based on the comparisons, parts **a–c**, do you think opinion on the fairness of a travel professional's salary differs for males and females?

e. Refer to part **d**. Conduct the appropriate statistical test using $\alpha = .10$.

f. Construct and interpret a 90% confidence interval for the difference between the proportions of part **a**.

10.28 Eyewitnesses and mugshots. Refer to the *Applied Psychology in Criminal Justice* (April 2010) study of mugshot choices by eyewitnesses to a crime, Exercise 9.78 (p. 583). Recall that a sample of 96 college students was shown a video of a simulated theft, then asked to select a mugshot that most closely resembled the thief. The students were randomly assigned to view either 3, 6, or 12 mugshots at a time, with 32 students in each group. The number of students in the 3-, 6-, and 12-photos-per-page groups who selected the target mugshot were 19, 19, and 15, respectively.

a. For each photo group, compute the proportion of students who selected the target mugshot. Which group yielded the lowest proportion?

b. Create a contingency table for these data, with photo group in the rows and whether or not the target mugshot was selected in the columns.

c. Analyze the contingency table, part **b**. Are there differences in the proportions who selected the target mugshot among the three photo groups? Test using $\alpha = .10$.

10.29 Package design influences taste. Can the package design of a food product, along with accompanying sounds, influence how the consumer will rate the taste of the product? A team of experimental psychologists reported on a study that examined how rounded or angular package shapes and high- or low-pitched sounds can convey information about the taste (sweetness and sourness) of a product (*Food Quality and Preference*, June 2014). Study participants were presented with one of two types of packaging displayed on a computer screen monitor: rounded shape with a low-pitched sound or angular shape with a high-pitched sound. Assume that half of the participants viewed the rounded packaging and half viewed the angular packaging. After viewing the product, each participant rated whether the packaging was more appropriate for either a sweet- or a sour-tasting food product. A summary of the results (numbers of participants) for a sample of 80 participants is shown in the following contingency table. (These data are simulated, based on the results reported in the article.)

		Package Design/Pitch	
		Angular/High	Rounded/Low
Taste	*Sweet*	35	7
Choice	*Sour*	5	33

a. Specify the null and alternative hypotheses for testing whether the package design and sound pitch combination influences the consumer's opinion on the product taste.

b. Assuming the null hypothesis is true, find the expected number in each cell of the table.

c. Use the expected numbers and observed counts in the table to compute the chi-square test statistic.

d. The observed significance level (*p*-value) of the test is approximately 0. (You can verify this result using statistical software.) For any reasonably chosen value of α, give the appropriate conclusion.

Applying the Concepts—Intermediate

10.30 Job satisfaction of women in construction. The hiring of women in construction and construction-related jobs has steadily increased over the years. A study was conducted to provide employers with information designed to reduce the potential for turnover of female employees (*Journal of Professional Issues in Engineering Education & Practice*, April 2013). A survey questionnaire was emailed to members of the National Association of Women in Construction (NAWIC). A total of 477 women responded to survey questions on job challenge and satisfaction with life as an employee. The results (number of females responding in the different categories) are summarized in the accompanying table. What conclusions can you draw from the data regarding the association between an NAWIC member's satisfaction with life as an employee and her satisfaction with job challenge?

		Life as an Employee	
		Satisfied	Dissatisfied
Job	*Satisfied*	364	33
Challenge	*Dissatisfied*	24	26

Source: E. K. Malone and R. A. Issa, "Work-Life Balance and Organizational Commitment of Women in the U.S. Construction Industry," *Journal of Professional Issues in Engineering Education & Practice*, Vol. 139, No. 2, April 2013 (Table 11).

10.31 Offshoring companies. Refer to *The Journal of Applied Business Research* (January/February 2011) study of offshoring companies, Exercise 10.10 (p. 607). In addition to U.S. firms, CEOs from international companies were also surveyed on their offshoring positions. The number of firms in each position category (adapted from the results of the actual study) is shown in the accompanying table. Does a firm's position on offshoring depend on the firm's nationality? Test using $\alpha = .05$.

Firm's Position	United States	Europe	South America	Asia-Pacific
Currently offshoring	126	75	35	93
Not currently offshoring, but plan to do so in the future	72	36	10	27
Offshored in the past, but no more	30	9	4	6
Offshoring not applicable	372	180	51	174
Totals	600	300	100	300

10.32 "Cry Wolf" effect in air traffic controlling. Researchers at Alion Science Corporation and New Mexico State University collaborated on a study of how air traffic controllers respond to false alarms (*Human Factors,* August 2009). The researchers theorize that the high rate of false alarms regarding mid-air collisions leads to the "cry wolf" effect, i.e., the tendency for air traffic controllers to ignore true alerts in the future. The investigation examined data on a random sample of 437 conflict alerts. Each alert was first classified as a "true" or "false" alert. Then, each was classified according to whether or not there was a human controller response to the alert. A summary of the responses is provided in the accompanying table. Do the data indicate that the response rate of air traffic controllers to mid-air collision alarms differs for true and false alerts? Test using $\alpha = .05$. What inference can you make concerning the "cry wolf" effect?

	No Response	Response	Totals
True alert	3	231	234
False alert	37	166	203
Totals	40	397	437

Source: Based on C. "False Alerts in Air Traffic Control Conflict Alerting System: Is There a 'Cry Wolf' Effect?" *Human Factors,* Vol. 51, No. 4, August 2009 (Table 2).

10.33 Mobile device typing strategies. Refer to the *Applied Ergonomics* (March 2012) study of mobile device typing strategies, Exercise 10.13 (p. 607). Recall that typing style of mobile device users was categorized as (1) device held with both hands/both thumbs typing, (2) device held with right hand/right thumb typing, (3) device held with left hand/left thumb typing, (4) device held with both hands/right thumb typing, (5) device held with left hand/right index finger typing, or (6) other. The researchers' main objective was to determine if there are gender differences in typing strategies. Typing strategy and gender were observed for each in a sample of 859 college students observed typing on their mobile devices. The data are summarized in the accompanying table. Is this sufficient evidence to conclude that the proportions of mobile device users in the six texting style categories depend on whether a male or a female is texting? Use $\alpha = .10$ to answer the question.

Typing Strategy	Number of Males	Number of Females
Both hands hold/both thumbs type	161	235
Right hand hold/right thumb type	118	193
Left hand hold/left thumb type	29	41
Both hands hold/right thumb type	10	29
Left hand hold/right index type	6	12
Other	11	14

Source: J. E. Gold et al., "Postures, Typing Strategies, and Gender Differences in Mobile Device Usage: An Observational Study," *Applied Ergonomics,* Vol. 43, No. 2, March 2012 (Table 2).

10.34 Twitter opinions of iPhone 6 features. Refer to the *Decision Analytics* (October 2015) study of the features of Apple's iPhone 6, Exercise 2.13 (p. 74). Recall that opinions were extracted from a sample of 552 tweets obtained from the social media site Twitter.com. The tweets originated in four cities: San Francisco (138 tweets), New York (182), Los Angeles (89), and Chicago (143). A summary

of the opinions on the iPhone 6 camera (Excellent, Good, or Bad) from tweets in each city is reproduced below. Conduct a test to compare the opinions on the iPhone 6 camera for tweets originating in the four cities. Is there evidence to conclude that the distribution of excellent, good, and bad opinions differs depending on the city? Use $\alpha = .05$.

City	Number of Tweets about iPhone 6 Camera		
	Excellent	Good	Bad
San Francisco	14	94	30
New York	18	113	51
Los Angeles	5	51	33
Chicago	0	94	49

Source: S. Hridoy, et al., "Localized Twitter Opinion Mining Using Sentiment Analysis," *Decision Analytics,* Vol. 2, No. 8, October 2015 (adapted from Figures 10-13).

10.35 Consumer recycling behavior. Refer to the *Journal of Consumer Research* (December 2013) study of consumer recycling behavior, Exercise 3.17 (p. 170). Recall that 78 college students were asked to dispose of cut paper they used during an exercise. Half the students were randomly assigned to list five uses for the cut paper (*usefulness is salient* condition), while the other half were asked to list their five favorite TV shows (*control* condition). The researchers kept track of which students recycled and which students disposed of their paper in the garbage. Assume that of the 39 students in the *usefulness is salient* condition, 26 recycled; of the 39 students in the *control* condition, 14 recycled. Recall that the researchers wanted to test the theory that students in the *usefulness is salient* condition will recycle at a higher rate than students in the *control* condition. Use a χ^2 test (at $\alpha = .05$) to either support or refute the theory.

10.36 Firefighter glove sizing. Refer to the *Human Factors* (December 2015) study on how well firefighter gloves fit, Exercise 3.38 (p. 181). Recall that in a sample of 586 firefighters who reported their glove size, the researchers classified firefighters according to whether the gloves fit well or poorly and by gender. A summary of the data (number of firefighters) is reproduced in the accompanying table. The researchers want to know whether the proportion of firefighters who wear a poorly fitting glove differs for males and females. Conduct an analysis that will answer the researchers' question. Use a test of hypothesis at $\alpha = .01$ and supplement your analysis with a 99% confidence interval on the difference in proportions for males and females.

	Glove Fits Well	Glove Fits Poorly	Totals
Males	415	132	547
Females	19	20	39
Totals	434	152	586

Source: H. Hsiao et al., "Firefighter Hand Anthropometry and Structural Glove Sizing: A New Perspective," *Human Factors,* Vol. 57, No. 8, December 2015 (Table 6).

10.37 Classifying air threats with heuristics. The *Journal of Behavioral Decision Making* (January 2007) published a study on the use of heuristics to classify the threat level of approaching aircraft. Of special interest was the use of a fast and frugal heuristic—a computationally simple procedure for making judgments with limited information—named "Take-the-Best-for-Classification" (TTBC). Subjects were 48 men and women; some were from a Canadian Forces reserve unit, and others were university students. Each subject was presented with a radar screen on which simulated approaching aircraft were identified with asterisks. By using the computer mouse to click on the asterisk, further information about the aircraft was provided. The goal was to identify the aircraft as "friend" or "foe" as fast as possible. Half the subjects were given cue-based instructions for determining the type of aircraft, while the other half were given pattern-based instructions. The researcher also classified the heuristic strategy used by the subject as TTBC, Guess, or Other. Data on the two variables, instruction type and strategy, measured for each of the 48 subjects are saved in the file. (Data for the first five and last five subjects are shown in the table below.) Do the data provide sufficient evidence (at $\alpha = .05$) to indicate that choice of heuristic strategy depends on type of instruction provided? At $\alpha = .01$?

Instruction	Strategy
Pattern	Other
Pattern	Other
Pattern	Other
Cue	TTBC
Cue	TTBC
⋮	⋮
Pattern	TTBC
Cue	Guess
Cue	TTBC
Cue	Guess
Pattern	Guess

Source: D. J. Bryant, "Classifying Simulated Air Threats with Fast and Frugal Heuristics," *Journal of Behavioral Decision Making,* Vol. 20, January 2007 (Appendix C).

10.38 Coupon user study. Refer to the study of a customer's motivation to use a technology-based self-service (TBSS) encounter developed for a firm's discount coupons, Exercise 10.15 (p. 608). Recall that the coupon users received the coupons in one of three ways—mail only (nontechnology user), Internet only (TBSS user), and both mail and Internet. The researcher wants to know if there are differences in customer characteristics—specifically gender (male or female) and coupon usage satisfaction (satisfied, unsatisfied, or indifferent)—among the three types of coupon users. That is, does type of coupon user depend on gender? Does type depend on coupon usage satisfaction level? Data on these categorical variables were collected

for a sample of 440 coupon users and are saved in the file. Conduct the appropriate analyses for the researcher. Use $\alpha = .01$ for each analysis. Present your conclusions in a professional report.

Applying the Concepts—Advanced

10.39 Examining the "Monty Hall Dilemma." In Exercise 3.133 (p. 210), you solved the game show problem of whether or not to switch your choice of three doors—one of which hides a prize—after the host reveals what is behind a door not chosen. (Despite the natural inclination of many to keep one's first choice, the correct answer is that you should switch your choice of doors.) This problem is sometimes called the "Monty Hall Dilemma," named for Monty Hall, the host of the popular TV game show *Let's Make a Deal.* In *Thinking & Reasoning* (August 2007), Wichita State University professors set up an experiment designed to influence subjects to switch their original choice of doors. Each subject participated in 23 trials. In trial #1, three doors (boxes) were presented on a computer screen, only one of which hid a prize. In each subsequent trial, an additional box was presented, so that in trial #23, 25 boxes were presented. After selecting a box in each trial, all the remaining boxes except for one were either (1) shown to be empty (*Empty* condition), (2) disappeared (*Vanish* condition), (3) disappeared and the chosen box enlarged (*Steroids* condition), or (4) disappeared and the remaining box not chosen enlarged (*Steroids2* condition). A total of 27 subjects were assigned to each condition. The number of subjects who ultimately switched boxes is tallied, by condition, in the table below for both the first trials and the last trial.

	First Trial (#1)		Last Trial (#23)	
Condition	Switch Boxes	No Switch	Switch Boxes	No Switch
Empty	10	17	23	4
Vanish	3	24	12	15
Steroids	5	22	21	6
Steroids2	8	19	19	8

Source: Based on J. N. Howard, C. G. Lambdin, and D. L. Datteri, "Let's Make a Deal: Quality and Availability of Second-Stage Information as a Catalyst for Change," *Thinking & Reasoning,* Vol. 13, No. 3, August 2007, pp. 248–272 (Table 2).

a. For a selected trial, does the likelihood of switching boxes depend on condition?

b. For a given condition, does the likelihood of switching boxes depend on trial number?

c. Based on the results, parts **a** and **b**, what factors influence a subject to switch choices?

10.4 A Word of Caution About Chi-Square Tests

Because the χ^2 statistic for testing hypotheses about multinomial probabilities is one of the most widely applied statistical tools, it is also one of the most abused statistical procedures. Consequently, the user should always be certain that the experiment satisfies the assumptions given with each procedure. Furthermore, the user should be certain that the sample is drawn from the correct population—that is, from the population about which the inference is to be made.

The use of the χ^2 probability distribution as an approximation to the sampling distribution for χ^2 should be avoided when the expected counts are very small. The approximation can become very poor when these expected counts are small, and thus the true α level may be quite different from the tabled value. As a rule of thumb, an expected cell count of at least 5 means that the χ^2 probability distribution can be used to determine an approximate critical value.

If the χ^2 value does not exceed the established critical value of χ^2, *do not accept the hypothesis of independence.* You would be risking a Type II error (accepting H_0 if it is false), and the probability β of committing such an error is unknown. The usual alternative hypothesis is that the classifications are dependent. Because the number of ways in which two classifications can be dependent is virtually infinite, it is difficult to calculate one or even several values of β to represent such a broad alternative hypothesis. Therefore, we avoid concluding that two classifications are independent, even when χ^2 is small.

Finally, if a contingency table χ^2 value does exceed the critical value, we must be careful to avoid inferring that a *causal* relationship exists between the classifications. Our alternative hypothesis states that the two classifications are statistically dependent—and a statistical dependence does not imply causality. Therefore, *the existence of a causal relationship cannot be established by a contingency table analysis.*

ETHICS in STATISTICS

Using the results of a chi-square analysis to make a desired influence when you are fully aware that the sample is too small or that the assumptions are violated is considered *unethical statistical practice.*

CHAPTER NOTES

Key Terms

Categories 601
Cell counts 601
Cells 601
Chi-square test 602
Classes 601
Contingency table 608
Contingency table with
   fixed marginals 615
Dependence 611
Dimensions of classification 608

Expected cell count 603
Fisher's exact test 616
Independence of two
   classifications 609
Marginal probabilities 609
Multinomial experiment 601
Observed count 610
One-way table 602
Two-way table 608

Key Symbols/Notation

$p_{i,0}$ Value of multinomial probability p_i hypothesized in H_0

χ^2 Chi-square test statistic used in analysis of categorical data

n_i Number of observed outcomes in cell i of a one-way table

E_i Expected number of outcomes in cell i of a one-way table

p_{ij} Probability of an outcome in row i and column j of a two-way table

n_{ij} Number of observed outcomes in row i and column j of a two-way table

$\hat{E}_{ij}$ Estimated expected number of outcomes in row i and column j of a two-way table

R_i Total number of outcomes in row i of a two-way table

C_j Total number of outcomes in column j of a two-way table

Key Ideas

Multinomial data

Qualitative data that fall into two or more categories (or classes)

Properties of a Multinomial Experiment

1. n identical trials
2. k possible outcomes to each trial
3. probabilities of the k outcomes $(p_1, p_2, \ldots, p_k)$ remain the same from trial to trial, where
$$p_1 + p_2 + \cdots + p_k = 1$$
4. trials are independent
5. variables of interest: *cell counts* (i.e., number of observations falling into each outcome category), denoted $n_1, n_2, \ldots, n_k$

One-way table
Summary table for a *single* qualitative variable

Two-way (contingency) table
Summary table for *two* qualitative variables

Chi-square (χ^2) statistic
used to test category probabilities in one-way and two-way tables

Chi-square tests for independence
should **not** be used to *infer a causal relationship between 2 qualitative variables*

Conditions Required for Valid χ^2 Tests

1. multinomial experiment
2. sample size n is large (expected cell counts are all greater than or equal to 5)

Categorical Data Analysis Guide

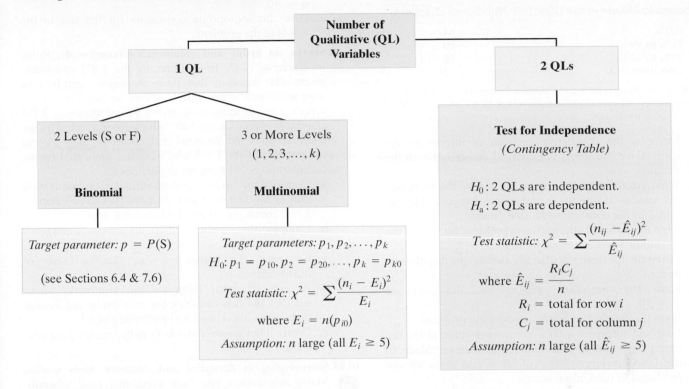

Number of Qualitative (QL) Variables

1 QL

2 Levels (S or F)

Binomial

Target parameter: $p = P(S)$

(see Sections 6.4 & 7.6)

3 or More Levels
$(1, 2, 3, \ldots, k)$

Multinomial

Target parameters: $p_1, p_2, \ldots, p_k$
$H_0: p_1 = p_{10}, p_2 = p_{20}, \ldots, p_k = p_{k0}$

Test statistic: $\chi^2 = \sum \dfrac{(n_i - E_i)^2}{E_i}$

where $E_i = n(p_{i0})$

Assumption: n large (all $E_i \geq 5$)

2 QLs

Test for Independence
(Contingency Table)

H_0: 2 QLs are independent.
H_a: 2 QLs are dependent.

Test statistic: $\chi^2 = \sum \dfrac{(n_{ij} - \hat{E}_{ij})^2}{\hat{E}_{ij}}$

where $\hat{E}_{ij} = \dfrac{R_i C_j}{n}$
R_i = total for row i
C_j = total for column j

Assumption: n large (all $\hat{E}_{ij} \geq 5$)

SUPPLEMENTARY EXERCISES 10.40–10.58

Learning the Mechanics

10.40 A random sample of 250 observations was classified according to the row and column categories shown in the table below.

L10040

		Column		
		1	2	3
	1	20	20	10
Row	2	10	20	70
	3	20	50	30

a. Do the data provide sufficient evidence to conclude that the rows and columns are dependent? Test using $\alpha = .05$.

b. Would the analysis change if the row totals were fixed before the data were collected?

c. Do the assumptions required for the analysis to be valid differ according to whether the row (or column) totals are fixed? Explain.

d. Convert the table entries to percentages by using each column total as a base and calculating each row response as a percentage of the corresponding column total. In addition, calculate the row totals and convert them to percentages of all 250 observations.

e. Create a bar graph with row 1 percentage on the vertical axis against the column number on the horizontal axis. Draw horizontal lines corresponding to the row 1 percentages. Does the graph support the result of the test conducted in part **a**?

10.41 A random sample of 150 observations was classified into the categories shown in the table below.

L10041

	Category				
	1	2	3	4	5
n_i	28	35	33	25	29

a. Do the data provide sufficient evidence that the categories are not equally likely? Use $\alpha = .10$.

b. Form a 90% confidence interval for p_2, the probability that an observation will fall in category 2.

Applying the Concepts—Basic

10.42 "Made in the USA" survey. Refer to the *Journal of Global Business* (Spring 2002) study of what "Made in the USA" on product labels means to the typical consumer, Exercise 2.154 (p. 143). Recall that 106 shoppers participated in the survey. Their responses, given as a percentage of U.S. labor and materials in four categories, are summarized in the table (p. 628). Suppose a consumer advocate group claims that half of all consumers believe that "Made in the USA" means "100%" of labor and materials are produced in the United States, one-fourth believe that "75% to 99%" are produced in the United States, one-fifth believe that "50% to 74%" are produced in the United States, and 5% believe that "less than 50%" are produced in the United States.

MIUSA

Table for Exercise 10.42

Response to "Made in the USA"	Number of Shoppers
100%	64
75% to 99%	20
50% to 74%	18
Less than 50%	4

Source: Based on "'Made in the USA': Consumer Perceptions, Deception and Policy Alternatives," *Journal of Global Business*, Vol. 13, No. 24, Spring 2002 (Table 3). Copyright year: 2002.

a. Describe the qualitative variable of interest in the study. Give the levels (categories) associated with the variable.

b. What are the values of $p_1, p_2, p_3,$ and p_4, the probabilities associated with the four response categories hypothesized by the consumer advocate group?

c. Give the null and alternative hypotheses for testing the consumer advocate group's claim.

d. Compute the test statistic for testing the hypotheses, part **c**.

e. Find the rejection region of the test at $\alpha = .10$.

f. State the conclusion in the words of the problem.

g. Find and interpret a 90% confidence interval for the true proportion of consumers who believe "Made in the USA" means "100%" of labor and materials are produced in the United States.

10.43 Survey on giving and volunteering. *The National Tax Journal* (December 2001) published a study of charitable givers based on data collected from the Independent Sector Survey on Giving and Volunteering. A total of 1,072 charitable givers reported that their charitable contributions were motivated by tax considerations. The number of these 1,072 givers in each of 10 household income categories (saved in the accompanying file) is shown in the table below.

Household Income Group	Number of Charitable Givers
Under $10,000	42
$10,000 – $20,000	93
$20,000 – $30,000	99
$30,000 – $40,000	153
$40,000 – $50,000	91
$50,000 – $60,000	114
$60,000 – $70,000	157
$70,000 – $80,000	101
$80,000 – $100,000	95
Over $100,000	127

Source: L. Tiehen, "Tax Policy and Charitable Contributions of Money," *National Tax Journal*, Vol. 54, No. 4, December 2001, p. 717 (adapted from Table 5). Copyright © 2001 by the National Tax Association. Reprinted with permission.

a. If the true proportions of charitable givers in each household income group are the same, how many of the 1,072 sampled givers would you expect to find in each income category?

b. Give the null hypothesis for testing whether the true proportions of charitable givers in each household income group are the same.

c. Compute the chi-square test statistic for testing the null hypothesis, part **b**.

d. Find the rejection region for the test if $\alpha = .10$.

e. Give the appropriate conclusion for the test in the words of the problem.

10.44 Survey on giving and volunteering (continued). Refer to Exercise 10.43. In addition to the 1,072 charitable givers who reported that their charitable contributions were motivated by tax considerations, another 1,693 givers reported no tax motivation, giving a total sample of 2,765 charitable givers. Of the 1,072 who were motivated by tax considerations, 691 itemized deductions on their income tax returns. Of the 1,693 who were not motivated by tax considerations, 794 itemized deductions.

a. Consider the two categorical variables, tax motivation (yes or no) and itemize deductions (yes or no). Form a 2×2 contingency table for these variables.

b. Compute the expected cell counts for the contingency table, part **a**.

c. Compute the value of χ^2 for a test of independence.

d. At $\alpha = .05$, what inference can you make about whether the two variables, tax motivation and itemize deductions, are related for charitable givers?

e. Create a bar graph that will visually support your conclusion in part **d**.

10.45 Stereotyping in deceptive and authentic news stories. Major newspapers lose their credibility (and subscribers) when they are found to have published deceptive or misleading news stories. In *Journalism and Mass Communication Quarterly* (Summer 2007), University of Texas researchers investigated whether certain stereotypes (e.g., negative references to certain nationalities) occur more often in deceptive news stories than in authentic news stories. The researchers analyzed 183 news stories that were proven to be deceptive in nature and 128 news stories that were considered authentic. Specifically, the researchers determined whether each story was negative, neutral, or positive in tone. The accompanying table gives the number of news stories found in each tone category.

	Authentic News Stories	Deceptive News Stories
Negative tone	59	111
Neutral tone	49	61
Positive tone	20	11
Totals	128	183

Source: Based on D. Lasorsa and J. Dai, "When News Reporters Deceive: The Production of Stereotypes," *Journalism and Mass Communication Quarterly*, Vol. 84, No. 2, Summer 2007 (Table 2).

a. Find the sample proportion of negative tone news stories that are deceptive.

b. Find the sample proportion of neutral news stories that are deceptive.

c. Find the sample proportion of positive news stories that are deceptive.

d. Compare the sample proportions, parts **a–c**. Does it appear that the proportion of news stories that are deceptive depends on story tone?

Tabulated statistics: TONE, STORY

Using frequencies in NUMBER

Rows: TONE   Columns: STORY

```
            Authentic   Deceptive    All

Negative          59        111       170
               69.97     100.03    170.00

Neutral           49         61       110
               45.27      64.73    110.00

Positive          20         11        31
               12.76      18.24     31.00

All              128        183       311
              128.00     183.00    311.00

Cell Contents:       Count
                     Expected count


Pearson Chi-Square = 10.427, DF = 2, P-Value = 0.005
Likelihood Ratio Chi-Square = 10.348, DF = 2, P-Value = 0.006
```

Minitab output for Exercise 10.45

e. Give the null hypothesis for testing whether the authenticity of a news story depends on tone.

f. Use the Minitab printout above to conduct the test, part **e.** Test at $\alpha = .05$.

10.46 Colors of M&M's candies. M&M's plain chocolate candies come in six different colors: dark brown, yellow, red, orange, green, and blue. According to the manufacturer (Mars, Inc.), the color ratio in each large production batch is 30% brown, 20% yellow, 20% red, 10% orange, 10% green, and 10% blue. To test this claim, a professor at Carleton College (Minnesota) had students count the colors of M&M's found in "fun size" bags of the candy. The results for 400 M&M's sampled in a similar study are displayed in the next table.

Brown	Yellow	Red	Orange	Green	Blue	Total
100	75	85	50	40	50	400

a. Assuming the manufacturer's stated percentages are accurate, calculate the expected numbers falling into the six categories.

b. Calculate the value of χ^2 for testing the manufacturer's claim.

c. Conduct a test to determine whether the true percentages of the colors produced differ from the manufacturer's stated percentages. Use $\alpha = .05$.

Applying the Concepts—Intermediate

10.47 Top Internet search engines. *Search Engine Land* reported on the "search" shares (i.e., percentage of all Internet searches) for the most popular search engines available on the Web. In December 2013, Google accounted for 65% of all worldwide searches, Baidu for 8%, Yahoo! for 5%, Yandex for 3%, MSN for 2.5%, and all other search engines for 16.5%. Suppose that in a random sample of 1,000 recent Internet searches, 648 used Google, 91 used Baidu, 45 used Yandex, 40 used Yahoo!, 21 used MSN, and 155 used another search engine.

a. Do the sample data disagree with the percentages reported by *Search Engine Land*? Test using $\alpha = .05$.

b. Find and interpret a 95% confidence interval for the percentage of all Internet searches that use the Google search engine.

10.48 Pig farm study. An article in *Sociological Methods & Research* (May 2001) analyzed the data presented in the table. A sample of 262 Kansas pig farmers was classified according to their education level (college or not) and size of their pig farm (number of pigs). Conduct a test to determine whether a pig farmer's education level has an impact on the size of the pig farm. Use $\alpha = .05$ and support your answer with a graph.

	Education Level		
Farm Size	No College	College	Totals
<1,000 pigs	42	53	95
1,000–2,000 pigs	27	42	69
2,000–5,000 pigs	22	20	42
>5,000 pigs	27	29	56
Totals	118	144	262

Source: Based on A. Agresti and I. Liu, "Strategies for Modeling a Categorical Variable Allowing Multiple Category Choices," *Sociological Methods & Research*, Vol. 29, No. 4, May 2001 (Table 1).

10.49 Management system failures. Refer to the *Process Safety Progress* (December 2004) and U.S. Chemical Safety and Hazard Investigation Board study of industrial accidents caused by management system failures, Exercise 2.150 (p. 142). The table below gives a breakdown of the root causes of a sample of 83 incidents. Are there significant differences in the percentage of incidents in the four cause categories? Test using $\alpha = .05$.

Management System Cause	Number of Incidents
Engineering & Design	27
Procedures & Practices	24
Management & Oversight	22
Training & Communication	10
Total	83

Source: Republished with permission of John Wiley & Sons, Inc. from A. S. Blair, "Management System Failures Identified in Incidents Investigated by the U.S. Chemical Safety and Hazard Investigation Board," *Process Safety Progress*, Vol. 23, No. 4, December 2004, pp. 232–236 (Table 1). Permission conveyed through Copyright Clearance Center, Inc.

10.50 History of corporate acquisitions. Refer to the *Academy of Management Journal* (August 2008) investigation of the performance and timing of corporate acquisitions, Exercise 2.12 (p. 74). Data on the number of firms sampled and the number that announced one or more acquisitions during the years from 1980 to 2000 are saved in the accompanying file. Suppose you want to determine if the proportion of firms with acquisitions differed annually from 1990 to 2000, that is, you want to determine if year and acquisition status were dependent from 1990 to 2000.

a. Identify the two qualitative variables (and their respective categories) to be analyzed.

b. Set up the null and alternative hypotheses for the test.

c. Use the Minitab printout at the top of next page to conduct the test at $\alpha = .5$.

Tabulated statistics: ACQUISITION, YEAR

```
Using frequencies in NUMBER

Rows: ACQUISITION    Columns: YEAR

      1990  1991  1992  1993  1994  1995  1996  1997  1998  1999  2000   All

No    1847  1891  1936  2050  2149  2238  2319  2300  2047  2049  2030  22856
      1689  1738  1817  1985  2134  2222  2360  2383  2240  2152  2136  22856

Yes    350   370   427   532   626   652   751   799   866   750   748   6871
       508   523   546   597   641   668   710   716   673   647   642   6871

All   2197  2261  2363  2582  2775  2890  3070  3099  2913  2799  2778  29727
      2197  2261  2363  2582  2775  2890  3070  3099  2913  2799  2778  29727

Cell Contents:        Count
                      Expected count

Pearson Chi-Square = 297.048, DF = 10, P-Value = 0.000
Likelihood Ratio Chi-Square = 303.612, DF = 10, P-Value = 0.000
```

Minitab output for Exercise 10.50

10.51 Creating menus to influence others. Refer to the *Journal of Consumer Research* (March 2003) study on influencing the choices of others by offering undesirable alternatives, Exercise 7.80 (p. 426). In another experiment conducted by the researcher, 96 subjects were asked to imagine that they had just moved to an apartment with two others and that they were shopping for a new appliance (e.g., television, microwave oven). Each subject was asked to create a menu of three brand choices for their roommates; then subjects were randomly assigned (in equal numbers) to one of three different "goal" conditions—(1) create the menu in order to influence roommates to buy a preselected brand, (2) create the menu in order to influence roommates to buy a brand of your choice, and (3) create the menu with no intent to influence roommates. The researcher theorized that the menus created to influence others would likely include undesirable alternative brands. Consequently, the number of menus in each goal condition that was consistent with the theory was determined. The data are summarized in the table below. Analyze the data for the purpose of determining whether the proportion of subjects who selected menus consistent with the theory depends on goal condition. Use $\alpha = .01$.

MENU3

Goal Condition	Number Consistent with Theory	Number Not Consistent with Theory	Totals
Influence/preselected brand	15	17	32
Influence/own brand	14	18	32
No influence	3	29	32

Source: Based on R. W. Hamilton, "Why Do People Suggest What They Do Not Want? Using Context Effects to Influence Others' Choices," *Journal of Consumer Research*, Vol. 29, No. 4, March 2003 (Table 2).

10.52 Attitudes toward top corporate managers. Scandals involving large U.S. corporations (e.g., Enron, WorldCom, and Adelphia) have had a major impact on the public's attitude toward business managers. In a Harris Poll administered immediately after the Enron scandal, a national sample of 2,023 adults were asked to agree or disagree with the following statement: "Top company managers have become rich at the expense of ordinary workers" (*The Harris Poll*,

TOPMGR

#55, Oct. 18, 2002). The response categories (and number of respondents in each) were strongly agree (1,173), somewhat agree (587), somewhat disagree (182), and strongly disagree (81). Suppose that prior to the Enron scandal, the percentages of all U.S. adults falling into the four response categories were 45%, 35%, 15%, and 5%, respectively. Is there evidence to infer that the percentages of all U.S. adults falling into the four response categories changed after the Enron scandal? Test using $\alpha = .01$.

10.53 Guilt in decision making. The effect of guilt emotion on how a decision maker focuses on a problem was investigated in the January 2007 issue of the *Journal of Behavioral Decision Making* (see Exercise 3.48, p. 183). A total of 171 volunteer students participated in the experiment, where each was randomly assigned to one of three emotional states (guilt, anger, or neutral) through a reading/writing task. Immediately after the task, students were presented with a decision problem where the stated option had predominantly negative features (e.g., spending money on repairing a very old car). The results (number responding in each category) are summarized in the accompanying table. Is there sufficient evidence (at $\alpha = .10$) to claim that the option choice depended on emotional state? Use the data saved to answer the question.

GUILT

Emotional State	Choose Stated Option	Do Not Choose Stated Option	Totals
Guilt	45	12	57
Anger	8	50	58
Neutral	7	49	56
Totals	60	111	171

Source: A. Gangemi and F. Mancini, "Guilt and Focusing in Decision-Making," *Journal of Behavioral Decision Making*, Vol. 20, January 2007 (Table 2).

10.54 "Fitness for use" of gasoline filters. Product or service quality is often defined as *fitness for use*. This means the product or service meets the customer's needs. Generally speaking, fitness for use is based on five quality characteristics: technological (e.g., strength, hardness), psychological (taste, beauty), time-oriented (reliability), contractual (guarantee provisions), and ethical (courtesy, honesty).

FILTER

The quality of a service may involve all these characteristics, while the quality of a manufactured product generally depends on technological and time-oriented characteristics (Schroeder, *Operations Management*, 2008). After a barrage of customer complaints about poor quality, a manufacturer of gasoline filters for cars had its quality inspectors sample 600 filters—200 per work shift—and check for defects. The data in the table resulted.

Shift	Defectives Produced
First	25
Second	35
Third	80

a. Do the data indicate that the quality of the filters being produced may be related to the shift producing the filter? Test using $\alpha = .05$.

b. Estimate the proportion of defective filters produced by the first shift. Use a 95% confidence interval.

10.55 Flight response of geese to helicopter traffic. Offshore oil drilling near an Alaskan estuary has led to increased air traffic—mostly large helicopters—in the area. The U.S. Fish and Wildlife Service commissioned a study to investigate the impact these helicopters have on the flocks of Pacific brant geese that inhabit the estuary in fall before migrating (*Statistical Case Studies: A Collaboration between Academe and Industry*, 1998). Two large helicopters were flown repeatedly over the estuary at different altitudes and lateral distances from the flock. The flight responses of the geese (recorded as "low" or "high"), altitude (hundreds of meters), and lateral distance (hundreds of meters) for each of the 464 helicopter overflights were recorded and are saved in the file. (The data for the first 10 overflights are shown in the table below.)

Overflight	Altitude	Lateral Distance	Flight Response
1	0.91	4.99	High
2	0.91	8.21	High
3	0.91	3.38	High
4	9.14	21.08	Low
5	1.52	6.60	High
6	0.91	3.38	High
7	3.05	0.16	High
8	6.10	3.38	High
9	3.05	6.60	High
10	12.19	6.60	High

Source: From W. Erickson, T. Nick, and D. Ward, "Investigating Flight Response of Pacific Brant to Helicopters at Izembek Lagoon, Alaska, by Using Logistic Regression," *Statistical Case Studies: A Collaboration Between Academe and Industry*, by Roxy Peck, Larry D. Haugh and Arnold Goodman. Copyright © 1998 Society for Industrial and Applied Mathematics. Used by permission of the Society for Industrial and Applied Mathematics.

a. The researchers categorized altitude as follows: less than 300 meters; 300–600 meters; and 600 or more meters; Summarize the data in the file by creating a contingency table for altitude category and flight response.

b. Conduct a test to determine if flight response of the geese depends on altitude of the helicopter. Test using $\alpha = .01$.

c. The researchers categorized lateral distance as follows: less than 1,000 meters; 1,000–2,000 meters; 2,000–3,000 meters; and 3,000 or more meters. Summarize the data in the file by creating a contingency table for lateral distance category and flight response.

d. Conduct a test to determine if flight response of the geese depends on lateral distance of the helicopter from the flock. Test using $\alpha = .01$.

e. The current Federal Aviation Authority (FAA) minimum altitude standard for flying over the estuary is 2,000 feet (approximately 610 meters). Based on the results, parts **a–d**, what changes to the FAA regulations do you recommend to minimize the effects to Pacific brant geese?

Applying the Concepts—Advanced

10.56 Software defects. The PROMISE Software Engineering Repository at the University of Ottawa provides researchers with data sets for building predictive software models. (See Exercise 2.160, p. 145.) Data on 498 modules of software code written in "C" language for a NASA spacecraft instrument are saved in the file. Recall that each module was analyzed for defects and classified as "true" if it contained defective code and "false" if not. One algorithm for predicting whether or not a module has defects is "essential complexity" (denoted EVG), where a module with at least 15 subflow graphs with D-structured primes is predicted to have a defect. When the method predicts a defect, the predicted EVG value is "yes"; otherwise, it is "no." Would you recommend the essential complexity algorithm as a predictor of defective software modules? Explain.

10.57 Goodness-of-fit test. A statistical analysis is to be done on a set of data consisting of 1,000 monthly salaries. The analysis requires the assumption that the sample was drawn from a normal distribution. A preliminary test, called the χ^2 *goodness-of-fit test*, can be used to help determine whether it is reasonable to assume that the sample is from a normal distribution. Suppose the mean and standard deviation of the 1,000 salaries are hypothesized to be $1,200 and $200, respectively. Using the standard normal table, we can approximate the probability of a salary being in the intervals listed in the table below. The third column represents the expected number of the 1,000 salaries to be found in each interval if the sample was drawn from a normal distribution with $\mu = \$1,200$ and $\Sigma = \$200$. Suppose the last column contains the actual observed frequencies in the sample. Large differences between the observed and expected frequencies cast doubt on the normality assumption.

Table for Exercise 10.57

Interval	Probability	Expected Frequency	Observed Frequency
Less than $800	.023	23	26
Between $800 and $1,000	.136	136	146
Between $1,000 and $1,200	.341	341	361
Between $1,200 and $1,400	.341	341	311
Between $1,400 and $1,600	.136	136	143
Above $1,600	.023	23	13

a. Compute the χ^2 statistic based on the observed and expected frequencies—just as you did in Section 10.2. $\alpha = .01$.

b. Find the tabulated χ^2 value when $\alpha = .05$ and there are 5 degrees of freedom. (There are $k - 1 = 5$ df associated with this χ^2 statistic.)

c. Based on the χ^2 statistic and the tabulated χ^2 value, is there evidence that the salary distribution is nonnormal?

d. Find an approximate observed significance level for the test in part c.

Critical Thinking Challenge

10.58 A "rigged" election? *Chance* (Spring 2004) presented data from a recent election held to determine the board of directors of a local community. There were 27 candidates for the board, and each of 5,553 voters was allowed to choose 6 candidates. The claim was that "a fixed vote with fixed percentages (was) assigned to each and every candidate making it impossible to participate in an honest election." Votes were tallied in six time periods: after 600 total votes were in, after 1,200, after 2,444, after 3,444, after 4,444, and after 5,553 votes. The data for three of the candidates (Smith, Coppin, and Montes) are shown in the following table. A residential organization believes that "there was nothing random about the count and tallies each time period and specific unnatural or rigged percentages were being assigned to each and every candidate." Give your opinion. Is the probability of a candidate receiving votes independent of the time period? If so, does this imply a rigged election?

	Time Period					
	1	2	3	4	5	6
Votes for Smith	208	208	451	392	351	410
Votes for Coppin	55	51	109	98	88	104
Votes for Montes	133	117	255	211	186	227
Total Votes	600	600	1,244	1,000	1,000	1,109

Source: Based on A. Gelman, "55,000 Residents Desperately Need Your Help!" *Chance*, Vol. 17, No. 2, Spring 2004, p. 32 (Figures 1 and 5, p. 34).

ACTIVITY 10.1 **Binomial vs. Multinomial Experiments**

In this activity, you will study the difference between binomial and multinomial experiments.

1. A television station has hired an independent research group to determine whether television viewers in the area prefer its local news program to the news programs of two other stations in the same city. Explain why a multinomial experiment would be appropriate and design a poll that satisfies the five properties of a multinomial experiment. State the null and alternative hypotheses for the corresponding χ^2 test.

2. Suppose the television station believes that a majority of local viewers prefer its news program to those of its two competitors. Explain why a binomial experiment would be appropriate to support this claim and design a poll that satisfies the five properties of a binomial experiment. State the null and alternative hypotheses for the corresponding test.

3. Generalize the situations in Exercises 1 and 2 to describe conditions under which a multinomial experiment can be rephrased as a binomial experiment. Is there any advantage in doing so? Explain.

ACTIVITY 10.2 **Contingency Tables**

In this Activity, you will revisit Activity 3.1, *Exit Polls* (p. 210). For convenience, the table shown in that activity is repeated here.

2012 Presidential Election, Vote by Gender

	Obama	Romney	Other
Male (47%)	45%	52%	3%
Female (53%)	55%	44%	1%

Source: Based on table "Presidential Election, Vote by Gender," from CNN Web site.

1. Determine whether the table above and the similar tables that you found for Activity 3.1 are contingency tables. If not, do you have enough information to create a contingency table for the data? If you need more information, state specifically what information you need.

2. Choose one of your examples from the previous activity if it contains a contingency table or enough information to create one, or use the Internet or some other source to find a new example with a contingency table given. Determine whether the conditions for a valid χ^2 test are met. If not, choose a different example where the conditions are met.

3. Perform a χ^2 test for independence for the example chosen in Exercise 2. Are the results what you would expect in the given situation? Explain.

References

Agresti, A. *Categorical Data Analysis*. New York: Wiley, 1990.

Cochran, W. G. "The χ^2 test of goodness of fit," *Annals of Mathematical Statistics*, 1952, 23.

Conover, W. J. *Practical Nonparametric Statistics*, 2nd ed. New York: Wiley, 1980.

DeGroot, M. H., Fienberg, S. E., and Kadane, J. B., eds. *Statistics and the Law*. New York: Wiley, 1986.

Fisher, R. A. "The logic of inductive inference (with discussion)," *Journal of the Royal Statistical Society*, Vol. 98, 1935, pp. 39–82.

Hollander, M., and Wolfe, D. A. *Nonparametric Statistical Methods*. New York: Wiley, 1973.

Savage, I. R. "Bibliography of nonparametric statistics and related topics," *Journal of the American Statistical Association*, 1953, 48.

USING TECHNOLOGY — Technology images shown here are taken from SPSS Statistics Professional 23.0, Minitab 17, XLSTAT, and Excel 2016.

SPSS: Chi-Square Analyses

SPSS can conduct chi-square tests for both one-way and two-way (contingency) tables.

One-Way Table

Step 1 Access the SPSS spreadsheet file that contains the variable with category values for each of the n observations in the data set. (*Note:* SPSS requires that these categories be specified numerically, e.g., 1, 2, 3.)

Step 2 Click on the "Analyze" button on the SPSS menu bar and then click on "Nonparametric Tests," "Legacy Dialogs," and "Chi-square," as shown in Figure 10.S.1. The resulting dialog box appears as shown in Figure 10.S.2.

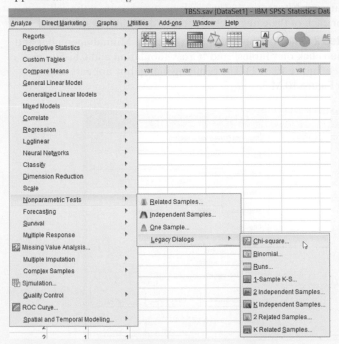

Figure 10.S.1 SPSS menu options for a one-way chi-square analysis

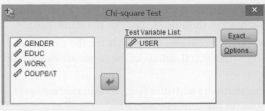

Figure 10.S.2 SPSS one-way chi-square dialog box

Step 3 Specify the qualitative variable of interest in the "Test Variable List" box.

Step 4 If you want to test for equal cell probabilities in the null hypothesis, then select the "All categories equal" option under the "Expected Values" box (as shown in Figure 10.S.2.). If the null hypothesis specifies unequal cell probabilities, then select the "Values" option under the "Expected Values" box. Enter the hypothesized cell probabilities in the adjacent box, one at a time, clicking "Add" after each specification.

Step 5 Click "OK" to generate the SPSS printout.

Two-Way Table

Step 1 Access the SPSS spreadsheet file that contains the sample data. The data file should contain two qualitative variables, with category values for each of the n observations in the data set.

Step 2 Click on the "Analyze" button on the SPSS menu bar and then click on "Descriptive Statistics" and "Crosstabs," as shown in Figure 10.S.3. The resulting dialog box appears as shown in Figure 10.S.4.

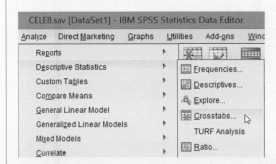

Figure 10.S.3 SPSS menu options for two-way chi-square analysis

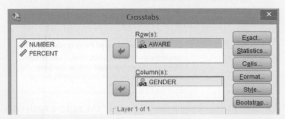

Figure 10.S.4 SPSS crosstabs dialog box

Step 3 Specify one qualitative variable in the "Row(s)" box and the other qualitative variable in the "Column(s)" box.

Step 4 Click the "Statistics" button and select the "Chi-square" option, as shown in Figure 10.S.5.

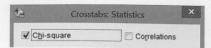

Figure 10.S.5 SPSS statistics menu selections for the two-way analysis

Step 5 Click "Continue" to return to the "Crosstabs" dialog box. If you want the contingency table to include expected values, row percentages, and/or column percentages, click the "Cells" button and make the appropriate menu selections.

Step 6 When you return to the "Crosstabs" menu screen, click "OK" to generate the SPSS printout.

Note: If your SPSS spreadsheet contains summary information (i.e., the cell counts for the contingency table) rather than the actual categorical data values for each observation, you must weight each observation in your data file by the cell count for that observation prior to running the chi-square analysis. Do this by selecting the "Data" button on the SPSS menu bar and then click on "Weight Cases" and specify the variable that contains the cell counts.

Minitab: Chi-Square Analyses

Minitab can conduct chi-square tests for both one-way and two-way (contingency) tables.

One-Way Table

Step 1 Access the Minitab worksheet file that contains the sample data for the qualitative variable of interest.

[*Note:* The data file can have actual values (levels) of the variable for each observation, or, alternatively, two columns—one column listing the levels of the qualitative variable and the other column with the observed counts for each level.]

Step 2 Click on the "Stat" button on the Minitab menu bar and then click on "Tables" and "Chi-Square Goodness-of-Fit Test (One Variable)," as shown in Figure 10.M.1. The resulting dialog box appears as shown in Figure 10.M.2.

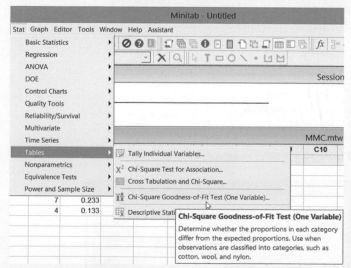

Figure 10.M.1 Minitab menu options for a one-way chi-square analysis

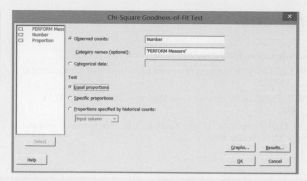

Figure 10.M.2 Minitab one-way chi-square dialog box

Step 3 If your data have one column of values for your qualitative variable, select "Categorical data" and specify the variable name (or column) in the box. If your data have summary information in two columns (see above), select "Observed counts" and specify the column with the counts and the column with the variable names in the respective boxes.

Step 4 Select "Equal proportions" for a test of equal proportions or select "Specific proportions" and enter the hypothesized proportion next to each level in the resulting box.

Step 5 Click "OK" to generate the Minitab printout.

Two-Way Table

Step 1 Access the Minitab worksheet file that contains the sample data. The data file should contain two qualitative variables, with category values for each of the *n* observations in the data set. Alternatively, the worksheet can contain the cell counts for each of the categories of the two qualitative variables.

Step 2 Click on the "Stat" button on the Minitab menu bar and then click on "Tables" and "Cross Tabulation and Chi-Square," (see Figure 10.M.1). The resulting dialog box appears as shown in Figure 10.M.3.

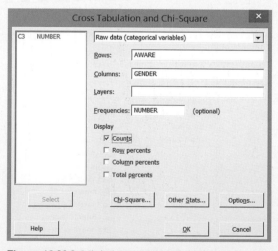

Figure 10.M.3 Minitab cross tabulation dialog box

Step 3 Specify one qualitative variable in the "For rows" box and the other qualitative variable in the "For columns" box.

[*Note:* If your worksheet contains cell counts for the categories, enter the variable with the cell counts in the "Frequencies are in" box.]

Step 4 Select the summary statistics (e.g., counts, percentages) you want to display in the contingency table.

Step 5 Click the "Chi-Square" button. The resulting dialog box is shown in Figure 10.M.4.

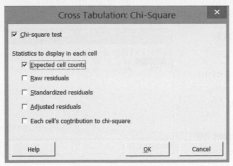

Figure 10.M.4 Minitab chi-square dialog box

Step 6 Select "Chi-Square analysis" and "Expected cell counts" and click "OK."

Step 7 When you return to the "Cross Tabulation" menu screen, click "OK" to generate the Minitab printout.

Note: If your Minitab worksheet contains only the cell counts for the contingency table in columns, click the "Chi-Square Test (Two-Way Table in Worksheet)" menu option (see Figure 10.M.1) and specify the columns in the "Columns containing the table" box. Click "OK" to produce the Minitab printout.

Excel/XLSTAT: Chi-Square Analyses

XLSTAT can conduct a chi-square analysis for both one-way and two-way (contingency) tables. The Excel workbook file should include a column for the quantitative dependent (response) variable, and columns for the qualitative factors.

One-Way Table

Step 1 First, create a workbook with columns representing the levels (categories) of the qualitative variable, the cell (category) counts, and the hypothesized proportions for the levels, as shown in Figure 10.E.1.

	A	B	C
1	Category	Number	Proportion
2	NONE	42	0.1
3	STANDARD	365	0.65
4	MERIT	193	0.25

Figure 10.E.1 Excel workbook format for one-way chi-square analysis

Step 2 Click the "XLSTAT" button on the Excel main menu bar, select "Parametric tests," then click "Multinomial goodness of fit test," as shown in Figure 10.E.2.

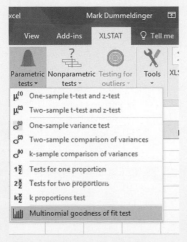

Figure 10.E.2 XLSTAT menu options for one-way chi-square test

Step 3 When the resulting dialog box appears (Figure 10.E.3), enter the column containing the cell counts in the "Frequencies" box. Check the "Proportions" option in the "Data format" area, then enter the column containing the hypothesized proportions in the "Expected proportions" box. Also, select the "Chi-square test" option.

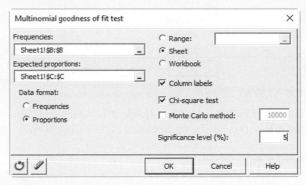

Figure 10.E.3 XLSTAT dialog box for one-way chi-square test

Step 4 Click "OK," then "Continue" to display the test results.

Two-Way Table

Step 1 Create a workbook with one column representing the levels (categories) of the first qualitative variable, a second column representing the levels (categories) of the second qualitative variable, and a third column containing the cell counts, as shown in Figure 10.E.4.

	A	B	C
1	Model	Claim	Number
2	Conventional	Injury	5364
3	Hybrid	Injury	1505
4	Conventional	No Injury	44768
5	Hybrid	No Injury	3859

Figure 10.E.4 Excel workbook format for two-way chi-square analysis

Step 2 Click the "XLSTAT" button on the Excel main menu bar, select "Correlation/Association tests," then click "Tests on contingency tables (Chi-square)," as shown in Figure 10.E.5.

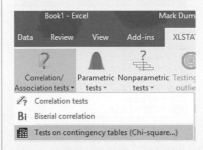

Figure 10.E.5 XLSTAT menu options for two-way chi-square test

Step 3 When the resulting dialog box appears (Figure 10.E.6), enter the column for one qualitative variable in the "Row variables" box and the column for the other qualitative variable in the "Column variables" box. Check the "Weights" option, then enter the column containing the cell counts in the appropriate box.

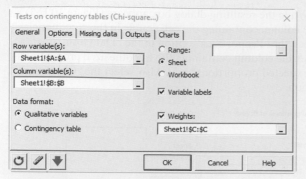

Figure 10.E.6 XLSTAT dialog box for two-way chi-square test

Step 4 Click the "Options" tab, then check "Chi-square test" in the resulting dialog box, as shown in Figure 10.E.7. Click "OK."

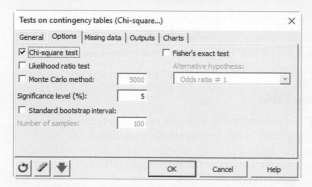

Figure 10.E.7 XLSTAT options for two-way chi-square test

Step 5 (Optional) Click the "Outputs" tab, then select the statistics you want to display in the contingency table (e.g., observed frequencies, expected frequencies). Click "OK."

Step 6 Click "OK," then "Continue" to display the test results.

TI-84 Graphing Calculator: Chi-Square Analyses

One-Way Table

Step 1 *Enter the data for the observed and expected values*

- Press **STAT** and select **1:Edit**
- Enter the observed category values in **L1** and the expected category values in **L2**

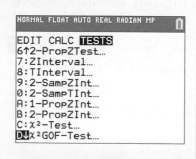

Step 2 *Access the statistical tests menu and perform the chi-square test*

- Press **STAT**
- Arrow right to **TESTS**
- Arrow down to χ^2: **GOF-Test**
- Press **ENTER**
- Arrow down to **Calculate**
- Press **ENTER**

Two-Way (Contingency) Table

Step 1 *Access the Matrix menu to enter the observed values*

- Press **2nd x⁻¹** for **MATRX**
- Arrow right to **EDIT**
- Press **ENTER**
- Use the **ARROW** key to enter the row and column dimensions of your observed Matrix
- Use the **ARROW** key to enter your observed values into Matrix [A]

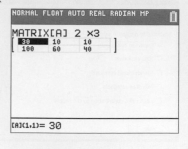

Step 2 *Access the Matrix menu to enter the expected values*

- Press **2nd x⁻¹** for **MATRX**
- Arrow right to **EDIT**
- Arrow down to **2:[B]**
- Press **ENTER**
- Use the **ARROW** key to enter the row and column dimensions of your expected matrix (The dimensions will be the same as in Matrix A)
- Use the **ARROW** key to enter your expected values into Matrix [B]

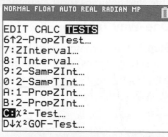

Step 3 *Access the Statistical Tests menu and perform the chi-square test*

- Press **STAT**
- Arrow right to **TESTS**
- Arrow down to χ^2 **Test**
- Press **ENTER**
- Arrow down to **Calculate**
- Press **ENTER**

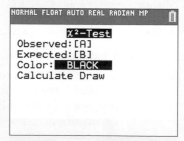

Discrimination in the Workplace

Title VII of the Civil Rights Act of 1964 prohibits discrimination in the workplace on the basis of race, color, religion, gender, or national origin. The Age Discrimination in Employment Act of 1967 (ADEA) protects workers age 40 to 70 against discrimination based on age. The potential for discrimination exists in such processes as hiring, promotion, compensation, and termination.

In 1971 the U.S. Supreme Court established that employment discrimination cases fall into two categories: **disparate treatment** and **disparate impact.** In the former, the issue is whether the employer intentionally discriminated against a worker. For example, if the employer considered an individual's race in deciding whether to terminate him, the case is one of disparate treatment. In a disparate impact case, the issue is whether employment practices have an adverse impact on a protected group or class of people, even when the employer does not intend to discriminate.

Part I: Downsizing at a Computer Firm

Disparate impact cases almost always involve the use of statistical evidence and expert testimony by professional statisticians. Attorneys for the plaintiffs frequently use hypothesis test results in the form of *p*-values in arguing the case for their clients.

Table C4.1 was recently introduced as evidence in a race case that resulted from a round of layoffs during the downsizing of a division of a computer manufacturer. The company had selected 51 of the division's 1,215 employees to lay off. The plaintiffs—in this case 15 of the 20 African Americans who were laid off—were suing the company for $20 million in damages.

The company's lawyers argued that the selections followed from a performance-based ranking of all employees. The plaintiffs' legal team

and their expert witnesses, citing the results of a statistical test of hypothesis, argued that the layoffs were a function of race.

The validity of the plaintiffs' interpretation of the data is dependent on whether the assumptions of the test are met in this situation. In particular, like all hypothesis tests presented in this text, the assumption of random sampling must hold. If it does not, the results of the test may be due to the violation of this assumption rather than to discrimination. In general, the appropriateness of the testing procedure is dependent on the test's ability to capture the relevant aspects of the employment process in question (DeGroot, Fienberg, and Kadane, *Statistics and the Law*, 1986).

Prepare a document to be submitted as evidence in the case (i.e., an exhibit) in which you evaluate the validity of the plaintiffs' interpretation of the data. Your evaluation should be based in part on your knowledge of the processes companies use to lay off employees and how well those processes are reflected in the hypothesis-testing procedure employed by the plaintiffs.

Table C4.1	Summary of Downsizing Data for Race Case		
		Decision	
		Retained	**Laid off**
Race	White	1,051	31
	Black	113	20

Source: P. George Benson.

 *Data Set:* LAYOFF

Part II: Age Discrimination—You Be the Judge

As part of a significant restructuring of product lines, AJAX Pharmaceuticals (a fictitious name for a real company) laid off 24 of 55 assembly line workers in its Pittsburgh manufacturing plant. Citing the ADEA, 11 of the laid-off workers claimed they were discriminated against on the basis of age and sued AJAX for $5,000,000. Management disputed the claim, saying that because the workers were essentially interchangeable, they had used random sampling to choose the 24 workers to be terminated.

Table C4.2 lists the 55 assembly line workers and identifies which were terminated and which remained active. Plaintiffs are denoted by an asterisk. These data were used by both the plaintiffs and the defendants to determine whether the layoffs had an adverse impact on workers age 40 and over and to establish the credibility of management's random sampling claim.

Table C4.2	Data for Age Discrimination Case		
Employee	Yearly Wages	Age	Employment Status
*Adler, C. J.	$41,200	45	Terminated
Alario, B. N.	39,565	43	Active
Anders, J. M.	30,980	41	Active
Bajwa, K. K.	23,225	27	Active
Barny, M. L.	21,250	26	Active
*Berger, R. W.	41,875	45	Terminated
Brenn, L. O.	31,225	41	Active
Cain, E. J.	30,135	36	Terminated
Carle, W. J.	29,850	32	Active
Castle, A. L.	21,850	22	Active
Chan, S. D.	43,005	48	Terminated
Cho, J. Y.	34,785	41	Active
Cohen, S. D.	25,350	27	Active
Darel, F. E.	36,300	42	Active
*Davis, D. E.	40,425	46	Terminated
*Dawson, P. K.	39,150	42	Terminated
Denker, U. H.	19,435	19	Active
Dorando, T. R.	24,125	28	Active
Dubois, A. G.	30,450	40	Active
England, N.	24,750	25	Active
Estis, K. B.	22,755	23	Active
Fenton, C. K.	23,000	24	Active
Finer, H. R.	42,000	46	Terminated
*Frees, O. C.	44,100	52	Terminated
Gary, J. G.	44,975	55	Terminated
Gillen, D. J.	25,900	27	Active
Harvey, D. A.	40,875	46	Terminated
Higgins, N. M.	38,595	41	Active
*Huang, T. J.	42,995	48	Terminated
Jatho, J. A.	31,755	40	Active
Johnson, C. H.	29,540	32	Active
Jurasik, T. B.	34,300	41	Active
Klein, K. L.	43,700	51	Terminated
Lang, T. F.	19,435	22	Active

Employee	Yearly Wages	Age	Employment Status
Liao, P. C.	28,750	32	Active
*Lostan, W. J.	44,675	52	Terminated
Mak, G. L.	35,505	38	Terminated
Maloff, V. R.	33,425	38	Terminated
McCall, R. M.	31,300	36	Terminated
*Nadeau, S. R.	42,300	46	Terminated
*Nguyen, O. L.	43,625	50	Terminated
Oas, R. C.	37,650	42	Active
*Patel, M. J.	38,400	43	Terminated
Porter, K. D.	32,195	35	Terminated
Rosa, L. M.	19,435	21	Active
Roth, J. H.	32,785	39	Terminated
Sayino, G. L.	37,900	42	Active
Scott, I. W.	29,150	30	Terminated
Smith, E. E.	35,125	41	Active
Teel, Q. V.	27,655	33	Active
*Walker, F. O.	42,545	47	Terminated
Wang, T. G.	22,200	32	Active
Yen, D. O.	40,350	44	Terminated
Young, N. L.	28,305	34	Active
Zeitels, P. W.	36,500	42	Active

Denotes plaintiffs

Using whatever statistical methods you think are appropriate, build a case that supports the plaintiffs' position. (Call documents related to this issue Exhibit A.) Similarly, build a case that supports the defendants' position. (Call these documents Exhibit B.) Then discuss which of the two cases is more convincing and why. [*Note:* The data for this case are available in the file, described in the table.]

Variable	Type
LASTNAME	QL
WAGES	QN
AGE	QN
STATUS	QL

(Number of observations: 55)

Data Set: DISCRM

CONTENTS

WHERE WE'VE BEEN

- Presented methods for estimating and testing population parameters
- Developed a test for relating two qualitative variables

WHERE WE'RE GOING

- Introduce the straight-line (*simple linear regression*) model as a means of relating one quantitative variable to another quantitative variable (11.1)
- Assess how well the simple linear regression model fits the sample data (11.2–11.4)
- Introduce the *correlation coefficient* as a means of relating one quantitative variable to another quantitative variable (11.5)
- Employ the simple linear regression model for predicting the value of one variable from a specified value of another variable (11.6–11.7)

Simple Linear Regression

STATISTICS IN ACTION   Legal Advertising—Does It Pay?

According to the American Bar Association, there are over 1 million lawyers competing for your business. To gain a competitive edge, these lawyers aggressively advertise their services. The advertising of legal services has long been a controversial subject, with many believing that it constitutes an unethical (and in some cases even illegal) practice. Nonetheless, legal advertisements appear in nearly all media, ranging from the covers of telephone directories to infomercials on television, as well as a significant presence on the Internet. In fact, Erickson Marketing, Inc., reports that "attorneys are the #1 category of advertising in the Yellow Pages."

For this *Statistics in Action*, we present an actual recent case involving two former law partners. One partner (A) sued the other (B) over who should pay what share of the expenses of their former partnership. Partner A handled personal injury (PI) cases, while partner B handled only worker's compensation (WC) cases. The firm's advertising was focused on personal injury only, but partner A claimed that the ads resulted in the firm getting more WC cases for partner B, and therefore partner B should share the advertising expenses.

Table SIA11.1 shows the firm's new PI and WC cases each month over a 48-month period for this partnership. Also shown is the total expenditure on advertising each month and over the previous 6 months. Do these data provide support for the hypothesis that increased advertising expenditures are associated with more PI cases? With more WC cases? If advertising expenditures have a statistically significant association with the number of cases, does this necessarily mean that there is a causal relationship, that is, that spending more on advertising causes an increase in the number of cases? Based on these data, should partner A or partner B bear the brunt of the advertising expenditures?

STATISTICS IN ACTION

(continued)

Table SIA11.1	Legal Advertising Data			
Month	Advertising Expenditure ($)	New PI Cases	New WC Cases	6 Months Cumulative Adv. Exp. ($)
1	9,221.55	7	26	n/a
2	6,684.00	9	33	n/a
3	200.00	12	18	n/a
4	14,546.75	27	15	n/a
5	5,170.14	9	19	n/a
6	5,810.30	13	26	n/a
7	5,816.20	11	24	41,632.74
8	8,236.38	7	22	38,227.39
9	−2,089.55	13	12	39,779.77
10	29,282.24	7	15	37,490.22
11	9,193.58	9	21	52,225.71
12	9,499.18	8	24	56,249.15
13	11,128.76	18	25	59,938.03
14	9,057.64	9	19	65,250.59
15	13,604.54	25	12	66,071.85
16	14,411.76	26	33	81,765.94
17	13,724.28	27	32	66,895.46
18	13,419.42	12	21	71,426.16
19	17,372.33	14	18	75,346.40
20	6,296.35	5	25	81,589.97
21	13,191.59	22	12	78,828.68
22	26,798.80	15	7	78,415.73
23	18,610.95	12	22	90,802.77
24	829.53	18	27	95,689.44
25	16,976.53	20	25	83,099.55
26	14,076.98	38	26	82,703.75
27	24,791.75	13	28	90,484.38
28	9,691.25	18	31	102,084.54
29	28,948.25	21	40	84,976.99
30	21,373.52	7	39	95,314.29
31	9,675.25	16	41	115,858.28
32	33,213.55	12	48	108,557.00
33	19,859.85	15	28	127,693.57
34	10,475.25	18	29	122,761.67
35	24,790.84	30	20	123,545.67
36	36,660.94	12	27	119,388.26
37	8,812.50	30	26	134,675.68
38	41,817.75	20	45	133,812.93
39	27,399.33	19	30	142,417.13
40	25,723.10	29	33	149,956.61
41	16,312.10	58	24	165,204.46
42	26,332.78	42	40	156,725.72
43	60,207.58	24	36	146,397.56
44	42,485.39	47	29	197,792.64
45	35,601.92	24	17	198,460.28
46	72,071.50	14	13	206,662.87
47	12,797.11	31	15	253,011.27
48	12,310.50	26	16	249,496.28

Source: Based on Legal Advertising Data from Info Tech, Inc.

 *Data Set:* LEGADV

The data for the case are saved in the **LEGADV** file. In the *Statistics in Action Revisited* sections of this chapter, we examine the relationship between monthly advertising expenditure and the number of new legal cases in an attempt to answer these questions.

STATISTICS IN ACTION REVISITED

- Estimating a Straight-Line Regression Model **(p. 651)**
- Assessing How Well a Straight-Line Regression Model Fits Data **(p. 667)**
- Using the Coefficient of Correlation and the Coefficient of Determination **(p. 677)**
- Prediction Using the Straight-Line Model **(p. 686)**

In Chapters 6–9, we described methods for making inferences about population means. The mean of a population was treated as a *constant*, and we showed how to use sample data to estimate or to test hypotheses about this constant mean. In many applications, the mean of a population is not viewed as a constant but rather as a variable. For example, the mean sale price of residences sold this year in a large city might be treated as a variable that depends on the square feet of living space in the residence. For example, the relationship might be

$$\text{Mean sale price} = \$30,000 + \$60 \text{ (living space size)}$$

This formula implies that the mean sale price of 1,000-square-foot homes is $90,000, the mean sale price of 2,000-square-foot homes is $150,000, and the mean sale price of 3,000-square-foot homes is $210,000.

In this chapter, we discuss situations in which the mean of the population is treated as a variable, dependent on the value of another variable. The dependence of residential sale price on the square feet of living space is one illustration. Other examples include the dependence of mean sales revenue of a firm on advertising expenditure, the dependence of mean starting salary of a college graduate on the student's GPA, and the dependence of mean monthly production of automobiles on the total number of sales in the previous month.

We begin our discussion with the simplest of all models relating a population mean to another variable—*the straight-line model*. We show how to use the sample data to estimate the straight-line relationship between the mean value of one variable, y, as it relates to a second variable, x. The methodology of estimating and using a straight-line relationship is referred to as *simple linear regression analysis*.

11.1 Probabilistic Models

An important consideration in merchandising a product is the amount of money spent on advertising. Suppose you want to model the monthly sales revenue of an appliance store as a function of the monthly advertising expenditure. The first question to be answered is this: "Do you think an exact relationship exists between these two variables?" That is, do you think it is possible to state the exact monthly sales revenue if the amount spent on advertising is known? We think you will agree with us that this is *not* possible for several reasons. Sales depend on many variables other than advertising expenditure—for example, time of year, the state of the general economy, inventory, and price structure. Even if many variables are included in a model (the topic of Chapter 12), it is still unlikely that we would be able to predict the monthly sales *exactly*. There will almost certainly be some variation in monthly sales due strictly to *random phenomena* that cannot be modeled or explained.

If we were to construct a model that hypothesized an exact relationship between variables, it would be called a **deterministic model.** For example, if we believe that y, the monthly sales revenue, will be exactly 15 times x, the monthly advertising expenditure, we write

$$y = 15x$$

This represents a *deterministic relationship* between the variables y and x. It implies that y can always be determined exactly when the value of x is known. *There is no allowance for error in this prediction.*

If, on the other hand, we believe there will be unexplained variation in monthly sales—perhaps caused by important but unincluded variables or by random phenomena—we discard the deterministic model and use a model that accounts for this **random error.** This **probabilistic model** includes both a deterministic component and a random error component. For example, if we hypothesize that the sales y are related to advertising expenditure x by

$$y = 15x + \text{Random error}$$

General Form of Probabilistic Models

$$y = \text{Deterministic component} + \text{Random error}$$

where y is the variable of interest. We always assume that the mean value of the random error equals 0. This is equivalent to assuming that the mean value of y, $E(y)$, equals the deterministic component of the model; that is,

$$E(y) = \text{Deterministic component}$$

---

we are hypothesizing a *probabilistic relationship* between y and x. Note that the deterministic component of this probabilistic model is $15x$.

Figure 11.1a shows the possible values of y and x for five different months, when the model is deterministic. All the pairs of (x, y) data points must fall exactly on the line because a deterministic model leaves no room for error.

Figure 11.1b shows a possible set of points for the same values of x when we are using a probabilistic model. Note that the deterministic part of the model (the straight line itself) is the same. Now, however, the inclusion of a random error component allows the monthly sales to vary from this line. Because we know that the sales revenue does vary randomly for a given value of x, the probabilistic model provides a more realistic model for y than does the deterministic model.

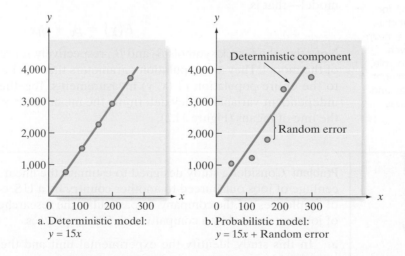

Figure 11.1

Possible sales revenues, y, for five different months, x

a. Deterministic model:
   $y = 15x$

b. Probabilistic model:
   $y = 15x + \text{Random error}$

In this chapter, we present the simplest of probabilistic models—the **straight-line model**—which derives its name from the fact that the deterministic portion of the model graphs as a straight line. Fitting this model to a set of data is an example of **regression analysis,** or **regression modeling.** The elements of the straight-line model are summarized in the next box.

A First-Order (Straight-Line) Probabilistic Model

$$y = \beta_0 + \beta_1 x + \varepsilon$$

where

$y = $ **Dependent** *or* **response variable** (quantitative variable to be modeled)

$x = $ **Independent** *or* **predictor variable** (quantitative variable used as a predictor of y)*

$E(y) = \beta_0 + \beta_1 x = $ Deterministic component

ε (epsilon) $= $ Random error component

β_0 (beta zero) $= $ **y-intercept of the line,** that is, the point at which the line *intercepts or cuts through the y-axis* (see Figure 11.2)

β_1 (beta one) $= $ **Slope of the line,** that is, the change (amount of increase or decrease) in the deterministic component of y for every 1-unit increase in x

[*Note:* A *positive* slope implies that $E(y)$ *increases* by the amount β_1 for each unit increase in x (see Figure 11.2). A *negative* slope implies that $E(y)$ *decreases* by the amount β_1.]

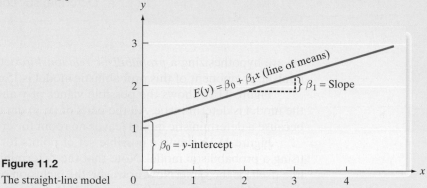

Figure 11.2
The straight-line model

In the probabilistic model, the deterministic component is referred to as the **line of means** because the mean of y, $E(y)$, is equal to the straight-line component of the model—that is,

$$E(y) = \beta_0 + \beta_1 x$$

Note that the Greek symbols β_0 and β_1, respectively, represent the y-intercept and slope of the model. They are population parameters that will be known only if we have access to the entire population of (x, y) measurements. Together with a specific value of the independent variable x, they determine the mean value of y, which is a specific point on the line of means (Figure 11.2).

EXAMPLE 11.1

Modeling Job Outsourcing Level of a U.S. Company

Problem Consider a study designed to estimate the linear relationship between the percentage of jobs outsourced to another country by a U.S. company and the size (number of employees) of the company. In particular, the researchers want to predict percentage of jobs outsourced by a company with 500 employees.

a. In this study, identify the experimental unit and the dependent and independent variables.

b. Explain why a probabilistic model is more appropriate than a deterministic model.

c. Write the equation of the straight-line, probabilistic model.

---

*The word *independent* should not be interpreted in a probabilistic sense, as defined in Chapter 3. The phrase *independent variable* is used in regression analysis to refer to a predictor variable for the response y.

Solution

a. Since the researchers want to predict (or model) percentage of jobs outsourced, then y = percentage of jobs outsourced to another country is the dependent variable. And, since the researchers want to use company size to make the prediction, x = size of the company is the independent variable. Note that both variables are measured for each U.S. company; therefore, a company is the experimental unit for this application.

b. It would be unrealistic to expect all U.S. companies of the same size (x) to yield the same percentage of outsourced jobs (y). That is, we don't expect company size to determine, exactly, the company's level of outsourcing due to company-to-company variation. Consequently, a probabilistic model is more appropriate than a deterministic model.

c. The probabilistic model takes the form $y = \beta_0 + \beta_1 x + \varepsilon$, where β_0 is the y-intercept of the line, β_1 is the slope of the line, and ε represents random error.

Look Ahead In the next section, we show how to estimate the y-intercept and slope of the line from the sample data.

● **Now Work Exercise 11.11**

The values of β_0 and β_1 will be unknown in almost all practical applications of regression analysis. The process of developing a model, estimating the unknown parameters, and using the model can be viewed as the five-step procedure shown in the next box.

Step 1: Hypothesize the deterministic component of the model that relates the mean, $E(y)$, to the independent variable x (Section 11.1).

Step 2: Use the sample data to estimate unknown parameters in the model (Section 11.2).

Step 3: Specify the probability distribution of the random error term and estimate the standard deviation of this distribution (Section 11.3).

Step 4: Statistically evaluate the usefulness of the model (Sections 11.4 and 11.5).

Step 5: When satisfied that the model is useful, use it for prediction, estimation, and other purposes (Section 11.6).

Exercises 11.1–11.13

Learning the Mechanics

11.1 In each case, graph the line that passes through the given points.
  a. $(1, 1)$ and $(5, 5)$ **b.** $(0, 3)$ and $(3, 0)$
  c. $(-1, 1)$ and $(4, 2)$ **d.** $(-6, -3)$ and $(2, 6)$

11.2 Give the slope and y-intercept for each of the lines graphed in Exercise 11.1.

11.3 The equation for a straight line (deterministic model) is

$$y = \beta_0 + \beta_1 x$$

If the line passes through the point $(-2, 4)$, then $x = -2$, $y = 4$ must satisfy the equation; that is,

$$4 = \beta_0 + \beta_1(-2)$$

Similarly, if the line passes through the point $(4, 6)$, then $x = 4$, $y = 6$ must satisfy the equation; that is,

$$6 = \beta_0 + \beta_1(4)$$

Use these two equations to solve for β_0 and β_1; then find the equation of the line that passes through the points $(-2, 4)$ and $(4, 6)$.

11.4 Refer to Exercise 11.3. Find the equations of the lines that pass through the points listed in Exercise 11.1.

11.5 Plot a linear graph $y = \beta_0 + \beta_1 x$ for each of the following cases.
  a. $\beta_0 = 8$ and $\beta_1 = 1$ **b.** $\beta_1 = -2$ and $(2, 4)$
  c. $\beta_0 = -3$ and $(5, 1)$ **d.** $\beta_0 = 0$ and $\beta_1 = 2$
  e. $\beta_0 = 4$ and $\beta_1 = 0$ **f.** $\beta_1 = -.5$ and $(3, 6)$

11.6 Identify the slope, y-intercept and x-intercept for the lines graphed in Exercise 11.5.

11.7 Why do we generally prefer a probabilistic model to a deterministic model? Give examples for when the two types of models might be appropriate.

11.8 What is the line of means?

11.9 If a straight-line probabilistic relationship relates the mean $E(y)$ to an independent variable x, does it imply that every value of the variable y will always fall exactly on the line of means? Why or why not?

Applying the Concepts—Basic

11.10 Congress voting on women's issues. The *American Economic Review* (March 2008) published research on how the gender mix of a U.S. legislator's children can influence the legislator's votes in Congress. The American Association of University Women (AAUW) uses voting records of each member of Congress to compute an AAUW score, where higher scores indicate more favorable voting for women's rights. The researcher wants to use the number of daughters a legislator has to predict the legislator's AAUW score.

a. In this study, identify the dependent and independent variables.

b. Explain why a probabilistic model is more appropriate than a deterministic model.

c. Write the equation of the straight-line, probabilistic model.

11.11 Best-paid CEOs. Refer to Glassdoor Economic Research
[NW] firm's 2015 ranking of the 40 best-paid CEOs in Table 2.1 (p. 65). Recall that data were collected on a CEO's age and ratio of salary to a typical worker's pay at the firm. One objective is to predict the ratio of salary to worker pay based on the CEO's age.

a. In this study, identify the dependent and independent variables.

b. Explain why a probabilistic model is more appropriate than a deterministic model.

c. Write the equation of the straight-line, probabilistic model.

11.12 Estimating repair and replacement costs of water pipes. Refer to Exercise 2.124 (p. 131). A team of civil engineers used simple linear regression analysis to model the ratio of repair to replacement cost of commercial pipe as a function of the pipe's diameter. (*IHS Journal of Hydraulic Engineering*, September 2012.)

a. In this study, identify the dependent and independent variables.

b. Explain why a probabilistic model is more appropriate than a deterministic model.

c. Write the equation of the straight-line, probabilistic model.

11.13 Forecasting movie revenues with Twitter. A study presented at the 2010 *IEEE International Conference on Web Intelligence and Intelligent Agent Technology* investigated whether the volume of chatter on Twitter.com could be used to forecast the box-office revenues of movies. For each in a sample of 24 recent movies, opening weekend box-office revenue (in millions of dollars) was measured, as well as the movie's *tweet rate* (the average number of tweets referring to the movie one week prior to the movie's release).

a. In this study, identify the dependent and independent variables.

b. Explain why a probabilistic model is more appropriate than a deterministic model.

c. Write the equation of the straight-line, probabilistic model.

11.2 Fitting the Model: The Least Squares Approach

After the straight-line model has been hypothesized to relate the mean $E(y)$ to the independent variable x, the next step is to collect data and to estimate the (unknown) population parameters, the y-intercept β_0 and the slope β_1.

To begin with a simple example, suppose an appliance store conducts a 5-month experiment to determine the effect of advertising on sales revenue. The results are shown in Table 11.1. (The number of measurements and the measurements themselves are unrealistically simple to avoid arithmetic confusion in this introductory example.) This set of data will be used to demonstrate the five-step procedure of regression modeling given in Section 11.1. In this section, we hypothesize the deterministic component of the model and estimate its unknown parameters (steps 1 and 2). The model assumptions and the random error component (step 3) are the subjects of Section 11.3, whereas Sections 11.4 and 11.5 assess the utility of the model (step 4). Finally, we use the model for prediction and estimation (step 5) in Section 11.6.

Step 1: *Hypothesize the deterministic component of the probabilistic model.* As stated before, we will consider only straight-line models in this chapter. Thus, the complete model to relate mean sales revenue $E(y)$ to advertising expenditure x is given by

$$E(y) = \beta_0 + \beta_1 x$$

Table 11.1	Advertising-Sales Data	
Month	Advertising Expenditure, x ($100s)	Sales Revenue, y ($1,000s)
1	1	1
2	2	1
3	3	2
4	4	2
5	5	4

Data Set: ADSALE

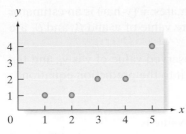

Figure 11.3

Scatterplot for data in Table 11.1

Step 2: *Use sample data to estimate unknown parameters in the model.* This step is the subject of this section—namely, how can we best use the information in the sample of five observations in Table 11.1 to estimate the unknown y-intercept β_0 and slope β_1?

To determine whether a linear relationship between y and x is plausible, it is helpful to plot the sample data in a **scatterplot** (or **scattergram**). Recall (Section 2.9) that a scatterplot locates each of the five data points on a graph, as shown in Figure 11.3. Note that the scatterplot suggests a general tendency for y to increase as x increases. If you place a ruler on the scatterplot, you will see that a line may be drawn through three of the five points, as shown in Figure 11.4. To obtain the equation of this visually fitted line, note that the line intersects the y-axis at $y = -1$, so the y-intercept is -1. Also, y increases exactly 1 unit for every 1-unit increase in x, indicating that the slope is $+1$. Therefore, the equation is

$$\tilde{y} = -1 + 1(x) = -1 + x$$

where $\tilde{y}$ is used to denote the predicted y from the visual model.

One way to decide quantitatively how well a straight line fits a set of data is to note the extent to which the data points deviate from the line. For example, to evaluate the model in Figure 11.4, we calculate the magnitude of the *deviations* (i.e., the differences between the observed and the predicted values of y). These deviations, or **errors of prediction,** are the vertical distances between observed and predicted values (see Figure 11.4).* The observed and predicted values of y, their differences, and their squared differences are shown in Table 11.2. Note that the *sum of errors* equals 0 and the *sum of squares of the errors* (SSE), which gives greater emphasis to large deviations of the points from the line, is equal to 2.

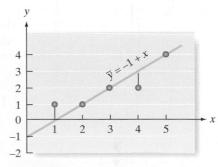

Figure 11.4

Visual straight line fitted to the data in Figure 11.3

Table 11.2	Comparing Observed and Predicted Values for the Visual Model			
x	y	$\tilde{y} = -1 + x$	$(y - \tilde{y})$	$(y - \tilde{y})^2$
1	1	0	$(1 - 0) = 1$	1
2	1	1	$(1 - 1) = 0$	0
3	2	2	$(2 - 2) = 0$	0
4	2	3	$(2 - 3) = -1$	1
5	4	4	$(4 - 4) = 0$	0
			Sum of errors $= 0$	Sum of squared errors (SSE) $= 2$

You can see by shifting the ruler around the graph that it is possible to find many lines for which the sum of errors is equal to 0, but it can be shown that there is one (and only one) line for which the SSE is a *minimum*. This line is called the **least squares line,** the **regression line,** or the **least squares prediction equation.** The methodology used to obtain this line is called the **method of least squares.**

Now Work Exercise 11.16a, b, c, d

To find the least squares prediction equation for a set of data, assume that we have a sample of n data points consisting of pairs of values of x and y, say (x_1, y_1), $(x_2, y_2), \dots, (x_n, y_n)$. For example, the $n = 5$ data points shown in Table 11.2 are $(1, 1)$, $(2, 1)$, $(3, 2)$, $(4, 2)$, and $(5, 4)$. The fitted line, which we will calculate based on the five data points, is written as

$$\hat{y} = \hat{\beta}_0 + \hat{\beta}_1 x$$

*In Chapter 12, we refer to these errors of prediction as **regression residuals.** There, we learn that an analysis of residuals is essential in establishing a useful regression model.

The "hats" indicate that the symbols below them are estimates: $\hat{y}$ (y-hat) is an estimator of the mean value of y, $E(y)$, and a predictor of some future value of y; and $\hat{\beta}_0$ and $\hat{\beta}_1$ are estimators of β_0 and β_1, respectively.

For a given data point, say the point (x_i, y_i), the observed value of y is y_i, and the predicted value of y would be obtained by substituting x_i into the prediction equation:

$$\hat{y}_i = \hat{\beta}_0 + \hat{\beta}_1 x_i$$

And the deviation of the ith value of y from its predicted value is

$$(y_i - \hat{y}_i) = [y_i - (\hat{\beta}_0 + \hat{\beta}_1 x_i)]$$

Then the sum of squares of the deviations of the y-values about their predicted values for all the n points is

$$\text{SSE} = \sum [y_i - (\hat{\beta}_0 + \hat{\beta}_1 x_i)]^2$$

The quantities $\hat{\beta}_0$ and $\hat{\beta}_1$ that make the SSE a minimum are called the **least squares estimates** of the population parameters β_0 and β_1, and the prediction equation $\hat{y} = \hat{\beta}_0 + \hat{\beta}_1 x$ is called the *least squares line*.

The **least squares line** $\hat{y} = \hat{\beta}_0 + \hat{\beta}_1 x$ is one that has the following two properties:

1. The sum of the errors equals 0, i.e., mean error = 0.
2. The sum of squared errors (SSE) is smaller than for any other straight-line model, i.e., the error variance is minimum.

The values of $\hat{\beta}_0$ and $\hat{\beta}_1$ that minimize the SSE are (proof omitted) given by the formulas in the box.*

Formulas for the Least Squares Estimates

$$\text{Slope: } \hat{\beta}_1 = \frac{\text{SS}_{xy}}{\text{SS}_{xx}}$$

$$\text{y-intercept: } \hat{\beta}_0 = \bar{y} - \hat{\beta}_1 \bar{x}$$

$$\text{where}^\dagger \quad \text{SS}_{xy} = \sum (x_i - \bar{x})(y_i - \bar{y})$$

$$\text{SS}_{xx} = \sum (x_i - \bar{x})^2$$

$$n = \text{Sample size}$$

EXAMPLE 11.2	
Applying the Method of Least Squares— Advertising-Sales Data	**Problem** Refer to the advertising–monthly sales data presented in Table 11.1. Consider the straight-line model, $E(y) = \beta_0 + \beta_1 x$, where y = sales revenue (thousands of dollars) and x = advertising expenditure (hundreds of dollars).

a. Use the method of least squares to estimate the values of β_0 and β_1.

b. Predict the sales revenue when advertising expenditure is $200 (i.e., when $x = 2$).

c. Find SSE for the analysis.

d. Give practical interpretations to β_0 and β_1.

*Students who are familiar with calculus should note that the values of β_0 and β_1 that minimize $\text{SSE} = \sum (y_i - \hat{y}_i)^2$ are obtained by setting the two partial derivatives $\partial \text{SSE}/\partial \beta_0$ and $\partial \text{SSE}/\partial \beta_1$ equal to 0. The solutions to these two equations yield the formulas shown in the box. Furthermore, we denote the *sample* solutions to the equations by $\hat{\beta}_0$ and $\hat{\beta}_1$, where the "hat" denotes that these are sample estimates of the true population intercept β_0 and true population slope β_1.

†Alternatively, you can use the following "shortcut" formulas:

$$\text{SS}_{xy} = \sum x_i y_i - \frac{(\sum x_i)(\sum y_j)}{n}; \quad \text{SS}_{xx} = \sum x_i^2 - \frac{(\sum x_i)^2}{n}$$

	A	B	C	D	E	F	G	H
1		AdvExp (X)	SalesRev (Y)	(X-3)	(Y-2)	(X-3)(Y-2)	(X-3)(X-3)	(Y-2)(Y-2)
2		1	1	-2	-1	2	4	1
3		2	1	-1	-1	1	1	1
4		3	2	0	0	0	0	0
5		4	2	1	0	0	1	0
6		5	4	2	2	4	4	4
7								
8	Totals	15	10	0	0	7	10	6
9	Mean	3	2					

Figure 11.5

Excel spreadsheet showing calculations for advertising-sales example

Solution

a. We used Excel to make the preliminary computations for finding the least squares line. The Excel spreadsheet is shown in Figure 11.5. Using the values on the spreadsheet, we find

$$\bar{x} = \frac{\sum x}{5} = \frac{15}{5} = 3$$

$$\bar{y} = \frac{\sum y}{5} = \frac{10}{5} = 2$$

$$SS_{xy} = \sum(x - \bar{x})(y - \bar{y}) = \sum(x - 3)(y - 2) = 7$$

$$SS_{xx} = \sum(x - \bar{x})^2 = \sum(x - 3)^2 = 10$$

Then the slope of the least squares line is

$$\hat{\beta}_1 = \frac{SS_{xy}}{SS_{xx}} = \frac{7}{10} = .7$$

and the y-intercept is

$$\hat{\beta}_0 = \bar{y} - \hat{\beta}_1\bar{x} = 2 - (.7)(3) = 2 - 2.1 = -.1$$

The least squares line is thus

$$\hat{y} = \hat{\beta}_0 + \hat{\beta}_1 x = -.1 + .7x$$

The graph of this line is shown in Figure 11.6.

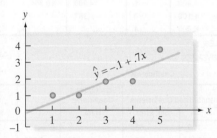

Figure 11.6

The line $\hat{y} = -.1 + .7x$ fitted to the data

b. The predicted value of y for a given value of x can be obtained by substituting into the formula for the least squares line. Substituting $x = 2$ into the least squares equation yields

$$\hat{y} = -.1 + .7x = -.1 + .7(2) = 1.3$$

Thus, when advertising expenditure is $200, we predict monthly sales revenue to be $1,300. We show how to find a prediction interval for y in Section 11.6.

c. The observed and predicted values of y, the deviations of the y-values about their predicted values, and the squares of these deviations are shown in the Excel spreadsheet, Figure 11.7. Note that SSE = 1.10, and (as we would expect) this is less than the SSE = 2.0 obtained in Table 11.2 for the visually fitted line.

d. The estimated y-intercept, $\hat{\beta}_0 = -.1$, appears to imply that the estimated mean sales revenue is equal to $-.1$, or $-$100, when the advertising expenditure, x, is equal to $0. Because negative sales revenues are not possible, this seems to make the model nonsensical. However, *the model parameters should be interpreted only within the sampled range of the independent variable*—in this case, for advertising expenditures between $100 and $500. Thus, the y-intercept—which is, by definition, at $x = 0$ ($0 advertising expenditure)—is not within the range of the sampled values of x and is not subject to meaningful interpretation.

Figure 11.7

Excel spreadsheet comparing observed and predicted values for advertising-sales example

	A	B	C	D	E
1	AdvExp (X)	SalesRev (Y)	Predicted Y=-.1+.7X	(Y-Yhat)	(Y-Yhat)(Y-Yhat)
2	1	1	0.6	0.4	0.16
3	2	1	1.3	-0.3	0.09
4	3	2	2	0	0
5	4	2	2.7	-0.7	0.49
6	5	4	3.4	0.6	0.36
7					
8			Sum	0	1.1

The slope of the least squares line, $\hat{\beta}_1 = .7$, implies that for every unit increase of x, the mean value of y is estimated to increase by .7 unit. In terms of this example, for every \$100 increase in advertising, the mean sales revenue is estimated to increase by \$700 *over the sampled range of advertising expenditures from \$100 to \$500.* Thus, the model does not imply that increasing the advertising expenditures from \$500 to \$1,000 will result in an increase in mean sales of \$3,500, because the range of x in the sample does not extend to \$1,000 ($x = 10$). Be careful to interpret the estimated parameters only within the sampled range of x.

Look Back The calculations required to obtain $\hat{\beta}_0$, $\hat{\beta}_1$, and SSE in simple linear regression, although straight-forward, can become rather tedious. Even with the use of an Excel spreadsheet, the process is laborious, especially when the sample size is large. Fortunately, a statistical software package can significantly reduce the labor involved in regression calculations. The SPSS, Minitab, and Excel/XLSTAT outputs for the simple linear regression of the data in Table 11.1 are displayed in Figures 11.8a–c. The values of $\hat{\beta}_0$ and $\hat{\beta}_1$ are

Model Summary

Model	R	R Square	Adjusted R Square	Std. Error of the Estimate
1	.904[a]	.817	.756	.606

a. Predictors: (Constant), ADVEXP_X

ANOVA[a]

Model		Sum of Squares	df	Mean Square	F	Sig.
1	Regression	4.900	1	4.900	13.364	.035[b]
	Residual	1.100	3	.367		
	Total	6.000	4			

a. Dependent Variable: SALES_Y

b. Predictors: (Constant), ADVEXP_X

Coefficients[a]

Model		Unstandardized Coefficients		Standardized Coefficients	t	Sig.
		B	Std. Error	Beta		
1	(Constant)	-.100	.635		-.157	.885
	ADVEXP_X	.700	.191	.904	3.656	.035

a. Dependent Variable: SALES_Y

Figure 11.8a

SPSS printout for the advertising-sales regression

Regression Analysis: SALES_Y versus ADVEXP_X

```
Analysis of Variance

Source        DF  Adj SS  Adj MS  F-Value  P-Value
Regression     1   4.900  4.9000    13.36    0.035
  ADVEXP_X     1   4.900  4.9000    13.36    0.035
Error          3   1.100  0.3667
Total          4   6.000


Model Summary

      S    R-sq  R-sq(adj)  R-sq(pred)
0.605530  81.67%    75.56%      26.11%


Coefficients

Term       Coef  SE Coef  T-Value  P-Value   VIF
Constant  -0.100   0.635    -0.16    0.885
ADVEXP_X   0.700   0.191     3.66    0.035  1.00


Regression Equation

SALES_Y = -0.100 + 0.700 ADVEXP_X
```

Figure 11.8b

Minitab printout for the advertising-sales regression

Regression of variable SALES_Y:

Goodness of fit statistics:

Observations	5.0000
Sum of weights	5.0000
DF	3.0000
R²	0.8167
Adjusted R²	0.7556
MSE	0.3667
RMSE	0.6055
DW	2.5091

Analysis of variance:

Source	DF	Sum of squares	Mean squares	F	Pr > F
Model	1	4.9000	4.9000	13.3636	0.0354
Error	3	1.1000	0.3667		
Corrected Total	4	6.0000			

Computed against model Y=Mean(Y)

Model parameters:

Source	Value	Standard error	t	Pr > |t|	Lower bound (95%)	Upper bound (95%)
Intercept	-0.1000	0.6351	-0.1575	0.8849	-2.1211	1.9211
ADVEXP_X	0.7000	0.1915	3.6556	0.0354	0.0906	1.3094

Equation of the model:

SALES_Y = -0.10000+0.70000*ADVEXP_X

Figure 11.8c

XLSTAT printout of sales-advertising regression model

highlighted on the printouts. These values, $\hat{\beta}_0 = -.1$ and $\hat{\beta}_1 = .7$, agree exactly with our calculated values. The value of SSE $= 1.10$ is also highlighted on the printouts.

 Now Work Exercise 11.19

Interpreting the Estimates of β_0 and β_1 in Simple Linear Regression

y-intercept: $\hat{\beta}_0$ represents the predicted value of y when $x = 0$ (*Caution:* This value will not be meaningful if the value $x = 0$ is non sensical or outside the range of the sample data.)

slope: $\hat{\beta}_1$ represents the increase (or decrease) in y for every 1-unit increase in x (*Caution:* This interpretation is valid only for x-values within the range of the sample data.)

Even when the interpretations of the estimated parameters in a simple linear regression are meaningful, we need to remember that they are only estimates based on the sample. As such, their values will typically change in repeated sampling. How much confidence do we have that the estimated slope, $\hat{\beta}_1$, accurately approximates the true slope, β_1? This requires statistical inference, in the form of confidence intervals and tests of hypotheses, which we address in Section 11.4.

To summarize, we defined the best-fitting straight line to be the one that minimizes the sum of squared errors around the line, and we called it the *least squares line*. We should interpret the least squares line only within the sampled range of the independent variable. In subsequent sections, we show how to make statistical inferences about the model.

STATISTICS
IN ACTION

REVISITED

Estimating a Straight-Line Regression Model

We return to the legal advertising case involving two former law partners (p. 640). Recall that partner A (who handled PI cases) sued partner B (who handled WC cases) over who should pay what share of the advertising expenses of their former partnership. Monthly data were collected on the number of new PI cases, number of new WC cases, and the total amount spent (in thousands of dollars) on advertising over the previous 6 months. These data (shown in Table SIA11.1, p. 641) are saved in the **LEGADV** file. Do these data provide support for the hypothesis that increased advertising expenditures are associated with more

PI cases? Define y as the number of new PI cases per month and x as the cumulative 6-month advertising expenditures (in thousands of dollars). One way to investigate the link between these two variables is to fit the straight-line model, $E(y) = \beta_0 + \beta_1 x$, to the data in Table SIA11.1.

A Minitab scatterplot of the data and a simple linear regression printout are shown in Figure SIA11.1. Note that the least squares line is also displayed on the scatterplot. You can see that the line has a positive slope and, although there is some variation of the data points around the line, it appears that advertising expenditure (x) is fairly strongly related to the number of new PI cases (y). The estimated slope of the line (highlighted on Figure SIA11.1) is $\hat{\beta}_1 = .113$. Thus, we estimate a .113 increase in the number of new PI cases for every \$1,000 increase in cumulative advertising expenditures.

Does such a relationship also exist between number of new WC cases and advertising expenditure? Now let y = number of new WC cases per month and x = cumulative 6-month advertising expenditures. A Minitab scatterplot and simple linear regression analysis for these two variables are shown in Figure SIA11.2. Compared with the previous scatterplot, the slope of the least squares line shown in Figure SIA11.2 is much flatter, and the variation of the data points around the line is much larger. Consequently, it does not appear that number of new WC cases is very strongly related to advertising expenditure. In fact, the estimated slope (highlighted in Figure SIA11.2) implies that a \$1,000 increase in cumulative advertising expenditures will lead to only a $\hat{\beta}_1 = .0098$ increase in the number of new WC cases per month.

Based on these descriptive statistics (scatterplots and least squares lines), it appears that partner A's argument that partner B should share the advertising expenses is weak, at best. In the *Statistics in Action Revisited* sections that follow, we will provide a measure of reliability to this inference and investigate the legal advertising data further.

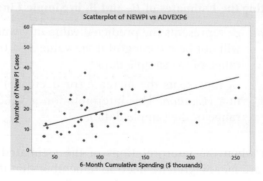

Regression Analysis: NEWPI versus ADVEXP6

Analysis of Variance

Source	DF	Adj SS	Adj MS	F-Value	P-Value
Regression	1	1530	1529.52	16.34	0.000
Error	40	3744	93.61		
Total	41	5274			

Model Summary

S	R-sq	R-sq(adj)
9.67521	29.00%	27.23%

Coefficients

Term	Coef	SE Coef	T-Value	P-Value
Constant	7.77	3.38	2.29	0.027
ADVEXP6	0.1129	0.0279	4.04	0.000

Regression Equation

NEWPI = 7.77 + 0.1129 ADVEXP6

Figure SIA11.1

Minitab analysis of new PI cases vs. 6-month cumulative advertising expenditure

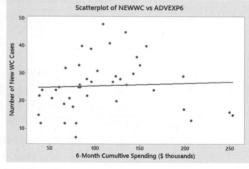

Regression Analysis: NEWWC versus ADVEXP6

Analysis of Variance

Source	DF	Adj SS	Adj MS	F-Value	P-Value
Regression	1	11.58	11.58	0.13	0.725
Error	40	3704.06	92.60		
Total	41	3715.64			

Model Summary

S	R-sq	R-sq(adj)
9.62296	0.31%	0.00%

Coefficients

Term	Coef	SE Coef	T-Value	P-Value
Constant	24.57	3.37	7.30	0.000
ADVEXP6	0.0098	0.0278	0.35	0.725

Regression Equation

NEWWC = 24.57 + 0.0098 ADVEXP6

Figure SIA11.2

Minitab analysis of new WC cases vs. 6-month cumulative advertising expenditure

Exercises 11.14–11.30

Learning the Mechanics

11.14 The following table is similar to Table 11.2. It is used for making the preliminary computations for finding the least squares line for the given pairs of x- and y-values.

x_i	y_i	x_i^2	$x_i y_i$
7	2		
4	4		
6	2		
2	5		
1	7		
1	6		
3	5		
Totals	$\sum x_i =$	$\sum y_i =$	$\sum x_i^2 =$	$\sum x_i y_i =$

a. Complete the table.
b. Find SS_{xy}.
c. Find SS_{xx}.
d. Find $\hat{\beta}_1$.
e. Find $\bar{x}$ and $\bar{y}$.
f. Find $\hat{\beta}_0$.
g. Find the least squares line.

11.15 Refer to Exercise 11.14. After the least squares line has been obtained, the table below (which is similar to Table 11.2) can be used for (1) comparing the observed and the predicted values of y and (2) computing SSE.

x	y	$\hat{y}$	$(y - \hat{y})$	$(y - \hat{y})^2$
7	2			
4	4			
6	2			
2	5			
1	7			
1	6			
3	5			
			$\sum(y - \hat{y}) =$	$SSE = \sum(y - \hat{y})^2 =$

a. Complete the table.
b. Plot the least squares line on a scatterplot of the data. Plot the following line on the same graph: $\hat{y} = 14 - 2.5x$.
c. Show that SSE is larger for the line in part **b** than it is for the least squares line.

11.16 Construct a scatterplot for the data in the following table.

x	.5	1	1.5
y	2	1	3

a. Plot the following two lines on your scatterplot:

$$y = 3 - x \quad \text{and} \quad y = 1 + x$$

b. Which of these lines would you choose to characterize the relationship between x and y? Explain.
c. Show that the sum of the errors of prediction for both of these lines equals 0.
d. Which of these lines has the smaller SSE?
e. Find the least squares line for the data and compare it with the two lines described in part **a**.

11.17 Consider the following pairs of measurements:

x	8	5	4	6	2	5	3
y	1	3	6	3	7	2	5

a. Construct a scatterplot for these data.
b. What does the scatterplot suggest about the relationship between x and y?
c. Find the least squares estimates of β_0 and β_1.
d. Plot the least squares line on your scatterplot. Does the line appear to fit the data well? Explain.

🔲 Applet Exercise 11.1

Use the applet *Regression by Eye* to explore the relationship between the pattern of data in a scatterplot and the corresponding least squares model.

a. Run the applet several times. For each time, attempt to move the green line into a position that appears to minimize the vertical distances of the points from the line. Then click *Show regression line* to see the actual regression line. How close is your line to the actual line? Click *New data* to reset the applet.
b. Click the trash can to clear the graph. Use the mouse to place five points on the scatterplot that are approximately in a straight line. Then move the green line to approximate the regression line. Click *Show regression line* to see the actual regression line. How close were you this time?
c. Continue to clear the graph and plot sets of five points with different patterns among the points. Use the green line to approximate the regression line. How close do you come to the actual regression line each time?
d. Based on your experiences with the applet, explain why we need to use more reliable methods of finding the regression line than just "eyeing" it.

Applying the Concepts—Basic

11.18 In business, do nice guys finish first or last? Refer to the *Nature* (March 20, 2008) study of whether "nice guys finish last" in the business world, Exercise 2.125 (p. 131). Recall that college students repeatedly played a version of the game "prisoner's dilemma," where competitors choose cooperation, defection, or costly punishment. (Cooperation meant paying 1 unit for the opponent to receive 2 units, defection meant gaining 1 unit at a cost of 1 unit for the opponent, and punishment meant paying 1 unit for the opponent to lose 4 units.) At the conclusion of the games, the researchers recorded the average payoff and the number of times cooperation, defection, and punishment were used for each player. The scatterplots on p. 654 plot average payoff (y) against level of cooperation use, defection use, and punishment use, respectively.

a. Consider cooperation use (x) as a predictor of average payoff (y). Based on the scatterplot, is there evidence of a linear trend?
b. Consider defection use (x) as a predictor of average payoff (y). Based on the scatterplot, is there evidence of a linear trend?
c. Consider punishment use (x) as a predictor of average payoff (y). Based on the scatterplot (reproduced from Exercise 2.125), is there evidence of a linear trend?
d. Refer to part **c**. Is the slope of the line relating punishment use (x) to average payoff (y) positive or negative?

Scatterplots for Exercise 11.18

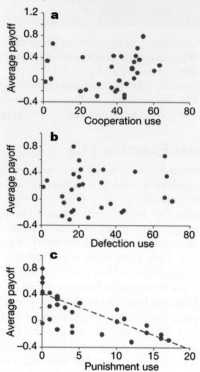

11.19 State Math SAT scores. Refer to the data on average state Math SAT scores for 2010 and 2014, Exercise 2.27 (p. 84). The first five observations and last two observations in the file are reproduced in the next table. In Exercise 2.128 (p. 132), you examined the relationship between the 2010 Math SAT scores and the 2014 Math SAT scores with a scatterplot.

State	2014	2010
Alabama	538	550
Alaska	503	513
Arizona	525	524
Arkansas	571	564
California	510	516
⋮		
Wisconsin	608	603
Wyoming	599	565

Coefficients[a]

Model		Unstandardized Coefficients		Standardized Coefficients		
		B	Std. Error	Beta	t	Sig.
1	(Constant)	-70.692	29.887		-2.365	.022
	MATH2010	1.132	.055	.946	20.417	.000

a. Dependent Variable: MATH2014

SPSS Output for Exercise 11.19

a. Write the equation of a straight-line model relating 2014 Math SAT score (y) to 2010 Math SAT score (x).
An SPSS simple linear regression printout for the data is shown. Find the least squares prediction equation.

b. Give a practical interpretation of the y-intercept of the least squares line. If a practical interpretation is not possible, explain why.

c. Give a practical interpretation of the slope of the least squares line. Over what range of x is the interpretation meaningful?

11.20 Lobster fishing study. Refer to the *Bulletin of Marine Science* (April 2010) study of teams of fishermen fishing for the red spiny lobster in Baja California Sur, Mexico, Exercise 2.126 (p. 131). Two variables measured for each of 15 teams from two fishing cooperatives were y = total catch of lobsters (in kilograms) during the season and x = average percentage of traps allocated per day to exploring areas of unknown catch (called *search frequency*). These data are listed in the table.

Total Catch	Search Frequency	Total Catch	Search Frequency
9,998	18	6,535	21
7,767	14	6,695	26
8,764	4	4,891	29
9,077	18	4,937	23
8,343	9	5,727	17
9,222	5	7,019	21
6,827	8	5,735	20
2,785	35		

Source: Based on G. G. Shester, "Explaining Catch Variation Among Baja California Lobster Fishers Through Spatial Analysis of Trap-Placement Decisions," *Bulletin of Marine Science*, Vol. 86, No. 2, April 2010 (Table 1).

a. Graph the data in a scatterplot. What type of trend, if any, do you observe?

b. A simple linear regression analysis was conducted using XLSTAT. A portion of the regression printout is shown below. Find the estimates of β_0 and β_1 on the printout.

c. If possible, give a practical interpretation of the estimate of β_0. If no practical interpretation is possible, explain why.

d. If possible, give a practical interpretation of the estimate of β_1. If no practical interpretation is possible, explain why.

Model parameters:

Source	Value	Standard error	t	Pr > |t|	Lower bound (95%)	Upper bound (95%)
Intercept	9877.8300	829.0411	11.9148	< 0.0001	8086.7957	11668.8643
SEARCHFR	-163.6024	41.9014	-3.9045	0.0018	-254.1249	-73.0799

Equation of the model:

CATCH = 9877.82997-163.60242*SEARCHFREQ

XLSTAT output for Exercise 11.20

11.21 Repair and replacement costs of water pipes. Refer to the *IHS Journal of Hydraulic Engineering* (September 2012) study of water pipes, Exercise 11.12 (p. 646). Recall that a team of civil engineers used regression analysis to estimate y = the ratio of repair to replacement cost of commercial pipe. The independent variable in the regression analysis was x = the diameter (in millimeters) of the pipe. Data for a sample of 13 different pipe sizes are provided in the table, followed by a Minitab simple linear regression printout.

Diameter (mm)	Ratio
80	6.58
100	6.97
125	7.39
150	7.61
200	7.78
250	7.92
300	8.20
350	8.42
400	8.60
450	8.97
500	9.31
600	9.47
700	9.72

Source: Based on ISH *Journal of Hydraulic Engineering*, Volume 18, Issue 3, pp. 241–251. Copyright: September 2012.

a. Find the least squares line relating ratio of repair to replacement cost (y) to pipe diameter (x) on the printout.

b. Locate the value of SSE on the printout. Is there another line with an average error of 0 that has a smaller SSE than the line, part **a**? Explain.

c. Interpret, practically, the values $\hat{\beta}_0$ and $\hat{\beta}_1$.

d. Use the regression line to predict the ratio of repair to replacement cost of pipe with a diameter of 800 millimeters.

e. Comment on the reliability of the prediction, part **d**.

Regression Analysis: RATIO versus DIAMETER

```
Analysis of Variance

Source       DF   Adj SS   Adj MS   F-Value   P-Value
Regression    1  10.8067  10.8067    221.20     0.000
  DIAMETER    1  10.8067  10.8067    221.20     0.000
Error        11   0.5374   0.0489
Total        12  11.3441

Model Summary

      S    R-sq  R-sq(adj)  R-sq(pred)
0.221034  95.26%     94.83%      92.09%

Coefficients

Term         Coef   SE Coef  T-Value  P-Value   VIF
Constant    6.678     0.121    55.29    0.000
DIAMETER  0.004786  0.000322    14.87    0.000  1.00

Regression Equation

RATIO = 6.678 + 0.004786 DIAMETER
```

Minitab Output for Exercise 11.21

11.22 Joint Strike Fighter program. The Joint Strike Fighter (JSF) program, operated by the U.S. Department of Defense, is a global defense program that involves acquisition of military fighter jets for participating allied countries. An article in the *Air & Space Power Journal* (March-April 2014) reported on the estimated annual cost of adding a military aircraft to the JSF program. The table below lists the year of initial operation and cost (in millions of dollars) for 12 JSF military aircraft models. For this problem, let y = estimated annual cost and x = year of initial operation for each aircraft model.

a. Fit the simple linear regression model, $E(y) = \beta_0 + \beta_1 x$, to the data.

b. If possible, give a practical interpretation of the y-intercept of the line.

c. Give an estimate of the increase in the cost of adding a military aircraft to the JSF program each year. (*Hint:* Practically interpret the slope of the line.)

Year	Model	Cost
1974	F-14	40
1975	F-15AB	28
1977	A-10	13
1978	FA-18AB	26
1978	F-15CD	30
1979	F-16AB	16
1981	F-16CD	20
1987	FA-18CD	29
1989	F-15E	31
1998	FA-18EF	55
2005	F-22	105
2012	F-35	80

11.23 Software millionaires and birthdays. In *Outliers: The Story of Success* (Little, Brown, 2008), the author notes that a disproportionate number of software millionaires were born around the year 1955. Is this a coincidence, or does birth year matter when gauging whether a software founder will be successful? On his Web blog (www.measuringusability.com), statistical consultant Jeff Sauro investigated this question by analyzing the data shown in the table on the next page.

a. Fit a simple linear regression model relating number (y) of software millionaire birthdays in a decade to total number (x) of U.S. births. Give the least squares prediction equation.

b. Practically interpret the estimated y-intercept and slope of the model, part **a**.

c. Predict the number of software millionaire birthdays that will occur in a decade where the total number of U.S. births is 35 million.

d. Fit a simple linear regression model relating number (y) of software millionaire birthdays in a decade to number (x) of CEO birthdays. Give the least squares prediction equation.

e. Practically interpret the estimated y-intercept and slope of the model, part **d**.

f. Predict the number of software millionaire birthdays that will occur in a decade in which the number of CEO birthdays (from a random sample of 70 companies) is 10.

Data for Exercise 11.23

Decade	Total U.S. Births (millions)	Number of Software Millionaire Birthdays	Number of CEO Birthdays (in a random sample of 70 companies from the *Fortune* 500 list)
1920	28.582	3	2
1930	24.374	1	2
1940	31.666	10	23
1950	40.530	14	38
1960	38.808	7	9
1970	33.309	4	0

Source: J. Sauro, "Were Most Software Millionaires Born Around 1955?" *Measuring Usability*, November 17, 2010. Copyright © 2010 by Measuring Usability LLC. Reprinted with permission.

Applying the Concepts—Intermediate

11.24 Public corruption and bad weather. The Federal Emergency Management Agency (FEMA) provides disaster relief for states impacted by natural disasters (e.g., hurricanes, tornados, floods). Do these bad weather windfalls lead to public corruption? This was the research question of interest in an article published in the *Journal of Law and Economics* (November 2008). Data on y = average annual number of public corruption convictions (per 100,000 residents) and x = average annual FEMA relief (in dollars) per capita for each of the 50 states were used in the investigation.

a. Access the data, saved in the file, and construct a scatterplot. Do you observe a trend?

b. Fit the simple linear regression model, $E(y) = \beta_0 + \beta_1 x$, to the data and obtain estimates of the y-intercept and slope.

c. Practically interpret the estimated y-intercept and estimated slope.

11.25 Ranking driving performance of professional golfers. Refer to *The Sport Journal* (Winter 2007) study of a method for ranking the total driving performance of golfers on the Professional Golf Association (PGA) tour, Exercise 2.52 (p. 97). Recall that the method computes a driving performance index based on a golfer's average driving distance (yards) and driving accuracy (percent of drives that land in the fairway). Data for the top 40 PGA golfers (as ranked by the new method) are saved in the file. (The first five and last five observations are listed in the table.)

Rank	Player	Driving Distance (yards)	Driving Accuracy (%)	Driving Performance Index
1	Woods	316.1	54.6	3.58
2	Perry	304.7	63.4	3.48
3	Gutschewski	310.5	57.9	3.27
4	Wetterich	311.7	56.6	3.18
5	Hearn	295.2	68.5	2.82
⋮	⋮	⋮	⋮	⋮
36	Senden	291	66	1.31
37	Mickelson	300	58.7	1.30
38	Watney	298.9	59.4	1.26
39	Trahan	295.8	61.8	1.23
40	Pappas	309.4	50.6	1.17

Source: From "A New Method for Ranking Total Driving Performance on the PGA Tour" by Frederick Wiseman, Mohamed Habibullah, and Mustafa Yilmaz in *The Sport Journal*, Vol. 10, No. 1. Copyright © 2010 by Sports Journal Entertainment. Used by permission of Sports Journal Entertainment.

a. Write the equation of a straight-line model relating driving accuracy (y) to driving distance (x).

b. Fit the model, part **a,** to the data using simple linear regression. Give the least squares prediction equation.

c. Interpret the estimated y-intercept of the line.

d. Interpret the estimated slope of the line.

e. In Exercise 2.134 (p. 133), you were informed that a professional golfer, practicing a new swing to increase his average driving distance, is concerned that his driving accuracy will be lower. Which of the two estimates, y-intercept or slope, will help you determine if the golfer's concern is a valid one? Explain.

11.26 Sweetness of orange juice. The quality of the orange juice produced by a manufacturer (e.g., Minute Maid, Tropicana) is constantly monitored. There are numerous sensory and chemical components that combine to make the best-tasting orange juice. For example, one manufacturer has developed a quantitative index of the "sweetness" of orange juice. (The higher the index, the sweeter the juice.) Is there a relationship between the sweetness index and a chemical measure such as the amount of water-soluble pectin (parts per million) in the orange juice? Data collected on these two variables for 24 production runs at a juice manufacturing plant are shown in the table below. Suppose a manufacturer wants to use simple linear regression to predict the sweetness (y) from the amount of pectin (x).

Run	Sweetness Index	Pectin (ppm)
1	5.2	220
2	5.5	227
3	6.0	259
4	5.9	210
5	5.8	224
6	6.0	215
7	5.8	231
8	5.6	268
9	5.6	239
10	5.9	212
11	5.4	410
12	5.6	256
13	5.8	306
14	5.5	259
15	5.3	284
16	5.3	383
17	5.7	271
18	5.5	264
19	5.7	227
20	5.3	263
21	5.9	232
22	5.8	220
23	5.8	246
24	5.9	241

Note: The data in the table are authentic. For confidentiality reasons, the manufacturer cannot be disclosed.

a. Find the least squares line for the data.

b. Interpret $\hat{\beta}_0$ and $\hat{\beta}_1$ in the words of the problem.

c. Predict the sweetness index if amount of pectin in the orange juice is 300 ppm. [*Note:* A measure of reliability of such a prediction is discussed in Section 11.6]

11.27 Forecasting movie revenues with Twitter. Marketers are keenly interested in how social media (e.g., Facebook, Twitter) may influence consumers who buy their products. Researchers investigated whether the volume of chatter on Twitter.com could be used to forecast the box office revenues of movies (*IEEE International Conference on Web Intelligence and Intelligent Agent Technology*, 2010). Opening weekend box office revenue data (in millions of dollars) were collected for a sample of 23 recent movies. In addition, the researchers computed each movie's *tweet rate*, i.e., the average number of tweets (at Twitter.com) referring to the movie per hour 1 week prior to the movie's release. The data (simulated based on information provided in the study) are listed in the accompanying table. Assuming that movie revenue and tweet rate are linearly related, how much do you estimate a movie's opening weekend revenue to change as the tweet rate for the movie increases by an average of 100 tweets per hour?

Tweet Rate	Revenue (millions)
1365.8	142
1212.8	77
581.5	61
310.1	32
455	31
290	30
250	21
680.5	18
150	18
164.5	17
113.9	16
144.5	15
418	14
98	14
100.8	12
115.4	11
74.4	10
87.5	9
127.6	9
52.2	9
144.1	8
41.3	2
2.75	0.3

11.28 Charisma of top-level leaders. According to a theory proposed in the *Academy of Management Journal* (August 2015), top leaders in business are selected based on their organization's performance as well as the leader's charisma. To test this theory, the researchers collected data on 24 U.S. presidential elections from 1916 to 2008. The dependent variable of interest was Democratic vote share (y), measured as the percentage of voters who voted for the Democratic candidate in the national election. The charisma of both the Democratic and Republican candidates was measured (on a 150-point scale) based on the candidates' acceptance speeches at their party's national

convention. One of the independent variables of interest was the difference (x) between the Democratic and Republican charisma values. These data are listed in the accompanying table.

a. Find the least squares line relating Democratic vote share (y) to charisma difference (x).

b. Graph the least squares line on a scatterplot of the data. Is there visual evidence of a linear relationship between the variables? Is the relationship positive or negative?

c. Interpret, practically, the estimated slope of the line.

Year	Vote Share	Charisma Difference
1916	51.68	−6.0
1920	36.15	−60.0
1924	41.74	18.0
1928	41.24	4.0
1932	59.15	−22.0
1936	62.23	−14.5
1940	54.98	−7.5
1944	53.78	−10.0
1948	52.32	−10.5
1952	44.71	2.0
1956	42.91	0.0
1960	50.09	−34.5
1964	61.20	−29.0
1968	49.43	−20.5
1972	38.21	−6.0
1976	51.05	14.0
1980	44.84	−12.0
1984	40.88	−42.0
1988	46.17	−34.0
1992	53.62	18.5
1996	54.74	−16.5
2000	50.26	−2.5
2004	48.77	48.5
2008	53.69	13.5

Source: Data from P. Jacquart and J. Antonakis, "When Does Charisma Matter for Top-Level Leaders? Effect of Attributional Ambiguity," *Academy of Management Journal*, Vol. 58, No. 4, August 2015 (Table 1).

11.29 Rankings of research universities. Refer to the College Choice *2015 Rankings of National Research Universities,* Exercise 2.43 (p. 95). Recall that data on academic reputation score, financial aid awarded, net cost to attend, median salary during early career, percentage of alumni who feel their work makes a better place in which to live, and percentage of science, technology, engineering, and math (STEM) degrees awarded for the top 50 research universities are saved in the file. Information on the top 10 schools are listed in the table on the next page.

a. Select one of the variables as the dependent variable, y, and another as the independent variable, x. Use your knowledge of the subject area and common sense to help you select the variables.

b. Fit the simple linear model, $E(y) = \beta_0 + \beta_1 x$, to the data for all 50 top-ranked schools. Interpret the estimates of the slope and y-intercept.

Data for Exercise 11.29

	Rank University	Academic Rep. Score	Financial Aid	Cost	Early Pay	Better Place	STEM
1	Harvard	99 pts.	$41,555	$14,455	$61,400	65%	28%
2	MIT	92	34,641	20,629	74,900	55	79
3	Stanford	94	38,522	19,233	65,900	62	29
4	Columbia	95	37,934	21,274	60,200	56	29
5	Yale	97	39,771	18,479	60,300	68	21
6	CalTech	91	31,445	22,645	72,600	66	93
7	Dartmouth	91	38,148	20,490	56,300	45	20
8	Penn	92	35,539	21,821	60,300	55	19
9	Duke	92	33,191	24,134	60,600	59	35
10	Johns Hopkins	89	34,469	22,973	57,500	63	26

Applying the Concepts—Advanced

11.30 Spreading rate of spilled liquid. Refer to the *Chemical Engineering Progress* (January 2005) study of the rate at which a spilled volatile liquid will spread across a surface, Exercise 2.130 (p. 132). Recall that a DuPont Corp. engineer calculated the mass (in pounds) of a 50-gallon methanol spill after a period of time ranging from 0 to 60 minutes. Do the data in the table below indicate that the mass of the spill tends to diminish as time increases? If so, how much will the mass diminish each minute?

Time (minutes)	Mass (pounds)	Time (minutes)	Mass (pounds)
0	6.64	22	1.86
1	6.34	24	1.60
2	6.04	26	1.37
4	5.47	28	1.17
6	4.94	30	0.98
8	4.44	35	0.60
10	3.98	40	0.34
12	3.55	45	0.17
14	3.15	50	0.06
16	2.79	55	0.02
18	2.45	60	0.00
20	2.14		

Source: Based on the source J. Barry, "Estimating Rates of Spreading and Evaporation of Volatile Liquids," *Chemical Engineering Progress*, Vol. 101, No. 1, January 2005.

11.3   Model Assumptions

In Section 11.2, we assumed that the probabilistic model relating the firm's sales revenue y to the advertising dollars is

$$y = \beta_0 + \beta_1 x + \varepsilon$$

We also recall that the least squares estimate of the deterministic component of the model, $\beta_0 + \beta_1 x$, is

$$\hat{y} = \hat{\beta}_0 + \hat{\beta}_1 x = -.1 + .7x$$

Now we turn our attention to the random component ε of the probabilistic model and its relation to the errors in estimating β_0 and β_1. We will use a probability distribution to characterize the behavior of ε. We will see how the probability distribution of ε determines how well the model describes the relationship between the dependent variable y and the independent variable x.

Step 3 in a regression analysis requires us to specify the probability distribution of the random error ε. We will make four basic assumptions about the general form of this probability distribution:

Assumption 1: The mean of the probability distribution of ε is 0—that is, the average of the values of ε over an infinitely long series of experiments is 0 for each setting of the independent variable x. This assumption implies that the mean value of y, $E(y)$, for a given value of x is $E(y) = \beta_0 + \beta_1 x$.

Assumption 2: The variance of the probability distribution of ε is constant for all settings of the independent variable x. For our straight-line model, this assumption means that the variance of ε is equal to a constant, say σ^2, for all values of x.

Assumption 3: The probability distribution of ε is normal.

Assumption 4: The values of ε associated with any two observed values of y are independent—that is, the value of ε associated with one value of y has no effect on the values of ε associated with other y-values.

The implications of the first three assumptions can be seen in Figure 11.9, which shows distributions of errors for three values of x, namely, x_1, x_2, and x_3. Note that the relative frequency distributions of the errors are normal with a mean of 0 and a constant variance σ^2. (All the distributions shown have the same amount of spread or variability.) The straight line shown in Figure 11.9 is the line of means. It indicates the mean value of y for a given value of x. We denote this mean value as $E(y)$. Then, the line of means is given by the equation

$$E(y) = \beta_0 + \beta_1 x$$

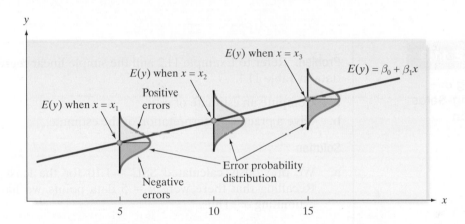

Figure 11.9

The probability distribution of ε

These assumptions make it possible for us to develop measures of reliability for the least squares estimators and to develop hypothesis tests for examining the usefulness of the least squares line. We have various techniques for checking the validity of these assumptions, and we have remedies to apply when they appear to be invalid. Several of these remedies are discussed in Chapter 12. Fortunately, the assumptions need not hold exactly in order for least squares estimators to be useful. The assumptions will be satisfied adequately for many applications encountered in practice.

It seems reasonable to assume that the greater the variability of the random error ε (which is measured by its variance σ^2), the greater will be the errors in the estimation of the model parameters β_0 and β_1 and in the error of prediction when $\hat{y}$ is used to predict y for some value of x. Consequently, you should not be surprised, as we proceed through this chapter, to find that σ^2 appears in the formulas for all confidence intervals and test statistics that we will be using.

In most practical situations, σ^2 is unknown, and we must use our data to estimate its value. The best estimate of σ^2, denoted by s^2, is obtained by dividing the sum of squares of the deviations of the y-values from the prediction line,

$$\text{SSE} = \sum (y_i - \hat{y}_i)^2$$

by the number of degrees of freedom associated with this quantity. We use 2 df to estimate the two parameters β_0 and β_1 in the straight-line model, leaving $(n - 2)$ df for the error variance estimation.

Estimation of σ^2 for a (First-Order) Straight-Line Model

$$s^2 = \frac{\text{SSE}}{\text{Degrees of freedom for error}} = \frac{\text{SSE}}{n - 2}$$

where $\text{SSE} = \Sigma(y_i - \hat{y}_i)^2 = \text{SS}_{yy} - \hat{\beta}_1\text{SS}_{xy}$

$$\text{SS}_{yy} = \Sigma(y_i - \bar{y})^2 *$$

To estimate the standard deviation σ of ε, we calculate

$$s = \sqrt{s^2} = \sqrt{\frac{\text{SSE}}{n - 2}}$$

We will refer to s as the **estimated standard error of the regression model.**

> ❗ **CAUTION** When performing these calculations, you may be tempted to round the calculated values of SS_{yy}, $\hat{\beta}_1$, and SS_{xy}. Be certain to carry at least six significant figures for each of these quantities to avoid substantial errors in calculation of the SSE.

EXAMPLE 11.3

Estimating σ — Advertising-Sales Regression

Problem Refer to Example 11.2 and the simple linear regression of the advertising-sales data in Table 11.1.

a. Compute an estimate of σ.

b. Give a practical interpretation of the estimate.

Solution

a. We previously calculated SSE = 1.10 for the least squares line $\hat{y} = -.1 + .7x$. Recalling that there were $n = 5$ data points, we have $n - 2 = 5 - 2 = 3$ df for estimating σ^2. Thus,

$$s^2 = \frac{\text{SSE}}{n - 2} = \frac{1.10}{3} = .367$$

is the estimated variance, and

$$s = \sqrt{.367} = .61$$

is the standard error of the regression model.

b. You may be able to grasp s intuitively by recalling the interpretation of a standard deviation given in Chapter 2 and remembering that the least squares line estimates the mean value of y for a given value of x. Because s measures the spread of the distribution of y-values about the least squares line, we should not be surprised to find that most of the observations lie within $2s$, or $2(.61) = 1.22$, of the least squares line. For this simple example (only five data points), all five sales revenue values fall within $2s$ (or \$1,220) of the least squares line. In Section 11.6, we use s to evaluate the error of prediction when the least squares line is used to predict a value of y to be observed for a given value of x.

Look Back The values of s^2 and s can also be obtained from a simple linear regression printout. The Minitab printout for the advertising-sales example is reproduced in Figure 11.10. The value of s^2 is highlighted at the bottom of the printout in the

---

* Alternatively, you can use the following "shortcut" formula:

$$\text{SS}_{yy} = \Sigma y^2 - \frac{(\Sigma y)^2}{n}$$

Regression Analysis: SALES_Y versus ADVEXP_X

Analysis of Variance

Source	DF	Adj SS	Adj MS	F-Value	P-Value
Regression	1	4.900	4.9000	13.36	0.035
ADVEXP_X	1	4.900	4.9000	13.36	0.035
Error	3	1.100	0.3667		
Total	4	6.000			

Model Summary

S	R-sq	R-sq(adj)	R-sq(pred)
0.605530	81.67%	75.56%	26.11%

Coefficients

Term	Coef	SE Coef	T-Value	P-Value	VIF
Constant	-0.100	0.635	-0.16	0.885	
ADVEXP_X	0.700	0.191	3.66	0.035	1.00

Regression Equation

SALES_Y = -0.100 + 0.700 ADVEXP_X

Figure 11.10
Minitab printout for the advertising-sales regression

MS (Mean Square) column in the row labeled **Residual Error**. (In regression, the estimate of σ^2 is called Mean Square for Error, or MSE.) The value, $s^2 = .3667$, agrees with the one calculated by hand. The value of s is also highlighted in Figure 11.10. This value, $s = .60553$, agrees (except for rounding) with our hand-calculated value.

● **Now Work Exercise 11.36**

Interpretation of s, the Estimated Standard Deviation of ε

We expect most ($\approx 95\%$) of the observed y-values to lie within $2s$ of their respective least squares predicted values, $\hat{y}$.

Exercises 11.31–11.44

Learning the Mechanics

11.31 Visually compare the scatterplots shown below. If a least squares line were determined for each data set, which do you think would have the smallest variance, s^2? Explain.

11.32 Calculate SSE and s^2 for each of the following cases:
  a. $n = 20$, $SS_{yy} = 95$, $SS_{xy} = 50$, $\hat{\beta}_1 = .75$
  b. $n = 40$, $\Sigma y^2 = 860$, $\Sigma y = 50$, $SS_{xy} = 2,700$, $\hat{\beta}_1 = .2$
  c. $n = 10$, $\Sigma(y_i - \bar{y})^2 = 58$, $SS_{xy} = 91$, $SS_{xx} = 170$

11.33 Suppose you fit a least squares line where $n = 20$, $\Sigma y = 176.11$, $\Sigma y^2 = 1,602.097$, $SS_{xy} = 5,365.0735$, and $\hat{\beta}_1 = .0087$.
  a. Calculate the estimated standard error for the regression model.
  b. Interpret the estimation value calculated in part **a**.

11.34 Refer to Exercise 11.14 (p. 653). Calculate SSE, s^2, and s for the least squares line. Use the value of s to determine where most of the errors of prediction lie.

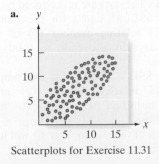
a.

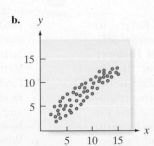
b.

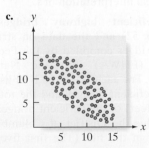
c.

Scatterplots for Exercise 11.31

Applying the Concepts—Basic

11.35 Do nice guys really finish last in business? Refer to the *Nature* (March 20, 2008) study of whether "nice guys finish last" in business, Exercise 11.18 (p. 653). Recall that college students repeatedly played a version of the game "prisoner's dilemma," where competitors choose cooperation, defection, or costly punishment. At the conclusion of the games, the researchers recorded the average payoff and the number of times punishment was used for each player. Based on a scatterplot of the data, the simple linear regression relating average payoff (y) to punishment use (x) resulted in SSE = 1.04.

    a. Assuming a sample size of $n = 28$, compute the estimated standard deviation of the error distribution, s.

    b. Give a practical interpretation of s.

11.36 State Math SAT scores. Refer to the simple linear regression relating $y = 2014$ Math SAT scores to $x = 2010$ Math SAT scores, Exercise 11.19 (p. 654). A portion of the SPSS printout of the analysis is shown below.

Model Summary

Model	R	R Square	Adjusted R Square	Std. Error of the Estimate
1	.946[a]	.895	.893	15.811

a. Predictors: (Constant), MATH2010

ANOVA[a]

Model		Sum of Squares	df	Mean Square	F	Sig.
1	Regression	104211.594	1	104211.594	416.853	.000[b]
	Residual	12249.817	49	249.996		
	Total	116461.412	50			

a. Dependent Variable: MATH2014

b. Predictors: (Constant), MATH2010

    a. Locate the values of SSE, s^2, and s on the SPSS printout.

    b. Give a practical interpretation of the value of s.

11.37 Repair and replacement costs of water pipes. Refer to the *IHS Journal of Hydraulic Engineering* (September 2012) study of water pipes, Exercise 11.21 (p. 655). Refer, again, to the Minitab simple linear regression printout (p. 655) relating $y =$ the ratio of repair to replacement cost of commercial pipe to $x =$ the diameter (in millimeters) of the pipe.

    a. Locate the value of s on the printout.

    b. Give a practical interpretation of s.

11.38 Joint Strike Fighter program. Refer to the *Air & Space Power Journal* (March-April 2014) study of the Joint Strike Fighter program, Exercise 11.22 (p. 655). You fit the simple linear regression model relating $y =$ estimated annual cost to $x =$ year of initial aircraft operation.

    a. Find s, the estimated standard deviation of the random error term, for the model.

    b. Give a practical interpretation of s.

11.39 Structurally deficient highway bridges. Refer to Exercise 1.30 (p. 52) and the data on structurally deficient highway bridges compiled by the Federal Highway Administration (FHWA) into the National Bridge Inventory (NBI). For each state, the NBI lists the number of structurally deficient bridges and the total area (thousands of square feet) of the deficient bridges. The data for the 50 states (plus the District of Columbia and Puerto Rico) are saved in the file. (The first five and last five observations are listed in the table in the next column.)

For future planning and budgeting, the FHWA wants to estimate the total area of structurally deficient bridges in a state based on the number of deficient bridges.

State	Number	Area (thousands of sq. ft.)
Alabama	1,899	432.7
Alaska	155	60.9
Arizona	181	110.5
Arkansas	997	347.3
California	3,140	5,177.9
⋮	⋮	⋮
Washington	400	502.0
West Virginia	1,058	331.5
Wisconsin	1,302	399.8
Wyoming	389	143.4
Puerto Rico	241	195.4

    a. Write the equation of a straight-line model relating total area (y) to number of structurally deficient bridges (x).

    b. The model, part **a**, was fit to the data using Minitab, as shown below. Find the least squares prediction equation on the printout.

    c. List the assumptions required for the regression analysis.

    d. Locate the estimated standard error of the regression model, s, on the printout.

    e. Use the value of s to find a range where most (about 95%) of the errors of prediction will fall.

Regression Analysis: SDArea versus NumberSD

```
Analysis of Variance

Source        DF    Adj SS     Adj MS    F-Value  P-Value
Regression     1  12710141   12710141    31.50    0.000
Error         50  20173111     403462
Total         51  32883252


Model Summary

      S   R-sq   R-sq(adj)
635.187  38.65%    37.43%


Coefficients

Term       Coef   SE Coef  T-Value  P-Value
Constant    120       123     0.97    0.335
NumberSD 0.3456    0.0616     5.61    0.000


Regression Equation

SDArea = 120 + 0.3456 NumberSD
```

Applying the Concepts—Intermediate

11.40 Software millionaires and birthdays. Refer to Exercise 11.23 (p. 655) and the study of software millionaires and their birthdays. The data are reproduced on p. 663.

    a. Find SSE, s^2, and s for the simple linear regression model relating number (y) of software millionaire birthdays in a decade to total number (x) of U.S. births.

    b. Find SSE, s^2, and s for the simple linear regression model relating number (y) of software millionaire birthdays in a decade to number (x) of CEO birthdays.

    c. Which of the two models' fit will have smaller errors of prediction? Why?

Data for Exercise 11.40

Decade	Total U.S. Births (millions)	Number of Software Millionaire Birthdays	Number of CEO Birthdays (in a random sample of 70 companies from the *Fortune* 500 list)
1920	28.582	3	2
1930	24.374	1	2
1940	31.666	10	23
1950	40.530	14	38
1960	38.808	7	9
1970	33.309	4	0

Source: J. Sauro, "Were Most Software Millionaires Born Around 1955?" *Measuring Usability*, November 17, 2010. Copyright © 2010 by Measuring Usability LLC. Reprinted with permission.

11.41 Public corruption and bad weather. Refer to the *Journal of Law and Economics* (November 2008) study of the link between Federal Emergency Management Agency (FEMA) disaster relief and public corruption, Exercise 11.24 (p. 656). You used the data in the file to fit a straight-line model relating a state's average annual number of public corruption convictions (y) to the state's average annual FEMA relief (x).
  a. Estimate σ^2, the variance of the random error term in the model.
  b. Estimate σ, the standard deviation of the random error term in the model.
  c. Which of the estimates, part **a** or **b**, can be interpreted practically? Why?
  d. Make a statement about how accurate the model is in predicting a state's average annual number of public corruption convictions.

11.42 Sweetness of orange juice. Refer to the study of the quality of orange juice produced at a juice manufacturing plant, Exercise 11.26 (p. 656). Recall that simple linear regression was used to predict the sweetness index (y) from the amount of pectin (x) in the orange juice.
  a. Find the values of SSE, s^2, and s for this regression.
  b. Explain why it is difficult to give a practical interpretation to s^2.
  c. Give a practical interpretation of the value of s.

11.43 Rankings of research universities. Refer to the College Choice *2015 Rankings of National Research Universities*, Exercise 11.29 (p. 657). From among the variables on the file—academic reputation score, financial aid awarded, net cost to attend, early career median salary, percent of alumni who feel their work makes a better place in which to live, and percentage of STEM degrees awarded—you selected one as the dependent variable, y, and another as the independent variable, x, and ran a simple linear

regression. Now select a different independent variable and run another simple linear regression. Which of the two independent variables is a more accurate predictor of your chosen dependent variable? Explain.

Applying the Concepts—Advanced

11.44 Life tests of cutting tools. To improve the quality of the output of any production process, it is necessary first to understand the capabilities of the process (Gitlow, *Quality Management*, 2004). In a particular manufacturing process, the useful life of a cutting tool is related to the speed at which the tool is operated. The data in the table below were derived from life tests for the two different brands of cutting tools currently used in the production process. For which brand would you feel more confident in using the least squares line to predict useful life for a given cutting speed? Explain.

Cutting Speed (meters per minute)	Useful Life (Hours)	
	Brand A	Brand B
30	4.5	6.0
30	3.5	6.5
30	5.2	5.0
40	5.2	6.0
40	4.0	4.5
40	2.5	5.0
50	4.4	4.5
50	2.8	4.0
50	1.0	3.7
60	4.0	3.8
60	2.0	3.0
60	1.1	2.4
70	1.1	1.5
70	.5	2.0
70	3.0	1.0

11.4 Assessing the Utility of the Model: Making Inferences About the Slope β_1

Now that we have specified the probability distribution of ε and found an estimate of the variance σ^2, we are ready to make statistical inferences about the model's usefulness for predicting the response y. This is step 4 in our regression modeling procedure.

Refer again to the data of Table 11.1 and suppose the appliance store's sales revenue is *completely unrelated* to the advertising expenditure. What could be said about the values of β_0 and β_1 in the hypothesized probabilistic model

$$y = \beta_0 + \beta_1 x + \varepsilon$$

if x contributes no information for the prediction of y? The implication is that the mean of y—that is, the deterministic part of the model $E(y) = \beta_0 + \beta_1 x$—does not change as x changes. In the straight-line model, this means that the true slope, β_1, is equal to 0 (see Figure 11.11). Therefore, to test the null hypothesis that the linear model contributes no information for the prediction of y against the alternative hypothesis that the linear model is useful in predicting y, we test

$$H_0: \beta_1 = 0 \text{ against } H_a: \beta_1 \neq 0$$

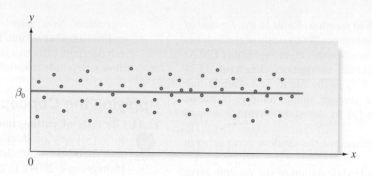

Figure 11.11

Graph of the straight-line model when slope is zero, i.e., $y = \beta_0 + \varepsilon$

If the data support the alternative hypothesis, we will conclude that x does contribute information for the prediction of y using the straight-line model (although the true relationship between $E[y]$ and x could be more complex than a straight line). Thus, in effect, this is a test of the usefulness of the hypothesized model.

The appropriate test statistic is found by considering the sampling distribution of $\hat{\beta}_1$, the least squares estimator of the slope β_1, as shown in the following box.

Sampling Distribution of $\hat{\beta}_1$

If we make the four assumptions about ε (see Section 11.3), the sampling distribution of the least squares estimator $\hat{\beta}_1$ of the slope will be normal with mean β_1 (the true slope) and standard deviation

$$\sigma_{\hat{\beta}_1} = \frac{\sigma}{\sqrt{SS_{xx}}} \quad \text{(see Figure 11.12)}$$

We estimate $\sigma_{\hat{\beta}_1}$ by $s_{\hat{\beta}_1} = \dfrac{s}{\sqrt{SS_{xx}}}$ and refer to this quantity as the **estimated standard error of the least squares slope $\hat{\beta}_1$.**

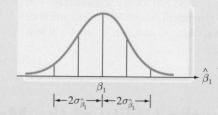

Figure 11.12

Sampling distribution of $\hat{\beta}_1$

Because σ is usually unknown, the appropriate test statistic is a *t*-statistic, formed as follows:

$$t = \frac{\hat{\beta}_1 - \text{Hypothesized value of } \beta_1}{s_{\hat{\beta}_1}} \quad \text{where } s_{\hat{\beta}} = \frac{s}{\sqrt{SS_{xx}}}$$

Thus,

$$t = \frac{\hat{\beta}_1 - 0}{s/\sqrt{SS_{xx}}}$$

Note that we have substituted the estimator s for σ and then formed the estimated standard error $s_{\hat{\beta}_1}$ by dividing s by $\sqrt{SS_{xx}}$. The number of degrees of freedom associated with this t-statistic is the same as the number of degrees of freedom associated with s. Recall that this number is $(n - 2)$ df when the hypothesized model is a straight line (see Section 11.3). The setup of our test of the usefulness of the straight-line model is summarized in the following boxes.

A Test of Model Utility: Simple Linear Regression

Test statistic: $t_c = \dfrac{\hat{\beta}_1}{s_{\hat{\beta}_1}} = \dfrac{\hat{\beta}_1}{(s/\sqrt{SS_{xx}})}$

	One-Tailed Tests		Two-Tailed Test
	$H_0: \beta_1 = 0$ $H_a: \beta_1 < 0$	$H_0: \beta_1 = 0$ $H_a: \beta_1 > 0$	$H_0: \beta_1 = 0$ $H_a: \beta_1 \neq 0$
Rejection region:	$t_c < -t_\alpha$	$t_c > t_\alpha$	$\lvert t_c \rvert > t_{\alpha/2}$
p-value:	$P(t < t_c)$	$P(t > t_c)$	$2P(t > t_c)$ if t_c is positive $2P(t < t_c)$ if t_c is negative

Decision: Reject H_0 if $\alpha > p$-value or if test statistic (t_c) falls in rejection region where $P(t > t_\alpha) = \alpha$, $P(t > t_{\alpha/2}) = \alpha/2$, and t is based on $(n - 2)$ degrees of freedom

---

Conditions Required for a Valid Test: Simple Linear Regression

Refer to the four assumptions about ε listed in Section 11.3.

EXAMPLE 11.4

Testing the Regression Slope, β_1—Sales Revenue Model

Problem Refer to the simple linear regression analysis of the advertising-sales data, Examples 11.2 and 11.3. Conduct a test (at $\alpha = .05$) to determine if sales revenue (y) is linearly related to advertising expenditure (x).

Solution As stated previously, we want to test $H_0: \beta_1 = 0$ against $H_a: \beta_1 \neq 0$. For this example, $n = 5$. Thus t will be based on $n - 2 = 3$ df, and the rejection region (at $\alpha = .05$) will be

$$\lvert t \rvert > t_{.025} = 3.182$$

We previously calculated $\hat{\beta}_1 = .7$, $s = .61$, and $SS_{xx} = 10$. Thus, the test statistic is

$$t = \frac{\hat{\beta}_1}{s/\sqrt{SS_{xx}}} = \frac{.7}{.61/\sqrt{10}} = \frac{.7}{.19} = 3.7$$

Because this calculated t-value falls into the upper-tail rejection region (see Figure 11.13), we reject the null hypothesis and conclude that the slope β_1 is not 0. The sample evidence indicates that advertising expenditure x contributes information for the production of sales revenue y when a linear model is used.

[*Note:* We can reach the same conclusion by using the observed significance level (*p*-value) of the test from a computer printout. The Minitab printout for the advertising-sales example is reproduced in Figure 11.14. The test statistic and *two-tailed p*-value are highlighted on the printout. Because the *p*-value is smaller than $\alpha = .05$, we will reject H_0.]

Figure 11.13

Rejection region and calculated *t*-value for testing H_0: $\beta_1 = 0$ versus H_a: $\beta_1 \neq 0$

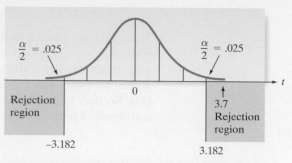

Figure 11.14

Minitab printout for the advertising-sales regression

Regression Analysis: SALES_Y versus ADVEXP_X

Analysis of Variance

Source	DF	Adj SS	Adj MS	F-Value	P-Value
Regression	1	4.900	4.9000	13.36	0.035
ADVEXP_X	1	4.900	4.9000	13.36	0.035
Error	3	1.100	0.3667		
Total	4	6.000			

Model Summary

S	R-sq	R-sq(adj)	R-sq(pred)
0.605530	81.67%	75.56%	26.11%

Coefficients

Term	Coef	SE Coef	T-Value	P-Value	VIF
Constant	-0.100	0.635	-0.16	0.885	
ADVEXP_X	0.700	0.191	3.66	0.035	1.00

Regression Equation

SALES_Y = -0.100 + 0.700 ADVEXP_X

Look Back What conclusion can be drawn if the calculated *t*-value does not fall in the rejection region or if the observed significance level of the test exceeds α? We know from previous discussions of the philosophy of hypothesis testing that such a *t*-value does *not* lead us to accept the null hypothesis—that is, we do not conclude that $\beta_1 = 0$. Additional data might indicate that β_1 differs from 0, or a more complex relationship may exist between *x* and *y*, requiring the fitting of a model other than the straight-line model. We discuss several such models in Chapter 12.

● **Now Work Exercise 11.50**

Interpreting *p*-Values for β Coefficients in Regression

Almost all statistical computer software packages report a *two-tailed p*-value for each of the β parameters in the regression model. For example, in simple linear regression, the *p*-value for the two-tailed test H_0: $\beta_1 = 0$ versus H_a: $\beta_1 \neq 0$ is given on the printout. If you want to conduct a *one-tailed* test of hypothesis, you will need to adjust the *p*-value reported on the printout as follows:

$$\text{Upper-tailed test } (H_a\text{: } \beta_1 > 0)\text{: } p\text{-value} = \begin{cases} p/2 & \text{if } t > 0 \\ 1 - p/2 & \text{if } t < 0 \end{cases}$$

$$\text{Lower-tailed test } (H_a\text{: } \beta_1 < 0)\text{: } p\text{-value} = \begin{cases} p/2 & \text{if } t < 0 \\ 1 - p/2 & \text{if } t > 0 \end{cases}$$

where *p* is the *p*-value reported on the printout and *t* is the value of the test statistic.

Another way to make inferences about the slope β_1 is to estimate it using a confidence interval. This interval is formed as shown in the next box.

A $100(1 - \alpha)$% Confidence Interval for the Simple Linear Regression Slope β_1

$$\hat{\beta}_1 \pm t_{\alpha/2}s_{\hat{\beta}_1}$$

where the estimated standard error $\hat{\beta}_1$ is calculated by

$$s_{\hat{\beta}_1} = \frac{s}{\sqrt{SS_{xx}}}$$

and $t_{\alpha/2}$ is based on $(n - 2)$ degrees of freedom.

Conditions Required for a Valid Confidence Interval: Simple Linear Regression

Refer to the four assumptions about ϵ listed in Section 11.3.

For the simple linear regression of sales revenue (Examples 11.1–11.3), $t_{\alpha/2}$ is based on $(n - 2) = 3$ degrees of freedom, and, for $\alpha = .05, t_{.025} = 3.182$. Therefore, a 95% confidence interval for the slope β_1, the expected change in sales revenue for a \$100 increase in advertising expenditure, is

$$\hat{\beta}_1 \pm (t_{.025})s_{\hat{\beta}_1} = .7 \pm 3.182\left(\frac{s}{\sqrt{SS_{xx}}}\right) = .7 \pm 3.182\left(\frac{.61}{\sqrt{10}}\right) = .7 \pm .61$$

Thus, the interval estimate of the slope parameter β_1 is .09 to 1.31. [*Note:* This interval can also be obtained using statistical software and is highlighted on the SPSS printout, Figure 11.15.] In terms of this example, the implication is that we can be 95% confident that the *true* mean increase in monthly sales revenue per additional \$100 of advertising expenditure is between \$90 and \$1,310. This inference is meaningful only over the sampled range of x—that is, from \$100 to \$500 of advertising expenditures.

Coefficients[a]

Model		Unstandardized Coefficients B	Std. Error	Standardized Coefficients Beta	t	Sig.	95.0% Confidence Interval for B Lower Bound	Upper Bound
1	(Constant)	-.100	.635		-.157	.885	-2.121	1.921
	ADVEXP_X	.700	.191	.904	3.656	.035	.091	1.309

a. Dependent Variable: SALES_Y

Figure 11.15

SPSS printout with 95% confidence intervals for the advertising-sales regression β's

Because all the values in this interval are positive, it appears that β_1 is positive and that the mean of y, $E(y)$, increases as x increases. However, the rather large width of the confidence interval reflects the small number of data points (and, consequently, a lack of information) in the experiment. Particularly bothersome is the fact that the lower end of the confidence interval implies that we are not even recovering our additional expenditure because a \$100 increase in advertising may produce as little as a \$90 increase in mean sales. If we wish to tighten this interval, we need to increase the sample size.

STATISTICS IN ACTION REVISITED

Assessing How Well a Straight-Line Regression Model Fits Data

In the previous *Statistics in Action Revisited*, we fit the straight-line model, $E(y) = \beta_0 + \beta_1x$, where x = cumulative 6-month advertising expenditures and y represents either the number of new PI cases or the number of new WC cases per month. The SPSS regression printouts for the two analyses are shown in Figure SIA11.3. (The regression for y = number of new PI cases is shown at the top, and the regression for y = number of new WC cases is shown at the bottom of the printout.) The objective is to determine whether one or both of the dependent variables are statistically linearly related to cumulative 6-month advertising expenditures.

The two-tailed p-values for testing the null hypothesis, $H_0: \beta_1 = 0$ (highlighted on the printouts), are p-value ≈ 0 for number of new PI cases and p-value $= .725$ for

STATISTICS IN ACTION

REVISITED

(continued)

Coefficients[a]

		Unstandardized Coefficients		Standardized Coefficients				95.0% Confidence Interval for B	
Model		B	Std. Error	Beta	t	Sig.		Lower Bound	Upper Bound
1	(Constant)	7.767	3.385		2.295	.027		.926	14.609
	CUM. ADV (thous)	.113	.028	.539	4.042	.000		.056	.169

a. Dependent Variable: New PI Cases

Coefficients[a]

		Unstandardized Coefficients		Standardized Coefficients				95.0% Confidence Interval for B	
Model		B	Std. Error	Beta	t	Sig.		Lower Bound	Upper Bound
1	(Constant)	24.574	3.367		7.299	.000		17.770	31.379
	CUM. ADV (thous)	.010	.028	.056	.354	.725		-.046	.066

a. Dependent Variable: New WC Cases

Figure SIA11.3

SPSS simple linear regressions for legal advertising data

number of new WC cases. For y = number of new PI cases, there is sufficient evidence to reject H_0 (at $\alpha = .01$) and conclude that the number of new PI cases is linearly related to cumulative 6-month advertising expenditures. In contrast, for y = number of WC cases, there is insufficient evidence to reject H_0 (at $\alpha = .01$); thus, there is no evidence of a linear relationship between the number of new WC cases and cumulative 6-month advertising expenditures.

We can gain further insight into this phenomenon by examining a 95% confidence interval for the slope, β_1. For y = number of new PI cases, the interval (highlighted on the SPSS printout) is (.056, .169). With 95% confidence, we can state that for every $1,000 increase in monthly advertising expenditures, the number of new PI cases each month will increase between .056 and .169. Now, a more realistic increase in cumulative 6-month advertising expenditures is, say, $20,000. Multiplying the endpoints of the interval by 20, we see that this increase in advertising spending leads to an increase of anywhere between 1 and 3 new PI cases.

Now, for y = number of new WC cases, the 95% confidence interval for the slope (also highlighted on the SPSS printout) is (−.046, .066). Because the interval spans the value 0, we draw the same conclusion as we did with the hypothesis test—there is no statistical evidence of a linear relationship between the number of new WC cases and cumulative 6-month advertising expenditures.

Recall that partner A (who handled the PI cases) sued partner B (who handled the WC cases) for not paying a fair share of the advertising expenses. These results do not support partner A's argument because there is no evidence that partner B benefitted from advertising.

Exercises 11.45–11.63

Learning the Mechanics

11.45 Ten pairs of variables x and y were collected to determine if there is sufficient evidence to indicate that x and y have a negative linear relationship at the 5% significance level. The regression analysis results in $\hat{\beta}_1 = 1.1909$, $s = 3.0018$, $SS_{xx} = 370.9$, and p-value = .0000607.

a. Specify the null and alternative hypotheses to test whether the data provide sufficient evidence to indicate that x and y have a negative linear relationship.

b. Make an appropriate conclusion for your analysis.

c. Construct a 95% confidence interval for the slope parameter. Interpret your result.

11.46 Consider the following pairs of observations:

L11046

x	1	4	3	2	5	6	0
y	1	3	3	1	4	7	2

a. Construct a scatterplot for the data.

b. Use the method of least squares to fit a straight line to the seven data points in the table.

c. Plot the least squares line on your scatterplot of part **a.**

d. Specify the null and alternative hypotheses you would use to test whether the data provide sufficient evidence to indicate that x contributes information for the (linear) prediction of y.

e. What is the test statistic that should be used in conducting the hypothesis test of part **d?** Specify the degrees of freedom associated with the test statistic.

f. Conduct the hypothesis test of part **d** using $\alpha = .05$.

11.47 Refer to Exercise 11.46. Construct an 80% and a 98% confidence interval for β_1.

11.48 Do the accompanying data provide sufficient evidence to conclude that a straight line is useful for characterizing the relationship between x and y?
L11048

x	4	2	4	3	2	4
y	1	6	5	3	2	4

Applying the Concepts—Basic

11.49 State Math SAT Scores. Refer to the SPSS simple linear regression relating y = average state SAT Math score in 2014 with x = average state SAT Math score in 2010, Exercise 11.19 (p. 654).

   a. Give the null and alternative hypotheses for determining whether a positive linear relationship exists between y and x.

   b. Locate the p-value of the test on the SPSS printout. Interpret the result if $\alpha = .05$.

   c. Find a 95% confidence interval for the slope, β_1. Interpret the result.

11.50 Lobster fishing study. Refer to the *Bulletin of Marine Science* (April 2010) study of teams of fishermen fishing for the red spiny lobster in Baja California Sur, Mexico, Exercise 11.20 (p. 654). A simple linear regression model relating y = total catch of lobsters (in kilograms) and x = average percentage of traps allocated per day to exploring areas of unknown catch (called *search frequency*) was fit to the data in the file. A portion of the XLSTAT printout is reproduced at the bottom of the page.

   a. Give the null and alternative hypotheses for testing whether total catch (y) is negatively linearly related to search frequency (x).

   b. Find the p-value of the test on the XLSTAT printout.

   c. Give the appropriate conclusion of the test, part **c**, using $\alpha = .05$.

11.51 Congress voting on women's issues. The *American Economic Review* (March 2008) published research on how the gender mix of a U.S. legislator's children can influence the legislator's votes in Congress. Specifically, the researcher investigated how having daughters influences voting on women's issues. The American Association of University Women (AAUW) uses voting records of each member of Congress to compute an AAUW score, where higher scores indicate more favorable voting for women's rights. The researcher modeled AAUW score (y) as a function of the number of daughters (x) a legislator has. Data collected for the 434 members of the 107th Congress were used to fit the straight-line model, $E(y) = \beta_0 + \beta_1 x$.

   a. If it is true that having daughters influences voting on women's issues, will the sign of β_1 be positive or negative? Explain.

   b. The following statistics were reported in the article: $\hat{\beta}_1 = .27$ and $s_{\hat{\beta}_1} = .74$. Find a 95% confidence interval for β_1.

   c. Use the result, part **b**, to make an inference about the model. [*Note:* We will return to this problem in Chapter 12 and consider a more complex model for AAUW score.]

11.52 Generation Y's entitlement mentality. The current workforce is dominated by "Generation Y"—people born between 1982 and 1999. These workers have a reputation as having an entitlement mentality (e.g., they believe they have a right to a high-paying job, without the work ethic). The reasons behind this phenomenon were investigated in *Proceedings of the Academy of Educational Leadership* (Vol. 16, 2011). A sample of 272 undergraduate business students was administered a questionnaire designed to capture the behaviors that lead to an entitlement mentality. The responses were used to measure the following two quantitative variables for each student: entitlement score (y)—where higher scores indicate a greater level of entitlement, and "helicopter parents" score (x)—where higher scores indicate that the student's parents had a higher level of involvement in his or her everyday experiences and problems.

   a. Give the equation of a simple linear regression model relating y to x.

   b. The researchers theorize that helicopter parents lead to an entitlement mentality. Based on this theory, would you expect β_0 to be positive or negative (or are you unsure)? Would you expect β_1 to be positive or negative (or are you unsure)? Explain.

   c. The p-value for testing $H_0: \beta_1 = 0$ versus $H_a: \beta_1 > 0$ was reported as .002. Use this result to test the researchers' entitlement theory at $\alpha = .01$.

11.53 Estimating repair and replacement costs of water pipes. Refer to the *IHS Journal of Hydraulic Engineering* (September 2012) study of water pipes susceptible to breakage, Exercises 11.21 (p. 655) and 11.37 (p. 662). Recall that civil engineers used simple linear regression to model the ratio of repair to replacement cost of commercial pipe (y) as a function of the diameter (x, in millimeters) of the pipe. The Minitab printout of the analysis is reproduced on the next page. Are the engineers able to conclude (at $\alpha = .05$) that the cost ratio increases linearly with pipe diameter? If so, provide a 95% confidence interval for the increase in cost ratio for every 1-millimeter increase in pipe diameter. (This interval is shown on the printout.)

Model parameters:

Source	Value	Standard error	t	Pr > |t|	Lower bound (95%)	Upper bound (95%)
Intercept	9877.8300	829.0411	11.9148	< 0.0001	8086.7957	11668.8643
SEARCHFR	−163.6024	41.9014	−3.9045	0.0018	−254.1249	−73.0799

Equation of the model:

CATCH = 9877.82997−163.60242*SEARCHFREQ

XLSTAT output for Exercise 11.50

```
Model Summary

       S    R-sq  R-sq(adj)    PRESS  R-sq(pred)
0.221034  95.26%     94.83%  0.897108      92.09%


Coefficients

Term         Coef    SE Coef           95% CI          T-Value  P-Value   VIF
Constant    6.678      0.121  (  6.412,    6.944)         55.29    0.000
DIAMETER  0.004786   0.000322  (0.004077, 0.005494)        14.87    0.000  1.00


Regression Equation

RATIO = 6.678 + 0.004786 DIAMETER
```

Minitab Output for Exercise 11.53

11.54 Sweetness of orange juice. Refer to the simple linear regression relating y = sweetness index of an orange juice sample with x = amount of water-soluble pectin, Exercise 11.26 (p. 656). Use the results of the regression to form a 95% confidence interval for the slope, β_1. Interpret the result.

Applying the Concepts—Intermediate

11.55 Software millionaires and birthdays. Refer to Exercise 11.23 (p. 655) and the study of whether birth decade can predict the number of software millionaires born in the decade.

a. Construct a 95% confidence interval for the slope of the model, $E(y) = \beta_0 + \beta_1 x$, where x = total number of U.S. births and y = number of software millionaire birthdays. Give a practical interpretation of the interval.

b. Construct a 95% confidence interval for the slope of the model, $E(y) = \beta_0 + \beta_1 x$, where x = number of CEO birthdays (in a sample of 70 companies) and y = number of software millionaire birthdays. Give a practical interpretation of the interval.

c. Can you conclude that number of software millionaires born in a decade is linearly related to total number of people born in the United States? Number of CEOs born in the decade?

11.56 Beauty and electoral success. Are good looks an advantage when running for political office? This was the question of interest in an article published in the *Journal of Public Economics* (February 2010). The researchers focused on a sample of 641 nonincumbent candidates for political office in Finland. Photos of each candidate were evaluated by non-Finnish subjects; each evaluator assigned a beauty rating—measured on a scale of 1 (lowest rating) to 5 (highest rating)—to each candidate. The beauty ratings for each candidate were averaged, then the average was divided by the standard deviation for all candidates to yield a beauty index for each candidate. (*Note:* A 1-unit increase in the index represents a 1-standard-deviation increase in the beauty rating.) The relative success (measured as a percentage of votes obtained) of each candidate was used as the dependent variable (y) in a regression analysis. One of the independent variables in the model was beauty index (x).

a. Write the equation of a simple linear regression relating y to x.

b. Does the y-intercept of the equation, part **a**, have a practical interpretation? Explain.

c. The article reported the estimated slope of the equation, part **a**, as 22.91. Give a practical interpretation of this value.

d. The standard error of the slope estimate was reported as 3.73. Use this information and the estimate from part **c** to conduct a test for a positive slope at $\alpha = .01$. Give the appropriate conclusion in the words of the problem.

11.57 Ranking driving performance of professional golfers. Refer to *The Sport Journal* (Winter 2007) study of a new method for ranking the total driving performance of golfers on the PGA tour, Exercise 11.25 (p. 656). You fit a straight-line model relating driving accuracy (y) to driving distance (x) to the data saved in the file.

a. Give the null and alternative hypotheses for testing whether driving accuracy (y) decreases linearly as driving distance (x) increases.

b. Find the test statistic and p-value of the test, part **a**.

c. Make the appropriate conclusion at $\alpha = .01$.

11.58 Public corruption and bad weather. Refer to the *Journal of Law and Economics* (November 2008) study of the link between Federal Emergency Management Agency (FEMA) disaster relief and public corruption, Exercise 11.24 (p. 656). Evaluate the overall adequacy of the straight-line model relating a state's average annual number of public corruption convictions (y) to the state's average annual FEMA relief (x). Use $\alpha = .01$.

11.59 Charisma of top-level leaders. Refer to the *Academy of Management Journal* (August 2015) study of the charisma of top-level leaders, Exercise 11.28 (p. 657). Recall that the researchers used data on 24 U.S. presidential election years to model Democratic vote share (y) as a function of the difference (x) between the Democratic and Republican candidates' charisma scores. Is there evidence to indicate that the simple linear regression model is statistically useful for predicting Democratic vote share? Test using $\alpha = .10$.

11.60 Joint Strike Fighter program. Refer to the *Air & Space Power Journal* (March-April 2014) study of the Joint Strike Fighter program, Exercises 11.22 and 11.38 (pp. 655 and 662). Recall that you fit the simple linear regression model relating y = estimated annual cost to x = year of initial aircraft operation. Find and interpret a 90% confidence interval for the increase in the cost of adding a military aircraft to the JSF program each year.

11.61 Rankings of research universities. Refer to the College Choice *2015 Rankings of National Research Universities*, Exercise 11.43 (p. 663). Now consider a simple linear regression model for a university's academic reputation score (y), using early career median salary (x) as the independent variable. Is there sufficient evidence of a positive linear relationship between academic reputation score and early career median salary? Test using $\alpha = .05$. Does your conclusion change if you use $\alpha = .01$?

Applying the Concepts—Advanced

11.62 Spreading rate of spilled liquid. Refer to the *Chemical Engineering Progress* (January 2005) study of the rate at which a spilled volatile liquid will spread across a surface, Exercise 11.30 (p. 658). Recall that the data on mass of the spill and elapsed time of the spill are saved in the file. Is there sufficient evidence (at $\alpha = .05$) to indicate that the mass of the spill tends to diminish linearly as time increases? If so, give an interval estimate (with 95% confidence) of the decrease in spill mass for each minute of elapsed time.

11.63 Does elevation impact hitting performance in baseball?
Refer to the *Chance* (Winter 2006) investigation of the effects of elevation on slugging percentage in Major League Baseball, Exercise 2.127 (p. 132). Recall that data were compiled on players' composite slugging percentage at each of 29 cities for a recent season, as well as each city's elevation (feet above sea level). The data are saved in the file. (Selected observations are shown in the table on the right.) Consider a straight-line model relating slugging percentage (*y*) to elevation (*x*).

a. Is there sufficient evidence (at $\alpha = .01$) of a positive linear relationship between elevation (*x*) and slugging percentage (*y*)?.

b. Construct a scatterplot for the data and draw the least squares line on the graph. Locate the data point for Denver on the graph. What do you observe?

c. You learned in Exercise 2.127 that the Colorado Rockies, who play their home games in Coors Field, Denver, typically lead the league in team slugging percentage. Many baseball experts attribute this to the "thin air" of Denver—called the "mile-high" city due to

Selected data for Exercise 11.63

City	Slug Pct.	Elevation
Anaheim	.480	160
Arlington	.605	616
Atlanta	.530	1,050
Baltimore	.505	130
Boston	.505	20
⋮	⋮	⋮
Denver	.625	5,277
⋮	⋮	⋮
Seattle	.550	350
San Francisco	.510	63
St. Louis	.570	465
Tampa	.500	10
Toronto	.535	566

Source: Based on Schaffer, J., & Heiny, E.L. "The effects of elevation on slugging percentage in Major League Baseball," *Chance*, Vol. 19, No. 1, Winter 2006 (adapted from Figure 2, p. 30).

its elevation. Remove the data point for Denver from the data set and refit the straight-line model to the remaining data. What conclusions can you draw about the "thin air" theory from this analysis?

11.5 The Coefficients of Correlation and Determination

In this section, we present two statistics that describe the adequacy of a model: the *coefficient of correlation* and the *coefficient of determination*.

Coefficient of Correlation

Recall (from Section 2.10) that a **bivariate relationship** describes a relationship—or correlation—between two variables, *x* and *y*. Scatterplots are used to graphically describe a bivariate relationship. In this section, we will discuss the concept of **correlation** and show how it can be used to measure the linear relationship between two variables *x* and *y*. A numerical descriptive measure of the linear association between *x* and *y* is provided by the *coefficient of correlation, r*.

The **coefficient of correlation,** * *r*, is a measure of the strength of the *linear* relationship between two variables *x* and *y*. It is computed (for a sample of *n* measurements on *x* and *y*) as follows:

$$r = \frac{SS_{xy}}{\sqrt{SS_{xx}SS_{yy}}} = \hat{\beta}_1 \sqrt{\frac{SS_{xx}}{SS_{yy}}}$$

where

$$SS_{xy} = \Sigma(x - \bar{x})(y - \bar{y})$$

$$SS_{xx} = \Sigma(x - \bar{x})^2$$

$$SS_{yy} = \Sigma(y - \bar{y})^2$$

Note that the computational formula for the correlation coefficient *r* given in the definition involves the same quantities that were used in computing the least squares prediction equation. In fact, you can see from the formula that $r = 0$ when $\hat{\beta}_1 = 0$ (the

*The value of *r* is often called the *Pearson correlation coefficient* to honor its developer, Karl Pearson. (See Biography, p. 579.)

case where x contributes no information for the prediction of y), and r is positive when the slope is positive and negative when the slope is negative. Unlike $\hat{\beta}_1$, the correlation coefficient r is *scaleless* and assumes a value between -1 and $+1$, regardless of the units of x and y.

A value of r near or equal to 0 implies little or no linear relationship between y and x. In contrast, the closer r comes to 1 or -1, the stronger the linear relationship between y and x. And if $r = 1$ or $r = -1$, all the sample points fall exactly on the least squares line. Positive values of r imply a positive linear relationship between y and x; that is, y increases as x increases. Negative values of r imply a negative linear relationship between y and x; that is, y decreases as x increases. Each of these situations is portrayed in Figure 11.16.

Now Work Exercise 11.64

We demonstrate how to calculate the coefficient of correlation r using the data in Table 11.1 for the advertising-sales example. The quantities needed to calculate r are SS_{xy}, SS_{xx}, and SS_{yy}. The first two quantities have been calculated previously as $SS_{xy} = 7$ and $SS_{xx} = 10$. The calculation for $SS_{yy} = \Sigma(y - \bar{y})^2$ is shown on the last column of the Excel spreadsheet, Figure 11.5 (p. 649). The result is $SS_{yy} = 6$.

We now find the coefficient of correlation:

$$r = \frac{SS_{xy}}{\sqrt{SS_{xx}SS_{yy}}} = \frac{7}{\sqrt{(10)(6)}} = \frac{7}{\sqrt{60}} = .904$$

The fact that r is positive and near 1 in value indicates that the sales revenue y tends to increase as advertising expenditure x increases—*for this sample of 5 months*. This is the same conclusion we reached when we found the calculated value of the least squares slope to be positive.

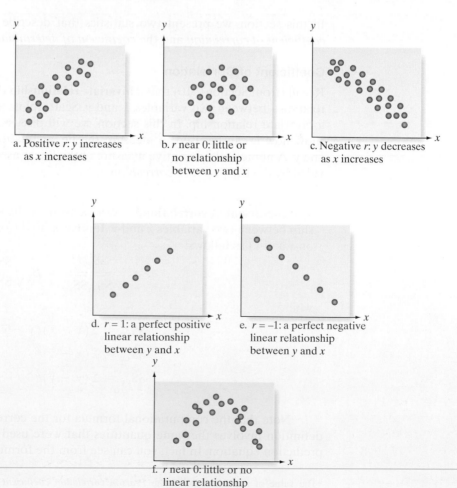

a. Positive r: y increases as x increases

b. r near 0: little or no relationship between y and x

c. Negative r: y decreases as x increases

d. $r = 1$: a perfect positive linear relationship between y and x

e. $r = -1$: a perfect negative linear relationship between y and x

f. r near 0: little or no linear relationship between y and x

Figure 11.16

Values of r and their implications

EXAMPLE 11.5

Using the Correlation Coefficient—Relating Crime Rate and Casino Employment

Problem Legalized gambling is available on several riverboat casinos operated by a city in Mississippi. The mayor of the city wants to know the correlation between the number of casino employees and the yearly crime rate. The records for the past 10 years are examined, and the results listed in Table 11.3 are obtained. Calculate the coefficient of correlation r for the data. Interpret the result.

Table 11.3	Data on Casino Employees and Crime Rate, Example 11.5	
Year	Number of Casino Employees, x (thousands)	Crime Rate, y (number of crimes per 1,000 population)
2006	15	1.35
2007	18	1.63
2008	24	2.33
2009	22	2.41
2010	25	2.63
2011	29	2.93
2012	30	3.41
2013	32	3.26
2014	35	3.63
2015	38	4.15

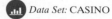 *Data Set:* CASINO

Solution Rather than use the computing formula for r given in the definition, we resort to using a statistical software package. The data of Table 11.3 were analyzed using Excel/XLSTAT, and the XLSTAT printout is shown in Figure 11.17.

The coefficient of correlation, highlighted at the top on the printout, is $r = .987$. Thus, the size of the casino workforce and crime rate in this city are very highly correlated—at least over the past 10 years. The implication is that a strong positive linear relationship exists between these variables (see the scatterplot at the bottom of Figure 11.17). We must be careful, however, not to jump to any unwarranted conclusions.

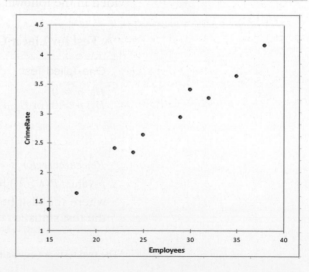

Figure 11.17
Excel/XLSTAT correlation printout for Example 11.5

For instance, the mayor may be tempted to conclude that hiring more casino workers next year will increase the crime rate—that is, that there is a *causal relationship* between the two variables. However, high correlation does not imply causality. The fact is, many things have probably contributed both to the increase in the casino workforce and to the increase in crime rate. The city's tourist trade has undoubtedly grown since riverboat casinos were legalized, and it is likely that the casinos have expanded both in services offered and in number. *We cannot infer a causal relationship on the basis of high sample correlation. When a high correlation is observed in the sample data, the only safe conclusion is that a linear trend may exist between* x *and* y.

Look Back Another variable, such as the increase in tourism, may be the underlying cause of the high correlation between x and y.

● **Now Work Exercise 11.81**

> ⚠ **CAUTION** When using the sample correlation coefficient, r, to infer the nature of the relationship between x and y, two caveats exist: (1) A *high correlation* does not necessarily imply that a causal relationship exists between x and y—only that a linear trend may exist; (2) a *low correlation* does not necessarily imply that x and y are unrelated—only that x and y are not strongly *linearly* related.

Keep in mind that the correlation coefficient r measures the linear association between x-values and y-values in the sample, and a similar linear coefficient of correlation exists for the population from which the data points were selected. The **population correlation coefficient** is denoted by the symbol ρ (rho). As you might expect, ρ is estimated by the corresponding sample statistic, r. Or, instead of estimating ρ, we might want to test the null hypothesis $H_0: \rho = 0$ against $H_a: \rho \neq 0$—that is, we can test the hypothesis that x contributes no information for the prediction of y by using the straight-line model against the alternative that the two variables are at least linearly related.

However, we already performed this *identical* test in Section 11.4 when we tested $H_0: \beta_1 = 0$ against $H_a: \beta_1 \neq 0$—that is, the null hypothesis $H_0: \rho = 0$ is equivalent to the hypothesis $H_0: \beta_1 = 0$.* When we tested the null hypothesis $H_0: \beta_1 = 0$ in connection with the advertising-sales example, the data led to a rejection of the null hypothesis at the $\alpha = .05$ level. This rejection implies that the null hypothesis of a 0 correlation between the two variables (sales revenue and advertising expenditure) can also be rejected at the $\alpha = .05$ level. The only real difference between the least squares slope $\hat{\beta}_1$ and the coefficient of correlation r is the measurement scale. Therefore, the information they provide about the usefulness of the least squares model is to some extent redundant. Consequently, we will use the slope to make inferences about the existence of a positive or negative linear relationship between two variables.

For the sake of completeness, a summary of the test for linear correlation is provided in the following boxes.

A Test for Linear Correlation

One-Tailed Test	Two-Tailed Test
$H_0: \rho = 0$	$H_0: \rho = 0$
$H_a: \rho > 0$ (or $H_a: \rho < 0$)	$H_a: \rho \neq 0$

$$\text{Test statistic: } t = \frac{r\sqrt{n-2}}{\sqrt{1-r^2}} = \frac{\hat{\beta}_1}{s_{\hat{\beta}_1}}$$

Rejection region: $t > t_\alpha$ (or $t < -t_\alpha$)	Rejection region: $\lvert t \rvert > t_{\alpha/2}$
p-value: $P(t > t_c)$ [or $P(t < -t_c)$]	p-value: $2P(t > t_c)$

where the distribution of t depends on $(n-2)$ df and t_c is the computed value of the test statistic.

---

*The two tests are equivalent in simple linear regression only.

Coefficient of Determination

Another way to measure the usefulness of the model is to measure the contribution of x in predicting y. To accomplish this, we calculate how much the errors of prediction of y were reduced by using the information provided by x. To illustrate, consider the sample shown in the scatterplot of Figure 11.18a. If we assume that x contributes no information for the prediction of y, the best prediction for a value of y is the sample mean $\bar{y}$, which is shown as the horizontal line in Figure 11.18b. The vertical line segments in Figure 11.18b are the deviations of the points about the mean $\bar{y}$. Note that the sum of squares of deviations for the prediction equation $\hat{y} = \bar{y}$ is

$$\text{SS}_{yy} = \sum (y_i - \bar{y})^2$$

Now suppose you fit a least squares line to the same set of data and locate the deviations of the points about the line as shown in Figure 11.18c. Compare the deviations about the prediction lines in Figures 11.18b and 11.18c. You can see that

1. If x contributes little or no information for the prediction of y, the sums of squares of deviations for the two lines,

$$\text{SS}_{yy} = \sum (y_i - \bar{y})^2 \quad \text{and} \quad \text{SSE} = \sum (y_i - \hat{y}_i)^2$$

will be nearly equal.

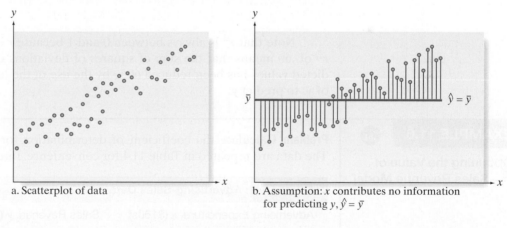

a. Scatterplot of data

b. Assumption: x contributes no information for predicting y, $\hat{y} = \bar{y}$

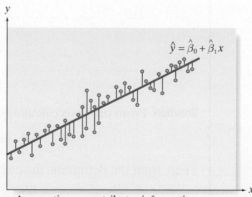

c. Assumption: x contributes information for predicting y, $\hat{y} = \hat{\beta}_0 + \hat{\beta}_1 x$

Figure 11.18

A comparison of the sum of squares of deviations for two models

2. If x does contribute information for the prediction of y, the SSE will be smaller than SS_{yy}. In fact, if all the points fall on the least squares line, then SSE $= 0$.

Then the reduction in the sum of squares of deviations that can be attributed to x, expressed as a proportion of SS_{yy}, is

$$\frac{SS_{yy} - SSE}{SS_{yy}}$$

Note that SS_{yy} is the "total sample variation" of the observations around the mean $\bar{y}$ and that SSE is the remaining "unexplained sample variability" after fitting the line $\bar{y}$. Thus, the difference $(SS_{yy} - SSE)$ is the "explained sample variability" attributable to the linear relationship with x. Then a verbal description of the proportion is

$$\frac{SS_{yy} - SSE}{SS_{yy}} = \frac{\text{Explained sample variability}}{\text{Total sample variability}}$$

$$= \text{Proportion of total sample variability explained by the linear relationship}$$

In simple linear regression, it can be shown that this proportion—called the *coefficient of determination*—is equal to the square of the simple linear coefficient of correlation r.

Coefficient of Determination

$$r^2 = \frac{SS_{yy} - SSE}{SS_{yy}} = 1 - \frac{SSE}{SS_{yy}}$$

It represents the proportion of the total sample variability around $\bar{y}$ that is explained by the linear relationship between y and x. (In simple linear regression, it may also be computed as the square of the coefficient of correlation r.)

Note that r^2 is always between 0 and 1 because r is between -1 and $+1$. Thus, an r^2 of .60 means that the sum of squares of deviations of the y-values about their predicted values has been reduced 60% by the use of the least squares equation $\hat{y}$, instead of $\bar{y}$, to predict y.

EXAMPLE 11.6

Obtaining the Value of r^2—Sales Revenue Model

Problem Calculate the coefficient of determination for the advertising-sales example. The data are repeated in Table 11.4 for convenience. Interpret the result.

Table 11.4	Advertising-Sales Data
Advertising Expenditure, x ($100s)	Sales Revenue, y ($1,000s)
1	1
2	1
3	2
4	2
5	4

.ıl *Data Set:* ADSALE

Solution From previous calculations,

$$SS_{yy} = 6 \quad \text{and} \quad SSE = \sum (y - \hat{y})^2 = 1.10$$

Then, from the definition, the coefficient of determination is given by

$$r^2 = \frac{SS_{yy} - SSE}{SS_{yy}} = \frac{6.0 - 1.1}{6.0} = \frac{4.9}{6.0} = .82$$

Another way to compute r^2 is to recall (Section 11.2) that $r = .904$. Then we have $r^2 = (.904)^2 = .82$. A third way to obtain r^2 is from a computer printout. This value is highlighted on the SPSS printout reproduced in Figure 11.19. Our interpretation is as follows: We know that using advertising expenditure, x, to predict y with the least squares line

$$\hat{y} = -.1 + .7x$$

Model Summary

Model	R	R Square	Adjusted R Square	Std. Error of the Estimate
1	.904[a]	.817	.756	.606

a. Predictors: (Constant), ADVEXP_X

Figure 11.19

Portion of SPSS printout for advertising-sales regression

accounts for 82% of the total sum of squares of deviations of the five sample y-values about their mean. Or, stated another way, 82% of the sample variation in sales revenue (y) can be "explained" by using advertising expenditure (x) in a straight-line model.

● Now Work Exercise 11.70a

Practical Interpretation of the Coefficient of Determination, r^2

About $100(r^2)\%$ of the sample variation in y (measured by the total sum of squares of deviations of the sample y-values about their mean $\bar{y}$) can be explained by (or attributed to) using x to predict y in the straight-line model.

STATISTICS IN ACTION

REVISITED

Using the Coefficient of Correlation and the Coefficient of Determination

In the previous *Statistics in Action Revisited* (p. 667), we discovered that cumulative 6-month advertising expenditures constituted a statistically useful linear predictor of number of new PI cases but not a useful linear predictor of number of new WC cases. Both the coefficients of correlation and determination (highlighted on the Minitab printouts in Figures SIA11.4 and SIA11.5) also support this conclusion.

```
Regression Analysis: NEWPI versus ADVEXP6

Analysis of Variance

Source      DF  Adj SS   Adj MS  F-Value  P-Value
Regression   1    1530  1529.52    16.34    0.000
  ADVEXP6    1    1530  1529.52    16.34    0.000
Error       40    3744    93.61
Total       41    5274

Model Summary

     S   R-sq  R-sq(adj)  R-sq(pred)
9.67521  29.00%    27.23%      20.37%

Coefficients

Term      Coef  SE Coef  T-Value  P-Value   VIF
Constant  7.77     3.38     2.29    0.027
ADVEXP6 0.1129   0.0279     4.04    0.000  1.00

Regression Equation

NEWPI = 7.77 + 0.1129 ADVEXP6
```

Figure SIA11.4

Minitab printout with coefficients of correlation and determination for y = number of new PI cases

Correlation: NEWPI, ADVEXP6

```
Pearson correlation of NEWPI and ADVEXP6 = 0.539
P-Value = 0.000
```

Regression Analysis: NEWWC versus ADVEXP6

```
Analysis of Variance

Source      DF   Adj SS  Adj MS  F-Value  P-Value
Regression   1    11.58   11.58    0.13    0.725
  ADVEXP6    1    11.58   11.58    0.13    0.725
Error       40  3704.06   92.60
Total       41  3715.64

Model Summary

     S   R-sq  R-sq(adj)  R-sq(pred)
9.62296  0.31%      0.00%       0.00%

Coefficients

Term        Coef  SE Coef  T-Value  P-Value   VIF
Constant   24.57     3.37     7.30    0.000
ADVEXP6   0.0098   0.0278     0.35    0.725  1.00

Regression Equation

NEWWC = 24.57 + 0.0098 ADVEXP6
```

Figure SIA11.5

Minitab printout with coefficients of correlation and determination for y = number of new WC cases

Correlation: NEWWC, ADVEXP6

```
Pearson correlation of NEWWC and ADVEXP6 = 0.056
P-Value = 0.725
```

For y = number of new PI cases, the correlation coefficient value of $r = .539$ is statistically significantly different from 0 and indicates a moderate positive linear relationship between the variables. The coefficient of determination, $r^2 = .29$, implies that almost 30% of the sample variation in number of new PI cases can be explained by using advertising expenditure (x) in the straight-line model. In contrast, for y = number of new WC cases, $r = .056$ is not statistically different from 0 and $r^2 = .003$ implies that only 0.3% of the sample variation in number of new WC cases can be explained by using advertising expenditure (x) in the straight-line model.

Exercises 11.64–11.81

Learning the Mechanics

11.64 Explain what each of the following sample correlation coefficients tells you about the relationship between the x- and y-values in the sample:
- **a.** $r = 1$
- **b.** $r = -1$
- **c.** $r = 0$
- **d.** $r = -.90$
- **e.** $r = .10$
- **f.** $r = -.88$

11.65 Answer the following questions based on the results of a simple regression analysis for the variables x and y.
- **a.** Determine the regression equation model if the slope = .5 and y-intercept = 1.
- **b.** Identify the direction of the regression model in part **a.**
- **c.** Interpret the coefficient of correlation $r = .9608$.
- **d.** Determine and interpret the coefficient of determination.
- **e.** Justify if there is any relationship between x and y at 1% significance level if the p-value for the regression is .000147.

11.66 Construct a scatterplot for each data set. Then calculate r and r^2 for each data set. Interpret their values.

a.

x	-2	-1	0	1	2
y	-2	1	2	5	6

b.

x	-2	-1	0	1	2
y	6	5	3	2	0

c.

x	1	2	2	3	3	3	4
y	2	1	3	1	2	3	2

d.

x	0	1	3	5	6
y	0	1	2	1	0

11.67 Calculate r^2 for the least squares line in each of the following exercises. Interpret their values.
- **a.** Exercise 11.14
- **b.** Exercise 11.17

📊 Applet Exercise 11.2

Use the applet *Correlation by Eye* to explore the relationship between the pattern of data in a scatterplot and the corresponding correlation coefficient.

- **a.** Run the applet several times. Each time, guess the value of the correlation coefficient. Then click *Show r* to see the actual correlation coefficient. How close is your value to the actual value of r? Click *New data* to reset the applet.
- **b.** Click the trash can to clear the graph. Use the mouse to place five points on the scatterplot that are approximately in a straight line. Then guess the value of the correlation coefficient. Click *Show r* to see the actual correlation coefficient. How close were you this time?
- **c.** Continue to clear the graph and plot sets of five points with different patterns among the points. Guess the value of r. How close do you come to the actual value of r each time?
- **d.** Based on your experiences with the applet, explain why we need to use more reliable methods of finding the correlation coefficient than just "eyeing" it.

Applying the Concepts—Basic

11.68 In business, do nice guys finish first or last? Refer to the *Nature* (March 20, 2008) study of the use of punishment in cooperation games, Exercise 11.18 (p. 653). Recall that college students repeatedly played a version of the game "prisoner's dilemma," and the researchers recorded the average payoff and the number of times cooperation, defection, and punishment were used for each player.

a. A test of no correlation between cooperation use (x) and average payoff (y) yielded a p-value of .33. Interpret this result.

b. A test of no correlation between defection use (x) and average payoff (y) yielded a p-value of .66. Interpret this result.

c. A test of no correlation between punishment use (x) and average payoff (y) yielded a p-value of .001. Interpret this result.

11.69 Going for it on fourth-down in the NFL. Each week coaches in the National Football League (NFL) face a decision during the game. On fourth-down, should the team punt the ball or go for a first-down? To aid in the decision-making process, statisticians developed a regression model for predicting the number of points scored (y) by a team that has a first-down with a given number of yards (x) from the opposing goal line (*Chance*, Winter 2009). One of the models fit to data collected on five NFL teams from a recent season was the simple linear regression model, $E(y) = \beta_0 + \beta_1 x$. The regression yielded the following results: $\hat{y} = 4.42 - 048x, r^2 = .18$.

a. Give a practical interpretation of the coefficient of determination, r^2.

b. Compute the value of the coefficient of correlation, r, from the value of r^2. Is the value of r positive or negative? Why?

11.70 Lobster fishing study. Refer to the *Bulletin of Marine Science* (April 2010) study of teams of fishermen fishing for the red spiny lobster in Baja California Sur, Mexico, Exercise 11.50 (p. 669). Recall that simple linear regression was used to model y = total catch of lobsters (in kilograms) during the season as a function of x = average

Correlation matrix (Pearson):

Variables	CATCH	SEARCHFREQ
CATCH	1	**-0.7347**
SEARCHFREQ	**-0.7347**	1

Values in bold are different from 0 with a significance level alpha=0.05

p-values:

Variables	CATCH	SEARCHFREQ
CATCH	0	**0.0018**
SEARCHFREQ	**0.0018**	0

Values in bold are different from 0 with a significance level alpha=0.05

Coefficients of determination (R²):

Variables	CATCH	SEARCHFREQ
CATCH	1	0.5397
SEARCHFREQ	0.5397	1

XLSTAT output for Exercise 11.70

percentage of traps allocated per day to exploring areas of unknown catch (called *search frequency*). Another portion of the XLSTAT printout of the analysis is shown at the bottom of the previous column.

NW a. Locate and interpret the coefficient of determination, r^2, on the printout.

b. Locate and interpret the coefficient of correlation, r, on the printout.

c. In Exercise 11.50, you conducted a test to determine that total catch (y) is negatively linearly related to search frequency (x). Which of the two statistics, r or r^2, can be used to partially support this inference? Explain.

11.71 RateMyProfessors.com. A popular Web site among college students is RateMyProfessors.com (RMP). RMP allows students to post quantitative ratings of their instructors. In *Practical Assessment, Research & Evaluation* (May 2007), researchers investigated whether instructor ratings posted on RMP are correlated with the formal in-class student evaluations of teaching (SET) that all universities are required to administer at the end of the semester. Data collected for $n = 426$ University of Maine instructors yielded a correlation between RMP and SET ratings of .68.

a. Give the equation of a linear model relating SET rating (y) to RMP rating (x).

b. Give a practical interpretation of the value $r = .68$.

c. Is the estimated slope of the line, part **a**, positive or negative? Explain.

d. A test of the null hypothesis $H_0: \rho = 0$ yielded a p-value of .001. Interpret this result.

e. Compute the coefficient of determination, r^2, for the regression analysis. Interpret the result.

11.72 Last name and acquisition timing. Refer to the *Journal of Consumer Research* (August 2011) study of the speed with which consumers decide to purchase a product, Exercise 8.13 (p. 466). Recall that the researchers theorized that consumers with last names that begin with letters later in the alphabet would tend to acquire items faster than those whose last names begin with letters earlier in the alphabet (i.e., the *last name effect*). Each in a sample of 50 MBA students was offered free tickets to an event for which there was a limited supply of tickets. The first letter of the last name of those who responded to an e-mail offer in time to receive the tickets was noted and given a numerical value (e.g., "A" = 1, "B" = 2, etc.). Each student's response time (measured in minutes) was also recorded.

a. The researchers computed the correlation between the two variables as $r = -.271$. Interpret this result.

b. The observed significance level for testing for a negative correlation in the population was reported as p-value = .018. Interpret this result for $\alpha = .05$.

c. Does this analysis support the researchers' *last name effect* theory? Explain.

11.73 Women in top management. An empirical analysis of women in upper management positions at U.S. firms was published in the *Journal of Organizational Culture, Communications and Conflict* (July 2007). Monthly data ($n = 252$ months) were collected for several variables, including the number of females in managerial positions, the number of females with a college degree, and the number of female high school graduates with no college degree. Similar data were collected for males.

a. The correlation coefficient relating number of females in managerial positions and number of females with a college degree was reported as $r = .983$. Interpret this result.

b. The correlation coefficient relating number of females in managerial positions and number of female high school graduates with no college degree was reported as $r = .074$. Interpret this result.

c. The correlation coefficient relating number of males in managerial positions and number of males with a college degree was reported as $r = .722$. Interpret this result.

d. The correlation coefficient relating number of males in managerial positions and number of male high school graduates with no college degree was reported as $r = .528$. Interpret this result.

Applying the Concepts—Intermediate

11.74 Taste testing scales. Refer to the *Journal of Food Science* (February 2014) taste testing study, Exercise 9.58 (p. 565). Recall that a sample of 200 college students and staff used a scale ranging from -100 (for strongest imaginable dislike) to $+100$ (for strongest imaginable like) to rate their most favorite and least favorite food. This rating was labeled *perceived hedonic intensity*. In addition, each taster rated the sensory intensity of four different solutions: salt, sucrose, citric acid, and hydrochloride. The average of these four ratings was used by the researchers to quantify individual variation in taste intensity—called *perceived sensory intensity*. These data are saved in the file. The accompanying Minitab printout shows the correlation between perceived sensory intensity (PSI) and perceived hedonic intensity for both favorite (PHI-F) and least favorite (PHI-L) foods.

a. Give practical interpretations of the values of r shown on the printout.

b. According to the researchers, "the palatability of the favorite and least favorite foods varies depending on the perceived intensity of taste: Those who experience the greatest taste intensity (that is, supertasters) tend to experience more extreme food likes and dislikes." Do you agree? Explain.

Results for: TASTE.mtw (Group = gLMS)

Correlation: PSI, PHI-F

```
Pearson correlation of PSI and PHI-F = 0.401
P-Value = 0.000
```

Correlation: PSI, PHI-L

```
Pearson correlation of PSI and PHI-L = -0.375
P-Value = 0.000
```

11.75 Software millionaires and birthdays. Refer to Exercise 11.23 (p. 655) and the study of the seemingly disproportionate number of software millionaires born around the year 1955.

a. Find the coefficient of determination for the simple linear regression model relating number (y) of software millionaire birthdays in a decade to total number (x) of U.S. births. Interpret the result.

b. Find the coefficient of determination for the simple linear regression model relating number (y) of software millionaire birthdays in a decade to number (x) of CEO birthdays. Interpret the result.

c. The consulting statistician argued that the software industry appears to be no different from any other industry with respect to producing millionaires in a decade. Do you agree? Explain.

11.76 Child labor in diamond mines. The role of child laborers on Africa's colonial-era diamond mines was the subject of research published in the *Journal of Family History* (Vol. 35, 2010). One particular mining company lured children to the mines by offering incentives for adult male laborers to relocate their families close to the diamond mine. The success of the incentive program was examined by determining the annual *accompaniment rate*, i.e., the percentage of wives (or sons, or daughters) who accompanied their husbands (or fathers) in relocating to the mine. Information from the journal article was used to simulate accompaniment rates for nine consecutive years. Those rates are shown in the table below.

a. Find the correlation coefficient relating the accompaniment rates for wives and sons. Interpret this value.

b. Find the correlation coefficient relating the accompaniment rates for wives and daughters. Interpret this value.

c. Find the correlation coefficient relating the accompaniment rates for sons and daughters. Interpret this value.

Year	Wives	Sons	Daughters
1	28.7	2.4	14.3
2	41.6	1.7	13.1
3	37.2	0.5	10
4	39.3	3.7	19.6
5	39.5	5.6	19.4
6	39.9	11.2	21.7
7	40.2	12.1	15.3
8	31.3	8.8	15.1
9	25.3	7.6	19.6

Source: Based on T. Cleveland, "Minors in Name Only: Child Laborers on the Diamond Mines of the *Companhia de Diamantes de Angola* (Diamang), 1917–1975," *Journal of Family History*, Vol. 35, No. 1, 2010 (Table 1).

11.77 Sweetness of orange juice. Refer to the simple linear regression relating y = sweetness index of an orange juice sample with x = amount of water-soluble pectin, Exercise 11.26 (p. 656) and the data saved in the file. Find and interpret the coefficient of determination, r^2, and the coefficient of correlation, r.

11.78 Performance ratings of government agencies. The U.S. Office of Management and Budget (OMB) requires government agencies to produce annual performance and accounting reports (PARS) each year. Refer to *The Public Manager* (Summer 2008) listing of PARS evaluation scores for 24 government agencies, Exercise 2.131 (p. 132). Recall that evaluation scores ranged from 12 (lowest) to 60 (highest). The PARS evaluation scores for two consecutive years are reproduced in the table on p. 681.

a. Calculate and interpret the coefficient of correlation between the PARS scores in year 1 and year 2.

b. Is there sufficient evidence of a positive linear relationship between year 2 PARS score (y) and year 1 PARS score (x)? Test using $\alpha = .05$.

Agency	Year 1	Year 2
Transportation	55	53
Labor	53	51
Veterans	51	51
NRC	39	34
Commerce	37	36
HHS	37	35
DHS	37	30
Justice	35	37
Treasury	35	35
GSA	34	40
Agriculture	33	35
EPA	33	36
Social Security	33	33
USAID	32	42
Education	32	36
Interior	32	31
NASA	32	32
Energy	31	34
HUD	31	30
NSF	31	31
State	31	50
OPM	27	28
SBA	22	31
Defense	17	32

Source: J. Ellig and H. Wray, "Measuring Performance Reporting Quality," *The Public Manager*, Vol. 37, No. 2, Summer 2008 (p. 66). Copyright © 2008 by Jerry Ellig. Reprinted with permission.

11.79 Evaluation of an imputation method for missing data. When analyzing *big data* (large data sets with many variables), business researchers often encounter the problem of missing data (e.g., non-response). Typically, an imputation method will be used to substitute in reasonable values (e.g., the mean of the variable) for the missing data. An imputation method that uses "nearest neighbors" as substitutes for the missing data was evaluated in *Data & Knowledge Engineering* (March 2013). Two quantitative assessment measures of the imputation algorithm are normalized root mean square error (NRMSE) and classification bias. The researchers applied the imputation method to a sample of 3,600 data sets with missing values and determined the NRMSE and classification bias for each data set. The correlation coefficient between the two variables was reported as $r = .2838$.

a. Conduct a test to determine if the true population correlation coefficient relating NRMSE and bias is positive. Interpret this result practically.

b. A scatterplot for the data (extracted from the journal article) is shown below. Based on the graph, would you recommend using NRMSE as a linear predictor of bias? Explain why your answer does not contradict the result in part **a**.

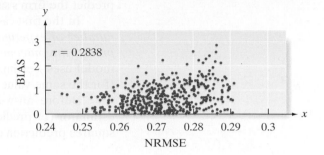

11.80 Spreading rate of spilled liquid. Refer to the *Chemical Engineering Progress* (January 2005) study of the rate at which a spilled volatile liquid will spread across a surface, Exercise 11.30 (p. 658) and the data saved in the file. Find and interpret r and r^2 for the simple linear regression y = mass of the spill and x = elapsed time of the spill.

Applying the Concepts—Advanced

11.81 Salary linked to height. Are short people short-changed when it comes to salary? According to researchers, tall people tend to earn more money over their careers than short people (*Journal of Applied Psychology*, June 2004). Using data collected from participants in the National Longitudinal Surveys, the researchers computed the correlation between average earnings (in dollars) and height (in inches) for several occupations. The results are given in the table. Are average earnings positively related to height? For all occupations? If so, can you conclude that a person taller than you will earn a higher salary? Explain.

Occupation	Correlation, r	Sample Size, n
Sales	.41	117
Managers	.35	455
Blue Collar	.32	349
Service Workers	.31	265
Professional/Technical	.30	453
Clerical	.25	358
Crafts/Forepersons	.24	250

Source: Copyright © 2004 by American Psychological Association. Reproduced with permission. "The Effect of Physical Height on Workplace Success and Income: Preliminary Test of a Theoretical Model" by Timothy A. Judge and Daniel M. Cable in *Journal of Applied Psychology*, Vol. 89, No. 3. The use of APA information does not imply endorsement by APA.

11.6 Using the Model for Estimation and Prediction

If we are satisfied that a useful model has been found to describe the relationship between x and y, we are ready for step 5 in our regression modeling procedure: using the model for estimation and prediction.

The most common uses of a probabilistic model for making inferences can be divided into two categories. The first is using the model to estimate the mean value of y, E(y), *for a specific value of* x. For our advertising-sales example, we may want to estimate the mean sales revenue for *all* months during which $400 ($x = 4$) is expended on advertising.

The second use of the model entails predicting a new individual y-value for a given x. That is, if we decide to expend $400 in advertising next month, we may want to predict the firm's sales revenue for that month.

In the first case, we are attempting to *estimate the mean value of* y *for a very large number of experimental units at the given x-value.* In the second case, we are trying to *predict the outcome for a single experimental unit at the given x-value.* Which of these model uses—estimating the mean value of y or predicting an individual new value of y (for the same value of x)—can be accomplished with the greater accuracy?

Before answering this question, we first consider the problem of choosing an estimator (or predictor) of the mean (or a new individual) y-value. We will use the least squares prediction equation

$$\hat{y} = \hat{\beta}_0 + \hat{\beta}_1 x$$

both to estimate the mean value of y and to predict a specific new value of y for a given value of x. For our example, we found

$$\hat{y} = -.1 + .7x$$

so that the estimated mean sales revenue for all months when $x = 4$ (advertising is $400) is

$$\hat{y} = -.1 + .7(4) = 2.7$$

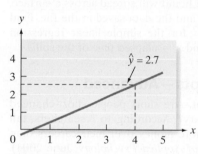

Figure 11.20

Estimated mean value and predicted individual value of sales revenue y for $x = 4$

or $2,700. (Recall that the units of y are thousands of dollars.) The same value is used to predict a new y-value when $x = 4$—that is, both the estimated mean and the predicted value of y are $\hat{y} = 2.7$ when $x = 4$, as shown in Figure 11.20.

The difference between these two model uses lies in the relative accuracy of the estimate and the prediction. These accuracies are best measured by using the sampling errors of the least squares line when it is used as an estimator and as a predictor, respectively. These errors are reflected in the standard deviations given in the next box.

Sampling Errors for the Estimator of the Mean of y and the Predictor of an Individual New Value of y

1. The *standard deviation* of the sampling distribution of the estimator $\hat{y}$ of the *mean value of y* at a specific value of x, say x_p, is

$$\sigma_{\hat{y}} = \sigma\sqrt{\frac{1}{n} + \frac{(x_\mathrm{p} - \bar{x})^2}{SS_{xx}}}$$

where σ is the standard deviation of the random error ε. We refer to $\sigma_{\hat{y}}$ as the **standard error of $\hat{y}$.**

2. The *standard deviation* of the prediction error for the predictor $\hat{y}$ of an individual *new y-value* at a specific value of x is

$$\sigma_{(y-\hat{y})} = \sigma\sqrt{1 + \frac{1}{n} + \frac{(x_\mathrm{p} - \bar{x})^2}{SS_{xx}}}$$

where σ is the standard deviation of the random error ε. We refer to $\sigma_{(y-\hat{y})}$ as the **standard error of the prediction.**

The true value of σ is rarely known, so we estimate σ by s and calculate the estimation and prediction intervals as shown in the next two boxes.

> **A $100(1 - \alpha)$% Confidence Interval for the Mean Value of y at $x = x_p$**
>
> $$\hat{y} \pm t_{\alpha/2} \text{ (Estimated standard error of } \hat{y})$$
>
> or
>
> $$\hat{y} \pm t_{\alpha/2} s \sqrt{\frac{1}{n} + \frac{(x_p - \bar{x})^2}{SS_{xx}}}$$
>
> where $t_{\alpha/2}$ is based on $(n - 2)$ degrees of freedom.

> **A $100(1 - \alpha)$% Prediction Interval* for an Individual New Value of y at $x = x_p$**
>
> $$\hat{y} \pm t_{\alpha/2} \text{ (Estimated standard error of prediction)}$$
>
> or
>
> $$\hat{y} \pm t_{\alpha/2} s \sqrt{1 + \frac{1}{n} + \frac{(x_p - \bar{x})^2}{SS_{xx}}}$$
>
> where $t_{\alpha/2}$ is based on $(n - 2)$ degrees of freedom.

EXAMPLE 11.7

Estimating the Mean of y—Sales Revenue Model

Problem Refer to the sales-appraisal simple linear regression in previous examples. Find a 95% confidence interval for the mean monthly sales when the appliance store spends $400 on advertising.

Solution Here, we desire a confidence interval for the mean, $E(y)$, for *all* months when the store spends $400 on advertising. For a $400 advertising expenditure, $x = 4$, and the confidence interval for the mean value of y is

$$\hat{y} \pm t_{\alpha/2} s \sqrt{\frac{1}{n} + \frac{(x_p - \bar{x})^2}{SS_{xx}}} = \hat{y} \pm t_{.025} s \sqrt{\frac{1}{5} + \frac{(4 - \bar{x})^2}{SS_{xx}}}$$

where $t_{.025}$ is based on $n - 2 = 5 - 2 = 3$ degrees of freedom. Recall that $\hat{y} = 2.7$, $s = .61, \bar{x} = 3$, and $SS_{xx} = 10$. From Table III in Appendix D, $t_{.025} = 3.182$. Thus, we have

$$2.7 \pm (3.182)(.61) \sqrt{\frac{1}{5} + \frac{(4 - 3)^2}{10}} = 2.7 \pm (3.182)(.61)(.55)$$

$$= 2.7 \pm (3.182)(.34)$$

$$= 2.7 \pm 1.1 = (1.6, 3.8)$$

Therefore, when the store spends $400 a month on advertising, we are 95% confident that the mean sales revenue for these months is between $1,600 and $3,800.

Look Back Note that we used a small amount of data (small in size) for purposes of illustration in fitting the least squares line. The interval would probably be narrower if more information had been obtained from a larger sample.

● **Now Work Exercise 11.82a–d**

---

*The term *prediction interval* is used when the interval formed is intended to enclose the value of a random variable. The term *confidence interval* is reserved for the estimation of population parameters (such as the mean).

EXAMPLE 11.8

Predicting an Individual value of y—Sales Revenue Model

Problem Refer, again, to the sales-appraisal regression. Predict the monthly sales for next month if $400 is spent on advertising. Use a 95% prediction interval.

Solution Here, our focus is on a *single* month when the store spends $400 on advertising. To predict the sales for a particular month for which $x_p = 4$, we calculate the 95% prediction interval as

$$\hat{y} \pm t_{\alpha/2}s\sqrt{1 + \frac{1}{n} + \frac{(x_p - \bar{x})^2}{SS_{xx}}} = 2.7 \pm (3.182)(.61)\sqrt{1 + \frac{1}{5} + \frac{(4-3)^2}{10}}$$

$$= 2.7 \pm (3.182)(.61)(1.14)$$

$$= 2.7 \pm (3.182)(.70)$$

$$= 2.7 \pm 2.2 = (.5, 4.9)$$

Therefore, we predict with 95% confidence that the sales revenue next month (a month in which we spend $400 in advertising) will fall in the interval from $500 to $4,900.

Look Back Like the confidence interval for the mean value of y, the prediction interval for y is quite large. This is because we have chosen a simple example (only five data points) to fit the least squares line. The width of the prediction interval could be reduced by using a larger number of data points.

• **Now Work Exercise 11.82e**

Both the confidence interval for $E(y)$ and prediction interval for y can be obtained using a statistical software package. Figure 11.21 is a Minitab printout showing the confidence interval and prediction interval for the data in the advertising-sales example. The 95% confidence interval for $E(y)$ when $x = 4$, highlighted under "95% CI" in Figure 11.21, is (1.645, 3.755). The 95% prediction interval for y when $x = 4$, highlighted in Figure 11.21 under "95% PI," is (.503, 4.897). Both intervals agree with the ones computed in Examples 11.6–11.7.

Figure 11.21

Minitab printout giving 95% confidence interval for $E(y)$ and 95% prediction interval for y

Prediction for SALES_Y

```
Regression Equation

SALES_Y = -0.100 + 0.700 ADVEXP_X


Variable  Setting
ADVEXP_X     4


Fit    SE Fit       95% CI                95% PI
2.7    0.331662  (1.64450, 3.75550)  (0.502806, 4.89719)
```

Note that the prediction interval for an individual new value of y is *always* wider than the corresponding confidence interval for the mean value of y. To see this, consider the following. The error in estimating the mean value of y, $E(y)$, for a given value of x, say x_p, is the distance between the least squares line and the true line of means, $E(y) = \beta_0 + \beta_1 x$. This error, $[\hat{y} - E(y)]$, is shown in Figure 11.22. In contrast, *the error* $(y_p - \hat{y})$ *in predicting some future value of* y *is the sum of two errors*—the error of estimating the mean of y, $E(y)$, plus the random error that is a component of the value of y to be predicted (see Figure 11.23). Consequently, the error of predicting a particular value of y will be larger than the error of estimating the mean value of y for a particular value of x. Note from their formulas that both the error of estimation and the error of prediction take their smallest values when $x_p = \bar{x}$. The farther x_p lies from $\bar{x}$, the larger will be the errors of estimation and prediction. You can see why this is true by noting the deviations for different values of x_p between the line of means $E(y) = \beta_0 + \beta_1 x$ and the predicted line of means $\hat{y} = \hat{\beta}_0 + \hat{\beta}_1 x$ shown in Figure 11.23. The deviation is larger at the extremes of the interval where the largest and smallest values of x in the data set occur.

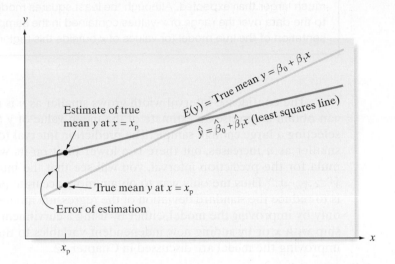

Figure 11.22

Error of estimating the mean value of y for a given value of x

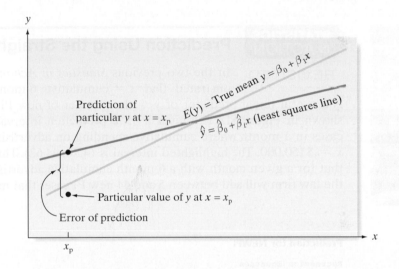

Figure 11.23

Error of predicting a future value of y for a given value of x

Both the confidence intervals for mean values and the prediction intervals for new values are depicted over the entire range of the regression line in Figure 11.24. You can see that the confidence interval is always narrower than the prediction interval, and they are both narrowest at the mean $\bar{x}$, increasing steadily as the distance $|x - \bar{x}|$ increases. In fact, when x is selected far enough away from $\bar{x}$ so that it falls outside the range of the sample data, it is dangerous to make any inferences about $E(y)$ or y.

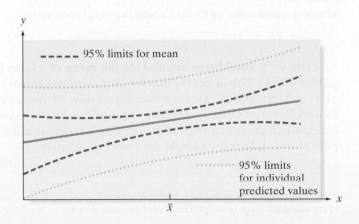

Figure 11.24

Confidence intervals for mean values and prediction intervals for new values

> **!** **CAUTION** Using the least squares prediction equation to estimate the mean value of y or to predict a particular value of y for values of x that fall *outside the range* of the values of x contained in your sample data may lead to errors of estimation or prediction that are much larger than expected. Although the least squares model may provide a very good fit to the data over the range of x-values contained in the sample, it could give a poor representation of the true model for values of x outside this region.

The confidence interval width grows smaller as n is increased; thus, in theory, you can obtain as precise an estimate of the mean value of y as desired (at any given x) by selecting a large enough sample. The prediction interval for a new value of y also grows smaller as n increases, but there is a lower limit on its width. If you examine the formula for the prediction interval, you will see that the interval can get no smaller than $\hat{y} \pm z_{\alpha/2}\sigma$.* Thus, the only way to obtain more accurate predictions for new values of y is to reduce the standard deviation of the regression model, σ. This can be accomplished only by improving the model, either by using a curvilinear (rather than linear) relationship with x or by adding new independent variables to the model, or both. Methods of improving the model are discussed in Chapter 12.

STATISTICS IN ACTION REVISITED
Prediction Using the Straight-Line Model

In the two previous *Statistics in Action Revisited* sections, we demonstrated that $x =$ cumulative 6-month advertising expenditures is a useful linear predictor of $y =$ the number of new PI cases. The Minitab printout shown in Figure SIA11.6 gives a 95% prediction interval for the number of new PI cases in a month where cumulative spending on advertising over the past 6 months is $x = \$150,000$. The highlighted interval is (4.78, 44.62). Thus, we can be 95% confident that for a given month with a 6-month cumulative advertising expenditure of $\$150,000$, the law firm will add between 5 and 44 new PI cases that month.

Prediction for NEWPI

```
Regression Equation

NEWPI = 7.77 + 0.1129 ADVEXP6


Variable  Setting
ADVEXP6      150


   Fit   SE Fit       95% CI              95% PI
24.7011  1.88524  (20.8909, 28.5113)  (4.77905, 44.6232)
```

Figure SIA11.6

Minitab prediction interval for legal advertising straight-line model

The 95% **confidence interval for the mean of y** (also highlighted on the printout) is (20.89, 28.51). This indicates that for all months with cumulative spending on advertising of $x = \$150,000$, the average number of new PI cases each month will range between 21 and 28 cases. Of course, if these projections are to be useful for future planning, other economic factors that may affect the firm's business must be similar to those during the period over which the sample data were generated.

---

*The result follows from the facts that, for large n, $t_{\alpha/2} \approx z_{\alpha/2}$, $s \approx \sigma$, and the last two terms under the radical in the standard error of the predictor are approximately 0.

Learning the Mechanics

11.82 Consider the following pairs of measurements:

NW							
L11082	x	−2	0	2	4	6	8	10
	y	0	3	2	3	8	10	11

a. Construct a scatterplot for these data.
b. Find the least squares line and plot it on your scatterplot.
c. Find s^2 and s.
d. Find a 90% confidence interval for the mean value of y when x = 3. Plot the upper and lower bounds of the confidence interval on your scatterplot.
e. Find a 90% prediction interval for a new value of y when x = 3. Plot the upper and lower bounds of the prediction interval on your scatterplot.
f. Compare the widths of the intervals you constructed in parts **d** and **e**. Which is wider and why?

11.83 Consider the pairs of measurements shown in the table. For these data, $SS_{xx} = 38.9$, $SS_{yy} = 33.6$, $SS_{xy} = 32.8$, and $\hat{y} = -.414 + .843x$.

L11083

x	4	6	0	5	2	3	2	6	2	1
y	3	5	−1	4	3	2	0	4	1	1

a. Construct a scatterplot for these data.
b. Plot the least squares line on your scatterplot.
c. Use a 95% confidence interval to estimate the mean value of y when $x_p = 6$. Plot the upper and lower bounds of the interval on your scatterplot.
d. Repeat part **c** for $x_p = 3.2$ and $x_p = 0$.
e. Compare the widths of the three confidence intervals you constructed in parts **c** and **d** and explain why they differ.

11.84 Refer to Exercise 11.83.
a. Using no information about x, estimate and calculate a 95% confidence interval for the mean value of y. [*Hint:* Use the one-sample t methodology of Section 5.4.]
b. Plot the estimated mean value and the confidence interval as horizontal lines on your scatterplot.
c. Compare the confidence intervals you calculated in parts **c** and **d** of Exercise 11.77 with the one you calculated in part **a** of this exercise. Does x appear to contribute information about the mean value of y?
d. Check the answer you gave in part **c** with a statistical test of the null hypothesis $H_0: \beta_1 = 0$ against $H_a: \beta_1 \neq 0$. Use $\alpha = .05$.

11.85 In fitting a least squares line to n = 10 data points, the following quantities were computed:

$$SS_{xx} = 50 \quad \bar{x} = 12 \quad SS_{yy} = 458 \quad \bar{y} = 45 \quad SS_{xy} = 145 \quad s = 2.5$$

a. Determine $\hat{\beta}_1$ and $\hat{\beta}_0$.
b. Determine the least squares model.
c. Estimate the standard deviation of the sampling distribution of $\hat{y}$ at x = 18.
d. Estimate the standard deviation of the prediction error of $\hat{y}$ at x = 18.

e. Find a 95% confidence interval for the mean value of y when x = 18.
f. Find a 95% confidence interval for y when x = 18.

Applying the Concepts—Basic

11.86 **In business, do nice guys finish first or last?** Refer to the *Nature* (March 20, 2008) study of the use of punishment in cooperation games, Exercise 11.18 (p. 653). Recall that simple linear regression was used to model a player's average payoff (y) as a straight-line function of the number of times punishment was used (x) by the player.
a. If the researchers want to predict average payoff for a single player who used punishment 10 times, how should they proceed?
b. If the researchers want to predict the mean of the average payoffs for all players who used punishment 10 times, how should they proceed?

11.87 **Lobster fishing study.** Refer to the *Bulletin of Marine Science* (April 2010) study of teams of fishermen fishing for the red spiny lobster in Baja California Sur, Mexico, Exercise 11.20 (p. 654). Recall that simple linear regression was used to model y = total catch of lobsters (in kilograms) during the season as a function of x = average percentage of traps allocated per day to exploring areas of unknown catch (called *search frequency*). A portion of the Minitab printout giving a 95% confidence interval for E(y) and a 95% prediction interval for y when x = 25 is shown below.

Prediction for CATCH

```
Regression Equation

CATCH = 9878 - 163.6 SEARCHFREQ


Variable    Setting
SEARCHFREQ     25


  Fit    SE Fit        95% CI            95% PI
5787.77  464.961  (4783.28, 6792.26)  (2643.02, 8932.52)
```

a. Locate and interpret the 95% confidence interval for E(y).
b. Locate and interpret the 95% prediction interval for y.

11.88 **Forecasting movie revenues with Twitter.** Refer to the *IEEE International Conference on Web Intelligence and Intelligent Agent Technology* (2010) study of how social media (e.g., Twitter.com) may influence the products consumers buy, Exercise 11.27 (p. 657). Recall that opening weekend box-office revenue (in millions of dollars) and *tweet rate* (average number of tweets referring to the movie per hour) were collected for a sample of 23 recent movies. You fit a simple linear regression model, with y = revenue and x = tweet rate. The results are shown in the accompanying Excel-XLSTAT printout on the next page.
a. Evaluate the adequacy of the simple linear regression model. Do you recommend using the model for prediction purposes?
b. Find a 95% prediction interval for the revenue (y) of a movie with a tweet rate (x) of 250 tweets per hour. Give a practical interpretation of the interval.

XLSTAT Output for Exercise 11.88

Regression of variable Revenue (millions):

Goodness of fit statistics:

Observations	23.0000
Sum of weights	23.0000
DF	21.0000
R²	0.8242
Adjusted R²	0.8159
MSE	177.3295
RMSE	13.3165
DW	2.3487

Model parameters:

Source	Value	Standard error	t	Pr > |t|	Lower bound (95%)	Upper bound (95%)
Intercept	1.1502	3.6761	0.3129	0.7575	-6.4947	8.7950
TweetRate	0.0788	0.0079	9.9233	< 0.0001	0.0623	0.0953

Predictions for the new observations:

TweetRate	Pred(Revenue (millions))	Lower bound 95% (Mean)	Upper bound 95% (Mean)	Lower bound 95% (Observation)	Upper bound 95% (Observation)
250	20.8420	15.0004	26.6836	-7.4606	49.1446

11.89 Sweetness of orange juice. Refer to the simple linear regression of sweetness index y and amount of pectin x for $n = 24$ orange juice samples, Exercise 11.26 (p. 656). A 90% confidence interval for the mean sweetness index, $E(y)$, for each of the first 5 runs is shown on the SPSS spreadsheet below. Select an observation and interpret this interval.

RUN	SWEET	PECTIN	LOWER90M	UPPER90M
1	5.2	220	5.65	5.84
2	5.5	227	5.64	5.82
3	6.0	259	5.58	5.73
4	5.9	210	5.66	5.87
5	5.8	224	5.64	5.83

11.90 Public corruption and bad weather. Refer to the *Journal of Law and Economics* (Nov. 2008) study of the link between Federal Emergency Management Agency (FEMA) disaster relief and public corruption, Exercise 11.58 (p. 670). You determined that the p-value for testing the adequacy of the straight-line model relating a state's average annual number of public corruption convictions (y) to the state's average annual FEMA relief (x) was $p = .102$. Based on this result, would you recommend using the model to predict the number of public corruption convictions in a state with an annual FEMA relief of $x = 5$ thousand dollars? Explain.

Applying the Concepts—Intermediate

11.91 Software millionaires and birthdays. Refer to Exercise 11.40 (p. 662) and the study of software millionaires and their birthdays. Recall that simple linear regression was used to model number (y) of software millionaire birthdays in a decade as a straight-line function of number (x) of CEO birthdays.
  a. Consider a future decade where the number of CEO birthdays (in a random sample of 70 companies) is 25. Find a 95% prediction interval for the number of

software millionaire birthdays in this decade. Interpret the result.
  b. Consider another future decade where the number of CEO birthdays (in a random sample of 70 companies) is 10. Will the 95% prediction interval for the number of software millionaire birthdays in this decade be narrower or wider than the interval, part **b**? Explain.

11.92 Ranking driving performance of professional golfers. Refer to *The Sport Journal* (Winter 2007) study of a new method for ranking the total driving performance of golfers on the PGA tour, Exercise 11.25 (p. 656). You fit a straight-line model relating driving accuracy (y) to driving distance (x) to the data saved in the file. Of interest is predicting y and estimating $E(y)$ when $x = 300$ yards.
  a. Find and interpret a 95% prediction interval for y.
  b. Find and interpret a 95% confidence interval for $E(y)$.
  c. If you are interested in knowing the average driving accuracy of all PGA golfers who have a driving distance of 300 yards, which of the intervals is relevant? Explain.

11.93 Spreading rate of spilled liquid. Refer to the *Chemical Engineering Progress* (January 2005) study of the rate at which a spilled volatile liquid will spread across a surface, Exercise 11.30 (p. 658). Recall that simple linear regression was used to model y = mass of the spill as a function of x = elapsed time of the spill.
  a. Find a 99% confidence interval for the mean mass of all spills with an elapsed time of 15 minutes. Interpret the result.
  b. Find a 99% prediction interval for the mass of a single spill with an elapsed time of 15 minutes. Interpret the result.
  c. Compare the intervals, parts **a** and **b**. Which interval is wider? Will this always be the case? Explain.

11.94 Removing nitrogen from toxic wastewater. Highly toxic wastewater is produced during the manufacturing of dry-spun acrylic fiber. One way to lessen toxicity is to remove the nitrogen from the wastewater. A group of environmental engineers investigated a promising method—called anaerobic ammonium oxidation—for nitrogen removal and reported the results in the *Chemical Engineering Journal* (April 2013). A sample of 120 specimens of toxic wastewater was collected and each specimen was treated with the nitrogen removal method. The amount of nitrogen removed (measured in milligrams per liter) was determined, as well as the amount of ammonium (milligrams per liter) used in the removal process. These data (simulated from information provided in the journal article) are saved in the file. The data for the first 5 specimens are shown below. Consider a simple linear regression analysis, where y = amount of nitrogen removed and x = amount of ammonium used.

a. Assess, statistically, the adequacy of the fit of the linear model. Do you recommend using the model for predicting nitrogen amount?

b. Find a 95% prediction interval for nitrogen amount when amount of ammonium used is 100 milligrams per liter. Practically interpret the result.

c. Will a 95% confidence interval for the mean nitrogen amount when amount of ammonium used is 100 milligrams per liter be wider or narrower than the interval, part **b**? Verify your answer by finding the 95% confidence interval for the mean.

d. Will a 90% confidence interval for the mean nitrogen amount when amount of ammonium used is 100 milligrams per liter be wider or narrower than the interval, part **c**? Verify your answer by finding the 90% confidence interval for the mean.

(first 5 observations of 120 shown)

Nitrogen	Ammonium
18.87	67.40
17.01	12.49
23.88	61.96
10.45	15.63
36.03	83.66

11.95 Predicting quit rates in manufacturing. The reasons given by workers for quitting their jobs generally fall into one of two categories: (1) worker quits to seek or take a different job, or (2) worker quits to withdraw from the labor force. Economic theory suggests that wages and quit rates are related. The next table lists quit rates (quits per 100 employees) and the average hourly wage in a sample of 15 manufacturing industries. Consider the simple linear regression of quit rate y on average wage x.

a. Do the data present sufficient evidence to conclude that average hourly wage rate contributes useful information for the prediction of quit rates? What does your model suggest about the relationship between quit rates and wages?

b. Find a 95% prediction interval for the quit rate in an industry with an average hourly wage of $9.00. Interpret the result.

c. Find a 95% confidence interval for the mean quit rate for industries with an average hourly wage of $9.00. Interpret this result.

Industry	Quit Rate, y	Average Wage, x
1	1.4	$ 8.20
2	.7	10.35
3	2.6	6.18
4	3.4	5.37
5	1.7	9.94
6	1.7	9.11
7	1.0	10.59
8	.5	13.29
9	2.0	7.99
10	3.8	5.54
11	2.3	7.50
12	1.9	6.43
13	1.4	8.83
14	1.8	10.93
15	2.0	8.80

Applying the Concepts—Advanced

11.96 Life tests of cutting tools. Refer to the data saved in the file, Exercise 11.44 (p. 663).

a. Use a 90% confidence interval to estimate the mean useful life of a brand A cutting tool when the cutting speed is 45 meters per minute. Repeat for brand B. Compare the widths of the two intervals and comment on the reasons for any difference.

b. Use a 90% prediction interval to predict the useful life of a brand A cutting tool when the cutting speed is 45 meters per minute. Repeat for brand B. Compare the widths of the two intervals with each other and with the two intervals you calculated in part **a**. Comment on the reasons for any differences.

c. Note that the estimation and prediction you performed in parts **a** and **b** were for a value of x that was not included in the original sample—that is, the value $x = 45$ was not part of the sample. However, the value is within the range of x-values in the sample, so the regression model spans the x-value for which the estimation and prediction were made. In such situations, estimation and prediction represent *interpolations*. Suppose you were asked to predict the useful life of a brand A cutting tool for a cutting speed of $x = 100$ meters per minute. Because the given value of x is outside the range of the sample x-values, the prediction is an example of **extrapolation**. Predict the useful life of a brand A cutting tool that is operated at 100 meters per minute and construct a 95% prediction interval for the actual useful life of the tool. What additional assumption do you have to make in order to ensure the validity of an extrapolation?

11.7 A Complete Example

In the preceding sections, we have presented the basic elements necessary to fit and use a straight-line regression model. In this section, we will assemble these elements by applying them in an example with the aid of a computer.

Suppose a fire insurance company wants to relate the amount of fire damage in major residential fires to the distance between the burning house and the nearest fire station. The study is to be conducted in a large suburb of a major city; a sample of 15 recent fires in this suburb is selected. The amount of damage, y, and the distance between the fire and the nearest fire station, x, are recorded for each fire. The results are shown in Table 11.5 and saved in the **RFIRES** file.

Table 11.5	Fire Damage Data
Distance from Fire Station, x (miles)	Fire Damage, y (thousands of dollars)
3.4	26.2
1.8	17.8
4.6	31.3
2.3	23.1
3.1	27.5
5.5	36.0
.7	14.1
3.0	22.3
2.6	19.6
4.3	31.3
2.1	24.0
1.1	17.3
6.1	43.2
4.8	36.4
3.8	26.1

 Data Set: RFIRES

Step 1: First, we hypothesize a model to relate fire damage, y, to the distance from the nearest fire station, x. We hypothesize a straight-line probabilistic model:

$$y = \beta_0 + \beta_1 x + \varepsilon$$

Step 2: Next, we open the **RFIRES** file and use a statistical software package to estimate the unknown parameters in the deterministic component of the hypothesized model. The Excel printout for the simple linear regression analysis is shown in Figure 11.25. The least squares estimates of the slope β_1 and intercept β_0, highlighted on the printout, are

$$\hat{\beta}_1 = 4.919331$$
$$\hat{\beta}_0 = 10.277929$$

and the least squares equation is (rounded)

$$\hat{y} = 10.278 + 4.919x$$

This prediction equation is graphed in the Minitab scatterplot, Figure 11.26.

The least squares estimate of the slope, $\hat{\beta}_1 = 4.919$, implies that the estimated mean damage increases by \$4,919 for each additional mile from the fire station. This interpretation is valid over the range of x, or from .7 to 6.1 miles from the station. The estimated y-intercept, $\hat{\beta}_0 = 10.278$, has the interpretation that a fire 0 miles from the fire station has an estimated mean damage of \$10,278. Although this would seem to apply to the fire station itself, remember that the y-intercept is meaningfully interpretable only if $x = 0$ is within the sampled range of the independent variable. Because $x = 0$ is outside the range in this case, $\hat{\beta}_0$ has no practical interpretation.

SUMMARY OUTPUT

Regression Statistics	
Multiple R	0.960977715
R Square	0.923478169
Adjusted R Square	0.917591874
Standard Error	2.316346184
Observations	15

ANOVA

	df	SS	MS	F	Significance F
Regression	1	841.766358	841.7664	156.8862	1.2478E-08
Residual	13	69.75097535	5.36546		
Total	14	911.5173333			

	Coefficients	Standard Error	t Stat	P-value	Lower 95%	Upper 95%
Intercept	10.27792855	1.420277811	7.236562	6.59E-06	7.209604884	13.34625221
DISTANCE	4.919330727	0.392747749	12.52542	1.25E-08	4.070850799	5.767810655

Figure 11.25

Excel printout for fire damage regression analysis

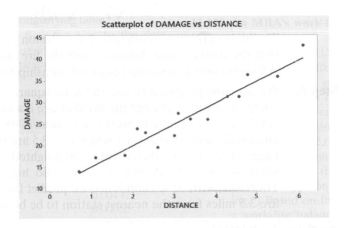

Figure 11.26

Minitab scatterplot with least squares line for fire damage regression analysis

Step 3: Now we specify the probability distribution of the random error component ε. The assumptions about the distribution are identical to those listed in Section 11.3. Although we know that these assumptions are not completely satisfied (they rarely are for practical problems), we are willing to assume they are approximately satisfied for this example. The estimate of the standard deviation σ of ε, highlighted on the Excel printout (Figure 11.25) is

$$s = 2.31635$$

This implies that most of the observed fire damage (y) values will fall within approximately $2s = 4.64$ thousand dollars of their respective predicted values when using the least squares line. [*Note:* A more precise prediction interval for y is given in step 5.]

Step 4: We can now check the usefulness of the hypothesized model—that is, whether x really contributes information for the prediction of y using the straight-line model. First, test the null hypothesis that the slope β_1 is 0—that is, that there is no linear relationship between fire damage and the distance from the nearest fire station, against the alternative hypothesis that fire damage increases as the distance increases. We test

$$H_0: \beta_1 = 0$$
$$H_a: \beta_1 > 0$$

The test statistic value (highlighted on the printout) is $t = 12.53$. Also, the two-tailed observed significance level for testing $H_a: \beta_1 \neq 0$, (highlighted on the printout) is approximately 0. When we divide this value in half, the p-value for our one-tailed test is also approximately 0. This small p-value leaves little doubt that mean fire damage and distance between the fire and station are at least linearly related, with mean fire damage increasing as the distance increases.

CHAPTER NOTES

Key Terms

Bivariate relationship 671
Coefficient of correlation 671
Coefficient of determination 676
Confidence interval for mean
  of y 686
Correlation 671
Dependent variable 644
Deterministic model 642
Errors of prediction 647
Estimated standard error
  of the least squares
  slope 664
Estimated standard error of
  regression model 660
Extrapolation 689
Independent variable 644
Least squares estimates 648
Least squares line 647
Least squares prediction
  equation 647
Line of means 644

Method of least squares 647
Population correlation
  coefficient 674
Prediction interval for y 683
Predictor variable 644
Probabilistic model 643
Random error 643
Regression analysis 643
Regression line 647
Regression modeling 643
Regression residuals 647
Response variable 644
Scattergram 647
Scatterplot 647
Slope of the line 644
Standard error of the
  prediction 682
Standard error of $\hat{y}$ 682
Straight-line (first-order)
  model 643
y-intercept of the line 644

Key Symbols/Notation

y	Dependent variable (variable to be predicted)
x	Independent variable (variable used to predict y)
$E(y)$	Expected value (mean) of y
β_0	y-intercept of true line
β_1	Slope of true line
$\hat{\beta}_0$	Least squares estimate of y-intercept
$\hat{\beta}_1$	Least squares estimate of slope
ε	Random error
$\hat{y}$	Predicted value of y for a given x-value
$(y - \hat{y})$	Estimated error of prediction
SSE	Sum of squared errors of prediction
r	Coefficient of correlation
r^2	Coefficient of determination
x_p	Value of x used to predict y

$$r^2 = \frac{SS_{yy} - SSE}{SS_{yy}} \qquad \text{Coefficient of determination}$$

$$\hat{y} \pm t_{\alpha/2}s\sqrt{\frac{1}{n} + \frac{(x_p - \bar{x})^2}{SS_{xx}}} \qquad \begin{array}{l}100\%(1 - \alpha) \text{ confidence} \\ \text{interval for } E(y) \text{ when} \\ x = x_p\end{array}$$

$$\hat{y} \pm t_{\alpha/2}s\sqrt{1 + \frac{1}{n} + \frac{(x_p - \bar{x})^2}{SS_{xx}}} \qquad \begin{array}{l}100\%(1 - \alpha) \text{ prediction} \\ \text{interval for } y \text{ when } x = x_p\end{array}$$

Key Ideas

Simple Linear Regression variables

$y =$ **Dependent** variable (quantitative)
$x =$ **Independent** variable (quantitative)

Method of Least Squares Properties

1. average error of prediction = 0
2. sum of squared errors is minimum

Practical Interpretation of y-Intercept

Predicted y-value when $x = 0$

(no practical interpretation if $x = 0$ is either nonsensical or outside range of sample data)

Practical Interpretation of Slope

Increase (or decrease) in mean y for every 1-unit increase in x

First-Order (Straight-Line) Model

$$E(y) = \beta_0 + \beta_1 x$$

where $E(y) = $ mean of y

    $\beta_0 = y$-**intercept** of line (point where line intercepts y-axis)
    $\beta_1 = $ **slope** of line (change in mean of y for every 1-unit change in x)

Coefficient of Correlation, r

1. ranges between -1 and $+1$
2. measures strength of *linear relationship* between y and x

Coefficient of Determination, r^2

1. ranges between 0 and 1
2. measures proportion of sample variation in y "explained" by the model

Practical Interpretation of Model Standard Deviation, s

Ninety-five percent of y-values fall within $2s$ of their respected predicted values

Width of *confidence interval for $E(y)$* will always be **narrower** than width of prediction interval for y

Guide to Simple Linear Regression

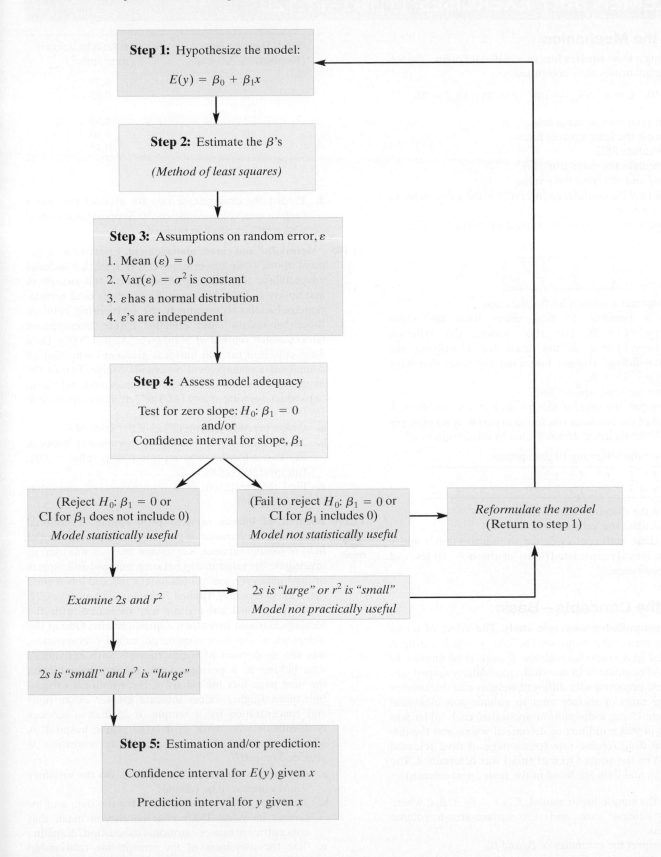

Step 1: Hypothesize the model:

$$E(y) = \beta_0 + \beta_1 x$$

Step 2: Estimate the β's

(Method of least squares)

Step 3: Assumptions on random error, ε

1. Mean $(\varepsilon) = 0$
2. $\text{Var}(\varepsilon) = \sigma^2$ is constant
3. ε has a normal distribution
4. ε's are independent

Step 4: Assess model adequacy

Test for zero slope: $H_0: \beta_1 = 0$
and/or
Confidence interval for slope, β_1

(Reject $H_0: \beta_1 = 0$ or
CI for β_1 does not include 0)
Model statistically useful

(Fail to reject $H_0: \beta_1 = 0$ or
CI for β_1 includes 0)
Model not statistically useful

Reformulate the model
(Return to step 1)

Examine 2s and r^2

2s is "large" or r^2 is "small"
Model not practically useful

2s is "small" and r^2 is "large"

Step 5: Estimation and/or prediction:

Confidence interval for $E(y)$ given x

Prediction interval for y given x

Learning the Mechanics

11.101 In fitting a least squares line to $n = 10$ data points, the following quantities were computed:

$$SS_{xx} = 10 \quad \bar{x} = 4 \quad SS_{yy} = 108 \quad \bar{y} = 28 \quad SS_{xy} = 25$$

a. Find the least squares line.
b. Graph the least squares line.
c. Calculate SSE.
d. Calculate the estimator of σ.
e. Find and interpret the r value.
f. Find a 95% confidence interval for the mean value of y at $x = 2$.
g. Find a 95% confidence interval for y when $x = 2$.

11.102 Consider the following sample data:

y	5	1	3
x	5	1	3

a. Construct a scatterplot for the data.
b. It is possible to find many lines for which $\Sigma(y - \hat{y}) = 0$. For this reason, the criterion $\Sigma(y - \hat{y}) = 0$. is not used for identifying the "best-fitting" straight line. Find two lines that have $\Sigma(y - \hat{y}) = 0$.
c. Find the least squares line.
d. Compare the value of SSE for the least squares line with that of the two lines you found in part **b**. What principle of least squares is demonstrated by this comparison?

11.103 Consider the following 10 data points:

L11103

x	3	5	6	4	3	7	6	5	4	7
y	4	3	2	1	2	3	3	5	4	2

a. Plot the data on a scatterplot.
b. Calculate the values of r and r^2.
c. Is there sufficient evidence to indicate that x and y are linearly correlated? Test at the $\alpha = .10$ level of significance.

Applying the Concepts—Basic

11.104 **Drug controlled-release rate study.** The effect of tablet surface area and volume on the rate at which a drug is released in a controlled-release dosage is of interest to chemical companies. In one study, six similarly shaped tablets were prepared with different weights and thicknesses, and the ratio of surface area to volume was measured for each. Using a dissolution apparatus, each tablet was placed in 900 milliliters of deionized water, and the diffusional drug release rate (percentage of drug released divided by the square root of time) was determined. The experimental data are listed in the table (next column).

a. Fit the simple linear model, $E(y) = \beta_0 + \beta_1 x$, where y = release rate and x = surface-area-to-volume ratio.
b. Interpret the estimates of β_0 and β_1.
c. Find the value of s for the straight-line model.
d. Give a practical interpretation of the value of s.
e. Form a 90% confidence interval for the slope, β_1. Interpret the result.

Drug Release Rate (% released/$\sqrt{\text{time}}$)	Surface Area to Volume (mm^2/mm^3)
40	1.30
32	0.85
26	0.70
22	0.55
20	0.40
19	0.45

f. Predict the drug release rate for a tablet that has a surface area/volume ratio of .50. Support your answer with a 90% prediction interval.

11.105 **"Metaskills" and career management.** Effective management of one's own career requires a skill set that includes adaptability, tolerance for ambiguity, self-awareness, and ability to identify change. Researchers used correlation coefficients to investigate the relationship between these "metaskills" and effective career management (*International Journal of Manpower*, August 2000). Data were collected for 446 business graduates who had all completed a management metaskills course. Two of the many variables measured were self-knowledge skill level (x) and goal-setting ability (y). The correlation coefficient for these two variables was $r = .70$.

a. Give a practical interpretation of the value of r.
b. The p-value for a test of no correlation between the two variables was reported as p-value = .001. Interpret this result.
c. Find the coefficient of determination, r^2, and interpret the result.

11.106 **Burnout of human services professionals.** Emotional exhaustion, or *burnout*, is a significant problem in the field of human services. Regression analysis was used to investigate the relationship between burnout and aspects of the human services professional's job and job-related behavior (*Journal of Applied Behavioral Science*, Vol. 22, 1986). Emotional exhaustion was measured with the Maslach Burnout Inventory, a questionnaire. One of the independent variables considered, called *concentration*, was the proportion of social contacts with individuals who belong to a person's work group. The table on the next page lists the values of the emotional exhaustion index (higher values indicate greater exhaustion) and concentration for a sample of 25 human services professionals who work in a large public hospital. A Minitab printout of the simple linear regression is provided on p. 697.

a. Construct a scatterplot for the data. Do the variables x and y appear to be related?
b. Find the correlation coefficient for the data and interpret its value. Does your conclusion mean that concentration causes emotional exhaustion? Explain.
c. Test the usefulness of the straight-line relationship with concentration for predicting burnout. Use $\alpha = .05$.
d. Find the coefficient of determination for the model and interpret it.

Data for Exercise 11.106

Exhaustion Index, y	Concentration, x	Exhaustion Index, y	Concentration, x
100	20%	493	86%
525	60	892	83
300	38	527	79
980	88	600	75
310	79	855	81
900	87	709	75
410	68	791	77
296	12	718	77
120	35	684	77
501	70	141	17
920	80	400	85
810	92	970	96
506	77		

Regression Analysis: EXINDEX versus CONCEN

```
Analysis of Variance

Source      DF   Adj SS   Adj MS   F-Value  P-Value
Regression   1  1102408  1102408   36.33    0.000
Error       23   698009    30348
Total       24  1800417

Model Summary

      S   R-sq  R-sq(adj)
174.207  61.23%   59.55%

Coefficients

Term      Coef  SE Coef  T Value  P Value
Constant   -29      107    -0.28    0.785
CONCEN    8.87     1.47     6.03    0.000
```

Prediction for EXINDEX

```
Regression Equation

EXINDEX = -29 + 8.87 CONCEN

Variable  Setting
CONCEN         80

Fit    SE Fit       95% CI              95% PI
679.741  38.6924  (599.700, 759.782)  (310.584, 1048.90)
```

Minitab output for Exercise 11.106

e. Find a 95% confidence interval for the slope β_1. Interpret the result.

f. Use a 95% confidence interval to estimate the mean exhaustion level for all professionals who have 80% of their social contacts within their work groups. Interpret the interval.

11.107 Retaliation against company "whistle-blowers." Individuals who report perceived wrongdoing of a corporation or public agency are known as *whistle-blowers*. Two researchers developed an index to measure the extent of retaliation against a whistle-blower (*Journal of Applied Psychology*, 1986). The index was based on the number of forms of reprisal actually experienced, the number of forms of reprisal threatened, and the number of people within the organization (e.g., coworkers or immediate supervisor) who retaliated against them. The table (next column) lists the retaliation index (higher numbers indicate more extensive retaliation) and salary for a sample of 15 whistle-blowers from federal agencies.

a. Construct a scatterplot for the data. Does it appear that the extent of retaliation increases, decreases, or stays the same with an increase in salary? Explain.

Retaliation Index	Salary
301	$62,000
550	36,500
755	21,600
327	$24,000
500	30,100
377	35,000
290	47,500
452	54,000
535	19,800
455	44,000
615	46,600
700	15,100
650	70,000
630	21,000
360	16,900

Source: Based on J. P. Near and M. P. Miceli, "Retaliation Against Whistle Blowers: Predictors and Effects," *Journal of Applied Psychology*, Vol. 71, No. 1, 1986, pp. 137–145.

b. Use the method of least squares to fit a straight line to the data.

c. Graph the least squares line on your scatterplot. Does the least squares line support your answer to the question in part **a**? Explain.

d. Interpret the y-intercept, $\hat{\beta}_0$ of the least squares line in terms of this application. Is the interpretation meaningful?

e. Interpret the slope, $\hat{\beta}_1$, of the least squares line in terms of this application. Over what range of x is this interpretation meaningful?

f. Test the adequacy of the model using $\alpha = .05$.

11.108 Extending the life of an aluminum smelter pot. An investigation of the properties of bricks used to line aluminum smelter pots was published in *The American Ceramic Society Bulletin* (February 2005). Six different commercial bricks were evaluated. The life length of a smelter pot depends on the porosity of the brick lining (the less porosity, the longer the life); consequently, the researchers measured the apparent porosity of each brick specimen, as well as the mean pore diameter of each brick. The data are given in the accompanying table.

Brick	Apparent Porosity (%)	Mean Pore Diameter (micrometers)
A	18.8	12.0
B	18.3	9.7
C	16.3	7.3
D	6.9	5.3
E	17.1	10.9
F	20.4	16.8

Source: Based on P. Bonadia, et al. "Aluminosilicate Refractories for Aluminum Cell Linings," *The American Ceramic Society Bulletin*, Vol. 84, No. 2, Feb. 2005, pp. 26–31 (Table II).

a. Find the least squares line relating porosity (y) to mean pore diameter (x).

b. Interpret the y-intercept of the line.

c. Interpret the slope of the line.

d. Conduct a test to determine whether porosity (y) and diameter (x) are positively linearly related. Use $\alpha = .01$.

11.109 Diamonds sold at retail. Refer to the *Journal of Statistics Education* study of 308 diamonds sold on the open market, Exercise 2.158 (p. 144). Recall that you related the size of the diamond (number of carats) to the asking price (dollars) using a scatterplot.

DIAMND

a. Write the equation of a straight-line model relating asking price (y) to number of carats (x).

b. An XLSTAT simple linear regression printout for the analysis is shown below. Find the equation of the least squares line.

c. Give a practical interpretation of the y-intercept of the least squares line. If a practical interpretation is not possible, explain why.

d. Locate a 95% confidence interval for the slope of the least squares line on the printout and practically interpret the result. Over what range is the interpretation meaningful?

e. Locate the estimated standard deviation of the random error on the printout and practically interpret this value.

f. Specify the null and alternative hypotheses for determining whether a positive linear relationship exists between asking price and size.

g. Locate the p-value of the test, part **f**, on the printout. Interpret the result if $\alpha = .05$.

h. Locate the coefficient of determination, r^2, on the printout and interpret the result.

i. Locate the coefficient of correlation, r, on the printout and interpret the result.

j. Locate a 95% prediction interval for the asking price when carat size is .5 on the printout and practically interpret the result.

k. Locate a 95% confidence interval for the mean asking price when carat size is .5 on the printout and practically interpret the result.

11.110 Sports news on local TV broadcasts. *The Sports Journal* (Winter 2004) published the results of a study conducted to assess the factors that impact the time allotted to sports news on local television news broadcasts. Information on total time (in minutes) allotted to sports and audience ratings of the TV news broadcast (measured on a 100-point scale) was obtained from a national sample of 163 news directors. A correlation analysis on the data yielded $r = .43$.

a. Interpret the value of the correlation coefficient, r.

b. Find and interpret the value of the coefficient of determination, r^2.

Applying the Concepts—Intermediate

11.111 Evaluating managerial success. An observational study of 19 managers from a medium-sized manufacturing plant investigated which activities *successful* managers actually perform (*Journal of Applied Behavioral Science*, August 1985). To measure success, the researchers devised an index based on the manager's length of time in the organization and his or her level within the firm; the higher the index, the more successful the manager. The table on the following page presents data that can be used to determine whether managerial success is related to the extensiveness of a manager's network-building interactions with people outside the manager's work unit. Such interactions include phone and face-to-face meetings with customers and suppliers, attending outside meetings, and doing public relations work.

MINDEX

Correlation matrix (Pearson):

Variables	CARAT	PRICE
CARAT	1	0.9447
PRICE	0.9447	1

Values in bold are different from 0 with a significance level alpha=0.05

Regression of variable PRICE:

Goodness of fit statistics:

Observations	308.0000
Sum of weights	308.0000
DF	306.0000
R²	0.8925
Adjusted R²	0.8922
MSE	1248949.7531
RMSE	1117.5642
DW	1.2156

Analysis of variance:

Source	DF	Sum of squares	Mean squares	F	Pr > F
Model	1	3173248722.4667	3173248722.4667	2540.7337	< 0.0001
Error	306	382178624.4521	1248949.7531		
Corrected Total	307	3555427346.9188			

Computed against model Y=Mean(Y)

Model parameters:

Source	Value	Standard error	t	Pr > |t|	Lower bound (95%)	Upper bound (95%)
Intercept	-2298.3576	158.5306	-14.4979	< 0.0001	-2610.3056	-1986.4096
CARAT	11598.8840	230.1106	50.4057	< 0.0001	11146.0846	12051.6834

Predictions for the new observations:

CARAT	Pred(PRICE)	Lower bound 95% (Mean)	Upper bound 95% (Mean)	Lower bound 95% (Observation)	Upper bound 95% (Observation)
0.5	4197.0174	4067.6649	4326.3700	1994.1331	6399.9018

XLSTAT output for Exercise 11.109

Data for Exercise 11.111

Manager	Manager Success Index, y	Number of Interactions with Outsiders, x
1	40	12
2	73	71
3	95	70
4	60	81
5	81	43
6	27	50
7	53	42
8	66	18
9	25	35
10	63	82
11	70	20
12	47	81
13	80	40
14	51	33
15	32	45
16	50	10
17	52	65
18	30	20
19	42	21

a. Construct a scatterplot for the data.
b. Find the prediction equation for managerial success.
c. Find s for your prediction equation. Interpret the standard deviation s in the context of this problem.
d. Plot the least squares line on your scatterplot of part **a.** Does it appear that the number of interactions with outsiders contributes information for the prediction of managerial success? Explain.
e. Conduct a formal statistical hypothesis test to answer the question posed in part **d.** Use $\alpha = .05$.
f. Construct a 95% confidence interval for β_1. Interpret the interval in the context of the problem.
g. A particular manager was observed for 2 weeks. She made 55 contacts with people outside her work unit. Predict the value of the manager's success index. Use a 90% prediction interval.
h. A second manager was observed for 2 weeks. This manager made 110 contacts with people outside his work unit. Why should caution be exercised in using the least squares model developed from the given data set to construct a prediction interval for this manager's success index?
i. In the context of this problem, determine the value of x for which the associated prediction interval for y is the narrowest.

11.112 Doctors and ethics. Refer to the *Journal of Medical Ethics* (Vol. 32, 2006) study of physicians' use of ethics consultation, Exercise 2.166 (p. 146). Recall that the medical researchers measured the *length of time in practice* (i.e., years of experience) and the *amount of exposure to ethics in medical school* (number of hours) for a sample of 118 physicians. Consider a straight-line regression model relating hours of exposure (y) to time in practice (x).
a. Fit the model to the data saved in the file and conduct a test (at $\alpha = .05$) for a linear relationship between the two variables.
b. In Exercise 2.166 you identified a highly suspect outlier for hours of exposure. Remove this outlier from the data set and rerun the analysis, part **a.** What do you observe?

11.113 FCAT scores and poverty. In the state of Florida, elementary school performance is based on the average score obtained by students on a standardized exam, called the Florida Comprehensive Assessment Test (FCAT). An analysis of the link between FCAT scores and sociodemographic factors was published in the *Journal of Educational and Behavioral Statistics* (Spring 2004). Data on average math and reading FCAT scores of third graders, as well as the percentage of students below the poverty level, for a sample of 22 Florida elementary schools are listed in the table below.

a. Propose a straight-line model relating math score (y) to percentage (x) of students below the poverty level.
b. Fit the model to the data using the method of least squares.
c. Graph the least squares line on a scatterplot of the data. Is there visual evidence of a relationship between the two variables? Is the relationship positive or negative?
d. Interpret the estimates of the y-intercept and slope in the words of the problem.
e. Conduct a test (at $\alpha = .05$) to determine if math score (y) and percentage (x) below the poverty level are linearly related.
f. Now consider a model relating reading score (y) to percentage (x) of students below the poverty level. Repeat parts **a–e** for this model.
g. Consider the simple linear regression relating math score (y) to percentage (x) of students below the poverty level. Find and interpret the value of s for this regression.
h. Consider the simple linear regression relating reading score (y) to percentage (x) of students below the poverty level. Find and interpret the value of s for this regression.
i. Which dependent variable, math score or reading score, can be more accurately predicted by percentage (x) of students below the poverty level? Explain.

Elementary School	FCAT-Math	FCAT-Reading	% Below Poverty
1	166.4	165.0	91.7
2	159.6	157.2	90.2
3	159.1	164.4	86.0
4	155.5	162.4	83.9
5	164.3	162.5	80.4
6	169.8	164.9	76.5
7	155.7	162.0	76.0
8	165.2	165.0	75.8
9	175.4	173.7	75.6
10	178.1	171.0	75.0
11	167.1	169.4	74.7
12	177.0	172.9	63.2
13	174.2	172.7	52.9
14	175.6	174.9	48.5
15	170.8	174.8	39.1
16	175.1	170.1	38.4
17	182.8	181.4	34.3
18	180.3	180.6	30.3
19	178.8	178.0	30.3
20	181.4	175.9	29.6
21	182.8	181.6	26.5
22	186.1	183.8	13.8

Source: Based on C. D. Tekwe, et al., "An Empirical Comparison of Statistical Models for Value-Added Assessment of School Performance," *Journal of Educational and Behavioral Statistics,* Vol. 29, No. 1, Spring 2004, pp. 11–36 (Table 2).

Data for Exercise 11.114

Rank	Team	Current Value ($mil)	1-Yr Value Change (%)	Debt/ Value (%)	Revenue ($mil)	Operating Income ($mil)
1	Dallas Cowboys	4,000	25	5	620	270
2	New England Patriots	3,200	23	7	494	195
3	Washington Redskins	2,850	19	8	439	124.9
4	New York Giants	2,800	33	18	400	105.2
5	San Francisco 49ers	2,700	69	21	427	123.7
6	New York Jets	2,600	44	23	383	118.4
7	Houston Texans	2,500	35	7	383	114.6
8	Chicago Bears	2,450	44	4	352	85.7
9	Philadelphia Eagles	2,400	37	8	370	88.7
10	Green Bay Packers	1,950	42	6	347	63.3
11	Denver Broncos	1,940	34	6	346	65.8
12	Baltimore Ravens	1,930	29	14	345	59.8
13	Pittsburgh Steelers	1,900	41	11	344	54
14	Indianapolis Colts	1,875	34	3	321	90.1
15	Seattle Seahawks	1,870	41	6	334	43.6
16	Miami Dolphins	1,850	42	19	322	41.5
17	Atlanta Falcons	1,670	48	51	303	25.4
18	Minnesota Vikings	1,590	38	31	281	34.5
19	Carolina Panthers	1,560	25	4	325	77.8
20	Arizona Cardinals	1,540	54	10	308	57.2
21	Kansas City Chiefs	1,530	39	5	307	48.6
22	San Diego Chargers	1,525	53	7	304	64.8
23	New Orleans Saints	1,515	36	5	322	70
24	Tampa Bay Buccaneers	1,510	23	12	313	55.2
25	Cleveland Browns	1,500	34	13	313	34.7
26	Tennessee Titans	1,490	28	10	318	50.5
27	Jacksonville Jaguars	1,480	53	7	315	67
28	St Louis Rams	1,450	56	8	290	34
29	Cincinnati Bengals	1,445	46	7	296	55.5
30	Detroit Lions	1,440	50	19	298	36.1
31	Oakland Raiders	1,430	47	14	285	39
32	Buffalo Bills	1,400	50	14	296	44.2

Source: Based on *Forbes* Magazine, "The Most Valuable Teams in the NFL," Copyright: September 14, 2015.

11.114 Monetary values of NFL teams. Refer to the *Forbes* magazine 2015 report on the financial standings of each team in the National Football League (NFL), Exercise 2.26 (p. 84). The table listing the current value (without deduction for debt, except stadium debt) and operating income for each team is reproduced above.

a. Propose a straight-line model relating an NFL team's current value (y) to its operating income (x).

b. Fit the model to the data using the method of least squares.

c. Interpret the least squares estimates of the slope and y-intercept in the words of the problem.

d. Statistically assess the adequacy of the model. Do you recommend using it to predict an NFL team's value?

11.115 Evaluating a truck weigh-in-motion program. The Minnesota Department of Transportation installed a state-of-the-art weigh-in-motion scale in the concrete surface of the eastbound lanes of Interstate 494 in Bloomington, Minnesota. After installation, a study was undertaken to determine whether the scale's readings correspond to the static weights of the vehicles being monitored. (Studies of this type are known as *calibration studies*.) After some preliminary comparisons using a two-axle, six-tire truck carrying different loads (see the accompanying table), calibration adjustments were made

in the software of the weigh-in-motion system, and the scales were reevaluated.

a. Construct two scatterplots, one of y_1 versus x and the other of y_2 versus x.

Trial Number	Static Weight of Truck, x (thousand pounds)	Weigh-in-Motion Reading Prior to Calibration Adjustment, y_1 (thousand pounds)	Weigh-in-Motion Reading After Calibration Adjustment, y_2 (thousand pounds)
1	27.9	26.0	27.8
2	29.1	29.9	29.1
3	38.0	39.5	37.8
4	27.0	25.1	27.1
5	30.3	31.6	30.6
6	34.5	36.2	34.3
7	27.8	25.1	26.9
8	29.6	31.0	29.6
9	33.1	35.6	33.0
10	35.5	40.2	35.0

Source: Based on J. L. Wright, F. Owen, and D. Pena, "Status of MN/ DOT's Weigh-in-Motion Program," St. Paul: Minnesota Department of Transportation, January 1983.

b. Use the scatterplots of part **a** to evaluate the performance of the weigh-in-motion scale both before and after the calibration adjustment.

c. Calculate the correlation coefficient for both sets of data and interpret their values. Explain how these correlation coefficients can be used to evaluate the weigh-in-motion scale.

d. Suppose the sample correlation coefficient for y_2 and x was 1. Could this happen if the static weights and the weigh-in-motion readings disagreed? Explain.

11.116 Energy efficiency of buildings. Firms conscious of the energy efficiency of proposed new structures are interested in the relation between yearly energy consumption and the number of square feet of building shell. The table below lists the energy consumption in British thermal units (a BTU is the amount of heat required to raise 1 pound of water 1°F) for 22 buildings that were all subjected to the same climatic conditions. Consider a straight-line model relating BTU consumption, y, to building shell area, x.

a. Find the least squares estimates of the intercept β_0 and the slope β_1.

b. Investigate the usefulness of the model you developed in part **a**. Is yearly energy consumption positively linearly related to the shell area of the building? Test using $\alpha = .10$.

c. Find the observed significance level of the test of part **b.** Interpret its value.

d. Find the coefficient of determination r^2 and interpret its value.

e. A company wishes to build a new warehouse that will contain 8,000 square feet of shell area. Find the predicted value of energy consumption and associated 95% prediction interval. Comment on the usefulness of this interval.

f. The application of the model you developed in part **a** to the warehouse problem of part **e** is appropriate only if certain assumptions can be made about the new warehouse. What are these assumptions?

BTU/Year (thousands)	Shell Area (square feet)
3,870,000	30,001
1,371,000	13,530
2,422,000	26,060
672,200	6,355
233,100	4,576
218,900	24,680
354,000	2,621
3,135,000	23,350
1,470,000	18,770
1,408,000	12,220
2,201,000	25,490
2,680,000	23,680
337,500	5,650
567,500	8,001
555,300	6,147
239,400	2,660
2,629,000	19,240
1,102,000	10,700
423,500	9,125
423,500	6,510
1,691,000	13,530
1,870,000	18,860

11.117 Forecasting managerial needs. Managers are an important part of any organization's resource base. Accordingly, the organization should be just as concerned about forecasting its future managerial needs as it is with forecasting its needs for, say, the natural resources used in its production process (Northcraft and Neale, *Organizational Behavior: A Management Challenge*, 2001). A common forecasting procedure is to model the relationship between sales and the number of managers needed. To develop this relationship, the data shown in the following table are collected from a firm's records.

a. Test the usefulness of the model. Use $\alpha = .05$. State your conclusion in the context of the problem.

b. The company projects that it will sell 39 units next month. Use the least squares model to construct a 90% prediction interval for the number of managers needed next month.

c. Interpret the interval in part **b.** Use the interval to determine the reliability of the firm's projection.

Units Sold, x	Managers, y
5	10
4	11
8	10
7	10
9	9
15	10
20	11
21	17
25	19
24	21
30	22
31	25
36	30
38	30
40	31
41	31
51	32
40	30
48	32
47	32

Applying the Concepts—Advanced

11.118 Regression through the origin. Sometimes it is known from theoretical considerations that the straight-line relationship between two variables, x and y, passes through the origin of the xy-plane. Consider the relationship between the total weight of a shipment of 50-pound bags of flour, y, and the number of bags in the shipment, x. Because a shipment containing $x = 0$ bags (i.e., no shipment at all) has a total weight of $y = 0$, a straight-line model of the relationship between x and y should pass through the point $x = 0$, $y = 0$. In such a case, you could assume $\beta_0 = 0$ and characterize the relationship between x and y with the following model:

$$y = \beta_1 x + \varepsilon$$

The least squares estimate of β_1 for this model is

$$\hat{\beta}_1 = \frac{\sum x_i y_i}{\sum x_i^2}$$

From the records of past flour shipments, 15 shipments were randomly chosen, and the data shown in the table below were recorded.

Weight of Shipment	Number of 50-Pound Bags in Shipment
5,050	100
10,249	205
20,000	450
7,420	150
24,685	500
10,206	200
7,325	150
4,958	100
7,162	150
24,000	500
4,900	100
14,501	300
28,000	600
17,002	400
16,100	400

a. Find the least squares line for the given data under the assumption that $\beta_0 = 0$. Plot the least squares line on a scatterplot of the data.

b. Find the least squares line for the given data using the model

$$y = \beta_0 + \beta_1 x + \varepsilon$$

(i.e., do not restrict β_0 to equal 0). Plot this line on the same scatterplot you constructed in part **a.**

c. Refer to part **b.** Why might $\hat{\beta}_0$ be different from 0 even though the true value of β_0 is known to be 0?

d. The estimated standard error of $\hat{\beta}_0$ is equal to

$$s\sqrt{\frac{1}{n} + \frac{\bar{x}^2}{SS_{xx}}}$$

Use the t-statistic

$$t = \frac{\hat{\beta}_0 - 0}{s\sqrt{(1/n) + (\bar{x}^2/SS_{xx})}}$$

to test the null hypothesis $H_0: \beta_0 = 0$ against the alternative $H_a: \beta_0 \neq 0$. Use $\alpha = .10$. Should you include β_0 in your model?

Critical Thinking Challenges

11.119 Comparing cost functions. Models of past cost behavior are called *cost functions*. Factors that influence costs are called *cost drivers* (Horngren, Datar, and Rajan, *Cost Accounting*, 2011). The cost data shown in the next column are from a rug manufacturer. Indirect manufacturing labor costs consist of machine maintenance costs and setup labor costs. Machine-hours and direct manufacturing labor-hours are cost drivers. Your task is to estimate and compare two alternative cost functions for indirect manufacturing labor costs. In the first, machine-hours is the independent variable; in the second, direct manufacturing labor-hours is the independent variable. Prepare a report that compares the two cost functions and recommends which should be used to explain and predict indirect manufacturing labor costs. Be sure to justify your choice.

Week	Indirect Manufacturing Labor Costs	Machine-Hours	Direct Manufacturing Labor-Hours
1	$1,190	68	30
2	1,211	88	35
3	1,004	62	36
4	917	72	20
5	770	60	47
6	1,456	96	45
7	1,180	78	44
8	710	46	38
9	1,316	82	70
10	1,032	94	30
11	752	68	29
12	963	48	38

Source: Based on C. T. Horngren, S. M. Datar, and M. Rajan, *Cost Accounting: A Managerial Emphasis*, 14th ed. Upper Saddle River, N.J.: Prentice Hall, 2011.

11.120 Spall damage in bricks. A civil suit revolved around a five-building brick apartment complex located in the Bronx, New York, which began to suffer *spalling* damage (i.e., a separation of some portion of the face of a brick from its body). The owner of the complex alleged that the bricks were defectively manufactured. The brick manufacturer countered that poor design and shoddy management led to the damage. To settle the suit, an estimate of the rate of damage per 1,000 bricks, called the *spall rate*, was required (*Chance*, Summer 1994). The owner estimated the spall rate using several *scaffold-drop* surveys. (With this method, an engineer lowers a scaffold down at selected places on building walls and counts the number of visible spalls for every 1,000 bricks in the observation area.) The brick manufacturer conducted its own survey by dividing the walls of the complex into 83 wall segments and taking a photograph of each wall segment. (The number of spalled bricks that could be made out from each photo was recorded, and the sum over all 83 wall segments was used as an estimate of total spall damage.) In this court case, the jury was faced with the following dilemma: The scaffold-drop survey provided the most accurate estimate of spall rates in a given wall segment. Unfortunately, the drop areas were not selected at random from the entire complex; rather, drops were made at areas with high spall concentrations, leading to an overestimate of the total damage. On the other hand, the photo survey was complete in that all 83 wall segments in the complex were checked for spall damage. But the spall rate estimated by the photos, at least in areas of high spall concentration, was biased low (spalling damage cannot always be seen from a photo), leading to an underestimate of the total damage.

Drop Location	Drop Spall Rate (per 1,000 bricks)	Photo Spall Rate (per 1,000 bricks)
1	0	0
2	5.1	0
3	6.6	0
4	1.1	.8
5	1.8	1.0
6	3.9	1.0
7	11.5	1.9
8	22.1	7.7
9	39.3	14.9
10	39.9	13.9
11	43.0	11.8

Source: Based on W. B. Fairley et al., "Bricks, Buildings, and the Bronx: Estimating Masonry Deterioration," *Chance*, Vol. 7. No. 3, Summer 1994, p. 36 (Figure 3). [*Note:* The data points are estimated from the points shown on a scatterplot.]

The data in the table are the spall rates obtained using the two methods at 11 drop locations. Use the data, as did expert statisticians who testified in the case, to help the jury estimate the true spall rate at a given wall segment. Then explain how this information, coupled with the data (not given here) on all 83 wall segments, can provide a reasonable estimate of the total spall damage (i.e., total number of damaged bricks).

ACTIVITY 11.1 Applying Simple Linear Regression to Your Favorite Data

Many dependent variables in business serve as the subjects of regression modeling efforts. We list five such variables here:

1. Rate of return of a stock
2. Annual unemployment rate
3. Grade point average of an accounting student
4. Gross domestic product of the United States
5. Salary cap space available for your favorite NFL team

Choose one of these dependent variables, or choose some other dependent variable, for which you want to construct a prediction model. There may be a large number of independent variables that should be included in a prediction equation for the dependent variable you choose. List three potentially important independent variables, x_1, x_2, and x_3, that you think might be (individually) strongly related to your dependent variable. Next, obtain 25 data values, each of which consists of a measure of your dependent variable y and the corresponding values of x_1, x_2, and x_3.

a. Use the least squares formulas given in this chapter to fit three straight-line models—one for each independent variable—for predicting y.

b. Interpret the sign of the estimated slope coefficient $\hat{\beta}_1$ in each case, and test the utility of each model by testing H_0: $\beta_1 = 0$ against H_a: $\beta_1 \neq 0$. What assumptions must be satisfied to ensure the validity of these tests?

c. Calculate the coefficient of determination, r^2, for each model. Which of the independent variables predicts y best for the 25 sampled sets of data? Is this variable necessarily best in general (i.e., for the entire population)? Explain.

Be sure to keep the data and the results of your calculations, since you will need them for the Activity section in Chapter 12.

References

Chatterjee, S., and Price, B. *Regression Analysis by Example*, 2nd ed. New York: Wiley, 1991.

Draper, N., and Smith, H. *Applied Regression Analysis*, 3rd ed. New York: Wiley, 1987.

Gitlow, H., Oppenheim, A., and Oppenheim, R. *Quality Management: Tools and Methods for Improvement*, 2nd ed. Burr Ridge, Ill.: Irwin, 1995.

Graybill, F. *Theory and Application of the Linear Model*. North Scituate, Mass.: Duxbury, 1976.

Kleinbaum, D., and Kupper, L. *Applied Regression Analysis and Other Multivariable Methods*, 2nd ed. North Scituate, Mass.: Duxbury, 1997.

Kutner, M., Nachtsheim, C., Neter, J., and Li, W. *Applied Linear Statistical Models*, 5th ed. New York: McGraw-Hill, 2006.

Mendenhall, W. *Introduction to Linear Models and the Design and Analysis of Experiments*. Belmont, CA.: Wadsworth, 1968.

Mendenhall, W., and Sincich, T. A. *Second Course in Statistics: Regression Analysis*, 7th ed. Upper Saddle River, N.J.: Prentice Hall, 2011.

Montgomery, D., Peck, E., and Vining, G. *Introduction to Linear Regression Analysis*, 3rd ed. New York: Wiley, 2001.

Mosteller, F., and Tukey, J. W. *Data Analysis and Regression: A Second Course in Statistics*. Reading, Mass.: Addison-Wesley, 1977.

Rousseeuw, P. J., and Leroy, A. M. *Robust Regression and Outlier Detection*. New York: Wiley, 1987.

Weisburg, S. *Applied Linear Regression*, 2nd ed. New York: Wiley, 1985.

SPSS: Simple Linear Regression

Regression Analysis

Step 1 Access the SPSS spreadsheet file that contains the two quantitative variables (dependent and independent variables).

Step 2 Click on the "Analyze" button on the SPSS menu bar and then click on "Regression" and "Linear," as shown in Figure 11.S.1.

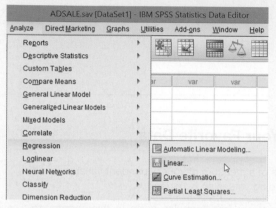

Figure 11.S.1 SPSS menu options for regression

Step 3 On the resulting dialog box (see Figure 11.S.2), specify the dependent variable in the "Dependent" box and the independent variable in the "Independent(s)" box. Be sure to select "Enter" in the "Method" box.

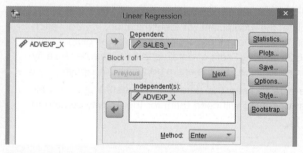

Figure 11.S.2 SPSS linear regression dialog box

Step 4 To produce confidence intervals for the model parameters, click the "Statistics" button and check the appropriate menu items in the resulting menu list.

Step 5 To obtain prediction intervals for y and confidence intervals for $E(y)$, click the "Save" button and check the appropriate items in the resulting menu list, as shown in Figure 11.S.3. (The prediction intervals will be added as new columns to the SPSS data spreadsheet.)

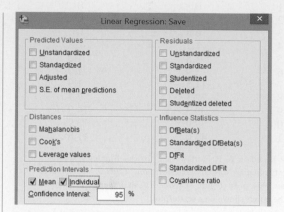

Figure 11.S.3 SPSS linear regression save dialog box

Step 6 To return to the main Regression dialog box from any of these optional screens, click "Continue." Click "OK" on the Regression dialog box to view the linear regression results.

Correlation Analysis

Step 1 Click on the "Analyze" button on the main menu bar and then click on "Correlate" (see Figure 11.S.1).

Step 2 Click on "Bivariate." The resulting dialog box appears in Figure 11.S.4.

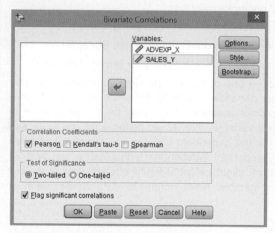

Figure 11.S.4 SPSS correlation dialog box

Step 3 Enter the variables of interest in the "Variables" box and check the "Pearson" option.

Step 4 Click "OK" to obtain a printout of the correlation.

Minitab: Simple Linear Regression

Regression Analysis

Step 1 Access the Minitab worksheet file that contains the two quantitative variables (dependent and independent variables).

Step 2 Click on the "Stat" button on the Minitab menu bar and then click on "Regression" twice and "Fit Regression Model," as shown in Figure 11.M.1.

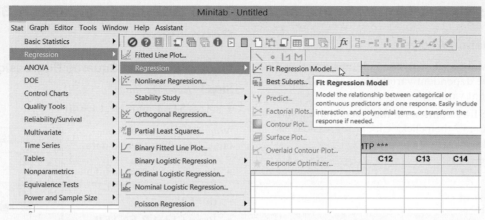

Figure 11.M.1 Minitab menu options for regression

Step 3 On the resulting dialog box (see Figure 11.M.2), specify the dependent variable in the "Responses" box and the independent variable in the "Continuous predictors" box. Click "OK" to produce the linear regression results.

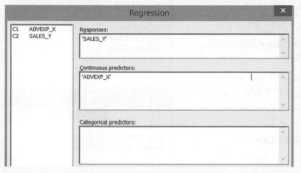

Figure 11.M.2   Minitab regression dialog box

Step 4 To produce prediction intervals for y and confidence intervals for $E(y)$, click "Stat", "Regression" twice, then "Predict". The resulting dialog box is shown in Figure 11.M.3.

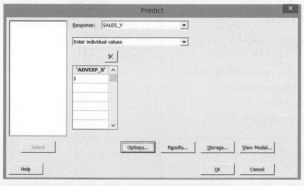

Figure 11.M.3   Minitab regression dialog box

Step 5 Enter the value of x in the appropriate box (under the independent variable), and click "OK."

[*Note:* The default confidence level is .95. To change the confidence level, click "Options" and change the value in the "Confidence Level" box.]

Correlation Analysis

Step 1 Click on the "Stat" button on the Minitab main menu bar, then click on "Basic Statistics," and then click on "Correlation," as shown in Figure 11.M.4.

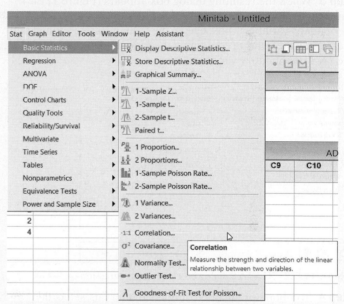

Figure 11.M.4 Minitab menu options for correlation

Step 2 On the resulting dialog box (see Figure 11.M.5), enter the two variables of interest in the "Variables" box.

Figure 11.M.5 Minitab correlation dialog box

Step 3 Click "OK" to obtain a printout of the correlation.

Excel/XLSTAT: Simple Linear Regression

Regression/Correlation Analysis

Step 1 First, create a workbook with two columns, one representing the quantitative dependent variable and the other the quantitative independent variable.

Step 2 Click the "XLSTAT" button on the Excel main menu bar, select "Modeling data," then click "Linear regression," as shown in Figure 11.E.1.

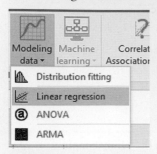

Figure 11.E.1 XLSTAT menu options for simple linear regression

Step 3 When the resulting dialog box appears (Figure 11.E.2), enter the column containing the dependent variable in the "Y / Dependent variables" box. Check the "Quantitative" option and then enter the column containing the independent variable in the "X / Explanatory variables" box.

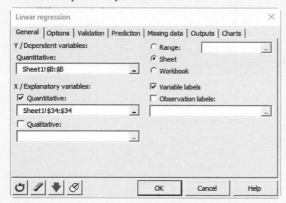

Figure 11.E.2 XLSTAT dialog box for linear regression

Step 4 To obtain prediction/confidence intervals, select the "Prediction" tab, then enter the column with the values of the independent variable for which you want to make predictions in the "X / Explanatory variables" and "Quantitative" box, as shown in Figure 11.E.3.

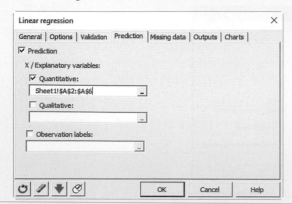

Figure 11.E.3 XLSTAT dialog box for predictions

Step 5 Click "OK," then "Continue" to display the test results.

TI-84 Graphing Calculator: Simple Linear Regression

Finding the Least Squares Regression Equation

Step 1 *Enter the data*

• Press **STAT** and select **1:Edit**

Note: If a list already contains data, clear the old data.

• Use the up arrow to highlight the list name, **"L1"** or **"L2"**

• Press **CLEAR ENTER**

• Enter your x-data in **L1** and your y-data in **L2**

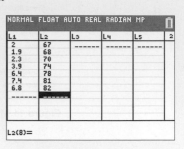

Step 2 *Find the equation*

• Press **STAT** and highlight **CALC**

• Press **4** for **LinReg(ax + b)**

• Press **ENTER**

• Select **Calculate**, press **ENTER**

• The screen will show the values for a and b in the equation $y = ax + b$.

Finding r and r^2

Use this procedure if r and r^2 do not already appear on the LinReg screen from part I:

Step 1 *Turn the diagnostics feature on*

• Press **2nd 0** for **CATALOG**

• Press the **ALPHA** key and x^{-1} for **D**

• Press the down **ARROW** until **DiagnosticsOn** is highlighted

• Press **ENTER** twice

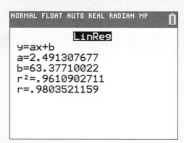

Step 2 *Find the regression equation as shown in part I above* The values for r and r^2 will appear on the screen as well.

Graphing the Least Squares Line with the Scatterplot

Step 1 *Enter the data as shown in Step 1 above*

Step 2 *Set up the data plot*

• Press **Y =** and **CLEAR** all functions from the Y registers

• Press **2ndY =** for **STAT PLOT**

• Press **1** for **Plot1**

• Set the cursor so that **ON** is flashing and press **ENTER**

- For **Type,** use the **ARROW** and **ENTER** keys to highlight and select the scatterplot (first icon in the first row)
- For **Xlist,** choose the column containing the *x*-data
- For **Ylist,** choose the column containing the *y*-data

Step 3 *Find the regression equation and store the equation in Y1*

- Press **STAT** and highlight **CALC**
- Press **4** for **LinReg(ax + b)** (Note: Don't press ENTER here because you want to store the regression equation in Y1.)

- Arrow down to **Store RegEq**
- Press **VARS**
- Use the right arrow to highlight **Y-VARS**
- Press **ENTER** to select **1:Function**
- Press **ENTER** to select **1:Y1**
- Arrow down to **Calculate**, then press **ENTER**

Step 4 *View the scatterplot and regression line*

- Press **ZOOM** and then press **9** to select **9:ZoomStat**

You should see the data graphed along with the regression line.

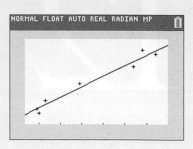

12

WHERE WE'VE BEEN

- Introduced the straight-line model relating a dependent variable y to a single independent variable x

- Demonstrated how to estimate the parameters of the straight-line model using the method of least squares

- Showed how to statistically assess the adequacy of the model

- Showed how to use the model to Estimate $E(y)$ and predict y for a given value of x

Multiple Regression and Model Building

STATISTICS IN ACTION — Bid Rigging in the Highway Construction Industry

In the United States, commercial contractors bid for the right to construct state highways and roads. A state government agency, usually the Department of Transportation (DOT), notifies various contractors of the state's intent to build a highway. Sealed bids are submitted by the contractors, and the contractor with the lowest bid (building cost) is awarded the road construction contract. The bidding process works extremely well in competitive markets but has the potential to increase construction costs if the markets are noncompetitive or if collusive practices are present. The latter occurred in the 1980s in Florida. Numerous road contractors either admitted or were found guilty of price fixing (i.e., setting the cost of construction above the fair, or competitive, cost through bid rigging or other means).

This *Statistics in Action* involves data collected by the Florida attorney general shortly following the price-fixing crisis. The attorney general's objective is to build a model for the cost (y) of a road construction contract awarded using the sealed-bid system. The **FLAG** file contains data for a sample of 235 road contracts. The variables measured for each contract are listed in Table SIA12.1. Ultimately, the attorney general wants to use the model to predict the costs of future road contracts in the state.

In several *Statistics in Action Revisited* sections in this chapter, we show how to analyze the data using a multiple regression analysis.

Table SIA12.1	**Variables in the FLAG Data File**	
Variable Name	Type	Description
CONTRACT	Quantitative	Road contract number
COST	Quantitative	Low bid contract cost (thousands of dollars)
DOTEST	Quantitative	DOT engineer's cost estimate (thousands of dollars)
STATUS	Qualitative	Bid status (1 = fixed, 0 = competitive)
B2B1RAT	Quantitative	Ratio of second lowest bid to low bid
B3B1RAT	Quantitative	Ratio of third lowest bid to low bid
BHB1RAT	Quantitative	Ratio of highest bid to low bid
DISTRICT	Qualitative	Location of road (1 = south Florida, 0 = north Florida)
BTPRATIO	Quantitative	Ratio of number of bidders to number of plan holders
DAYSEST	Quantitative	DOT engineer's estimate of number of workdays required

 *Data Set:* FLAG

STATISTICS IN **ACTION** REVISITED

- Evaluating a First-Order Model **(p. 730)**
- Variable Screening and Model Building **(p. 778)**
- A Residual Analysis **(p. 795)**

12.1 Multiple Regression Models

Most practical applications of regression analysis employ models that are more complex than the simple straight-line model. For example, a realistic probabilistic model for monthly sales revenue would include more than just the amount of advertising expenditure. Factors such as last month's sales, number of sales competitors, and advertising medium are some of the many variables that might be related to sales revenue. Thus, we would want to incorporate these and other potentially important independent variables into the model in order to make accurate predictions.

Probabilistic models that include more than one independent variable are called **multiple regression models.** The general form of these models is

$$y = \beta_0 + \beta_1 x_1 + \beta_2 x_2 + \cdots + \beta_k x_k + \varepsilon$$

The dependent variable y is now written as a function of k independent variables, $x_1, x_2, \ldots, x_k$. The random error term is added to make the model probabilistic rather than deterministic. The value of the coefficient β_i determines the contribution of the independent variable x_i, and β_0 is the y-intercept. The coefficients $\beta_0, \beta_1, \ldots, \beta_k$ are usually unknown because they represent population parameters.

At first glance it might appear that the regression model shown above would not allow for anything other than straight-line relationships between y and the independent variables, but this is not true. Actually, $x_1, x_2, \ldots, x_k$ can be functions of variables as long as the functions do not contain unknown parameters. For example, the monthly sales revenue, y, could be a function of the independent variables

$$x_1 = \text{Advertising expenditure}$$
$$x_2 = \text{Number of sales competitors}$$
$$x_3 = (x_1)^2$$
$$x_4 = 1 \text{ if TV advertising, 0 if not}$$

The x_3 term is called a **higher-order term** because it is the value of a quantitative variable (x_1) squared (i.e., raised to the second power). The x_4 term is a **coded variable** representing a qualitative variable (advertising medium). The multiple regression model is quite versatile and can be made to model many different types of response variables.

The General Multiple Regression Model*

$$y = \beta_0 + \beta_1 x_1 + \beta_2 x_2 + \cdots + \beta_k x_k + \varepsilon$$

where

y is the dependent variable.

$x_1, x_2, \ldots, x_k$ are the independent variables.

$E(y) = \beta_0 + \beta_1 x_1 + \beta_2 x_2 + \cdots + \beta_k x_k$ is the deterministic portion of the model.

β_i determines the contribution of the independent variable x_i.

Note: The symbols $x_1, x_2, \ldots, x_k$ may represent higher-order terms for quantitative predictors or terms that represent qualitative predictors.

As shown in the box, the steps used to develop the multiple regression model are similar to those used for the simple linear regression model.

Analyzing a Multiple Regression Model

Step 1 Hypothesize the deterministic component of the model. This component relates the mean, $E(y)$, to the independent variables $x_1, x_2, \ldots, x_k$. This involves the choice of the independent variables to be included in the model (Sections 12.2, 12.5–12.10).

Step 2 Use the sample data to estimate the unknown model parameters $\beta_0, \beta_1, \beta_2, \ldots, \beta_k$ in the model (Section 12.2).

Step 3 Specify the probability distribution of the random error term, ε, and estimate the standard deviation of this distribution, σ (Section 12.3).

Step 4 Check that the assumptions on ε are satisfied and make model modifications if necessary (Section 12.11).

Step 5 Statistically evaluate the usefulness of the model (Section 12.3).

Step 6 When satisfied that the model is useful, use it for prediction, estimation, and other purposes (Section 12.4).

The assumptions we make about the random error ε of the multiple regression model are also similar to those in a simple linear regression (see Section 11.3). These are summarized below.

Assumptions for Random Error ε

For any given set of values of $x_1, x_2, \ldots, x_k$, the random error ε has a probability distribution with the following properties:

1. Mean equal to 0
2. Variance equal to σ^2
3. Normal distribution
4. Random errors are independent (in a probabilistic sense).

This chapter is divided into three parts. In Part I, we consider the most basic multiple regression model involving only quantitative independent variables, called a *first-order model.* In Part II, we introduce several other different types of models that form the foundation of **model building** (i.e., useful model construction). Finally, in Part III, we discuss how to check the validity of the model assumptions on the random error term—called a *residual analysis.*

---

*Technically, this model is referred to as a general multiple *linear* regression model since the equation is a linear function of the β's.

PART I: FIRST-ORDER MODELS WITH QUANTITATIVE INDEPENDENT VARIABLES

12.2 Estimating and Making Inferences About the β Parameters

GEORGE U. YULE (1871–1951)
Yule Processes

Born on a small farm in Scotland, George Yule received an extensive childhood education. After graduating from University College (London), where he studied civil engineering, Yule spent a year employed in engineering workshops. However, he made a career change in 1893, accepting a teaching position back at University College under the guidance of statistician Karl Pearson (see p. 603). Inspired by Pearson's work, Yule produced a series of important articles on the statistics of regression and correlation. Yule is considered the first to apply the method of least squares in regression analysis, and he developed the theory of multiple regression. He eventually was appointed a lecturer in statistics at Cambridge University and later became the president of the prestigious Royal Statistical Society. Yule made many other contributions to the field, including the invention of time series analysis and the development of Yule processes and the Yule distribution.

A model that includes terms only for *quantitative* independent variables, called a **first-order model,** is described in the box. Note that the first-order model does not include any higher-order terms (such as x_1^2).

A First-Order Model in Five Quantitative Independent (Predictor) Variables*

$$E(y) = \beta_0 + \beta_1 x_1 + \beta_2 x_2 + \beta_3 x_3 + \beta_4 x_4 + \beta_5 x_5$$

where $x_1, x_2, \ldots, x_5$ are all quantitative variables that *are not* functions of other independent variables.

Note: β_i represents the slope of the line relating y to x_i when all the other x's are held fixed.

The method of fitting first-order models—and multiple regression models in general—is identical to that of fitting the simple straight-line model: the **method of least squares**—that is, we choose the estimated model

$$\hat{y} = \hat{\beta}_0 + \hat{\beta}_1 x_1 + \cdots + \hat{\beta}_k x_k$$

that   (1) has an average error of prediction of 0, i.e., $\Sigma(y - \hat{y}) = 0$
and   (2) minimizes SSE $= (y - \hat{y})^2$

As in the case of the simple linear model, the sample estimates $\hat{\beta}_0, \hat{\beta}_1, \ldots, \hat{\beta}_k$ are obtained as a solution to a set of simultaneous linear equations.[†]

The primary difference between fitting the simple and multiple regression models is computational difficulty. The $(k + 1)$ simultaneous linear equations that must be solved to find the $(k + 1)$ estimated coefficients $\hat{\beta}_0, \hat{\beta}_1, \ldots, \hat{\beta}_k$ cannot be written in simple equation form; rather, the estimates are obtained using matrices and matrix algebra. Instead of presenting the complex matrix algebra required to fit the models, we resort to statistical software and present output from SPSS, Minitab, and Excel.

EXAMPLE 12.1

Fitting a First-Order Model: Price of an Antique Clock

Problem A collector of antique grandfather clocks sold at auction believes that the price received for the clocks depends on both the age of the clocks and the number of bidders at the auction. Thus, he hypothesizes the first-order model

$$y = \beta_0 + \beta_1 x_1 + \beta_2 x_2 + \varepsilon$$

where

$$
\begin{aligned}
y &= \text{Auction price (dollars)} \\
x_1 &= \text{Age of clock (years)} \\
x_2 &= \text{Number of bidders}
\end{aligned}
$$

A sample of 32 auction prices of grandfather clocks, along with their age and the number of bidders, is given in Table 12.1.

a. Use scatterplots to plot the sample data. Interpret the plots.

b. Use the method of least squares to estimate the unknown parameters β_0, β_1, and β_2 of the model.

---

*The terminology *first order* is derived from the fact that each x in the model is raised to the first power.

[†]Students who are familiar with calculus should note that $\hat{\beta}_0, \hat{\beta}_1, \ldots, \hat{\beta}_k$ are the solutions to the set of equations $\partial\text{SSE}/\partial\hat{\beta}_0 = 0, \partial\text{SSE}/\partial\hat{\beta}_1 = 0, \ldots, \partial\text{SSE}/\partial\hat{\beta}_k = 0$. The solution is usually given in matrix form, but we do not present the details here. See the references for details.

Table 12.1	Auction Price Data				
Age, x_1	Number of Bidders, x_2	Auction Price, y	Age, x_1	Number of Bidders, x_2	Auction Price, y
127	13	$1,235	170	14	$2,131
115	12	1,080	182	8	1,550
127	7	845	162	11	1,884
150	9	1,522	184	10	2,041
156	6	1,047	143	6	845
182	11	1,979	159	9	1,483
156	12	1,822	108	14	1,055
132	10	1,253	175	8	1,545
137	9	1,297	108	6	729
113	9	946	179	9	1,792
137	15	1,713	111	15	1,175
117	11	1,024	187	8	1,593
137	8	1,147	111	7	785
153	6	1,092	115	7	744
117	13	1,152	194	5	1,356
126	10	1,336	168	7	1,262

 *Data Set:* CLOCKS

c. Find the value of SSE that is minimized by the least squares method.

d. Estimate σ, the standard deviation of the model, and interpret the result.

Solution

a. Minitab side-by-side scatterplots for examining the bivariate relationships between y and x_1, and between y and x_2, are shown in Figure 12.1. Of the two variables, age (x_1) appears to have the stronger linear relationship with auction price (y).

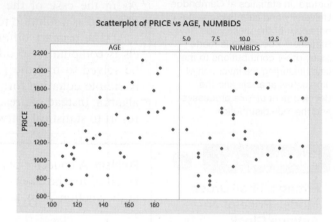

Figure 12.1

Minitab side-by-side scatterplots for the data of Table 12.1

b. The model hypothesized is fit to the data of Table 12.1 with Excel/XLSTAT. A portion of the printout is reproduced in Figure 12.2. The least squares estimates of the β parameters (highlighted at the bottom of the printout) are $\hat{\beta}_0 = -1,339$, $\hat{\beta}_1 = 12.74$, and $\hat{\beta}_2 = 85.95$. Therefore, the equation that minimizes SSE for this data set (i.e., the **least squares prediction equation**) is

$$\hat{y} = -1,339 + 12.74x_1 + 85.95x_2$$

c. The minimum value of the sum of the squared errors, also highlighted in Figure 12.2, is SSE = 516,727.

d. Recall that the estimator of σ^2 for the straight-line model is $s^2 = \text{SSE}/(n - 2)$, and note that the denominator is (n − number of estimated β parameters), which is $(n - 2)$ in the straight-line model. Because we must estimate the three parameters β_0, β_1, and β_2 for the first-order model, the estimator of σ^2 is

$$s^2 = \frac{\text{SSE}}{n - 3} = \frac{\text{SSE}}{32 - 3} = \frac{516,727}{29} = 17,818$$

Regression of variable PRICE:					
Goodness of fit statistics:					
Observations	32.0000				
Sum of weights	32.0000				
DF	29.0000				
R²	0.8923				
Adjusted R²	0.8849				
MSE	17818.1565				
RMSE	133.4847				
DW	1.8720				

Analysis of variance:

Source	DF	Sum of squares	Mean squares	F	Pr > F
Model	2	4283062.9601	2141531.4801	120.1882	< 0.0001
Error	29	516726.5399	17818.1565		
Corrected Total	31	4799789.5000			

Computed against model Y=Mean(Y)

Model parameters:

Source	Value	Standard error	t	Pr > |t|	Lower bound (90%)	Upper bound (90%)
Intercept	-1338.9513	173.8095	-7.7036	< 0.0001	-1634.2757	-1043.6270
AGE	12.7406	0.9047	14.0820	< 0.0001	11.2033	14.2778
NUMBIDS	85.9530	8.7285	9.8474	< 0.0001	71.1221	100.7839

Equation of the model:
PRICE = -1339+12.74057*AGE+85.95298*NUMBIDS

Figure 12.2

Excel-XLSTAT Analysis of the Action Price Model

This value, often called the **mean square for error (MSE)**, is also highlighted on Figure 12.2. The estimate of σ, then, is

$$s = \sqrt{17{,}818} = 133.5$$

which is highlighted at the top of the printout in Figure 12.2. One useful interpretation of the estimated standard deviation s is that the interval $\pm 2s$ will provide a rough approximation to the accuracy with which the model will predict future values of y for given values of x. Thus, we expect the model to provide predictions of auction price to within about $\pm 2s = \pm 2(133.5) = \pm 267$ dollars.*

Look Back As with simple linear regression, we will use the estimator of σ^2 both to check the utility of the model (Section 12.3) and to provide a measure of reliability of predictions and estimates when the model is used for those purposes (Section 12.4). Thus, you can see that the estimation of σ^2 plays an important part in the development of a regression model.

● **Now Work Exercise 12.2a–c**

Estimator of σ^2 for a Multiple Regression Model with k Independent Variables

$$s^2 = \frac{\text{SSE}}{n - \text{number of estimated } \beta \text{ parameters}} = \frac{\text{SSE}}{n - (k + 1)}$$

After obtaining the least squares prediction equation, the analyst will usually want to make meaningful interpretations of the β estimates. Recall that in the straight-line model (Chapter 11)

$$y = \beta_0 + \beta_1 x + \varepsilon$$

β_0 represents the y-intercept of the line, and β_1 represents the slope of the line. From our discussion in Chapter 11, β_1 has a practical interpretation—it represents the mean change in y for every 1-unit increase in x. When the independent variables are quantitative, the β parameters in the first-order model specified in Example 12.1 have similar interpretations. The difference is that when we interpret the β that multiplies one of the variables (e.g., x_1), we must be certain to hold the values of the remaining independent variables (e.g., x_2, x_3) fixed.

*The $\pm 2s$ approximation will improve as the sample size is increased. We will provide more precise methodology for the construction of prediction intervals in Section 12.4.

To see this, suppose that the mean $E(y)$ of a response y is related to two quantitative independent variables, x_1 and x_2, by the first-order model

$$E(y) = 1 + 2x_1 + x_2$$

In other words, $\beta_0 = 1$, $\beta_1 = 2$, and $\beta_2 = 1$.

Now, when $x_2 = 0$, the relationship between $E(y)$ and x_1 is given by

$$E(y) = 1 + 2x_1 + (0) = 1 + 2x_1$$

A Minitab graph of this relationship (a straight line) is shown in Figure 12.3. Similar graphs of the relationship between $E(y)$ and x_1 for $x_2 = 1$,

$$E(y) = 1 + 2x_1 + (1) = 2 + 2x_1$$

and for $x_2 = 2$,

$$E(y) = 1 + 2x_1 + (2) = 3 + 2x_1$$

also are shown in Figure 12.3. Note that the slopes of the three lines are all equal to $\beta_1 = 2$, the coefficient that multiplies x_1.

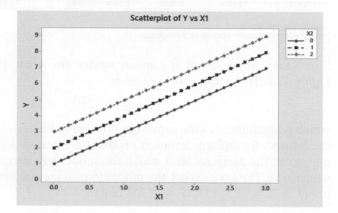

Figure 12.3

Minitab graph of
$E(y) = 1 + 2x_1 + x_2$ for
$x_2 = 0, 1, 2$

Figure 12.3 exhibits a characteristic of all first-order models: If you graph $E(y)$ versus any one variable—say, x_1—for fixed values of the other variables, the result will always be a *straight line* with slope equal to β_1. If you repeat the process for other values of the fixed independent variables, you will obtain a set of *parallel* straight lines. This indicates that the effect of the independent variable x_i on $E(y)$ is independent of all the other independent variables in the model, and this effect is measured by the slope β_i (see the box on page 711).

EXAMPLE 12.2

Interpreting the β Estimates: Clock Auction Price Model

Problem Refer to the first-order model for auction price *(y)* considered in Example 12.1. Interpret the estimates of the β parameters in the model.

Solution The least squares prediction equation, as given in Example 12.1, is $\hat{y} = -1{,}339 + 12.74x_1 + 85.95x_2$. We know that with first-order models, β_1 represents the slope of the line relating y to x_1 for fixed x_2. That is, β_1 measures the change in $E(y)$ for every 1-unit increase in x_1 when the other independent variable in the model is held fixed. A similar statement can be made about β_2: β_2 measures the change in $E(y)$ for every 1-unit increase in x_2 when the other x in the model is held fixed. Consequently, we obtain the following interpretations:

$\hat{\beta}_1 = 12.74$: We estimate the mean auction price $E(y)$ of an antique clock to increase \$12.74 for every 1-year increase in age (x_1) when the number of bidders (x_2) is held fixed.

$\hat{\beta}_2 = 85.95$: We estimate the mean auction price $E(y)$ of an antique clock to increase \$85.95 for every 1-bidder increase in the number of bidders (x_2) when age (x_1) is held fixed.

The value $\hat{\beta}_0 = -1{,}339$ does not have a meaningful interpretation in this example. To see this, note that $\hat{y} = \hat{\beta}_0$ when $x_1 = x_2 = 0$. Thus, $\hat{\beta}_0 = -1{,}339$ represents the estimated mean auction price when the values of all the independent variables are set equal to 0. Because an antique clock with these characteristics—an age of 0 years and 0 bidders on the clock—is not practical, the value of $\hat{\beta}_0$ has no meaningful interpretation.

Look Back In general, $\hat{\beta}_0$ will not have a practical interpretation unless it makes sense to set the values of the x's simultaneously equal to 0.

● **Now Work Exercise 12.14a, b**

> **⊗ CAUTION** The interpretation of the β parameters in a multiple regression model will depend on the terms specified in the model. The interpretations above are for a first-order linear model only. In practice, you should be sure that a first-order model is the correct model for $E(y)$ before making these β interpretations. (We discuss alternative models for $E(y)$ in Sections 12.5–12.8.)

Inferences about the individual β parameters in a model are obtained using either a confidence interval or a test of hypothesis, as outlined in the following two boxes.*

A 100$(1 - \alpha)$% Confidence Interval for a β Parameter

$$\hat{\beta}_i \pm t_{\alpha/2}s_{\hat{\beta}_i}$$

where $t_{\alpha/2}$ is based on $n - (k + 1)$ degrees of freedom and

$n =$ Number of observations

$k + 1 =$ Number of β parameters in the model

Test of an Individual Parameter Coefficient in the Multiple Regression Model

One-Tailed Test	Two-Tailed Test
$H_0: \beta_i = 0$	$H_0: \beta_i = 0$
$H_a: \beta_i < 0$ [or $H_a: \beta_i > 0$]	$H_a: \beta_i \neq 0$

$$\text{Test statistic: } t = \frac{\hat{\beta}_i}{s_{\hat{\beta}_i}}$$

One-Tailed Test	Two-Tailed Test
Rejection region: $t < -t_\alpha$ [or $t > t_\alpha$ when $H_a: \beta_i > 0$]	*Rejection region:* $|t| > t_{\alpha/2}$
p-value: $P(t < t_c)$ [or $P(t > t_c)$ when $H_a: \beta_i > 0$]	*p*-value: $2P(t > |t_c|)$

where t_α and $t_{\alpha/2}$ are based on $n - (k + 1)$ degrees of freedom and

$n =$ Number of observations

$k + 1 =$ Number of β parameters in the model

---

*The formulas for computing $\hat{\beta}_i$ and its standard error are so complex that the only reasonable way to present them is by using matrix algebra. We do not assume a prerequisite of matrix algebra for this text, and, in any case, we think the formulas can be omitted in an introductory course without serious loss. They are programmed into almost all statistical software packages with multiple regression routines and are presented in some of the texts listed in the references.

Conditions Required for Valid Inferences About the β Parameters

Refer to the four assumptions about the probability distribution for the random error ε. (p. 710).

We illustrate these methods with another example.

EXAMPLE 12.3

Inferences about the β Parameters—Auction Price Model

Problem Refer to Examples 12.1 and 12.2. The collector of antique grandfather clocks knows that the price (y) received for the clocks increases linearly with the age (x_1) of the clocks. Moreover, the collector hypothesizes that the auction price (y) will increase linearly as the number of bidders (x_2) increases. Use the information on the XLSTAT printout shown in Figure 12.2 (p. 713) to

a. Test the hypothesis that the mean auction price of a clock increases as the number of bidders increases when age is held constant, that is, test $\beta_2 > 0$. Use $\alpha = .05$.

b. Form a 90% confidence interval for β_1 and interpret the result.

Solution

a. The hypotheses of interest concern the parameter β_2. Specifically,

$$H_0: \beta_2 = 0$$
$$H_a: \beta_2 > 0$$

The test statistic is a t-statistic formed by dividing the sample estimate $\hat{\beta}_2$ of the parameter β_2 by the estimated standard error of $\hat{\beta}_2$ (denoted $s_{\hat{\beta}_2}$). These estimates, $\hat{\beta}_2 = 85.953$ and $s_{\hat{\beta}_2} = 8.729$, as well as the calculated t-value,

$$\text{Test statistic: } t = \frac{\hat{\beta}_2}{s_{\hat{\beta}_2}} = \frac{85.953}{8.729} = 9.85$$

are highlighted on the Minitab printout in Figure 12.2.

The rejection region for the test is found in exactly the same way as the rejection regions for the t-tests in previous chapters—that is, we consult Table III in Appendix D to obtain an upper-tail value of t. This is a value t_α such that $P(t > t_\alpha) = \alpha$. We can then use this value to construct rejection regions for either one-tailed or two-tailed tests.

For $\alpha = .05$ and $n - (k + 1) = 32 - (2 + 1) = 29$ df, the critical t-value obtained from Table III is $t_{.05} = 1.699$. Therefore,

Rejection region: $t > 1.699$ (see Figure 12.4)

Because the test statistic value, $t = 9.85$, falls in the rejection region, we have sufficient evidence to reject H_0. Thus, the collector can conclude that the mean auction price of a clock increases as the number of bidders increases, when age is held constant. Note that the two-tailed observed significance level of the test is also highlighted on the printout. Because the one-tailed p-value (half this value) is p-value $< (.0001/2) = .00005$, any nonzero α (e.g., $\alpha = .01$) will lead us to reject H_0.

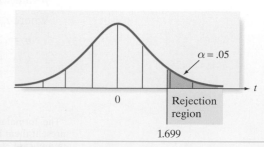

Figure 12.4

Rejection region for $H_0: \beta_2 = 0$ vs. $H_a: \beta_2 > 0$

b. A 90% confidence interval for β_1 is:

$$\hat{\beta}_1 \pm t_{\alpha/2}s_{\hat{\beta}_1} = \hat{\beta}_1 \pm t_{.05}s_{\hat{\beta}_1}$$

Substituting $\hat{\beta}_1 = 12.74$, $s_{\hat{\beta}_1} = .905$ (both obtained from the XLSTAT printout, Figure 12.2), and $t_{.05} = 1.699$ (from part **a**) into the equation, we obtain

$$12.74 \pm 1.699(.905) = 12.74 \pm 1.54 = (11.20, 14.28)$$

[Note: This interval is also highlighted on the XLSTAT printout.] Thus, we are 90% confident that β_1 falls between 11.20 and 14.28. Because β_1 is the slope of the line relating auction price (y) to age of the clock (x_1), we conclude that the price increases between \$11.20 and \$14.28 for every 1-year increase in age, holding number of bidders (x_2) constant.

Look Back When interpreting the β multiplied by one x, be sure to hold fixed the values of the other x's in the model.

> ● **Now Work Exercise 12.14c, d**

12.3 Evaluating Overall Model Utility

In Section 12.2, we demonstrated the use of t-tests in making inferences about β parameters in the multiple regression model. There are caveats, however, with conducting these t-tests for the purposes of determining which x's are useful for predicting y. Several of these are listed next.

Use Caution When Conducting t-Tests on the β Parameters

It is dangerous to conduct t-tests on the individual β parameters in a *first-order linear model* for the purpose of determining which independent variables are useful for predicting y and which are not. If you fail to reject H_0: $\beta_i = 0$, several conclusions are possible:

1. There is no relationship between y and x_i.
2. A straight-line relationship between y and x exists (holding the other x's in the model fixed), but a Type II error occurred.
3. A relationship between y and x_i (holding the other x's in the model fixed) exists but is more complex than a straight-line relationship (e.g., a curvilinear relationship may be appropriate). The most you can say about a β parameter test is that there is either sufficient (if you reject H_0: $\beta_i = 0$) or insufficient (if you do not reject H_0: $\beta_i = 0$) evidence of a *linear* (*straight-line*) relationship between y and x_i.

In addition, conducting t-tests on each β parameter in a model is *not* the best way to determine whether the overall model is contributing information for the prediction of y. If we were to conduct a series of t-tests to determine whether the independent variables are contributing to the predictive relationship, we would be very likely to make one or more errors in deciding which terms to retain in the model and which to exclude.

For example, suppose you fit a first-order model in 10 quantitative x variables and decide to conduct t-tests on all 10 of the individual β's in the model, each at $\alpha = .05$. Even if all the β parameters (except β_0) are equal to 0, approximately 40% of the time you will incorrectly reject the null hypothesis at least once and conclude that some β parameter differs from 0.* Thus, in multiple regression models for which a large number

*The proof of this result (assuming independence of tests) proceeds as follows:

$P(\text{Reject } H_0 \text{ at least once} \mid \beta_1 = \beta_2 = \cdots = \beta_{10} = 0)$
$= 1 - P(\text{Reject } H_0 \text{ no times} \mid \beta_1 = \beta_2 = \cdots = \beta_{10} = 0)$
$\leq 1 - [P(\text{Accept } H_0\text{: } \beta_1 = 0 \mid \beta_1 = 0) \cdot P(\text{Accept } H_0\text{: } \beta_2 = 0 \mid \beta_2 = 0) \cdots \cdot P(\text{Accept } H_0\text{: } \beta_{10} = 0 \mid \beta_{10} = 0)]$
$= 1 - [(1 - \alpha)^{10}] = 1 - (.95)^{10} = .401$

For dependent tests, the Bonferroni inequality states that
$P(\text{Reject } H_0 \text{ at least once} \mid \beta_1 = \beta_2 = \cdots = \beta_{10} = 0) \leq 10(\alpha) = 10(.05) = .50.$

of independent variables are being considered, conducting a series of t-tests may include a large number of insignificant variables and exclude some useful ones. To test the utility of a multiple regression model, we need a *global test* (one that encompasses all the β parameters). We would also like to find some statistical quantity that measures how well the model fits the data.

We commence with the easier problem—finding a measure of how well a linear model fits a set of data. For this we use the multiple regression equivalent of r^2, the coefficient of determination for the straight-line model (Chapter 11), as shown in the box.

> The **multiple coefficient of determination, R^2,** is defined as
>
> $$R^2 = 1 - \frac{SSE}{SS_{yy}} = \frac{SS_{yy} - SSE}{SS_{yy}} = \frac{\text{Explained variability}}{\text{Total variability}}$$

Just like r^2 in the simple linear model, R^2 represents the fraction of the sample variation of the y-values (measured by SS_{yy}) that is explained by the least squares prediction equation. Thus, $R^2 = 0$ implies a complete lack of fit of the model to the data, and $R^2 = 1$ implies a perfect fit, with the model passing through every data point. In general, the larger the value of R^2, the better the model fits the data.

To illustrate, the value $R^2 = .892$ for the auction price model of Examples 12.1–12.3 is highlighted on the SPSS printout for the analysis shown in Figure 12.5. This high value of R^2 implies that using the independent variables age and number of bidders in a first-order model explains 89.2% of the total *sample variation* (measured by SS_{yy}) in auction price (y). Thus, R^2 is a sample statistic that tells how well the model fits the data and thereby represents a measure of the usefulness of the entire model.

Model	R	R Square	Adjusted R Square	Std. Error of the Estimate
1	.945[a]	.892	.885	133.485

a. Predictors: (Constant), NUMBIDS, AGE

ANOVA[a]

Model		Sum of Squares	df	Mean Square	F	Sig.
1	Regression	4283062.960	2	2141531.480	120.188	.000[b]
	Residual	516726.540	29	17818.157		
	Total	4799789.500	31			

a. Dependent Variable: PRICE

b. Predictors: (Constant), NUMBIDS, AGE

Coefficients[a]

Model		Unstandardized Coefficients B	Std. Error	Standardized Coefficients Beta	t	Sig.
1	(Constant)	-1338.951	173.809		-7.704	.000
	AGE	12.741	.905	.887	14.082	.000
	NUMBIDS	85.953	8.729	.620	9.847	.000

a. Dependent Variable: PRICE

Figure 12.5

SPSS analysis of the auction price model

A large value of R^2 computed from the *sample* data does not necessarily mean that the model provides a good fit to all of the data points in the *population*. For example, a first-order linear model that contains three parameters will provide a perfect fit to a sample of three data points, and R^2 will equal 1. Likewise, you will always obtain a perfect fit $(R^2 = 1)$ to a set of n data points if the model contains exactly n parameters. Consequently, if you want to use the value of R^2 as a measure of how useful the model will be for predicting y, it should be based on a sample that contains substantially more data points than the number of parameters in the model.

> **! CAUTION** In a multiple regression analysis, use the value of R^2 as a measure of how useful a linear model will be for predicting y only if the sample contains substantially more data points than the number of β parameters in the model.

As an alternative to using R^2 as a measure of model adequacy, the *adjusted multiple coefficient of determination*, denoted R_a^2, is often reported. The formula for R_a^2 is shown in the box.

The **adjusted multiple coefficient of determination** is given by

$$R_a^2 = 1 - \left[\frac{(n-1)}{n-(k+1)} \right]\left(\frac{\text{SSE}}{\text{SS}_{yy}} \right)$$

$$= 1 - \left[\frac{(n-1)}{n-(k+1)} \right](1 - R^2)$$

Note: $R_a^2 \leq R^2$

R^2 and R_a^2 have similar interpretations. However, unlike R^2, R_a^2 takes into account ("adjusts" for) both the sample size n and the number of β parameters in the model. R_a^2 will always be smaller than R^2 and, more importantly, cannot be "forced" to 1 by simply adding more and more independent variables to the model. Consequently, analysts prefer the more conservative R_a^2 when choosing a measure of model adequacy. The value of R_a^2 is also highlighted in Figure 12.5. Note that $R_a^2 = .885$, a value only slightly smaller than R^2.

Despite their utility, R^2 and R_a^2 are only sample statistics. Therefore, it is dangerous to judge the global usefulness of a model based solely on these values. A better method is to conduct a test of hypothesis involving *all* the β parameters (except β_0) in a model. In particular, for the general multiple regression model $E(y) = \beta_0 + \beta_1 x_1 + \beta_2 x_2 + \cdots + \beta_k x_k$, we would test

$$H_0: \beta_1 = \beta_2 = \cdots = \beta_k = 0$$

H_a: At least one of the coefficients is nonzero.

The test statistic used to test this hypothesis is an F-statistic, and several equivalent versions of the formula can be used (although we will usually rely on the computer to calculate the F-statistic):

$$\textit{Test statistic: } F = \frac{(\text{SS}_{yy} - \text{SSE})/k}{\text{SSE}/[n-(k+1)]}$$

$$= \frac{\text{Mean Square (Model)}}{\text{Mean Square (Error)}} = \frac{R^2/k}{(1-R^2)/[n-(k+1)]}$$

These formulas indicate that the F-statistic is the ratio of the *explained* variability divided by the model degrees of freedom to the *unexplained* variability divided by the error degrees of freedom. Thus, the larger the proportion of the total variability accounted for by the model, the larger the F-statistic.

To determine when the ratio becomes large enough that we can confidently reject the null hypothesis and conclude that the model is more useful than no model at all for predicting y, we compare the calculated F-statistic to a tabulated F-value with k df in the numerator and $[n - (k + 1)]$ df in the denominator. Recall that tabulations of the F-distribution for various values of α are given in Tables V, VI, VII, and VIII in Appendix D.

> *Rejection region:* $F > F_\alpha$, where F is based on k numerator and $n - (k + 1)$ denominator degrees of freedom.

The analysis of variance F-test for testing the usefulness of the model is summarized in the next box.

Testing Global Usefulness of the Model: The Analysis of Variance F-Test

$H_0: \beta_1 = \beta_2 = \cdots = \beta_k = 0$ (All model terms are unimportant for predicting y.)

$H_a:$ At least one $\beta_i \neq 0$ (At least one model term is useful for predicting y.)

$$\textit{Test statistic: } F = \frac{(\text{SS}_{yy} - \text{SSE})/k}{\text{SSE}/[n - (k + 1)]} = \frac{R^2/k}{(1 - R^2)/[n - (k + 1)]}$$

$$= \frac{\text{Mean Square (Model)}}{\text{Mean Square (Error)}}$$

where n is the sample size and k is the number of terms in the model.

Rejection region: $F > F_\alpha$, with k numerator degrees of freedom and $[n - (k + 1)]$ denominator degrees of freedom.

p-value: $P(F > F_c)$, where F_c is the calculated value of the test statistic.

Conditions Required for the Global F-Test in Regression to Be Valid

refer to the standard regression assumptions about the random error component (Section 12.1).

> ❗ **CAUTION** A rejection of the null hypothesis $H_0: \beta_1 = \beta_2 = \cdots = \beta_k$ in the *global F-test* leads to the conclusion [with $100(1 - \alpha)\%$ confidence] that the model is statistically useful. However, statistically "useful" does not necessarily mean "best." Another model may prove even more useful in terms of providing more reliable estimates and predictions. This global F-test is usually regarded as a test that the model *must* pass to merit further consideration.

EXAMPLE 12.4

Assessing Overall Adequacy—Clock Auction Price Model

Problem Refer to Examples 12.1–12.3, in which an antique collector modeled the auction price (y) of grandfather clocks as a function of the age of the clock (x_1) and the number of bidders (x_2). Recall that the hypothesized first-order model is

$$y = \beta_0 + \beta_1 x_1 + \beta_2 x_2 + \varepsilon$$

The SPSS printout for the analysis is shown in Figure 12.5 (p. 718).

a. Find and interpret the adjusted coefficient of determination R_a^2.
b. Conduct the global F-test of model usefulness at the $\alpha = .05$ level of significance.

Solution

a. The R_a^2 value (highlighted in Figure 12.5) is .885. This implies that the least squares model has explained about 88.5% of the total sample variation in y-values (auction prices), after adjusting for sample size and number of independent variables in the model.

b. The elements of the global test of the model follow:

$H_0: \beta_1 = \beta_2 = 0$ (*Note: k = 2*)

H_a: At least one of the two model coefficients, β_1 and β_2, is nonzero.

Test statistic: $F = \dfrac{\text{MS (Model)}}{\text{MSE}} = \dfrac{2{,}141{,}531}{17{,}818} = 120.19$ (see Figure 12.5)

p-value ≈ 0

Conclusion: Because $\alpha = .05$ exceeds the observed significance level, $(p \approx 0)$, the data provide strong evidence that at least one of the model coefficients is nonzero. The overall model appears to be statistically useful for predicting auction prices.

Look Back Can we be sure that the best prediction model has been found if the global F-test indicates that a model is useful? Unfortunately, we cannot. The addition of other independent variables may improve the usefulness of the model. (See the box on p. 720.) We consider more complex multiple regression models in Sections 12.5–12.8.

● **Now Work Exercise 12.15d-h**

In this section, we discussed several different statistics for assessing the utility of a multiple regression model: t-tests on individual β parameters, R^2, R_a^2, and the global F-test. Both R^2 and R_a^2 are indicators of how well the prediction equation fits the data. Intuitive evaluations of the contribution of the model based on R^2 must be examined with care. Unlike R_a^2, the value of R^2 increases as more and more variables are added to the model. Consequently, you could force R^2 to take a value very close to 1 even though the model contributes no information for the prediction of y. In fact, R^2 equals 1 when the number of terms in the model (including β_0) equals the number of data points. Therefore, you should not rely solely on the value of R^2 (or even R_a^2) to tell you whether the model is useful for predicting y.

Conducting t-tests on all of the individual β parameters is also not the best method of testing the global utility of the model because these multiple tests result in a high probability of making at least one Type I error. Use the F-test for testing the global utility of the model.

After we have determined that the overall model is useful for predicting y using the F-test, we may elect to conduct one or more t-tests on the individual β parameters. However, the test (or tests) to be conducted should be decided a priori—that is, prior to fitting the model. Also, we should limit the number of t-tests conducted to avoid the potential problem of making too many Type I errors. Generally, the regression analyst will conduct t-tests only on the "most important" β's. We provide insight in identifying the most important β's in a linear model in Sections 12.5–12.8.

Recommendation for Checking the Utility of a Multiple Regression Model

1. First, conduct a test of overall model adequacy using the F-test—that is, test

$$H_0: \beta_1 = \beta_2 = \cdots = \beta_k = 0$$

If the model is deemed adequate (that is, if you reject H_0), then proceed to step 2. Otherwise, you should hypothesize and fit another model. The new model may include more independent variables or higher-order terms.

2. Conduct t-tests on those β parameters in which you are particularly interested (that is, the "most important" β's). As we will see in Sections 12.5 and 12.6, these usually involve only the β's associated with higher-order terms (x^2, x_1x_2, etc.). However, it is a safe practice to limit the number of β's that are tested. Conducting a series of t-tests leads to a high overall Type I error rate α.

Exercises 12.1–12.24

Learning the Mechanics

12.1 Write a first-order model relating $E(y)$ to
   a. two quantitative independent variables.
   b. four quantitative independent variables.
   c. five quantitative independent variables.

12.2 Minitab was used to fit the model
NW $E(y) = \beta_0 + \beta_1 x_1 + \beta_2 x_2$ to $n = 20$ data points, and the printout shown below was obtained.
   a. What are the sample estimates of β_0, β_1, and β_2?
   b. What is the least squares prediction equation?
   c. Find SSE, MSE, and s. Interpret the standard deviation in the context of the problem.
   d. Test $H_0: \beta_1 = 0$ against $H_0: \beta_1 \neq 0$. Use $\alpha = .05$.
   e. Use a 95% confidence interval to estimate β_2.
   f. Find R^2 and R_a^2 and interpret these values.
   g. Find the test statistic for testing $H_0: \beta_1 = \beta_2 = 0$.
   h. Find the observed significance level of the test, part **g**. Interpret the result.

Regression Analysis: Y versus X1, X2

Analysis of Variance

Source	DF	Adj SS	Adj MS	F-Value	P-Value
Regression	2	128329	64165	7.22	0.005
Error	17	151016	8883		
Total	19	279345			

Model Summary

S	R-sq	R-sq(adj)
94.251	45.9%	39.6%

Coefficients

Term	Coef	SE Coef	T-Value	P-Value
Constant	506.35	45.17	11.21	0.000
X1	-941.90	275.08	-3.42	0.003
X2	-429.06	379.83	-1.13	0.275

Regression Equation

Y = 506.35 - 941.9 X1 - 429.1 X2

12.3 Suppose you fit the multiple regression model
$$y = \beta_0 + \beta_1 x_1 + \beta_2 x_2 + \beta_3 x_3 + \varepsilon$$
to $n = 30$ data points and obtain the following result:
$$\hat{y} = 3.4 - 4.6x_1 + 2.7x_2 + .93x_3$$
The estimated standard errors of $\hat{\beta}_2$ and $\hat{\beta}_3$ are 1.86 and .29, respectively.
   a. Test the null hypothesis $H_0: \beta_2 = 0$ against the alternative hypothesis $H_a: \beta_2 \neq 0$. Use $\alpha = .05$.
   b. Test the null hypothesis $H_0: \beta_3 = 0$ against the alternative hypothesis $H_a: \beta_3 \neq 0$. Use $\alpha = .05$.
   c. The null hypothesis $H_0: \beta_2 = 0$ is not rejected. In contrast, the null hypothesis $H_0: \beta_3 = 0$ is rejected. Explain how this can happen even though $\hat{\beta}_2 > \hat{\beta}_3$.

12.4 Suppose you fit the first-order multiple regression model
$$y = \beta_0 + \beta_1 x_1 + \beta_2 x_2 + \varepsilon$$
to $n = 25$ data points and obtain the prediction equation
$$\hat{y} = 6.4 + 3.1x_1 + .92x_2$$
The estimated standard deviations of the sampling distributions of $\hat{\beta}_1$ and $\hat{\beta}_2$ are 2.3 and .27, respectively.

   a. Test $H_0: \beta_1 = 0$ against $H_a: \beta_1 > 0$. Use $\alpha = .05$.
   b. Test $H_0: \beta_2 = 0$ against $H_a: \beta_2 \neq 0$. Use $\alpha = .05$.
   c. Find a 90% confidence interval for β_1. Interpret the interval.
   d. Find a 99% confidence interval for β_2. Interpret the interval.

12.5 How is the number of degrees of freedom available for estimating σ^2 (the variance of ε) related to the number of independent variables in a regression model?

12.6 Consider the first-order model equation in three quantitative independent variables
$$E(y) = 2 - 3x_1 + 5x_2 - x_3$$
   a. Graph the relationship between y and x_3 for $x_1 = 2$ and $x_2 = 1$.
   b. Repeat part **a** for $x_1 = 1$ and $x_2 = -2$.
   c. How do the graphed lines in parts **a** and **b** relate to each other? What is the slope of each line?
   d. If a linear model is first-order in three independent variables, what type of geometric relationship will you obtain when $E(y)$ is graphed as a function of one of the independent variables for various combinations of the other independent variables?

12.7 Suppose you fit the first-order model
$$y = \beta_0 + \beta_1 x_1 + \beta_2 x_2 + \beta_3 x_3 + \beta_4 x_4 + \beta_5 x_5 + \varepsilon$$
to $n = 30$ data points and obtain
$$\text{SSE} = .33 \quad R^2 = .92$$
   a. Do the values of SSE and R^2 suggest that the model provides a good fit to the data? Explain.
   b. Is the model of any use in predicting y? Test the null hypothesis $H_0: \beta_1 = \beta_2 = \beta_3 = \beta_4 = \beta_5 = 0$ against the alternative hypothesis H_a: At least one of the parameters $\beta_1, \beta_2, \ldots, \beta_5$ is nonzero. Use $\alpha = .05$.

12.8 If the analysis of variance F-test leads to the conclusion that at least one of the model parameters is nonzero, can you conclude that the model is the best predictor for the dependent variable y? Can you conclude that all of the terms in the model are important for predicting y? What is the appropriate conclusion?

Applying the Concepts—Basic

12.9 **Ambiance of 5-star hotels.** Although invisible and intangible, ambient conditions such as air quality (x_1), temperature (x_2), odor/aroma (x_3), music (x_4), noise level (x_5), and overall image (x_6) may affect guests' satisfaction with their stay at a hotel. A study in the *Journal of Hospitality Marketing & Management* (Vol. 24, 2015) was designed to assess the effect of each of these ambient factors on customer satisfaction with the hotel (y). Using a survey, researchers collected data for a sample of 422 guests at 5-star hotels. All variables were measured as an average of several 5-point questionnaire responses. The results of the multiple regression are summarized in the table on the next page.
   a. Write the equation of a first-order model for hotel image (y) as a function of the six ambient conditions.

Table for Exercise 12.9

Variable	β Estimate	Std. Error	t-Value
Air Quality (x_1)	.122	.0486	2.51
Temperature (x_2)	.018	.0545	.33
Odor/Aroma (x_3)	.124	.0446	2.78
Music (x_4)	.119	.0372	3.20
Noise/Sound Level (x_5)	.101	.0380	2.66
Overall Image (x_6)	.463	.0438	10.56

$R^2 = .508$, $R_{adj}^2 = .501$, $F = 71.42$

Source: Based on M. Suh, et al. "Invisible and Intangible, but Undeniable: Role of Ambient Conditions in Building Hotel Guests' Loyalty," *Journal of Hospitality Marketing & Management*, Vol. 24, No. 7, 2015 (Table 4). Copyright: 2015.

b. Give a practical interpretation of each of the β-estimates shown.

c. A 99% confidence interval for β_6 is (.350, .576). Give a practical interpretation of this result.

d. Interpret the value of adjusted R^2.

e. Is there sufficient evidence that the overall model is statistically useful for predicting hotel image (y)? Test using $\alpha = .01$.

12.10 Forecasting movie revenues with Twitter. Refer to the *IEEE International Conference on Web Intelligence and Intelligent Agent Technology* (2010) study on using the volume of chatter on Twitter.com to forecast movie box office revenue, Exercise 11.27 (p. 657). Recall that opening weekend box office revenue data (in millions of dollars) were collected for a sample of 24 recent movies. In addition to each movie's *tweet rate*, i.e., the average number of tweets referring to the movie per hour 1 week prior to the movie's release, the researchers also computed the ratio of positive to negative tweets (called the *PN-ratio*).

a. Give the equation of a first-order model relating revenue (y) to both tweet rate (x_1) and PN-ratio (x_2).

b. Which β in the model, part **a,** represents the change in revenue (y) for every 1-tweet increase in the tweet rate (x_1), holding PN-ratio (x_2) constant?

c. Which β in the model, part **a,** represents the change in revenue (y) for every 1-unit increase in the PN-ratio (x_2), holding tweet rate (x_1) constant?

d. The following coefficients were reported: $R^2 = .945$ and $R_a^2 = .940$. Give a practical interpretation for both R^2 and R_a^2.

e. Conduct a test of the null hypothesis, $H_0: \beta_1 = \beta_2 = 0$. Use $\alpha = .05$.

f. The researchers reported the *p*-values for testing $H_0: \beta_1 = 0$ and $H_0: \beta_2 = 0$ as both less than .0001. Interpret these results (use $\alpha = .01$).

12.11 Accounting and Machiavellianism. Refer to the *Behavioral Research in Accounting* (January 2008) study of Machiavellian traits (e.g., manipulation, cunning, duplicity, deception, and bad faith) in accountants, Exercise 9.8 (p. 529). Recall that a Mach rating score was determined for each in a sample of accounting alumni of a large

southwestern university. For one portion of the study, the researcher modeled an accountant's Mach score (y) as a function of age, gender, education, and income. Data on $n = 198$ accountants yielded the results shown in the table.

Independent Variable	t-Value for $H_0: \beta_i = 0$	p-Value
Age (x_1)	0.10	> .10
Gender (x_2)	−0.55	> .10
Education (x_3)	1.95	< .01
Income (x_4)	0.52	> .10

Overall model: $R^2 = .13$, $F = 4.74$ (*p*-value < .01)

a. Conduct a test of overall model utility. Use $\alpha = .05$.

b. Interpret the coefficient of determination, R^2.

c. Is there sufficient evidence (at $\alpha = .05$) to say that income is a statistically useful predictor of Mach score?

12.12 Characteristics of lead users. "Lead users" describe creative individuals who are on the leading edge of an important market trend. *Creativity and Innovation Management* (February 2008) published an article on identifying the social network characteristics of lead users of children's computer games. Data were collected for $n = 326$ children, and the following variables were measured: lead-user rating (y, measured on a 5-point scale), gender ($x_1 = 1$ if female, 0 if male), age (x_2, years), degree of centrality (x_3, measured as the number of direct ties to other peers in the network), and betweenness centrality (x_4, measured as the number of shortest paths between peers). A first-order model for y was fit to the data, yielding the following least squares prediction equation:

$$\hat{y} = 3.58 + .01x_1 - .06x_2 - .01x_3 + .42x_4$$

a. Give two properties of the errors of prediction that result from using the method of least squares to obtain the parameter estimates.

b. Give a practical interpretation of the estimate of β_4 in the model.

c. A test of $H_0: \beta_4 = 0$ resulted in a *p*-value of .002. Make the appropriate conclusion at $\alpha = .05$.

12.13 Predicting elements in aluminum alloys. Aluminum scraps that are recycled into alloys are classified into three categories: soft-drink cans, pots and pans, and automobile crank chambers. A study of how these three materials affect the metal elements present in aluminum alloys was published in *Advances in Applied Physics* (Vol. 1, 2013). Data on 126 production runs at an aluminum plant were used to model the percentage (y) of various elements (e.g., silver, boron, iron) that make up the aluminum alloy. Three independent variables were used in the model: $x_1 = $ proportion of aluminum scraps from cans, $x_2 = $ proportion of aluminum scraps from pots/pans, and $x_3 = $ proportion of aluminum scraps from crank chambers. The first-order model, $E(y) = \beta_0 + \beta_1 x_1 + \beta_2 x_2 + \beta_3 x_3$, was fit to the data for several elements. The estimates of the model parameters (*p*-values in parentheses) for silver and iron are shown in the accompanying table.

Element (y)	β_0	β_1	β_2	β_3	F p-value	R^2
Silver	.0020 (.001)	−.0000141 (.015)	−.0000123 (.035)	−.0000357 (.009)	.049	.075
Iron	−5.958 (<.001)	.079 (<.001)	.084 (<.001)	.054 (<.001)	<.001	.783

a. Is the overall model statistically useful (at $\alpha = .05$) for predicting the percentage of silver in the alloy? If so, give a practical interpretation of R^2.

b. Is the overall model statistically useful (at $\alpha = .05$) for predicting the percentage of iron in the alloy? If so, give a practical interpretation of R^2.

c. Based on the parameter estimates, sketch the relationship between percentage of silver (y) and proportion of aluminum scraps from cans (x_1). Conduct a test to determine if this relationship is statistically significant at $\alpha = .05$.

d. Based on the parameter estimates, sketch the relationship between percentage of iron (y) and proportion of aluminum scraps from cans (x_1). Conduct a test to determine if this relationship is statistically significant at $\alpha = .05$.

12.14 Predicting runs scored in baseball. Consider a multiple regression model for predicting the total number of runs scored by a Major League Baseball (MLB) team during a season. Using data on number of walks (x_1), singles (x_2), doubles (x_3), triples (x_4), home runs (x_5), stolen bases (x_6), times caught stealing (x_7), strike outs (x_8), and ground outs (x_9) for each of the 30 teams during the 2014 MLB season, a first-order model for total number of runs scored (y) was fit. The results are shown in the accompanying Minitab printout.

a. Write the least squares prediction equation for $y =$ total number of runs scored by a team during the 2014 season.

b. Give practical interpretations of the β estimates.

c. Conduct a test of $H_0: \beta_7 = 0$ against $H_a: \beta_7 < 0$ at $\alpha = .05$. Interpret the results.

d. Locate a 95% confidence interval for β_5 on the printout. Interpret the interval.

e. Predict the number of runs scored in 2014 by your favorite Major League Baseball team. How close is the predicted value to the actual number of runs scored by your team? (*Note:* You can find data on your favorite team on the Internet at www.mlb.com.)

Applying the Concepts—Intermediate

12.15 Novelty of a vacation destination. Many tourists choose a vacation destination based on the newness or uniqueness (i.e., the novelty) of the itinerary. The relationship between novelty and vacationing golfers' demographics was investigated in the *Annals of Tourism Research* (Vol. 29, 2002). Data were obtained from a mail survey of 393 golf vacationers to a large coastal resort in the southeastern United States. Several measures of novelty level (on a numerical scale) were obtained for each vacationer, including "change from routine," "thrill," "boredom-alleviation," and "surprise." The researcher employed four independent variables in a regression model to predict each of the novelty measures. The independent variables were $x_1 =$ number of rounds of golf per year, $x_2 =$ total number of golf vacations taken, $x_3 =$ number of years played golf, and $x_4 =$ average golf score.

a. Give the hypothesized equation of a first-order model for $y =$ change from routine.

b. A test of $H_0: \beta_3 = 0$ versus $H_a: \beta_3 < 0$ yielded a p-value of .005. Interpret this result if $\alpha = .01$.

c. The estimate of β_3 was found to be negative. Based on this result (and the result of part **b**), the researcher concluded that "those who have played golf for more years

Minitab Output for Exercise 12.14

```
Analysis of Variance

Source          DF    Adj SS   Adj MS   F-Value  P-Value
Regression       9   84174.4   9352.7    24.77    0.000
  Walks          1    3488.9   3488.9     9.24    0.006
  Singles        1    5653.8   5653.8    14.97    0.001
  Doubles        1    6221.4   6221.4    16.48    0.001
  Triples        1    3376.7   3376.7     8.94    0.007
  HomeRuns       1   11913.7  11913.7    31.55    0.000
  StolenBases    1      29.5     29.5     0.08    0.783
  CaughtStealing 1       3.1      3.1     0.01    0.929
  StrikeOuts     1    1847.7   1847.7     4.89    0.039
  GroundOuts     1    1498.9   1498.9     3.97    0.060
Error           20    7551.9    377.6
Total           29   91726.3


Model Summary

      S    R-sq  R-sq(adj)  R-sq(pred)
19.4318  91.77%     88.06%      82.38%


Coefficients

Term              Coef  SE Coef        95% CI          T-Value  P-Value   VIF
Constant            40      156  (   -285,     364)       0.25    0.801
Walks           0.2538   0.0835  ( 0.0796,  0.4280)       3.04    0.006   1.55
Singles          0.407    0.105  (  0.188,   0.627)       3.87    0.001   2.18
Doubles          0.841    0.207  (  0.409,   1.273)       4.06    0.001   1.92
Triples          1.633    0.546  (  0.494,   2.772)       2.99    0.007   1.23
HomeRuns         1.092    0.194  (  0.687,   1.498)       5.62    0.000   1.84
StolenBases      0.050    0.179  ( -0.323,   0.422)       0.28    0.783   1.54
CaughtStealing  -0.044    0.484  ( -1.054,   0.966)      -0.09    0.929   1.89
StrikeOuts     -0.0911   0.0412  (-0.1771, -0.0052)      -2.21    0.039   1.55
GroundOuts     -0.1218   0.0612  (-0.2494,  0.0057)      -1.99    0.060   2.27


Regression Equation

Runs = 40 + 0.2538 Walks + 0.407 Singles + 0.841 Doubles + 1.633 Triples + 1.092 HomeRuns
       + 0.050 StolenBases - 0.044 CaughtStealing - 0.0911 StrikeOuts - 0.1218 GroundOuts
```

are less apt to seek change from their normal routine in their golf vacations." Do you agree with this statement? Explain.

d. The regression results for three dependent novelty measures, based on data collected for $n = 393$ golf vacationers, are summarized in the table below. Give the null hypothesis for testing the overall adequacy of the first-order regression model.

e. Give the rejection region for the test, part **d,** for $\alpha = .01$.

f. Use the test statistics reported in the table and the rejection region from part **e** to conduct the test for each of the dependent measures of novelty.

g. Verify that the p-values reported in the table support your conclusions in part **f.**

h. Interpret the values of R^2 reported in the table.

Dependent Variable	F-Value	p-Value	R^2
Thrill	5.56	< .001	.055
Change from routine	3.02	.018	.030
Surprise	3.33	.011	.023

Source: Based on J. F. Petrick, "An Examination of Golf Vacationers' Novelty," *Annals of Tourism Research*, Vol. 29, No. 2, 2002, pp. 384–400.

12.16 Arsenic in groundwater. *Environmental Science & Technology* (January 2005) reported on a study of the reliability of a commercial kit to test for arsenic in groundwater. The field kit was used to test a sample of 328 groundwater wells in Bangladesh. In addition to the arsenic level (micrograms per liter), the latitude (degrees), longitude (degrees), and depth (feet) of each well were measured. The data are saved in the file. (The first and last 5 observations are listed in the table below.)

Well ID	Latitude	Longitude	Depth	Arsenic
10	23.7887	90.6522	60	331
14	23.7886	90.6523	45	302
30	23.7880	90.6517	45	193
59	23.7893	90.6525	125	232
85	23.7920	90.6140	150	19
⋮	⋮	⋮	⋮	⋮
7353	23.7949	90.6515	40	48
7357	23.7955	90.6515	30	172
7890	23.7658	90.6312	60	175
7893	23.7656	90.6315	45	624
7970	23.7644	90.6303	30	254

a. Write a first-order model for arsenic level (y) as a function of latitude, longitude, and depth.

b. Fit the model to the data using the method of least squares.

c. Give practical interpretations of the β estimates.

d. Find the model standard deviation, s, and interpret its value.

e. Find and interpret the values of R^2 and R_a^2.

f. Conduct a test of overall model utility at $\alpha = .05$.

g. Based on the results, parts **d–f,** would you recommend using the model to predict arsenic level (y)? Explain.

12.17 Reality TV and cosmetic surgery. How much influence does the media have on one's decision to undergo cosmetic surgery? This was the question of interest in *Body Image:*

An International Journal of Research (March 2010). In the study, 170 college students answered questions about their impressions of reality TV shows featuring cosmetic surgery. The five variables analyzed in the study were measured as follows:

DESIRE—scale ranging from 5 to 25, where the higher the value, the greater the interest in having cosmetic surgery
GENDER—1 if male, 0 if female
SELFESTM—scale ranging from 4 to 40, where the higher the value, the greater the level of self-esteem
BODYSAT—scale ranging from 1 to 9, where the higher the value, the greater the satisfaction with one's own body
IMPREAL—scale ranging from 1 to 7, where the higher the value, the more one believes reality television shows featuring cosmetic surgery are realistic

The data for the study (simulated based on statistics reported in the journal article) are saved in the file. Selected observations are listed in the accompanying table. Multiple regression was used to model desire to have cosmetic surgery (y) as a function of gender (x_1), self-esteem (x_2), body satisfaction (x_3), and impression of reality TV (x_4).

STUDENT	DESIRE	GENDER	SELFESTM	BODYSAT	IMPREAL
1	11	0	24	3	4
2	13	0	20	3	4
3	11	0	25	4	5
4	11	1	22	9	4
5	18	0	8	1	6
⋮	⋮	⋮	⋮	⋮	⋮
166	18	0	25	3	5
167	13	0	26	4	5
168	9	1	13	5	6
169	14	0	20	3	2
170	6	1	27	8	3

a. Fit the first-order model, $E(y) = \beta_0 + \beta_1 x_1 + \beta_2 x_2 + \beta_3 x_3 + \beta_4 x_4$, to the data in the file. Give the least squares prediction equation.

b. Interpret the β estimates in the words of the problem.

c. Is the overall model statistically useful for predicting desire to have cosmetic surgery? Test using $\alpha = .01$.

d. Which statistic, R^2 or R_a^2, is the preferred measure of model fit? Practically interpret the value of this statistic.

e. Conduct a test to determine whether desire to have cosmetic surgery decreases linearly as level of body satisfaction increases. Use $\alpha = .05$.

f. Find a 95% confidence interval for β_4. Practically interpret the result.

12.18 Contamination from a plant's discharge. Refer to the U.S. Army Corps of Engineers data (Example 1.5, p. 38) on fish contaminated from the toxic discharges of a chemical plant located on the banks of the Tennessee River in Alabama. Recall that the engineers measured the length (in centimeters), weight (in grams), and DDT level (in parts per million) for 144 captured fish. In addition, the number of miles upstream from the river was recorded. The data are saved in the file. (The first and last five observations are shown in the table on the next page.)

a. Fit the first-order model, $E(y) = \beta_0 + \beta_1 x_1 + \beta_2 x_2 + \beta_3 x_3$, to the data, where $y = $ DDT level, $x_1 = $ mile, $x_2 = $ length, and $x_3 = $ weight. Report the least squares prediction equation.

Data for Exercise 12.18

River	Mile	Species	Length	Weight	DDT
FC	5	CHANNELCATFISH	42.5	732	10.00
FC	5	CHANNELCATFISH	44.0	795	16.00
FC	5	CHANNELCATFISH	41.5	547	23.00
FC	5	CHANNELCATFISH	39.0	465	21.00
FC	5	CHANNELCATFISH	50.5	1,252	50.00
⋮	⋮	⋮	⋮	⋮	⋮
TR	345	LARGEMOUTHBASS	23.5	358	2.00
TR	345	LARGEMOUTHBASS	30.0	856	2.20
TR	345	LARGEMOUTHBASS	29.0	793	7.40
TR	345	LARGEMOUTHBASS	17.5	173	0.35
TR	345	LARGEMOUTHBASS	36.0	1,433	1.90

b. Find the estimate of the standard deviation of ε for the model and give a practical interpretation of its value.

c. Conduct a test of the global utility of the model. Use $\alpha = .05$.

d. Do the data provide sufficient evidence to conclude that DDT level increases as length increases? Report the observed significance level of the test and reach a conclusion using $\alpha = .05$.

e. Find and interpret a 95% confidence interval for β_3.

12.19 Cooling method for gas turbines. Refer to the *Journal of Engineering for Gas Turbines and Power* (January 2005) study of a high-pressure inlet fogging method for a gas turbine engine, Exercise 7.94 (p. 431). Recall that the heat rate (kilojoules per kilowatt per hour) was measured for each in a sample of 67 gas turbines augmented with high-pressure inlet fogging. In addition, several other variables were measured, including cycle speed (revolutions per minute), inlet temperature (°C), exhaust gas temperature (°C), cycle pressure ratio, and air mass flow rate (kilograms per second). The data are saved in the file. (The first and last five observations are listed in table below.)

RPM	CP Ratio	Inlet Temp.	Exhaust Temp.	Airflow	Heat Rate
27,245	9.2	1,134	602	7	14,622
14,000	12.2	950	446	15	13,196
17,384	14.8	1,149	537	20	11,948
11,085	11.8	1,024	478	27	11,289
14,045	13.2	1,149	553	29	11,964
⋮	⋮	⋮	⋮	⋮	⋮
18,910	14.0	1,066	532	8	12,766
3,600	35.0	1,288	448	152	8,714
3,600	20.0	1,160	456	84	9,469
16,000	10.6	1,232	560	14	11,948
14,600	13.4	1,077	536	20	12,414

Source: Based on R. Bhargava and C. B. Meher-Homji, "Parametric Analysis of Existing Gas Turbines with Inlet Evaporative and Overspray Fogging," *Journal of Engineering for Gas Turbines and Power*, Vol. 127, No. 1, January 2005, pp. 145–158.

a. Write a first-order model for heat rate (y) as a function of speed, inlet temperature, exhaust temperature, cycle pressure ratio, and airflow rate.

b. Fit the model to the data using the method of least squares.

c. Give practical interpretations of the β estimates.

d. Find the model standard deviation, s, and interpret its value.

e. Conduct a test for overall model utility using $\alpha = .01$.

f. Find and interpret R_a^2.

g. Is there sufficient evidence (at $\alpha = .01$) to indicate that heat rate (y) is linearly related to inlet temperature?

12.20 Rankings of research universities. Refer to the College Choice *2015 Rankings of National Research Universities*, Exercise 11.29 (p. 657). Data on academic reputation score, average financial aid awarded, average net cost to attend, median salary during early career, percentage of alumni who feel their work makes a better place, and percentage of science, technology, engineering, and math (STEM) degrees awarded for the top 50 research universities are saved in the file. Information on the top 10 schools are reproduced in the table. Consider a first-order multiple regression model to predict academic reputation score (y) using financial aid awarded (x_1), net cost (x_2), early career salary (x_3), work makes a better place percentage (x_4), and percentage of STEM degrees (x_5).

Rank University	Academic Rep. Score	Financial Aid	Cost	Early Pay	Better Place	STEM
1 Harvard	99 pts.	$41,555	$14,455	$61,400	65%	28%
2 MIT	92	34,641	20,629	74,900	55	79
3 Stanford	94	38,522	19,233	65,900	62	29
4 Columbia	95	37,934	21,274	60,200	56	29
5 Yale	97	39,771	18,479	60,300	68	21
6 CalTech	91	31,445	22,645	72,600	66	93
7 Dartmouth	91	38,148	20,490	56,300	45	20
8 Penn	92	35,539	21,821	60,300	55	19
9 Duke	92	33,191	24,134	60,600	59	35
10 Johns Hopkins	89	34,469	22,973	57,500	63	26

a. Use statistical software to fit the model to the data. Give the least squares prediction equation.

b. Find and give a practical interpretation of the standard deviation of the model, s.

c. Find and give a practical interpretation of the coefficient of determination, R^2.

d. Conduct a test of the overall adequacy of the model using $\alpha = .05$.

e. Find a 90% confidence interval for the β coefficient associated with work makes a better place percentage (x_4). Interpret the result.

12.21 Bubble behavior in subcooled flow boiling. In industry cooling applications (e.g., cooling of nuclear reactors), a process called subcooled flow boiling is often employed. Subcooled flow boiling is susceptible to small bubbles that occur near the heated surface. The characteristics of these bubbles were investigated in *Heat Transfer Engineering* (Vol. 34., 2013). A series of experiments was conducted to measure two important bubble behaviors—bubble diameter (millimeters) and bubble density (liters per meters squared). The mass flux (kilograms per meters squared per second) and heat flux (megawatts per meters squared) were varied for each experiment. The data obtained at a set pressure are listed in the following table.

Bubble	Mass Flux	Heat Flux	Diameter	Density
1	406	0.15	0.64	13103
2	406	0.29	1.02	29117
3	406	0.37	1.15	123021
4	406	0.62	1.26	165969
5	406	0.86	0.91	254777
6	406	1.00	0.68	347953
7	811	0.15	0.58	7279
8	811	0.29	0.98	22566
9	811	0.37	1.02	106278
10	811	0.62	1.17	145587
11	811	0.86	0.86	224204
12	811	1.00	0.59	321019
13	1217	0.15	0.49	5096
14	1217	0.29	0.80	18926
15	1217	0.37	0.93	90992
16	1217	0.62	1.06	112102
17	1217	0.86	0.81	192903
18	1217	1.00	0.43	232211

Source: U. Puli, A. K. Rajvanshi, and S. K. Das, "Investigation of Bubble Behavior in Subcooled Flow Boiling of Water in a Horizontal Annulus Using High-Speed Flow Visualization," *Heat Transfer Engineering*, Vol. 34, No. 10, 2013 (Table 8). Copyright © 2013 by Taylor & Francis.

a. Consider the multiple regression model, $E(y_1) = \beta_0 + \beta_1 x_1 + \beta_2 x_2$, where y_1 = bubble diameter, x_1 = mass flux, and x_2 = heat flux. Use statistical software to fit the model to the data and test the overall adequacy of the model.

b. Consider the multiple regression model, $E(y_2) = \beta_0 + \beta_1 x_1 + \beta_2 x_2$, where y_2 = bubble density, x_1 = mass flux, and x_2 = heat flux. Use statistical software to fit the model to the data and test the overall adequacy of the model.

c. Which of the two dependent variables, diameter (y_1) or density (y_2), is better predicted by mass flux (x_1) and heat flux (x_2)?

12.22 R^2 and model fit. Because the coefficient of determination R^2 always increases when a new independent variable is

added to the model, it is tempting to include many variables in a model to force R^2 to be near 1. However, doing so reduces the degrees of freedom available for estimating σ^2, which adversely affects our ability to make reliable inferences. Suppose you want to use 18 economic indicators to predict next year's gross domestic product (GDP). You fit the model

$$y = \beta_0 + \beta_1 x_1 + \beta_2 x_2 + \cdots + \beta_{17} x_{17} + \beta_{18} x_{18} + \varepsilon$$

where y = GDP and $x_1, x_2, \ldots, x_{18}$ are the economic indicators. Only 20 years of data $(n = 20)$ are used to fit the model, and you obtain $R^2 = .95$. Test to see whether this impressive-looking R^2 is large enough for you to infer that the model is useful—that is, that at least one term in the model is important for predicting GDP. Use $\alpha = .05$.

Applying the Concepts—Advanced

12.23 Bordeaux wine sold at auction. The uncertainty of the weather during the growing season, the phenomenon that wine tastes better with age, and the fact that some vineyards produce better wines than others encourage speculation concerning the value of a case of wine produced by a certain vineyard during a certain year (or vintage). The publishers of a newsletter titled *Liquid Assets: The International Guide to Fine Wine* discussed a multiple regression approach to predicting the London auction price of red Bordeaux wine. The natural logarithm of the price y (in dollars) of a case containing a dozen bottles of red wine was modeled as a function of weather during growing season and age of vintage. Consider the multiple regression results for hypothetical data collected for 30 vintages (years) shown below.

a. Conduct a t-test (at $\alpha = .05$) for each of the β parameters in the model. Interpret the results.

b. When the natural log of y is used as a dependent variable, the antilogarithm of a β coefficient minus 1—that is $e^{\beta_i} - 1$—represents the percentage change in y for every 1-unit increase in the associated x-value. Use this information to interpret each of the β estimates.

c. Interpret the values of R^2 and s. Do you recommend using the model for predicting Bordeaux wine prices? Explain.

12.24 Cost analysis for a shipping department. Multiple regression is used by accountants in cost analysis to shed light on the factors that cause costs to be incurred and the

Results for Exercise 12.23

Independent Variables	Beta Estimate	Standard Error
x_1 = Vintage year	.03	.006
x_2 = Average growing season temperature (°C)	.60	.120
x_3 = Sept./Aug. rainfall (cm)	−.004	.001
x_4 = Rainfall in months preceding vintage (cm)	.0015	.0005
x_5 = Average Sept. temperature (°C)	.008	.550
	$R^2 = .85$	
	$s = .30$	

Data for Exercise 12.24

Week	Labor, y (hr)	Pounds Shipped, x_1 (1,000s)	Percentage of Units Shipped by Truck, x_2	Average Shipment Weight, x_3 (lb)
1	100	5.1	90	20
2	85	3.8	99	22
3	108	5.3	58	19
4	116	7.5	16	15
5	92	4.5	54	20
6	63	3.3	42	26
7	79	5.3	12	25
8	101	5.9	32	21
9	88	4.0	56	24
10	71	4.2	64	29
11	122	6.8	78	10
12	85	3.9	90	30
13	50	3.8	74	28
14	114	7.5	89	14
15	104	4.5	90	21
16	111	6.0	40	20
17	110	8.1	55	16
18	100	2.9	64	19
19	82	4.0	35	23
20	85	4.8	58	25

magnitudes of their effects. Sometimes, it is desirable to use physical units instead of cost as the dependent variable in a cost analysis (e.g., if the cost associated with the activity of interest is a function of some physical unit, such as hours of labor). The advantage of this approach is that the regression model will provide estimates of the number of labor hours required under different circumstances, and these hours can then be costed at the current labor rate (Horngren and Datar, *Cost Accounting*, 2014). The sample data shown in the table above have been collected from a firm's accounting and production records to provide cost information about the firm's shipping department. These data are saved in the file. Consider the model

$$y = \beta_0 + \beta_1 x_1 + \beta_2 x_2 + \beta_3 x_3 + \varepsilon$$

a. Find the least squares prediction equation.
b. Use an F-test to investigate the usefulness of the model specified in part **a**. Use $\alpha = .01$ and state your conclusion in the context of the problem.

c. Test $H_0: \beta_2 = 0$ versus $H_a: \beta_2 \neq 0$ using $\alpha = .05$. What do the results of your test suggest about the magnitude of the effects of x_2 on labor costs?
d. Find R^2 and interpret its value in the context of the problem.
e. If shipping department employees are paid $7.50 per hour, how much less, on average, will it cost the company per week if the average number of pounds per shipment increases from a level of 20 to 21? Assume that x_1 and x_2 remain unchanged. Your answer is an estimate of what is known in economics as the *expected marginal cost* associated with a 1-pound increase in x_3.
f. With what approximate precision can this model be used to predict the hours of labor? [*Note:* The precision of multiple regression predictions is discussed in Section 12.4.]
g. Can regression analysis alone indicate what factors *cause* costs to increase? Explain.

12.4 Using the Model for Estimation and Prediction

In Section 11.6, We discussed the use of the least squares line for estimating the mean value of y, $E(y)$, for some particular value of x, say, $x = x_p$. We also showed how to use the same fitted model to predict, when $x = x_p$, some new value of y to be observed in the future. Recall that the least squares line yielded the same value for both the estimate of $E(y)$ and the prediction of some future value of y—that is, both are the result of substituting x_p into the prediction equation $\hat{y} = \hat{\beta}_0 + \hat{\beta}_1 x$ and calculating $\hat{y}_p$. There the equivalence ends. The confidence interval for the mean $E(y)$ is narrower than the prediction interval for y because of the additional uncertainty attributable to the random error ε when predicting some future value of y.

These same concepts carry over to the multiple regression model. Consider a first-order model relating sale price (y) of a residential property to land value (x_1), appraised improvements value (x_2), and home size (x_3). Suppose we want to estimate the mean sale price for a given property with $x_1 = \$15,000$, $x_2 = \$50,000$, and $x_3 = 1,800$ square feet. Assuming that the first-order model represents the true relationship between sale price and the three independent variables, we want to estimate

$$E(y) = \beta_0 + \beta_1 x_1 + \beta_2 x_2 + \beta_3 x_3 = \beta_0 + \beta_1(15,000) + \beta_2(50,000) + \beta_3(1,800)$$

After obtaining the least squares estimates $\hat{\beta}_0, \hat{\beta}_1, \hat{\beta}_2$, and $\hat{\beta}_3$, the estimate of $E(y)$ will be

$$\hat{y} = \hat{\beta}_0 + \hat{\beta}_1(15,000) + \hat{\beta}_2(50,000) + \hat{\beta}_3(1,800)$$

To form a confidence interval for the mean, we need to know the standard deviation of the sampling distribution for the estimator $\hat{y}$. For multiple regression models, the form of this standard deviation is rather complex. However, the regression routines of statistical computer software packages allow us to obtain the confidence intervals for mean values of y for any given combination of values of the independent variables. We illustrate with an example.

EXAMPLE 12.5

Estimating E(y) and Predicting y—Auction Price Model

Problem Refer to Examples 12.1–12.4 and the first-order model, $E(y) = \beta_0 + \beta_1 x_1 + \beta_2 x_2$, where y = auction price of a grandfather clock, x_1 = age of the clock, and x_2 = number of bidders.

a. Estimate the average auction price for all 150-year-old clocks sold at auction with 10 bidders using a 95% confidence interval. Interpret the result.

b. Predict the auction price for a single 150-year-old clock sold at an auction with 10 bidders using a 95% prediction interval. Interpret the result.

c. Suppose you want to predict the auction price for one clock that is 50 years old and has 2 bidders. How should you proceed?

Solution

a. Here, the key words *average* and *for all* imply we want to estimate the mean of y, $E(y)$. We want a 95% confidence interval for $E(y)$ when $x_1 = 150$ years and $x_2 = 10$ bidders. A Minitab printout for this analysis is shown in Figure 12.6. The confidence interval (highlighted under **"95% CI"**) is (1,381.4, 1,481.9). Thus, we are 95% confident that the mean auction price for all 150-year-old clocks sold at an auction with 10 bidders lies between $1,381.40 and $1,481.90.

b. The key words *predict* and *for a single* imply that we want a 95% prediction interval for y when $x_1 = 150$ years and $x_2 = 10$ bidders. This interval (highlighted under **"95% PI"** on the Minitab printout, Figure 12.6) is (1,154.1, 1,709.3). We say, with 95% confidence, that the auction price for a single 150-year-old clock sold at an auction with 10 bidders falls between $1,154.10 and $1,709.30.

c. Now, we want to predict the auction price, y, for a single (*one*) grandfather clock when $x_1 = 50$ years and $x_2 = 2$ bidders. Consequently, we desire a 95% prediction interval for y. However, before we form this prediction interval, we should check to make sure that the selected values of the independent variables, $x_1 = 50$ and $x_2 = 2$, are both reasonable and within their respective sample ranges. If you

---

Figure 12.6

Minitab printout with 95% confidence intervals for grandfather clock model

Prediction for PRICE

Regression Equation

PRICE = -1339 + 12.741 AGE + 85.95 NUMBIDS

Variable	Setting
AGE	150
NUMBIDS	10

Fit	SE Fit	95% CI	95% PI
1431.66	24.5774	(1381.40, 1481.93)	(1154.07, 1709.26)

examine the sample data shown in Table 12.1 (p. 712), you will see that the range for age is $108 \leq x_1 \leq 194$, and the range for number of bidders is $5 \leq x_2 \leq 15$. Thus, both selected values fall well *outside* their respective ranges. Recall the *Caution* box in Section 11.6 (p. 686) warning about the dangers of using the model to predict y for a value of an independent variable that is not within the range of the sample data. Doing so may lead to an unreliable prediction.

Look Back If we want to make the prediction requested in part **c**, we would need to collect additional data on clocks with the requested characteristics (i.e., $x_1 = 50$ years and $x_2 = 2$ bidders) and then refit the model.

● **Now Work Exercise 12.29**

STATISTICS IN ACTION **Evaluating a First-Order Model**

REVISITED The Florida attorney general wants to develop a model for the cost (y) of a road construction contract awarded using the sealed-bid system and to use the model to predict the costs of future road contracts in the state. In addition to contract cost, the **FLAG** file contains data on eight potential predictor variables for a sample of 235 road contracts. (See Table SIA12.1 on p. 709.) Minitab scatterplots (with the dependent variable, COST, plotted against each of the potential predictors) for the data are shown in Figure SIA12.1. From the scatterplots, it appears that the DOT engineer's cost estimate (DOTEST) and estimate of work days (DAYSEST) would be good predictors of contract cost. [In a future *Statistics in Action Revisited* section (p. 778), we will learn that the two best predictors of contract cost are actually DOTEST and the fixed or competitive status (STATUS) of the contract.] However, in this section, we will fit the first-order regression model using all eight independent variables.

The Minitab printout for the regression analysis is shown in Figure SIA12.2. The global F-statistic ($F = 1,166.68$) and associated p-value (.000) shown on the printout

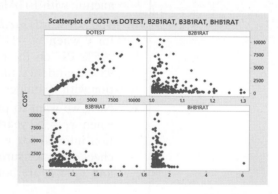

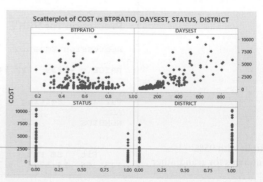

Figure SIA12.1

Minitab scatterplots for **FLAG** data

```
Analysis of Variance

Source       DF    Adj SS      Adj MS    F-Value  P-Value
Regression    8  865909963   108238745   1166.71    0.000
Error       226   20966676       92773
Total       234  886876639


Model Summary

      S    R-sq  R-sq(adj)
304.586  97.64%     97.55%


Coefficients

Term        Coef   SE Coef   T-Value  P-Value
Constant     124       427      0.29    0.772
DOTEST    0.9065    0.0166     54.64    0.000
B2B1RAT     -147       419     -0.35    0.726
B3B1RAT      -84       245     -0.34    0.733
BHB1RAT    -59.1      54.9     -1.08    0.283
STATUS     148.2      51.5      2.88    0.004
DISTRICT    37.8      43.1      0.88    0.382
BTPRATIO     218       140      1.56    0.121
DAYSEST    0.344     0.180      1.91    0.058


Regression Equation

COST = 124 + 0.9065 DOTEST - 147 B2B1RAT - 84 B3B1RAT - 59.1 BHB1RAT + 148.2 STATUS
       + 37.8 DISTRICT + 218 BTPRATIO + 0.344 DAYSEST
```

Figure SIA12.2

Minitab regression output for first-order model of road construction cost

indicate that the overall model is statistically useful for predicting construction cost. The value of R^2 indicates that the model can explain 97.6% of the sample variation in contract cost. Both of these results provide strong statistical support for using the model for estimation and prediction.

[*Note:* Not all of the independent variables have statistically significant *t*-values. However, we caution against dropping the insignificant variables from the model at this stage. One reason (discussed in Section 12.3) is that performing a large number of *t*-tests will yield an inflated probability of at least one Type I error. In later sections of this chapter, we develop other reasons for why the multiple *t*-test approach is not a good strategy for determining which independent variables to keep in the model.]

The Minitab printout shown in Figure SIA12.3 gives a 95% prediction interval for cost and a 95% confidence interval for the mean cost for the *x*-values associated with the last observation (contract) in the **FLAG** file. These *x*-values are engineer's cost estimate (DOTEST) = 497 thousand dollars, ratio of second lowest bid to lowest bid (B2B1RAT) = 1.07, ratio of third lowest bid to lowest bid (B3B1RAT) = 1.08, ratio of highest bid to lowest bid (BHB1RAT) = 1.19, competitive bid (STATUS = 0), south Florida contract (DISTRICT = 1), bidders to planholders ratio (BTPRATIO) = 0.5, and estimated work days (DAYSEST) = 90. The 95% confidence interval of (339.2, 528.2) implies that for all road contracts with these *x*-values, the mean contract cost falls between 339.2 and 528.2 thousand dollars, with 95% confidence.

Prediction for COST

```
Regression Equation

COST = 124 + 0.9065 DOTEST - 147 B2B1RAT - 84 B3B1RAT - 59.1 BHB1RAT + 148.2 STATUS
       + 37.8 DISTRICT + 218 BTPRATIO + 0.344 DAYSEST


Variable   Setting
DOTEST         497
B2B1RAT       1.07
B3B1RAT       1.08
BHB1RAT       1.19
STATUS           0
DISTRICT         1
BTPRATIO       0.5
DAYSEST         90
```

Figure SIA12.3

Minitab printout with 95% confidence and prediction intervals

```
   Fit   SE Fit       95% CI              95% PI
433.641  47.9459  (339.163, 528.119)  (-173.942, 1041.22)
```

STATISTICS
IN ACTION
REVISED
(continued)

The 95% prediction interval of $(-173.9, 1,041.2)$ implies that for an individual road contract with these x-values, the contract cost falls between 0 (because cost cannot be negative) and 1,041.2 thousand dollars, with 95% confidence. Note the wide range of the prediction interval. This is due to the large magnitude of the model standard deviation, $s = 305$ thousand dollars. Although the model is deemed statistically useful for predicting contract cost, it may not be "practically" useful. To reduce the magnitude of s, we will need to improve the model's predictive ability. (We consider such a model in the next *Statistics in Action Revisited* section.)

 Data Set: FLAG

Exercises 12.25–12.34

Applying the Concepts—Basic

12.25 Characteristics of lead users. Refer to the *Creativity and Innovation Management* (February 2008) study of lead users of children's computer games, Exercise 12.12 (p. 723). Recall that the researchers modeled lead-user rating (y, measured on a 5-point scale) as a function of gender ($x_1 = 1$ if female, 0 if male), age (x_2, years), degree of centrality (x_3, measured as the number of direct ties to other peers in the network), and betweenness centrality (x_4, measured as the number of shortest paths between peers). The least squares prediction equation was $\hat{y} = 3.58 + .01x_1 - .06x_2 - .01x_3 + .42x_4$.

a. Compute the predicted lead-user rating of a 10-year-old female child with 5 direct ties to other peers in her social network and with 2 shortest paths between peers.

b. Compute an estimate for the mean lead-user rating of all 8-year-old male children with 10 direct ties to other peers and with 4 shortest paths between peers.

12.26 User experience professionals salary survey. The User Experience Professionals Association (UXPA) supports people who research, design, and evaluate the user experience of products and services. The UXPA periodically conducts a salary survey of its members (e.g., *UXPA Salary Survey*, November 2014). One of the authors of the report, Jeff Sauro, investigated how much having a Ph.D. affects salaries in this profession and discussed his analysis on the blog, www.measuringusability.com. Sauro fit a first-order multiple regression model for salary (y, in dollars) as a function of years of experience (x_1), PhD status ($x_2 = 1$ if PhD, 0 if not), and manager status ($x_3 = 1$ if

manager, 0 if not). The following prediction equation was obtained:

$$\hat{y} = 52,484 + 2,941x_1 + 16,880x_2 + 11,108x_3$$

a. Predict the salary of a UXPA member with 10 years of experience, who does not have a PhD, but is a manager.

b. Predict the salary of a UXPA member with 10 years of experience, who does have a PhD, but is not a manager.

c. Why is a 95% prediction interval preferred over the predicted values given in parts **a** and **b**?

12.27 Reality TV and cosmetic surgery. Refer to the *Body Image: An International Journal of Research* (March 2010) study of the impact of reality TV shows on one's desire to undergo cosmetic surgery, Exercise 12.17 (p. 725). Recall that psychologists used multiple regression to model desire to have cosmetic surgery (y) as a function of gender (x_1), self-esteem (x_2), body satisfaction (x_3), and impression of reality TV (x_4). The SPSS printout below shows a confidence interval for $E(y)$ for each of the first five students in the study.

a. Interpret the confidence interval for $E(y)$ for student 1.

b. Interpret the confidence interval for $E(y)$ for student 4.

12.28 Chemical plant contamination. Refer to Exercise 12.18 (p. 725) and the U.S. Army Corps of Engineers study. You fit the first-order model, $E(y) = \beta_0 + \beta_1 x_1 + \beta_2 x_2 + \beta_3 x_3$, to the data, where y = DDT level (parts per million), x_1 = number of miles upstream, x_2 = length (centimeters), and x_3 = weight (grams). Use the Excel/XLSTAT printout below to predict, with 90% confidence, the DDT level of a fish caught 300 miles upstream with a length of 40 centimeters and a weight of 1,000 grams. Interpret the result.

	STUDENT	DESIRE	GENDER	SELFESTM	BODYSAT	IMPREAL	Lower95CL_Mean	Upper95CL_Mean
1	1	11	0	24	3	4	13.42	14.31
2	2	13	0	20	3	4	13.56	14.55
3	3	11	0	25	4	5	13.42	14.56
4	4	11	1	22	9	4	8.79	10.89
5	5	18	0	8	1	6	15.18	17.34

SPSS output for Exercise 12.27

Predictions for the new observations:

Observation	Pred(DDT)	Lower bound 90% (Mean)	Upper bound 90% (Mean)	Lower bound 90% (Observation)	Upper bound 90% (Observation)
MILE=300, LNGTH=40, WT=1000	18.8803	3.8650	33.8956	-143.2178	180.9784

XLSTAT output for Exercise 12.28

12.29 Cooling method for gas turbines. Refer to the *Journal of Engineering for Gas Turbines and Power* (January 2005) study of a high-pressure inlet fogging method for a gas turbine engine, Exercise 12.19 (p. 726). Recall that you fit a first-order model for heat rate (y) as a function of speed (x_1), inlet temperature (x_2), exhaust temperature (x_3), cycle pressure ratio (x_4), and airflow rate (x_5). A Minitab printout with both a 95% confidence interval for $E(y)$ and prediction interval for y for selected values of the x's is shown below.

a. Interpret the 95% prediction interval for y in the words of the problem.

b. Interpret the 95% confidence interval for $E(y)$ in the words of the problem.

c. Will the confidence interval for $E(y)$ always be narrower than the prediction interval for y? Explain.

Prediction for HEATRATE

```
Regression Equation

HEATRATE = 13614 + 0.0888 RPM - 9.20 INLET-TEMP + 14.39 EXH-TEMP + 0.4 CPRATIO)
         - 0.848 AIRFLOW


Variable    Setting
RPM         7500
INLET-TEMP  1000
EXH-TEMP    525
CPRATIO     13.5
AIRFLOW     10


  Fit    SE Fit      95% CI            95% PI
12632.5  237.342  (12157.9, 13107.1)  (11599.6, 13665.5)
```

Applying the Concepts—Intermediate

12.30 Arsenic in groundwater. Refer to the *Environmental Science & Technology* (Jan. 2005) study of the reliability of a commercial kit to test for arsenic in groundwater, Exercise 12.16 (p. 725). You fit a first-order model for arsenic level (y) as a function of latitude, longitude, and depth. Based on the model statistics, the researchers concluded that the arsenic level is highest at a low latitude, high longitude, and low depth. Do you agree? If so, find a 95% prediction interval for arsenic level for the lowest latitude, highest longitude, and lowest depth that are within the range of the sample data. Interpret the result.

12.31 Predicting runs scored in baseball. Refer to the study of runs scored in Major League Baseball games, Exercise 12.14 (p. 724). Multiple regression was used to model total number of runs scored (y) of a team during the season as a function of number of walks (x_1), number of singles (x_2), number of doubles (x_3), number of triples (x_4), number of home runs (x_5), number of stolen bases (x_6), number of times caught stealing (x_7), number of strikeouts (x_8), and total number of outs (x_9). Using the β estimates given in Exercise 12.14, predict the number of runs scored by your favorite Major League Baseball team last year. [*Note:* You can find data on your favorite team on the Internet at www.mlb.com.] Use statistical software to form a 95% prediction interval for your prediction. Does the actual number of runs scored by your team fall within the interval?

12.32 Rankings of research universities. Refer to the analysis of data from College Choice *2015 Rankings of National Research Universities*, Exercise 12.20 (p. 726). You fit a first-order multiple regression model to predict academic reputation score (y) using financial aid awarded (x_1), net cost (x_2), early career salary (x_3), work makes a better place percentage (x_4), and percentage of STEM degrees

(x_5). Now use statistical software to find and interpret a 95% prediction interval for the academic reputation score of a university with the following characteristics: $x_1 = \$23,368$, $x_2 = \$32,868$, $x_3 = \$49,100$, $x_4 = 46\%$, and $x_5 = 12\%$. [*Note:* These values correspond to Wake Forest University, which had an academic reputation score of 76. Does this score fall within the interval?]

12.33 Emotional intelligence and team performance. The *Engineering Project Organizational Journal* (Vol. 3, 2013) published the results of an exploratory study designed to gain a better understanding of how the emotional intelligence of individual team members relate directly to the performance of their team during an engineering project. Undergraduate students enrolled in the course, Introduction to the Building Industry, participated in the study. All students completed an emotional intelligence test and received an interpersonal score, stress management score, and mood score. Students were grouped in to $n = 23$ teams and assigned a group project. However, each student received an individual project score. These scores were averaged to obtain the dependent variable in the analysis—mean project score (y). Three independent variables were determined for each team: range of interpersonal scores (x_1), range of stress management scores (x_2), and range of mood scores (x_3). Data (simulated from information provided in the article) are listed in the table.

Team	Intrapersonal (Range)	Stress (Range)	Mood (Range)	Project (Average)
1	14	12	17	88.0
2	21	13	45	86.0
3	26	18	6	83.5
4	30	20	36	85.5
5	28	23	22	90.0
6	27	24	28	90.5
7	21	24	38	94.0
8	20	30	30	85.5
9	14	32	16	88.0
10	18	32	17	91.0
11	10	33	13	91.5
12	28	43	28	91.5
13	19	19	21	86.0
14	26	31	26	83.0
15	25	31	11	85.0
16	40	35	24	84.0
17	27	12	14	85.5
18	30	13	29	85.0
19	31	24	28	84.5
20	25	26	16	83.5
21	23	28	12	85.0
22	20	32	10	92.5
23	35	35	17	89.0

a. Hypothesize a first-order model for project score (y) as a function of x_1, x_2, and x_3.

b. Fit the model, part **a**, to the data using statistical software.

c. Is there sufficient evidence to indicate the overall model is statistically useful for predicting y? Test using $\alpha = .10$.

d. Evaluate the model statistics R_a^2 and $2s$.

e. Find and interpret a 95% prediction interval for y when $x_1 = 20$, $x_2 = 30$, and $x_3 = 25$.

12.34 Boiler drum production. In a production facility, an accurate estimate of man-hours needed to complete a task is required. A manufacturer of boiler drums used regression to predict the number of man-hours needed to erect the drums in future projects. To accomplish this, data for 35 boilers were collected. In addition to man-hours (y), the variables measured were boiler capacity (x_1 = lb/hr), boiler design pressure (x_2 = pounds per square inch or psi), boiler type (x_3 = 1 if industry field erected, 0 if utility field erected), and drum type (x_4 = 1 if steam, 0 if mud). The data are saved in the file. (The first five and last five observations are listed in the accompanying table.)

a. Fit the model $E(y) = \beta_0 + \beta_1 x_1 + \beta_2 x_2 + \beta_3 x_3 + \beta_4 x_4$ to the data. Give the estimates of the β's.

b. Conduct a test for the global utility of the model. Use $\alpha = .01$.

c. Find a 95% confidence interval for $E(y)$ when $x_1 = 150,000$, $x_2 = 500$, $x_3 = 1$, and $x_4 = 0$. Interpret the result.

Man-Hours, y	Boiler Capacity, x_1	Design Pressure, x_2	Boiler Type, x_3	Drum Type, x_4
3,137	120,000	375	1	1
3,590	65,000	750	1	1
4,526	150,000	500	1	1
10,825	1,073,877	2,170	0	1
4,023	150,000	325	1	1
⋮	⋮	⋮	⋮	⋮
4,206	441,000	410	1	0
4,006	441,000	410	1	0
3,728	627,000	1,525	0	0
3,211	610,000	1,500	0	0
1,200	30,000	325	1	0

Source: Dr. Kelly Uscategui.

PART II: MODEL BUILDING IN MULTIPLE REGRESSION

12.5 Interaction Models

In Section 12.2, we demonstrated the relationship between $E(y)$ and the independent variables in a first-order model. When $E(y)$ is graphed against any one variable (say, x_1) for fixed values of the other variables, the result is a set of *parallel* straight lines (see Figure 12.3, p. 714). When this situation occurs (as it always does for a first-order model), we say that the relationship between $E(y)$ and any one independent variable *does not depend* on the values of the other independent variables in the model.

However, if the relationship between $E(y)$ and x_1 does, in fact, depend on the values of the remaining x's held fixed, then the first-order model is not appropriate for predicting y. In this case, we need another model that will take into account this dependence. Such a model includes the *cross products* of two or more x's.

For example, suppose that the mean value $E(y)$ of a response y is related to two quantitative independent variables, x_1 and x_2, by the model

$$E(y) = 1 + 2x_1 - x_2 + 3x_1 x_2$$

A graph of the relationship between $E(y)$ and x_1 for $x_2 = 0, 1$, and 2 is displayed in the Minitab graph, Figure 12.7.

Note that the graph shows three nonparallel straight lines. You can verify that the slopes of the lines differ by substituting each of the values $x_2 = 0, 1$, and 2 into the equation.

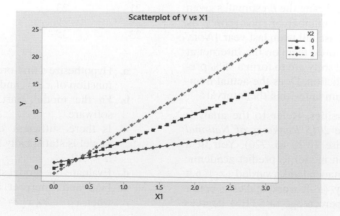

Figure 12.7

Minitab graphs of $1 + 2x_1 - x_2 + 3x_1 x_2$ for $x_2 = 0, 1, 2$

For $x_2 = 0$:

$$E(y) = 1 + 2x_1 - (0) + 3x_1(0) = 1 + 2x_1 \qquad (\text{slope} = 2)$$

For $x_2 = 1$,

$$E(y) = 1 + 2x_1 - (1) + 3x_1(1) = 0 + 5x_1 \qquad (\text{slope} = 5)$$

For $x_2 = 2$,

$$E(y) = 1 + 2x_1 - (2) + 3x_1(2) = -1 + 8x_1 \qquad (\text{slope} = 8)$$

Note that the slope of each line is represented by $\beta_1 + \beta_3 x_2 = 2 + 3x_2$. Thus, the effect on $E(y)$ of a change in x_1 (i.e., the slope) now *depends* on the value of x_2. When this situation occurs, we say that x_1 and x_2 **interact.** The cross-product term, x_1x_2, is called an **interaction term,** and the model $E(y) = \beta_0 + \beta_1 x_1 + \beta_2 x_2 + \beta_3 x_1 x_2$ is called an **interaction model** with two quantitative variables.

An Interaction Model Relating $E(y)$ to Two Quantitative Independent Variables

$$E(y) = \beta_0 + \beta_1 x_1 + \beta_2 x_2 + \beta_3 x_1 x_2$$

where

$(\beta_1 + \beta_3 x_2)$ represents the change in $E(y)$ for every 1-unit increase in x_1, holding x_2 fixed

$(\beta_2 + \beta_3 x_1)$ represents the change in $E(y)$ for every 1-unit increase in x_2, holding x_1 fixed

---

An interaction model is appropriate when the linear relationship between y and one independent variable depends on the value of another independent variable. The next example illustrates this idea.

EXAMPLE 12.6

Evaluating an Interaction Model— Clock Auction Prices

Problem Refer to Examples 12.1–12.4. Suppose the collector of grandfather clocks, having observed many auctions, believes that the *rate of increase* of the auction price with age will be driven upward by a large number of bidders. Thus, instead of a relationship like that shown in Figure 12.8a, in which the rate of increase in price with age is the same for any number of bidders, the collector believes the relationship is like that shown in Figure 12.8b. Note that as the number of bidders increases from 5 to 15, the slope of the price versus age line increases.

Consequently, the interaction model is proposed:

$$y = \beta_0 = \beta_1 x_1 + \beta_2 x_2 + \beta_3 x_1 x_2 + \varepsilon$$

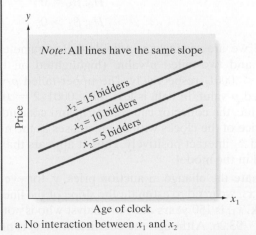 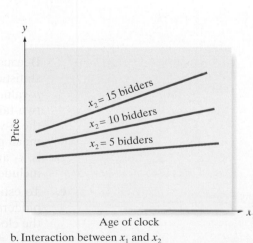

Figure 12.8

Examples of no-interaction and interaction models

a. No interaction between x_1 and x_2 b. Interaction between x_1 and x_2

The 32 data points listed in Table 12.1 (p. 712) were used to fit the model with interaction. A portion of the Excel/XLSTAT printout is shown in Figure 12.9.

Regression of variable PRICE:

Goodness of fit statistics:

Observations	32.0000
Sum of weights	32.0000
DF	28.0000
R²	0.9539
Adjusted R²	0.9489
MSE	7905.7905
RMSE	88.9145
DW	2.4190

Analysis of variance:

Source	DF	Sum of squares	Mean squares	F	Pr > F
Model	3	4578427.3668	1526142.4556	193.0411	< 0.0001
Error	28	221362.1332	7905.7905		
Corrected Total	31	4799789.5000			
Computed against model Y=Mean(Y)					

Model parameters:

Source	Value	Standard error	t	Pr > |t|	Lower bound (95%)	Upper bound (95%)
Intercept	320.4580	295.1413	1.0858	0.2868	-284.1115	925.0275
AGE	0.8781	2.0322	0.4321	0.6690	-3.2845	5.0408
NUMBIDS	-93.2648	29.8916	-3.1201	0.0042	-154.4950	-32.0346
AGE-BID	1.2978	0.2123	6.1123	< 0.0001	0.8629	1.7328

Equation of the model:
PRICE = 320.45799+0.87814*AGE-93.26482*NUMBIDS+1.29785*AGE-BID

Figure 12.9

Excel/XLSTAT Printout for Interaction Model of Auction Price

a. Test the overall utility of the model using the global F-test at $\alpha = .05$.

b. Test the hypothesis (at $\alpha = .05$) that the price-age slope increases as the number of bidders increases—that is, that age and number of bidders, x_2, interact positively.

c. Estimate the change in auction price of a 150-year-old grandfather clock, y, for each additional bidder.

Solution

a. The global F-test is used to test the null hypothesis

$$H_0: \beta_1 = \beta_2 = \beta_3 = 0$$

The test statistic and p-value of the test (highlighted on the printout) are $F = 193.04$ and p-value $< .0001$, respectively. Because $\alpha = .05$ exceeds the p-value, there is sufficient evidence to conclude that the model fit is a statistically useful predictor of auction price, y.

b. The hypotheses of interest to the collector concern the interaction parameter β_3. Specifically,

$$H_0: \beta_3 = 0$$
$$H_a: \beta_3 > 0$$

Because we are testing an individual β parameter, a t-test is required. The test statistic and two-tailed p-value (highlighted on the printout) are $t = 6.11$ and p-value $< .0001$, respectively. The upper-tailed p-value, obtained by dividing the two-tailed p-value in half, is less than $.0001/2 = .00005$. Because $\alpha = .05$ exceeds the p-value, the collector can reject H_0 and conclude that the rate of change of the mean price of the clocks with age increases as the number of bidders increases; that is, x_1 and x_2 interact positively. Thus, it appears that the interaction term should be included in the model.

c. To estimate the change in auction price, y, for every 1-unit increase in number of bidders, x_2, we need to estimate the slope of the line relating y to x_2 when the age of the clock, x_1, is 150 years old. An analyst who is not careful may estimate this slope as $\hat{\beta}_2 = -93.26$. Although the coefficient of x_2 is negative, this does *not* imply that auction price decreases as the number of bidders increases. Since interaction is present, the rate of change (slope) of mean auction price with the number of bidders *depends* on x_1, the age of the clock. For a fixed value of age (x_1), we can rewrite the interaction model as follows:

$$E(y) = \beta_0 + \beta_1 x_1 + \beta_2 x_2 + \beta_3 x_1 x_2 = \underbrace{(\beta_0 + \beta_1 x_1)}_{y\text{-intercept}} + \underbrace{(\beta_2 + \beta_3 x_1)}_{\text{slope}} x_2$$

Thus, the estimated rate of change of y for a 1-unit increase in x_2 (one new bidder) for a 150-year-old clock is

$$\text{Estimated slope of the } y \text{ versus } x_2 \text{ line} = \hat{\beta}_2 + \hat{\beta}_3 x_1$$
$$= -93.26 + 1.30(150) = 101.74$$

In other words, we estimate that the auction price of a 150-year-old clock will *increase* by about \$101.74 for every additional bidder.

Look Back Although the rate of increase will vary as x_1 is changed, it will remain positive for the range of values of x_1 included in the sample. Extreme care is needed in interpreting the signs and sizes of coefficients in a multiple regression model.

→ **Now Work Exercise 12.40**

Example 12.6 illustrates an important point about conducting t-tests on the β parameters in the interaction model. The key β parameter in this model is the interaction β, β_3. [Note that this β is also the one associated with the highest-order term in the model, $x_1 x_2$.]* Consequently, we will want to test H_0: $\beta_3 = 0$ after we have determined that the overall model is useful for predicting y. Once interaction is detected (as in Example 12.6), however, tests on the first-order terms x_1 and x_2 should *not* be conducted because they are meaningless tests; the presence of interaction implies that both x's are important.

> **! CAUTION** Once interaction has been deemed important in the model $E(y) = \beta_0 + \beta_1 x_1 + \beta_2 x_2 + \beta_3 x_1 x_2$, do not conduct t-tests on the β coefficients of the first-order terms x_1 and x_2. These terms should be kept in the model regardless of the magnitude of their associated p-values shown on the printout.

Exercises 12.35–12.48

Learning the Mechanics

12.35 Suppose the mean value $E(y)$ of a response y is related to the quantitative independent variables x_1 and x_2

$$E(y) = 2 + x_1 - 3x_2 - x_1 x_2$$

a. Identify and interpret the slope for x_2.
b. Plot the linear relationship between $E(y)$ and x_2 for $x_1 = 0, 1, 2$, where $1 \leq x_2 \leq 3$.
c. How would you interpret the estimated slopes?
d. Use the lines you plotted in part **b** to determine the changes in $E(y)$ for each $x_1 = 0, 1, 2$.
e. Use your graph from part **b** to determine how much $E(y)$ changes when $3 \leq x_1 \leq 5$ and $1 \leq x_2 \leq 3$.

12.36 Suppose you fit the interaction model

$$y = \beta_0 + \beta_1 x_1 + \beta_2 x_2 + \beta_3 x_1 x_2 + \varepsilon$$

to $n = 32$ data points and obtain the following results:

$$SS_{yy} = 479 \quad SSE = 21 \quad \hat{\beta}_3 = 10 \quad s_{\hat{\beta}_3} = 4$$

a. Find R^2 and interpret its value.
b. Is the model adequate for predicting y? Test at $\alpha = .05$.
c. Use a graph to explain the contribution of the $x_1 x_2$ term to the model.
d. Is there evidence that x_1 and x_2 interact? Test at $\alpha = .05$.

*The order of a term is equal to the sum of the exponents of the quantitative variables included in the term. Thus, when x_1 and x_2 are both quantitative variables, the cross product, $x_1 x_2$, is a second-order term.

12.37 The Minitab printout below was obtained from fitting the model

$$y = \beta_0 + \beta_1 x_1 + \beta_2 x_2 + \beta_3 x_1 x_2 + \varepsilon$$

to $n = 15$ data points.

Regression Analysis: Y versus X1, X2, X1X2

```
Analysis of Variance

Source        DF    Adj SS    Adj MS   F-Value   P-Value
Regression     3    33.149    11.050     21.75     0.000
Error         11     5.587     0.508
Total         14    38.736


Model Summary

      S   R-sq   R-sq(adj)
  0.713  85.6%       81.6%


Coefficients

Term       Coef   SE Coef   T-Value   P-Value
Constant  -2.550    1.142     -2.23     0.043
X1         3.815    0.529      7.22     0.000
X2         2.630    0.344      7.64     0.000
X1X2      -1.285    0.159     -8.06     0.000


Regression Equation

Y = -2.55 + 3.815 X1 + 2.63 X2 - 1.285 X1X2
```

a. What is the prediction equation?

b. Give an estimate of the slope of the line relating y to x_1 when $x_2 = 10$.

c. Plot the prediction equation for the case when $x_2 = 1$. Do this twice more on the same graph for the cases when $x_2 = 3$ and $x_2 = 5$.

d. Explain what it means to say that x_1 and x_2 interact. Explain why your graph of part **c** suggests that x_1 and x_2 interact.

e. Specify the null and alternative hypotheses you would use to test whether x_1 and x_2 interact.

f. Conduct the hypothesis test of part **e** using $\alpha = .01$.

Applying the Concepts—Basic

12.38 Tipping behavior in restaurants. Can food servers increase their tips by complimenting the customers they are waiting on? To answer this question, researchers collected data on the customer tipping behavior for a sample of 348 dining parties and reported their findings in the *Journal of Applied Social Psychology* (Vol. 40, 2010). Tip size (y, measured as a percentage of the total food bill) was modeled as a function of size of the dining party (x_1) and whether or not the server complimented the customers' choice of menu items (x_2). One theory states that the effect of size of the dining party on tip size is independent of whether or not the server compliments the customers' menu choices. A second theory hypothesizes that the effect of size of the dining party on tip size is greater when the server compliments the customers' menu choices as opposed to when the server refrains from complimenting menu choices.

a. Write a model for $E(y)$ as a function of x_1 and x_2 that corresponds to Theory 1.

b. Write a model for $E(y)$ as a function of x_1 and x_2 that corresponds to Theory 2.

c. The researchers summarized the results of their analysis with the following graph. Based on the graph, which of the two models would you expect to fit the data better? Explain.

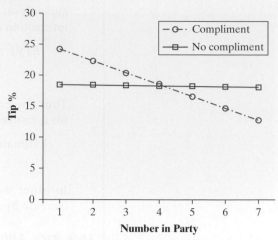

12.39 Forecasting movie revenues with Twitter. Refer to the *IEEE International Conference on Web Intelligence and Intelligent Agent Technology* (2010) study on using the volume of chatter on Twitter.com to forecast movie box office revenue, Exercise 12.10 (p. 723). The researchers modeled a movie's opening weekend box office revenue (y) as a function of tweet rate (x_1) and ratio of positive to negative tweets (x_2) using a first-order model.

a. Write the equation of an interaction model for $E(y)$ as a function of x_1 and x_2.

b. In terms of the β's in the model, part **a**, what is the change in revenue (y) for every 1-tweet increase in the tweet rate (x_1), holding PN-ratio (x_2) constant at a value of 2.5?

c. In terms of the β's in the model, part **a**, what is the change in revenue (y) for every 1-tweet increase in the tweet rate (x_1), holding PN-ratio (x_2) constant at a value of 5.0?

d. In terms of the β's in the model, part **a**, what is the change in revenue (y) for every 1-unit increase in the PN-ratio (x_2), holding tweet rate (x_1) constant at a value of 100?

e. Give the null hypothesis for testing whether tweet rate (x_1) and PN-ratio (x_2) interact to affect revenue (y).

12.40 Role of retailer interest on shopping behavior. Retail interest is defined by marketers as the level of interest a consumer has in a given retail store. Marketing professors investigated the role of retailer interest in consumers' shopping behavior (*Journal of Retailing*, Summer 2006). Using survey data collected for $n = 375$ consumers, the professors developed an interaction model for $y =$ willingness of the consumer to shop at a retailer's store in the future (called *repatronage intentions*) as a function of $x_1 =$ consumer satisfaction and $x_2 =$ retailer interest. The regression results are shown below.

Variable	$\hat{\beta}$	t-Value	p-Value
Satisfaction (x_1)	.426	7.33	< .01
Retailer interest (x_2)	.044	0.85	> .10
Interaction ($x_1 x_2$)	−.157	−3.09	< .01

$R^2 = .65, F = 226.35, p$-value $< .001$

a. Is the overall model statistically useful for predicting y? Test using $\alpha = .05$.

b. Conduct a test for interaction at $\alpha = .05$.

c. Use the β estimates to sketch the estimated relationship between repatronage intentions (y) and satisfaction (x_1) when retailer interest is $x_2 = 1$ (a low value).

d. Repeat part **c** when retailer interest is $x_2 = 7$ (a high value).

e. Sketch the two lines, parts **c** and **d**, on the same graph to illustrate the nature of the interaction.

12.41 Tilting in online poker. In poker, making bad decisions due to negative emotions is known as *tilting*. A study in the *Journal of Gambling Studies* (March, 2014) investigated the factors that affect the severity of tilting for online poker players. A survey of 214 online poker players produced data on the dependent variable, severity of tilting (y), measured on a 30-point scale (where higher values indicate a higher severity of tilting). Two independent variables measured were poker experience (x_1, measured on a 30-point scale) and perceived effect of experience on tilting (x_2, measured on a 28-point scale). The researchers fit the interaction model, $E(y) = \beta_0 + \beta_1 x_1 + \beta_2 x_2 + \beta_3 x_1 x_2$. The results are shown below (p-values in parentheses).

$\hat{\beta}_1 = .22$	$\hat{\beta}_2 = -.25$	$\hat{\beta}_3 = -.11$	$R^2 = .18$	$F = 31.98$
$t = 5.75$	$t = -5.44$	$t = -5.61$		$(<.001)$
$(<.001)$	$(<.001)$	$(<.001)$		

a. Evaluate the overall adequacy of the model using $\alpha = .01$.

b. The researchers hypothesize that the rate of change of severity of tilting (y) with perceived effect of experience on tilting (x_2) depends on poker experience (x_1). Do you agree? Test using $\alpha = .01$.

12.42 Consumer behavior while waiting in line. The *Journal of Consumer Research* (November 2003) published a study

of consumer behavior while waiting in a queue. A sample of $n = 148$ college students was asked to imagine that they were waiting in line at a post office to mail a package and that the estimated waiting time is 10 minutes or less. After a 10-minute wait, students were asked about their level of negative feelings (annoyed, anxious) on a scale of 1 (strongly disagree) to 9 (strongly agree). Before answering, however, the students were informed about how many people were ahead of them and behind them in the line. The researchers used regression to relate negative feelings score (y) to number ahead in line (x_1) and number behind in line (x_2).

a. The researchers fit an interaction model to the data. Write the hypothesized equation of this model.

b. In the words of the problem, explain what it means to say that "x_1 and x_2 interact to affect y."

c. A t-test for the interaction β in the model resulted in a p-value greater than .25. Interpret this result.

d. From their analysis, the researchers concluded that "the greater the number of people ahead, the higher the negative feeling score" and "the greater the number of people behind, the lower the negative feeling score." Use this information to determine the signs of β_1 and β_2 in the model.

Applying the Concepts—Intermediate

12.43 Reality TV and cosmetic surgery. Refer to the *Body Image: An International Journal of Research* (March 2010) study of the impact of reality TV shows on a college student's decision to undergo cosmetic surgery, Exercise 12.17 (p. 725). Recall that the data for the study (simulated based on statistics reported in the journal article) are saved in the file. Consider the interaction model, $E(y) = \beta_0 + \beta_1 x_1 + \beta_2 x_4 + \beta_3 x_1 x_4$, where $y =$ desire to have cosmetic surgery (25-point scale), $x_1 = \{1$ if male, 0 if female$\}$, and $x_4 =$ impression of reality TV (7-point scale). The model was fit to the data and the resulting SPSS printout appears below.

a. Give the least squares prediction equation.

Model Summary

Model	R	R Square	Adjusted R Square	Std. Error of the Estimate
1	.670[a]	.449	.439	2.350

a. Predictors: (Constant), GENDER_IMPREAL, IMPREAL, GENDER

ANOVA[a]

Model		Sum of Squares	df	Mean Square	F	Sig.
1	Regression	747.001	3	249.000	45.086	.000[b]
	Residual	916.787	166	5.523		
	Total	1663.788	169			

a. Dependent Variable: DESIRE

b. Predictors: (Constant), GENDER_IMPREAL, IMPREAL, GENDER

Coefficients[a]

Model		Unstandardized Coefficients B	Std. Error	Standardized Coefficients Beta	t	Sig.
1	(Constant)	11.779	.674		17.486	.000
	GENDER	-1.972	1.179	-.303	-1.672	.096
	IMPREAL	.585	.162	.258	3.617	.000
	GENDER_IMPREAL	.663	.276	-.378	-2.004	.047

a. Dependent Variable: DESIRE

SPSS output for Exercise 12.43

b. Find the predicted level of desire (y) for a male college student with an impression-of-reality-TV-scale score of 5.

c. Conduct a test of overall model adequacy. Use $\alpha = .10$.

d. Give a practical interpretation of R_a^2.

e. Give a practical interpretation of s.

f. Conduct a test (at $\alpha = .10$) to determine if gender (x_1) and impression of reality TV show (x_4) interact in the prediction of level of desire for cosmetic surgery (y).

12.44 Factors that impact an auditor's judgment. A study was conducted to determine the effects of linguistic delivery style and client credibility on auditors' judgments (*Advances in Accounting and Behavioral Research*, 2004). Two hundred auditors from Big 5 accounting firms were each asked to perform an analytical review of a fictitious client's financial statement. The researchers gave the auditors different information on the client's credibility and linguistic delivery style of the client's explanation. Each auditor then provided an assessment of the likelihood that the client-provided explanation accounted for the fluctuation in the financial statement. The three variables of interest—credibility (x_1), linguistic delivery style (x_2), and likelihood (y)—were all measured on a numerical scale. Regression analysis was used to fit the interaction model, $y = \beta_0 + \beta_1 x_1 + \beta_2 x_2 + \beta_3 x_1 x_2 + \varepsilon$. The results are summarized in the table at the bottom of page.

a. Interpret the phrase *client credibility and linguistic delivery style interact* in the words of the problem.

b. Give the null and alternative hypotheses for testing the overall adequacy of the model.

c. Conduct the test, part **b,** using the information in the table.

d. Give the null and alternative hypotheses for testing whether client credibility and linguistic delivery style interact.

e. Conduct the test, part **d,** using the information in the table.

f. The researchers estimated the slope of the likelihood–linguistic delivery style line at a low level of client credibility $(x_1 = 22)$. Obtain this estimate and interpret it in the words of the problem.

g. The researchers also estimated the slope of the likelihood–linguistic delivery style line at a high level of client credibility $(x_1 = 46)$. Obtain this estimate and interpret it in the words of the problem.

12.45 Service workers and customer relations. A study in *Industrial Marketing Management* (February 2016) investigated the impact of service workers' (e.g., waiters and waitresses) personal resources on the quality of the firm's relationship with customers. The study focused on four types of personal resources: flexibility in dealing with customers (x_1), service worker reputation (x_2), empathy for the customer (x_3), and service worker's task alignment (x_4). A multiple regression model was employed to relate these four independent variables to relationship quality (y). Data were collected for $n = 220$ customers who had recent dealings with a service worker. (All variables were measured on a quantitative scale, based on responses to a questionnaire.)

a. Write a first-order model for $E(y)$ as a function of the four independent variables.

b. Refer to part **a.** Which β coefficient measures the effect of flexibility (x_1) on relationship quality (y), independently of the other independent variables in the model?

c. Repeat part **b** for reputation (x_2), empathy (x_3), and task alignment (x_4).

d. The researchers theorize that task alignment (x_4) "moderates" the effect of each of the other x's on relationship quality (y) — that is, the impact of each x $(x_1, x_2,$ or $x_3)$ on y depends on x_4. Write an interaction model for $E(y)$ that matches the researchers' theory.

e. Refer to part **d.** What null hypothesis would you test to determine if the effect of flexibility (x_1) on relationship quality (y) depends on task alignment (x_4)?

f. Repeat part **e** for the effect of reputation (x_2) and the effect of empathy (x_3).

g. None of the t-tests for interaction were found to be "statistically significant." Given these results, the researchers concluded that their theory was not supported. Do you agree?

12.46 Bubble behavior in subcooled flow boiling. Refer to the *Heat Transfer Engineering* (Vol. 34, 2013) study of bubble behavior in subcooled flow boiling, Exercise 12.21 (p. 726). Recall that bubble density (liters per meters squared) was modeled as a function of mass flux (kilograms per meters squared per second) and heat flux (megawatts per meters squared) using data saved in the file.

a. Write an interaction model for bubble density (y) as a function of $x_1 = $ mass flux and $x_2 = $ heat flux.

b. Fit the interaction model, part **a,** to the data using statistical software. Give the least squares prediction equation.

c. Evaluate overall model adequacy by conducting a global F test (at $\alpha = .05$) and interpreting the model statistics, R_a^2 and $2s$.

d. Conduct a test (at $\alpha = .05$) to determine whether mass flux and heat flux interact.

Results for Exercise 12.44

	Beta Estimate	Std Error	t-Statistic	p-Value
Constant	15.865	10.980	1.445	0.150
Client credibility (x_1)	0.037	0.339	0.110	0.913
Linguistic delivery style (x_2)	−0.678	0.328	−2.064	0.040
Interaction $(x_1 x_2)$	0.036	0.009	4.008	< 0.005

F-statistic $= 55.35$ $(p < 0.0005)$: $R_a^2 = .450$

e. How much do you expect bubble density to decrease for every 1 kg/m^2-sec increase in mass flux, when heat flux is set at .5 megawatt/m^2?

12.47 Arsenic in groundwater. Refer to the *Environmental Science & Technology* (January 2005) study of the reliability of a commercial kit to test for arsenic in groundwater, Exercise 12.16 (p. 725). Recall that you fit a first-order model for arsenic level (y) as a function of latitude (x_1), longitude (x_2), and depth (x_3).

a. Write a model for arsenic level (y) that includes first-order terms for latitude, longitude, and depth, as well as terms for interaction between latitude and depth and interaction between longitude and depth.

b. Use statistical software to fit the interaction model, part **a**, to the data. Give the least squares prediction equation.

c. Conduct a test (at $\alpha = .05$) to determine whether latitude and depth interact to affect arsenic level.

d. Conduct a test (at $\alpha = .05$) to determine whether longitude and depth interact to affect arsenic level.

e. Practically interpret the results of the tests, parts **c** and **d**.

12.48 Cooling method for gas turbines. Refer to the *Journal of Engineering for Gas Turbines and Power* (January 2005) study of a high-pressure inlet fogging method for a gas turbine engine, Exercise 12.19 (p. 726). Recall that you fit a first-order model for heat rate (y) as a function of speed (x_1), inlet temperature (x_2), exhaust temperature (x_3), cycle pressure ratio (x_4), and airflow rate (x_5).

a. Researchers hypothesize that the linear relationship between heat rate (y) and temperature (both inlet and exhaust) depends on airflow rate. Write a model for heat rate that incorporates the researchers' theories.

b. Use statistical software to fit the interaction model, part **a**, to the data. Give the least squares prediction equation.

c. Conduct a test (at $\alpha = .05$) to determine whether inlet temperature and airflow rate interact to affect heat rate.

d. Conduct a test (at $\alpha = .05$) to determine whether exhaust temperature and airflow rate interact to affect heat rate.

e. Practically interpret the results of the tests, parts **c** and **d**.

12.6 Quadratic and Other Higher-Order Models

All of the models discussed in the previous sections proposed straight-line relationships between $E(y)$ and each of the independent variables in the model. In this section, we consider models that allow for curvature in the two-dimensional relationship between y and an independent variable. Each of these models is a **second-order model** because it will include an x^2 term.

First, we consider a model that includes only one independent variable x. The form of this model, called the **quadratic model,** is

$$y = \beta_0 + \beta_1 x + \beta_2 x^2 + \varepsilon$$

The term involving x^2, called a **quadratic term** (or **second-order term**), enables us to hypothesize curvature in the graph of the response model relating y to x. Graphs of the quadratic model for two different values of β_2 are shown in Figure 12.10. When the curve opens upward, the sign of β_2 is positive (see Figure 12.10a); when the curve opens downward, the sign of β_2 is negative (see Figure 12.10b).

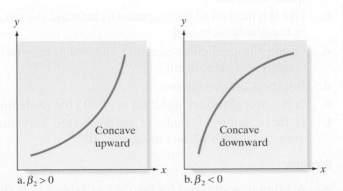

Figure 12.10
Graphs for two quadratic models

a. $\beta_2 > 0$ Concave upward

b. $\beta_2 < 0$ Concave downward

> **A Quadratic (Second-Order) Model in a Single Quantitative Independent Variable**
>
> $$E(y) = \beta_0 + \beta_1 x + \beta_2 x^2$$
>
> where
>
> β_0 is the y-intercept of the curve.
>
> β_1 is a shift parameter.
>
> β_2 is the rate of curvature.

EXAMPLE 12.7

Analyzing a Quadratic Model—Predicting Electrical Usage

Problem In all-electric homes, the amount of electricity expended is of interest to consumers, builders, and groups involved with energy conservation. Suppose we wish to investigate the monthly electrical usage, y, in all-electric homes and its relationship to the size, x, of the home. Moreover, suppose we think that monthly electrical usage in all-electric homes is related to the size of the home by the quadratic model

$$y = \beta_0 + \beta_1 x + \beta_2 x^2 + \varepsilon$$

To fit the model, the values of y and x are collected for 15 homes during a particular month. The data are shown in Table 12.2.

Table 12.2	Home Size–Electrical Usage Data
Size of Home, x (sq. ft.)	**Monthly Usage, y (kilowatt-hours)**
1,290	1,182
1,350	1,172
1,470	1,264
1,600	1,493
1,710	1,571
1,840	1,711
1,980	1,804
2,230	1,840
2,400	1,986
2,710	2,007
2,930	1,984
3,000	1,960
3,210	2,001
3,240	1,928
3,520	1,945

 *Data Set:* KWHRS

a. Construct a scatterplot for the data. Is there evidence to support the use of a quadratic model?

b. Use the method of least squares to estimate the unknown parameters β_0, β_1, and β_2 in the quadratic model.

c. Graph the prediction equation and assess how well the model fits the data, both visually and numerically.

d. Interpret the β estimates.

e. Is the overall model useful (at $\alpha = .01$) for predicting electrical usage y?

f. Is there sufficient evidence of downward curvature in the home size–electrical usage relationship? Test using $\alpha = .01$.

Solution

a. A Minitab scatterplot for the data in Table 12.2 is shown in Figure 12.11. The figure illustrates that electrical usage appears to increase in a curvilinear manner with the size of the home. This provides some support for the inclusion of the quadratic term x^2 in the model.

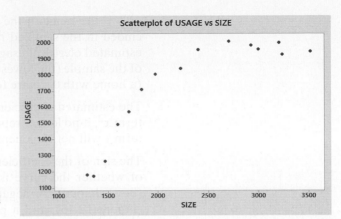

Figure 12.11

Minitab scatterplot for electrical usage data

b. We used Excel to fit the model to the data in Table 12.2. Part of the Excel regression output is displayed in Figure 12.12. The least squares estimates of the β parameters (highlighted) are $\hat{\beta}_0 = -806.7$, $\hat{\beta}_1 = 1.9616$, and $\hat{\beta}_2 = -.00034$. Therefore, the equation that minimizes the SSE for the data is

$$\hat{y} = -806.7 + 1.9616x - .00034x^2$$

SUMMARY OUTPUT

Regression Statistics	
Multiple R	0.988576
R Square	0.977283
Adjusted R Square	0.973496
Standard Error	50.19975
Observations	15

ANOVA

	df	SS	MS	F	Significance F
Regression	2	1300900.218	650450.1	258.1135719	0.0000000001
Residual	12	30240.18169	2520.015		
Total	14	1331140.4			

	Coefficients	Standard Error	t Stat	P-value	Lower 95%	Upper 95%
Intercept	–806.717	166.8720911	–4.83434	0.0004089596	–1170.299712	–443.134
SIZE	1.961617	0.152524384	12.861	0.0000000223	1.629294434	2.293939
SIZESQ	–0.00034	0.00003212	–10.599	0.0000001903	–0.000410426	–0.00027

Figure 12.12

Excel regression output for electrical usage model

c. Figure 12.13 is a Minitab graph of the least squares prediction equation. Note that the graph provides a good fit to the data of Table 12.2. A numerical measure of fit is obtained with the adjusted coefficient of determination, R_a^2. This value (shown on both Figures 12.12 and 12.13) is $R_a^2 = .973$. This implies that about 97% of the sample variation in electrical usage (y) can be explained by the quadratic model (after adjusting for sample size and degrees of freedom).

d. The interpretation of the estimated coefficients in a quadratic model must be undertaken cautiously. First, the estimated y-intercept, $\hat{\beta}_0$, can be meaningfully interpreted

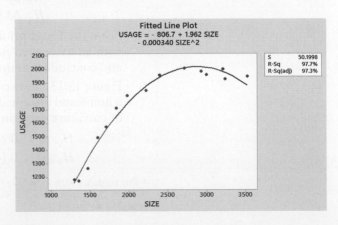

Figure 12.13

Minitab plot of least squares model for electrical usage

only if the range of the independent variable includes zero—that is, if $x = 0$ is included in the sampled range of x. Although $\hat{\beta}_0 = -806.7$ seems to imply that the estimated electrical usage is negative when $x = 0$, this zero point is not in the range of the sample (the lowest value of x is 1,290 square feet), and the value is nonsensical (a home with 0 square feet); thus the interpretation of $\hat{\beta}_0$ is not meaningful.

The estimated coefficient of x is $\hat{\beta}_1 = 1.9616$, but in the presence of the quadratic term x^2, it no longer represents a slope.* The estimated coefficient of the first-order term x will not, in general, have a meaningful interpretation in the quadratic model.

The sign of the coefficient, $\hat{\beta}_2 = -.00034$, of the quadratic term, x^2, is the indicator of whether the curve is concave downward (mound-shaped) or concave upward (bowl-shaped). A negative $\hat{\beta}_2$ implies downward concavity, as in this example (Figure 12.13), and a positive $\hat{\beta}_2$ implies upward concavity. Rather than interpreting the numerical value of $\hat{\beta}_2$ itself, we employ a graphical representation of the model, as in Figure 12.13, to describe the model.

Note that Figure 12.13 implies that the estimated electrical usage is leveling off as the home sizes increase beyond 2,500 square feet. In fact, the convexity of the model would lead to decreasing usage estimates if we were to display the model out to 4,000 square feet and beyond (see Figure 12.14). However, model interpretations are not meaningful outside the range of the independent variable, which has a maximum value of 3,520 square feet in this example. Thus, although the model appears to support the hypothesis that the *rate of increase* per square foot *decreases* for home sizes near the high end of the sampled values, the conclusion that usage will actually begin to decrease for very large homes would be a *misuse* of the model because no homes of 3,600 square feet or more were included in the sample.

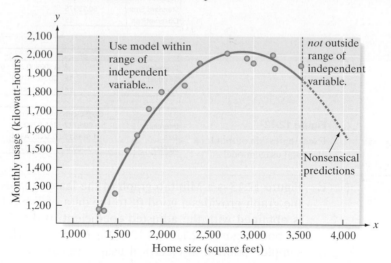

Figure 12.14

Potential misuse of quadratic model

e. To test whether the quadratic model is statistically useful, we conduct the global *F*-test:

$$H_0: \beta_1 = \beta_2 = 0$$

H_a: At least one of the above coefficients is nonzero.

From the Excel printout, Figure 12.12, the test statistic (highlighted) is $F = 258.11$ with an associated p-value of approximately 0. For any reasonable α, we reject H_0 and conclude that the overall model is a useful predictor of electrical usage, y.

f. Figure 12.13 shows concave downward curvature in the relationship between size of a home and electrical usage in the sample of 15 data points. To determine if this type of curvature exists in the population, we want to test

$$H_0: \beta_2 = 0 \text{ (no curvature in the response curve)}$$

$$H_a: \beta_2 < 0 \text{ (downward concavity exists in the response curve)}$$

---

* For students with knowledge of calculus, note that the slope of the quadratic model is the first derivative $\partial y/\partial x = \beta_1 + 2\beta_2 x$. Thus, the slope varies as a function of x, rather than the constant slope associated with the straight-line model.

The test statistic for testing β_2, highlighted on the printout, is $t = -10.599$, and the associated two-tailed p-value is .0000002. Because this is a one-tailed test, the appropriate p-value is $(.0000002)/2 = .0000001$. Now $\alpha = .01$ exceeds this p-value. Thus, there is very strong evidence of downward curvature in the population—that is, electrical usage increases more slowly per square foot for large homes than for small homes.

Look Back Note that the Excel printout in Figure 12.12 also provides the t-test statistic and corresponding two-tailed p-values for the tests of $H_0: \beta_0 = 0$ and $H_0: \beta_1 = 0$. Because the interpretation of these parameters is not meaningful for this model, the tests are not of interest.

● **Now Work Exercise 12.56**

When two or more quantitative independent variables are included in a second-order model, we can incorporate squared terms for each x in the model, as well as the interaction between the two independent variables. A model that includes all possible second-order terms in two independent variables—called a **complete second-order model**—is given in the box below. When one of the x's is held fixed, this model proposes a parabolic shape relating y to the other x.

Complete Second-Order Model with Two Quantitative Independent Variables

$$E(y) = \beta_0 + \beta_1 x_1 + \beta_2 x_2 + \beta_3 x_1 x_2 + \beta_4 x_1^2 + \beta_5 x_2^2$$

Comments on the Parameters

β_0: the value of $E(y)$ when $x_1 = x_2 = 0$

$\beta_1, \beta_2, \beta_3$: control the magnitude of the shift of the parabola when holding one x fixed

β_4: the rate of curvature of the parabola relating y to x_1 when x_2 is held fixed

β_5: the rate of curvature of the parabola relating y to x_2 when x_1 is held fixed

---

EXAMPLE 12.8

A More Complex Second-Order Model— Predicting Hours Worked per Week

Problem A social scientist would like to relate the number of hours worked per week (outside the home) by a married woman to the number of years of formal education she has completed and the number of children in her family.

a. Identify the dependent variable and the independent variables.

b. Write the first-order model for this example.

c. Modify the model in part **b** to include an interaction term.

d. Write a complete second-order model for $E(y)$.

Solution

a. The dependent variable is

$$y = \text{Number of hours worked per week by a married woman}$$

The two independent variables, both quantitative in nature, are

$x_1 = $ Number of years of formal education completed by the woman

$x_2 = $ Number of children in the family

b. The first-order model is

$$E(y) = \beta_0 + \beta_1 x_1 + \beta_2 x_2$$

This model would probably not be appropriate in this situation because x_1 and x_2 may interact and/or curvature terms corresponding to x_1^2 and x_2^2 may be needed to obtain a good model for $E(y)$.

c. Adding the interaction term, we obtain

$$E(y) = \beta_0 + \beta_1 x_1 + \beta_2 x_2 + \beta_3 x_1 x_2$$

This model should be better than the model in part **b** because we have now allowed for interaction between x_1 and x_2.

d. The complete second-order model is

$$E(y) = \beta_0 + \beta_1 x_1 + \beta_2 x_2 + \beta_3 x_1 x_2 + \beta_4 x_1^2 + \beta_5 x_2^2$$

Because it would not be surprising to find curvature relating hours worked (y) to either years of education (x_1) or number of children (x_2), the complete second-order model would be preferred to the models in parts **b** and **c**.

Look Back How can we tell whether the complete second-order model really does provide better predictions of hours worked than the models in parts **b** and **c**? The answers to these and similar questions are examined in Section 12.9.

● **Now Work Exercise 12.59**

Most relationships between $E(y)$ and two or more quantitative independent variables are second order and require the use of either the interactive or the complete second-order model to obtain a good fit to a data set. As in the case of a single quantitative independent variable, however, the curvature may be very slight over the range of values of the variables in the data set. When this happens, a first-order model may provide a good fit to the data.

Exercises 12.49–12.65

Learning the Mechanics

12.49 Write a second-order model relating the mean of y, $E(y)$, to
  a. one quantitative independent variable
  b. two quantitative independent variables
  c. three quantitative independent variables [*Hint:* Include all possible two-way cross-product terms and squared terms.]

12.50 Suppose you fit the second-order model

$$y = \beta_0 + \beta_1 x + \beta_2 x^2 + \varepsilon$$

to $n = 25$ data points. Your estimate of β_2 is $\hat{\beta}_2 = .47$, and the estimated standard error of the estimate is .15.
  a. Test $H_0: \beta_2 = 0$ against $H_a: \beta_2 \neq 0$. Use $\alpha = .05$.
  b. Suppose you want to determine only whether the quadratic curve opens upward; that is, as x increases, the slope of the curve increases. Give the test statistic and the rejection region for the test for $\alpha = .05$. Do the data support the theory that the slope of the curve increases as x increases? Explain.

12.51 Suppose you fit the quadratic model

$$E(y) = \beta_0 + \beta_1 x + \beta_2 x^2$$

to a set of $n = 20$ data points and found $R^2 = .91$, $SS_{yy} = 29.94$, and SSE $= 2.63$.
  a. Is there sufficient evidence to indicate that the model contributes information for predicting y? Test using $\alpha = .05$.

  b. What null and alternative hypotheses would you test to determine whether upward curvature exists?
  c. What null and alternative hypotheses would you test to determine whether downward curvature exists?

12.52 Consider the following data that fit the quadratic model $E(y) = \beta_0 + \beta_1 x + \beta_2 x^2$:

x	y	x	y
0	8	4	5.2
1	7.3	5	6.5
2	5.6	6	8.8
3	5.9	7	12.1

  a. Construct a scatterplot for this data. Give the prediction equation and calculate R^2 based on the model above.
  b. Interpret the value of R^2.
  c. Justify whether the overall model is significant at the 1% significance level if the data result into a p-value of .000514.

12.53 Minitab was used to fit the complete second-order model

$$E(y) = \beta_0 + \beta_1 x_1 + \beta_2 x_2 + \beta_3 x_1 x_2 + \beta_4 x_1^2 + \beta_5 x_2^2$$

to $n = 39$ data points. The printout is shown on the next page.
  a. Is there sufficient evidence to indicate that at least one of the parameters—β_1, β_2, β_3, β_4, and β_5—is nonzero? Test using $\alpha = .05$.
  b. Test $H_0: \beta_4 = 0$ against $H_a: \beta_4 \neq 0$. Use $\alpha = .01$.
  c. Test $H_0: \beta_5 = 0$ against $H_a: \beta_5 \neq 0$. Use $\alpha = .01$.
  d. Use graphs to explain the consequences of the tests in parts **b** and **c**.

Minitab output for Exercise 12.53

```
Analysis of Variance

Source      DF  Adj SS  Adj MS  F-Value  P-Value
Regression   5  989.30  197.86    25.93    0.000
Error       33  251.81    7.63
Total       38 1241.11

Model Summary

    S    R-sq  R-sq(adj)
2.762   79.7%     76.6%

Coefficients

Term        Coef   SE Coef  T-Value  P-Value
Constant  24.563    6.531    -3.76    0.001
X1         1.198    0.110    10.86    0.000
X2        27.988   79.489     0.35    0.727
X1X2      -0.539    1.033    -0.52    0.605
X1SQ     -0.0043    0.0004  -10.74    0.000
X2SQ      0.0020    0.0033     0.60    0.550

Regression Equation

Y = 24.56 + 1.20 X1 + 27.99 X2 - 0.54 X1X2 - .004 X1SQ + .002 X2SQ
```

Applying the Concepts—Basic

12.54 Personality traits and job performance. When attempting to predict job performance using personality traits, researchers typically assume that the relationship is linear. A study published in the *Journal of Applied Psychology* (Jan. 2011) investigated a curvilinear relationship between job task performance and a specific personality trait—conscientiousness. Using data collected for 602 employees of a large public organization, task performance was measured on a 30-point scale (where higher scores indicate better performance) and conscientiousness was measured on a scale of -3 to $+3$ (where higher scores indicate a higher level of conscientiousness).

a. The coefficient of correlation relating task performance score to conscientiousness score was reported as $r = .18$. Explain why the researchers should not use this statistic to investigate the curvilinear relationship between task performance and conscientiousness.

b. Give the equation of a curvilinear (quadratic) model relating task performance score (y) to conscientiousness score (x).

c. The researchers theorized that task performance increases as level of conscientiousness increases, but at a decreasing rate. Draw a sketch of this relationship.

d. If the theory in part **c** is supported, what is the expected sign of β_2 in the model, part **b**?

e. The researchers reported $\hat{\beta}_2 = -.32$ with an associated p-value of less than .05. Use this information to test the researchers' theory at $\alpha = .05$.

12.55 Going for it on fourth-down in the NFL. Refer to the *Chance* (Winter 2009) study of fourth-down decisions by coaches in the National Football League (NFL), Exercise 11.69 (p. 679). Recall that statisticians at California State University, Northridge, fit a straight-line model for predicting the number of points scored (y) by a team that has a first-down with a given number of yards (x) from the opposing goal line. A second model fit to data collected on five NFL teams from a recent season was the quadratic regression model, $E(y) = \beta_0 + \beta_1 x + \beta_2 x^2$. The regression yielded the following results: $\hat{y} = 6.13 + .141x - .0009x^2$, $R^2 = .226$.

a. If possible, give a practical interpretation of each of the β estimates in the model.

b. Give a practical interpretation of the coefficient of determination, R^2.

c. In Exercise 11.63, the coefficient of correlation for the straight-line model was reported as $R^2 = .18$. Does this statistic alone indicate that the quadratic model is a better fit than the straight-line model? Explain.

d. What test of hypothesis would you conduct to determine if the quadratic model is a better fit than the straight-line model?

12.56 Catalytic converters in cars. A quadratic model was applied to motor vehicle toxic emissions data collected in Mexico City (*Environmental Science & Engineering*, Sept. 1, 2000). The following equation was used to predict the percentage (y) of motor vehicles without catalytic converters in the Mexico City fleet for a given year (x):

$$\hat{y} = 325{,}790 - 321.67x + .0794x^2.$$

a. Explain why the value $\hat{\beta}_0 = 325{,}790$ has no practical interpretation.

b. Explain why the value $\hat{\beta}_1 = -321.67$ should not be interpreted as a slope.

c. Examine the value of $\hat{\beta}_2$ to determine the nature of the curvature (upward or downward) in the sample data.

d. The researchers used the model to estimate "that just after the year 2021 the fleet of cars with catalytic converters will completely disappear." Comment on the danger of using the model to predict y in the year 2021. (*Note:* The model was fit to data collected between 1984 and 1999.)

12.57 Commercial refrigeration systems. The role of maintenance in energy saving in commercial refrigeration was the topic of an article in the *Journal of Quality in Maintenance Engineering* (Vol. 18, 2012). The authors provided the following illustration of data relating the efficiency (relative performance) of a refrigeration system to the fraction of total charges for cooling the system required for optimal performance. Based on the data shown in the graph (next page), hypothesize an appropriate model for relative performance (y) as a function of fraction of charge (x). What is the hypothesized sign (positive or negative) of the β_2 parameter in the model?

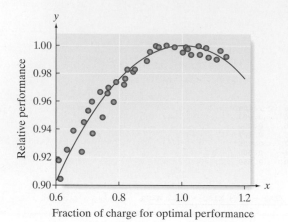

Fraction of charge for optimal performance

12.58 Assertiveness and leadership. Management professors at Columbia University examined the relationship between assertiveness and leadership (*Journal of Personality and Social Psychology,* February 2007). The sample represented 388 people enrolled in a full-time MBA program. Based on answers to a questionnaire, the researchers measured two variables for each subject: assertiveness score (x) and leadership ability score (y). A quadratic regression model was fit to the data, with the following results:

Independent Variable	β Estimate	t-Value	p-Value
x	.57	2.55	.01
x^2	−.088	−3.97	< .01
Model R^2 = .12			

a. Conduct a test of overall model utility. Use $\alpha = .05$.

b. The researchers hypothesized that leadership ability increases at a decreasing rate with assertiveness. Set up the null and alternative hypotheses to test this theory.

c. Use the reported results to conduct the test, part b. Give your conclusion (at $\alpha = .05$) in the words of the problem.

12.59 Goal congruence in top management teams. Do chief executive officers (CEOs) and their top managers always agree on the goals of the company? Goal importance congruence between CEOs and vice presidents (VPs) was studied in the *Academy of Management Journal* (Feb. 2008). The researchers used regression to model a VP's attitude toward the goal of improving efficiency (y) as a function of the two quantitative independent variables level of CEO leadership (x_1) and level of congruence between the CEO and the VP (x_2). A complete second-order model in x_1 and x_2 was fit to data collected for $n = 517$ top management team members at U.S. credit unions.

a. Write the complete second-order model for $E(y)$.

b. The coefficient of determination for the model, part a, was reported as $R^2 = .14$. Interpret this value.

c. The estimate of the β-value for the $(x_2)^2$ term in the model was found to be negative. Interpret this result, practically.

d. A t-test on the β-value for the interaction term in the model, x_1x_2, resulted in a p-value of .02. Practically interpret this result, using $\alpha = .05$.

Applying the Concepts—Intermediate

12.60 Shopping on Black Friday. Refer to the *International Journal of Retail and Distribution Management* (Vol. 39, 2011) study of shopping on Black Friday (the day after Thanksgiving), Exercise 6.16 (p. 340). Recall that researchers conducted interviews with a sample of 38 women shopping on Black Friday to gauge their shopping habits. Two of the variables measured for each shopper were age (x) and number of years shopping on Black Friday (y). Data on these two variables for the 38 shoppers are listed in the accompanying table.

a. Fit the quadratic model, $E(y) = \beta_0 + \beta_1 x + \beta_2 x^2$, to the data using statistical software. Give the prediction equation.

b. Conduct a test of the overall adequacy of the model. Use $\alpha = .01$.

c. Conduct a test to determine if the relationship between age (x) and number of years shopping on Black Friday (y) is best represented by a linear or quadratic function. Use $\alpha = .01$.

Age	Years	Age	Years
32	5	21	5
27	3	52	10
40	12	40	18
62	35	38	5
47	20	56	8
53	30	60	5
24	8	35	15
27	2	50	25
47	24	56	10
40	25	20	2
45	11	20	4
22	11	21	4
25	5	22	5
60	35	50	10
22	3	30	6
50	15	28	16
70	22	25	7
50	10	30	6
21	6	49	30

Source: Republished with permission of Emerald Group Publishing Limited, from J. B. Thomas and C. Peters, "An Exploratory Investigation of Black Friday Consumption Rituals," *International Journal of Retail and Distribution Management,* Vol. 39, No. 7, 2011 (Table I). Permission conveyed through Copyright Clearance Center, Inc.

12.61 Revenues of popular movies. The *Internet Movie Database* (www.imdb.com) monitors the gross revenues for all major motion pictures. The table on the next page gives both the domestic (United States and Canada) and international gross revenues for a sample of 25 popular movies.

Movie Title (year)	Domestic Gross ($ millions)	International Gross ($ millions)
Star Wars VII (2015)	936.4	1122
Avatar (2009)	760.5	2023.4
Jurassic World (2015)	652.2	1018.1
Titanic (1997)	658.7	1548.9
The Dark Knight (2008)	533.3	469.5
Pirates of the Caribbean (2006)	423.3	642.9
E.T. (1982)	434.9	357.9
Spider Man (2002)	403.7	418
Frozen (2013)	400.7	873.5
Jurassic Park (1993)	395.7	643.1
Furious 7 (2015)	351	1163
Lion King (1994)	422.8	564.7
Harry Potter and the Sorcerer's Stone (2001)	317.6	657.2
Inception (2010)	292.6	540
Sixth Sense (1999)	293.5	379.3
The Jungle Book (2016)	292.6	491.2
The Hangover (2009)	277.3	201.6
Jaws (1975)	260	210.6
Ghost (1990)	217.6	300
Saving Private Ryan (1998)	216.1	263.2
Gladiator (2000)	187.7	268.6
Dances with Wolves (1990)	184.2	240
The Exorcist (1973)	204.6	153
My Big Fat Greek Wedding (2002)	241.4	115.1
Rocky IV (1985)	127.9	172.6

Source: Based on information from *The Internet Movie Database* (http://www.imdb.com).

a. Write a first-order model for foreign gross revenues (y) as a function of domestic gross revenues (x).

b. Write a second-order model for international gross revenues y as a function of domestic gross revenues x.

c. Construct a scatterplot for these data. Which of the models from parts **a** and **b** appears to be the better choice for explaining the variation in foreign gross revenues?

d. Fit the model of part **b** to the data and investigate its usefulness. Is there evidence of a curvilinear relationship between international and domestic gross revenues? Try using $\alpha = .05$.

e. Based on your analysis in part **d**, which of the models from parts **a** and **b** better explains the variation in international gross revenues? Compare your answer with your preliminary conclusion from part **c**.

12.62 Company donations to charity. The amount a company donates to a charitable organization is often restricted by financial inflexibility at the firm. One measure of financial inflexibility is the ratio of restricted assets to total firm assets. A study published in the *Journal of Management Accounting Research* (Vol. 27, 2015) investigated the link between donation amount and this ratio. Data were collected on donations to 115,333 charities over a recent 10-year period, resulting in a sample of 419,225 firm-years. The researchers fit the quadratic model, $E(y) = \beta_0 + \beta_1 x + \beta_2 x^2$, where y = natural logarithm of total donations to charity by a firm in a year and x = ratio of restricted assets to the firm's total assets in the previous year. [*Note:* This model is a simplified version of the actual model fit by the researchers.]

a. The researchers' theory is that as a firm's restricted assets increase, donations will initially increase. However, there is a point at which donations will not only diminish, but also decline as restricted assets increase. How should the researchers use the model to test this theory?

b. The results of the multiple regression are shown in the table below. Use this information to test the researchers' theory at $\alpha = .01$. What do you conclude?

$\hat{\beta}_0 = 11.24$	$\hat{\beta}_1 = .365$	$\hat{\beta}_2 = -.279$	$R^2_{adj} = .833$
$s_{\hat{\beta}_0} = .017$	$s_{\hat{\beta}_1} = .033$	$s_{\hat{\beta}_2} = .039$	$n = 419{,}225$

12.63 Failure times of silicon wafer microchips. Researchers at National Semiconductor experimented with tin-lead solder bumps used to manufacture silicon wafer integrated circuit chips (*International Wafer Level Packaging Conference*, November 3–4, 2005). The failure times of the microchips (in hours) was determined at different solder temperatures (degrees Celsius). The data for one experiment are given in the table. The researchers want to predict failure time (y) based on solder temperature (x).

a. Construct a scatterplot for the data. What type of relationship, linear or curvilinear, appears to exist between failure time and solder temperature?

b. Fit the model, $E(y) = \beta_0 + \beta_1 x + \beta_2 x^2$, to the data. Give the least squares prediction equation.

c. Conduct a test to determine if there is upward curvature in the relationship between failure time and solder temperature. (Use $\alpha = .05$.)

Temperature (°C)	Time to Failure (hours)
165	200
162	200
164	1,200
158	500
158	600
159	750
156	1,200
157	1,500
152	500
147	500
149	1,100
149	1,150
142	3,500
142	3,600
143	3,650
133	4,200
132	4,800
132	5,000
134	5,200
134	5,400
125	8,300
123	9,700

Source: S. Gee and L. Nguyen, "Mean Time to Failure in Wafer Level-CSP Packages with SnPb and SnAgCu Solder Bumps," International Wafer Level Packaging Conference, San Jose, CA, November 3–4, 2005 (adapted from Figure 7). © 2005 by Surface Mount Technology Association (SMTA). Used by permission of the Surface Mount Technology Association (SMTA).

12.64 Estimating repair and replacement costs of water pipes. Refer to the *IHS Journal of Hydraulic Engineering* (September, 2012) study of the repair and replacement of water pipes, Exercise 11.21 (p. 655). Recall that a team of civil engineers used regression analysis to model y = the ratio of repair to replacement cost of commercial pipe as a function of x = the diameter (in millimeters) of the pipe. Data for a sample of 13 different pipe sizes are reproduced in the accompanying table. In Exercise 11.21, you fit a straight-line model to the data. Now consider the quadratic model, $E(y) = \beta_0 + \beta_1 x + \beta_2 x^2$. A Minitab printout of the analysis follows (next column).

Diameter	Ratio
80	6.58
100	6.97
125	7.39
150	7.61
200	7.78
250	7.92
300	8.20
350	8.42
400	8.60
450	8.97
500	9.31
600	9.47
700	9.72

Source: C. R. Suribabu and T. R. Neelakantan, "Sizing of Water Distribution Pipes Based on Performance Measure and Breakage-Repair Replacement Economics," *IHS Journal of Hydraulic Engineering*, Vol. 18, No. 3, September 2012 (Table 1). Copyright: September 2012

a. Give the least squares prediction equation relating ratio of repair to replacement cost (y) to pipe diameter (x).

b. Conduct a global F-test for the model using $\alpha = .01$. What do you conclude about overall model adequacy?

c. Evaluate the adjusted coefficient of determination, R^2_a, for the model.

Minitab Output for Exercise 12.64

Regression Analysis: RATIO versus DIAMETER, DIAMSQ

```
Analysis of Variance

Source       DF   Adj SS   Adj MS   F-Value   P-Value
Regression    2  11.0810  5.54049   210.56     0.000
Error        10   0.2631  0.02631
Total        12  11.3441
```

```
Model Summary

       S   R-sq  R-sq(adj)
0.162211  97.68%    97.22%
```

```
Coefficients

Term          Coef   SE Coef  T-Value  P-Value
Constant     6.266     0.155    40.31    0.000
DIAMETER  0.007914  0.000997     7.93    0.000
DIAMSQ   -0.000004  0.000001    -3.23    0.009
```

```
Regression Equation
RATIO = 6.266 + 0.007914 DIAMETER - 0.000004 DIAMSQ
```

Prediction for RATIO

```
Variable  Setting
DIAMETER      250
DIAMSQ      62500
```

```
     Fit    SE Fit         95% CI             95% PI
 7.97855  0.0579790  (7.84936, 8.10773)  (7.59472, 8.36237)
```

d. Give the null and alternative hypotheses for testing if the rate of increase of ratio (y) with diameter (x) is slower for larger pipe sizes.

e. Carry out the test, part **d**, using $\alpha = .01$.

f. Locate, on the printout, a 95% prediction interval for the ratio of repair to replacement cost for a pipe with a diameter of 240 millimeters. Interpret the result.

12.65 Orange juice demand study. A chilled orange juice warehousing operation in New York City was experiencing too many out-of-stock situations with its 96-ounce containers. To better understand current and future demand for this product, the company examined the last 40 days of sales, which are shown in the table below. One of the company's

Data for Exercise 12.65

Sale Day, x	Demand for 96 oz. Containers, y (in cases)	Sale Day, x	Demand for 96 oz. Containers, y (in cases)
1	4,581	21	5,902
2	4,239	22	2,295
3	2,754	23	2,682
4	4,501	24	5,787
5	4,016	25	3,339
6	4,680	26	3,798
7	4,950	27	2,007
8	3,303	28	6,282
9	2,367	29	3,267
10	3,055	30	4,779
11	4,248	31	9,000
12	5,067	32	9,531
13	5,201	33	3,915
14	5,133	34	8,964
15	4,211	35	6,984
16	3,195	36	6,660
17	5,760	37	6,921
18	5,661	38	10,005
19	6,102	39	10,153
20	6,099	40	11,520

Source: Tom Metzler and Rick Campbell.

objectives is to model demand, y, as a function of sale day, x (where $x = 1, 2, 3, \ldots, 40$).

a. Construct a scatterplot for these data.

b. Does it appear that a second-order model might better explain the variation in demand than a first-order model? Explain.

c. Fit a first-order model to these data.

d. Fit a second-order model to these data.

e. Compare the results in parts **c** and **d** and decide which model better explains variation in demand. Justify your choice.

12.7 Qualitative (Dummy) Variable Models

Multiple regression models can also be written to include **qualitative** (or **categorical**) **independent variables**. Qualitative variables, unlike quantitative variables, cannot be measured on a numerical scale. Therefore, we must code the values of the qualitative variables (called **levels**) as numbers before we can fit the model. These coded qualitative variables are called **dummy** (or **indicator) variables** because the numbers assigned to the various levels are arbitrarily selected.

To illustrate, suppose a female executive at a certain company claims that male executives earn higher salaries, on average, than female executives with the same education, experience, and responsibilities. To support her claim, she wants to model the salary y of an executive using a qualitative independent variable representing the gender of an executive (male or female).

A convenient method of coding the values of a qualitative variable at two levels involves assigning a value of 1 to one of the levels and a value of 0 to the other. For example, the dummy variable used to describe gender could be coded as follows:

$$x = \begin{cases} 1 & \text{if male} \\ 0 & \text{if female} \end{cases}$$

The choice of which level is assigned to 1 and which is assigned to 0 is arbitrary. The model then takes the following form:

$$E(y) = \beta_0 + \beta_1 x$$

The advantage of using a 0–1 coding scheme is that the β coefficients are easily interpreted. The model above allows us to compare the mean executive salary $E(y)$ for males with the corresponding mean for females.

$$\text{Males } (x = 1): E(y) = \beta_0 + \beta_1(1) = \beta_0 + \beta_1$$
$$\text{Females } (x = 0): E(y) = \beta_0 + \beta_1(0) = \beta_0$$

These two means are illustrated in the bar graph in Figure 12.15.

First note that β_0 represents the mean salary for females (say, μ_F). When a 0–1 coding convention is used, β_0 will always represent the mean response associated with the level of the qualitative variable assigned the value 0 (called the **base level**). The difference between the mean salary for males and the mean salary for females, $\mu_M - \mu_F$, is represented by β_1—that is,

$$\mu_M - \mu_F = (\beta_0 + \beta_1) - (\beta_0) = \beta_1$$

This difference is shown in Figure 12.15.* With a 0–1 coding convention, β_1 will always represent the difference between the mean response for the level assigned the value 1 and the mean for the base level. Thus, for the executive salary model, we have

$$\beta_0 = \mu_F$$
$$\beta_1 = \mu_M - \mu_F$$

The model relating a mean response $E(y)$ to a qualitative independent variable at two levels is summarized in the following box.

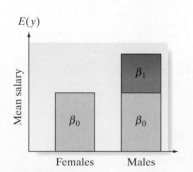

Figure 12.15

Bar graph comparing $E(y)$ for males and females

*Note that β_1 could be negative. If β_1 were negative, the height of the bar corresponding to males would be *reduced* (rather than increased) from the height of the bar for females by the amount β_1. Figure 12.15 is constructed assuming that β_1 is a positive quantity.

A Model Relating $E(y)$ to a Qualitative Independent Variable with Two Levels

$$E(y) = \beta_0 + \beta_1 x$$

where

$$x = \begin{cases} 1 & \text{if level A} \\ 0 & \text{if level B} \end{cases}$$

Interpretation of β's:

$$\beta_0 = \mu_B \ \text{(mean for base level)}$$
$$\beta_1 = \mu_A - \mu_B$$

Note: μ_i represents the mean of y, $E(y)$, for level i of the dummy variable.

Now carefully examine the model with a single qualitative independent variable at two levels; we will use exactly the same pattern for any number of levels. Moreover, the interpretation of the parameters will always be the same. One level (say, level A) is selected as the base level. Then for the 0–1 coding* for the dummy variables,

$$\mu_A = \beta_0$$

The coding for all dummy variables is as follows: To represent the mean value of y for a particular level, let that dummy variable equal 1; otherwise, the dummy variable is set equal to 0. Using this system of coding,

$$\mu_B = \beta_0 + \beta_1$$
$$\mu_C = \beta_0 + \beta_2$$

and so on. Because $\mu_A = \beta_0$, any other model parameter will represent the difference between means for that level and the base level:

$$\beta_1 = \mu_B - \mu_A$$
$$\beta_2 = \mu_C - \mu_A$$

and so on. Consequently, each β multiplied by a dummy variable represents the difference between $E(y)$ at one level of the qualitative variable and $E(y)$ at the base level.

A Model Relating $E(y)$ to One Qualitative Independent Variable with k Levels

Always use a number of dummy variables that is one less than the number of levels of the qualitative variable. Thus, for a qualitative variable with k levels, use $k - 1$ dummy variables:

$$E(y) = \beta_0 + \beta_1 x_1 + \beta_2 x_2 + \cdots + \beta_{k-1} x_{k-1}$$

where x_i is the dummy variable for level $i + 1$ and

$$x_i = \begin{cases} 1 & \text{if } y \text{ is observed at level } i + 1 \\ 0 & \text{otherwise} \end{cases}$$

Then, for this system of coding

$$\mu_A = \beta_0 \qquad \text{and} \qquad \beta_1 = \mu_B - \mu_A$$
$$\mu_B = \beta_0 + \beta_1 \qquad\qquad\qquad \beta_2 = \mu_C - \mu_A$$
$$\mu_C = \beta_0 + \beta_2 \qquad\qquad\qquad \beta_3 = \mu_D - \mu_A$$
$$\mu_D = \beta_0 + \beta_3 \qquad\qquad\qquad \vdots$$

Note: μ_i represents the mean of y, $E(y)$, for level i of the qualitative variable.

*You do not have to use a 0–1 system of coding for the dummy variables. Any two-value system will work, but the interpretation given to the model parameters will depend on the code. Using the 0–1 system makes the model parameters easy to interpret.

EXAMPLE 12.9

A Model with One Qualitative Independent Variable—Credit Card Debt

Problem Suppose an economist wants to compare the mean dollar amounts owed by delinquent credit card customers in three different socioeconomic classes: (1) lower class, (2) middle class, and (3) upper class. A sample of 10 customers with delinquent accounts is selected from each group, and the amount owed by each is recorded, as shown in Table 12.3.

Table 12.3	Dollars Owed, Example 12.9	
Group 1 (lower class)	Group 2 (middle class)	Group 3 (upper class)
$148	$513	$335
76	264	643
393	433	216
520	94	536
236	535	128
134	327	723
55	214	258
166	135	380
415	280	594
153	304	465

 *Data Set:* CCDEBT

a. Hypothesize a regression model for amount owed (y) using socioeconomic class as an independent variable.

b. Interpret the β's in the model.

c. Fit the model to the data and give the least squares prediction equation.

d. Use the model to determine if the mean dollar amounts owed by customers differ significantly for the three socioeconomic groups at $\alpha = .05$.

Solution

a. Note that socioeconomic status (low, middle, upper class) is a qualitative variable (measured on an ordinal scale). For a three-level qualitative variable, we need two dummy variables in the regression model. The model relating $E(y)$ to this single qualitative variable, socioeconomic group, is

$$E(y) = \beta_0 + \beta_1 x_1 + \beta_2 x_2$$

where (arbitrarily choosing group 1 as the base level)

$$x_1 = \begin{cases} 1 & \text{if group 2} \\ 0 & \text{if not} \end{cases} \qquad x_2 = \begin{cases} 1 & \text{if group 3} \\ 0 & \text{if not} \end{cases}$$

b. For this model

$$\beta_0 = \mu_1$$
$$\beta_1 = \mu_2 - \mu_1$$
$$\beta_2 = \mu_3 - \mu_1$$

where μ_1, μ_2, and μ_3 are the mean responses for socioeconomic groups 1, 2, and 3, respectively—that is, β_0 represents the mean amount owed for group 1 (lower class), β_1 represents the mean difference in amounts owed for group 2 (middle) and group 1 (lower), and β_2 represents the mean difference in amounts owed for group 3 (upper) and group 1 (lower).

c. The Minitab printout of the regression analysis is shown in Figure 12.16. The least squares estimates of the β's are highlighted on the printout, yielding the following least squares prediction equation:

$$\hat{y} = 229.6 + 80.3x_1 + 198.2x_2$$

```
Regression Analysis: Amount versus X1, X2

Analysis of Variance

Source        DF   Adj SS   Adj MS   F-Value   P-Value
Regression     2   198772    99386      3.48     0.045
Error         27   770671    28543
Total         29   969443

Model Summary

      S    R-sq   R-sq(adj)
168.948   20.50%     14.62%

Coefficients

Term       Coef   SE Coef   T-Value   P-Value
Constant  229.6      53.4      4.30     0.000
X1         80.3      75.6      1.06     0.297
X2        198.2      75.6      2.62     0.014

Regression Equation

Amount = 229.6 + 80.3 X1 + 198.2 X2
```

Descriptive Statistics: Amount

```
Variable  Class   N    Mean    StDev   Minimum   Maximum
Amount      L     10   229.6   158.2      55.0     520.0
            M     10   309.9   147.9      94.0     535.0
            U     10   427.8   196.8     128.0     723.0
```

Figure 12.16

Minitab output for model with dummy variables

The interpretations of the β's in part **b** allow us to obtain the β estimates from the sample means associated with the different levels of the qualitative variable.*

Because $\beta_0 = \mu_1$, then the estimate of β_0 is the estimated mean delinquent amount for the lower-class group. This sample mean, highlighted at the bottom of the Minitab printout, is 229.6; thus $\hat{\beta}_0 = 229.6$.

Now $\beta_1 = \mu_2 - \mu_1$; therefore, the estimate of β_1 is the difference between the sample mean delinquent amounts for the middle- and lower-class groups. Based on the sample means highlighted at the bottom of the Minitab printout, we have $\hat{\beta}_1 = 309.9 - 229.6 = 80.3$.

Similarly, the estimate of $\beta_2 = \mu_3 - \mu_1$ is the difference between the sample mean delinquent amounts for the upper- and lower-class groups. From the sample means highlighted at the bottom of the Minitab printout, we have $\hat{\beta}_2 = 427.8 - 229.6 = 198.2$.

d. Testing the null hypothesis that the means for the three groups are equal—that is, $\mu_1 = \mu_2 = \mu_3$—is equivalent to testing

$$H_0: \beta_1 = \beta_2 = 0$$

You can see this by observing that if $\beta_1 = \mu_2 - \mu_1 = 0$, then $\mu_1 = \mu_2$. Similarly, if $\beta_2 = \mu_3 - \mu_1 = 0$, then $\mu_3 = \mu_1$. Thus, if H_0 is true, then μ_1, μ_2, and μ_3 must be equal. The alternative hypothesis is

H_a: At least one of the parameters, β_1 and β_2, differs from 0, which implies that at least two of the three means (μ_1, μ_2, and μ_3) differ.

To test this hypothesis, we conduct the global F-test for the model. The value of the F-statistic for testing the adequacy of the model, $F = 3.48$, and the observed significance level of the test, p-value $= .045$, are both highlighted on Figure 12.16. Because $\alpha = .05$ exceeds the p-value, we reject H_0 and conclude that at least one of the parameters, β_1 and β_2, differs from 0. Or, equivalently, we conclude that the data provide sufficient evidence to indicate that the mean indebtedness does vary from one socioeconomic group to another.

Look Back This global F-test is equivalent to the analysis of variance F-test for a completely randomized design of Chapter 9.

● **Now Work Exercise 12.78**

*The least squares method and the sample means method will yield equivalent β estimates when the sample sizes associated with the different levels of the qualitative variable are equal.

CAUTION A common mistake of regression analysts is to use a single dummy variable x for a qualitative variable at k levels, where $x = 1, 2, 3, \ldots, k$. Such a regression model will have unestimable β's and β's that are difficult to interpret. Remember, when modeling $E(y)$ with a single qualitative independent variable, the number of 0–1 dummy variables to include in the model will always be one less than the number of levels of the qualitative variable.

Exercises 12.66–12.81

Learning the Mechanics

12.66 Write a regression model relating the mean value of y to a qualitative independent variable that can assume two levels. Interpret all the terms in the model.

12.67 Write a regression model relating $E(y)$ to a qualitative independent variable that can assume three levels. Interpret all the terms in the model.

12.68 The Excel printout below resulted from fitting the following model to $n = 15$ data points:

$$y = \beta_0 + \beta_1 x_1 + \beta_2 x_2 + \varepsilon$$

where

$$x_1 = \begin{cases} 1 \text{ if level } 2 \\ 0 \text{ if not} \end{cases} \quad x_2 = \begin{cases} 1 \text{ if level } 3 \\ 0 \text{ if not} \end{cases}$$

a. Report the least squares prediction equation.
b. Interpret the values of β_1 and β_2.
c. Interpret the following hypotheses in terms of μ_1, μ_2, and μ_3:

$H_0: \beta_1 = \beta_2 = 0$
$H_a:$ At least one of the parameters β_1 and β_2 differs from 0

d. Conduct the hypothesis test of part **c.**

Regression Statistics	
Multiple R	0.897
R Square	0.805
Adjusted R Square	0.772
Standard Error	9.129
Observations	15

ANOVA

	df	SS	MS	F	Significance F
Regression	2	4118.9	2060	24.72	0
Residual	12	1000	83.3		
Total	14	5118.9			

	Coefficients	Standard Error	t Stat	P-value
Intercept	80	4.082	19.6	0
X1	16.8	5.774	2.91	0.013
X2	40.4	5.774	7	0

12.69 The following model was used to relate $E(y)$ to a single qualitative variable with four levels:

$$E(y) = \beta_0 + \beta_1 x_1 + \beta_2 x_2 + \beta_3 x_3$$

where

$$x_1 = \begin{cases} 1 \text{ if level } 2 \\ 0 \text{ if not} \end{cases} \quad x_2 = \begin{cases} 1 \text{ if level } 3 \\ 0 \text{ if not} \end{cases} \quad x_3 = \begin{cases} 1 \text{ if level } 4 \\ 0 \text{ if not} \end{cases}$$

This model was fit to $n = 30$ data points, and the following result was obtained:

$$\hat{y} = 10.2 - 4x_1 + 12x_2 + 2x_3$$

a. Use the least squares prediction equation to find the estimate of $E(y)$ for each level of the qualitative independent variable.
b. Specify the null and alternative hypotheses you would use to test whether $E(y)$ is the same for all four levels of the independent variable.

Applying the Concepts—Basic

12.70 Can money spent on gifts buy love? Refer to the *Journal of Experimental Social Psychology* (Vol. 45, 2009) study of whether buying gifts truly buys love, Exercise 9.9 (p. 529). Recall that study participants were randomly assigned to play the role of gift-giver or gift-receiver. Gift-receivers were asked to provide the level of appreciation (measured on a 7-point scale where 1 = "not at all" and 7 = "to a great extent") they had for the last birthday gift they received from a loved one. Gift-givers were asked to recall the last birthday gift they gave to a loved one and to provide the level of appreciation the loved one had for the gift.
a. Write a dummy variable regression model that will allow the researchers to compare the average level of appreciation for birthday gift-givers (μ_G) with the average for birthday gift-receivers (μ_R).
b. Express each of the model's β parameters in terms of μ_G and μ_R.
c. The researchers hypothesize that the average level of appreciation is higher for birthday gift-givers than for birthday gift-receivers. Explain how to test this hypothesis using the regression model.

12.71 Production technologies, terroir, and quality of Bordeaux wine. In addition to state-of-the-art technologies, the production of quality wine is strongly influenced by the natural endowments of the grape-growing region—called the "terroir." *The Economic Journal* (May 2008) published an empirical study of the factors that yield a quality Bordeaux wine. A quantitative measure of wine quality (y) was modeled as a function of several qualitative independent variables, including grape-picking method (manual or automated), soil type (clay, gravel, or sand), and slope orientation (east, south, west, southeast, or southwest).
a. Create the appropriate dummy variables for each of the qualitative independent variables.
b. Write a model for wine quality (y) as a function of grape-picking method. Interpret the β's in the model.

c. Write a model for wine quality (y) as a function of soil type. Interpret the β's in the model.

d. Write a model for wine quality (y) as a function of slope orientation. Interpret the β's in the model.

12.72 Impact of race on football card values. University of Colorado sociologists investigated the impact of race on the value of professional football players' "rookie" cards (*Electronic Journal of Sociology*, 2007). The sample consisted of 148 rookie cards of National Football League (NFL) players who were inducted into the Football Hall of Fame. The price of the card (in dollars) was modeled as a function of several qualitative independent variables: race of player (black or white), card availability (high or low), and player position (quarterback, running back, wide receiver, tight end, defensive lineman, linebacker, defensive back, or offensive lineman).

a. Create the appropriate dummy variables for each of the qualitative independent variables.

b. Write a model for price (y) as a function of race. Interpret the β's in the model.

c. Write a model for price (y) as a function of card availability. Interpret the β's in the model.

d. Write a model for price (y) as a function of position. Interpret the β's in the model.

12.73 Ascorbic acid reduces goat stress. Refer to the *Animal Science Journal* (May, 2014) study on the use of ascorbic acid (AA) to reduce stress in goats during transportation from farm to market, Exercise 9.12 (p. 529). Recall that 24 healthy goats were randomly divided into four groups (A, B, C, and D) of six animals each. Goats in group A were administered a dosage of AA 30 minutes prior to transportation; goats in group B were administered a dosage of AA 30 minutes following transportation; group C goats were not given any AA prior to or following transportation; and, goats in group D were not given any AA and were not transported. Weight was measured before and after transportation and the weight loss (in kilograms) determined for each goat.

a. Write a model for mean weight loss, $E(y)$, as a function of the AA dosage group (A, B, C, or D). Use group D as the base level.

b. Interpret the β's in the model, part **a.**

c. Recall that the researchers discovered that mean weight loss is reduced in goats administered AA compared to goats not given any AA. On the basis of this result, determine the sign (positive or negative) of as many of the β's in the model, part **a,** as possible.

12.74 Buy-side vs. sell-side analysts' earnings forecasts. Refer to the *Financial Analysts Journal* (July/August 2008) comparison of earnings forecasts of buy-side and sell-side analysts, Exercise 2.86 (p. 112). The Harvard Business School professors used regression to model the relative optimism (y) of the analysts' 3-month horizon forecasts. One of the independent variables used to model forecast optimism was the dummy variable $x = \{1$ if the analyst worked for a buy-side firm, 0 if the analyst worked for a sell-side firm$\}$.

a. Write the equation of the model for $E(y)$ as a function of type of firm.

b. Interpret the value of β_0 in the model, part **a.**

c. The professors write that the value of β_1 in the model, part **a,** "represents the mean difference in relative forecast optimism between buy-side and sell-side analysts." Do you agree?

d. The professors also argue that "if buy-side analysts make less optimistic forecasts than their sell-side counterparts, the [estimated value of β_1] will be negative." Do you agree?

12.75 Do blondes raise more funds? During fundraising, does the physical appearance of the solicitor impact the level of capital raised? An economist at the University of Nevada-Reno designed an experiment to answer this question and published the results in *Economic Letters* (Vol. 100, 2008). Each in a sample of 955 households was contacted by a female solicitor and asked to contribute to the Center for Natural Hazards Mitigation Research. The level of contribution (in dollars) was recorded as well as the hair color of the solicitor (blond Caucasian, brunette Caucasian, or minority female).

a. Consider a model for the mean level of contribution, $E(y)$, that allows for different means depending on the hair color of the solicitor. Create the appropriate number of dummy variables for hair color. (Use minority female as the base level.)

b. Write the equation of the model, part **a,** incorporating the dummy variables.

c. In terms of the β's in the model, what is the mean level of contribution for households contacted by a blond Caucasian solicitor?

d. In terms of the β's in the model, what is the difference between the mean level of contribution for households contacted by a blond solicitor and those contacted by a minority female?

e. One theory posits that blond solicitors will achieve the highest mean contribution level, but that there will be no difference between the mean contribution levels attained by brunette Caucasian and minority females. If this theory is true, give the expected signs of the β's in the model.

f. The researcher found the β estimate for the dummy variable for blond Caucasian to be positive and significantly different from 0 (p-value $< .01$). The β estimate for the dummy variable for brunette Caucasian was also positive, but not significantly different from 0 (p-value $> .10$). Do these results support the theory, part **e?**

Applying the Concepts—Intermediate

12.76 Charisma of top-level leaders. Refer to the *Academy of Management Journal* (August, 2015) study of the charisma of top leaders in business, Exercise 11.28 (p. 657). Recall that data were collected on 24 U.S. presidential elections from 1916 to 2008. The dependent variable of interest was Democratic vote share (y), measured as the percentage of voters who voted for the Democratic candidate in the national election. One of the independent variables of interest was a categorical variable that represented whether or not the presidential election was affected by a World War. A second qualitative variable of interest was whether a Democrat or Republican incumbent was running for president. This incumbent variable was recorded at three levels: Democrat incumbent, Republican incumbent, or no incumbent running.

a. Write a model relating Democratic vote share (y) to the qualitative independent predictor, World War. Use "no World War" as the base level.

b. In terms of the β's of the model, part **a,** give an expression for the mean Democratic vote share during all years when there is no World War.

c. In terms of the β's of the model, part **a,** give an expression for the mean Democratic vote share during all years when there is a World War.

d. Fit the model, part **a,** to the data in the file. Is there sufficient evidence to indicate that the mean Democratic vote share during all years when there is a World War differs from the mean when there is no World War? Test using $\alpha = .10$.

e. Write a model relating Democratic vote share (y) to the qualitative independent predictor, incumbent running. Use "no incumbent running" as the base level.

f. In terms of the β's of the model, part **e,** give an expression for the mean Democratic vote share during all years when there is no incumbent running.

g. In terms of the β's of the model, part **e,** give an expression for the mean Democratic vote share during all years when a Republican incumbent is running.

h. In terms of the β's of the model, part **e,** give an expression for the difference between the mean Democratic vote share for all years when a Democratic incumbent is running and when there is no incumbent running.

i. Fit the model, part **e,** to the data in the file. Is there sufficient evidence to indicate that the mean Democratic vote share differs depending on the incumbent running? Test using $\alpha = .10$.

12.77 Corporate sustainability and firm characteristics. Refer to the *Business and Society* (March 2011) study on how firm size and firm type impact corporate sustainability behaviors, Exercise 9.7 (p. 528). Recall that Certified Public Accountants (CPAs) were surveyed on their firms' likelihood of reporting sustainability policies (measured as a probability between 0 and 1). The CPAs were divided into four groups depending on firm size (large or small) and firm type (public or private): large/public, large/private, small/public, and small/private. One goal of the analysis is to determine whether the mean likelihood of reporting sustainability policies differs depending on firm size and firm type.

a. Consider a single qualitative variable representing the four size/type categories. Create the appropriate dummy variables for representing this qualitative variable as an independent variable in a regression model for predicting likelihood of reporting sustainability policies (y).

b. Give the equation of the model, part **a,** and interpret each of the model parameters.

c. The global F-test for the model resulted in p-value $< .001$. Give a practical interpretation of this result.

d. Now consider treating firm size and firm type as two different qualitative independent variables in a model for likelihood of reporting sustainability policies (y). Create the appropriate dummy variables for representing these qualitative variables in the model.

e. Refer to part **d.** Write a model for $E(y)$ as a function of firm size and firm type, but do not include interaction. (This model is called the *main effects* model.)

f. Refer to the model, part **e.** For each combination of firm size and firm type (e.g., large/public), write $E(y)$ as a function of the model parameters.

g. Use the results, part **f,** to show that for the main effects model, the difference between the mean likelihoods for large and small firms does not depend on firm type.

h. Write a model for $E(y)$ as a function of firm size, firm type, and size $\times$ type interaction.

i. Refer to the model, part **h.** For each combination of firm size and firm type (e.g., large/public), write $E(y)$ as a function of the model parameters.

j. Use the results, part **i,** to show that for the interaction model, the difference between the mean likelihoods for large and small firms does depend on firm type.

12.78 Homework assistance for accounting students. Refer to the *Journal of Accounting Education* (Vol. 25, 2007) study of assisting accounting students with their homework, Exercise 9.30 (p. 545). Recall that 175 accounting students took a pretest on a topic not covered in class and then each was given a homework problem to solve on the same topic. The students were assigned to one of three homework assistance groups. Some students received the completed solution, some were given check figures at various steps of the solution, and some received no help at all. After finishing the homework, the students were all given a posttest on the subject. The dependent variable of interest was the knowledge gain (or test score improvement). These data are saved in the file.

a. Propose a model for the knowledge gain (y) as a function of the qualitative variable, homework assistance group.

b. In terms of the β's in the model, give an expression for the difference between the mean knowledge gains of students in the "completed solution" and "no help" groups.

c. Fit the model to the data and give the least squares prediction equation.

d. Conduct the global F-test for model utility using $\alpha = .05$. Interpret the results, practically.

e. Show that the results, part **d,** agree with the conclusions reached in Exercise 9.30.

12.79 Improving driving performance while fatigued. Refer to the *Human Factors* (May, 2014) study of driving performance while fatigued, Exercise 9.31 (p. 545). Recall that the researchers had 40 college students drive a long distance in a simulator. While driving, each student performed a task. One group of student-drivers performed a verbal task continuously (*continuous verbal condition*); another group performed the task only at the end of the drive (*late verbal condition*); a third group did not perform the task at all (*no verbal condition*); and, the fourth group listened to a program on the car radio (*radio show condition*). The dependent variable of interest was the percentage of billboards recalled by the student-driver. The data are listed in the table on the next page.

a. Write a model for mean recall percentage, $E(y)$, as a function of task group (continuous verbal, late verbal, no verbal, and radio show). Use radio show as the base level for the qualitative independent variable, task group.

b. Measures of central tendency for the recall percentage measurements of each task group are displayed

Data for Exercise 12.79

Continuous Verbal	Late Verbal	No Verbal	Radio Show
14	57	64	37
63	64	83	45
10	66	54	87
29	18	59	62
37	95	60	14
60	52	39	46
43	58	56	59
4	92	73	45
36	85	78	45
47	47	73	50

in the accompanying Minitab printout. Use this information to estimate the β parameters of the model, part **a**.

c. Fit the model, part **a**, to the data in the file. Use the output to verify your β estimates in part **b**.

d. Refer to the output, part **c**. Conduct a test (at $\alpha = .01$) to determine if the mean recall percentage differs for student-drivers in the four groups. Your answer should agree with that of Exercise 9.31.

Descriptive Statistics: NoVerb, LateVerb, ContVerb, Radio

```
                                      N for
Variable    N    Mean   Median   Mode   Mode
NoVerb     10   63.90   62.00     73     2
LateVerb   10   63.40   61.00      *     0
ContVerb   10   34.30   36.50      *     0
Radio      10   49.00   45.50     45     3
```

Applying the Concepts—Advanced

12.80 Manipulating rates of return with stock splits. Some firms have been accused of using stock splits to manipulate their stock prices before being acquired by another firm. An article in *Financial Management* (Winter 2008) investigated the impact of stock splits on long-run stock performance for acquiring firms. A simplified version of the model fit by the researchers follows:

$$E(y) = \beta_0 + \beta_1 x_1 + \beta_2 x_2 + \beta_3 x_1 x_2,$$

where

y = Firm's 3-year buy-and-hold return rate (%)
$x_1 = \{1$ if stock split prior to acquisition, 0 if not$\}$
$x_2 = \{1$ if firm's discretionary accrual is high, 0 if discretionary accrual is low$\}$

a. In terms of the β's in the model, what is the mean buy-and-hold return rate (BAR) for a firm with no stock split and a high discretionary accrual (DA)?

b. In terms of the β's in the model, what is the mean BAR for a firm with no stock split and a low DA?

c. For firms with no stock split, find the difference between the mean BAR for firms with high and low DA. (*Hint:* Use your answers to parts **a** and **b**.)

d. Repeat part **c** for firms with a stock split.

e. Note that the differences, parts **c** and **d**, are not the same. Explain why this illustrates the notion of interaction between x_1 and x_2.

f. A test for $H_0: \beta_3 = 0$ yielded a p-value of .027. Using $\alpha = .05$, interpret this result.

g. The researchers reported that the estimated values of both β_2 and β_3 are negative. Consequently, they conclude that "high-DA acquirers perform worse compared with low-DA acquirers. Moreover, the underperformance is even greater if high-DA acquirers have a stock split before acquisition." Do you agree?

12.81 Banning controversial sports team sponsors. Refer to the *Journal of Marketing Research* (October. 2015) study of the impact of banning a controversial sponsor on a sports team's success, Exercise 9.34 (p. 546). Recall that markets for English soccer clubs were classified as one of four types: (1) banned alcohol sponsors but now have other sponsors, (2) banned alcohol sponsors and now have no other sponsors, (3) did not ban alcohol sponsors but now have other sponsors, and (4) did not ban alcohol sponsors and now have no other sponsors. To assess the impact of an alcohol ban in a market, the researchers computed the *matching value loss* (*MVL*) for each market and treated this as the dependent variable in the analysis. The data (simulated from information provided in the study) are saved in the file. Consider a model for mean MVL as a function of the qualitative independent variable, market type.

a. Give the equation of the model for $E(MVL)$. Use market type "no ban/no other" as the base level for the qualitative independent variable.

b. Fit the model, part **a**, to the data. Give the least squares prediction equation.

c. Provide a practical interpretation of each of the estimated β's in the model.

d. Conduct the global F-test for the model using $\alpha = .05$. What inference can you make about the mean MVL values for the four markets?

e. The sample mean MVL values for the four markets were 8.52, 8.55, 6.63, and 6.38, respectively. Show how to find these sample means using only the β estimates obtained in part **b**.

12.8 Models with Both Quantitative and Qualitative Variables

Suppose you want to relate the mean monthly sales $E(y)$ of a company to monthly advertising expenditure x for three different advertising media (say, internet, mobile device, and television) and you wish to use first-order (straight-line) models to model the responses for all three media. Graphs of these three relationships might appear as shown in Figure 12.17.

Because the lines in Figure 12.17 are hypothetical, a number of practical questions arise. Is one advertising medium as effective as any other? That is, do the three mean sales lines differ for the three advertising media? Do the increases in mean sales per dollar input in advertising differ for the three advertising media? That is, do the slopes of the three lines differ? Note that the two practical questions have been rephrased into questions about the parameters that define the three lines in Figure 12.17. To answer them, we must write a single regression model that will characterize the three lines of Figure 12.17 and that, by testing hypotheses about the lines, will answer the questions.

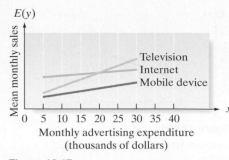

Figure 12.17

Graphs of the relationship between mean sales $E(y)$ and advertising expenditure x

The response described previously, monthly sales, is a function of *two* independent variables, one quantitative (advertising expenditure x_1) and one qualitative (type of medium). We will proceed, in stages, to build a model relating $E(y)$ to these variables and will show graphically the interpretation we would give to the model at each stage. This will help you to see the contributions of the various terms in the model.

1. The straight-line relationship between mean sales $E(y)$ and advertising expenditure is the same for all three media—that is, a single line will describe the relationship between $E(y)$ and advertising expenditure x_1 for all the media (see Figure 12.18).

$$E(y) = \beta_0 + \beta_1 x \qquad \text{where } x_1 = \text{advertising expenditure}$$

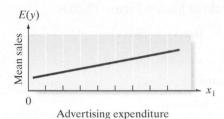

Figure 12.18

The relationship between $E(y)$ and x_1 is the same for all media

2. The straight lines relating mean sales $E(y)$ to advertising expenditure x_1 differ from one medium to another, but the rate of increase in mean sales per increase in dollar advertising expenditure x_1 is the same for all media—that is, the lines are parallel but possess different y-intercepts (see Figure 12.19).

$$E(y) = \beta_0 + \beta_1 x_1 + \beta_2 x_2 + \beta_3 x_3$$

where

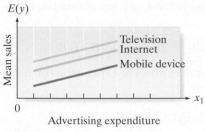

Figure 12.19

Parallel response lines for the three media

$$x_1 = \text{advertising expenditure}$$

$$x_2 = \begin{cases} 1 & \text{if mobile device medium} \\ 0 & \text{if not} \end{cases}$$

$$x_3 = \begin{cases} 1 & \text{if television medium} \\ 0 & \text{if not} \end{cases}$$

(Advertising medium base level = Internet)

Notice that this model is essentially a combination of a first-order model with a single quantitative variable and the model with a single qualitative variable:

First-order model with a single quantitative variable: $\qquad E(y) = \beta_0 + \beta_1 x_1$

Model with single qualitative variable at three levels: $\qquad E(y) = \beta_0 + \beta_2 x_2 + \beta_3 x_3$

where x_1, x_2, and x_3 are as just defined. The model described here implies no interaction between the two independent variables, which are advertising expenditure x_1 and the qualitative variable (type of advertising medium). The change in $E(y)$ for a 1-unit increase in x_1 is identical (the slopes of the lines are equal) for all three advertising media. The terms corresponding to each of the independent variables are called **main effect terms** because they imply no interaction.

3. The straight lines relating mean sales $E(y)$ to advertising expenditure x_1 differ for the three advertising media—that is, both the line intercepts and the slopes

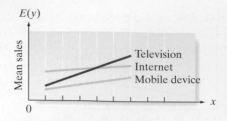

Figure 12.20

Different response lines for the three media

differ (see Figure 12.20). As you will see, this interaction model is obtained by adding terms involving the cross-product terms, one each from each of the two independent variables:

$$E(y) = \overbrace{\beta_0 + \beta_1 x_1}^{\substack{\text{Main effect,}\\ \text{advertising}\\ \text{expenditure}}} + \overbrace{\beta_2 x_2 + \beta_3 x_3}^{\substack{\text{Main effect,}\\ \text{type of}\\ \text{medium}}} + \overbrace{\beta_4 x_1 x_2 + \beta_5 x_1 x_3}^{\text{Interaction}}$$

Note that each of the preceding models is obtained by adding terms to model 1, the single first-order model used to model the responses for all three media. Model 2 is obtained by adding the main effect terms for type of medium, the qualitative variable. Model 3 is obtained by adding the interaction terms to model 2.

EXAMPLE 12.10

Interpreting the β's in a Model with Mixed Independent Variables

Problem Substitute the appropriate values of the dummy variables in model 3 (above) to obtain the equations of the three response lines in Figure 12.20.

Solution The complete model that characterizes the three lines in Figure 12.20 is

$$E(y) = \beta_0 + \beta_1 x_1 + \beta_2 x_2 + \beta_3 x_3 + \beta_4 x_1 x_2 + \beta_5 x_1 x_3$$

where

$$x_1 = \text{advertising expenditure}$$

$$x_2 = \begin{cases} 1 & \text{if mobile device medium} \\ 0 & \text{if not} \end{cases}$$

$$x_3 = \begin{cases} 1 & \text{if television medium} \\ 0 & \text{if not} \end{cases}$$

Examining the coding, you can see that $x_2 = x_3 = 0$ when the advertising medium is the Internet. Substituting these values into the expression for $E(y)$, we obtain the newspaper medium line:

$$E(y) = \beta_0 + \beta_1 x_1 + \beta_2(0) + \beta_3(0) + \beta_4 x_1(0) + \beta_5 x_1(0) = \beta_0 + \beta_1 x_1$$

Similarly, we substitute the appropriate values of x_2 and x_3 into the expression for $E(y)$ to obtain the mobile device medium line ($x_2 = 1, x_3 = 0$):

$$E(y) = \beta_0 + \beta_1 x_1 + \beta_2(1) + \beta_3(0) + \beta_4 x_1(1) + \beta_5 x_1(0)$$

$$= \underbrace{(\beta_0 + \beta_2)}_{y\text{-intercept}} + \underbrace{(\beta_1 + \beta_4)}_{Slope} x_1$$

and the television medium line: ($x_2 = 0, x_3 = 1$):

$$E(y) = \beta_0 + \beta_1 x_1 + \beta_2(0) + \beta_3(1) + \beta_4 x_1(0) + \beta_5 x_1(1)$$

$$= \underbrace{(\beta_0 + \beta_3)}_{y\text{-intercept}} + \underbrace{(\beta_1 + \beta_5)}_{Slope} x_1$$

Look Back If you were to fit model 3, obtain estimates of $\beta_0, \beta_1, \beta_2, \ldots, \beta_5$, and substitute them into the equations for the three media lines, you would obtain exactly the same prediction equations as you would obtain if you were to fit three separate straight lines, one to each of the three sets of media data. You may ask why we would not fit the three lines separately. Why bother fitting a model that combines all three lines (model 3) into the same equation? The answer is that you need to use this procedure if you wish to use statistical tests to compare the three media lines. We need to be able to express a practical question about the lines in terms of a hypothesis that a set of parameters in the model equals 0. (We demonstrate this procedure in the next section.) You could not do this if you were to perform three separate regression analyses and fit a line to each set of media data.

• **Now Work Exercise 12.82**

EXAMPLE 12.11

Testing for Two Different Slopes—Worker Productivity

Problem An industrial psychologist conducted an experiment to investigate the relationship between worker productivity and a measure of salary incentive for two manufacturing plants: One plant operates under "disciplined management practices," and the other plant uses a traditional management style. The productivity y per worker was measured by recording the number of machined castings that a worker could produce in a 4-week period of 40 hours per week. The incentive was the amount x_1 of bonus (in cents per casting) paid for all castings produced in excess of 1,000 per worker for the 4-week period. Nine workers were selected from each plant, and three from each group of nine were assigned to receive a 20¢ bonus per casting, three a 30¢ bonus, and three a 40¢ bonus. The productivity data for the 18 workers, three for each plant type and incentive combination, are shown in Table 12.4.

Table 12.4	Productivity Data for Example 12.11							
Management style	Incentive							
	20¢/casting			30¢/casting			40¢/casting		
Traditional	1,435	1,512	1,491	1,583	1,529	1,610	1,601	1,574	1,636
Disciplined	1,575	1,512	1,488	1,635	1,589	1,661	1,645	1,616	1,689

 Data Set: CAST

a. Write a model for mean productivity, $E(y)$, assuming that the relationship between $E(y)$ and incentive x_1 is first-order.

b. Fit the model and graph the prediction equations for the disciplined and traditional management styles.

c. Do the data provide sufficient evidence to indicate that the rate of increase of worker productivity is different for disciplined and traditional plants? Test at $\alpha = .10$.

Solution

a. If we assume that a first-order model* is adequate to detect a change in mean productivity as a function of incentive x_1, then the model that produces two straight lines, one for each plant, is

$$E(y) = \beta_0 + \beta_1 x_1 + \beta_2 x_2 + \beta_3 x_1 x_2$$

where

$$x_1 = \text{incentive} \qquad x_2 = \begin{cases} 1 & \text{if disciplined management style} \\ 0 & \text{if traditional management style} \end{cases}$$

b. The SPSS printout for the regression analysis is shown in Figure 12.21. Reading the parameter estimates highlighted at the bottom of the printout, you can see that

$$\hat{y} = 1,365.833 + 6.217x_1 + 47.778x_2 + .033x_1 x_2$$

---

*Although the model contains a term involving $x_1 x_2$, it is first-order (graphs as a straight line) in the quantitative variable x_1. The variable x_2 is a dummy variable that introduces or deletes terms in the model. The order of a model is determined only by the quantitative variables that appear in the model.

Model Summary

Model	R	R Square	Adjusted R Square	Std. Error of the Estimate
1	.843[a]	.711	.649	40.839

a. Predictors: (Constant), INC_PDUM, INCENTIVE, PDUMMY

ANOVA[a]

Model		Sum of Squares	df	Mean Square	F	Sig.
1	Regression	57332.389	3	19110.796	11.459	.000[b]
	Residual	23349.222	14	1667.802		
	Total	80681.611	17			

a. Dependent Variable: CASTING

b. Predictors: (Constant), INC_PDUM, INCENTIVE, PDUMMY

Coefficients[a]

Model		Unstandardized Coefficients		Standardized Coefficients	t	Sig.
		B	Std. Error	Beta		
1	(Constant)	1365.833	51.836		26.349	.000
	INCENTIVE	6.217	1.667	.758	3.729	.002
	PDUMMY	47.778	73.308	.357	.652	.525
	INC_PDUM	.033	2.358	.008	.014	.989

a. Dependent Variable: CASTING

Figure 12.21

SPSS printout of the complete model for the casting data

The prediction equation for the plant using a traditional management style can be obtained (see the coding) by substituting $x_2 = 0$ into the general prediction equation. Then

$$\hat{y} = \hat{\beta}_0 + \hat{\beta}_1 x_1 + \hat{\beta}_2(0) + \hat{\beta}_3 x_1(0) = \hat{\beta}_0 + \hat{\beta}_1 x_1$$
$$= 1{,}365.833 + 6.217 x_1$$

Similarly, the prediction equation for the plant with a disciplined management style can be obtained by substituting $x_2 = 1$ into the general prediction equation. Then

$$\hat{y} = \hat{\beta}_0 + \hat{\beta}_1 x_1 + \hat{\beta}_2 x_2 + \hat{\beta}_3 x_1 x_2$$
$$= \hat{\beta}_0 + \hat{\beta}_1 x_1 + \hat{\beta}_2(1) + \hat{\beta}_3 x_1(1)$$
$$= \underbrace{(\beta_0 + \beta_2)}_{y\text{-intercept}} + \underbrace{(\beta_1 + \beta_3)}_{Slope} x_1$$
$$= (1{,}365.833 + 47.778) + (6.217 + .033) x_1$$
$$= 1{,}413.611 + 6.250 x_1$$

A Minitab graph of these prediction equations is shown in Figure 12.22. Note that the slopes of the two lines are nearly identical (6.217 for traditional and 6.250 for disciplined).

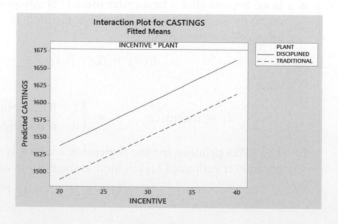

Figure 12.22

Minitab plot of prediction equations for two plants

c. If the rate of increase of productivity with incentive (i.e., the slope) for plants with the disciplined management style is different from the corresponding slope for traditional plants, then the interaction β (i.e., β_3) will differ from 0. Consequently, we want to test

$$H_0: \beta_3 = 0$$
$$H_a: \beta_3 \neq 0$$

This test is conducted using the t-test of Section 12.3. From the SPSS printout, the test statistic and corresponding p-value are

$$t = .014 \qquad p = .989$$

Because $\alpha = .10$ is less than the p-value, we fail to reject H_0. There is insufficient evidence to conclude that the traditional and disciplined shapes differ. Thus, the test supports our observation of two nearly identical slopes in part **b**.

Look Back Because interaction is not significant, we will drop the x_1x_2 term from the model and use the simpler model, $E(y) = \beta_0 + \beta_1x_1 + \beta_2x_2$, to predict productivity.

> ● **Now Work Exercise 12.88**

Models with both quantitative and qualitative x's may also include higher-order (e.g., second-order) terms. In the problem of relating mean monthly sales $E(y)$ of a company to monthly advertising expenditure x_1 and type of medium, suppose we think that the relationship between $E(y)$ and x_1 is curvilinear. We will construct the model, stage by stage, to enable you to compare the procedure with the stage-by-stage construction of the first-order model in the beginning of this section. The graphical interpretations will help you understand the contributions of the model terms.

1. The mean sales curves are identical for all three advertising media—that is, a single second-order curve will suffice to describe the relationship between $E(y)$ and x_1 for all the media (see Figure 12.23):

$$E(y) = \beta_0 + \beta_1x_1 + \beta_2x_1^2$$

   where $x_1 =$ advertising expenditure

2. The response curves possess the same shapes but different y-intercepts (see Figure 12.24):

$$E(y) = \beta_0 + \beta_1x_1 + \beta_2x_1^2 + \beta_3x_2 + \beta_4x_3$$

   where

$$x_1 = \text{advertising expenditure}$$

$$x_2 = \begin{cases} 1 & \text{if mobile device medium} \\ 0 & \text{if not} \end{cases}$$

$$x_3 = \begin{cases} 1 & \text{if television medium} \\ 0 & \text{if not} \end{cases}$$

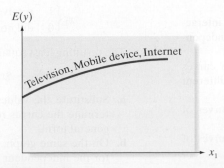

Figure 12.23

The relationship between $E(y)$ and x_1 is the same for all media

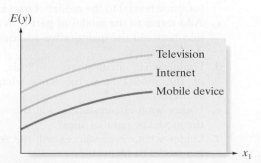

Figure 12.24

The response curves have the same shapes but different y-intercepts

3. The response curves for the three advertising media are different (i.e., advertising expenditure and type of medium interact), as shown in Figure 12.25:

$$E(y) = \beta_0 + \beta_1 x_1 + \beta_2 x_1^2 + \beta_3 x_2 + \beta_4 x_3 + \beta_5 x_1 x_2 + \beta_6 x_1 x_3 + \beta_7 x_1^2 x_2 + \beta_8 x_1^2 x_3$$

Now that you know how to write a model with two independent variables—one qualitative and one quantitative—we ask, Why do it? Why not write a separate second-order model for each type of medium where $E(y)$ is a function of only advertising expenditure? As stated earlier, one reason we wrote the single model representing all three response curves is so that we can test to determine whether the curves are different. We illustrate this procedure in Section 12.9. A second reason for writing a single model is that we obtain a pooled estimate of σ^2, the variance of the random error component ε. If the variance of ε is truly the same for each type of medium, the pooled estimate is superior to three separate estimates calculated by fitting a separate model for each type of medium.

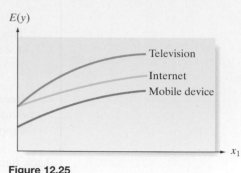

Figure 12.25

The response curves for the three media differ

Exercises 12.82–12.96

Learning the Mechanics

12.82 Consider a multiple regression model for a response y, [NW] with one quantitative independent variable x_1 and one qualitative variable at three levels.
 a. Write a first-order model that relates the mean response $E(y)$ to the quantitative independent variable.
 b. Add the main effect terms for the qualitative independent variable to the model of part **a**. Specify the coding scheme you use.
 c. Add terms to the model of part **b** to allow for interaction between the quantitative and qualitative independent variables.
 d. Under what circumstances will the response lines of the model in part **c** be parallel?
 e. Under what circumstances will the model in part **c** have only one response line?

12.83 Refer to Exercise 12.82.
 a. Write a complete second-order model that relates $E(y)$ to the quantitative variable.
 b. Add the main effect terms for the qualitative variable (at three levels) to the model of part **a**.
 c. Add terms to the model of part **b** to allow for interaction between the quantitative and qualitative independent variables.
 d. Under what circumstances will the response curves of the model have the same shape but different y-intercepts?
 e. Under what circumstances will the response curves of the model be parallel lines?
 f. Under what circumstances will the response curves of the model be identical?

12.84 Consider the model:

$$y = \beta_0 + \beta_1 x_1 + \beta_2 x_2 + \beta_3 x_3 + \varepsilon$$

where x_1 is a quantitative variable and x_2 and x_3 are dummy variables describing a qualitative variable at three levels using the coding scheme

$$x_2 = \begin{cases} 1 & \text{if level 2} \\ 0 & \text{otherwise} \end{cases} \qquad x_3 = \begin{cases} 1 & \text{if level 3} \\ 0 & \text{otherwise} \end{cases}$$

The resulting least squares prediction equation is

$$\hat{y} = 44.8 + 2.2x_1 + 9.4x_2 + 15.6x_3$$

 a. What is the response line (equation) for $E(y)$ when $x_2 = x_3 = 0$? When $x_2 = 1$ and $x_3 = 0$? When $x_2 = 0$ and $x_3 = 1$?
 b. What is the least squares prediction equation associated with level 1? Level 2? Level 3? Plot these on the same graph.

12.85 Consider the model:

$$E(y) = \beta_0 + \beta_1 x_1 + \beta_2 x_2 + \beta_3 x_2^2 + \beta_4 x_3 + \beta_5 x_1 x_2^2$$

where x_2 is a quantitative model and

$$x_1 \begin{cases} 1 & \text{received treatment} \\ 0 & \text{did not receive treatment} \end{cases}$$

The resulting least squares prediction equation is

$$\hat{y} = 2 + x_1 - 5x_2 + 3x_2^2 - 4x_3 + x_1 x_2^2$$

 a. Substitute the values for the dummy variables to determine the curves relating to the mean value $E(y)$ in general form.
 b. On the same graph, plot the curves obtained in part **a** for the independent variable between 0 and 3. Use the least squares prediction equation.

12.86 Write a model that relates $E(y)$ to two independent variables—one quantitative and one qualitative at four levels. Construct a model that allows the associated response curves to be second-order but does not allow for interaction between the two independent variables.

Applying the Concepts—Basic

12.87 Reality TV and cosmetic surgery. Refer to the *Body Image: An International Journal of Research* (March 2010) study of the impact of reality TV shows on a college student's decision to undergo cosmetic surgery, Exercise 12.43 (p. 739). The data saved in the file were used to fit the interaction model, $E(y) = \beta_0 + \beta_1 x_1 + \beta_2 x_4 + \beta_3 x_1 x_4$, where y = desire to have cosmetic surgery (25-point scale), $x_1 = \{1$ if male, 0 if female$\}$, and x_4 = impression of reality TV (7-point scale). From the SPSS printout (p. 739), the estimated equation is:

BDYIMG

$$\hat{y} = 11.78 - 1.97x_1 + .58x_4 - .55x_1 x_4$$

a. Give an estimate of the change in desire (y) for every 1-point increase in impression of reality TV show (x_4) for female students.

b. Repeat part **a** for male students.

12.88 Do blondes raise more funds? Refer to the *Economic Letters* (Vol. 100, 2008) study of whether the color of a female solicitor's hair impacts the level of capital raised, Exercise 12.75 (p. 756). Recall that 955 households were contacted by a female solicitor to raise funds for hazard mitigation research. In addition to the household's level of contribution (in dollars) and the hair color of the solicitor (blond Caucasian, brunette Caucasian, or minority female), the researcher also recorded the beauty rating of the solicitor (measured quantitatively, on a 10-point scale).

NW

a. Write a first-order model (with no interaction) for mean contribution level, $E(y)$, as a function of a solicitor's hair color and her beauty rating.

b. Refer to the model, part **a**. For each hair color, express the change in contribution level for each 1-point increase in a solicitor's beauty rating in terms of the model parameters.

c. Write an interaction model for mean contribution level, $E(y)$, as a function of a solicitor's hair color and her beauty rating.

d. Refer to the model, part **c**. For each hair color, express the change in contribution level for each 1-point increase in a solicitor's beauty rating in terms of the model parameters.

e. Refer to the model, part **c**. Illustrate the interaction with a graph.

12.89 Job performance under time pressure. Time pressure is common at firms that must meet hard and fast deadlines. How do employees working in teams perform when they perceive time pressure? And, can this performance improve with a strong team leader? These were the research questions of interest in a study published in the *Academy of Management Journal* (October, 2015). Data were collected on $n = 139$ project teams working for a software company in India. Among the many variables recorded were team performance (*y*, measured on a 7-point scale), perceived time pressure (x_1, measured on a 7-point scale),

and whether or not the team had a strong and effective team leader ($x_2 = 1$ if yes, 0 if no). The researchers hypothesized a curvilinear relationship between team performance (y) and perceived time pressure (x_1), with different-shaped curves depending on whether or not the team had an effective leader (x_2). A model for $E(y)$ that supports this theory is the complete second-order model:

$$E(y) = \beta_0 + \beta_1 x_1 + \beta_2 x_1^2 + \beta_3 x_2 + \beta_4 x_1 x_2 + \beta_5 x_1^2 x_2$$

a. Write the equation for $E(y)$ as a function of x_1 when the team leader is not effective ($x_2 = 0$).

b. Write the equation for $E(y)$ as a function of x_1 when the team leader is effective ($x_2 = 1$).

c. The researchers reported the following β-estimates: $\hat{\beta}_0 = 4.5$, $\hat{\beta}_1 = -.13$, $\hat{\beta}_2 = -.17$, $\hat{\beta}_3 = .15$, $\hat{\beta}_4 = .15$, and $\hat{\beta}_5 = .29$. Use these estimates to sketch the two equations, parts **a** and **b**. What is the nature of the curvilinear relationship when the team leaders is not effective? Effective?

12.90 Buy-side vs. sell-side analysts' earnings forecasts. Refer to the *Financial Analysts Journal* (July/August 2008) comparison of earnings forecasts of buy-side and sell-side analysts, Exercise 12.74 (p. 756). Recall that the Harvard Business School professors used regression to model the relative optimism (y) of the analysts' 3-month horizon forecasts. The following model was fit to data collected on 11,121 forecasts: $E(y) = \beta_0 + \beta_1 x_1 + \beta_2 x_2 + \beta_3 x_3$, where

$x_1 = \{1$ if the analyst worked for a buy-side firm, 0 if the analyst worked for a sell-side firm$\}$

x_2 = number of days between forecast and fiscal year-end (i.e., forecast horizon)

x_3 = natural logarithm of the number of quarters the analyst had worked with the firm

a. The coefficient of determination for the model was reported as $R^2 = .069$. Interpret this value.

b. Use the value of R^2 in part **a** to conduct a test of the global utility of the model. Use $\alpha = .01$.

c. The value of β_1 was estimated as 1.07, with an associated t-value of 4.3. Use this information to test ($\alpha = .01$.) whether x_1 contributes significantly to the prediction of y.

d. The professors concluded that "after controlling for forecast horizon and analyst experience, earnings forecasts by the analysts at buy-side firms are more optimistic than forecasts made by analysts at sell-side firms." Do you agree?

12.91 Workplace bullying and intention to leave. Workplace bullying has been shown to have a negative psychological effect on victims, often leading the victim to quit or resign. In *Human Resource Management Journal* (October 2008), researchers employed multiple regression to examine whether perceived organizational support (POS) would moderate the relationship between workplace bullying and victims' intention to leave the firm. The dependent variable in the analysis, intention to leave (y), was measured on a quantitative scale. The two key independent variables in the study were bullying (x_1, measured on a quantitative scale) and perceived organizational support (measured qualitatively as "low," "neutral," or "high").

a. Set up the dummy variables required to represent POS in the regression model.

b. Write a model for $E(y)$ as a function of bullying and POS that hypothesizes three parallel straight lines, one for each level of POS.

c. Write a model for $E(y)$ as a function of bullying and POS that hypothesizes three nonparallel straight lines, one for each level of POS.

d. The researchers discovered that the effect of bullying on intention to leave was greater at the low level of POS than at the high level of POS. Which of the two models, parts **b** and **c**, support these findings?

Applying the Concepts—Intermediate

12.92 Agreeableness, gender, and wages. Do agreeable individuals get paid less, on average, than those who are less agreeable on the job? And is this gap greater for males than for females? These questions were addressed in the *Journal of Personality and Social Psychology* (February 2012). Several variables were measured for each in a sample of individuals enrolled in the National Survey of Midlife Development in the U.S. Three of these variables are: (1) level of agreeableness score (where higher scores indicate a greater level of agreeableness), (2) gender (male or female), and (3) annual income (dollars). The researchers modeled mean income, $E(y)$, as a function of both agreeableness score (x_1) and a dummy variable for gender ($x_2 = 1$ if male, 0 if female). Data for a sample of 100 individuals (simulated, based on information provided in the study) are saved in the file. The first 10 observations are listed in the accompanying table.

Data for First 10 Individuals in Study

Income	Agree Score	Gender
44,770	3.0	1
51,480	2.9	1
39,600	3.3	1
24,370	3.3	0
15,460	3.6	0
43,730	3.8	1
48,330	3.2	1
25,970	2.5	0
17,120	3.5	0
20,140	3.2	0

a. Consider the model, $E(y) = \beta_0 + \beta_1 x_1 + \beta_2 x_2$. The researchers theorized that for either gender, income would decrease as agreeableness score increases. If this theory is true, what is the expected sign of β_1 in the model?

b. The researchers also theorized that the rate of decrease of income with agreeableness score would be steeper for males than for females (i.e., the income gap between males and females would be greater the less agreeable the individuals are). Can this theory be tested using the model, part **a**? Explain.

c. Consider the interaction model, $E(y) = \beta_0 + \beta_1 x_1 + \beta_2 x_2 + \beta_3 x_1 x_2$. If the theory, part **b**, is true, give the expected sign of β_1. The expected sign of β_3.

d. Fit the model, part **c**, to the sample data. Check the signs of the estimated β coefficients. How do they compare with the expected values, part **c**?

e. Refer to the interaction model, part **c.** Give the null and alternative hypotheses for testing whether the rate of decrease of income with agreeableness score is steeper for males than for females.

f. Conduct the test, part **e.** Use $\alpha = .05$. Is the researchers' theory supported?

12.93 Chemical plant contamination. Refer to Exercise 12.18 (p. 725) and the model relating the mean DDT level $E(y)$ of contaminated fish to $x_1 =$ miles captured upstream, $x_2 =$ length, and $x_3 =$ weight. Now consider a model for $E(y)$ as a function of both weight and species (channel catfish, largemouth bass, and smallmouth buffalo).

a. Set up the appropriate dummy variables for species.

b. Write the equation of a model that proposes parallel straight-line relationships between mean DDT level $E(y)$ and weight, one line for each species.

c. Write the equation of a model that proposes nonparallel straight-line relationships between mean DDT level $E(y)$ and weight, one line for each species.

d. Fit the model, part **b**, to the data saved in the file. Give the least squares prediction equation.

e. Refer to part **d**. Interpret the value of the least squares estimate of the beta coefficient multiplied by weight.

f. Fit the model, part **c**, to the data saved in the file. Give the least squares prediction equation.

g. Refer to part **f**. Find the estimated slope of the line relating DDT level (y) to weight for the channel catfish species.

12.94 Personality traits and job performance. Refer to the *Journal of Applied Psychology* (Jan. 2011) study of the relationship between task performance and conscientiousness, Exercise 12.54 (p. 747). Recall that the researchers used a quadratic model to relate $y =$ task performance score (measured on a 30-point scale) to $x_1 =$ conscientiousness score (measured on a scale of -3 to $+3$). In addition, the researchers included job complexity in the model, where $x_2 = \{1$ if highly complex job, 0 if not$\}$. The complete model took the form

$$E(y) = \beta_0 + \beta_1 x_1 + \beta_2 (x_1)^2 + \beta_3 x_2 + \beta_4 x_1 x_2 + \beta_5 (x_1)^2 x_2$$

a. For jobs that are not highly complex, write the equation of the model for $E(y)$ as a function of x_1. (Substitute $x_2 = 0$ into the equation.)

b. Refer to part **a**. What do each of the β's represent in the model?

c. For highly complex jobs, write the equation of the model for $E(y)$ as a function of x_1. (Substitute $x_2 = 1$ into the equation.)

d. Refer to part **c**. What do each of the β's represent in the model?

e. Does the model support the researchers' theory that the curvilinear relationship between task performance score (y) and conscientiousness score (x_1) depends on job complexity (x_2)? Explain.

12.95 Recently sold, single-family homes. The National Association of Realtors maintains a database consisting of sales information on homes sold in the United States. The next table lists the sale prices for a sample of 28 recently sold, single-family homes. The table also identifies the region of the country in which the home is located and the total number of homes sold in the region during the month the home sold.

Data for Exercise 12.95

Home Price	Region	Sales Volume
$218,200	NE	55,156
235,900	NE	61,025
192,888	NE	48,991
200,990	NE	55,156
345,300	NE	60,324
178,999	NE	51,446
240,855	NW	61,025
183,200	NW	94,166
165,225	NW	92,063
160,633	NW	89,485
173,900	NW	91,772
241,000	NW	99,025
188,950	NW	94,166
192,880	NW	95,688
193,000	S	155,666
211,980	S	160,000
179,500	S	153,540
185,650	S	148,668
250,900	S	163,210
190,990	S	141,822
242,790	S	163,611
258,900	W	109,083
202,420	W	101,111
365,900	W	116,983
219,900	W	108,773
228,250	W	105,106
235,300	W	107,839
269,800	W	109,026

Source: Based on information from National Association of Realtors, www.realtor.org.

a. Propose a complete second-order model for the sale price of a single-family home as a function of region and sales volume.

b. Give the equation of the curve relating sale price to sales volume for homes sold in the West.

c. Repeat part **b** for homes sold in the Northwest.

d. Which β's in the model, part **a**, allow for differences among the mean sale prices for homes in the four regions?

e. Fit the model, part **a**, to the data using an available statistical software package. Is the model statistically useful for predicting sale price? Test using $\alpha = .01$.

12.96 Charisma of top-level leaders. Refer to the *Academy of Management Journal* (August, 2015) study of the charisma of top leaders in business, Exercise 12.76 (p. 756). The researchers analyzed data collected for 24 U.S. presidential elections where the dependent variable of interest was Democratic vote share (y), measured as the percentage of voters who voted for the Democratic candidate in the national election. One potential quantitative predictor of vote share was the difference (x_1) between the Democratic and Republican candidates' charisma values. (Recall that charisma was measured on a 150-point scale based on the candidates' acceptance speeches at their party's national convention.) One potential qualitative predictor was whether or not the election was affected by a World War: $x_2 = \{1$ if war, 0 if not$\}$.

a. Propose a model that describes the relationship between Democratic vote share (y) and charisma difference (x_1) as two nonparallel straight-lines, one for each level of World War status (x_2).

b. In terms of the β's of the model, part **a**, what is the slope of the line relating Democratic vote share (y) to charisma difference (x_1) for election years affected by a World War?

c. In terms of the β's of the model, part **a**, what is the slope of the line relating Democratic vote share (y) to charisma difference (x_1) for election years not affected by a World War?

d. In terms of the β's of the model, part **a**, what is the effect of a World War on mean Democratic vote share, $E(y)$, for all election years when there is no charisma difference (i.e., $x_1 = 0$)?

e. In terms of the β's of the model, part **a**, what is the effect of a World War on mean Democratic vote share, $E(y)$, for all election years when there the charisma difference is $x_1 = 50$?

f. Fit the model, part **a**, to the data in the file. Is there sufficient evidence to indicate that the linear effect of the charisma difference on mean Democratic vote share depends on World War status? Test using $\alpha = .10$.

12.9 Comparing Nested Models

To be successful model builders, we require a statistical method that will allow us to determine (with a high degree of confidence) which one among a set of candidate models best fits the data. In this section, we present such a technique for *nested models*.

Two models are **nested** if one model contains all the terms of the second model and at least one additional term. The more complex of the two models is called the **complete** (or **full**) model, and the simpler of the two is called the **reduced** model.

To illustrate the concept of nested models, consider the straight-line interaction model for the mean auction price $E(y)$ of a grandfather clock as a function of two quantitative variables: age of the clock (x_1) and number of bidders (x_2). The interaction model, fit in Example 12.6, is

$$E(y) = \beta_0 + \beta_1 x_1 + \beta_2 x_2 + \beta_3 x_1 x_2$$

If we assume that the relationship between auction price (y), age (x_1), and bidders (x_2) is curvilinear, then the complete second-order model is more appropriate:

$$E(y) = \overbrace{\beta_0 + \beta_1 x_1 + \beta_2 x_2 + \beta_3 x_1 x_2}^{\text{Terms in interaction model}} + \overbrace{\beta_4 x_1^2 + \beta_5 x_2^2}^{\text{Quadratic terms}}$$

Note that the curvilinear model contains quadratic terms for x_1 and x_2, as well as the terms in the interaction model. Therefore, the models are nested models. In this case, the interaction model is nested within the more complex curvilinear model. Thus, the curvilinear model is the *complete* model, and the interaction model is the *reduced* model.

Suppose we want to know whether the more complex curvilinear model contributes more information for the prediction of y than the straight-line interaction model. This is equivalent to determining whether the quadratic terms β_4 and β_5 should be retained in the model. To test whether these terms should be retained, we test the null hypothesis

H_0: $\beta_4 = \beta_5 = 0$ (i.e., quadratic terms are not important for predicting y)

against the alternative hypothesis

H_a: At least one of the parameters β_4 and β_5 is nonzero (i.e., at least one of the quadratic terms is useful for predicting y).

Note that the terms being tested are those additional terms in the complete (curvilinear) model that are not in the reduced (straight-line interaction) model.

In Section 12.3, we presented the t-test for a single β coefficient and the global F-test for *all* the β parameters (except β_0) in the model. We now need a test for a *subset*

F-Test for Comparing Nested Models

Reduced model: $E(y) = \beta_0 + \beta_1 x_1 + \cdots + \beta_g x_g$

Complete model: $E(y) = \beta_0 + \beta_1 x_1 + \cdots + \beta_g x_g + \beta_{g+1} x_{g+1} + \cdots + \beta_k x_k$

H_0: $\beta_{g+1} = \beta_{g+2} = \cdots = \beta_k = 0$

H_a: At least one of the β parameters under test is nonzero.

$$\text{Test statistic: } F = \frac{(\text{SSE}_R - \text{SSE}_C)/(k - g)}{\text{SSE}_C/[n - (k + 1)]}$$

$$= \frac{(\text{SSE}_R - \text{SSE}_C)/\#\beta\text{'s tested in } H_0}{\text{MSE}_C}$$

where

SSE_R = Sum of squared errors for the reduced model

SSE_C = Sum of squared errors for the complete model

MSE_C = Mean square error (s^2) for the complete model

$k - g$ = Number of β parameters specified in H_0 (i.e., number of β parameters tested)

$k + 1$ = Number of β parameters in the complete model (including β_0)

n = Total sample size

Rejection region: $F > F_\alpha$

p-value: $P(F > F_c)$

where F is based on $v_1 = k - g$ numerator degrees of freedom and $v_2 = n - (k + 1)$ denominator degrees of freedom and F_c is the computed value of the test statistic.

of the β parameters in the complete model. The test procedure is intuitive. First, we use the method of least squares to fit the reduced model and calculate the corresponding sum of squares for error, SSE_R (the sum of squares of the deviations between observed and predicted y-values). Next, we fit the complete model and calculate its sum of squares for error, SSE_C. Then we compare SSE_R with SSE_C by calculating the difference, $SSE_R - SSE_C$. If the additional terms in the complete model are significant, then SSE_C should be much smaller than SSE_R, and the difference $SSE_R - SSE_C$ will be large.

Because SSE will always decrease when new terms are added to the model, the question is whether the difference $SSE_R - SSE_C$ is large enough to conclude that it is due to more than just an increase in the number of model terms and to chance. The formal statistical test uses an F-statistic, as shown in the box.

When the assumptions listed in Section 12.1 about the random error term are satisfied, this F-statistic has an F-distribution with ν_1 and ν_2 df. Note that ν_1 is the number of β parameters being tested, and ν_2 is the number of degrees of freedom associated with s^2 in the complete model.

EXAMPLE 12.12
Analyzing a Complete Second-Order Model— Auction Price Data

Problem Refer to the problem of modeling the auction price (y) of an antique grandfather clock, Examples 12.1–12.6. In these examples, we discovered that price was related to both age (x_1) of the clock and number of bidders (x_2), and age and number of bidders had an interactive effect on price. Both the first-order model of Example 12.1 and the interaction model of Example 12.6, however, propose only straight-line (linear) relationships. We did not consider the possibility that the relationship between price (y) and age (x_1) is curvilinear, or that the relationship between price (y) and number of bidders (x_2) is curvilinear.

a. Propose a complete second-order model for price (y) as a function of age (x_1) and number of bidders (x_2).

b. Fit the model to the data for the 32 clocks in Table 12.1 and give the least squares prediction equation.

c. Do the data provide sufficient evidence to indicate that the quadratic terms in the model contribute information for the prediction of price (y)? That is, is there evidence of curvature in the price-age and price-bidders relationships?

Solution

a. Because both age (x_1) and number of bidders (x_2) are quantitative variables, we write the complete second-order model as follows:

$$E(y) = \beta_0 + \beta_1 x_1 + \beta_2 x_2 + \beta_3 x_1 x_2 + \beta_4 (x_1)^2 + \beta_5 (x_2)^2$$

Note that we have added two quadratic terms, $\beta_4 (x_1)^2$ and $\beta_5 (x_2)^2$, to the interaction model of Example 12.6.

b. We used Minitab to fit the model to the data in Table 12.2. The Minitab output is shown in Figure 12.26. The least squares prediction equation, highlighted on the printout, is

$$\hat{y} = -332 + 3.21x_1 + 14.8x_2 + 1.12x_1 x_2 - .003(x_1)^2 - 4.18(x_2)^2$$

Note that the estimates of the quadratic terms, β_4 and β_5, are both negative, implying downward curvature in both the price-age and price-bidders relationships.

c. To determine whether the quadratic terms are useful for predicting price (y), we want to test

$$H_0: \beta_4 = \beta_5 = 0$$
$$H_a: \text{At least one of the parameters, } \beta_4 \text{ and } \beta_5, \text{ differs from 0.}$$

Because the null hypothesis involves a subset of β's, we will need to perform a nested model F-test. The complete model is the complete second-order model of

Regression Analysis: PRICE versus AGE, NUMBIDS, AGE-BID, AGESQ, NUMBIDSQ

```
Analysis of Variance

Source       DF    Adj SS    Adj MS   F-Value   P-Value
Regression    5   4607038    921408    124.29     0.000
Error        26    192752      7414
Total        31   4799790

Model Summary

       S    R-sq   R-sq(adj)
 86.1019   95.98%     95.21%

Coefficients

Term         Coef   SE Coef   T-Value   P-Value
Constant     -332       765     -0.43     0.668
AGE          3.21      8.95      0.36     0.723
NUMBIDS      14.8      62.2      0.24     0.814
AGE-BID     1.123     0.232      4.85     0.000
AGESQ     -0.0030    0.0275     -0.11     0.914
NUMBIDSQ    -4.18      2.15     -1.95     0.062

Regression Equation

PRICE = -332 + 3.21 AGE + 14.8 NUMBIDS + 1.123 AGE-BID - 0.0030 AGESQ - 4.18 NUMBIDSQ
```

Figure 12.26

Minitab analysis of complete second-order model for auction price

part **a**. The reduced model is obtained by dropping the quadratic terms out of the complete model. Doing so yields:

$$Reduced\ model: E(y) = \beta_0 + \beta_1 x_1 + \beta_2 x_2 + \beta_3 x_1 x_2$$

We fit this model in Example 12.6. The Minitab printout for this reduced model is reproduced in Figure 12.27.

To conduct this test, we first obtain the SSE values for the complete and reduced models. These values (highlighted, respectively, on Figures 12.26 and 12.27) are

$$SSE_C = 192{,}752 \text{ and } SSE_R = 221{,}362$$

Also, s^2 for the complete model (highlighted on Figure 12.26) is

$$s^2 = MSE_C = 7{,}414$$

Recall that $n = 32$ and that there are $k = 5$ terms in the complete model and $g = 3$ terms in the reduced model. Therefore, the calculated value of the test statistic is

$$Test\ statistic: F = \frac{(SSE_R - SSE_C)/(k - g)}{MSE_C} = \frac{(221{,}362 - 192{,}752)/2}{7{,}414} = 1.93$$

The critical F-value for the rejection region is based on $\nu_1 = (k - g) = 2$ numerator df and $\nu_2 = [n - (k + 1)] = 26$ denominator df. If we choose $\alpha = .05$, this critical value is $F_{.05} = 3.37$ and the rejection region is

$$Rejection\ region: F > 3.37$$

Regression Analysis: PRICE versus AGE, NUMBIDS, AGE-BID

```
Analysis of Variance

Source       DF    Adj SS    Adj MS   F-Value   P-Value
Regression    3   4578427   1526142    193.04     0.000
Error        28    221362      7906
Total        31   4799790

Model Summary

       S    R-sq   R-sq(adj)
 88.9145   95.39%     94.89%

Coefficients

Term        Coef   SE Coef   T-Value   P-Value
Constant     320       295      1.09     0.287
AGE         0.88      2.03      0.43     0.669
NUMBIDS    -93.3      29.9     -3.12     0.004
AGE-BID    1.298     0.212      6.11     0.000

Regression Equation

PRICE = 320 + 0.88 AGE - 93.3 NUMBIDS + 1.298 AGE-BID
```

Figure 12.27

Minitab analysis of reduced model for auction price

Because the test statistic, $F = 1.93$, falls outside the rejection region, we fail to reject H_0. That is, there is insufficient evidence (at $\alpha = .05$) to conclude that at least one of the quadratic terms contributes information for the prediction of auction price (y). Consequently, there is no evidence of curvature in either the price-age or price-bidders relationship. It appears that the first-order, interaction (reduced) model is adequate for predicting auction price.

Look Back Some statistical software packages will perform the desired nested model F-test if requested. The test statistic and p-value for the test above are highlighted on the SPSS printout, Figure 12.28. Note that p-value $= .165$ exceeds $\alpha = .05$; thus, there is insufficient evidence to reject H_0.

● **Now Work Exercise 12.100**

Model Summary

Model	R	R Square	Adjusted R Square	Std. Error of the Estimate	R Square Change	F Change	df1	df2	Sig. F Change
						Change Statistics			
1	.977ᵃ	.954	.949	88.915	.954	193.041	3	28	.000
2	.980ᵇ	.960	.952	86.102	.006	1.930	2	26	.165

a. Predictors: (Constant), AGE_BID, AGE, NUMBIDS
b. Predictors: (Constant), AGE_BID, AGE, NUMBIDS, NUMBIDSQ, AGESQ

Figure 12.28

SPSS printout of nested model F-test for auction price

The nested model F-test can be used to determine whether *any* subset of terms should be included in a complete model by testing the null hypothesis that a particular set of β parameters simultaneously equals 0. For example, we may want to test to determine whether a set of interaction terms for quantitative variables or a set of main effect terms for a qualitative variable should be included in a model. If we reject H_0, the complete model is the better of the two nested models. If we fail to reject H_0, as in Example 12.12, we favor the reduced model. Although we must be cautious about accepting H_0, most practitioners of regression analysis adopt the principle of *parsimony*—that is, in situations where two competing models are found to have essentially the same predictive power (as in Example 12.12), the model with the fewer number of β's (i.e., the more parsimonious model) is selected. Based on this principle, we would drop the two quadratic terms and select the first-order, interaction (reduced) model over the second-order (complete) model.

A **parsimonious model** is a general linear model with a small number of β parameters. In situations where two competing models have essentially the same predictive power (as determined by an F-test), choose the more parsimonious of the two.

Guidelines for Selecting Preferred Model in a Nested Model F-Test

Conclusion		*Preferred Model*
Reject H_0	$\rightarrow$	Complete Model
Fail to reject H_0	$\rightarrow$	Reduced Model

When the candidate models in model building are nested models, the F-test developed in this section is the appropriate procedure to apply to compare the models. However, if the models are not nested, this F-test is not applicable. In this situation, the analyst must base the choice of the best model on statistics such as R_a^2 and s. It is important to remember that decisions based on these and other numerical descriptive measures of model adequacy cannot be supported with a measure of reliability and are often very subjective in nature.

Exercises 12.97–12.110

Learning the Mechanics

12.97 Determine which pairs of the following models are "nested" models. For each pair of nested models, identify the complete and reduced model.

a. $E(y) = \beta_0 + \beta_1 x_1 + \beta_2 x_2$
b. $E(y) = \beta_0 + \beta_1 x_1$
c. $E(y) = \beta_0 + \beta_1 x_1 + \beta_2 x_1^2$
d. $E(y) = \beta_0 + \beta_1 x_1 + \beta_2 x_2 + \beta_3 x_1 x_2$
e. $E(y) = \beta_0 + \beta_1 x_1 + \beta_2 x_2 + \beta_3 x_1 x_2 + \beta_4 x_1^2 + \beta_5 x_2^2$

12.98 Suppose you fit the regression model

$$y = \beta_0 + \beta_1 x_1 + \beta_2 x_2 + \beta_3 x_1 x_2 + \beta_4 x_1^2 + \beta_5 x_2^2 + \varepsilon$$

to $n = 30$ data points and wish to test

$$H_0: \beta_3 = \beta_4 = \beta_5 = 0$$

a. State the alternative hypothesis H_a.
b. Give the reduced model appropriate for conducting the test.
c. What are the numerator and denominator degrees of freedom associated with the F-statistic?
d. Suppose the SSE's for the reduced and complete models are $SSE_R = 1,250.2$ and $SSE_C = 1,125.2$. Conduct the hypothesis test and interpret the results of your test. Test using $\alpha = .05$.

12.99 The complete model

$$y = \beta_0 + \beta_1 x_1 + \beta_2 x_2 + \beta_3 x_3 + \beta_4 x_4 + \varepsilon$$

was fit to $n = 20$ data points, with SSE = 152.66. The reduced model, $y = \beta_0 + \beta_1 x_1 + \beta_2 x_2 + \varepsilon$, was also fit, with SSE = 160.44.

a. How many β parameters are in the complete model? The reduced model?
b. Specify the null and alternative hypotheses you would use to investigate whether the complete model contributes more information for the prediction of y than the reduced model.
c. Conduct the hypothesis test of part **b**. Use $\alpha = .05$.

Applying the Concepts—Basic

12.100 Shared leadership in airplane crews. Refer to the *Human Factors* (March 2014) study of shared leadership by the cockpit and cabin crews of a commercial airplane, Exercise 8.14 (p. 466). Recall that simulated flights were taken by 84 six-person crews, where each crew consisted of a 2-person cockpit (captain and first officer) and a 4-person cabin team (three flight attendants and a purser.) During the simulation, smoke appeared in the cabin and the reactions of the crew were monitored for teamwork. One key variable in the study was the team goal attainment score, measured on a 0 to 60 point scale. Multiple regression analysis was used to model team goal attainment (y) as a function of the independent variables job experience of purser (x_1), job experience of head flight attendant (x_2), gender of purser (x_3), gender of head flight attendant (x_4), leadership score of purser (x_5), and leadership score of head flight attendant (x_6).

a. Write a complete, first-order model for $E(y)$ as a function of the six independent variables.

b. Consider a test of whether the leadership score of either the purser or the head flight attendant (or both) is statistically useful for predicting team goal attainment. Give the null and alternative hypotheses as well as the reduced model for this test.

c. The two models were fit to the data for the $n = 60$ successful cabin crews with the following results: $R^2 = .02$ for reduced model, $R^2 = .25$ for complete model. On the basis of this information only, give your opinion regarding the null hypothesis for successful cabin crews.

d. The p-value of the subset F-test for comparing the two models for successful cabin crews was reported in the article as $p < .05$. Formally test the null hypothesis using $\alpha = .05$. What do you conclude?

e. The two models were also fit to the data for the $n = 24$ unsuccessful cabin crews with the following results: $R^2 = .14$ for reduced model, $R^2 = .15$ for complete model. On the basis of this information only, give your opinion regarding the null hypothesis for unsuccessful cabin crews.

f. The p-value of the subset F-test for comparing the two models for unsuccessful cabin crews was reported in the article as $p < .10$. Formally test the null hypothesis using $\alpha = .05$. What do you conclude?

12.101 Buy-side vs. sell-side analysts' earnings forecasts. Refer to the *Financial Analysts Journal* (July/August 2008) comparison of earnings forecasts of buy-side and sell-side analysts, Exercise 12.90 (p. 765). Recall that the professors used regression to model the relative optimism (y) of the analysts' 3-month horizon forecasts as a function of $x_1 = \{1$ if the analyst worked for a buy-side firm, 0 if the analyst worked for a sell-side firm} and $x_2 =$ number of days between forecast and fiscal year-end (i.e., forecast horizon). Consider the complete second-order model

$$E(y) = \beta_0 + \beta_1 x_1 + \beta_2 x_2 + \beta_3 x_1 x_2 + \beta_4 (x_2)^2 + \beta_5 x_1 (x_2)^2$$

a. What null hypothesis would you test to determine whether the quadratic terms in the model are statistically useful for predicting relative optimism (y)?
b. Give the complete and reduced models for conducting the test, part **a**.
c. What null hypothesis would you test to determine whether the interaction terms in the model are statistically useful for predicting relative optimism (y)?
d. Give the complete and reduced models for conducting the test, part **c**.
e. What null hypothesis would you test to determine whether the dummy variable terms in the model are statistically useful for predicting relative optimism (y)?
f. Give the complete and reduced models for conducting the test, part **e**.

12.102 Workplace bullying and intention to leave. Refer to the *Human Resource Management Journal* (October 2008) study of workplace bullying, Exercise 12.91 (p. 765). Recall that multiple regression was used to model an employee's intention to leave (y) as a function of bullying

(x_1, measured on a quantitative scale) and perceived organizational support (measured qualitatively as "low POS," "neutral POS," or "high POS"). In Exercise 12.91b, you wrote a model for $E(y)$ as a function of bullying and POS that hypothesizes three parallel straight lines, one for each level of POS. In Exercise 12.91c, you wrote a model for $E(y)$ as a function of bullying and POS that hypothesizes three nonparallel straight lines, one for each level of POS.

a. Explain why the two models are nested. Which is the complete model? Which is the reduced model?

b. Give the null hypothesis for comparing the two models.

c. If you reject H_0 in part **b**, which model do you prefer? Why?

d. If you fail to reject H_0 in part **b**, which model do you prefer? Why?

12.103 Cooling method for gas turbines. Refer to the *Journal of Engineering for Gas Turbines and Power* (January 2005) study of a high-pressure inlet fogging method for a gas turbine engine, Exercise 12.19 (p. 726). Consider a model for heat rate (kilojoules per kilowatt per hour) of a gas turbine as a function of cycle speed (revolutions per minute) and cycle pressure ratio. The data are saved in the file.

a. Write a complete second-order model for heat rate (y).

b. Give the null and alternative hypotheses for determining whether the curvature terms in the complete second-order model are statistically useful for predicting heat rate (y).

c. For the test in part **b**, identify the complete and reduced model.

d. The complete and reduced models were fit and compared using SPSS. A summary of the results are shown in the accompanying SPSS printout. Locate the value of the test statistic on the printout.

e. Find the rejection region for $\alpha = .10$ and locate the *p*-value of the test on the printout.

f. State the conclusion in the words of the problem.

12.104 Personality traits and job performance. Refer to the *Journal of Applied Psychology* (January 2011) study of the relationship between task performance and conscientiousness, Exercise 12.94 (p. 766). Recall that y = task performance score (measured on a 30-point scale) was modeled as a function of x_1 = conscientiousness score (measured on a scale of -3 to $+3$) and x_2 = {1 if highly complex job, 0 if not} using the complete model

$$E(y) = \beta_0 + \beta_1 x_1 + \beta_2 (x_1)^2 + \beta_3 x_2 + \beta_4 x_1 x_2 + \beta_5 (x_1)^2 x_2$$

a. Specify the null hypothesis for testing the overall adequacy of the model.

b. Specify the null hypothesis for testing whether task performance score (y) and conscientiousness score (x_1) are curvilinearly related.

c. Specify the null hypothesis for testing whether the curvilinear relationship between task performance score (y) and conscientiousness score (x_1) depends on job complexity (x_2).

d. Explain how each of the tests, parts **a–c**, should be conducted (i.e., give the forms of the test statistic and the reduced model).

Applying the Concepts—Intermediate

12.105 Reality TV and cosmetic surgery. Refer to the *Body Image: An International Journal of Research* (March 2010) study of the influence of reality TV shows on one's desire to undergo cosmetic surgery, Exercise 12.17 (p. 725). Recall that psychologists modeled desire to have cosmetic surgery (y) as a function of gender (x_1), self-esteem (x_2), body satisfaction (x_3), and impression of reality TV (x_4). The psychologists theorized that one's impression of reality TV will "moderate" the impact that each of the first three independent variables has on one's desire to have cosmetic surgery. If so, then x_4 will interact with each of the other independent variables.

a. Give the equation of the model for $E(y)$ that matches the theory.

b. Fit the model, part **a**, to the simulated data saved in the file. Evaluate the overall utility of the model.

c. Give the null hypothesis for testing the psychologists' theory.

d. Conduct a nested model *F*-test to test the theory. What do you conclude?

12.106 Study of supervisor-targeted aggression. "Moonlighters" are workers who hold two jobs at the same time. What are the factors that impact the likelihood of a moonlighting worker becoming aggressive toward his/her supervisor? This was the research question of interest in the *Journal of Applied Psychology* (July 2005). Completed questionnaires were obtained from $n = 105$ moonlighters, and the data were used to fit several multiple regression models for supervisor-directed aggression score (y). Two of the models (with R^2-values in parentheses) are given below:

Model 1: $E(y) = \beta_0 + \beta_1(\text{Age}) + \beta_2(\text{Gender}) +$
$\beta_3(\text{Interactional injustice at 2nd job}) +$
$\beta_4(\text{Abusive supervisor at 2nd job})$

$(R^2 = .101)$

Model 2: $E(y) = \beta_0 + \beta_1(\text{Age}) + \beta_2(\text{Gender}) +$
$\beta_3(\text{Interactional injustice at 2nd job}) +$
$\beta_4(\text{Abusive supervisor at 2nd job}) +$
$\beta_5(\text{Self-esteem}) + \beta_6(\text{History of aggression}) +$
$\beta_7(\text{Interactional injustice at primary job}) +$
$\beta_8(\text{Abusive supervisor at primary job})$

$(R^2 = .555)$

SPSS Output for Exercise 12.103

Model Summary

Model	R	R Square	Adjusted R Square	Std. Error of the Estimate	R Square Change	F Change	df1	df2	Sig. F Change
1	.922ª	.849	.842	633.842	.849	118.303	3	63	.000
2	.941ᵇ	.885	.875	563.513	.035	9.353	2	61	.000

a. Predictors: (Constant), RPM_CPR, CPRATIO, RPM
b. Predictors: (Constant), RPM_CPR, CPRATIO, RPM, CPRSQ, RPMSQ

a. Interpret the R^2-values for the models.

b. Give the null and alternative hypotheses for comparing the fits of models 1 and 2.

c. Are the two models nested? Explain.

d. The nested F-test for comparing the two models resulted in $F = 42.13$ and p-value $< .001$. What can you conclude from these results?

e. A third model was fit, one that hypothesizes all possible pairs of interactions between self-esteem, history of aggression, interactional injustice at primary job, and abusive supervisor at primary job. Give the equation of this model (model 3).

f. A nested F-test to compare models 2 and 3 resulted in a p-value $> .10$. What can you conclude from this result?

12.107 Agreeableness, gender, and wages. Refer to the *Journal of Personality and Social Psychology* (February 2012) study of on-the-job agreeableness and wages, Exercise 12.92 (p. 766). The researchers modeled mean income, $E(y)$, as a function of both agreeableness score (x_1) and a dummy variable for gender ($x_2 = 1$ if male, 0 if female). Suppose the researchers theorize that for either gender, income will decrease at a decreasing rate as agreeableness score increases. Consequently, they want to fit a second-order model.

a. Consider the model, $E(y) = \beta_0 + \beta_1 x_1 + \beta_2 (x_1)^2 + \beta_3 x_2$. If the researchers' belief is true, what is the expected sign of β_2 in the model?

b. Draw a sketch of the model, part **a,** showing how gender impacts the income-agreeableness score relationship.

c. Write a complete second-order model for $E(y)$ as a function of x_1 and x_2.

d. Draw a sketch of the model, part **c,** showing how gender impacts the income-agreeableness score relationship.

e. What null hypothesis would you test in order to compare the two models, parts **a** and **c?**

f. Fit the models to the sample data saved in the file and carry out the test, part **e.** What do you conclude? (Test using $\alpha = .10$.)

12.108 Recently sold, single-family homes. Refer to the National Association of Realtors data on sales price (y), region (NE, NW, S, or W), and sales volume for 28 recently sold, single-family homes, Exercise 12.95 (p. 766). You fit a complete second-order model for $E(y)$ as a function of region and sales volume.

a. Conduct a nested-model F-test to determine whether the quadratic terms in the model are statistically useful for predicting sales price (y). Use $\alpha = .05$.

b. Based on the result, part **a,** which of the nested models (the complete or the reduced model) do you prefer to use in predicting sales price (y)? Explain.

c. Refer to part **b.** Treat the preferred model as the complete model and conduct a nested model F-test to determine whether region and sales volume interact to affect sales price (y). Use $\alpha = .05$.

d. Based on the result, part **c,** which of the nested models (the complete or the reduced model) do you prefer to use in predicting sales price (y)? Explain.

12.109 Glass as a waste encapsulant. Because glass is not subject to radiation damage, encapsulation of waste in glass is considered to be one of the most promising solutions to the problem of low-level nuclear waste in the environment. However, chemical reactions may weaken the glass. This concern led to a study undertaken jointly by the Department of Materials Science and Engineering at the University of Florida and the U.S. Department of Energy to assess the utility of glass as a waste encapsulant.* Corrosive chemical solutions (called *corrosion baths*) were prepared and applied directly to glass samples containing one of three types of waste (TDS-3A, FE, and AL); the chemical reactions were observed over time. A few of the key variables measured were

$y =$ Amount of silicon (in parts per million) found in solution at end of experiment. (This is both a measure of the degree of breakdown in the glass and a proxy for the amount of radioactive species released into the environment.)

$x_1 =$ Temperature (°C) of the corrosion bath

$x_2 = 1$ if waste type TDS-3A, 0 if not

$x_3 = 1$ if waste type FE, 0 if not

(Waste type AL is the base level.) Suppose we want to model amount y of silicon as a function of temperature (x_1) and type of waste (x_2, x_3).

a. Write a model that proposes parallel straight-line relationships between amount of silicon and temperature, one line for each of the three waste types.

b. Add terms for the interaction between temperature and waste type to the model of part **a.**

c. Refer to the model of part **b.** For each waste type, give the slope of the line relating amount of silicon to temperature.

d. Explain how you could test for the presence of temperature–waste type interaction.

Applying the Concepts—Advanced

12.110 Job performance under time pressure. Refer to the *Academy of Management Journal* (October 2015) study of how time pressure affects team job performance, Exercise 12.89 (p. 765). Recall that the researchers hypothesized a complete second-order model relating team performance (y) to perceived time pressure (x_1), and whether or not the team had an effective leader ($x_2 = 1$ if yes, 0 if no):

$$E(y) = \beta_0 + \beta_1 x_1 + \beta_2 x_1^2 + \beta_3 x_2 + \beta_4 x_1 x_2 + \beta_5 x_1^2 x_2$$

a. How would you determine whether the rate of increase of team performance with time pressure depends on effectiveness of the team leader?

b. For fixed time pressure, how would you determine whether the mean team performance differs for teams with effective and noneffective team leaders?

*The background information for this exercise was provided by Dr. David Clark, Department of Materials Science and Engineering, University of Florida.

12.10 Stepwise Regression

Consider the problem of predicting the salary y of an executive. Perhaps the biggest problem in building a model to describe executive salaries is choosing the important independent variables to be included in the model. The list of potentially important independent variables is extremely long (e.g., age, experience, tenure, education level, etc.), and we need some objective method of screening out those that are not important.

The problem of deciding which of a large set of independent variables to include in a model is a common one. For example, we may try to determine which variables influence the profit of a firm, affect the Dow Jones Industrial average, or are related to a student's performance in college.

A systematic approach to building a model with a large number of independent variables is difficult because the interpretation of multivariable interactions and higher-order terms is tedious. We therefore turn to a screening procedure, available in most statistical software packages, known as **stepwise regression.**

The most commonly used stepwise regression procedure works as follows. The user first identifies the response, y, and the set of potentially important independent variables, $x_1, x_2, \ldots, x_k$, where k is generally large. [*Note:* This set of variables could include both first-order and higher-order terms. However, we may often include only the main effects of both quantitative variables (first-order terms) and qualitative variables (dummy variables) because the inclusion of second-order terms greatly increases the number of independent variables.] The response and independent variables are then entered into the computer software, and the stepwise procedure begins.

Step 1: The software program fits all possible one variable models of the form

$$E(y) = \beta_0 + \beta_1 x_i$$

to the data, where x_i is the ith independent variable, $i = 1, 2, \ldots, k$. For each model, the test of the null hypothesis

$$H_0: \beta_1 = 0$$

against the alternative hypothesis

$$H_a: \beta_1 \neq 0$$

is conducted using the t-test (or the equivalent F-test) for a single β parameter. The independent variable that produces the largest (absolute) t-value is declared the best one-variable predictor of y.* Call this independent variable x_1.

Step 2: The stepwise program now begins to search through the remaining $(k-1)$ independent variables for the best two-variable model of the form

$$E(y) = \beta_0 + \beta_1 x_1 + \beta_2 x_i$$

This is done by fitting all two-variable models containing x_1 and each of the other $(k-1)$ options for the second variable x_i. The t-values for the test $H_0: \beta_2 = 0$ are computed for each of the $(k-1)$ models (corresponding to the remaining independent variables, x_i, $i = 2, 3, \ldots, k$), and the variable having the largest t is retained. Call this variable x_2.

At this point, some software packages diverge in methodology. The better packages now go back and check the t-value of $\hat{\beta}_1$ after $\hat{\beta}_2 x_2$ has been added to the model. If the t-value has become nonsignificant at some specified α level (say $\alpha = .10$), the variable x_1 is removed and a search is made for the independent variable with a β parameter that will yield the most significant t-value in the presence of $\hat{\beta}_2 x_2$. Other packages do not recheck the significance of $\hat{\beta}_1$ but proceed directly to step 3.†

---

*In step 1, note that the variable with the largest t-value is also the one with the largest (absolute) Pearson product moment correlation, r (Section 11.5), with y.

†*Forward selection* is the name given to stepwise routines that *do not* recheck the significance of each previously entered independent variable. This is in contrast to *stepwise selection* routines, which perform the rechecks. A third approach is to use *backward selection*, where initially, all terms are entered and then eliminated one by one.

The reason the t-value for x_1 may change from step 1 to step 2 is that the meaning of the coefficient $\hat{\beta}_1$ changes. In step 2, we are approximating a complex response surface in two variables with a plane. The best-fitting plane may yield a different value for $\hat{\beta}_1$ than that obtained in step 1. Thus, both the value of $\hat{\beta}_1$ and its significance usually change from step 1 to step 2. For this reason, the software packages that recheck the t-values at each step are preferred.

Step 3:   The stepwise procedure now checks for a third independent variable to include in the model with x_1 and x_2—that is, we seek the best model of the form

$$E(y) = \beta_0 + \beta_1 x_1 + \beta_2 x_2 + \beta_3 x_i$$

To do this, we fit all the $(k-2)$ models using x_1, x_2, and each of the $(k-2)$ remaining variables, x_i, as a possible x_3. The criterion is again to include the independent variable with the largest t-value. Call this best third variable x_3.

The better programs now recheck the t-values corresponding to the x_1 and x_2 coefficients, removing the variables with t-values that have become nonsignificant. This procedure is continued until no further independent variables can be found that yield significant t-values (at the specified α level) in the presence of the variables already in the model.

The result of the stepwise procedure is a model containing only those terms with t-values that are significant at the specified α level. Thus, in most practical situations, only several of the large number of independent variables remain. However, it is very important *not* to jump to the conclusion that all the independent variables important for predicting y have been identified or that the unimportant independent variables have been eliminated. Remember, the stepwise procedure is using only *sample estimates* of the true model coefficients (β's) to select the important variables. An extremely large number of single β parameter t-tests have been conducted, and the probability is very high that one or more errors have been made in including or excluding variables—that is, we have very probably included some unimportant independent variables in the model (Type I errors) and eliminated some important ones (Type II errors).

There is a second reason why we might not have arrived at a good model. When we choose the variables to be included in the stepwise regression, we may often omit higher-order terms (to keep the number of variables manageable). Consequently, we may have initially omitted several important terms from the model. Thus, we should recognize stepwise regression for what it is: an **objective variable screening procedure.**

Successful model builders will now consider second-order terms (for quantitative variables) and other interactions among variables screened by the stepwise procedure. It would be best to develop this response surface model with a second set of data independent of that used for the screening, so that the results of the stepwise procedure can be partially verified with new data. This is not always possible, however, because in many modeling situations only a small amount of data is available.

Do not be deceived by the impressive-looking t-values that result from the stepwise procedure—it has retained only the independent variables with the largest t-values. Also, be certain to consider second-order terms in systematically developing the prediction model. Finally, if you have used a first-order model for your stepwise procedure, remember that it may be greatly improved by the addition of higher-order terms.

> ⓘ **CAUTION**   Be wary of using the results of stepwise regression to make inferences about the relationship between $E(y)$ and the independent variables in the resulting first-order model. First, an extremely large number of t-tests have been conducted, leading to a high probability of making one or more Type I or Type II errors. Second, the stepwise model does not include any higher-order or interaction terms. Stepwise regression should be used only when necessary—that is, when you want to determine which of a large number of potentially important independent variables should be used in the model-building process.

EXAMPLE 12.13

Running a Stepwise Regression—Modeling Executive Salary

Problem An international management consulting company develops multiple regression models for executive salaries of its client firms. The consulting company has found that models that use the natural logarithm of salary as the dependent variable have better predictive power than those using salary as the dependent variable.* A preliminary step in the construction of these models is the determination of the most important independent variables. For one firm, 10 potential independent variables (7 quantitative and 3 qualitative) were measured in a sample of 100 executives. The data, described in Table 12.5, are saved in the file. Because it would be very difficult to construct a complete second-order model with all of the 10 independent variables, use stepwise regression to decide which of the 10 variables should be included in the building of the final model for the natural log of executive salaries.

Table 12.5	Independent Variables in the Executive Salary Example	
Independent Variable	Description	Type
x_1	Experience (years)	Quantitative
x_2	Education (years)	Quantitative
x_3	Bonus eligibility (1 if yes, 0 if no)	Qualitative
x_4	Number of employees supervised	Quantitative
x_5	Corporate assets (millions of dollars)	Quantitative
x_6	Board member (1 if yes, 0 if no)	Qualitative
x_7	Age (years)	Quantitative
x_8	Company profits (past 12 months, millions of dollars)	Quantitative
x_9	Has international responsibility (1 if yes, 0 if no)	Qualitative
x_{10}	Company's total sales (past 12 months, millions of dollars)	Quantitative

Data Set: EXSAL

Solution We will use stepwise regression with the main effects of the 10 independent variables to identify the most important variables. The dependent variable y is the natural logarithm of the executive salaries. The Excel/XLSTAT stepwise regression printout is shown in Figure 12.29.

Regression of variable Y:

Summary of the variables selection:

Nbr. of variables	Variables	Variable IN/OUT	Status	MSE	R²	Adjusted R²
1	X1	X1	IN	0.0260	0.6190	0.6151
2	X1 / X3	X3	IN	0.0173	0.7492	0.7440
3	X1 / X3 / X4	X4	IN	0.0112	0.8391	0.8341
4	X1 / X2 / X3 / X4	X2	IN	0.0065	0.9075	0.9036
5	X1 / X2 / X3 / X4 / X5	X5	IN	0.0056	0.9206	0.9164

Goodness of fit statistics:

Observations	100.0000
Sum of weights	100.0000
DF	94.0000
R²	0.9206
Adjusted R²	0.9164
MSE	0.0056
RMSE	0.0751
DW	2.0763

Analysis of variance:

Source	DF	Sum of squares	Mean squares	F	Pr > F
Model	5	6.1523	1.2305	218.0606	< 0.0001
Error	94	0.5304	0.0056		
Corrected Total	99	6.6827			

Computed against model Y=Mean(Y)

Model parameters:

Source	Value	Standard error	t	Pr > |t|
Intercept	9.9619	0.1011	98.5777	< 0.0001
X1	0.0273	0.0010	26.5005	< 0.0001
X2	0.0291	0.0033	8.7188	< 0.0001
X3	0.2247	0.0164	13.7424	< 0.0001
X4	0.0005	0.0000	11.0643	< 0.0001
X5	0.0020	0.0005	3.9469	0.0002

Figure 12.29

Excel/XLSTAT stepwise regression printout for executive salary data

*This is probably because salaries tend to be incremented in *percentages* rather than dollar values. When a response variable undergoes percentage changes as the independent variables are varied, the logarithm of the response variable will be more suitable as a dependent variable.

Looking at the top of the printout, note that the first variable included in the model is x_1, years of experience. At the second step, x_3, a dummy variable for the qualitative variable, bonus eligibility or not, is brought into the model. In steps 3, 4, and 5, the variables x_4 (number of employees supervised), x_2 (years of education), and x_5 (corporate assets), respectively, are selected for model inclusion. The procedure stops after five steps because no other independent variables met the criterion for admission into the model. As a default, Excel/XLSTAT uses $\alpha = .05$ in the t-tests conducted. In other words, if the p-value associated with a β coefficient exceeds $\alpha = .05$, the variable is *not* included in the model.*

The results of the stepwise regression suggest that we should concentrate on these five independent variables. Models with second-order terms and interactions should be proposed and evaluated to determine the best model for predicting executive salaries.

• **Now Work Exercise 12.113**

✓ **RECOMMENDATION** Do *not* use the stepwise regression model as the *final* model for predicting y. Recall that the stepwise procedure tends to perform a large number of t-tests, inflating the overall probability of a Type I error, and does not automatically include higher-order terms (e.g., interactions and squared terms) in the final model. Use stepwise regression as a variable screening tool when there exist a large number of potentially important independent variables. Then begin building models for y using the variables identified by stepwise.

STATISTICS IN ACTION

REVISITED

Variable Screening and Model Building

In the previous *Statistics in Action Revisited* section (p. 730), we used all eight of the independent variables in Table SIA12.1 to fit a first-order model for the cost (y) of a road construction contract awarded using the sealed-bid system. Although the model was deemed statistically useful for predicting y, the standard deviation of the model ($s = 305$ thousand dollars) was probably too large for the model to be practically useful. A more complex model—one involving higher-order terms (interactions and squared terms)—needs to be considered. A complete second-order model involving all eight of the independent variables, however, would require over 100 terms! Consequently, we'll use stepwise regression to select the best subset of independent variables and then form a complete second-order model with just these variables.

Figure SIA12.4 is a Minitab printout of the stepwise regression. You can see that the DOT engineer's cost estimate (DOTEST) is the first variable selected, followed by bid status (STATUS), estimated work days (DAYSEST), and bids to plan holders ratio (BTPRATIO). Minitab uses a default α level of .15. If we reduce the significance level for entry to $\alpha = .05$, only DOTEST and STATUS are selected because the p-values (highlighted on the printout) for DAYSEST and BTPRATIO are both greater than .05.

Because bid status is a qualitative variable ($x_2 = 1$ if fixed and 0 if competitive), a complete second-order model for contract cost (y) using DOTEST (x_1) and STATUS (x_2) is given by the equation

$$E(y) = \beta_0 + \beta_1 x_1 + \beta_2 (x_1)^2 + \beta_3 x_2 + \beta_4 x_1 x_2 + \beta_5 (x_1)^2 x_2$$

The Minitab printout for this model is shown in Figure SIA12.5. Note that the global F-test for the model is statistically significant (p-value = .000), and the model standard deviation, $s = 296.6$, is smaller than the standard deviation of the first-order model.

---

*Other software (e.g., Minitab) uses $\alpha = .15$ as the default significance level. Although the probability of a Type I error is increased, the chance of excluding an important independent variable (i.e., a Type II error) is decreased.

```
Stepwise Selection of Terms

Candidate terms: DOTEST, B2B1RAT, B3B1RAT, BHB1RAT, STATUS, DISTRICT, BTPRATIO, DAYSEST

              -----Step 1-----   -----Step 2-----   -----Step 3----   -----Step 4----
                 Coef      P         Coef      P        Coef      P        Coef      P
Constant         20.9               -20.5             -55.2            -212.8
DOTEST        0.92629   0.000     0.93078   0.000    0.9110   0.000    0.9132   0.000
STATUS                             166.3   0.001     166.9   0.001     171.2   0.001
DAYSEST                                              0.274   0.122     0.330   0.065
BTPRATIO                                                                 241   0.072

S              313.085            306.329           305.401           303.918
R-sq            97.42%             97.55%            97.57%            97.60%
R-sq(adj)       97.41%             97.52%            97.54%            97.56%
R-sq(pred)      97.25%             97.36%            97.32%            97.34%
Mallows' Cp      15.18               5.66              5.24              3.99

α to enter = 0.15, α to remove = 0.15

Analysis of Variance

Source       DF    Adj SS      Adj MS   F-Value   P-Value
Regression    4  865632473  216408118   2342.94     0.000
Error       230   21244166      92366
Total       234  886876639

Model Summary

       S    R-sq  R-sq(adj)
 303.918  97.60%     97.56%

Coefficients

Term       Coef   SE Coef   T-Value   P-Value
Constant  -212.8     93.9     -2.27     0.024
DOTEST    0.9132    0.0160    57.11     0.000
STATUS     171.2      49.0      3.50     0.001
BTPRATIO     241       133      1.81     0.072
DAYSEST    0.330     0.178      1.85     0.065
```

Figure SIA12.4

Minitab stepwise regression for the road cost data

Are the second-order terms in the model, $\beta_2(x_1)^2$ and $\beta_5(x_1)^2 x_2$, necessary? If not, we can simplify the model by dropping these curvature terms. The hypothesis of interest is $H_0: \beta_2 = \beta_5 = 0$. To test this subset of β's, we compare the complete second-order model to a model without the curvilinear terms. The reduced model takes the form

$$E(y) = \beta_0 + \beta_1 x_1 + \beta_3 x_2 + \beta_4 x_1 x_2$$

The results of this nested model (or partial) F-test are shown at the bottom of the SPSS printout, Figure SIA12.6. The p-value of the test (highlighted on the SPSS printout) is .355. Because this p-value is greater than $\alpha = .05$, there is insufficient evidence to reject H_0—that is, there is no evidence to indicate that the two curvature terms are useful

Regression Analysis: COST versus DOTEST, DOTEST2, STATUS, STA_DOT, STA_DOT2

```
Analysis of Variance

Source       DF    Adj SS      Adj MS    F-Value   P-Value
Regression    5  866725402  173345080   1969.91     0.000
Error       229   20151237      87997
Total       234  886876639

Model Summary

       S    R-sq  R-sq(adj)
 296.642  97.73%     97.68%

Coefficients

Term          Coef    SE Coef   T-Value   P-Value
Constant      -3.0       30.9     -0.10     0.923
DOTEST      0.9155     0.0292     31.39     0.000
DOTEST2   0.000001   0.000003      0.21     0.833
STATUS       -36.7       74.8     -0.49     0.624
STA_DOT      0.324      0.119      2.72     0.007
STA_DOT2  -0.000036   0.000025    -1.44     0.150

Regression Equation

COST = -3.0 + 0.9155 DOTEST + 0.000001 DOTEST2 - 36.7 STATUS + 0.324 STA_DOT
       - 0.000036 STA_DOT2
```

Figure SIA12.5

Minitab regression printout for the complete second-order model of contract cost

Model Summary

Model	R	R Square	Adjusted R Square	Std. Error of the Estimate	R Square Change	F Change	df1	df2	Sig. F Change
1	.988[a]	.977	.977	296.69515	.977	3281.312	3	231	.000
2	.989[b]	.977	.977	296.64238	.000	1.041	2	229	.355

a. Predictors: (Constant), STA_DOT, DOTEST, STATUS
b. Predictors: (Constant), STA_DOT, DOTEST, STATUS, DOTEST2, STA_DOT2

Figure SIA12.6

SPSS printout of test to compare the complete second-order model of contract cost to the reduced model

predictors of road construction cost. Consequently, the reduced model is selected as the better predictor of cost.

The Minitab printout for the reduced model is shown in Figure SIA12.7. The overall model is statistically useful (p-value $= .000$ for global F-test), explaining about 98% of the sample variation in contract costs. The model standard deviation, $s = 296.7$, implies that we can predict costs to within about 593 thousand dollars. Also, the t-test for the interaction term, $\beta_4 x_1 x_2$, is significant (p-value $= .000$), implying that the relationship between contract cost (y) and DOT cost estimate depends on bid status (fixed or competitive).

Regression Analysis: COST versus DOTEST, STATUS, STA_DOT

```
Analysis of Variance

Source       DF      Adj SS     Adj MS   F-Value   P-Value
Regression    3   866542162  288847387   3281.31     0.000
Error       231    20334478      88028
Total       234   886876639

Model Summary

      S    R-sq   R-sq(adj)
296.695   97.71%     97.60%

Coefficients

Term        Coef  SE Coef  T-Value  P-Value
Constant    -6.4     26.2    -0.25    0.807
DOTEST   0.92134  0.00972    94.75    0.000
STATUS      28.7     58.7     0.49    0.626
STA_DOT  0.1633   0.0404     4.04    0.000

Regression Equation

COST = -6.4 + 0.92134 DOTEST + 28.7 STATUS + 0.1633 STA_DOT
```

Figure SIA12.7

Minitab regression printout for the reduced model of contract cost

The nature of the interaction is illustrated in the Minitab graph of the least squares prediction equation for the reduced model, Figure SIA12.8. You can see that the rate of increase of contract cost (y) with the DOT engineer's estimate of cost (x_1) is steeper for fixed contracts than for competitive contracts.

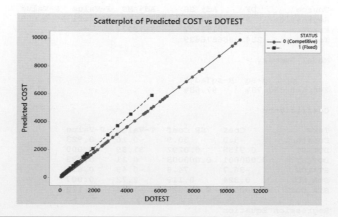

Figure SIA12.8

Minitab plot of least squares prediction equation for the reduced model of contract cost

Exercises 12.111–12.119

Learning the Mechanics

12.111 There are six independent variables, x_1, x_2, x_3, x_4, x_5, and x_6, that might be useful in predicting a response y. A total of $n = 50$ observations is available, and it is decided to employ stepwise regression to help in selecting the independent variables that appear to be useful. The software fits all possible one-variable models of the form

$$E(y) = \beta_0 + \beta_1 x_i$$

where x_i is the ith independent variable, $i = 1, 2, \ldots, 6$. The information in the table is provided from the computer printout.

Independent Variable	$\hat{\beta}_i$	$s_{\hat{\beta}_i}$
x_1	1.6	.42
x_2	−.9	.01
x_3	3.4	1.14
x_4	2.5	2.06
x_5	−4.4	.73
x_6	.3	.35

a. Which independent variable is declared the best one-variable predictor of y? Explain.

b. Would this variable be included in the model at this stage? Explain.

c. Describe the next phase that a stepwise procedure would execute.

Applying the Concepts—Basic

12.112 Teacher pay and pupil performance. In *Economic Policy* (January 2011), researchers from the London School of Economics conducted a cross-country analysis of the relationship between teacher's pay and pupils' performance. Data collected for 39 countries were used to model $y =$ the country's average standardized score of its pupils. The independent variables under consideration were: $x_1 =$ country's total teaching staff as a percentage of the country's labor force, $x_2 =$ percentage of women on country's total teaching staff, $x_3 =$ country's pupil-teacher ratio, $x_4 =$ average teacher's salary after 15 years on staff, $x_5 =$ average teaching hours per year, $x_6 =$ GDP growth of country (%), $x_7 =$ country's educational spending per year, and $x_8 =$ percentile position of country's teachers' salaries after 15 years on staff. Consider a stepwise regression run on the data.

a. What is the form of the model fit in step 1? How many models are fit? How is the "best" independent variable selected in this step?

b. What is the form of the model fit in step 2? How many models are fit? How is the "best" independent variable selected in this step?

c. What is the form of the model fit in step 3? How many models are fit? How is the "best" independent variable selected in this step?

d. The variables x_3, x_4, and x_6 were deemed the best variables for predicting y. How do you recommend the researchers proceed from here? Why?

12.113 Risk management performance. An article in the *International Journal of Production Economics* (Vol. 171, 2016) investigated the factors associated with a firm's supply chain risk management performance (y). Five potential independent variables (all measured quantitatively) were considered: (1) firm size, (2) supplier orientation, (3) supplier dependency, (4) customer orientation, and (5) systemic purchasing. Consider running a stepwise regression to find the best subset of predictors for risk management performance.

a. How many 1-variable models are fit in step 1 of the stepwise regression?

b. Assume supplier orientation is selected in step 1. How many 2-variable models are fit in step 2 of the stepwise regression?

c. Assume systemic purchasing is selected in step 2. How many 3-variable models are fit in step 3 of the stepwise regression?

d. Assume customer orientation is selected in step 3. How many 4-variable models are fit in step 4 of the stepwise regression?

e. Through the first 4 steps of the stepwise regression, determine the total number of t-tests performed. Assuming each test uses an $\alpha = .05$ level of significance, give an estimate of the probability of at least one Type I error in the stepwise regression.

12.114 Accuracy of software effort estimates. Periodically, software engineers must provide estimates of their effort in developing new software. In the *Journal of Empirical Software Engineering* (Vol. 9, 2004), multiple regression was used to predict the accuracy of these effort estimates. The dependent variable, defined as the relative error in estimating effort,

$$y = (\text{Actual effort} - \text{Estimated effort})/(\text{Actual effort})$$

was determined for each in a sample of $n = 49$ software development tasks. Eight independent variables were evaluated as potential predictors of relative error using stepwise regression. Each of these was formulated as a dummy variable, as shown in the table.

Company role of estimator:	$x_1 = 1$ if developer, 0 if project leader
Task complexity:	$x_2 = 1$ if low, 0 if medium/high
Contract type:	$x_3 = 1$ if fixed price, 0 if hourly rate
Customer importance:	$x_4 = 1$ if high, 0 if low/medium
Customer priority:	$x_5 = 1$ if time of delivery, 0 if cost or quality
Level of knowledge:	$x_6 = 1$ if high, 0 if low/medium
Participation:	$x_7 = 1$ if estimator participates in work, 0 if not
Previous accuracy:	$x_8 = 1$ if more than 20% accurate, 0 if less than 20% accurate

a. In step 1 of the stepwise regression, how many different one-variable models are fit to the data?

b. In step 1, the variable x_1 is selected as the best one-variable predictor. How is this determined?

c. In step 2 of the stepwise regression, how many different two-variable models (where x_1 is one of the variables) are fit to the data?

d. The only two variables selected for entry into the stepwise regression model were x_1 and x_8. The stepwise regression yielded the following prediction equation:

$$\hat{y} = .12 - .28x_1 + .27x_8$$

Give a practical interpretation of the β estimates multiplied by x_1 and x_8.

e. Why should a researcher be wary of using the model, part **d**, as the final model for predicting effort (y)?

Applying the Concepts—Intermediate

12.115 Diet of ducks bred for broiling. Corn is high in starch content; consequently, it is considered excellent feed for domestic chickens. Does corn possess the same potential in feeding ducks bred for broiling? This was the subject of research published in *Animal Feed Science and Technology* (April 2010). The objective of the study was to establish a prediction model for the true metabolizable energy (TME) of corn regurgitated from ducks. The researchers considered 11 potential predictors of TME: dry matter (DM), crude protein (CP), ether extract (EE), ash (ASH), crude fiber (CF), neutral detergent fiber (NDF), acid detergent fiber (ADF), gross energy (GE), amylose (AM), amylopectin (AP), and amylopectin/amylose (AMAP). Stepwise regression was used to find the best subset of predictors. The final stepwise model yielded the following results:

$$\widehat{TME} = 7.70 + 2.14(AMAP) + .16(NDF), R^2 = .988,$$
$$s = .07, \text{Global } F \text{ } p\text{-value} = .001$$

a. Determine the number of t-tests performed in step 1 of the stepwise regression.

b. Determine the number of t-tests performed in step 2 of the stepwise regression.

c. Give a full interpretation of the final stepwise model regression results.

d. Explain why it is dangerous to use the final stepwise model as the "best" model for predicting TME.

e. Using the independent variables selected by the stepwise routine, write a complete second-order model for TME.

f. Refer to part **e.** How would you determine if the terms in the model that allow for curvature are statistically useful for predicting TME?

12.116 Reality TV and cosmetic surgery. Refer to the *Body Image: An International Journal of Research* (March 2010) study of the influence of reality TV shows on one's desire to undergo cosmetic surgery, Exercise 12.17 (p. 725). Recall that psychologists modeled desire to have cosmetic surgery (y) as a function of gender (x_1), self-esteem (x_2), body satisfaction (x_3), and impression of reality TV (x_4). Suppose you want to determine which subset of these four independent variables is best for predicting one's desire to have cosmetic surgery. Consequently, you will run a stepwise regression.

a. In step 1 of the stepwise regression, how many t-tests will be performed?

b. In step 2 of the stepwise regression, how many t-tests will be performed?

c. Access the data saved in the file and run the stepwise regression. Which independent variables comprise the best subset of variables for predicting one's desire to have cosmetic surgery?

d. Do you recommend using the resulting stepwise regression model for predicting one's desire to have cosmetic surgery or do you recommend further analysis? Explain your reasoning.

12.117 Bus Rapid Transit study. Bus Rapid Transit (BRT) is a rapidly growing trend in the provision of public transportation in America. The Center for Urban Transportation Research (CUTR) at the University of South Florida conducted a survey of BRT customers in Miami (*Transportation Research Board* Annual Meeting, January 2003). Data on the following variables (all measured on a 5-point scale, where 1 = very unsatisfied and 5 = very satisfied) were collected for a sample of over 500 bus riders: overall satisfaction with BRT (y), safety on bus (x_1), seat availability (x_2), dependability (x_3), travel time (x_4), cost (x_5), information/maps (x_6), convenience of routes (x_7), traffic signals (x_8), safety at bus stops (x_9), hours of service (x_{10}), and frequency of service (x_{11}). CUTR analysts used stepwise regression to model overall satisfaction (y).

a. How many models are fit at step 1 of the stepwise regression?

b. How many models are fit at step 2 of the stepwise regression?

c. How many models are fit at step 11 of the stepwise regression?

d. The stepwise regression selected the following eight variables to include in the model (in order of selection): $x_{11}, x_4, x_2, x_7, x_{10}, x_1, x_9,$ and x_3. Write the equation for $E(y)$ that results from stepwise regression.

e. The model, part **d**, resulted in $R^2 = .677$. Interpret this value.

f. Explain why the CUTR analysts should be cautious in concluding that the best model for $E(y)$ has been found.

12.118 Adverse effects of hot-water runoff. The Environmental Protection Agency (EPA) wants to determine whether the hot-water runoff from a particular power plant located near a large gulf is having an adverse effect on the marine life in the area. The goal is to acquire a prediction equation for the number of marine animals located at certain designated areas, or stations, in the gulf. Based on past experience, the EPA considered the following environmental factors as predictors for the number of animals at a particular station:

$x_1 =$ Temperature of water (TEMP)
$x_2 =$ Salinity of water (SAL)
$x_3 =$ Dissolved oxygen content of water (DO)
$x_4 =$ Turbidity index, a measure of the turbidity of the water (TI)
$x_5 =$ Depth of the water at the station (ST_DEPTH)
$x_6 =$ Total weight of sea grasses in sampled area (TGRSWT)

As a preliminary step in the construction of this model, the EPA used a stepwise regression procedure to identify the most important of these six variables. A total of

716 samples were taken at different stations in the gulf, producing the SPSS printout shown below. (The response measured was y, the logarithm of the number of marine animals found in the sampled area.)

a. According to the SPSS printout, which of the six independent variables should be used in the model? (Use $\alpha = .10$.)

b. Are we able to assume that the EPA has identified all the important independent variables for the prediction of y? Why?

c. Using the variables identified in part **a**, write the first-order model with interaction that may be used to predict y.

d. How would the EPA determine whether the model specified in part **c** is better than the first-order model?

e. Note the small value of R^2. What action might the EPA take to improve the model?

12.119 After-death album sales. When a popular music artist dies, sales of the artist's albums often increase dramatically. A study of the effect of after-death publicity on album sales was published in *Marketing Letters* (March 2016). The following data were collected weekly for each of 446 albums of artists who died a natural death: album publicity (measured as the total number of printed articles in which the album was mentioned at least once during the week), artist death status (before or after death), and album sales (dollars). Suppose you want to use the data to model weekly album sales (y) as a function of album publicity and artist death status. Do you recommend using stepwise regression to find the "best" model for predicting y? Explain. If not, outline a strategy for finding the best model.

Variables Entered/Removed[a]

Model	Variables Entered	Variables Removed	Method
1	ST_DEPTH	.	Stepwise (Criteria: Probability-of-F-to-enter <= .050, Probability-of-F-to-remove >= .100).
2	TGRSWT	.	Stepwise (Criteria: Probability-of-F-to-enter <= .050, Probability-of-F-to-remove >= .100).
3	TI	.	Stepwise (Criteria: Probability-of-F-to-enter <= .050, Probability-of-F-to-remove >= .100).

a. Dependent Variable: LOGNUM

Model Summary

Model	R	R Square	Adjusted R Square	Std. Error of the Estimate
1	.329[a]	.122	.121	.7615773
2	.427[b]	.182	.180	.7348470
3	.432[c]	.187	.184	.7348469

a. Predictors: (Constant), ST_DEPTH

b. Predictors: (Constant), ST_DEPTH, TGRSWT

c. Predictors: (Constant), ST_DEPTH, TGRSWT, TI

PART III: MULTIPLE REGRESSION DIAGNOSTICS

12.11 Residual Analysis: Checking the Regression Assumptions

When we apply regression analysis to a set of data, we never know for certain whether the assumptions of Section 12.1 are satisfied. How far can we deviate from the assumptions and still expect regression analysis to yield results that will have the reliability stated in this chapter? How can we detect departures (if they exist) from the assumptions, and what can we do about them? We provide some answers to these questions in this section.

Recall from Section 12.1 that for any given set of values of $x_1, x_2, \ldots, x_k$, we assume that the random error term ε has the following properties:

1. mean equal to 0
2. constant variance (σ^2)
3. normal probability distribution
4. probabilistically independent

It is unlikely that these assumptions are ever satisfied exactly in a practical application of regression analysis. Fortunately, experience has shown that least squares regression analysis produces reliable statistical tests, confidence intervals, and prediction intervals as long as the departures from the assumptions are not too great. In this section, we present some methods for determining whether the data indicate significant departures from the assumptions.

Because the assumptions all concern the random error component, ε, of the model, the first step is to estimate the random error. Because the actual random error associated with a particular value of y is the difference between the actual y-value and its unknown mean, we estimate the error by the difference between the actual y-value and the *estimated* mean. This estimated error is called the *regression residual*, or simply the **residual**, and is denoted by $\hat{\varepsilon}$. The actual error ε and residual $\hat{\varepsilon}$ are shown in Figure 12.30.

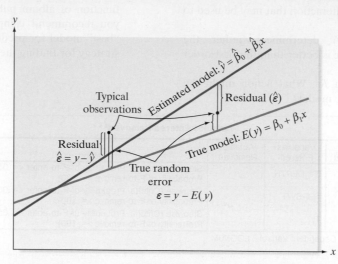

Figure 12.30

Actual random error ε and regression residual $\hat{\varepsilon}$

A **regression residual**, $\hat{\varepsilon}$, is defined as the difference between an observed y-value and its corresponding predicted value:

$$\hat{\varepsilon} = (y - \hat{y}) = y - (\hat{\beta}_0 + \hat{\beta}_1 x_1 + \hat{\beta}_2 x_2 + \cdots + \hat{\beta}_k x_k)$$

Because the true mean of y (that is, the true regression model) is not known, the actual random error cannot be calculated. However, because the residual is based on the estimated mean (the least squares regression model), it can be calculated and used to estimate the random error and to check the regression assumptions. Such checks are generally referred to as **residual analyses.** Two useful properties of residuals are given in the next box.

Properties of Regression Residuals

1. The mean of the residuals is equal to 0. This property follows from the fact that the sum of the differences between the observed y-values and their least squares predicted $\hat{y}$-values is equal to 0.

$$\sum (\text{Residuals}) = \sum (y - \hat{y}) = 0$$

2. The standard deviation of the residuals is equal to the standard deviation of the fitted regression model, s. This property follows from the fact that the sum of the squared residuals is equal to SSE, which when divided by the error degrees of freedom is equal to the variance of the fitted regression model, s^2. The square root of the variance is both the standard deviation of the residuals and the standard deviation of the regression model.

$$\sum (\text{Residuals})^2 = \sum (y - \hat{y})^2 = \text{SSE}$$

$$s = \sqrt{\frac{\sum (\text{Residuals})^2}{n - (k + 1)}} = \sqrt{\frac{\text{SSE}}{n - (k + 1)}}$$

FRANCIS J. ANSCOMBE (1918–2001)
Anscombe's Data

British citizen Frank Anscombe grew up in a small town near the English Channel. He attended Trinity College in Cambridge, England, on a merit scholarship, graduating with first class honors in mathematics in 1939. He later earned his master's degree in 1943. During World War II, Anscombe worked for the British Ministry of Supply, developing a mathematical solution for aiming antiaircraft rockets at German bombers and buzz bombs. Following the war, Anscombe worked at the Rothamsted Experimental Station, applying statistics to agriculture. There, he formed his appreciation for solving problems with social relevance. During his career as a professor of statistics, Anscombe served on the faculty of Cambridge, Princeton, and Yale universities. He was a pioneer in the application of computers to statistical analysis and was one of the original developers of residual analysis in regression. Anscombe is famous for a paper he wrote in 1973, in which he showed that one regression model could be fit by four very different data sets ("Anscombe's data"). While Anscombe published 50 research articles on statistics, he also had serious interests in classical music, poetry, and art.

The following examples show how a graphical analysis of regression residuals can be used to verify the assumptions associated with the model and to support improvements to the model when the assumptions do not appear to be satisfied. We rely on statistical software to generate the appropriate graphs in the examples and exercises.

Checking Assumption #1: Mean $\varepsilon = 0$

First, we demonstrate how a residual plot can detect a model in which the hypothesized relationship between $E(y)$ and an independent variable x is misspecified. The assumption of mean error of 0 is violated in these types of models.*

EXAMPLE 12.14

Analyzing Residuals— Electrical Usage Model

Problem Refer to the problem of modeling the relationship between home size (x) and electrical usage (y) in Example 12.7 (p. 742). The data for $n = 15$ homes are repeated in Table 12.6. Minitab printouts for a straight-line model and a quadratic model fitted to the data are shown in Figures 12.31a and 12.31b, respectively. The residuals from these models are highlighted in the printouts. The residuals are then plotted on the vertical axis against the variable x, size of home, on the horizontal axis in Figures 12.32a and 12.32b, respectively.

a. Verify that each residual is equal to the difference between the observed y-value and the estimated mean value, $\hat{y}$.

b. Analyze the residual plots.

Table 12.6	Home Size-Electrical Usage Data
Size of Home, x (sq. ft.)	Monthly Usage, y (kilowatt-hours)
1,290	1,182
1,350	1,172
1,470	1,264
1,600	1,493
1,710	1,571
1,840	1,711
1,980	1,804
2,230	1,840
2,400	1,956
2,710	2,007
2,930	1,984
3,000	1,960
3,210	2,001
3,240	1,928
3,520	1,945

---

*For a misspecified model, the hypothesized mean of y, denoted by $E_h(y)$, will not equal the true mean of y, $E(y)$. Because $y = E_h(y) + \varepsilon$, then $\varepsilon = y - E_h(y)$ and $E(\varepsilon) = E[y - E_h(y)] = E(y) - E_h(y) \neq 0$.

Regression Analysis: USAGE versus SIZE

Analysis of Variance

Source	DF	Adj SS	Adj MS	F-Value	P-Value
Regression	1	1017803	1017803	42.23	0.000
Error	13	313338	24103		
Total	14	1331140			

Model Summary

S	R-sq	R-sq(adj)
155.251	76.46%	74.65%

Coefficients

Term	Coef	SE Coef	T-Value	P-Value
Constant	903	132	6.83	0.000
SIZE	0.3559	0.0548	6.50	0.000

Regression Equation
USAGE = 903 + 0.3559 SIZE

Fits and Diagnostics for All Observations

Obs	USAGE	Fit	Resid	Std Resid
1	1182.0	1362.2	-180.2	-1.29
2	1172.0	1383.5	-211.5	-1.50
3	1264.0	1426.2	-162.2	-1.13
4	1493.0	1472.5	20.5	0.14
5	1571.0	1511.7	59.3	0.41
6	1711.0	1557.9	153.1	1.04
7	1804.0	1607.8	196.2	1.32
8	1840.0	1696.8	143.2	0.96
9	1956.0	1757.3	198.7	1.33
10	2007.0	1867.6	139.4	0.94
11	1984.0	1945.9	38.1	0.26
12	1960.0	1970.8	-10.8	-0.07
13	2001.0	2045.6	-44.6	-0.32
14	1928.0	2056.3	-128.3	-0.91
15	1945.0	2155.9	-210.9	-1.57

Figure 12.31a

Minitab printout for straight-line model of electrical usage

Regression Analysis: USAGE versus SIZE, SIZESQ

Analysis of Variance

Source	DF	Adj SS	Adj MS	F-Value	P-Value
Regression	2	1300900	650450	258.11	0.000
Error	12	30240	2520		
Total	14	1331140			

Model Summary

S	R-sq	R-sq(adj)
50.1998	97.73%	97.35%

Coefficients

Term	Coef	SE Coef	T-Value	P-Value
Constant	-807	167	-4.83	0.000
SIZE	1.962	0.153	12.86	0.000
SIZESQ	-0.000340	0.000032	-10.60	0.000

Regression Equation
USAGE = -807 + 1.962 SIZE - 0.000340 SIZESQ

Fits and Diagnostics for All Observations

Obs	USAGE	Fit	Resid	Std Resid
1	1182.0	1157.2	24.8	0.61
2	1172.0	1221.0	-49.0	-1.14
3	1264.0	1341.2	-77.2	-1.70
4	1493.0	1460.3	32.7	0.70
5	1571.0	1552.2	18.8	0.40
6	1711.0	1650.1	60.9	1.30
7	1804.0	1742.6	61.4	1.32
8	1840.0	1874.7	-34.7	-0.76
9	1956.0	1940.2	15.8	0.35
10	2007.0	2009.0	-2.0	-0.04
11	1984.0	2018.2	-34.2	-0.73
12	1960.0	2014.1	-54.1	-1.16
13	2001.0	1982.1	18.9	0.42
14	1928.0	1975.1	-47.1	-1.05
15	1945.0	1880.0	65.0	1.87

Figure 12.31b

Minitab printout for quadratic model of electrical usage

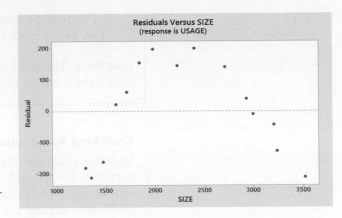

Figure 12.32a

Minitab residual plot for straight-line model of electrical usage

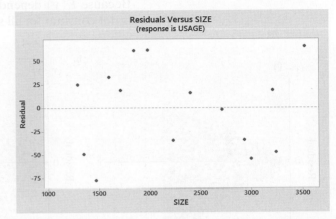

Figure 12.32b

Minitab residual plot for quadratic model of electrical usage

Solution

a. For the straight-line model, the residual is calculated for the first y-value as follows:

$$\hat{\varepsilon} = (y - \hat{y}) = 1{,}182 - 1{,}362.2 = -180.2$$

where $\hat{y}$ is the first number in the column labeled **Fit** on the Minitab printout in Figure 12.31a. Similarly, the residual for the first y-value using the quadratic model (Figure 12.31b) is

$$\hat{\varepsilon} = 1{,}182 - 1{,}157.2 = 24.8$$

Both residuals agree with the first values given in the column labeled **Residual** in Figures 12.31a and Figure 12.31b, respectively. Although the residuals both correspond to the same observed y-value, 1,182, they differ because the predicted mean value changes depending on whether the straight-line model or quadratic model is used. Similar calculations produce the remaining residuals.

b. The Minitab plot of the residuals for the straight-line model (Figure 12.32a) reveals a nonrandom pattern. The residuals exhibit a curved shape, with the residuals for the small values of x below the horizontal 0 (mean of the residuals) line, the residuals corresponding to the middle values of x above the 0 line, and the residuals for the largest values of x again below the 0 line. The indication is that the mean value of the random error ε *within* each of these ranges of x (small, medium, large) may not be equal to 0. Such a pattern usually indicates that curvature needs to be added to the model.

When the second-order term is added to the model, the nonrandom pattern disappears. In Figure 12.32b, the residuals appear to be randomly distributed around the 0 line, as expected. Note, too, that the residuals on the quadratic residual plot vary between -75 and 50, compared with between -200 and 200 on the straight-line plot. In fact, $s \approx 50$ for the quadratic model is much smaller than $s \approx 155$ for the straight-line model. The implication is that the quadratic model provides a considerably better model for predicting electrical usage.

Look Back The residual analysis verifies our conclusions from Example 12.7, where we found the t-test for the quadratic term, $\beta_2 x^2$, to be statistically significant.

● **Now Work Exercise 12.120a**

Checking Assumption #2: Constant Error Variance

Residual plots can also be used to detect violations of the assumption of constant error variance. For example, a plot of the residuals versus the predicted value $\hat{y}$ may display one of the patterns shown in Figure 12.33. In these figures, the range in values of the residuals increases (or decreases) as $\hat{y}$ increases, thus indicating that the variance of the random error, ε, becomes larger (or smaller) as the estimate of $E(y)$ increases in value. Because $E(y)$ depends on the x-values in the model, this implies that the variance of ε is not constant for all settings of the x's.

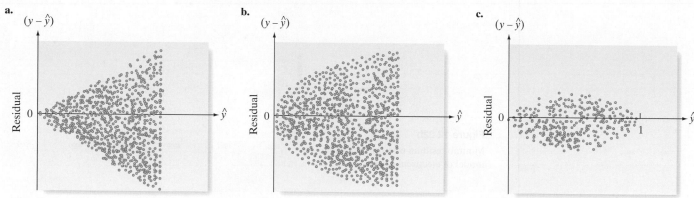

Figure 12.33

Residual plots showing changes in the variance of ε

In the next example, we demonstrate how to use this plot to detect a nonconstant variance and suggest a useful remedy.

EXAMPLE 12.15

Using Residuals to Check Equal Variances—Social Workers' Salaries

Problem The data in Table 12.7 are the salaries, y, and years of experience, x, for a sample of 50 social workers. The first-order model $E(y) = \beta_0 + \beta_1 x$ was fitted to the data using SPSS. The SPSS printout is shown in Figure 12.34, followed by a plot of the residuals versus $\hat{y}$ in Figure 12.35. Interpret the results. Make model modifications, if necessary.

Solution The SPSS printout, Figure 12.34, suggests that the first-order model provides an adequate fit to the data. The R^2-value indicates that the model explains 78.7% of the sample variation in salaries. The t-value for testing β_1, 13.31, is highly significant (p-value ≈ 0) and indicates that the model contributes information for the prediction of y. However, an examination of the residuals plotted against $\hat{y}$ (Figure 12.35) reveals a potential problem. Note the "cone" shape of the residual variability; the size of the residuals increases as the estimated mean salary increases, implying that the constant variance assumption is violated.

One way to stabilize the variance of ε is to refit the model using a transformation on the dependent variable y. With economic data (e.g., salaries), a useful **variance-stabilizing transformation** is the natural logarithm of y, denoted $\ln(y)$.* We fit the model

$$\ln(y) = \beta_0 + \beta_1 x + \varepsilon$$

*Other variance-stabilizing transformations that are used successfully in practice are $\sqrt{y}$ and $\sin^{-1}\sqrt{y}$. Consult the references for more details on these transformations.

Table 12.7	Salary Data for Example 12.15					
Years of Experience, x	Salary, y	Years of Experience, x	Salary, y	Years of Experience, x	Salary, y
7	$26,075	21	$43,628	28	$99,139
28	79,370	4	16,105	23	52,624
23	65,726	24	65,644	17	50,594
18	41,983	20	63,022	25	53,272
19	62,308	20	47,780	26	65,343
15	41,154	15	38,853	19	46,216
24	53,610	25	66,537	16	54,288
13	33,697	25	67,447	3	20,844
2	22,444	28	64,785	12	32,586
8	32,562	26	61,581	23	71,235
20	43,076	27	70,678	20	36,530
21	56,000	20	51,301	19	52,745
18	58,667	18	39,346	27	67,282
7	22,210	1	24,833	25	80,931
2	20,521	26	65,929	12	32,303
18	49,727	20	41,721	11	38,371
11	33,233	26	82,641		

📊 *Data Set*: SOCIAL

Model Summary

Model	R	R Square	Adjusted R Square	Std. Error of the Estimate
1	.887[a]	.787	.782	8642.441

a. Predictors: (Constant), EXPER

ANOVA[a]

Model		Sum of Squares	df	Mean Square	F	Sig.
1	Regression	1.324E+10	1	1.324E+10	177.257	.000[b]
	Residual	3585206077	48	74691793.28		
	Total	1.682E+10	49			

a. Dependent Variable: SALARY

b. Predictors: (Constant), EXPER

Coefficients[a]

Model		Unstandardized Coefficients		Standardized Coefficients	t	Sig.
		B	Std. Error	Beta		
1	(Constant)	11368.721	3160.317		3.597	.001
	EXPER	2141.381	160.839	.887	13.314	.000

a. Dependent Variable: SALARY

Figure 12.34

SPSS regression printout for first-order model of salary

to the data of Table 12.7. Figure 12.36 shows the SPSS regression analysis printout for the $n = 50$ measurements, while Figure 12.37 shows a plot of the residuals from the log model.

You can see that the logarithmic transformation has stabilized the error variances. Note that the cone shape is gone; there is no apparent tendency of the residual variance to increase as mean salary increases. We therefore are confident that inferences using the $\ln(y)$ model are more reliable than those using the untransformed model.

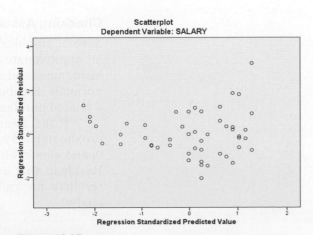

Figure 12.35

SPSS residual plot for first-order model of salary

Model Summary

Model	R	R Square	Adjusted R Square	Std. Error of the Estimate
1	.929[a]	.864	.861	.1541127

a. Predictors: (Constant), EXPER

ANOVA[a]

Model		Sum of Squares	df	Mean Square	F	Sig.
1	Regression	7.212	1	7.212	303.660	.000[b]
	Residual	1.140	48	.024		
	Total	8.352	49			

a. Dependent Variable: LNSALARY

b. Predictors: (Constant), EXPER

Coefficients[a]

Model		Unstandardized Coefficients		Standardized Coefficients	t	Sig.
		B	Std. Error	Beta		
1	(Constant)	9.841	.056		174.631	.000
	EXPER	.050	.003	.929	17.426	.000

a. Dependent Variable: LNSALARY

Figure 12.36

SPSS regression printout for model of log salary

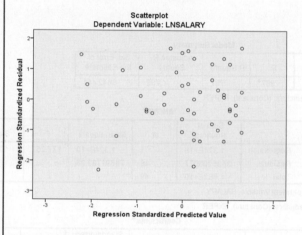

Figure 12.37

SPSS residual plot for model of ln(salary)

Look Back With transformed models, the analyst should be wary when interpreting model statistics such as $\hat{\beta}_1$ and s. These interpretations must take into account that the dependent variable is not some function of y. For example, the antilogarithm of $\hat{\beta}_1$ in the $\ln(y)$ model for salary (y) represents the percentage change in salary for every 1 year increase in experience (x).

● **Now Work Exercise 12.120b**

Checking Assumption #3: Errors Normally Distributed

Several graphical methods are available for assessing whether the random error ε has an approximate normal distribution. Recall (Section 4.7) that stem-and-leaf displays, histograms, and normal probability plots are useful for checking whether the data are normally distributed. We illustrate these techniques in an example. But first, we discuss a related problem—using residuals to check for *outliers*.

If the assumption of normally distributed errors is satisfied, then we expect approximately 95% of the residuals to fall within 2 standard deviations of the mean of 0, and almost all of the residuals to lie within 3 standard deviations of the mean of 0. Residuals that are extremely far from 0 and disconnected from the bulk of the other residuals are called *regression outliers* and should receive special attention from the analyst.

A **regression outlier** is a residual that is larger than $3s$ (in absolute value).

EXAMPLE 12.16

Identifying Outliers—
Grandfather Clock Price
Model

Problem Refer to Example 12.6 (p. 735) in which we modeled the auction price (y) of a grandfather clock as a function of age (x_1) and number of bidders (x_2). The data for this example are repeated in Table 12.8, with one important difference: The auction price of the clock at the top of the sixth column has been changed from \$2,131 to \$1,131 (highlighted in Table 12.8). The interaction model

$$E(y) = \beta_0 + \beta_1 x_1 + \beta_2 x_2 + \beta_3 x_1 x_2$$

is again fit to these (modified) data, with the Minitab printout shown in Figure 12.38. The residuals are shown highlighted in the printout and then plotted against the number of bidders, x_2, in Figure 12.39. Analyze the residual plot.

Table 12.8	Altered Auction Price Data				
Age, x_1 (years)	Number of Bidders, x_2	Auction Price, y (\$)	Age, x_1 (years)	Number of Bidders, x_2	Auction Price, y (\$)
127	13	1,235	170	14	1,131
115	12	1,080	182	8	1,550
127	7	845	162	11	1,884
150	9	1,522	184	10	2,041
156	6	1,047	143	6	845
182	11	1,979	159	9	1,483
156	12	1,822	108	14	1,055
132	10	1,253	175	8	1,545
137	9	1,297	108	6	729
113	9	946	179	9	1,792
137	15	1,713	111	15	1,175
117	11	1,024	187	8	1,593
137	8	1,147	111	7	785
153	6	1,092	115	7	744
117	13	1,152	194	5	1,356
126	10	1,336	168	7	1,262

 *Data Set*: CLOCK2

Solution The residual plot dramatically reveals the one altered measurement. Note that one of the two residuals at $x_2 = 14$ bidders falls more than 3 standard deviations below 0. (This observation is highlighted on Figure 12.38.) Note that no other residual falls more than 2 standard deviations from 0.

What do we do with outliers once we identify them? First, we try to determine the cause. Were the data entered into the computer incorrectly? Was the observation recorded incorrectly when the data were collected? If so, we correct the observation and rerun the analysis. Another possibility is that the observation is not representative of the conditions we are trying to model. For example, in this case the low price may be attributable to extreme damage to the clock or to a clock of inferior quality compared with the others. In these cases, we probably would exclude the observation from the analysis. In many cases, you may not be able to determine the cause of the outlier. Even so, you may want to rerun the regression analysis excluding the outlier in order to assess the effect of that observation on the results of the analysis.

Figure 12.40 shows the printout when the outlier observation is excluded from the grandfather clock analysis, and Figure 12.41 shows the new plot of the residuals against the number of bidders. Now only one of the residuals lies beyond 2 standard deviations from 0, and none of them lies beyond 3 standard deviations. Also, the model statistics indicate a much better model without the outlier. Most notably, the s has decreased from 200.6 to 85.83, indicating a model that will provide more precise estimates and predictions (narrower confidence and prediction intervals) for clocks that are similar to those in the reduced sample.

Regression Analysis: PRICE versus AGE, NUMBIDS, AGE_BIDS

Analysis of Variance

Source	DF	Adj SS	Adj MS	F-Value	P-Value
Regression	3	3033587	1011196	25.13	0.000
Error	28	1126703	40239		
Total	31	4160289			

Model Summary

S	R-sq	R-sq(adj)
200.598	72.92%	70.02%

Coefficients

Term	Coef	SE Coef	T-Value	P-Value
Constant	-513	666	-0.77	0.448
AGE	8.17	4.58	1.78	0.086
NUMBIDS	19.9	67.4	0.29	0.770
AGE_BIDS	0.320	0.479	0.67	0.510

Regression Equation
PRICE = -513 + 8.17 AGE + 19.9 NUMBIDS + 0.320 AGE_BIDS

Fits and Diagnostics for All Observations

Obs	PRICE	Fit	Resid	Std Resid	
1	1235.0	1310.4	-75.4	-0.39	
2	1080.0	1105.9	-25.9	-0.14	
3	845.0	947.5	-102.5	-0.54	
4	1522.0	1322.5	199.5	1.01	
5	1047.0	1179.5	-132.5	-0.69	
6	1979.0	1831.9	147.1	0.81	
7	1822.0	1598.0	224.0	1.17	
8	1253.0	1185.8	67.2	0.34	
9	1297.0	1178.9	118.1	0.60	
10	946.0	913.9	32.1	0.17	
11	1713.0	1561.0	152.0	0.82	
12	1024.0	1072.6	-48.6	-0.25	
13	1147.0	1115.2	31.8	0.16	
14	1092.0	1149.2	-57.2	-0.30	
15	1152.0	1187.2	-35.2	-0.19	
16	1336.0	1117.6	218.4	1.12	
17	1131.0	1914.4	-783.4	-4.80	R
18	1550.0	1597.7	-47.7	-0.25	
19	1884.0	1598.3	285.7	1.49	
20	2041.0	1776.6	264.4	1.41	
21	845.0	1048.4	-203.4	-1.06	
22	1483.0	1421.8	61.2	0.31	
23	1055.0	1130.7	-75.7	-0.43	
24	1545.0	1522.7	22.3	0.12	
25	729.0	695.5	33.5	0.19	
26	1792.0	1642.7	149.3	0.78	
27	1175.0	1224.0	-49.0	-0.29	
28	1593.0	1651.3	-58.3	-0.31	
29	785.0	781.1	3.9	0.02	
30	744.0	822.7	-78.7	-0.42	
31	1356.0	1480.7	-124.7	-0.83	X
32	1262.0	1374.0	-112.0	-0.58	

R Large residual
X Unusual X

Figure 12.38

Minitab regression printout for altered grandfather clock data

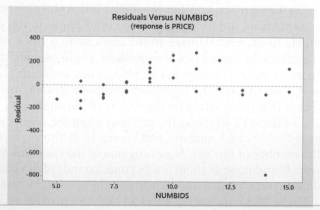

Figure 12.39

Minitab residual plot for altered grandfather clock data

```
Analysis of Variance

Source         DF   Adj SS   Adj MS   F-Value   P-Value
Regression      3  3933417  1311139    177.99     0.000
Error          27   198897     7367
Total          30  4132314

Model Summary

      S   R-sq  R-sq(adj)
85.8286  95.19%     94.65%

Coefficients

Term       Coef  SE Coef  T-Value  P-Value
Constant    474      298     1.59    0.124
AGE       -0.46     2.11    -0.22    0.827
NUMBIDS  -114.1     31.2    -3.65    0.001
AGE_BIDS  1.478    0.229     6.44    0.000

Regression Equation
PRICE = 474 - 0.46 AGE - 114.1 NUMBIDS + 1.478 AGE_BIDS
```

Figure 12.40

Minitab regression printout when outlier is deleted

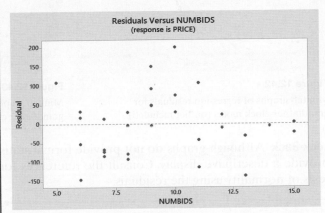

Figure 12.41

Minitab residual plot when outlier is deleted

ETHICS in STATISTICS

Removing observations from a sample data set for the sole purpose of improving the fit of a regression model without investigating whether the observations are outliers or legitimate data points is considered *unethical statistical practice*.

Look Back Remember that if the outlier is removed from the analysis when in fact it belongs to the same population as the rest of the sample, the resulting model may provide misleading estimates and predictions.

● **Now Work Exercise 12.120c**

The next example checks the assumption of the normality of the random error component.

EXAMPLE 12.17

Using Residuals to Check for Normal Errors—Grandfather Clock Prices

Problem Refer to Example 12.16. Analyze the distribution of the residuals in the grandfather clock example, both before and after the outlier residual is removed. Determine whether the assumption of a normally distributed error term is reasonable.

Solution A histogram and normal probability plot for the two sets of residuals are constructed using Minitab and are shown in Figures 12.42 and 12.43. Note that the outlier appears to skew the histogram in Figure 12.42, whereas the histogram in Figure 12.43 appears to be more mound-shaped. Similarly, the pattern of residuals in the normal probability plot in Figure 12.43 (outlier deleted) is more nearly a straight line than the pattern in Figure 12.42 (outlier included). Thus, the normality assumption appears to be more plausible after the outlier is removed.

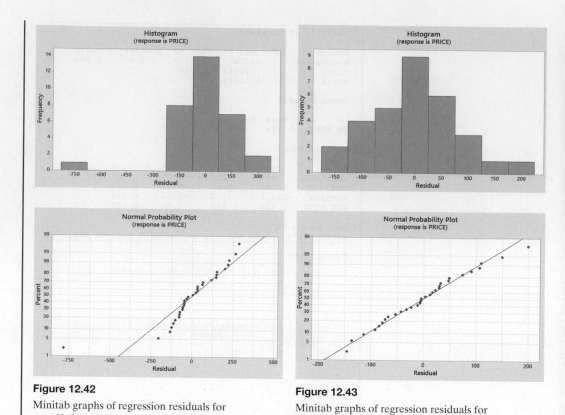

Figure 12.42

Minitab graphs of regression residuals for grandfather clock model (outlier included)

Figure 12.43

Minitab graphs of regression residuals for grandfather clock model (outlier deleted)

Look Back Although graphs do not provide formal statistical tests of normality, they do provide a descriptive display. Consult the references for methods to conduct statistical tests of normality using the residuals.

● **Now Work Exercise 12.120d**

Of the four assumptions in Section 12.1, the assumption that the random error is normally distributed is the least restrictive when we apply regression analysis in practice—that is, moderate departures from a normal distribution have very little effect on the validity of the statistical tests, confidence intervals, and prediction intervals presented in this chapter. In this case, we say that regression analysis is **robust** with respect to nonnormal errors. However, great departures from normality cast doubt on any inferences derived from the regression analysis.

Checking Assumption #4: Errors Independent

The assumption of independent errors is violated when successive errors are correlated. This typically occurs when the data for both the dependent and independent variables are observed sequentially over a period of time—called **time series data**. Time series data have a unique characteristic; the experimental unit represents a unit of time (e.g., a year, a month, a quarter). There are both graphical and formal statistical tests available for checking the assumption of independent regression errors. For example, a simple graph is to plot the residuals against time. If the residuals tend to group alternately into positive and negative clusters (as shown in Figure 12.44), then it is likely that the errors are correlated and the assumption is violated. If correlated errors are detected, one solution is to construct a **time series model** for $E(y)$. These methods are discussed in detail in Chapter 14.

Summary

Residual analysis is a useful tool for the regression analyst, not only to check the assumptions but also to provide information about how the model can be improved. A summary of the residual analyses presented in this section to check the assumption that the random error ε is normally distributed with mean 0 and constant variance is presented in the next box.

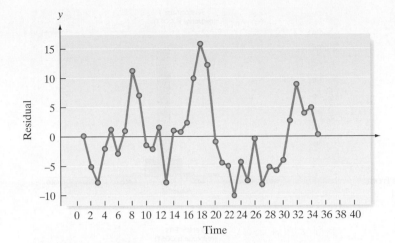

Figure 12.44

Hypothetical residual plot for time series data

Steps in a Residual Analysis

1. Check for a misspecified model by plotting the residuals against each of the quantitative independent variables. Analyze each plot, looking for a curvilinear trend. This shape signals the need for a quadratic term in the model. Try a second-order term in the variable against which the residuals are plotted.

2. Examine the residual plots for outliers. Draw lines on the residual plots at 2- and 3-standard-deviation distances below and above the 0 line. Examine residuals outside the 3-standard-deviation lines as potential outliers and check to see that no more than 5% of the residuals exceed the 2-standard-deviation lines. Determine whether each outlier can be explained as an error in data collection or transcription, corresponds to a member of a population different from that of the remainder of the sample, or simply represents an unusual observation. If the observation is determined to be an error, fix it or remove it. Even if you cannot determine the cause, you may want to rerun the regression analysis without the observation to determine its effect on the analysis.

3. Check for nonnormal errors by plotting a frequency distribution of the residuals, using a stem-and-leaf display or a histogram. Check to see if obvious departures from normality exist. Extreme skewness of the frequency distribution may be due to outliers or could indicate the need for a transformation of the dependent variable. (Normalizing transformations are beyond the scope of this book, but you can find information in the references.)

4. Check for unequal error variances by plotting the residuals against the predicted values, $\hat{y}$. If you detect a cone-shaped pattern or some other pattern that indicates that the variance of ε is not constant, refit the model using an appropriate variance-stabilizing transformation on y, such as $\ln(y)$. (Consult the references for other useful variance-stabilizing transformations.)

STATISTICS IN ACTION

REVISITED

A Residual Analysis

In the previous *Statistics in Action Revisited* section (p. 778), we found the interaction model, $E(y) = \beta_0 + \beta_1 x_1 + \beta_3 x_2 + \beta_4 x_1 x_2$, to be both a statistically and practically useful model for predicting the cost (y) of a road construction contract. Recall that the two independent variables are the DOT engineer's estimate of cost (x_1) and bid status, where $x_2 = 1$ if a fixed bid and $x_2 = 0$ if a competitive bid. Before actually using the model in practice, we need to examine the residuals to be sure that the standard regression assumptions are reasonably satisfied.

Figures SIA12.9 and SIA12.10 are Minitab graphs of the residuals from the interaction model. The histogram shown in Figure SIA12.9 appears to be approximately

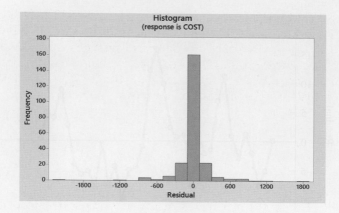

Figure SIA12.9

Minitab histogram of residuals from interaction model for road cost

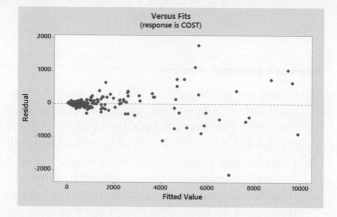

Figure SIA12.10

Minitab plot of residuals versus predicted values from interaction model for road cost

normally distributed; consequently the assumption of normal errors is reasonably satisfied. The scatterplot of the residuals against $\hat{y}$ shown in Figure SIA12.10, however, shows a distinct "funnel" pattern; this indicates that the assumption of a constant error variance is likely to be violated. One way to modify the model to satisfy this assumption is to use a variance-stabilizing transformation (such as the natural log) on cost (y). When both the y and x variables in a regression equation are economic variables (prices, costs, salaries, etc.), it is often advantageous to transform the x variable also. Consequently, we'll modify the model by making a log transform on both cost (y) and DOTEST (x_1).

Our modified (log-log) interaction model takes the form

$$E(y^*) = \beta_0 + \beta_1 x_1^* + \beta_2 x_2 + \beta_3 (x_1^*) x_2$$

where $y^* = \ln(\text{COST})$ and $x_1^* = \ln(\text{DOTEST})$. The Minitab printout for this model is shown in Figure SIA12.11, followed by graphs of the residuals in Figures SIA12.12 and

Regression Analysis: LNCOST versus LNDOTEST, STATUS, STA_LNDOT

Analysis of Variance

Source	DF	Adj SS	Adj MS	F-Value	P-Value
Regression	3	439.622	146.541	6108.16	0.000
Error	231	5.542	0.024		
Total	234	445.164			

Model Summary

S	R-sq	R-sq(adj)
0.154890	98.76%	98.74%

Coefficients

Term	Coef	SE Coef	T-Value	P-Value
Constant	-0.1618	0.0519	-3.12	0.002
LNDOTEST	1.00778	0.00798	126.25	0.000
STATUS	0.324	0.136	2.39	0.018
STA_LNDOT	-0.0176	0.0218	-0.81	0.422

Figure SIA12.11

Minitab regression printout for modified (log-log) model of road construction cost

Regression Equation
LNCOST = -0.1618 + 1.00778 LNDOTEST + 0.324 STATUS - 0.0176 STA_LNDOT

SIA12.13. The histogram shown in Figure SIA12.12 is approximately normal, and, more important, the scatterplot of the residuals shown in Figure SIA12.13 has no distinct trend. It appears that the log transformations successfully stabilized the error variance. Note, however, that the t-test for the interaction term in the model (highlighted in Figure SIA12.11) is no longer statistically significant (p-value = .420). Consequently, we will drop the interaction term from the model and use the simpler modified model,

$$E(y^*) = \beta_0 + \beta_1 x_1^* + \beta_2 x_2$$

to predict road construction cost.

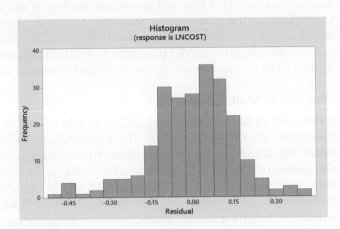

Figure SIA12.12

Minitab histogram of residuals from modified (log-log) model for road construction cost

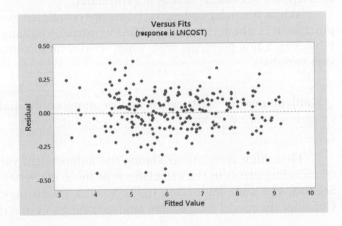

Figure SIA12.13

Minitab plot of residuals versus predicted values from modified (log-log) model for road construction cost

12.12 Some Pitfalls: Estimability, Multicollinearity, and Extrapolation

You should be aware of several potential problems when constructing a prediction model for some response y. A few of the most important are discussed in this final section.

Problem 1: Parameter Estimability

Suppose you want to fit a model relating annual crop yield y to the total expenditure for fertilizer x. We propose the first-order model

$$E(y) = \beta_0 + \beta_1 x$$

Now suppose we have 3 years of data and $1,000 is spent on fertilizer each year. The data are shown in Figure 12.45. You can see the problem: The parameters of the model cannot be estimated when all the data are concentrated at a single x-value. Recall that it takes two points (x-values) to fit a straight line. Thus, the parameters are not estimable when only one x is observed.

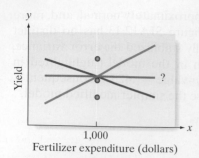

Figure 12.45

Yield and fertilizer expenditure data: Three years

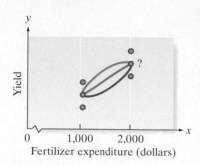

Figure 12.46

Only two x-values observed: Quadratic model not estimable

A similar problem would occur if we attempted to fit the quadratic model

$$E(y) = \beta_0 + \beta_1 x + \beta_2 x^2$$

to a set of data for which only one or two different x-values were observed (see Figure 12.46). At least three different x-values must be observed before a quadratic model can be fit to a set of data (that is, before all three parameters are estimable).

In general, the number of levels of observed x-values must be one more than the order of the polynomial in x that you want to fit.

For controlled experiments, the researcher can select one of the experimental designs in Chapter 9 that will permit estimation of the model parameters. Even when the values of the independent variables cannot be controlled by the researcher, the independent variables are almost always observed at a sufficient number of levels to permit estimation of the model parameters. When the statistical software you use suddenly refuses to fit a model, however, the problem is probably inestimable parameters.

Problem 2: Multicollinearity

Often, two or more of the independent variables used in a regression model contribute redundant information—that is, the independent variables are correlated with each other. For example, suppose we want to construct a model to predict the gas mileage rating of a truck as a function of its load, x_1 (in tons), and the horsepower, x_2 (in foot-pounds per second), of its engine. We would expect heavy loads to require greater horsepower and to result in lower mileage ratings. Thus, although both x_1 and x_2 contribute information for the prediction of mileage rating, y, some of the information is overlapping because x_1 and x_2 are correlated.

When the independent variables are correlated, we say *multicollinearity* exists. In practice, it is not uncommon to observe correlations among the independent variables. However, a few problems arise when serious multicollinearity is present in the regression variables.

> **Multicollinearity** exists when two or more of the independent variables used in regression are correlated.

First, high correlations among the independent variables increase the likelihood of rounding errors in the calculations of the β estimates, standard errors, and so forth. Second, and more important, the regression results may be confusing and misleading. Consider the model for gasoline mileage rating (y) of a truck:

$$E(y) = \beta_0 + \beta_1 x_1 + \beta_2 x_2$$

where x_1 = load and x_2 = horsepower. Fitting the model to a sample data set, we might find that the t-tests for testing β_1 and β_2 are both nonsignificant at the $\alpha = .05$ level, while the F-test for $H_0: \beta_1 = \beta_2 = 0$ is highly significant ($p = .001$). The tests may seem to be contradictory, but really they are not. The t-tests indicate that the contribution of one variable, say x_1 = load, is not significant after the effect of x_2 = horsepower has been accounted for (because x_2 is also in the model). The significant F-test, on the other hand, tells us that at least one of the two variables is making a contribution to the prediction of y (i.e., either β_1 or β_2 or both differ from 0). In fact, both are probably contributing, but the contribution of one overlaps with that of the other.

Multicollinearity can also have an effect on the signs of the parameter estimates. More specifically, a value of β_i may have the opposite sign from what is expected. In the truck gasoline mileage example, we expect heavy loads to result in lower mileage ratings, and we expect higher horsepowers to result in lower mileage ratings; consequently, we expect the signs of both the parameter estimates to be negative. Yet we may actually see a positive value of β_1 and be tempted to claim that heavy loads result in *higher* mileage ratings. This is the danger of interpreting a β coefficient when the independent variables are correlated. Because the variables contribute redundant information, the effect of x_1 = load on y = mileage rating is measured only partially by β_1.

How can you avoid the problems of multicollinearity in regression analysis? One way is to conduct a designed experiment (Chapter 9) so that the levels of the x variables are uncorrelated. Unfortunately, time and cost constraints may prevent you from collecting data in this manner. Consequently, most data are collected observationally. Because observational data frequently consist of correlated independent variables, you will need to recognize when multicollinearity is present and, if necessary, make modifications in the regression analysis.

Several methods are available for detecting multicollinearity in regression. A simple technique is to calculate the coefficient of correlation, r, between each pair of independent variables in the model and use the procedure outlined in Section 11.5 to test for significantly correlated variables. If one or more of the r-values are statistically different from 0, the variables in question are correlated, and a multicollinearity problem may exist.* The degree of multicollinearity will depend on the magnitude of the value of r, as shown in the box.

Using the Correlation Coefficient r to Detect Multicollinearity

Extreme multicollinearity: $|r| \geq .8$

Moderate multicollinearity: $.2 \leq |r| < .8$

Low multicollinearity: $|r| < .2$

Other indications of the presence of multicollinearity include those mentioned above—namely, non-significant t-tests for the individual parameter estimates when the F-test for overall model adequacy is significant and estimates with opposite signs from what is expected.[†]

Detecting Multicollinearity in the Regression Model

1. Significant correlations between pairs of independent variables (see box above)
2. Nonsignificant t-tests for all (or nearly all) of the individual β parameters when the F-test for overall model adequacy is significant
3. Signs opposite from what is expected in the estimated β parameters

---

EXAMPLE 12.18

Detecting Multicollinearity— Modeling Carbon Monoxide in Cigarette Smoke

Problem The Federal Trade Commission (FTC) annually ranks varieties of domestic cigarettes according to their tar, nicotine, and carbon monoxide contents. The U.S. Surgeon General considers each of these three substances hazardous to a smoker's health. Past studies have shown that increases in the tar and nicotine contents of a cigarette are accompanied by an increase in the carbon monoxide emitted from the cigarette smoke. Table 12.9 presents data on tar, nicotine, and carbon monoxide contents (in milligrams) and weight (in grams) for a sample of 25 (filter) brands tested in a recent year. Suppose

---

*Remember that r measures only the pairwise correlation between x-values. Three variables, x_1, x_2, and x_3, may be highly correlated as a group but may not exhibit large pairwise correlations. Thus, multicollinearity may be present even when all pairwise correlations are not significantly different from 0.

[†]More formal methods for detecting multicollinearity, such as variance-inflation factors (VIFs), are available. Independent variables with a VIF of 10 or above are usually considered to be highly correlated with one or more of the other independent variables in the model. Calculation of VIFs are beyond the scope of this introductory text. Consult the chapter references for a discussion of VIFs and other formal methods of detecting multicollinearity.

we want to model carbon monoxide content, y, as a function of tar content, x_1, nicotine content, x_2, and weight, x_3, using the model

$$E(y) = \beta_0 + \beta_1 x_1 + \beta_2 x_2 + \beta_3 x_3$$

The model is fit to the 25 data points in Table 12.9, and a portion of the Minitab printout is shown in Figure 12.47. Examine the printout. Do you detect any signs of multicollinearity?

Table 12.9	FTC Cigarette Data for Example 12.18		
Tar, x_1	Nicotine, x_2	Weight, x_3	Carbon Monoxide, y
14.1	.86	.9853	13.6
16.0	1.06	1.0938	16.6
29.8	2.03	1.1650	23.5
8.0	.67	.9280	10.2
4.1	.40	.9462	5.4
15.0	1.04	.8885	15.0
8.8	.76	1.0267	9.0
12.4	.95	.9225	12.3
16.6	1.12	.9372	16.3
14.9	1.02	.8858	15.4
13.7	1.01	.9643	13.0
15.1	.90	.9316	14.4
7.8	.57	.9705	10.0
11.4	.78	1.1240	10.2
9.0	.74	.8517	9.5
1.0	.13	.7851	1.5
17.0	1.26	.9186	18.5
12.8	1.08	1.0395	12.6
15.8	.96	.9573	17.5
4.5	.42	.9106	4.9
14.5	1.01	1.0070	15.9
7.3	.61	.9806	8.5
8.6	.69	.9693	10.6
15.2	1.02	.9496	13.9
12.0	.82	1.1184	14.9

Source: Federal Trade Commission   📊 *Data Set:* FTC

Regression Analysis: CO versus TAR, NICOTINE, WEIGHT

```
Analysis of Variance

Source       DF  Adj SS   Adj MS   F-Value  P-Value
Regression    3  495.26  165.086    78.98    0.000
Error        21   43.89    2.090
Total        24  539.15

Model Summary

      S   R-sq  R-sq(adj)
1.44573  91.86%   90.70%

Coefficients

Term       Coef  SE Coef  T-Value  P-Value
Constant   3.20     3.46     0.93    0.365
TAR       0.963    0.242     3.97    0.001
NICOTINE  -2.63     3.90    -0.67    0.507
WEIGHT    -0.13     3.89    -0.03    0.974

Regression Equation
CO = 3.20 + 0.963 TAR - 2.63 NICOTINE - 0.13 WEIGHT
```

Correlation: TAR, NICOTINE, WEIGHT

```
            TAR  NICOTINE
NICOTINE  0.977
          0.000

WEIGHT    0.491   0.500
          0.013   0.011

Cell Contents: Pearson correlation
               P-Value
```

Figure 12.47

Minitab printout for model of carbon monoxide content, Example 12.18

Solution First, note that the F-test for overall model utility is highly significant. The test statistic ($F = 78.98$) and observed significance level (p-value $= .000$) are highlighted on the Minitab printout, Figure 12.47. Therefore, at, say $\alpha = .01$, we can conclude that at least one of the parameters—$\beta_1, \beta_2,$ or β_3—in the model is nonzero. The t-tests for two of three individual β's, however, are nonsignificant. (The p-values for these tests are highlighted on the printout.) Unless tar (x_1) is the only one of the three variables useful for predicting carbon monoxide content, these results are the first indication of a potential multicollinearity problem.

The negative values for β_2 and β_3 (highlighted on the printout) are a second clue to the presence of multicollinearity. From past studies, the FTC expects carbon monoxide content (y) to increase when either nicotine content (x_2) or weight (x_3) increases—that is, the FTC expects *positive* relationships between y and x_2 and between y and x_3, not negative ones.

All signs indicate that a serious multicollinearity problem exists.

Look Back To confirm our suspicions, we had Minitab produce the coefficient of correlation, r, for each of the three pairs of independent variables in the model. The resulting output is shown (highlighted) at the bottom of Figure 12.47. You can see that tar (x_1) and nicotine (x_2) are highly correlated ($r = .977$), while weight (x_3) is moderately correlated with the other two x's ($r \approx .5$). All three correlations have p-values $\approx .01$ or less; consequently, all three are significantly different from 0 at, say, $\alpha = .05$.

● **Now Work Exercise 12.119**

Once you have detected that multicollinearity exists, there are several alternative measures available for solving the problem. The appropriate measure to take depends on the severity of the multicollinearity and the ultimate goal of the regression analysis.

Some researchers, when confronted with highly correlated independent variables, choose to include only one of the correlated variables in the final model. If you are interested in using the model only for estimation and prediction (step 6), you may decide not to drop any of the independent variables from the model. In the presence of multicollinearity, we have seen that it is dangerous to interpret the individual β parameters. However, confidence intervals for $E(y)$ and prediction intervals for y generally remain unaffected *as long as the values of the x's used to predict* y *follow the same pattern of multicollinearity exhibited in the sample data*—that is, you must take strict care to ensure that the values of the x variables fall within the range of the sample data.

Solutions to Some Problems Created by Multicollinearity in Regression*

1. Drop one or more of the correlated independent variables from the model. One way to decide which variables to keep in the model is to employ stepwise regression (Section 12.10).

2. If you decide to keep all the independent variables in the model,

   a. Avoid making inferences about the individual β parameters based on the t-tests.

   b. Restrict inferences about $E(y)$ and future y-values to values of the x's that fall within the range of the sample data.

Problem 3: Prediction Outside the Experimental Region

Many research economists had developed highly technical models to relate the state of the economy to various economic indices and other independent variables. Many of these models were multiple regression models, where, for example, the dependent

---

*Several other solutions are available. For example, in the case where higher-order regression models are fit, the analyst may want to code the independent variables so that higher-order terms (e.g., x^2) for a particular x variable are not highly correlated with x. One transformation that works is $z = (x - \bar{x})/s$. Other, more sophisticated procedures for addressing multicollinearity (such as *ridge regression*) are beyond the scope of the text. Consult the references at the end of this chapter.

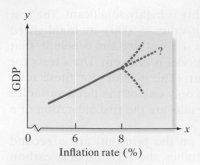

Figure 12.48

Using a regression model outside the experimental region

variable y might be next year's gross domestic product (GDP) and the independent variables might include this year's rate of inflation, this year's consumer price index (CPI), and so on. In other words, the model might be constructed to predict next year's economy using this year's knowledge.

Unfortunately, these models were almost all unsuccessful in predicting the recession in the early 1970s and the late 1990s. What went wrong? One of the problems was that many of the regression models were used to **extrapolate** (i.e., predict y-values of the independent variables that were outside the region in which the model was developed). For example, the inflation rate in the late 1960s, when the models were developed, ranged from 6% to 8%. When the double-digit inflation of the early 1970s became a reality, some researchers attempted to use the same models to predict future growth in GDP. As you can see in Figure 12.48, the model may be very accurate for predicting y when x is in the range of experimentation, but using the model outside that range is a dangerous practice.

Exercises 12.120–12.133

Learning the Mechanics

12.120 Identify the problem(s) in each of the residual plots
[NW] shown below.

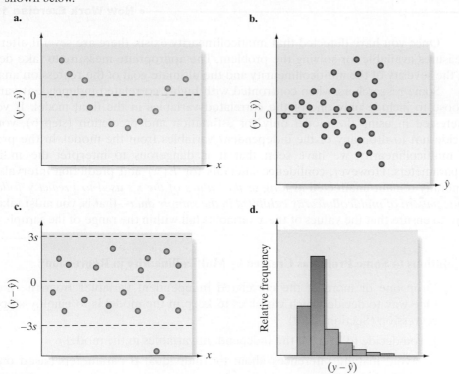

12.121 Consider fitting the multiple regression model
[NW]
$$E(y) = \beta_0 + \beta_1 x_1 + \beta_2 x_2 + \beta_3 x_3 + \beta_4 x_4 + \beta_5 x_5$$

A matrix of correlations for all pairs of independent variables is given below. Do you detect a multicollinearity problem? Explain.

	x_1	x_2	x_3	x_4	x_5
x_1	—	.17	.02	−.23	.19
x_2		—	.45	.93	.02
x_3			—	.22	−.01
x_4				—	.86
x_5					—

Applying the Concepts—Basic

12.122 **Emotional intelligence and team performance.** Refer to
 the *Engineering Project Organizational Journal* (Vol. 3, **TEAMPERF** 2013) study of the relationship between emotional intelligence of individual team members and their performance during an engineering project, Exercise 12.33 (p. 733). Using data on $n = 23$ teams, you fit a first-order model for mean project score (y) as a function of range of interpersonal scores (x_1), range of stress management scores (x_2), and range of mood scores (x_3). The regression results, as well as a correlation matrix for the independent variables, are displayed in the accompanying Minitab printout. Do you detect any signs

Minitab Output for Exercise 12.122

Regression Analysis: Project versus IntraPers, StressMan, Mood

Analysis of Variance

```
Source      DF  Adj SS  Adj MS  F-Value  P-Value
Regression   3   70.29  23.429    2.66    0.077
Error       19  167.08   8.794
Total       22  237.37
```

Model Summary

```
     S   R-sq  R-sq(adj)
2.96544  29.61%   18.50%
```

Coefficients

```
Term        Coef  SE Coef  T-Value  P-Value
Constant   86.90     3.20    27.17    0.000
IntraPers -0.2099   0.0936   -2.24    0.037
StressMan  0.1515   0.0769    1.97    0.063
Mood       0.0733   0.0671    1.09    0.289
```

Regression Equation
Project = 86.90 - 0.2099 IntraPers + 0.1515 StressMan + 0.0733 Mood

Correlation: IntraPers, StressMan, Mood

```
           IntraPers  StressMan
StressMan      0.083
               0.705

Mood           0.201     -0.198
               0.359      0.366
```

Cell Contents: Pearson correlation
              P-Value

of multicollinearity in the data? [*Note:* The researchers expect the linear relationship between project score and each independent variable to be negative for range of interpersonal scores and positive for both range of stress management scores and mood scores.]

12.123 State casket sales restrictions. Some states permit only licensed firms to sell funeral goods (e.g., caskets, urns) to the consumer, while other states have no restrictions. States with casket sales restrictions are being challenged in court to lift these monopolistic restrictions. A paper in the *Journal of Law and Economics* (February 2008) used multiple regression to investigate the impact of lifting casket sales restrictions on the cost of a funeral. Data collected for a sample of 1,437 funerals were used to fit the model. A simpler version of the model estimated by the researchers is $E(y) = \beta_0 + \beta_1 x_1 + \beta_2 x_2 + \beta_3 x_1 x_2$, where y is the price (in dollars) of a direct burial, $x_1 = $ {1 if funeral home is in a restricted state, 0 if not}, and $x_2 = $ {1 if price includes a basic wooden casket, 0 if no casket}. The estimated equation (with standard errors in parentheses) is:

$$\hat{y} = 1,432 + 793x_1 - 252x_2 + 261x_1x_2, R^2 = .78$$
$$(70) \quad (134) \quad (109)$$

a. Calculate the predicted price of a direct burial with a basic wooden casket at a funeral home in a restricted state.

b. The data include a direct burial funeral with a basic wooden casket at a funeral home in a restricted state that costs $2,200. Assuming the standard deviation of the model is $50, is this data value an outlier?

c. The data also include a direct burial funeral with a basic wooden casket at a funeral home in a restricted state that costs $2,500. Again, assume that the standard deviation of the model is $50. Is this data value an outlier?

12.124 Personality traits and job performance. Refer to the *Journal of Applied Psychology* (January 2011) study of the determinants of task performance, Exercise 12.94 (p. 766). In addition to $x_1 = $ conscientiousness score and $x_2 = $ {1 if highly complex job, 0 if not}, the researchers also used $x_3 = $ emotional stability score, $x_4 = $ organizational citizenship behavior score, and $x_5 = $ counterproductive work behavior score to model $y = $ task performance score. One of their concerns is the level of multicollinearity in the data. Below is a matrix of correlations for all possible pairs of independent variables. Based on this information, do you detect a moderate or high level of multicollinearity? If so, what are your recommendations?

	x_1	x_2	x_3	x_4
Conscientiousness (x_1)				
Job complexity (x_2)	.13			
Emotional stability (x_3)	.62	.14		
Organizational citizenship (x_4)	.24	.03	.24	
Counterproductive work (x_5)	−.23	−.02	−.25	−.62

12.125 Women in top management. Refer to the *Journal of Organizational Culture, Communications and Conflict* (July 2007) study on women in upper management positions at U.S. firms, Exercise 11.73 (p. 679). Monthly data ($n = 252$ months) were collected for several variables in an attempt to model the number of females in managerial positions (y). The independent variables included the number of females with a college degree (x_1), the number of female high school graduates with no college degree (x_2), the number of males in managerial positions (x_3), the number of males with a college degree (x_4), and the number of male high school graduates with no college degree (x_5). The correlations provided in Exercise 11.67 are given in each part. Determine which of the correlations results in a potential multicollinearity problem for the regression analysis.

a. The correlation relating number of females in managerial positions and number of females with a college degree: $r = .983$.

b. The correlation relating number of females in managerial positions and number of female high school graduates with no college degree: $r = .074$.

c. The correlation relating number of males in managerial positions and number of males with a college degree: $r = .722$.

d. The correlation relating number of males in managerial positions and number of male high school graduates with no college degree: $r = .528$.

12.126 Accuracy of software effort estimates. Refer to the *Journal of Empirical Software Engineering* (Vol. 9, 2004) study of the accuracy of new software effort estimates, Exercise 12.114 (p. 781). Recall that stepwise regression was used to develop a model for the relative error in estimating effort (y) as a function of company role of estimator ($x_1 = 1$ if developer, 0 if project leader) and previous accuracy ($x_8 = 1$ if more than 20% accurate, 0 if less than 20% accurate). The stepwise regression yielded the prediction equation $\hat{y} = .12 - .28x_1 + .27x_8$. The researcher is concerned that the sign of the estimated β multiplied by x_1 is the opposite from what is expected. (The researcher expects a project leader to have a smaller relative error of estimation than a developer.) Give at least one reason why this phenomenon occurred.

Applying the Concepts—Intermediate

12.127 Arsenic in groundwater. Refer to the *Environmental Science & Technology* (January 2005) study of the reliability of a commercial kit to test for arsenic in groundwater, Exercise 12.16 (p. 725). Recall that you fit a first-order model for arsenic level (y) as a function of latitude (x_1), longitude (x_2), and depth (x_3) to data saved in the file. Conduct a residual analysis of the data. Based on the results, comment on each of the following:
a. assumption of mean error = 0
b. assumption of constant error variance
c. outliers
d. assumption of normally distributed errors
e. multicollinearity

12.128 Reality TV and cosmetic surgery. Refer to the *Body Image: An International Journal of Research* (March 2010) study of the influence of reality TV shows on one's desire to undergo cosmetic surgery, Exercise 12.17 (p. 725). Simulated data for the study are saved in the file. In Exercise 12.17, you fit the first-order model, $E(y) = \beta_0 + \beta_1 x_1 + \beta_2 x_2 + \beta_3 x_3 + \beta_4 x_4$, where y = desire to have cosmetic surgery, x_1 is a dummy variable for gender, x_2 = level of self-esteem, x_3 = level of body satisfaction, and x_4 = impression of reality TV.
a. Check the data for multicollinearity. If you detect multicollinearity, what modifications to the model do you recommend?
b. Conduct a complete residual analysis for the model. Do you detect any violations of the assumptions? If so, what modifications to the model do you recommend?

12.129 Failure times of silicon wafer microchips. Refer to the National Semiconductor study of manufactured silicon wafer integrated circuit chips, Exercise 12.63 (p. 749). Recall that the failure times of the microchips (in hours) was determined at different solder temperatures (degrees Celsius). The data are repeated in the table below.

Temperature (°C)	Time to Failure (hours)	Temperature (°C)	Time to Failure (hours)
165	200	149	1,150
162	200	142	3,500
164	1,200	142	3,600
158	500	143	3,650
158	600	133	4,200
159	750	132	4,800
156	1,200	132	5,000
157	1,500	134	5,200
152	500	134	5,400
147	500	125	8,300
149	1,100	123	9,700

Source: S. Gee and L. Nguyen, "Mean Time to Failure in Wafer Level-CSP Packages with SnPb and SnAgCu Solder Bumps," International Wafer Level Packaging Conference, San Jose, CA, November 3–4, 2005 (adapted from Figure 7). Copyright: 2005.

a. Fit the straight-line model $E(y) = \beta_0 + \beta_1 x$ to the data, where y = failure time and x = solder temperature.
b. Compute the residual for a microchip manufactured at a temperature of 149°C.
c. Plot the residuals against solder temperature (x). Do you detect a trend?
d. In Exercise 12.63c, you determined that failure time (y) and solder temperature (x) were curvilinearly related. Does the residual plot, part c, support this conclusion?

12.130 Bubble behavior in subcooled flow boiling. Refer to the *Heat Transfer Engineering* (Vol. 34, 2013) study of bubble behavior in subcooled flow boiling, Exercise 12.46 (p. 740). Using data saved in the file, you fit an interaction model for bubble density (y) as a function of x_1 = mass flux and x_2 = heat flux. Conduct a complete residual analysis for the model. Do you recommend any model modifications?

12.131 Banning controversial sports team sponsors. Refer to the *Journal of Marketing Research* (October 2015) study of the impact of banning a controversial sponsor on a sports team's success, Exercise 12.81 (p. 758). Recall that markets for English soccer clubs were classified as one of four types: (1) banned alcohol sponsors but now have other sponsors, (2) banned alcohol sponsors and now have no other sponsors, (3) did not ban alcohol sponsors but now have other sponsors, and (4) did not ban alcohol sponsors and now have no other sponsors. To assess the impact of an alcohol ban in a market, you fit a main effects model for the *matching value loss* (y) as a function of the qualitative independent variable market type. Conduct a complete residual analysis for the multiple regression model. Are the standard regression assumptions reasonably satisfied?

12.132 Cooling method for gas turbines. Refer to the *Journal of Engineering for Gas Turbines and Power* (January 2005) study of a high-pressure inlet fogging method for a gas turbine engine, Exercise 12.103 (p. 773). Now consider the interaction model for heat rate (y) of a gas turbine as a function of cycle speed (x_1) and cycle pressure ratio (x_2), $E(y) = \beta_0 + \beta_1 x_1 + \beta_2 x_2 + \beta_3 x_1 x_2$. Use the data saved in the file to conduct a complete residual analysis for the model. Do you recommend making model modifications?

12.133 Agreeableness, gender, and wages. Refer to the *Journal of Personality and Social Psychology* (Feb. 2012) study of on-the-job agreeableness and wages, Exercise 12.107 (p. 774). Recall that the researchers modeled mean income, $E(y)$, as a function of both agreeableness score (x_1) and a dummy variable for gender ($x_2 = 1$ if male, 0 if female). Use the data saved in the file to analyze the residuals of the model,

$$E(y) = \beta_0 + \beta_1 x_1 + \beta_2 (x_1)^2 + \beta_3 x_2$$

What model modifications, if any, do you recommend?

CHAPTER NOTES

Key Terms

Adjusted multiple coefficient of determination 719
Base level 751
Categorical variable 751
Coded variable 709
Complete model 767
Complete second-order model 745
Dummy variable 751
Extrapolation 802
First-order model 711
Full model 767
General multiple regression model 710
Higher-order term 709
Indicator variable 751
Interaction 735
Interaction model 735
Interaction term 735
Least squares prediction equation 712
Level of a variable 751
Main effect terms 759
Mean square for error (MSE) 713
Method of least squares 711
Model building 710

Multicollinearity 798
Multiple coefficient of determination (R^2) 718
Multiple regression model 709
Nested model 767
Nested model F-test 771
Objective variable screening procedure 776
Parameter estimability 797
Parsimonious model 771
Quadratic model 741
Quadratic term 741
Qualitative variable 751
Reduced model 767
Regression outlier 790
Regression residual 784
Residual 784
Residual analysis 784
Robust method 794
Second-order model 741
Second-order term 741
Stepwise regression 775
Time series data 794
Time series model 794
Variance-stabilizing transformation 788

Key Formulas

$$s^2 = \text{MSE} = \frac{\text{SSE}}{n - (k + 1)}$$

Estimator of σ^2 for a model with k independent variables

$$t = \frac{\hat{\beta}_i}{s_{\hat{\beta}_i}}$$

Test statistic for testing $H_0: \beta_i$

$\hat{\beta}_i \pm (t_{\alpha/2})s_{\hat{\beta}_i}$, where $t_{\alpha/2}$ depends on $n - (k + 1)$ df

$100(1 - \alpha)\%$ confidence interval for β_i

$$R^2 = \frac{\text{SS}_{yy} - \text{SSE}}{\text{SS}_{yy}}$$

Multiple coefficient of determination

$$R_a^2 = 1 - \left[\frac{(n - 1)}{n - (k + 1)}\right](1 - R^2)$$

Adjusted multiple coefficient of determination

$$F = \frac{\text{MS (Model)}}{\text{MSE}}$$
$$= \frac{R^2/k}{(1 - R^2)/[n - (k + 1)]}$$

Test statistic for testing $H_0: \beta_1 = \beta_2 = \cdots = \beta_k = 0$

$$F = \frac{(\text{SSE}_R - \text{SSE}_C)/\text{number of } \beta\text{'s tested}}{\text{MSE}_C}$$

Test statistic for comparing reduced and complete models

$y \quad \hat{y}$

Regression residual

Key Symbols

x_1^2	Quadratic form for a quantitative x
$x_1 x_2$	Interaction term
MSE	Mean square for error (estimates σ^2)
$\hat{\varepsilon}$	Estimated random error (residual)
SSE_R	Sum of squared errors, reduced model
SSE_C	Sum of squared errors, complete model
MSE_C	Mean squared error, complete model
$\ln(y)$	Natural logarithm of dependent variable

Key Ideas

Multiple regression variables

y = **Dependent** variable (quantitative)

$x_1, x_2, \ldots, x_k$ are **independent** variables (quantitative or qualitative)

First-order model in k quantitative x's

$$E(y) = \beta_0 + \beta_1 x_1 + \beta_2 x_2 + \cdots + \beta_k x_k$$

Each β_i represents the change in $E(y)$ for every 1-unit increase in x_i, holding all other x's fixed.

Interaction model in 2 quantitative x's

$$E(y) = \beta_0 + \beta_1 x_1 + \beta_2 x_2 + \beta_3 x_1 x_2$$

$(\beta_1 + \beta_3 x_2)$ represents the change in $E(y)$ for every 1-unit increase in x_1, for fixed value of x_2

$(\beta_2 + \beta_3 x_1)$ represents the change in $E(y)$ for every 1-unit increase in x_2, for fixed value of x_1

Quadratic model in 1 quantitative x

$$E(y) = \beta_0 + \beta_1 x + \beta_2 x^2$$

β_2 represents the rate of curvature in $E(y)$ for x

($\beta_2 > 0$ implies *upward* curvature)

($\beta_2 < 0$ implies *downward* curvature)

Complete second-order model in 2 quantitative x's

$$E(y) = \beta_0 + \beta_1 x_1 + \beta_2 x_2 + \beta_3 x_1 x_2 + \beta_4 x_1^2 + \beta_5 x_2^2$$

β_4 represents the rate of curvature in $E(y)$ for x_1, holding x_2 fixed

β_5 represents the rate of curvature in $E(y)$ for x_2, holding x_1 fixed

Dummy variable model for 1 qualitative x

$$E(y) = \beta_0 + \beta_1 x_1 + \beta_2 x_2 + \cdots + \beta_{k-1} x_{k-1}$$

$x_1 = \{1 \text{ if level 1, 0 if not}\}$

$x_2 = \{1 \text{ if level 2, 0 if not}\}$

$x_{k-1} = \{1 \text{ if level } k - 1, 0 \text{ if not}\}$

$\beta_0 = E(y)$ for level k (base level) $= \mu_k$

$\beta_1 = \mu_1 - \mu_k$

$\beta_2 = \mu_2 - \mu_k$

Complete second-order model in 1 quantitative x and 1 qualitative x (two levels, A and B)

$$E(y) = \beta_0 + \beta_1 x_1 + \beta_2 x_1^2 + \beta_3 x_2 + \beta_4 x_1 x_2 + \beta_5 x_1^2 x_2$$

$x_2 = \{1 \text{ if level A, 0 if level B}\}$

Adjusted coefficient of determination, R_a^2

Cannot be "forced" to 1 by adding independent variables to the model.

Interaction between x_1 and x_2

Implies that the relationship between y and one x depends on the other x.

Parsimonious model
A model with a small number of β parameters.

Recommendation for Assessing Model Adequacy
1. Conduct global F-test; if significant, then:
2. Conduct t-tests on only the most important β's (*interaction* or *squared terms*)
3. Interpret value of $2s$
4. Interpret value of R_a^2

Recommendation for Testing Individual β's
1. If *curvature* (x^2) deemed important, do not conduct test for first-order (x) term in the model.
2. If *interaction* (x_1x_2) deemed important, do not conduct tests for first-order terms $(x_1$ and $x_2)$ in the model.

Extrapolation
Occurs when you predict y for values of x's that are outside of range of sample data.

Nested models
Are models where one model (the *complete model*) contains all the terms of another model (the *reduced model*) plus at least one additional term.

Multicollinearity
Occurs when two or more x's are correlated.
Indicators of multicollinearity:
1. Highly correlated x's
2. Significant global F-test, but all t-tests nonsignificant
3. Signs on β's opposite from expected

Problems with Using Stepwise Regression Model as the "Final" Model
1. *Extremely large number of* t-*tests* inflate overall probability of at least one Type I error.
2. *No higher-order terms* (interactions or squared terms) are included in the model.

Analysis of Residuals
1. Detect **misspecified model:** *plot residuals vs. quantitative x* (look for trends, e.g., curvilinear trend)
2. Detect **nonconstant error variance:** *plot residuals vs.* $\hat{y}$ (look for patterns, e.g., cone shape)
3. Detect **nonnormal errors:** *histogram, stem-leaf, or normal probability plot of residuals* (look for strong departures from normality)
4. Identify **outliers:** *residuals greater than 3s in absolute value* (investigate outliers before deleting)

Guide to Multiple Regression

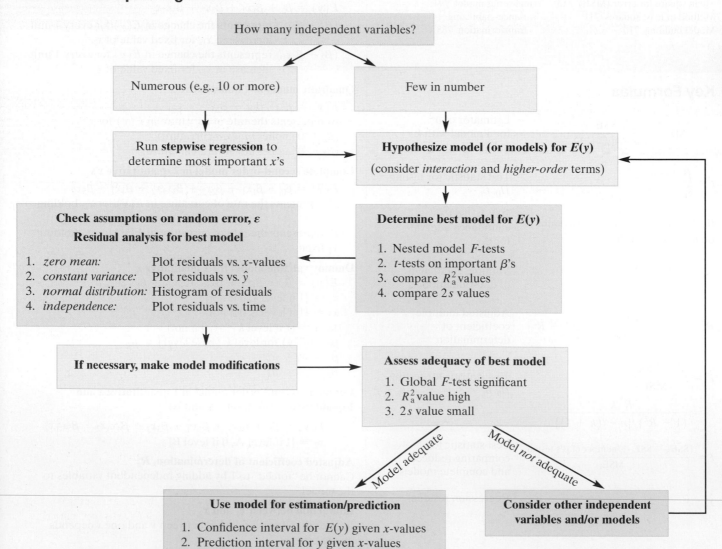

SUPPLEMENTARY EXERCISES 12.134–12.174

Learning the Mechanics

12.134 Suppose you have developed a regression model to explain the relationship between y and x_1, x_2, and x_3. The ranges of the variables you observed were as follows: $10 \le y \le 100$, $5 \le x_1 \le 55$, $.5 \le x_2 \le 1$, and $1,000 \le x_3 \le 2,000$. Will the error of prediction be smaller when you use the least squares equation to predict y when $x_1 = 30$, $x_2 = .6$, and $x_3 = 1,300$, or when $x_1 = 60$, $x_2 = .4$, and $x_3 = 900$? Why?

12.135 When a multiple regression model is used for estimating the mean of the dependent variable and for predicting a new value of y, which will be narrower—the confidence interval for the mean or the prediction interval for the new y-value? Why?

12.136 Suppose you fit the model

$$y = \beta_0 + \beta_1 x_1 + \beta_2 x_1^2 + \beta_3 x_2 + \beta_4 x_1 x_2 + \varepsilon$$

to $n = 25$ data points with the following results:

$$\hat{\beta}_0 = 1.26 \quad \hat{\beta}_1 = -2.43 \quad \hat{\beta}_2 = .05 \quad \hat{\beta}_3 = .62 \quad \hat{\beta}_4 = 1.81$$

$$s_{\hat{\beta}_1} = 1.21 \quad s_{\hat{\beta}_2} = .16 \quad s_{\hat{\beta}_3} = .26 \quad s_{\hat{\beta}_4} = 1.49$$

$$SSE = .41 \quad R^2 = .83$$

a. Is there sufficient evidence to conclude that at least one of the parameters $\beta_1, \beta_2, \beta_3$, or β_4 is nonzero? Test using $\alpha = .05$.
b. Test $H_0: \beta_1 = 0$ against $H_a: \beta_1 < 0$. Use $\alpha = .05$.
c. Test $H_0: \beta_2 = 0$ against $H_a: \beta_2 > 0$. Use $\alpha = .05$.
d. Test $H_0: \beta_3 = 0$ against $H_a: \beta_3 \neq 0$. Use $\alpha = .05$.

12.137 Suppose you used Minitab to fit the model

$$y = \beta_0 + \beta_1 x_1 + \beta_2 x_2 + \varepsilon$$

to $n = 15$ data points and obtained the printout shown below.

```
The regression equation is
Y = 90.1 - 1.84 X1 + .285 X2


Predictor   Coef   SE Coef    T      P
Constant    90.10   23.10    3.90   0.002
X1          -1.836   0.367   -5.01  0.001
X2           0.285   0.231    1.24  0.465


S = 10.68    R-Sq = 91.6%    R-Sq(adj) = 90.2%

Analysis of Variance

Source           DF    SS     MS      F      P
Regression        2   14801   7400   64.91  0.001
Residual Error   12    1364    114
Total            14   16165
```

a. What is the least squares prediction equation?
b. Find R^2 and interpret its value.
c. Is there sufficient evidence to indicate that the model is useful for predicting y? Conduct an F-test using $\alpha = .05$.
d. Test the null hypothesis $H_0: \beta_1 = 0$ against the alternative hypothesis $H_a: \beta_1 \neq 0$. Test using $\alpha = .05$. Draw the appropriate conclusions.

e. Find the standard deviation of the regression model and interpret it.

12.138 The first-order model $E(y) = \beta_0 + \beta_1 x_1$ was fit to $n = 19$ data points. A residual plot for the model is provided below. Is the need for a quadratic term in the model evident from the residual plot? Explain.

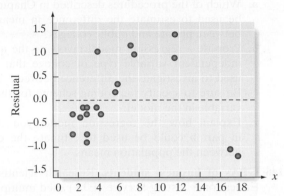

12.139 Write a model relating $E(y)$ to one qualitative independent variable that is at four levels. Define all the terms in your model.

12.140 It is desired to relate $E(y)$ to a quantitative variable x_1 and a qualitative variable at three levels.
a. Write a first-order model.
b. Write a model that will graph as three different second-order curves—one for each level of the qualitative variable.

12.141 Explain why stepwise regression is used. What is its value in the model-building process?

12.142 Consider relating $E(y)$ to two quantitative independent variables x_1 and x_2.
a. Write a first-order model for $E(y)$.
b. Write a complete second-order model for $E(y)$.

12.143 To model the relationship between y, a dependent variable, and x, an independent variable, a researcher has taken one measurement on y at each of three different x-values. Drawing on his mathematical expertise, the researcher realizes that he can fit the second-order model

$$E(y) = \beta_0 + \beta_1 x + \beta_2 x^2$$

and it will pass exactly through all three points, yielding $SSE = 0$. The researcher, delighted with the excellent fit of the model, eagerly sets out to use it to make inferences. What problems will he encounter in attempting to make inferences?

12.144 Suppose you fit the regression model

$$E(y) = \beta_0 + \beta_1 x_1 + \beta_2 x_2 + \beta_3 x_2^2 + \beta_4 x_1 x_2 + \beta_5 x_1 x_2^2$$

to $n = 35$ data points and wish to test the null hypothesis $H_0: \beta_4 = \beta_5 = 0$.
a. State the alternative hypothesis.
b. Explain in detail how to compute the F-statistic needed to test the null hypothesis.
c. What are the numerator and denominator degrees of freedom associated with the F-statistic in part **b**?
d. Give the rejection region for the test if $\alpha = .05$.

Applying the Concepts—Basic

12.145 Comparing private and public college tuition. According to the *Chronicle of Higher Education Almanac*, 4-year private colleges charge, on average, five times as much for tuition and fees than 4-year public colleges. In order to estimate the true difference in the mean amounts charged for an academic year, random samples of 40 private colleges and 40 public colleges were contacted and questioned about their tuition structures.

   a. Which of the procedures described in Chapter 8 could be used to estimate the difference in mean charges between private and public colleges?

   b. Propose a regression model involving the qualitative independent variable type of college that could be used to investigate the difference between the means. Be sure to specify the coding scheme for the dummy variable in the model.

   c. Explain how the regression model you developed in part **b** could be used to estimate the difference between the population means.

12.146 GPAs of business students. Research scientists at the Educational Testing Service (ETS) used multiple regression analysis to model y, the final grade point average (GPA) of business and management doctoral students. A list of the potential independent variables measured for each doctoral student in the study follows:

   (1) Quantitative Graduate Management Aptitude Test (GMAT) score

   (2) Verbal GMAT score

   (3) Undergraduate GPA

   (4) First-year graduate GPA

   (5) Student cohort (i.e., year in which student entered doctoral program: year 1, year 3, or year 5)

   a. Identify the variables as quantitative or qualitative.

   b. For each quantitative variable, give your opinion on whether the variable is positively or negatively related to final GPA.

   c. For each of the qualitative variables, set up the appropriate dummy variable.

   d. Write a first-order, main effects model relating final GPA, y, to the five independent variables.

   e. Interpret the β's in the model, part **d**.

   f. Write a first-order model for final GPA, y, that allows for a different slope for each student cohort.

   g. For each quantitative independent variable in the model, part **f**, give the slope of the line (in terms of the β's) for the year 1 cohort.

12.147 Comparing two orange juice extractors. The Florida Citrus Commission is interested in evaluating the performance of two orange juice extractors, brand A and brand B. It is believed that the size of the fruit used in the test may influence the juice yield (amount of juice per pound of oranges) obtained by the extractors. The commission wants to develop a regression model relating the mean juice yield $E(y)$ to the type of orange juice extractor (brand A or brand B) and the size of orange (diameter), x_1.

   a. Identify the independent variables as qualitative or quantitative.

   b. Write a model that describes the relationship between $E(y)$ and size of orange as two parallel lines, one for each brand of extractor.

   c. Modify the model of part **b** to permit the slopes of the two lines to differ.

   d. Sketch typical response lines for the model of part **b**. Do the same for the model of part **c**. Carefully label your graphs.

   e. Specify the null and alternative hypotheses you would use to determine whether the model in part **c** provides more information for predicting yield than does the model in part **b**.

   f. Explain how you would obtain the quantities necessary to compute the *F*-statistic that would be used in testing the hypotheses you described in part **e**.

12.148 Highway crash data analysis. Researchers at Montana State University have written a tutorial on an empirical method for analyzing before and after highway crash data (Montana Department of Transportation, Research Report, May 2004). The initial step in the methodology is to develop a Safety Performance Function (SPF)—a mathematical model that estimates crash occurrence for a given roadway segment. Using data collected for over 100 roadway segments, the researchers fit the model, $E(y) = \beta_0 + \beta_1 x_1 + \beta_2 x_2$, where y = number of crashes per 3 years, x_1 = roadway length (miles), and x_2 = AADT = average annual daily traffic (number of vehicles). The results are shown in the following tables.

Interstate Highways

Variable	Parameter Estimate	Standard Error	*t*-Value
Intercept	1.81231	.50568	3.58
Length (x_1)	.10875	.03166	3.44
AADT (x_2)	.00017	.00003	5.19

Noninterstate Highways

Variable	Parameter Estimate	Standard Error	*t*-Value
Intercept	1.20785	.28075	4.30
Length (x_1)	.06343	.01809	3.51
AADT (x_2)	.00056	.00012	4.86

   a. Give the least squares prediction equation for the interstate highway model.

   b. Give practical interpretations of the β estimates, part **a**.

   c. Refer to part **a**. Find a 99% confidence interval for β_1 and interpret the result.

   d. Refer to part **a**. Find a 99% confidence interval for β_2 and interpret the result.

   e. Repeat parts **a–d** for the noninterstate highway model.

   f. Write a first-order model for $E(y)$ as a function of x_1 and x_2 that allows the slopes to differ depending on whether the roadway segment is Interstate or non-interstate. [*Hint*: Create a dummy variable for Interstate/non-interstate.]

12.149 Defects in nuclear missile housing parts. The technique of multivariable testing (MVT) was discussed in the *Journal of the Reliability Analysis Center* (First Quarter, 2004). MVT was shown to improve the quality of carbon-foam rings used in nuclear missile housings. The rings are produced via a casting process that involves mixing ingredients, oven curing, and carving the finished part. One type of defect analyzed was the number y of black streaks in the manufactured ring. Two variables found to impact the number of defects were turntable speed (revolutions per minute), x_1, and cutting-blade position (inches from center), x_2.

a. The researchers discovered "an interaction between blade position and turntable speed." Hypothesize a regression model for $E(y)$ that incorporates this interaction.

b. The researchers reported a positive linear relationship between number of defects (y) and turntable speed (x_1) but found that the slope of the relationship was much steeper for lower values of cutting-blade position (x_2). What does this imply about the interaction term in the model, part **a**? Explain.

12.150 Mental health of a community. An article in the *Community Mental Health Journal* (August 2000) used multiple regression analysis to model the level of community adjustment of clients of the Department of Mental Health and Addiction Services in Connecticut. The dependent variable, community adjustment (y), was measured quantitatively based on staff ratings of the clients. (Lower scores indicate better adjustment.) The complete model was a first-order model with 21 independent variables. The independent variables were categorized as Demographic (4 variables), Diagnostic (7 variables), Treatment (4 variables), and Community (6 variables).

a. Write the equation of $E(y)$ for the complete model.

b. Give the null hypothesis for testing whether the 7 Diagnostic variables contribute information for the prediction of y.

c. Give the equation of the reduced model appropriate for the test, part **b**.

d. The test, part **b**, resulted in a test statistic of $F = 59.3$ and p-value $< .0001$. Interpret this result in the words of the problem.

12.151 Urban population estimation using satellite images. Can the population of an urban area be estimated without taking a census? *Geographical Analysis* (January 2007) demonstrated the use of satellite image maps for estimating urban population. A portion of Columbus, Ohio, was partitioned into $n = 125$ census block groups, and satellite imagery was obtained. For each census block, the following variables were measured: population density (y), proportion of block with low-density residential areas (x_1), and proportion of block with high-density residential areas (x_2). A first-order model for y was fit to the data with the following results:

$$\hat{y} = -.0304 + 2.006x_1 + 5.006x_2, R^2 = .686$$

a. Give a practical interpretation of each β estimate in the model.

b. Give a practical interpretation of the coefficient of determination, R^2.

c. State H_0 and H_a for a test of overall model adequacy.

d. Refer to part **c**. Compute the value of the test statistic.

e. Refer to parts **c** and **d**. Make the appropriate conclusion at $\alpha = .01$.

12.152 Testing tires for wear. Underinflated or overinflated tires can increase tire wear. A new tire was tested for wear at different pressures, with the results shown in the following table.

Pressure, x (pounds per square inch)	Mileage, y (thousands)
30	29
31	32
32	36
33	38
34	37
35	33
36	26

a. Plot the data on a scatterplot.

b. If you were given only the information for $x = 30, 31, 32, 33$, what kind of model would you suggest? For $x = 33, 34, 35, 36$? For all the data?

12.153 Impact of race on football card values. Refer to the *Electronic Journal of Sociology* (2007) study of the impact of race on the value of professional football players' "rookie" cards, Exercise 12.72 (p. 756). Recall that the sample consisted of 148 rookie cards of NFL players who were inducted into the Football Hall of Fame (HOF). The researchers modeled the natural logarithm of card price (y) as a function of the following independent variables:

Race:	$x_1 = 1$ if black, 0 if white
Card availability:	$x_2 = 1$ if high, 0 if low
Card vintage:	$x_3 =$ year card printed
Finalist:	$x_4 =$ natural logarithm of number of times player on final HOF ballot
Position-QB:	$x_5 = 1$ if quarterback, 0 if not
Position-RB:	$x_7 = 1$ if running back, 0 if not
Position-WR:	$x_8 = 1$ if wide receiver, 0 if not
Position-TE:	$x_9 = 1$ if tight end, 0 if not
Position-DL:	$x_{10} = 1$ if defensive lineman, 0 if not
Position-LB:	$x_{11} = 1$ if linebacker, 0 if not
Position-DB:	$x_{12} = 1$ if defensive back, 0 if not

[*Note:* For position, offensive lineman is the base level.]

a. The model $E(y) = \beta_0 + \beta_1 x_1 + \beta_2 x_2 + \beta_3 x_3 + \beta_4 x_4 + \beta_5 x_5 + \beta_6 x_6 + \beta_7 x_7 + \beta_8 x_8 + \beta_9 x_9 + \beta_{10} x_{10} + \beta_{11} x_{11} + \beta_{12} x_{12}$ was fit to the data with the following results: $R^2 = .705$, $R_a^2 = .681$, $F = 26.9$. Interpret the results, practically. Make an inference about the overall adequacy of the model.

b. Refer to part **a**. Statistics for the race variable were reported as follows: $\hat{\beta}_1 = -.147$, $s_{\hat{\beta}_1} = .145$, $t = -1.014$, p-value $= .312$. Use this information to make an inference about the impact of race on the value of professional football players' rookie cards.

c. Refer to part **a**. Statistics for the card vintage variable were reported as follows: $\hat{\beta}_3 = -.074$, $s_{\hat{\beta}_3} = .007$, $t = -10.92$, p-value $= .000$. Use this information to make an inference about the impact of card vintage on the value of professional football players' rookie cards.

d. Write a first-order model for $E(y)$ as a function of card vintage (x_3) and position $(x_5 - x_{12})$ that allows for the relationship between price and vintage to vary depending on position.

12.154 Factors identifying urban counties. The *Professional Geographer* (February 2000) published a study of urban and rural counties in the western United States. Six independent variables—total county population (x_1), population density (x_2), population concentration (x_3), population growth (x_4), proportion of county land in farms (x_5), and 5-year change in agricultural land base (x_6)—were used to model the urban/rural rating (y) of a county, where rating was recorded on a scale of 1 (most rural) to 10 (most urban). Prior to running the multiple regression analysis, the researchers were concerned about possible multicollinearity in the data. Below is a correlation matrix for data collected on $n = 256$ counties.

Independent Variable	x_1	x_2	x_3	x_4	x_5
x_1: Total population					
x_2: Population density	.20				
x_3: Population concentration	.45	.43			
x_4: Population growth	−.05	−.14	−.01		
x_5: Farm land	−.16	−.15	−.07	−.20	
x_6: Agricultural change	−.12	−.12	−.22	−.06	−.06

Source: Based on K. A. Berry et al., "Interpreting What Is Rural and Urban for Western U.S. Counties," *Professional Geographer*, Vol. 52, No. 1, February 2000, pp. 93–105 (Table 2). Copyright: Feb. 2000.

a. Based on the correlation matrix, is there any evidence of extreme multicollinearity?

b. The first-order model with all six independent variables was fit, and the results are shown in the next table. Based on the reported tests, is there any evidence of extreme multicollinearity?

Independent Variable	β Estimate	p-Value
x_1: Total population	0.110	0.045
x_2: Population density	0.065	0.230
x_3: Population concentration	0.540	0.000
x_4: Population growth	−0.009	0.860
x_5: Farm land	−0.150	0.003
x_6: Agricultural change	−0.027	0.580

Overall model: $R_a^2 = .43$ $F = 32.47$ p-value $< .001$
$R^2 = .44$

Source: K. A. Berry et al., "Interpreting What Is Rural and Urban for Western U.S. Counties," *Professional Geographer*, Vol. 52, No. 1, February 2000 (Table 2).

12.155 Entry-level job preferences. *Benefits Quarterly* published a study of entry-level job preferences. A number of independent variables were used to model the job preferences (measured on a 10-point scale) of 164 business school graduates. Suppose stepwise regression is used to build a model for job preference score (y) as a function of the following independent variables:

$$x_1 = \begin{cases} 1 & \text{if flextime position} \\ 0 & \text{if not} \end{cases}$$

$$x_2 = \begin{cases} 1 & \text{if day care support required} \\ 0 & \text{if not} \end{cases}$$

$$x_3 = \begin{cases} 1 & \text{if spousal transfer support required} \\ 0 & \text{if not} \end{cases}$$

$x_4 = $ Number of sick days allowed

$$x_5 = \begin{cases} 1 & \text{if applicant married} \\ 0 & \text{if not} \end{cases}$$

$x_6 = $ Number of children of applicant

$$x_7 = \begin{cases} 1 & \text{if male applicant} \\ 0 & \text{if female applicant} \end{cases}$$

a. How many models are fit to the data in step 1? Give the general form of these models.

b. How many models are fit to the data in step 2? Give the general form of these models.

c. How many models are fit to the data in step 3? Give the general form of these models.

d. Explain how the procedure determines when to stop adding independent variables to the model.

e. Describe two major drawbacks to using the final stepwise model as the best model for job preference score y.

12.156 A CEO's impact on corporate profits. Can a corporation's annual profit be predicted from information about the company's CEO? Each year *Forbes* publishes data on company profit (in \$ millions), CEO's annual income (in \$ thousands), and percentage of the company's stock owned by the CEO. Consider a model relating company profit (y) to CEO income (x_1) and stock percentage (x_2). Explain what it means to say that "CEO income x_1 and stock percentage x_2 interact to affect company profit y."

12.157 Deferred tax allowance study. A study was conducted to identify accounting choice variables that influence a manager's decision to change the level of the deferred tax asset allowance at the firm (*The Engineering Economist*, January/February 2004). Data were collected for a sample of 329 firms that reported deferred tax assets in 2000. The dependent variable of interest (DTVA) is measured as the change in the deferred tax asset valuation allowance divided by the deferred tax asset. The independent variables used as predictors of DTVA are listed as follows:

LEVERAGE: $x_1 = $ ratio of debt book value to shareholder's equity

BONUS: $x_2 = 1$ if firm maintains a management bonus plan, 0 if not

MVALUE: $x_3 = $ market value of common stock

BBATH: $x_4 = 1$ if operating earnings negative and lower than last year, 0 if not

EARN: $x_5 = $ change in operating earnings divided by total assets

A first-order model was fit to the data with the following results (*p*-values in parentheses):

$$R_a^2 = .280$$

$$\hat{y} = .044 + .006x_1 − .035x_2 − .001x_3 + .296x_4 + .010x_5$$

$$(.070) \quad (.228) \quad (.157) \quad (.678) \quad (.001) \quad (.869)$$

a. Interpret the estimate of the β coefficient for x_4.

b. The "Big Bath" theory proposed by the researchers states that the mean DTVA for firms with negative earnings and earnings lower than last year will exceed the mean DTVA of other firms. Is there evidence to support this theory? Test using $\alpha = .05$.

c. Interpret the value of R_a^2.

Applying the Concepts—Intermediate

12.158 Promotion of supermarket vegetables. A supermarket chain is interested in exploring the relationship between the sales of its store-brand canned vegetables (y), the amount spent on promotion of the vegetables in local newspapers (x_1), and the amount of shelf space allocated to the brand (x_2). One of the chain's supermarkets was randomly selected, and over a 20-week period x_1 and x_2 were varied, as reported in the table.

CANVEG

Week	Sales ($)	Advertising Expenditures ($)	Shelf Space (sq. ft.)
1	2,010	201	75
2	1,850	205	50
3	2,400	355	75
4	1,575	208	30
5	3,550	590	75
6	2,015	397	50
7	3,908	820	75
8	1,870	400	30
9	4,877	997	75
10	2,190	515	30
11	5,005	996	75
12	2,500	625	50
13	3,005	860	50
14	3,480	1,012	50
15	5,500	1,135	75
16	1,995	635	30
17	2,390	837	30
18	4,390	1,200	50
19	2,785	990	30
20	2,989	1,205	30

a. Fit the following model to the data:

$$y = \beta_0 + \beta_1 x_1 + \beta_2 x_2 + \beta_3 x_1 x_2 + \varepsilon$$

b. Conduct an F-test to investigate the overall usefulness of this model. Use $\alpha = .05$.

c. Test for the presence of interaction between advertising expenditures and shelf space. Use $\alpha = .05$.

d. Explain what it means to say that advertising expenditures and shelf space interact.

e. Explain how you could be misled by using a first-order model instead of an interaction model to explain how advertising expenditures and shelf space influence sales.

f. Based on the type of data collected, comment on the assumption of independent errors.

12.159 Yield strength of steel alloy. Industrial engineers at the University of Florida used regression modeling as a tool to reduce the time and cost associated with developing new metallic alloys (*Modelling and Simulation in Materials Science and Engineering*, Vol. 13, 2005). To illustrate, the engineers built a regression model for the tensile yield strength (y) of a new steel alloy. The potentially important predictors of yield strength are listed in the accompanying table.

x_1 = Carbon amount (% weight)
x_2 = Manganese amount (% weight)
x_3 = Chromium amount (% weight)
x_4 = Nickel amount (% weight)
x_5 = Molybdenum amount (% weight)
x_6 = Copper amount (% weight)
x_7 = Nitrogen amount (% weight)
x_8 = Vanadium amount (% weight)
x_9 = Plate thickness (millimeters)
x_{10} = Solution treating (milliliters)
x_{11} = Aging temperature (degrees, Celsius)

a. The engineers discovered that the variable Nickel (x_4) was highly correlated with the other potential independent variables. Consequently, Nickel was dropped from the model. Do you agree with this decision? Explain.

b. The engineers used stepwise regression on the remaining 10 potential independent variables in order to search for a parsimonious set of predictor variables. Do you agree with this decision? Explain.

c. The stepwise regression selected the following independent variables: x_1 = Carbon, x_2 = Manganese, x_3 = Chromium, x_5 = Molybdenum, x_6 = Copper, x_8 = Vanadium, x_9 = Plate thickness, x_{10} = Solution treating, and x_{11} = Aging temperature. All these variables were statistically significant in the step-wise model, with $R^2 = .94$. Consequently, the engineers used the estimated stepwise model to predict yield strength. Do you agree with this decision? Explain.

12.160 Estimating change-point dosage. A standard method for studying toxic substances and their effects on humans is to observe the responses of rodents exposed to various doses of the substance over time. In the *Journal of Agricultural, Biological, and Environmental Statistics* (June 2005), researchers used least squares regression to estimate the *change-point* dosage—defined as the largest dose level that has no adverse effects. Data were obtained from a dose-response study of rats exposed to the toxic substance aconiazide. A sample of 50 rats was evenly divided into five dosage groups: 0, 100, 200, 500, and 750 milligrams per kilogram of body weight. The dependent variable y measured was the weight change (in grams) after a 2-week exposure. The researchers fit the quadratic model $E(y) = \beta_0 + \beta_1 x + \beta_2 x^2$, where x = dosage level, with the following results: $\hat{y} = 10.25 + .0053x - .0000266x^2$.

a. Construct a rough sketch of the least squares prediction equation. Describe the nature of the curvature in the estimated model.

b. Estimate the weight change (y) for a rat given a dosage of 500 mg/kg of aconiazide.

c. Estimate the weight change (y) for a rat given a dosage of 0 mg/kg of aconiazide. (This dosage is called the *control* dosage level.)

d. Of the five dosage groups in the study, find the largest dosage level x that yields an estimated weight change that is closest to but below the estimated weight change for the control group. This value is the *change-point* dosage.

12.161 Modeling peak-hour roadway traffic. Traffic forecasters at the Minnesota Department of Transportation (MDOT) use regression analysis to estimate weekday peak-hour

MNDOT

traffic volumes on existing and proposed roadways. In particular, they model y, the peak-hour volume (typically, the volume between 7:00 and 8:00 A.M.), as a function of x_1, the road's total volume for the day. For one project involving the redesign of a section of Interstate 494, the forecasters collected $n = 72$ observations of peak-hour traffic volume and 24-hour weekday traffic volume using electronic sensors that count vehicles. The data are saved in the file. (The first and last five observations are listed in the table.)

Observation Number	Peak-Hour Volume	24-Hour Volume	I-35
1	1,990.94	20,070	0
2	1,989.63	21,234	0
3	1,986.96	20,633	0
4	1,986.96	20,676	0
5	1,983.78	19,818	0
⋮	⋮	⋮	⋮
68	2,147.93	22,948	1
69	2,147.85	23,551	1
70	2,144.23	21,637	1
71	2,142.41	23,543	1
72	2,137.39	22,594	1

Source: Traffic and Commodities Studies Section, Minnesota Department of Transportation, St. Paul, Minnesota.

a. Construct a scatterplot for the data, plotting peak-hour volume y against 24-hour volume x_1. Note the isolated group of observations at the top of the scatterplot. Investigators discovered that all of these data points were collected at the intersection of Interstate 35W and 46th Street. (These are observations 55–72 in the table.) While all other locations in the sample were three-lane highways, this location was unique in that the highway widens to four lanes just north of the electronic sensor. Consequently, the forecasters decided to include a dummy variable to account for a difference between the I-35W location and all other locations.

b. Knowing that peak-hour traffic volumes have a theoretical upper bound, the forecasters hypothesized that a second-order model should be used to explain the variation in y. Propose a complete second-order model for $E(y)$ as a function of 24-hour volume x_1 and the dummy variable for location.

c. Using an available statistical software package, fit the model of part b to the data. Interpret the results. Specifically, is the curvilinear relationship between peak-hour volume and 24-hour volume different at the two locations?

d. Conduct a residual analysis of the model, part **b**. Evaluate the assumptions of normality and constant error variance and determine whether any outliers exist.

12.162 Improving Math SAT scores. Refer to the *Chance* (Winter 2001) study of students who paid a private tutor (or coach) to help them improve their Scholastic Assessment Test (SAT) scores, Exercise 2.88 (p. 113). Multiple regression was used to estimate the effect of coaching on SAT–Mathematics scores. Data on 3,492 students (573 of whom were coached) were used to fit the model, $E(y) = \beta_0 + \beta_1 x_1 + \beta_2 x_2$, where

$y = $ SAT–Math score, $x_1 = $ score on PSAT, and $x_2 = \{1$ if student was coached, 0 if not$\}$.

a. The fitted model had an adjusted R^2-value of .76. Interpret this result.

b. The estimate of β_2 in the model was 19, with a standard error of 3. Use this information to form a 95% confidence interval for β_2. Interpret the interval.

c. Based on the interval, part **b**, what can you say about the effect of coaching on SAT–Math scores?

d. As an alternative model, the researcher added several "control" variables, including dummy variables for student ethnicity (x_3, x_4, and x_5), a socioeconomic status index variable (x_6), two variables that measured high school performance (x_7 and x_8), the number of math courses taken in high school (x_9), and the overall GPA for the math courses (x_{10}). Write the hypothesized equation for $E(y)$ for the alternative model.

e. Give the null hypothesis for a nested model F-test comparing the initial and alternative models.

f. The nested model F-test, part **e**, was statistically significant at $\alpha = .05$. Practically interpret this result.

g. The alternative model, part **d**, resulted in $R_a^2 = .79$, $\hat{\beta}_2 = 14$, and $s_{\hat{\beta}_2} = 3$. Interpret the value of R_a^2.

h. Refer to part **g**. Find and interpret a 95% confidence interval for β_2.

i. The researcher concluded that "the estimated effect of SAT coaching decreases from the baseline model when control variables are added to the model." Do you agree? Justify your answer.

j. As a modification to the model of part **d**, the researcher added all possible interactions between the coaching variable (x_2) and the other independent variables in the model. Write the equation for $E(y)$ for this modified model.

k. Give the null hypothesis for comparing the models, parts **d** and **j**. How would you perform this test?

12.163 Impact of advertising on market share. The audience for a product's advertising can be divided into four segments according to the degree of exposure received as a result of the advertising. These segments are groups of consumers who receive very high (VH), high (H), medium (M), or low (L) exposure to the advertising. A company is interested in exploring whether its advertising effort affects its product's market share. Accordingly, the company identifies 24 sample groups of consumers who have been exposed to its advertising, six groups at each exposure level. Then, the company determines its product's market share within each group.

Market Share within Group	Exposure Level	Market Share within Group	Exposure Level
10.1	L	12.2	H
10.3	L	12.1	H
10.0	L	11.8	H
10.3	L	12.6	H
10.2	L	11.9	H
10.5	L	12.9	H
10.6	M	10.7	VH
11.0	M	10.8	VH
11.2	M	11.0	VH
10.9	M	10.5	VH
10.8	M	10.8	VH
11.0	M	10.6	VH

a. Write a regression model that expresses the company's market share as a function of advertising exposure level. Define all terms in your model and list any assumptions you make about them.

b. Did you include interaction terms in your model? Why or why not?

c. The data in the table (previous page) were obtained by the company. Fit the model in part **a** to the data.

d. Is there evidence to suggest that the firm's expected market share differs for different levels of advertising exposure? Test using $\alpha = .05$.

12.164 Comparing mosquito repellents. Which insect repellents protect best against mosquitoes? *Consumer Reports* (June 2000) tested 14 products that all claim to be an effective mosquito repellent. Each product was classified as either lotion/cream or aerosol/spray. The cost of the product (in dollars) was divided by the amount of the repellent needed to cover exposed areas of the skin (about 1/3 ounce) to obtain a cost-per-use value. Effectiveness was measured as the maximum number of hours of protection (in half-hour increments) provided when human testers exposed their arms to 200 mosquitoes. The data from the report are listed in the table.

Insect Repellent	Type	Cost/Use	Maximum Protection
Amway Hour Guard 12	Lotion/Cream	$2.08	13.5 hours
Avon Skin-So-Soft	Aerosol/Spray	0.67	0.5
Avon BugGuard Plus	Lotion/Cream	1.00	2.0
Ben's Backyard Formula	Lotion/Cream	0.75	7.0
Bite Blocker	Lotion/Cream	0.46	3.0
BugOut	Aerosol/Spray	0.11	6.0
Cutter Skinsations	Aerosol/Spray	0.22	3.0
Cutter Unscented	Aerosol/Spray	0.19	5.5
Muskoll Ultra6Hours	Aerosol/Spray	0.24	6.5
Natrapel	Aerosol/Spray	0.27	1.0
Off! Deep Woods	Aerosol/Spray	1.77	14.0
Off! Skintastic	Lotion/Cream	0.67	3.0
Sawyer Deet Formula	Lotion/Cream	0.36	7.0
Repel Permanone	Aerosol/Spray	2.75	24.0

Source: Based on "Buzz off and Insect Repellants: Which Keep Bugs at Bay?" *Consumer Reports*, June 2000.

a. Suppose you want to use repellent type to model the cost per use (y). Create the appropriate number of dummy variables for repellent type and write the model.

b. Fit the model, part a, to the data.

c. Give the null hypothesis for testing whether repellent type is a useful predictor of cost per use (y).

d. Conduct the test, part **c**, and give the appropriate conclusion. Use $\alpha = .10$.

e. Repeat parts **a–d** if the dependent variable is the maximum number of hours of protection (y).

12.165 Forecasting daily admission of a water park. To determine whether extra personnel are needed for the day, the owners of a water adventure park would like to find a model that would allow them to predict the day's

attendance each morning before opening based on the day of the week and weather conditions. The model is of the form

$$E(y) = \beta_0 + \beta_1 x_1 + \beta_2 x_2 + \beta_3 x_3$$

where

y = Daily admission

$$x_1 = \begin{cases} 1 & \text{if weekend} \\ 0 & \text{otherwise} \end{cases} \quad \text{(dummy variable)}$$

$$x_2 = \begin{cases} 1 & \text{if sunny} \\ 0 & \text{if overcast} \end{cases} \quad \text{(dummy variable)}$$

x_3 = predicted daily high temperature (°F)

These data were recorded for a random sample of 30 days, and a regression model was fitted to the data. The least squares analysis produced the following results:

$$\hat{y} = -105 + 25x_1 + 100x_2 + 10x_3$$

with

$$s_{\hat{\beta}_1} = 10 \quad s_{\hat{\beta}_2} = 30 \quad s_{\hat{\beta}_3} = 4 \quad R^2 = .65$$

a. Interpret the estimated model coefficients.

b. Is there sufficient evidence to conclude that this model is useful for the prediction of daily attendance? Use $\alpha = .05$.

c. Is there sufficient evidence to conclude that the mean attendance increases on weekends? Use $\alpha = .10$.

d. Use the model to predict the attendance on a sunny weekday with a predicted high temperature of 95°F.

e. Suppose the 90% prediction interval for part **d** is (645, 1,245). Interpret this interval.

12.166 Forecasting daily admission of a water park (cont'd). Refer to Exercise 12.165. The owners of the water adventure park are advised that the prediction model could probably be improved if interaction terms were added. In particular, it is thought that the *rate* at which mean attendance increases as predicted high temperature increases will be greater on weekends than on weekdays. The following model is therefore proposed:

$$E(y) = \beta_0 + \beta_1 x_1 + \beta_2 x_2 + \beta_3 x_3 + \beta_4 x_1 x_3$$

The same 30 days of data used in Exercise 12.165 are again used to obtain the least squares model

$$\hat{y} = 250 - 700x_1 + 100x_2 + 5x_3 + 15x_1 x_3$$

with

$$s_{\hat{\beta}_4} = 3.0 \quad R^2 = .96$$

a. Graph the predicted day's attendance, y, against the day's predicted high temperature, x_3, for a sunny weekday and for a sunny weekend day. Plot both on the same graph for x_3 between 70°F and 100°F. Note the increase in slope for the weekend day. Interpret this.

b. Do the data indicate that the interaction term is a useful addition to the model? Use $\alpha = .05$.

c. Use this model to predict the attendance for a sunny weekday with a predicted high temperature of 95°F.

d. Suppose the 90% prediction interval for part **c** is (800, 850). Compare this result with the prediction interval for the model without interaction in Exercise 12.165, part **e**. Do the relative widths of the confidence intervals support or refute your conclusion about the utility of the interaction term (part **b**)?

e. The owners, noting that the coefficient $\hat{\beta}_1 = -700$, conclude the model is ridiculous because it seems to imply that the mean attendance will be 700 less on weekends than on weekdays. Explain why this is *not* the case.

12.167 Sale prices of apartments. A Minneapolis, Minnesota, real estate appraiser used regression analysis to explore the relationship between the sale prices of apartment buildings and various characteristics of the buildings. The file contains data for a random sample of 25 apartment buildings. *Note:* Physical condition of each apartment building is coded E (excellent), G (good), or F (fair). Data for selected observations are shown in the table below.

a. Write a model that describes the relationship between sale price and number of apartment units as three parallel lines, one for each level of physical condition. Be sure to specify the dummy variable coding scheme you use.

b. Plot y against x_1 (number of apartment units) for all buildings in excellent condition. On the same graph, plot y against x_1 for all buildings in good condition. Do this again for all buildings in fair condition. Does it appear that the model you specified in part **a** is appropriate? Explain.

c. Fit the model from part **a** to the data. Report the least squares prediction equation for each of the three building condition levels.

d. Plot the three prediction equations of part **c** on a scatterplot of the data.

e. Do the data provide sufficient evidence to conclude that the relationship between sale price and number of units differs depending on the physical condition of the apartments? Test using $\alpha = .05$.

f. Check the data set for multicollinearity. How does this impact your choice of independent variables to use in a model for sale price?

g. Conduct a complete residual analysis for the model to check the assumptions on ε.

12.168 Volatility of foreign stocks. The relationship between country credit ratings and the volatility of the countries' stock markets was examined in the *Journal of Portfolio Management* (Spring 1996). The researchers point out that this volatility can be explained by two factors: the countries' credit ratings and whether the countries in question have developed or emerging markets. Data on the volatility (measured as the standard deviation of stock returns), credit rating (measured as a percentage), and market type (developed or emerging) for a sample of 30 fictitious countries are saved in the file. (Selected observations are shown in the table below.)

a. Write a model that describes the relationship between volatility (y) and credit rating (x_1) as two nonparallel lines, one for each type of market. Specify the dummy variable coding scheme you use.

b. Plot volatility y against credit rating x_1 for all the developed markets in the sample. On the same graph, plot y against x_1 for all emerging markets in the sample. Does it appear that the model specified in part a is appropriate? Explain.

c. Fit the model, part **a**, to the data using a statistical software package. Report the least squares prediction equation for each of the two types of markets.

d. Plot the two prediction equations of part **c** on a scatterplot of the data.

e. Is there evidence to conclude that the slope of the linear relationship between volatility y and credit rating x_1 depends on market type? Test using $\alpha = .01$.

Country	Volatility (standard deviation of return), y	Credit Rating, x_1	Developed (D) or Emerging (E), x_2
1	56.9	9.5	E
2	25.1	72.4	D
3	28.4	58.2	E
4	56.2	9.9	E
5	21.5	92.1	D
:	:	:	:
26	47.5	16.9	E
27	22.0	89.0	D
28	21.5	91.9	D
29	38.1	30.7	E
30	37.4	32.2	E

Data for Exercise 12.167 (selected observations)

Code No.	Sale Price, y ($)	No. of Apartments, x_1	Age of Structure, x_2 (years)	Lot Size, x_3 (sq. ft.)	No. of On-Site Parking Spaces, x_4	Gross Building Area, x_5 (sq. ft.)	Condition of Apartment Building
0229	90,300	4	82	4,635	0	4,266	F
0094	384,000	20	13	17,798	0	14,391	G
0043	157,500	5	66	5,913	0	6,615	G
0079	676,200	26	64	7,750	6	34,144	E
0134	165,000	5	55	5,150	0	6,120	G
:	:	:	:	:	:	:	:
0019	93,600	4	82	6,864	0	3,840	F
0074	110,000	4	50	4,510	0	3,092	G
0057	573,200	14	10	11,192	0	23,704	E
0104	79,300	4	82	7,425	0	3,876	F
0024	272,000	5	82	7,500	0	9,542	E

Source: Robinson Appraisal Co., Inc., Mankato, Minnesota.

12.169 Forecasting a job applicant's merit rating. A large research and development firm rates the performance of each member of its technical staff on a scale of 0 to 100, and this merit rating is used to determine the size of the person's pay raise for the coming year. The firm's personnel department is interested in developing a regression model to help them forecast the merit rating that an applicant for a technical position will receive after being employed 3 years. The firm proposes to use the following second-order model to forecast the merit ratings of applicants who have just completed their graduate studies and have no prior related job experience:

$$E(y) = \beta_0 + \beta_1 x_1 + \beta_2 x_2 + \beta_3 x_1 x_2 + \beta_4 x_1^2 + \beta_5 x_2^2$$

where

y = Applicant's merit rating after 3 years
x_1 = Applicant's GPA in graduate school
x_2 = Applicant's total score (verbal plus quantitative) on the Graduate Record Examination (GRE)

The model, fit to data collected for a random sample of $n = 40$ employees, resulted in SSE = 1,830.44 and SS(model) = 4,911.5. The reduced model $E(y) = \beta_0 + \beta_1 x_1 + \beta_2 x_2$ is also fit to the same data, resulting in SSE = 3,197.16.

a. Identify the appropriate null and alternative hypotheses to test whether the complete (second-order) model contributes information for the prediction of y.

b. Conduct the test of hypothesis given in part **a**. Test using $\alpha = .05$. Interpret the results in the context of this problem.

c. Identify the appropriate null and alternative hypotheses to test whether the complete model contributes more information than the reduced (first-order) model for the prediction of y.

d. Conduct the test of hypothesis given in part **c**. Test using $\alpha = .05$. Interpret the results in the context of this problem.

e. Which model, if either, would you use to predict y? Explain.

12.170 Household food consumption. The data in the table below were collected for a random sample of 26 households in Washington, D.C. An economist wants to relate DCFOOD

household food consumption, y, to household income, x_1, and household size, x_2, with the first-order model

$$E(y) = \beta_0 + \beta_1 x_1 + \beta_2 x_2$$

a. Fit the model to the data. Do you detect any signs of multicollinearity in the data? Explain.

b. Is there visual evidence (from a residual plot) that a second-order model may be more appropriate for predicting household food consumption? Explain.

c. Comment on the assumption of constant error variance, using a residual plot. Does it appear to be satisfied?

d. Are there any outliers in the data? If so, identify them.

e. Based on a graph of the residuals, does the assumption of normal errors appear to be reasonably satisfied? Explain.

12.171 State casket sales restrictions. Refer to the *Journal of Law and Economics* (February 2008) study of the impact of lifting casket sales restrictions on the cost of a funeral, Exercise 12.123 (p. 803). Recall that data collected for a sample of 1,437 funerals were used to fit the model, $E(y) = \beta_0 + \beta_1 x_1 + \beta_2 x_2 + \beta_3 x_1 x_2$, where y is the price (in dollars) of a direct burial, $x_1 = \{1$ if funeral home is in a restricted state, 0 if not$\}$, and $x_2 = \{1$ if price includes a basic wooden casket, 0 if no casket$\}$. The estimated equation (with standard errors in parentheses) is:

$$\hat{y} = 1,432 + 793x_1 - 252x_2 + 261x_1x_2, R^2 = .78$$
$$\quad\quad\quad (70) \quad\quad (134) \quad\quad (109)$$

a. Interpret the reported value of R^2.

b. Use the value of R^2 to compute the F-statistic for testing the overall adequacy of the model. Test at $\alpha = .05$.

c. Compute the predicted price of a direct burial with a basic wooden casket for a funeral home in a restrictive state.

d. Estimate the difference between the mean price of a direct burial with a basic wooden casket and the mean price of a burial with no casket for a funeral home in a restrictive state.

e. Estimate the difference between the mean price of a direct burial with a basic wooden casket and the mean price of a burial with no casket for a funeral home in a nonrestrictive state.

Data for Exercise 12.170

Household	Food Consumption ($1,000s)	Income ($1,000s)	Household Size	Household	Food Consumption ($1,000s)	Income ($1,000s)	Household Size
1	4.2	41.1	4	14	4.1	95.2	2
2	3.4	30.5	2	15	5.5	45.6	9
3	4.8	52.3	4	16	4.5	78.5	3
4	2.9	28.9	1	17	5.0	20.5	5
5	3.5	36.5	2	18	4.5	31.6	4
6	4.0	29.8	4	19	2.8	39.9	1
7	3.6	44.3	3	20	3.9	38.6	3
8	4.2	38.1	4	21	3.6	30.2	2
9	5.1	92.0	5	22	4.6	48.7	5
10	2.7	36.0	1	23	3.8	21.2	3
11	4.0	76.9	3	24	4.5	24.3	7
12	2.7	69.9	1	25	4.0	26.9	5
13	5.5	43.1	7	26	7.5	7.3	5

f. Is there sufficient evidence to indicate that the difference between the mean price of a direct burial with a basic wooden casket and the mean price of a burial with no casket depends on whether the funeral home is in a restrictive state? Test using $\alpha = .05$.

Applying the Concepts—Advanced

12.172 Modeling monthly collision claims. A medium-sized automobile insurance company is interested in developing a regression model to help predict the monthly collision claims of its policyholders. A company analyst has proposed modeling monthly collision claims (y) in the Middle Atlantic states as a function of the percentage of claims by drivers under age 30 (x_1) and the average daily temperature during the month (x_2). She believes that as the percentage of claims by drivers under age 30 increases, claims will rise because younger drivers are usually involved in more serious accidents than older drivers. She also believes that claims will rise as the average daily temperature decreases because lower temperatures are associated with icy, hazardous driving conditions. In order to develop a preliminary model, data were collected for the state of New Jersey over a 3-year period. The data are saved in the file. (The first and last five observations are listed in the table below.)

a. Use a statistical software package to fit the complete second-order model

$$E(y) = \beta_0 + \beta_1 x_1 + \beta_2 x_2 + \beta_3 x_1 x_2 + \beta_4 x_1^2 + \beta_5 x_2^2$$

b. Test the hypothesis $H_0: \beta_4 = \beta_5 = 0$ using $\alpha = .05$. Interpret the results in practical terms.

c. Do the results support the analysts' beliefs? Explain. (You may need to conduct further tests of hypotheses to answer this question.)

12.173 Developing a model for college GPA. Many colleges and universities develop regression models for predicting the GPA of incoming freshmen. This predicted GPA can then be used to make admission decisions. Although most models use many independent variables to predict GPA, we will illustrate by choosing two variables:

x_1 = Verbal score on college entrance examination (percentile)

x_2 = Mathematics score on college entrance examination (percentile)

The file contains data on these variables for a random sample of 40 freshmen at one college. (Selected observations are shown in the table.) Use the data to develop a useful prediction equation for college freshman GPA (y). Be sure to conduct a residual analysis for the model.

Verbal, x_1	Mathematics, x_2	GPA, y
81	87	3.49
68	99	2.89
57	86	2.73
100	49	1.54
54	83	2.56
⋮	⋮	⋮
74	67	2.83
87	93	3.84
90	65	3.01
81	76	3.33
84	69	3.06

Critical Thinking Challenge

12.174 IQs and *The Bell Curve*. *The Bell Curve* (Free Press, 1994), written by Richard Herrnstein and Charles Murray (H&M), is a controversial book about race, genes, IQ, and economic mobility. The book heavily employs statistics and statistical methodology in an attempt to support the authors' positions on the relationships among these variables and their social consequences. The main theme of *The Bell Curve* can be summarized as follows:

(1) Measured intelligence (IQ) is largely genetically inherited.
(2) IQ is correlated positively with a variety of socioeconomic status success measures, such as prestigious job, high annual income, and high educational attainment.
(3) From 1 and 2, it follows that socioeconomic successes are largely genetically caused and therefore resistant to educational and environmental interventions (such as affirmative action).

The statistical methodology (regression) employed by the authors and the inferences derived from the statistics were critiqued in *Chance* (Summer 1995) and *The Journal of the American Statistical Association* (December 1995). The following are just a few of the problems with H&M's use of regression that are identified:

Data for Exercise 12.172 (first and last 5 months)

Month	Monthly Collision Claims, y ($)	Percentage of Monthly Claimants Under the Age of 30, x_1	Newark, N.J., Average Daily Temperature During the Month, x_2 (°F)
1	116,250	50.0	31.5
2	217,180	60.8	33.0
3	43,436	45.1	45.0
4	159,265	56.4	53.9
5	130,308	53.3	63.9
⋮	⋮	⋮	⋮
44	136,528	53.1	76.6
45	193,608	59.8	68.6
46	38,722	45.6	62.4
47	212,309	63.9	50.0
48	118,796	52.3	42.3

Source: New Jersey Department of Insurance; *Weather of U.S. Cities*, 4th ed., Gale Research Inc., Detroit, copyright 1992.

Problem 1 H&M consistently use a trio of independent variables—IQ, socioeconomic status, and age—in a series of first-order models designed to predict dependent social outcome variables such as income and unemployment. (Only on a single occasion are interaction terms incorporated.) Consider, for example, the model

$$E(y) = \beta_0 + \beta_1 x_1 + \beta_2 x_2 + \beta_3 x_3$$

where y = income, x_1 = IQ, x_2 = socioeconomic status, and x_3 = age. H&M employ t-tests on the individual β parameters to assess the importance of the independent variables. As with most of the models considered in *The Bell Curve*, the estimate of β_1 in the income model is positive and statistically significant at $\alpha = .05$, and the associated t-value is larger (in absolute value) than the t-values associated with the other independent variables. Consequently, *H&M claim that IQ is a better predictor of income than the other two independent variables.* No attempt was made to determine whether the model was properly specified or whether the model provides an adequate fit to the data.

Problem 2 In an appendix, the authors describe multiple regression as a "mathematical procedure that yields coefficients for each of [the independent variables], indicating how much of a change in [the dependent variable] can be anticipated for a given change in any particular [independent] variable, with all the others held constant." Armed with this information and the fact that the estimate of β_1 in the model above is positive, *H&M infer that a high IQ necessarily implies (or causes) a high income, and a low IQ inevitably leads to a low income.*

(Cause-and-effect inferences like this are made repeatedly throughout the book.)

Problem 3 The title of the book refers to the normal distribution and its well-known "bell-shaped" curve. There is a misconception among the general public that scores on intelligence tests (IQ) are normally distributed. In fact, most IQ scores have distributions that are decidedly skewed. Traditionally, psychologists and psychometricians have transformed these scores so that the resulting numbers have a precise normal distribution. H&M make a special point to do this. Consequently, *the measure of IQ used in all the regression models is normalized (i.e., transformed so that the resulting distribution is normal), despite the fact that regression methodology does not require predictor (independent) variables to be normally distributed.*

Problem 4 A variable that is not used as a predictor of social outcome in any of the models in *The Bell Curve* is level of education. H&M purposely omit education from the models, arguing that IQ causes education, not the other way around. Other researchers who have examined H&M's data report that *when education is included as an independent variable in the model, the effect of IQ on the dependent variable (say, income) is diminished.*

a. Comment on each of the problems identified. Why do each of these problems cast a shadow on the inferences made by the authors?

b. Using the variables specified in the model above, describe how you would conduct the multiple regression analysis. (Propose a more complex model and describe the appropriate model tests, including a residual analysis.)

ACTIVITY 12.1   *Insurance Premiums:* **Collecting Data for Several Variables**

Premiums for life insurance, health insurance, homeowners insurance, and car insurance are based on more than one factor. In this activity, you will consider factors that influence the price that an individual pays for insurance and how you might collect data that would be useful in studying insurance premiums. You may wish to look over statements from your own insurance policies to determine how much coverage you have and how much it costs you.

1. Suppose that you host an independent Web site that provides information about insurance coverage and costs. You would like to add a feature to your site where a person answers a few simple questions in order to receive an estimate of what that person should expect to pay for insurance with a major carrier. Pick one type of insurance and determine what five questions you would most like to ask the person in order to prepare an estimate.

2. Use your five questions from Exercise 1 to define five independent variables. What is the dependent variable in this situation? What would a first-order model for this situation look like?

3. The estimates provided on your Web site will be based on a random sample of policies recently purchased through major carriers. Because insurance rates change frequently, your Web site will need to be frequently updated through new samples. Design a sampling method that can easily be repeated as needed. Be specific as to how you will identify people who have recently purchased policies, how you will choose your sample, what data you will gather, and what method you will use to gather the data.

4. Once the data are collected, describe how you will organize them and use them to complete the model in Exercise 3.

ACTIVITY 12.2 Collecting Data and Fitting a Multiple Regression Model

Note: The use of statistical software is required for this project. This is a continuation of the Activity section in Chapter 11, in which you selected three independent variables as predictors of a dependent variable of your choice and obtained at least 25 data values. Now, by means of an available software package, fit the multiple regression model

$$y = \beta_0 + \beta_1 x_1 + \beta_2 x_2 + \beta_3 x_3 + \varepsilon$$

where

y = Dependent variable you chose

x_1 = First independent variable you chose

x_2 = Second independent variable you chose

x_3 = Third independent variable you chose

1. Compare the coefficients $\hat{\beta}_1$, $\hat{\beta}_2$, and $\hat{\beta}_3$ with their corresponding slope coefficients in the Activity of Chapter 11, where you fit three separate straight-line models. How do you account for the differences?

2. Calculate the coefficient of determination, R^2, and conduct the F-test of the null hypothesis $H_0: \beta_1 = \beta_2 = \beta_3 = 0$. What is your conclusion?

3. Check the data for multicollinearity. If multicollinearity exists, how should you proceed?

4. Now increase your list of 3 variables to include approximately 10 that you think would be useful in predicting the dependent variable. With the aid of statistical software, employ a stepwise regression program to choose the important variables among those you have listed. To test your intuition, list the variables in the order you think they will be selected before you conduct the analysis. How does your list compare with the stepwise regression results?

5. After the group of 10 variables has been narrowed to a smaller group of variables by the stepwise analysis, try to improve the model by including interactions and quadratic terms. Be sure to consider the meaning of each interaction or quadratic term before adding it to the model. (A quick sketch can be very helpful.) See if you can systematically construct a useful model for prediction. If you have a large data set, you might want to hold out the last observations to test the predictive ability of your model after it is constructed. (As noted in Section 12.10, using the same data to construct and to evaluate predictive ability can lead to invalid statistical tests and a false sense of security.)

References

Barnett, V., and Lewis, T. *Outliers in Statistical Data.* New York: Wiley, 1978.

Belsley, D. A., Kuh, E., and Welsch, R. E. *Regression Diagnostics: Identifying Influential Data and Sources of Collinearity.* New York: Wiley, 1980.

Chatterjee, S., and Price, B. *Regression Analysis by Example,* 2nd ed. New York: Wiley, 1991.

Draper, N., and Smith, H. *Applied Regression Analysis,* 2nd ed. New York: Wiley, 1981.

Graybill, F. *Theory and Application of the Linear Model.* North Scituate, Mass.: Duxbury, 1976.

Kutner, M., Nachtsheim, C., Neter, J., and Li, W. *Applied Linear Statistical Models,* 5th ed. New York: McGraw-Hill/Irwin, 2005.

Mendenhall, W. *Introduction to Linear Models and the Design and Analysis of Experiments.* Belmont, Calif.: Wadsworth, 1968.

Mendenhall, W., and Sincich, T. *A Second Course in Statistics: Regression Analysis,* 7th ed. Upper Saddle River, N.J.: Prentice Hall, 2011.

Mosteller, F., and Tukey, J. W. *Data Analysis and Regression: A Second Course in Statistics.* Reading, Mass.: Addison-Wesley, 1977.

Rousseeuw, P. J., and Leroy, A. M. *Robust Regression and Outlier Detection.* New York: Wiley, 1987.

Weisberg, S. *Applied Linear Regression,* 2nd ed. New York: Wiley, 1985.

USING TECHNOLOGY

Technology images shown here are taken from SPSS Statistics Professional 23.0, Minitab 17, XLSTAT, and Excel 2016.

Note: Automated commands for generating combinations and permutations are not available in SPSS.

SPSS: Multiple Regression

Step 1 Access the SPSS spreadsheet file that contains the dependent and independent variables.

Step 2 Click on the "Analyze" button on the SPSS menu bar and then click on "Regression" and "Linear," as shown in Figure 12.S.1. The resulting dialog box appears as shown in Figure 12.S.2.

Step 3 Specify the dependent variable in the "Dependent" box and the independent variables in the "Independent(s)" box. [*Note:* If your model includes interaction and/or squared terms, you must create and add these higher-order variables to the SPSS spreadsheet file *prior* to running a regression analysis. You can do this by clicking the "Transform" button on the SPSS main menu and selecting the "Compute" option.]

Step 4 To perform a standard regression analysis, select "Enter" in the "Method" box. To perform a stepwise regression analysis, select "Stepwise" in the "Method" box.

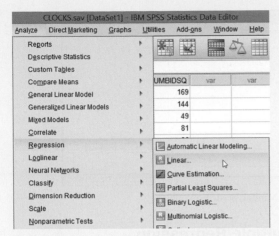

Figure 12.S.1 SPSS menu options for regression

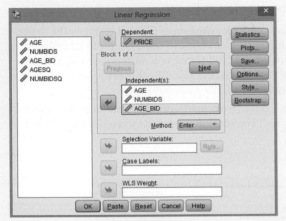

Figure 12.S.2 SPSS linear regression dialog box

Step 5 To perform a nested model F-test for additional model terms, click the "Next" button and enter the terms you want to test in the "Independent(s)" box. [*Note:* These terms, plus the terms you entered initially, form the complete model for the nested F-test.] Next, click the "Statistics" button and select "R squared change." Click "Continue" to return to the main SPSS regression dialog box.

Step 6 To produce confidence intervals for the model parameters, click the "Statistics" button and check the appropriate menu items in the resulting menu list (see Figure 12.S.3).

Step 7 To obtain prediction intervals for y and confidence intervals for $E(y)$, click the "Save" button and check the appropriate

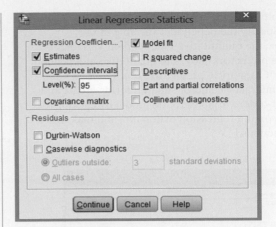

Figure 12.S.3 SPSS linear regression save options

items in the resulting menu list. (The prediction intervals will be added as new columns to the SPSS data spreadsheet.)

Step 8 Residual plots are obtained by clicking the "Plots" button and making the appropriate selections on the resulting menu (see Figure 12.S.4).

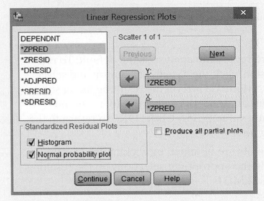

Figure 12.S.4 SPSS linear regression plots options

Step 9 To return to the main Regression dialog box from any of these optional screens, click "Continue." Click "OK" on the Regression dialog box to view the multiple regression results.

Minitab: Multiple Regression

Step 1 Access the Minitab worksheet file that contains the dependent and independent variables.

Step 2 Click on the "Stat" button on the Minitab menu bar and then click on "Regression," "Regression" again and "Fit Regression Model," as shown in Figure 12.M.1.

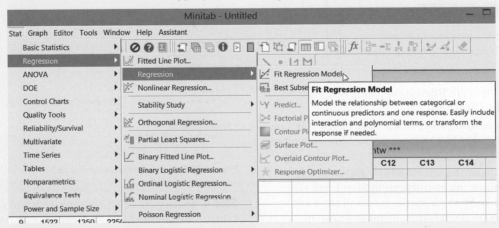

Figure 12.M.1 Minitab menu options for regression

Step 3 The resulting dialog box appears as shown in Figure 12.M.2. Specify the dependent variable in the "Responses" box, the quantitative independent variables in the "Continuous predictors" box, and qualitative independent variables in the "Categorical predictors" box. [*Note:* If your model includes interaction and/or squared terms, create and add these higher-order variables to the model by clicking the "Model" button on the regression dialog box and making the appropriate selections.]

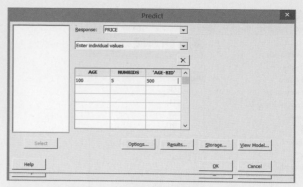

Figure 12.M.4 Minitab prediction options

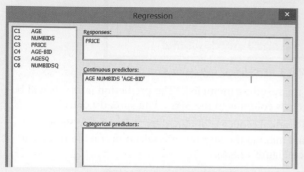

Figure 12.M.2 Minitab regression dialog box

Excel: Multiple Regression

Multiple Regression in Excel

Step 1 Access the Excel worksheet file that contains the dependent and independent variables. [*Note:* If your model includes interaction and/or squared terms, you must create and add these higher-order variables to the Excel worksheet *prior* to running a regression analysis.]

Step 4 A standard regression analysis is the default. To run a stepwise regression, click the "Stepwise" button and select "Stepwise" in the "Method" box on the resulting menu screen. (As an option, you can select the value of α to use in the analysis. The default value is .15.) Click "OK" to return to the Regression dialog box.

Step 5 Residual plots are obtained by clicking the "Graphs" button and making the appropriate selections on the resulting menu (see Figure 12.M.3).

Step 2 Click "Data" from the Excel menu bar and then select "Data Analysis." The resulting menu is shown in Figure 12.E.1.

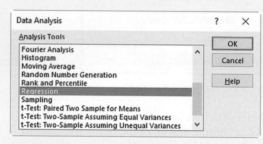

Figure 12.E.1 Excel data analysis menu options for regression

Step 3 Select "Regression" from the drop-down menu and then click "OK." The resulting dialog box is shown in Figure 12.E.2.

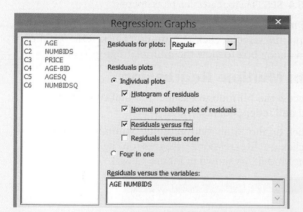

Figure 12.M.3 Minitab regression graphs options

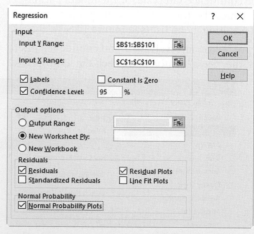

Figure 12.E.2 Excel regression dialog box

Step 6 To return to the main Regression dialog box from any of these optional screens, click "OK."

Step 7 When you have made all your selections, click "OK" on the main Regression dialog box to produce the Minitab multiple regression printout.

Step 8 To produce prediction intervals for y and confidence intervals for $E(y)$, follow the instructions in Step 1, but select "Predict" (see Figure 12.M.1). Enter the values of the x's in the appropriate boxes on the resulting menu as shown in Figure 12.M.4, then click "OK."

Step 4 Specify the cell ranges for the y and x variables in the "Input" area of the Multiple Regression dialog box. [*Note:* The x variables must be in adjacent columns on the Excel worksheet.]

Step 5 Select the confidence level for confidence intervals for the model parameters.

Step 6 To produce graphs of the regression residual, select the "Residual Plots" and "Normal probability plots" options.

Step 7 After making all your selections, click "OK" to produce the multiple regression results.

Multiple Regression with Excel/XLSTAT

Step 1 Within XLSTAT, open the Excel spreadsheet with the data for the dependent and independent variables.

Step 2 Click the "XLSTAT" button on the Excel main menu bar, select "Modeling data," then click "Linear regression," as shown in Figure 12.E.3.

Figure 12.E.3 XLSTAT menu options for multiple regression

Step 3 When the resulting dialog box appears (Figure 12.E.4), enter the column containing the dependent variable in the "Y / Dependent variables" box. Depending on the type of independent variables, check either the "Quantitative" or "Qualitative" option (or both) and then enter the columns containing the independent variables in the appropriate "X / Explanatory variables" boxes.

Figure 12.E.4 XLSTAT dialog box for linear regression

Step 4 To obtain prediction/confidence intervals, select the "Prediction" tab, then enter the column with the values of the independent variables for which you want to make predictions in the "X / Explanatory variables" and "Quantitative" or "Qualitative" boxes, as shown in Figure 12.E.5.

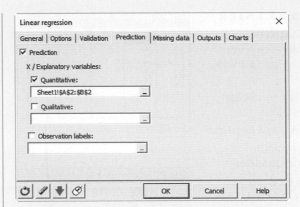

Figure 12.E.5 XLSTAT dialog box for predictions

Step 5 Click "OK," then "Continue" to display the test results.

Stepwise Regression with Excel/XLSTAT

Step 1 Within XLSTAT, open the Excel spreadsheet with the data for the dependent and independent variables.

Step 2 Click the "XLSTAT" button on the Excel main menu bar, select "Modeling data," then click "Linear regression," as shown in Figure 12.E.3.

Step 3 When the resulting dialog box appears (Figure 12.E.4), enter the column containing the dependent variable in the "Y / Dependent variables" box. Depending on the type of independent variables, check either the "Quantitative" or "Qualitative" option (or both) and then enter the columns containing the independent variables in the appropriate "X / Explanatory variables" boxes.

Step 4 Select the "Options" tab, then check the "Stepwise" option under "Model selection," as shown in Figure 12.E.6.

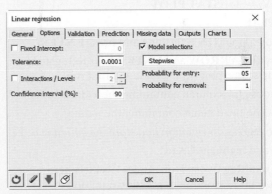

Figure 12.E.6 XLSTAT regression options dialog box

Step 5 Click "OK," then "Continue" to display the stepwise results.

TI-84 Graphing Calculator:

Multiple Regression

Note: Only simple linear and quadratic regression models can be fit using the TI-84 graphing calculator.

Quadratic Regression

I. Finding the quadratic regression equation

Step 1 *Enter the data*

- Press **STAT** and select **1:Edit**

  Note: If a list already contains data, clear the old data. Use the up **ARROW** to highlight "**L1**" or "**L2**."

- Press **CLEAR ENTER**
- Use the **ARROW** and **ENTER** keys to enter the data set into **L1** and **L2**

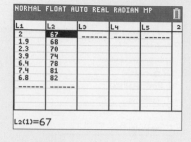

Step 2 *Find the quadratic regression equation*

- Press **STAT** and highlight **CALC**
- Press **5** for **QuadReg**
- Press **ENTER**, arrow down to **CALCULATE**, then press **ENTER** again
- The screen will show the values for a, b, and c in the equation
- If the diagnostics are on, the screen will also give the value for r^2

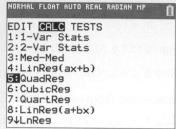

- To turn the diagnostics feature on:
- Press **2nd 0** for **CATALOG**
- Press the **ALPHA** key and x^{-1} for **D**
- Press the down **ARROW** until **DiagnosticsOn** is highlighted
- Press **ENTER** twice

II. Graphing the Quadratic Curve with the Scatterplot

Step 1 *Enter the data as shown in part I above*

Step 2 *Set up the data plot*

- Press **Y =** and **CLEAR** all functions from the Y registers
- Press **2nd Y =** for **STAT PLOT**
- Press **1** for **Plot1**
- Set the cursor so that **ON** is flashing and press **ENTER**
- For **Type**, use the **ARROW** and **ENTER** keys to highlight and select the scatterplot (first icon in the first row)
- For **Xlist**, choose the column containing the *x*-data
- For **Ylist**, choose the column containing the *y*-data

Step 3 *Find the regression equation and store the equation in Y1*

- Press **STAT** and highlight **CALC**
- Press **5** for **QuadReg** (*Note:* Don't press ENTER here because you want to store the regression equation in Y1)
- Arrow down to **Store RegEq**
- Press **VARS**
- Use the right **ARROW** to highlight **Y-VARS**
- Press **ENTER** to select **1:Function**
- Press **ENTER** to select **1:Y1**

QuadReg
y=ax²+bx+c
a=-.1696102447
b=4.038782195
c=60.69357156
R²=.966971885

- Arrow down to **Calculate**, then press **ENTER**

Step 4 *View the scatterplot and regression line*

- Press **ZOOM** and then press **9** to select **9:ZoomStat**

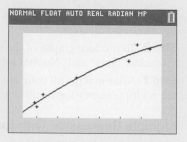

Plotting Residuals

When computing a regression equation on the TI-84, the residuals are automatically computed and saved to a list called **RESID**. **RESID** can be found under the **LIST menu** (**2nd STAT**).

Step 1 *Enter the data*

- Press **STAT** and select **1:Edit**
- *Note:* If the list already contains data, clear the old data. Use the up **ARROW** to highlight "L1" or "L2."
- Press **CLEAR ENTER**
- Use the **ARROW** and **ENTER** keys to enter the data set into **L1** and **L2**

Step 2 *Compute the regression equation*

- Press **STAT** and highlight **CALC**
- Press **4** for **LinReg(ax + b)**
- Press **ENTER**

Step 3 *Set up the data plot*

- Press **Y =** and **CLEAR** all functions from the Y registers
- Press **2nd Y =** for **STATPLOT**
- Press **1** for **Plot1**
- Set the cursor so that **ON** is flashing and press **ENTER**
- For **Type**, use the **ARROW** and **ENTER** keys to highlight and select the scatterplot (first icon in the first row).
- Move the cursor to **Xlist** and choose the column containing the *x*-data
- Move the cursor to **Ylist** and press **2nd STAT** for **LIST**
- Use the down **ARROW** to highlight the list-name **RESID** and press **ENTER**

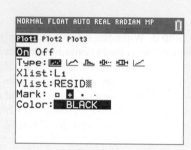

Step 4 *View the scatterplot of the residuals*

- Press **ZOOM 9** for **ZoomStat**

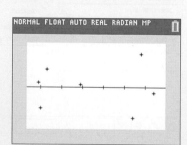

The Condo Sales Case

This case involves an investigation of the factors that affect the sale price of oceanside condominium units. It represents an extension of an analysis of the same data by Herman Kelting. Although condo sale prices have increased dramatically over the past 20 years, the relationship between these factors and sale price remains about the same. Consequently, the data provide valuable insight into today's condominium sales market.

The sales data were obtained for a new oceanside condominium complex consisting of two adjacent and connected eight-floor buildings. The complex contains 200 units of equal size (approximately 500 square feet each). The locations of the buildings relative to the ocean, the swimming pool, the parking lot, etc., are shown in the accompanying figure. There are several features of the complex that you should note:

1. The units facing south, called *ocean view*, face the beach and ocean. In addition, units in building 1 have a good view of the pool. Units to the rear of the building, called *bay-view*, face the parking lot and an area of land that ultimately borders a bay. The view from the upper floors of these units is primarily of wooded, sandy terrain. The bay is very distant and barely visible.

2. The only elevator in the complex is located at the east end of building 1, as are the office and the game room. People moving to or from the higher floor units in building 2 would likely use the elevator and move through the passages to their units. Thus, units on the higher floors and at a greater distance from the elevator would be less convenient; they would require greater effort in moving baggage, groceries, and so on and would be farther away from the game room, the office, and the swimming pool. These units also possess an advantage: there would be the least amount of traffic through the hallways in the area and hence they are the most private.

3. Lower-floor oceanside units are most suited to active people; they open onto the beach, ocean, and pool. They are within easy reach of the game room, and they are easily reached from the parking area.

4. Checking the layout of the condominium complex, you discover that some of the units in the center of the complex, units ending in numbers 11 and 14, have part of their view blocked.

5. The condominium complex was completed at the time of the 1975 recession; sales were slow, and the developer was forced to sell most of the units at auction approximately 18 months after opening. Consequently, the auction data are completely buyer specified and hence consumer oriented in contrast to most other real estate sales

data that are, to a high degree, seller and broker specified.

6. Many unsold units in the complex were furnished by the developer and rented prior to the auction. Consequently, some of the units bid on and sold at auction had furniture; others did not.

This condominium complex is obviously unique. For example, the single elevator located at one end of the complex produces a remarkably high level of both inconvenience and privacy for the people occupying units on the top floors in building 2. Consequently, the developer is unsure of how the height of the unit (floor number), distance of the unit from the elevator, presence or absence of an ocean view, etc., affect the prices of the units sold at auction. To investigate these relationships, the following data (saved in the data file) were recorded for each of the 106 units sold at the auction:

1. *Sale price.* Measured in hundreds of dollars (adjusted for inflation).

2. *Floor height.* The floor location of the unit; the variable levels are 1, 2, . . . , 8.

3. *Distance from elevator.* This distance, measured along the length of the complex, is expressed in number of condominium units. An additional two units of distance was added to the units in building 2 to account for the walking distance in the connecting area between the two buildings. Thus, the distance of unit 105 from the elevator would

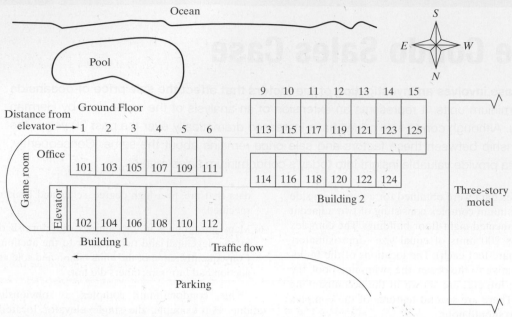

Figure C5.1 Layout of condominium complex

be 3, and the distance between unit 113 and the elevator would be 9. The variable levels are 1, 2, . . . , 15.

4. *View of ocean.* The presence or absence of an ocean view is recorded for each unit and specified with a dummy variable (1 if the unit possesses an ocean view and 0 if not). Note that units not possessing an ocean view face the parking lot.

5. *End unit.* We expect the partial reduction of view of end units on the ocean side (numbers ending in 11) to reduce their sale price. The ocean view of these end units is partially blocked by building 2. This qualitative variable is also specified with a dummy variable (1 if the unit has a unit number ending in 11 and 0 if not).

6. *Furniture.* The presence or absence of furniture is recorded for each unit and is represented with a single dummy variable (1 if the unit was furnished and 0 if not).

Your objective for this case is to build a regression model that accurately predicts the sale price of a condominium unit sold at auction. Prepare a professional document that presents the results of your analysis. Include graphs that demonstrate how each of the independent variables in your model affects auction price. A layout of the data file is described below.

Variable	Type
PRICE	QN
FLOOR	QN
DISTANCE	QN
VIEW	QL
ENDUNIT	QL
FURNISH	QL

(Number of Observations: 106)  *Data Set:* CONDO

Coventry University London

Appendix A: Summation Notation

Denote the measurements of a quantitative data set as follows: $x_1, x_2, x_3, \ldots, x_n$, where x_1 is the first measurement in the data set, x_2 is the second measurement in the data set, x_3 is the third measurement in the data set, $\ldots$, and x_n is the nth (and last) measurement in the data set. Thus, if we have five measurements in a set of data, we will write x_1, x_2, x_3, x_4, x_5 to represent the measurements. If the actual numbers are 5, 3, 8, 5, and 4, we have $x_1 = 5, x_2 = 3, x_3 = 8, x_4 = 5$, and $x_5 = 4$.

Most of the formulas used in this text require a summation of numbers. For example, one sum is the sum of all the measurements in the data set, or $x_1 + x_2 + x_3 + \cdots + x_n$. To shorten the notation, we use the symbol Σ for the summation–that is, $x_1 + x_2 + x_3 + \cdots + x_n = \sum_{i=1}^{n} x_i$. Verbally translate $\sum_{i=1}^{n} x_i$ as follows:

"The sum of the measurements, whose typical member is x_i, beginning with the member x_1 and ending with the member x_n."

Suppose, as in our earlier example, that $x_1 = 5, x_2 = 3, x_3 = 8, x_4 = 5$, and $x_5 = 4$. Then the sum of the five measurements, denoted $\sum_{i=1}^{n} x_i$, is obtained as follows:

$$\sum_{i=1}^{5} x_i = x_1 + x_2 + x_3 + x_4 + x_5$$
$$= 5 + 3 + 8 + 5 + 4 = 25$$

Another important calculation requires that we square each measurement and then sum the squares. The notation for this sum is $\sum_{i=1}^{n} x_i^2$. For the preceding five measurements, we have

$$\sum_{i=1}^{5} x_i^2 = x_1^2 + x_2^2 + x_3^2 + x_4^2 + x_5^2$$
$$= 5^2 + 3^2 + 8^2 + 5^2 + 4^2$$
$$= 25 + 9 + 64 + 25 + 16 = 139$$

In general, the symbol following the summation sign represents the variable (or function of the variable) that is to be summed.

The Meaning of Summation Notation $\sum_{i=1}^{n} x_i$

Sum the measurements on the variable that appears to the right of the summation symbol, beginning with the 1st measurement and ending with the nth measurement.

EXAMPLE A.1
Finding a Sum

Problem A sample data set contains the following six measurements: 5, 1, 3, 0, 2, 1. Find

$$\sum_{i=1}^{n} x_i$$

Solution For these data, the sample size $n = 6$. The measurements are denoted $x_1 = 5$, $x_2 = 1, x_3 = 3, x_4 = 0, x_5 = 2$, and $x_6 = 5$. Then

$$\sum_{i=1}^{n} x_i = x_1 + x_2 + x_3 + x_4 + x_5 + x_6 = 5 + 1 + 3 + 0 + 2 + 1 = 12$$

EXAMPLE A.2

Finding a Sum of Squares

Problem Refer to Example A.1. Find

$$\sum_{i=1}^{n} x_i^2$$

Solution Now we desire the sum of squares of the six measurements.

$$\sum_{i=1}^{n} x_i^2 = x_1^2 + x_2^2 + x_3^2 + x_4^2 + x_5^2 + x_6^2 = 5^2 + 1^2 + 3^2 + 0^2 + 2^2 + 1^2$$

$$= 25 + 1 + 9 + 0 + 4 + 1 = 40$$

EXAMPLE A.3

Finding a Sum of Differences

Problem Refer to Example A.1. Find

$$\sum_{i=1}^{n} (x_i - 2)$$

Solution Here, we subtract 2 from each measurement, then sum the six differences.

$$\sum_{i=1}^{n} (x_i - 2) = (x_1 - 2) + (x_2 - 2) + (x_3 - 2) + (x_4 - 2) + (x_5 - 2) + (x_6 - 2)$$

$$= (5 - 2) + (1 - 2) + (3 - 2) + (0 - 2) + (2 - 2) + (1 - 2)$$

$$= 3 + (-1) + 1 + (-2) + 0 + (-1) = 0$$

Appendix B: Basic Counting Rules

Sample points associated with many experiments have identical characteristics. If you can develop a counting rule to count the number of sample points, it can be used to aid in the solution of many probability problems. For example, many experiments involve sampling n elements from a population of N. Then, as explained in Section 3.1, we can use the formula

$$\binom{N}{n} = \frac{N!}{n!(N-n)!}$$

to find the number of different samples of n elements that could be selected from the total of N elements. This gives the number of sample points for the experiment.

Here, we give you a few useful counting rules. You should learn the characteristics of the situation to which each rule applies. Then, when working a probability problem, carefully examine the experiment to see whether you can use one of the rules.

Learning how to decide whether a particular counting rule applies to an experiment takes patience and practice. If you want to develop this skill, try to use the rules to solve some of the exercises in Chapter 3. Proofs of the rules below can be found in the text by W. Feller listed in the references to Chapter 3.

Multiplicative Rule

You have k sets of different elements, n_1 in the first set, n_2 in the second set, ..., and n_k in the kth set. Suppose you want to form a sample of k elements by *taking one element from each of the* k *sets*. The number of different samples that can be formed is the product

$$n_1 \cdot n_2 \cdot n_3 \cdot \cdots \cdot n_k$$

EXAMPLE B.1

Applying the Multiplicative Rule

Problem A product can be shipped by four airlines, and each airline can ship via three different routes. How many distinct ways exist to ship the product?

Solution A method of shipment corresponds to a pairing of one airline and one route. Therefore, $k = 2$, the number of airlines is $n_1 = 4$, the number of routes is $n_2 = 3$, and the number of ways to ship the product is

$$n_1 \cdot n_2 = (4)(3) = 12$$

Look Back How the multiplicative rule works can be seen by using a tree diagram, introduced in Section 3.6. The airline choice is shown by three branching lines in Figure B.1.

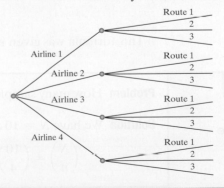

Figure B.1

Tree diagram for airline example

827

EXAMPLE B.2

Applying the Multiplicative Rule

Problem You have 20 candidates for three different executive positions, E_1, E_2, and E_3. How many different ways could you fill the positions?

Solution For this example, there are $k = 3$ sets of elements:

Set 1: The candidates available to fill position E_1
Set 2: The candidates remaining (after filling E_1) that are available to fill E_2
Set 3: The candidates remaining (after filling E_1 and E_2) that are available to fill E_3

The numbers of elements in the sets are $n_1 = 20$, $n_2 = 19$, and $n_3 = 18$. Thus, the number of different ways to fill the three positions is

$$n_1 \cdot n_2 \cdot n_3 = (20)(19)(18) = 6,480$$

Partitions Rule

You have a *single* set of N distinctly different elements, and you want to partition it into k sets, the first set containing n_1 elements, the second containing n_2 elements, ..., and the kth containing n_k elements. The number of different partitions is

$$\frac{N!}{n_1! n_2! \cdot \cdots \cdot n_k!} \quad \text{where } n_1 + n_2 + n_3 + \cdots + n_k = N$$

EXAMPLE B.3

Applying the Partitions Rule

Problem You have 12 construction workers available for 3 job sites. Suppose you want to assign 3 workers to job 1, 4 to job 2, and 5 to job 3. How many different ways could you make this assignment?

Solution For this example, $k = 3$ (corresponding to the $k = 3$ job sites), $N = 12$, and $n_1 = 3$, $n_2 = 4$, $n_3 = 5$. Then the number of different ways to assign the workers to the job sites is

$$\frac{N!}{n_1! n_2! n_3!} = \frac{12!}{3!4!5!} = \frac{12 \cdot 11 \cdot 10 \cdot \cdots \cdot 3 \cdot 2 \cdot 1}{(3 \cdot 2 \cdot 1)(4 \cdot 3 \cdot 2 \cdot 1)(5 \cdot 4 \cdot 3 \cdot 2 \cdot 1)} = 27,720$$

Combinations Rule

The combinations rule given in Chapter 3 is a special case $(k = 2)$ of the partitions rule–that is, sampling is equivalent to partitioning a set of N elements into $k = 2$ groups: elements that appear in the sample and those that do not. Let $n_1 = n$, the number of elements in the sample, and $n_2 = N - n$, the number of elements remaining. Then the number of different samples of n elements that can be selected from N is

$$\frac{N!}{n_1! n_2!} = \frac{N!}{n!(N - n)!} = \binom{N}{n}$$

This formula was given in Section 3.1.

EXAMPLE B.4

Applying the Combinations Rule

Problem How many samples of 4 firefighters can be selected from a group of 10?

Solution We have $N = 10$ and $n = 4$; then

$$\binom{N}{n} = \binom{10}{4} = \frac{10!}{4!6!} = \frac{10 \cdot 9 \cdot 8 \cdot \cdots \cdot 3 \cdot 2 \cdot 1}{(4 \cdot 3 \cdot 2 \cdot 1)(6 \cdot 5 \cdot \cdots \cdot 2 \cdot 1)} = 210$$

Permutations Rule

The permutations rule is a generalization of the combinations rule where the order of the elements selected from the sample is important. (It can also be viewed as a special case of the multiplicative rule.) A particular order is called a *permutation*. The number of different permutations of n elements that can be selected from a population of N elements is

$$\frac{N!}{(N-n)!} = N(N-1)(N-2)\cdots(N-n+1)$$

EXAMPLE B.5

Applying the Permutations Rule

Problem There are three different entrances to a burning building. A fire captain must select three firefighters to enter the building, one for each entrance. The first firefighter selected will enter through the front door, the second through the back door, and the third one through a hole in the roof. How many permutations of three firefighters can be selected from a crew of 10 firefighters?

Solution Here we have $N = 10$ and $n = 3$. Since the order of selection is important, we apply the permutations rule:

$$\frac{N!}{(N-n)!} = \frac{10!}{(10-3)!} = \frac{10!}{7!} = \frac{10\cdot9\cdot8\cdot7\cdot6\cdot5\cdot4\cdot3\cdot2\cdot1}{7\cdot6\cdot5\cdot4\cdot3\cdot2\cdot1} = 10\cdot9\cdot8 = 720$$

Appendix C: Calculation Formulas for Analysis of Variance

C.1   Formulas for the Calculations in the Completely Randomized Design

$$CM = \text{Correction for mean}$$

$$= \frac{(\text{Total of all observations})^2}{\text{Total number of observations}} = \frac{\left(\sum\limits_{i=1}^{n} y_i \right)^2}{n}$$

$$SS(\text{Total}) = \text{Total sum of squares}$$

$$= (\text{Sum of squares of all observations}) - CM = \sum_{i=1}^{n} y_i^2 - CM$$

$$SST = \text{Sum of squares for treatments}$$

$$= \left(\begin{array}{c} \text{Sum of squares of treatment totals with} \\ \text{each square divided by the number of} \\ \text{observations for that treatment} \end{array} \right) - CM$$

$$= \frac{T_1^2}{n_1} + \frac{T_2^2}{n_2} + \cdots + \frac{T_k^2}{n_k} - CM$$

$$SSE = \text{Sum of squares for error} = SS(\text{Total}) - SST$$

$$MST = \text{Mean square for treatments} = \frac{SST}{k-1}$$

$$MSE = \text{Mean square for error} = \frac{SSE}{n-k}$$

$$F = \text{Test statistic} = \frac{MST}{MSE}$$

where

$$n = \text{Total number of observations}$$

$$k = \text{Number of treatments}$$

$$T_i = \text{Total for treatment } i \ (i = 1, 2, \ldots, k)$$

C.2   Formulas for the Calculations in the Randomized Block Design

$$CM = \text{Correction for mean}$$

$$= \frac{(\text{Total of all observations})^2}{\text{Total number of observations}} = \frac{\left(\sum y_i\right)^2}{n}$$

$$SS(\text{Total}) = \text{Total sum of squares}$$

$$= (\text{Sum of squares of all observations}) - CM = \sum y_i^2 - CM$$

$$SST = \text{Sum of squares for treatments}$$

$$= \left(\begin{array}{c}\text{Sum of squares of treatment totals with} \\ \text{each square divided by } b, \text{ the number of} \\ \text{observations for that treatment}\end{array}\right) - CM$$

$$= \frac{T_1^2}{b} + \frac{T_2^2}{b} + \cdots + \frac{T_p^2}{b} - CM$$

$$SST = \text{Sum of squares for blocks}$$

$$= \left(\begin{array}{c}\text{Sum of squares of block totals with} \\ \text{each square divided by } k, \text{ the number} \\ \text{of observations in that block}\end{array}\right) - CM$$

$$= \frac{B_1^2}{k} + \frac{B_2^2}{k} + \cdots + \frac{B_b^2}{k} - CM$$

$$SSE = \text{Sum of squares for error} = SS(\text{Total}) - SST - SSB$$

$$MST = \text{Mean square for treatments} = \frac{SST}{k - 1}$$

$$MSB = \text{Mean square for blocks} = \frac{SSB}{b - 1}$$

$$MSE = \text{Mean square for error} = \frac{SSE}{n - k - b + 1}$$

$$F = \text{Test statistic} = \frac{MST}{MSE}$$

where

$$n = \text{Total number of observations}$$

$$b = \text{Number of blocks}$$

$$k = \text{Number of treatments}$$

$$T_i = \text{Total for treatment } i \ (i = 1, 2, \ldots, k)$$

$$B_i = \text{Total for block } i \ (i = 1, 2, \ldots, b)$$

C.3 Formulas for the Calculations for a Two-Factor Factorial Experiment

$$CM = \text{Correction for mean}$$

$$= \frac{(\text{Total of all } n \text{ measurements})^2}{n} = \frac{\left(\sum_{i=1}^{n} y_i\right)^2}{n}$$

$$SS(\text{Total}) = \text{Total sum of squares}$$

$$= (\text{Sum of squares of all } n \text{ measurements}) - CM = \sum_{i=1}^{n} y_i^2 - CM$$

$$SS(A) = \text{Sum of squares for main effects, factor } A$$

$$= \left(\begin{array}{c} \text{Sum of squares of the totals } A_1, A_2, \ldots, A_a \\ \text{divided by the number of measurements} \\ \text{in a single total, namely } br \end{array} \right) - CM$$

$$= \frac{\sum_{i=1}^{a} A_i^2}{br} - CM$$

$$SS(B) = \text{Sum of squares for main effects, factor } B$$

$$= \left(\begin{array}{c} \text{Sum of squares of the totals } B_1, B_2, \ldots, B_b \\ \text{divided by the number of measurements} \\ \text{in a single total, namely } ar \end{array} \right) - CM$$

$$= \frac{\sum_{i=1}^{b} B_i^2}{ar} - CM$$

$$SS(AB) = \text{Sum of squares for } AB \text{ interaction}$$

$$= \left(\begin{array}{c} \text{Sum of squares of the cell totals} \\ AB_{11}, AB_{12}, \ldots, AB_{ab} \text{ divided by} \\ \text{the number of measurements} \\ \text{in a single total, namely } r \end{array} \right) - SS(A) - SS(B) - CM$$

$$= \frac{\sum_{j=1}^{b} \sum_{i=1}^{a} AB_{ij}^2}{r} - SS(A) - SS(B) - CM$$

$$SSE = \text{Sum of squares for error} = SS(\text{total}) - SS(A) - SS(B) - SS(AB)$$

$$MS(A) = \frac{SS(A)}{a-1} = \text{Mean square for } A$$

$$MS(B) = \frac{SS(B)}{b-1} = \text{Mean square for } B$$

$$MS(AB) = \frac{SS(AB)}{(a-1)(b-1)} = \text{Mean square for } AB$$

$$MSE = \frac{SSE}{ab(r-1)} = \text{Mean square for error}$$

$$F(A) = \text{Test statistic for } A = \frac{MS(A)}{MSE}$$

$$F(B) = \text{Test statistic for } B = \frac{MS(B)}{MSE}$$

$$F(AB) = \text{Test statistic for } AB = \frac{MS(AB)}{MSE}$$

where

a = Number of levels of factor A

b = Number of levels of factor B

r = Number of replicates (observations per treatment)

A_i = Total for level i of factor A ($i = 1, 2, \ldots, a$)

B_j = Total for level j of factor B ($j = 1, 2, \ldots, b$)

AB_{ij} = Total for treatment (i, j), i.e., for ith level of factor A and jth level of factor B

C.4 Tukey's Multiple Comparisons Procedure (Equal Sample Sizes)

Step 1 Select the desired experimentwise error rate, α

Step 2 Calculate

$$\omega = q_\alpha(k, v) \frac{s}{\sqrt{n_t}}$$

where

k = Number of sample means (i.e., number of treatments)

$s = \sqrt{MSE}$

v = Number of degrees of freedom associated with MSE

n_t = Number of observations in each of the k samples (i.e., number of observations per treatment)

$q_\alpha(k, v)$ = Critical value of the Studentized range (Table XV in Appendix D)

Step 3 Calculate and rank the k sample means.

Step 4 Place a bar over those pairs of treatment means that differ by less than ω. A pair of treatments not connected by an overbar (i.e., differing by more than ω) implies a difference in the corresponding population means.

Note: The confidence level associated with all inferences drawn from the analysis is $(1 - \alpha)$.

C.5 Bonferroni Multiple Comparisons Procedure (Pairwise Comparisons)

Step 1 Calculate for each treatment pair (i, j)

$$B_{ij} = t_{\alpha/(2c)} s \sqrt{\frac{1}{n_i} + \frac{1}{n_j}}$$

where

k = Number of sample (treatment) means in the experiment

c = Number of pairwise comparisons

[*Note:* If all pairwise comparisons are to be made, then $c = k(k-1)/2$]

$s = \sqrt{\text{MSE}}$

v = Number of degrees of freedom associated with MSE

n_i = Number of observations in sample for treatment i

n_j = Number of observations in sample for treatment j

$t_{\alpha/(2c)}$ = Critical value of t distribution with v df and tail area $\alpha/(2c)$ (Table III in Appendix D)

Step 2 Rank the sample means and place a bar over any treatment pair (i, j) whose sample means differ by less than B_{ij}. Any pair of means not connected by an overbar implies a difference in the corresponding population means.

Note: The level of confidence associated with all inferences drawn from the analysis is at least $(1 - \alpha)$.

C.6 Scheffé's Multiple Comparisons Procedure (Pairwise Comparisons)

Step 1 Calculate Scheffé's critical difference for each pair of treatments (i, j):

$$S_{ij} = \sqrt{(k-1)(F_\alpha)(\text{MSE})\left(\frac{1}{n_1} + \frac{1}{n_j}\right)}$$

where

k = Number of sample (treatment) means

MSE = Mean squared error

n_i = Number of observations in sample for treatment i

n_j = Number of observations in sample for treatment j

F_α = Critical value of F-distribution with $k - 1$ numerator df and v denominator df (Tables V, VI, VII, and VIII in Appendix D)

v = Number of degrees of freedom associated with MSE

Step 2 Rank the k sample means and place a bar over any treatment pair (i, j) that differs by less than S_{ij}. Any pair of sample means not connected by an overbar implies a difference in the corresponding population means.

Appendix D: Tables

Table I	Binomial Probabilities

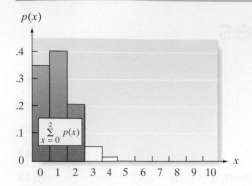

Tabulated values are $\sum_{x=0}^{k} p(x)$. *(Computations are rounded at the third decimal place.)*

a. $n = 5$

p k	.01	.05	.10	.20	.30	.40	.50	.60	.70	.80	.90	.95	.99
0	.951	.774	.590	.328	.168	.078	.031	.010	.002	.000	.000	.000	.000
1	.999	.977	.919	.737	.528	.337	.188	.087	.031	.007	.000	.000	.000
2	1.000	.999	.991	.942	.837	.683	.500	.317	.163	.058	.009	.001	.000
3	1.000	1.000	1.000	.993	.969	.913	.812	.663	.472	.263	.081	.023	.001
4	1.000	1.000	1.000	1.000	.998	.990	.969	.922	.832	.672	.410	.226	.049

b. $n = 6$

p k	.01	.05	.10	.20	.30	.40	.50	.60	.70	.80	.90	.95	.99
0	.941	.735	.531	.262	.118	.047	.016	.004	.001	.000	.000	.000	.000
1	.999	.967	.886	.655	.420	.233	.109	.041	.011	.002	.000	.000	.000
2	1.000	.998	.984	.901	.744	.544	.344	.179	.070	.017	.001	.000	.000
3	1.000	1.000	.999	.983	.930	.821	.656	.456	.256	.099	.016	.002	.000
4	1.000	1.000	1.000	.998	.989	.959	.891	.767	.580	.345	.114	.033	.001
5	1.000	1.000	1.000	1.000	.999	.996	.984	.953	.882	.738	.469	.265	.059

c. $n = 7$

p k	.01	.05	.10	.20	.30	.40	.50	.60	.70	.80	.90	.95	.99
0	.932	.698	.478	.210	.082	.028	.008	.002	.000	.000	.000	.000	.000
1	.998	.956	.850	.577	.329	.159	.063	.019	.004	.000	.000	.000	.000
2	1.000	.996	.974	.852	.647	.420	.227	.096	.029	.005	.000	.000	.000
3	1.000	1.000	.997	.967	.874	.710	.500	.290	.126	.033	.003	.000	.000
4	1.000	1.000	1.000	.995	.971	.904	.773	.580	.353	.148	.026	.004	.000
5	1.000	1.000	1.000	1.000	.996	.981	.937	.841	.671	.423	.150	.044	.002
6	1.000	1.000	1.000	1.000	1.000	.998	.992	.972	.918	.790	.522	.302	.068

d. $n = 8$

p k	.01	.05	.10	.20	.30	.40	.50	.60	.70	.80	.90	.95	.99
0	.923	.663	.430	.168	.058	.017	.004	.001	.000	.000	.000	.000	.000
1	.997	.943	.813	.503	.255	.106	.035	.009	.001	.000	.000	.000	.000
2	1.000	.994	.962	.797	.552	.315	.145	.050	.011	.001	.000	.000	.000
3	1.000	1.000	.995	.944	.806	.594	.363	.174	.058	.010	.000	.000	.000
4	1.000	1.000	1.000	.990	.942	.826	.637	.406	.194	.056	.005	.000	.000
5	1.000	1.000	1.000	.999	.989	.950	.855	.685	.448	.203	.038	.006	.000
6	1.000	1.000	1.000	1.000	.999	.991	.965	.894	.745	.497	.187	.057	.003
7	1.000	1.000	1.000	1.000	1.000	.999	.996	.983	.942	.832	.570	.337	.077

(continued)

Table I	(continued)

e. n = 9

k \ p	.01	.05	.10	.20	.30	.40	.50	.60	.70	.80	.90	.95	.99
0	.914	.630	.387	.134	.040	.010	.002	.000	.000	.000	.000	.000	.000
1	.997	.929	.775	.436	.196	.071	.020	.004	.000	.000	.000	.000	.000
2	1.000	.992	.947	.738	.463	.232	.090	.025	.004	.000	.000	.000	.000
3	1.000	.999	.992	.914	.730	.483	.254	.099	.025	.003	.000	.000	.000
4	1.000	1.000	.999	.980	.901	.733	.500	.267	.099	.020	.001	.000	.000
5	1.000	1.000	1.000	.997	.975	.901	.746	.517	.270	.086	.008	.001	.000
6	1.000	1.000	1.000	1.000	.996	.975	.910	.768	.537	.262	.053	.008	.000
7	1.000	1.000	1.000	1.000	1.000	.996	.980	.929	.804	.564	.225	.071	.003
8	1.000	1.000	1.000	1.000	1.000	1.000	.998	.990	.960	.866	.613	.370	.086

f. n = 10

k \ p	.01	.05	.10	.20	.30	.40	.50	.60	.70	.80	.90	.95	.99
0	.904	.599	.349	.107	.028	.006	.001	.000	.000	.000	.000	.000	.000
1	.996	.914	.736	.376	.149	.046	.011	.002	.000	.000	.000	.000	.000
2	1.000	.988	.930	.678	.383	.167	.055	.012	.002	.000	.000	.000	.000
3	1.000	.999	.987	.879	.650	.382	.172	.055	.011	.001	.000	.000	.000
4	1.000	1.000	.998	.967	.850	.633	.377	.166	.047	.006	.000	.000	.000
5	1.000	1.000	1.000	.994	.953	.834	.623	.367	.150	.033	.002	.000	.000
6	1.000	1.000	1.000	.999	.989	.945	.828	.618	.350	.121	.013	.001	.000
7	1.000	1.000	1.000	1.000	.998	.988	.945	.833	.617	.322	.070	.012	.000
8	1.000	1.000	1.000	1.000	1.000	.998	.989	.954	.851	.624	.264	.086	.004
9	1.000	1.000	1.000	1.000	1.000	1.000	.999	.994	.972	.893	.651	.401	.096

g. n = 15

k \ p	.01	.05	.10	.20	.30	.40	.50	.60	.70	.80	.90	.95	.99
0	.860	.463	.206	.035	.005	.000	.000	.000	.000	.000	.000	.000	.000
1	.990	.829	.549	.167	.035	.005	.000	.000	.000	.000	.000	.000	.000
2	1.000	.964	.816	.398	.127	.027	.004	.000	.000	.000	.000	.000	.000
3	1.000	.995	.944	.648	.297	.091	.018	.002	.000	.000	.000	.000	.000
4	1.000	.999	.987	.838	.515	.217	.059	.009	.001	.000	.000	.000	.000
5	1.000	1.000	.998	.939	.722	.403	.151	.034	.004	.000	.000	.000	.000
6	1.000	1.000	1.000	.982	.869	.610	.304	.095	.015	.001	.000	.000	.000
7	1.000	1.000	1.000	.996	.950	.787	.500	.213	.050	.004	.000	.000	.000
8	1.000	1.000	1.000	.999	.985	.905	.696	.390	.131	.018	.000	.000	.000
9	1.000	1.000	1.000	1.000	.996	.966	.849	.597	.278	.061	.002	.000	.000
10	1.000	1.000	1.000	1.000	.999	.991	.941	.783	.485	.164	.013	.001	.000
11	1.000	1.000	1.000	1.000	1.000	.998	.982	.909	.703	.352	.056	.005	.000
12	1.000	1.000	1.000	1.000	1.000	1.000	.996	.973	.873	.602	.184	.036	.000
13	1.000	1.000	1.000	1.000	1.000	1.000	1.000	.995	.965	.833	.451	.171	.010
14	1.000	1.000	1.000	1.000	1.000	1.000	1.000	1.000	.995	.965	.794	.537	.140

(continued)

Table I   (*continued*)

h. $n = 20$

k \ p	.01	.05	.10	.20	.30	.40	.50	.60	.70	.80	.90	.95	.99
0	.818	.358	.122	.012	.001	.000	.000	.000	.000	.000	.000	.000	.000
1	.983	.736	.392	.069	.008	.001	.000	.000	.000	.000	.000	.000	.000
2	.999	.925	.677	.206	.035	.004	.000	.000	.000	.000	.000	.000	.000
3	1.000	.984	.867	.411	.107	.016	.001	.000	.000	.000	.000	.000	.000
4	1.000	.997	.957	.630	.238	.051	.006	.000	.000	.000	.000	.000	.000
5	1.000	1.000	.989	.804	.416	.126	.021	.002	.000	.000	.000	.000	.000
6	1.000	1.000	.998	.913	.608	.250	.058	.006	.000	.000	.000	.000	.000
7	1.000	1.000	1.000	.968	.772	.416	.132	.021	.001	.000	.000	.000	.000
8	1.000	1.000	1.000	.990	.887	.596	.252	.057	.005	.000	.000	.000	.000
9	1.000	1.000	1.000	.997	.952	.755	.412	.128	.017	.001	.000	.000	.000
10	1.000	1.000	1.000	.999	.983	.872	.588	.245	.048	.003	.000	.000	.000
11	1.000	1.000	1.000	1.000	.995	.943	.748	.404	.113	.010	.000	.000	.000
12	1.000	1.000	1.000	1.000	.999	.979	.868	.584	.228	.032	.000	.000	.000
13	1.000	1.000	1.000	1.000	1.000	.994	.942	.750	.392	.087	.002	.000	.000
14	1.000	1.000	1.000	1.000	1.000	.998	.979	.874	.584	.196	.011	.000	.000
15	1.000	1.000	1.000	1.000	1.000	1.000	.994	.949	.762	.370	.043	.003	.000
16	1.000	1.000	1.000	1.000	1.000	1.000	.999	.984	.893	.589	.133	.016	.000
17	1.000	1.000	1.000	1.000	1.000	1.000	1.000	.996	.965	.794	.323	.075	.001
18	1.000	1.000	1.000	1.000	1.000	1.000	1.000	.999	.992	.931	.608	.264	.017
19	1.000	1.000	1.000	1.000	1.000	1.000	1.000	1.000	.999	.988	.878	.642	.182

i. $n = 25$

k \ p	.01	.05	.10	.20	.30	.40	.50	.60	.70	.80	.90	.95	.99
0	.778	.277	.072	.004	.000	.000	.000	.000	.000	.000	.000	.000	.000
1	.974	.642	.271	.027	.002	.000	.000	.000	.000	.000	.000	.000	.000
2	.998	.873	.537	.098	.009	.000	.000	.000	.000	.000	.000	.000	.000
3	1.000	.966	.764	.234	.033	.002	.000	.000	.000	.000	.000	.000	.000
4	1.000	.993	.902	.421	.090	.009	.000	.000	.000	.000	.000	.000	.000
5	1.000	.999	.967	.617	.193	.029	.002	.000	.000	.000	.000	.000	.000
6	1.000	1.000	.991	.780	.341	.074	.007	.000	.000	.000	.000	.000	.000
7	1.000	1.000	.998	.891	.512	.154	.022	.001	.000	.000	.000	.000	.000
8	1.000	1.000	1.000	.953	.677	.274	.054	.004	.000	.000	.000	.000	.000
9	1.000	1.000	1.000	.983	.811	.425	.115	.013	.000	.000	.000	.000	.000
10	1.000	1.000	1.000	.994	.902	.586	.212	.034	.002	.000	.000	.000	.000
11	1.000	1.000	1.000	.998	.956	.732	.345	.078	.006	.000	.000	.000	.000
12	1.000	1.000	1.000	1.000	.983	.846	.500	.154	.017	.000	.000	.000	.000
13	1.000	1.000	1.000	1.000	.994	.922	.655	.268	.044	.002	.000	.000	.000
14	1.000	1.000	1.000	1.000	.998	.966	.788	.414	.098	.006	.000	.000	.000
15	1.000	1.000	1.000	1.000	1.000	.987	.885	.575	.189	.017	.000	.000	.000
16	1.000	1.000	1.000	1.000	1.000	.996	.946	.726	.323	.047	.000	.000	.000
17	1.000	1.000	1.000	1.000	1.000	.999	.978	.846	.488	.109	.002	.000	.000
18	1.000	1.000	1.000	1.000	1.000	1.000	.993	.926	.659	.220	.009	.000	.000
19	1.000	1.000	1.000	1.000	1.000	1.000	.998	.971	.807	.383	.033	.001	.000
20	1.000	1.000	1.000	1.000	1.000	1.000	1.000	.991	.910	.579	.098	.007	.000
21	1.000	1.000	1.000	1.000	1.000	1.000	1.000	.998	.967	.766	.236	.034	.000
22	1.000	1.000	1.000	1.000	1.000	1.000	1.000	1.000	.991	.902	.463	.127	.002
23	1.000	1.000	1.000	1.000	1.000	1.000	1.000	1.000	.998	.973	.729	.358	.026
24	1.000	1.000	1.000	1.000	1.000	1.000	1.000	1.000	1.000	.996	.928	.723	.222

Table II	Normal Curve Areas

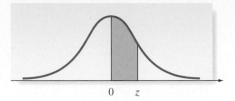

z	.00	.01	.02	.03	.04	.05	.06	.07	.08	.09
.0	.0000	.0040	.0080	.0120	.0160	.0199	.0239	.0279	.0319	.0359
.1	.0398	.0438	.0478	.0517	.0557	.0596	.0636	.0675	.0714	.0753
.2	.0793	.0832	.0871	.0910	.0948	.0987	.1026	.1064	.1103	.1141
.3	.1179	.1217	.1255	.1293	.1331	.1368	.1406	.1443	.1480	.1517
.4	.1554	.1591	.1628	.1664	.1700	.1736	.1772	.1808	.1844	.1879
.5	.1915	.1950	.1985	.2019	.2054	.2088	.2123	.2157	.2190	.2224
.6	.2257	.2291	.2324	.2357	.2389	.2422	.2454	.2486	.2517	.2549
.7	.2580	.2611	.2642	.2673	.2704	.2734	.2764	.2794	.2823	.2852
.8	.2881	.2910	.2939	.2967	.2995	.3023	.3051	.3078	.3106	.3133
.9	.3159	.3186	.3212	.3238	.3264	.3289	.3315	.3340	.3365	.3389
1.0	.3413	.3438	.3461	.3485	.3508	.3531	.3554	.3577	.3599	.3621
1.1	.3643	.3665	.3686	.3708	.3729	.3749	.3770	.3790	.3810	.3830
1.2	.3849	.3869	.3888	.3907	.3925	.3944	.3962	.3980	.3997	.4015
1.3	.4032	.4049	.4066	.4082	.4099	.4115	.4131	.4147	.4162	.4177
1.4	.4192	.4207	.4222	.4236	.4251	.4265	.4279	.4292	.4306	.4319
1.5	.4332	.4345	.4357	.4370	.4382	.4394	.4406	.4418	.4429	.4441
1.6	.4452	.4463	.4474	.4484	.4495	.4505	.4515	.4525	.4535	.4545
1.7	.4554	.4564	.4573	.4582	.4591	.4599	.4608	.4616	.4625	.4633
1.8	.4641	.4649	.4656	.4664	.4671	.4678	.4686	.4693	.4699	.4706
1.9	.4713	.4719	.4726	.4732	.4738	.4744	.4750	.4756	.4761	.4767
2.0	.4772	.4778	.4783	.4788	.4793	.4798	.4803	.4808	.4812	.4817
2.1	.4821	.4826	.4830	.4834	.4838	.4842	.4846	.4850	.4854	.4857
2.2	.4861	.4864	.4868	.4871	.4875	.4878	.4881	.4884	.4887	.4890
2.3	.4893	.4896	.4898	.4901	.4904	.4906	.4909	.4911	.4913	.4916
2.4	.4918	.4920	.4922	.4925	.4927	.4929	.4931	.4932	.4934	.4936
2.5	.4938	.4940	.4941	.4943	.4945	.4946	.4948	.4949	.4951	.4952
2.6	.4953	.4955	.4956	.4957	.4959	.4960	.4961	.4962	.4963	.4964
2.7	.4965	.4966	.4967	.4968	.4969	.4970	.4971	.4972	.4973	.4974
2.8	.4974	.4975	.4976	.4977	.4977	.4978	.4979	.4979	.4980	.4981
2.9	.4981	.4982	.4982	.4983	.4984	.4984	.4985	.4985	.4986	.4986
3.0	.4987	.4987	.4987	.4988	.4988	.4989	.4989	.4989	.4990	.4990
3.1	.49903	.49906	.49910	.49913	.49916	.49918	.49921	.49924	.49926	.48829
3.2	.49931	.49934	.49936	.49938	.49940	.49942	.49944	.49946	.49948	.49950
3.3	.49952	.49953	.49955	.49957	.49958	.49960	.49961	.49962	.49964	.49965
3.4	.49966	.49968	.49969	.49970	.49971	.49972	.49973	.49974	.49975	.49976
3.5	.49977	.49978	.49978	.49979	.49980	.49981	.49981	.49982	.49983	.49983
3.6	.49984	.49985	.49985	.49986	.49986	.49987	.49987	.49988	.49988	.49989
3.7	.49989	.49990	.49990	.49990	.49991	.49991	.49992	.49992	.49992	.49992
3.8	.49993	.49993	.49993	.49994	.49994	.49994	.49994	.49995	.49995	.49995
3.9	.49995	.49995	.49996	.49996	.49996	.49996	.49996	.49996	.49997	.49997

Source: Abridged from Table I of A. Hald. *Statistical Tables and Formulas* (New York: Wiley), 1952.

Table III   **Critical Values of *t***

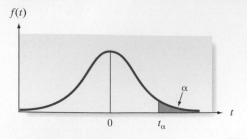

Degrees of Freedom	$t_{.100}$	$t_{.050}$	$t_{.025}$	$t_{.010}$	$t_{.005}$	$t_{.001}$	$t_{.0005}$
1	3.078	6.314	12.706	31.821	63.657	318.31	636.62
2	1.886	2.920	4.303	6.965	9.925	22.326	31.598
3	1.638	2.353	3.182	4.541	5.841	10.213	12.924
4	1.533	2.132	2.776	3.747	4.604	7.173	8.610
5	1.476	2.015	2.571	3.365	4.032	5.893	6.869
6	1.440	1.943	2.447	3.143	3.707	5.208	5.959
7	1.415	1.895	2.365	2.998	3.499	4.785	5.408
8	1.397	1.860	2.306	2.896	3.355	4.501	5.041
9	1.383	1.833	2.262	2.821	3.250	4.297	4.781
10	1.372	1.812	2.228	2.764	3.169	4.144	4.587
11	1.363	1.796	2.201	2.718	3.106	4.025	4.437
12	1.356	1.782	2.179	2.681	3.055	3.930	4.318
13	1.350	1.771	2.160	2.650	3.012	3.852	4.221
14	1.345	1.761	2.145	2.624	2.977	3.787	4.140
15	1.341	1.753	2.131	2.602	2.947	3.733	4.073
16	1.337	1.746	2.120	2.583	2.921	3.686	4.015
17	1.333	1.740	2.110	2.567	2.898	3.646	3.965
18	1.330	1.734	2.101	2.552	2.878	3.610	3.922
19	1.328	1.729	2.093	2.539	2.861	3.579	3.883
20	1.325	1.725	2.086	2.528	2.845	3.552	3.850
21	1.323	1.721	2.080	2.518	2.831	3.527	3.819
22	1.321	1.717	2.074	2.508	2.819	3.505	3.792
23	1.319	1.714	2.069	2.500	2.807	3.485	3.767
24	1.318	1.711	2.064	2.492	2.797	3.467	3.745
25	1.316	1.708	2.060	2.485	2.787	3.450	3.725
26	1.315	1.706	2.056	2.479	2.779	3.435	3.707
27	1.314	1.703	2.052	2.473	2.771	3.421	3.690
28	1.313	1.701	2.048	2.467	2.763	3.408	3.674
29	1.311	1.699	2.045	2.462	2.756	3.396	3.659
30	1.310	1.697	2.042	2.457	2.750	3.385	3.646
40	1.303	1.684	2.021	2.423	2.704	3.307	3.551
50	1.299	1.676	2.009	2.403	2.678	3.261	3.496
60	1.296	1.671	2.000	2.390	2.660	3.232	3.460
70	1.294	1.667	1.994	2.381	2.648	3.211	3.435
80	1.292	1.664	1.990	2.374	2.639	3.195	3.416
90	1.291	1.662	1.987	2.369	2.632	3.183	3.402
100	1.290	1.660	1.984	2.364	2.629	3.174	3.390
120	1.289	1.658	1.980	2.358	2.617	3.160	3.373
150	1.287	1.655	1.976	2.351	2.609	3.145	3.357
∞	1.282	1.645	1.960	2.326	2.576	3.090	3.291

Table IV Critical Values of χ^2

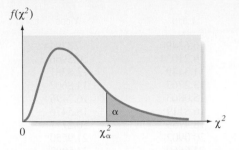

$f(\chi^2)$

Degrees of Freedom	$\chi^2_{.995}$	$\chi^2_{.990}$	$\chi^2_{.975}$	$\chi^2_{.950}$	$\chi^2_{.900}$
1	.0000393	.0001571	.0009821	.0039321	.0157908
2	.0100251	.0201007	.0506356	.102587	.210720
3	.0717212	.114832	.215795	.351846	.584375
4	.206990	.297110	.484419	.710721	1.063623
5	.411740	.554300	.831211	1.145476	1.61031
6	.675727	.872085	1.237347	1.63539	2.20413
7	.989265	1.239043	1.68987	2.16735	2.83311
8	1.344419	1.646482	2.17973	2.73264	3.48954
9	1.734926	2.087912	2.70039	3.32511	4.16816
10	2.15585	2.55821	3.24697	3.94030	4.86518
11	2.60321	3.05347	3.81575	4.57481	5.57779
12	3.07382	3.57056	4.40379	5.22603	6.30380
13	3.56503	4.10691	5.00874	5.89186	7.04150
14	4.07468	4.66043	5.62872	6.57063	7.78953
15	4.60094	5.22935	6.26214	7.26094	8.54675
16	5.14224	5.81221	6.90766	7.96164	9.31223
17	5.69724	6.40776	7.56418	8.67176	10.0852
18	6.26481	7.01491	8.23075	9.39046	10.8649
19	6.84398	7.63273	8.90655	10.1170	11.6509
20	7.43386	8.26040	9.59083	10.8508	12.4426
21	8.03366	8.89720	10.28293	11.5913	13.2396
22	8.64272	9.54249	10.9823	12.3380	14.0415
23	9.26042	10.19567	11.6885	13.0905	14.8479
24	9.88623	10.8564	12.4011	13.8484	15.6587
25	10.5197	11.5240	13.1197	14.6114	16.4734
26	11.1603	12.1981	13.8439	15.3791	17.2919
27	11.8076	12.8786	14.5733	16.1513	18.1138
28	12.4613	13.5648	15.3079	16.9279	18.9392
29	13.1211	14.2565	16.0471	17.7083	19.7677
30	13.7867	14.9535	16.7908	18.4926	20.5992
40	20.7065	22.1643	24.4331	26.5093	29.0505
50	27.9907	29.7067	32.3574	34.7642	37.6886
60	35.5346	37.4848	40.4817	43.1879	46.4589
70	43.2752	45.4418	48.7576	51.7393	55.3290
80	51.1720	53.5400	57.1532	60.3915	64.2778
90	59.1963	61.7541	65.6466	69.1260	73.2912
100	67.3276	70.0648	74.2219	77.9295	82.3581
150	109.142	112.668	117.985	122.692	128.275
200	152.241	156.432	162.728	168.279	174.835
300	240.663	245.972	253.912	260.878	269.068
400	330.903	337.155	346.482	354.641	364.207
500	422.303	429.388	439.936	449.147	459.926

(continued)

Table IV (continued)

Degrees of Freedom	$\chi^2_{.100}$	$\chi^2_{.050}$	$\chi^2_{.025}$	$\chi^2_{.010}$	$\chi^2_{.005}$
1	2.70554	3.84146	5.02389	6.63490	7.87944
2	4.60517	5.99147	7.37776	9.21034	10.5966
3	6.25139	7.81473	9.34840	11.3449	12.8381
4	7.77944	9.48773	11.1433	13.2767	14.8602
5	9.23635	11.0705	12.8325	15.0863	16.7496
6	10.6446	12.5916	14.4494	16.8119	18.5476
7	12.0170	14.0671	16.0128	18.4753	20.2777
8	13.3616	15.5073	17.5346	20.0902	21.9550
9	14.6837	16.9190	19.0228	21.6660	23.5893
10	15.9871	18.3070	20.4831	23.2093	25.1882
11	17.2750	19.6751	21.9200	24.7250	26.7569
12	18.5494	21.0261	23.3367	26.2170	28.2995
13	19.8119	22.3621	24.7356	27.6883	29.8194
14	21.0642	23.6848	26.1190	29.1413	31.3193
15	22.3072	24.9958	27.4884	30.5779	32.8013
16	23.5418	26.2962	28.8454	31.9999	34.2672
17	24.7690	27.5871	30.1910	33.4087	35.7185
18	25.9894	28.8693	31.5264	34.8053	37.1564
19	27.2036	30.1435	32.8523	36.1908	38.5822
20	28.4120	31.4104	34.1696	37.5662	39.9968
21	29.6151	32.6705	35.4789	38.9321	41.4010
22	30.8133	33.9244	36.7807	40.2894	42.7956
23	32.0069	35.1725	38.0757	41.6384	44.1813
24	33.1963	36.4151	39.3641	42.9798	45.5585
25	34.3816	37.6525	40.6465	44.3141	46.9278
26	35.5631	38.8852	41.9232	45.6417	48.2899
27	36.7412	40.1133	43.1944	46.9630	49.6449
28	37.9159	41.3372	44.4607	48.2782	50.9933
29	39.0875	42.5569	45.7222	49.5879	52.3356
30	40.2560	43.7729	46.9792	50.8922	53.6720
40	51.8050	55.7585	59.3417	63.6907	66.7659
50	63.1671	67.5048	71.4202	76.1539	79.4900
60	74.3970	79.0819	83.2976	88.3794	91.9517
70	85.5271	90.5312	95.0231	100.425	104.215
80	96.5782	101.879	106.629	112.329	116.321
90	107.565	113.145	118.136	124.116	128.299
100	118.498	124.342	129.561	135.807	140.169
150	172.578	179.581	185.800	193.208	198.360
200	226.021	233.994	241.058	249.445	255.264
300	331.789	341.395	349.874	359.906	366.844
400	436.649	447.632	457.305	468.724	476.606
500	540.930	553.127	563.852	576.493	585.207

Table V	Percentage Points of the *F*-Distribution, $\alpha = .10$

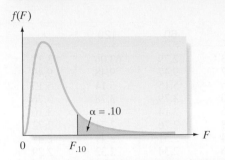

	ν_1	Numerator Degrees of Freedom								
ν_2		1	2	3	4	5	6	7	8	9
	1	39.86	49.50	53.59	55.83	57.24	58.20	58.91	59.44	59.86
	2	8.53	9.00	9.16	9.24	9.29	9.33	9.35	9.37	9.38
	3	5.54	5.46	5.39	5.34	5.31	5.28	5.27	5.25	5.24
	4	4.54	4.32	4.19	4.11	4.05	4.01	3.98	3.95	3.94
	5	4.06	3.78	3.62	3.52	3.45	3.40	3.37	3.34	3.32
	6	3.78	3.46	3.29	3.18	3.11	3.05	3.01	2.98	2.96
	7	3.59	3.26	3.07	2.96	2.88	2.83	2.78	2.75	2.72
	8	3.46	3.11	2.92	2.81	2.73	2.67	2.62	2.59	2.56
	9	3.36	3.01	2.81	2.69	2.61	2.55	2.51	2.47	2.44
	10	3.29	2.92	2.73	2.61	2.52	2.46	2.41	2.38	2.35
	11	3.23	2.86	2.66	2.54	2.45	2.39	2.34	2.30	2.27
	12	3.18	2.81	2.61	2.48	2.39	2.33	2.28	2.24	2.21
	13	3.14	2.76	2.56	2.43	2.35	2.28	2.23	2.20	2.16
	14	3.10	2.73	2.52	2.39	2.31	2.24	2.19	2.15	2.12
	15	3.07	2.70	2.49	2.36	2.27	2.21	2.16	2.12	2.09
	16	3.05	2.67	2.46	2.33	2.24	2.18	2.13	2.09	2.06
	17	3.03	2.64	2.44	2.31	2.22	2.15	2.10	2.06	2.03
	18	3.01	2.62	2.42	2.29	2.20	2.13	2.08	2.04	2.00
	19	2.99	2.61	2.40	2.27	2.18	2.11	2.06	2.02	1.98
	20	2.97	2.59	2.38	2.25	2.16	2.09	2.04	2.00	1.96
	21	2.96	2.57	2.36	2.23	2.14	2.08	2.02	1.98	1.95
	22	2.95	2.56	2.35	2.22	2.13	2.06	2.01	1.97	1.93
	23	2.94	2.55	2.34	2.21	2.11	2.05	1.99	1.95	1.92
	24	2.93	2.54	2.33	2.19	2.10	2.04	1.98	1.94	1.91
	25	2.92	2.53	2.32	2.18	2.09	2.02	1.97	1.93	1.89
	26	2.91	2.52	2.31	2.17	2.08	2.01	1.96	1.92	1.88
	27	2.90	2.51	2.30	2.17	2.07	2.00	1.95	1.91	1.87
	28	2.89	2.50	2.29	2.16	2.06	2.00	1.94	1.90	1.87
	29	2.89	2.50	2.28	2.15	2.06	1.99	1.93	1.89	1.86
	30	2.88	2.49	2.28	2.14	2.05	1.98	1.93	1.88	1.85
	40	2.84	2.44	2.23	2.09	2.00	1.93	1.87	1.83	1.79
	60	2.79	2.39	2.18	2.04	1.95	1.87	1.82	1.77	1.74
	120	2.75	2.35	2.13	1.99	1.90	1.82	1.77	1.72	1.68
	∞	2.71	2.30	2.08	1.94	1.85	1.77	1.72	1.67	1.63

Denominator Degrees of Freedom

(continued)

Table V	(continued)									

ν_2	\multicolumn{10}{c}{Numerator Degrees of Freedom ν_1}
	10	12	15	20	24	30	40	60	120	∞
1	60.19	60.71	61.22	61.74	62.00	62.26	62.53	62.79	63.06	63.33
2	9.39	9.41	9.42	9.44	9.45	9.46	9.47	9.47	9.48	9.49
3	5.23	5.22	5.20	5.18	5.18	5.17	5.16	5.15	5.14	5.13
4	3.92	3.90	3.87	3.84	3.83	3.82	3.80	3.79	3.78	3.76
5	3.30	3.27	3.24	3.21	3.19	3.17	3.16	3.14	3.12	3.10
6	2.94	2.90	2.87	2.84	2.82	2.80	2.78	2.76	2.74	2.72
7	2.70	2.67	2.63	2.59	2.58	2.56	2.54	2.51	2.49	2.47
8	2.54	2.50	2.46	2.42	2.40	2.38	2.36	2.34	2.32	2.29
9	2.42	2.38	2.34	2.30	2.28	2.25	2.23	2.21	2.18	2.16
10	2.32	2.28	2.24	2.20	2.18	2.16	2.13	2.11	2.08	2.06
11	2.25	2.21	2.17	2.12	2.10	2.08	2.05	2.03	2.00	1.97
12	2.19	2.15	2.10	2.06	2.04	2.01	1.99	1.96	1.93	1.90
13	2.14	2.10	2.05	2.01	1.98	1.96	1.93	1.90	1.88	1.85
14	2.10	2.05	2.01	1.96	1.94	1.91	1.89	1.86	1.83	1.80
15	2.06	2.02	1.97	1.92	1.90	1.87	1.85	1.82	1.79	1.76
16	2.03	1.99	1.94	1.89	1.87	1.84	1.81	1.78	1.75	1.72
17	2.00	1.96	1.91	1.86	1.84	1.81	1.78	1.75	1.72	1.69
18	1.98	1.93	1.89	1.84	1.81	1.78	1.75	1.72	1.69	1.66
19	1.96	1.91	1.86	1.81	1.79	1.76	1.73	1.70	1.67	1.63
20	1.94	1.89	1.84	1.79	1.77	1.74	1.71	1.68	1.64	1.61
21	1.92	1.87	1.83	1.78	1.75	1.72	1.69	1.66	1.62	1.59
22	1.90	1.86	1.81	1.76	1.73	1.70	1.67	1.64	1.60	1.57
23	1.89	1.84	1.80	1.74	1.72	1.69	1.66	1.62	1.59	1.55
24	1.88	1.83	1.78	1.73	1.70	1.67	1.64	1.61	1.57	1.53
25	1.87	1.82	1.77	1.72	1.69	1.66	1.63	1.59	1.56	1.52
26	1.86	1.81	1.76	1.71	1.68	1.65	1.61	1.58	1.54	1.50
27	1.85	1.80	1.75	1.70	1.67	1.64	1.60	1.57	1.53	1.49
28	1.84	1.79	1.74	1.69	1.66	1.63	1.59	1.56	1.52	1.48
29	1.83	1.78	1.73	1.68	1.65	1.62	1.58	1.55	1.51	1.47
30	1.82	1.77	1.72	1.67	1.64	1.61	1.57	1.54	1.50	1.46
40	1.76	1.71	1.66	1.61	1.57	1.54	1.51	1.47	1.42	1.38
60	1.71	1.66	1.60	1.54	1.51	1.48	1.44	1.40	1.35	1.29
120	1.65	1.60	1.55	1.48	1.45	1.41	1.37	1.32	1.26	1.19
∞	1.60	1.55	1.49	1.42	1.38	1.34	1.30	1.24	1.17	1.00

Denominator Degrees of Freedom ν_2

Table VI   Percentage Points of the *F*-Distribution, $\alpha = .05$

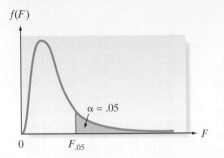

ν_1	Numerator Degrees of Freedom								
ν_2	1	2	3	4	5	6	7	8	9
1	161.4	199.5	215.7	224.6	230.2	234.0	236.8	238.9	240.5
2	18.51	19.00	19.16	19.25	19.30	19.33	19.35	19.37	19.38
3	10.13	9.55	9.28	9.12	9.01	8.94	8.89	8.85	8.81
4	7.71	6.94	6.59	6.39	6.26	6.16	6.09	6.04	6.00
5	6.61	5.79	5.41	5.19	5.05	4.95	4.88	4.82	4.77
6	5.99	5.14	4.76	4.53	4.39	4.28	4.21	4.15	4.10
7	5.59	4.74	4.35	4.12	3.97	3.87	3.79	3.73	3.68
8	5.32	4.46	4.07	3.84	3.69	3.58	3.50	3.44	3.39
9	5.12	4.26	3.86	3.63	3.48	3.37	3.29	3.23	3.18
10	4.96	4.10	3.71	3.48	3.33	3.22	3.14	3.07	3.02
11	4.84	3.98	3.59	3.36	3.20	3.09	3.01	2.95	2.90
12	4.75	3.89	3.49	3.26	3.11	3.00	2.91	2.85	2.80
13	4.67	3.81	3.41	3.18	3.03	2.92	2.83	2.77	2.71
14	4.60	3.74	3.34	3.11	2.96	2.85	2.76	2.70	2.65
15	4.54	3.68	3.29	3.06	2.90	2.79	2.71	2.64	2.59
16	4.49	3.63	3.24	3.01	2.85	2.74	2.66	2.59	2.54
17	4.45	3.59	3.20	2.96	2.81	2.70	2.61	2.55	2.49
18	4.41	3.55	3.16	2.93	2.77	2.66	2.58	2.51	2.46
19	4.38	3.52	3.13	2.90	2.74	2.63	2.54	2.48	2.42
20	4.35	3.49	3.10	2.87	2.71	2.60	2.51	2.45	2.39
21	4.32	3.47	3.07	2.84	2.68	2.57	2.49	2.42	2.37
22	4.30	3.44	3.05	2.82	2.66	2.55	2.46	2.40	2.34
23	4.28	3.42	3.03	2.80	2.64	2.53	2.44	2.37	2.32
24	4.26	3.40	3.01	2.78	2.62	2.51	2.42	2.36	2.30
25	4.24	3.39	2.99	2.76	2.60	2.49	2.40	2.34	2.28
26	4.23	3.37	2.98	2.74	2.59	2.47	2.39	2.32	2.77
27	4.21	3.35	2.96	2.73	2.57	2.46	2.37	2.31	2.25
28	4.20	3.34	2.95	2.71	2.56	2.45	2.36	2.29	2.24
29	4.18	3.33	2.93	2.70	2.55	2.43	2.35	2.28	2.22
30	4.17	3.32	2.92	2.69	2.53	2.42	2.33	2.27	2.21
40	4.08	3.23	2.84	2.61	2.45	2.34	2.25	2.18	2.12
60	4.00	3.15	2.76	2.53	2.37	2.25	2.17	2.10	2.04
120	3.92	3.07	2.68	2.45	2.29	2.17	2.09	2.02	1.96
∞	3.84	3.00	2.60	2.37	2.21	2.10	2.01	1.94	1.88

(continued)

Table VI	(continued)								

ν_1	Numerator Degrees of Freedom								
ν_2	10	12	15	20	24	30	40	60	120	∞

Denominator Degrees of Freedom

ν_2	10	12	15	20	24	30	40	60	120	∞
1	241.9	243.9	245.9	248.0	249.1	250.1	251.1	252.2	253.3	254.3
2	19.40	19.41	19.43	19.45	19.45	19.46	19.47	19.48	19.49	19.50
3	8.79	8.74	8.70	8.66	8.64	8.62	8.59	8.57	8.55	8.53
4	5.96	5.91	5.86	5.80	5.77	5.75	5.72	5.69	5.66	5.63
5	4.74	4.68	4.62	4.56	4.53	4.50	4.46	4.43	4.40	4.36
6	4.06	4.00	3.94	3.87	3.84	3.81	3.77	3.74	3.70	3.67
7	3.64	3.57	3.51	3.44	3.41	3.38	3.34	3.30	3.27	3.23
8	3.35	3.28	3.22	3.15	3.12	3.08	3.04	3.01	2.97	2.93
9	3.14	3.07	3.01	2.94	2.90	2.86	2.83	2.79	2.75	2.71
10	2.98	2.91	2.85	2.77	2.74	2.70	2.66	2.62	2.58	2.54
11	2.85	2.79	2.72	2.65	2.61	2.57	2.53	2.49	2.45	2.40
12	2.75	2.69	2.62	2.54	2.51	2.47	2.43	2.38	2.34	2.30
13	2.67	2.60	2.53	2.46	2.42	2.38	2.34	2.30	2.25	2.21
14	2.60	2.53	2.46	2.39	2.35	2.31	2.27	2.22	2.18	2.13
15	2.54	2.48	2.40	2.33	2.29	2.25	2.20	2.16	2.11	2.07
16	2.49	2.42	2.35	2.28	2.24	2.19	2.15	2.11	2.06	2.01
17	2.45	2.38	2.31	2.23	2.19	2.15	2.10	2.06	2.01	1.96
18	2.41	2.34	2.27	2.19	2.15	2.11	2.06	2.02	1.97	1.92
19	2.38	2.31	2.23	2.16	2.11	2.07	2.03	1.98	1.93	1.88
20	2.35	2.28	2.20	2.12	2.08	2.04	1.99	1.95	1.90	1.84
21	2.32	2.25	2.18	2.10	2.05	2.01	1.96	1.92	1.87	1.81
22	2.30	2.23	2.15	2.07	2.03	1.98	1.94	1.89	1.84	1.78
23	2.27	2.20	2.13	2.05	2.01	1.96	1.91	1.86	1.81	1.76
24	2.25	2.18	2.11	2.03	1.98	1.94	1.89	1.84	1.79	1.73
25	2.24	2.16	2.09	2.01	1.96	1.92	1.87	1.82	1.77	1.71
26	2.22	2.15	2.07	1.99	1.95	1.90	1.85	1.80	1.75	1.69
27	2.20	2.13	2.06	1.97	1.93	1.88	1.84	1.79	1.73	1.67
28	2.19	2.12	2.04	1.96	1.91	1.87	1.82	1.77	1.71	1.65
29	2.18	2.10	2.03	1.94	1.90	1.85	1.81	1.75	1.70	1.64
30	2.16	2.09	2.01	1.93	1.89	1.84	1.79	1.74	1.68	1.62
40	2.08	2.00	1.92	1.84	1.79	1.74	1.69	1.64	1.58	1.51
60	1.99	1.92	1.84	1.75	1.70	1.65	1.59	1.53	1.47	1.39
120	1.91	1.83	1.75	1.66	1.61	1.55	1.50	1.43	1.35	1.25
∞	1.83	1.75	1.67	1.57	1.52	1.46	1.39	1.32	1.22	1.00

Table VII	Percentage Points of the *F*-Distribution, $\alpha = .025$

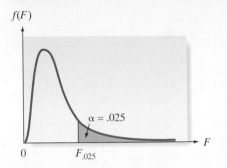

$f(F)$

$\alpha = .025$

$F_{.025}$

F

0

ν_2 \ ν_1	Numerator Degrees of Freedom								
	1	2	3	4	5	6	7	8	9
1	647.8	799.5	864.2	899.6	921.8	937.1	948.2	956.7	963.3
2	38.51	39.00	39.17	39.25	39.30	39.33	39.36	39.37	39.39
3	17.44	16.04	15.44	15.10	14.88	14.73	14.62	14.54	14.47
4	12.22	10.65	9.98	9.60	9.36	9.20	9.07	8.98	8.90
5	10.01	8.43	7.76	7.39	7.15	6.98	6.85	6.76	6.68
6	8.81	7.26	6.60	6.23	5.99	5.82	5.70	5.60	5.52
7	8.07	6.54	5.89	5.52	5.29	5.12	4.99	4.90	4.82
8	7.57	6.06	5.42	5.05	4.82	4.65	4.53	4.43	4.36
9	7.21	5.71	5.08	4.72	4.48	4.32	4.20	4.10	4.03
10	6.94	5.46	4.83	4.47	4.24	4.07	3.95	3.85	3.78
11	6.72	5.26	4.63	4.28	4.04	3.88	3.76	3.66	3.59
12	6.55	5.10	4.47	4.12	3.89	3.73	3.61	3.51	3.44
13	6.41	4.97	4.35	4.00	3.77	3.60	3.48	3.39	3.31
14	6.30	4.86	4.24	3.89	3.66	3.50	3.38	3.29	3.21
15	6.20	4.77	4.15	3.80	3.58	3.41	3.29	3.20	3.12
16	6.12	4.69	4.08	3.73	3.50	3.34	3.22	3.12	3.05
17	6.04	4.62	4.01	3.66	3.44	3.28	3.16	3.06	2.98
18	5.98	4.56	3.95	3.61	3.38	3.22	3.10	3.01	2.93
19	5.92	4.51	3.90	3.56	3.33	3.17	3.05	2.96	2.88
20	5.87	4.46	3.86	3.51	3.29	3.13	3.01	2.91	2.84
21	5.83	4.42	3.82	3.48	3.25	3.09	2.97	2.87	2.80
22	5.79	4.38	3.78	3.44	3.22	3.05	2.93	2.84	2.76
23	5.75	4.35	3.75	3.41	3.18	3.02	2.90	2.81	2.73
24	5.72	4.32	3.72	3.38	3.15	2.99	2.87	2.78	2.70
25	5.69	4.29	3.69	3.35	3.13	2.97	2.85	2.75	2.68
26	5.66	4.27	3.67	3.33	3.10	2.94	2.82	2.73	2.65
27	5.63	4.24	3.65	3.31	3.08	2.92	2.80	2.71	2.63
28	5.61	4.22	3.63	3.29	3.06	2.90	2.78	2.69	2.61
29	5.59	4.20	3.61	3.27	3.04	2.88	2.76	2.67	2.59
30	5.57	4.18	3.59	3.25	3.03	2.87	2.75	2.65	2.57
40	5.42	4.05	3.46	3.13	2.90	2.74	2.62	2.53	2.45
60	5.29	3.93	3.34	3.01	2.79	2.63	2.51	2.41	2.33
120	5.15	3.80	3.23	2.89	2.67	2.52	2.39	2.30	2.22
∞	5.02	3.69	3.12	2.79	2.57	2.41	2.29	2.19	2.11

Denominator Degrees of Freedom

(continued)

Table VII	(continued)									
	ν_1				Numerator Degrees of Freedom					
ν_2	10	12	15	20	24	30	40	60	120	∞
1	968.6	976.7	984.9	993.1	997.2	1,001	1,006	1,010	1,014	1,018
2	39.40	39.41	39.43	39.45	39.46	39.46	39.47	39.48	39.49	39.50
3	14.42	14.34	14.25	14.17	14.12	14.08	14.04	13.99	13.95	13.90
4	8.84	8.75	8.66	8.56	8.51	8.46	8.41	8.36	8.31	8.26
5	6.62	6.52	6.43	6.33	6.28	6.23	6.18	6.12	6.07	6.02
6	5.46	5.37	5.27	5.17	5.12	5.07	5.01	4.96	4.90	4.85
7	4.76	4.67	4.57	4.47	4.42	4.36	4.31	4.25	4.20	4.14
8	4.30	4.20	4.10	4.00	3.95	3.89	3.84	3.78	3.73	3.67
9	3.96	3.87	3.77	3.67	3.61	3.56	3.51	3.45	3.39	3.33
10	3.72	3.62	3.52	3.42	3.37	3.31	3.26	3.20	3.14	3.08
11	3.53	3.43	3.33	3.23	3.17	3.12	3.06	3.00	2.94	2.88
12	3.37	3.28	3.18	3.07	3.02	2.96	2.91	2.85	2.79	2.72
13	3.25	3.15	3.05	2.95	2.89	2.84	2.78	2.72	2.66	2.60
14	3.15	3.05	2.95	2.84	2.79	2.73	2.67	2.61	2.55	2.49
15	3.06	2.96	2.86	2.76	2.70	2.64	2.59	2.52	2.46	2.40
16	2.99	2.89	2.79	2.68	2.63	2.57	2.51	2.45	2.38	2.32
17	2.92	2.82	2.72	2.62	2.56	2.50	2.44	2.38	2.32	2.25
18	2.87	2.77	2.67	2.56	2.50	2.44	2.38	2.32	2.26	2.19
19	2.82	2.72	2.62	2.51	2.45	2.39	2.33	2.27	2.20	2.13
20	2.77	2.68	2.57	2.46	2.41	2.35	2.29	2.22	2.16	2.09
21	2.73	2.64	2.53	2.42	2.37	2.31	2.25	2.18	2.11	2.04
22	2.70	2.60	2.50	2.39	2.33	2.27	2.21	2.14	2.08	2.00
23	2.67	2.57	2.47	2.36	2.30	2.24	2.18	2.11	2.04	1.97
24	2.64	2.54	2.44	2.33	2.27	2.21	2.15	2.08	2.01	1.94
25	2.61	2.51	2.41	2.30	2.24	2.18	2.12	2.05	1.98	1.91
26	2.59	2.49	2.39	2.28	2.22	2.16	2.09	2.03	1.95	1.88
27	2.57	2.47	2.36	2.25	2.19	2.13	2.07	2.00	1.93	1.85
28	2.55	2.45	2.34	2.23	2.17	2.11	2.05	1.98	1.91	1.83
29	2.53	2.43	2.32	2.21	2.15	2.09	2.03	1.96	1.89	1.81
30	2.51	2.41	2.31	2.20	2.14	2.07	2.01	1.94	1.87	1.79
40	2.39	2.29	2.18	2.07	2.01	1.94	1.88	1.80	1.72	1.64
60	2.27	2.17	2.06	1.94	1.88	1.82	1.74	1.67	1.58	1.48
120	2.16	2.05	1.94	1.82	1.76	1.69	1.61	1.53	1.43	1.31
∞	2.05	1.94	1.83	1.71	1.64	1.57	1.48	1.39	1.27	1.00

Denominator Degrees of Freedom

Table VIII	Percentage Points of the *F*-Distribution, $\alpha = .01$

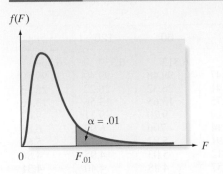

ν_2 \ ν_1	Numerator Degrees of Freedom								
	1	2	3	4	5	6	7	8	9
1	4,052	4,999.5	5,403	5,625	5,764	5,859	5,928	5,982	6,022
2	98.50	99.00	99.17	99.25	99.30	99.33	99.36	99.37	99.39
3	34.12	30.82	29.46	28.71	28.24	27.91	27.67	27.49	27.35
4	21.20	18.00	16.69	15.98	15.52	15.21	14.98	14.80	14.66
5	16.26	13.27	12.06	11.39	10.97	10.67	10.46	10.29	10.16
6	13.75	10.92	9.78	9.15	8.75	8.47	8.26	8.10	7.98
7	12.25	9.55	8.45	7.85	7.46	7.19	6.99	6.84	6.72
8	11.26	8.65	7.59	7.01	6.63	6.37	6.18	6.03	5.91
9	10.56	8.02	6.99	6.42	6.06	5.80	5.61	5.47	5.35
10	10.04	7.56	6.55	5.99	5.64	5.39	5.20	5.06	4.94
11	9.65	7.21	6.22	5.67	5.32	5.07	4.89	4.74	4.63
12	9.33	6.93	5.95	5.41	5.06	4.82	4.64	4.50	4.39
13	9.07	6.70	5.74	5.21	4.86	4.62	4.44	4.30	4.19
14	8.86	6.51	5.56	5.04	4.69	4.46	4.28	4.14	4.03
15	8.68	6.36	5.42	4.89	4.56	4.32	4.14	4.00	3.89
16	8.53	6.23	5.29	4.77	4.44	4.20	4.03	3.89	3.78
17	8.40	6.11	5.18	4.67	4.34	4.10	3.93	3.79	3.68
18	8.29	6.01	5.09	4.58	4.25	4.01	3.84	3.71	3.60
19	8.18	5.93	5.01	4.50	4.17	3.94	3.77	3.63	3.52
20	8.10	5.85	4.94	4.43	4.10	3.87	3.70	3.56	3.46
21	8.02	5.78	4.87	4.37	4.04	3.81	3.64	3.51	3.40
22	7.95	5.72	4.82	4.31	3.99	3.76	3.59	3.45	3.35
23	7.88	5.66	4.76	4.26	3.94	3.71	3.54	3.41	3.30
24	7.82	5.61	4.72	4.22	3.90	3.67	3.50	3.36	3.26
25	7.77	5.57	4.68	4.18	3.85	3.63	3.46	3.32	3.22
26	7.72	5.53	4.64	4.14	3.82	3.59	3.42	3.29	3.18
27	7.68	5.49	4.60	4.11	3.78	3.56	3.39	3.26	3.15
28	7.64	5.45	4.57	4.07	3.75	3.53	3.36	3.23	3.12
29	7.60	5.42	4.54	4.04	3.73	3.50	3.33	3.20	3.09
30	7.56	5.39	4.51	4.02	3.70	3.47	3.30	3.17	3.07
40	7.31	5.18	4.31	3.83	3.51	3.29	3.12	2.99	2.89
60	7.08	4.98	4.13	3.65	3.34	3.12	2.95	2.82	2.72
120	6.85	4.79	3.95	3.48	3.17	2.96	2.79	2.66	2.56
∞	6.63	4.61	3.78	3.32	3.02	2.80	2.64	2.51	2.41

(continued)

Table VIII	(continued)									
ν_1	Numerator Degrees of Freedom									
ν_2	10	12	15	20	24	30	40	60	120	∞
1	6,056	6,106	6,157	6,209	6,235	6,261	6,287	6,313	6,339	6,366
2	99.40	99.42	99.43	99.45	99.46	99.47	99.47	99.48	99.49	99.50
3	27.23	27.05	26.87	26.69	26.60	26.50	26.41	26.32	26.22	26.13
4	14.55	14.37	14.20	14.02	13.93	13.84	13.75	13.65	13.56	13.46
5	10.05	9.89	9.72	9.55	9.47	9.38	9.29	9.20	9.11	9.02
6	7.87	7.72	7.56	7.40	7.31	7.23	7.14	7.06	6.97	6.88
7	6.62	6.47	6.31	6.16	6.07	5.99	5.91	5.82	5.74	5.65
8	5.81	5.67	5.52	5.36	5.28	5.20	5.12	5.03	4.95	4.86
9	5.26	5.11	4.96	4.81	4.73	4.65	4.57	4.48	4.40	4.31
10	4.85	4.71	4.56	4.41	4.33	4.25	4.17	4.08	4.00	3.91
11	4.54	4.40	4.25	4.10	4.02	3.94	3.86	3.78	3.69	3.60
12	4.30	4.16	4.01	3.86	3.78	3.70	3.62	3.54	3.45	3.36
13	4.10	3.96	3.82	3.66	3.59	3.51	3.43	3.34	3.25	3.17
14	3.94	3.80	3.66	3.51	3.43	3.35	3.27	3.18	3.09	3.00
15	3.80	3.67	3.52	3.37	3.29	3.21	3.13	3.05	2.96	2.87
16	3.69	3.55	3.41	3.26	3.18	3.10	3.02	2.93	2.84	2.75
17	3.59	3.46	3.31	3.16	3.08	3.00	2.92	2.83	2.75	2.65
18	3.51	3.37	3.23	3.08	3.00	2.92	2.84	2.75	2.66	2.57
19	3.43	3.30	3.15	3.00	2.92	2.84	2.76	2.67	2.58	2.49
20	3.37	3.23	3.09	2.94	2.86	2.78	2.69	2.61	2.52	2.42
21	3.31	3.17	3.03	2.88	2.80	2.72	2.64	2.55	2.46	2.36
22	3.26	3.12	2.98	2.83	2.75	2.67	2.58	2.50	2.40	2.31
23	3.21	3.07	2.93	2.78	2.70	2.62	2.54	2.45	2.35	2.26
24	3.17	3.03	2.89	2.74	2.66	2.58	2.49	2.40	2.31	2.21
25	3.13	2.99	2.85	2.70	2.62	2.54	2.45	2.36	2.27	2.17
26	3.09	2.96	2.81	2.66	2.58	2.50	2.42	2.33	2.23	2.13
27	3.06	2.93	2.78	2.63	2.55	2.47	2.38	2.29	2.20	2.10
28	3.03	2.90	2.75	2.60	2.52	2.44	2.35	2.26	2.17	2.06
29	3.00	2.87	2.73	2.57	2.49	2.41	2.33	2.23	2.14	2.03
30	2.98	2.84	2.70	2.55	2.47	2.39	2.30	2.21	2.11	2.01
40	2.80	2.66	2.52	2.37	2.29	2.20	2.11	2.02	1.92	1.80
60	2.63	2.50	2.35	2.20	2.12	2.03	1.94	1.84	1.73	1.60
120	2.47	2.34	2.19	2.03	1.95	1.86	1.76	1.66	1.53	1.38
∞	2.32	2.18	2.04	1.88	1.79	1.70	1.59	1.47	1.32	1.00

Denominator Degrees of Freedom

Table IX	Control Chart Constants				
Number of Observations in Subgroup, n	A_2	d_2	d_3	D_3	D_4
2	1.880	1.128	.853	.000	3.267
3	1.023	1.693	.888	.000	2.574
4	.729	2.059	.880	.000	2.282
5	.577	2.326	.864	.000	2.114
6	.483	2.534	.848	.000	2.004
7	.419	2.704	.833	.076	1.924
8	.373	2.847	.820	.136	1.864
9	.337	2.970	.808	.184	1.816
10	.308	3.078	.797	.223	1.777
11	.285	3.173	.787	.256	1.744
12	.266	3.258	.778	.283	1.717
13	.249	3.336	.770	.307	1.693
14	.235	3.407	.762	.328	1.672
15	.223	3.472	.755	.347	1.653
16	.212	3.532	.749	.363	1.637
17	.203	3.588	.743	.378	1.622
18	.194	3.640	.738	.391	1.608
19	.187	3.689	.733	.403	1.597
20	.180	3.735	.729	.415	1.585
21	.173	3.778	.724	.425	1.575
22	.167	3.819	.720	.434	1.566
23	.162	3.858	.716	.443	1.557
24	.157	3.895	.712	.451	1.548
25	.153	3.931	.709	.459	1.541

| Table X | Critical Values for the Durbin-Watson d-Statistic, $\alpha = .05$ | | | | | | | | | |

	$k = 1$		$k = 2$		$k = 3$		$k = 4$		$k = 5$	
n	d_L	d_U	d_L	d_U	d_L	d_U	d_L	d_U	d_L	d_U
15	1.08	1.36	.95	1.54	.82	1.75	.69	1.97	.56	2.21
16	1.10	1.37	.98	1.54	.86	1.73	.74	1.93	.62	2.15
17	1.13	1.38	1.02	1.54	.90	1.71	.78	1.90	.67	2.10
18	1.16	1.39	1.05	1.53	.93	1.69	.92	1.87	.71	2.06
19	1.18	1.40	1.08	1.53	.97	1.68	.86	1.85	.75	2.02
20	1.20	1.41	1.10	1.54	1.00	1.68	.90	1.83	.79	1.99
21	1.22	1.42	1.13	1.54	1.03	1.67	.93	1.81	.83	1.96
22	1.24	1.43	1.15	1.54	1.05	1.66	.96	1.80	.96	1.94
23	1.26	1.44	1.17	1.54	1.08	1.66	.99	1.79	.90	1.92
24	1.27	1.45	1.19	1.55	1.10	1.66	1.01	1.78	.93	1.90
25	1.29	1.45	1.21	1.55	1.12	1.66	1.04	1.77	.95	1.89
26	1.30	1.46	1.22	1.55	1.14	1.65	1.06	1.76	.98	1.88
27	1.32	1.47	1.24	1.56	1.16	1.65	1.08	1.76	1.01	1.86
28	1.33	1.48	1.26	1.56	1.18	1.65	1.10	1.75	1.03	1.85
29	1.34	1.48	1.27	1.56	1.20	1.65	1.12	1.74	1.05	1.84
30	1.35	1.49	1.28	1.57	1.21	1.65	1.14	1.74	1.07	1.83
31	1.36	1.50	1.30	1.57	1.23	1.65	1.16	1.74	1.09	1.83
32	1.37	1.50	1.31	1.57	1.24	1.65	1.18	1.73	1.11	1.82
33	1.38	1.51	1.32	1.58	1.26	1.65	1.19	1.73	1.13	1.81
34	1.39	1.51	1.33	1.58	1.27	1.65	1.21	1.73	1.15	1.81
35	1.40	1.52	1.34	1.58	1.28	1.65	1.22	1.73	1.16	1.80
36	1.41	1.52	1.35	1.59	1.29	1.65	1.24	1.73	1.18	1.80
37	1.42	1.53	1.36	1.59	1.31	1.66	1.25	1.72	1.19	1.80
38	1.43	1.54	1.37	1.59	1.32	1.66	1.26	1.72	1.21	1.79
39	1.43	1.54	1.38	1.60	1.33	1.66	1.27	1.72	1.22	1.79
40	1.44	1.54	1.39	1.60	1.34	1.66	1.29	1.72	1.23	1.79
45	1.48	1.57	1.43	1.62	1.38	1.67	1.34	1.72	1.29	1.78
50	1.50	1.59	1.46	1.63	1.42	1.67	1.38	1.72	1.34	1.77
55	1.53	1.60	1.49	1.64	1.45	1.68	1.41	1.72	1.38	1.77
60	1.55	1.62	1.51	1.65	1.48	1.69	1.44	1.73	1.41	1.77
65	1.57	1.63	1.54	1.66	1.50	1.70	1.47	1.73	1.44	1.77
70	1.58	1.64	1.55	1.67	1.52	1.70	1.49	1.74	1.46	1.77
75	1.60	1.65	1.57	1.68	1.54	1.71	1.51	1.74	1.49	1.77
80	1.61	1.66	1.59	1.69	1.56	1.72	1.53	1.74	1.51	1.77
85	1.62	1.67	1.60	1.70	1.57	1.72	1.55	1.75	1.52	1.77
90	1.63	1.68	1.61	1.70	1.59	1.73	1.57	1.75	1.54	1.78
95	1.64	1.69	1.62	1.71	1.60	1.73	1.58	1.75	1.56	1.78
100	1.65	1.69	1.63	1.72	1.61	1.74	1.59	1.76	1.57	1.78

Table XI — Critical Values for the Durbin-Watson d-Statistic, $\alpha = .01$

	k = 1		k = 2		k = 3		k = 4		k = 5	
n	d_L	d_U	d_L	d_U	d_L	d_U	d_L	d_U	d_L	d_U
15	.81	1.07	.70	1.25	.59	1.46	.49	1.70	.39	1.96
16	.84	1.09	.74	1.25	.63	1.44	.53	1.66	.44	1.90
17	.87	1.10	.77	1.25	.67	1.43	.57	1.3	.48	1.85
18	.90	1.12	.80	1.26	.71	1.42	.61	1.60	.52	1.80
19	.93	1.13	.83	1.26	.74	1.41	.65	1.58	.56	1.77
20	.95	1.15	.86	1.27	.77	1.41	.68	1.57	.60	1.74
21	.97	1.16	.89	1.27	.80	1.41	.72	1.55	.63	1.71
22	1.00	1.17	.91	1.28	.83	1.40	.75	1.54	.66	1.69
23	1.02	1.19	.94	1.29	.86	1.40	.77	1.53	.70	1.67
24	1.04	1.20	.96	1.30	.88	1.41	.80	1.53	.72	1.66
25	1.05	1.21	.98	1.30	.90	1.41	.83	1.52	.75	1.65
26	1.07	1.22	1.00	1.31	.93	1.41	.85	1.52	.78	1.64
27	1.09	1.23	1.02	1.32	.95	1.41	.88	1.51	.81	1.63
28	1.10	1.24	1.04	1.32	.97	1.41	.90	1.51	.83	1.62
29	1.12	1.25	1.05	1.33	.99	1.42	.92	1.51	.85	1.61
30	1.13	1.26	1.07	1.34	1.01	1.42	.94	1.51	.88	1.61
31	1.15	1.27	1.08	1.34	1.02	1.42	.96	1.51	.90	1.60
32	1.16	1.28	1.10	1.35	1.04	1.43	.98	1.51	.92	1.60
33	1.17	1.29	1.11	1.36	1.05	1.43	1.00	1.51	.94	1.59
34	1.18	1.30	1.13	1.36	1.07	1.43	1.01	1.51	.95	1.59
35	1.19	1.31	1.14	1.27	1.08	1.44	1.03	1.51	.97	1.59
36	1.21	1.32	1.15	1.38	1.10	1.44	1.04	1.51	.99	1.59
37	1.22	1.32	1.16	1.38	1.11	1.45	1.06	1.51	1.00	1.59
38	1.23	1.33	1.18	1.39	1.12	1.45	1.07	1.52	1.02	1.58
39	1.24	1.34	1.19	1.39	1.14	1.45	1.09	1.52	1.03	1.58
40	1.25	1.34	1.20	1.40	1.15	1.46	1.10	1.52	1.05	1.58
45	1.29	1.38	1.24	1.42	1.20	1.48	1.16	1.53	1.11	1.58
50	1.32	1.40	1.28	1.45	1.24	1.49	1.20	1.54	1.16	1.59
55	1.36	1.43	1.32	1.47	1.28	1.51	1.25	1.55	1.21	1.59
60	1.38	1.45	1.35	1.48	1.32	1.52	1.28	1.56	1.25	1.60
65	1.41	1.47	1.38	1.50	1.35	1.53	1.31	1.57	1.28	1.61
70	1.43	1.49	1.40	1.52	1.37	1.55	1.34	1.58	1.31	1.61
75	1.45	1.50	1.42	1.53	1.39	1.56	1.37	1.59	1.34	1.62
80	1.47	1.52	1.44	1.54	1.42	1.57	1.39	1.60	1.36	1.62
85	1.48	1.53	1.46	1.55	1.43	1.58	1.41	1.60	1.39	1.63
90	1.50	1.54	1.47	1.56	1.45	1.59	1.43	1.61	1.41	1.64
95	1.51	1.55	1.49	1.57	1.47	1.60	1.45	1.62	1.42	1.64
100	1.52	1.56	1.50	1.58	1.48	1.60	1.46	1.63	1.44	1.65

| Table XII | Critical Values of T_L and T_U for the Wilcoxon Rank Sum Test: Independent Samples |

Test statistic is the rank sum associated with the smaller sample (if equal sample sizes, either rank sum can be used).

a. $\alpha = .025$ one-tailed; $\alpha = .05$ two-tailed

n_2 \ n_1	3		4		5		6		7		8		9		10	
	T_L	T_U	T_L	T_U	T_L	T_U	T_L	T_U	T_L	T_U	T_L	T_U	T_L	T_U	T_L	T_U
3	5	16	6	18	6	21	7	23	7	26	8	28	8	31	9	33
4	6	18	11	25	12	28	12	32	13	35	14	38	15	41	16	44
5	6	21	12	28	18	37	19	41	20	45	21	49	22	53	24	56
6	7	23	12	32	19	41	26	52	28	56	29	61	31	65	32	70
7	7	26	13	35	20	45	28	56	37	68	39	73	41	78	43	83
8	8	28	14	38	21	49	29	61	39	73	49	87	51	93	54	98
9	8	31	15	41	22	53	31	65	41	78	51	93	63	108	66	114
10	9	33	16	44	24	56	32	70	43	83	54	98	66	114	79	131

b. $\alpha = .05$ one-tailed; $\alpha = .10$ two-tailed

n_2 \ n_1	3		4		5		6		7		8		9		10	
	T_L	T_U	T_L	T_U	T_L	T_U	T_L	T_U	T_L	T_U	T_L	T_U	T_L	T_U	T_L	T_U
3	6	15	7	17	7	20	8	22	9	24	9	27	10	29	11	31
4	7	17	12	24	13	27	14	30	15	33	16	36	17	39	18	42
5	7	20	13	27	19	36	20	40	22	43	24	46	25	50	26	54
6	8	22	14	30	20	40	28	50	30	54	32	58	33	63	35	67
7	9	24	15	33	22	43	30	54	39	66	41	71	43	76	46	80
8	9	27	16	36	24	46	32	58	41	71	52	84	54	90	57	95
9	10	29	17	39	25	50	33	63	43	76	54	90	66	105	69	111
10	11	31	18	42	26	54	35	67	46	80	57	95	69	111	83	127

Source: From Wilcoxon, F., & Wilcox, R. A. "Some rapid approximate statistical procedures," 1964, 20–23. Courtesy of Lederle Laboratories Division of American Cyanamid Company, Madison, NJ.

Table XIII	Critical Values of T_0 in the Wilcoxon Paired Difference Signed Rank Test						
One-Tailed	Two-Tailed	$n = 5$	$n = 6$	$n = 7$	$n = 8$	$n = 9$	$n = 10$
$\alpha = .05$	$\alpha = .10$	1	2	4	6	8	11
$\alpha = .025$	$\alpha = .05$		1	2	4	6	8
$\alpha = .01$	$\alpha = .02$			0	2	3	5
$\alpha = .005$	$\alpha = .01$				0	2	3
		$n = 11$	$n = 12$	$n = 13$	$n = 14$	$n = 15$	$n = 16$
$\alpha = .05$	$\alpha = .10$	14	17	21	26	30	36
$\alpha = .025$	$\alpha = .05$	11	14	17	21	25	30
$\alpha = .01$	$\alpha = .02$	7	10	13	16	20	24
$\alpha = .005$	$\alpha = .01$	5	7	10	13	16	19
		$n = 17$	$n = 18$	$n = 19$	$n = 20$	$n = 21$	$n = 22$
$\alpha = .05$	$\alpha = .10$	41	47	54	60	68	75
$\alpha = .025$	$\alpha = .05$	35	40	46	52	59	66
$\alpha = .01$	$\alpha = .02$	28	33	38	43	49	56
$\alpha = .005$	$\alpha = .01$	23	28	32	37	43	49
		$n = 23$	$n = 24$	$n = 25$	$n = 26$	$n = 27$	$n = 28$
$\alpha = .05$	$\alpha = .10$	83	92	101	110	120	130
$\alpha = .025$	$\alpha = .05$	73	81	90	98	107	117
$\alpha = .01$	$\alpha = .02$	62	69	77	85	93	102
$\alpha = .005$	$\alpha = .01$	55	61	68	76	84	92
		$n = 29$	$n = 30$	$n = 31$	$n = 32$	$n = 33$	$n = 34$
$\alpha = .05$	$\alpha = .10$	141	152	163	175	188	201
$\alpha = .025$	$\alpha = .05$	127	137	148	159	171	183
$\alpha = .01$	$\alpha = .02$	111	120	130	141	151	162
$\alpha = .005$	$\alpha = .01$	100	109	118	128	138	149
		$n = 35$	$n = 36$	$n = 37$	$n = 38$	$n = 39$	
$\alpha = .05$	$\alpha = .10$	214	228	242	256	271	
$\alpha = .025$	$\alpha = .05$	195	208	222	235	250	
$\alpha = .01$	$\alpha = .02$	174	186	198	211	224	
$\alpha = .005$	$\alpha = .01$	160	171	183	195	208	
		$n = 40$	$n = 41$	$n = 42$	$n = 43$	$n = 44$	$n = 45$
$\alpha = .05$	$\alpha = .10$	287	303	319	336	353	371
$\alpha = .025$	$\alpha = .05$	264	279	295	311	327	344
$\alpha = .01$	$\alpha = .02$	238	252	267	281	297	313
$\alpha = .005$	$\alpha = .01$	221	234	248	262	277	292
		$n = 46$	$n = 47$	$n = 48$	$n = 49$	$n = 50$	
$\alpha = .05$	$\alpha = .10$	389	408	427	446	466	
$\alpha = .025$	$\alpha = .05$	361	379	397	415	434	
$\alpha = .01$	$\alpha = .02$	329	345	362	380	398	
$\alpha = .005$	$\alpha = .01$	307	323	339	356	373	

Source: From Wilcoxon, F., & Wilcox, R. A. "Some rapid approximate statistical procedures," 1964, p. 28. Courtesy of Lederle Laboratories Division of American Cyanamid Company, Madison, NJ.

| Table XIV | Critical Values of Spearman's Rank Correlation Coefficient |

The values correspond to a one-tailed test of $H_0: p = 0$. The value should be doubled for two-tailed tests.

n	$\alpha = .05$	$\alpha = .025$	$\alpha = .01$	$\alpha = .005$	n	$\alpha = .05$	$\alpha = .025$	$\alpha = .01$	$\alpha = .005$
5	.900	–	–	–	18	.399	.476	.564	.625
6	.829	.886	.943	–	19	.388	.462	.549	.608
7	.714	.786	.893	–	20	.377	.450	.534	.591
8	.643	.738	.833	.881	21	.368	.438	.521	.576
9	.600	.683	.783	.833	22	.359	.428	.508	.562
10	.564	.648	.745	.794	23	.351	.418	.496	.549
11	.523	.623	.736	.818	24	.343	.409	.485	.537
12	.497	.591	.703	.780	25	.336	.400	.475	.526
13	.475	.566	.673	.745	26	.329	.392	.465	.515
14	.457	.545	.646	.716	27	.323	.385	.456	.505
15	.441	.525	.623	.689	28	.317	.377	.448	.496
16	.425	.507	.601	.666	29	.311	.370	.440	.487
17	.412	.490	.582	.645	30	.305	.364	.432	.478

Table XV	Critical Values of the Studentized Range, $\alpha = .05$									
k ν	2	3	4	5	6	7	8	9	10	11
1	17.97	26.98	32.82	37.08	40.41	43.12	45.40	47.36	49.07	50.59
2	6.08	8.33	9.80	10.88	11.74	12.44	13.03	13.54	13.99	14.39
3	4.50	5.91	6.82	7.50	8.04	8.48	8.85	9.18	9.46	9.72
4	3.93	5.04	5.76	6.29	6.71	7.05	7.35	7.60	7.83	8.03
5	3.64	4.60	5.22	5.67	6.03	6.33	6.58	6.80	6.99	7.17
6	3.46	4.34	4.90	5.30	5.63	5.90	6.12	6.32	6.49	6.65
7	3.34	4.16	4.68	5.06	5.36	5.61	5.82	6.00	6.16	6.30
8	3.26	4.04	4.53	4.89	5.17	5.40	5.60	5.77	5.92	6.05
9	3.20	3.95	4.41	4.76	5.02	5.24	5.43	5.59	5.74	5.87
10	3.15	3.88	4.33	4.65	4.91	5.12	5.30	5.46	5.60	5.72
11	3.11	3.82	4.26	4.57	4.82	5.03	5.20	5.35	5.49	5.61
12	3.08	3.77	4.20	4.51	4.75	4.95	5.12	5.27	5.39	5.51
13	3.06	3.73	4.15	4.45	4.69	4.88	5.05	5.19	5.32	5.43
14	3.03	3.70	4.11	4.41	4.64	4.83	4.99	5.13	5.25	5.36
15	3.01	3.67	4.08	4.37	4.60	4.78	4.94	5.08	5.20	5.31
16	3.00	3.65	4.05	4.33	4.56	4.74	4.90	5.03	5.15	5.26
17	2.98	3.63	4.02	4.30	4.52	4.70	4.86	4.99	5.11	5.21
18	2.97	3.61	4.00	4.28	4.49	4.67	4.82	4.96	5.07	5.17
19	2.96	3.59	3.98	4.25	4.47	4.65	4.79	4.92	5.04	5.14
20	2.95	3.58	3.96	4.23	4.45	4.62	4.77	4.90	5.01	5.11
24	2.92	3.53	3.90	4.17	4.37	4.54	4.68	4.81	4.92	5.01
30	2.89	3.49	3.85	4.10	4.30	4.46	4.60	4.72	4.82	4.92
40	2.86	3.44	3.79	4.04	4.23	4.39	4.52	4.63	4.73	4.82
60	2.83	3.40	3.74	3.98	4.16	4.31	4.44	4.55	4.65	4.73
120	2.80	3.36	3.68	3.92	4.10	4.24	4.36	4.47	4.56	4.64
∞	2.77	3.31	3.63	3.86	4.03	4.17	4.29	4.39	4.47	4.55

k ν	12	13	14	15	16	17	18	19	20
1	51.96	53.20	54.33	55.36	56.32	57.22	58.04	58.83	59.56
2	14.75	15.08	15.38	15.65	15.91	16.14	16.37	16.57	16.77
3	9.95	10.15	10.35	10.52	10.69	10.84	10.98	11.11	11.24
4	8.21	8.37	8.52	8.66	8.79	8.91	9.03	9.13	9.23
5	7.32	7.47	7.60	7.72	7.83	7.93	8.03	8.12	8.21
6	6.79	6.92	7.03	7.14	7.24	7.34	7.43	7.51	7.59
7	6.43	6.55	6.66	6.76	6.85	6.94	7.02	7.10	7.17
8	6.18	6.29	6.39	6.48	6.57	6.65	6.73	6.80	6.87
9	5.98	6.09	6.19	6.28	6.36	6.44	6.51	6.58	6.64
10	5.83	5.93	6.03	6.11	6.19	6.27	6.34	6.40	6.47
11	5.71	5.81	5.90	5.98	6.06	6.13	6.20	6.27	6.33
12	5.61	5.71	5.80	5.88	5.95	6.02	6.09	6.15	6.21
13	5.53	5.63	5.71	5.79	5.86	5.93	5.99	6.05	6.11
14	5.46	5.55	5.64	5.71	5.79	5.85	5.91	5.97	6.03
15	5.40	5.49	5.57	5.65	5.72	5.78	5.85	5.90	5.96
16	5.35	5.44	5.52	5.59	5.66	5.73	5.79	5.84	5.90
17	5.31	5.39	5.47	5.54	5.61	5.67	5.73	5.79	5.84
18	5.27	5.35	5.43	5.50	5.57	5.63	5.69	5.74	5.79
19	5.23	5.31	5.39	5.46	5.53	5.59	5.65	5.70	5.75
20	5.20	5.28	5.36	5.43	5.49	5.55	5.61	5.66	5.71
24	5.10	5.18	5.25	5.32	5.38	5.44	5.49	5.55	5.59
30	5.00	5.08	5.15	5.21	5.27	5.33	5.38	5.43	5.47
40	4.90	4.98	5.04	5.11	5.16	5.22	5.27	5.31	5.36
60	4.81	4.88	4.94	5.00	5.06	5.11	5.15	5.20	5.24
120	4.71	4.78	4.84	4.90	4.95	5.00	5.04	5.09	5.13
∞	4.62	4.68	4.74	4.80	4.85	4.89	4.93	4.97	5.01

Answers to Selected Exercises

Chapter 1

1.3 Population/sample; variable(s); tables/graphs; identify patterns **1.5** Published source; designed experiment; observationally **1.13** Qualitative; qualitative **1.15** Interviewee position and type of organization—qualitative; experience—quantitative **1.17 a.** Entire set of students **b.** 250 students **c.** Single student **d.** Parking time **1.19 a.** Fulfilling orders **b.** Whether an order has been pulled correctly **c.** Set of all orders checked **d.** Proportion of all orders that are pulled **e.** Answers may vary **1.21** Descriptive **1.23 b.** College student **c.** Type of condition and type of disposal—both qualitative **1.25 a.** Single-family residential property **b.** Sale price and the Zillow estimated value; quantitative **c.** If the 2,045 properties were all the properties sold in Arlington, Texas, in the past 6 months of 2006 **d.** All the single-family residential properties sold in the last 6 months in Arlington, Texas **e.** No **1.27 a.** All who took the GMAT **b.** Survey **c.** No; self-selection **1.29 a.** Quantitative **b.** Quantitative **c.** Qualitative **d.** Quantitative **e.** Qualitative **f.** Quantitative **g.** Qualitative **1.31 b.** Speed of the deliveries; accuracy of the invoices; quality of the packaging **c.** Customers surveyed **1.33 a.** All accounting alumni of the large university **b.** Quantitative: age, income, job satisfaction score, Machiavellian rating; qualitative: gender, education level **c.** 198 alumni who returned the questionnaire **d.** Survey **e.** Machiavellian behavior is not required to achieve success in business. **f.** Nonrespondents may be more Machiavellian in nature, biasing the results. **1.35 b.** All bank presidents in the United States **1.37 a.** All persons older than 14 years in United States **b.** Unemployment status; qualitative **c.** Inferential

Chapter 2

2.1 48, .15, .4, .2, .05 **2.3 a.** .615 **b.** .328 **c.** .057 **d.** 221.4, 118.1, 20.5 **2.5 a.** Bar graph **b.** Type of robotic limb **c.** Legs only **d.** None: .142; both: .075; legs only: .594; wheels only: .189 **2.7 a.** Explorer with .12 **b.** Remote code execution **2.9** Most had first degree (54.7%) and only 10.1% had postgraduate degree. **2.11** Most (84%) malls have small or small standard tenants. **2.13 d.** In all cities, most tweets rate iPhone as good. **2.15 a.** Response time **c.** 3,570 **d.** No **2.17 d.** Most aquifers are bedrock; most MTBE levels are below limit; 79% of private wells and 60% of public wells are not contaminated. **2.19** 36, 180, 120, 90, 84, 60, 30 **2.21 a.** Frequency histogram **b.** 14 **c.** 49 **2.23 a.** Relative frequency **b.** 12% **2.25 b.** Years 1996-2000 had the highest number of firms with at least one acquisition. **2.27 a.** Very little change **c.** 34; Wyoming **2.29** Yes **2.31** Yes **2.33** "Inside job" is not likely, since histogram appears similar to frequency distribution. **2.35** $\bar{x} = 2.72$; $m = 2.65$ **2.37** mean > median: skewed right; mean < median: skewed left; mean = median: symmetric **2.39** mode − 15; $\bar{x} = 14.55$; $m = 15$ **2.41 a.** mean < median **b.** mean > median **c.** mean = median **2.43 a.** Population mean **b.** Sample mean **2.45 a.** $\bar{x} = 17.8235$ **b.** $m = 20$ **c.** mode = 30 **2.47 a.** Average permeability of Group A slices is 73.62; half of Group A slices have permeability above 70.45. **b.** Average permeability of

Group B slices is 128.54; half of Group B slices have permeability above 139.30. **c.** Average permeability of Group C slices is 83.07; half of Group C slices have permeability above 78.65. **d.** Most frequent permeability score of Group C is 70.9. **e.** Type B **2.49 a.** 11 **b.** 9 **c.** 7 **d.** Honey dosage leads to greatest improvement. **2.51 a.** Skewed right **b.** Skewed left **c.** Skewed right **d.** Skewed right **e.** Symmetric **f.** Skewed left **2.53** Joint: $\bar{x} = 2.65$, $m = 1.5$; no prefiling: $\bar{x} = 4.24$, $m = 3.2$; prepack: $\bar{x} = 1.82$, $m = 1.4$; 3 centers **2.55 a.** Median **b.** Mean **2.57 a.** $R = 4$, $s^2 = 2.3$, $s = 1.52$ **b.** $R = 6$, $s^2 = 3.619$, $s = 1.90$ **c.** $R = 10$, $s^2 = 7.111$, $s = 2.67$ **d.** $R = 5$, $s^2 = 1.624$, $s = 1.274$ **2.59 a.** $\bar{x} = 5.6$, $s^2 = 17.3$, $s = 4.16$ **b.** $\bar{x} = 13.75$ feet, $s^2 = 152.25$ square feet, $s = 12.34$ feet **c.** $\bar{x} = -2.5$, $s^2 = 4.3$, $s = 2.07$ **d.** $x = .33$ ounce, $s^2 = .0587$ square ounce, $s = .24$ ounce **2.61** Data set 1: 0, 1, 2, 3, 4, 5, 6, 7, 8, 9; data set 2: 0, 0, 1, 1, 2, 2, 3, 3, 9, 9 **2.63 a.** $R = 3$, $s^2 = 1.3$, $s = 1.14$ **b.** $R = 3$, $s^2 = 1.3$, $s = 1.14$ **c.** $R = 3$, $s^2 = 1.3$, $s = 1.14$ **d.** No effect **2.65 a.** $R = 62.20$ **b.** $s = 14.48$ **c.** B **2.67 a.** 155; accurate **b.** 722.036; inaccurate **c.** 26.871; less **d.** Standard deviation **2.69 a.** $R = 5$, $s^2 = 1.72$, $s = 1.311$ **b.** $R = 4$, $s^2 = 1.209$, $s = 1.100$ **c.** $R = 8$, $s^2 = 5.06$, $s = 2.25$; variation decreases. **2.71 a.** Dollars; quantitative **b.** At least 3/4; at least 8/9; nothing; nothing **2.73** Approx. 68%; approx. 95%; essentially all **2.75** Between $R/6 = 104.17$ and $R/4 = 156.25$; no **2.77 a.** Chebyshev's Rule, data not symmetric; 73 $\pm$ 43.44 **b.** 128.54 $\pm$ 65.91 **c.** 83.07 $\pm$ 60.15 **d.** Type B **2.81 a.** $\bar{x} = 94.8$, $s = 4.99$ **b.** (89.81, 99.79), (84.82, 104.78), (79.83, 107.77) **c.** 73.3%, 96.9%, 97.9%; Chebyshev's Rule **2.83** 3.967 $\pm$ 1.7 **2.85 a.** Flexed: $\bar{x} \pm 2s = (51, 67)$; extended: $\bar{x} \pm 2s = (39, 47)$; yes **b.** Flexed: $\bar{x} \pm 2s = (39, 79)$; extended: $\bar{x} \pm 2s = (13, 73)$; no **2.87** Do not buy **2.89** 11:30 and 4:00 **2.91 a.** 25%, 75% **b.** 50%, 50% **c.** 80%, 20% **d.** 16%, 84% **2.93 a.** $z = 2$ **b.** $z = -3$ **c.** $z = -2$ **d.** $z = 1.67$ **2.95** Average score is 282; 25% score below 258; 75% score below 308; 90% score below 329 **2.97** Average current salary of graduates is $57,000; half of the graduates had mid-career salaries less than $48,000; 90% of graduates had mid-career salaries less than $131,000. **2.99** No **2.101** Average ROE is 13.93; 50% of firms have ROE below 14.86; 5% of firms have ROE below −19.64; 25% of firms have ROE below 7.59; 75% of firms have ROE below 21.32; 95% of firms have ROE below 38.42; most observations will fall within 2s or 43.30 units of mean. **2.103 a.** Harvard's productivity score falls 5.08 standard deviations above the mean. **b.** Howard's productivity score falls .81 standard deviation below the mean. **c.** Yes **2.105** Not necessarily, since the standard deviation will be large for right-skewed data **2.107** IQR = 25 **2.109 a.** Sample A: IQR = 22; sample B: IQR = 15 **b.** Sample A: 84; sample B: 140 and 206 **2.111 a.** $z = 1.57$; no **b.** $z = -3.36$; yes **2.113 a.** 50% of expenditures are less than $6,232; 25% are less than $5,309; 75% are less than $7,216. **b.** $1,907 **c.** $.75 - .25 = .50$ **2.115 b.** Joint: 1.5; none firms: 3.2; prepack: 1.4 **d.** No **e.** Yes **2.117 a.** 4 outliers: 69, 73, 76, 78 **b.** 4 outliers: 69, 73, 76, 78 **c.** Yes **2.119 a.** 3 outliers: 117.3, 118.5, 122.4 **b.** 1 outlier: 50.4 **c.** No outliers **d.** In **a**, mean and standard deviation decrease, and median slightly decreases; in **b**, mean increases, standard deviation decreases, and median slightly increases. **2.121** 102 is suspect outlier; agree with claim **2.125** Yes; yes, negative association between punishment use and average payoff **2.127** No **2.129** Positive trend **2.131 a.** Yes **b.** USAID and State **2.133 a.** Weak negative trend **b.** Highly suspect outlier is 1951. **c.** Strength of association is stronger. **2.135** Vertical axis is cut off; width of bars increases. **2.137 a.** Scales on two vertical axes differ. **b.** Craigslist revenue is much lower than newspaper ad sales. **2.141 a.** $-2, 2, 10$ **b.** $-2, 0, 4$ **c.** $-4, -2, 2$ **d.** $-1, -0.5, 0.5$ **2.143 a.** 465 **b.** 450 **c.** 250 **d.** 99.37 **2.149 a.** Companies and employees created 73% of blogs/forums. **b.** $(0, 28.29)$ **c.** Skewed right **2.151 a.** .082, .173, .167, .174, .139, .098, .074, .046, .048; 16.7% of articles published were in the Buyer Behavior area. **b.** Lower percentage for Marketing Research **2.153 a.** 60% of cars with 4-star rating **b.** Average driver's severity of head injury in head-on collisions is 603.7. **c.** $(232.9, 974.5)$ **d.** $z = -1.06$ **2.155 a.** Body defect **b.** Paint or dents **2.157 a.** Mean is 653; average amount of sparkling wine exported by the 30 countries is $653,000. **b.** Median is 231; half the 30 export values are above $231,000. **c.** Mean is 481; average change in amount exported by the 30 countries is 481%. **d.** Median is 156; half the 30 percentage changes are above 156%. **e.** 4,882 **f.** 1,113 **g.** 1,238,769. **h.** $(0, 2879)$ **2.159 a.** Grounding and fire **b.** $\bar{x} = 66.19, s = 56.05; (0, 234.34)$ **2.161 a.** At least 8/9 of the velocities fall within $(906, 966)$. **b.** No **2.163 b.** Info for 2006 is incomplete. **c.** Complete data for 2006 and data for 2007–2011 **2.165 a.** Skewed right **c.** ≈ 38 **d.** No, $z = 3.333$ **2.167 a.** Both height and width of bars change. **2.169** Laid off: $m = 40.5$; not laid off: $m = 40$; company probably not vulnerable **2.171** Yes; no observations were recorded in the interval just below the interval centered at 1.000 cm.

Chapter 3

3.1 a. .4 **b.** .25 **c.** .4 **3.3** $P(A) = .55, P(B) = .50, P(C) = .70$ **3.5 a.** 10 **b.** 20 **c.** 15,504 **3.7 a.** (HHH), (HHT), (HTH), (THH), (HTT), (THT), (TTH), (TTT) **b.** 1/8 **c.** $P(A) = 1/10$, $P(B) = 3/5, P(C) = 3/10$ **3.9 a.** (economy), (national security), (not sure) **b.** $P(R) = .76, P(N) = .09, P(C) = .15$ **c.** .8 **3.11 a.** Brown, yellow, red, blue, orange, and green **b.** $P(\text{Br}) = 0.13, P(Y) = 0.14, P(R) = 0.13, P(\text{Bl}) = 0.24$, $P(O) = 0.2, P(G) = 0.16$ **c.** .13 **d.** .43 **e.** .76 **3.13 a.** .61 **b.** .39 **3.15 a.** 11/17 **b.** 9/17 **3.17** Those in usefulness is salient condition recycled (26/39) at almost twice the rate as those in control condition (14/39). **3.19 a.** .01 **b.** .0095; yes **3.21 a.** 1/8 **b.** 70 **c.** .5 **3.23** 455 **3.25 a.** 27 **b.** 351 **3.27 a.** 1 to 2 **b.** 1/2 **c.** 2/5 **3.29 a.** 32 **b.** 1/32 **c.** 12 **d.** .375 **e.** .5 **3.31 a.** $(1, 2, 3, 4, 5, 6, 8, 10)$ **b.** $\{2, 4, 6\}$ **c.** $A \cup B$ **d.** $A \cap B$ **3.33 a.** 3/4 **b.** 13/20 **c.** 1 **d.** 2/5 **e.** 1/4 **f.** 7/20 **g.** 1 **h.** 1/4 **3.35 a.** .65 **b.** .72 **c.** .25 **d.** .08 **e.** .35 **f.** .72 **g.** 0 **h.** A and C, B and C, C and D **3.37** .858 **3.39 a.** $A \cap B$ **b.** A^C **c.** $C \cup B$ **d.** $B^C \cap A^C$ **3.41** .133 **3.43 a.** .6 **b.** .84 **c.** .44 **d.** 1 **3.45 a.** 127/244 **b.** 7/244 **c.** 117/244 **d.** 148/244 **3.47 a.** .531 **b.** .75 **c.** .094 **3.49 a.** .0086 **b.** .9914 **c.** .0135 **d.** .9865 **3.53 a.** .5 **b.** .25 **c.** No **3.55 a.** .08 **b.** .4 **c.** .52 **3.57 a.** .8, .7, .6 **b.** .25, .375, .375 **d.** No **3.59 a.** A and C, B and C **b.** None **c.** .65, .90 **3.61** .444 **3.63 a.** .75 **b.** .30 **3.65** .1558 **3.67 a.** .055 **b.** .139 **c.** No **3.69 a.** .371 **b.** .209 **c.** Yes **3.71 a.** .406 **b.** .294 **3.73** .35 **3.75 a.** .23 **b.** .729 **3.77 a.** 1 **b.** .0588 **c.** 17 **3.79 a.** $(.05)^{10} = .000977$ **b.** .00195 **c.** .99805 **3.81 a.** .225 **b.** .125 **c.** .35 **d.** .643 **e.** .357 **3.85 a.** .0788 **b.** .2545 **c.** Novice **3.87 a.** .52, .39, .09 **b.** .516 **3.89** No; $P(D \mid G > 60) = .1075$

3.91 a. .5 **b.** .0028 **3.95 a.** .7 **b.** .9 **3.97 a.** Yes **b.** No **3.99** .5 **3.101 a.** 0, .2, .9, 1, .7, .3, .4, 0 **b.** No; yes **c.** No; no **3.103 a.** E and D, P and P, M and O, T and C **b.** .325 **c.** .711 **3.105** .73 **3.107 a.** False **b.** True **c.** True **d.** False **3.109 a.** 6; $(G_1G_2G_3)$, $(G_1G_2G_4), (G_1G_2G_5), (G_2G_3G_4), (G_2G_3G_5), (G_3G_4G_5)$ **b.** .282, .065, .339, .032, .008, .274 **c.** .686 **3.111 a.** Certification mark on label **b.** .60 **c.** .16 **d.** .94 **3.113 a.** .684 **b.** .124 **c.** No **d.** .316 **e.** .717 **f.** .091 **3.115 a.** .00000625 **b.** .0135 **c.** Doubt validity of the manufacturer's claim **d.** No **3.117 a.** .09 **b.** .09 **c.** .84 **d.** No **e.** Column events not mutually exclusive **3.119 a.** .157 **b.** .029 **c.** .291 **d.** .222 **e.** .183 **3.121** .79 **3.123 a.** LLLL, LLLU, LLUL, LULL, ULLL, LLUU, LULU, LUUL, ULLU, ULUL, UULL, LUUU, ULUU, UULU, UUUL, UUUU **b.** 1/16 **c.** 5/16 **3.125 a.** 12 **b.** No **3.127** $P(A \mid B) = 0$ **3.129** .526 **3.131 a.** .0362 **b.** .0352 **3.133** Marilyn

Chapter 4

4.1 a. Discrete **b.** Continuous **c.** Continuous **d.** Continuous **e.** Discrete **4.3** Discrete **4.5** Continuous **4.7** Inflation rate **4.9** Number of returns per day; number of new salespeople hired **4.11 a.** .25 **b.** .35 **d.** .80 **4.13 a.** .3 **b.** .40 **c.** 5.7, 2.532 **4.15 a.** $p(x) = 1/6$ for all x values **4.17 a.** $\mu = 0$, $\sigma^2 = 2.94, \sigma = 1.72$ **c.** .96 **4.19 a.** 1; 1 **b.** x **c.** $\mu = 1$, $\sigma^2 = .6; \mu = 1, \sigma^2 = .2$ **4.21 a.** $p(1) = 0$, $p(2) = .0408, p(3) = .1735, p(4) = .6020, p(5) = .1837$ **b.** .1837 **c.** .0408 **d.** 3.93 **4.23 c.** .95 **d.** .90; .85 **4.25 a.** 0, 2, 3, 4 **b.** $p(0) = .3302, p(2) = .5472, p(3) = .0472$, $p(4) = .0755$ **c.** 1.538 **4.27 b.** $p(0) = .0053, p(1) = .0488$, $p(2) = .1811, p(3) = .3364, p(4) = .3124, p(5) = .1160$ **d.** .4284 **4.29 a.** .23 **b.** .0809 **c.** .77 **4.31 a.** .508 **b.** .391 **c.** .094 **d.** .007 **4.33** $p(8.5) = .4622, p(9) = .2888, p(9.5) = .1417$, $p(10) = .0700, p(10.5) = .0252, p(11) = .0117$, $p(12) = .00052$ **4.35 a.** $p(\$300,000) = .3, p(\$0) = .7$ **b.** $90,000 **4.37 a.** 30, 40, 50, 60 **b.** .10 **c.** $p(30) = .10$, $p(40) = .2333, p(50) = .30, p(60) = .3667$ **d.** .6667 **4.39** $.25 **4.41 a.** Discrete **b.** Binomial **d.** 3.5; 1.02 **4.43 a.** .1536 **b.** .027 **c.** .0081 **d.** .027 **e.** .1890 **f.** .3456 **4.45 a.** 12.5, 6.25, 2.5 **b.** 16, 12.8, 3.578 **c.** 60, 24, 4.899 **d.** 63, 6.3, 2.510 **e.** 48, 9.6, 3.098 **f.** 40, 38.4, 6.197 **4.47 a.** Adult who does not work in the summer **c.** .22 **d.** .2244 **e.** .6169 **4.49 b.** .772 **c.** .714 **4.51 a.** 1 **b.** .0005 **c.** 1; 0 **4.53 a.** .6591 **b.** .2373 **4.55 a.** .055 **b.** In 2020, more than 9% of Denver bridges will have a rating of 4 or below. **4.57 a.** 680, 10.1 **b.** No, $z = -27.72$ **4.59 b.** $\mu = 2.4, \sigma = 1.47$ **c.** $p = .90, q = .10, n = 24$, $\mu = 21.60, \sigma = 1.47$ **4.61 a.** Discrete **b.** Poisson **d.** $\mu = 3$, $\sigma = 1.73$ **4.63 a.** .3 **b.** .119 **c.** .167 **d.** .167 **4.65 a.** .9197 **b.** .6767 **c.** .4232 **d.** Decreases **4.67 a.** Hypergeometric **b.** Binomial **4.69 c.** $\mu = 1.415, \sigma = 1.054$ **d.** .280 **4.71 a.** .368 **b.** .368 **c.** 1, 1 **4.73** .2693 **4.75** .1848 **4.77** .1931 **4.79** .5507 **4.81** no; P(only 5 females selected) ≈ 0 **4.83 a.** .333 **b.** .133 **4.85 a.** .0721 **b.** .0594 **c.** .2434 **d.** .3457 **e.** .5 **f.** .9233 **4.87 a.** .6826 **b.** .9500 **c.** .90 **d.** .9544 **4.89 a.** $-.81$ **b.** .55 **c.** 1.43 **d.** .21 **e.** -2.05 **f.** .50 **4.91 a.** -2.5 **b.** 0 **c.** -6.81 **d.** -3.75 **e.** 1.25 **f.** -1.25 **4.93 a.** .3830 **b.** .3023 **c.** .1525 **d.** .7333 **e.** .1314 **f.** .9545 **4.95 a.** Yes **b.** 10, 6 **c.** .726 **d.** .7291 **4.97 a.** .5328 **b.** .6915 **c.** .5 **4.99 a.** .0331 **b.** .4677 **c.** 99.9 **4.101 a.** .4207 **b.** .000337 **4.103 a.** 175 **b.** 11.4564 **c.** 2.23 **d.** .9871 **4.105** -4.256% **4.107** .8664 **4.109 a.** $p = .12$ for this hotel **b.** p much greater than .12 for this hotel **4.111 a.** 25.14% **b.** 90.375 **4.113 b.** 59; 2 **c.** .9732; 0 **4.115** $z = -.588$ if no coaching, $z = 2.4$ if coaching; more likely that leader did not

receive coaching **4.117 a.** .68 **b.** .95 **c.** 1.00 **4.119** Plot c
4.121 a. Yes, $IQR/s = 1.62$ **b.** Yes, $IQR/s = 1.46$
4.123 a. Approx. normal **b.** Approx. normal
4.125 b. $\bar{x} = 67.76$, $s = 26.87$; 94.5% of observations within
$\bar{x} \pm 2s$ **c.** $IQR = 37$, $IQR/s = 1.38$ **4.127** No **4.129** None
4.131 $z = -1.06$ for minimum value of 0 **4.133 a.** $f(x) = .04$
$(20 \leq x \leq 45)$, 0 otherwise **b.** 32.5, 7.22 **4.135 a.** .367879
b. .950213 **c.** .223130 **d.** .993262 **4.139 a.** .333 **b.** .133 **c.** 113.5
4.141 a. .133; .571 **b.** .267; 0 **4.143 a.** .449329 **b.** .864665
4.145 a. .5 **b.** .3 **c.** Only 1 possible connection
4.147 a. Continuous **c.** 7, .2887, (6.422, 7.577) **d.** .5 **e.** 0 **f.** .75
g. .0002 **4.149 a.** .753403 **b.** .667 **c.** .811 **4.151** .4444
4.153 $-\theta \ln(.5) = .6931470\theta$ **4.157 a.** .2734 **b.** .4096 **c.** .3432
4.159 a. .192 **b.** .228 **c.** .772 **d.** .987 **e.** .960 **f.** 14, 4.2, 2.049 **g.** .975
4.161 a. Poisson **b.** Binomial **c.** Binomial **4.163 a.** Discrete
b. Continuous **c.** Continuous **d.** Continuous **4.165 a.** .9821
b. .0179 **c.** .9505 **d.** .3243 **e.** .9107 **f.** .0764 **4.167 a.** . Exponential
b. Uniform **c.** Normal **4.169 a.** .6915 **b.** .1587 **c.** .1915 **d.** .3085
e. 0 **f.** 1 **4.171** 47.68 **b.** 47.68 **c.** 30.13 **d.** 41.5 **e.** 30.13
4.173 b. .14 **c.** $\mu = 4.655$, $\sigma^2 = 19.856$ **d.** $(-4.26, 13.57)$
4.175 .25 **4.177 a.** .221199 **b.** .002394 **c.** .082085
4.179 b. $n = 20, p = .8$ **c.** .175 **d.** .804 **e.** 16 **4.181 a.** .367869
b. .606531 **c.** .135335; .135335 **d.** .814046 **4.183 a.** .383 **b.** .0002
4.185 No **4.187 a.** .8264 **b.** 17 times **c.** .6217 **d.** 0, -157
4.189 a. 1.25, 1.09; no **b.** .007 **c.** Not applicable **4.191 a.** .3413
b. .0026 **c.** .3830 **4.193 b.** .85 **c.** .6, .7, 0 **d.** A1: 2.4; A2: 1.5; A3:
1.65; A4: .10 **e.** A1: .86; A2: .67; A3: .57; A4: .3 **4.195** Unlikely,
$p = .0548$ **4.197 a.** 7,667 **b.** 45.62% **4.199 a.** 69.2 **b.** 42.2
4.201 292 **4.203 a.** $p(x) = .05$ for all x-values **b.** 52.5
c. $(-5.16, 110.16)$ **f.** 33.25, 38.3577 **g.** .525 **i.** .20 **j.** .65
4.205 a. $\sigma = 1$: .6826; $\sigma = 2$: .4260; $\sigma = 4$: .3734
b. $\sigma = 1$; .6945; $\sigma = 2$: .42; $\sigma = 4$: .3709 **c.** $\sigma = 1$; $\sigma = 2$

Chapter 5

5.1 a. $(0, 0), (0, 2), (0, 4), (0, 6), (2, 0), (2, 2), (2, 4), (2, 6),$
$(4, 0), (4, 2), (4, 4), (4, 6), (6, 0), (6, 2), (6, 4), (6, 6)$
b. 0, 1, 2, 3, 1, 2, 3, 4, 2, 3, 4, 5, 3, 4, 5, 6 **c.** 1/16 **d.** $p(0) = 1/16$,
$p(1) = 2/16, p(2) = 3/16, p(3) = 4/16, p(4) = 3/16,$
$p(5) = 2/16, p(6) = 1/16$ **5.3 a.** $p(1) = .04, p(1.5) = .12,$
$p(2) = .17, p(2.5) = .20, p(3) = .20, p(3.5) = .14,$
$p(4) = .08, p(4.5) = .04, p(5) = .01$ **c.** .05 **d.** No
5.5 a. Same as Exercise 5.3a **5.9 a.** 5 **b.** $E(\bar{x}) = 5$
c. $E(m) = 4.778$ **d.** $\bar{x}$ **5.11 a.** Yes **b.** median **5.13 b.** 1.61
c. $E(s^2) = 1.61$ **e.** $E(s) = 1.004$ **5.15** No **5.17 a.** 100, 5
b. 100, 2 **c.** 100, 1 **d.** 100, 1.414 **e.** 100, .447 **f.** 100, .316
5.19 a. .0228 **b.** .0668 **c.** .0062 **d.** .8185 **e.** .0013 **5.21 a.** .8944
b. .0228 **c.** .1292 **d.** .9699 **5.23 a.** 353 **b.** 20 **c.** $\approx$ normal **d.** 0
5.25 a. 68 **b.** 4.02 **c.** $\approx$ normal **d.** .7734 **5.27** No;
$P(\bar{x} < 103) = .0107$ **5.29 a.** $\approx$ normal with $\mu_{\bar{x}} = .53$;
$\sigma_{\bar{x}} = .0273$ **b.** .0336 **c.** Before: $p = .0139$; after: $p = .3557$; after
5.31 a. .0034 **b.** ≈ 0; true mean is larger than 6 ppb
5.33 a. Skewed right **b.** $\mu = 95.52$, $\sigma = 91.37$ **c.** Normal;
$\mu_{\bar{x}} = 95.52$ and $\sigma_{\bar{x}} = 14.47$ **d.** .3520 **5.35** Handrubbing:
$p = .2743$; handwashing: $p = .0047$; handrubbing
5.37 a. $\mu_{\hat{p}} = .1, \sigma_{\hat{p}} = .0134$ **b.** $\mu_{\hat{p}} = .5, \sigma_{\hat{p}} = .0224$
c. $\mu_{\hat{p}} = .7, \sigma_{\hat{p}} = .0205$ **5.39 a.** $E(\hat{p}) = .85, \sigma_{\hat{p}} = .0226$
b. $\approx$ normal **c.** .9864 **5.41 d.** As n increases, $\sigma_{\hat{p}}$
decreases; distributions all $\approx$ normal **5.43 a.** $E(\hat{p}) = .15$
b. $\sigma_{\hat{p}} = .016$ **c.** $\approx$ normal **d.** .0301 **e.** ≈ 1 **5.45 a.** .9774
b. ≈ 0 **5.47** .2676 **5.49 a.** .92 **b.** .0099 **5.51** True percent less
than 90% **5.53 b.** $E(A) = \theta$ **c.** Choose estimator with smaller
variance **5.55 a.** .5 **b.** .0606 **c.** .0985 **d.** .8436 **5.57 a.** .9032

b. .9850 **c.** .3328 **5.63** .0838 **5.65 a.** .0019 **b.** True, $p > .4$
c. Sample not representative of target population
5.67 a. $\approx$ normal **b.** .0091 **c.** .9544 **5.69** .9772 **5.71 a.** $\mu_{\hat{p}} = .2$,
$\sigma_{\hat{p}} = .0253$ **b.** (.1494, .2596) **c.** .9544 **5.73 a.** .01; .002
b. (.00164, .00236) **5.75** Not likely; $P(\bar{x} > 42) \approx 0$

Chapter 6

6.1 a. 1.645 **b.** 2.576 **c.** 1.96 **d.** 1.282 **6.3 a.** $28 \pm .784$
b. $102 \pm .65$ **c.** $15 \pm .0588$ **d.** $4.05 \pm .163$ **e.** No
6.5 a. $26.2 \pm .96$ **b.** In repeated sampling, 95% of all confidence
intervals constructed will include μ. **c.** 26.2 ± 1.26 **d.** Increases
e. Yes **6.7** Point estimator is a single number. **6.9** Yes
6.11 112 ± 21.46; 95% confident true mean tipping point is between 90.54 and 133.46. **6.13 a.** 3.11 **b.** (3.02, 3.30) **c.** Incorrect
d. No impact—CLT applies **6.15 a.** $2.42 \pm .504$ **b** 90%
confident the mean intention to comply score for all entry-level
accountants is between 1.916 and 2.924 **c.** .90 **d.** 2.42 ± 5.68;
$\approx$ 95% of all scores will fall in the interval **6.17 a.** μ = mean
salary of all 4110 CEOs **6.19 a.** 99.6 **b.** 99.6 ± 2.24 **c.** 95%
confident that true Mach rating score of all purchasing managers
is between 97.36 and 101.84. **d.** Yes **6.21** SAT—Math
6.23 a. $z_{.10} = 1.282, t_{.10} = 1.533$ **b.** $z_{.05} = 1.645, t_{.05} = 2.132$
c. $z_{.025} = 1.96, t_{.025} = 2.776$ **d.** $z_{.01} = 2.326, 3.747$
e. $z_{.005} = 2.576, t_{.005} = 4.604$ **6.25 a.** 2.228 **b.** 2.228 **c.** -1.812
d. 1.725 **e.** 4.032 **6.27 a.** 5 ± 1.88 **b.** 5 ± 2.39 **c.** 5 ± 3.75
d. $5 \pm .78, 5 \pm .94, 5 \pm 1.28$; decreased width **6.29 a.** μ =
mean trap spacing for the population of red spiny lobster
fishermen **b.** 89.86 **c.** Sampling distribution of $\bar{x}$ is unknown.
d. (79.10, 100.62) **e.** 95% confident that true mean trap spacing is between 79.10 and 100.62 meters **f.** Population of trap
spacings is normally distributed. **6.31 a.** (2.55, 3.98) **b.** 99%
confident that true mean number of wheels on all social robots
is between 2.55 and 3.98 **c.** .99 **6.33 a.** (7.64, 8.81) **b.** No
c. Population of ratios is normally distributed. **6.35 a.** (.24281,
.28135), 95% confident that true mean bubble rising velocity is
between .24281 and .28135 **b.** No, $\mu = .338$ is not in the confidence interval **6.37 a.** (303.4, 413.6) **b.** 95% confident that true
mean skidding distance falls between 303.4 and 413.6 meters
c. $\approx$ normal **d.** No **6.39 a.** All 216 firms in *Forbes* Largest
Private Companies list **b.** (2.45, 12.42) **c.** 98% confident that
true mean revenue is between $2.45 and $12.42 billion.
d. $\approx$ normal **e.** Yes **6.41 a.** Yes **b.** No **c.** No **d.** No
6.43 a. Yes **b.** $.46 \pm .065$ **c.** 95% confident p is between .395
and .525 **d.** 95% of all similarly constructed intervals contain
the true value of p. **6.45 a.** .5 **b.** (.448, .552) **c.** We are 90%
confident that the true proportion of all U.S adults who would
agree to participate in the store loyalty card program, despite
the potential for information sharing, is between .448 and .552.
6.47 a. .4 **b.** $\approx$ normal **c.** (.38, .42) **d.** 95% confident that true
proportion of Arlington homes with market values that are overestimated by more than 10% falls between .38 and .42 **e.** No
6.49 a. All American adults **b.** 1,000 adults surveyed
c. Proportion of all American adults who think Starbucks coffee
is overpriced **d.** $.73 \pm .028$ **6.51** (.797, .843) 90% of all intervals constructed in this manner will contain the true mean.
6.53 (.08, .22) No **6.55 a.** No **b.** (0, .019) **6.57 a.** True proportion of all fillets that are red snapper **c.** $.27 \pm .17$ **d.** 95%
confident that true proportion of all fillets that are red snapper
is between .10 and .44 **6.59** 95% CI for p: (.849, .851); actual
performance is below claim of $p = .95$. **6.61 a.** 68 **b.** 31
6.63 34 **6.65 a.** 098, 0.784, 0.56, 0.392, 0.196 **6.67** 1,692
6.69 84 **6.71** $\approx$ 286 **6.73** 14,735 **6.75** 43; 171; 385 **6.77** 271

6.79 a. 1,083 **b.** Wider **c.** 38.3%   **6.81 a.** 4.90 **b.** 5.66 **c.** 6.00
d. 6.293   **6.83 a.** 1.00 **b.** .6124 **c.** 0 **d.** As n increases, standard
error decreases.   **6.85** .42 $\pm$ .021   **6.87 a.** .56 $\pm$ .012 **c.** 95%
confident that true proportion of active NFL players who select
a professional coach as most influential is between .548 and .572
6.89 a. 156.46 **b.** 18.70 **c.** 156.46 $\pm$ 37.405 **d.** Not reasonable
6.91 1 $\pm$ 41.43   **6.93 a.** 11.0705, 1.1455 **b.** 24.7356, 5.0088
c. 44.4608, 15.3079 **d.** 29.8195, 3.5650   **6.95 a.** (2.13, 2.97)
b. (.016, .029) **c.** (25.34, 42.53) **d.** (.974, 3.559)   **6.97 a.** σ^2, the
variance of the interval oil content measurements for sweet po-
tato chips **b.** (47.15, 727.85) **c.** 95% of all intervals constructed
in the same manner will contain the true variance. **d.** $\approx$ normal
f. (6.87, 26.98)   **6.99 a.** (.13, .19); 95% confident that true standard deviation of facial WHR for CEOs is between .13 and .19
b. $\approx$ normal   **6.101** (6.25, 17.74); 99% confident that true variance in drug concentrations is between 6.67 and 17.74
6.103 (43.72, 1199.95)   **6.105 a.** (2.39, 3.58) **b.** (2.71, 4.11)
c. Cannot conclude the variances differ because the intervals
overlap   **6.107 a.** .6912 **b.** 1.3968 **c.** 1.7291 **d.** 2.0639
6.109 a. 32.5 $\pm$ 5.15 **b.** 23,871 **c.** (714.2, 1163.7)
6.111 a. 19.0228; 2.70039 **b.** 32.8523; 8.90655 **c.** 79.49; 27.9907
6.113 (1) p = proportion with excellent health; **(2), (3),** and
(4) μ = mean number of days health not good   **6.115 a.** .11
b. .11 $\pm$ .050   **6.117** 97   **6.119** .694 $\pm$ .092
6.121 6,563 $\pm$ 97.65   **6.123** .667 $\pm$ .065   **6.125 a.** (1.64, 2.13)
b. No   **6.127** (1203, 1743) 90% confident that the true mean
threshold compensation level for all major airlines is between
\$1,203.46 and \$1,742.54   **6.129 a.** .867 **b.** (.781, .953) **c.** 95%
confident that true proportion of Walmart stores with more than
2 inaccurately scanned items is between .781 and .953 **d.** Not
believable **e.** No **f.** 126   **6.131 a.** .60 **b.** (.58, .62) **c.** 95% confident that true proportion of all adults who use cell phones while
driving falls between .58 and .62 **d.** .015   **6.133** 818
6.137 99% confidence interval is (959.99, 1011.21); 1,000 in
interval, not out of control   **6.139 a.** Yes **b.** Missing measure of
reliability **c.** 95% CI for μ: .932 $\pm$ .037

Chapter 7

7.1 Null; alternative   **7.3** α **7.5** Reject H_0 when H_0 is true;
accept H_0 when H_0 is true. Reject H_0 when H_0 is false; accept
H_0 when H_0 is false.   **7.7** No   **7.9** H_0: p = .4, H_a: $p \neq$ .4
7.11 H_0: p = .12, H_a: $p <$ .12   **7.13** H_0: μ = 863, H_a: $\mu <$ 863
7.15 a. Unsafe; safe **c.** α **7.17 c.** α **e.** Decrease **f.** Increase
7.19 a. .1151 **b.** .1151 **c.** .2302   **7.21 a.** Do not reject H_0.
b. Reject H_0. **c.** Reject H_0. **d.** Do not reject H_0. **e.** Do not
reject H_0.   **7.23** .0150   **7.25** .03   **7.27** .06   **7.29 a.** $z >$ 2.14
b. .0162   **7.31 a.** $z =$ −1.61, reject H_0. **b.** $z =$ −1.61, do not reject
H_0.   **7.33 a.** $z =$ 5.71, reject H_0. **b.** Test is valid due to CLT.
7.35 H_0: μ = 2.2, H_a: $\mu \neq$ 2.2, p-value $\approx$ 0, reject H_0 for any
reasonable α.   **7.37 a.** H_0: μ = .250, H_a: $\mu \neq$ .250 **b.** $\bar{x}$ = .25248,
s = .00223 **c.** z = 7.03 **d.** p-value $\approx$ 0 **e.** $|z| >$ 2.576 **f.** Yes,
reject H_0.   **7.39 a.** Yes; z = 1.85, p-value = .0322, reject H_0.
b. Yes; z = −1.85, p-value = .0322, reject H_0. **c.** No; apply CLT.
7.41 z = −1.86, do not reject H_0.   **7.43 a.** z = 26.15, p-value $\approx$ 0,
reject H_0. **b.** z = −14.24, p-value $\approx$ 0, reject H_0.
7.45 a. z = 4.12, reject H_0. **b.** 10.82 $\pm$ .152 **c.** 10.5 not in interval implies reject H_0.   **7.47 a.** Small n, data normal **b.** Mound-
shaped and symmetric; t is flatter than z.   **7.49 a.** $|t| >$ 2.160
b. $t >$ 2.500 **c.** $t >$ 1.397 **d.** $t <$ −2.718 **e.** $|t| >$ 1.729
f. $t <$ −2.353   **7.51 b.** Reject H_0 at α = .05. **c.** Do not reject
null hypothesis   **7.53 a.** H_0: μ = 70, H_a: $\mu <$ 70 **b.** $t <$ −6.965

c. t = −.29 **d.** Fail to reject H_0. **e.** Population $\approx$ normal
7.55 H_0: μ = 6,000; H_a: $\mu <$ 6,000; t = −1.82;
p-value = .048; α = .10; reject H_0 **7.57 a.** H_0: μ = .338,
H_a: $\mu \neq$ .338, t = −8.13, p-value $\approx$ 0, reject H_0. **b.** No
7.59 Yes, t = −2.53   **7.61** H_0: μ = 76, H_a: $\mu >$ 76, t = 3.93,
p-value = .03, reject H_0, yes.   **7.63** Yes, using α = .05;
Plant 1: p-value = .197; Plant 2: p-value = .094   **7.65 a.** −2.33
c. Reject H_0. **d.** .0099   **7.67 a.** z = 1.13, do not reject H_0.
b. .1292   **7.69 a.** $\hat{p}$ = .9 **b.** H_0: p = .8, H_a: $p >$ .8 **c.** z = 3.95
d. $z >$ 2.326 **e.** p-value $\approx$ 0 **f.** Reject H_0. **g.** Reject H_0.
7.71 H_0: p = 1/3, H_a: $p \neq$ 1/3, z = 1.69, reject H_0 if $|z| >$ 1.645,
reject H_0.   **7.73 a.** H_0: p = .5, H_a: $p <$ .5 **b.** .188 **c.** Do not
reject H_0.   **7.75** No; z = −.89   **7.77 a.** No, z = 1.49 **b.** .0681
7.79 Population: all U.S. households in \$75,000 income bracket;
experimental unit: individual household; variable: whether or
not the household owns Smart TV with Internet and video
streaming access; parameter: p = proportion all households with
Smart TV with Internet and video streaming access; H_0: p = .29,
H_a: $p \neq$ .29; test statistic $z = (\hat{p} - .29)/\sqrt{(.29)(.71)/n}$
7.81 z = 1.20, do not reject H_0.   **7.83 a.** $\chi^2 <$ 6.26214 or
$\chi^2 >$ 27.4884 **b.** $\chi^2 >$ 40.2894 **c.** $\chi^2 >$ 21.0642 **d.** $\chi^2 <$ 3.57056
e. $\chi^2 <$ 1.63539 or $\chi^2 >$ 12.5916 **f.** $\chi^2 <$ 13.8484
7.85 a. χ^2 = 479.16, reject H_0.   **7.87 a.** H_0: σ^2 = 100,
H_a: $\sigma^2 <$ 100 **b.** $\chi^2 <$ 167.361 **c.** Chance of concluding $\sigma <$ 10
when σ = 10 is .05. **d.** χ^2 = 154.71, p-value = .009 **e.** Reject H_0.
f. Rates of return $\approx$ normal   **7.89 a.** H_0: σ^2 = .000004,
H_a: $\sigma^2 \neq$ .000004 **b.** χ^2 = 48.49, do not reject H_0. **c.** Tee
weights $\approx$ normal   **7.91** H_0: σ^2 = 25, H_a: $\sigma^2 <$ 25, χ^2 = 10.94,
p-value = .552, do not reject H_0.   **7.93** No, χ^2 = 13.77
7.95 a. With large s, test statistic will be small. **b.** 1.76
c. Yes; χ^2 − 99 **d.** Inference about μ is valid; inference about σ
is not valid.   **7.97 b.** 532.9 **d.** .1949 **e.** .8051   **7.99 a.** Approx.
normal with $\mu_{\bar{x}}$ = 75 and $\sigma_{\bar{x}}$ = 2.14 **b.** Approx. normal with
$\mu_{\bar{x}}$ = 70 and $\sigma_{\bar{x}}$ = 2.14 **c.** .1469 **d.** .8531   **7.101 a.** Approx.
normal **b.** .0426 **c.** 41.29% of chance of an incorrect acceptance
of null hypothesis. **d.** 99.63% chance of incorrect acceptance of
null hypothesis.   **7.103 a.** .1949, Type II error **b.** .05, Type I
error **c.** .8051   **7.105** .7764   **7.107** .1075   **7.109** Alternative
7.111 Large   **7.113 a.** t = −2, reject H_0. **b.** Fail to reject H_0.
7.115 a. z = −1.78, reject H_0. **b.** z = −1.78, do not reject H_0.
7.117 a. χ^2 = 63.48, reject H_0. **b.** χ^2 = 63.48, reject H_0.
7.119 Yes, z = −3.54   **7.121 a.** $\chi^2 <$ 24.3 or $\chi^2 >$ 73.1
b. χ^2 = 63.72 **c.** Do not reject H_0.   **7.123 a.** H_0: μ = 1,
H_a: $\mu >$ 1 **b.** Reject H_0 if $t >$ 1.345. **d.** t = 2.41
e. .01 < p-value < .025, reject H_0. **f.** χ^2 = 12.78, do not
reject H_0.   **7.125 a.** $\hat{p}$ = .67 **b.** H_0: p = .7, H_a: $p >$ .7
c. z = −1.80 **d.** $z >$ 2.326 **e.** p-value = .9641 **f.** Do not reject
H_0. **g.** Do not reject H_0.   **7.127 a.** H_0: μ = 85, H_a: $\mu \neq$ 85
b. Reject H_0 if $z >$ 1.645 or $z <$ −1.645. **c.** z = 12.80
d. Reject H_0.   **7.129 a.** H_0: No disease, H_a: Disease **b.** Type I
error = false positive; Type II error = false negative
c. Type II error; β **7.131** χ^2 = 187.9, do not reject H_0.
7.133 a. z = −3.22 **b.** p-value $\approx$ 1 **c.** .8159
7.135 a. Concluding that percentage of shoplifters turned over
to police is 50% when, in fact, the percentage is higher than 50%
b. .8461 **c.** Decreases to .7389   **7.137 a.** No, z = 1.41 **b.** Small
c. .0793   **7.139 a.** No **b.** β = .5910, power = .4090 **c.** Increases
7.141 At α = .05, yes; χ^2 = 133.90   **7.143 a.** H_0: μ = 1.4, H_a:
$\mu >$ .4 **b.** Chance of concluding $\mu >$ .4 when μ = 1.4 is .10.
c. $\bar{x}$ = 5.243, s = .192 **d.** t = 34.67 **e.** p-value = 0 **f.** Reject H_0.
7.145 a. z = 2.73, reject H_0. **c.** Sampling distribution of $\bar{x}$ is
approx. normal by CLT.   **7.147** z = 7.83, reject H_0.

Chapter 8

8.1 a. 150 ± 6 **b.** 150 ± 8 **c.** $0; 5$ **d.** 0 ± 10 **e.** Variability of the difference is greater. **8.3 a.** 35 ± 24.5 **b.** $z = 2.8$, p-value $= .0052$, reject H_0. **c.** p-value $= .0026$ **d.** $z = .8$, p-value $= .4238$, do not reject H_0. **e.** Independent random samples **8.5 a.** No **b.** No **c.** No **d.** Yes **e.** No **8.7 a.** .5989 **b.** Yes, $t = -2.39$ **c.** $-1.24 \pm .98$ **d.** Confidence interval **8.9 a.** Do not reject H_0. **b.** .0575 **8.11 a.** $t = -1.646$, do not reject H_0. **b.** -2.50 ± 3.12 **8.13 a.** 5.70 ± 5.07 **b.** R–Z group; yes **8.15 a.** $H_0: \mu_C = \mu_G, H_a: \mu_C < \mu_G$ **b.** $p = .045$, reject H_0. **8.17 a.** $.90 \pm .064$ **b.** Buy-side **c.** Large, independent random samples **8.19 a.** None **b.** A, C, and D **c.** Large samples, CLT applies. **8.21** $z = -2.81$, reject $H_0: \mu_C = \mu_R$. **8.23** Yes, $z = 3.20$, sufficient evidence to conclude $\mu_{Honey} > \mu_{DM}$ **8.25 a.** No sample variances **b.** s_1^2 and s_2^2 **c.** $z < -2.326$ **d.** $.24$ **e.** Smaller **8.27 a.** $t > 1.796$ **b.** $t > 1.319$ **c.** $t > 3.182$ **d.** $t > 2.374$ **8.29 a.** $H_0: \mu_d = 0, H_a: \mu_d < 0$ **b.** $t = -5.29$, p-value $= .0003$, reject H_0. **c.** $(-4.98, -2.42)$ **d.** Population of differences is normal. **8.31 a.** $H_0: \mu_d = 0, H_a: \mu_d > 0$ **b.** Paired test **c.** $z = 3.10$ **d.** $z = 19.18$ **e.** Paired test **f.** Reject H_0. **g.** No **h.** $(2.86, 3.74)$ **8.33 a.** Two hole measurements at each location **c.** $\bar{d} = .14, s_d = 1.26$ **d.** $(-.435, .715)$ **e.** Yes **8.35 a.** Response rates observed twice for each survey **b.** No, $t = .53$ **c.** Reject H_0. **8.37 a.** Yes, $t = 2.864$ **8.39** Yes, $(-390.9, -176.3)$ **8.41** $t = .46$, p-value $= .65$, do not reject H_0. **8.43 a.** Binomial distributions **b.** Distribution is approx. normal for large n's **8.45 a.** No **b.** No **c.** No **d.** No **e.** No **8.47 a.** $z = -4.02$, reject H_0. **b.** $z = -4.02$, reject H_0. **c.** $z = -4.02$, reject H_0. **d.** $.1 \pm .041$ **8.49 a.** .153 **b.** .215 **c.** $(-.132, .008)$ **d.** No evidence of a difference **8.51 a.** $p_1 - p_2$ **b.** $H_0: p_1 - p_2 = 0, H_a: p_1 - p_2 \neq 0$ **c.** $z = -2.67$ **d.** $|z| > 2.576$ **e.** .008 **f.** Reject H_0. **8.53 a.** All January patients; all May patients **b.** .083 **c.** $(.033, .133)$ **d.** Yes **8.55** No, $z = 1.68$ **8.57** Yes; 95% CI for $(p_{AA} - p_{White}) = (.089, .131)$, $z = 14.64$ **8.59** $z = -2.60$, client-flow website more likely to be vulnerable to impersonation attack **8.61 a.** 29,954 **b.** 2,165 **c.** 1,113 **8.63** 34 **8.65** 156 **8.67 a.** $p_{Server} - p_{Client}$ **b.** .95 **c.** .15 **d.** 86 **e.** $n_1 = 128, n_2 = 64$ **8.69** $n_S = 320, n_U = 160$ **8.71 a.** 5,051 **8.73 a.** 4.10 **b.** 3.57 **c.** 8.81 **d.** 3.21 **8.75 a.** $F > 3.2927$ **b.** $F > 5.613$ **c.** $F > 3.2927$ **d.** $F > 4.20$ **8.77 a.** $F > 2.11$ **b.** $F > 3.01$ **c.** $F > 2.04$ **d.** $F > 2.30$ **e.** $F > 5.27$ **8.79 a.** $F = 4.29$, do not reject H_0. **b.** $.05 < p$-value $< .10$, **8.81 a.** $H_0: \sigma_1^2/\sigma_2^2 = 1, H_a: \sigma_1^2/\sigma_2^2 \neq 1$ **b.** $F = .8963$ **c.** p-value $= .9617$, **d.** Fail to reject H_0. **8.83** $F = .844$, p-value $= .681$, fail to reject H_0. **8.85 a.** No, $F = 2.27$ **b.** $.05 < p$-value $< .10$, **8.87** In scenario with $s_1 = 4$ and $s_2 = 2$ **8.91 a.** $t = -1.015$, fail to reject H_0. **b.** -6.9 ± 14.0631 **c.** 46 **8.93 a.** $3.90 \pm .311$ **b.** $p \approx 0$, reject H_0. **c.** 346 **8.95 a.** $p_{Male} - p_{Female}$, independent samples **b.** $\mu_{Crestor} - \mu_{Mevacor}$, independent samples **c.** μ_d, population of differences approx. normal **d.** $\sigma_{High}^2/\sigma_{Low}^2$, populations approx. normal and independent samples **8.97 a.** $.29 \pm 1.45$ **b.** $F = 1.06$, do not reject H_0. **c.** No significant difference **8.99 a.** $\mu_1 - \mu_2$ **b.** $H_0: \mu_1 - \mu_2 = 0, H_a: \mu_1 - \mu_2 > 0$ **c.** Yes **8.101 a.** $\mu_1 - \mu_2$ **c.** $-.561 \pm 1.438$ **d.** No **e.** Random sample of pairs **8.103 a.** $H_0: \mu_1 - \mu_2 = 0, H_a: \mu_1 - \mu_2 \neq 0$ **b.** $t = .62$ **c.** $|t| > 1.684$ **d.** Do not reject H_0. **e.** Do not reject H_0. **f.** Independent random samples, both populations normal, $\sigma_1^2 = \sigma_2^2$ **8.105 a.** $H_0: p_1 - p_2 = 0, H_a: p_1 - p_2 > 0$ **b.** $z = 3.16$ **c.** Reject H_0 if $z > 2.33$. **d.** p-value ≈ 0, **d.** Reject H_0. **8.107 a.** Male and female smartphone users **b.** $.48, .60$ **c.** $(-.19, -.05)$ **d.** Yes **e.** $.42, .35$ **f.** $z = 1.66$, reject H_0. **8.109 a.** Yes, $t = -1.96$ **c.** .058.

d. -7.4 ± 6.38 **8.111 a.** $z = 94.35$, reject H_0. **b.** $(-.155, -.123)$ **8.113** 4,802 **8.115** No, $F = 2.79$ **8.117** $n_1 = n_2 = 293$ **8.119** Aad: no, at $\alpha = .05$; Ab: yes, at $\alpha = .05$; Intention: no, at $\alpha = .05$ **8.121 a.** Yes, $z = -2.79$ **b.** 95% CI: $-.011 \pm .0077$ **8.123** Yes; 95% confidence interval for μ_d: $(-242.29, -106.96)$

Chapter 9

9.1 A, B, C, D **9.5 a.** Observational **b.** Designed **c.** Observational **d.** Observational **e.** Observational **9.7 a.** CPAs **b.** Likelihood of reporting sustainability policies **c.** Firm size; firm type **d.** Size: large or small; type: public or private **e.** large/public, large/private, small/public, and small/private **9.9 a.** Experimental units randomly assigned to treatments **b.** Exp. unit: participant; response: level of appreciation; factor: role; treatments: gift-giver, gift-receiver **9.11 a.** 4 **b.** (Within-store/home), (Within-store/in store), (Between-store/home), (Between-store/in store) **9.13 a.** Experimental units randomly assigned to treatments **b.** Exp. unit: participant; dep. var.: number of words spoken by women **c.** Gender composition (0, 1, 2, 3, 4, 5 women); decision rule (unanimous, majority rule) **d.** 12: $(0, U), (1, U), (2, U), (3, U), (4, U), (5, U), (0, M), (1, M), (2, M), (3, M), (4, M), (5, M)$ **9.15 a.** 6.39 **b.** 15.98 **c.** 1.54 **d.** 3.18 **9.17 a.** Plot 2 **b.** $\bar{x}_1 = 9$ and $\bar{x}_2 = 14$ for both plots **c.** SST $= 75$ for both plots **d.** Plot 1: SSE $= 20$; Plot 2: SSE $= 144$ **e.** Plot 1: SS(Total) $= 95$ (78.95%); Plot 2: SS(Total) $= 219$ (34.25%) **f.** Plot 1: $F = 37.5$; Plot 2: $F = 5.21$ **g.** Reject H_0 for both plots. **h.** Both populations are normal with equal variances. **9.19** Plot 1: df(Treatments) $= 1$, df(Error) $= 10$, df(Total) $= 11$, SST $= 75$, SSE $= 20$, SS(Total) $= 95$, MST $= 75$, MSE $= 2, F = 37.5$; Plot 2: df(Treatments) $= 1$, df(Error) $= 10$, df(Total) $= 11$, SST $= 75$, SSE $= 144$, SS(Total) $= 219$, MST $= 75$, MSE $= 14.4, F = 5.21$ **9.21 a.** df(Treatments) $= 2$, df(Error) $= 9$, df(Total) $= 11$, SST $= 12.30$, SSE $= 18.89$, SS(Total) $= 31.19$, MST $= 6.15$, MSE $= 2.10, F = 2.93$ **b.** Fail to reject H_0. **9.23 a.** Responses: # tweets, # tweets, continue use, continue use; trt.: twitter skill level, $H_0: \mu_1 = \mu_2 = \mu_3 = \mu_4 = \mu_5, H_a$: At least two treatment means differ. **b.** Male, # tweets: $F = 1.17, p = .331$, fail to reject H_0; Female, # tweets: $F = .56, p = .731$, fail to reject H_0.; Male, continue use: $F = 2.21, p = .062$, fail to reject H_0; Female, continue use: $F = 3.34, p = .006$, reject H_0. **9.25 a.** Completely randomized design; exp. units: bus customers; dependent variable: performance score; factor: bus depot; treatments: Depot 1, Depot 2, and Depot 3 **b.** Yes; $p = .0001$ **9.27 a.** $H_0: \mu_1 = \mu_2 = \mu_3 = \mu_4 = \mu_5 = \mu_6 = \mu_7, H_a$: At least two treatment means differ. **b.** $F = 1.60, p = .174$, fail to reject H_0. **9.29 a.** Completely randomized design **b.** Exp. units: students; dependent variable: tanning attitude; treatments: models with a tan, models with no tan, and no model **c.** H_0: $\mu_{Tan} = \mu_{NoTan} = \mu_{NoModel}$ **d.** No measure of variance **e.** Reject H_0. **f.** Independent random samples from normal populations with equal variances **9.31** $F = 5.388, p = .004$, reject H_0. **9.33** Reject $H_0: \mu_1 = \mu_2 = \mu_3 = \mu_4$ for shell thickness and whipping capacity **9.35 a.** 3 **b.** 10 **c.** 6 **d.** 45 **9.37** $P(\text{Type I error})$ for a single comparison **9.39** $(\mu_1, \mu_4) > (\mu_2, \mu_3)$ **9.41** Highest: μ_8 or μ_{14}, lowest: μ_{12} **9.43** $\mu_1 > \mu_2 > \mu_3$ **9.45 a.** 7 cheeses **b.** Color change index **c.** Reject $H_0: \mu_1 = \mu_2 = \mu_3 = \mu_4 = \mu_5 = \mu_6 = \mu_7$. **d.** 21 **e.** $\mu_M > \mu_P > (\mu_{Ch}, \mu_G) > (\mu_{Ed}, \mu_{Em}) > \mu_{Co}$ **9.47** $\mu_{NL} > (\mu_{AC}, \mu_{EO}); \mu_{IE} > \mu_{EO}$ **9.49 a.** $(-.125, -.032); \mu_{Barn} > \mu_{Cage}$ **b.** $(-.1233, -.0307);$

$\mu_{Free} > \mu_{Cage}$ **c.** $(-.105, -.0123)$; $\mu_{Organic} > \mu_{Cage}$
d. $(-.0501, .0535)$; no difference **e.** $(-.0318, .0718)$;
no difference **f.** $(-.0335, .0701)$; no difference
g. $(\mu_{Barn}, \mu_{Free}, \mu_{Organic}) > \mu_{Cage}$; .05 **9.51 a.** SSB = .8889,
SSE = 7.7778, MST = 10.7778, MSB = .4445, MSE = 1.9445,
$F(\text{Treatments}) = 5.54$, $F(\text{Blocks}) = .23$ **b.** $H_0: \mu_1 = \mu_2 = \mu_3$
c. $F = 5.54$ **e.** Do not reject H_0. **9.53 a.** $F = 3.20$; $F = 1.80$
b. $F = 13.33$; $F = 2.00$ **c.** $F = 5.33$; $F = 5.00$ **d.** $F = 16.00$;
$F = 6.00$ **e.** $F = 2.67$; $F = 1.00$ **9.55 a.** Blocks: employees;
treatments: time periods **b.** p-values given
c. $H_0: \mu_{Before} = \mu_{2months} = \mu_{2days}$ **d.** Mean competence levels
differ for three time periods. **e.** $\mu_{Before} < (\mu_{2months}, \mu_{2days})$
9.57 a. 8 activities **b.** 15 adults **c.** Reject H_0: All treatment
means are equal. **d.** $(\mu_{rest}, \mu_{ga\,min\,g}) > (\mu_{balance}, \mu_{muscle},$
$\mu_{arobics}) > (\mu_{walking}, \mu_{jogging})$ **9.59** $H_0: \mu_1 = \mu_2 = \mu_3 =$
$\mu_4 = \mu_5$ **c.** $p = .319$, fail to reject H_0 **d.** No differences; yes
e. $P(\text{at least one Type I error}) = .05$ **9.61** $F = 5.04$,
$p = .018$, reject H_0; highest mean rating: either neutral or
high **9.63** Yes, $F = 34.12$; S4 and S1 **9.67 a.** $(1, 1), (1, 2),$
$(1, 3), (2, 1), (2, 2), (2, 3)$ **b.** Yes, $F = 21.62$ **c.** Yes; $F = 36.62$,
reject H_0. **d.** No **9.69 a.** $F(AB) = .75$, $F(A) = 3.00$,
$F(B) = 1.50$ **b.** $F(AB) = 7.50$, $F(A) = 3.00$, $F(B) = 3.00$
c. $F(AB) = 3.00$, $F(A) = 12.00$, $F(B) = 3.00$
d. $F(AB) = 4.50$, $F(A) = 36.00$, $F(B) = 36.00$
9.71 a. (male, STEM), (female, STEM), (male, non-STEM),
(female, non-STEM) **b.** Effect of gender on satisfaction
depends on level of discipline **c.** Yes **d.** df(Gender) = 1,
df(Discipline) = 1, df(Gender × Discipline) = 1,
df(Error) = 211 **e.** Reject H_0; significant interaction between
gender and discipline **9.73 a.** Factors: statement type and
information order; treatments: concrete/statement first, concrete/
behavior first, abstract/statement first, abstract/behavior first
b. Reject H_0: no interaction **d.** No main effect tests
9.75 a. df(Order) = 1, df(Menu) = 1, df(Order × Menu) = 1,
df(Error) = 176 **b.** Reject H_0. **c.** No **9.77 a.** (cut,
extra-large), (no cut, extra-large), (cut, half-sheet),
(no cut, half-sheet) **b.** Yes; effect of paper size on response
depends on paper distortion. **c.** No **d.** $\mu_{C, H} > (\mu_{C, E}, \mu_{NC, H},$
$\mu_{NC, E})$ **9.79** Do not reject H_0: no interaction, $p = .289$; reject
$H_0: \mu_V = \mu_S = \mu_N$ ($p = .000$); do not reject $H_0: \mu_{yes} = \mu_{no}$
($p = .145$). **9.81 a.** 450; 152.5; 195; 157.5 **b.** 9,120.25 **c.** 1,222.25;
625; 676 **d.** 225; 90.25; 90.25; 100 **e.** 12,132 **f.** 14,555.25
g.

Source	df	SS	MS	F
Load	1	1,122.25	1,122.25	8.88
Name	1	625.00	625.00	4.95
Load × Name	1	676.00	676.00	5.35
Error	96	12,132.00	126.375	
Total	99	14,555.25		

h. Yes **i.** Evidence of interaction **j.** Normal distributions for
each treatment, with equal variances
9.87 a.

Source	df	SS	MS	F
Treatment	3	11.332	3.777	157.39
Block	4	10.688	2.672	111.33
Error	12	0.288	0.024	
Total	19	22.308		

b. Yes, $F = 157.39$ **c.** Yes, 6 **d.** Yes, $F = 111.33$
9.89 a. Completely randomized design **b.** Treatments: 3, 6, 9,

and 12 robots; dependent variable: energy expended **c.** H_0:
$\mu_3 = \mu_6 = \mu_9 = \mu_{12}$ **d.** Reject H_0 **e.** 6 **f.** $(\mu_3, \mu_6, \mu_9) > \mu_{12}$
9.91 a. 2×2 factorial; factors: color and question; treatments:
(red/simple), (red/difficult), (blue/simple), (blue/difficult) **b.** Difference between red and blue exam means depends on question
difficulty **9.93 b.** No **c.** Yes **d.** No **e.** $\mu_{Large} > \mu_{Small}$; no other
significant differences **f.** 95% confidence
9.95 a. Yes, $F = 3.90$ **b.** Probability of claiming at least
2 means are different when they are not is .01. **c.** 3
d. $(\mu_{Under30} - \mu_{30to60})$; $(\mu_{Under30} - \mu_{Over60})$ **9.97 a.** 8
b. Interaction significant; effect of type of yeast on mean autolysis depends on level of temperature. **c.** Yeast: $H_0: \mu_{Ba} = \mu_{Br}$,
$H_a: \mu_{Ba} \neq \mu_{Br}$; Temperature: $H_0: \mu_{45} = \mu_{48} = \mu_{51} = \mu_{54}$,
H_a: At least two temperature means differ. **d.** Interaction
significant; may cover up main effects **e.** Baker's yeast:
$(\mu_{45}, \mu_{48}, \mu_{51}) > \mu_{54}$; Brewer's yeast: $(\mu_{45}, \mu_{48}, \mu_{51}) > \mu_{54}$
9.99 a. Factor = Group; treatments = 5 levels of Group;
response variable = ethics score; experimental units =
employees **b.** $H_0 \mu_1 = \mu_2 = \mu_3 = \mu_4 = \mu_5$, H_a: At least two
treatment means differ. **c.** Yes; $F = 9.85$, $p = 0$ **d.** Assumption
of constant variance is violated. **e.** Unequal sample sizes
f. 10 **g.** Implementer's/survivors and formulators
9.101 $H_0: \mu_1 = \mu_2 = \mu_3 = \mu_4 = \mu_5 = \mu_6$ **b.** No **d.** Designed
9.103 a. $H_0: \mu_D = \mu_E = \mu_F = \mu_G = \mu_H$ **b.** $F = 2.11$, $p = .064$,
reject H_0 **c.** No differences at $\alpha = .05$ **9.105 a.** Low/BC,
low/PC, low/NA, medium/BC, medium/PC, medium/NA,
high/BC, high/PC, high/NA **b.** df(Trust) = 2, SSE = 149.5641,
MS(PES) = 1.0887, MS(Trust) = 3.81835,
MS(PES × Trust) = .4345, F(PES) = 1.4995,
$F(\text{Trust}) = 5.2592$, $F(\text{PES} \times \text{Trust}) = .5984$ **c.** Do not reject
H_0. **d.** Yes **e.** Yes **9.107 a.** 2×2 factorial experiment
b. Factors: tent type and location; 4 treatments: (treated/inside),
(treated/outside), (untreated/inside), and (untreated/outside)
c. Number of mosquito bites received in a 20-minute interval
d. Effect of tent type on mean number of bites depends on
location. **9.109 a.** $t_{A-D} = 2.83$, $p = .016$; $t_{B-D} = -.65$,
$p = .539$ **b.** Too many t-tests inflate alpha value. **c.** Run
ANOVA; PAH Ratio 1: $F = 2.61$, $p = .083$, fail to reject H_0,
no difference among location means for PAH1; PAH Ratio 2:
$F = 4.45$, $p = .017$, reject H_0, $\mu_A < \mu_B$, no other differences
among location means

Chapter 10

10.1 a. $< .025$ **b.** $< .1$ **c.** $< .005$ **10.3** $E(n_i) \geq 5$
10.5 a. $\chi^2 = 3.29$ **c.** $(.226, .350)$
10.7 b. $H_0: p_1 = .50, p_2 = .30, p_3 = .10, p_4 = .10$ H_a: At least
one of the probabilities differs from the hypothesized value.
c. 53, 31.8, 10.6, 10.6 **d.** $\chi^2 = 8.73$ **e.** Reject H_0. **10.9 a.** No;
$\chi^2 = 1.67$, $p = .797$ **b.** $(.134, .400)$ **10.11** No; $\chi^2 = 266.17$
10.13 Yes, $\chi^2 = 963.4$ **10.15** $\chi^2 = 164.9$, reject H_0.
10.17 $\chi^2 = 12.37$, do not reject H_0. **10.21 a.** column 1: 36%,
64%; column 2: 53%, 47%; column 3: 68%, 32%; row 1: 9.4%,
35.4%, 55.2%; row 2: 22.5%, 42.3%, 35.2% **c.** Yes **10.23 a.** B_1:
30%, 47%, 23%; B_2: 44%, 33%, 23%; B_3: 30%, 49%, 21% **b.** A_1:
35%; A_2: 42%; A_3: 23% **c.** Yes **10.25 a.** Yes **b.** Always/Male:
240; Always/Female: 476; Often/Male: 405; Often/Female: 527;
Occasional/Male: 525; Occasional/Female: 493; Never/Male: 330;
Never/Female: 204 **c.** H_0: Gender and Purchasing are
independent. **d.** $\chi^2 = 112.43$, p-value ≈ 0 **e.** Reject H_0.
10.27 a. .316; .488 **b.** .500; .401 **c.** .184; .110 **d.** Yes **e.** $\chi^2 = 6.95$,

reject H_0. **f.** $(-.280, -.064)$ **10.29 a.** H_0: Design/pitch and Taste are independent, H_a: Design/pitch and Taste are dependent.
b. Sweet/angular/high: 21, sweet/rounded/low: 21, sour/angular/high: 19, sour/rounded/low: 19 **c.** $\chi^2 = 39.3$ **d.** Reject H_0.
10.31 Yes; $\chi^2 = 21.24$ **10.33** No; $\chi^2 = 4.21$ **10.35** $\chi^2 = 7.39$, reject H_0. **10.37** Yes, $\chi^2 = 7.38$, $p = .025$; no **10.39 a.** No for first trial: $\chi^2 = 5.88$; Yes for last trial: $\chi^2 = 12.00$ **b.** Yes for all conditions: Empty ($\chi^2 = 13.17$), Vanish ($\chi^2 = 7.48$), Steriods ($\chi^2 = 18.99$), Steriods2 ($\chi^2 = 8.96$) **c.** Condition and Trial **10.41 a.** No; $\chi^2 = 2.133$ **b.** $.233 \pm .057$ **10.43 a.** 107.2
b. $H_0: p_1 = p_2 = \cdots p_{10} = .10$ **c.** 93.15 **d.** $\chi^2 > 14.6837$
e. Reject H_0. **10.45 a.** .653 **b.** .555 **c.** .355 **d.** yes **e.** Authenticity and Tone are independent **f.** $\chi^2 = 10.43$, reject H_0
10.47 a. No, $\chi^2 = 6.60$ **b.** $(.62, .68)$ **10.49** Yes, $\chi^2 = 8.04$
10.51 $\chi^2 = 12.47$, reject H_0. **10.53** Yes, $\chi^2 = 72.23$
10.55 a. Low/<300: 85; Low/300–600: 77; Low/>600: 17; High/<300: 105; High/300–600: 121; High/>600: 59
b. $\chi^2 = 11.48$, reject H_0. **c.** Low/$<1,000$: 37; Low/1,000–2,000: 68; Low/2,000–3,000: 44; Low/$>3,000$: 30; High/$<1,000$: 243; High/1,000–2,000: 37; High/2,000–3,000: 4; High/$>3,000$: 1
d. $\chi^2 = 207.81$, reject H_0 **e.** Maximum height: 300 m; minimum distance: 3,000 m **10.57 a.** 9.65 **b.** 11.0705 **c.** No
d. $.05 < p$-value $< .10$

Chapter 11

11.3 $\beta_1 = 1/3, \beta_0 = 14/3, y = 14/3 + (1/3)x$ **11.9** No
11.11 a. Dep. Variable: ratio of salary to worker pay; Indep. Variable: CEO's age **c.** $y = \beta_0 + \beta_1 x + \varepsilon$ **11.13 a.** Dep. Variable: opening weekend box-office revenue; Indep. Variable: movie's twitter rate **c.** $y = \beta_0 + \beta_1 x + \varepsilon$ **11.15 a.** $\sum(y - \hat{y}) = 0.02$, SSE $= 1.2204$ **c.** SSE $= 108.00$ **11.17 b.** Negative linear relationship **c.** $8.54, -.994$ **11.19 a.** $y = \beta_0 + \beta_1 x + \varepsilon$
b. $\hat{y} = -70.7 + 1.132x$ **c.** No practical interpretation **d.** For every 1-point increase in 2010 Math SAT score, estimate 2014 Math SAT score to increase 1.132 points. **11.21 a.** $\hat{y} = 6.68 + .0048x$
b. .5374; no **c.** $\hat{\beta}_0$: no practical interpretation; $\hat{\beta}_1$: For every 1 mm increase in diameter, the mean ratio is estimated to increase by .0048. **d.** 10.5 **e.** Not reliable **11.23 a.** $\hat{y} = -14.14 + .63x$
b. For each additional 1 million births, estimate number of software millionaire birthdays to increase by .63. **c.** 7.83
d. $\hat{y} = 2.72 + .31x$ **e.** For each additional CEO birthday, estimate number of software millionaire birthdays to increase by .63. **f.** 5.79 **11.25 a.** $E(y) = \beta_0 + \beta_1 x$ **b.** $\hat{y} = 250.14 - .629x$
c. No practical interpretation **d.** For every 1-yard increase in driving distance, driving accuracy is to decrease .629%. **e.** Slope
11.27 \$7.88 million **11.31** Plot b **11.33 a.** .5101
11.35 a. .2 **b.** About 95% of the observed payoffs fall within .4 unit of their predicted values. **11.37 a.** .22 **b.** About 95% of the observed ratios fall within .44 units of their predicted values.
11.39 a. $y = \beta_0 + \beta_1 x + \varepsilon$ **b.** $\hat{y} = 119.863 + .3456x$ **c.** ε's are independent and normally distributed with mean of 0 and constant variance for each level of the independent variable.
d. 635.187 **e.** Most will fall within 1270.4 units of predicted values. **11.41 a.** .02225 **b.** .149176 **c.** Part b
11.47 80% CI: $.82 \pm .33$; 98% CI: $.82 \pm .76$ **11.49 a.** $H_0: \beta_1 = 0$, $H_a: \beta_1 > 0$ **b.** Reject $H_0, p \approx 0$ **c.** $(1.09, 1.29)$ **11.51 a.** Positive
b. $(-1.18, 1.72)$ **c.** Insufficient evidence of a linear relationship
11.53 Yes; $t = 14.87, p = 0$; $(.004077, .005494)$ **11.55 a.** $(-.048, 1.304)$ **b.** $(.179, .434)$ **c.** No; yes **11.57 a.** $H_0: \beta_1 = 0, H_a: \beta_1 < 0$
b. $t = -13.23, p \approx 0$ **c.** Reject H_0. **11.59** No; $t = .42, p = .676$
11.61 Yes; $t = 2.34, p = .0115$; Decision changes if we use

$\alpha = .01$. **11.63 a.** Yes, $p = .008/2 = .004$ **b.** Possible outlier
c. $p = .332/2 = .166$, do not reject H_0. **11.65 b.** Positive
c. Positive **d.** Reject null hypothesis **11.67 a.** .944
b. .802 **11.69 a.** 18% of sample variation in points scored is explained by the linear relationship with yards from goal line.
b. $-.424$; negative **11.71 a.** $E(y) = \beta_0 + \beta_1 x$ **b.** Moderately strong positive linear relationship between RMP and SET ratings **c.** Positive **d.** Reject $H_0: \rho = 0$. **e.** .4624 **11.73 a.** Strong positive linear relationship between number of females in managerial positions and number of females with college degree
b. Very weak positive linear relationship between number of females in managerial positions and number of female HS graduates with no college **c.** Moderately strong positive linear relationship between number of males in managerial positions and number of males with college degree **d.** Moderate positive linear relationship between number of males in managerial positions and number of male HS graduates with no college
11.75 a. .624; 62.4% of sample variation in software millionaire birthdays is explained by the linear relationship with number of U.S. births. **b.** .917; 91.7% of sample variation in software millionaire birthdays is explained by the linear relationship with number of CEO births. **c.** Yes **11.77** $r^2 = .2286, r = -.478$
11.79 a. $t = 17.75, p \approx 0$, do not reject H_0. **11.81** Yes, reject $H_0: \rho = 0$ for all occupations; no **11.83 c.** 4.64 ± 1.12
d. $2.28 \pm .63$; $-.41 \pm 1.17$ **11.85 a.** 2.9, 10.2 **b.** $\hat{y} = 10.2 + 2.9x$
c. 2.2981 **d.** 3.3958 **e.** $(56.7768, 65.0232)$ **f.** $(59.0042, 65.7958)$
11.87 a. $(4783, 6792)$ **b.** $(2643, 8933)$ **11.89** For run $= 1$: 90% confident that mean sweetness index of all runs with pectin value of 220 falls between 5.65 and 5.84 **11.91 a.** $(5.44, 15.32)$ **b.** Narrower **11.93 a.** $(2.955, 4.066)$; 99% confident that the mean mass of all spills with elapsed time of 15 minutes is between 2.995 and 4.066 **b.** $(1.02, 6.00)$; 99% confident that the actual mass of a single spill with elapsed time of 15 minutes is between 1.02 and 6.0
c. Prediction interval for y; yes **11.95 a.** Yes, $t = -5.91$; negative **b.** $(.656, 2.829)$ **c.** $(1.467, 2.018)$ **11.97** $\hat{y} = -32.35 + 4.82x$;
$t = 16.60, p = 0$, reject H_0; $r^2 = .69$ **11.99 a.** $t = 6.73, p = 0$, reject H_0; $r^2 = .8047$ **b.** $t = -4.13, p = .002$, reject H_0;
$r^2 = .6079$ **11.103 b.** $r = -.1245, r^2 = .0155$ **c.** No; $t = -.35$
11.105 a. Moderately strong positive linear relationship between skill level and goal-setting ability **b.** Reject H_0 at $\alpha = .01$. **c.** .49
11.107 b. $\hat{y} = 569.58 - .0019x$ **e.** Range of x: \$15,100 to \$70,000
f. $t = -.82$, do not reject H_0. **11.109 a.** $E(y) = \beta_0 + \beta_1 x$
b. $\hat{y} = -2,298.4 + 11,598.9x$ **c.** No practical interpretation
d. $(11,146.1, 12,051.7)$ **e.** 1,117.6 **f.** $H_0: \beta_1 = 0, H_a: \beta_1 > 0$
g. $p < .0001$ **h.** .8925 **i.** .9447 **j.** $(1,297.6, 5,704.6)$ **k.** $(3,362.5, 3,639.7)$ **11.111 b.** $\hat{y} = 44.13 + .237x$ **c.** 19.40 **d.** Possibly
e. $t = 1.27$, do not reject H_0. **f.** $(-.16, .63)$ **g.** 57.143 ± 34.818
h. $x = 110$ outside range **i.** $\bar{x} = 44.1579$ **11.113 a.**
$E(y) = \beta_0 + \beta_1 x$ **b.** $\hat{y} = 189.8 - .305x$ **c.** Yes; negative **d.** $\hat{\beta}_0$:
no practical interpretation; $\hat{\beta}_1$: For each 1 percent increase in the % below poverty, the mean FCAT-Math score is estimated to decrease by .305 **e.** $t = -6.42, p = .000$, reject H_0. **f. (a).**
$E(y) = \beta_0 + \beta_1 x$ **(b).** $\hat{y} = 187.01 - .2708x$ **(c).** Yes; negative **(d).** $\hat{\beta}_0$: no practical interpretation; $\hat{\beta}_1$: For each 1 percent increase in the % below poverty, the mean FCAT-Reading score is estimated to decrease by .27085. **(e).** $t = -8.92$,
$p = .000$, reject H_0 **g.** $s = 5.37$ **h.** $s = 3.42$ **i.** Reading
11.115 c. $r_1 = .965, r_2 = .996$ **d.** Yes **11.117 a.** $t = 15.35$
b. 28.18 ± 4.63 **11.119** Machine-hours: $t = 3.30, p = .008$
, reject $H_0, r^2 = .521$; labor-hours: $t = 1.43, p = .183$, do not reject $H_0, r^2 = .170$

Chapter 12

12.1 a. $E(y) = \beta_0 + \beta_1 x_1 + \beta_2 x_2$
b. $E(y) = \beta_0 + \beta_1 x_1 + \beta_2 x_2 + \beta_3 x_3 + \beta_4 x_4$
c. $E(y) = \beta_0 + \beta_1 x_1 + \beta_2 x_2 + \beta_3 x_3 + \beta_4 x_4 + \beta_5 x_5$
12.3 a. $t = 1.45$, do not reject H_0. **b.** $t = 3.21$, reject H_0.
12.5 $n - (k + 1)$ **12.7 a.** Yes, $s = .117$ **b.** Yes, $F = 55.2$
12.9 a. $E(y) = \beta_0 + \beta_1 x_1 + \beta_2 x_2 + \beta_3 x_3 + \beta_4 x_4 + \beta_5 x_5 + \beta_6 x_6$
b. $\hat{\beta}_1$:estimate mean satisfaction score will increase by .122 for each unit increase in air quality, holding other variables fixed; $\hat{\beta}_2$: estimate mean satisfaction score will increase by .018 for each unit increase in temperature, holding other variables fixed; $\hat{\beta}_3$: estimate mean satisfaction score will increase by .124 for each unit increase in odor/aroma, holding other variables fixed; $\hat{\beta}_4$: estimate mean satisfaction score will increase by .119 for each unit increase in music, holding other variables fixed; $\hat{\beta}_5$: estimate mean satisfaction score will increase by .101 for each unit increase in noise/sound level, holding other variables fixed; $\hat{\beta}_6$: estimate mean satisfaction score will increase by .463 for each unit increase in overall image, holding other variables fixed **c.** 99% confident that for each additional unit increase in overall image, mean satisfaction will increase between .350 and .576, holding all other variables constant **d.** $R_a^2 = .501$:50.1% of sample variation in satisfaction is explained by the model, adjusted for the sample size and number of variables in the model. **e.** Yes, $F = 71.42$, $p = 0$ **12.11 a.** $F = 4.74$, $p < .01$, reject H_0. **b.** 13% of sample variation in Mach score can be explained by the model. **c.** No **12.13 a.** Yes, $p = .049$; $R^2 = .075$:7.5% of sample variation in amount of silver is explained by the model. **b.** Yes, $p < .001$; $R^2 = .783$:78.3% of sample variation in amount of iron is explained by the model. **c.** $p = .015$, reject H_0. **d.** $p < .001$, reject H_0.
12.15 a. $E(y) = \beta_0 + \beta_1 x_1 + \beta_2 x_2 + \beta_3 x_3 + \beta_4 x_4$ **b.** Reject H_0. **c.** Yes **d.** $H_0: \beta_1 = \beta_2 = \beta_3 = \beta_4 = 0$ **e.** $F > 3.37$ **f.** Thrill: reject H_0; Change: do not reject H_0.; Surprise: do not reject H_0.
12.17 a. $\hat{y} = 14.0107 - 2.1865 x_1 - .04794 x_2 - .3223 x_3 + .493 x_4$ **c.** Yes, $F = 40.85$ **d.** R_a^2 **e.** $t = -2.25$, reject H_0. **f.** (.24, .74)
12.19 a. $E(x) = \beta_0 + \beta_1 x_1 + \beta_2 x_2 + \beta_3 x_3 + \beta_4 x_4 + \beta_5 x_5$
b. $\hat{y} = 13,614.5 + .0888 x_1 - 9.201 x_2 + 14.394 x_3 + .35 x_4 - .848 x_5$ **d.** 458.83 **e.** $F = 147.3$, $p < .001$, reject H_0. **f.** .917
g. Yes, $t = -6.14$ **12.21 a.** $\hat{y} = 1.088 - .000234 x_1 - .080 x_2$; $F = 1.00$, $p = .391$, fail to reject H_0.
b. $\hat{y} = -1030 - 57.9 x_1 + 332,037 x_2$; $F = 121.31$, $p = .000$, reject H_0. **c.** Density **12.23 a.** $t = 5.00$, reject $H_0: \beta_1 = 0$; $t = 5.00$, reject $H_0: \beta_2 = 0$; $t = -4.00$, reject $H_0: \beta_3 = 0$; $t = 3.00$, reject $H_0: \beta_4 = 0$; $t = .015$, fail to reject $H_0: \beta_5 = 0$
c. $R^2 = .85$: 85% of the sample variation in the natural logarithm of price is explained by the model; $s = .30$:Approximately 95% of the natural logarithms of price fall within .60 units of their predicted values. **12.25 a.** -3 **12.27 a.** 95% confident that mean desire is between 13.42 and 14.31 for all females with a self-esteem of 24, body satisfaction of 3, and impression of reality TV of 4 **b.** 95% confident that mean desire is between 8.79 and 10.89 for all males with a self-esteem of 22, body satisfaction of 9, and impression of reality TV of 4
12.29 a. (11,599.6, 13,665.5) **b.** (12,157.9, 13,107.1) **c.** Yes
12.33 a. $E(y) = \beta_0 + \beta_1 x_1 + \beta_2 x_2 + \beta_3 x_3$
b. $\hat{y} = 86.9 - .21 x_1 + .15 x_2 + .073 x_3$ **c.** Yes, $F = 2.66$, $p = .077$
d. $R_a^2 = .185$; $2s = 5.93$ **e.** (82.6, 95.6) **12.35 c.** Interaction is present. **12.37 a.** $\hat{y} = -2.55 + 3.815 x_1 + 2.63 x_2 - 1.285 x_1 x_2$
b. -9.08 **c.** $x_2 = 1$: $\hat{y} = .08 + 2.53 x_1$; $x_2 = 3$: $\hat{y} = 5.34 - .05 x_1$; $x_2 = 5$: $\hat{y} = 10.6 - 2.63 x_1$ **e.** $H_0: \beta_3 = 0$ vs. $H_a: \beta_3 \neq 0$
f. $t = -8.06$, reject H_0. **12.39 a.** $E(y) = \beta_0 + \beta_1 x_1 +$

$\beta_2 x_2 + \beta_3 x_1 x_2$ **b.** $(\beta_1 + 2.5\beta_3)$ **c.** $(\beta_1 + 5\beta_3)$ **d.** $(\beta_2 + 100\beta_3)$
e. $H_0: \beta_3 = 0$ **12.41 a.** $F = 31.98$, $p < .001$, reject H_0.
b. Yes, $t = -5.61$, $p < .001$ **12.43 a.** $\hat{y} = 11.779 - 1.972 x_1 + .585 x_4 - .553 x_1 x_4$ **b.** 9.97 **c.** $F = 45.1$, reject H_0. **d.** .439 **e.** 2.35
f. $t = -2.00$, reject H_0. **12.45 a.** $E(y) = \beta_0 + \beta_1 x_1 + \beta_2 x_2 + \beta_3 x_3 + \beta_4 x_4$ **b.** β_1 **c.** β_2; β_3; β_4 **d.** $E(y) = \beta_0 + \beta_1 x_1 + \beta_2 x_2 + \beta_3 x_3 + \beta_4 x_4 + \beta_5 x_1 x_4 + \beta_6 x_2 x_4 + \beta_7 x_3 x_4$ **e.** $H_0: \beta_5 = 0$
f. $H_0: \beta_6 = 0$; $H_0: \beta_7 = 0$ **g.** Yes **12.47 a.** $E(y) = \beta_0 + \beta_1 x_1 + \beta_2 x_2 + \beta_3 x_3 + \beta_4 x_1 x_3 + \beta_5 x_2 x_3$ **b.** $\hat{y} = 10,769 - 1,288 x_1 + 218.8 x_2 - 1,550.1 x_3 - 10.99 x_1 x_3 + 19.99 x_2 x_3$ **c.** $t = -.93$, do not reject H_0. **d.** $t = 1.78$, do not reject H_0.
12.49 a. $E(y) = \beta_0 + \beta_1 x + \beta_2 x^2$ **b.** $E(y) = \beta_0 + \beta_1 x_1 + \beta_2 x_2 + \beta_3 x_1 x_2 + \beta_4 x_1^2 + \beta_5 x_2^2$ **c.** $E(y) = \beta_0 + \beta_1 x_1 + \beta_2 x_2 + \beta_3 x_3 + \beta_4 x_1 x_2 + \beta_5 x_1 x_3 + \beta_6 x_2 x_3 + \beta_7 x_1^2 + \beta_8 x_2^2 + \beta_9 x_3^2$
12.51 a. Yes, $F = 85.94$ **b.** $H_0: \beta_2 = 0$ vs. $H_a: \beta_2 > 0$ **c.** $H_0: \beta_2 = 0$ vs. $H_a: \beta_2 < 0$ **12.53 a.** Yes, $F = 25.93$ **b.** $t = -10.74$, reject H_0.
c. $t = .60$, do not reject H_0. **12.55 b.** 22.6% of the sample variation in points scored is explained by the quadratic model.
c. No **d.** $H_0: \beta_2 = 0$ **12.57** $E(y) = \beta_0 + \beta_1 x + \beta_2 x^2$; negative
12.59 a. $E(y) = \beta_0 + \beta_1 x_1 + \beta_2 x_2 + \beta_3 x_1 x_2 + \beta_4 x_1^2 + \beta_5 x_2^2$
b. 14% of sample variation in attitude toward improving efficiency can be explained by the model **c.** Downward curvature in the relationship between attitude and congruence
d. Evidence of interaction **12.61 a.** $E(y) = \beta_0 + \beta_1 x$
b. $E(y) = \beta_0 + \beta_1 x + \beta_2 x^2$ **c.** Linear model **d.** $F = 19.85$, overall model is statistically useful; $t = -.77$, $p = .452$ insufficient evidence of curvature **e.** Linear model **12.63 a.** Curvilinear
b. $\hat{y} = 154,243 - 1,908.9 x + 5.93 x^2$ **c.** $t = 5.66$, reject H_0.
12.65 b. Possibly **c.** $\hat{y} = 2,802.4 + 122.95 x$ **d.** $\hat{y} = 4,944.2 - 183.03 x + 7.46 x^2$ **e.** $t = 3.38$, reject $H_0: \beta_2 = 0$; 2nd-order
12.67 $E(y) = \beta_0 + \beta_1 x_1 + \beta_2 x_2$, where $x_1 = $ {1 level 1, 0 if not}, $x_2 = $ {1 level 2, 0 if not}; $\beta_0 = \mu_3$, $\beta_1 = \mu_1 - \mu_3$, $\beta_2 = \mu_2 - \mu_3$ **12.69 a.** Level 1: 10.2; Level 2: 6.2; Level 3: 22.2; Level 4: 12.2 **b.** $H_0: \beta_1 = \beta_2 = \beta_3 = 0$
12.71 a. Method: $x_1 = $ {1 manual, 0 if automated}; Soil: $x_2 = $ {1 if clay, 0 if not}, $x_3 = $ {1 if gravel, 0 if not}; Slope: $x_4 = $ {1 if East, 0 if not}, $x_5 = $ {1 if South, 0 if not}, $x_6 = $ {1 if West, 0 if not}, $x_7 = $ {1 if Southeast, 0 if not} **b.** $E(y) = \beta_0 + \beta_1 x_1$
c. $E(y) = \beta_0 + \beta_1 x_2 + \beta_2 x_3$ **d.** $E(y) = \beta_0 + \beta_1 x_4 + \beta_2 x_5 + \beta_3 x_6 + \beta_4 x_7$ **12.73 a.** $E(y) = \beta_0 + \beta_1 x_1 + \beta_2 x_2 + \beta_3 x_3$
b. $\beta_0 = $ mean weight loss of group D; $\beta_1 = $ difference in mean weight loss between groups A and D; $\beta_2 = $ difference in mean weight loss between groups B and D; $\beta_3 = $ difference in mean weight loss between groups C and D **c.** $\beta_1 < 0$; $\beta_2 < 0$
12.75 a. $x_1 = $ {1 if blond Caucasian, 0 if not}, $x_2 = $ {1 if brunette Caucasian, 0 if not} **b.** $E(y) = \beta_0 + \beta_1 x_1 + \beta_2 x_2$ **c.** $\beta_0 + \beta_1$
d. β_1 **e.** $\beta_0 > 0$; $\beta_1 > 0$; $\beta_2 \approx 0$ **f.** Yes **12.77 a.** $x_1 = $ {1 if large/private, 0 if not}, $x_2 = $ {1 if small/public, 0 if not}, $x_3 = $ {1 if small/private, 0 if not} **b.** $E(y) = \beta_0 + \beta_1 x_1 + \beta_2 x_2 + \beta_3 x_3$
c. Differences in mean likelihood of reporting sustainability policies among the four groups **d.** $x_1 = $ {1 if small, 0 if large}, $x_2 = $ {1 if private, 0 if public} **e.** $E(y) = \beta_0 + \beta_1 x_1 + \beta_2 x_2$
f. Large/public: β_0; large/private: $\beta_0 + \beta_2$; small/public: $\beta_0 + \beta_1$; small/private: $\beta_0 + \beta_1 + \beta_2$ **g.** Public: $\mu_S - \mu_L = \beta_1$; private: $\mu_S - \mu_L = \beta_1$ **h.** $E(y) = \beta_0 + \beta_1 x_1 + \beta_2 x_2 + \beta_3 x_1 x_2$
i. Large/public: β_0; large/private: $\beta_0 + \beta_2$; small/public: $\beta_0 + \beta_1$; small/private: $\beta_0 + \beta_1 + \beta_2 + \beta_3$ **j.** Public: $\mu_S - \mu_L = \beta_1$; private: $\mu_S - \mu_L = \beta_1 + \beta_3$ **12.79 a.** $E(y) = \beta_0 + \beta_1 x_1 + \beta_2 x_2 + \beta_3 x_3$ **b.** 49; -14.7; 14.4; 14.9 **d.** $F = 5.39$, reject H_0.
12.81 a. $E(MVL) = \beta_0 + \beta_1 x_1 + \beta_2 x_2 + \beta_3 x_3$
b. $\widehat{MVL} = 6.38 + 2.14 x_1 + 2.17 x_2 + .25 x_3$ **c.** $\hat{\beta}_0 = 6.38$: estimate of mean MVL for "no ban/no other"; $\hat{\beta}_1 = 2.14$: estimate of difference in mean MVL between "banned/other" and "no

ban/no other"; $\hat{\beta}_2 = 2.17$: estimate of difference in mean MVL between "banned/no other" and "no ban/no other"; $\hat{\beta}_3 = .25$: estimate of difference in mean MVL between "no ban/other" and "no ban/no other" **d.** $F = 105.37$, reject H_0.
12.83 a. $E(y) = \beta_0 + \beta_1 x_1 + \beta_2 x_1^2$ **b.** $E(y) = \beta_0 + \beta_1 x_1 + \beta_2 x_1^2 + \beta_3 x_2 + \beta_4 x_3$, where x_2 and x_3 are dummy variables
c. Add terms: $\beta_5 x_1 x_2 + \beta_6 x_1 x_3 + \beta_7 x_1^2 x_2 + \beta_8 x_1^2 x_3$
d. $\beta_5 = \beta_6 = \beta_7 = \beta_8 = 0$ **e.** $\beta_2 = \beta_5 = \beta_6 = \beta_7 = \beta_8 = 0$
f. $\beta_3 = \beta_4 = \beta_5 = \beta_6 = \beta_7 = \beta_8 = 0$ **12.87 a.** .58
b. .03 **12.89 a.** $E(y) = \beta_0 + \beta_1 x_1 + \beta_2 x_1^2$
b. $E(y) = (\beta_0 + \beta_3) + (\beta_1 + \beta_4)x_1 + (\beta_2 + \beta_5)x_1^2$
c. Downward curvature; upward curvature **12.91 a.** $x_2 = \{1$ if low, 0 if not$\}$, $x_3 = \{1$ if neutral, 0 if not$\}$ **b.** $E(y) = \beta_0 + \beta_1 x_1 + \beta_2 x_2 + \beta_3 x_3$ **c.** $E(y) = \beta_0 + \beta_1 x_1 + \beta_2 x_2 + \beta_3 x_3 + \beta_4 x_1 x_2 + \beta_5 x_1 x_3$ **d.** Part **c** **12.93 a.** $x_1 = \{1$ if channel catfish, 0 if not$\}$, $x_2 = \{1$ if largemouth bass, 0 if not$\}$ **b.** $E(y) = \beta_0 + \beta_1 x_1 + \beta_2 x_2 + \beta_3 x_3$, where $x_3 = $ weight **c.** $E(y) = \beta_0 + \beta_1 x_1 + \beta_2 x_2 + \beta_3 x_3 + \beta_4 x_1 x_3 + \beta_5 x_2 x_3$ **d.** $\hat{y} = 3.1 + 26.5 x_1 + 4.1 x_2 + .0037 x_3$
f. $\hat{y} = 3.5 + 25.6 x_1 - 3.47 x_2 + .0034 x_3 + .0008 x_1 x_3 - .0013 x_2 x_3$
g. .0042 **12.95 a.** $E(y) = \beta_0 + \beta_1 x_1 + \beta_2 x_1^2 + \beta_3 x_2 + \beta_4 x_3 + \beta_5 x_4 + \beta_6 x_1 x_2 + \beta_7 x_1 x_3 + \beta_8 x_1 x_4 + \beta_9 x_1^2 x_2 + \beta_{10} x_1^2 x_3 + \beta_{11} x_1^2 x_4$, where $x_1 = $ sales volume and $x_2 - x_4$ are dummy variables for region **b.** $E(y) = (\beta_0 + \beta_5) + (\beta_1 + \beta_8)x_1 + (\beta_2 + \beta_{11})x_1^2$
c. $E(y) = (\beta_0 + \beta_3) + (\beta_1 + \beta_6)x_1 + (\beta_2 + \beta_9)x_1^2$
d. β_3 through β_{11} **e.** Yes, $F = 8.21$, $p = .000$ **12.97** a and b, a and d, a and e, b and c, b and d, b and e, c and e, d and e
12.99 a. 5; 3 **b.** $H_0: \beta_3 = \beta_4 = 0$ **c.** $F = .38$, do not reject H_0.
12.101 a. $H_0: \beta_4 = \beta_5 = 0$ **b.** Complete model:
$E(y) = \beta_0 + \beta_1 x_1 + \beta_2 x_2 + \beta_3 x_1 x_2 + \beta_4 x_2^2 + \beta_5 x_1 x_2^2$;
reduced model: $E(y) = \beta_0 + \beta_1 x_1 + \beta_2 x_2 + \beta_3 x_1 x_2$
c. $H_0: \beta_3 = \beta_5 = 0$ **d.** Complete model: $E(y) = \beta_0 + \beta_1 x_1 + \beta_2 x_2 + \beta_3 x_1 x_2 + \beta_4 x_2^2 + \beta_5 x_1 x_2^2$; reduced model: $E(y) = \beta_0 + \beta_1 x_1 + \beta_2 x_2 + \beta_4 x_2^2$ **e.** $H_0: \beta_1 = \beta_3 = \beta_5 = 0$ **f.** Complete model: $E(y) = \beta_0 + \beta_1 x_1 + \beta_2 x_2 + \beta_3 x_1 x_2 + \beta_4 x_2^2 + \beta_5 x_1 x_2^2$; reduced model: $E(y) = \beta_0 + \beta_2 x_2 + \beta_4 x_2^2$ **12.103 a.** $E(y) = \beta_0 + \beta_1 x_1 + \beta_2 x_2 + \beta_3 x_1 x_2 + \beta_4 x_1^2 + \beta_5 x_2^2$ **b.** $H_0: \beta_4 = \beta_5 = 0$
c. Complete model: $E(y) = \beta_0 + \beta_1 x_1 + \beta_2 x_2 + \beta_3 x_1 x_2 + \beta_4 x_1^2 + \beta_5 x_2^2$; reduced model: $E(y) = \beta_0 + \beta_1 x_1 + \beta_2 x_2 + \beta_3 x_1 x_2$
d. $F = 9.35$ **e.** $F > 2.39$; $p = .000$ **e.** Reject H_0.
12.105 a. $E(y) = \beta_0 + \beta_1 x_1 + \beta_2 x_2 + \beta_3 x_3 + \beta_4 x_4 + \beta_5 x_1 x_4 + \beta_6 x_2 x_4 + \beta_7 x_3 x_4$ **b.** $F = 24.40$, reject H_0. **c.** $H_0: \beta_5 = \beta_6 = \beta_7 = 0$
d. $F = 1.74$, do not reject H_0. **12.107 a.** Positive
c. $E(y) = \beta_0 + \beta_1 x_1 + \beta_2 x_1^2 + \beta_3 x_2 + \beta_4 x_1 x_2 + \beta_5 x_1^2 x_2$
e. $H_0: \beta_4 = \beta_5 = 0$ **f.** $F = .83$, do not reject H_0.
12.109 a. $E(y) = \beta_0 + \beta_1 x_1 + \beta_2 x_2 + \beta_3 x_3$ **b.** Add terms: $\beta_4 x_1 x_2 + \beta_5 x_1 x_3$ **c.** AL: β_1; TDS-3A: $\beta_1 + \beta_4$; FE: $\beta_1 + \beta_5$
d. Test $H_0: \beta_4 = \beta_5 = 0$ using a nested model F-test
12.111 a. x_2 **b.** Yes **c.** Fit all models of the form $E(y) = \beta_0 + \beta_1 x_2 + \beta_2 x_i$ **12.113 a.** 5 **b.** 4 **c.** 3 **d.** 2 **e.** 14; .51 **12.115 a.** 11 **b.** 10
d. No interactions or squared terms; inflated Type I error rate
e. $E(y) = \beta_0 + \beta_1(\text{AMAP}) + \beta_2(\text{NDF}) + \beta_3(\text{AMAP})(\text{NDF}) + \beta_4(\text{AMAP})^2 + \beta_5(\text{NDF})^2$
f. Test $H_0: \beta_3 = \beta_4 = \beta_5 = 0$ **12.117 a.** 11 **b.** 10 **c.** 1
d. $E(y) = \beta_0 + \beta_1 x_{11} + \beta_2 x_4 + \beta_3 x_2 + \beta_4 x_7 + \beta_5 x_{10} + \beta_6 x_1 + \beta_7 x_9 + \beta_8 x_3$ **e.** 67.7% of sample variation in overall satisfaction can be explained by the model. **f.** No interactions or squared terms in model; high probability of making at least one Type I error **12.121** Yes **12.123 a.** 2,234 **b.** No
c. Yes, $z = 5.32$ **12.125 a.** No **b.** No **c.** Yes **d.** Possibly
12.127 a. Satisfied **b.** Violated **c.** Some outliers **d.** Violated
e. No **12.129 a.** $\hat{y} = 30,856 - 191.57x$ **b.** -1162.07
c. Yes, curvilinear trend **d.** Yes **12.131** No, nonnormal error, nonconstant error variance **12.133** Nonconstant error variance

12.135 Confidence interval **12.137 a.** $\hat{y} = 90.1 - 1.836 x_1 + .285 x_2$ **b.** .916 **c.** Yes, $F = 64.91$ **d.** $t = -5.01$, reject H_0. **e.** 10.68
12.139 $E(y) = \beta_0 + \beta_1 x_1 + \beta_2 x_2 + \beta_3 x_3$, where $x_1 = \{1$ if level 2, 0 otherwise$\}$, $x_2 = \{1$ if level 3, 0 otherwise$\}$, $x_3 = \{1$ if level 4, 0 otherwise$\}$ **12.143** No degrees of freedom for error
12.145 a. Confidence interval for $(\mu_1 - \mu_2)$ **b.** $E(y) = \beta_0 + \beta_1 x$, $x = \{1$ if public college, 0 if private college$\}$ **12.147 a.** Type of extractor is qualitative; size is quantitative **b.** $E(y) = \beta_0 + \beta_1 x_1 + \beta_2 x_2$, where $x_1 = $ diameter of orange, $x_2 = \{1$ if brand B, 0 if not$\}$ **c.** $E(y) = \beta_0 + \beta_1 x_1 + \beta_2 x_2 + \beta_3 x_1 x_2$
e. $H_0: \beta_3 = 0$ **12.149 a.** $E(y) = \beta_0 + \beta_1 x_1 + \beta_2 x_2 + \beta_3 x_1 x_2$
b. $\beta_3 < 0$ **12.151 a.** β_0: no practical interpretation; β_1: for every 1-unit increase in proportion of block with low-density areas, estimate density to increase 2.006 units, holding other variable constant; β_2: for every 1-unit increase in proportion of block with high-density areas, estimate density to increase 5.006 units, holding other variable constant **b.** 68.6% of sample variation in population density can be explained by the model.
c. $H_0: \beta_1 = \beta_2 = 0$ **d.** $F = 133.3$ **e.** Reject H_0. **12.153 a.** Model is statistically useful; reject $H_0: \beta_1 = \beta_2 = \cdots = \beta_{12} = 0$
b. No significant impact; do not reject $H_0: \beta_1 = 0$ **c.** Positive impact; reject $H_0: \beta_3 = 0$ **d.** $E(y) = \beta_0 + \beta_1 x_3 + \beta_2 x_5 + \beta_3 x_6 + \cdots + \beta_9 x_{12} + \beta_{10} x_3 x_5 + \beta_{11} x_3 x_6 + \cdots + \beta_{17} x_3 x_{12}$
12.155 a. 7; $E(y) = \beta_0 + \beta_1 x_i$ **b.** 6; $E(y) = \beta_0 + \beta_1 x_1 + \beta_2 x_i$
c. 5; $E(y) = \beta_0 + \beta_1 x_1 + \beta_2 x_2 + \beta_3 x_i$ **12.157 a.** $\beta_4 = .296$; the difference in the mean value of DTVA between when the operating earnings are negative and lower than last year and when the operating earnings are not negative and lower than last year is estimated to be .296, holding all other variables constant.
b. $p = .0005$, yes **c.** $R_a^2 = .280$, 28% of the variability in the DTVA scores is explained by the model containing the 5 independent variables, adjusted for the number of variables in the model and the sample size. **12.159 a.** Possibly **b.** Yes **c.** No
12.161 b. $E(y) = \beta_0 + \beta_1 x_1 + \beta_2 x_1^2 + \beta_3 x_2 + \beta_4 x_1 x_2 + \beta_5 x_1^2 x_2$, where $x_2 = \{1$ if I-35W, 0 if not$\}$ **c.** Yes, $F = 457.73$ **d.** Assumptions satisfied **12.163 a.** $E(y) = \beta_0 + \beta_1 x_1 + \beta_2 x_2 + \beta_3 x_i$, where $x_1 = \{1$ if VH, 0 otherwise$\}$, $x_2 = \{1$ if H, 0 otherwise$\}$, $x_3 = \{1$ if M, 0 otherwise$\}$ **b.** No **c.** $\hat{y} = 10.2 + .5 x_1 + 2.02 x_2 + .683 x_3$ **d.** Yes, $F = 63.09$ **12.165 b.** Yes, $F = 16.10$ **c.** Yes, $t = 2.5$
d. 945 **12.167 a.** $E(y) = \beta_0 + \beta_1 x_1 + \beta_2 x_6 + \beta_3 x_7$, where $x_6 = \{1$ if good, 0 otherwise$\}$, $x_7 = \{1$ if fair, 0 otherwise$\}$
c. Excellent: $\hat{y} = 188,875 + 15,617 x_1$; good: $\hat{y} = 85,829 + 15,617 x_1$; fair: $\hat{y} = 36,388 + 15,617 x_1$
e. Yes, $F = 8.43$ **f.** $(x_1$ and $x_3)$, $(x_1$ and $x_5)$, $(x_3$ and $x_5)$ highly correlated **g.** Assumptions satisfied
12.169 a. $H_0: \beta_1 = \beta_2 = \beta_3 = \beta_4 = \beta_5 = 0$ **b.** $F = 18.24$, reject H_0. **c.** $H_0: \beta_3 = \beta_4 = \beta_5 = 0$ **d.** $F = 8.46$, reject H_0.
e. Second-order model **12.171 a.** 78% of sample variation in price is explained by the model. **b.** $F = 1,693.55$, reject H_0. **c.** $2,234 **d.** $9 **e.** $-$252 **f.** Yes, $t = 2.39$
12.173 $\hat{y} = -11.5 + .189 x_1 + .159 x_2 - .00114 x_1^2 - .000871 x_2^2$

Chapter 13

13.7 Out of control **13.9 a.** 1.023 **b.** 0.308 **c.** 0.167
13.11 b. $\bar{\bar{x}} = 20.11625$, $\bar{R} = 3.31$ **c.** UCL $= 22.529$, LCL $= 17.703$ **d.** Upper A–B: 21.725, Lower A–B: 18.507, Upper B–C: 20.920, Lower B–C: 19.312 **e.** Yes
13.13 a. $\bar{x} = 100.59$, $s = .454$ **b.** $\bar{\bar{x}} = 100.59$, UCL $= 101.952$, LCL $= 99.228$ **c.** No **13.15 a.** 70 **b.** 32.5 **c.** UCL $= 80.01$, LCL $= 59.99$ **d.** Yes **f.** Yes **13.17 c.** 15.1 **c.** No **d.** No **e.** Yes
13.19 a. $\bar{\bar{x}} = 13.05$, Upper A–B: 13.55, Lower A–B: 12.55,

Upper B–C: 13.3, Lower B–C: 12.8 **b.** Out of control
c. Under-reporting likely   **13.21 a.** $\bar{\bar{x}} = 100.08$, $\bar{R} = .8065$,
UCL $= 100.91$, LCL $= 99.26$, Upper A–B: 100.63, Lower A–B:
99.53, Upper B–C: 100.36, Lower B–C: 99.81; in control
b. $\bar{\bar{x}} = 100.08$, $\bar{R} = .75$, UCL $= 100.86$, LCL $= 99.33$,
Upper A–B: 100.61, Lower A–B: 99.58, Upper B–C: 100.35,
Lower B–C: 99.84; out of control   **13.23** Variation
13.2 5 a. 0, 2.282 **b.** .283, 1.717 **c.** .451, 1.548   **13.27a.** UCL $= 7.553$
b. Upper A–B: 6.139, Lower A–B: .481, Upper B–C: 4.725,
Lower B–C: 1.895 **c.** In control   **13.29 a.** 40 samples of size
$n = 5$ **b.** No   **13.31 a.** 32.5 **b.** UCL $= 57.75$, LCL $= 7.259$ **c.** Yes
e. Out of control   **13.33 a.** $\bar{R} = .0238$, UCL $= .0778$, LCL $= 0$,
Upper A–B: .0598, Lower A–B: .0122, Upper B–C: .0418, Lower
B–C: .0058; in control **b.** $\bar{\bar{x}} = .2214$, UCL $= .2661$, LCL $= .1767$,
Upper A–B: .2512, Lower A–B: .1916, Upper B–C: .2363, Lower
B–C: .2065; in control **c.** In control; .2214   **13.35 a.** $\bar{R} = .8065$,
UCL $= 2.076$; yes **b.** $\bar{R} = .75$, UCL $= 1.931$; out of control
13.37 $\bar{R} = .1868$, UCL $= .4263$, LCL $= 0$, Upper A–B: .346,
Lower A–B: .027, Upper B–C: .267, Lower B–C: .107; in control
13.39 Proportion   **13.41** 104   **13.43 a.** $p = .0575$, UCL $= .1145$,
LCL $= .0005$, Upper A–B: .0955, Lower A–B: .0195, Upper
B–C: .0765, Lower B–C: .0385 **d.** No **e.** No   **13.45 a.** Postopera-
tive complication **b.** Months **c.** .10 **e.** UCL $= .191$, LCL $= .009$,
Upper A–B: .161, Lower A–B: .039, Upper B–C: .130, Lower
B–C: .070 **g.** Out of control   **13.47 a.** Yes **b.** UCL $= .0202$,
LCL $= .0008$ **c.** In control   **13.49 a.** $p = .04$, UCL $= .099$,
LCL $= 0$, Upper A–B: .079, Lower A–B: .001, Upper B–C: .060,
Lower B–C: .020 **b.** No **c.** No   **13.51** $p = .06$, UCL $= .092$,
LCL $= .028$, Upper A–B: .081, Lower A–B: .039, Upper B–C: .071,
Lower B–C: .049; out of control   **13.59 a.** 126 **b.** 31.2 **c.** 660.36
d. .0144   **13.61** 6s   **13.63** .377   **13.65 b.** .51 **c.** 3.9967 **d.** Yes
13.67 $Cp = 29.08$, capable   **13.73** Yes   **13.83 a.** $\bar{x} = 6.4$
b. Increasing variance   **13.85** Out of control (Rule 2)
13.87 a. $\bar{R} = 2.76$, UCL $= 5.83$ **b.** $\bar{\bar{x}} = 54.26$, UCL $= 55.85$,
LCL $= 52.67$ **c.** Mean chart out of control **d.** No
13.89 a. $\bar{R} = 5.455$, UCL $= 11.532$, Upper A–B: 9.508,
Lower A–B: 1.402, Upper B–C: 7.481, Lower B–C: 3.429
b. In control **d.** $\bar{\bar{x}} = 3.867$, UCL $= 7.013$, LCL $= .721$,
Upper A–B: 5.965, Lower A–B: 1.769, Upper B–C: 4.916,
Lower B–C: 2.818 **e.** In control **f.** Yes **h.** No **i.** .381
13.91 a. LSL $= 3.12$, USL $= 3.72$ **b.** .152 **c.** $Cp = .505$
13.93 No

Chapter 14

14.5 a. 127.63 **b.** 116.37   **14.7 a.** $I_{2015} = 420.58$; beer
production in 2010 increased by 320.58% over the beer
production in 2004. **b.** Quantity **c.** $I_{2015} = 242.05$
14.9 a. $I_{1997} = 100.00$, $I_{1998} = 83.94, \ldots, I_{2015} = 105.22$
c. Price   **14.11 a.** $I_{1970} = 100.00$, $I_{1975} = 157.94, \ldots$,
$I_{2015} = 1,5891.53$ **b.** $I_{1970} = 36.98$, $I_{1975} = 58.40, \ldots$,
$I_{2015} = 699.49$ **c.** Flattens the graph
14.13 a. Men: $I_{2007} = 100.00$, $I_{2008} = 104.18, \ldots, I_{2015} = 116.71$;
Women: $I_{2007} = 100.00$, $I_{2008} = 103.91, \ldots, I_{2015} = 118.24$
c. $I_{2000} = 100.00$, $I_{2008} = 104.06, \ldots, I_{2015} = 117.39$
14.15 $w = .2$ **14.17 a.** $E_{2004} = 5.830$, $E_{2005} = 5.992, \ldots$,
$E_{2014} = 13.019$, $E_{2015} = 15.319$ **b.** $E_{2004} = 5.830$, $E_{2005} = 6.198$,
$\ldots, E_{2014} = 20.722$, $E_{2015} = 23.760$ **c.** $w = .2$ series
14.19 a. $E_{1990} = 384.00$, $E_{1991} = 366.40, \ldots, E_{2014} = 1304.70$,
$E_{2015} = 1188.94$ **14.21 a.** $w = .1$: $E_{1995} = 1,544.0$,
$E_{1996} = 1,543.7, \ldots, E_{2014} = 1,698.6$, $E_{2015} = 1,634.5$;
$w = .9$: $E_{1995} = 1,544.0$, $E_{1996} = 1,541.3, \ldots, E_{2014} = 1,200.9$,
$E_{2015} = 1,072.3$ **b.** $w = .9$ series   **14.25 a.** $w = .3$: $F_{2014} =$

$F_{2015} = 12.043$; $w = .7$: $F_{2014} = F_{2015} = 14.622$ **b.** $w = .7$
and $v = .3$: $F_{2014} = 16.481$, $F_{2015} = 17.903$; $w = .3$ and
$v = .7$: $F_{2014} = 15.799$, $F_{2015} = 17.468$ **14.27 a.** Yes
b. $F_{2016} = 233.19$ **c.** $F_{2016} = 242.64$ **14.29 a.** Forecast for
all four quarters $= 1,989.9$ **b.** Forecast for all four quarters
$= 1,869.8$ **14.31 a.** Forecast for all 12 months $= 1,701.20$
b. $F_{Jan} = 1,701.20$, $F_{Feb} = 1,1676.70$, $F_{Mar} = 1,1709.40, \ldots$,
$F_{Dec} = 1,7117.59$ **c.** Forecasts: $F_{Jan} = 1,742.88$, $F_{Feb} = 1,753.23$,
$F_{Mar} = 1,763.59, \ldots, F_{Dec} = 1,856.76$; one-step-ahead
forecasts: $F_{Jan} = 1,742.88$, $F_{Feb} = 1,685.22$, $F_{Mar} = 1,715.56$, c,
$F_{Dec} = 1,780.26$ **14.33 a.** 5.68, 6.62 **b.** 6.36, 7.05 **c.** MAD $= 6.15$,
MAPE $= 26.31$, RMSE $= 6.17$ **d.** MAD $= 6.71$, MAPE $= 28.73$,
RMSE $= 6.72$ **14.35 a.** MAD $= 147.98$, MAPE $= 7.22$,
RMSE $= 171.23$ **b.** MAD $= 103.99$, MAPE $= 5.08$,
RMSE $= 131.45$ **c.** Holt's model with $w = .7$ and $v = .5$
14.37 a. Forecasts for all 3 years $= 78,862.5$
b. $F_{2012} = 80,404.1$, $F_{2013} = 81,490.4$, $F_{2014} = 82,576.7$
c. Exponential smoothing: MAD $= 1,058.5$, MAPE $= 1.4$,
RMSE $= 1,168.7$; Holt's: MAD $= 3,686.4$, MAPE $= 4.75$,
RMSE $= 3,936.9$; Exponential smoothing model
14.39 a. $E(Y_t) = \beta_0 + \beta_1 t + \beta_2 x_1 + \beta_3 x_2 + \beta_4 x_3$,
where $x_1 = \{1$ if Qtr. 1, 0 if not$\}$, $x_2 = \{1$ if Qtr. 2, 0 if not$\}$,
$x_3 = \{1$ if Qtr. 3, 0 if not$\}$ **b.** $\hat{Y}_t = 11.49 + .51t - 3.95x_1 -$
$2.09x_2 - 4.52x_3$; $F = 1,275.44$, reject H_0. **c.** Qtr. 1: (27.22, 29.67);
Qtr. 2: (29.59, 32.04); Qtr. 3: (27.67, 30.12); Qtr. 4: (32.70, 35.15)
14.41 a. $\hat{Y}_t = 9.372 - .223t$ **b.** 3.57; (2.00, 5.15)
14.43 a. $E(Y_t) = \beta_0 + \beta_1 X_t$ **b.** $E(Y_t) = \beta_0 + \beta_1 X_t +$
$\beta_2 x_1 + \beta_3 x_2 + \cdots + \beta_{12} x_{11}$, where $x_1 = \{1$ if Jan., 0 if not$\}$,
$x_2 = \{1$ if Feb., 0 if not$\}, \ldots, x_{11} = \{1$ if Nov., 0 if not$\}$
c. Subset F-test; H_0: $\beta_2 = \beta_3 = \cdots = \beta_{12} = 0$
d. $\hat{\beta}_0 + \hat{\beta}_1 (180) + \hat{\beta}_2$ **14.45 a.** $\hat{Y}_t = 409.19 - 3.533t$
b. $F_{2015} = 299.68$, $F_{2016} = 296.15$ **c.** F_{2015}: (245.07, 354.29);
F_{2016}: (241.19, 351.10)   **14.47 a.** $E(Y_t) = \beta_0 + \beta_1 X_{1,t-1}$
b. Add $\beta_2 X_{2,t-1} + \beta_3 X_{3,t-1} + \beta_4 X_{4,t-1}$. **c.** Add
$\beta_2 Q_1 + \beta_3 Q_2 + \beta_4 Q_3$, where Q_1, Q_2, Q_3 are dummy variables
for quarter.   **14.49 a.** Inconclusive **b.** Inconclusive **c.** Reject H_0.
d. Fail to reject H_0.   **14.51 a.** H_0: No autocorrelation; H_a: Positive
autocorrelation **b.** Reject H_0.   **14.53** No; do not reject H_0.
14.55 a. Yes **b.** $d = .75$, reject H_0. **c.** Invalid   **14.57 b.** Models
statistically useful for Banks 1, 2, 3, 4, and 7 **c.** No evidence
of positive autocorrelation for all nine banks
14.59 a. $E_{2000} = 140.9$, $E_{2001} = 141.9, \ldots, E_{2014} = 165.5$,
$E_{2015} = 167.5$ **c.** $E_{2016} = 167.5$, $E_{2017} = 167.5$
14.61 a. $\hat{Y}_t = 38.17 + 7.32t$; forecasts: 118.68, 126.00, 133.32
b. Year 11: (100.61, 136.75); Year 12: (107.06, 144.94); Year 13:
(113.40, 153.24)   **14.63 a.** $E_{1995} = 41.08$, $E_{1996} = 48.81, \ldots$,
$E_{2014} = 44.68$, $E_{2015} = 44.86$; $F_{2016} = 44.86$, $F_{2017} = 44.86$,
loss .05 **b.** $E_{1996} = 50.75$, $E_{1997} = 64.49, \ldots, E_{2014} = 43.52$,
$E_{2015} = 43.75$; $F_{2016} = 42.05$, $F_{2017} = 40.25$, loss 4.66
14.65 a. Other: $I_{1995} = 65.0$, $I_{2000} = 100.0, \ldots, I_{2014} = 173.3$;
DC: $I_{1995} = 56.7$, $I_{2000} = 100.0, \ldots, I_{2014} = 226.7$;
IRA: $I_{1995} = 50.0$, $I_{2000} = 100.0, \ldots, I_{2014} = 284.6$
14.67 a. $F_{2016,1} = 18,321.5$, (18,162.8, 18,480.3);
$F_{2016,2} = 18,473.5$, (18,312.6, 18,634.4); $F_{2016,3} = 18,625.4$,
(18,462.2, 18,788.6); $F_{2016,4} = 18,777.3$, (18,611.7, 18,943.0)
b. $F = .84$, yes **c.** $F_{2016,1} = 18,272.6$, (18,095.9, 18,449.4);
$F_{2016,2} = 18,474.0$, (18,297.2, 18,650.7); $F_{2016,3} = 18,640.3$,
(18,463.5, 18,817.0;) $F_{2016,4} = 18,779.5$, (18,602.7, 18,956.2)
d. $d = 1.12$; fail to reject H_0.   **14.69 a.** $F_{2016} = 998.78$,
(830.86, 1,166.69); $F_{2017} = 1,020.14$, (850.16, 1,190.13)
b. $F_{2016} = 971.19$; $F_{2017} = 1,012.18$ **14.71 a.** $F_{Oct} =$
$F_{Nov} = F_{Dec} = 150.34$; $E_{Oct} = -10.26$, $E_{Nov} = -10.92$,
$E_{Dec} = -12.72$ **b.** $\hat{Y}_t = 166.12 - 1.35t$ **c.** ± 17.56

d. $F_{\text{Oct}} = 152.59$, $(126.94, 178.25)$; $F_{\text{Nov}} = 151.24$, $(124.09, 178.39)$; $F_{\text{Dec}} = 149.89$, $(121.07, 178.71)$
e. Exp. smoothed: MAD $= 11.30$, MAPE $= 8.13$, RMSE $= 11.35$; Regression: MAD $= 12.20$, MAPE $= 8.77$. RMSE $= 12.20$ **f.** Independent **g.** $d = .82$, reject H_0.

Chapter 15

15.1 Nonnormal data **15.3 a.** .035 **b.** .363 **c.** .004 **d.** .151; .151 **e.** .2122; .2119 **15.5** $p = .054$; reject H_0. **15.7 a.** H_0: $\eta = 125{,}000$ $125{,}000$, H_a: $\eta > 125{,}000$ **b.** $S = 9$, p-value $= .304$, do not reject H_0. **c.** Random sample **15.9** No; $S = 11$, $p = .322$ **15.11** $S = 11$, $p = .023$, reject H_0. **15.13** $S = 9$, $p = .073$, reject H_0. **15.15** Yes, $z = -2.47$ **15.17 a.** H_0: Two sampled populations have identical probability distributions, H_a: The probability distribution for population B is shifted to the right of that for population A. **b.** $T_B = 42.5$, reject H_0. **15.19 a.** H_0: Two sampled populations have identical probability distributions, H_a: The probability distribution for nontexting group is shifted to the right or left of that for texting group. **b.** Reject H_0; texting group has preference for face-to-face meetings. **15.21 b.** $T_1 = 104$ **c.** $T_2 = 106$ **d.** $T_1 = 104$ **e.** Do not reject H_0. **15.23 a.** Wilcoxon rank sum test **b.** H_a: Distribution of X-Factors for low-handicapped golfers is shifted to the right of distribution for high-handicapped golfers. **c.** $T_2 \leq 41$ **d.** Do not reject H_0. **15.25** $T_1 = 39.5$, $p = .080$, fail to reject H_0; data not normal **15.27 b.** $z = 2.43$, reject H_0. **c.** Sample sizes large, Central Limit Theorem applies. **15.29 a.** Smaller of T_+ or T_-; $T \leq 152$ **b.** T_-; $T_- \leq 60$ **c.** T_+; $T_+ \leq 0$ **15.31 a.** H_0: Two sampled populations have identical probability distributions. **b.** $T_- = 3.5$, reject H_0. **15.33 a.** Nonnormal differences **b.** Signed rank test **e.** $T_+ = 65$; $T_- = 55$ **f.** Yes **15.35 a.** $z = -4.64$ **b.** Yes, $p \approx 0$ **15.37** $p = .011$, reject H_0 at $\alpha = .05$; enforcement program is effective. **15.39** $T_- = 3.5$,

reject H_0. **15.41** $T_+ = 0$, reject H_0. **15.43** $n \geq 5$ for each sample **15.45 a.** Completely randomized **b.** H_0: 3 probability distributions are identical. **c.** $H > 9.21034$ **d.** $H = 13.85$, reject H_0. **15.47 a.** H_0: The 5 probability distributions are identical, H_a: At least 2 probability distributions differ in location. **c.** Reject H_0. **15.49** $H = 12.846$, $p = .005$, reject H_0. **15.51 b.** Normal data and equal variances **c.** $H = .07$, do not reject H_0. **15.53** $H = 26.82$, reject H_0. **15.55 a.** H_0: Distributions for three treatments are identical. **b.** $F_r > 4.60517$ **c.** $F_r = 6.93$, reject H_0. **15.57 a.** Data are not independent (blocked on subject). **b.** $F_r = 14.37$, $p = .002$ **c.** Reject H_0. **15.59 a.** $R_1 = 35$, $R_2 = 32$, $R_3 = 23$ **b.** $F_r = 5.20$ **c.** $p = .074$ **d.** Reject H_0 at $\alpha = .10$. **15.61** $F_r = 29.11$, $p = .001$, reject H_0. **15.63** No, $F_r = .20$ **15.65** $F_r = 7.85$, fail to reject H_0. **15.67 a.** $|r_s| > .648$ **b.** $r_s > .45$ **c.** $r_s < -.432$ **15.69 a.** .4 **b.** $-.9$ **c.** $-.2$ **d.** .2 **15.71 a.** .8286 **b.** No **c.** .8117 **d.** No **15.73 b.** Navigability: do not reject H_0; transactions: reject H_0; locatability: reject H_0; information: do not reject H_0; files: do not reject H_0. **15.75** Yes; $r_s = -.829$, reject H_0. **15.77** $r_s = .572$ **15.79** No, $r_s = .089$ **15.81 a.** No, $r_s = .40$ **b.** Yes, $T_- = 1.5$ **15.83** Yes, $F_r = 14.9$ **15.85 a.** H_0: Two sampled populations have identical probability distributions. **b.** $z = -.66$ **c.** $|z| > 1.645$ **d.** Do not reject H_0. **15.87 a.** 43 **b.** H_0: $\eta = 37$, H_a: $\eta > 37$ **c.** $S = 11$, $p = .059$, reject H_0 at $\alpha = .10$. **15.89 a.** .657 **b.** No **15.91 a.** No, at $\alpha = .05$; $S = 20$, $z = -3.71$ **b.** No; sample collected in Boston only **15.93 a.** $T_- = 4$, reject H_0. **b.** Yes **15.27 b.** $p = .3431$, do not reject H_0. **15.97 a.** H_0: $\eta = .75$, H_a: $\eta \neq .75$ **d.** $p = .044$, reject H_0. **15.99** $F_r = 6.21$, do not reject H_0. **15.101** Moderate positive rank correlation between Methods I and III; all other pairs have weak positive rank correlation. **15.103** Evidence of difference in distributions (at $\alpha = .05$) for creative ideas and good use of skills

Selected Formulas

CHAPTER 2

Relative Frequency $=$ (frequency)$/n$

$$\bar{x} = \frac{\Sigma x}{n}$$

$$s^2 = \frac{\Sigma (x - \bar{x})^2}{n - 1} = \frac{\Sigma x^2 - \frac{(\Sigma x)^2}{n}}{n - 1}$$

$$s = \sqrt{s^2}$$

$$z = \frac{x - \mu}{\sigma} = \frac{x - \bar{x}}{s}$$

Chebyshev $=$ At least $\left(1 - \dfrac{1}{k^2}\right)100\%$

$\text{IQR} = Q_U - Q_L$

CHAPTER 3

$$P(A^c) = 1 - P(A)$$

$$P(A \cup B) = P(A) + P(B) - P(A \cap B)$$
$$= P(A) + P(B) \text{ if } A \text{ and } B \text{ mutually exclusive}$$

$$P(A \cap B) = P(A|B) \cdot P(B) = P(B|A) \cdot P(A)$$
$$= P(A) \cdot P(B) \text{ if } A \text{ and } B \text{ independent}$$

$$P(A|B) = \frac{P(A \cap B)}{P(B)}$$

$$\binom{N}{n} = \frac{N!}{n!(N - n)!}$$

Bayes's: $P(S_i|A) =$

$$\frac{P(S_i)P(A|S_i)}{P(S_1)P(A|S_1) + P(S_2)P(A|S_2) + \cdots + P(S_k)P(A|S_k)}$$

CHAPTER 6

CI for μ: $\bar{x} \pm (z_{\alpha/2})\sigma/\sqrt{n}$ (large n)
$\bar{x} \pm (t_{\alpha/2})s/\sqrt{n}$ (small n, σ unknown)

CI for p: $\hat{p} \pm z_{\alpha/2}\sqrt{\dfrac{\hat{p}\hat{q}}{n}}$

Estimating μ: $n = (z_{\alpha/2})^2(\sigma^2)/(\text{SE})^2$

Estimating p: $n = (z_{\alpha/2})^2(pq)/(\text{SE})^2$

CI for σ^2: $= \dfrac{(n - 1)s^2}{\chi^2_{\alpha/2}} < \sigma^2 < \dfrac{(n - 1)s^2}{\chi^2_{1 - \alpha/2}}$

CHAPTER 4

Key Formulas

Random Variable	Prob. Dist'n	Mean	Variance
General Discrete:	Table, formula, or graph for $p(x)$	$\sum\limits_{\text{all } x} x \cdot p(x)$	$\sum\limits_{\text{all } x} (x - \mu)^2 \cdot p(x)$
Binomial:	$p(x) = \binom{n}{x}p^x q^{n-x}$ $x = 0, 1, 2, \ldots, n$	np	npq
Poisson:	$p(x) = \dfrac{\lambda^x e^{-\lambda}}{x!}$ $x = 0, 1, 2, \ldots$	λ	λ
Uniform:	$f(x) = 1/(d - c)$ $(c \leq x \leq d)$	$(c + d)/2$	$(d - c)^2/12$
Normal:	$f(x) = \dfrac{1}{\sigma\sqrt{2\pi}} e^{-\frac{1}{2}[(x-\mu)/\sigma]^2}$	μ	σ^2
Standard Normal:	$f(z) = \dfrac{1}{\sqrt{2\pi}} e^{-\frac{1}{2}(z)^2}$ $z = (x - \mu)/\sigma$	$\mu = 0$	$\sigma^2 = 1$

CHAPTER 5

Sample Mean (large n):	Approx. normal	$\mu_{\bar{x}} = \mu$	$\sigma^2_{\bar{x}} = \sigma^2/n$
Sample Proportion (large n):	Approx. normal	$\mu_p = p$	$\sigma^2_{\hat{p}} = p(1 - p)/n$

CHAPTER 7

Test for μ: $z = \dfrac{\bar{x} - \mu}{\sigma/\sqrt{n}}$ (large n)

$t = \dfrac{\bar{x} - \mu}{s/\sqrt{n}}$ (small n, σ unknown)

Test for p: $z = \dfrac{\hat{p} - p_0}{\sqrt{p_0 q_0 / n}}$

Test for σ^2: $\chi^2 = (n-1)s^2/(\sigma_0)^2$

CHAPTER 8

CI for $\mu_1 - \mu_2$:

$\left.(\bar{x}_1 - \bar{x}_2) \pm z_{\alpha/2}\sqrt{\dfrac{\sigma_1^2}{n_1} + \dfrac{\sigma_2^2}{n_2}}\right\}$ (large n_1 and n_2)

Test for $\mu_1 - \mu_2$:

$\left. z = \dfrac{(\bar{x}_1 - \bar{x}_2) - (\mu_1 - \mu_2)}{\sqrt{\dfrac{\sigma_1^2}{n_1} + \dfrac{\sigma_2^2}{n_2}}}\right\}$ (large n_1 and n_2)

$s_p^2 = \dfrac{(n_1 - 1)s_1^2 + (n_2 - 1)s_2^2}{n_1 + n_2 - 2}$

CI for $\mu_1 - \mu_2$:

$\left.(\bar{x}_1 - \bar{x}_2) \pm t_{\alpha/2}\sqrt{s_p^2\left(\dfrac{1}{n_1} + \dfrac{1}{n_2}\right)}\right\}$ (small n_1 and/or n_2)

Test for $\mu_1 - \mu_2$:

$\left. t = \dfrac{(\bar{x}_1 - \bar{x}_2) - (\mu_1 - \mu_2)}{\sqrt{s_p^2\left(\dfrac{1}{n_1} + \dfrac{1}{n_2}\right)}}\right\}$ (small n_1 and/or n_2)

CI for μ_d: $\bar{x}_d \pm t_{\alpha/2} \dfrac{s_d}{\sqrt{n}}$

Test for μ_d: $t = \dfrac{\bar{x}_d - \mu_d}{s_d/\sqrt{n}}$

CI for $p_1 - p_2$: $(\hat{p}_1 - \hat{p}_2) \pm z_{\alpha/2}\sqrt{\dfrac{\hat{p}_1\hat{q}_1}{n_1} + \dfrac{\hat{p}_2\hat{q}_2}{n_2}}$

Test for $p_1 - p_2$: $z = \dfrac{(\hat{p}_1 - \hat{p}_2) - (p_1 - p_2)}{\sqrt{\hat{p}\hat{q}\left(\dfrac{1}{n_1} + \dfrac{1}{n_2}\right)}}$

$\hat{p} = \dfrac{x_1 + x_2}{n_1 + n_2}$

Test for (σ_1^2/σ_2^2): $F = (s_1^2/s_2^2)$

Estimating $\mu_1 - \mu_2$: $n_1 = n_2 = (z_{\alpha/2})^2(\sigma_1^2 + \sigma_2^2)/(\text{ME})^2$

Estimating $p_1 - p_2$: $n_1 = n_2 = (z_{\alpha/2})^2(p_1q_1 + p_2q_2)/(\text{ME})^2$

CHAPTER 9

ANOVA Test for completely randomized design:
$F = \text{MST}/\text{MSE}$

ANOVA Test for randomized block design:
$F = \text{MST}/\text{MSE}$

ANOVA Test for factorial design interaction:
$F = \text{MS}(\text{A} \times \text{B})/\text{MSE}$

Pairwise comparisons: $c = k(k - 1)/2$

CHAPTER 10

Multinomial test: $\chi^2 = \Sigma \dfrac{(n_i - E_i)^2}{E_i}$

$E_i = n(p_{i0})$

Contingency table test: $\chi^2 = \Sigma \dfrac{(n_{ij} - E_{ij})^2}{E_{ij}}$

$E_{ij} = \dfrac{R_i C_j}{n}$

CHAPTER 11

$\text{SS}_{xx} = \Sigma(x - \bar{x})^2 = \Sigma x^2 - \dfrac{(\Sigma x)^2}{n}$

$\text{SS}_{yy} = \Sigma(y - \bar{y})^2 = \Sigma y^2 - \dfrac{(\Sigma y)^2}{n}$

$\text{SS}_{xy} = \Sigma(x - \bar{x})(y - \bar{y}) = \Sigma xy - \dfrac{(\Sigma x)(\Sigma y)}{n}$

$\hat{y} = \hat{\beta}_0 + \hat{\beta}_1 x$

$\hat{\beta}_1 = \dfrac{\text{SS}_{xy}}{\text{SS}_{xx}}$

$\hat{\beta}_1 = \bar{y} - \hat{\beta}_1 \bar{x}$

$r = \dfrac{\text{SS}_{xy}}{\sqrt{\text{SS}_{xx}}\sqrt{\text{SS}_{yy}}}$

CHAPTER 11 (cont'd)

$$s^2 = \frac{SSE}{n-2}$$

$$s = \sqrt{s^2}$$

$$r^2 = \frac{SS_{yy} - SSE}{SS_{yy}}$$

CI for β_1: $\hat{\beta}_1 \pm (t_{\alpha/2})s/\sqrt{SS_{xx}}$

Test for β_1: $t = \dfrac{\hat{\beta}_1 - 0}{s/\sqrt{SS_{xx}}}$

CI for $E(y)$ when $x = x_p$: $\hat{y} \pm t_{\alpha/2}s\sqrt{\dfrac{1}{n} + \dfrac{(x_p - \bar{x})^2}{SS_{xx}}}$

CI for y when $x = x_p$: $\hat{y} \pm t_{\alpha/2}s\sqrt{1 + \dfrac{1}{n} + \dfrac{(x_p - \bar{x})^2}{SS_{xx}}}$

CHAPTER 12

First-Order Model (QN x's):
$$E(y) = \beta_0 + \beta_1 x_1 + \beta_2 x_2 + \ldots + \beta_k x_k$$

Interaction Model (QN x's):
$$E(y) = \beta_0 + \beta_1 x_1 + \beta_2 x_2 + \beta_3 x_1 x_2$$

Quadratic Model (QN x):
$$E(y) = \beta_0 + \beta_1 x + \beta_2 x^2$$

Complete 2nd-Order Model (QN x's):
$$E(y) = \beta_0 + \beta_1 x_1 + \beta_2 x_2 + \beta_3 x_1 x_2 + \beta_4 x_1^2 + \beta_5 x_2^2$$

Dummy Variable Model (QL x):
$$E(y) = \beta_0 + \beta_1 x_1 + \beta_2 x_2$$
where $x_1 = \{1$ if A, 0 if not$\}$, $x_2 = \{1$ if B, 0 if not$\}$

$$MSE = s^2 = \frac{SSE}{n - (k+1)}$$

$$R^2 = \frac{SS_{yy} - SSE}{SS_{yy}}$$

$$R_a^2 = 1 - \left[\frac{(n-1)}{n - (k+1)}\right](1 - R^2)$$

Test for overall model: $F = \dfrac{MS(\text{Model})}{MSE}$

Test for individual β: $t = \dfrac{\hat{\beta}_i - 0}{s_{\hat{\beta}_i}}$

CI for β_i: $\hat{\beta}_i \pm (t_{\alpha/2})s_{\hat{\beta}_i}$

Nested model F test: $F = \dfrac{(SSE_R - SSE_C)/\# \beta\text{'s tested}}{MSE_C}$

CHAPTER 13

Key Formulas

Control Chart	Centerline	Control Limits	A–B Boundary	B–C Boundary
$\bar{x}$-chart	$\bar{\bar{x}} = \dfrac{\sum_{i=1}^{k} \bar{x}_i}{k}$	$\bar{\bar{x}} \pm A_2\bar{R}$ or $\bar{\bar{x}} \pm 2\dfrac{(\bar{R}/d_2)}{\sqrt{n}}$	$\bar{\bar{x}} \pm \dfrac{2}{3}(A_2\bar{R})$ or $\bar{\bar{x}} \pm 2\dfrac{(\bar{R}/d_2)}{\sqrt{n}}$	$\bar{\bar{x}} \pm \dfrac{1}{3}(A_2\bar{R})$
R-chart	$\bar{R} = \dfrac{\sum_{i=1}^{k} R_i}{k}$	$(\bar{R}D_3, \bar{R}D_4)$	$\bar{R} \pm 2d_3\left(\dfrac{\bar{R}}{d_2}\right)$	$\bar{R} \pm d_3\left(\dfrac{\bar{R}}{d_2}\right)$
p-chart	$\bar{p} = \dfrac{\text{Total number defectives}}{\text{Total number units sampled}}$	$\bar{p} \pm 3\sqrt{\dfrac{\bar{p}(1-\bar{p})}{n}}$	$\bar{p} \pm 2\sqrt{\dfrac{\bar{p}(1-\bar{p})}{n}}$	$\bar{p} \pm \sqrt{\dfrac{\bar{p}(1-\bar{p})}{n}}$

Capability index: $C_p = (\text{USL} - \text{LSL})/6\sigma$

Index

Note: Page numbers followed by n indicate footnotes.

Photo Credits